Great Lakes
2003

ExxonMobil Travel Publications

ACKNOWLEDGMENTS

We gratefully acknowledge the help of our representatives for their efficient and perceptive inspection of the lodging and dining establishments listed; the establishments' proprietors for their cooperation in showing their facilities and providing information about them; the many users of previous editions of the Mobil Travel Guides who have taken the time to share their experiences; and for their time and information, the thousands of chambers of commerce, convention and visitors bureaus, city, state, and provincial tourism offices, and government agencies who assisted in our research.

PHOTO CREDITS

D. Dvorak, Jr.Photography: 238, 486; FPG/Getty Images: Gene Ahrens: 458; Willard Clay: 109, 296; Richard Laird: 50; Terry Qing: 445; Jerry Sieve: 419, 618; Travelpix: 65; Ray F. Hillstrom Photography: 582; Layne Kennedy/Corbis: 629; James P. Rowan Photography: 9, 33, 84, 89, 130, 137, 170, 193, 264, 269, 285, 305, 327, 527, 574; SuperStock: 25, 149, 153, 200, 271, 277, 281, 405, 423, 427, 459, 474, 518, 540, 554, 591, 599.

Maps © MapQuest 2002, www.mapquest.com

Printed by Publications International, Ltd.
7373 North Cicero Avenue
Lincolnwood, Illinois 60712

info@mobiltravelguide.com

ISBN 0-7627-2612-1

Manufactured in China.

10 9 8 7 6 5 4 3 2 1

CONTENTS

Welcome A-25
A Word to Our Readers A-26
How to Use This Book A-29
Making the Most of Your Trip A-37
Important Toll-Free Numbers and Online Information A-41
Four- and Five-Star Establishments in the Great Lakes A-43

Great Lakes

Mileage Chart A-6	Wisconsin 504
Illinois 1	Appendix A: Attraction List .635
Indiana 162	Appendix B: Lodging List . .674
Michigan 243	Appendix C: Restaurant List 696
Ohio 385	City Index 706

Maps

Map Legend A-22	Ohio A-18
Interstate Highway Map of the United States A-4	Wisconsin A-20
	Chicago, IL 26
Great Lakes Region A-8	Indianapolis, IN 195
Distance and Driving Time A-10	Detroit, MI 274
Illinois A-12	Cincinnati, OH 410
Indiana A-14	Milwaukee, WI 572
Michigan A-16	

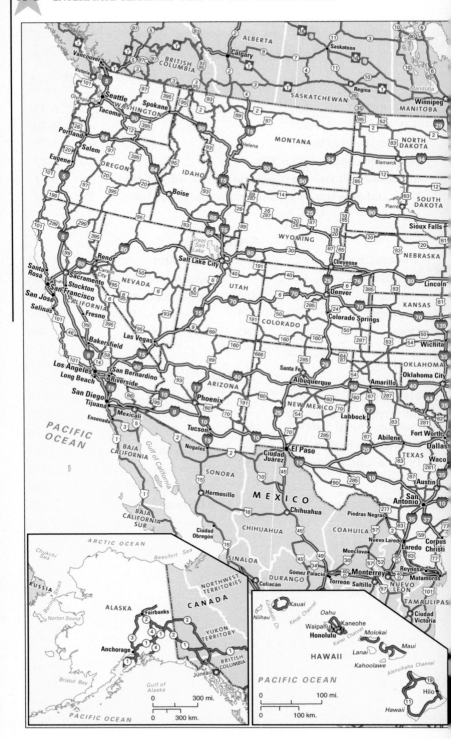

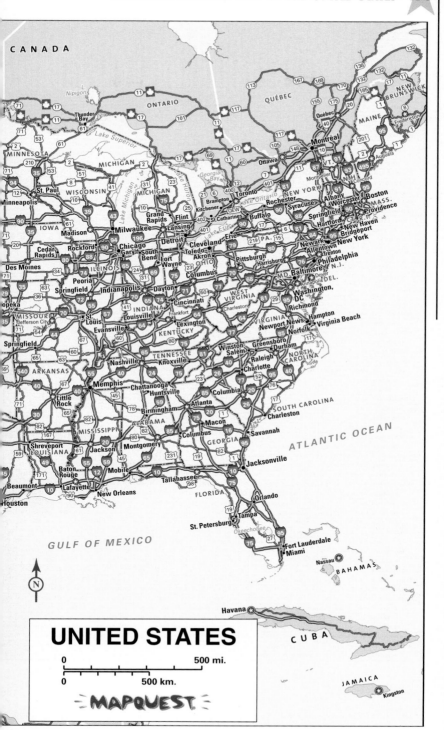

UNITED STATES

0   500 mi.

0   500 km.

MAPQUEST

A-6 Mileage Chart

Distances in chart are in miles. To convert miles to kilometers, multiply the distance in miles by 1.609 Example: New York, NY to Boston, MA = 215 miles or 346 kilometers (215 x 1.609)	ALBUQUERQUE, NM	ATLANTA, GA	BALTIMORE, MD	BILLINGS, MT	BIRMINGHAM, AL	BISMARCK, ND	BOISE, ID	BOSTON, MA	BUFFALO, NY	BURLINGTON, VT	CHARLESTON, SC	CHARLESTON, WV	CHARLOTTE, NC	CHEYENNE, WY	CHICAGO, IL	CINCINNATI, OH	CLEVELAND, OH	DALLAS, TX	DENVER, CO	DES MOINES, IA	DETROIT, MI	EL PASO, TX	HOUSTON, TX	INDIANAPOLIS, IN	JACKSON, MS	KANSAS CITY, MO	LAS VEGAS, NV
ALBUQUERQUE, NM		1490	1902	991	1274	1333	966	2240	1808	2178	1793	1568	1649	538	1352	1409	1619	754	438	1091	1608	263	994	1298	1157	894	578
ATLANTA, GA	1490		679	1889	150	1559	2218	1100	910	1158	317	503	238	1482	717	476	726	792	1403	967	735	1437	800	531	386	801	2067
BALTIMORE, MD	1902	679		1959	795	1551	2401	422	370	481	583	352	441	1665	708	521	377	1399	1690	1031	532	2045	1470	600	1032	1087	2445
BILLINGS, MT	991	1889	1959		1839	413	626	2254	1796	2181	2157	1755	2012	455	1246	1552	1597	1433	554	1007	1534	1255	1673	1432	1836	1088	965
BIRMINGHAM, AL	1274	150	795	1839		1509	2170	1215	909	1241	466	578	389	1434	667	475	725	647	1356	919	734	1292	678	481	241	753	1852
BISMARCK, ND	1333	1559	1551	413	1509		1039	1846	1388	1773	1749	1347	1604	594	838	1144	1189	1342	693	675	1126	1597	1582	1024	1548	801	1378
BOISE, ID	966	2218	2401	626	2170	1039		2697	2239	2624	2520	2182	2375	737	1708	1969	2040	1711	833	1369	1977	1206	1952	1852	2115	1376	760
BOSTON, MA	2240	1100	422	2254	1215	1846	2697		462	214	1003	741	861	1961	1003	862	654	1819	2004	1326	741	2465	1890	940	1453	1427	2757
BUFFALO, NY	1808	910	370	1796	909	1388	2239	462		375	899	431	695	1502	545	442	197	1393	1546	868	277	2039	1513	508	1134	995	2299
BURLINGTON, VT	2178	1158	481	2181	1241	1773	2624	214	375		1061	782	919	1887	930	817	567	1763	1931	1253	652	2409	1916	878	1479	1366	2684
CHARLESTON, SC	1793	317	583	2157	466	1749	2520	1003	899	1061		468	204	1783	907	622	724	1109	1705	1204	879	1754	1110	721	703	1102	2371
CHARLESTON, WV	1568	503	352	1755	578	1347	2182	741	431	782	468		265	1445	506	209	255	1072	1367	802	410	1718	1192	320	816	764	2122
CHARLOTTE, NC	1649	238	441	2012	389	1604	2375	861	695	919	204	265		1637	761	476	520	1031	1559	1057	675	1677	1041	575	625	956	2225
CHEYENNE, WY	538	1482	1665	455	1434	594	737	1961	1502	1887	1783	1445	1637		972	1233	1304	979	100	633	1241	801	1220	1115	1382	640	843
CHICAGO, IL	1352	717	708	1246	667	838	1708	1003	545	930	907	506	761	972		302	346	936	1015	337	283	1543	1108	184	750	532	1768
CINCINNATI, OH	1409	476	521	1552	475	1144	1969	862	442	817	622	209	476	1233	302		253	958	1200	599	261	1605	1079	116	700	597	1955
CLEVELAND, OH	1619	726	377	1597	725	1189	2040	654	197	567	724	255	520	1304	346	253		1208	1347	669	171	1854	1328	319	950	806	2100
DALLAS, TX	754	792	1399	1433	647	1342	1711	1819	1393	1763	1109	1072	1031	979	936	958	1208		887	752	1218	647	241	913	406	554	1331
DENVER, CO	438	1403	1690	554	1356	693	833	2004	1546	1931	1705	1367	1559	100	1015	1200	1347	887		676	1284	701	1127	1088	1290	603	756
DES MOINES, IA	1091	967	1031	1007	919	675	1369	1326	868	1253	1204	802	1057	633	337	599	669	752	676		606	1283	992	481	931	194	1429
DETROIT, MI	1608	735	532	1534	734	1126	1977	741	277	652	879	410	675	1241	283	261	171	1218	1284	606		1799	1338	318	960	795	2037
EL PASO, TX	263	1437	2045	1255	1292	1597	1206	2465	2039	2409	1754	1718	1677	801	1543	1605	1854	647	701	1283	1799		758	1489	1051	1085	717
HOUSTON, TX	994	800	1470	1673	678	1582	1952	1890	1513	1916	1110	1192	1041	1220	1108	1079	1328	241	1127	992	1338	758		1033	445	795	1474
INDIANAPOLIS, IN	1298	531	600	1432	481	1024	1852	940	508	878	721	320	575	1115	184	116	319	913	1088	481	318	1489	1033		675	485	1843
JACKSON, MS	1157	386	1032	1836	241	1548	2115	1453	1134	1479	703	816	625	1382	750	700	950	406	1290	931	960	1051	445	675		747	1735
KANSAS CITY, MO	894	801	1087	1088	753	801	1376	1427	995	1366	1102	764	956	640	532	597	806	554	603	194	795	1085	795	485	747		1358
LAS VEGAS, NV	578	2067	2445	965	1852	1378	760	2757	2299	2684	2371	2122	2225	843	1768	1955	2100	1331	756	1429	2037	717	1474	1843	1735	1358	
LITTLE ROCK, AR	900	528	1072	1530	381	1183	1808	1493	1066	1437	900	745	754	1076	662	632	882	327	984	567	891	974	447	587	269	382	1478
LOS ANGELES, CA	806	2237	2705	1239	2092	1702	1033	3046	2572	2957	2554	2374	2453	1116	2042	2215	2374	1446	1029	1703	2310	801	1558	2104	1851	1632	274
LOUISVILLE, KY	1320	419	602	1547	369	1139	1933	964	545	915	610	251	464	1197	299	106	356	852	1118	595	366	1499	972	112	594	516	1874
MEMPHIS, TN	1033	389	933	1625	241	1337	1954	1353	927	1297	760	606	614	1217	539	493	742	466	1116	720	752	1112	586	464	211	536	1611
MIAMI, FL	2155	661	1109	2554	812	2224	2883	1529	1425	1587	583	994	730	2147	1382	1141	1250	1367	2069	1632	1401	1959	1201	1196	915	1466	2733
MILWAUKEE, WI	1426	813	805	1175	763	767	1748	1100	642	1027	1003	601	857	1012	89	398	443	1010	1055	378	380	1617	1193	279	835	573	1808
MINNEAPOLIS, MN	1339	1129	1121	839	1079	431	1465	1417	958	1343	1319	918	1173	881	409	714	760	999	924	246	697	1530	1240	596	1151	441	1677
MONTRÉAL, QC	2172	1241	564	2093	1289	1685	2535	313	397	92	1145	822	1003	1799	841	815	588	1772	1843	1165	564	2363	1892	872	1514	1359	2596
NASHVILLE, TN	1248	242	716	1648	194	1315	1976	1136	716	1086	543	395	397	1240	474	281	531	681	1162	725	541	1328	801	287	423	559	1826
NEW ORLEANS, LA	1276	473	1142	1955	351	1734	2234	1563	1254	1588	783	926	713	1502	935	820	1070	525	1409	1117	1079	1118	360	826	185	932	1854
NEW YORK, NY	2015	869	192	2049	985	1641	2491	215	400	299	773	515	631	1755	797	636	466	1589	1799	1121	622	2235	1660	715	1223	1202	2552
OKLAHOMA CITY, OK	546	944	1354	1227	729	1136	1506	1694	1262	1632	1248	1022	1102	773	807	863	1073	209	681	546	1062	737	449	752	612	348	1124
OMAHA, NE	973	989	1168	904	941	616	1234	1463	1005	1390	1290	952	1144	497	474	736	806	669	541	136	743	1236	910	618	935	188	1294
ORLANDO, FL	1934	440	904	2333	591	2003	2662	1324	1221	1383	379	790	525	1926	1161	920	1045	1146	1847	1411	1180	1738	980	975	694	1245	2512
PHILADELPHIA, PA	1954	782	104	2019	897	1611	2462	321	414	371	685	454	543	1725	768	576	437	1501	1744	1091	592	2147	1572	655	1135	1141	2500
PHOENIX, AZ	466	1868	2366	1199	1723	1662	993	2706	2274	2644	2184	2035	2107	1004	1819	1876	2085	1077	904	1558	2074	432	1188	1764	1482	1360	285
PITTSBURGH, PA	1670	676	246	1719	763	1311	2161	592	217	587	642	217	438	1425	467	292	136	1246	1460	791	292	1893	1366	370	988	857	2215
PORTLAND, ME	2338	1197	520	2352	1313	1944	2795	107	560	233	1101	839	959	2059	1101	960	751	1917	2102	1424	838	2563	1988	1038	1550	1525	2855
PORTLAND, OR	1395	2647	2830	889	2599	1301	432	3126	2667	3052	2948	2610	2802	1166	2137	2398	2469	2140	1261	1798	2405	1767	2381	2280	2544	1805	1188
RAPID CITY, SD	841	1511	1626	379	1463	320	930	1921	1463	1848	1824	1422	1678	305	913	1219	1264	1077	404	629	1201	1105	1318	1101	1458	710	1035
RENO, NV	1020	2440	2623	960	2392	1372	430	2919	2460	2845	2741	2403	2595	959	1930	2191	2262	1933	1054	1591	2198	1315	2072	2073	2337	1598	442
RICHMOND, VA	1876	527	152	2053	678	1645	2496	572	485	630	428	322	289	1760	802	530	471	1309	1688	1126	627	1955	1330	641	914	1085	2444
ST. LOUIS, MO	1051	549	841	1341	501	1053	1628	1181	749	1119	850	512	704	892	294	350	560	635	855	436	549	1242	863	239	505	252	1610
SALT LAKE CITY, UT	624	1916	2100	548	1868	960	342	2395	1936	2322	2218	1880	2072	436	1406	1667	1738	1410	531	1067	1675	864	1650	1549	1813	1074	417
SAN ANTONIO, TX	818	1000	1671	1500	878	1599	1761	2092	1665	2036	1310	1344	1241	1046	1270	1231	1481	271	946	1009	1490	556	200	1186	644	812	1272
SAN DIEGO, CA	825	2166	2724	1302	2021	1765	1096	3065	2632	3020	2483	2393	2405	1179	2105	2234	2437	1375	1092	1766	2373	730	1487	2122	1780	1695	337
SAN FRANCISCO, CA	1111	2618	2840	1176	2472	1749	646	3135	2677	3062	2934	2620	2759	1176	2146	2407	2478	1827	1271	1807	2415	1181	1938	2290	2232	1814	575
SEATTLE, WA	1463	2705	2775	816	2657	1229	500	3070	2612	2997	2973	2571	2827	1234	2062	2368	2413	2208	1329	1822	2350	1944	2449	2249	2612	1872	1256
TAMPA, FL	1949	455	960	2348	606	2018	2677	1380	1276	1438	434	845	581	1941	1176	935	1101	1161	1862	1426	1194	1753	995	990	709	1259	2526
TORONTO, ON	1841	958	565	1762	958	1354	2204	570	106	419	1006	537	802	1468	510	484	303	1441	1512	834	233	2032	1561	541	1183	1028	2265
VANCOUVER, BC	1597	2838	2908	949	2791	1362	633	3204	2745	3130	3106	2705	2960	1368	2196	2501	2547	2342	1463	1956	2483	2087	2583	2383	2746	2007	1390
WASHINGTON, DC	1896	636	38	1953	758	1545	2395	458	384	517	539	346	397	1659	701	517	370	1362	1686	1025	526	2008	1433	596	996	1083	2441
WICHITA, KS	707	989	1276	1067	838	934	1346	1616	1184	1554	1291	953	1145	613	728	785	995	367	521	390	984	898	608	674	771	192	1276

LITTLE ROCK, AR	LOS ANGELES, CA	LOUISVILLE, KY	MEMPHIS, TN	MIAMI, FL	MILWAUKEE, WI	MINNEAPOLIS, MN	MONTRÉAL, QC	NASHVILLE, TN	NEW ORLEANS, LA	NEW YORK, NY	OKLAHOMA CITY, OK	OMAHA, NE	ORLANDO, FL	PHILADELPHIA, PA	PHOENIX, AZ	PITTSBURGH, PA	PORTLAND, ME	PORTLAND, OR	RAPID CITY, SD	RENO, NV	RICHMOND, VA	SALT LAKE CITY, UT	SAN ANTONIO, TX	SAN DIEGO, CA	SAN FRANCISCO, CA	SEATTLE, WA	ST. LOUIS, MO	TAMPA, FL	TORONTO, ON	VANCOUVER, BC	WASHINGTON, DC	WICHITA, KS
00	806	1320	1033	2155	1426	1339	2172	1248	1276	2015	546	973	1934	1954	466	1670	2338	1395	841	1020	1876	1051	624	818	825	1111	1463	1949	1841	1597	1896	707
28	2237	419	389	661	813	1129	1241	242	473	869	944	989	440	782	1868	676	1197	2647	1511	2440	527	549	1916	1000	2166	2618	2705	455	958	2838	636	989
072	2705	602	933	1109	805	1121	564	716	1142	192	1354	1168	904	104	2366	246	520	2830	1626	2623	152	841	2100	1671	2724	2840	2775	960	565	2908	38	1276
30	1239	1547	1625	2554	1175	839	2093	1648	1955	2049	1227	904	2333	2019	1199	1719	2352	889	379	960	2053	1341	548	1500	1302	1176	816	2348	1762	949	1953	1067
81	2092	369	241	812	763	1079	1289	194	351	985	729	941	591	897	1723	763	1313	2599	1463	2392	678	501	1868	878	2021	2472	2657	606	958	2791	758	838
83	1702	1139	1337	2224	767	431	1685	1315	1734	1641	1136	616	2003	1611	1662	1311	1944	1301	320	1372	1645	1053	960	1599	1765	1749	1229	2018	1354	1362	1545	934
08	1033	1933	1954	2883	1748	1465	2535	1976	2234	2491	1506	1234	2662	2462	993	2161	2795	432	930	430	2496	1628	342	1761	1096	646	500	2677	2204	633	2395	1346
93	3046	964	1353	1529	1100	1417	313	1136	1563	215	1694	1463	1324	321	2706	592	107	3126	1921	2919	572	1181	2395	2092	3065	3135	3070	1380	570	3204	458	1616
66	2572	545	927	1425	642	958	397	716	1254	400	1262	1005	1221	414	2274	217	560	2667	1463	2460	485	749	1936	1665	2632	2677	2612	1276	106	2745	384	1184
37	2957	915	1297	1587	1027	1343	92	1086	1588	299	1632	1390	1383	371	2644	587	233	3052	1848	2845	630	1119	2322	2036	3020	3062	2997	1438	419	3130	517	1554
00	2554	610	760	583	1003	1319	1145	543	783	773	1248	1290	379	685	2184	642	1101	2948	1824	2741	428	850	2218	1310	2483	2934	2973	434	1006	3106	539	1291
45	2374	251	606	994	601	918	822	395	926	515	1022	952	790	454	2035	217	839	2610	1422	2403	322	512	1880	1344	2393	2620	2571	845	537	2705	346	953
54	2453	464	614	730	857	1173	1003	397	713	631	1102	1144	525	543	2107	438	959	2802	1678	2595	289	704	2072	1241	2405	2759	2827	581	802	2960	397	1145
76	1116	1197	1217	2147	1012	881	1799	1240	1502	1755	773	497	1926	1725	1004	1425	2059	1166	305	959	1760	892	436	1046	1179	1176	1234	1941	1468	1368	1659	613
62	2042	299	539	1382	89	409	841	474	935	797	807	474	1161	768	1819	467	1101	2137	913	1930	802	294	1406	1270	2105	2146	2062	1176	510	2196	701	728
32	2215	106	493	1141	398	714	815	281	820	636	863	736	920	576	1876	292	960	2398	1219	2191	530	350	1667	1231	2234	2407	2368	935	484	2501	517	785
82	2374	356	742	1250	443	760	588	531	1070	466	1073	806	1045	437	2085	136	751	2469	1264	2262	471	560	1738	1481	2437	2478	2413	1101	303	2547	370	995
27	1446	852	466	1367	1010	999	1772	681	525	1589	209	669	1146	1501	1077	1246	1917	2140	1077	1933	1309	635	1410	271	1375	1827	2208	1161	1441	2342	1362	367
34	1029	1118	1116	2069	1055	924	1843	1162	1409	1799	681	541	1847	1744	904	1460	2102	1261	404	1054	1688	855	531	946	1092	1271	1329	1862	1512	1463	1686	521
57	1703	595	720	1632	378	246	1165	725	1117	1121	546	136	1411	1091	1558	791	1424	1798	629	1591	1126	436	1067	1009	1766	1807	1822	1426	834	1956	1025	390
91	2310	366	752	1401	380	697	564	541	1079	622	1062	743	1180	592	2074	292	838	2405	1201	2198	627	549	1675	1490	2373	2415	2350	1194	233	2483	526	984
74	801	1499	1112	1959	1617	1530	2363	1328	1118	2235	737	1236	1738	2147	432	1893	2563	1767	1105	1315	1955	1242	864	556	730	1181	1944	1753	2032	2087	2008	898
47	1558	972	586	1201	1193	1240	1892	801	360	1660	449	910	980	1572	1188	1366	1988	2381	1318	2072	1330	863	1650	200	1487	1938	2449	995	1561	2583	1433	608
37	2104	112	464	1196	279	596	872	287	826	715	752	618	975	655	1764	370	1038	2280	1101	2073	641	239	1549	1186	2122	2290	2249	990	541	2383	596	674
59	1851	594	211	915	835	1151	1514	423	185	1223	612	935	694	1135	1482	988	1550	2544	1458	2337	914	505	1813	644	1780	2232	2612	709	1183	2746	996	771
32	1632	516	536	1466	573	441	1359	559	932	1202	348	188	1245	1141	1360	857	1525	1805	710	1598	1085	252	1074	812	1695	1814	1872	1259	1028	2007	1083	192
78	274	1874	1611	2733	1808	1677	2596	1826	1854	2552	1124	1294	2512	2500	285	2215	2855	1188	1035	442	2444	1610	417	1272	337	575	1256	2526	2265	1390	2441	1276
	1706	526	140	1190	747	814	1446	355	455	1262	355	570	969	1175	1367	920	1590	2237	1093	2030	983	416	1507	600	1703	2012	2305	984	1115	2439	1036	464
06		2126	1839	2759	2082	1951	2869	2054	1917	2820	1352	1567	2538	2760	369	2476	3144	971	1309	519	2682	1856	691	1356	124	385	1148	2553	2538	1291	2702	1513
6	2126		386	1084	394	711	920	175	714	739	774	704	863	678	1786	394	1062	2362	1215	2155	572	264	1631	1125	2144	2372	2364	878	589	2497	596	705
0	1839	386		1051	624	940	1306	215	396	1123	487	724	830	1035	1500	780	1451	2382	1247	2175	843	294	1652	739	1841	2144	2440	845	975	2574	896	597
90	2759	1084	1051		1478	1794	1671	907	874	1299	1609	1654	232	1211	2390	1167	1627	3312	2176	3105	954	1214	2581	1401	2688	3140	3370	274	1532	3504	1065	1655
7	2082	394	624	1478		337	939	569	1020	894	880	514	1257	865	1892	564	1198	2063	842	1970	899	367	1446	1343	2145	2186	1991	1272	607	2124	799	769
4	1951	711	940	1794	337		1255	886	1337	1211	793	383	1573	1181	1805	881	1515	1727	606	1839	1216	621	1315	1257	2014	2055	1654	1588	924	1788	1115	637
46	2869	920	1306	1671	939	1255		1094	1632	383	1625	1300	1466	454	2637	607	282	2963	1758	2756	714	1112	2232	2043	2931	2972	2907	1522	330	3041	600	1547
5	2054	175	215	907	569	886	1094		539	906	703	747	686	818	1715	569	1234	2405	1269	2198	626	307	1675	954	2056	2360	2463	701	764	2597	679	748
5	1917	714	396	874	1020	1337	1632	539		1332	731	1121	653	1245	1548	1108	1660	2663	1643	2431	1002	690	1932	560	1846	2298	2731	668	1302	2865	1106	890
52	2820	739	1123	1299	894	1211	383	906	1332		1469	1258	1094	91	2481	367	313	2920	1716	2713	342	956	2189	1861	2839	2929	2864	1150	507	2998	228	1391
5	1352	774	487	1609	880	793	1625	703	731	1469		463	1388	1408	1012	1124	1792	1934	871	1727	1331	505	1204	466	1370	1657	2002	1403	1295	2136	1350	161
0	1567	704	724	1654	514	383	1300	747	1121	1258	463		1433	1228	1440	928	1561	1662	525	1455	1263	440	932	927	1630	1672	1719	1448	971	1853	1162	307
9	2538	863	830	232	1257	1573	1466	686	653	1094	1388	1433		1006	2169	963	1422	3091	1955	2884	750	993	2360	1180	2467	2918	3149	82	1327	3283	860	1434
5	2760	678	1035	1211	865	1181	454	818	1245	91	1408	1228	1006		2420	306	419	2890	1686	2683	254	895	2160	1774	2779	2900	2835	1062	522	2968	140	1330
57	369	1786	1500	2390	1892	1805	2637	1715	1548	2481	1012	1440	2169	2420		2136	2804	1335	1308	883	2343	1517	651	987	358	750	1513	2184	2307	1655	2362	1173
0	2476	394	780	1167	564	881	607	569	1108	367	1124	928	963	306	2136		690	2590	1386	2383	341	611	1859	1519	2494	2599	2534	1019	321	2668	240	1046
0	3144	1062	1451	1627	1198	1515	282	1234	1660	313	1792	1561	1422	419	2804	690		3223	2019	3016	670	1279	2493	2189	3162	3233	3168	1478	668	3301	556	1714
37	971	2362	2382	3312	2063	1727	2963	2405	2663	2920	1934	1662	3091	2890	1335	2590	3223		1268	578	2925	2057	771	2322	1093	638	170	3106	2633	313	2824	1775
3	1309	1215	1247	2176	842	606	1758	1269	1643	1716	871	525	1955	1686	1308	1386	2019	1268		1151	1720	963	628	1335	1372	1368	1195	1970	1429	1328	1620	712
0	519	2155	2175	3105	1970	1839	2756	2198	2431	2713	1727	1455	2884	2683	883	2383	3016	578	1151		2718	1850	524	1870	642	217	755	2899	2426	898	2617	1568
3	2682	572	843	954	899	1216	714	626	1002	342	1331	1263	750	254	2343	341	670	2925	1720	2718		834	2194	1530	2684	2934	2869	805	660	3003	108	1274
5	1856	264	294	1214	367	621	1112	307	690	956	505	440	993	895	1517	611	1279	2057	963	1850	834		1326	968	1875	2066	2125	1008	782	2259	837	441
7	691	1631	1652	2581	1446	1315	2232	1675	1932	2189	1204	932	2360	2160	651	1859	2493	771	628	524	2194	1326		1419	754	740	839	2375	1902	973	2094	1044
)	1356	1125	739	1401	1343	1257	2043	954	560	1861	466	927	1180	1774	987	1519	2189	2322	1335	1870	1530	968	1419		1285	1737	2275	1195	1714	2410	1635	624
3	124	2144	1841	2688	2145	2014	2931	2056	1846	2839	1370	1630	2467	2779	358	2494	3162	1093	1372	642	2684	1875	754	1285		508	1271	2481	2601	1414	2720	1531
2	385	2372	2144	3140	2186	2055	2972	2360	2298	2929	1657	1672	2918	2900	750	2599	3233	638	1368	217	2934	2066	740	1737	508		816	2933	2643	958	2834	1784
5	1148	2364	2440	3370	1991	1654	2907	2463	2731	2864	2002	1719	3149	2835	1513	2534	3168	170	1195	755	2869	2125	839	2275	1271	816		3164	2577	140	2769	1843
	2553	878	845	274	1272	1588	1522	701	668	1150	1403	1448	82	1062	2184	1019	1478	3106	1970	2899	805	1008	2375	1195	2481	2933	3164		1383	3297	916	1448
	2538	589	975	1532	607	924	330	764	1302	507	1295	971	1327	522	2307	321	668	2633	1429	2426	660	782	1902	1714	2601	2643	2577	1383		2711	563	1217
9	1291	2497	2574	3504	2124	1788	3041	2597	2865	2998	2136	1853	3283	2968	1655	2668	3301	313	1328	898	3003	2259	973	2410	1414	958	140	3297	2711		2902	1977
5	2702	596	896	1065	799	1115	600	679	1106	228	1350	1162	860	140	2362	240	556	2824	1620	2617	108	837	2094	1635	2720	2834	2769	916	563	2902		1272
	1513	705	597	1655	769	637	1547	748	890	1391	161	307	1434	1330	1173	1046	1714	1775	712	1568	1274	441	1044	624	1531	1784	1843	1448	1217	1977	1272	

MAPQUEST

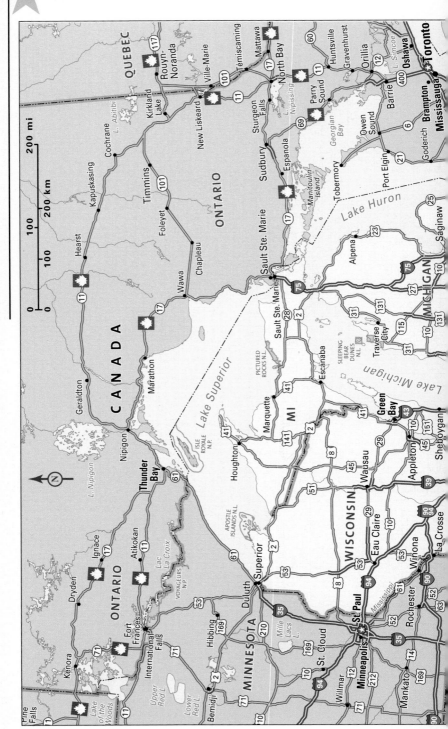

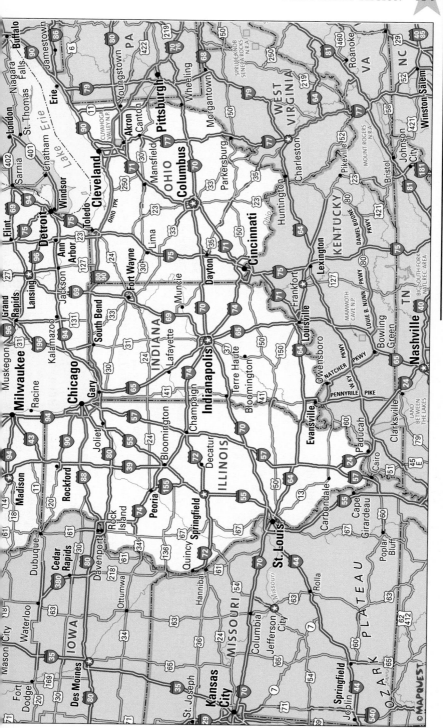

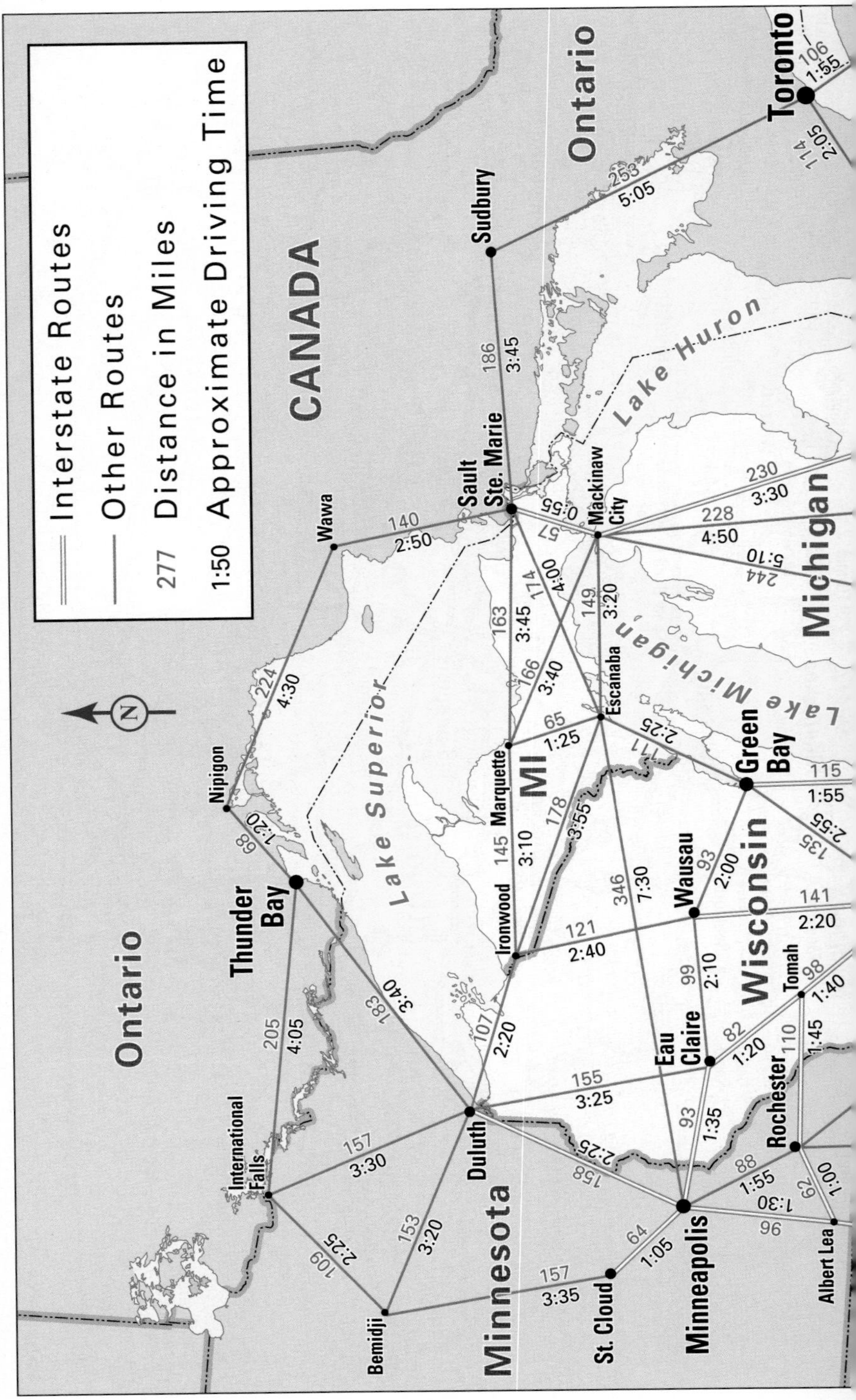
Interstate Routes
Other Routes
277 Distance in Miles
1:50 Approximate Driving Time
CANADA
Ontario
Ontario
Minnesota
Wisconsin
Michigan
MI
Lake Superior
Lake Michigan
Lake Huron
Thunder Bay
Nipigon
Wawa
Sault Ste. Marie
Sudbury
Toronto
Mackinaw City
Marquette
Escanaba
Green Bay
Ironwood
Wausau
Tomah
Eau Claire
Rochester
Albert Lea
Minneapolis
St. Cloud
Bemidji
Duluth
International Falls
88 1:20
224 4:30
140 2:50
186 3:45
253 5:05
106 1:55
114 2:05
0:55 57
230 3:30
228 4:50
244 5:10
163 3:45
174 4:00
149 3:20
166 3:40
65 1:25
111 2:25
115 1:55
135 2:55
145 3:10
178 3:55
346 7:30
93 2:00
121 2:40
141 2:20
99 2:10
98 1:40
82 1:20
110 1:45
205 4:05
183 3:40
107 2:20
155 3:25
158 2:25
93 1:35
157 3:30
153 3:20
109 2:25
157 3:35
64 1:05
88 1:55
96 1:30
62 1:00

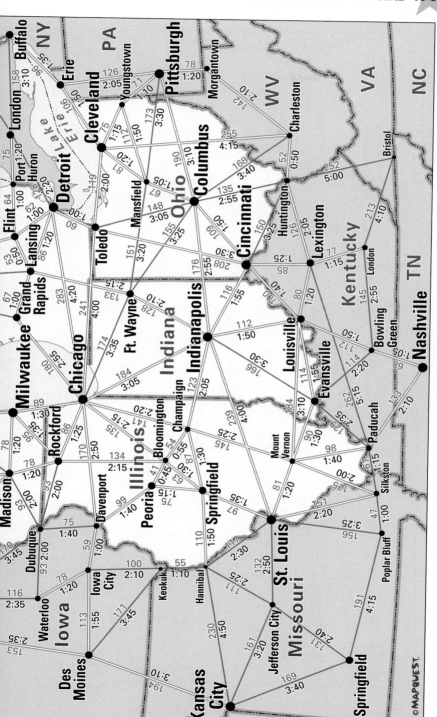

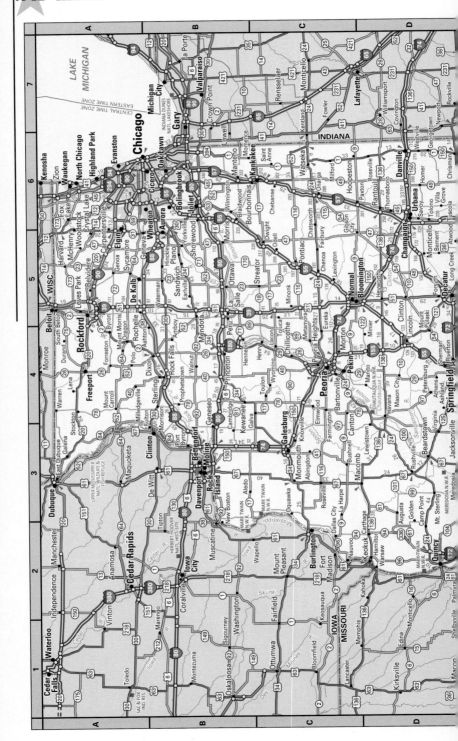

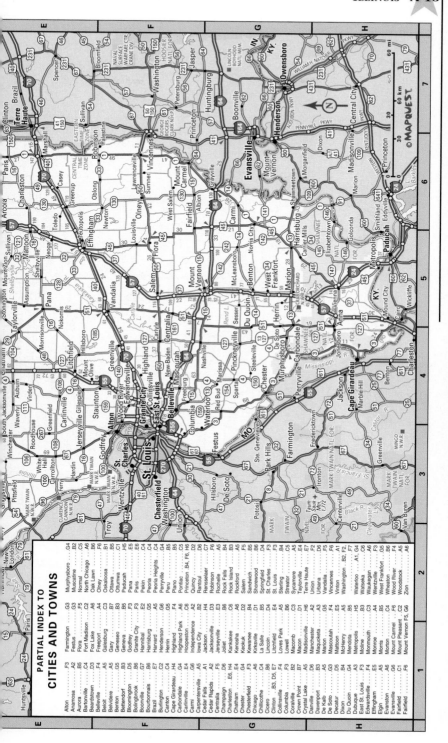

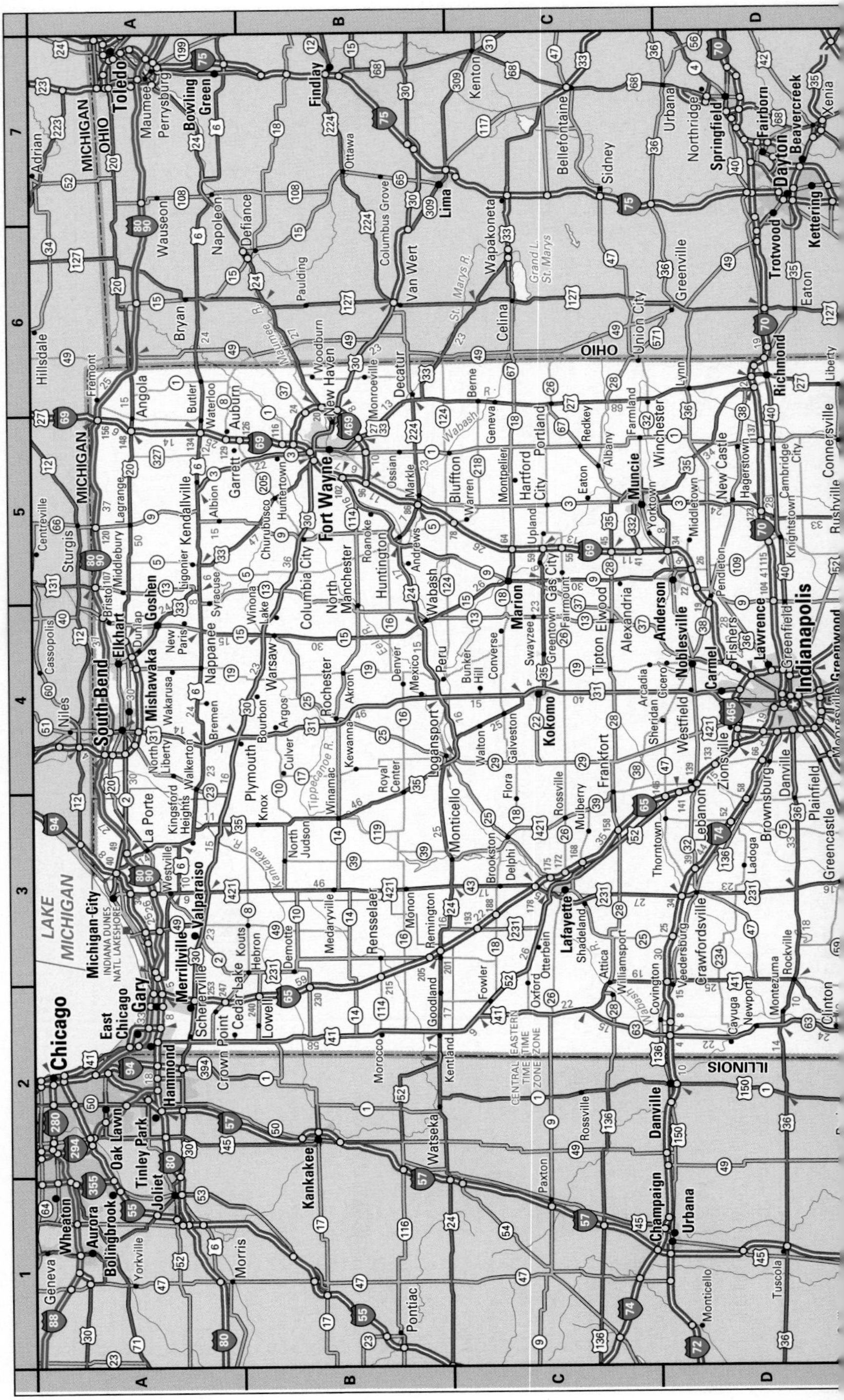
LAKE MICHIGAN
MICHIGAN
OHIO
INDIANA DUNES NATL. LAKESHORE
CENTRAL TIME ZONE
EASTERN TIME ZONE
ILLINOIS
Chicago
East Chicago
Gary
Hammond
Michigan City
Merrillville
Valparaiso
La Porte
South Bend
Mishawaka
Elkhart
Goshen
Niles
Sturgis
Kendallville
Angola
Auburn
Garrett
Fort Wayne
New Haven
Huntington
Wabash
Warsaw
Plymouth
Rochester
Logansport
Peru
Kokomo
Marion
Muncie
Anderson
Noblesville
Carmel
Lawrence
Indianapolis
Lafayette
Frankfort
Lebanon
Crawfordsville
Danville
Champaign
Urbana
Kankakee
Joliet
Toledo
Bowling Green
Findlay
Defiance
Lima
Van Wert
Decatur
Celina
Wapakoneta
Sidney
Springfield
Dayton
Richmond
Kettering

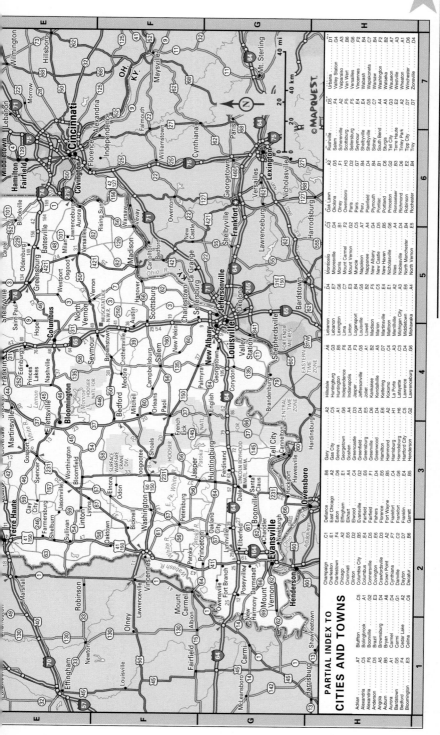

PARTIAL INDEX TO
CITIES AND TOWNS

Adrian	H6
Albion	H5
Allendale	G4
Alma	G5
Alpena	D6
Amherstburg	H7
Angola	H5
Ann Arbor	H5
Battle Creek	G5
Bay City	F6
Belding	G5
Bellevue	G5
Benton Harbor	G4
Big Rapids	F4
Brighton	G6
Burton	G6
Cadillac	E4
Calumet City	H2
Charlotte	G5
Chicago	H2
Cicero	H2
Coldwater	H5
Connorville	B7
Cutlerville	G4
Davison	F6
Dearborn	E2
Detroit	G7
Dowagiac	H4

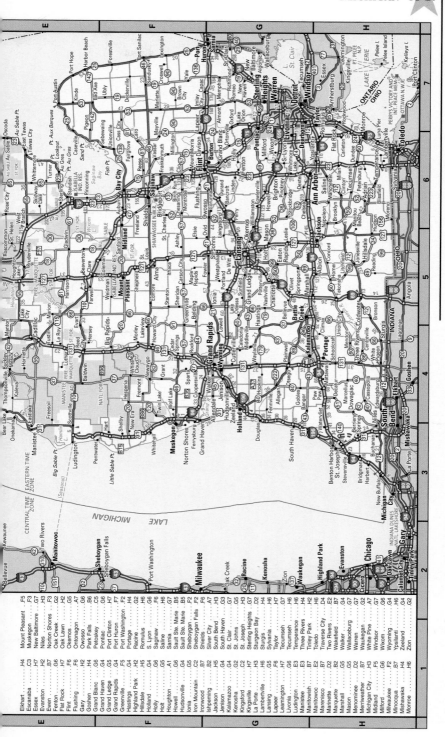

Elkhart F5
Escanaba C3
Essex H7
Evanston H2
Ewen B2
Fenton G6
Flat Rock H7
Flint F6
Flushing F6
Gary A7
Goshen F5
Grand Blanc G6
Grand Haven G4
Grand Ledge G5
Grand Rapids F5
Greenville F5
Hastings H4
Highland Park H2
Hillsdale G6
Holland G4
Holly G5
Holt F6
Houghton A1
Howell G6
Hudsonville G4
Ionia G5
Iron Mountain C2
Ironwood B2
Ishpeming B2
Jackson H5
Jenison G4
Kalamazoo G6
Kenosha H2
Kingsford C2
Kingsville H7
La Porte H3
Lambertville H6
Lansing F6
Lapeer F6
Leamington H7
Livonia H6
Ludington E4
Manistee E3
Manistique C3
Manitowoc E2
Marinette D4
Marlette B7
Marquette B2
Marshall G5
Mason G5
Menominee D2
Merriweather B2
Michigan City H3
Midland F5
Milford G6
Milwaukee F2
Minocqua A7
Mishawaka H4
Monroe H6

Mount Pleasant F5
Muskegon F3
New Baltimore H3
Niles H3
Norton Shores G4
Oak Creek F3
Oak Lawn G2
Okemos G5
Ontonagon A7
Owosso F6
Park Falls B6
Petoskey C5
Pontiac G6
Port Clinton G5
Port Huron F7
Port Washington F2
Portage G4
Racine G2
Romulus H6
S. Lyon G6
Saginaw F6
Saline H6
Sarnia G6
Sault Ste. Marie A5
Sault Ste. Marie B5
Sheboygan E2
Sheboygan Falls F2
Shields F6
Silver City B7
South Bend H3
South Haven G3
St. Clair G7
St. Joseph H3
Sterling Heights H3
Sturgis H5
Sturgeon Bay D2
Sylvania H6
Taylor F6
Tecumseh H7
Temperance H6
Three Rivers H4
Tinley Park H2
Toledo H6
Traverse City D4
Two Rivers E2
Walkerville B7
Walker F5
Wallaceburg G7
Warren H6
Waukegan H2
White Pine B7
Windsor H6
Wixom G6
Wyoming G4
Ypsilanti H6
Zeeland G4
Zion H6

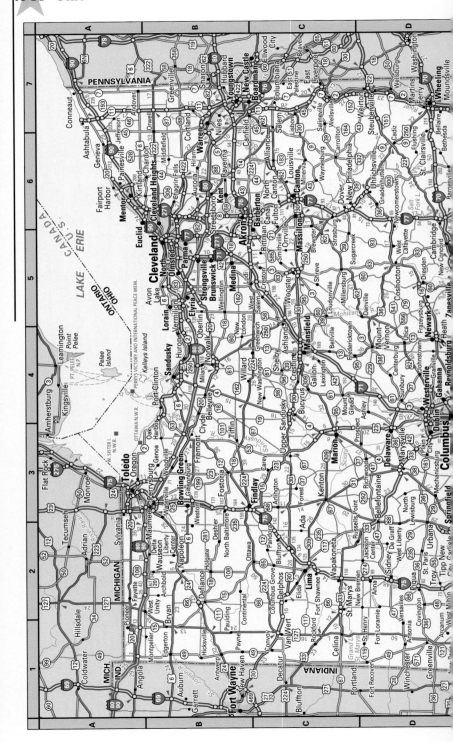

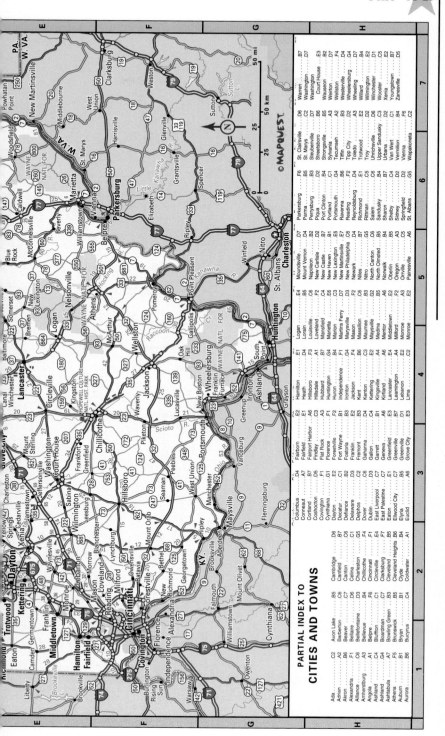

PARTIAL INDEX TO
CITIES AND TOWNS

Ada	C2	Cambridge	D6	Columbus	D4	Fairborn	D4	Hamilton	E2	Logan	E4	Parkersburg	D7	St. Clairsville	F6	Warren	B7
Adrian	A2	Canfield	B7	Conneaut	A7	Fairfield	E1	Heath	D4	Lorain	B5	Parma	B5	St. Marys	C2	Washington	D4
Akron	B6	Canton	C6	Cortland	B7	Fairport Harbor	A6	Hillsboro	F3	Louisville	C6	Perrysburg	B2	Steubenville	D7	Washington
Alexandria	D4	Celina	C1	Coshocton	D5	Findlay	C3	Hillsdale	C3	Loveland	E2	Piqua	D2	Strongsville	B6	Court House	D4
Alliance	C6	Charleston	G5	Covington	D2	Flat Rock	A3	Hubbard	B7	Mansfield	C4	Port Clinton	B4	Sylvania	A2	Wauseon	E3
Amherstburg	A3	Chillicothe	E4	Cynthiana	G1	Florence	G1	Huntington	G4	Marietta	E5	Portland	C1	Tecumseh	A2	Weirton	D7
Angola	B1	Cincinnati	E1	Dayton	D2	Forestville	F2	Huron	B4	Marion	C3	Portsmouth	F4	Tiffin	B3	Wellston	F4
Ashland	A3	Circleville	D4	Decatur	F2	Fort Wayne	C1	Independence	B5	Martins Ferry	D7	Ravenna	B6	Tippe City	D2	Wellsville	C6
Ashland	G4	Clarksburg	F7	Defiance	B2	Fostoria	B3	Ironton	G4	Martinsville	F1	Reading	E2	Toledo	A3	West Union	F3
Ashtabula	A7	Cleveland	B5	Delaware	D3	Franklin	D3	Jackson	F4	Marysville	C3	Reynoldsburg	D4	Trotwood	D2	Wheelersburg	G4
Athens	F5	Cleveland Heights	B6	Delphos	C2	Fremont	B3	Kent	B6	Mason	E2	Richmond	D4	Troy	D2	Wheeling	D7
Auburn	B4	Clyde	B4	Dover	C6	Gahanna	D4	Kenton	C3	Massillon	C6	Rittman	C5	Upper Sandusky	C3	Willard	B4
Aurora	B6	Coldwater	C4	East Liverpool	C7	Gallipolis	F5	Kettering	D2	Massillon	B6	Salem	C6	Urbana	D3	Wilmington	E3
Avon Lake	B5			East Palestine	C7	Garrett	C1	Kingsville	A6	Maumee	B3	Sandusky	B4	Van Wert	C1	Winchester	F3
Barberton	B6			Eaton	D1	Geneva	A6	Kirtland	A6	Mentor	A6	Sharon	B7	Vermilion	B4	Wooster	C5
Beaver	C7			Ellwood City	B7	Greenfield	E3	Lancaster	E4	Middletown	E2	Shelby	C4	Vienna	D2	Xenia	D3
Bellaire	F1			Elyria	B5	Greenville	D1	Leamington	A4	Milford	E2	Sidney	D2	Vienna	B7	Youngstown	B7
Bellefontaine	D2			Euclid	B5	Greenville	C1	Lebanon	E2	Monroe	A3	Springfield	D3	Wapakoneta	C2	Zanesville	D5
Belpre	D6					Grove City	D4	Lima	C2	Monroe	C2	St. Albans	G5		
Bluffton	C2														
Boardman	B7														
Bowling Green	B3														
Brunswick	B6														
Bryan	A1														
Bucyrus	C4														

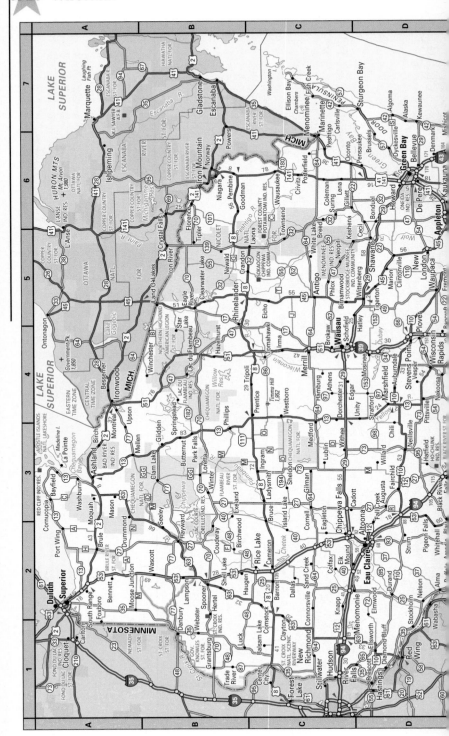

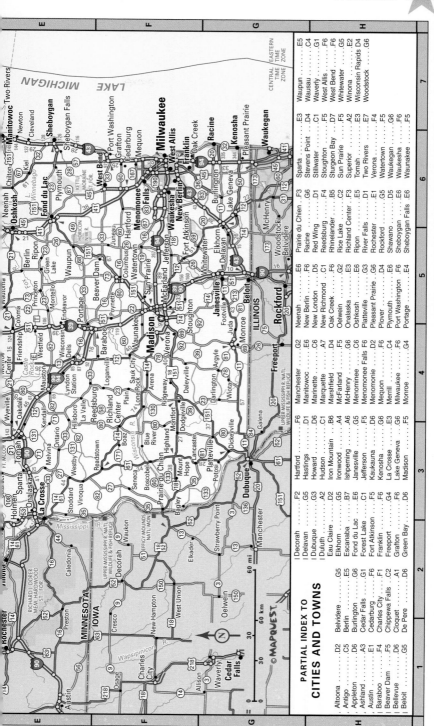

MAP LEGEND

TRANSPORTATION

CONTROLLED ACCESS HIGHWAYS

- Free
- Toll; Toll Booth
- Under Construction
- Interchange and Exit Number
- Ramp
  Downtown maps only

OTHER HIGHWAYS

- Primary Highway
- Secondary Highway
- Multilane Divided Highway
  Primary and secondary highways only
- Other Paved Road
- Unpaved Road
  Check conditions locally

HIGHWAY MARKERS

- Interstate Route
- US Route
- State or Provincial Route
- County or Other Route
- Business Route
- Trans-Canada Highway
- Canadian Provincial Autoroute
- Mexican Federal Route

OTHER SYMBOLS

- Distances Along Major Highways
  Miles in US; kilometers in Canada and Mexico
- Tunnel; Pass
- One-Way Street
- Airport
- Railroad
  Downtown maps only
- Auto Ferry; Passenger Ferry

RECREATION AND FEATURES OF INTEREST

- National Park
- National Forest; National Grassland
- Other Large Park or Recreation Area
- Military Lands
- Indian Reservation
- Small State Park with and without Camping
- Public Campsite
- Trail
- Point of Interest
- Golf Course
  Professional tournament location
- Hospital
  City maps only
- Ski Area

CITIES AND TOWNS

- National Capital; State or Provincial Capital
- County Seat
  State maps only
- Cities, Towns, and Populated Places
  Type size indicates relative importance
- Urban Area
  State and province maps only
- Large Incorporated Cities

OTHER MAP FEATURES

- County Boundary and Name
  JEFFERSON
- Time Zone Boundary
- Mountain Peak; Elevation
  Feet in US; meters in Canada and Mexico
  + Mt. Olympus
    7,965
- Perennial; Intermittent River
- Perennial; Intermittent or Dry Water Body
- Dam
- Swamp

It pays for all kinds of fuel.

Speedpass: today's way to pay. Don't go on the road without *Speedpass*. You can pay for gas at the pump or just about anything inside our store. It's fast, free, and links to a check card or major credit card you already have. To join the millions who use *Speedpass*, call **1-87-SPEEDPASS** or visit speedpass.com.

We're drivers too.

With the right gas, a kid could go pretty far.

Next time you stop at an Exxon or Mobil station, consider a new destination: college. ExxonMobil is working with Upromise to help you save for a child's education. How do you start saving? Just join at upromise.com and register your credit cards. It's FREE to join. Then when you buy Exxon or Mobil gas with a credit card registered with Upromise, one cent per gallon will be contributed to your Upromise account.* This account helps you pay for the college education of any child you choose. Contributions from other Upromise participants, like GM, AT&T and Toys"R"Us, are also added to this account.** One more thing: be sure to register the credit card you linked to your *Speedpass*. That way, *Speedpass* gasoline purchases can also contribute to your account. To get your FREE *Speedpass*, go to speedpass.com or call toll free 1-87-SPEEDPASS. Upromise is an easy way to help you save for a child's education. How do we know? We're drivers too.

Join Upromise for FREE at upromise.com
For your FREE *Speedpass*, call 1-87-SPEEDPASS
or visit speedpass.com.

 Mobil

We're drivers too.

WELCOME

Dear Traveler,

Since its inception in 1958, Mobil Travel Guide has served as a trusted aid to auto travelers in search of value in lodging, dining, and destinations. Now in its 45th year, Mobil Travel Guide is the hallmark of our ExxonMobil family of travel publications, and we're proud to offer an array of products and services from our Mobil, Exxon, and Esso brands in North America to facilitate life on the road.

Whether business or pleasure venues, our nationwide network of independent, professional evaluators offers their expertise on thousands of travel options, allowing you to plan a quick family getaway, a full-service business meeting, or an unforgettable Five-Star celebration.

Your feedback is important to us as we strive to improve our product offerings and better meet today's travel needs. Whether you travel once a week or once a year, please take the time to complete the customer feedback form at the back of this book. Or, contact us at www.mobiltravelguide.com. We hope to hear from you soon.

Best wishes for safe and enjoyable travels.

Lee R. Raymond
Chairman
Exxon Mobil Corporation

A WORD TO
OUR READERS

In this day and age the travel industry is ever-changing, and having accurate, reliable travel information is indispensable. Travelers are back on the roads in enormous numbers. They are going on day trips, long weekends, extended family vacations, and business trips. They are traveling across the country- stopping at National Parks, major cities, small towns, monuments, and landmarks. And for 45 years, the Mobil Travel Guide has been providing this invaluable service to the traveling consumer and is committed to continuing this service well into the future.

You, the traveler, deserve the best food and accommodations available in every city, town, or village you visit. But finding suitable accommodations can be problematic. You could try to meet and ask local residents about appropriate places to stay and eat, but that time-consuming option comes with no guarantee of getting the best advice.

The Mobil Travel Guide One- to Five-Star rating system is the oldest and most respected lodging and restaurant inspection and rating program in North America. This trusted, well-established tool directs you to satisfying places to eat and stay, as well as to interesting events and attractions in thousands of locations. Mobil Corporation (now known as Exxon Mobil Corporation, following a 1999 merger) began producing the Mobil Travel Guides in 1958, following the introduction of the US Highway system in 1956. The first edition covered only 5 southwestern states. Since then, the Mobil Travel Guide has become the premier travel guide in North America, covering the 48 contiguous states and major cities in Canadian provinces. Now, ExxonMobil presents the latest edition of our annual Travel Guides series.

For the past 45 years, Mobil Travel Guide has been inspecting and rating lodging and restaurants throughout the United States and Canada. Each restaurant, motel, hotel, inn, resort, guest ranch, etc., is inspected and must meet the basic requirements of cleanliness and service to be included in the Mobil Travel Guide. Highly trained quality assurance team members travel across the country generating exhaustive inspections reports. Mobil Travel Guide management's careful scrutiny of findings detailed in the inspection reports, incognito inspections, where we dine in the restaurant and stay overnight at the lodging to gauge the level of service of the hotel and restaurant, review of our extensive files of reader comments and letters are all used in the final ratings determinations. All of this information is used to arrive at fair, accurate, and useful assessments of lodgings and restaurants. Based upon these elements, Mobil Travel Guide determines those establishments eligible for listing. Only facilities meeting Mobil Travel Guide standards of cleanliness, maintenance and stable management are listed in the Guide. Deteriorating, poorly managed establishments are deleted. A listing in the Mobil Travel Guide constitutes a positive quality recommendation; every rating is an accolade; a recognition of achievement. Once an establishment is chosen for a listing, Mobil's respected and world-famous one- to five-star rating system highlights their distinguishing characteristics.

Although the ten-book set allows us to include many more hotels, restaurants, and attractions than in past years, space limitations still make it impossible for us to include every hotel, motel, and restaurant in America. Instead, our database consists of a generous, representative sampling, with information about places that are above-average in their type. In essence, you can confidently patronize any of the restaurants, places of lodging, and attractions contained in the *Mobil Travel Guide* series.

What do we mean by "representative sampling"? You'll find that the *Mobil Travel Guide* books include information about a great variety of establishments. Perhaps you favor rustic lodgings and restaurants, or perhaps you're most comfortable with elegance and high style. Money may be no object or, like most of us, you may be on a budget. Some travelers place a high premium on 24-hour room service or special menu items. Others look for quiet seclusion. Whatever your travel needs and desires, they will be reflected in the *Mobil Travel Guide* listings.

Allow us to emphasize that we have charged no establishment for inclusion in our guides. We have no relationship with any of the businesses and attractions we list and act only as a consumer advocate. In essence, we do the investigative legwork so you won't have to.

Look over the "How to Use This Book" section that follows. You'll discover just how simple it is to quickly and easily gather all the information you need—before your trip or while on the road. For terrific tips on saving money, travel safety, and other ways to get the most out of your travels, be sure to read our special section, "Making the Most of Your Trip."

Keep in mind that the hospitality business is ever-changing. Restaurants and places of lodging—particularly small chains or stand-alone establishments—can change management or even go out of business with surprising quickness. Although we have made every effort to double-check information during our annual updates, we nevertheless recommend that you call ahead to be sure a place you have selected is open and still offers all the features you want. Phone numbers are provided, and, when available, we also list fax and Web site information.

We hope that all your travel experiences are easy and relaxing. If any aspects of your accommodations or dining motivate you to comment, please drop us a line. We depend a great deal on our readers' remarks, so you can be assured that we will read and assimilate your comments into our research. General comments about our books are also welcome. You can write us at Mobil Travel Guides,

1460 Renaissance Drive, Suite 401, Park Ridge, IL 60068, or send email to info@mobiltravelguide.com.

Take your *Mobil Travel Guide* books along on every trip. You'll be pleased by their convenience, ease of use, and breadth of dependable coverage.

Happy travels in the new millennium!

EDITORIAL CONTRIBUTOR AND CONSULTANT FOR DRIVING TOURS, WALKING TOURS, ATTRACTIONS, EVENTS, AND PHOTOGRAPHY:

Mike Michaelson is a writer and editor whose specialty is Midwest travel. His weekly travel page "Around the Midwest" appears in the Sunday Travel section of the *Daily Herald, Post-Tribune,* and *The Des Moines Register.* He is the author of several travel titles including the *Weekend Getaway* series and the *Best-Kept Secrets* series (with titles for Chicago, New York, and London). His travel articles appear regularly in national magazines, including *National Geographic Traveler* and *Midwest Living.*

How to Use This Book

The *Mobil Travel Guides* are designed for ease of use. Each state has its own chapter. The chapter begins with a general introduction, which provides both a general geographical and historical orientation to the state; it also covers basic statewide tourist information, from state recreation areas to seatbelt laws. The remainder of each chapter is devoted to the travel destinations within the state—cities and towns, state and national parks, and tourist areas—which, like the states, are arranged alphabetically.

The following is an explanation of the wealth of information you'll find regarding those travel destinations—information on the area, on things to see and do there, and on where to stay and eat.

Maps and Map Coordinates

Next to most destinations is a set of map coordinates. These are referenced to the appropriate state map in the front of this book. In addition, we have provided maps of selected larger cities.

Destination Information

Because many travel destinations are close to other cities and towns where visitors might find additional attractions, accommodations, and restaurants, cross-references to those places are included whenever possible. Also listed are addresses and phone numbers for travel information resources—usually the local chamber of commerce or office of tourism—as well as pertinent vital statistics and a brief introduction to the area.

What to See and Do

Almost 20,000 museums, art galleries, amusement parks, universities, historic sites and houses, plantations, churches, state parks, ski areas, and other attractions are described in the *Mobil Travel Guides*. A white star on a red background ✪ signals that the attraction is one of the best in the state. Because municipal parks, public tennis courts, swimming pools, and small educational institutions are common to most towns, they are generally not represented within the city.

Following the attraction's description, you'll find the months and days it's open, address/location and phone number, and admission costs (see the inside front cover for an explanation of the cost symbols). Note that directions are given from the center of the town under which the attraction is listed, which may not necessarily be the town in which the attraction is located. Zip codes are listed only if they differ from those given for the town.

Driving and Walking Tours

The driving tours are usually day trips—though they can be longer—that make for interesting side trips. This is a way to get off the beaten track and visit an area often overlooked. These trips frequently cover areas of natural beauty or historical significance. The walking tours focus on a particularly interesting area of a city or town. Again, these can be a break from more everyday tourist attractions. The tours often include places to stop for a meal or snack.

Special Events

Special events can either be annual events that last only a short time, such as festivals and fairs, or longer, seasonal events such as horse racing, summer theater and concerts, and professional sports. Special event listings might also include an infrequently occurring occasion that marks a certain date or event, such as a centennial or other commemorative celebration.

Major Cities

Additional information on airports and ground transportation, and suburbs may be included for large cities.

Lodging and Restaurant Listings

ORGANIZATION

For both lodgings and restaurants, when a property is in a town that does not have its own heading, the listing appears under the town nearest its location with the address and town immediately after the establishment name. In large cities, lodgings located within five miles of major commercial airports are listed under a separate "Airport" heading, following the city listings.

LODGING CLASSIFICATIONS

Each property is classified by type according to the characteristics below. Because the following features and services are found at most motels and hotels, they are not shown in those listings:

- Year-round operation with a single rate structure unless otherwise quoted
- European plan (meals not included in room rate)
- Bathroom with tub and/or shower in each room
- Air-conditioned/heated, often with individual room control
- Cots
- Daily maid service
- In-room phones
- Elevators

Motels/Motor Lodges. Accommodations are in low-rise structures with rooms easily accessible to parking (which is usually free). Properties have outdoor room entry and small, functional lobbies. Service is often limited, and dining may not be offered in lower-rated motels and lodges. Shops and businesses are found only in higher-rated properties, as are bellhops, room service, and restaurants serving three meals daily.

Hotels. To be categorized as a hotel, an establishment must have most of the following facilities and services: multiple floors, a restaurant and/or coffee shop, elevators, room service, bellhops, a spacious lobby, and recreational facilities. In addition, the following features and services not shown in listings are also found:

- Valet service (one-day laundry/cleaning service)
- Room service during hours restaurant is open
- Bellhops
- Some oversize beds

Resorts. These specialize in stays of three days or more and usually offer American plan and/or housekeeping accommodations. Their emphasis is on recreational facilities, and a social director is often available. Food services are of primary importance, and guests must be able to eat three meals a day on the premises, either in restaurants or by having access to an on-site grocery store and preparing their own meals.

All Suites. All Suites' guest rooms consist of two rooms, one bedroom and one living room. Higher rated properties offer facilities and services comparable to regular hotels.

B&Bs/Small Inns. Frequently thought of as a small hotel, a bed-and-breakfast or an inn is a place of homelike comfort and warm hospitality. It is often a structure of historic significance, with an equally interesting setting. Meals are a special occasion, and refreshments are frequently served in late afternoon. Rooms are usually individually decorated, often with antiques or furnishings representative of the locale. Phones, bathrooms, or TVs may not be available in every room.

Guest Ranches. Like resorts, guest ranches specialize in stays of three days or more. Guest ranches also offer meal plans and extensive outdoor activities. Horseback riding is usually a feature; there are stables and trails on the ranch property, and trail rides and daily instruction are part of the program. Many guest ranches are working ranches, ranging from casual to rustic, and guests are encouraged to participate in ranch life. Eating is often family style and may also include cookouts. Western saddles are assumed; phone ahead to inquire about English saddle availability.

Extended Stay. These hotels specialize in stays of three days or more and usually offer weekly room rates. Service is often limited and dining might not be offered at lower-rated extended-stay hotels.

Villas/Condos. Similar to Cottage Colonies, these establishments are usually found in recreational areas. They are often separate houses, often luxuriously furnished, and rarely offer restaurants and only a small variety of services on the premises.

Conference Centers. Conference Centers are hotels with extended meeting space facilities designed to house multiday conferences and seminars. Amenities are often geared toward groups staying for longer than one night and often include restaurants and fitness facilities. Larger Conference Center Hotels are often referred to as Convention Center Hotels.

Casinos. Casino Hotels incorporate areas that offer games of chance like Blackjack, Poker, Slot machines, etc. and are only found in states that legalize gambling. Casino Hotels offer a wide range of services and amenities, comparable to regular hotels.

Cottage Colonies. These are housekeeping cottages and cabins that are usually found in recreational areas. Any dining or recreational facilities are noted in our listing.

DINING CLASSIFICATIONS

Restaurants. Most dining establishments fall into this category. All have a full kitchen and offer table service and a complete menu. Parking on or near the premises, in a lot or garage, is assumed. When a property offers valet or other special parking features, or when only street parking is available, it is noted in the listing.

Unrated Dining Spots. These places, listed after Restaurants in many cities, are chosen for their unique atmosphere, specialized menu, or local flavor. They include delis, ice-cream parlors, cafeterias, tearooms, and pizzerias. Because they may not have a full kitchen or table service, they are not given a *Mobil Travel Guides* rating. Often they offer extraordinary value and quick service.

QUALITY RATINGS

The *Mobil Travel Guides* have been rating lodgings and restaurants on a national basis since the first edition was published in 1958. For years the guide was the only source of such ratings, and it remains among the few guidebooks to rate restaurants across the country.

All listed establishments were inspected by experienced field representatives or evaluated by a senior staff member. Ratings are based upon their detailed inspection reports of the individual properties, on written evaluations of staff members who stay and dine anonymously, and on an extensive review of comments from our readers.

You'll find a key to the rating categories, ★ through ★★★★★, on the inside front cover. All establishments in the book are recommended. Even a ★ place is clean, convenient, limited service, usually providing a basic, informal experience. Rating categories reflect both the features the property offers and its quality in relation to similar establishments.

For example, lodging ratings take into account the number and quality of facilities and services, the luxury of appointments, and the attitude and professionalism of staff and management. A ★ establishment provides a comfortable night's lodging. A ★★ property offers more than a facility that rates one star, and the decor is well planned and integrated. Establishments that rate ★★★ are well-appointed, with full service and amenities; the lodging experience is truly excellent, and the range of facilities is extensive. Properties that have been given ★★★★ not only offer many services but also have their own style and personality; they are luxurious, creatively decorated, and superbly maintained. The ★★★★★ properties are among the best in North America, superb in every respect and entirely memorable, year in and year out.

Restaurant evaluations reflect the quality of the food and the ingredients, preparation, presentation, service levels, as well as the property's decor and ambience. A restaurant that has fairly simple goals for menu and decor but that achieves those goals superbly might receive the same number of stars as a restaurant with somewhat loftier ambitions, but the execution of which falls short of the mark. In general, ★ indicates a restaurant that's a good choice in its area, usually fairly simple and perhaps catering to a clientele of locals and families; ★★ denotes restaurants that are more highly recommended in their area;

★★★ restaurants are of national caliber, with professional and attentive service and a skilled chef in the kitchen; ★★★★ reflect superb dining choices, where remarkable food is served in equally remarkable surroundings; and ★★★★★ represent that rare group of the best restaurants in the country, where in addition to near perfection in every detail, there's that special something extra that makes for an unforgettable dining experience.

A list of the four-star and five-star establishments in each region is located just before the state listings.

Each rating is reviewed annually and each establishment must work to maintain its rating (or improve it). Every effort is made to assure that ratings are fair and accurate; the designated ratings are published purely as an aid to travelers. In general, properties that are very new or have recently undergone major management changes are considered difficult to assess fairly and are often listed without ratings.

LODGINGS

Each listing gives the name, address, directions (when there is no street address), neighborhood and/or directions from downtown (in major cities), phone number (local and 800), fax number, number and type of rooms available, room rates, and seasons open (if not year-round). Also included are details on recreational and dining facilities on the property or nearby, the presence of a luxury level, and credit card information. A key to the symbols at the end of each listing is on the inside front cover. (Note that Exxon or Mobil Corporation credit cards cannot be used for payment of meals and room charges.)

All prices quoted in the *Mobil Travel Guide* publications are expected to be in effect at the time of publication and during the entire year; however, prices cannot be guaranteed. In some localities there may be short-term price variations because of special events or holidays. Whenever possible, these price charges are noted. Certain resorts have complicated rate structures that vary with the time of year; always confirm listed rates when you make your plans.

RESTAURANTS

Each listing gives the name, address, directions (when there is no street address), neighborhood and/or directions from downtown (in major cities), phone number, hours and days of operation (if not open daily year-round), reservation policy, cuisine (if other than American), price range for each meal served, children's menu (if offered), specialties, and credit card information. In addition, special features such as chef ownership, ambience, and entertainment are noted. By carefully reading the detailed restaurant information and comparing prices, you can easily determine whether the restaurant is formal and elegant or informal and comfortable for families.

TERMS AND ABBREVIATIONS IN LISTINGS

The following terms and abbreviations are used throughout the listings:

A la carte entrees With a price, refers to the cost of entrees/main dishes that are not accompanied by side dishes.

AP American plan (lodging plus all meals).

Bar Liquor, wine, and beer are served in a bar or cocktail lounge and usually with meals unless otherwise indicated (e.g., "wine, beer").

Business center The property has a designated area accessible to all guests with business services.

Business servs avail The property can perform/arrange at least two of the following services for a guest: audiovisual equipment rental, binding, computer rental, faxing, messenger services, modem availability, notary service, obtaining office supplies, photocopying, shipping, and typing.

Cable Standard cable service; "premium" indicates that HBO, Disney, Showtime, or similar cable services are available.

Ck-in, ck-out Check-in time, check-out time.

Coin lndry Self-service laundry.

Complete meal Soup and/or salad, entree, and dessert, plus nonalcoholic beverage.

Continental bkfst Usually coffee and a roll or doughnut.

Cr cds: A, American Express; C, Carte Blanche; D, Diners Club; DS, Discover; ER, enRoute; JCB, Japanese Credit Bureau; MC, MasterCard; V, Visa.

D Followed by a price, indicates room rate for a "double"—two people in one room in one or two beds (the charge may be higher for two double beds).

Downhill/X-country ski Downhill and/or cross-country skiing within 20 miles of property.

Each addl Extra charge for each additional person beyond the stated number of persons at a reduced price.

Early-bird dinner A meal served at specified hours, typically around 4:30-6:30 pm.

Exc Except.

Exercise equipt Two or more pieces of exercise equipment on the premises.

Exercise rm Both exercise equipment and room, with an instructor on the premises.

Fax Facsimile machines available to all guests.

Golf privileges Privileges at a course within ten miles.

Hols Holidays.

In-rm modem link Every guest room has a connection for a modem that's separate from the phone line.

Kit. or **Kits.** A kitchen or kitchenette that contains stove or microwave, sink, and refrigerator and that is either part of the room or a separate room. If the kitchen is not fully equipped, the listing will indicate "no equipt" or "some equipt."

Luxury level A special section of a lodging, covering at least an entire floor, that offers increased luxury accommodations. Management must provide no less than three of these four services: separate check-in and check-out, concierge, private lounge, and private elevator service (key access). Complimentary breakfast and snacks are commonly offered.

MAP Modified American plan (lodging plus two meals).

Movies Prerecorded videos are available for rental.

No cr cds accepted No credit cards are accepted.

No elvtr In hotels with more than two stories, it's assumed there are elevators; only their absence is noted.

No phones Phones, too, are assumed; only their absence is noted.

Parking There is a parking lot on the premises.

Private club A cocktail lounge or bar available to members and their guests. In motels and hotels where these clubs exist, registered guests can usually use the club as guests of the management; the same is frequently true of restaurants.

Prix fixe A full meal for a stated price; usually one price is quoted.

Res Reservations.

S Followed by a price, indicates room rate for a "single," i.e., one person.

Serv bar A service bar, where drinks are prepared for dining patrons only.

Serv charge Service charge is the amount added to the restaurant check in lieu of a tip.

Table d'hôte A full meal for a stated price, dependent upon entree selection; no a la carte options are available.

Tennis privileges Privileges at tennis courts within five miles.

TV Indicates color television.

Under certain age free Children under that age are not charged if staying in room with a parent.

Valet parking An attendant is available to park and retrieve a car.

VCR VCRs in all guest rooms.

VCR avail VCRs are available for hookup in guest rooms.

Special Information for Travelers with Disabilities

The *Mobil Travel Guides* D symbol shown in accommodation and restaurant listings indicates establishments that are at least partially accessible to people with mobility problems.

The *Mobil Travel Guides* criteria for accessibility are unique to our publication. Please do not confuse them with the universal symbol for wheelchair accessibility. When the D symbol appears following a listing, the establishment is equipped with facilities to accommodate people using wheelchairs or crutches or otherwise needing easy access to doorways and rest rooms. Travelers with severe mobility problems or with hearing or visual impairments may or may not find facilities they need. Always phone ahead to make sure that an establishment can meet your needs.

All lodgings bearing our D symbol have the following facilities:

- ISA-designated parking near access ramps
- Level or ramped entryways to building
- Swinging building entryway doors minimum 39"
- Public rest rooms on main level with space to operate a wheelchair; handrails at commode areas
- Elevators equipped with grab bars and lowered control buttons
- Restaurants with accessible doorways; rest rooms with space to operate wheelchair; handrails at commode areas
- Minimum 39" width entryway to guest rooms
- Low-pile carpet in rooms
- Telephone at bedside and in bathroom
- Bed placed at wheelchair height

- Minimum 39" width doorway to bathroom
- Bath with open sink—no cabinet; room to operate wheelchair
- Handrails at commode areas; tub handrails
- Wheelchair-accessible peephole in room entry door
- Wheelchair-accessible closet rods and shelves

All restaurants bearing our D symbol offer the following facilities:

- ISA-designated parking beside access ramps
- Level or ramped front entryways to building
- Tables to accommodate wheelchairs
- Main-floor rest rooms; minimum 39" width entryway
- Rest rooms with space to operate wheelchair; handrails at commode areas

In general, the newest properties are apt to impose the fewest barriers.

To get the kind of service you need and have a right to expect, do not hesitate when making a reservation to question the management in detail about the availability of accessible rooms, parking, entrances, restaurants, lounges, or any other facilities that are important to you, and confirm what is meant by "accessible." Some guests with mobility impairments report that lodging establishments' housekeeping and maintenance departments are most helpful in describing barriers. Also inquire about any special equipment, transportation, or services you may need.

MAKING THE MOST OF YOUR TRIP

A few hardy souls might look with fondness upon the trip where the car broke down and they were stranded for a week. Or maybe even the vacation that cost twice what it was supposed to. For most travelers, though, the best trips are those that are safe, smooth, and within their budget. To help you make your trip the best it can be, we've assembled a few tips and resources.

Saving Money

ON LODGING

After you've seen the published rates, it's time to look for discounts. Many hotels and motels offer them—for senior citizens, business travelers, families, you name it. It never hurts to ask—politely, that is. Sometimes, especially in late afternoon, desk clerks are instructed to fill beds, and you might be offered a lower rate, or a nicer room, to entice you to stay. Look for bargains on stays over multiple nights, in the off-season, and on weekdays or weekends (depending on location). Many hotels in major metropolitan areas, for example, have special weekend package plans that offer considerable savings on rooms; they may include breakfast, cocktails, and meal discounts. Prices can change frequently throughout the year, so phone ahead.

Another way to save money is to choose accommodations that give you more than just a standard room. Rooms with kitchen facilities enable you to cook some meals for yourself, reducing restaurant costs. A suite might save money for two couples traveling together. Even hotel luxury levels can provide good value, as many include breakfast or cocktails in the price of the room.

State and city sales taxes, as well as special room taxes, can increase your room rates as much as 25 percent per day. We are unable to include this specific information in the listings, but we strongly urge that you ask about these taxes when placing reservations to understand the total cost of your lodgings.

Watch out for telephone-usage charges that hotels frequently impose on long-distance calls, credit-card calls, and other phone calls—even those that go unanswered. Before phoning from your room, read the information given to you at check-in, and then be sure to read your bill carefully before checking out. You won't be expected to pay for charges that they did not spell out. (On the other hand, it's not unusual for a hotel to bill you for your calls after you return home.) Consider using your cell phone; or, if public telephones are available in the hotel lobby, your cost savings may outweigh the inconvenience.

ON DINING

There are several ways to get a less expensive meal at a more expensive restaurant. Early-bird dinners are popular in many parts of the country and offer considerable savings. If you're interested in sampling a 4- or 5-star establishment, consider going at lunchtime. While the prices then are probably relatively high, they may be half of those at dinner and come with the same ambience, service, and cuisine.

ON PARK PASSES

Although many national parks, monuments, seashores, historic sites, and recreation areas may be used free of charge, others charge an entrance fee (ranging from $1 to $6 per person to $5 to $15 per carload) and/or a "use fee" for special services and facilities. If you plan to make several visits to federal recreation areas, consider one of the following National Park Service money-saving programs:

Park Pass. This is an annual entrance permit to a specific unit in the National Park Service system that normally charges an entrance fee. The pass admits the permit holder and any accompanying passengers in a private noncommercial vehicle or, in the case of walk-in facilities, the holder's spouse, children, and parents. It is valid for entrance fees only. A Park Pass may be purchased in person or by mail from the National Park Service unit at which the pass will be honored. The cost is $15 to $20, depending upon the area.

Golden Eagle Passport. This pass, available to people who are between 17 and 61, entitles the purchaser and accompanying passengers in a private noncommercial vehicle to enter any outdoor National Park Service unit that charges an entrance fee and admits the purchaser and family to most walk-in fee-charging areas. Like the Park Pass, it is good for one year and does not cover use fees. It may be purchased from the National Park Service, Office of Public Inquiries, Room 1013, US Department of the Interior, 18th and C sts NW, Washington, D.C. 20240, phone 202/208-4747; at any of the ten regional offices throughout the country; and at any National Park Service area that charges a fee. The cost is $50.

Golden Age Passport. Available to citizens and permanent residents of the United States 62 years or older, this is a lifetime entrance permit to fee-charging recreation areas. The fee exemption extends to those accompanying the permit holder in a private noncommercial vehicle or, in the case of walk-in facilities, to the holder's spouse and children. The passport also entitles the holder to a 50 percent discount on use fees charged in park areas but not to fees charged by concessionaires. Golden Age Passports must be obtained in person. The applicant must show proof of age, i.e., a driver's license, birth certificate, or signed affidavit attesting to age (Medicare cards are not acceptable proof). These passports are available at most park service units where they're used, at National Park Service headquarters (see above), at park system regional offices, at National Forest Supervisors' offices, and at most Ranger Station offices. The cost is $10.

Golden Access Passport. Issued to citizens and permanent residents of the United States who are physically disabled or visually impaired, this passport is a free lifetime entrance permit to fee-charging recreation areas. The fee exemption extends to those accompanying the permit holder in a private noncommercial vehicle or, in the case of walk-in facilities, to the holder's spouse and children. The passport also entitles the holder to a 50 percent discount on use fees charged in park areas but not to fees charged by concessionaires. Golden Access Passports must be obtained in person. Proof of eligibility to receive federal benefits is required (under programs such as Disability Retirement, Compensation for Military Service-Connected Disability, Coal Mine Safety and Health Act, etc.), or an affidavit must be signed attesting to eligibility. These passports are available at the same outlets as Golden Age Passports.

FOR SENIOR CITIZENS

Look for the senior-citizen discount symbol in the lodging and restaurant listings. Always call ahead to confirm that the discount is being offered, and be sure to carry proof of age. At places not listed in the book, it never hurts to ask if a senior-citizen discount is offered. Additional information for mature travelers is available from the American Association of Retired Persons (AARP), 601 E St NW, Washington, D.C. 20049, phone 202/434-2277.

Tipping

Tipping is an expression of appreciation for good service, and often service workers rely on tips as a significant part of their income. However, you never need to tip if service is poor.

IN HOTELS

Door attendants in major city hotels are usually given $1 for getting you a cab. Bellhops expect $1 per bag, usually $2 if you have only one bag. Concierges are tipped according to the service they perform. It's not mandatory to tip when you've asked for suggestions on sightseeing or restaurants or help in making reservations for dining. However, when a concierge books you a table at a restaurant known to be difficult to get into, a gratuity of $5 is appropriate. For obtaining theater or sporting event tickets, $5-$10 is expected. Maids, often overlooked by guests, may be tipped $1-$2 per days of stay.

AT RESTAURANTS

Coffee shop and counter service waitstaff are usually given 8 percent–10 percent of the bill. In full-service restaurants, tip 15 percent of the bill, before sales tax. In fine restaurants, where the staff is large and shares the gratuity, 18 percent–20 percent for the waiter is appropriate. In most cases, tip the maitre d' only if service has been extraordinary and only on the way out; $20 is the minimum in upscale properties in major metropolitan areas. If there is a wine steward, tip him or her at least $6 a bottle, more if the wine was decanted or if the bottle was very expensive. If your bus person has been unusually attentive, $2 pressed into his hand on departure is a nice gesture. An increasing number of restaurants automatically add a service charge to the bill instead of a gratuity. Before tipping, carefully review your check. If you are in doubt, ask your server.

AT AIRPORTS

Curbside luggage handlers expect $1 per bag. Car-rental shuttle drivers who help with your luggage appreciate a $1 or $2 tip.

Staying Safe

The best way to deal with emergencies is to be prepared enough to avoid them. However, unforeseen situations do happen, and you can prepare for them.

IN YOUR CAR

Before your trip, make sure your car has been serviced and is in good working order. Change the oil, check the battery and belts, and make sure tires are inflated properly (this can also improve gas mileage). Other inspections recommended by the car's manufacturer should be made, too.

Next, be sure you have the tools and equipment to deal with a routine breakdown: jack, spare tire, lug wrench, repair kit, emergency tools, jumper cables, spare fan belt, auto fuses, flares and/or reflectors, flashlights, first-aid kit, and, in winter, windshield wiper fluid, a windshield scraper, and snow shovel.

Bring all appropriate and up-to-date documentation—licenses, registration, and insurance cards—and know what's covered by your insurance. Also bring an extra set of keys, just in case.

En route, always buckle up! In most states it is required by law.

If your car does break down, get out of traffic as soon as possible—pull well off the road. Raise the hood and turn on your emergency flashers or tie a white cloth to the roadside door handle or antenna. Stay near your car. Use flares or reflectors to keep your car from being hit.

IN YOUR LODGING

Chances are slim that you will encounter a hotel or motel fire. The 🏨 in a listing indicates that there were smoke detectors and/or sprinkler systems in the rooms we inspected. Once you've checked in, make sure that any smoke detector in your room is working properly. Ascertain the locations of fire extinguishers and at least two fire exits. Never use an elevator in a fire.

For personal security, use the peephole in your room's door.

PROTECTING AGAINST THEFT

To guard against theft wherever you go, don't bring anything of more value than you need. If you do bring valuables, leave them at your hotel rather than in your car, and if you have something very expensive, lock it in a safe. Many hotels have one in each room; others will store your valuables in the hotel's safe. And of course, don't carry more money than you need; use traveler's checks and credit cards, or visit cash machines.

For Travelers with Disabilities

A number of publications can provide assistance. The most complete listing of published material for travelers with disabilities is available from The Disability Bookshop, Twin Peaks Press, Box 129, Vancouver, WA 98666, phone 360/694-2462.

The Reference Section of the National Library Service for the Blind and Physically Handicapped (Library of Congress, Washington, D.C. 20542, phone 202/707-9276 or 202/707-5100) provides information and resources for persons with mobility problems and hearing and vision impairments, as well as information about the NILS talking program (or visit your local library).

IMPORTANT TOLL-FREE NUMBERS AND ONLINE INFORMATION

Hotels and Motels

Adams Mark   800 444-2326
   www.adamsmark.com
Amerisuites   800 833-1516
   www.amerisuites.com
AMFA Parks & Resorts   800 236-7916
   www.amfac.com
Baymont Inns   800 229-6668
   www.baymontinns.com
Best Western   800 780-7234
   www.bestwestern.com
Budget Host Inn   800 283-4678
   www.budgethost.com
Candlewood Suites   888 226-3539
   www.candlewoodsuites.com
Clarion Hotels   800 252-7466
   www.choicehotels.com
Clubhouse Inns   800 258-2466
   www.clubhouseinn.com
Coast Hotels & Resorts 800 663-1144
   www.coasthotels.com
Comfort Inns   800 252-7466
   www.choicehotels.com
Concorde Hotels   800 888-4747
   www.concorde-hotel.com
Country Hearth Inns   800 848-5767
   www.countryhearth.com
Country Inns   800 456-4000
   www.countryinns.com
Courtyard by Marriott 888 236-2437
   www.courtyard.com
Crown Plaza Hotels   800 227-6963
   www.crowneplaza.com
Days Inn   800 544-8313
   www.daysinn.com
Delta Hotels   800 268-1133
   www.deltahotels.com
Destination Hotels & Resorts
   800 434-7347
   www.destinationhotels.com
Doubletree   800 222-8733
   www.doubletree.com
Drury Inns   800 378-7946
   www.druryinn.com
Econolodge   800 553-2666
   www.econolodge.com
Embassy Suites   800 362-2779
   www.embassysuites.com
Fairfield Inns   800 228-2800
   www.fairfieldinn.com
Fairmont Hotels   800 441-1414
   www.fairmont.com
Family Inns of America 800 251-9752
   www.familyinnsofamerica.com

Forte Hotels   800 300-9147
   www.fortehotels.com
Four Points by Sheraton
   888 625-5144   www.starwood.com
Four Seasons   800 545-4000
   www.fourseasons.com
Hampton Inns   800 426-7866
   www.hamptoninn.com
Hilton   800 774-1500
   www.hilton.com
Holiday Inn   800 465-4329
   www.holiday-inn.com
Homestead Studio Suites 888 782-9473
   www.stayhsd.com
Homewood Suites   800 225-5466
   www.homewoodsuites.com
Howard Johnson   800 406-1411
   www.hojo.com
Hyatt   800 633-7313
   www.hyatt.com
Inn Suites Hotels & Suites
   800 842-4242   www.innsuites.com
Inter-Continental   888 567-8725
   www.interconti.com
Jameson Inns   800 526-3766
   www.jamesoninns.com
Kempinski Hotels   800-426-3135
   www.kempinski.com
Kimpton Hotels   888-546-7866
   www.kimptongroup.com
La Quinta   800-531-5900
   www.laquinta.com
Leading Hotels of the World
   800-223-6800   www.lhw.com
Loews Hotels   800-235-6397
   www.loewshotels.com
Mainstay Suites   800-660-6246
   www.choicehotels.com
Mandarin Oriental   800-526-6566
   www.mandarin-oriental.com
Marriott   888-236-2427
   www.marriott.com
Nikko Hotels   800-645-5687
   www.nikkohotels.com
Omni Hotels   800-843-6664
   www.omnihotels.com
Preferred Hotels & Resorts Worldwide
   www.preferredhotels.com
   800-323-7500
Quality Inn   800-228-5151
   www.qualityinn.com
Radisson Hotels   800-333-3333
   www.radisson.com

Ramada 888-298-2054
www.ramada.com
Red Lion Inns 800-733-5466
www.redlion.com
Red Roof Inns 800-733-7663
www.redroof.com
Regal Hotels 800-222-8888
www.regal-hotels.com
Regent International 800-545-4000
www.regenthotels.com
Renaissance Hotels 888-236-2427
www.renaissancehotels.com
Residence Inns 888-236-2427
www.residenceinn.com
Ritz Carlton 800-241-3333
www.ritzcarlton.com
Rodeway Inns 800-228-2000
www.rodeway.com
Rosewood Hotels & Resorts
888-767-3966
www.rosewood-hotels.com
Sheraton 888-625-5144
www.sheraton.com
Shilo Inns 800-222-2244
www.shiloinns.com
Shoney's Inns 800-552-4667
www.shoneysinn.com
Sleep Inns 800-453-3746
www.sleepinn.com
Small Luxury Hotels 800-525-4800
www.slh.com
Sofitel 800-763-4835
www.sofitel.com
Sonesta Hotels & Resorts
800-766-3782 www.sonesta.com
SRS Worldhotels 800-223-5652
www.srs-worldhotels.com
Summerfield Suites 800-833-4353
www.summerfieldsuites.com
Summit International 800-457-4000
www.summithotels.com
Swissotel 800-637-9477
www.swissotel.com
The Peninsula Group
www.peninsula.com
Travelodge 800-578-7878
www.travelodge.com
Westin Hotels & Resorts
800-937-8461 www.westin.com
Wingate Inns 800-228-1000
www.wingateinns.com
Woodfin Suite Hotels
www.woodfinsuitehotels.com
800-966-3346
Wyndham Hotels & Resorts
800-996-3426 www.wyndham

Airlines
Air Canada 888-247-2262
www.aircanada.ca
Alaska 800-252-7522
www.alaska-air.com

American 800-433-7300
www.aa.com
America West 800-235-9292
www.americawest.com
British Airways 800-247-9297
www.british-airways.com
Continental 800-523-3273
www.flycontinental.com
Delta 800-221-1212
www.delta-air.com
Island Air 800-323-3345
www.islandair.com
Mesa 800-637-2247
www.mesa-air.com
Northwest 800-225-2525
www.nwa.com
Southwest 800-435-9792
www.southwest.com
United 800-241-6522
www.ual.com
US Air 800-428-4322
www.usair.com

Car Rentals
Advantage 800-777-5500
www.arac.com
Alamo 800-327-9633
www.goalamo.com
Allstate 800-634-6186
www.bnm.com/as.htm
Avis 800-831-2847
www.avis.com
Budget 800-527-0700
www.budgetrentacar.com
Dollar 800-800-4000
www.dollarcar.com
Enterprise 800-325-8007
www.pickenterprise.com
Hertz 800-654-3131
www.hertz.com
National 800-227-7368
www.nationalcar.com
Payless 800-729-5377
www.800-payless.com
Rent-A-Wreck.com 800-535-1391
www.rent-a-wreck.com
Sears 800-527-0770
www.budget.com
Thrifty 800-847-4389
www.thrifty.com

FOUR-STAR AND FIVE-STAR ESTABLISHMENTS IN THE GREAT LAKES

Illinois

★★★★★ **Lodgings**
Four Seasons Hotel Chicago, *Chicago*
The Peninsula, Chicago, *Chicago*
The Ritz-Carlton, Chicago, A Four Seasons Hotel, *Chicago*

★★★★★ **Restaurant**
Charlie Trotter's, *Chicago*

★★★★ **Lodgings**
Park Hyatt Chicago, *Chicago*
The Westin Chicago River North, *Chicago*

★★★★ **Restaurants**
Ambria, *Chicago*
Carlos', *Highland Park*
Everest, *Chicago*
Le Francias, *Wheeling*
Les Nomades, *Chicago*
The Ritz-Carlton Dining Room, *Chicago*
Seasons, *Chicago*
Trio, *Evanston*
Tru, *Chicago*

Michigan

★★★★ **Lodgings**
Amway Grand Plaza Hotel, *Grand Rapids*
The Townsend Hotel, *Birmingham*

★★★★ **Restaurants**
The Lark, *Bloomfield Hills*
Tapawingo, *Charlevoix*

Ohio

★★★★★ **Restaurant**
Maisonette, *Cincinnati*

★★★★ **Lodgings**
The Ritz-Carlton, Cleveland, *Cleveland*
The Cincinnatian Hotel, *Cincinnati*

★★★★ **Restaurant**
L'auberge, *Dayton*

Wisconsin

★★★★ **Lodgings**
The American Club, *Kohler*
Canoe Bay, *Rice Lake*

ILLINOIS

Illinois extends from Chicago, on the shores of Lake Michigan, to the vast woodlands of Shawnee National Forest. It is a major transportation center, and its resources include wheat, corn, soybeans, livestock, minerals, coal, oil, and an immense diversity of manufactured goods. The growth of this industrial-agricultural giant has been remarkable. In a century and a half it has evolved from a frontier to a vast empire of cities, farms, mines, and mills. There are nearly one million factory workers; more than 90 percent of its land is cultivated, producing more than 40 different crops with an annual value of $4.2 billion. Livestock value averages more than $1 billion annually.

Population: 12,419,293
Area: 55,646 square miles
Elevation: 279-1,235 feet
Peak: Charles Mound (Jo Daviess County)
Entered Union: December 3, 1818 (21st state)
Capital: Springfield
Motto: State Sovereignty-National Union
Nickname: Land of Lincoln
Flower: Violet
Bird: Cardinal
Tree: White Oak
Fair: Mid-August, 2003, in Springfield
Time Zone: Central
Web Site: www.enjoyillinois.com

The state takes its name from the confederated tribes who called themselves the Iliniwek ("superior men") and inhabited the valley of the Illinois River. In 1673 the first known white men entered the land of the Iliniwek. Father Jacques Marquette and Louis Jolliet paddled down the Mississippi, returned up the Illinois, and carried their canoes across the portage where Chicago now stands. Five years later, Robert Cavelier de La Salle established Fort Créve Coeur, near Peoria Lake. French interest then shifted to the area around Cahokia and Kaskaskia. Fort de Chartres was built in 1720, and trappers and traders soon followed. The district was designated Illinois, the first official use of the name.

French rule ended when the British seized Fort de Chartres in 1765, but the British stayed in Illinois only briefly. The region was important to the American cause and was won by George Rogers Clark in 1778-1779. For a while Illinois was claimed as a county by Virginia, but it was ceded to the federal government; in 1787 it became part of the Northwest Territory. This territory was variously subdivided; Illinois, first part of Indiana Territory, became Illinois Territory in 1809, with Ninian Edwards as its first governor. Nine years later it was admitted as the 21st state.

Through the early years of the 19th century, the Sauk (or Sac) and Fox tribes struggled to retain their lands. They were moved across the Mississippi by a treaty that touched off the Black Hawk War of 1832. The defeat of the Sauk and Fox, and a later treaty forcing the Potawatomi to cede their lands, virtually removed Native Americans from the state. Settlers then surged into the fertile country.

A young backwoods lawyer named Abraham Lincoln returned from the Black Hawk War and entered politics. As leader of the Sangamon County delegation in the state legislature, he was successful in moving the capital from Vandalia to Springfield. Lincoln supported projects for waterway improvements, which resulted in canals and interstate railroads. The new transportation system helped build commercial centers and contributed to the state's eventual industrialization. The Civil War sparked broad industrialization and rapid growth which, together with vast agricultural riches, have carried the state through many economic crises.

Illinois stretches 385 miles from north to south. As a vacation area, it offers lakes and rivers with excellent fishing, beautiful parks and recreation areas, historic and archeological sites, landmark buildings, prairie lands, and canyons. The attractions in Chicago and the surrounding area are endless, as are the hundreds of festivals and events sponsored by cities and towns year-round throughout the state.

When to Go/Climate

Illinois weather can be extreme and unpredictable. Winters can bring heavy snows; summers are often hot, hazy, and humid. Summer thunderstorms are frequent and magnificent. Tornadoes have been recorded from spring through fall.

AVERAGE HIGH/LOW TEMPERATURES (°F)

CHICAGO

Jan 29/13	**May** 70/48	**Sept** 75/54
Feb 34/17	**June** 80/58	**Oct** 63/42
Mar 46/29	**July** 84/63	**Nov** 48/32
Apr 59/39	**Aug** 82/62	**Dec** 34/19

SPRINGFIELD

Jan 33/16	**May** 75/52	**Sept** 79/56
Feb 37/20	**June** 84/62	**Oct** 67/44
Mar 50/32	**July** 87/66	**Nov** 52/34
Apr 64/43	**Aug** 84/63	**Dec** 37/22

Parks and Recreation Finder

Directions to and information about the parks and recreation areas below are given under their respective town/city sections. Please refer to those sections for details.

NATIONAL PARK AND RECREATION AREAS

Key to abbreviations. I.H.S. = International Historic Site; I.P.M. = International Peace Memorial; N.B. = National Battlefield; N.B.P. = National Battlefield Park; N.B.C. = National Battlefield and Cemetery; N.C.A. = National Conservation Area; N.E.M. = National Expansion Memorial; N.F. = National Forest; N.G. = National Grassland; N.H.P. = National Historical Park; N.H.C. = National Heritage Corridor; N.H.S. = National Historic Site; N.L. = National Lakeshore; N.M. = National Monument; N.M.P. = National Military Park; N.Mem. = National Memorial; N.P. = National Park; N.Pres. = National Preserve; N.R.A. = National Recreational Area; N.R.R. = National Recreational River; N.Riv. = National River; N.S. = National Seashore; N.S.R. = National Scenic Riverway; N.S.T. = National Scenic Trail; N.Sc. = National Scientific Reserve; N.V.M. = National Volcanic Monument.

Place Name	Listed Under
Lincoln Home N.H.S.	SPRINGFIELD
Shawnee N.F.	CARBONDALE

STATE PARK AND RECREATION AREAS

Key to abbreviations. I.P. = Interstate Park; S.A.P. = State Archaeological Park; S.B. = State Beach; S.C.A. = State Conservation Area; S.C.P. = State Conservation Park; S.Cp. = State Campground; S.F. = State Forest; S.G. = State Garden; S.H.A. = State Historic Area; S.H.P. = State Historic Park; S.H.S. = State Historic Site; S.M.P. = State Marine Park; S.N.A. = State Natural Area; S.P. = State Park; S.P.C. = State Public Campground; S.R. = State Reserve; S.R.A. = State Recreation Area; S.Res. = State Reservoir; S.Res.P. = State Resort Park; S.R.P. = State Rustic Park.

CALENDAR HIGHLIGHTS

FEBRUARY

Chicago Auto Show (Chicago). McCormick Place. Hundreds of foreign and domestic cars are displayed. Phone 312/791-7000.

MARCH

St. Patrick's Day Parade (Chicago). The Chicago River is dyed green in honor of the Irish saint. City parade Saturday before holiday; South Side parade Sunday before holiday. Phone 312/744-3315.

JUNE

Swedish Days (Geneva). Six-day festival with parade, entertainment, arts and crafts, music, food. Also includes the state's largest music competition and Swedish rosemaling (painting). Phone 630/232-6060.

JULY

Taste of Chicago (Chicago). Grant Park. Showcase of Chicago's diverse culinary scene. Selected Chicago restaurants offer sample-size specialties. Phone 312/744-3315.

Western Open Golf Tournament (Lockport). A major tournament on the PGA tour. Cog Hill Golf Course. Phone 630/257-5872.

Bagelfest (Mattoon). World's biggest bagel breakfast. Bagelfest Queen Pageant, Beautiful Bagel Baby Contest. Parade, talent show, music. Phone 217/235-5661.

Illinois Shakespeare Festival (Bloomington). Ewing Manor. Shakespearean performances preceded by Elizabethan-era music and entertainment. Phone 309/438-2535.

AUGUST

Illinois State Fair (Springfield). Ilinois State Fairgrounds. Baking contests, livestock competitions, agricultural displays, food, entertainment. Phone 217/782-6661.

OCTOBER

Spoon River Scenic Drive (Havana and Peoria). A 140-mile autumn drive through small towns and rolling, wooded countryside noted for fall color; 19th- and early 20th-century crafts, exhibits, demonstrations; antiques, collectibles; produce, food. Phone 309/547-3234.

Scarecrow Festival (St. Charles). Lincoln Park. Display of up to 100 scarecrows; entertainment, food, crafts. Phone 630/377-6161 or 800/777-4373.

Place Name	Listed Under
Argyle Lake S.P.	MACOMB
Bishop Hill S.H.S.	BISHOP HILL
Black Hawk S.H.S.	ROCK ISLAND
Buffalo Rock S.P.	OTTAWA
Cahokia Courthouse S.H.S.	CAHOKIA
Cahokia Mounds S.H.S.	CAHOKIA
Carl Sandburg S.H.S.	GALESBURG
Castle Rock S.P.	OREGON
Chain O'Lakes S.P.	ANTIOCH
Dana-Thomas House S.H.S.	SPRINGFIELD
Ferne Clyffe S.P.	MARION

Fort Defiance S.P.	CAIRO
Fort Kaskaskia S.H.S.	same
Fox Ridge S.P.	CHARLESTON
Gebhard Woods S.P.	MORRIS
Giant City S.P.	CARBONDALE
Horseshoe Lake S.C.	CAIRO
Illinois Beach S.P.	same
Johnson Sauk Trail S.P.	KEWANEE
Jubilee College S.H.S.	PEORIA
Jubilee College S.P.	PEORIA
Kankakee River S.P.	KANKAKEE
Kickapoo S.P.	DANVILLE
Lincoln Log Cabin S.H.S.	CHARLESTON
Lincoln Tomb S.H.S.	SPRINGFIELD
Lincoln Trail S.P.	MARSHALL
Lincoln's New Salem S.H.S.	PETERSBURG
Lowden Memorial S.P.	OREGON
Matthiessen S.P.	PERU
Metamora Courthouse S.H.S.	PEORIA
Moore Home S.H.S.	CHARLESTON
Moraine Hills S.P.	McHENRY
Mount Pulaski Courthouse S.H.S.	LINCOLN
Nauvoo S.P.	NAUVOO
Old State Capitol S.H.S.	SPRINGFIELD
Père Marquette S.P.	same
Postville Courthouse S.H.S.	LINCOLN
Ramsey Lake S.P.	VANDALIA
Rock Cut S.P.	ROCKFORD
Starved Rock S.P.	same
Stephen A. Forbes S.P.	SALEM
Ulysses S. Grant Home S.H.S.	GALENA
Vandalia Statehouse S.H.S.	VANDALIA
Wayne Fitzgerrell S.R.A.	BENTON
White Pines Forest S.P.	OREGON

Water-related activities, hiking, riding, various other sports, picnicking, and visitor centers are available in many of these areas. Camping is permitted in more than 60 areas ($8-$15/site/night) only by permit from the park ranger, obtainable for overnight or a maximum of 14 nights. Pets on leash only. State parks are open daily, weather permitting, except January 1 and December 25. For full information about state parks, tent camping, and other facilities, contact the Department of Natural Resources, Division of Land Management and Education, 600 N Grand Ave W, Springfield 62706, phone 217/782-6752.

SKI AREAS

Place Name	Listed Under
Chestnut Mountain Resort	GALENA
Wilmot Mountain Ski Area	ANTIOCH

FISHING AND HUNTING

Lakes, streams, and rivers provide fishing to suit every freshwater angler. The Illinois shoreline of Lake Michigan is 63 miles long. Nonresident season fishing license $26.50; ten-day license $15; 24-hour fishing license $7.50; resident season license $15. Licenses and further information may be obtained from the Department of Natural Resources, License Section, 524 S 2nd St, Springfield 62701-1787, phone 217/782-7305, or department vendors throughout the state.

Many areas of the state provide good hunting, with Canada geese, ducks, quail, rabbits, and squirrels plentiful. Deer and turkey hunting is by permit only. Nonresident season hunting license $55.75; five-day license $32.75. Additional stamps required for waterfowl ($12.50), habitat game ($7.50). The Department of Natural Resources maintains shooting areas at numerous places throughout the state. For more information concerning fishing and hunting in Illinois, contact the Department of Natural Resources, 524 S 2nd St, Springfield 62701, phone 217/782-6302. Licenses may be obtained from department vendors throughout the state.

Driving Information

Safety belts are mandatory for all persons in front seat of vehicle. Children under seven years must be in an approved passenger restraint anywhere in vehicle: ages five or six may use a regulation safety belt; age four and under must use an approved safety seat.

INTERSTATE HIGHWAY SYSTEM

The following alphabetical listing of Illinois towns in *Mobil Travel Guide* shows that these cities are within ten miles of the indicated Interstate highways. A highway map, however, should be checked for the nearest exit.

Highway Number	Cities/Towns within ten miles
Interstate 39	Peru, Rockford.
Interstate 55	Bloomington, Brookfield, Chicago, Cicero, Collinsville, Downers Grove, Edwardsville, Hinsdale, Joliet, La Grange, Lincoln, Lockport, Naperville, Oak Lawn, Springfield.
Interstate 57	Arcola, Benton, Cairo, Champaign/Urbana, Charleston, Chicago, Effingham, Homewood, Kankakee, Marion, Mattoon, Mount Vernon, Oak Lawn, Salem.
Interstate 64	Belleville, Collinsville, Mount Vernon.
Interstate 70	Altamont, Collinsville, Edwardsville, Effingham, Greenville, Marshall, Vandalia.
Interstate 72	Champaign/Urbana, Decatur, Springfield.
Interstate 74	Bloomington, Champaign/Urbana, Danville, Galesburg, Moline, Peoria.
Interstate 80	Chicago, Homewood, Joliet, Lockport, Moline, Morris, Ottawa, Peru, Rock Island.
Interstate 88	Aurora, Brookfield, Chicago, Chicago O'Hare Airport Area, Cicero, De Kalb, Dixon, Downers Grove, Elmhurst, Geneva, Glen Ellyn, Hillside, Hinsdale, Itasca, La Grange, Moline, Naperville, Oak Brook, Oak Park, St. Charles, Wheaton.
Interstate 90	Arlington Heights, Chicago, Chicago O'Hare Airport Area, Cicero, Elgin, Elmhurst, Hillside, Itasca, Oak Park, Rockford, Schaumburg, Union.
Interstate 94	Chicago, Chicago O'Hare Airport Area, Evanston, Glenview, Grayslake, Gurnee, Highland Park, Highwood, Libertyville, Northbrook, Skokie, Waukegan, Wheeling, Wilmette.
Interstate 290	Arlington Heights, Chicago, Chicago O'Hare Airport Area, Cicero, Elmhurst, Glen Ellyn, Hillside, Itasca, Libertyville, Northbrook, Oak Brook, Oak Park, Schaumburg.
Interstate 294	Arlington Heights, Chicago, Chicago O'Hare Airport Area, Cicero, Elmhurst, Evanston, Glen Ellyn, Glenview, Highland Park, Highwood, Hillside, Itasca,

	Libertyville, Northbrook, Oak Brook, Oak Park, Skokie, Wheeling, Wilmette.
Interstate 355 (North-South Tollway)	Chicago O'Hare Airport Area, Downers Grove, Elmhurst, Glen Ellyn, Hillside, Hinsdale, Itasca, La Grange, Lockport, Naperville, Oak Brook, Schaumburg, Wheaton.

Additional Visitor Information

For specific information about Illinois attractions, activities, and travel counseling, contact the Illinois Bureau of Tourism, phone 800/2-CONNECT or 800/406-6418 (TTY).

Locations of Illinois tourist information centers (April-October): off I-80 (eastbound) near Rapid City; off I-57 near Monee; off I-24 (westbound) near Metropolis; off I-57 near Whittington; off I-57 (northbound) near Anna; off I-64 (eastbound) near New Baden; off I-70 (eastbound) near Highland; off I-70 (westbound) near Marshall; off I-74 (westbound) near Oakwood; off I-80 (eastbound) near South Holland; off I-90 (southbound) near South Beloit.

THE GREAT RIVER ROAD

Illinois has more than 500 miles of distinctive state, county, and US highways comprising its Great River Road, which runs along the Mississippi River from East Dubuque to Cairo. One of the most scenic drives in Illinois, the Great River Road entices travelers with a glimpse into laid-back life along Old Man River. Natural beauty alternates with river history; something is always on the offer. The route is meandering to say the least; it winds back and forth over the river, changes direction frequently, and wanders in and out of towns long since forgotten. That being said, this is the perfect trip for those looking to get lost for a little while. However, you don't have to worry about getting *too* lost. The portion of the route that runs through Illinois (the Great River Road also runs through nine other states) is particularly well marked. Keep your eyes peeled for the green-and-white signs with a steamboat design in the middle, and you're sure to stay on the right road. You can also contact the Mississippi Parkway Commission (Pioneer Building, Suite 1513, 336 N Robert St, St. Paul, MN 56101) for a detailed map (a $1 donation is requested).

From Rockford, take Highway 20 to Route 84, the starting point for this tour. If you're looking for a little action, East Dubuque has paddleboat gambling. Otherwise, head first to Galena, one of Illinois' most treasured historic towns. When it comes to tourist attractions, Galena has much to satisfy a range of interests. Spend some time exploring the many mansions and buildings listed on the National Historic Register, poke through tiny antique stores, or take a guided walking tour. If these options don't inspire you, try a tour and wine tasting at the Galena Cellars Winery, a river cruise, or a visit to the Galena/Jo Daviess County History Museum. Farther south on our route along the Big Muddy is the historic Mormon town of Nauvoo. Architecture is the big draw here; you'll find 25 historic sites (circa 1840) to explore. Heading south once again, you will eventually come upon the town of Grafton, home to Pere Marquette, Illinois' largest state park. Grafton is also where you'll find some of the prettiest stretches of the Great River Road. If you are traveling during the winter, you'll want to stop next in nearby Alton to do some eagle watching. About 200 to 400 bald eagles winter in this area every year. The Cahokia Native American village reconstruction (a World Heritage Site) near Collinsville is also worth a stop. South of Carbondale, the cool woods of Shawnee National Forest provide a welcome respite from the dead heat of an Illinois summer. Acres of hiking trails are available if you're interested in stretching your legs a bit. When you are ready to return to Rockford, keep in mind that sticking to main interstates and highways (rather than returning via the Great River Road) will allow for a much speedier trip.
(APPROX 500 MI)

Altamont

See also Effingham, Vandalia

Pop 2,283 **Elev** 619 ft **Area code** 618
Zip 62411
Information Chamber of Commerce,
PO Box 141; 618/483-5714

Motel/Motor Lodge

★ **SUPER 8 MOTEL.** *I-70 & SR 26 S
(62411). 618/483-6300; fax 618/483-
3323; toll-free 800/800-8000. www.
super8.com.* 25 rms, 2 story. S, D $39-
$60; each addl $4; under 12 free.
Crib $5. Pet accepted, some restric-
tions; $8. TV; cable (premium). Play-
ground. Restaurant adj 6 am-9 pm.
Meeting rms. Ck-out 11 am. Coin
lndry. Cr cds: A, C, D, DS, MC, V.
🅓 🐾 🖂 🔥 SC

Alton

(F-3) *See also Cahokia, Collinsville,
Edwardsville*

Pop 30,496 **Elev** 500 ft **Area code** 618
Zip 62002
Information Greater Alton/Twin
Rivers Convention & Visitor's
Bureau, 200 Piasa St; 618/465-6676
or 800/258-6645
Web www.altoncvb.org

Alton is located on the bluffs just
above the confluence of the Mississippi and Missouri rivers. It has three
historic districts, four square blocks
of antique stores, and many opulent
houses, the former residences of
steamboat captains, industrialists,
and railroad barons. Here in 1837,
Elijah Lovejoy, the abolitionist editor, died protecting his press from a
proslavery mob. In the Alton Cemetery there is a 93-foot monument to
Lovejoy. A sandbar in the river was
the scene of the projected Lincoln-
Shields duel of 1842, which was settled without bloodshed. The final
Lincoln-Douglas debate was held in
Alton on October 15, 1858. Alton
was the home of Robert Wadlow, the
tallest man in history; a life-size

nine-foot statue of Wadlow is on
College Avenue.

What to See and Do

Alton Belle Riverboat Casino. Entertainment complex includes slots,
showrooms, lounges, and restaurants. (Daily) On waterfront at 1
Front St. Phone 800/711-GAME.

Alton Museum of History and Art.
Displays on local history and culture,
include exhibit on Alton's Robert
Wadlow, the world's tallest man. 2809
College Ave. Phone 618/462-2763. ¢¢

Brussels Ferry. Ferry boat navigates
the Illinois River at the confluence of
the Mississippi River. (Daily) 20 mi
W on Great River Rd (IL 100), near
Grafton. Phone 618/786-3636. **FREE**

Confederate Soldiers' Cemetery.
Monument lists names of soldiers
who died in Illinois's first state
prison, which was a prisoner-of-war
camp during the Civil War. Rozier St,
W of State St. Phone 800/258-6645.

Pere Marquette State Park. (see)
Approx 23 mi W on IL 100. Phone
618/786-3323.

Piasa Bird Painting Reproduction.
According to Native American legend, a monster bird frequented these
bluffs and preyed on all who came
near. When Marquette sailed down
the Mississippi in 1673, he spotted
"high rocks with hideous monsters
painted on them" at this spot. The
paintings, destroyed by quarrying in
the 19th century, were reproduced in
1934. These reproductions in turn
were destroyed by the construction
of Great River Rd. They were reproduced a second time on a bluff farther up the river. On bluffs NW of
town, best seen from the river and IL
100. Phone 800/258-6645.

Raging Rivers Waterpark. Is 20 acres
and includes Tree House Harbor, an
interactive family play area; Lazy
River float ride; body flumes; giant
wave pool; whitewater rapids ride.
(Memorial Day wkend-Labor Day
wkend) 15 mi NW on IL 100 to
Grafton, at 100 Palisades Pkwy.
Phone 800/548-7573. ¢¢¢

Village of Elsah. Many buildings are
more than 100 yrs old. Museum
(Apr-Nov, Thurs-Sun afternoons). 11
mi W on Great River Rd (IL 100).
Phone 618/374-1059. **FREE**

Motels/Motor Lodges

★★ **HOLIDAY INN - ALTON.** 3800 Homer Adams Pkwy (62002). 618/462-1220; fax 618/462-0906. www.holiday-inn.com. 137 rms, 4 story. S, D $103.50-$117.50; each addl $10; under 18 free. Crib free. TV; cable (premium), VCR (movies). Indoor pool; whirlpool. Complimentary bkfst buffet, coffee in rms. Restaurant 6 am-2 pm, 5-10 pm; Sun from 7 am. Rm serv. Bar 1 pm-1 am; Sun to 10 pm; entertainment. Ck-out noon. Meeting rms. Business servs avail. In-rm modem link. Coin lndry. Valet serv. Bellhops. Free airport, RR station transportation. Exercise equipt; sauna. Health club privileges. Game rm. Balconies. Cr cds: A, C, D, DS, JCB, MC, V.

🄳 ⌦ 🛪 ✈ 🖄 🔥

★ **PERE MARQUETTE LODGE.** 100 Great River Rd, Grafton (62037). 618/786-2331; fax 618/786-3498. 72 rms, 2 story. S $67; D $82; each addl $10; under 17 free. Crib free. TV; cable, VCR avail (movies). Indoor pool; whirlpool. Complimentary coffee in rms. Restaurant 6:30 am-9 pm; wkends to 10 pm. Bar 4 pm-1 am. Ck-out noon. Meeting rms. Business servs avail. Lighted tennis. Exercise equipt, sauna. Playground. Game rm. Rec rm. Gift shop. Lawn games. Some balconies. Picnic tables, grills. On Mississippi River. Cr cds: A, MC, V.

🄳 ⌦ 🛪 🖊 🖄 🔥

★ **SUPER 8.** 1800 Homer Adams Pkwy (62002). 618/465-8885; fax 618/465-8964; res 800/800-8000. www.super8.com. 61 rms, 3 story. S, D $44-$65; each addl $6; suites $50-$56; under 12 free; package plans; higher rates races. Crib free. Pet accepted, some restrictions. TV; cable (premium). Complimentary continental bkfst. Restaurant nearby. Complimentary coffee in lobby. Ck-out 11 am. Business servs avail. In-rm modem link. Health club privileges. Cr cds: A, C, D, DS, MC, V.

🄳 🐾 🖄 🔥

B&B/Small Inn

★ **THE HOMERIDGE BED AND BREAKFAST.** 1470 N State St, Jerseyville (62052). 618/498-3442; fax 618/498-5662. www.homeridge.com. 5 rms, 3 story. No rm phones. S, D $95, wkly rates. Complimentary full bkfst. Ck-out 11 am, ck-in 4-6 pm. Pool. Game rm. Lawn games. Built in 1867; Italianate Victorian decor. Previous home of Senator Theodore S. Chapman. Totally nonsmoking. Cr cds: A, MC, V.

⌦ 🖄 🔥

Restaurant

★★ **TONY'S.** 312 Piasa St (62002). 618/462-8384. www.tonyssteaks.com. Hrs: 4:30-10:30 pm; Fri, Sat to 11:30 pm; Sun to 10 pm. Closed hols. Res accepted. Italian menu. Bar. Dinner $8.95-$32. Child's menu. Specializes in pepperloin steak, pasta, pizzas. Valet parking. Outdoor dining. Six dining rms. Cr cds: A, D, DS, MC, V.

🄳 🖃

Antioch

See also Gurnee, Waukegan

Settled 1836 **Pop** 8,788 **Elev** 772 ft
Area code 847 **Zip** 60002
Information Chamber of Commerce, 884 Main St; 847/395-2233
Web www.lake-online.com/antioch

What to See and Do

Chain O'Lakes Area. Yr-round recreational facilities, includes fishing, ice fishing, boating; x-country skiing and snowmobiling.

Chain O'Lakes State Park. Encompasses 6,063 acres. Fishing, boating (ramp, rentals, motors); hiking and bridle trails (rentals), hunting, x-country skiing, snowmobiling, picnicking, concession, camping. Standard hrs, fees. (Daily) 6 mi W on IL 173 in Spring Grove. Phone 847/587-5512. **FREE**

Hiram Butrick Sawmill. Replica of water-powered sawmill (1839) around which the community grew. Tours (by appt). 790 Cunningham Dr, at Gage Brothers Park on Sequoit Creek. Phone 847/395-2160. **FREE**

Wilmot Mountain Ski Area. (see LAKE GENEVA, WI) 3 mi N on IL 83, then W on WI County C; 1 mi S of Wilmot, WI, near IL state line.

Motel/Motor Lodge

★★ **BEST WESTERN REGENCY INN.** *350 Hwy 173 (60002). 847/395-3606; fax 847/395-3606. www.best western.com.* 68 rms, 3 story, 24 suites. May-Sept: S, D $80-$95; suites $94-$114; under 17 free; lower rates rest of yr. Crib $7. Pet accepted, some restrictions; $25 deposit. TV; cable (premium), VCR avail. Complimentary continental bkfst. Restaurant adj. Complimentary coffee in rms. Bar 3 pm-1 am. Ck-out 11 am. Meeting rms. Business servs avail. In-rm modem link. Coin lndry. Valet serv. Health club privileges. Heated indoor pool; whirlpool. Refrigerator, wet bar in suites. Some whirlpools. Cr cds: A, C, D, DS, MC, V.

Illinois Prairie

Arcola

(E-6) *See also Champaign/Urbana, Decatur, Mattoon*

Pop 2,652 **Elev** 678 ft **Area code** 217 **Zip** 61910

Information Chamber of Commerce, 135 N Oak, PO Box 274; 217/268-4530 or 800/336-5456

Web www.arcola-il.org

Arcola is located in Illinois' Amish Country, where it is not unusual to see horse-drawn carriages traveling the highways.

What to See and Do

Amish Country Tours. Museum dedicated to central Illinois' Amish community, the first museum of its kind. Exhibits include antique buggies, quilts, and handicrafts. Local tours avail. (Apr-Nov, Mon-Sat; Dec-Mar, Wed-Sat) 111 S Locust St. Phone 217/268-3599. ¢¢

Rockome Gardens. Native rocks inlaid in concrete to form fences, arches, ornamental designs; landscaped gardens, ponds; petting zoo; train and buggy rides; lookout tower, treehouse; Amish-style restaurant, shops; replica of Amish house. Re-creation of Illinois frontier village on 15 acres, including craft guild shop, blacksmith shop, old country store, calico shop, bakery, and furniture and candle shops; antique museum; special wkend events. Admission includes all attractions exc buggy ride. (Memorial Day-Oct, daily; mid-Apr-Memorial Day, days vary) 5 mi W on IL 133. Phone 217/268-4106. ¢¢¢

Special Event

Raggedy Ann Festival. Honors local man Johnny Gruelle, creator of Raggedy Ann and Andy. Includes carnival and petting zoo. Phone 217/268-4530. Third wk May.

Motel/Motor Lodge

★ **COMFORT INN.** *610 E Springfield Rd (61910). 217/268-4000; fax 217/268-4001. www.comfortinn.com.* 41 rms, 2 story. Apr-Nov: S $55.99-$75.99; D $59.99-$79.99; each addl $7; wkend, hol rates; lower rates rest of yr. Crib $7. TV; cable (premium). Pool. Complimentary continental

bkfst. Coffee in rms. Restaurant opp
6 am-10 pm. Ck-out 11 am. Business
servs avail. In-rm modem links.
Refrigerators avail. Cr cds: A, D, DS,
MC, V.

D ⇌ ⬚ 🔥 SC

Restaurants

★ **DUTCH KITCHEN.** *127 E Main
(61910).* 217/268-3518. Hrs: 7:30 am-
7 pm. Closed 2 wks Jan. Amish,
American menu. Bkfst $1.95-$5,
lunch, dinner $5.25-$7.50. Child's
menu. Specializes in shoofly pie,
Dutch sausage, apple butter. Salad
bar. Family-owned. Cr cds: C, D,
MC, V.

D ⬚

★ **ROCKOME FAMILY STYLE.** *125
N County Rd, 425E (61910).* 217/268-
4106. *www.rockome.com.* Hrs: 11 am-
7 pm; hrs vary mid-Apr-mid-May.
Closed Mon, Tues mid-Sept-Oct; also
Nov-mid-Apr. Complete meals:
lunch, dinner $10.80. Child's menu.
Specializes in Amish cooking. Own
baking. Season open is the same as
Rockome Gardens. Cr cds: C, D,
MC, V.

D ⬚

Arlington Heights

*See also Chicago O'Hare Airport Area,
Wheeling*

Settled 1836 **Pop** 76,031 **Elev** 700 ft
Area code 847
Information Chamber of Commerce,
180 N Arlington Heights Rd, 60004;
847/253-1703
Web www.arlingtonhtschamber.com

What to See and Do

Historical Museum. Complex consists of 1882 house, 1907 house, a
coach house, and a reconstructed log
cabin. (Sat-Sun, also first Fri of
month; closed hols) Also here is a
heritage gallery (Thurs-Sun). 500 N
Vail Ave. Phone 847/255-1225.
Museum ¢

Long Grove Village. Restored 19th-
century German village with more
than 90 antique shops, boutiques,
and restaurants. Seasonal festivals.
(Daily) 1 mi N, at jct IL 53, 83 in
Long Grove. Phone 847/634-0888.
FREE

Motels/Motor Lodges

★ ★ **AMERISUITES.** *2111 S Arlington
Heights Rd (60005).* 847/956-1400; fax
847/956-0804. *www.amerisuites.com.*
103 suites, 6 story. S, D $115-$125;
each addl $10; under 12 free. Crib
free. Pet accepted. TV; cable (premium). Complimentary buffet
bkfst, coffee in rms. Restaurant opp
open 24 hrs. Ck-out noon. Meeting
rms. Business center. Valet serv.
Exercise equipt. Health club privileges. Whirlpool. Refrigerators,
microwaves. Cr cds: A, C, D, DS,
JCB, MC, V.

D 🐾 🕺 ⬚ 🔥 SC 🚶

★ ★ **COURTYARD BY MARRIOTT.**
100 W Algonquin Rd (60005).
847/437-3344; fax 847/437-3367; toll-
free 800/321-2211. *www.courtyard.
com.* 147 rms, 3 story. S, D $114-
$124; suites $144; under 12 free. Crib
free. TV; cable (premium). Indoor
pool; whirlpool. Complimentary coffee in rms. Restaurant 6:30 am-10
pm; Sat, Sun 7 am-11 pm. Rm serv.
Bar 4-11 pm. Ck-out noon. Coin
lndry. Meeting rms. Business servs
avail. In-rm modem link. Valet serv.
Sundries. Exercise equipt. Health
club privileges. Refrigerator,
microwave in suites. Some private
patios, balconies. Cr cds: A, C, D, DS,
JCB, MC, V.

D ⇌ 🕺 ⬚ 🔥 SC

★ ★ **HOLIDAY INN EXPRESS.** *2120
S Arlington Heights Rd (60005).*
847/593-9400; fax 847/593-3632.
www.holiday-inn.com. 125 rms, 3
story. S, D $104-$114; suite $129;
under 18 free. TV; cable (premium).
Complimentary continental bkfst.
Restaurant opp open 24 hrs. Ck-out
noon. Meeting rms. Business servs
avail. In-rm modem link. Valet serv.
Refrigerators in suites. Some balconies. Cr cds: A, C, D, DS, JCB,
MC, V.

D ⬚ 🔥 SC

★ ★ **LA QUINTA INN.** *1415 W
Dundee Rd (60004).* 847/253-8777; fax

847/818-9167; toll-free 800/531-5900. www.laquinta.com. 121 rms, 4 story. S $96.99; D $102.99; suites $123.99-$129.99; under 18 free. Crib free. Pet accepted, some restrictions. TV; cable (premium). Heated pool. Complimentary continental bkfst, coffee in rms. Restaurant adj 11-1 am. Ck-out noon. Meeting rms. Business servs avail. In-rm modem link. Coin lndry. Valet serv. Sundries. Exercise equipt. Cr cds: A, C, D, DS, MC, V.

★★ **WYNDHAM GARDEN HOTEL.** 900 W Lake Cook Rd, Buffalo Grove (60089). 847/215-8883; fax 847/215-9304. www.wyndham.com. 155 rms, 2 story. S, D $99-$109; wkend rates. Crib free. TV; cable (premium). Indoor pool; whirlpool. Coffee in rms. Restaurant 6:30 am-10 pm. Rm serv. Bar 5-10 pm. Ck-out 11 am. Coin lndry. Meeting rms. Business servs avail. In-rm modem link. Valet serv. Sundries. Airport transportation (Sun, Mon). Lighted tennis. Exercise equipt. Some balconies, patios. Cr cds: A, D, DS, MC, V.

Hotels

★★★ **RADISSON HOTEL.** 75 W Algonquin Rd (60005). 847/364-7600; fax 847/364-7665; toll-free 800/333-3333. www.radisson.com. 247 rms, 6 story. S, D $109-$139; each addl $10; suites $195-$350; under 18 free; wkend rates. Crib free. TV; cable (premium). Indoor pool; whirlpool. Coffee in rms. Restaurant 6:30 am-11 pm. Bar 11-1 am. Ck-out noon. Meeting rms. Business servs avail. In-rm modem link. Gift shop. Airport transportation. Exercise equipt; sauna. Some bathrm phone, refrigerator in suites. Cr cds: A, C, D, DS, MC, V.

★★★ **SHERATON ARLINGTON PARK.** 3400 W Euclid Ave (60005). 847/394-2000; fax 847/394-2095; toll-free 800/325-3535. www.sheraton.com. 429 rms, 13 story. S $105-$195; D $125-$215; each addl $20; suites $250-$675; family, wkend rates. Crib free. TV; cable (premium). Heated indoor pool; whirlpool. Complimentary coffee in rms. Restaurant 6:30

am-10:30 pm. Bar 11-1 am; Sun from noon. Ck-out 11 am. Convention facilities. Business center. In-rm modem link. Gift shop. Tennis. Volleyball. Exercise equipt; sauna. Massage. Some bathrm phones. Luxury level. Cr cds: A, D, DS, JCB, MC, V.

Restaurants

★★★ **LE TITI DE PARIS.** 1015 W Dundee Rd (60004). 847/506-0222. www.letitideparis.com. Hrs: 11:30 am-3 pm, 5:30-10 pm; Sat from 5:30 pm. Closed Sun, Mon; July 4, Thanksgiving, Dec 24, 25. Res accepted. French menu. Serv bar. Wine list. A la carte entrees: lunch $11.50-$18, dinner $19.75-$26.50. Prix fixe: dinner $47. Child's menu. Specialties: pigeon with roasted sweet garlic; lobster with warm champagne chive sauce; Norwegian salmon with cider sauce and apples. Own pastries. Menu changes seasonally. Parking. Cr cds: A, D, DS, MC, V.

★★ **PALM COURT.** 1912 N Arlington Heights Rd (60004). 847/870-7770. www.palmcourtah.com. Hrs: 11 am-midnight; Fri to 1 am; Sat 5 pm-1 am; Sun noon-10 pm. Closed July 4, Dec 25. Res accepted. Continental menu. Bar. Lunch $5.95-$9.95, dinner $9.95-$19.95. Specialties: Dover sole, veal Oscar, rack of lamb. Pianist (dinner) exc Sun. Parking. Cr cds: A, D, DS, MC, V.

★★ **RETRO BISTRO.** 1746 W Golf Rd, Mt Prospect (60056). 847/439-2424. Hrs: 11:30 am-3 pm, 5:30-10:30 pm; Sat from 5 pm. Closed Sun; some major hols. Res accepted. Continental menu. Bar. A la carte entrees: lunch $6-$10.50, dinner $12-$16.50. Child's menu. Specialties: Ahi tuna, pork tenderloin, ostrich medallions. Own pastries. Contemporary bistro. Cr cds: A, C, D, DS, MC, V.

Aurora

(B-5) *See also Geneva, Joliet, Naperville, St. Charles*

Settled 1834 **Pop** 142,990 **Elev** 676 ft
Area code 630
Information Aurora Area Convention & Tourism Council, 44 W Downer Pl, 60507; 630/897-5581 or 800/477-4369
Web www.ci.aurora.il.us

Potawatomi chief Waubonsie and his tribe inhabited this area on the Fox River when, in the 1830s, pioneers arrived from the East. Water power and fertile lands attracted more settlers, and two villages united as Aurora. Today, the city prospers because of its location along a high-tech corridor.

What to See and Do

Aurora Historical Museum. In restored Ginsberg Building, the museum contains displays of 19th-century life, collection of mastodon bones, history center and research library, and public art displays. (Wed-Sun afternoons) 20 W Downer Pl. Phone 630/897-9029. ¢¢

Blackberry Historical Farm Village. An 1840s to 1920 living history museum and working farm; children's animal farm; craft demonstrations; wagon rides, discovery barn, pony rides, peddle tracker, farm play area, train. (May-Labor Day, daily; after Labor Day-Oct, Fri-Sun) W on I-88 (East-West Tollway) to Orchard Rd, S to Galena Blvd, then W to Barnes Rd. Phone 630/892-1550. ¢¢

Fermi National Accelerator Laboratory. World's highest energy particle accelerator is on a 6,800-acre site. Also on grounds are hiking trails and a buffalo herd. Obtain brochures for self-guided tours in atrium of 15-story Wilson Hall. Art and cultural events, films in auditorium. Call for hours. 2 mi N on IL 31, 2½ mi E on Butterfield Rd (IL 56), then N on Kirk Rd, at Pine St in Batavia. Phone 630/840-3351. **FREE**

Michael Jordan Golf Center. Facilities include covered and heated tee stations, short-game area, three-tiered putting green, 18-hole miniature golf. Clinics, youth programs, lessons, and golf schools. Clubhouse with golf shop, equipment, video imaging; restaurant. (Daily) 2 mi S of I-88, W of IL 59 at 4523 Michael Jordan Dr. Phone 630/851-0023.

Paramount Arts Centre. (1931) Theater designed by Rapp and Rapp to compete with opulent movie palaces of the area; restored to its original appearance, it offers a variety of productions throughout the yr. Guided backstage tours. (Mon-Fri) 23 E Galena Blvd, along river. Phone 630/896-7676. Tours ¢

Schingoethe Center for Native American Cultures. Private collection, thousands of Native American artifacts; jewelry, textiles, pottery, baskets. (Tues-Fri, Sun; closed hols, also Jan) 347 S Gladstone Ave. Phone 630/844-5402. **FREE**

SciTech—Science and Technology Interactive Center. In historic post office building, this interactive center provides more than 150 hands-on learning exhibits using motion, light, sound, and fun to teach science principles. (Tues-Sun) 18 W Benton. Phone 630/859-3434. ¢¢

Motels/Motor Lodges

★★ **BEST WESTERN FOX VALLEY INN.** *2450 N Farnsworth Ave (60504). 630/851-2000; fax 630/851-8885; toll-free 800/937-8376. www.bestwestern. com.* 114 rms, 2 story. S, D $72-$85; each addl $5; under 12 free. Crib $5. TV; cable (premium). Pool. Restaurant adj 5 am-11 pm. Bar; entertainment Fri, Sat. Coffee in lobby, rms. Ck-out noon. Meeting rms. Business servs avail. Coin lndry. Sundries. Exercise equipt. Game rm. Cr cds: A, C, D, DS, MC, V.

[icons]

★★ **COMFORT INN.** *4005 Gabrielle Dr (60504). 630/820-3400; fax 630/820-7081; toll-free 800/228-5150. www.comfortinn.com.* 51 rms, 2 story. S $69-$76; D $79-$86; each addl $7; under 18 free. Crib free. TV; cable (premium); VCR. Complimentary continental bkfst. Restaurant nearby. Ck-out 11 am. Meeting rm. Business servs avail. Coin lndry. Valet serv. Exercise equipt. Cr cds: A, C, D, DS, ER, JCB, MC, V.

[icons]

★★ **COMFORT SUITES.** *111 N Broadway (60505). 630/896-2800; fax 630/896-2887; toll-free 800/517-4000. www.comfortsuites.com.* 82 suites, 3 story. S $109-$159; D $119-$199; under 18 free; wkend rates; higher rates Dec 31. Crib free. TV; cable (premium), VCR (movies). Heated indoor pool; whirlpool. Complimentary continental bkfst. Coffee in rms. Restaurant adj 11 am-midnight. Ck-out 11 am. Coin lndry. Meeting rms. Business center. In-rm modem link. Sundries. Gift shop. Exercise equipt. Game rm. Playground. Refrigerators, micro-waves. Some whirlpools, fireplaces. Cr cds: A, C, D, DS, JCB, MC, V.

[D] ⌖ 木 ⊠ 🔥 太

Belleville (F-4)

Founded 1814 **Pop** 42,785 **Elev** 529 ft
Area code 618
Information Belleville Tourism, Inc, 216 East A St, 62220; 618/233-6769 or 800/677-9255

Named Belleville (beautiful city) by its early French settlers, the city today is largely populated by people of German descent. The governmental, financial, and medical center of southern Illinois, Belleville is also the headquarters of Scott Air Force Base.

What to See and Do

National Shrine of Our Lady of the Snows. Unique architecture and imaginative landscaping on 200 acres; features replica of Lourdes Grotto in France. Visitor center, restaurant, lodging, gift shop. (Daily) 9500 W IL 15. Phone 618/397-6700. **FREE**

Motels/Motor Lodges

★ **BELLEVILLE INN.** *2120 W Main St (62226). 618/234-9400; fax 618/234-6142; toll-free 800/329-7466.* 80 rms, 2 story. Mid-May-mid-Sept: S $61-$67; D $69-$81; each addl $6; suites $85-$150; under 13 free; lower rates rest of yr. Crib free. TV; cable (premium). Pool. Complimentary continental bkfst. Restaurant 7 am-

midnight. Bar 11:30-1 am; wkends to 2 am. Ck-out noon. Meeting rms. In-rm modem link. Valet serv. Gift shop. Refrigerators, microwaves. Cr cds: A, C, D, DS, MC, V.

[D] ⌖ ⊠ 🔥 SC

★★ **HAMPTON INN.** *150 Ludwig Dr, Fairview Heights (62208). 618/397-9705; fax 618/397-7829; res 800/426-7866. www.hamptoninn.com.* 55 rms, 3 story, 8 suites. Apr-Sep: S, D $69-$79; suites $64-$88; each addl $7; under 18 free; wkend rates; lower rates rest of yr. Crib avail. TV; cable (premium). Indoor pool; whirlpool. Complimentary bkfst. Coffee in rms, lobby. Restaurant nearby. Ck-out noon. Meeting rms. Business servs avail. Coin lndry. Valet serv. In-rm modem link. Refrigerators, micro-waves in suites. Cr cds: A, C, D, DS, ER, JCB, MC, V.

[D] ⌖ ⊠ 🔥 SC

★★ **RAMADA INN - FAIRVIEW HEIGHTS.** *6900 N Illinois, Fairview Heights (62208). 618/632-4747; fax 618/632-9428; toll-free 888/298-2054. www.ramada.com.* 159 rms, 5 story. May-Aug: S, D $68-$77; each addl $9; suites $165-$185; under 18 free; higher rates special events; lower rates rest of yr. Crib avail. Pet accepted; $10. 2 pools; 1 indoor. TV; cable (premium). Complimentary continental bkfst buffet; coffee in rms. Rm serv. Restaurant 11 am-11 pm; Fri, Sat to midnight. Ck-out noon. Meeting rms. Business servs avail. In-rm modem link. Valet serv. Coin lndry. Exercise equipt. Game rm. Some refrigerators, microwaves, wet bars, whirlpools. Cr cds: A, C, D, JCB, MC, V.

[D] 🐾 木 ⊠ 🔥 SC ⌖

★★ **RAMADA LIMITED.** *1320 Park Plaza Dr, O'Fallon (62260). 618/628-9700; fax 618/628-9740; res 800/272-6232. www.ramada.com.* 64 rms, 3 story. S, D $59-$79; under 18 free. Crib avail. Pet accepted; $10. TV; cable; coffee in rms. Restaurant adj 6 am-10 pm. Ck-out noon. Meeting rm. Business servs avail. In-rm modem link. Exercise equipt; sauna. Indoor pool. Cr cds: A, MC, V.

🐾 ⌖ 木 ⊠ 🔥 SC

★ **TOWN HOUSE MOTEL.** *400 S Illinois St (62220). 618/233-7881; fax*

618/233-7885. 55 rms, 2 story. S $39.45; D $42.45; each addl $5; under 12 free. Crib free. Pet accepted, some restrictions. TV; cable (premium). Restaurant 6 am-9 pm. Rm serv from 8 am. Bar 5 pm-2 am; entertainment. Whirlpool. Ck-out noon. Meeting rms. Business servs avail. In-rm modem link. Health club privileges. Refrigerators, microwaves avail. Cr cds: A, C, D, DS, MC, V.

B&B/Small Inn

★ ★ **SWAN'S COURT BED & BREAKFAST.** 421 Court St (62220). 618/233-0779; fax 618/277-3150; toll-free 800/840-1058. 4 rms, 2 share bath. S $45; D $65-$90; wkly rates. TV in common rm. Complimentary full bkfst. Restaurant nearby. In-rm modem link. Free guest lndry. Built in 1883; some original furnishing, period antiques. Totally nonsmoking. Cr cds: A, DS, MC, V.

Restaurants

★ **FISCHER'S.** 2100 W Main St (62226). 618/233-1131. Hrs: 7 am-midnight. Closed July 4, Dec 24 evening. Res accepted. Continental menu. Bar 10-2 am. Lunch $4.95-$8.95, dinner $5.95-$17.50. Child's menu. Specializes in seafood, veal, steak. Contemporary restaurant with a touch of elegance. Family-owned. Cr cds: A, D, DS, MC, V.

★ **LOTAWATA CREEK.** 311 Salem Pl, Fairview Heights (62208). 618/628-7373. www.lotawata.com. Hrs: 11 am-10 pm; Fri, Sat to 11 pm. Closed Thanksgiving, Dec 25. Bar. Lunch, dinner $7.25-$17.95. Child's menu. Specialties: prime rib, country fried steak. Parking. Warehouse atmosphere. Cr cds: A, D, DS, MC, V.

Benton (G-5)

Pop 6,880 **Elev** 470 ft **Area code** 618 **Zip** 62812

Information Benton/West City Area Chamber of Commerce, 500 W Main St, PO Box 574; 618/438-2121

What to See and Do

Rend Lake. Created from the Big Muddy and Casey Fork rivers, the Y-shaped Rend Lake covers 19,000 acres adj to 21,000 acres of public land with six recreation areas. Two beaches; fishing for bass, crappie, and catfish; boating (launches, marina); hiking, biking, and horseback riding trails; hunting, trap range; golf course. Restaurant. Five campgrounds; amphitheaters, programs. Visitor center at main dam. (Apr-Oct) Fee for some activities. 5 mi N via I-57, exit IL 154. Phone 618/724-2493. On the E shore, off I-57 exit 77, is

> **Wayne Fitzgerrell State Recreation Area.** Approx ⅓ of the 3,300 acres used for hunting and dog field trial grounds. Swimming, waterskiing, fishing, boating (ramps, dock); hiking and bridle trails, hunting, picnicking (shelters), camping, tent and trailer sites (dump station, hookups), cabins, playground, grocery, restaurant. Standard hrs, fees. Phone 618/629-2320.

Southern Illinois Arts & Crafts Marketplace. Houses Illinois artisan shops and galleries. Special events, demonstrations. (Daily; closed hols) 6 mi N on I-57 then W on IL 154. Phone 618/629-2220. **FREE**

Special Event

Rend Lake Water Festival. Second wk May. Phone 618/724-2493.

Motel/Motor Lodge

★ **DAYS INN.** 711 W Main St (62812). 618/439-3183; fax 618/439-3183; toll-free 800/329-7466. www.daysinn.com. 57 rms, 2 story. S $49.88; D $58.88; each addl $5; suite $90-$95; under 12 free; higher rates special events. Crib avail. Pet accepted. TV; cable, VCR avail (movies). Restaurant 6 am-10 pm. Rm serv. Bar 3-10 pm; entertainment. Ck-out noon. Meeting rms. Business servs avail. Barber/beauty shop. Coin lndry. Valet serv. Refrigerators, microwaves avail. Picnic tables. Cr cds: A, C, D, DS, JCB, V.

D ◣ ⬧ ▨ ▨ SC

Resort

★ ★ **REND LAKE RESORT.** *11712 E Windy Ln, Whittington (62897). 618/629-2211; fax 618/629-2584; toll-free 800/633-3341. www.dnr.state.il.us/ lodges/rendlake.htm.* 90 units, 20 rms in lodge, 22 cottages. Mar-mid-Nov: S, D $78-$103; each addl $9; cottages $93; under 18 free; wkends, hols (2-day min); lower rates rest of yr; package plans. Crib free. TV. Pool; wading pool. Playground. Dining rm 8 am-9 pm. Ck-out 11 am. Meeting rms. Business servs avail. Gift shop. Bicycle rental. Lighted tennis. 27-hole golf privileges, greens fee $32, pro. Health club privileges. Some refrigerators, whirlpools, fireplaces. On Rend Lake. Cr cds: A, D, DS, MC, V.

D ⬧ ⟐ ▥ ▨ ▨ ▨ ▨

Bishop Hill

See also Galesburg, Kewanee

Settled 1846 **Pop** 125 **Elev** 780 ft
Area code 309 **Zip** 61419

What to See and Do

◪ **Bishop Hill State Historic Site.** Settled in 1846 by Swedish immigrants seeking religious freedom, the communal-utopian colony was led by Erik Jansson until his assassination in 1850. In 1861, communally owned property was divided and the colony dissolved. Descendants of the settlers still live in the community. The state-owned Colony Hotel and Colony Church still stand, as do 15 of the original 21 buildings. (Daily; closed hols; hrs vary) Phone 309/927-3345. **FREE** Among the restorations are

Bishop Hill Museum. Houses collection of paintings by Olof Krans, whose primitive folk art depicts the Bishop Hill colony of his childhood.

Colony Blacksmith Shop. Traditional craftsmen selling and

demonstrating crafts. Phone 309/927-3390.

Colony Church. (1848) This gambrel-roofed building houses a collection of Bishop Hill artifacts. Second floor features restored sanctuary with original walnut pews.

Colony Store. (1853) Restored general store with original shelving and counters. (Daily; closed Thanksgiving, Dec 25) Phone 309/927-3596.

Steeple Building. (1854) This three-story Greek Revival edifice is of handmade brick covered with plaster. The clock, in its wooden steeple, was designed with only one hand. Heritage Museum houses displays of the community's history. The Bishop Hill Heritage collection of late 19th-century Bishop Hill memorabilia is here; slide show daily in season. (Apr-Dec, daily; closed Thanksgiving, Dec 25) Phone 309/927-3899. **DONATION**

Village tours. The Bishop Hill Heritage Association conducts tours of the village (Apr-mid-Dec, by appt). Phone 309/927-3899. ¢¢

Special Events

Midsommar. Sun afternoon concerts. June.

Bishop Hill Jordbruksdagarna. Agricultural celebration features harvesting demonstrations, children's games, "colony stew," hayrack rides. Late Sept. Phone 309/927-3345.

Julmarknad. Christmas market with decorated shops; Swedish foods; "Juletomte" (Christmas elf) and "Julbok" (Christmas goat) roam the village. Late Nov and early Dec. Phone 309/927-3345.

Lucia Nights. Festival of lights. "Lucia" girls with candle crowns serve coffee and sweets to guests; choral programs, carolers, sleigh rides. Mid-Dec. Phone 309/927-3345.

Bloomington

(D-5) *See also Peoria*

Founded 1843 **Pop** 64,808 **Elev** 829 ft
Area code 309
Information Bloomington-Normal
Area Convention & Visitors Bureau,
210 S East St; 309/829-1641 or
800/433-8226
Web www.visitbloomingtonnormal.
org

Bloomington, the McLean County
seat, took its name from the original
settlement of Blooming Grove.

The Illinois Republican party was
formed here in 1856 at the Anti-
Nebraska convention, at which
Abraham Lincoln made the famous
"lost speech" spelling out the principles that were to elect him president. Bloomington was also the
home of Adlai E. Stevenson, vice
president under Grover Cleveland.
His grandson, Illinois Governor
Adlai E. Stevenson II, twice Democ-
ratic candidate for president and US
Ambassador to the United Nations,
is buried here. Along with agriculture, the founding of Illinois Wesleyan University and the selection
of North Bloomington (now the
twin city of Normal) as the site for
Illinois State University helped
determine the town's economic
future.

What to See and Do

Funk Prairie Home. (1863) Built by
LaFayette Funk with lumber and
timber felled in Funk's Grove, the
large Italianate house with wrap-
around porches features an elaborately decorated parlor with a
Chickering piano, Italian marble
fireplace, and gold valance boards
above windows. Guided tours (allow
1½-2 hrs; res advised) includes adj
Gem and Mineral Museum. (Mar-
Dec, Tues-Sat; closed hols) Call for
directions. Phone 309/827-6792.
FREE

Illinois State University. (1857)
22,000 students. The first state
university in Illinois. Tours

arranged. 1 mi S of jct US 51, I-55
in Normal. Phone 309/438-2181.
On campus is

**Adlai E. Stevenson Memorial
Room.** Contains personal memora-
bilia, photographs. (Mon-Fri)
Phone 309/438-5669. **FREE**

Illinois Wesleyan University. (1850)
2,000 students. North side residential area on US 51, I-55 Business,
and IL 9. Liberal arts college. E University St. Phone 309/556-3034. On
campus are

Sheean Library. Contains the
papers of former US Congressman
Leslie Arends and the Gernon Collection of 19th- and 20th-century
literature. Also on display is a collection of Native American pottery
of Major John Wesley Powell, former faculty member at Wesleyan
and credited with the first exploration of the Colorado River and
Grand Canyon. Phone 309/556-
3350. **FREE**

Miller Park Zoo. Big cats, river otters
in natural settings; sea lions; tropical
rain forest; children's zoo. Other
activities in Miller Park include
swimming, fishing, boating; picnicking, tennis, and miniature golf (some
fees). There is a playground and a
steam locomotive display. Band concerts are held in season. (Daily) On
Morris Ave, ½ mi N of I-55 Business.
Phone 309/434-2250. **¢¢**

Old Courthouse Museum. Maintained by McLean County Historical
Society and housed in 1903 courthouse. Exhibits include area history,
farming, an authentic courtroom,
hands-on displays, and a research
library. Museum store. (Mon-Sat;
closed hols) 200 N Main St. Phone
309/827-0428. **¢**

Special Events

The American Passion Play. Scottish
Rite Temple, 110 E Mulberry St. A
cast of more than 300; presented
annually since 1924. Sat and Sun,
late-Mar-mid-May. Phone 309/829-
3903.

Illinois Shakespeare Festival. Shake-
spearean performances preceded by
Elizabethan-era music and entertainment. June-early-Aug. Ewing Manor,
Emerson and Towanda sts. Phone
309/438-2535.

Motels/Motor Lodges

★★ **BEST INNS.** *1905 W Market St (61701). 309/827-5333; fax 309/827-5333; toll-free 800/237-8466. www. bestinn.com.* 106 rms, 2 story. S $42-$56; D $49-$63; each addl $7; under 18 free. Crib free. Pet accepted. TV; cable. Pool. Complimentary bkfst buffet. Restaurant adj 10 am-midnight. Ck-out 1 pm. Business servs avail. In-rm modem link. Cr cds: A, D, DS, MC, V.

⬛ 🍴 🏊 🚳 🔥 SC

★★ **BEST WESTERN UNIVERSITY INN.** *6 Traders Cir, Normal (61761). 309/454-4070; fax 309/888-4505; toll-free 800/780-7234. www.bestwestern. com.* 102 rms, 2 story. S, D $69-$74; under 16 free. Crib free. Pet accepted. TV; cable (premium). Indoor pool. Complimentary continental bkfst. Restaurant nearby. Ck-out 11 am. Exercise equipt. Meeting rms. Business servs avail. Valet serv. Free airport, RR station, bus depot transportation. Sauna. Game rm. Cr cds: A, C, D, DS, MC, V.

⬛ 🍴 🏊 🏋 ✈ 🚳 🔥

★★ **EASTLAND SUITES.** *1801 Eastland Dr (61704). 309/662-0000; fax 309/663-6668; res 800/53-SUITE. www.eastland-suites.com.* 88 kit. suites, 3 story. S $79; D $89; under 18 free; wkly rates; higher rates graduation. Crib free. TV; cable (premium). Indoor pool; whirlpool. Complimentary continental bkfst, coffee in rms. Restaurant nearby. Ck-out noon. Coin lndry. Valet serv. Meeting rms. Business center. In-rm modem link. Bellhops. Free airport, RR station, bus depot transportation. Exercise equipt; sauna. Balconies. Picnic tables, grills. Cr cds: A, D, DS, MC, V.

⬛ 🏊 🏋 ✈ 🚳 🔥 🚶

★★ **FAIRFIELD INN** . *202 Landmark Dr, Normal (61761). 309/454-6600; fax 309/454-6600. www.fairfieldinn. com.* 128 rms, 3 story. S, D $74; each addl $7; under 18 free. Crib free. TV; cable (premium). Heated pool. Complimentary continental bkfst. Restaurant nearby. Ck-out noon. Meeting rms. Business servs avail. Valet serv. In-rm modem link. Some refrigerators, microwaves. Cr cds: A, C, D, DS, MC, V.

⬛ 🏊 🚳 🚳 SC

★★ **HAMPTON INN.** *604½ IAA Dr (61701). 309/662-2800; fax 309/662-2811; res 800/426-7866. www.hamptoninn.com.* 108 rms, 3 story. S $81; D $83; under 18 free; higher rates special events. Crib free. TV; cable (premium). Heated pool. Complimentary continental bkfst. Coffee in rms. Restaurant adj open 24 hrs. Ck-out noon. Meeting rm. Business servs avail. In-rm modem link. Valet serv. Sundries. Free airport, RR station, bus depot transportation. Health club privileges. Cr cds: A, C, D, DS, ER, JCB, MC, V.

⬛ 🏊 🚳 🔥

★★ **HOLIDAY INN-NORMAL.** *8 Traders Cir, Normal (61761). 309/452-8300; fax 309/454-6722; toll-free 800/465-4329. www.holiday-inn.com.* 160 rms, 5 story. S $68.50-$72.50; D $78.50-$82.50; each addl $9; under 18 free. Crib free. Pet accepted, some restrictions. TV; cable (premium), VCR avail (movies). Indoor pool; whirlpool. Coffee in rms. Restaurant 6:30 am-2 pm, 5-10 pm. Rm serv. Bar 3 pm-midnight. Ck-out noon. Meeting rms. Business center. Bellhops. Valet serv. Free airport, railroad station, bus depot transportation. Exercise equipt; sauna. Game rm. Cr cds: A, MC, V.

⬛ 🍴 🏊 🏋 🚳 SC 🚶

Hotel

★★★ **JUMER CHATEAU.** *1601 Jumer Dr (61704). 309/662-2020; fax 309/662-2020; res 800/285-8637. www.jumers.com.* 180 rms, 5 story, 26 suites. S $85-$100; D $94-$103; each addl $10; suites $107-$154; under 18 free; wkend rates; golf plans. Crib free. Pet accepted. TV; cable (premium). Indoor pool; whirlpool. Coffee in rms, lobby. Restaurant 6:30 am-10 pm; Fri, Sat to 11 pm; Sun 7 am-10 pm. Rm serv. Bar 11:30-1 am; Sun noon-midnight; entertainment. Ck-out noon. Meeting rms. Business servs avail. Gift shop. Free airport, RR station, bus depot transportation. Exercise equipt; sauna. Game rm. Rec rm. Refrigerator, minibar in suites.

Some fireplaces. French decor. Library, antiques. Cr cds: A, MC, V.

[icons]

Restaurants

★★ **CENTRAL STATION CAFE.** *220 E Front St (61701). 309/828-2323. www.centralstation.cc.* Hrs: 11 am-midnight. Closed Mon (Memorial Day-Labor Day); major hols. Continental, American menu. Bar. Lunch $4.95-$6.95, dinner $6.95-$15.95. Specializes in mesquite-grilled fresh seafood, prime rib, barbecued ribs. Entertainment Thurs-Sat. In former fire station (1902). Cr cds: A, DS, MC, V.

[icons]

★★ **JIM'S STEAK HOUSE.** *2307 E Washington St (61704). 309/663-4142.* Hrs: 11 am-midnight; Mon to 10 pm; Sat, Sun from 4 pm. Closed Dec 25. Res accepted. Bar. Lunch $4.25-$8.95, dinner $9.50-$26.95. Specializes in dry-aged steak, prime rib, fresh fish. Pianist Tues-Sat. Rustic decor. Cr cds: A, D, DS, MC, V.

[icons]

Brookfield

See also Cicero, La Grange

Pop 19,085 **Elev** 620 ft **Area code** 708 **Zip** 60513

Information Chamber of Commerce, 3724 Grand Blvd; 708/485-1434

What to See and Do

⭐ **Brookfield Zoo.** (Chicago Zoological Park) One of the finest zoos in the country, it has barless, naturally landscaped enclosures housing more than 2,800 exotic and familiar animals. Exhibits include Hamill Family Play Zoo, an interactive nature environment; The Fragile Kingdom, an introduction to Asia and Africa with emphasis on how the regions' animals—including large cats—relate to each other and to their environment; Tropic World, a simulated rain forest; Habitat Africa!, a five-acre savannah exhibit; Seven Seas Panorama (dolphin shows several times daily; fee); Children's Zoo (animal demonstrations June-Aug, daily; fee); and Motor

Safari Tours (early spring-late fall; fee); free winter shuttle; picnic areas, concessions. Special events throughout the yr, including National Pig Day (early Mar), Teddy Bear Picnic (mid-June), Boo! at the Zoo (Oct), and Holiday Magic Festival (Dec eves). Parking (fee). (Daily) 31st St and 1st Ave. Phone 708/485-0263. ¢¢

Motel/Motor Lodge

★ **COLONY.** *9232 W Ogden Ave (60513). 708/485-0300; fax 708/485-0300.* 36 rms, 1-2 story, 6 kits. S $31.95; D $31.95-$33.95; each addl $3; kit. units $51.95-$53.95. TV; cable (premium). Complimentary coffee. Restaurant nearby. Ck-out 11 am. Cr cds: A, D, DS, MC, V.

[icon]

Cahokia

See also Belleville, Collinsville, Edwardsville

Founded 1699 **Pop** 16,391 **Elev** 411 ft **Area code** 618 **Zip** 62206

Information Cahokia Area Chamber of Commerce, 905 Falling Springs Rd; 618/332-1900

Cahokia, the oldest town in Illinois, was once the center of a vast French missionary area that included what is now Chicago, more than 260 miles northeast. The first church in Illinois was built here by Father St. Cosme in 1699, and a trading post developed around the mission. Cahokia came under the British flag in 1765 and under the American flag in 1778.

What to See and Do

Cahokia Courthouse State Historic Site. Believed to be the oldest house (ca 1735) in the state. Former house of François Saucier, son of the builder of Fort de Chartres. Sold in 1793, it was used as a territorial courthouse and jail until 1814. Museum display of courtroom and period lifestyle; interpretive program. (Tues-Sat) 107 Elm St, just off IL 3. Phone 618/332-1782. **FREE**

⭐ **Cahokia Mounds State Historic Site.** This site preserves the central section of the only prehistoric city N of Mexico. Archaeological finds indicate that the Cahokia site was first inhabited around AD 700. Eventually a very complex community developed; the city of Cahokia covered six sq mi and had a population of tens of thousands. The earthen mounds, used primarily for ceremonial activities of the living, originally numbered more than 100. Only 68 are currently preserved. Monks Mound, the great platform mound named for Trappist monks who once lived near it (1809-1813), is the largest mound north of Mexico and also the largest prehistoric earthen construction in the New World. Its base covers 14 acres, and it rises in four terraces to a height of 100 ft. Two other types of mounds, conical and ridgetop, are also found here. Archaeological excavations have partially uncovered remains of four circular sun calendars, which once consisted of large, evenly spaced log posts probably used to predict the changing seasons. One has been reconstructed in the original location. The 2,000-acre site has a resident archaeologist. Activities include hiking and picnicking. Self-guided tours avail. A museum displays artifacts from the nearby mounds and village areas (Daily; closed some hols). I-255 exit 24, W on Collinsville Rd. Contact Public Relations, 30 Ramey St, Collinsville 62234. Phone 618/346-5160. **FREE**

Historic Holy Family Mission Log Church. Completed in 1799; restored in 1949; the original walnut logs stand upright in Canadian fashion. The old cemetery is behind the church. (June-Aug, daily; 10 am-4 pm) At jct IL 3, 157. Phone 618/337-4548. **DONATION**

Cairo

(H-5) *See also Carbondale*

Settled 1837 **Pop** 3,632 **Elev** 314 ft
Area code 618 **Zip** 62914
Information Chamber of Commerce, 220 8th St; 618/734-2737

Farther south than Richmond, Virginia, Cairo (CARE-o), a city of magnolia trees, is located at the confluence of the Ohio and Mississippi rivers. Settlement was attempted in 1818 by a St. Louis merchant who named the site Cairo because he thought it resembled the Egyptian capital. Cairo and the southern tip of Illinois are still locally referred to as "Little Egypt." Dominating rail and river traffic, spearheading the thrust of free territory into the South, and harboring citizens with Southern sympathies, strategic Cairo was immediately fortified after the outbreak of the Civil War. Cairo served as headquarters, fortress, supply depot, and hospital for Grant's Army of the Tennessee. After the Civil War, the town had the highest per capita commercial valuation in the United States. Rich with war profits, citizens lavished money on both public and private building projects that, according to the National Register of Historic Places, remain as "individual works of architectural brilliance."

Bridges at Cairo connect three states: Illinois, Missouri, and Kentucky. Local legend has it that a penny tossed into the confluence of the rivers at Point Cairo will bring one back again. The levee, rising from the river delta, and the streets along it retain the flavor of the steamboat era.

What to See and Do

Custom House Museum. 19th-century Federal building contains artifacts and replicas from Cairo's past. (Mon-Fri) 1400 Washington Ave. **FREE**

Fort Defiance State Park. Splendid view of the confluence of Ohio and Mississippi rivers on 39 acres; site of Civil War fort. On US 51 at S edge of town.

Horseshoe Lake State Conservation Area. Large flocks of Canada geese migrate to these 10,336 acres in winter. Fishing, boating (ramp; ten-hp motor limit mid-Mar-mid-Nov); hunting, hiking, picnicking, concession, camping. Standard hrs, fees. 7 mi NW on IL 3. Phone 618/776-5689.

Magnolia Manor. (1869) Italianate Victorian mansion (14 rms) built for wealthy flour merchant contains period furnishings, items of local historical interest. View of Mississippi and Ohio rivers from tower. (Daily; closed hols) 2700 Washington Ave. Phone 618/734-0201. ¢¢

Carbondale

(G-4) *See also Cairo, Du Quoin, Marion*

Founded 1852 **Pop** 20,681 **Elev** 415 ft
Area code 618 **Zip** 62901
Information Convention and Tourism Bureau, 1245 E Main St, Suite A32; 618/529-4451 or 800/526-1500
Web www.cctb.org

Carbondale is surrounded by lakes and rivers, including Crab Orchard and Little Grassy lakes and the Big Muddy River. Railroad yards, Southern Illinois University, and surrounding coal fields give the community a unique personality.

What to See and Do

Bald Knob. View of three states from this high point in the Illinois Ozarks. 16 mi S on US 51 to Cobden, then 4 mi W to Alto Pass. Phone 618/529-4451.

Ferne Clyffe State Park. Hawk's cave, a shelter bluff, gorges, canyons on 1,125 acres. Fishing; hunting, hiking, and riding trails; picnicking, camping, equestrian camping. Nature preserve. Standard fees. (Daily) 15 mi S of Marion on IL 37, in Goreville. Phone 618/995-2411. **FREE**

Giant City State Park. Picturesque rock formations and a prehistoric "stone fort" on 4,055 acres. Fishing; hunting, hiking and riding trails, picnicking, concession, lodge, dining room. Camping, cabins, horse campground. Standard hrs, fees. (Daily) 10 mi S on US 51, then E on Old Rt 51, in Makanda. Phone 618/457-4836. **FREE**

Southern Illinois University. (1869) 19,500 students. S on Illinois Ave, US 51. Phone 618/453-2121. On campus is

    University Museum. Exhibits include southern Illinois history, nationally known artists, local collections; changing exhibits. Gift shop. (Tues-Sat, by appt; Sun 1-4 pm; closed school hols) N end of

Faner Hall. Phone 618/453-5388. **FREE**

Motels/Motor Lodges

★ **BEST INNS.** *1345 E Main St (62901). 618/529-4801; fax 618/529-7212; toll-free 800/237-8466. www.bestinn.com.* 82 rms, 2 story. S $42-$50; D $49-$57; each addl $7; under 18 free; higher rates special university events. Crib free. Pet accepted. TV; cable. Pool. Complimentary continental bkfst. Restaurant adj 3 pm-midnight. Business servs avail. Ck-out 1 pm. Refrigerators avail. Cr cds: A, C, D, DS, MC, V.
D ⚡ ≋ ⊠ 🐾 SC

★ **SUPER 8.** *1180 E Main St (62901). 618/457-8822; fax 618/457-4186; res 800/800-8000. www.super8.com.* 63 rms, 3 story. No elvtr. S, D $40-$85; under 12 free. Crib free. Pet accepted. TV; cable (premium). Restaurant adj 6 am-midnight. Coffee in rms. Ck-out 11 am. Cr cds: A, C, D, DS, MC, V.
D ⚡ ⊠ 🔥

Cottage Colony

★ **GIANT CITY STATE PARK LODGE.** *460 Giant City Lodge Rd, Makanda (62958). 618/457-4921.* 34 cottages. S, D $49-$90; each addl $5. Closed mid-Dec-Jan. Crib $5. TV. Pool. Dining rm 8 am-8:30 pm; Sun to 8 pm. Bar to 9 pm. Meeting rms. Gift shop. Some wet bars. In Giant City State Park. Cr cds: A, MC, V.
D 🐾 📺 ≋

Restaurants

★ **MARY LOU'S GRILL.** *114 S Illinois Ave (62901). 618/457-5084.* Hrs: 7 am-2 pm. Closed Sun, Mon; most major hols. Bkfst $1.95-$5, lunch $3-$4.75. Specialties: cream pies, biscuits and gravy. Family-owned. Cr cds: MC, V.
D 🍴

★ **TRES HOMBRES.** *119 N Washington St (62901). 618/457-3308.* Hrs: 11 am-10 pm. Closed most major hols. Res accepted. Mexican menu. Bar. Lunch $3-$7, dinner $5-$10. Specializes in fajitas. Entertainment Thurs.

Southwestern atmosphere. Extensive beer selection. Cr cds: A, D, MC, V.

[D] [⊐]

Unrated Dining Spot

BOOBY'S. *406 S Illinois Ave (62901). 618/549-3366.* Hrs: 11 am-10 pm; Fri, Sat to midnight. Closed major hols. Bar. Deli menu. Lunch, dinner $2.79-$5.99. Specializes in submarine sandwiches, deli fare. Beer garden. Cr cds: D, MC, V.

[D] [⊐]

Centralia

(F-5) *See also Edwardsville, Mount Vernon, Salem*

Founded 1853 **Pop** 14,136 **Elev** 499 ft **Area code** 618 **Zip** 62801
Information Chamber of Commerce, 130 S Locust St; 618/532-6789

Centralia, named for the Illinois Central Railroad, and its neighbors, Central City and Wamac, form a continuous urban area that is the trading center and labor pool for four counties in south central Illinois.

What to See and Do

Centralia Carillon. This 160-ft tower houses 65 bells. Concerts; tours (by appt). 114 N Elm at Noleman. Phone 618/533-4381. **FREE**

Fairview Park. Site of Engine 2500. One of the largest steam locomotives ever built (225 tons), the engine was donated to the city by the Illinois Central Railroad. Swimming; picnicking, playgrounds. (Daily) W on IL 161, at W Broadway.

Lake Centralia. Swimming, fishing, boating; picnicking. 8 mi NE on Green Street Rd.

Raccoon Lake. Fishing, boating (ramp). (Apr-Oct) 3 mi E on IL 161, then ½ mi N on Country Club Rd.

Special Event

Balloon Fest. Foundation Park. Hot-air balloons, races, crafters, food, children's activities, cardboard boat races. Mid-Aug. Phone 618/532-6789.

Motel/Motor Lodge

★ **MOTEL CENTRALIA.** *215 S Poplar St (62801). 618/532-7357; fax 618/533-4304.* 57 rms, 1-2 story. S $35; D $39-$50; each addl $5; under 12 free. Crib $5. TV; cable. Complimentary coffee in lobby. Restaurant nearby. Ck-out 11 am. Business servs avail. Cr cds: A, D, DS, MC, V.

[D] [⊠] [♿]

Restaurant

★ ★ **CENTRALIA HOUSE.** *111 N Oak St (62801). 618/532-9754.* Hrs: 4-11 pm. Closed Sun; hols. Res accepted. Cajun, American menu. Bar. Dinner $18-$25. Specializes in shrimp, pepper steak. Turn-of-the-century elegance. Cr cds: A, D, DS, MC, V.

[SC] [⊐]

Champaign/ Urbana

(D-6) *See also Arcola, Danville*

Settled Urbana, 1822 **Pop** 67,518 **Elev** Champaign, 742 ft; Urbana, 727 ft **Area code** 217 **Zip** Urbana, 61801
Information Convention & Visitors Bureau, 1817 S Neil St, Ste 201, Champaign 61820-7234; 217/351-4133 or 800/369-6151
Web www.cupartnership.org

Champaign and Urbana, separately incorporated, are united as the home of the University of Illinois. Champaign started as West Urbana when the Illinois Central Railroad ran its line two miles west of Urbana, the county seat. Defying annexation by Urbana in 1855, the new community was incorporated in 1860 as Champaign and prospered as a trade center. Today the two communities are geographically one; Champaign continues as a commercial and industrial center, with the larger part of the university falling within the boundaries of Urbana.

Urbana became the seat of Champaign County in 1833, but its anticipated growth was interrupted when the railroad bypassed it. In 1867, the Industrial University opened in Urbana. Now the University of Illinois, it extends into the "twin city" of Champaign. Lincoln Square, the second downtown covered mall in the US, is a forerunner in the revitalization of downtown districts.

What to See and Do

Champaign County Historical Museum. Located in the Historical Cattle Bank (1857); many original items. (Wed-Sat, Sun; closed some hols) 102 E University Ave, Champaign. Phone 217/356-1010. ¢

Lake of the Woods County Preserve. Swimming, boating (rentals), fishing; golf (fee), picnicking, playground. Also Early American Museum and botanical gardens (Memorial Day-Labor Day, daily; after Labor Day-early Oct, wkends). Visitor center. Park (daily). 10 mi W on I-74, then ¼ mi N on IL 47, in Mahomet. Phone 586/218-3586. **FREE**

Orpheum Children's Science Museum. Located in historic Orpheum Theatre. Hands-on exhibits include Dino Dig, Kinderblocks, water tornado, and ghost images. (Wed-Sun, afternoons) 346 N Neil St, Champaign. Phone 217/352-5895. ¢¢

University of Illinois. (1867) 37,000 students. Included among the 200 major buildings on campus are the main library, the third largest academic library in the US (daily); the undergraduate library, built underground to prevent throwing a shadow on the Morrow Plots, the oldest experimental plot of land still in use; Mumford House, the oldest building on campus (1870); Altgeld Hall with a carillon that plays tunes periodically throughout the day; Krannert Center for the Performing Arts; the 69,200-seat Memorial Stadium; and the domed Assembly Hall, which hosts basketball games and concerts. Campus walking tour avail. Information desk at Illini Union, Wright and Green Sts. Campus Visitors Center, Levis Faculty Center, 919 W Illinois (Mon-Fri). Phone 217/333-6241. Phone 217/333-0824. Also on campus

> **Krannert Art Museum.** (Tues-Sat; also Sun afternoons) Peabody St, between 4th and 6th Sts. Phone 217/333-1860. **FREE**

Museum of Natural History. (Mon-Sat, also Sun afternoons) Green St, adj Illini Union. Phone 217/333-2517. **FREE**

World Heritage Museum. (Academic yr, Mon-Fri, also Sun afternoons) Lincoln Hall, Wright St. Phone 217/333-2360. **FREE**

William M. Staerkel Planetarium. Second largest planetarium in Illinois projects 7,600 visible stars on a 50-ft dome. Multimedia shows, lectures. (Thurs-Sat) 2400 W Bradley Ave, in Parkland College Cultural Center, Champaign. Phone 217/351-2446. ¢¢

Motels/Motor Lodges

★ ★ **BEST WESTERN PARADISE INN.** *1001 N Dunlap St, Savoy (61874). 217/356-1824; fax 217/356-1824; 800/780-7234. www.bestwestern. com.* 62 rms, 1-2 story. S $55-$66; D $59-$67; each addl $4; under 12 free. Crib $5. Pet accepted, some restrictions; $5/day. TV; cable (premium). Heated pool; wading pool. Playground. Complimentary continental bkfst, coffee in rms. Restaurant nearby. Ck-out 11 am. Coin lndry. Meeting rm. Business servs avail. In-rm modem link. Exercise equipt. Free airport transportation. Cr cds: A, C, D, DS, MC, V.
⊠ ⊠ ☝ ⬤ D ⧖

★ **COMFORT INN.** *305 W Marketview Dr, Champaign (61821). 217/352-4055; fax 217/352-4055; toll-free 800/228-5150. www.comfortinn. com.* 67 rms, 2 story. Mar-Oct: S, D $59.99; each addl $6; suites $64.99; under 18 free; lower rates rest of yr. Crib free. Pet accepted, some restrictions. TV; cable (premium). Heated indoor pool; whirlpool. Complimentary continental bkfst. Restaurant nearby. Ck-out 11 am. Meeting rm. Business servs avail. Health club privileges. Microwave, refrigerator in suites. Cr cds: A, C, D, DS, MC, V.
D ⬤ ⊠ ⊠ ☝ SC

★ ★ **EAST LAND SUITES.** *1907 N Cunningham, Urbana (61802). 217/367-8331; fax 217/384-3370; toll-free 800/253-8331. www.eastlandsuites urbana.com.* 127 rms, 2 story, 75 suites. S, D $65-$199; each addl $10; under 18 free. Crib free. Pet accepted, some restrictions. TV; cable (premium). Indoor lap pool. Complimentary full bkfst. Bar 5:30-8 pm, closed Sat, Sun. Ck-out 11 am. Meeting rms. Business servs avail. Bellhops. Valet serv. Free airport transportation. Exercise equipt; sauna. Some refrigerators, microwaves, kitchenettes. Private patios, balconies. Cr cds: A, C, D, DS, MC, V.

★ ★ HAWTHORN SUITE HOTEL & CONFERENCE CENTER. *101 Trade Centre Dr, Champaign (61820). 217/398-3400; fax 217/398-6147; toll-free 800/527-1133. www.hawthorn. com.* 199 suites, 4-5 story. S $89-$119; D $99-$129; each addl $10; under 18 free. Crib free. TV; cable (premium), VCR avail. Indoor pool; whirlpool. Complimentary full bkfst, coffee in rms. Restaurant adj 11-1 am. Ck-out noon. Coin lndry. Valet serv. Meeting rms. Business center. In-rm modem link. Bellhops. Sundries. Free airport, RR station, bus depot transportation. Exercise equipt. Health club privileges. Refrigerators, wet bars, microwaves in rms. Cr cds: A, D, DS, JCB, MC, V.

★ ★ LA QUINTA INN. *1900 Center Dr, Champaign (61820). 217/356-4000; fax 217/352-7783; toll-free 800/531-5900. www.laquinta.com.* 122 rms, 2 story. S, D $59.99-$79.99; each addl $7; under 18 free. Crib free. Pet accepted, some restrictions. TV; cable (premium). Heated pool. Complimentary bkfst. Restaurant adj open 24 hrs. Ck-out noon. Coin lndry. In-rm modem link. Valet serv. Cr cds: A, C, D, DS, MC, V.

★ ★ LINCOLN LODGE. *403 W University Ave, Urbana (61801). 217/367-1111; fax 217/367-8233.* 31 rms, 1-2 story. S $48.95; D $54.95; each addl $6; under 12 free. Crib free. TV; cable (premium). Pool. Ck-out noon. Business servs avail. Cr cds: A, D, DS, MC, V.

★ RED ROOF INN. *212 W Anthony Dr, Champaign (61820). 217/352-0101; fax 217/352-1891; toll-free 800/RED-ROOF. www.redroof.com.* 112 rms, 2 story. June-Oct: S $36.99-$51.99; each addl $5; under 18 free.

Crib avail. Pet accepted. TV; cable (premium). Complimentary coffee in lobby. Restaurant nearby. Ck-out noon. Business servs avail. Cr cds: A, D, DS, MC, V.

★ SUPER 8 MOTEL. *202 Marketview Dr, Champaign (61820). 217/359-2388; fax 217/359-2388; toll-free 800/800-8000. www.super8.com.* 61 rms, 2 story. S, D $40-$76; each addl $5; under 12 free. Crib free. Pet accepted; $5 deposit. TV; cable (premium). Complimentary continental bkfst. Restaurants nearby. Ck-out 11 am. Business servs avail. Cr cds: A, C, D, DS, MC, V.

Hotels

★ ★ CHANCELLOR INN. *1501 S Neil St, Champaign (61820). 217/352-7891; fax 217/352-8108.* 224 rms, 4-7 story. S $89; D $99; suites $100-$200; under 18 free. Crib free. Pet accepted. TV; cable. 2 pools, 1 indoor; wading pool. Complimentary continental bkfst. Restaurant adj 6 am-11 pm; to 2 am wkends. Bar 4 pm-1 am; closed Sun. Ck-out 1 pm. Meeting rms. Business servs avail. In-rm modem link. Gift shop. Health club privileges. Free airport, RR, bus transportation. Some refrigerators; microwaves. Dinner theater. Cr cds: A, C, D, DS, MC, V.

★ ★ ★ JUMERS CASTLE LODGE. *209 S Broadway, Urbana (61801). 217/384-8800; fax 217/384-9001.* 130 rms, 4 story. S $82-$127; D $92-$127; each addl $10; suites $107-$170; under 12 free; wkend rates. Crib free. Pet accepted, some restrictions; $25 deposit. TV; cable (premium). Indoor pool; whirlpool. Complimentary coffee in lobby. Restaurant 6:30 am-10 pm; Fri, Sat to 11 pm. Bar 4 pm-1 am. Ck-out noon. Meeting rms. Business servs avail. In-rm modem link. Shopping arcade. Free airport transportation. Health club privileges. Some fireplaces. Cr cds: A, DS, MC, V.

Restaurants

★ **NED KELLY'S.** *1601 N Cunningham Ave, Urbana (61801). 217/344-8201. www.nedkellyssteakhouse.com.* Hrs: 11 am-10 pm; Fri, Sat to 11 pm; Sun to 9 pm. Closed Dec 25. Res accepted. Bar. Lunch $6-$10, dinner $8-$18. Child's menu. Specializes in steak, prime rib, pasta. Multi-level dining with Australian theme. Cr cds: A, DS, MC, V.
D ⊒

★ ★ **TIMPONE'S.** *710 S Goodwin Ave, Urbana (61801). 217/344-7619.* Hrs: 11 am-10 pm; Fri, Sat to 11 pm. Closed Sun; major hols. Res accepted. Contemporary Italian, American menu. Bar. Lunch $3.75-$9.95, dinner $8.95-$19.95. Specializes in fresh seafood, pasta, pizza. Own desserts. Cr cds: MC, V.
D ⊒

Charleston

(E-6) *See also Arcola, Mattoon*

Pop 20,398 **Elev** 686 ft **Area code** 217 **Zip** 61920
Information Charleston Area Chamber of Commerce, 501 Jackson St, PO Box 77; 217/345-7041
Web www.charlestonchamber.com

One of the great Lincoln/Douglas debates was held here on September 18, 1858. As an itinerate lawyer riding the circuit, Abraham Lincoln practiced law in the area. His father, Thomas Lincoln, and stepmother once lived in a cabin eight miles south of Charleston.

What to See and Do

Coles County Courthouse. (1898) Courthouse sits on Charleston Sq, where Lincoln practiced law in an earlier courthouse, and where Charleston Riot took place; riot involved 300 men in armed conflict during the Civil War.

Eastern Illinois University. (1895) 10,000 students. Tarble Arts Center on S 9th St at Cleveland Ave houses visual arts exhibits; changing displays. (Tues-Sun; closed hols) (See SPECIAL EVENTS) Phone 217/581-2787. **FREE**

Fox Ridge State Park. A rugged area of 1,500 acres with Ridge Lake maintained by Illinois Natural History Survey. Fishing (permit from Survey required), boating (no motors); hiking, picnicking, camping (standard fees). 7 mi S on IL 130. Phone 217/345-6416.

Lincoln Log Cabin State Historic Site. This 86-acre site contains the Thomas Lincoln Log Cabin, reconstructed on the original foundation as it was when Abraham Lincoln's father built it in 1840; a reconstructed 1840s farm surrounds the cabin. In nearby Shiloh Cemetery are the graves of Thomas Lincoln and Sarah Bush Lincoln, the president's stepmother. Interpretive program offered May-Oct. Picnicking. (Daily; closed Jan 1, Thanksgiving, Dec 25) (See SPECIAL EVENTS) 8 mi S of Charleston on 4th. Phone 217/345-1845. **FREE**

Moore Home State Historic Site. Before leaving for his inauguration, Lincoln ate his last meal here with his stepmother and her daughter, Mrs. Matilda Moore. (June-Aug, limited hrs) 7 mi S of Charleston on 4th St. Phone 217/345-1845. **FREE**

Special Events

Coles County Fair. Fairgrounds, on Madison Ave. Late July. Phone 217/345-2656.

Celebration: A Festival of the Arts. Eastern Illinois University. Exhibits include paintings, crafts, pottery, and sculpture; plays, music, dancing; foods from around the world; children's activities. Late Aug. Phone 217/581-2113.

Harvest Frolic and Trades Fair. Lincoln Log Cabin State Historic Site. Festival based on central Illinois' agricultural history; exhibits, entertainment. First wkend Oct. Phone 217/345-1845.

Motels/Motor Lodges

★ ★ **BEST WESTERN WORTHINGTON INN.** *920 W Lincoln Ave (61920). 217/348-8161; fax 217/348-8165; toll-free 800/528-8161. www.bestwestern.com.* 67 rms, 1-2 story. S, D $57-$72; each addl $5; suites $116-$126; under 12 free; wkly rates. Crib free. Pet accepted, some restrictions. TV; cable. Heated pool. Complimentary continental bkfst. Restaurants 11 am-8 pm, Sat 7 am-8 pm, Sun 8 am-2 pm. Ck-out 11 am. Meeting rms. Business servs avail. Free airport transportation. Health club privileges. Refrigerators, microwaves avail. Cr cds: A, C, D, DS, MC, V.

John Hancock Building

★ **DAYS INN.** *810 W Lincoln Hwy (61920). 217/345-7689; fax 217/345-7697. www.daysinn.com.* 53 rms, 2 story. S $38-$79; D $42-$85; under 12 free. Crib $5. Pet accepted; $10 deposit. TV; cable (premium), VCR avail. Complimentary continental bkfst. Restaurant nearby. Coffee in rms. Ck-out 11 am. Business servs avail. Refrigerators, microwaves avail. Cr cds: A, C, D, MC, V.

Chicago (A-6)

Settled 1803 **Pop** 2,896,016 **Elev** 596 ft **Area code** 312, 773

Information Chicago Office of Tourism, Chicago Cultural Center, 78 E Washington St, 60602; 312/744-2400 or 800/226-6632

Web www.ci.chi.il.us/tourism

Suburbs *North:* Evanston, Glenview, Gurnee, Highland Park, Highwood, Northbrook, Skokie, Wilmette; *Northwest:* Arlington Heights, Itasca, Schaumburg, Wheeling; *West:* Brookfield, Cicero, Downers Grove, Elmhurst, Geneva, Glen Ellyn, Hillside, Hinsdale, La Grange, Naperville, Oak Brook, Oak Park, St Charles, Wheaton; *South:* Homewood, Oak Lawn.

"I have struck a city—a real city—and they call it Chicago," wrote Rudyard Kipling. For poet Carl Sandburg, it was the "City of the Big Shoulders"; for writer A.J. Liebling, a New Yorker, it was the "Second City." Songwriters have dubbed it a "toddlin' town," and "my kind of town." Boosters say it's "the city that works"; and to most people it is "the windy city." But over and above all the words and slogans is the city itself and the people who helped make it what it is today.

The people of Chicago represent a varied ethnic and racial mix. From the Native Americans who gave the city its name—*Checagou*—to the restless Easterners who traveled west in search of land and opportunity to the hundreds of thousands of venturesome immigrants from Europe, Asia, and Latin America who brought with them the foods and customs of the Old World to the Southern blacks and Appalachians who came in hope of finding better jobs and housing, all have contributed to the strength, vitality, and cosmopolitan ambience that makes Chicago a distinctive and unique experience for the visitor.

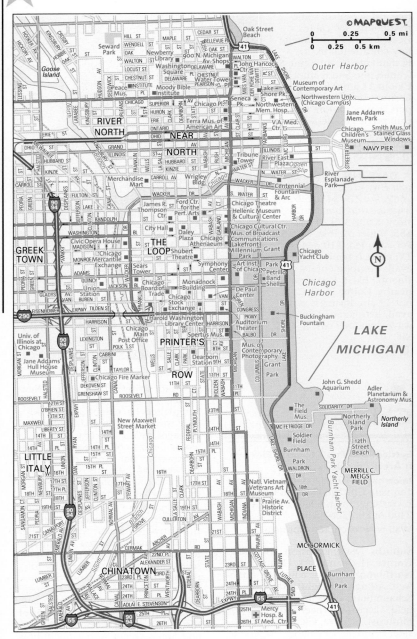

Chicago's past is equally distinctive, built on adversity and contradiction. The first permanent settler was a black man, Jean Baptiste Point du Sable. The city's worst tragedy, the Great Fire of 1871, was the basis for its physical and cultural renaissance. In the heart of one of the poorest ethnic neighborhoods, two young women of means, Jane Addams and Ellen Gates Starr, created Hull House, a social service institution that has been copied throughout the world. A city of neat frame cottages and bulky stone mansions, it produced the geniuses of the Chicago School of Architecture (Louis Sullivan, Daniel Burnham, Dankmar Adler, William LeBaron Jenney, John Willborn Root), whose innovative tradition was carried on by Frank Lloyd Wright and Ludwig Mies van der Rohe. Even its most famous crooks provide a study in contrasts: Al Capone, the Prohibition gangster, and Samuel Insull, the financial finagler whose stock manipulations left thousands of small investors penniless in the late twenties.

Chicago's early merchants resisted the intrusion of the railroad, yet the city became the rail center of the nation. Although Chicago no longer boasts a stockyard, its widely diversified economy makes it one of the most stable cities in the country. Metropolitan Chicago has more than 12,000 factories with a $20-billion annual payroll and ranks first in the United States in the production of canned and frozen foods, metal products, machinery, railroad equipment, letterpress printing, office equipment, musical instruments, telephones, housewares, candy, and lampshades. It has one of the world's busiest airports, largest grain exchange, and biggest mail-order business. It is a great educational center (58 institutions of higher learning); one of the world's largest convention and trade show cities; a showplace, marketplace, shopping, and financial center; and a city of skyscrapers, museums, parks, and churches, with more than 2,700 places of worship.

Chicago turns its best face toward Lake Michigan, where a green fringe of parks forms an arc from Evanston to the Indiana border. The Loop is a city within a city, with many corporate headquarters, banks, stores, and other enterprises. To the far south are the docks along the Calumet River, used by ocean vessels since the opening of the St. Lawrence Seaway and servicing a belt of factories, steel mills, and warehouses. Behind these lies a maze of industrial and shopping areas, schools, and houses.

Although Louis Jolliet mapped the area as early as 1673 and du Sable and a compatriot, Antoine Ouilmette, had established a trading post by 1796, the real growth of the city did not begin until the 19th century and the advent of the Industrial Revolution.

In 1803, the fledging US government took possession of the area and sent a small military contingent from Detroit to select the site for a fort. Fort Dearborn was built at a strategic spot on the mouth of the Chicago River; on the opposite bank, a settlement slowly grew. Fort and settlement were abandoned when the British threatened them during the War of 1812. On their way to Fort Wayne, soldiers and settlers were attacked and killed or held captive by Native Americans who had been armed by the British. The fort was rebuilt in 1816; a few survivors returned, new settlers arrived, but there was little activity until Chicago was selected as the terminal site of the proposed Illinois and Michigan Canal. This started a land boom.

Twenty thousand Easterners swept through on their way to the riches of the West. Merchants opened stores; land speculation was rampant. Although 1837—the year Chicago was incorporated as a city—was marked by financial panic, the pace of expansion and building did not falter. In 1841, grain destined for world ports began to pour into the city; almost immediately, Chicago became the largest grain market in the world. In the wake of the grain came herds of hogs and cattle for the Chicago slaughterhouses. Tanneries, packing plants, mills, and factories soon sprang up.

The Illinois and Michigan Canal, completed in 1848, quadrupled imports and exports. Railroads fanned out from the city, transporting merchandise throughout the nation and bringing new produce to Chicago. During the slump that followed the panic of 1857, Chicago built a huge wooden shed (the Wigwam) at the southeast corner of Wacker and Lake to house the Republican National Convention. Abraham Lincoln was nominated Republican candidate for president here in 1860. The Civil War doubled grain shipments from Chicago. In 1865, the mile-square Union Stock Yards were established. Chicago was riotously prosperous; its population skyrocketed. Then, on October 8, 1871, fire erupted in a cow barn and roared through the city, destroying 15,768 buildings, killing almost 300 people, and leaving a third of the population homeless. But temporary and permanent rebuilding started at once, and Chicago emerged from the ashes to take advantage of the rise of industrialization. The labor unrest of the period produced the Haymarket bombing and the Pullman and other strikes. The 1890s were noteworthy for cultural achievements: orchestras, libraries, universities, and the new urban architectural form for which the term "skyscraper" was coined. The Columbian Exposition of 1893, a magnificent success, was followed by depression and municipal corruption.

Chicago's fantastic rate of growth continued into the 20th century. Industries boomed during World War I, and in the 1920s the city prospered as never before—unruffled by dizzying financial speculation and notorious gang warfare, an outgrowth of Prohibition. The stock market crash of 1929 brought down the shakier financial pyramids; the repeal of Prohibition virtually ended the rackets; and a more sober Chicago produced the Century of Progress Exposition in 1933. Chicago's granaries and steel mills helped carry the country through WWII. The past several decades have seen a reduction of manufacturing jobs in the area and an increase of jobs in service industries and in the fields of finance, law, advertising, and insurance. The 1996 relocation of Lake Shore Drive made it possible to create the Museum Campus, a 57-acre extension of Burnham Park. The Museum Campus provides an easier and more scenic route to the Adler Planetarium, Field Museum, and Shedd Aquarium, and surrounds these three institutions with one continuous park featuring terraced gardens and broad walkways.

Although in the eyes of some Chicago evokes the image of an industrial giant, it is also a city in which the arts flourish. Chicagoans are proud of their world-famous symphony orchestra, their Lyric Opera, and their numerous and diverse dance companies. Since 1912,

Chicago has been the home of *Poetry* magazine. Chicago's theater community is vibrant, with more than 100 off-Loop theaters presenting quality drama. The collections at the Art Institute, Museum of Contemporary Art, Terra Museum of American Art, and many galleries along Michigan Ave and in the River North area are among the best in the country.

Other museums are equally renowned: the Museum of Science and Industry, the Field Museum of Natural History, the Chicago Children's Museum at Navy Pier, and the various specialty museums that reflect the ethnic and civic interests of the city.

The zoos, planetarium, and aquarium, as well as many parks and beaches along the lakefront, afford pleasure for visitors of any age. Chicago's attractions are many, and sightseeing tours can be taken by boat, bus, car, bicycle, or foot.

Buses and rapid transit lines are integrated into one system—the most extensive in the nation—with interchangeable transfers. Elevated lines run through the Loop. Subway trains run under State and Dearborn streets and run on elevated structures to both the north and south. Rapid transit lines also serve the West Side as well as O'Hare and Midway airports. Commuter trains stretch out to the far western and southern suburbs and near the Wisconsin and Indiana borders.

Driving and parking in Chicago are no more difficult than in any other major city. There are indoor and outdoor parking areas near and in the Loop; some provide shuttle bus service to the Loop or to the Merchandise Mart.

The attractions decribed under CHICAGO are arranged topically, and most contain neighborhood designations following their addresses. The Loop is considered the center of the city, with State Street running north and south and Madison Street east and west as the baselines. Attractions contain the following designations: The Loop, Near North, North, Near South, South, and West. The eastern border of the city is Lake Michigan. In addition, some attractions in outlying areas are listed.

Additional Visitor Information

For additional attractions and accommodations, see CHICAGO O'HARE AIRPORT AREA, which follows CHICAGO.

When avail, half-price, day-of-performance tickets are offered, with a slight service charge, at HOT TIX ticket booths, Chicago Place at 700 N Michigan Ave, 108 N State St, 1616 Sherman Ave in Evanston, and Oak Park Visitor Center at 158 Forest Ave in Oak Park. (Tues-Sat; Sun tickets sold on Sat) For avail tickets phone 312/977-1755.

Chicago magazine is helpful for anyone visiting Chicago; avail at most newsstands. *Key-This Week in Chicago* and *Where,* at major hotels, provide up-to-date information. For additional info see any of the daily newspapers; special sections to look at are: *Friday* in the Friday *Chicago Tribune;* the *Arts & Entertainment* section in the Sunday *Chicago Tribune;* and the *Weekend Plus* section of the Friday Chicago *Sun-Times.* A free weekly newspaper, *The Reader,* provides information on local events, art, and entertainment.

There are five Illinois Travel Information centers, located at 310 S Michigan Ave, at the Sears Tower, at the James R. Thompson Center (100 W Randolph St), and at Midway and O'Hare Airports. (Mon-Fri).

The Pumping Station, at the corner of Chicago and Michigan Aves, houses a visitor information center that provides brochures and information on points of interest and transportation. (Daily).

Contact the Chicago Office of Tourism, Chicago Cultural Center, 78 E Washington St, 60602; 312/744-2400 or 800/226-6632. The Office of Tourism distributes an event calendar, maps and museum guides, and hotel and restaurant guides, plus other info concerning the Chicago area. (Mon-Sat, also Sun afternoons).

Transportation

Airport. *O'Hare Intl Airport,* Mannheim Rd & Kennedy Expy, 19 mi NW of Loop (see CHICAGO O'HARE AIRPORT AREA), phone 773/686-2200; *Chicago Midway Airport,* 5700 S Cicero Ave (approx 8 mi S of Loop), phone 773/838-0600.

Car Rental Agencies. See IMPORTANT TOLL-FREE NUMBERS.

Public Transportation. Chicago Transit Authority/Regional Transit Authority, phone 312/836-7000.

Rail Passenger Service. Amtrak 800/872-7245.

What to See and Do

Adler Planetarium & Astronomy Museum. (1930) Bronze sundial by sculptor Henry Moore in entry plaza. Two-part Sky Show in Universe and Sky theaters, Zeiss VI projector, and horizon projection system; Sat and Sun morning children's shows. Exhibits on modern astronomy and astronomical techniques; Race to the Moon exhibit features videotape of first manned landing on the moon; 2.6-oz moon rock; early scientific instruments; displays on the *Voyager* probes, satellites; navigation and the use of telescopes (includes the telescope William Herschel used to discover Uranus); computerized observing station linked with Apache Point observatory in New Mexico; solar telescope. Museum (daily; closed Thanksgiving, Dec 25). 1300 S Lake Shore Dr, on a peninsula in Lake Michigan, Near S Side. Phone 312/322-0300. ¢¢

☆ **Architectural tours.** View the city's architecture by bus, boat, bike, or on foot. Sponsored by the Chicago Architecture Foundation; approx 50 different architectural tours of the city's neighborhoods and suburbs. (Days vary; no tours hols) Contact Chicago Architecture Foundation, 224 S Michigan Ave, 60604. Among tours offered are

Chicago Highlights Bus Tour. This 4-hr bus tour covers the Loop, the Gold Coast, Hyde Park, three historic districts, and three university campuses; includes interior of Frank Lloyd Wright's Robie House. (Sat and Sun) Res required. 224 S Michigan Ave. Phone 312/922-3432. ¢¢¢¢

Chicago River Boat Tour. This 1½-hr tour covers north and south branches of the Chicago River with views of the city's celebrated riverfront architecture; historic 19th-century railroad bridges and ware-houses, 20th-century bridgehouses, and magnificent Loop skyscrapers. (May-Sept, daily; Oct, Tues, Thurs, Sat, and Sun; no tours Labor Day) Res required. 455 E Illinois. Phone 312/942-3432. ¢¢¢¢

Graceland Cemetery Tour. View burial sites and monuments of Chicago's famous historical figures. Headstones of businessmen Marshall Field and Philip Armour, detective Allan Pinkerton, heavy-weight boxing champions Jack Johnson and Robert Fitzsimmons, baseball's National League founder William Hulbert. Cemetery at Clark St and Irving Park Rd on North Side. (Sept-Oct, Sun) Contact Chicago Architecture Foundation. Phone 312/922-TOUR. ¢¢

Loop Walking Tours. Each tour two hrs long. *Early Skyscrapers* traces origins of Chicago School of Architecture and skyscrapers built 1880-1940. Includes the Monadnock and the Rookery. *Modern & Beyond* reviews important newer buildings, including the Federal Center, IBM Building, and the James R. Thompson Center; also public murals and sculptures by Calder, Chagall, Miro, Picasso, Henry Moore, and Dubuffet. (Daily) Depart from Tour Center, 224 S Michigan Ave. Phone 312/922-3432. ¢¢

★ **The Art Institute of Chicago.** (1879) World-renowned collection of American and European paintings, sculpture, prints, and drawings; classical art, Asian art, European and American decorative arts; textiles; primitive art; photography; architectural drawings and fragments; stained-glass windows by Marc Chagall; 68 Thorne miniature rooms; reconstructed Chicago Stock Exchange Trading Room, Arthur Rubloff's paperweight collection; Kraft Education Center. The School of the Art Institute is also located here; gift shop, garden restaurant (summer), cafeteria and dining room (all yr). (Daily; closed Thanksgiving, Dec 25) Free admission Tues. Michigan Ave and Adams St, in Grant Park. Phone 312/443-3600. ¢¢¢

Auditorium Building. (1889) Landmark structure designed by Louis Sullivan and Dankmar Adler. Interior is noted for its intricate system of iron

framing, breathtaking ornamentation, and near-perfect acoustics. Now houses Roosevelt University. 430 S Michigan Ave, in the Loop.

Balzekas Museum of Lithuanian Culture. Antiques, art, children's museum, memorabilia, and literature spanning 1,000 yrs of Lithuanian history. Exhibits include amber, armor and antique weapons, rare maps, textiles, dolls, stamps, coins; research library. (Daily; closed Jan 1, Thanksgiving, Dec 25) Free admission Mon. 6500 S Pulaski Rd, S Side. Phone 773/582-6500. ¢

Brookfield Zoo. (see BROOKFIELD)

Carson Pirie Scott. (1899) Landmark department store building is considered architect Louis Sullivan's masterpiece. Extraordinary cast iron ornamentation on first and second floors frames display windows like paintings. (Mon-Sat and selected Sun; closed hols) State and Madison Sts, in the Loop. Phone 312/641-7000.

Chicago Academy of Sciences' Peggy Notebaert Nature Museum. Environmental museum features six interactive permanent exhibits about Midwestern biodiversity. Gift shop and Butterfly Cafe. (Daily; closed Jan 1, Thanksgiving, Dec 25) Free admission Tues. Phone 773/755-5100. ¢

Chicago Botanic Garden. (see).

Chicago Cultural Center. Landmark building, formerly a library, with Tiffany glass domes, mosaics, marble walls and stairs; houses visitor center. Free programs and changing exhibits sponsored by Chicago Dept of Cultural Affairs. (Daily; closed hols) 78 E Washington St, at Michigan Ave, in the Loop. Phone 312/346-3278. **FREE** Also here is

> **Museum of Broadcast Communications.** Collection of antique radios and televisions; archives of vintage and current radio and television series and events; Radio Hall of Fame; special screenings in Kraft TeleCenter. (Daily; closed hols) Phone 312/629-6000. **FREE**

Chicago Fire Academy. Built on site where the Great Fire of 1871 is believed to have started. 558 W DeKoven St, W Side. Phone 312/747-8151. **FREE**

Chicago Historical Society. Changing exhibits focus on history and devel-

ART DECO THE CHICAGO WAY

Chicago is a textbook of Art Deco design. Look up at the facades of historic high rises, peek into the lobbies of landmark office buildings, ride an elevator or two. Begin at the Chicago Board of Trade (141 West Jackson Boulevard), home to the world's oldest and largest futures exchange, formed in 1848. Ceres, the Roman goddess of grain and harvest, receives due homage with a 31-foot-tall statue atop the original 1930 building and a monumental mural in the atrium added in the 1980s. A massive clock is ornamented with a distinctive agrarian motif. The three-story lobby, a dazzling Art Deco masterpiece, gleams with contrasting black- and buff-colored marble trimmed with silver; elevator doors are silver and black. Light fixtures behind translucent panels throw out a diffused glow, and stylized figures are abundant. Take a free guided tour and watch the frenetic trading in the "pits."

Walk a couple of blocks west for breakfast at Lou Mitchell's (563 West Jackson Boulevard), known for egg dishes served in sizzling skillets. The restaurant presents boxes of Milk Duds to waiting female patrons. Then head north to the American National Bank Building (1 North LaSalle Street). This 49-story limestone building, with typical Art Deco setbacks and dominant vertical lines, occupies an entire block of Chicago's financial district. A stunning Art Deco lobby features dark marble contrasted by gleaming metalwork and exquisite carved wood sconces. Outside, at the fifth-floor level, relief panels chronicle the 17th-century explorations of René Robert de La Salle (Vitzhum & Burns, 1930).

Turn east to the former Chicago Daily News Building (400 West Madison Street). Horace Greeley, Joseph Pulitzer, and other famous journalists, as well as events from Chicago's rich newspaper history, are chronicled with stylized bas-relief figures carved by Alvin Meyer. Originally, the limestone building with dramatic setbacks and an open riverfront plaza was designed to house the newspaper's offices and plant. Inside are ornate metal elevator doors, grillwork, and terrazzo floors in a geometric pattern. Travel north to the Carbide and Carbon Building (230 North Michigan Avenue). Now being renovated, this Art Deco skyscraper is as dramatically dark as its eponymous minerals. Offsetting piles of black polished granite are dark green masonry and gold terra-cotta trim. The stunning two-story lobby features marble walls, elegant bronze grillwork, gold-and-white plaster, and recessed lights of frosted glass. Just a block or two southwest, Heaven on Seven is tucked away on the seventh floor of the Garland Building (111 North Washington Street). Notable Cajun and Creole cooking includes gumbo, po' boy sandwiches, spicy jambalaya, sweet potato pie, and bread pudding.

Divert your attention from the chocolate goodies at Fanny May's street-level outlet and focus on the fifth-floor of this limestone building at 333 North Michigan Avenue. Seven-foot-high carved panels depicting settlers and Native Americans commemorate the site of Fort Dearborn, which overlooked the Chicago River at this spot. The lobby has terrazzo floors of black, russet, and green and brass elevator doors decorated with stylized figures. Farther north on the Magnificent Mile, look up above chic storefronts at the former Palmolive/Playboy Building (919 North Michigan Avenue). Notice the dark bas-relief designs between windows of this massive, stepped building. Turn the corner onto Walton and check out the lobby. It features Art Deco lights and handsome walnut elevator doors sculpted with bas-relief figures. Ride an elevator and note that the ornate carvings continue inside. The Saloon (200 East Chestnut) is a warm, cheery steakhouse with high-quality, flavorful meat, suitably marbled and dry-aged. Be sure to try a side of bacon-scallion mashed potatoes. Decor features stenciled earth-tone walls, parchment sconces, and Native American murals.

opment of Chicago. Selected aspects of Illinois and US history including galleries devoted to costumes, decorative arts, and architecture. Pioneer craft demonstrations; hands-on gallery. (Daily; closed Jan 1, Thanksgiving, Dec 25) Free admission Mon. Additional charges for special exhibits. Clark St at North Ave, Near N Side. Phone 312/642-4600. ¢¢

Chicago Loop Synagogue. (1957) The eastern wall of this building is a unique example of contemporary stained glass, depicting ancient Hebraic symbols whirling through the cosmos. 16 S Clark St, in the Loop. Phone 312/346-7370.

Chicago Temple. (First Methodist Episcopal Church, 1923) At 568 ft from street level to the tip of its Gothic tower, this is the highest church spire in the world. Tours (Mon-Sat at 2 pm; tours Sun after 8:30 am and 11 am services; no tours hols). 77 W Washington St, in the Loop. Phone 312/236-4548.

Chicago Tribune Tower. (1925) Essentially, this is a *moderne* building (36 story) with a Gothic-detailed base and crown; it does exactly what publisher Joseph Medill intended: it "thames" the Chicago river. The tower's once strong foundation has been loosening in recent yrs, and structural engineers have noted that the edifice has been slowly sinking at the rate of almost a ft a yr due to seepage from a sublevel bog just west along the riverbank. Bits and pieces of historic structures from around the world are embedded in the exterior walls of the lower floors. 435 N Michigan Ave, Near N Side. Phone 312/222-3994.

Civic Opera Building. (1929) On the lower levels, under 45 floors of commercial office space, is the richly Art Deco, 3,600-seat Civic Opera House, home of the Lyric Opera of Chicago. 20 N Wacker Dr, in the Loop. Phone 312/332-2244.

DePaul University. 20,500 students. The north campus, with its blend of modern and Gothic architecture, is an integral part of Chicago's historic Lincoln Park neighborhood. The Blue Demons, DePaul's basketball team, play home games at the Allstate Arena in Rosemont (see). Tours (by appt). Lincoln Park campus, Fullerton and Sheffield St, Near North

Side; Loop campus, 1 E Jackson Blvd. Phone 312/362-8300.

Donald E. Stevens Convention Center. 5555 N River Rd, Rosemont. Phone 847/692-2220.

DuSable Museum of African-American History. African and African-American art objects; displays of black history in Africa and the US. Extensive collection includes paintings, sculpture, artifacts, textiles, books, and photographs. (Daily; closed Jan 1, Thanksgiving, Dec 25) Free admission Sun. 740 E 56th Pl, S Side. Phone 773/947-0600. ¢¢

★ **Field Museum.** (1920) One of the largest natural history museums in the world. Includes world culture, history, animal, and gem exhibits. Egyptian tomb complex with burial shaft, chamber, and mummies. Touchable displays in the Place for Wonder; Traveling the Pacific features exhibits on Pacific natural history and cultures. Special exhibits, films, lectures, demonstrations, and performances; restaurants and gift shop. (Daily; closed Jan 1, Dec 25) List of touchables for visually impaired avail. Free admission (Sept-Feb, Mon-Tues). 1400 S Lake Shore Dr, Near S Side. Phone 312/922-9410. ¢¢¢

Fourth Presbyterian Church. Completed in 1914, this beautiful church is a fine example of Gothic design. One of its architects, Ralph A. Cram, was a leader of the Gothic Revival in the US. Tours avail by appt or after Sun services.(Daily) 126 E Chestnut, Near N Side. Phone 312/787-4570.

Garfield Park and Conservatory. Outdoor formal gardens. Conservatory has eight houses and propagating houses on more than five acres. Permanent exhibits. Four major shows annually at Horticultural Hall and Show House. (Daily) 300 N Central Park Ave, W Side. Phone 312/746-5100. **FREE**

Grant Park. Chicago's downtown park. Contains the James C. Petrillo Music Shell. (See SPECIAL EVENTS) Stretching from Randolph St to McFetridge Dr, in the Loop. Also in Grant Park is

   Buckingham Fountain. Carved of pink Georgia marble; formal gardens nearby. Waters rise 135 ft; color display and water spectacle (May-Oct 1, daily). Foot of Congress St.

The Ferris Wheel at Navy Pier.

Petrillo Music Shell. Columbus Dr and Jackson Blvd in Grant Park. Phone 312/742-7530.

Haymarket Riot Monument. Commemorates the riot that killed seven policemen when a bomb exploded during a labor strike May 4, 1886. Statue still stirs passions over labor issues. 1300 W Jackson St.

Holy Name Cathedral. (Roman Catholic) Neo-Gothic architecture. (Daily) Guided tours, res required. 735 N State St, Near N Side. Phone 312/787-8040.

Horse racing.

Balmoral Park Race Track. Harness racing. (All yr, days vary) 25 mi S on 1-94 to IL 394, continue S to Elmscourt Ln in Crete. Phone 708/672-1414.

Hawthorne Race Course. (see).

Maywood Park Race Track. Parimutuel harness racing. Nightly Mon, Wed, Fri. Also TV simulcast thoroughbred racing (daily). 8600 W North Ave, in Maywood, I-290, exit 1st Ave N. Phone 708/343-4800.

Sportsman's Park Race Track. (see CICERO) Approx 7 mi W. Phone 773/242-1121.

Illinois Institute of Technology. (1892) 6,000 students. Campus designed by Mies van der Rohe. 3300 S Federal St, S Side. Phone 312/567-3000.

International Museum of Surgical Science. Housed in an old mansion, museum features exhibits on the history of surgery. Main exhibit on surgical implements ca 1900. (Tues-Sat) 1524 N Lake Shore Dr. Phone 312/642-6502. ¢¢

Jane Addams' Hull House. Two original Hull House buildings, restored Hull Mansion (1856) and dining hall (1905), which formed the nucleus of the 13-building settlement complex founded in 1889 by Jane Addams and Ellen Gates Starr, social welfare pioneers. Exhibits and presentations on the history of Hull House, the surrounding neighborhood, ethnic groups, and women's history. (Mon-Fri, also Sun afternoons; closed hols) 800 S Halsted St, on campus of University of Illinois at Chicago, W Side. Phone 312/413-5353. **FREE**

John G. Shedd Aquarium. (1930) The world's largest indoor aquarium features more than 8,000 freshwater and marine animals displayed in 200 naturalistic habitats; divers hand-feed fish, sharks, eels, and turtles several times daily in 90,000-gallon Caribbean Reef exhibit. The Oceanarium re-creates a Pacific Northwest ecosystem with whales, dolphins, sea otters, and seals. A colony of penguins inhabit a Falkland Islands exhibit; Seahorse Symphony exhibit. Food service and gift shops. (Daily; closed Jan 1, Dec 25) Free admission Mon, Tues (Sept-Feb only). 1200 S Lake Shore Dr, at Roosevelt Rd, Near S Side. Phone 312/939-2438. ¢¢¢

John Hancock Center. (1969) World's tallest office/residential skyscraper (100 stories); ¼-mi high. Observatory, at 1,030 ft, offers an excellent view of the city, the Chicago lakefront, and four states. (Daily; cashier located on concourse level) Parking garage in building (fee). 875 N

Michigan Ave, Near N Side. Phone 312/751-3681. ¢¢¢

Lincoln Park. Largest in Chicago, stretches almost the entire length of the north end of the city along the lake. Contains statues of Lincoln, Hans Christian Andersen, Shakespeare, and others; nine-hole golf course, driving range, miniature golf, bike and jogging paths, obstacle course, protected beaches. Near N Side. Phone 312/742-7529. In park are

> **Lincoln Park Conservatory.** Has four glass buildings, 18 propagating houses, and three acres of cold frames; formal and rock gardens; extensive collection of orchids. Four major flower shows annually at Show House. (Daily) Stockton Dr near Fullerton. Phone 312/742-7736. **FREE**

> **Lincoln Park Zoological Gardens.** The zoo is situated on 35 acres and houses more than 1,600 animals, including many exotic and endangered species; one of the largest collections in US. Regenstein Small Mammal and Reptile House is a glass-domed facility housing over 200 animals, including endangered species. A well-known gorilla collection is housed in a spectacular naturalistic habitat, and thousands of migrant and resident birds are sheltered in a wooded area. Also here is a five-acre farm-in-the-zoo and children's zoo with Discovery Center. Guided tours, zoo films and lectures, talks at animal habitats. (Daily) W entrance, Webster Ave and Stockton Dr; E entrance, Cannon Dr off Fullerton Ave. Phone 312/742-2000. **FREE**

Loyola University. (1870) 14,300 students. Martin d'Arcy Museum of Art (Tues-Sat; closed hols, semester breaks). Fine Arts Gallery of the Edward Crown Center; exhibits (Mon-Fri; closed hols). Lake Shore campus, 6525 N Sheridan Rd. Downtown campus, 820 N Michigan Ave, N Side.

Marina City. (1959-67). Condominium and commercial building complex with marina and boat storage. Includes two 550-ft-tall cylindrical buildings; home of House of Blues club and hotel. Designed by Bertrand Goldberg Associates; one of the most unusual downtown living-

working complexes in the US. 300 N State St, N side of Chicago River, Near N Side.

Marshall Field's. (1902, 1907) Landmark for more than a century; one of the most famous stores in the country. A traditional Chicago meeting place is under its clock, which projects over the sidewalk. On one side is an inner court rising 13 stories, on the other is a six-story rotunda topped by a Tiffany dome made of 1.6 million pieces of glass. (Daily; closed Thanksgiving, Dec 25) 111 N State St, in the Loop. Phone 312/781-4483.

McCormick Place Convention Complex. Nation's largest exposition and meeting complex. Exhibits, special shows, Arie Crown Theatre, and restaurant facilities. E 23rd St and S Lake Shore Dr, S Side. Phone 312/791-7000.

Merchandise Mart. (1930) The world's largest commercial building; restaurants and shopping; Apparel Center adj. Wells St at Chicago River, Near N Side. Phone 312/527-7600.

Mexican Fine Arts Center Museum. Showcase of Mexican art and heritage; museum features revolving exhibits of contemporary and classical works by renowned Mexican artists. (Tues-Sun) 1852 W 19th St. Phone 312/738-1503. **FREE**

⭐ **Michigan Avenue.** Michigan Ave, between the Chicago River on the south and Oak St on the north, is one of the world's great shopping areas, with representative branches of many national and international specialty and department stores. Near N Side. Also on the "Magnificent Mile" are

> **Chicago Place.** Eight-story vertical mall with more than 50 stores and seven restaurants. (Daily; closed Jan 1, Easter, Dec 25) 700 N Michigan Ave. Phone 312/642-4811.

> **Nike Town.** Since opening in 1993, the five-story sports store has become a tourist attraction. Includes Nike Museum, a video theater, display of athletic gear worn by Michael Jordan, and a basketball court with a 28-ft likeness of the basketball star. (Daily; closed hols) 669 N Michigan Ave. Phone 312/642-6363.

> **900 North Michigan Shops.** More than 60 shops and restaurants

around marble atrium. (Daily; closed hols) Phone 312/915-3916.

Water Tower Place. Atrium mall with more than 125 shops, 11 restaurants, seven movie theaters, and the Ritz-Carlton Hotel. (Daily; closed hols) 835 N Michigan Ave. Phone 312/440-3165.

Monadnock Building. (1889-91) Highest wall-bearing building in Chicago was, at the time of its construction, the tallest and largest office building in the world. It is now considered one of the masterworks of the Chicago school of architecture. Designed by Burnham & Root; south addition by Holabird & Roche (1893). 53 W Jackson Blvd, in the Loop.

Museum of Contemporary Art. Changing exhibits of contemporary art; paintings, sculpture, video, performance, films, lectures. (Tues-Sun; closed Jan 1, Thanksgiving, Dec 25) Free admission Tues. 220 E Chicago Ave, Near N Side. Phone 312/280-2660. ¢¢

Museum of Contemporary Photography. Museum focuses on photography from 1950-present. (Mon-Sat) 600 S Michigan Ave. Phone 312/663-5554. **FREE**

Museum of Holography/Chicago. Permanent collection of holograms (three-dimensional images made with lasers) featuring pieces from the US and many European and Asian countries. (Wed-Sun, afternoons; closed hols) 1134 W Washington Blvd, W Side. Phone 312/226-1007. ¢¢

⭐ **Museum of Science and Industry.** More than 2,000 exhibit units use visitor interaction to illustrate scientific principles and industrial concepts. Among the many displays are the "Idea Factory"; Apollo 8 spacecraft; miniature circus with 22,000 hand-carved pieces; chick incubator; coal mine; captured German U-boat; and 16-ft-tall, walk-through human heart model. (Daily; closed Dec 25) Free admission Thurs. 57th St and Lake Shore Dr, S Side. Phone 773/684-1414. ¢¢¢ Also here is

Crown Space Center. This 35,000-sq-ft space center houses the latest in space exhibitions; 334-seat Omnimax Theater in a 76-ft diameter projection dome. Omnimax ¢¢¢

National Vietnam Veterans Art Museum. Houses more than 500 pieces of fine art created by artists who served in the Vietnam War. Interactive dioramas, artifacts; museum store, cafe. (Tues-Sun; closed hols). 1801 S Indiana, S Side. Phone 312/326-0270. ¢

Navy Pier. This landmark extends more than ½ mi into the lake. Renovated in 1995, the pier features a 150-ft-high Ferris wheel, carousel, children's museum, four-masted schooner, shops, restaurants, and arcades. The Skyline Stage offers a variety of music in the summertime. 600 E Grand Ave, Near N Side. Phone 312/595-7437. Also here is

Chicago Children's Museum. Interactive exhibits focus on the arts, science, and humanities. Includes a fully-equiped art studio. (Daily) Phone 312/527-1000.

The Newberry Library. (1887) Houses more than 1.4 million volumes and several million manuscripts. Internationally famous collections on the Renaissance, Native Americans, the Chicago Renaissance, the American West, local and family history, music history, history of printing, calligraphy, cartography, others. Exhibits open to the public. Admission to reading rooms by registration. (Tues-Sat; closed hols) Tours (Thurs, Sat). 60 W Walton St, Near N Side. Phone 312/943-9090. **FREE**

North Pier Chicago. Three-blk-long warehouse (1905) converted into marketplace with more than 50 shops; restaurants, bars, nightclubs, video arcades, miniature golf. Parking (fee). (Daily; closed Jan 1, Thanksgiving, Dec 25) 435 E Illinois St, 4 blks E of N Michigan Ave, Near N Side. Phone 312/836-4300. **FREE**

Northwestern University Chicago Campus. (1920) 5,400 students. Schools of Medicine, Law, Dentistry, and University College. (See also EVANSTON) Lake Shore Dr and Chicago Ave, Near N Side. Phone 312/503-8649.

Oak Street. The blk between Michigan Ave and N Rush St is lined with small shops that specialize in high fashion and the avant-garde from around the world. Near N Side.

Oriental Institute Museum. Outstanding collection of archaeological material illustrating the art, architecture, religion, and literature from the ancient Near East. Lectures, workshops, free films (Sun; limited hrs). Museum (Tues-Sun; closed Jan 1, Thanksgiving, Dec 25). 1155 E 58th St, on University of Chicago campus, S Side. Phone 773/702-9514. **FREE**

Our Lady of Sorrows Basilica. (1890-1902) Worth seeing are the Shrine Altar of the Seven Holy Founders of the Servites (main altar of Carrara marble) and the beautiful English Baroque steeple, chapels, paintings, and other architectural ornamentations (daily). Tours (by res). 3121 W Jackson Blvd, W Side. Phone 773/638-0159.

Outdoor Art.

Batcolumn. (1977) Designed by artist Claes Oldenburg. This 100-ft-tall, 20-ton welded steel sculpture resembles a baseball bat, set in a concrete base. 600 W Madison St, outside the Harold Washington Social Security Administration Building plaza, in the Loop.

Flamingo. (1974) Sculptor Alexander Calder's stabile is 53 ft high and weighs 50 tons. Federal Center Plaza, Adams and Dearborn Sts, in the Loop.

The Four Seasons. (1974) This 3,000-sq-ft mosaic designed by Marc Chagall contains more than 320 different shades and hues of marble, stone, granite, and glass. First National Plaza, Monroe and Dearborn Sts, in the Loop.

Miro's Chicago. (1981) The structure, made of steel, wire mesh, concrete, bronze, and ceramic tile, is 39 ft tall. The Brunswick Building, 69 W Washington, in the Loop.

Untitled. (1967) Created by Pablo Picasso, the structure is 50 ft high and weighs 162 tons. Richard J. Daley Plaza, Washington St, in the Loop.

Untitled Sounding Sculpture. (1975) Unique "sounding sculpture" set in reflecting pool. Designed by Harry Bertoia. Amoco Building, 200 E Randolph, in the Loop.

Performing arts—City.

Chicago Symphony Orchestra. Symphony Center. 220 S Michigan Ave. Phone 312/294-3333.

Lyric Opera of Chicago. Civic Opera House. 20 N Wacker Dr. Phone 312/419-0033.

Peace Museum. Exhibits focusing on the role of the arts, the sciences, labor, women, minorities, and religious institutions on issues of war and peace and on the contributions of individual peacemakers. (Tues-Fri; schedule varies) Garfield Park Dome, 100 N Central Park Ave. 1 blk E and 4 blks N of Independence St exit of Eisenhower Expressway. Phone 773/638-6450. ¢¢

Performing arts—Outlying Areas.

Marriott Lincolnshire Resort Theater. (see WHEELING) Lincolnshire. Phone 847/634-0200.

North Shore Center for the Performing Arts. (see SKOKIE) 9501 Skokie Blvd. Phone 847/673-6300.

Pheasant Run Dinner Theatre. W on IL 64 in St. Charles. Phone 630/584-6300.

Ravinia Festival. (see HIGHLAND PARK) Phone 847/266-5000.

Polish Museum of America. Polish culture, folklore, immigration; art gallery, archives, and library; Paderewski and Kosciuszko rooms. (Closed Thurs; Jan 1, Good Friday, Dec 25) 984 N Milwaukee Ave, Near N Side. Phone 773/384-3352. **DONATION**

Prairie Avenue Historic District. Area where millionaires lived during the 1800s. The **Clarke House** (ca 1835), the oldest house still standing in the city, has been restored and now stands at a site near its original location. The **Glessner House** (1886), 1800 S Prairie Ave, is owned and maintained by the Chicago Architecture Foundation. Designed by architect Henry Hobson Richardson, the house has 35 rooms, many of which are restored with original furnishings; interior courtyard. Two-hr guided tour of both houses (Wed-Sun). Other houses on the cobblestone street are **Kimball House** (1890), 1801 S Prairie Ave, replica of a French chateau; **Coleman House** (ca 1885), 1811 S Prairie Ave, and **Keith House** (ca 1870), 1900 S

Prairie Ave. Architectural tours. Free admission on Wed. Prairie Ave, between 18th and Cullerton Sts, S Side. Phone 312/326-1480. One-house tour ¢¢ Two-house tour ¢¢¢

Professional sports.

Chicago Blackhawks (NHL). United Center, 1901 W Madison St. Phone 312/455-4500.

Chicago Bulls (NBA). United Center, 1901 W Madison St. Phone 312/455-4000.

Chicago Cubs (MLB). Wrigley Field, 1060 W Addison St. Phone 773/404-2827.

Chicago White Sox (MLB). Comiskey Park. 333 W 35th St. Phone 312/674-1000.

Chicago Wolves (IHL). Allstate Arena. 6920 Mannheim Rd. Rosemont, IL. 800/THE-WOLVES.

Richard J. Daley Center and Plaza. This 31-story, 648-ft building houses county and city courts and administrative offices. In the plaza is the Chicago Picasso sculpture; across Washington St is the Chicago Miro sculpture. Randolph and Clark Sts, in the Loop. Phone 312/603-7980.

Robie House. (1909) Designed by Frank Lloyd Wright, this may be the ultimate example of the Prairie house. Tours (daily; closed hols). 5757 S Woodlawn Ave, near University of Chicago campus, S Side. Phone 773/834-1847. ¢¢

Rockefeller Memorial Chapel. Designed by Bertram Grosvenor Goodhue Associates; noted for its Gothic construction, vaulted ceiling, 8,600-pipe organ and 72-bell carillon. Guided tours by appt. 5850 S Woodlawn Ave, on University of Chicago campus. Phone 773/702-2100.

The Rookery. (1886) Oldest remaining steel-skeleton skyscraper in the world. Designed by Burnham & Root, the remarkable glass-encased lobby was remodeled in 1905 by Frank Lloyd Wright. 209 S La Salle St, in the Loop.

Roosevelt University. (1945) 6,400 students. Auditorium Building designed by Louis Sullivan and engineered by Dankmar Adler in 1889. Entrance at 430 S Michigan Ave, in the Loop. Phone 312/341-3500.

⭐ **Sears Tower.** (1974) This 110-story office building, designed by Skidmore, Owings & Merrill, is the Northern Hemisphere's tallest, rising 1,454 ft over the city. Skydeck observation area on 103rd floor (daily) with optional "Chicago Experience" multimedia presentation. *Universe,* a motorized, kinetic mobile by Alexander Calder, is located in the Wacker Dr lobby. More than 15 shops and restaurants are in the building. Skydeck entrance on Jackson Blvd, between Franklin and Wacker. 233 S Wacker Dr, in the Loop. Phone 312/875-9696. Skydeck ¢¢

Sightseeing boat tours.

Mercury, the Skyline Cruiseline. Offers 1-hr, 1½-hr, and 2-hr lake and river cruises; also Sun brunch, dinner, and luncheon cruises. (May-Oct) Wacker Dr and Michigan Ave (S side of Michigan Ave Bridge). Phone 312/332-1353. ¢¢¢¢

Shoreline Marine Company. Thirty-min tour of lakefront. (May-Sept, daily) Departures from Shedd Aquarium, afternoons, and Buckingham Fountain, eves. Phone 312/222-9328. ¢¢

Spirit of Chicago. Lunch, brunch, dinner, and moonlight cruises; entertainment. (Yr-round) Navy Pier. Phone 312/836-7899. ¢¢¢¢

Wendella. One-, 1½-, and 2-hr lake and river cruises. (Apr-mid-Oct, daily) 400 N Michigan Ave, at the Wrigley Building (NW side of Michigan Ave Bridge). Phone 312/337-1446. ¢¢¢

Sightseeing bus tours.

American Sightseeing Tours. Depart from Palmer House Hotel, 17 E Monroe St. Phone 312/251-3100.

Chicago Motor Coach Company. Double-decker tours depart from Sears Tower at Jackson and Wacker, Field Museum, Michigan and Pearson, and Michigan and Wacker. Phone 312/922-8919.

Chicago Neighborhood Tours. Departs from the Chicago Cultural Center. Narrated tours visit ten different neighborhoods via motor coach bus. Tours on Sat only. Reservations strongly recommended. Phone 312/742-1190.

Chicago Trolley Company. One-fee, all-day ride, with ability to hop on and off at major sites. Phone 312/663-0260. ¢¢¢¢

Gray Line Tours. Tours depart from 17 E Monroe St. Phone 312/251-3107.

Untouchable Tours. Guided tour of gangster hot spots of 1920s and '30s. Departs from 610 N Clark St. Tour with dinner and revue also avail. (Daily; res strongly recommended) Phone 773/881-1195. ¢¢¢¢

Six Flags Great America. (see).

Spertus Museum. Permanent collection of ceremonial objects from many parts of the world; sculpture, graphic arts, and paintings; ethnic materials spanning centuries; changing exhibits in fine arts; documentary films and photographs. Rosenbaum Artifact Center has hands-on exhibits on ancient Near East archaeology. (Mon-Fri, Sun; closed Sat, hols and Jewish hols) Free admission Fri. At Spertus Institute of Jewish Studies, 618 S Michigan Ave, in the Loop. Phone 312/322-1747. ¢¢

State Street. Besides many specialty stores, shopping on State St including Marshall Field's and Carson Pirie Scott department stores and some of the world's most renowned architecture. Recent renovations have returned State St to its 1920s glamour, with period lampposts, ornamental subway kiosks, landscaped planters, and multicolored sidewalks. A self-guided tour of 20 historically significant State St buildings is avail. In the Loop.

Swedish-American Museum Center. Pays tribute to Swedish heritage and history. Exhibits on Swedish memorabilia. (Tues-Sun) 5211 N Clark St. Phone 773/728-8111.

Symphony Center. (1904) Historic Symphony Center is home of the Chicago Symphony Orchestra and stage for the Civic Orchestra of Chicago, chamber music groups, diverse musical attractions, and children's programs. Includes Buntrock Hall, a ballroom, rehearsal space, and restaurant. 220 S Michigan Ave, in the Loop.

Terra Museum of American Art. Collection of 19th-, and 20th-century paintings by American artists. (Tues-Sun; closed hols) Free admission

Thurs, 1st Sun of month. 664 N Michigan Ave, Near N Side. Phone 312/664-3939. ¢¢

Theaters.

Apollo. 2540 N Lincoln Ave. Phone 773/935-6100.

Arie Crown. McCormick Place, E 23rd St and S Lake Shore Dr. Phone 312/791-6000.

Auditorium. 50 E Congress Pkwy. Phone 312/922-2110.

Briar Street. 3133 N Halsted St. Phone 773/348-4000.

Chicago. 175 N State St. Phone 312/443-1130.

Civic Opera House. Owned and operated by the Lyric Opera of Chicago, 20 N Wacker Dr. Phone 312/419-0033.

Goodman. 170 N Dearborn. Phone 312/443-3800.

Royal George. 1641 N Halsted St. Phone 312/988-9000.

Second City. 1616 and 1608 N Wells St. Phone 337/399-2161 or 642/818-9160.

Shubert. 22 W Monroe St. Phone 312/977-1710.

Steppenwolf. 1650 N Halsted St. Phone 312/335-1650.

Theatre Building. 1225 W Belmont Ave. Phone 773/327-5252.

Victory Gardens. 2257 N Lincoln Ave. Phone 773/549-5788.

United Center. 1901 W Madison St. Phone 312/455-4500.

United States Post Office. (1933) Largest in the world under one roof. Individuals may join 1½-hr guided group tours (Mon-Fri, three tours daily; no tours hols and Dec). No cameras, pkgs, or purses. Res required. 433 W Harrison, in the Loop. Phone 312/983-7550 or 312/983-7527. **FREE**

University of Chicago. (1892) 12,750 students. It was on this campus that Enrico Fermi produced the first sustained nuclear reaction. The University of Chicago also has had one of the highest number of Nobel Prize winners of any institution. The campus includes the Oriental Institute, Robie House, Rockefeller Memorial Chapel, and David and Alfred Smart Museum of Art, on Greenwood Ave (Tues-Sun; free; phone 773/702-0200). Guided one-hr campus tours leave from 1212 E 59th St. 5801 S

Ellis Ave, S Side. Phone 773/702-8374.

University of Illinois at Chicago.
(1965) 25,000 students. Comprehensive urban university. On campus is Jane Addams' Hull House. Near I-94 and I-290, W Side. 1200 W Harrison. Phone 312/996-4350.

Wabash Avenue. This unique street, always in the shadow of elevated train tracks, is known for its many specialty stores—books, music, musical instruments, records, men's clothing, tobacco, etc.—as well as being the center of the wholesale and retail jewelry trade. S of the river to Congress Ave, in the Loop.

⭐ **Walking tours of Pullman Historic District.** Built in 1880-1884 to house the workers at George M. Pullman's Palace Car Company, the original town was a complete model community with many civic and recreational facilities. Unlike most historic districts, 9/10 of the original buildings still stand. The 1½-hr tours start at the Historic Pullman Center, 614 E 113th St. Tours (May-Oct, first Sun of month; two departures). Phone 773/785-3828. ¢¢

Water Tower. (1869) Fanciful, Gothic Revival tower that survived the Great Chicago Fire of 1871. 806 N Michigan Ave, Near N Side.

Wrigley Building. (1924) One of the most beloved buildings in the city, the white terra-cotta Spanish Renaissance-style tower is actually two structures connected by bridges. Headquarters of the chewing gum empire; illuminated nightly. 400 N Michigan Ave, Near N Side.

Special Events

Navy Pier Art Fair. At Navy Pier. Month-long exhibit of local artists' work. Jan. Phone 312/744-3370.

Chicago Auto Show. McCormick Place. Hundreds of foreign and domestic cars are displayed. Second wkend Feb. Phone 312/744-3370.

Winter Delights. Citywide. Includes snow carving contests. First 2 wks Feb. Phone 312/744-3315.

St. Patrick's Day Parade. City parade Sat before hol; S Side parade Sun before hol. Wkend closest Mar 17. Phone 312/744-3370.

Spring Flower Show. Citywide, most notably at the Lincoln Park Conservatory. Apr. Phone 312/746-5100.

Art Chicago. Navy Pier. Worldwide artists' exhibition. Mid-May. Phone 312/587-3300.

Chicago Blues Festival. Grant Park. Three-day festival featuring concerts from blues artists worldwide. June. Phone 312/744-3370.

Ravinia Festival. (see HIGHLAND PARK) Early June-mid-Sept.

Taste of Chicago. Grant Park. Selected Chicago restaurants offer sample-size specialties. Late June-early July. Phone 312/744-3370.

Grant Park Music Festival. James C. Petrillo Music Shell. Concerts Wed, Fri, Sat, late June-Sept. Phone 312/742-4763. **FREE**

Grant Park July 3 Concert. At Petrillo Music Shell. Lakefront blazes with cannon flashes as the Grant Park Symphony welcomes Independence Day with Tchaikovsky's *1812 Overture;* fireworks. July 3. Phone 312/744-3370.

Chicago to Mackinac Races. On Lake Michigan. Third wkend July. Phone 312/744-3370.

Venetian Night. Monroe St Harbor. Venetian aquatic parade, fireworks. Late July. Phone 312/747-2474.

Air & Water Show. North Ave Beach. Dazzling display of air/sea virtuosity by US Navy Blue Angels Flight Squadron and Golden Knights Parachute team. Mid Aug. Phone 312/744-3370.

Jazz Festival. Grant Park. Late Aug-early Sept. Phone 312/744-3370.

Chicago International Film Festival. New films shown throughout city. Phone 312/425-9400 (24-hr hotline). Three wks Oct.

Motels/Motor Lodges

★★ **BEST WESTERN INN OF CHICAGO.** *162 E Ohio St (60610). 312/787-3100; fax 312/573-3136; res 800/557-2378. www.bestwestern.com.* 354 rms, 22 story. S, D $101-$119; suites $195-$325; under 17 free; package plans. Self parking $22. Valet parking $24. TV; cable. Restaurant 6:30 am-10:30 pm. Bar 11-2 am. Ck-out noon. Business servs avail. Meeting rms. Gift shop. Bellhops. Airport transportation. Health club privileges. Cr cds: A, C, D, DS, MC, V.

⊡ ⊠ ⊠

★ **BEST WESTERN RIVER NORTH HOTEL.** *125 W Ohio St (60610). 312/467-0800; fax 312/467-1665; toll-free 800/727-0800. www.bestwestern. com/rivernorthhotel.* 150 rms, 7 story. S, D $157-$167; each addl $8; suites $250; under 18 free; wkend rates; higher rates special events. Crib free. TV; cable (premium). Indoor pool. Complimentary coffee in rms. Restaurant 6 am-midnight. Rm serv. Ck-out noon. In-rm modem link. Bellhops. Exercise equipt. Sun deck. Some refrigerators. Free parking. Cr cds: A, C, D, DS, JCB, MC, V.

⊠ ⊼ ⊠ ⊠

★ **COMFORT INN.** *601 W Diversey Pkwy (60614). 773/348-2810; fax 773/348-1912. www.comfortinn.com.* 74 rms, 5 story. S $95-$225; D $99-$225; each addl $10; suites $205-$225; under 18 free. TV; cable (premium). Complimentary continental bkfst. Restaurant nearby. Coffee in rms. Ck-out noon. Meeting rm. Business servs avail. Saunas. Health club privileges. Some in-rm whirlpools. Cr cds: A, C, D, DS, MC, V.

⊡ ⊠ ⊠ SC

★★ **COURTYARD BY MARRIOTT.** *6610 S Cicero Ave, Bedford Park (60638). 708/563-0200; fax 708/728-2841. www.courtyard.com.* 174 rms, 5 story. S, D $149-$189; each addl $10; under 16 free. Crib avail. TV; cable (premium). Complimentary coffee in rms. Restaurant. Bar 4-9:30 pm. Ck-out noon. Meeting rms. Business center. In-rm modem link. Coin lndry. Free airport transportation. Exercise equipt. Indoor pool; whirlpool. Some balconies. Cr cds: A, C, D, DS, JCB, MC, V.

⊡ ⊠ ⊼ ⊠ ⊠ ⊼

★★ **COURTYARD BY MARRIOTT.** *30 E Hubbard St (60611). 312/329-2500; fax 312/329-0293; toll-free 800/321-2211. www.courtyard.com.* 337 rms, 15 story. S, D $239; suites $279; under 18 free; wkly, wkend rates. Crib free. Garage parking, in/out $29. TV; cable (premium). Indoor pool; whirlpool. Complimentary coffee in rms. Restaurant 6:30-10:30 am, 4-11 pm. Rm serv. Bar 2

pm-midnight. Ck-out 1 pm. Coin lndry. Valet serv. Meeting rms. Business servs avail. In-rm modem link. Gift shop. Exercise equipt; sauna. Health club privileges. Refrigerators in suites; microwaves avail. Cr cds: A, C, D, DS, JCB, MC, V.

⊡ ⊠ ⊼ ⊠ ⊠ SC

★★ **FAIRFIELD INN .** *6630 S Cicero Ave, Bedford Park (60638). 708/594-0090; fax 708/728-2842; res 800/228-2800. www.fairfieldinn.com.* 113 rms, 5 story. S, D $109-$135; under 18 free. Crib free. TV; cable (premium). Indoor pool; whirlpool. Complimentary continental bkfst. Restaurant adj 11 am-10 pm. Ck-out noon. Meeting rm. Business servs avail. In-rm modem link. Valet serv. Free airport transportation. Exercise equipt. Some refrigerators, microwaves. Cr cds: A, C, D, DS, MC, V.

⊠ ⊡ ⊠ ⊠ SC ⊼

★★ **HAMPTON INN AT MIDWAY AIRPORT.** *6540 S Cicero Ave, Bedford Park (60638). 708/496-1900; fax 708/496-1997; toll-free 800/426-7866. www.hamptoninn.com.* 171 rms, 5 story. S, D $129; under 18 free. Crib free. TV; cable (premium). Complimentary continental bkfst. Restaurant nearby. Rm serv. Ck-out noon. Meeting rms. Business servs avail. In-rm modem link. Valet serv. Free airport transportation. Health club privileges. Exercise equipt. Cr cds: A, C, D, DS, ER, JCB, MC, V.

⊡ ⊠ SC ⊠ ⊼

★ **RAMADA INN LAKESHORE.** *4900 S Lake Shore Dr (60615). 773/288-5800; fax 773/288-5745; toll-free 800/237-4933. www.ramada.com.* 184 rms, 2-4 story. S $99; D $104; each addl $10; suites $170; under 18 free; wkend rates. Crib free. TV; cable (premium). Pool; poolside serv. Restaurant 6:30 am-10 pm. Rm serv. Bar noon-1 am. Ck-out noon. Meeting rms. Business center. Bellhops. Health club privileges. Many rms with view of Lake Michigan. Cr cds: A, C, D, DS, MC, V.

⊡ ⊠ ⊠ ⊠ SC ⊼

★★ **SHERATON FOUR POINTS.** *7353 S Cicero Ave (60629). 773/581-5300; fax 773/581-8421; toll-free 800/325-3535. www.fourpoints.com.* 157 rms, 5 story. S, D $109; each addl $10; under 18 free. Crib free. TV;

cable (premium). Pool. Restaurant 6 am-10 pm. Rm serv. Bar 5 pm-1 am. Ck-out noon. Meeting rms. Business servs avail. Bellhops. Free airport transportation. Exercise equipt. Cr cds: A, C, D, DS, JCB, MC, V.

[D] [≈] [⟨] [✕] [≒] [⬚] [SC]

★ **SLEEP INN CHICAGO/MIDWAY.** *6650 S Cicero Ave (60638). 708/594-0001; fax 708/594-0058. www.midinns.com.* 120 rms, 118 with shower only, 3 story. S $79-$159; D $85; each addl $10; under 18 free. Crib free. TV; cable (premium). Complimentary continental bkfst. Ck-out noon. Meeting rms. Business servs avail. In-rm modem link. Free airport transportation. Exercise equipt. Whirlpool. Cr cds: A, D, DS, MC, V.

[D] [⟨] [≒] [⬚]

Hotels

★★★ **ALLERTON CROWNE PLAZA HOTEL.** *701 N Michigan Ave (60611). 312/440-1500; fax 312/440-1819. www.allertoncrowneplaza.com.* 443 rms, 25 story. S, D $175-$275; each addl $25; under 16 free. Crib avail. TV; cable (premium), VCR avail. Restaurant 6 am-10 pm. Bar noon-midnight. Ck-out noon. Meeting rms. Business center. Gift shop. Exercise rm. Refrigerators avail. Minibars. Cr cds: A, C, D, DS, MC, V.

[⟨] [≒] [⬚] [⚲] [⟨]

★★ **BELDEN-STRATFORD.** *2300 W Lincoln Park West (60614). 773/281-2900; fax 773/880-2039; toll-free 800/800-8301. www.beldenstratford.com.* 29 kit. units in 17-story landmark bldg. S, D $139-$199; wkly, wkend rates. Crib. Valet parking $25. TV; cable, VCR avail. Complimentary coffee in rms. Restaurant (see also AMBRIA). Bar 6-11 pm. Ck-out noon. Coin lndry. Business servs avail. In-rm modem link. Barber, beauty shop. Exercise equipt. Microwaves. Views of park, Lake Michigan and skyline. Cr cds: A, D, DS, JCB, MC, V.

[D] [⟨] [≒] [⬚] [SC]

★★ **CITY SUITES.** *933 W Belmont Ave (60657). 773/404-3400; fax 773/404-3405. www.cityinns.com.* 45 rms, 4 story, 29 suites. S $139; D $159; each addl $10; suites $179; under 12 free. Crib free. Garage parking $7. TV; cable (premium), VCR

avail. Complimentary continental bkfst. Restaurant adj 24 hrs. Ck-out noon. Health club privileges. Refrigerators avail. Cr cds: A, D, DS, MC, V.

[D] [≒] [⬚] [⚲] [SC]

★★★ **CLARIDGE.** *1244 N Dearborn Pkwy (60610). 312/787-4980; fax 312/787-4069; toll-free 800/245-1258. www.claridgehotel.com.* 164 rms, 14 story. S $165; D $225; each addl $15; suites $250-$450; under 18 free; wkend rates. Crib free. Pet accepted, some restrictions. Valet parking $31. TV. Complimentary continental bkfst. Restaurant 6:30 am-10:30 pm. Bar 4:30 pm-2 am. Ck-out noon. Meeting rms. Business servs avail. Concierge. Airport transportation. Health club privileges. Minibars. Fireplace in some suites. In historic residential area. Cr cds: A, C, D, DS, ER, JCB, MC, V.

[D] [🐾] [≒] [⚲]

★★ **CLARION HOTEL EXECUTIVE PLAZA.** *71 E Wacker Dr (60601). 312/346-7100; fax 312/346-1721; toll-free 800/621-4005. www.executive-plaza.com.* 421 rms, 39 story. S $159-$199; D $179-$219; each addl $20; suites $295-$850; under 18 free; wkend rates; package plans. Crib free. Garage, in/out $28. TV; cable. Coffee in rms. Restaurant 6:30 am-11 pm. Bar to 2 am. Ck-out noon. Meeting rms. Business center. Concierge. Gift shop. Exercise equipt. Health club privileges. Bathrm phones, minibars. Some wet bars in suites. Cr cds: A, C, D, DS, JCB, MC, V.

[D] [⟨] [≒] [⚲] [SC] [⟨]

★★ **CONGRESS PLAZA.** *520 S Michigan Ave (60605). 312/427-3800; fax 312/427-3972; toll-free 800/635-1666. www.congressplazahotel.com.* 851 rms, 6-14 story. S $105-$165; D $105-$165; each addl $25; suites $250-$750; under 17 free. Crib free. Valet parking $23; garage $20. TV. Complimentary coffee in rms. Restaurant 6:30 am-10:30 pm. Bar 4 pm-2 am. Ck-out noon. Convention facilities. Business servs avail. Concierge. Gift shop. Barber. Exercise equipt. Cr cds: A, D, DS, JCB, MC, V.

[D] [⟨] [≒] [⚲]

★★★ **CROWNE PLAZA CHICAGO - THE SILVERSMITH.** *10 S Wabash Ave (60603). 312/372-7696; fax*

312/372-7320. www.crowneplaza.com.
143 rms, 10 story. S, D $159-$300;
each addl $20; under 17 free. Crib
avail. TV; cable (premium), VCR
avail. Complimentary coffee in rms.
Restaurant 6 am-midnight. Ck-out 11
am. Meeting rms. Business center.
Exercise rm. Refrigerators. Cr cds: A,
C, D, DS, MC, V.

★ ★ ★ **THE DRAKE.** 140 E Walton Pl
(60611). 312/787-2200; fax 312/787-
1431; toll-free 800/553-7253. www.
thedrakehotel.com. 537 rms, 10 story.
S, D $275-$365; suites $395-$2,450;
family, wkend rates. Crib free. Valet
parking $32/night; in/out privileges.
TV; cable (premium), VCR avail.
Restaurant 6:30 am-11 pm (see also
CAPE COD ROOM). Rm serv 24 hrs.
Bar 11-2 am; piano bar. Ck-out noon.
Convention facilities. Business center. In-rm modem link. Concierge.
Shopping arcade. Barber. Exercise
equipt. Health club privileges. Minibars; wet bar in some suites. Overlooks Lake Michigan. Luxury level.
Cr cds: A, C, D, DS, JCB, MC, V.

★ ★ ★ **THE FAIRMONT CHICAGO.**
200 N Columbus Dr (60601). 312/565-
8000; fax 312/861-3656. www.
fairmont.com. 692 rms, 37 story. S, D
$199-$359; each addl $35; suites
$500-$3,600. Crib free. Valet parking,
in/out $28. Pet accepted, some
restrictions. TV; cable (premium),
VCR avail. Restaurants. Rm serv 24
hrs. Bar 11-2 am; entertainment Tues-
Sat. Ck-out 1 pm. Convention facilities. Business center. In-rm modem
link. Concierge. Bellhop. Gift shop.
Health club privileges. Golf, tennis
nearby. Bathrm phones, minibars. Cr
cds: A, C, D, DS, ER, JCB, MC, V.

★ ★ ★ ★ ★ **FOUR SEASONS HOTEL
CHICAGO.** 120 E Delaware Pl
(60611). 312/280-8800; fax 312/280-
1748; toll-free 800/332-3442. www.
fourseasons.com. Within the exclusive
shopping building of 900 N Michigan Ave, this luxury hotel offers 191
rooms and 152 suites, all with
breathtaking views of the city and
Lake Michigan. The marble-floored
lobby is quiet and airy, comple-
mented by soft colors and sparkling
chandeliers. Visit the Roman-
columned, skylit pool in the health

club or dine on contemporary American cuisine at the elegant Seasons
restaurant. 343 rms, 66-story bldg
(guest rms on floors 30-46), 152
suites. S $385-$465; D $425-$505;
each addl $30; suites $515-$1,175;
wkend rates; package plans. Crib
free. Pet accepted. Valet parking $32.
TV; cable (premium), VCR avail
(movies). Indoor pool; whirlpool.
Restaurant (see also SEASONS). Rm
serv 24 hrs. Bar 11:30-1 am; entertainment. Ck-out noon. Convention
facilities. Business center. In-rm
modem link. Concierge. Barber,
beauty shop. Exercise rm; sauna,
steam rm. Bathrm phones, minibars;
some wet bars. Lake 3 blks. Cr cds: A,
C, D, DS, ER, JCB, MC, V.

★ ★ ★ **HILTON CHICAGO.** 720 S
Michigan Ave (60605). 312/922-4400;
fax 312/922-5240. www.chicagohilton.
com. 1,544 rms, 25 story. S $149-$339;
D $174-$364; each addl $25; suites
from $325; wkend rates. Crib free.
Garage $23; valet parking $28. TV;
cable (premium). Indoor pool;
whirlpools. Complimentary coffee in
rms. Restaurants 5:30-1:30 am (see
also BUCKINGHAM'S). Rm serv. Bars
to 2 am; entertainment. Ck-out 11
am. Convention facilities. Business
center. Concierge. Shopping arcade.
Barber, beauty shop. Exercise rm;
sauna. Massage. Minibars. Luxury
level. Cr cds: A, C, D, DS, ER, JCB,
MC, V.

★ ★ **HOLIDAY INN.** 350 N Orleans St
(60654). 312/836-5000; fax 312/222-
9508; toll-free 800/465-4329. www.
holiday-inn.com. 521 rms, 23 story;
guest rms on floors 16-23. S $135-
$175; D $155-$195; each addl $16;
suites $475-$625; under 18 free;
wkend rates; package plans. Crib
free. Pet accepted, some restrictions.
Garage $18/day. TV. Indoor pool.
Restaurant 6:30 am-2 pm, 5-10:30
pm. Bars noon-2 am. Ck-out noon.
Coin lndry. Convention facilities.
Shopping arcade. Barber, beauty
shop. Airport transportation. Exercise equipt. Cr cds: A, C, D, DS, JCB,
MC, V.

★ ★ **HOLIDAY INN.** 300 E Ohio St
(60611). 312/787-6100; fax 312/787-
6259; toll-free 800/465-4329. www.

holiday-inn.com. 500 rms, 26 story. S $129-$179, D $149-$199; each addl $20; suites $400-$700; under 18 free; wkend rates. Crib free. Garage adj $20. TV; cable (premium), VCR avail. Pool; whirlpools, lifeguard. Restaurant 6:30 am-11 pm. Bars 11:30-2 am. Ck-out noon. Coin lndry. Meeting rms. Business center. In-rm modem link. Tennis privileges. Health club privileges; sauna. Massage. Sauna in suites. Cr cds: A, C, D, DS, ER, JCB, MC, V.

⊡ ⛱ 🎿 ⛷ 🐾 SC 🏃

★ ★ ★ **HOTEL ALLEGRO.** *171 W Randolph St (60601). 312/236-0123; fax 312/236-0917; res 800/643-1500. www.allegrochicago.com.* 483 rms, 19 story. S, D $175-$279; each addl $10; suites $239-$399; under 18 free. Crib free. Valet parking $28. TV; cable (premium), VCR avail. Restaurant (see 312 CHICAGO). Bar 5 pm-12:30 am. Ck-out noon. Convention facilities. Business center. In-rm modem link. Concierge. Gift shop. Barber, beauty shop. Exercise equipt. Health club privileges. Refrigerators, minibars; some in-rm whirlpools. Cr cds: A, C, D, DS, ER, JCB, MC, V.

⊡ 🎿 ⛷ 🐾 🏃

★ ★ ★ **HOTEL BURNHAM.** *1 W Washington (60602). 312/782-1111. www.burnhamhotel.com.* 122 rms, 15 story, 19 suites. Mar-Nov: S, D $275; each addl $15; suites $425; under 17 free; lower rates rest of yr. Crib avail. Pet accepted. TV; cable (premium), VCR avail. Restaurant 7 am-10 pm. Rm serv 24 hrs. Bar. Ck-out noon, ck-in 3 pm. Business serv avail. Exercise rm. Some refrigerators, minibars. Cr cds: A, C, D, DS, JCB, MC, V.

⊡ 🐾 🎿 ⛷ 🐾

★ ★ ★ **HOTEL INTER-CONTINENTAL.** *505 N Michigan Ave (60611). 312/944-4100; fax 312/944-1320. www.chicago.interconti.com.* 814 rms, 2 bldgs, 26 and 42 story, 42 suites. S, D $189-$349; each addl $25; suites from $375; under 14 free. Crib free. Covered parking $32/day. TV; cable, VCR avail. Indoor pool; poolside serv. Coffee in rms. Restaurants. Rm serv 24 hrs. Afternoon tea 2-5 pm. Bar 11-1 am; entertainment Thurs-Sun. Ck-out noon. Convention facilities. Business center. In-rm modem link. Concierge. Gift shop. Exercise

rm; sauna. Massage. Minibars, bathrm phones; microwaves avail. Two buildings, one of which was originally constructed (1929) as the Medinah Athletic Club. Cr cds: A, C, D, DS, ER, JCB, MC, V.

⊡ ⛱ 🎿 ⛷ 🐾 🏃

★ ★ ★ **HOTEL MONACO CHICAGO.** *225 N Wabash (60601). 312/960-8500; fax 312/960-1883. www.monaco-chicago.com.* 192 rms, 14 story. S, D $195-$350; each addl $25; under 17 free. Crib avail. Pet accepted. TV; cable (premium), VCR avail. Complimentary coffee in rms. Restaurant 6 am-10 pm. Ck-out noon. Meeting rms. Business center. Gift shop. Exercise rm. Some refrigerators, minibars. Cr cds: A, C, D, DS, MC, V.

⊡ 🐾 🎿 ⛷ 🐾 🏃

★ ★ ★ **HOUSE OF BLUES.** *222 N Dearborn (60610). 312/245-0333; fax 312/923-2458. www.loewshotels.com.* 367 rms, 15 story. S, D $225-$375; each addl $20; under 18 free. Crib avail. TV; cable (premium), VCR avail. Complimentary coffee in rms. Restaurant 6 am-11 pm. Ck-out noon. Meeting rms. Business center. Gift shop. Exercise rm. Some refrigerators, minibars. Cr cds: A, C, D, DS, MC, V.

🎿 ⛷ 🐾 🏃

★ ★ ★ **HYATT AT UNIVERSITY VILLAGE.** *625 S Ashland Ave (60607). 312/491-1234; fax 312/529-6095. www.hyatt.com.* 114 rms, 4 story. S $145-$295; D $170-$320; each addl $25; suites $395-$795; under 18 free; package plans. Crib free. TV; cable (premium), VCR avail. Pool privileges. Restaurant 6 am-10 pm. Rm serv. Bar 11 am-midnight. Ck-out noon. Meeting rms. Business center. Valet serv. Valet parking. Tennis privileges. Exercise equipt. Health club privileges. Some refrigerators; microwaves avail. Near University of Illinois Chicago campus. Cr cds: A, D, DS, JCB, MC, V.

⊡ 🎿 🎿 ⛷ 🐾 🏃

★ ★ ★ **HYATT ON PRINTER'S ROW.** *500 S Dearborn St (60605). 312/986-1234; fax 312/939-2468; toll-free 800/233-1234. www.hyatt.com.* 161 rms, 7-12 story. S $225-$325; D $250-$350; each addl $25; suites

$650; wkend rates. Crib free. Valet parking $31; self-park $18. TV; cable (premium), VCR avail. Restaurant 6:30 am-10 pm (see also PRAIRIE). Bar 6:30 am-10 pm. Ck-out noon. Meeting rms. Business servs avail. Airport transportation. Exercise equipt. Health club privileges. Bathrm phones, minibars. Financial district nearby. Cr cds: A, D, DS, JCB, MC, V.

D ⟨symbols⟩ SC

★★★ **HYATT REGENCY.** *151 E Wacker Dr (60601). 312/565-1234; fax 312/565-2966; toll-free 800/233-1234. www.hyatt.com.* 2,019 rms, 34 story (East Tower), 36 story (West Tower). S $139-$295; D $139-$320; each addl $25; suites $565-$3,600; under 18 free; package plans. Crib free. Garage, in/out $33. TV; cable (premium), VCR avail (movies). Restaurant (see also STETSON'S CHOPHOUSE). Rm serv 24 hrs. Bar 11-2 am. Ck-out noon. Convention facilities. Business center. In-rm modem link. Concierge. Shopping arcade. Barber, beauty shop. Health club privileges. Minibars; some in-rm steam baths, whirlpools. Bathrm phone, refrigerator in suites. Luxury level. Cr cds: A, C, D, DS, ER, JCB, MC, V.

D ⟨symbols⟩ SC ⟨symbol⟩

★★★ **HYATT REGENCY MCCORMICK PLACE.** *2233 S Martin Luther King Dr (60616). 312/567-1234; fax 312/528-4000; res 800/233-1234. www.hyatt.com.* 800 rms, 33 story. S $199; D $224; each addl $25; suites $1,100-$3,300; family rates; package plans; higher rates citywide conventions. Crib avail. Valet parking $27; garage parking $22. TV; cable (premium), VCR avail. Indoor pool. Restaurant 6:30 am-10 pm. Rm serv 24 hrs. Bar 11-1 am. Ck-out noon. Convention facilities. Business center. In-rm modem link. Concierge. Gift shop. Drugstore. Coin lndry. Exercise equipt; sauna. Refrigerator, wet bar in suites; microwaves avail. Cr cds: A, C, D, DS, ER, JCB, MC, V.

D ⟨symbols⟩

★★★ **LE MERIDIEN CHICAGO.** *520 N Michigan Ave (60611). 312/645-1500; fax 312/645-1550. www.lemeridien.com.* 311 rms, 12 story. S, D $250-$425; each addl $40; under 12 free. Crib avail. Pet accepted, some restrictions. 2 heated pools. TV; cable (premium), VCR avail. Complimentary coffee in rms. Restaurant 6:30 am-10 pm. Rm serv 24 hrs. Ck-out noon. Meeting rms. Business center. Gift shop. Exercise rm. Refrigerators, minibars. Cr cds: A, C, D, DS, ER, JCB, MC, V.

⟨symbols⟩

★★ **MAJESTIC HOTEL.** *528 W Brompton Ave (60657). 773/404-3499; fax 773/404-3495; res 800/727-5108. www.cityinns.com.* 52 rms, 4 story, 22 kit. suites. S $139; D $159; each addl $10; under 12 free; wkend rates. Crib free. Garage parking $18. TV; cable (premium). Complimentary continental bkfst. Restaurant nearby. Ck-out noon. Bellhops. Health club privileges. Refrigerator, microwave, wet bar in suites. Cr cds: A, D, DS, MC, V.

⟨symbols⟩ SC

★★★ **MARRIOTT DOWNTOWN CHICAGO.** *540 N Michigan Ave (60611). 312/836-0100; fax 312/836-6139. www.marriott.com.* 1,192 rms, 46 story. S, D $159-$329; suites $590-$1,150; under 18 free; wkend rates. Crib free. Pet accepted, some restrictions. Valet parking $32. TV; cable (premium), VCR avail. Indoor pool; whirlpool, poolside serv. Coffee in rms. Restaurant 6 am-11 pm. Bar 11-2 am. Ck-out noon. Convention facilities. Business center. In-rm modem link. Concierge. Barber, beauty shop. Exercise rm; sauna. Massage. Basketball courts. Game rm. Bathrm phone in suites; microwaves avail. Cr cds: A, C, D, DS, ER, JCB, MC, V.

D ⟨symbols⟩ SC ⟨symbol⟩

★★★ **MILLENNIUM KNICKERBOCKER.** *163 E Walton Pl (60611). 312/751-8100; fax 312/751-9205; toll-free 800/621-8140. www.millenniumhotels.com.* 305 rms, 14 story. S, D $119-$249; each addl $20; suites $285-$1,200; under 18 free; wkend rates. Crib free. Valet parking, in/out $32. TV; cable (premium) VCR avail. Pool privileges. Restaurant (see also NIX). Rm serv 24 hrs. Bar 11-2 am. Ck-out noon. Meeting rms. Business servs avail. In-rm modem link. Concierge. Indoor tennis privileges. Exercise equipt. Health club privi-

leges. Minibars. Luxury level. Cr cds:
A, C, D, DS, ER, JCB, MC, V.

⬛ 🖼 🏋 🛏 🔥 SC

★ ★ ★ **OMNI AMBASSADOR EAST.**
1301 N State Pkwy (60610). 312/787-
7200; fax 312/787-4760; toll-free
800/843-6664. www.omnihotels.com.
285 rms, 17 story. S $149-$229; D
$159-$239; each addl $20; suites
$375-$1000; under 17 free; wkend
rates. Crib free. Valet parking $34.
TV; cable (premium). Restaurant (see
also PUMP ROOM). Rm serv 24 hrs.
Bar 11-1 am. Ck-out noon. Meeting
rms. Business servs avail. Concierge.
Airport transportation. Exercise
equipt. Health club privileges. Minibars; microwaves avail. Cr cds: A, C,
D, DS, ER, JCB, MC, V.

⬛ 🏋 🛏 🔥

★ ★ ★ **OMNI CHICAGO HOTEL.**
676 N Michigan Ave (60611). 312/944-
6664; fax 312/266-3015. www.omni
hotels.com. 347 rms, 25 story. S, D
$199-$399; suites $249-$1,500; under
12 free. Crib free. Pet accepted; $50.
Parking in/out $32. Valet parking
avail. TV; cable (premium), VCR
avail. Heated indoor pool; whirlpool;
poolside serv. Supervised children's
activities. Coffee in rms. Restaurant
(see also CIELO). Rm serv 24 hrs.
Bar 11 am-midnight. Ck-out noon.
Meeting rms. Business center. In-rm
modem link. Concierge. Bellhops.
Valet serv. Exercise equipt; sauna.
Health club privileges. Refrigerators,
minibars, wet bars; microwaves avail.
Sundeck. Cr cds: A, C, D, DS, ER,
JCB, MC, V.

⬛ 🍴 ➰ 🏋 🛏 🔥 🏃

★ ★ ★ **PALMER HOUSE HILTON.**
17 E Monroe St (60603). 312/726-
7500; fax 312/917-1707; toll-free
800/445-8667. www.hilton.com. 1,639
rms, 25 story. S $159-$329; D $184-
$354; each addl $25; suites over
$600; family, wkend rates. Crib free.
Pet accepted. Garage $21, valet $31.
TV; cable (premium), VCR avail.
Indoor pool; whirlpool. Complimentary coffee in rms. Restaurant 6:30-2
am (see also BIG DOWNTOWN).
Bars 11-2 am; entertainment. Ck-out
11 am. Convention facilities. Business center. In-rm modem link.
Concierge. Shopping arcade. Barber,
beauty shop. Airport transportation.
Exercise rm; sauna, steam rm. Mas-

sage. Minibars. Refrigerator in suites.
Luxury level. Cr cds: A, C, D, DS, ER,
JCB, MC, V.

⬛ 🍴 ➰ 🏋 🛏 🔥 SC 🏃

★ ★ ★ ★ **PARK HYATT CHICAGO.**
800 N Michigan Ave (60611). 312/335-
1234; fax 312/239-4000. www.park
hyatt.com. This hotel off Michigan
Avenue gives its luxury competitors a
run for their money. A great value,
the comfortable rooms are fresh and
modernly decorated, and the bathrooms large and luxurious. Guests
will enjoy the professional, personal-
ized service. The hotel restaurant,
NoMi, is delightful and a "must
visit." 202 rms, 18 story. S, D $250-
$535; each addl $20; under 17 free.
Crib avail. Indoor pool. TV; cable
(premium), VCR avail. Complimentary coffee in rms. Restaurant 6 am-
10 pm (see also NOMI). Rm serv 24
hrs. Ck-out noon. Meeting rms. Business center. Exercise rm. Refrigerators,
minibars. Cr cds: A, C, D, DS, MC, V.

➰ 🏋 🛏 🔥 🏃

★ ★ ★ ★ ★ **THE PENINSULA**
CHICAGO. *108 E Superior St (60611).*
312/337-2888; fax 312/751-2888.
www.peninsula.com. Located in the
heart of the "Magnificent Mile"
shopping district and steps from the
historic Water Tower, this illustrious
hotel brings classic haute service and
guest facilities to the Midwest. Each
room is equipped with a bedside,
multifunctional electronic control
panel; marble bathroom with separate shower and soaking tub, television, and hands-free telephone; and
a 27-inch flat-screen television. The
Lobby Restaurant, decorated with 20
foot, floor-to-ceiling windows overlooking North Michigan Avenue, is
the perfect location for a romantic
meal. The state-of-the-art Peninsula
Spa, featuring seven treatment
rooms, exercise equipment, a lap
pool, hydrotherapy shower, and
multiple exercise classes, is the perfect place to be pampered after a
long day of work or sightseeing. 338
rms, 20 story. S, D $445-$535; each
addl $40; suites $475-$4,500. Crib
avail. Pet accepted. Heated pools.
TV; cable (premium), VCR avail.
Restaurant 6 am-10 pm. Rm serv 24
hrs. Valet parking $34. Ck-out noon.
Meeting rms. Business center. Gift
shop. Exercise rm. Spa. Valet serv.

Refrigerators, minibars. Cr cds: A, C, D, DS, JCB, MC, V.

★ ★ **RAPHAEL.** *201 E Delaware Pl (60611). 312/943-5000; fax 312/943-9483; toll-free 800/983-7870. www.raphaelchicago.com.* 172 rms, 17 story, 72 suites. S, D $99-$289; each addl $20; under 12 free; suites $170-$269; wkend rates. Crib free. Valet parking, in/out $32. TV; cable (premium), VCR avail. Restaurant 6:30-11 am, 11:30 am-2 pm, 5-10 pm; Sun 5-9 pm. Bar 11-1:30 am; entertainment Fri, Sat. Ck-out noon. Meeting rms. Health club privileges. Minibars. Cr cds: A, D, DS, MC, V.

★ **RED ROOF INN.** *162 E Ontario St (60611). 312/787-3580; fax 312/787-1299. www.redroofinn.com.* 195 rms, 15 story. 13 suites. S $79-$129, D $85-$139; each addl $7; suites $91-$149; under 17 free; wkend rates; higher rate: New Year's Eve, special events; lower rates rest of yr. Crib free. Valet parking $24-$30. TV; cable. Restaurant 11:30 am-10 pm. No rm serv. Ck-out noon. Health club privileges. Cr cds: A, C, D, DS, MC, V.

★ ★ ★ **RENAISSANCE CHICAGO HOTEL.** *1 W Wacker Dr (60601). 312/372-7200; fax 312/372-0093; toll-free 800/468-3571. www.renaissance hotels.com.* Situated between the offices of the Loop and the shops of Michigan Ave, this corner property affords great views of the city lights, Lake Michigan, and the Chicago River. The 27-floor structure holds 553 rooms, all with relaxing gray and rose tones and polished woods. The 13 conference rooms and 10,000-square-foot Grand Ballroom are popular for both social and corporate events. 553 units, 40 suites, 27 story. S, D $149-$319; each addl $20 up to 2; suites $389-$519; under 18 free; wkend rates. Crib free. Pet accepted, some restrictions. Garage; valet parking in/out $28. TV; cable (premium), VCR avail. Indoor pool; whirlpool, poolside serv. Restaurants 6 am-10 pm (see also CUISINES). Rm serv 24 hrs. Bar 3 pm-12:30 am; pianist. Coffee, tea in rms. Ck-out 1 pm. Convention facilities. Business center. In-rm modem link. Concierge. Shop-

ping arcade. Exercise rm; sauna. Massage. Shoe shine. Minibars; bathrm phone in suites. Luxury level. Cr cds: A, C, D, DS, MC, V.

★ ★ ★ ★ ★ **THE RITZ-CARLTON, CHICAGO.** *160 E Pearson St (60611). 312/266-1000; fax 312/266-1194; toll-free 800/621-6906. www.four seasons.com.* Rising above the energy of Michigan Avenue, this opulent hotel sits atop Water Tower Place, the well-known shopping center, and across the street from the Museum of Contemporary Art. The fountain in the lobby provides a dramatic entrance to the 435-room property, which boasts a private spa and a renowned contemporary French restaurant. 435 rms, 31 story, 91 suites. S, D $355-$455; each addl $40; suites $475-$1,950; under 12 free; wkend rates; package plans. Crib free. Pet accepted. Parking in/out, $32/day. TV; cable (premium), VCR avail. Heated pool; whirlpool. Restaurant 6:30 am-11 pm (see also THE RITZ-CARLTON DINING ROOM). Rm serv 24 hrs. Bar from 11:30 am; Fri, Sat to 2 am. Ck-out noon. Convention facilities. Business center. In-rm modem link. Concierge. Tennis privileges. Exercise rm; sauna, steam rm. Bathrm phones, minibars; refrigerators avail. Cr cds: A, MC, V.

★ ★ **SENECA.** *200 E Chestnut (60611). 312/787-8900; fax 312/988-4438; toll-free 800/800-6261. www.senecahotel.com.* 141 rms, 17 story, 135 kit. suites. S $149-$245; D $169-$265; each addl $20; under 12 free; wkend, hol rates. Crib $15. Valet parking $30. TV; cable (premium), VCR avail. Complimentary coffee in rms. Restaurants 7:30 am-10:30 pm. Bar from 11:30 am. Ck-out noon. Coin lndry. Meeting rms. Business servs avail. In-rm modem link. Beauty shop. Exercise equipt. Refrigerators, microwaves. Cr cds: A, C, D, DS, ER, JCB, MC, V.

★ ★ ★ **SHERATON CHICAGO HOTEL & TOWERS.** *301 E North Water St (60611). 312/464-1000; fax 312/464-9140; toll-free 800/233-4100. www.sheratonchicago.com.* 1,209 rms, 34 story, 34 suites. S $199-$269; D

$219-$289; each addl $25; suites $450-$3,500; under 17 free. Pet accepted, some restrictions. Garage, in/out $32. TV; cable (premium), VCR avail. Indoor pool. Complimentary coffee in rms. Restaurant 6-1 am. Rm serv 24 hrs. Bar 11-1:30 am; pianist. Ck-out noon. Convention facilities. Business center. In-rm modem link. Concierge. Gift shop. Exercise equipt; sauna. Massage. Minibars. On Chicago River, near Navy Pier. Views of Lake Michigan and skyline. Luxury level. Cr cds: A, D, DS, MC, V.

★ ★ ★ **SUTTON PLACE.** *21 E Bellevue Pl (60611). 312/266-2100; fax 312/266-2103; toll-free 800/810-6888. www.suttonplace.com.* 246 rms, 22 story, 40 suites. S $305-$360; D $330-$385; each addl $25; suites $395-$1,500; under 16 free; wkend rates. Crib free. Pet accepted, some restrictions; $200 refundable. Valet parking $32. TV; cable (premium), VCR avail. Restaurant. Rm serv 24 hrs. Bar 11:30-1 am. Ck-out noon. Meeting rms. Business center. In-rm modem link. Concierge. Airport transportation. Exercise equipt. Health club privileges. Bathrm phones, minibars. Penthouse suites with garden terrace. Cr cds: A, C, D, DS, JCB, MC, V.

★ ★ ★ **SWISSOTEL CHICAGO.** *323 E Wacker Dr (60601). 312/565-0565; fax 312/565-0540; toll-free 800/654-7263. www.swissotel.com.* 632 rms, 43 story. S $399-$439; D $419-$459; suites $395-$2,500; under 14 free. Covered parking, in/out $33. TV; cable (premium), VCR avail. Indoor pool; whirlpool. Coffee in rms. Restaurant 6 am-10:30 pm. Rm serv 24 hrs. Bar 11-2 am. Ck-out 1 pm. Convention facilities. Business center. In-rm modem link. Concierge. Gift shop. Exercise rm; sauna. Health club privileges. Massage. Spa. Bathrm phones, minibars. Panoramic views of city and Lake Michigan. Cr cds: A, C, D, DS, JCB, MC, V.

★ ★ ★ **THE TALBOTT HOTEL.** *20 E Delaware Pl (60611). 312/944-4970; fax 312/944-7241. www.talbotthotel. com.* 149 rms, 15 story. S, D $250-

$350; each addl $20; under 17 free. Crib avail. TV; cable (premium), VCR avail. Restaurant 6 am-10 pm. Ck-out noon. Meeting rms. Business servs avail. Exercise rm. Minibars. Cr cds: A, C, D, DS, JCB, MC, V.

★ ★ **TREMONT.** *100 E Chestnut St (60611). 312/751-1900; fax 312/751-8691. www.tremontchicago.com.* 130 rms, 16 story. S, D $199-$279; suites $299-$650; under 18 free; wkend rates. Crib free. Parking $32. TV; cable (premium), VCR (movies). Restaurant (see also MIKE DITKA'S). Rm serv 24 hrs. Bar 11 am-midnight. Ck-out noon. Meeting rms. Business servs avail. In-rm modem link. Concierge. Exercise equipt. Bathrm phones, minibars. Cr cds: A, C, D, DS, MC, V.

★ ★ ★ **W CHICAGO - CITY CENTER.** *172 W Adams St (60603). 312/332-1200.* 390 rms, 20 story. S, D $250-$475; each addl $35; under 17 free. Crib avail. TV; cable (premium), VCR. Complimentary coffee in rms. Restaurant 6 am-10 pm. Bar 4:30 pm-2 am; entertainment Tues-Sat. Ck-out noon. Meeting rms. Business servs avail. Exercise rm. Minibars. Cr cds: A, C, D, DS, MC, V.

★ ★ ★ **W CHICAGO - LAKESHORE.** *644 N Lakeshore Dr (60611). 312/943-9200.* 578 rms, 33 story. S, D $250-$375; each addl $25; under 17 free. Crib avail. Pet accepted. TV; cable (premium), VCR avail. Complimentary coffee in rms. Restaurant 6 am-10 pm. Ck-out noon. Meeting rms. Business center. Exercise rm. Some refrigerators, minibars. Cr cds: A, C, D, DS, MC, V.

★ ★ ★ **WESTIN MICHIGAN AVENUE.** *909 N Michigan Ave (60611). 312/943-7200; fax 312/397-5580; toll-free 800/228-3000. www. westinmichiganave.com.* 751 rms, 27 story. S, D $179-$399; each addl $20; suites $350-$1,500; under 18 free; package plans. Crib free. Pet accepted, some restrictions. Valet parking, in/out $32. TV; cable (premium). Restaurant 6:30 am-10 pm. Rm serv 24 hrs. Bar 11-1:30 am. Ck-out noon. Convention facilities. Business center. In-rm modem link. Concierge. Gift shop. Exercise equipt; sauna. Massage. Minibars; many bathrm phones; microwaves avail. Luxury level. Cr cds: A, C, D, DS, ER, JCB, MC, V.

⬜ 🎿 🏋 ⬜ 🔥 SC 🏃

★ ★ ★ ★ **WESTIN RIVER NORTH CHICAGO.** *320 Dearborn (60610). 312/744-1900; fax 312/527-2650. www.westinchicago.com.* Overlooking the Chicago River, this 424-room property is near the Merchandise Mart and a short ride to Michigan Avenue shops and the Loop's theaters and corporations. Accommodations have a relaxed, residential feel with spacious work areas, fax machines, and marble bathrooms. The 28,000 square feet of meeting space and the views from the Astor Ballroom attract many special-event clients. 424 rms, 20 story. S, D $159-$399; suites $650-$2,500; under 18 free; package plans. Crib free. Valet parking $33 in/out. TV; cable (premium), VCR avail. Coffee in rms. Restaurant 6:30 am-11 pm (see also CELEBRITY CAFE). Rm serv 24 hrs. Bar 11-1:30 am. Ck-out noon. Convention facilities. Business center. In-rm modem link. Concierge. Exercise rm; sauna. Massage. Bathrm phones, minibars. Cr cds: A, C, D, DS, JCB, MC, V.

⬜ 🏋 🔥 🏃

★ ★ ★ **THE WHITEHALL HOTEL.** *105 E Delaware Pl (60611). 312/944-6300; fax 312/944-8552; toll-free 800/948-4255. www.thewhitehallhotel. com.* 221 rms, 21 story. S, D $229-$359; each addl $25; suites $550-$1,575; under 12 free; wkly, wkend rates. Crib free. Valet parking $32.50. Restaurant 7-1 am. Rm serv 24 hrs. Bar from 11 am. Ck-out noon. Meeting rms. Business servs avail. In-rm modem link. Concierge. Exercise equipt. Health club privileges. Minibars. Luxury level. Cr cds: A, D, DS, MC, V.

⬜ 🏋 ⬜ 🔥

★ **THE WILLOWS.** *555 W Surf St (60657). 773/528-8400; fax 773/528-8483; res 800/787-3108. www.cityinns. com.* 55 rms, 4 story. S $139; D $159; each addl $10; suites $179; under 12 free; wkends (2-day min). Crib free. Garage parking $15. TV; cable. Com-

plimentary continental bkfst. Restaurant nearby. No rm serv. Ck-out noon. In-rm modem link. Bellhops. Concierge. Health club privileges. Cr cds: A, C, D, DS, MC, V.

⬜ 🐾 SC

★ ★ ★ **WYNDHAM CHICAGO.** *633 N St. Clair St (60611). 312/573-0300; fax 312/274-0164. www.wyndham. com.* 417 rms, 17 story. S, D $225-$350; each addl $20; under 17 free. Crib avail. Indoor pool. TV; cable (premium), VCR avail. Complimentary coffee in rms. Restaurant 6 am-10 pm. Ck-out noon. Meeting rms. Business center. Gift shop. Exercise rm. Some refrigerators, minibars. Cr cds: A, C, D, DS, MC, V.

🏊 🏋 ⬜ 🔥 🏃

B&Bs/Small Inns

★ ★ **GOLD COAST GUEST HOUSE.** *113 W Elm St (60610). 312/337-0361; fax 312/337-0362.* 4 rms, 3 story. S, D $119-$199. Children over 12 yrs only. TV; VCR avail. Complimentary continental bkfst. Restaurant nearby. Ck-out noon. Business servs avail. Health club privileges. Renovated brick townhome built in 1873. Cr cds: A, DS, MC, V.

⬜ 🐾

★ ★ ★ **OLD TOWN BED & BREAKFAST.** *1442 N North Park Ave (60610). 312/440-9268. www.oldtownchicago. com.* 4 rms, 4 story. S, D $139-$199. TV; cable (premium), VCR. Complimentary continental bkfst. Exercise rm. Ck-out 11 am. Art deco mansion. Cr cds: A, MC, V.

🏋 🐾

All Suites

★ ★ ★ **DOUBLETREE GUEST SUITES.** *198 E Delaware Pl (60611). 312/664-1100; fax 312/664-9881. www.doubletreehotels.com.* 345 suites, 30 story. S, D $129-$399; each addl $25; under 18 free; wkend rates. Crib free. Valet parking, in/out $32. TV; cable (premium), VCR avail. Indoor pool; whirlpool. Coffee in rms. Restaurant (see also PARK AVENUE CAFE). Rm serv 24 hrs. Bar 11-2 am. Ck-out noon. Meeting rms. Business center. In-rm modem link. Concierge. Gift shop. Exercise equipt; sauna. Game rm. Refrigerators, microwaves avail. Minibars. Cr cds: A, D, DS, JCB, MC, V.

⊡ ⇌ 🕅 ⊠ 🔥 SC 🕅

★ ★ ★ **EMBASSY SUITES CHICAGO - DOWNTOWN.** *600 N State St (60610). 312/943-3800; fax 312/943-7629; toll-free 800/362-2779. www.embassysuiteschicago.com.* 358 suites, 11 story. S $189-$399; D $299-$439; under 12 free. Crib free. Garage, in/out $32. TV; cable (premium). Indoor pool; whirlpool. Complimentary full bkfst, coffee in rms. Restaurant (see also PAPAGUS GREEK TAVERNA). Bar. Ck-out noon. Meeting rms. Business servs avail. In-rm modem link. Concierge. Gift shop. Exercise equipt; sauna. Refrigerators, microwaves, minibars, wet bars. Cr cds: A, C, D, DS, JCB, MC, V.

⊡ ⇌ 🕅 ⊠ 🔥 SC

★ ★ **FITZPATRICK CHICAGO HOTEL.** *166 E Superior St (60611). 312/787-6000; fax 312/787-4331. www.fitzpatrickhotels.com.* 143 suites, 29 story. Mar-Dec: S, D $139-$209; each addl $30; under 16 free; wkend, hol rates; lower rates rest of yr. Crib free. Garage parking $23; valet $32. TV; cable (premium), VCR (movies). Heated pool. Complimentary full bkfst, coffee in rms. Ck-out noon. Coin lndry. Meeting rms. Business servs avail. In-rm modem link. Concierge. Barber. Exercise equipt. Health club privileges. Microwaves. Cr cds: A, D, DS, JCB, MC, V.

⊡ ⇌ 🕅 ⊠ 🔥 SC

★ ★ **LENOX SUITES HOTEL.** *616 N Rush St (60611). 312/337-1000; fax 312/337-7217; toll-free 800/445-3669. www.lenoxsuites.com.* 324 kit. units, 17 story. S $149-$199; D $159-$299; each addl $15; under 16 free; wkend, monthly rates. Crib free. Valet parking $32. TV; cable (premium), VCR avail. Complimentary continental bkfst. Restaurants 6 am-11 pm. Rm serv. Bar 11-2 am. Ck-out noon. Coin lndry. Meeting rms. Business servs avail. In-rm modem link. Concierge. Gift shop. Exercise equipt. Health club privileges. Microwaves. Cr cds: A, C, D, DS, ER, JCB, MC, V.

⊡ 🕅 ⊠ 🔥

★ ★ ★ **RADISSON HOTEL & SUITES.** *160 E Huron (60611). 312/787-2900; fax 312/787-5158. www.radisson.com.* 350 rms, 40 story, 100 suites. Apr-Dec: S $139-$239; D $159-$259; each addl $20; suites $179-$279; under 17 free; wkend rates; lower rates rest of yr. Crib free. Pet accepted, some restrictions. Valet parking $31. TV; cable (premium), VCR avail. Pool; poolside serv. Complimentary coffee in rms. Restaurant 6 am-10 pm. Rm serv 24 hrs. Bar noon-midnight. Ck-out noon. Convention facilities. Business center. In-rm modem link. Concierge. Exercise equipt. Refrigerators; microwaves avail. Cr cds: A, D, DS, MC, V.

⊡ ⇌ ⊠ 🕅 ⊠ 🔥 SC 🕅

Extended Stay

★ ★ **RESIDENCE INN BY MARRIOTT.** *201 E Walton St (60611). 312/943-9800; fax 312/943-8579. www.marriott.com.* 221 kit. suites, 19 story. Suites $169-$429; package plans. Crib free. Pet accepted, some restrictions; $15. Valet parking, in/out $30. TV; cable (premium). Pool privileges. Complimentary full bkfst; afternoon refreshments. Complimentary coffee in rms. Restaurant adj 6:30 am-9:30 pm, Sat-Sun 7 am-10:30 pm. Ck-out noon. Coin lndry. Business servs avail. In-rm modem link. Exercise equipt. Health club privileges. Microwaves. One blk from Oak St beach. Cr cds: A, C, D, DS, JCB, MC, V.

⊡ ⇌ 🕅 ⊠ 🔥

Restaurants

★ ★ ★ **312 CHICAGO.** *136 N LaSalle (60602). 312/696-2420. www.312 chicago.citysearch.com.* Menu changes seasonally. Hrs: 7-10 am 11 am-3 pm, 5-10 pm; Fri to 11 pm; Sat 7 am-noon, 5-11 pm; Sun 8 am-3 pm, 5-10 pm. Closed hols. Res accepted. Wine, beer. Lunch $3.50-$22.95; dinner $13.95-$22.95. Brunch $3.50-$22.95. Cr cds: A, C, D, DS, MC, V.

⊡

★ ★ **ADOBO GRILL.** *1610 N Wells (60614). 312/266-7999. www.adobo grill.com.* Specializes in enchiladas, en chipotole, camarones al mojo de ajo en mole pipian. Hrs: 5:30-10:30 pm;

Fri to 11:30 pm; Sat 10:30 am-2:30 pm, 5:30-11:30 pm; Sun 10:30 am-2:30 pm, 3:30-9:30 pm. Res required. Wine, beer. Dinner $11.95-$18.95. Brunch $4.50-$11.95. Child's menu. Entertainment. Two vintage bars. Cr cds: A, D, MC, V.
D

★ **ALBERT'S CAFE & PATISSERIE.** *52 W Elm St (60610). 312/751-0666.* Hrs: 10 am-9 pm. Closed Mon; major hols. Contemporary American menu. A la carte entrees: lunch, dinner $6.95-$12.95. Specializes in European-style pastries and desserts, steak. Valet parking. Outdoor dining. Totally nonsmoking. Cr cds: A, D, DS, MC, V.

★★★★ **AMBRIA.** *2300 N Lincoln Park W (60614). 773/472-5959. www. lettuceentertainyou.com.* Opened in 1980, this refined establishment offers impeccable, old-school service with an expertly trained, perfectly synchronized staff that is completely without airs. The restaurant's Belden-Stratford location (in a upscale residential high-rise) makes guests feel they've found a hidden gem. And they have, one with a daily changing menu of exquisite, classic French offerings and a choice from the breathtaking, seven-ft-tall dessert cart. French, continental menu. Specializes in fresh seafood, seasonal offerings. Menu changes seasonally; daily specialties. Own baking. Hrs: 6-9:30 pm; Fri 6-10:30 pm; Sat from 5 pm. Closed Sun; hols. Res accepted. Bar. Wine list. A la carte entrees: dinner $29-$35. Prix fixe: dinner $75. Valet parking. Chef-owned. Cr cds: A, C, D, DS, MC, V.
D

★★★ **ARUN'S.** *4156 N Kedzie Ave (60618). 773/539-1909.* Miles apart from the typical neighborhood Thai restaurant, this destination is a bastion of artistry. Chef Arun Sampanthavivat instructs servers to conduct "interviews" so that tasting menus can be individually designed for each diner; no two tables receive the same meal. Dishes are intricate with intelligently balanced flavors and textures, all presented without pretense in a comfortable art-filled room. Thai menu; special chef-designed menus. Specialties: pad Thai, three-flavored red snapper, spicy roast eggplant.

Hrs: 5-10 pm. Closed Mon; hols. Res required. Bar. Prix fixe: 12-course dinner $75. Cr cds: A, D, DS, MC, V.
D

★ **ATHENIAN ROOM.** *807 W Webster (60611). 773/348-5155.* Specializes in chicken Kalamata. Hrs: 11 am-10 pm. Lunch, dinner $6-$12. Entertainment. Cr cds: MC, V.
D

★★★ **ATLANTIQUE.** *5101 N Clark (60640). 773/275-9191.* Specializes in seafood, steak. Menu changes seasonally. Hrs: 5:30-10 pm; Fri, Sat to 11 pm; Sun 5-9 pm. Res accepted. Wine,

Die-hard Cubs fans

beer. Dinner $16.95-$23.95. Entertainment. Cr cds: A, D, MC, V.
D ⏎

★★★ **ATWOOD CAFE.** *1 W Washington (60602). 312/368-1900.* Specializes in Atwood Cafe potpie, New York strip steak, salmon. Hrs: 7-10 am, 11:30 am-3:30 pm, 5-10 pm; Sat, Sun 8 am-11 pm. Closed hols. Res accepted. Wine, beer. Lunch $15-$20; dinner $25-$35. Brunch $10-$15. Entertainment. Cr cds: A, D, DS, MC, V.
D

★★★ **AUBRIOT.** *1962 N Halsted St (60614). 773/281-4211.* Hrs: 5-10:30 pm; Fri, Sat to 11:30 pm. Closed Mon; hols. Res accepted. French menu. Bar. Dinner $15-$24. Specialties: fricasse of Florida frog legs and roasted veal kidney beans, potato-wrapped goat cheese with romaine lettuce and croutons, sauteed sweetbreads and foie gras with artichokes and oven-roasted tomatoes. Valet parking. Eclectic decor with original artwork. Totally nonsmoking. Cr cds: A, D, MC, V.

D

★★ **BANDERA.** *535 N Michigan (60610). 312/644-3524.* Specializes in Seattle-style BBQ salmon, wood-fire rotisserie chicken. Hrs: 11:30 am-10 pm; Fri, Sat to 11 pm. Closed Sun; hols. Res accepted. Wine, beer. Lunch $6.95-$20; dinner $7.95-$25. Children's menu. Cr cds: A, D, MC, V.

D

★ **BAR LOUIE.** *226 W Chicago (60610). 312/337-3313. www.barlouie america.com.* Specializes in Louie steak sandwich. Hrs: 11:30 am-2 am; Thurs-Fri to 4 am; Sat, noon-5 am; Sun 5 pm-2 am. Wine, beer. Lunch, dinner $6.99-$9.99. Entertainment. Cr cds: A, D, MC, V.

D

★★ **BASTA PASTA.** *6733 Olmstead St (60631). 773/763-0667.* Specializes in rigatoni and sausage, splendido, mama breaded chicken. Hrs: 4:30-10 pm; Fri 11:30 am-2 pm, 4:30-11 pm; Sat 4:30-11 pm; Sun 4-9 pm. Closed Mon. Res accepted. Wine, beer. Lunch $4.95-$12.95; dinner $6.95-$26.95. Cr cds: A, D, MC, V.

D

★★★ **BELLA NOTTE.** *1372 W Grand Ave (60622). 312/733-5136.* Menu changes biannually. Hrs: 11 am-10 pm, Fri to 11:30 pm; Sat 5-11:30 pm; Sun 4-9:30 pm. Closed hols. Res accepted. Wine, beer. Lunch $4.95-$15.95; dinner $4.95-$29.95. Entertainment. Cr cds: A, C, D, DS, MC, V.

D

★ **BEN PAO.** *52 W Illinois St (60610). 312/222-1888. www.leye.com.* Hrs: 11:30 am-2 pm, 5-10 pm; Fri to 11 pm; Sat 5-11 pm; Sun 4-9 pm. Closed major hols. Res accepted. Chinese menu. Bar. A la carte entrees: lunch $7.95-$13.95, dinner $8.95-$17.95.

Child's menu. Specialties: grilled satays, black peppered scallops, seven-flavored chicken. Own desserts. Valet parking. Outdoor dining. Dramatic Chinese decor with waterfall columns. Cr cds: A, D, DS, MC, V.

D

★ **BERGHOFF.** *17 W Adams St (60603). 312/427-3170. www.berghoff. com.* Hrs: 11 am-9 pm; Fri to 9:30 pm; Sat to 10 pm. Closed Sun; major hols. Res accepted. German, American menu. Lunch $6.50-$11, dinner $9-$17. Child's menu. Specialties: Wiener schnitzel, chicken Dijon, sauerbraten. In 1881 building. Family-owned since 1898. Cr cds: A, MC, V.

D

★★ **BICE.** *158 E Ontario St (62611). 312/664-1474.* Hrs: 11:30 am-10:30 pm; Fri, Sat to 11:30 pm. Closed Jan 1, Dec 25. Res accepted. Northern Italian menu. Bar. A la carte entrees: lunch $11-$20, dinner $14-$25. Own pastries, desserts, pasta. Valet parking (dinner). Outdoor dining. Contemporary Italian decor. Cr cds: A, D, DS, MC, V.

SC

★★ **BIG BOWL CAFE.** *159 W Erie St (60610). 312/787-8297. www. bigbowl.com.* Hrs: 11:30 am-10 pm; Fri, Sat to 11 pm. Closed Sun; Thanksgiving, Dec 25. Wine, beer. Lunch, dinner $1.95-$6.95. Specializes in Asian cuisine. Casual, informal atmosphere. Cr cds: A, D, DS, MC, V.

D

★★ **BIG DOWNTOWN.** *124 S Wabash Ave (60603). 312/917-7399. www.hilton.com.* Hrs: 11-2 am. Res accepted (dinner). Bar. Lunch $8-$16, dinner $10-$22. Specialties: barbecue ribs, rotisserie chicken. Own baking. Blues Wed night. 1940s-style diner with jazz memorabilia, miniature replica of the Chicago El. Cr cds: A, D, DS, MC, V.

D SC

★★ **BIGGS.** *1150 N Dearborn St (60610). 312/787-0900.* Hrs: 5-10 pm. Closed major hols. Res accepted. Continental menu. Bar. Wine cellar. A la carte entrees: dinner $18.95-

$32.95. Specialties: beef Wellington, rack of lamb, caviar. Valet parking. Entertainment. Outdoor dining. Formal dining in mansion built 1874. Original oil paintings. Cr cds: A, D, DS, MC, V.

★ ★ **BIN 36.** *339 N Dearborn St (60610).* 312/755-9463. *www.bin36. com.* Menu changes seasonally. Hrs: 6:30 am-10 pm. Res accepted. Wine, beer. Lunch $9-$17; dinner $16-$28. Entertainment. Cr cds: A, D, DS, MC, V.
D ⊐

★ ★ **BISTRO 110.** *110 E Pearson St (60611).* 312/266-3110. *www.bistro 110restaurant.com.* Hrs: 11:30 am-11 pm; Fri, Sat to midnight; Sun brunch 11 am-4 pm. Closed major hols. Res accepted. French, American menu. Bar. A la carte entrees: lunch $7.95-$15.95, dinner $10.95-$24.95. Sun Jazz brunch $6.95-$14.95. Specializes in chicken prepared in wood-burning oven, fish. Valet parking. Outdoor dining. French bistro atmosphere. Cr cds: A, C, D, DS, MC, V.
D ⊐

★ ★ ★ **BISTROT ZINC.** *3443 N Southport Ave (60657).* 773/281-3443. French menu. Specializes in steak frites, roasted chicken. Hrs: 11:30 am-3 pm, 5:30-10 pm; Fri 5:30-11 pm; Sat 10 am-11 pm; Sun 10 am-9 pm. Closed Mon. Res accepted. Wine, beer. Lunch $6.95-$10.95; dinner $12.95-$18.95. Brunch $4.95-$9.95. Child's menu. Cr cds: A, C, D, MC, V.
D

★ ★ ★ **BLACKBIRD.** *619 W Randolph St (60606).* 312/715-0708. *www.blackbirdrestaurant.com.* Contemporary American menu. Hrs: 11:30 am-2 pm, 5:30-10:30 pm; Fri, Sat 5:30-11:30 pm. Closed Sun. A la carte: $15-$26. Valet. Res strongly recommended. Cr cds: A, D, DS, MC, V.
D

★ **BLACKHAWK LOUNGE.** *41 E Superior St (60611).* 312/280-4080. *www.levyrestaurants.com.* Hrs: 11 am-3 pm, 5-10 pm; Fri, Sat to 11 pm; Bluegrass Sun brunch 11 am-3 pm. Closed major hols. Res accepted. Bar. Lunch $13-$17, dinner $25-$29. Sun brunch $12-$17. Specializes in fresh fish, smoked tenderloin of beef, sea-

sonal game. Valet parking. Outdoor dining. Lodge atmosphere; eclectic artifacts. Cr cds: A, D, DS, MC, V.
D ⊐

★ ★ **BLUE MESA.** *1729 N Halsted (60614).* 312/944-5990. Hrs: 11:30 am-10:30 pm; Fri, Sat to 11:30 pm; Sun, Mon 4-10 pm; Sun brunch 11 am-3 pm. Closed Thanksgiving, Dec 25. Res accepted. Southwestern menu. Bar. Lunch, dinner $6.95-$13.95. Sun brunch $6.95-$12.95. Child's menu. Specialties: blue corn chicken enchilada, grilled shrimp and corn cake with chipotle butter sauce. Valet parking. Outdoor dining. Cr cds: A, D, DS, MC, V.
D

★ ★ **BLUE POINT OYSTER BAR.** *741 W Randolph (60661).* 312/207-1222. *www.rdg.com.* Specializes in seafood, steak. Hrs: 11:30 am-10:30 pm, Fri, Sat to midnight; Sun 5-10:30 pm. Closed hols. Res accepted. Wine, beer. Lunch $7.95-$21.95; dinner $17.95-$28.95. Entertainment. Cr cds: A, D, DS, MC, V.
D ⊐

★ ★ ★ **BRASSERIE JO.** *59 W Hubbard St (60610).* 312/595-0800. *www. lettuceentertainyou.com.* Hrs: 11:30 am-4 pm, 5-10 pm; Fri, Sat 5-11 pm. Closed Thanksgiving, Dec 24, 25. Res accepted. French menu. Bar. Wine cellar. Lunch $7.95-$15.95, dinner $9.50-$19.95. Specialties: smoked salmon, onion tart Uncle Hansi, Brasserie steak pomme frites. Own baking, pasta. Valet parking. Outdoor dining. Authentic French brasserie decor; casual European elegance. Cr cds: A, D, DS, MC, V.
D ⊐

★ ★ **BRETT'S.** *2011 W Roscoe (60618).* 773/248-0999. *www.bretts restaurant.com.* Menu changes seasonally. Hrs: 5-10 pm; Sat, Sun 9 am-2 pm. Closed hols. Res accepted. Wine, beer. Dinner $9.95-$21.95. Brunch $3.95-$8.95. Entertainment. Cr cds: A, D, MC, V.
D

★ ★ **BRICKS.** *1909 N Lincoln (60614).* 312/255-0851. *www.bricks pizza.com.* Specializes in thin crust pizza. Hrs: 5-11 pm. Closed hols. Res accepted. Wine, beer. Dinner $5.95-

$17.50. Entertainment. Cr cds: A, D, DS, JCB, MC, V.

🖃

★ **BUCA DI BEPPO.** *2941 N Clark St (60657). 773/348-7673.* Italian menu. Specializes in pasta, chicken cacciatore, tiramisu. Hrs: 5-10 pm; Fri to 11 pm; Sat, Sun from 4 pm. Closed Thanksgiving, Dec 24, 25. Res accepted. Bar. Dinner a la carte entrees: $7.95-$19.95. Eclectic decor. Cr cds: A, D, DS, MC, V.

★★ **BUCKINGHAM'S.** *720 S Michigan Ave (60605). 312/922-4400. www. hilton.com.* Hrs: 5:30-10 pm. Res accepted. Bar. Wine list. A la carte entrees: dinner $18.95-$29.95. Child's menu. Specialties: Australian lamb chops, Buckingham's porterhouse, Maryland crab cakes. Own baking. Valet parking. Elegant decor; cherrywood pillars, Italian marble; original artwork. Cr cds: A, C, D, DS, ER, JCB, MC, V.

★★ **CAFE ABSINTHE.** *1954 W North Ave (60622). 773/278-4488.* Specializes in grilled rack of lamb, tandori quail, grilled New York Strip with foie gras. Hrs: 5:30-10 pm; Fri, Sat 5:30-11 pm; Sun 5:30-9:30 pm. Closed hols. Res accepted. Wine, beer. Dinner $17.50-$28. Entertainment. Open kitchen viewing. Cr cds: A, D, MC, V.

Ⓓ 🖃

★ **CAFE BA-BA-REEBA!.** *2024 N Halsted St (60614). 773/935-5000. www.lettuceentertainyou.com.* Hrs: 11:30 am-10:30 pm; Fri, Sat to midnight; Sun noon-10 pm. Spanish tapas menu. Bar. A la carte entrees: lunch, dinner $1.95-$9.95. Specialties: baked goat cheese, paella, hot and cold tapas. Valet parking. Outside patio. Authentic Spanish tapas bar. Cr cds: A, C, D, DS, ER, MC, V.

Ⓓ 🖃

★★ **CAFE BERNARD.** *2100 N Halstead (60614). 773/871-2100. www. cafebernard.com.* Specializes in grilled salmon. Hrs: 5-10:30 pm; Fri, Sat to 11:30 pm; Sun 5-10 pm. Closed Dec 25. Res accepted. Wine, beer. Dinner $12.95-$21. Entertainment. Cr cds: A, D, DS, MC, V.

🖃

★★ **CAFI IBERICO.** *739 N LaSalle (60610). 312/573-1510. www.cafii berico.com.* Specializes in paella, pollo a la brasa, tapas. Hrs: 11 am-11:30 pm; Fri to 1:30 am; Sat noon-1:30 am; Sun noon-11:30 pm. Res accepted. Wine, beer. Lunch, dinner $9-$13. Entertainment. Cr cds: A, D, DS, MC, V.

🖃

★★★ **CALITERRA.** *633 N St. Clair (60611). 312/274-4444. www. wyndham.com.* Specializes in shrimp cigars, seared wild salmon, veal ribeye chop. Hrs: 6:30 am-10 pm. Res accepted. Wine, beer. Lunch $12-$18; dinner $17-$35. Child's menu. Cr cds: A, D, DS, MC, V.

Ⓓ 🖃

★★ **CAPE COD ROOM.** *140 E Walton (60611). 312/440-8486. www. hilton.com.* Hrs: noon-11 pm. Closed Dec 25. Res accepted. Seafood menu. Bar. Lunch, dinner $19-$37. Specialties: Maryland crab cakes, turbot, bookbinder's soup. Own baking. Valet parking. Nautical decor. View of Lake Michigan. Cr cds: A, D, DS, MC, V.

Ⓓ 🖃

★★★ **THE CAPITAL GRILLE.** *633 N St. Clair St (60611). 312/337-9400. www.thecapitalgrille.com.* Hrs: 11:30 am-2:30 pm, 5-10 pm; Fri to 11 pm; Sat 5-11 pm; Sun 5-10 pm. Closed July 4, Thanksgiving, Dec 25. Res accepted. Steak menu. Res accepted. Bar. Wine cellar. A la carte entrees: lunch $8.95-$16.95, dinner $16.95-$31.95. Specializes in steak, seafood, chops. Valet parking. Antiques; original oil paintings. Cr cds: A, D, DS, MC, V.

Ⓓ 🖃

★★ **CARMINE'S.** *1043 N Rush St (60611). 312/988-7676. www.rosebud restaurants.com.* Specializes in rigatoni alla vodka, pappardelle marinara, lamb chop oreganato. Hrs: 11 am-10 pm; Fri to midnight; Sat 8 am-midnight; Sun 8-10 pm. Res accepted. Wine, beer. Lunch $8.95-$15.95; dinner $10.95-$31.95. Brunch $6.95-$13.95. Entertainment. Cr cds: A, D, DS, MC, V.

Ⓓ 🖃

★★★ **CELEBRITY CAFE.** *320 N Dearborn St (60610). 312/836-5499.* Hrs: 6:30-11 am, 11:30 am-3 pm; 5:30-10 pm; Res accepted. Bar. A la carte entrees: bkfst $7-$13, lunch $6-$14, dinner $14-$25. Child's menu. Specialties: grilled salmon with honey-mustard glaze. Menu changes seasonally. Own pastries. Valet parking. Cr cds: A, D, DS, MC, V.
D

★ **CENTRO.** *710 N Wells St (60610). 312/988-7775. www.rosebud restaurants.com.* Hrs: 11 am-11 pm; Fri, Sat to 11:30 pm; Sun 4-10 pm. Closed Easter, Dec 25. Res accepted. Italian menu. Bar. A la carte entrees: lunch $6-$12, dinner $7.50-$25. Specialties: pappardelle, chicken Vesuvio, baked cavatelli. Valet parking. Outdoor dining. Bistro atmosphere. Cr cds: A, D, DS, MC, V.
D

★★★★★ **CHARLIE TROTTER'S.** *816 W Armitage Ave (60614). 773/248-6228. www.charlietrotters.com.* Famous for his perfectionist approach, it's no wonder superstar chef Charlie Trotter draws global admiration for his eponymous restaurant's stunning cuisine. The dining room is almost hidden in a meticulously maintained, ivy-covered brownstone on an energetic Lincoln Park street. The menu is prix fixe, constantly changes, and offers artistic presentations of painstakingly selected ingredients enriched without the use of excessive butter or cream. American menu with French and Asian influences. Specialties: aged veal strip loin, European turbot, Maine lobster, Canadian foie gras. Two degustation menus available nightly. Own baking. Hrs: 6-10 pm. Closed Sun, Mon; major hols. Res required. Bar. Wine cellars. Prix fixe: 6-course dinner $90-$100. Valet parking. Chef-owned. Jacket. Totally nonsmoking. Cr cds: A, D, DS, MC, V.
D

★★★ **CHEZ JOEL.** *1119 W Taylor St (60607). 312/226-6479.* Specializes in coq au vin, steak frites, bouillabaisse. Hrs: 11 am-3 pm, 5-10 pm; Fri, Sat to 11 pm. Closed Sun. Res accepted. Wine, beer. Lunch $6.95-$14.95; dinner $12.95-$23.95. Entertainment. Cr cds: A, C, D, DS, MC, V.

★★ **CHICAGO CHOP HOUSE.** *60 W Ontario St (60610). 312/787-7100. www.chicagochophouse.com.* Hrs: 11:30 am-11 pm; Fri to 11:30 pm; Sat 4-11:30 pm; Sun 4-11 pm. Closed major hols. Res accepted. Bar. Lunch $5.95-$18.95, dinner $15.95-$28.95. Specializes in prime rib, NY strip steak, lamb chops. Valet parking. Entertainment. Turn-of-the-century Chicago decor. Cr cds: A, C, D, DS, MC, V.
D

★★★ **CIELO.** *676 N Michigan Ave (60611). 312/944-6664. www.omni hotels.com.* Hrs: 6:30 am-10 pm; Fri, Sat to 11 pm; Sun brunch 11 am-2 pm. Res accepted. American with Italian accents. Bar to midnight. Wine list. A la carte entrees: bkfst $6.95-$15.95, lunch $8.25-$15.50, dinner $12-$30. Sun brunch $28.95. Cr cds: A, D, DS, MC, V.
D

★★ **CLUB GENE & GEORGETTI.** *500 N Franklin St (60610). 312/527-3718.* Hrs: 11:30 am-midnight. Closed Sun; major hols; also 1st wk July. Res accepted. Italian, American menu. Bar. Lunch $7-$18, dinner $14-$33.50. Specialties: prime strip steak, filet mignon, chicken Vesuvio. Valet parking. Chicago saloon atmosphere. Family-owned. Cr cds: A, DS, MC, V.
D

★★ **CLUB LUCKY.** *1824 W Wabansia (60622). 773/227-2300. www.club luckychicago.com.* Specializes in eggplant parmigiana, chicken vesuvio, 8 finger cavatelli. Hrs: 11:30 am-11 pm; Fri, Sat to midnight; Sun to 10 pm. Closed hols. Res accepted. Wine, beer. Lunch $6.95-$11.95; dinner $7.50-$17.95. Child's menu. Entertainment. Open kitchen viewing. 1940 supper club. Cr cds: A, D, DS, JCB, MC, V.

★★★ **COCO PAZZO.** *300 W Hubbard St (60610). 312/836-0900. www.tribads.com/cocopazzo.* Hrs: 11:30 am-2:30 pm, 5:30-10:30 pm; Fri to 11 pm; Sat 5:30-11 pm; Sun 5-10 pm. Closed major hols. Res accepted. Italian menu. Serv bar. Lunch $10.95-$16, dinner $12-$27. Specialties: cacciucco, bistecca alla Florentina. Own baking. Valet parking. Outdoor dining. Contemporary decor. Cr cds: A, DS, MC, V.

D 🖵

★ ★ ★ **CROFTON ON WELLS.** *535 N Wells St (60610). 312/755-1790. www.croftononwells.com.* Hrs: 11:30 am-2:30 pm, 5-10 pm; Fri to 11 pm; Sat 5-11 pm. Closed Sun; major hols. Res accepted. Contemporary American menu. Bar. A la carte entrees: lunch $6.75-$12.25, dinner $16-$24. Specialties: grilled foie gras, smoked pork loin, venison. Valet parking. Outdoor dining. Contemporary, intimate decor. Totally nonsmoking. Cr cds: A, D, DS, MC, V.

D

★ ★ **CUISINES.** *1 W Wacker Dr (60601). 312/372-4459. www.renaissancehotels.com.* Hrs: 11:30 am-2 pm, 5:30-10:30 pm; Sat, Sun from 5:30 pm. Closed major hols. Res accepted. Mediterranean menu. Bar. Wine cellar. Lunch $9.25-$17.25, dinner $6.95-$24.95. Specialties: seared sea scallops with wild mushrooms, fettucine with artichokes, roasted peppers with Barese sausage. Valet parking. Cr cds: A, D, DS, MC, V.

D

★ ★ ★ **CYRANO'S BISTRO AND WINE BAR.** *546 N Wells (60610). 312/467-0546.* Specializes in rotisserie duck, chicken, and rabbit; coq au vin. Hrs: 11:30 am-2:30 pm, 5:30-10:30 pm. Closed Sun; hols. Res accepted. Wine, beer. Lunch $6.95-$11.95; dinner $10.95-$25. Entertainment. Cr cds: A, C, D, DS, MC, V.

D 🖵

★ **DON JUAN.** *6730 N Northwest Hwy (60631). 773/775-6438.* Mexican menu. Menu changes seasonally. Hrs: 11 am-10 pm; Fri, Sat to 11 pm; Sun noon-9 pm. Closed hols. Res accepted. Wine, beer. Lunch $5.95-$15; dinner $6.95-$27. Child's menu. Entertainment. Cr cds: A, D, DS, MC, V.

D

★ ★ **ELI'S THE PLACE FOR STEAK.** *215 E Chicago Ave (60611). 312/642-1393. www.eliplaceforsteak.com.* Hrs: 11 am-3 pm, 5-10:30 pm; Fri to 11 pm; Sat, Sun from 5 pm. Closed major hols. Res accepted. Bar to 11 pm. Lunch $8.95-$12.95, dinner $19.95-$32.95. Specializes in steak, liver. Own cheesecake. Piano bar. Valet parking. Club-like atmosphere; original artwork of Chicago scenes. Cr cds: A, D, DS, MC, V.

D 🖵

★ ★ **EMILIO'S TAPAS.** *444 W Fullerton St (60614). 773/327-5100. www.emiliostapas.com.* Hrs: 11:30 am-10 pm; Fri, Sat to 11 pm. Closed major hols. Res accepted. Spanish tapas menu. Bar. A la carte entrees: lunch $3.50-$7.95, dinner $3.50-$16.95. Specialties: garlic potato salad, baked goat cheese, paella de mariscos. Own pastries. Valet parking. Outdoor dining. Casual Spanish garden atmosphere; overlooks courtyard. Cr cds: A, C, DS, MC, V.

D 🖵

★ **EMPEROR'S CHOICE.** *2238 S Wentworth Ave (60616). 312/225-8800.* Hrs: 11:45-12:30 am; Sun to 11:30 pm. Cantonese seafood menu. Serv bar. A la carte entrees: lunch, dinner $6.95-$19.95. (Mon-Fri): lunch $5.95-$9.95. Prix fixe: dinner for two $38-$58. Specialties: whole steamed oysters with black bean sauce, lobster, poached shrimp in shell with soy dip. Chinese artifacts including Ching dynasty emperor's robe; ink drawings of emperors from each dynasty. Cr cds: A, MC, V.

D 🖵

★ ★ ★ **ENTRE NOUS.** *200 N Columbus Dr (60601). 312/565-7997. www.fairmont.com.* Hrs: 5:30-10:30 pm; Sat to 11 pm. Closed Sun, Mon. Res accepted. Continental menu. Bar. Wine list. Dinner $18-$38. Specializes in regional American cuisine, seasonal dishes. Pianist. Valet parking. Elegant dining. Cr cds: A, D, DS, MC, V.

D 🖵

★ ★ ★ **ERWIN'S.** *2925 N Halsted St (60657). 773/528-7200. www.erwin cafe.com.* Hrs: 5:30-10 pm; Fri, Sat to 11 pm; Sun 5-9:30 pm; Sun brunch 10:30 am-2:30 pm. Closed Mon; major hols. Res accepted. Bar. Dinner $12.95-$16.95. Sun brunch $3.95-$9.95. Specializes in smoked trout appetizers, wood-grilled pork tenderloin, fresh seafood. Valet parking.

Casual bistro atmosphere. Cr cds: A, D, DS, MC, V.

[D]

★ ★ ★ ★ **EVEREST.** *440 S La Salle St (60605). 312/663-8920. www.lettuce entertainyou.com.* Famed Alsatian chef Jean Joho presents spectacularly unfussy cuisine at this fine French restaurant. The seven-course tasting menu is a decadent pleasure, but a la carte offerings are just as enticing, with five "reputation-making" dishes listed on the menu, including a roasted Maine lobster in Alsace Gewurztraminer, butter, and ginger. Window seats offer stunning city-light views from the 40th floor office-building location. Creative French menu with Alsatian influence. Specialties: marbre of cold bouillabaisse, seafood and shellfish; Maine lobster with Alsace Gewurztraminer and ginger; poached tenderloin of beef, pot-au-feu style, with horseradish cream. Hrs: 5:30-9 pm (last sitting); Fri, Sat to 10 pm (last sitting). Closed Sun, Mon; major hols. Res required. Serv bar. Extensive wine list; specializes in wines from Alsace. A la carte entrees: dinner $28-$38. Prix fixe: multicourse dinner $79. Free valet parking. Chef-owned. Jacket recommended. Cr cds: A, D, DS, MC, V.

[D]

★ ★ **FAHRENHEIT.** *695 N Milwaukee Ave (60622). 312/733-7400. www. fahrenheitchicago.com.* Menu changes seasonally. Hrs: 5:30-10:30 pm, Fri, Sat to 11:30 pm. Res accepted. Wine list. Dinner $12-$35. Entertainment. Open kitchen viewing. Cr cds: A, D, DS, MC, V.

[D] [⊷]

★ ★ ★ **FRONTERA GRILL.** *445 N Clark St (60610). 312/661-1434. www.fronterakitchens.com.* Hrs: 11:20 am-2 pm, 5:30-9:30 pm; Fri to 10:30 pm; Sat 5-11 pm; Sat brunch 10:30 am-2:30 pm. Closed Sun, Mon. Mexican menu. Bar. A la carte entrees: lunch $8-$12, dinner $9-$18.95. Sat brunch $5.95-$9.50. Specialties: grilled fresh fish, duck breast adobo, carne asada. Valet parking. Outdoor dining. Regional Mexican cuisine; casual dining. Cr cds: A, D, DS, MC, V.

[D]

★ **GEJA'S CAFE.** *340 W Armitage Ave (60614). 773/281-9101. www. gejascafe.com.* Hrs: 5-10:30 pm; Fri to midnight; Sat to 12:30 am; Sun 4:30-10 pm. Closed major hols. Res accepted Sun-Thurs. Fondue menu. Bar. Complete meals: dinner $18.50-$29.95. Specializes in cheese, meat, seafood and dessert fondues. Flamenco and classical guitarist nightly. Variety of wines, sold by the glass. Cr cds: A, D, DS, MC, V.

[⊷]

★ ★ **GIBSON'S STEAKHOUSE.** *1028 N Rush St (60611). 312/266-8999. www.gibsonssteakhouse.com.* Hrs: 3 pm-2 am. Closed major hols. Bar 3 pm-2 am. Wine list. Dinner $11-$33.25. Specializes in prime-aged steak, Chicago-cut steak, fresh seafood. Pianist in bar nightly. Valet parking. Art Deco decor. Cr cds: A, D, DS, MC, V.

[D] [⊷]

★ ★ **GIOCO.** *1312 S Wabash (60605). 312/939-3870. www. metromix.com.* Menu changes seasonally. Hrs: 11:30 am-2:30 pm, 5-10 pm; Thurs to 11 pm; Fri, Sat to midnight; Sun 4-9 pm. Closed hols. Res accepted. Wine, beer. Lunch $10-$18; dinner $9-$31. Entertainment. Cr cds: A, D, MC, V.

[D] [⊷]

★ ★ **GRACE.** *623 W Randolph St (60661). 312/928-9200. www.grace restaurant.com.* American contemporary menu. Specializes in venison loin stuffed with blackberry thyme, venison demiglaze. Hrs: 10 am-10 pm. Closed Sun. Res accepted. Wine list. Lunch $9-$22; dinner $15-$32. Entertainment. Hanging globes in restaurant. Cr cds: A, D, DS, MC, V.

[D] [⊷]

★ ★ **GREEK ISLANDS.** *200 S Halsted St (60661). 312/782-9855.* Hrs: 11 am-midnight; Fri, Sat to 1 am. Closed Thanksgiving, Dec 25. Res accepted Sun-Thurs. Greek, American menu. Bar. A la carte entrees: lunch $5-$8.50, dinner $5.95-$15.95. Complete meals: lunch, dinner $9.95-$16.95. Specialties: lamb with artichoke, broiled red snapper, saganaki. Valet parking. Greek decor; 5 dining areas. Family-owned. Cr cds: A, D, DS, MC, V.

[D] [⊷]

★★ **HARRY CARAY'S.** *33 W Kinzie St (60610).* 312/828-0966. *www.harry carays.com.* Hrs: 11:30 am-2:30 pm, 5-10:30 pm; Fri, Sat to 11 pm; Sun 4-10 pm. Closed Dec 25. Res accepted. Italian, American menu. Bar. A la carte entrees: lunch, dinner $8.95-$39.95. Specializes in chicken Vesuvio, lamb chop Oreganato, steak. Valet parking. Baseball memorabilia. Cr cds: A, DS, MC, V.
D

★★★ **HARVEST ON HURON.** *217 W Huron St (60610).* 312/587-9600. *www.harvestchicago.com.* Specializes in budakhan tuna san, seared sea scallops, sauted venison. Hrs: 11:30 am-2:30 pm, 5:30-10 pm; Fri to midnight; Sat 5:30 pm-midnight. Closed Sun. Res accepted. Wine, beer. Lunch $9-$18; dinner $14-$29. Entertainment. Cr cds: A, DS, MC, V.
D

★★ **HATSUHANA.** *160 E Ontario St (60611).* 312/280-8808. *www. hatsuhana-sushi.com.* Hrs: 11:45 am-2 pm, 5:30-10 pm; Sat from 5 pm. Closed Sun; major hols. Res accepted. Japanese menu. Serv bar. A la carte entrees: lunch $9-$19, dinner $11-$30. Complete meals: dinner $14-$26. Specialties: tempura, Hatsuhana and sushi specials. Sushi bar. Traditional Japanese decor. Cr cds: A, C, D, DS, MC, V.
D

★★ **INDIAN GARDEN.** *2546 W Devon Ave (60659).* 773/338-2929. *www.theindiangarden.com.* Hrs: 11:30 am-3 pm, 5-9:45 pm; Fri, Sat to 10:15 pm. Res accepted. Indian menu. Bar. Lunch buffet $6.95. A la carte entrees: dinner $7.95-$15.95. Specialties: chicken tikka masala, boti kebab masala, navrattan korma. Parking. Casual dining. Cr cds: A, D, MC, V.
D SC

★★★ **IXCAPUZALCO.** *2919 N Milwaukee (60618).* 773/486-7340. *www. citysearch.com.* Menu changes seasonally. Hrs: 10:30 am-2:30 pm, 5:30-10 pm; Fri, Sat to 11 pm. Res accepted. Wine, beer. Lunch $7.50-$12.95; dinner $16-$22.50. Brunch $6.50-$9. Entertainment. Cr cds: A, D, DS, MC, V.
D

★★ **JANE'S.** *1655 W Cortland (60622).* 773/862-5263. Menu changes seasonally. Hrs: 5-10 pm; Fri to 11 pm; Sat 11 am-11 pm; Sun 11 am-10 pm. Closed hols. Res accepted. Wine, beer. Lunch $6.95-$19.95; dinner $7.95-$19.95. Brunch $6.95-$19.95. Entertainment. Open kitchen viewing. Cr cds: D, MC, V.
D

★ **JOE'S BE-BOP CAFE.** *600 E Grand Ave (60611).* 312/595-5299. *www. joesbebop.com.* Hrs: 11 am-11 pm; Fri, Sat to midnight. Closed Thanksgiving, Dec 25. Res accepted. Barbecue menu. Bar. A la carte entrees: lunch, dinner $7.50-$17.95. Child's menu. Specializes in southern-style barbecue entrees. Jazz. Valet parking. Outdoor dining. Murals of Chicago jazz artists dating from 1940s to current era. Cr cds: A, D, DS, MC, V.
D

★★ **JOHN'S PLACE.** *1202 W Webster (60614).* 773/525-6670. Specializes in half-roasted chicken, turkey meatloaf. Hrs: 11 am-10 pm; Fri to 11 pm; Sat 8 am-11 pm. Sun 8 am-9 pm. Closed Mon. Res accepted. Wine, beer. Lunch $5.95-$8.95; dinner $17.95-$54.95. Brunch $6.95-$8.95. Child's menu. Entertainment. Cr cds: A, D, DS, MC, V.
D

★★★ **KIKI'S BISTRO.** *900 N Franklin (60610).* 312/335-5454. *www. opentable.com.* Hrs: 11:30 am-10 pm; Fri to 11 pm; Sat 5-11 pm. Closed Sun; major hols. Res accepted. French Provençale menu. Bar. Lunch $7-$14.50, dinner $12-$17. Specialties: roasted chicken, sauteed duck breast with leg confit, sauteed calf's liver with pearl onions. Own desserts, ice cream. Rustic, country-French decor with unfinished woodwork, brick walls. Cr cds: A, D, DS, MC, V.
D

★★ **KLAY OVEN.** *414 N Orleans St (60610).* 312/527-3999. Hrs: 11:30 am-2:30 pm, 5:30-10:30 pm. Closed major hols. Res accepted. Indian menu. Bar. A la carte entrees: lunch buffet $7.95, dinner $6.95-$25.95. Specialties: sikandari champa, tandoori batera, jheenga bemisaal. Tableside preparation in elegant sur-

roundings. Modern Indian art display. Cr cds: A, DS, MC, V.
[D]

★★ **LA BOCCA DELLA VERITA.**
4618 N Lincoln (60618). 773/784-6222. Specializes in spigola sale, ravoili ana tra. Hrs: 5-11 pm; Sun 3-10 pm. Closed Mon; hols. Res accepted. Wine, beer. Dinner $14.95-$24.95. Entertainment. Cr cds: A, D, DS, MC, V.
[D] [⬛]

★ **LA PAILLOTTE.** *2470 N Clark St (60659). 773/935-4005.* Specializes in steamed seabass, five-spice duck. Hrs: 5-11 pm; Sat 11:30 am-11 pm; Sun noon-10 pm. Closed Tues. Res accepted. Wine, beer. Lunch, dinner $7.95-$12.95. Entertainment. Cr cds: A, DS, MC, V.
[D]

★★★ **LA SARDINE.** *111 N Carpenter (60607). 312/421-2800. www.lasardine.com.* Specializes in bouillabaisse, fresh fish. Hrs: 11:30 am-2:30 pm, 5-11 pm. Closed Sun; hols. Res accepted. Wine, beer. Lunch $8.50-$13.50; dinner $11.75-$18.50. Entertainment. Cr cds: A, C, D, DS, MC, V.
[D] [⬛]

★★ **LA STRADA.** *155 N Michigan Ave (60601). 312/565-2200. www.lastradaristorante.com.* Hrs: 11:30 am-10 pm; Fri to 11 pm, Sat 5-11 pm; early-bird dinner 5-6:30 pm. Closed Sun; major hols. Res accepted. Northern Italian menu. Bar. Wine cellar. A la carte entrees: lunch $12-$18, dinner $14-$32, 7 course $75. Specialties: Applewood-smoked bacon, smoked monkfish, artichoke gaeta, olive-crusted lamb, veal chop valdostana. Own baking. Pianist from 5 pm. Valet parking. Tableside cooking. Cr cds: A, D, DS, MC, V.
[D] [⬛]

★★ **LAWRY'S PRIME RIB.** *100 E Ontario St (60611). 312/787-5000. www.lawrysonline.com.* Hrs: 11:30 am-2 pm, 5-11 pm; Fri, Sat to midnight; Sun 3-10 pm. Closed July 4, Dec 25. Res accepted. Bar. Wine list. Lunch $5.75-$10.95, dinner $19.95-$29.95. Child's menu. Specialties: prime rib, English trifle. Own baking. Valet parking (dinner). In 1896 McCormick mansion. Chicago coun-

terpart of famous California restaurant. Cr cds: A, D, DS, MC, V.
[SC] [⬛]

★★ **LE BOUCHON.** *1958 N Damen Ave (60647). 773/862-6600.* Hrs: 5:30-11 pm; Fri, Sat 5 pm-midnight. Closed Sun; major hols. Res accepted. French menu. Bar. Dinner $11-$14.95. Specialties: roast duck for two, Jean Claude onion tart, marquis au choclat. Own pastries, desserts. French bistro decor with lace curtains, pressed-tin ceiling. Cr cds: A, C, D, DS, MC, V.
[D] [⬛]

★★★ **LES NOMADES.** *222 E Ontario St (60611). 312/649-9010.* This restaurant was a private club for business, political, and social leaders from 1978 until 1996, when renowned culinary couple Roland and Mary Beth Liccioni opened the restaurant to the public. Tranquility is one of the dining room's marked traits, continuing a strict tradition of "no table-hopping." The three-story 1887 brownstone building is a splendid backdrop for the wonderful French meals. French menu. Hrs: 5-9:30 pm; Fri, Sat to 10:30 pm. Closed Sun, Mon; hols. Res accepted. Bar. Wine list. Prix fixe $60, 4 courses. Specialties: Jonah crabcake les nomades, roasted rack of lamb with crispy polenta. Own baking, pasta. Valet parking. Nonsmoking. Cr cds: A, C, D, MC, V.
[D]

★★ **LOUISIANA KITCHEN.** *2666 N Halsted (60614). 773/529-1666.* Specializes in shrimp jambalaya, etouffee, blackened catfish. Hrs: 5-10 pm; Fri to midnight; Sat 3 pm-midnight; Sun 10 am-10 pm. Closed Mon. Res accepted. Wine, beer. Lunch $4.95-$10.95; dinner $9.95-$22.95. Brunch $4.95-$10.95; dinner $9.95-$22.95. Brunch $4.95-$10.95. Entertainment. Cr cds: A, D, DS, MC, V.
[D] [⬛]

★ **MAGGIANO'S.** *516 N Clark St (60610). 312/644-7700. www.brinker.com.* Hrs: 11:30 am-2 pm, 5-10 pm; Fri to 11 pm; Sat 11:30 am-11 pm; Sun noon-10 pm. Closed Thanksgiving, Dec 25. Res accepted. Southern Italian menu. Bar. A la carte entrees: lunch $7.95-$14.95, dinner $9.95-$29.95. Specialties: Maggiano's salad, country-style rigatoni, roasted chicken with rosemary. Own baking. Valet parking. Outdoor dining. 1940s, family-style decor with wood columns and bistro-style seating. Cr cds: A, C, D, DS, MC, V.

D ⎽⫶

★ ★ **MARCHE.** 833 W Randolph St (60607). 312/226-8399. www.marche-chicago.com. Hrs: 11:30 am-2 pm, 5:30-10 pm; Thurs to 11 pm; Fri to midnight; Sat 5:30 pm-midnight; Sun from 5:30 pm. Closed hols. Res accepted. French menu. Bar. Wine list. A la carte entrees: lunch $8-$15, dinner $13-$29. Specialties: spit-roasted chicken with pommes frites, braised lamb shank with garlic whipped potatoes, seasonal fish. Own baking. Valet parking. Contemporary decor with custom-crafted furnishings, open kitchens. Cr cds: A, D, MC, V.

D ⎽⫶

★ ★ **MAZA.** 2743 N Lincoln Ave (60657). 773/929-9600. Lebanese menu. Specializes in seafood couscous, chicken brouchette, lamb chops. Hrs: 5-11 pm; Fri, Sat to midnight. Res accepted. Wine list. Dinner $9-$17. Entertainment. Wall paintings. Cr cds: A, MC, V.

D

★ ★ ★ **MERITAGE.** 2118 N Damen (60647). 773/235-6434. www.meritage cafe.com. Contemporary American menu. Specilaizs in beef tenderloin, seared sugar spiced tuna. Hrs: 5:30-10 pm; Fri, Sat to midnight; Sun 5-10 pm. Res accepted. Wine, beer. Dinner $16-$29. Entertainment. Cr cds: A, MC, V.

D

★ ★ ★ **MIA FRANCESCA.** 3311 N Clark St (60657). 773/281-3310. www.miafrancesca.com. Hrs: 5-10:30 pm; Fri, Sat to 11 pm; Sun to 10:30 pm. Closed major hols. Italian menu. Bar. A la carte entrees: dinner $7.95-$18.95. Child's menu. Specialties: linguine Sugo di scampi, skatewing al Balsamic, penne Siciliana. Valet parking. Marble colonnades; photographs of Rome. Cr cds: A, MC, V.

D ⎽⫶

★ ★ ★ **MIKE DITKA'S.** 100 E Chestnut (60611). 312/587-8989. www.mike ditkaschicago.com. Specializes in steak, chops, seafood. Hrs: 7:30-10 pm; Fri, Sat to 11 pm. Res accepted. Wine, beer. Lunch $7.95-$14.95; dinner $10-$32. Brunch $7.95-$14.95. Entertainment Wed-Sat. Cr cds: A, C, D, DS, MC, V.

D ⎽⫶

★ ★ ★ **MIRAI SUSHI.** 2020 W Division (60622). 773/862-8500. Specializes in Kani nigiri. Hrs: 5-10 pm; Thurs-Sat to 11 pm. Res accepted. Wine, beer. Dinner $9-$21. Entertainment. Cr cds: A, D, DS, MC, V.

D ⎽⫶

★ ★ ★ **MK.** 868 N Franklin St (60610). 312/482-9179. www.mkchicago.com. Specializes in pan-seared tuna, New York strip. Hrs: 11:30 am-10 pm; Fri to 11 pm; Sat 5:30-11 pm; Sun 5:30-10 pm. Closed hols. Res accepted. Wine list. Lunch $10-$17; dinner $16-$32. Entertainment. Cr cds: A, C, D, JCB, MC, V.

D ⎽⫶

★ ★ ★ **MOD.** 1520 N Damen Ave (60622). 773/252-1500. American menu. Menu changes seasonally. Specializes in organic produce and poultry. Hrs: 5:30-11 pm; Fri, Sat to midnight. Res accepted. Bar. A la carte entrees: dinner $12.95-$25.95. Eclectic decor. Cr cds: A, D, DS, MC, V.

★ ★ **MON AMI GABI.** 2300 N Lincoln Park W (60614). 773/348-8886. www. lettusentertainyou.com. Specializes in steak classique, New York Roquefort, fish. Hrs: 5:30-10 pm; Sat 5-11 pm; Sun 5-9 pm. Res accepted. Wine, beer. Dinner $12.95-$27.95. Entertainment. Cr cds: A, D, DS, MC, V.

D ⎽⫶

★ ★ ★ **MORTON'S OF CHICAGO.** 1050 N State St (60610). 312/266-4820. www.mortons.com. Hrs: 5:30-11 pm; Sun 5-10 pm. Closed major hols. Res accepted. Bar. Wine cellar. A la carte entrees: dinner $17-$30. Specialties: Maine lobster, prime dry-aged porterhouse steak, Sicilian veal chops. Valet parking. Menu on blackboard. English club atmosphere, decor. Cr cds: A, C, D, DS, MC, V.

D ⎽⫶

★★ **MOSSANT BISTRO.** *225 N Wabash (60601).* 312/236-9300. Menu changes seasonally. Hrs: 7-10 am, 11:30 am-2:30 pm. Wine, beer. Lunch $4-$21; dinner $6-$30. Cr cds: A, D, MC, V.
D

★★★ **NICK'S FISHMARKET.** *51 S Clark (60603).* 312/621-0200. Hrs: 11:30 am-3 pm, 5:30-11 pm; Fri to midnight; Sat 5:30 pm-midnight. Closed Sun; major hols. Res accepted. Bar 11-2 am. A la carte entrees: lunch $15-$46, dinner $14-$55. Specializes in fresh seafood, live Maine lobster, veal. Pianist exc Mon (dinner). Valet parking. Braille menu. Cr cds: A, D, DS, MC, V.
D **⇥**

★★ **NINE.** *440 W Randolph St (60606).* 312/575-9900. American menu. Specializes in Chilean sea bass wrapped in pancetta, seafood, steak. Hrs: 11 am-2 pm, 5:30-10 pm; Fri to midnight; Sat 5:30 pm-midnight. Res accepted. Bar. Dinner a la carte entrees: $15.95-$27.95. Modern decor. Cr cds: A, D, DS, MC, V.

★★ **NIX.** *163 E Walton Pl (60611).* 312/867-7575. www.millenium-hotels.com. Hrs: 6:30 am-2 pm; 5-10 pm. Sun brunch 9 am-2 pm. Res accepted. Bar. A la carte entrees: bkfst $6-$14.50, lunch $8-$17, dinner $14-$32. Sun brunch $15.95. Child's menu. Specialties: fajita egg rolls, roast duck and cherry pirogi, Moroccan-inspired lamb rack. Own desserts. Valet parking. Outdoor dining. Crisp, contemporary decor; casual dining. Cr cds: A, C, D, DS, MC, V.
D **SC** **⇥**

★ **N.N. SMOKEHOUSE.** *1465 W Irving Park (60613).* 773/868-4700. www.bigbookdirect.net/nnsmokehouse. Hrs: 4-10 pm; Mon to 9 pm; Fri 11:30 am-11 pm; Sat noon-11 pm; Sun noon-10 pm. Closed major hols. Wine, beer. Lunch $4.75-$9.50, dinner $5.85-$14.75. Child's menu. Specialties: spare ribs, Memphis pulled pork, Mississippi fried catfish. Own baking. Casual southern smokehouse atmosphere. Cr cds: C, D, DS, MC, V.
D **SC** **⇥**

★★★ **NOMI.** *800 N Michigan Ave (60611).* 312/239-4030. www.park hyatt.com. Contemporary French menu. Specializes in sushi, Carnaroli risotto, seafood. Hrs: 11:30-1 am; Fri, Sat to 2 am. Res accepted. Bar. Lunch, dinner a la carte entrees: $24-$39. Views of Lake Michigan. Cr cds: A, D, DS, MC, V.

★★★ **NORTH POND CAFE.** *2610 N Cannon Dr (60614).* 773/477-5845. www.northpondcafe.com. Menu changes seasonally. Hrs: 11:30 am-2 pm, 5:30-10 pm; Sun 11 am-2 pm, 5:30-10 pm. Closed Mon; hols. Res accepted. Wine, beer. Lunch $10-$13; dinner $23-$27. Entertainment. Cr cds: A, D, MC, V.
D **SC**

★ **NORTHSIDE CAFE.** *1635 N Damen (60647).* 773/384-3555. Specializes in Cajun catfish, burgers, Northside salad. Hrs: 11-2 am. Closed hols. Wine, beer. Lunch, dinner $6-$12. Entertainment. Cr cds: A, D, DS, MC, V.
D **⇥**

★ **OAK TREE.** *900 N Michigan Ave (60611).* 312/751-1988. Specializes in Texas chicken, chin chin. Hrs: 7:30 am-5:30 pm. Closed hols. Lunch $5.95-$15.95 Entertainment. Cr cds: A, D, DS, MC, V.
D **⇥**

★★★ **ONE SIXTYBLUE.** *160 N Loomis (60607).* 312/850-0303. Menu changes seasonally. Hrs: 5-10 pm; Fri, Sat to 11 pm. Closed Sun; hols. Res accepted. Wine, beer. Dinner $20-$30. Entertainment. Open kitchen viewing. Cr cds: A, D, MC, V.
D

★★ **PALM.** *323 E Wacker Dr (60601).* 312/616-1000. Hrs: 11:30 am-11 pm. Res accepted. Bar. A la carte entrees: lunch $8-$15, dinner $14-$32. Specializes in prime-aged beef, jumbo Nova Scotia lobsters, fresh seafood. Own desserts. Valet parking. Outdoor dining. Casual, energetic atmosphere; caricatures of celebrities and regular customers line walls. Family-owned. Cr cds: A, C, D, DS, MC, V.
D **⇥**

★ **PAPAGUS GREEK TAVERNA.** *620 N State St (60610).* 312/642-8450. www.leye.com. Hrs: 11:30 am-10 pm; Sat 11:30 am-midnight; Sun 2:30-10 pm. Res accepted. Greek menu. Bar. A la carte entrees: lunch $3.95-$14, dinner $7.75-$24.95. Specialties:

lamb chops, Greek chicken, whole fish fileted tableside. Valet parking. Outdoor dining. Rustic, country taverna atmosphere. Cr cds: A, C, D, DS, MC, V.

D ⌐

★ ★ ★ **PARK AVENUE CAFE.** *199 E Walton Pl (60611). 312/944-4414.* Hrs: 5-10 pm; Fri, Sat to 11 pm; Sun brunch 10:30 am-2 pm. Closed Mon. Res accepted. Contemporary American menu. Bar. Wine list. A la carte entrees: dinner $18.50-$32. Tasting menu: dinner; 3 course $49.50; 5 course $59.50. Sun brunch $38. Specialties: Hand-rolled cavatelli with wild mushrooms and white truffle oil, braised pork shank with voignier mustard reduction. Own baking, pasta. Valet parking. Warm atmosphere with antique barber poles and American folk art. Cr cds: A, D, DS, JCB, MC, V.

D ⌐

★ **PARTHENON.** *314 S Halsted St (60661). 312/726-2407. www.the parthenon.com.* Hrs: 11-1 am; Sat to 2 am. Closed Thanksgiving, Dec 25. Greek, American menu. A la carte entrees: lunch $4.95-$9.95, dinner $5.95-$10. Child's menu. Specialties: broiled whole fresh fish, saganaki, lamb. Free valet parking. Ancient Greek decor. Family-owned. Cr cds: A, C, D, DS, MC, V.

D ⌐

★ ★ **PASTEUR.** *5525 N Broadway (60640). 773/878-1061.* Vietnamese menu. Specialties: minced shrimp formed around sugar cane, grilled portobello mushrooms caps stuffed with ground pork, crepe filled with chicken, shrimp, mushroom. Hrs: noon-10 pm; Fri, Sat to 11 pm. Res accepted. Bar. Lunch, dinner a la carte entrees: $9.95-$29.95. Cr cds: A, MC, V.

★ **PENNY'S NOODLE SHOP.** *3400 N Sheffield (60657). 773/281-8222.* Specializes in pad se eu, pad thai, chicken or beef dishes. Hrs: 11 am-10 pm; Fri, Sat to 10:30 pm. Lunch, dinner $4-$5.75. Entertainment. No cr cds accepted.

D

★ **PIZZA D.O.C.** *2251 W Lawrence (60625). 773/784-8777.* Specializes in pizza. Hrs: 5-11 pm. Closed Tues;

hols. Res accepted. Wine, beer. Dinner $10.75-$16.75 Entertainment. Cr cds: A, C, D, MC, V.

D ⌐

★ ★ ★ **PRAIRIE.** *500 S Dearborn St (60605). 312/663-1143. www.hyatt. com.* Hrs: 6:30-10 am, 11:30 am-2 pm, 5-10 pm; Sat, Sun 11 am-2 pm. Res accepted. Bar. A la carte entrees: bkfst $5-$11, lunch, dinner $14-$26. Sun brunch $9-$16. Specialties: pan-roasted sturgeon with red wine butter sauce. Own pastries. Seasonal menu. Valet parking. Décor in the style of Frank Lloyd Wright; oak trim, architectural photographs and drawings. Cr cds: A, D, DS, MC, V.

D ⌐

★ ★ **PRINTER'S ROW.** *550 S Dearborn St (60605). 312/461-0780.* Hrs: 11:30 am-2:30 pm, 5-10 pm; Fri to 11 pm; Sat 5-11 pm. Closed Sun; major hols. Res accepted. Continental menu. Bar. Wine list. A la carte entrees: lunch $8.75-$12.95, dinner $14.95-$25.95. Specializes in fresh seafood, duck, seasonal game. Own pastries, desserts. In old printing building (1897). Cr cds: A, D, DS, MC, V.

D ⌐

★ ★ ★ **PUMP ROOM.** *1301 N State Pkwy (60610). 312/266-0360.* Hrs: 6:30-9:30 am, 6-10 pm; Sat, Sun 7-11 am, 6-10 pm. Res accepted. Bar. Wine list. Bkfst $4-$13.50, dinner $27-$39. Own desserts, sorbet. Entertainment Thurs-Sat. Valet parking. Famous dining rm; was once haunt of stars, celebrities; celebrity photographs. Cr cds: A, C, D, DS, MC, V.

D ⌐

★ **QUINCY GRILLE ON THE RIVER.** *200 S Wacker Dr (60606). 312/627-1800. www.quincygrille.com.* Hrs: 6:30-9:30 am, 11:30 am-2 pm, 5-8 pm. Closed Sun; major hols; also June-Aug (dinner). Res required (dinner). Contemporary American menu. Liqour, wine, beer. Buffet: bkfst $6.50. A la carte entrees: lunch $9.75-$23, dinner $16-$26. Child's menu. Specializes in duck, seafood, risotto. Valet parking. Outdoor dining. Riverside view. Cr cds: A, D, DS, MC, V.

D ⌐

★ **REDFISH.** *400 N State St (60610). 312/467-1600.* Hrs: 11:30 am-10 pm; Fri to 11 pm; Sat noon-11 pm; Sun noon-10 pm. Closed most major hols. Res accepted. Cajun/Creole menu. Bar to midnight. Lunch $10-$18, dinner $15-$18. Child's menu. Specialties: redfish, jambalaya. Jazz and blues Thurs-Sat. Valet parking. Outdoor dining. Louisiana roadhouse with Mardi Gras decor; masks, voodoo doll displays. Cr cds: A, D, DS, MC, V.
D ⌐

★ ★ **REDLIGHT.** *820 W Randolph St (60607). 312/733-8880. www.redlight-chicago.com.* Hrs: 5:30-10 pm; Thurs to 11 pm; Fri, Sat to midnight. Closed major hols. Res accepted. Chinese, Thai menu. Bar. Wine list. A la carte entrees: dinner $9-$28. Child's menu. Specialties: Wai Chi's duck, Taiwanese crispy whole catfish, Hong Kong steak. Valet parking. Outdoor dining. Contemporary decor. Cr cds: A, C, D, MC, V.
D ⌐

★ ★ ★ ★ **THE RITZ-CARLTON DINING ROOM.** *160 E Pearson St (60611). 312/266-1000. www.ritz-carlton.com.* In characteristic Ritz style, this contemporary French dining room ranks among some of the best in the country. Crystal chandeliers, plush booths, and impeccable service combine for a lush, old-fashioned romantic atmosphere. Plate presentations are as beautiful as the flavors they hold, and diners can choose from a la carte or tasting menus. The Sunday brunch is outstanding. French-inspired menu. Specialties: Maine lobster with mushrooms and lobster cake, Colorado rack of lamb glazed with thyme and honey. Own pastries. Hrs: 6-11 pm; Sun to 10:30 pm; Sun brunch 10:30 am-2:30 pm. Res accepted. Bar. A la carte entrees: dinner $30-$36. Prix fixe: 6-course dinner $75. Sun brunch $51. Pianist. Valet parking. Menu changes daily. Cr cds: A, C, D, DS, MC, V.
D

★ ★ **RIVA.** *700 E Grand Ave (60611). 312/644-7482.* Hrs: 11:30 am-3 pm, 5-11 pm; Fri, Sat to midnight; Sun noon-9 pm. Res accepted. Continental menu. Bar. Wine list. A la carte entrees: lunch $12.95-$26.95, dinner $14.95-$31.95. Specialties: filet of tuna, cedar plank fish, Chilean sea bass. Own baking, pasta. Valet parking. Casual atmosphere with striking views of Lake Michigan and Chicago skyline. Cr cds: A, C, D, DS, MC, V.
D ⌐

★ **ROSEBUD.** *1500 W Taylor (60607). 312/942-1117. www.rosebud restaurants.com.* Specializes in pasta, chicken, veal. Hrs: 11 am-10:30 pm; Sat 5-11:30 pm; Sun 4-10 pm. Res accepted. Wine, beer. Lunch $5.95-$12.95; dinner $7.95-$28.95. Entertainment. Cr cds: A, D, DS, MC, V.
D SC ⌐

★ ★ **RUSSIAN TEA CAFE.** *77 E Adams St (60603). 312/360-0000. www.russianteatime.com.* Hrs: 11 am-11 pm; Mon to 4 pm; Fri to midnight; Sat noon-midnight; Sun 1-9 pm. Closed Jan 1, Memorial Day. Res accepted. Russian, Ukrainian menu. Bar. Lunch $7-$13, dinner $18-$27. Specialties: borscht, shashlik, wild game. Traditional caviar service. Russian dolls on display. Cr cds: A, D, DS, MC, V.
D

★ ★ **SALOON.** *200 E Chestnut St (60611). 312/280-5454.* Hrs: 11 am-11 pm. Closed major hols. Res accepted. Bar. Lunch $5.95-$11.95, dinner $14.95-$27.95. Specializes in steak, prime rib, fresh seafood. Modern steakhouse atmosphere. Cr cds: A, C, D, DS, MC, V.
D ⌐

★ ★ **SALPICON.** *1252 N Wells St (60610). 312/988-7811. www.salpicon. com.* Hrs: 5-10 pm; Fri, Sat to 11 pm; early-bird dinner to 6:30 pm; Sun brunch 11 am-2:30 pm. Closed Thanksgiving, Dec 25. Res accepted. Mexican menu. Bar. Dinner $12.95-$21.95. Complete meal: dinner $19.95. 7-course tasting menu: $44. Sun brunch $8.95-$15.95. Specialties: shrimp with garlic sauce, beef tenderloin with wild mushrooms, lamb loin chops with garlic pasilla chile sauce. Own desserts. Valet parking. Outdoor dining. Totally nonsmoking. Cr cds: A, D, DS, MC, V.
D

★ ★ **SANTORINI.** *800 W Adams St (60607). 312/829-8820. www.santorini seafood.com.* Hrs: 11 am-midnight;

Fri, Sat to 1 am. Closed Thanksgiving, Dec 25. Res accepted. Greek menu. Bar. A la carte entrees: lunch $6.50-$13.95, dinner $9.95-$22.95. Specializes in fresh seafood, grilled lamb chops, Greek-style chicken. Valet parking. Simulated Greek town. Cr cds: A, D, DS, MC, V.
[D] [≡]

★ **SAYAT NOVA.** *157 E Ohio St (60611). 312/644-9159.* Hrs: 11:30 am-10:30 pm; Sat noon-11 pm; Sun 3-10 pm. Closed major hols. Res accepted. Armenian menu. Bar. Lunch $6.95-$11.95, dinner $9.90-$16.95. Specialties: lamb chops, char-broiled kebab, cous cous. Family-owned. Cr cds: A, C, D, DS, MC, V.
[D] [≡]

★★ **SCOOZI.** *410 W Huron (60610). 312/943-5900. www.lettuceenterain you.com.* Hrs: 11:30 am-2 pm, 5-9:30 pm; Fri to 10:30 pm; Sat 5-10:30 pm; Sun 4-9 pm. Closed Thanksgiving, Dec 25. Res accepted. Italian menu. Bar. A la carte entrees: lunch $7-$15, dinner $7-$21. Specializes in wood-burning-oven pizza, antipasti. Own pasta, desserts. Valet parking. Outdoor dining. Casual atmosphere with loft-style ceilings, woodburning oven and antipasti bar. Cr cds: A, D, DS, MC, V.
[D]

★★★★ **SEASONS.** *120 E Delaware Pl (60611). 312/649-2349. www.four seasons.com.* This elegant, luxuriously appointed dining room at the Four Seasons Hotel is refreshingly friendly and unpretentious for such an upscale establishment. The contemporary American dining room, which boasts views of Michigan Avenue, offers three prix-fixe menus each evening, including vegetarian, five-course, and eight-course options. The Sunday brunch is award-winning with an amazing selection and six different themed buffet stations. Hrs: 6:30-10 am, 11:30 am-2 pm, 6-10 pm; Sun brunch 10:30 am-1:30 pm. Res accepted. Bar 11:30-1 am. A la carte entrees: bkfst $12-$17, lunch $13-$25, dinner $26-$38. Prix fixe: 3-course lunch $23.50, 5-course dinner $76. Sun brunch $51.

Child's menu. Pianist, jazz trio Sat. Valet parking $25; validated self-parking $7. Cr cds: A, C, D, DS, ER, MC, V.
[D] [≡]

★★ **SHALLOTS.** *2324 N Clark St (60614). 773/755-5205.* Menu changes seasonally. Hrs: 11:30 am-1:30 pm, 5:30-9:30 pm. Closed Fri, Sat. Res required. Wine, beer. Lunch $16.50-$23; dinner $22-$45. Entertainment. Cr cds: A, D, DS, MC, V.
[D]

★★ **SHAW'S CRAB HOUSE.** *21 E Hubbard St (60611). 312/527-2722. www.shaws-chicago.com.* Hrs: 11:30 am-10 pm; Fri, Sat to 11 pm; Sun from 5 pm. Closed Thanksgiving, Dec 25. Res accepted. A la carte entrees: lunch $7.95-$14.95, dinner $13.95-$23.95. Specializes in grilled fish, crab cakes, oysters. Entertainment Tues, Thurs 7-10 pm. Valet parking. Décor re-creates look and atmosphere of 1940s seafood house. Cr cds: A, C, D, DS, MC, V.
[D] [≡]

★★ **SIGNATURE ROOM AT THE 95TH.** *875 N Michigan Ave (60611). 312/787-9596. www.signatureroom. com.* Hrs: 11 am-2:30 pm, 5-11 pm; Sat 11 am-2:30 pm, 5:30-11 pm; Sun brunch 10:30 am-2 pm. Closed Jan 1, Dec 25. Res accepted. Bar 11-12:30 am; Fri, Sat to 1:30 am. Lunch $5.95-$15.95. Buffet: lunch $9.50. A la carte entrees: dinner $21-$29.95. Specializes in seafood, lamb, beef. Pianist, Sun-Fri; jazz trio Sat. Magnificent views of city and lake from 95th floor. Cr cds: A, D, DS, MC, V.
[D] [≡]

★★★ **SOUK.** *1552 N Milwaukee Ave (60622). 773/227-1818.* Specializes in lamb chops, mahi-mahi, swordfish, filet mignon, vegetarian dishes. Hrs: 5:30-10:30 pm; Fri, Sat to 11:30 pm. Res accepted. Wine, beer. Dinner $15-$22. Open kitchen viewing. Cr cds: A, D, DS, MC, V.
[D] [≡]

★★★ **SOUL KITCHEN.** *1576 N Milwaukee (60622). 773/342-9742.* Menu changes seasonally. Hrs: 5-10:30 pm; Sun brunch 10 am-2 pm. Closed hols. Res accepted. Wine, beer. Dinner $12-$20. Brunch $7-$16. Entertainment. Cr cds: A, C, D, DS, JCB, MC, V.

D

★★★ **SPAGO.** *520 N Dearborn St (60610). 312/527-3700. www.wolfgang puck.com.* Hrs: 11:30 am-2 pm; 5:30-10 pm; Fri, Sat to 11 pm. Closed hols. Res accepted. Bar. A la carte entrees: lunch $11.50-$16.75, dinner $18.75-$28.50. Specializes in pasta, seafood, pizza with duck sausage. Own baking. Valet parking. Contemporary decor with light woods, vibrant colors. Cr cds: A, D, MC, V.

D

★★★ **SPIAGGIA.** *980 N Michigan Ave (60611). 312/280-2750.* In a city full of Italian food, this establishment remains a star with regional, seasonally inspired preparations. The upscale atmosphere of the airy, bilevel room offers stunning views of Lake Michigan and the beach. Try neighboring Cafe Spiaggia for more casual excursions. Italian menu. Seasonal specialties: wood-roasted veal chops, skewered boneless quail, scallops with porcini mushrooms. Own pastries, pasta. Hrs: 11:30 am-2 pm, 5:30-9:30 pm; Fri, Sat to 10:30 pm; Sun 5:30-9 pm. Closed hols. Res accepted. Bar to 11 pm; Fri, Sat to midnight; Sun to 10 pm. Extensive wine list. A la carte entrees: lunch $8.95-$17.95, dinner $16.95-$32.95. Pianist (dinner). Valet parking. Jacket (dinner). Cr cds: A, D, DS, MC, V.

D

★★★ **STETSON'S CHOPHOUSE.** *151 E Wacker Dr (60601). 312/565-1234.* Hrs: 4:30-10 pm. Res accepted. Steakhouse menu. Bar. Wine list. A la carte entrees: dinner $16-$30. Child's menu. Specializes in steak, seafood. Valet parking. Cr cds: A, D, DS, MC, V.

★★ **STREETERVILLE GRILLE.** *301 E North Water St (60611). 312/670-0788.* Hrs: 11:30 am-2 pm, 5:30-10 pm; Fri to 10:30 pm; Sat 5-10:30 pm. Closed Sun; Jan 1, Dec 25. Res accepted. Serv bar. Lunch $8-$17. A la carte entrees: dinner $18-$30. Specializes in steak, prime rib,

pasta. Valet parking. Cr cds: A, D, DS, MC, V.

D

★ **SU CASA.** *49 E Ontario St (60611). 312/943-4041.* Hrs: 11:30 am-11 pm; Fri, Sat to midnight. Closed Thanksgiving, Dec 25. Res accepted. Mexican menu. Bar. Lunch, dinner $4.95-$12.95. Specialties: chicken poblano, shrimp a la Veracruzana, pan-fried red snapper. Valet parking. Outdoor dining. 16th-century Mexican decor; Mexican artifacts. Cr cds: A, D, DS, MC, V.

D

★★ **SUSHI WABI.** *842 W Randolph St (60607). 312/563-1224.* Sushi menu. Specializes in dragon roll, spider. Hrs: 11:30 am-2 pm, 5 pm-midnight; Sun 5-11 pm. Closed hols. Res accepted. Wine, beer. Lunch $12-$15; dinner $24-$30. Entertainment: Wed, Fri, Sat. Cr cds: A, D, DS, MC, V.

D

★★ **SZECHWAN EAST.** *340 E Ohio St (60611). 312/255-9200. www. chicagobestchinesefood.com.* Hrs: 11:30 am-10 pm; Sun brunch to 2 pm. Closed Thanksgiving. Res accepted. Chinese menu. Bar to 1 am. Buffet: lunch $8.95. A la carte entrees: dinner $7.95-$23.95. Sun brunch $15.95. Specialties: Governor's chicken, steamed black sea bass with ginger and scallions, orange beef. Valet parking. Outdoor dining. Chinese decor with large golden Buddha, etched glass. Cr cds: A, C, D, DS, MC, V.

★★ **TIZI MELLOUL.** *531 N Wells (60610). 312/670-4338.* Menu changes seasonally. Hrs: 5:30-11 pm; Thurs 5-10 pm; Fri, Sat 5-11 pm; Sun 5:30-10 pm. Res accepted. Wine, beer. Dinner $12-$18. Entertainment. Cr cds: A, C, D, DS, MC, V.

D

★★★ **TOPOLOBAMPO.** *445 N Clark St (60610). 312/661-1434.* Regional Mexican menu. Specializes in gourmet cuisine featuring complex sauces, exotic wild game. Own pastries. Hrs: 11:30 am-2 pm, 5:30-9:30 pm; Fri, Sat 5:30-10:30 pm. Closed Sun, Mon. Res accepted. Bar. Wine list. A la carte entrees: lunch $8-$14, dinner $15.50-$23. Valet parking. Intimate dining. Cr cds: A, D, DS, MC, V.

D

★ ★ ★ **TRATTORIA NO. 10.** *10 N Dearborn St (60602). 312/984-1718. www.trattoriaten.com.* Hrs: 11:30 am-2 pm, 5:30-9 pm; Fri to 10 pm; Sat 5:30-10 pm. Closed Sun; major hols. Res accepted. Italian menu. Bar. Wine list. A la carte entrees: lunch, dinner $10.95-$22.95. Specializes in ravioli, rack of lamb, pastas. Own pastries. Valet parking. Dining in grotto-style trattoria. Cr cds: A, C, D, DS, MC, V.

D ⊐

★ ★ **TRATTORIA PARMA.** *400 N Clark St (60610). 312/245-9933.* Hrs: 11:30 am-2 pm, 5:30-10:30 pm; Sat 5:30-11 pm; Sun 4-9:30 pm. Closed some major hols. Res accepted. Italian menu. Bar. A la carte entrees: lunch $5.95-$11.95, dinner $9.95-$15.95. Specialties: stuffed rigatoni with tomato cream sauce, grilled pork chop with ricotto whipped potatoes. Valet parking (dinner). Outdoor dining. Murals of Venice, artwork. Cr cds: A, D, MC, V.

D ⊐

★ ★ ★ **TRU.** *676 N St. Clair (60611). 312/202-0001. www trurestaurant.com.* Contemporary French, richly intricate cuisine and a sleek white interior has made this restaurant the buzz of the town. Traces of color show up in strategically placed objets d'art (including one Andy Warhol piece), artistic plate presentations, and the chic crowd. Progressive French menu. Hrs: 5:30-10 pm; Fri, Sat 5-11 pm. Prix fixe: $75-$125. Dinner $45-$65. Valet. Res required. Jacket. Totally nonsmoking. Cr cds: A, D, DS, MC, V.

D

★ **TUCCI BENUCCH.** *900 N Michigan Ave (60611). 312/266-2500.* Hrs: 11:30 am-10 pm; Fri, Sat to 11 pm; Sun noon-9 pm. Closed Thanksgiving, Dec 25. Northern Italian menu. Bar. A la carte entrees: lunch, dinner $8.95-$13.95. Child's menu. Specializes in pasta, thin-crust pizza, salads. Own desserts. Replica of Italian country villa. Totally nonsmoking. Cr cds: A, D, DS, MC, V.

D

★ ★ **TUSCANY.** *1014 W Taylor St (60612). 312/829-1990. www.tuscany restaurnt.com.* Hrs: 11 am-3:30 pm, 5-11 pm; Fri to midnight; Sat 5 pm-midnight; Sun 2-9:30 pm. Closed major hols. Res accepted. Northern Italian menu. Bar. Lunch $8.95-$15, dinner $8.75-$30. Specialties: grilled baby octopus, ravioli pera, New Zealand lamb. Valet parking. Storefront windows, wood-burning pizza oven. Cr cds: A, D, DS, MC, V.

D ⊐

★ ★ **VINCI.** *1732 N Halsted St (60614). 312/266-1199. www.vinci-*

The Chicago River

group.com. Hrs: 5:30-10:30 pm; Fri, Sat to 11:30 pm; Sun 3:30-9:30 pm; Sun brunch 10:30 am-2:30 pm. Closed major hols. Res accepted. Italian menu. Bar. A la carte entrees: dinner $6.95-$17.95. Child's menu. Specialties: polenta con funghi, grilled duck breast, linguine della Nonna. Valet parking (dinner). Warm, rustic atmosphere. Cr cds: A, D, DS, MC, V.

D ⊐

★★ **VIVERE.** *71 W Monroe St (60603). 312/332-4040. www.italian village-chicago.com.* Hrs: 11:30 am-2:30 pm, 5-10 pm; Fri to 11 pm; Sat 5-11 pm. Closed Sun; major hols. Res accepted. Regional Italian menu. Bar. Extensive wine list. A la carte entrees: lunch $11-$21, dinner $16-$35. Specialties: tortelli di pecorino dolce, pesce del giorno come volete, medaglione di vitello. Valet parking. One of 3 restaurants in the Italian Village complex. Elegant dining in a contemporary Baroque setting; marble mosaic flooring. Family-owned. Cr cds: A, D, DS, MC, V.
[D]

★★ **VIVO.** *838 W Randolph (60607). 312/733-3379.* Hrs: 11:30 am-2:30 pm, 5:30-10 pm; Thurs to 11 pm; Fri to midnight; Sat, Sun 5:30 pm-midnight. Closed major hols. Res accepted. Southern Italian menu. Bar. A la carte entrees: lunch $6-$14, dinner $10-$26. Specialties: black linguine with crabmeat, baked whole snapper, risotto with white asparagus. Own baking, pasta. Valet parking. Outdoor dining. Dramatic, contemporary decor with unique artwork and lighting. Cr cds: A, D, MC, V.
[D] [⊿]

★★★ **WATUSI.** *1540 W North Ave (60622). 773/862-1540. www.watusi chicago.com.* Specializes in grilled octopus, blue crab claws, roasted pork. Hrs: 5:30-10 pm; Fri, Sat 5:30-11 pm. Res accepted. Wine, beer. Dinner $14-$19. Entertainment: Wed. Cr cds: A, D, DS, MC, V.
[D]

★★ **WISHBONE.** *1001 W Washington (60607). 312/850-2663. www. wishbonechicago.com.* Specializes in blackened catfish, shrimp and grits, Louisiana salad. Hrs: 7 am-3 pm, 5-10 pm; Sat, Sun from 8 am. Closed hols. Res accepted. Wine, beer. Lunch $3.50-$13; dinner $7-$15. Brunch $4-$12. Child's menu. Entertainment. Cr cds: A, C, D, DS, MC, V.
[D] [⊿]

★★★ **ZEALOUS.** *419 W Superior (60610). 312/475-9112.* Menu changes seasonally. Hrs: 5:30-10:30 pm. Closed Sun. Res required. Bar.

Dinner a la carte entrees: $18-$29. Entertainment. Cr cds: A, DS, MC, V.
[D]

★★★ **ZINFANDEL.** *59 W Grand Ave (60610). 312/527-1818. www. zinfandelrestaurant.com.* Hrs: 5-10 pm; Fri, Sat to 11 pm. Sat brunch 10:30 am-2 pm. Closed Sun, Mon; major hols. Res accepted. Bar. Wine list. Lunch $7-$14, dinner $16-$20. Sat brunch $6-$11. Specializes in regional American cuisine. Menu changes monthly with emphasis on different regions. Valet parking. Eclectic art. Cr cds: A, D, MC, V.
[D] [⊿]

Unrated Dining Spots

AMERICAN GIRL PLACE CAFE. *111 E Chicago Ave (60611). 312/943-9400.* American menu. Specializes in quiche lorraine, chicken Caesar salad, tic-tac-toe pizza. Sittings: 11 am, 12:30 pm, 2:30 pm, 4 pm, 5:30 pm; Sun also 7:30 pm. Res accepted. Lunch $16; dinner $18. American Girl retail emporium. Cr cds: A, D, DS, MC, V.

ANN SATHER. *929 W Belmont Ave (60657). 773/348-2378. www.ann sather.com.* Hrs: 7 am-10 pm; Fri, Sat to 11 pm. Swedish, American menu. Bar. A la carte entrees: bkfst $3.75-$6.75, lunch and dinner $4.25-$6.95. Complete meals: lunch, dinner $6.95-$10.95. Specializes in Swedish pancakes, fresh fish. Bkfst menu avail all day. Opened 1945. Cr cds: A, DS, MC, V.
[D] [SC] [⊿]

ARCO DE CUCHILLEROS. *3445 N Halsted St (60657). 773/296-6046.* Hrs: 4-11 pm; Fri, Sat to midnight; Sun noon-10 pm; Sun brunch to 3 pm. Closed Mon; major hols. Spanish tapas menu. Bar. A la carte entrees: lunch, dinner $1.95-$5.95. Specialties: fish cheeks sauteed with garlic and white wine, mussels in white wine and cream sauce, boiled potatoes in fresh garlic mayonnaise. Patio dining. Casual atmosphere. Cr cds: A, D, DS, MC, V.
[⊿]

ED DEBEVIC'S. *640 N Wells St (60610). 312/664-1707.* Hrs: 11 am-10 pm; Fri and Sat to midnight. Closed Thanksgiving, Dec 24-25. Bar.

Lunch, dinner $1.50-$6.95. Specializes in chili, hamburgers, meat loaf. Own desserts. Valet parking. Replica of 1950s diner. Cr cds: A, C, D, DS, ER, MC, V.

HARD ROCK CAFE. *63 W Ontario St (60610). 312/943-2252. www.hardrock. com.* Hrs: 11:30 am-11 pm; Fri to midnight; Sat 11 am-midnight; Sun to 10 pm. Closed Thanksgiving, Dec 25. Bar to 12:30 am; Fri, Sat to 1:30 am; Sun to midnight. Lunch, dinner $5.95-$11.95. Specialties: lime barbecue chicken, watermelon ribs. Valet parking. Rock memorabilia. Cr cds: A, D, DS, MC, V.

LUTZ'S CONTINENTAL CAFE & PASTRY SHOP. *2458 W Montrose Ave (60618). 773/478-7785. www.lutzcafe. com.* Hrs: 11 am-10 pm. Closed Mon; major hols. Wine, beer. A la carte entrees: lunch, dinner $5.50-$10.50. Specialties: whipped cream tortes, hand-dipped truffles. Own candy, ice cream. Outdoor dining. Bakeshop. Continental café atmosphere. Family-owned. Cr cds: MC, V.

PIZZERIA UNO. *29 E Ohio St (60611). 312/321-1000. www.unos. com.* Hrs: 11:30-1 am; Sat to 2 am; Sun to midnight. Closed Thanksgiving, Dec 25. Bar. Limited menu. Lunch, dinner $2.95-$8. Specialty: deep-dish pizza. Cr cds: A, C, D, DS, ER, MC, V.

POCKETS. *2618 N Clark St (60614). 773/404-7587. www.pocketsonline.com.* Hrs: 11 am-11 pm; Fri, Sat to midnight; Sun to 10 pm. Closed Thanksgiving, Dec 24-25. A la carte entrees: lunch, dinner $3.50-$6.25. Specializes in sandwiches, calzone, pizza. Cr cds: MC, V.

TAZA. *39 S Wabash Ave (60603). 312/425-9988.* Hrs: 7 am-9 pm; Sun 11 am-9 pm. Closed Thanksgiving, Dec 25. A la carte entrees: lunch, dinner $4.79-$5.89. Specializes in chicken, salads. Street parking. High tech decor; murals.

Chicago O'Hare Airport Area

See also Arlington Heights, Chicago, Elmhurst, Itasca, Schaumburg

Information Des Plaines Chamber of Commerce, 1401 Oakton St, 60018; 847/824-4200

Known as the "world's busiest airport," O'Hare is surrounded by an array of hotels, restaurants, and entertainment facilities—a city unto itself, crossing municipal boundaries.

Services and Information

Information. 312/686-2200.
Lost and Found. 312/686-2200.
Weather. 312/976-2300.
Cash Machines. Terminals 1, 2, 3.
Airlines. Aer Lingus, Aeroflot, Air Canada, Air France, Air India, Air Jamaica, Alitalia, America West, American, ATA, Austrian, British Airways, Canadian Arlns International, Casino Express, China Eastern, Continental, Delta, El Al, Japan Arlns, KLM, Korean Air, Kuwait Airways, LOT, Lufthansa, Mexicana, Northwest, Reno Air, Royal Jordanian, SABENA, SAS, Swissair, Taesa, TAROM, TWA, United, United Express, USAir.

What to See and Do

Allstate Arena. Auditorium with 18,500 seating capacity hosts concerts, sports and other events. Box office (Mon-Sat). Off Northwest Tollway (I-90) Lee St exit, at 6920 Mannheim Rd in Rosemont. Phone 847/635-6601 or 847/768-1285.

Cernan Earth and Space Center. Unique domed theater providing "wraparound" multimedia programs on astronomy, geography, and other topics; free exhibits on space exploration; gift shop. Show (Thurs-Sat eves, matinee Sat; no shows hols). 4 mi S via River Rd, at 2000 N 5th Ave in River Grove, on campus of Triton College. Phone 708/583-3100. ¢¢¢

Motels/Motor Lodges

★★ **BEST WESTERN MIDWAY HOTEL ELK GROVE.** *1600 Oakton St, Elk Grove Village (60007). 847/981-0010; fax 847/364-7365. www.best western.com.* 165 rms, 3 story. S, D $59-$149; each addl $10; suites from $120; under 12 free. Crib free. TV; cable (premium). Pool; whirlpool. Complimentary continental bkfst, coffee in rms. Restaurant 6 am-2 pm, 5-10 pm. Rm serv. Bar 4 pm-midnight. Ck-out noon. Meeting rms. Business servs avail. In-rm modem link. Bellhops. Free airport transportation. Exercise equipt; sauna. Game rm. Some refrigerators. Cr cds: A, C, D, DS, ER, JCB, MC, V.

⬛ 🛏 ✈ 🔽 🔥 SC

★★ **COMFORT INN O'HARE.** *2175 E Touhy Ave, Des Plaines (60018). 847/635-1300; fax 847/635-7572; toll-free 800/222-7666. www.comfortinn-ohare.com.* 145 rms, 3 story. S, D $99-$140; each addl $10; under 18 free. Crib free. TV; cable (premium). Complimentary continental bkfst. Coffee in rms. Restaurant adj 5:30-2 am. Bar 11-1 am. Rm serv 5:30-2 am. Ck-out 1 pm. Meeting rms. Business servs avail. Valet serv. Free airport transportation. Exercise equipt. Whirlpool. Cr cds: A, C, D, DS, ER, JCB, MC, V.

⬛ ✈ 🔽 🔥 SC

★★ **COURTYARD BY MARRIOTT O'HARE.** *2950 S River Rd, Des Plaines (60018). 847/824-7000; fax 847/824-4574; toll-free 800/321-2211. www. courtyard.com.* 180 rms, 5 story. S, D $129-$159; suites from $179; under 12 free; wkend rates. Crib free. TV; cable (premium). Indoor pool; whirlpool. Complimentary coffee in rms. Restaurant 6-9:30 am, 5-10 pm, Sat, Sun 7-11 am. Rm serv Mon-Thurs 5-10 pm. Bar 5-10 pm. Ck-out noon. Coin lndry. Meeting rms. Business servs avail. In-rm modem link. Valet serv. Sundries. Gift shop. Free airport transportation. Exercise equipt. Refrigerator, microwave in suites. Some balconies. Cr cds: A, D, DS, MC, V.

⬛ 🛏 ✈ 🔽 🔥 SC

★ **EXEL INN.** *2881 Touhy Ave, Elk Grove Village (60007). 847/803-9400; fax 847/803-9771; toll-free 800/367-3935. www.exelinns.com.* 123 rms, 3 story. S $65-$76; D $71-$82; under 18 free. Crib avail. Pet accepted, some restrictions. TV; cable. Complimentary continental bkfst. Coffee in rms. Restaurant nearby. Ck-out noon. Coin lndry. Business servs avail. In-rm modem link. Free airport transportation. Exercise equipt. Refrigerators, microwaves avail. Cr cds: A, C, D, DS, JCB, MC, V.

⬛ 🔽 ✈ 🔽 🔥 SC

★★ **HAMPTON INN.** *100 Busse Rd, Elk Grove (60007). 847/593-8600; fax 847/593-8607; toll-free 800/426-7866. www.hamptoninn.com.* 125 rms, 4 story. S $99; D $109; under 18 free; wkend rates. Crib free. TV; cable (premium). Complimentary continental bkfst. Restaurant nearby. Ck-out noon. Meeting rm. Business servs avail. In-rm modem link. Free airport transportation. Health club privileges. Cr cds: A, C, D, DS, ER, JCB, MC, V.

⬛ ✈ 🔽 🔥

★★ **LA QUINTA INN.** *1900 E Oakton St, Elk Grove Village (60007). 847/439-6767; fax 847/439-5464; toll-free 800/531-5900. www.laquinta.com.* 142 rms, 4 story. S, D $109; each addl $10; under 18 free. Crib free. Pet accepted, some restrictions. TV; cable (premium). Heated pool. Complimentary continental bkfst. Restaurant opp 7 am-11 pm. Ck-out noon. Business servs avail. In-rm modem link. Valet serv. Free airport transportation. Health club privileges. Some refrigerators. Cr cds: A, C, D, DS, MC, V.

⬛ 🔽 🛏 🔽 🔥 SC

★★ **RAMADA PLAZA HOTEL O'HARE.** *6600 N Mannheim Rd, Rosemont (60018). 847/827-5131; fax 847/827-5659; toll-free 800/272-6232. www.ramada.com.* 723 rms, 2-9 story. S, D $119-$179; each addl $10; suites $225-$800; studio rms $145; under 18 free; wkend rates. Crib free. Parking. TV; cable (premium). Indoor/outdoor pools; whirlpool, poolside serv. Coffee in rms. Restaurants 6 am-11 pm. Bars 11-2 am. Ck-out noon. Convention facilities. Business center. In-rm modem link. Gift shop. Free airport transportation. Tennis. Lighted 9-hole par-3 golf, putting green. Exercise equipt; sauna. Health club privileges. Game rm. Refrigerator in some suites. Many private patios, balconies. Mini-bars. Cr cds: A, C, D, DS, JCB, MC, V.

Hotels

★★ **HOLIDAY INN.** 5440 N River Rd, Rosemont (60018). 847/671-6350; fax 847/671-1378; toll-free 888/642-7344. www.chi-ohare.holiday-inn.com. 507 rms, 14 story. S, D $149-$189; each addl $20; suites $275-$475; under 18 free; wkend rates. Crib free. TV; cable (premium). Pool; whirlpool. Restaurant 6:30 am-midnight. Bars 5 pm-2 am; wkends to 4 am; entertainment. Ck-out noon. Coin lndry. Meeting rms. Business center. In-rm modem link. Free airport transportation. Exercise equipt. Game rm. Refrigerators avail. Mini-bars. Cr cds: A, C, D, DS, MC, V.

★★ **HOLIDAY INN SELECT.** 10233 W Higgins Rd, Rosemont (60018). 847/954-8600; fax 847/954-8800; toll-free 800/465-4329. www.hiselect.com/rosemontil. 300 rms, 11 story. S, D $89-$189; each addl $20; under 18 free. Crib avail. Pet accepted. TV; cable (premium), VCR avail. Complimentary coffee in rms. Restaurant 6:30 am-10:30 pm. Ck-out noon. Meeting rms. Business center. Gift shop. Exercise rm. Refrigerators, minibars. Cr cds: A, C, D, DS, MC, V.

★★★ **HYATT REGENCY O'HARE.** 9300 W Bryn Mawr Ave, Rosemont (60018). 847/696-1234; fax 847/698-0139. www.hyatt.com. 1,099 rms, 10 story. S, D $155-$260. Crib free. Parking $13. TV; cable (premium). Indoor pool. Restaurants 6 am-midnight. Rm serv 24 hrs. Bars 11-2 am. Ck-out 11 am. Convention facilities. Business center. In-rm modem link. Free airport transportation. Exercise equipt; sauna, steam rm. Massage. Many balconies. 12-story atrium lobby. Luxury level. Cr cds: A, C, D, DS, JCB, MC, V.

★★★ **HYATT ROSEMONT.** 6350 N River Rd, Rosemont (60018). 847/518-1234; toll-free 800/233-1234. www.hyatt.com. 206 rms, 8 story. S, D $219-$550; each addl $25; under 17

free. Crib avail. Indoor pool. TV; cable (premium), VCR avail. Complimentary coffee in rms. Restaurant 6 am-10 pm. Ck-out noon. Meeting rms. Exercise rm. Refrigerators. Cr cds: A, C, D, DS, MC, V.

★★★ **MARRIOTT CHICAGO O'HARE.** 8535 W Higgins Rd, Chicago (60631). 773/693-4444; fax 773/693-3164; toll-free 800/228-9290. www.marriott.com. 681 rms, 22 suites, 12 story. S, D $139-$204; suites $179-$450; under 18 free; wkend plans. Crib free. TV; cable (premium). 2 pools, 1 indoor/outdoor; wading pool, whirlpool, poolside serv. Restaurants 6:30 am-10 pm. Rm serv to midnight. Bars 11:30-1 am. Ck-out noon. Coin lndry. Convention facilities. Business center. In-rm modem link. Concierge. Gift shop. Valet parking. Free airport transportation. Exercise equipt. Health club privileges. Refrigerators. Private patios, balconies. Luxury level. Cr cds: A, C, D, DS, ER, JCB, MC, V.

★★★ **SOFITEL CHICAGO O'HARE.** 5550 N River Rd, Rosemont (60018). 847/678-4488; fax 847/678-4244; toll-free 800/233-5959. www.sofitel.com. 300 rms, 10 story. S $129-$245; D $149-$265; each addl $20; suites $300-$425; under 18 free. Crib free. Pet accepted, some restrictions. Valet parking $16. TV; cable (premium). Indoor pool. Restaurants 6:30-12:30 am. Rm serv 24 hrs. Bar 11-1 am. Ck-out noon. Convention facilities. Business center. In-rm modem link. Concierge. Gift shop. Free airport transportation. Exercise equipt; sauna. Bathrm phones, mini-bars; refrigerators avail. Traditional European-style hotel. Cr cds: A, C, D, DS, JCB, MC, V.

★★ **WESTIN.** 6100 N River Rd, Rosemont (60018). 847/698-6000; fax 847/698-4591; toll-free 800/937-8461. www.westin.com. 525 rms, 12 story. S $169-$239; D $189-$259; each addl $20; suites $195-$950; under 18 free; wkend rates. Valet parking $14. TV; cable (premium). Indoor pool; whirlpool. Coffee in rms. Restaurant 6 am-11 pm. Rm serv 24 hrs. Bar 5 pm to midnight. Ck-out 1 pm. Convention facilities. Business center. Gift shop. Free airport transportation. Exercise equipt; sauna. Minibars; some bathrm phones. Luxury level. Cr cds: A, C, D, DS, JCB, MC, V.

D ≈ 🏋 ≥ 🔥 SC 🚶

All Suites

★★★ **EMBASSY SUITES HOTEL O'HARE-ROSEMONT.** *5500 N River Rd, Rosemont (60018). 847/678-4000; fax 847/928-7659. www.embassy-ohare.com.* 293 suites, 8 story. S, D $130-$250; under 12 free; wkend rates. Crib free. TV; cable (premium). Indoor pool; whirlpool. Complimentary full bkfst. Restaurant 11 am-2 pm; 5-10 pm. Rm serv 6-1 am. Bar to 1 am. Ck-out noon. Meeting rms. Business center. In-rm modem link. Gift shop. Free airport, RR station transportation. Exercise equipt. Health club privileges. Refrigerators, microwaves, minibars, wet bars. Opp Donald E. Stephens Convention Center. Cr cds: A, C, D, DS, JCB, MC, V.

D ≈ 🏋 ≥ 🔥 🚶

★★★ **MARRIOTT SUITES CHICAGO O'HARE.** *6155 N River Rd, Rosemont (60018). 847/696-4400; fax 847/696-2122. www.marriott.com.* 256 suites, 11 story. S $199-$219; wkend rates. Crib free. TV; cable (premium), VCR avail. Indoor pool; whirlpool. Coffee in rms. Restaurant 6:30 am-10:30 pm. Bar 11:30 am-midnight. Ck-out 1 pm. Meeting rms. Business servs avail. In-rm modem link. Gift shop. Free airport transportation. Exercise equipt; sauna. Health club privileges. Refrigerators, wet bars; microwaves avail. Cr cds: A, D, DS, JCB, MC, V.

D ≈ 🏋 ≥ 🔥

★★ **SHERATON GATEWAY SUITES.** *6501 N Mannheim Rd, Rosemont (60018). 847/699-6300; fax 847/699-0391; toll-free 800/325-3535. www.sheraton.com.* 297 suites, 11 story. Sept-Dec: S, D $89-$239; each addl $20; under 18 free; wkend rates. Crib free. TV; cable (premium). Indoor pool; whirlpool. Complimentary coffee in rms. Restaurant 6 am-2 pm, 5-10 pm. Rm serv 24 hrs. Bar 11 am-midnight. Ck-out noon. Convention facilities. Business center. In-rm modem link. Gift shop. Free airport transportation. Exercise equipt;

sauna. Health club privileges. Refrigerators; some microwaves. Mini-bars. Cr cds: A, MC, V.

D ≈ 🏋 SC 🚶

★★★ **SHERATON SUITES.** *121 Northwest Point Blvd, Elk Grove Village (60007). 847/290-1600; fax 847/290-1129; toll-free 800/325-3535. www.sheraton.com.* 253 rms, 7 story. S, D $169-$219. Crib free. TV; cable (premium). 2 pools, 1 indoor; whirlpool. Complimentary coffee in rms. Restaurant 6:30 am-10 pm. Bar 4-11 pm. Ck-out 1 pm. Coin lndry. Meeting rms. Business servs avail. In-rm modem link. Gift shop. Free airport transportation. Exercise equipt. Refrigerators; microwaves avail. Cr cds: A, C, D, DS, ER, JCB, MC, V.

D ≈ 🏋 ≥ 🔥

Extended Stay

★★ **RESIDENCE INN BY MARRIOTT.** *9450 W Lawrence Ave, Schiller Park (60176). 847/725-2210; fax 847/725-2211; toll-free 800/331-3131. www.marriott.com.* 166 kit. suites, 3-6 story. 1-bedrm $99-$189; 2-bedrm $109-$189; 3-bedrm $275; monthly rates. Crib free. Pet accepted; $7/day. TV; cable (premium). Pool; whirlpool. Complimentary full bkfst. Coffee in rms. Restaurant adj. Ck-out noon. Coin lndry. Meeting rms. Business center. In-rm modem link. Valet serv. Free airport transportation. Health club privileges. Refrigerators, microwaves. Balconies. Cr cds: A, C, D, DS, JCB, MC, V.

D 🐾 ≈ ✈ ≥ 🔥 SC 🚶

Restaurants

★★ **BLACK RAM.** *1414 Oakton St, Des Plaines (60018). 847/824-1227. www.blackram.com.* Hrs: 11 am-11 pm; Sat from 4 pm; Sun 1-10 pm. Closed hols. Res accepted. Bar. Lunch $8-$15, dinner $15-$29. Specializes in steak, veal, fresh seafood. Own pastries. Entertainment Fri, Sat. Parking. Family-owned. Cr cds: A, C, D, DS, ER, MC, V.

D ≥

★★ **CAFE LA CAVE.** *2777 Mannheim Rd, Des Plaines (60018). 847/827-7818. www.cafelacave.com.* Hrs: 11:30 am-11:30 pm; Sat from 5 pm; Sun 5-9:30 pm. Closed hols. Res accepted. French, continental menu. Bar. Wine list. Lunch $6-$14.95, dinner $18.95-$33.95. Specialties: steak Diane prepared tableside, Dover sole, medallions of lobster. Valet parking. Cr cds: A, D, DS, MC, V.

D ⊟

★★ **CARLUCCI.** *6111 N River Rd, Rosemont (60018). 847/518-0990. www.carluccirestaurant.com.* Hrs: 11:30 am-10 pm; Fri, Sat to 11 pm. Closed hols. Res accepted. Tuscan, Italian menu. Bar to 1 am. A la carte entrees: lunch $7.95-$12.95, dinner $10.95-$22.95. Specializes in fresh pasta, seafood, rotisserie items. Own pastries. Valet parking. Outdoor dining. Tuscan decor; traditional trattoria setting; frescos. Cr cds: A, D, DS, MC, V.

D

★★★ **MORTON'S OF CHICAGO.** *9525 W Bryn Mawr Ave (60018). 847/678-5155. www.mortons.com.* Specializes in prime dry-aged porterhouse steak, Sicilian veal chops, Maine lobster. Hrs: 5:30-11 pm; Sun 5-10 pm. Closed hols. Res accepted. Bar. Dinner a la carte entrees: $17-$30. Valet parking. English club atmosphere. Menu on blackboard. Cr cds: A, C, D, DS, MC, V.

★★★ **NICK'S FISHMARKET.** *10275 W Higgins Rd, Rosemont (60018). 847/298-8200. www.harman-nickolas. com.* Hrs: 5:30-10 pm; Fri, Sat to 11 pm; Sun to 9 pm. Closed major hols. Res accepted. Continental menu. Bar to 2 am. Wine list. A la carte entrees: dinner $14-$46. Specializes in fresh seafood, steak, veal. Own pastries. Jazz combo Fri, Sat. Valet parking. Braille, Japanese menu. 3 large saltwater aquariums. Cr cds: A, D, DS, MC, V.

D ⊟

★★★ **WALTER'S.** *28 Main, Park Ridge (60068). 847/825-2240.* Hrs: 11:30 am-8:30 pm. Closed Sun; hols. Res accepted. Serv bar. Wine list. A la carte entrees: lunch, dinner $4.95-$26.95. Specializes in grilled seafood, rack of lamb, steak. Own baking, pasta. Parking. In 1890s building; atrium dining; 30-ft skylight. Seasonal menu. Cr cds: A, D, MC, V.

D ⊟

Cicero

(B-6) *See also Chicago*

Founded 1867 **Pop** 85,616 **Elev** 606 ft **Area code** 708 **Zip** 60650

Information Chamber of Commerce, 4937 W 25th St, Rm 209; 708/863-6000

Cicero, named after the Roman orator, is second only to Chicago as a manufacturing center; nearly 200 industrial plants are located here. Many fine ethnic bakeries and restaurants can be found along Cermak Road.

What to See and Do

Horse racing.

Hawthorne Race Course. Thoroughbred racing (Oct-Dec) and harness racing (Jan-Feb) on a one-mi track. (Daily) 3501 S Laramie Ave. Phone 708/780-3700. Grandstand ¢¢

Sportsman's Park. Thoroughbred racing (Feb-May), harness racing (May-Oct). 3301 S Laramie Ave. Phone 708/242-1121. **FREE**

Collinsville

(F-4) *See also Belleville, Cahokia, Edwardsville*

Pop 24,707 **Elev** 550 ft **Area code** 618 **Zip** 62234

Information Chamber of Commerce, 221 W Main St, phone 618/344-2884; or the Convention & Tourism Bureau, 1 Gateway Dr, phone 618/345-4999

What to See and Do

Fairmount Park. Thoroughbred racing Sun-Tues 1 pm; Fri, Sat 7:30 pm (mid-Apr-Oct). 2 mi W on US 40 at jct I-255. Phone 618/345-4300. Grandstand ¢

Special Event

Italian Fest. Main St, downtown. Entertainment, food, bocce ball tournament, 10K run. Usually mid-late Sept. Phone 618/345-5598.

Motels/Motor Lodges

★★ **BEST WESTERN HERITAGE INN.** *2003 Mall Rd (62234). 618/345-5660; fax 618/345-8135; toll-free 800/780-7234. www.bestwestern.com.* 80 rms, 2 story. May-Sept: S $55-$69; D $62-$75; each addl $10; suite $120; under 17 free; lower rates rest of yr. Crib free. TV; cable (premium), VCR avail (movies). Indoor pool; whirlpool; Complimentary continental bkfst. Ck-out noon. Meeting rm. Business servs avail. Coin lndry. Exercise equipt. Refrigerators, microwaves avail. Cr cds: A, D, DS, MC, V.
🄳 ⬌ 🏌 📶 🔥

★★ **DRURY INN.** *602 N Bluff Rd (62234). 618/345-7700; fax 618/345-7700. www.druryinn.com.* 123 rms, 4 story. S $75.99-$87.99; D $85.99-$97.99; each addl $10; under 18 free. Crib free. TV; cable (premium). Indoor pool. Complimentary bkfst. Restaurant adj 6 am-11 pm. Coffee in rms. Ck-out noon. In-rm modem link. Meeting rm. Exercise equipt. Cr cds: A, C, D, DS, MC, V.
🄳 ⬌ 🏌 📶 🔥

★ **ECONO LODGE.** *2701 Maryville Rd, Maryville (62062). 618/345-5720; fax 618/345-5721. www.econolodge.com.* 40 rms, 2 story. Apr-early Sept: S, D $52; each addl $5; lower rates rest of yr. TV; cable (premium), VCR avail (movies). Pool. Complimentary continental bkfst. Restaurant nearby. Ck-out 11 am. Business servs avail. Health club privileges. In-rm modem link. Refrigerators, microwaves. Picnic tables, grills. Cr cds: A, D, DS, MC, V.
🄳 ⬌ 📶 🔥 SC

★★ **HOLIDAY INN COLLINSVILLE/ ST. LOUIS.** *1000 Eastport Plaza Dr (62234). 618/345-2800; fax 618/345-9804; toll-free 800/551-5133. www.holiday-inn.com.* 229 rms, 5 story. S, D $129.95-$139.95; each addl $10; suites $129.95-$500. Crib free. Pet accepted, some restrictions. TV; cable (premium), Indoor pool; whirlpool. Complimentary full bkfst. Coffee,tea in rms. Restaurant 6:15 am-10:30 pm; wkend hrs vary. Rm serv 24 hrs. Bar 3 pm-midnight, Fri, Sat to 1 am. Ck-out noon. Coin lndry. Valet serv. Meeting rms. Business servs avail. In-rm modem link. Exercise equipt; sauna. Health club privileges. Volleyball. Sundeck. Game rm. Some refrigerators, microwaves avail. Free airport transportation. Cr cds: A, C, D, DS, JCB, MC, V.
🄳 🏊 ⬌ 🏌 ✈ 📶 🔥 SC

★ **HOWARD JOHNSON EXPRESS INN.** *301 N Bluff Rd (62234). 618/345-1530; fax 618/345-1321. www.hojo.com.* 88 rms, 2 story. June-Aug: S $40-$50; D $55-$65; each addl $5; under 10 free; lower rates rest of yr. Crib free. TV; cable (premium). Pool; wading pool. Restaurant adj 10 am-10 pm. Bar noon-1 am; Sat to 2 am. Ck-out 11 am. Coin lndry. Meeting rms. Business servs avail. Private patios. Cr cds: A, C, D, DS, MC, V.
⬌ 📶 🔥 SC

B&B/Small Inn

★ **MAGGIE'S BED & BREAKFAST.** *2102 N Keebler Rd (62234). 618/344-8283.* 5 rms, 3 story. No rm phones. S, D $35-$85; each addl $10. Pet accepted, some restrictions. TV; cable, VCR (movies). Complimentary full bkfst. Ck-out noon, ck-in 4-6 pm. Indoor pool; whirlpool. Game rm. Built in 1900; former boarding house. Totally nonsmoking.
🄳 🏊 ⬌ 📶 🔥

Danville

(D-6) *See also Champaign/Urbana*

Founded 1827 **Pop** 33,904 **Elev** 597 ft
Area code 217 **Zip** 61832
Information Danville Area Convention & Visitors Bureau, 100 W Main St, Rm 146, PO Box 992, 61834; 217/442-2096 or 800/383-4386
Web www.danvillecvb.com

The site of Danville is mentioned in old French records as Piankeshaw, "center of more Native American trails than any spot within a six-day journey." Named for Dan Beckwith, its first settler, it has been under the flags of France, Great Britain, and the United States and was the scene of a battle between Spanish forces and the Kickapoo. It has approximately 150 industries and is the center of a wide trade area.

What to See and Do

Forest Glen Preserve. Nature preserve, wildlife refuge. Observation tower overlooks Vermilion River. Picnicking, camping (fee). Pioneer homestead, trails, arboretum. (Daily) 10 mi SE, in Westville. Phone 217/662-2142. **FREE**

Kickapoo State Park. Several lakes on 2,843 acres. Fishing, boating (ramp, electric motors), rentals; hunting, hiking, horseback riding (rentals), picnicking, concession, camping. Standard hrs, fees. (Daily) 4 mi W on I-74, exit 210. Phone 217/442-4915. **FREE**

Vermilion County Museum. House built in 1855 by William Fithian, physician and statesman; Lincoln stayed here Sept 21, 1858; period furnishings, natural history room, art gallery; carriage house, herb garden. (Tues-Sun; closed hols) 116 N Gilbert St. Phone 217/442-2922. ¢¢

Special Event

Hoopeston Sweet Corn Festival. 15 mi N in Hoopeston. Twenty-nine tons of corn-on-the-cob, tractor pulls, antique auto show, horse show, National Sweetheart Pageant. Labor Day wkend. Phone 217/283-7873.

Motels/Motor Lodges

★ ★ **COMFORT INN.** *383 Lynch Dr (61834). 217/443-8004; fax 217/443-8004; toll-free 800/228-5150. www. comfortinn.com.* 56 rms, 2 story, 14 suites. S, D $24.99-$59.99; each addl $5; suites $64.99; under 18 free; higher rates special events. Crib free. Pet accepted. TV; cable (premium); VCR (movies). Heated indoor pool; whirlpool. Restaraunt nearby. Complimentary continental bkfst. Ck-out 11 am. Business servs avail. In-rm modem link. Refrigerators, microwaves in suites. Valet serv. Game rm. Cr cds: A, D, DS, MC, V.
D 🐾 ➣ 🖨 🔥 SC

★ **DAYS INN.** *77 N Gilbert St (61832). 217/443-6600; fax 217/443-2345; toll-free 800/329-7466. www. daysinn.com.* 95 rms, 6 story. S, D $76-$86; under 18 free; each addl $10. Crib free. TV; cable (premium). Pool. Complimentary coffee in lobby. Restaurant 6:30 am-1:30 pm, 5-9 pm;

Sun to 1:30 pm. Rm serv. Bar 3 pm-2 am; entertainment Tues-Sat. Ck-out 11 am. Meeting rms. Exercise equipt. Valet serv. Microwaves avail. Cr cds: A, C, D, DS, JCB, MC, V.
D ➣ 🖨 ➤ 🐾 SC

★ ★ **FAIRFIELD INN .** *389 Lynch Rd (61834). 217/443-3388; fax 217/443-3388; toll-free 800/228-2800. www. fairfield.com.* 55 rms, 3 story. S, D $64.99; each addl $6; under 18 free; higher rates special events. Crib free. TV; cable (premium). Indoor pool; whirlpool. Complimentary continental bkfst. Restaurant nearby. Ck-out noon. Meeting rm. Business servs avail. In-rm modem link. Game rm. Health club privileges. Cr cds: A, C, D, DS, MC, V.
D ➣ ➤ 🐾 SC

★ ★ **RAMADA INN.** *388 Eastgate Dr (61834). 217/446-2400; fax 217/446-3878. www.ramada.com.* 131 rms, 2 story. S $60-$64; D $62-$68; each addl $6; suites $98; under 18 free; wkend rates. Crib free. Pet accepted, some restrictions. TV; cable (premium). Pool. Complimentary continental bkfst, coffee in rms. Restaurant 6 am-9 pm. Rm serv. Bar 11-1 am, Sun 1-11 pm. Ck-out noon. Coin lndry. Meeting rms. Business servs avail. Valet serv. Sundries. Free airport transportation. Exercise equipt. Minibar in suites. Refrigerators avail. Cr cds: A, C, D, DS, MC, V.
D 🐾 ➣ 🖨 ➤ 🐾 ✈

Decatur

(D-5) *See also Lincoln, Springfield*

Founded 1829 **Pop** 81,860 **Elev** 670 ft **Area code** 217

Information Decatur Area Convention & Visitors Bureau, 202 E North St, 62523; 217/423-7000 or 800/331-4479

Web www.decaturcvb.com

In 1830, 21-year-old Abraham Lincoln drove through what would later become Decatur with his family to settle on the Sangamon River, a few miles west. He worked as a farmer and railsplitter and made his first political speech in what is now

Decatur's Lincoln Square. Today, agri-business, manufacturing, Richland Community College, and Millikin University provide a varied economy.

What to See and Do

Birks Museum. Decorative arts museum with more than 1,000 pieces of china, crystal, and pottery; some from 15th and 16th centuries. (Daily, Sept-June; June-Aug by appt only) 1184 W Main St, in Gorin Hall, on campus of Millikin University. Phone 217/424-6337. **FREE**

Fairview Park. Approx 180 acres. Swimming pool (fee); tennis, biking trail, picnicking, playground, baseball diamonds, horseshoe pits. (Daily) Jct US 36, IL 48. For further details on recreational facilities in the city's 1,967 acres of municipal parks, contact the Decatur Park District, 620 E Riverside, 62521. Phone 217/422-5911. **FREE**

Friends Creek Regional Park. Nature trails, picnicking, playground, camping (showers, dump station; fee). 16 mi NE via I-72, Argenta exit. Phone 217/423-7708.

Lake Decatur. Shoreline drive; boating, fishing. SE edge of town, on the Sangamon River. Phone 217/424-2837.

Macon County Historical Society Museum. Exhibit Center with displays of local artifacts; 1890s Victorian farmhouse exhibit; also Prairie Village with 1860s schoolhouse, 1850s printing shop, 1880s log cabin, blacksmith shop, 1890s train depot, and Macon County's first courthouse, where Lincoln once practiced law. (Tues-Sun afternoons; closed hols) 5580 North Fork Rd. Phone 217/422-4919. **DONATION**

Millikin Place. Housing development (1909) laid out and landscaped by Walter Burley Griffin, who designed Australia's capital, Canberra, in an international competition. Street features Prairie School entrance, naturalized landscaping; and houses by Marion Mahony, Griffin's wife, and Frank Lloyd Wright, for whom both Griffin and Mahony worked at the famous Oak Park Studio. Numbers 1 and 3 Millikin Place are by Mahony; 2 Millikin Place attributed to Wright. (Houses private) Entrance adj to 125 N Pine St.

Rock Springs Center for Environmental Discovery. Approx 1,320 acres with hiking and self-guided interpretive trails; picnic area, shelter, restrooms, asphalt bike trail. Ecocenter hands-on educational exhibits. Visitor Center with scheduled events and programs throughout yr. (Daily; closed Easter, Thanksgiving, Dec 25) S on IL 48, W 2 mi on Rock Spring Rd. 3939 Nearing Ln. Phone 217/423-7708. **DONATION**

Scovill Family Park Complex. E shore of Lake Decatur, S of US 36, on S Country Club Rd. Phone 217/422-5911. Complex includes

    Children's Museum. Features hands-on exhibits of the arts, science, and technology. (Tues-Sat, also Sun afternoons; closed hols) 55 S Country Club Dr. Phone 217/423-KIDS. ¢¢

    Hieronymus Mueller Museum. Exhibits include inventions of "Decatur's unsung genius," whose work revolutionized everyday lives. (Apr-Sept, Thurs-Sun afternoons; rest of yr, Fri-Sun afternoons) Phone 217/423-6161. ¢

    Oriental Garden. Greenery, rocks, sand, and water ornamented with sculpture. Chinese Fu dog guards entrance. (Daily) Phone 217/422-5911. **FREE**

Scovill Park and Zoo. Zoo has more than 500 animals. ZO & O Express Train takes visitors around zoo. Picnicking, playground. (Apr-Oct, daily) Phone 217/421-7435. Zoo ¢

Motels/Motor Lodges

★ **BAYMONT INN.** *5100 Hickory Point Frontage Rd (62526). 217/875-5800; fax 217/875-7537. www.baymontinns.com.* 102 rms, 2 story. S, D $49-$89; under 18 free. Crib free. Pet accepted, some restrictions. TV; cable (premium). Complimentary continental bkfst, coffee in rms. Restaurant nearby. Rm serv. Ck-out noon. Meeting rms. Business servs avail. In-rm modem link. Some refrigerators, microwaves. Cr cds: A, C, D, DS, MC, V.

[D] 🐾 ▨ 🐾

★ ★ **FAIRFIELD INN .** *1417 Hickory Point Dr, Forsyth (62535). 217/875-3337; fax 217/875-3337; toll-free 800/228-2800. www.fairfieldinn.com.*

62 rms, 3 story. S, D $60-$69.99; suites $72.99; under 18 free. Crib free. TV; cable (premium). Indoor pool; whirlpool. Complimentary continental bkfst. Restaurant nearby. Ck-out noon. Meeting rm. Business servs avail. Health club privileges. Refrigerator, microwave in suites. Cr cds: A, C, D, DS, MC, V.

★ ★ ★ **HOLIDAY INN SELECT.** *4191 US 36 and Wyckles Rd (62522). 217/422-8800; fax 217/422-9690; toll-free 800/465-4329. www.holiday-inn. com.* 370 rms, 2-4 story. S, D $89; each addl $10; suites $110-$250; under 19 free. Crib free. TV; cable, VCR avail. Indoor pool; wading pool; whirlpool. Playground. Restaurants 6 am-11 pm. Rm serv 6 am-10 pm. Bar noon-1 am; Sun to 10 pm; entertainment exc Sun. Coffee in rms. Ck-out noon. Convention facilities. Business center. In-rm modem link. Concierge. Bellhops. Gift shop. Florist. Free airport transportation. Lighted tennis. Exercise equipt; sauna. Health club privileges. Game rm. Picnic tables, fishing pond. Luxury level. Cr cds: A, C, D, DS, JCB, MC, V.

De Kalb

(A-5) *See also Aurora, Geneva, Oregon, St. Charles*

Pop 39,018 **Elev** 880 ft **Area code** 815 **Zip** 60115
Information Nehring Cultural & Tourism Center, 164 E Lincoln Hwy; 815/756-6306
Web www.dekalb.org

What to See and Do

Ellwood House Museum. Victorian mansion built by Isaac Ellwood, early manufacturer of barbed wire; restored interiors 1880-1915; horse-drawn vehicles, barbed wire, and farm implements; 1890s playhouse; extensive grounds and gardens. Visitor center with historical gallery and special exhibits. Guided tours. (Mar-early Dec, Tues-Sun, afternoons; closed hols) Entrance at rear, off Augusta Ave. 509 N 1st St. Phone 815/756-4609. ¢¢

Northern Illinois University. (1895) 22,000 students. Anthropology museum in Stevens Building has Native American and Southeast Asian displays (free). Art galleries in several locations; displays change frequently. One-hr guided tour of campus leaves Office of Admissions, Williston Hall, once a day (Mon-Sat; no tours hols). Also self-guided walking tour booklets. W Lincoln Hwy (IL 38). Phone 815/753-0446.

Special Events

Stage Coach Theater. 2 mi N, then ½ mi E on Barber Greene Rd. Summer community theater. Res suggested. Mid-June-mid-Sept. Phone 815/758-1940 for current show and dates.

Corn Fest. Downtown business district. Three-day street festival. Last full wkend Aug. Phone 815/748-CORN.

Motels/Motor Lodges

★ **HOWARD JOHNSON EXPRESS INN.** *1321 W Lincoln Hwy (60115). 815/756-1451; fax 815/756-7260. www.hojo.com.* 60 rms, 2 story. S $39-$50; D $45-$56; under 12 free; wkly, monthly rates. Crib free. TV; cable (premium). Complimentary continental bkfst. Ck-out noon. Business servs avail. Cr cds: A, C, D, DS, MC, V.

★ **SUPER 8 MOTEL.** *800 Fairview Dr (60115). 815/748-4688; fax 815/748-4688; toll-free 800/800-8000. www. super8.com.* 44 rms, 2 story. S, D $44-$88; each addl $7; suites $96-$119; under 12 free; higher rates NIU graduation, Cornfest. Crib $5. TV; cable (premium). Heated indoor pool; whirlpool. Restaurant nearby. Complimentary continental bkfst. Ck-out 11 am. Coin lndry. Meeting rm. Business servs avail. Microwave avail. Cr cds: A, C, D, DS, MC, V.

Des Plaines

(see Chicago O'Hare Airport Area)

Dixon

(B-4) *See also Oregon*

Settled 1830 **Pop** 15,941 **Elev** 659 ft
Area code 815 **Zip** 61021
Information Dixon Area Chamber of
Commerce, 101 W Second St;
815/284-3361
Web www.dixonil.com

At the southernmost point of the
Black Hawk Trail, Dixon sits on the
banks of the Rock River. Established
as a trading post and tavern by John
Dixon, it now is a center for light
industry. The 40th president of the
United States, Ronald Reagan, was
born in nearby Tampico and grew up
in Dixon.

What to See and Do

John Deere Historic Site. Site where
first self-scouring steel plow was
made in 1837; reconstructed blacksmith shop (demonstrations Wed-
Sun); restored house and gardens;
two-acre natural prairie. (Apr-Oct,
daily) 8393 S Main; 6 mi NE on IL 2
in Grand Detour. Phone 815/652-
4551. ¢¢

Lincoln Statue Park. Park includes
the site of Fort Dixon, around which
the town was built, and a statue of
Lincoln as a young captain in the
Black Hawk War of 1832. A plaque
summarizes Lincoln's military career;
at the statue's base is a bas-relief of
John Dixon. Along north bank of
river between Galena and Peoria
aves. Phone 815/288-3404. **FREE**
Also in the park is

    Old Settlers' Memorial Log Cabin.
    Built in 1894 and dedicated to the
    area's early settlers; period furnish-
    ings. (Memorial Day-Labor Day, Sat
    and Sun; rest of yr, by appt) Phone
    815/284-1134. **FREE**

Ronald Reagan's Boyhood Home.
Two-story, three-bedroom house with
1920s furnishings; memorabilia connected with the former president's
childhood and acting and political
careers. Visitor center adj. (Mar-Nov,
daily; rest of yr, Sat and Sun) 816 S
Hennepin. Phone 815/288-3404.
FREE

Special Event

Petunia Festival. Carnival, parade,
arts and crafts, bicycle race, tennis
tournament, festival garden, fireworks. July 4 wk. Phone 815/284-
3361.

Motel/Motor Lodge

★★ **BEST WESTERN REAGAN
HOTEL.** *443 Il Rte 2 (61021).
815/284-1890; fax 815/284-1174; toll-
free 800/780-7234. www.bestwestern.
com.* 91 rms, 2 story. S $63-$67; D
$70-$74; each addl $7; suites $60-
$160; under 18 free. Crib free. Pet
accepted, some restrictions; $25
deposit. Heated pool; whirlpool. TV;
cable, VCR avail (movies). Restaurant
6:30 am-9 pm; Sun to 2 pm; Mon
from 11 am. Rm serv. Bar 11 am-9
pm. Complimentary continental
bkfst (Mon-Fri). Coffee in rms. Ck-
out noon. Meeting rms. Business
servs avail. Exercise equipt. Cr cds: A,
C, D, DS, MC, V.
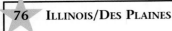

B&B/Small Inn

★★ **HILLENDALE BED & BREAK-
FAST.** *600 W Lincolnway, Morrison
(61270). 815/772-3454; fax 815/772-
7023. www.hillend.com.* 10 rms, 3
with shower only, 8 with private
bath, 3 story. S, D $85-$160; each
addl $5; package plans. Children
over 12 yrs only. TV in some rms;
cable, VCR avail (movies). Complimentary full bkfst. Restaurant
nearby. Ck-out 11 am, ck-in 3 pm.
X-country ski 3 mi. Exercise equipt.
Some whirlpools, fireplaces. Built in
1891; antiques. Totally nonsmoking.
Cr cds: A, D, DS, MC, V.

Downers Grove

See also Hinsdale, Oak Brook

Settled 1832 **Pop** 48,724 **Elev** 725 ft
Area code 630 **Zip** 60515
Information Visitors Bureau, 5202 Washington St, Suite 2; 800/934-0615
Web www.vil.downers-grove.il.us

What to See and Do

Historical Museum. Victorian house (1892) contains eight rooms of period furnishings, antiques, and artifacts; changing exhibits. (Sun-Fri 1-3 pm) 831 Maple Ave. Phone 630/963-1309. **FREE**

Morton Arboretum. On 1,700 acres. Native trees and woody plants collected from around the world and grown for use in landscapes, research, and education; wetlands; nature trails; prairie restoration. Visitor center. Restaurant. Library (Mon-Sat; closed hols). Grounds (daily). W on I-88 to jct IL 53, then 1 mi N, in Lisle. Phone 630/719-2400. Per vehicle ¢¢¢

Motels/Motor Lodges

★★ **COMFORT INN.** *3010 Finley Rd (60515). 630/515-1500; fax 630/515-1595. www.comfortinn.com.* 121 rms, 3 story. S, D $84; each addl $5; under 18 free. Crib free. TV; cable (premium). Heated pool; whirlpool. Complimentary continental bkfst. Restaurant nearby. Coffee in rms. Ckout noon. Meeting rm. Business servs avail. In-rm modem link. Valet serv. Exercise equipt. Health club privileges. Some microwaves. Cr cds: A, C, D, DS, JCB, MC, V.
🅳 ⇌ 🏋 ⊠ 🔥 SC

★★ **HOLIDAY INN EXPRESS.** *3031 Finley Rd (60515). 630/810-9500; fax 630/810-0059; toll-free 800/465-4329. www.hiexpress.com/chi-downers.* 123 rms, 3 story. S, D $99-$114; suites $129-$139; under 18 free. Crib free. TV; cable (premium). Complimentary continental bkfst. Restaurant nearby. Ck-out noon. Meeting rms. Business servs avail. Coin lndry. Valet serv. Conceirge. In-rm modem link. Health club privileges, $6. Some refrigerators, wet bars. Cr cds: A, C, D, DS, JCB, MC, V.
🅳 ⊠ 🔥 SC

★ **RED ROOF INN.** *1113 Butterfield Rd (60515). 630/963-4205; fax 630/963-4425; toll-free 800/733-7663. www.redroof.com.* 135 rms, 2 story. S, D $49.99-$54.99; suite $69.99; under 18 free. Crib free. Pet accepted. TV; cable (premium). Complimentary coffee in lobby. Ck-out noon. Meeting rm. Business servs avail. In-rm modem link. Cr cds: A, C, D, DS, MC, V.
🅳 🐾 ⊠ 🔥 SC

All Suites

★★★ **DOUBLETREE GUEST SUITES.** *2111 Butterfield Rd (60515). 630/971-2000; fax 630/971-1168; toll-free 800/222-8733. www.doubletree.com.* 247 suites, 7 story. Suites $189; under 12 free; wknd packages. Crib free. TV; cable (premium), VCR avail. Indoor pool; whirlpool. Coffee in rms. Restaurant 6 am-10 pm. Rm serv. Bar 4 pm-midnight. Ck-out noon. Convention facilities. Business servs avail. In-rm modem link. Coin lndry. Valet serv. Gift shop. RR station, bus depot transportation. Exercise equipt; sauna. Refrigerators, microwaves, wet bars. Racquetball. 2 lighted tennis courts. Luxury level. Cr cds: A, C, D, DS, ER, JCB, MC, V.
🅳 💺 🏋 ⊠ 🔥 SC ⇌

★★★ **EMBASSY SUITES.** *707 E Butterfield Rd, Lombard (60148). 630/969-7500; fax 630/969-8776; toll-free 800/362-2779. www.embassysuites.com.* 262 suites, 10 story. S, D $179-$225; each addl $20; under 18 free; wknd rates. Crib free. TV; cable (premium). Indoor/outdoor pool; whirlpool. Complimentary full bkfst. Coffee in rms. Restaurant 11:30 am-10 pm; Fri, Sat to 11 pm. Rm serv. Bar. Ck-out noon. Meeting rms. Business servs avail. In-rm modem link. Coin lndry. Valet serv. Gift shop. Exercise equipt; sauna. Refrigerators, microwaves. Cr cds: A, C, D, DS, ER, JCB, MC, V.
🅳 ⇌ 🏋 ⊠ 🔥 SC

★ ★ ★ **MARRIOTT SUITES.** *1500 Opus Pl (60515). 630/852-1500; fax 630/852-6527; toll-free 800/228-9290. www.marriott.com.* 254 suites, 7 story. S $124-$154; D $134-$164; wkend rates. Crib free. TV; cable (premium), VCR avail (movies $8.99). 2 pools; 1 indoor; whirlpool. Coffee in rms. Restaurant 7 am-10 pm. Rm serv. Bar from 11:30 am. Ck-out noon. Meeting rms. Business center. In-rm modem link. Coin lndry. Valet serv. Gift shop. Exercise equipt; sauna. Refrigerators, wet bars. Balconies. Cr cds: A, C, D, DS, ER, JCB, MC, V.

D ⚊ 🏃 ⤵ 🔥 🏃

Restaurant

★ ★ ★ **BISTRO BANLIEUE.** *44 Yorktown Convenience Center, Lombard (60148). 630/629-6560.* Specializes in roasted salmon, scallops, steak frites, pear and roquefort. Hrs: 11:30 am-9 pm; Fri to 10 pm; Sat 5-10 pm; Sun 4-8 pm. Closed hols. Res accepted. Wine, beer. Lunch $8.95-$14.95; dinner $10.95-$24.95. Entertainment. Cr cds: A, C, D, DS, MC, V.

D ⤵

Dundee

See also Elgin

Settled 1835 **Pop** 3,550 **Elev** 750 ft
Area code 847 **Zip** 60118

Two Potawatomi villages were nearby when settlers first arrived in 1835. A Scotsman won a lottery and was permitted to name the settlement after his hometown in Scotland, Dundee.

What to See and Do

Haeger Factory Outlet. Ceramic Museum. Factory outlet store (Mon, Thurs-Sun; closed hols). Van Buren St, 2 blks S of IL 72. Phone 847/426-3441. **FREE**

Racing Rapids Action Park. Features water slides, tube slide, go-carts, bumper boats, lazy river, and children's pool area. (June-Aug and Labor Day wkend, daily) Free parking. IL 25 and IL 72. Phone 847/426-5525. ¢¢¢

Santa's Village Theme Park. More than 30 rides; live shows and petting zoo. Picnic areas. Polar Dome Ice Arena for skating (late Sept-Mar, Sat, Sun, and hols; fee). (June-Aug, daily; Mother's Day-Memorial Day and Sept, wkends only) Free parking. At jct IL 25, 72. Phone 847/426-6751. ¢¢¢¢

B&B/Small Inn

★ ★ **VICTORIAN ROSE GARDEN BED & BREAKFAST.** *314 Washington St, Algonquin (60102). 847/854-9667; fax 847/854-3236; res 888/854-9667. www.sleepandeat.com.* 4 rms, 3 with shower only, 2 story. No rm phones. S, D $79-$139; each addl $10; package plans. Children over 12 years only. TV in sitting rm. Complimentary full bkfst. Restaurant nearby. Meeting rm. Business servs avail. Ck-out 11 am (noon on Sun), ck-in 4 pm. Bicycle trail. Built in 1886. Totally nonsmoking. Cr cds: A, MC, V.

⤵ 🏃

Restaurants

★ **CHA CHA CHA.** *16 E Main St (IL 72) (60118). 847/428-4774.* Hrs: 11:30 am-10 pm; Fri, Sat to 11 pm; Sun noon-9 pm. Closed Thanksgiving, Dec 25. Res accepted. Mexican menu. Bar. Lunch $5.50-$8.75, dinner $6.50-$12.25. Specialties: chicken, beef and seafood fajitas. Mexican village decor. Cr cds: A, C, D, DS, MC, V.

D ⤵

★ ★ **DURAN'S OF DUNDEE.** *8 S River St, East Dundee (60118). 847/428-0033.* Hrs: 11 am-2 pm, 5-8:30 pm; Fri, Sat 5-9:30 pm; Sun 4-8 pm. Closed major hols. Res accepted. Lunch $3.95-$8.95, dinner $7.95-$23.95. Child's menu. Specialties: filet mignon, broiled fish, veal. Own cheesecakes. Dining in restored house. Cr cds: A, D, DS, MC, V.

⤵

★ ★ **MILK PAIL.** *14 N 630 IL 25 (Milk Pail Village) (60118). 847/742-5040.* Hrs: 11 am-9 pm; Fri, Sat 10 am-10 pm; Sun 10 am-8 pm. Closed Dec 25. Res accepted. Bar. Lunch $5.75-$10.95, dinner $8.95-$19.95. Sun buffet $14.95. Child's menu. Specializes in turkey, chicken, trout.

Seasonal theatre productions. Own bakery. Country atmosphere. Cr cds: A, C, D, DS, ER, MC, V.

D ⟶

★★ **PORT EDWARD.** *20 W Algonquin Rd, Algonquin (60102). 847/658-5441.* Hrs: 11:30 am-10 pm; Fri to 11 pm; Sat 5-11 pm; Sun (brunch) 9:30 am-1 pm, 5-9 pm. Closed July 4, Thanksgiving, Dec 25. Res accepted. Bar. Lunch $3.50-$12.95, dinner $11.95-$32.95. Buffet: dinner $23.95 (Fri). Sun brunch $16.95. Child's menu. Specializes in seafood, steaks. Piano Wed, Fri, Sat. Parking. Boat and windmill in middle of restaurant. Cr cds: A, D, DS, MC, V.

D ⟶

Du Quoin

(G-4) *See also Benton, Carbondale, Marion*

Pop 6,448 **Elev** 468 ft **Area code** 618 **Zip** 62832

Du Quoin, in the fertile agricultural and mining region southeast of St. Louis, is a shipping point for coal, grain, livestock, and fruit.

Special Event

Du Quoin State Fair. 655 Executive Dr. Farm, house, art, and livestock shows; concerts; auto, harness racing; World Trotting Derby. Late Aug-Labor Day. Phone 618/542-9373.

B&B/Small Inn

★ **OXBOW BED & BREAKFAST.** *3967 IL 13 and 127, Pinckneyville (62274). 618/357-9839; res 800/929-6888. www.bbonline.com/il/oxbow.* 6 rms, 3 story. No rm phones. S, D $50-$65; each addl $15; under 6 free; wkly rates. Indoor pool; whirlpool. Complimentary full bkfst. Ck-out 11 am, ck-in noon. Built in 1929. Cr cds: MC, V.

≈ ⊠ SC

Restaurant

★★ **TO PERFECTION.** *1664 S Washington (62832). 618/542-2002.*

Hrs: 11 am-2 pm, 4-9 pm; Fri to 10 pm; Sat 4-10 pm. Closed Sun. Bar. Lunch $3.95-$6.95, dinner $8.95-$14.95. Specializes in prime rib, fresh seafood, hand-cut steak. Cr cds: MC, V.

D ⟶

Edwardsville

(F-4) *See also Alton, Belleville, Cahokia, Collinsville*

Pop 21,491 **Elev** 552 ft **Area code** 618 **Zip** 62025

Information Edwardsville/Glen Carbon Chamber of Commerce, 200 University Park Dr, Suite 260; 618/656-7600

Web www.ci.edwardsville.il.us

What to See and Do

Madison County Historical Museum. Ten-room house (1836) contains period rooms, history and genealogy reference library, pioneer and Native American artifacts; seasonal exhibits. (Wed-Fri, Sun; closed hols) 715 N Main St. Phone 618/656-7562. **FREE**

Southern Illinois University at Edwardsville. (1957) 11,800 students. Louis Sullivan Architectural Ornament collection on second floor of Lovejoy Library (daily). Campus tours (Mon-Fri, by appt). Phone 618/650-2000.

Motel/Motor Lodge

★★ **COMFORT INN & CONFERENCE CENTER.** *3080 S SR 157 (62025). 618/656-4900; toll-free 800/228-5150. www.comfortinn.com.* 68 rms, 3 story. S $64-$72; D $69-$77; suite $135-$145; each addl $5; under 18 free; higher rates special events. Crib free. Pet accepted. TV; cable (premium). Complimentary continental bkfst. Coffee in rms. Ck-out noon. Meeting rms. Business servs avail. Heated indoor pool. Exercise equipt. Refrigerator, microwave, whirlpool in suites. Game rm. Cr cds: A, D, DS, MC, V.

D 🐾 ≈ 🏋 ⊠ 🦽 SC

Restaurant

★ ★ **RUSTY'S.** *1201 N Main St (62025). 618/656-1113.* Hrs: 11 am-1:30 pm, 5-9 pm; Fri, Sat 5-11 pm; Sun brunch 11 am-2 pm. Closed hols. Res accepted. Italian, American menu. Bar. Lunch $4.50-$9.50, dinner $9.50-$24.50. Buffet: lunch $6.50. Sun brunch $7.25. Child's menu. Specializes in seafood, prime rib, veal. Entertainment Fri, Sat. Former trading post built 1819. Cr cds: A, D, DS, MC, V.

[D] [⤳]

Effingham

(E-5) *See also Altamont, Mattoon*

Settled 1853 **Pop** 12,384 **Elev** 592 ft
Area code 217 **Zip** 62401
Information Convention and Visitors Bureau, 201 E Jefferson Ave, PO Box 648; 217/342-5305 or 800/772-0750
Web www.effinghamil.com

This town is a regional center and seat of Effingham County. Industry includes housing and furniture components, graphic arts, and refrigeration. Outdoor recreation is popular here, with Lake Sara offering fishing, boating, and golfing opportunities.

Motels/Motor Lodges

★ **BEST INNS OF AMERICA.** *1209 N Keller Dr (62401). 217/347-5141; fax 217/347-5141; res 800/237-8466.* www.bestinn.com. 83 rms, 2 story. Mid-May-Oct: S $39.99-$45.99; D $46.99-$52.99; each addl $7; under 18 free; lower rates rest of yr. Crib free. Pet accepted, some restrictions. TV; cable. Pool. Complimentary bkfst. Restaurant nearby open 24 hrs. Ck-out 1 pm. Cr cds: A, C, D, DS, MC, V.

[D] [🐾] [⤳] [🔥] [SC] [⤳]

★ ★ **BEST WESTERN RAINTREE INN.** *1809 W Fayette Ave (62401). 217/342-4121; fax 217/342-4121; res 800/780-7234.* www.bestwestern.com. 65 rms, 2 story. May-Oct: S $49.95; D $59.95; each addl $5; under 12 free; higher rates special events; lower rates rest of yr. Crib free. Pet accepted, some restrictions. TV; cable

(premium). Pool. Complimentary continental bkfst. Coffee in lobby. Restaurant. Bar. Ck-out 11 am. Business servs avail. Some balconies. Cr cds: A, C, D, DS, MC, V.

[🐾] [⤳] [⤳] [🔥] [SC]

★ ★ ★ **COMFORT SUITES.** *1310 W Fayette Rd (62401). 217/342-3151; fax 217/342-3555; toll-free 800/228-5150.* www.comfortsuites.com. 65 rms, 3 story. S $74.95-$125.95; D $84.95-$125.95; each addl $6; under 18 free; higher rates special events. Crib avail. Pet accepted. TV; cable (premium). Indoor pool. Complimentary continental bkfst. Coffee in rms. Restaurant, bar adj 7-1 am. Ck-out 11 am. Business servs avail. In-rm modem link. Coin lndry. Sauna. Refrigerators, microwaves. Some whirlpools, fireplace. Health club privileges. Cr cds: A, D, DS, MC, V.

[D] [🐾] [🐾] [⤳] [⤳] [🔥]

★ **DAYS INN.** *1412 W Fayette Ave (62401). 217/342-9271; fax 217/342-5850; toll-free 800/687-4941.* www.daysinn.com. 109 rms, 2 story. Apr-mid-Sept: S, D $60-$70 each addl $5; under 13 free; lower rates rest of yr. Crib free. Pet accepted; $60. TV; cable (premium). Pool. Complimentary continental bkfst. Coffee in rms. Restaurant adj 6-1 am. Bar 11-1 am. Ck-out 11 am. Refrigerators, microwaves avail. Cr cds: A, C, D, DS, JCB, MC, V.

[D] [🐾] [⤳] [🔥] [SC] [⤳]

★ ★ **HAMPTON INN.** *1509 Hampton Dr (62401). 217/342-4499; fax 217/347-2828; toll-free 800/426-7866.* www.hamptoninn.com. 62 rms, 2 story. S $67-$78; D $71-$82; suites $79; under 18 free; higher rates special events. Crib free. Pet accepted. TV; cable (premium). Indoor pool. Complimentary continental bkfst. Coffee in rms. Restaurant nearby. Ck-out noon. Meeting rms. Business servs avail. In-rm modem link. Coin lndry. Valet serv. Health club privileges. Refrigerators, microwaves avail. Cr cds: A, C, D, DS, ER, JCB, MC, V.

[⤳] [D] [🐾] [⤳] [🔥] [SC]

★ ★ **HOLIDAY INN EXPRESS.** *1103 Ave of Mid-America (62401). 217/540-1111; fax 217/347-7341; toll-free 888/232-2525.* www.holiday-inn.com. 122 rms, 4 story, 14 suites. S, D $69-$74; suites $89.95; under 18 free;

wkly rates; higher rates special events. Crib free. TV; cable. Indoor pool. Complimentary continental bkfst, coffee in rms. Restaurant adj 6 am-10 pm. Ck-out noon. Meeting rms. Business servs avail. Coin lndry. Health club privileges. Cr cds: A, C, D, DS, JCB, MC, V.

★ ★ **QUALITY INN.** *1600 W Fayette Ave (62401).* 217/342-4161; fax 217/342-4164; toll-free 800/465-4329. *www.qualityinn.com.* 135 rms, 2 story. S $45-$55; D $50-$60; each addl $5; suites $95; under 17 free. Crib free. Pet accepted. TV; cable. Pool. Complimentary continental bkfst. Restaurant 6 am-9 pm; Fri, Sat to 10 pm. Rm serv. Bar 3 pm-1 am; Sun to 10 pm. Ck-out noon. Meeting rms. Business servs avail. Airport, RR station, bus depot transportation. Cr cds: A, C, D, DS, JCB, MC, V.

★ ★ **RAMADA INN AND CONVENTION CENTER.** *I-70/57 and Rte 32-33 (62401).* 217/347-8757; fax 217/347-8757; res 800/535-0546. *www.ramada.com.* 169 rms, 2 story, 8 condo units. S $52-$89; D $60-$89; each addl $7; suites $89-$129; condos $109-$129; under 18 free. Crib free. Pet accepted, some restrictions. TV; cable. 2 pools, 1 indoor; whirlpool. Playground. Complimentary continental bkfst. Restaurant 6 am-10 pm. Rm serv. Bar 4 pm-midnight; entertainment. Ck-out noon. Meeting rms. Valet serv. Gift shop. Free RR station, bus depot transportation. Exercise rm; sauna, steam rm. Bowling alley. Miniature golf. Game rm. Some in-rm whirlpools. Balconies. Cr cds: A, C, D, DS, MC, V.

★ **SUPER 8.** *1400 Thelma Keller Ave (62401).* 217/342-6888; fax 217/347-2863; toll-free 800/800-8000. *www.super8.com.* 49 rms, 2 story. S, D $43-$50; suites $49-$55; each addl $5; under 12 free. Crib free. Pet accepted, some restrictions. TV; cable (premium). Complimentary bkfst, coffee in lobby. Ck-out 11 am. Refrigerators, microwaves in suites. Cr cds: A, C, D, DS, MC, V.

Restaurants

★ **CHINA BUFFET.** *1500 W Fayette Ave (62401).* 217/342-3188. Hrs: 11 am-10 pm; Fri, Sat to 11 pm. Res accepted. Chinese menu. Lunch $4.15-$6.25, dinner $4.95-$12.99. Child's menu. Specialties: General Tso's chicken, sweet and sour pork, shrimp lo mein. Own baking. Chinese decor; photos of Great Wall of China. Cr cds: MC, V.

★ **EL RANCHERITO.** *1313 Keller Dr (62401).* 217/342-4753. Hrs: 11 am-10 pm; Fri, Sat to 11 pm. Closed Thanksgiving. Res accepted. Mexican menu. Serv bar. Lunch $2.99-$5.79, dinner $4.99-$9.99. Child's menu. Specialties: fajitas, chimichangas, burritos Mexicanos. Own baking. Authentic Mexican decor. Cr cds: A, C, MC, V.

★ **NIEMERG'S STEAK HOUSE.** *1410 W Fayette Ave (62401).* 217/342-3921. Hrs: 6-2 am; Sun to midnight. Closed Dec 25. Res accepted (lunch, dinner). Bar 11-1 am. Bkfst $1.90-$4.95, lunch $2.95-$7.65, dinner $4-$12.75. Child's menu. Specializes in chicken, steak, seafood. Own baking, pasta. Casual, family-style dining. Cr cds: A, D, MC, V.

Elgin

(A-5) *See also Dundee, Union*

Founded 1835 **Pop** 94,487 **Elev** 752 ft **Area code** 847

Information Elgin Area Convention and Visitors Bureau, 77 Riverside Dr, 60120; 847/695-7540 or 800/217-5362

Web www.enjoyelgin.com

It was here that the famous Elgin watch was produced. It was also here that the process of packing milk for long transport, or "condensing" it, was invented right after the Civil War by a young man named Gail Borden. Located in the heart of the Fox River Valley, Elgin has many interesting turn-of-the-century houses. The scenic Fox River divides the town and is used primarily for canoeing, fishing, and cycling along the Fox River Bicycle Trail.

What to See and Do

Elgin Area Historical Society Museum. In Old Main, a mid-19th century school building once known as Elgin Academy; contains artifacts of area history. (Mar-Dec, Sept, Wed-Sat; closed Jan (Sun-Tues), Feb) 360 Park St, between College St and Academy Pl. Phone 847/742-4248. ¢

Forest preserves.

Blackhawk. On 186 acres. Historic burial mound. Fishing, boating (ramp), canoeing; hiking, bicycle, and bridle trails; picnicking (shelter). S on IL 31 at the Fox River, in South Elgin.

Burnidge. On 484 acres. Hiking, x-country skiing, picnicking. Coombs Rd.

Tyler Creek. On 50 acres. Hiking trails, picnicking. IL 31 on Davis Rd.

Voyageurs Landing. On 16 acres. Boat ramp; picnic shelter. Frontage Rd via IL 31.

Fox River Trolley Museum. Historic and antique railway equipment displays; oldest interurban railcar in America. Optional three-mi ride along the scenic Fox River on interurban railcars and trolleys of the early 1900s. (See SPECIAL EVENTS) (July-Aug, Sat and Sun; mid-May-June and Sept-Oct, Sun; also Memorial Day, July 4, Labor Day) S on IL 31 in South Elgin. Phone 847/697-4676. Museum **FREE** Train ride ¢¢

Grand Victoria Riverboat Casino. Leaves shore. (Daily) 250 S Grove Ave. Phone 847/888-1000. **FREE**

Lords Park. On 120 acres; includes zoo, tennis courts, pool, lagoons, playgrounds, and picnic areas. 325 Hiawatha Dr. Phone 847/931-6120. Also here is

Elgin Public Museum. Displays include stuffed birds, fish, animals; local and regional history, anthropology, and natural history; discovery room. (Apr-Oct, daily; rest of yr, Sat-Mon) 225 Grand Blvd. Phone 847/741-6655. ¢

Special Events

Trolley Fest. Fox River Trolley Museum. Features once-a-yr operation of historic and antique rail equipt; also model trolley displays. Aug. Phone 847/697-4676.

Historic Cemetery Walk. Historical Society conducts tours of Bluff City Cemetery. Actors in period costumes stand at gravesites and tell stories of past lives. Late Sept. Phone 847/742-4248.

Elgin Symphony Orchestra. Classical and pops concerts. Oct-May. Phone 847/888-4000.

Touching on Traditions. Lords Park pavilion. Display honors over 50 countries whose people who have made their homes in Elgin. Costumes, decorations, objects of traditional importance. Sat after Thanksgiving-first Sat Jan. Phone 847/741-6655.

Motel/Motor Lodge

★ **DAYS INN.** *1585 Dundee Ave (60120).* 847/695-2100; fax 847/697-9114; toll-free 800/329-7466. *www. daysinn.com.* 97 rms, 2 story. S $54-$68; D $60-$74; each addl $6; under 18 free. Crib free. Pet accepted. TV; cable (premium). Indoor pool. Complimentary continental bkfst. Restaurant nearby. Coffee in rm. Ck-out 11 am. Meeting rms. Business servs avail. In-rm modem link. Sundries. Some whirlpools. Refrigerators, microwaves avail. Private patios, balconies. Cr cds: A, D, DS, MC, V.

D 🐾 ⊠ ⊠ 🔥

Elk Grove Village

(see Chicago O'Hare Airport Area)

Elmhurst

See also Chicago O'Hare Airport Area, Hillside, Oak Brook

Settled 1843 **Pop** 42,762 **Elev** 680 ft **Area code** 630 **Zip** 60126

Information Chamber of Commerce & Industry, 113 Adell Pl; 630/834-6060

Web www.elmhurst.org

What to See and Do

Elmhurst Historical Museum. Housed in 1892 building; changing exhibits on suburbanization and local history. Research and genealogy collections. Self-guided architectural walking tours. (Tues-Sun, afternoons; also by appt; closed hols) 120 E Park Ave. Phone 630/833-1457. **FREE**

Lizzadro Museum of Lapidary Art. Large collection of jade and other hardstone carvings, include displays of minerals, animal dioramas, fossils, and gemstones. (Tues-Sat, also Sun afternoons; closed hols) 220 Cottage Hill Ave, in Wilder Park. Phone 630/833-1616. ¢¢

Motels/Motor Lodges

★★ **COURTYARD BY MARRIOTT.** *370 N Rt 83 (60126). 630/941-9444; fax 630/941-3539; res 800/321-2211. www.courtyard.com.* 140 units, 7 story, 14 suites. S $59-$119; D $69-$129; suites $129-$145; under 18 free. Crib free. TV; cable (premium). Indoor pool; whirlpool. Coffee in rms, lobby. Restaurant nearby 10 am-10 pm. Bar 4-10 pm; closed Sun. Ck-out noon. Coin lndry. Meeting rms. Business servs avail. In-rm modem link. Valet serv. Exercise equipt; sauna. Minibars. Cr cds: A, D, DS, MC, V.

⊡ 🏋 ⛴ 🔥 SC ⊠

★★★ **HOLIDAY INN.** *624 N York Rd (60126). 630/279-1100; fax 630/279-4038; toll-free 800/465-4329. www.holiday-inn.com.* 237 rms, 4 story. S, D $119; suite $199; under 18 free. Crib free. Pet accepted, some restrictions; $20 deposit. TV; cable (premium). Indoor pool; whirlpool. Restaurant 7 am-2 pm, 5-10 pm. Rm serv. Bar 11 am-midnight; Fri, Sat to 2 am. Coffee, tea in rms. Ck-out 11 am. Coin lndry. Meeting rms. Business center. In-rm modem link. Concierge. Valet serv. Free airport transportation. Exercise equipt; sauna. Game rm. Balconies. Cr cds: A, C, D, DS, JCB, MC, V.

🐾 ⊠ 🏋 ✈ ⛴ 🔥 SC 🏋

Restaurant

★ **LAS BELLAS ARTES.** *112 W Park Ave (60126). 630/530-7725. www.lasbellasartes.com.* Hrs: 5:30-10 pm; Sun brunch 10 am-2 pm. Closed Mon; hols; 2 wks summer. Res accepted. Mexican cuisine. Bar. Dinner $15-$25. Prix fixe: dinner $35. Sun brunch $6-$15. Specializes in seafood, game, beef tenderloin. Own baking. European-style decor. Cr cds: DS, MC, V.

Evanston

See also Chicago, Skokie, Wilmette

Settled 1853 **Pop** 74,239 **Elev** 600 ft **Area code** 847

Information Convention and Visitors Bureau, One Rotary Center, 1560 Sherman Ave, Suite 860, 60201; 847/328-1500

Web www.cityofevanston.org

Located on the shores of Lake Michigan and adjoining the northern limits of Chicago, Evanston boasts five institutions of higher learning. In 1674, Marquette landed in the natural harbor of what was later the village of Gross Point, important as a lake port. In 1853 the village was renamed Evanston in honor of John Evans, one of the founders of Northwestern University.

What to See and Do

Charles Gates Dawes House. (1895) The 28-room house of General Charles G. Dawes, Nobel Peace Prize winner (1926) and vice president under Calvin Coolidge. National landmark with original furnishings and artifacts in restored rooms; local history exhibits; large research collection. Gift shop. Tours. (Tues-Sat afternoons; closed hols) 225 Greenwood St, off Sheridan Rd. Phone 847/475-3410. ¢¢

Frances E. Willard Home/National Woman's Christian Temperance Union. House where Frances E. Willard, founder of the worldwide WCTU, lived with her family;

Charles Gates Dawes House

authentically preserved house contains many souvenirs of her career. Administration building on grounds houses Willard Memorial Alcohol Research Library. (Mon-Fri by appt; closed one wk July-Aug, hols) 1730 Chicago Ave. Phone 847/328-7500. **Donation**

Gross Point Lighthouse. (1873) Constructed after a Lake Michigan wreck near Evanston cost 300 lives. Guided tours of keeper's quarters, museum, tower avail 2-4 pm on first come basis (June-Sept, Sat-Sun; closed hol wkends). Call for more detailed info. No children under 8 permitted. Sheridan Rd and Central St. Phone 847/328-6961. ¢

Ladd Arboretum. International Friendship Garden. (Daily) McCormick Blvd between Golf and Green Bay Rds. Phone 847/864-5181. **FREE** Also here is

Evanston Ecology Center. Home of Evanston Environmental Association. Nature education and activities. Environmental educational programs; greenhouse; library. (Mon-Sat) 2024 McCormick Blvd. Phone 847/864-5181. **FREE**

Merrick Rose Garden. Seasonal displays; All-American Test Garden; 1,200 rose bushes, 65 varieties. Lake Ave and Oak St. **FREE**

Mitchell Museum of the American Indian. Collection of more than 3,000 items of Native American art and artifacts; baskets, pottery, jewelry, Navajo rugs, beadwork, clothing, weapons, tools, stoneware. (Tues-Sun; closed hols) Kendall College, 2600 Central Park. Phone 847/475-1030. ¢

Northwestern University. (founded 1851, opened 1855) 11,700 students. Undergraduate and graduate schools in Evanston, professional schools in Chicago; John Evans Center, 1800 Sheridan Rd, has information (Mon-Fri). Dearborn Observatory (1888), 2131 Sheridan Rd, has free public viewing (Fri; two viewings, res only, phone 847/491-7650) Other places of interest are the Shakespeare Garden; University Library; Norris University Center; Alice Millar Religious Center; Theatre, and Interpretation Center; Mary and Leigh Block Museum of Art (Tues-Sun); Pick-Staiger Concert Hall (many free performances); Ryan Field (football); Welsh-Ryan Arena (basketball). Guided walking tours of the lakefront campus leave 1801 Hinman Ave (academic yr, one departure Mon-Sat; July-Aug, two departures Mon-Fri; res, phone 847/491-7271). Clark St at Sheridan Rd. Phone 847/491-3741.

Special Event

Custer's Last Stand Festival of Arts. Jct Main St and Chicago Ave. Festival featuring over 400 artists and crafters. Wkend Mid-June. Phone 847/328-2204.

Motel/Motor Lodge

★★ **HOLIDAY INN.** *1501 Sherman Ave (60201). 847/491-6400; fax 847/328-3090. www.holiday-inn.com.* 159 rms, 12 story. S, D $109-$189; each addl $10; suites $159-$215; under 18 free. TV; cable (premium), VCR avail. Heated pool; wading pool. Complimentary coffee in rms. Restaurant 6:30 am-2 pm, 5-10 pm. Rm serv. Bar 4 pm-1 am. Ck-out noon. Coin lndry. Meeting rms. Business servs avail. In-rm modem link. Bellhops. Exercise equipt; sauna. Health club privileges. Refrigerators avail. Cr cds: A, D, DS, MC, V.

D ⇌ 🏋 ⇘ 🔥

Hotel

★★ **OMNI ORRINGTON HOTEL.** *1710 Orrington Ave (60201). 847/866-8700; fax 847/866-8724. www.omni hotels.com.* 277 rms, 9 story. S $135-$165; D $135-$185; each addl $10; suites $250-$550; under 18 free; wkend rates; higher rates NU graduation (3-day min). Crib free. Pet accepted, some restriction; $50. Valet, covered parking $15. TV; cable, VCR avail. Concierge. Valet serv. Beauty shop. Restaurant 6:30 am-11 pm. Bar 11 am-midnight. Convention facilities. Business servs avail. In-rm modem link. Ck-out noon. Gift shop. Health club privileges. Exercise equipt. Refigerators. Cr cds: A, D, DS, JCB, MC, V.

D ◀ 🏋 ⇘

B&B/Small Inn

★ **THE MARGARITA EUROPEAN.** *1566 Oak Ave (60201). 847/869-2273; fax 847/869-2353. www.margaritainn. com.* 42 rms, 18 share bath, 6 story. 11 suites. No A/C. S, D $78-$120; each addl $10; suites $135-$145; higher rates university graduation; lower rates rest of yr. Crib $10. TV. Complimentary continental bkfst. Restaurant 5:30-9 pm; Fri, Sat to 10 pm. Ck-out 11 am, ck-in 2 pm. Meeting rms. Business servs avail. In-rm modem link. Built in 1927; originally used as a woman's club. Antique furniture, rooftop garden. Library. Cr cds: A, D, MC, V.

D ⇘ 🔥

Restaurants

★★★ **CAMPAGNOLA.** *815 Chicago Ave (60202). 847/475-6100.* Specializes in turbot with tuscan pazanella, organic beef tenderloin. Hrs: 5:30-9:30 pm; Fri, Sat to 10:30 pm; Sun 5-9 pm. Closed Mon, hols. Res accepted. Wine, beer. Dinner $14-$29. Entertainment. Cr cds: A, D, DS, MC, V.

D

★★ **THE DINING ROOM AT KENDALL COLLEGE.** *2408 Orrington Ave (60201). 847/866-1399. www. kendall.edu.* Hrs: noon-1:30 pm, 6-8 pm; Sat 6-8:30 pm. Closed Sun; hols. Res required. Complete meal: lunch $14.95. A la carte entrees: dinner $14.95-$17.95. Specializes in regional American and French cuisine. Own baking. Open kitchen. Kitchen and dining rm staffed by Culinary School of Kendall College students. Totally nonsmoking. Cr cds: A, DS, MC, V.

D

★ **JILLY'S CAFE.** *2614 Green Bay Rd (60201). 847/869-7636.* Hrs: 11:30 am-2 pm, 5-9 pm; Fri, Sat to 10 pm; Sun 5-8 pm; Sun brunch 10:30 am-2 pm. Closed Mon; hols. Res accepted. Wine. Lunch $5-$8, dinner $9-$17. Sun brunch $16.50. Menu changes quarterly. Specializes in fresh fish, seasonal game. Own pastries. Cr cds: A, D, MC, V.

SC

★ **KUNI'S JAPANESE RESTAURANT.** *511 Main St (60202). 847/328-2004.* Hrs: 11:30 am-2 pm, 5-10 pm; Sun from 5 pm. Closed Tues; hols. Japanese menu. Sushi bar. A la carte entrees: lunch $6-$10, dinner $10-$25. Specializes in sushi, sashimi, tempura. Cr cds: A, MC, V.

★ **LAS PALMAS.** *817 University Pl (60201). 847/328-2555.* Hrs: 11 am-10 pm; Fri, Sat to 11 pm; Sun from 1 pm. Closed Thanksgiving, Dec 25. Res accepted. Mexican menu. Bar. Lunch $3.50-$6.25, dinner $5.95-$12.95. Specializes in steak and chicken fajitas, grilled jumbo shrimp with garlic sauce. Harpist Thurs, Sat. Parking. Mexican decor. Cr cds: A, MC, V.

D

★ **LUCKY PLATTER.** *514 Main St (60202). 847/869-4064.* Hrs: 7 am-10 pm. Continental menu. Bkfst $3.95-$7.95, lunch, dinner $6-$15. Specializes in grilled fish, vegetarian entrees, chef-made pizzas. Own baking. Street parking. Informal, traditional, family-style dining area; knickknacks and local art throughout. Totally nonsmoking. Cr cds: DS, MC, V.

★★ **NEW JAPAN.** *1322 Chicago Ave (60201). 847/475-5980. www.city search.com.* Hrs: 11:30 am-2:15 pm, 5-9:15 pm; Fri, Sat to 10:15 pm; Sun 4:30-8:45 pm. Closed Mon; hols. Res accepted. Japanese menu; also French menu (dinner). Serv bar. A la carte entrees: lunch $6.25-$6.95. Complete meals: dinner $11.50-$18.50. Specializes in sushi, tempura, sukiyaki. Cr cds: A, D, MC, V.

D

★★★ **OCEANIQUE.** *505 Main St (60202). 847/864-3435. www. oceanique.com.* Hrs: 5:30-9:30 pm; Fri, Sat to 10:30 pm. Closed Sun; hols. Res accepted. French, American menu. Extensive wine list. Dinner $18-$24. Complete meal: dinner $50-$60. Specializes in fresh fish, sirloin steak, lamb. Own pastries, desserts. In historic building (1929). Southern European decor. Cr cds: A, C, D, DS, MC, V.

D ➘

★★ **PETE MILLER'S STEAK-HOUSE.** *1557 Sherman Ave (60201). 847/328-0399.* Hrs: 11:30 am-2 pm, 5-10 pm; Fri to 11 pm; Sat 5-11 pm; Sun 4:30-10 pm. Closed July 4, Thanksgiving, Dec 25. Res accepted. Bar to 12:30 am, Sun to 11:30 pm. Lunch $6.95-$18, dinner $18-$33. Specializes in prime-aged steak. Salad bar (lunch). Jazz nightly. Valet parking Thurs-Sat. Separate billiard rm. Cr cds: D, DS, MC, V.

D ➘

★ **SIAM SQUARE.** *622 Davis St (60201). 847/475-0860.* Hrs: 11:30 am-10 pm; Fri, Sat to 10:30 pm; Sun to 9 pm. Closed Thanksgiving, Dec 25. Res accepted. Wine, beer. Thai menu. A la carte entrees: lunch, din-

ner $5.50-$9.95; buffet: lunch $6.95-$9.95. Complete meal: dinner $8.95-$13.95. Specializes in seafood and duck, seasonal Thai dishes. Outdoor dining. 18th-century Thai decor. Cr cds: A, DS, MC, V.

★★★★ **TRIO.** *1625 Hinman Ave (60201). 847/733-8746. www.trio-restaurant.com.* At this dining room tucked away on a residential street in an affluent Chicago suburb, Chef Grant Achatz creates an impressive menu of progressive French cuisine. Artistic dishes, often presented on surfaces such as glass, marble, and mirror, use familiar ingredients that are prepared in an unusual way. Since 1993, service at every level has remained flawless and attitude-free. Continental menu. Own baking. Hrs: 6-9:30 pm; Fri also noon-1 pm; Sat 5-10:30 pm; Sun 11-1 pm, 5-9 pm. Closed Mon; hols. Res recommended. Serv bar. Wine cellar. Complete meal: lunch $26-$32, dinner $60-$75. Prix fixe: $75. Jacket. Totally nonsmoking. Cr cds: A, D, DS, MC, V.

D

★★ **VA PENSIERO.** *1566 Oak Ave (60201). 847/475-7779.* Hrs: 5:30-9 pm; Fri, Sat to 10 pm. Closed hols. Res accepted. Italian menu. Bar. Dinner $16-$23. Specialties: arrosta di salmone senape, gamberi con salsa di pistacchi, seafood brodetto. Own pastries. Outdoor dining. Cr cds: A, D, DS, MC, V.

D

Unrated Dining Spots

CARMEN'S. *1012 Church St (60201). 847/328-0031.* Hrs: 11 am-11 pm; Fri to midnight; Sat 4 pm-midnight; Sun 4-11 pm. Closed hols. Res accepted. Bar. A la carte entrees: lunch, dinner $4-$20. Specializes in stuffed pizza, pasta, Italian beef sandwiches. Parking. Cr cds: A, D, MC, V.

D ➘

MERLE'S #1 BARBECUE. *1727 Benson St (60201). 847/475-7766.* Hrs: 11:30 am-10:30 pm; Fri, Sat to 11:30 pm; Sun noon-10 pm. Closed Thanksgiving, Dec 25. Southwestern menu. Bar. Lunch $4.50-$7.95, dinner $8.95-$13.95. Child's menu. Specialties: pulled pork, baby back ribs, chicken barbecue. Cr cds: A, C, D, DS, MC, V.

D ⊒

Fort Kaskaskia State Historic Site

See also Carbondale

(6 mi NW of Chester, near Ellis Grove, off IL 3)

This 275-acre park includes the earthworks of the old fort, built in 1733, rebuilt in 1736 by the French, and finally destroyed to prevent British occupation after the Treaty of Paris. As a result of post-Revolutionary War anarchy (1784), the ruins of the fort, while in the hands of Connecticut renegade John Dodge, were the scene of murders and revelry. Nearby is Garrison Hill Cemetery, where 3,800 old settlers' remains rest, removed from the original graveyard when floodwaters threatened to wash them away. The Pierre Menard mansion, at the base of bluffs along the Mississippi, was built in 1802 in the style of a French Colonial house. The home has been called the "Mount Vernon of the West." Some original furnishings have been reclaimed and reinstalled by the state; tours (daily). The park provides hiking, picnicking, tent and trailer camping (dump station; hookups; standard fees). For information contact Site Manager, 4372 Park Rd, Ellis Grove 62241; phone 618/859-3741 or 618/859-3031 (Menard Mansion).

Freeport

(A-4) *See also Rockford*

Settled 1838 **Pop** 26,443 **Elev** 780 ft
Area code 815 **Zip** 61032
Information Stephenson County Convention & Visitors Bureau, 2047 AYP Rd; 815/233-1357 or 800/369-2955
Web www.stephenson-county-il.org

According to legend, Freeport is named for the generosity of its pioneer settler, William Baker, who was chided by his wife for running a "free port" for everyone coming along the trail. It was the scene of the second Lincoln-Douglas debate; the site is marked by a memorial boulder and a life-size statue of Lincoln and Douglas in debate. Freeport, an agricultural and industrial center, is the seat of Stephenson County.

What to See and Do

Freeport Arts Center. Collection includes Asian and Native American art; European painting and sculpture; Egyptian, Greek, and Roman antiquities; contemporary exhibits. (Tues-Sun, afternoons; closed hols) 121 N Harlem Ave. Phone 815/235-9755. ¢

Krape Park. Merry-go-round (mid-May-mid-Sept), garden, waterfall, duck pond. Boat rentals; tennis courts, miniature golf, picnicking, playground, concession (mid-May-mid-Sept). (Daily) Park Blvd. Phone 815/235-6114. **FREE**

Silvercreek and Stephenson Railroad. Trips on a 1912, 36-ton steam locomotive with three antique cabooses and a flat car. Also historical museum. (Memorial Day-Labor Day, periodic wkends) Walnut and Lamm Rds. Phone 815/232-2306. ¢¢

Stephenson County Historical Museum. In the 1857 Oscar Taylor house, museum features 19th-century furnishings and changing exhibits. On grounds with arboretum are 1840 log cabin, turn-of-the-century schoolhouse, blacksmith shop, and farm museum. (May-Oct, Wed-Sun; rest of yr, Fri-Sun, afternoons; closed hols). 1440 S Carroll Ave. Phone 815/232-8419. ¢

Special Event

Stephenson County Fair. Seven days mid-Aug. Phone 815/235-2918.

Motel/Motor Lodge

★★ **GUESTHOUSE HOTEL.** *1300 E South St (61032). 815/235-3121; fax 815/297-9701; toll-free 800/272-6232.* 90 rms, 2 story. S $66; D $72; each addl $6; under 8 free. Crib free. Pet accepted. TV; cable (premium).

Heated pool. Complimentary coffee in rms. Restaurant 6 am-2 pm, 5-10 pm. Bar 4 pm-1 am. Ck-out noon. Meeting rms. Business servs avail. Exercise equipt. Game rm. Cr cds: A, C, D, DS, MC, V.

[D] [⟲] [≈] [⚊] [⟲] [⟲] [SC]

Restaurant

★ **BELTLINE CAFE.** *325 W South St (61032).* 815/232-5512. Hrs: 5:30 am-2 pm. Closed Easter, Thanksgiving, Dec 25. Bkfst $2.25-$4.75, lunch $2.25-$5.25. Specializes in home-made soups, pies. Built 1890. Cr cds: A, MC, V.

[D] [SC] [⟲]

Galena

(A-3) *Also see Platteville, WI*

Founded 1826 **Pop** 3,460 **Elev** 609 ft
Area code 815 **Zip** 61036
Information Galena/Jo Daviess County Convention & Visitors Bureau, 720 Park Ave; 800/747-9377
Web www.galena.org

A quiet town of historical and architectural interest set on terraces cut by the old Fever River, Galena was once a major crossroads for French exploration of the New World and the commercial and cultural capital of the Northwest Territory. Deposits of lead were discovered in the region by the mid-18th century; when the town was laid out, it was named for the ore. By 1845, the area was producing nearly all the nation's lead, and Galena was the richest and most important city in the state. With wealth came opulence; the grand mansions standing today were built on fortunes acquired from the lead and steamboat business. However, the mining of lead peaked just before the outbreak of the Civil War. After the war, the city's importance declined rapidly. Although Galena's sympathies were divided at the outbreak of the Civil War, two companies were formed to support the Union. Ulysses S. Grant, who had recently come to Galena from St. Louis, accompanied local troops to Springfield as drillmaster.

The town has changed little since the middle of the last century. To walk the streets of Galena today is to take a step back in time. The 19th-century architecture varies from Federal to Greek Revival and from Italianate to Queen Anne. Ninety percent of the town's buildings are listed on the National Register of Historic Places. A favorite destination of weekend travelers from surrounding areas, especially Chicago, Galena is also a mecca for antique hunters and specialty shoppers.

What to See and Do

Belvedere Mansion. (1857) Italianate/Steamboat Gothic mansion (22 rooms) restored and furnished with antiques, including pieces used on set of *Gone With the Wind.* (Memorial Day-Oct, daily) Combination ticket with Dowling House. 1008 Park Ave. Phone 815/777-0747. ¢¢

Dowling House. (ca 1826) Restored stone house, oldest in Galena, is authentically furnished as a trading post with primitive living quarters. Guided tours. (May-Dec, daily; rest of yr, limited hrs) Combination ticket with Belvedere Mansion. 220 N Diagonal St. Phone 815/777-1250. ¢¢

Galena-Jo Daviess County History Museum. Located in 1858 Italianate house, museum displays Civil War artifacts, decorative arts; *A Ripple in Time,* a color slide tape presentation on the way of life of the town's earliest settlers; original *Peace in Union,* Thomas Nast's version of the surrender at Appomattox. (Daily; closed Jan 1, Easter, Thanksgiving, Dec 24, 25, 31) 211 S Bench St. Phone 815/777-9129. ¢¢

Galena Post Office & Customs House. Named a "Great American Post Office" by the Smithsonian Institution, the first post office to receive the honor; built in 1859, it is the second-oldest post office in the US still in use. (Mon-Sat) 110 Green St. Phone 815/777-0225.

Grace Episcopal Church. (1848) Gothic Revival church was later remodeled by William LeBaron Jenney, father of the skyscraper. Contains Belgian stained-glass windows; eagle lecturn carved by early Galena crafter; one-manual organ in use since 1838, brought from New York

City to New Orleans and then by steamboat to Galena. (Sun; also by appt) Hill and Prospect Sts. Phone 815/777-2590. **DONATION**

Old Market House State Historic 1846 Site. Recently restored building once housed a vast marketplace on the ground floor, the city council upstairs, and a jail in the basement. Permanent exhibit on the building's history; seasonal exhibitions. (Thurs-Sun) 123 N Commerce St. Phone 815/777-2570. **DONATION**

Sightseeing. Several trolley tours are avail. Contact the Convention and Visitors Bureau.

Skiing. Chestnut Mountain Resort. Two quads, three triple chairlifts, three surface lifts; patrol, school, rentals, snowmaking; restaurants, cafeteria, bars, lodge, nursery. Longest run 3,500 ft; vertical drop 475 ft. (Mid-Nov-mid-Mar, daily) 8700 W Chestnut Rd, 8 mi SE. Phone 815/777-1320 or 800/397-1320. ¢¢¢¢

Ulysses S. Grant Home State Historic Site. Italianate house was given to General Grant upon his return from the Civil War (1865); original furnishings and Grant family items. Interpretive tours. Picnicking. (Apr-Dec, daily; closed hols) 500 Bouthillier St. Phone 815/777-3310. ¢¢

Vinegar Hill Lead Mine & Museum. Guided tour of old mine showing early mining techniques. (June-Aug, daily; May, appt only; and Sept-Oct, wkends) 6 mi N on IL 84, then E on Furlong Rd, to 8885 N Three Pines Rd. Phone 815/777-0855. ¢¢

Special Events

June Tour of Historic Homes. Five houses open to public. Second wkend June. Phone 815/777-9129.

Stagecoach Trail Festival. A celebration of pioneer and Native American history. Fourth wkend June. Phone 815/369-2786.

Antique Town Rods Car Show. Pre-1949 vehicles. July. Phone 815/777-2088.

Galena Arts Festival. Third wkend July. Phone 815/777-9341.

Ladies' Getaway. Entertainment and demonstrations especially for women. Mid-Sept. Phone 815/777-9050.

Fall Tour of Homes. Last full wkend Sept. Phone 815/777-0229.

Galena Country Fair. Grant City Park. Exhibits, entertainment, country food. Columbus Day wkend. Phone 815/777-1048.

Grant's Home

Motels/Motor Lodges

★ **ALLEN'S VICTORIAN PINES LODGING.** *11383 US 20W (61036). 815/777-2043; fax 815/777-2625; toll-free 866/847-4637. www.victorian pineslodging.com.* 51 rms in motel, guest houses, 1-2 story. Some rm phones. S $35; D $59; suites $110-$225; rms in Ryan and Bedford houses $85-$175. Crib $5. Pet accepted, some restrictions. TV. Indoor whirlpool. Sauna. Spa. Massage. Complimentary continental bkfst. Coffee in lobby. Ck-out 11 am. Conference facilities. Downhill ski 9 mi; x-country ski 6 mi. Complex consists of motel; Ryan House (1876), a 24-rm Italianate/Victorian mansion with antiques; and Bedford House (1850), an Italianate structure with original chandeliers, leaded glass and walnut staircase. Cr cds: A, MC, V.

⬛ 🖼 🔥 SC

★★ **BEST WESTERN QUIET HOUSE & SUITES.** *9923 IL 20E (61036). 815/777-2577; fax 815/777-0584; toll-free 800/780-7234. www. bestwestern.com.* 42 suites, 3 story. S, D $114-$181; each addl $10; under 12 free; higher rates: special events, wkends. Pet accepted, some restrictions; $15. TV; cable (premium). Heated indoor/outdoor pool; whirlpool. Complimentary coffee in lobby, rms. Restaurant adj 7 am-11 pm. Ck-out 11 am. Business servs avail. Exercise equipt. Downhill/x-country ski 12 mi. Refrigerators, microwaves. Some balconies, whirlpools. Cr cds: A, D, DS, MC, V.

D ⬛ 🖼 🎿 🔥 SC

★★ **LONGHOLLOW POINT RESORT.** *5129 Longhollow Rd (61036). 815/777-6010; fax 815/777-2348; res 800/551-5129. www. longhollowpoint.com.* 67 suites, 3 story, 39 kit. units. May-Oct: S, D $125-$215; kit. units $159-$229; under 12 free. Crib avail. TV, VCR (movies). Complimentary coffee in rms. Restaurant nearby. Ck-out 11 am, ck-in 3 pm. Coin lndry. Meeting rms. Business servs avail. Downhill ski 15 mi; x-country ski 2 mi. Exercise equipt. Indoor pool; whirlpool. Sauna. Game rm. In-rm whirlpools, refrigerators, fireplaces; microwaves avail. Balconies. Cr cds: A, DS, MC, V.

D 🔥 🎿 🖼 🎿 🖼 SC

Hotel

★ **DESOTO HOUSE HOTEL.** *230 S Main St (61036). 815/777-0090; fax 815/777-9529; toll-free 800/343-6562.* 55 rms, 4 story. Apr-Oct: S, D $119-$140; each addl $10; suites $150-$165; under 18 free; package plans; lower rates rest of yr. Crib free. TV; cable (premium). Coffee in rms. Restaurant 7 am-2 pm, 5-9 pm. Bar 11 am-11 pm. Ck-out 11 am. Meeting rms. Business servs avail. Free covered parking. Downhill ski 8 mi; x-country ski 9 mi. Fireplace in suites. Renovated historic hotel built 1855. Cr cds: A, MC, V.

D 🎿 🖼 🔥 SC

Resort

★★★ **EAGLE RIDGE INN & RESORT.** *444 Eagle Ridge Dr (61036). 815/777-2444; fax 815/777-0445; toll-free 800/998-6338. www.eagleridge. com.* 80 rms, 2 story. May-Oct: S, D $199-$259; each addl $10; under 18 free; villas $239-$379; wkly rates; golf plan; lower rates rest of yr. Crib free. TV; cable (premium), VCR (movies $4). Indoor pool; whirlpool. Playground. Supervised child's activities; ages 4-12. Complimentary coffee in rms. Dining rm 6 am-2 pm, 5-11 pm. Rm serv. Bar 11-1 am. Entertainment exc Mon. Ck-out noon, ck-in 4 pm. Meeting rms. Business servs avail. Bellhops. Sundries. Gift shop. Free airport, bus depot transportation. Tennis. 9-hole golf course, three 18-hole golf courses, greens fee $77, pro, putting green, driving range, pro shop. Canoes, pontoon-boats. Bike rental. Sand beach, private lake, marina. Downhill ski 10 mi; x-country ski on site. Trail rides. Hayrides, sleigh rides. Soc dir. Game rm. Exercise equipt; sauna. Massage. Minibars, fireplaces, whirlpools; some refrigerators. Private patios, balconies. Located on a bluff, overlooking a lake. Cr cds: A, D, DS, MC, V.

D 🔥 🎿 🖼 🎿 🎿 🖼 🎿 🎿 🖼 🔥

B&Bs/Small Inns

★★ **ALDRICH GUEST HOUSE.** *900 3rd St (61036). 815/777-3323; fax*

815/777-3323. www.aldrichguesthouse. com. 5 rms, 2 story. No rm phones. S, D $85-$150; each addl $20. Children over 12 yrs only. TV in sitting rm; cable (premium), VCR. Complimentary full bkfst. Restaurant nearby. Ck-out 11 am, ck-in 4 pm. Street parking. Downhill/x-country ski 8 mi. Antiques. Library/sitting rm, fireplace. Screened porch. Built in 1845. Totally nonsmoking. Cr cds: DS, MC, V.

⊠ ⊠ ⊠ SC

★ **ANNIE WIGGINS GUEST HOUSE.** 1004 Park Ave (61036). 815/777-0336. www.anniewiggins.com. 7 rms, some A/C, 3 story. No rm phones. S, D $125-$175; each addl $15; package plans. Crib free. TV; cable. Complimentary continental bkfst. Ck-out 11 am, ck-in 2 pm. Downhill/x-country ski 7 mi. Refrigerators, microwaves. Screened porches. Antiques. Built 1826. Cr cds: A, MC, V.

⊠ ⊠ ⊠ SC

★★ **HELLMAN GUEST HOUSE.** 318 Hill St (61036). 815/777-3638. www.galena.com/hellman. 4 rms, 3 with shower only, 3 story. No rm phones. S, D $99-$149. Children over 12 only; package plans. Complimentary full bkfst. Ck-out 11 am, ck-in 4-6 pm. Downhill ski 10 mi; x-country ski 8 mi. Queen Anne-style house (1895). Totally nonsmoking. Cr cds: DS, MC, V.

⊠ ⊠

★ **LOGAN HOUSE.** 301 N Main St (61036). 815/777-0033; fax 815/777-0049. 6 rms, 2 story. No rm phones. May-Dec: S, D $75; each addl $7; suites $90; lower rates rest of yr. TV; cable (premium), VCR avail (free movies). Complimentary continental bkfst. Restaurant (see also CAFE ITALIA/TWISTED TACO CAFE). Ck-out 11 am, ck-in 2 pm. Street parking. In 1855 building constructed as one of town's first hotels. Country decor in guest rms. Cr cds: A, C, D, DS, MC, V.

⊠ ⊠

★★ **PARK AVENUE GUEST HOUSE.** 208 Park Ave (61036). 815/777-1075; toll-free 800/359-0743. www.galena.com/parkave. 4 rms, 3 with shower only, 3 story. No rm phones. S $105; D $105-$115; family rates 2-day min, wkends. Children over 12 yrs only. TV; cable (premium), VCR avail (movies). Complimentary full bkfst. Restaurant nearby. Ck-out 11 am, ck-in 4 pm. Some fireplaces. Downhill/x-country ski 7 mi. Built in 1893; antiques. Totally nonsmoking. Cr cds: DS, MC, V.

⊠ ⊠ ⊠

★★ **PINE HOLLOW INN BED & BREAKFAST.** 4700 N Council Hill Rd (61036). 815/777-1071. www.pine hollowinn.com. 5 rms, 2 story. No rm phones. S, D $95-$135. Children over 12 yrs only. Complimentary continental bkfst. Restaurant nearby. Ck-out 11 am, ck-in 3 pm. On 120-acre evergreen tree farm. Country decor. Fireplaces. Some whirlpools. Totally nonsmoking. Cr cds: DS, MC, V.

⊠ ⊠

Restaurants

★ **BUBBA GUMP'S.** 300 N Main St (61036). 815/777-8030. www.vinni vanucci.com. Hrs: 4-10 pm. Closed Easter, Thanksgiving, Dec 25. Seafood menu. Bar. Dinner $4.50-$15.95. Specialties: New Orleans jambalaya, grilled swordfish with shallots, filet mignon. Former ice cream parlor (1895). Smoking in bar only. Cr cds: A, C, D, DS, MC, V.

D ⊠

★★ **CAFE ITALIA/TWISTED TACO CAFE.** 301 N Main St (61036). 815/777-0033. Hrs: 11 am-3 pm, 5-10 pm; Sat and Sun from 4:30 pm. Res accepted. Italian, American, Mexican menu. Bar. Lunch $4.95-$8.95, dinner $8.95-$17.95. Child's menu. Specializes in pasta, barbecued ribs, fajitas. Built 1855. Cr cds: A, C, D, DS, MC, V.

D ⊠

★★ **FRIED GREEN TOMATOES.** 1301 Irish Hollow Rd (61036). 815/777-3938. www.friedgreen.com. Hrs: 11 am-2 pm, 5-10 pm; Fri, Sat 5-9:30 pm. Closed Thanksgiving, Dec 25. Res accepted. Italian, American menu. Bar. Lunch $5.95-$9.95, dinner $10.95-$24.95. Specialties: Chilean sea bass, pasta aglio, fried green tomatoes. Pianist Fri, Sat.

Three dining levels in historic (1851) rural setting. Cr cds: DS, MC, V.
D

★ **LOG CABIN.** *201 N Main St (61036). 815/777-0393.* Hrs: 11 am-10 pm; Fri, Sat to 11 pm. Closed Mon; Thanksgiving, Dec 24-25. Res accepted. Bar. Lunch $2.95-$7.95, dinner $4.75-$15. Child's menu. Specializes in steak, seafood. Pianist Fri, Sat. Cr cds: A, V.
D ➘

Galesburg

(C-3) *See also Bishop Hill, Moline, Monmouth*

Settled 1837 **Pop** 33,706 **Elev** 773 ft
Area code 309 **Zip** 61401
Information Convention & Visitors Bureau, 2163 E Main St; 309/343-2585
Web www.visitgalesburg.com

Eastern pioneers came to this area on the prairie to establish a community centering around a school for the training of ministers, Knox College. The town was named for their leader, G.W. Gale. Galesburg was an important station on the Underground Railroad. It is also the birth and burial place of poet Carl Sandburg.

What to See and Do

Carl Sandburg State Historic Site. (1860) Restored birthplace cottage; antique furnishings, some from Sandburg family; adj museum contains memorabilia. Remembrance Rock, named for Sandburg's historical novel, is a granite boulder under which his ashes were placed. (Daily; closed Jan 1, Thanksgiving, Dec 25) 331 E 3rd St. Phone 309/342-2361. ¢

Knox College. (1837) 1,100 students. Old Main (1856), original college building and site of Lincoln-Douglas debate. Fine Arts Center houses exhibits by students and faculty. Tours (when school is in session). Cherry and South Sts, 2 blks S of Public Sq. Phone 309/341-7313.

Lake Storey Recreational Area. Waterpark (Memorial Day-Labor Day), boat rentals; 18-hole golf (late Mar-Nov; fee), tennis, picnicking (Apr-Oct), playground, gardens, concessions, camping (mid-Apr-mid-Oct; fee; hookups, dump station, two-wk max). Pets on leash only. (Daily) ¼ mi N on US 150, then ½ mi W on S Lake Storey Rd. Phone 309/345-3683.

Special Events

Sandburg Days Festival. Three-day festival includes literary, history, sporting, and children's events. Apr 23-25. Phone 309/343-2485.

Railroad Days. Tour of train, yards, depot; memorabilia displays, carnival, fun runs, street fair. Fourth wkend June. Phone 309/343-2485.

Stearman Fly-In Days. Airport. Air shows, exhibits, Stearman contests. First wkend after Labor Day. Phone 309/343-2485.

Motels/Motor Lodges

★ ★ **COMFORT INN.** *907 W Carl Sandburg Dr (61401). 309/344-5445; fax 309/344-5445. www.comfortinn. com.* 46 rms, 2 story. May-Sept: S, D $69.95; suites $79.95; each addl $5; under 18 free; higher rates: Railroad Days, Stearman Fly-In wkend; lower rates rest of yr. Crib free. Pet accepted. TV; cable (premium), VCR avail. Complimentary continental bkfst. Restaurant nearby. Coffee in rms. Ck-out 11 am. Meeting rm. Business servs avail. Cr cds: A, C, D, DS, MC, V.
D ➤ ⚅ ⊠ ⚆ SC

★ ★ ★ **JUMERS CONTINENTAL INN.** *260 S Soangetaha Rd (61401). 309/343-7151; fax 309/343-7151. www.jumers.com.* 148 rms, 2 story. S $72; D $63; each addl $9; suites $130; under 18 free; wkend rates. Crib free. Pet accepted. TV; cable (premium), VCR avail (movies $8). Indoor pool; whirlpool. Saunas. Complimentary coffee in lobby. Restaurant 6:30 am-10 pm. Rm serv. Bar 11 am-midnight; Sun from noon; entertainment. Ck-out noon. Coin lndry. Meeting rms. Business servs avail. Bellhops. Valet serv. Sundries. Free airport, RR station transportation. Golf privileges. Health club privileges. Putting green. Many private patios. In-rm whirlpool. Some refrigerators, microwaves. Cr cds: A, D, DS, MC, V.

★★ **RAMADA INN.** *29 Public Sq (61401). 309/343-9161; fax 309/343-0157; toll-free 888/298-2054. www. ramada.com.* 96 rms, 7 story. S $50-$55; D $55-$60; each addl $5. Crib free. Pet accepted. TV; cable (premium), VCR avail (movies $6). Heated indoor pool; whirlpool. Complimentary coffee in lobby. Restaurant open 24 hrs. Bar. Ck-out noon. Meeting rms. Business servs avail. In-rm modem link. Balconies. Some refrigerators, microwaves. Near Knox College campus. Cr cds: A, C, D, DS, JCB, MC, V.

Restaurants

★ **LANDMARK CAFE & CREPERIE.** *62 S Seminary St (61401). 309/343-5376. www.seminarystreet.com.* Hrs: 11 am-10 pm; Fri to 10 pm; Sat 9 am-10 pm; Sun 9 am-9 pm. Closed some hols. Res accepted. French, American menu. A la carte entrees: bkfst $3.95-$7.50. Lunch, dinner $4.95-$12.95. Specializes in European-style crepes, pasta, health foods. Own desserts. Patio dining. Cr cds: A, DS, MC, V.

★ **OOGIE'S.** *1721 N Henderson (US 150W) (61401). 309/344-1259.* Hrs: 6 am-11 pm. Closed Dec 25. Res accepted. Serv bar. Bkfst $2.50-$6, lunch $4-$7, dinner $5-$11. Child's menu. Specializes in home-cooking, ribs, fish. Cr cds: DS, MC, V.

★ **PACKINGHOUSE.** *441 Mulberry (61401). 309/342-6868. www. seminarystreet.com.* Hrs: 11 am-2 pm, 5-9 pm; Fri, Sat to 10 pm; Sun noon-8 pm. Closed hols. Res accepted. Serv bar. Lunch $5.50-$6.95, dinner $11.95-$16.95. Child's menu. Specializes in prime rib, steak, seafood. Salad bar. Own baking. In former meat packing plant (1912). Cr cds: A, D, MC, V.

★★ **THE STEAK HOUSE.** *951 N Henderson (US 150) (61401). 309/343-9994.* Hrs: 5-10 pm. Closed Sun; hols. Res accepted. Bar 2 pm-1 am; Fri, Sat to 2 am. Dinner $8.95-$25. Specializes in aged prime beef, seafood. Cr cds: A, DS, MC, V.

Geneva

(B-5) *See also Aurora, St. Charles*

Settled 1833 **Pop** 19,515 **Elev** 720 ft
Area code 630 **Zip** 60134
Information Chamber of Commerce, 8 S 3rd St, PO Box 481; 630/232-6060
Web www.genevachamber.com

Lured by the stories of soldiers returning from the Black Hawk War, Easterners settled here on both sides of the Fox River. Geneva became a rallying place and supply point for pioneers continuing farther west. The first retail establishment was a hardware and general store; the second sold satin and lace, which began Geneva's unique tradition as a place hospitable to highly specialized retailing. Today, the town has more than 100 specialty stores. Geneva's greatest asset, however, is its historic district, which has more than 200 buildings listed on the National Register of Historic Places. Cyclists and hikers enjoy the trails that wind through the parks adjacent to the Fox River.

What to See and Do

Garfield Farm Museum. This 281-acre living history farm (currently under restoration) includes 1846 brick tavern, 1842 haybarn, and 1849 horse barn; poultry, oxen, sheep; gardens and prairie. Special events throughout the yr. Grounds (June-Sept, Wed, Sun; other times by appt). 5 mi W on IL 38 to Garfield Rd, near La Fox. Phone 630/584-8485. ¢¢

Wheeler Park. This 57-acre park features flower and nature gardens, hiking, tennis, ball fields, access to riverside bicycle trail, picnicking, miniature golf (late May-early Sept, daily; rest of May and Sept, Fri-Sun;

fee). Park (daily). Off IL 31, N of IL 38. **FREE** Also in park is

Geneva Historical Society Museum. Open daily. Phone 630/232-4951. **FREE**

Special Events

Swedish Days. Six-day festival with parade, entertainment, arts and crafts, music, food. Begins Tues after Father's Day. Phone 630/232-6060.

Festival of the Vine. Autumn harvest celebration. Food, wine tasting. Music, craft show, antique carriage rides. Second wkend Sept. Phone 630/232-6060.

Christmas Walk. First Fri and Sat Dec. Phone 630/232-6060.

B&B/Small Inn

★ ★ **THE HERRINGTON INN.** *15 S River Ln (60134). 630/208-7433; fax 630/208-8930; res 800/216-2466. www.herringtoninn.com.* 63 rms, 3 story. S, D $159-$385; each addl $15; under 12 free; higher rates wkends, hols. Crib free. TV; cable (premium), VCR avail (movies). Complimentary continental bkfst, coffee in rms. Restaurant (see also ATWATER'S). Rm serv. Ck-out noon, ck-in 4 pm. Business center. Luggage handling. Valet serv. Concierge serv. Airport transportation. Exercise equipt. Health club priviliges. Golf, green fee $22-$44. Bicycle rentals $6/hr. Bathrm phones, in-rm whirlpools, refrigerators, minibars, fireplaces. Many balconies. Some stereos, DVDs. On river. Built in late 1800s. Cr cds: A, C, D, DS, MC, V.

Restaurants

★ ★ ★ **302 WEST.** *302 W State St (60134). 630/232-9302.* Contemporary American menu. Menu changes daily. Specializes in pasta, seafood, steak. Hrs: 6-9 pm; Fri, Sat to 10 pm. Closed Sun, Mon; Thanksgiving, Dec 24, 25. Res accepted. Bar. Dinner a la carte entrees: $12.95-$23.95. Contemporary decor. Cr cds: A, MC, V. Cr cds: A, MC, V.

★ ★ **ATWATER'S.** *15 S River Ln (60134). 630/208-8920. www.the harringtoninn.com.* Hrs: 7-10:30 am, 11 am-2 pm, 5:30-9:30 pm; Sun brunch 11 am-2 pm. Closed Jan 1, Dec 25. Res accepted. Continental menu. Bar from noon. Bkfst $6-$9. A la carte entrees: lunch $5-$13, dinner $5-$33. Sun brunch $7-$11. Specialties: Asian tuna, Floridian red snapper, broasted chestnut chicken. Parking. Outdoor dining. Adj to river. Jacket. Cr cds: A, D, DS, MC, V.

★ ★ **MILL RACE INN.** *4 E State St (60134). 630/232-2030. www.themill raceinn.com.* Hrs: 11:30 am-3 pm, 5-9 pm; Fri, Sat to 10 pm; Sun brunch 10 am-2 pm. Closed Dec 25. Res accepted. Bar. Lunch $6.25-$11.95, dinner $13.95-$23.95. Sun brunch $7.95-$12.95. Child's menu. Specializes in seafood, prime rib. Own pastries, desserts. Entertainment Wed, Fri, Sat. Valet parking. Gazebo dining. Country decor. 1842 blacksmith shop; fireplaces. On Fox River. Family-owned. Cr cds: A, D, MC, V.

Unrated Dining Spot

LITTLE TRAVELER ATRIUM CAFE. *404 S 3rd St (60134). 630/232-4200. www.littletraveler.com.* Hrs: 9:30 am-5 pm; Sat to 5:30 pm; buffet (exc Sat) 1 pm sitting. Closed Sun; also hols. Res accepted; required buffet lunch. A la carte entrees: lunch $2-$5. Buffet: lunch $7.50. Specialties: tea sandwich plate, seafood salad, Shanghai chicken salad. English-type tea room within Victorian mansion with boutique and specialty shops. Fashion show during wkday lunch buffet. Family-owned. Cr cds: DS, MC, V.

Glen Ellyn

See also Wheaton

Pop 26,999 **Elev** 750 ft **Area code** 630 **Zip** 60137

Information Chamber of Commerce, 490 Pennsylvania Ave; 630/469-0907

Web www.glen-ellyn.com

Glen Ellyn contains over 24 houses that are more than 100 years old and are listed as historic sites. Although not open to the public, these houses are identified by plaques and make for a pleasant walking tour. Most can be found between the 300 and 800 blocks on Main Street as well as on Forest and Park Streets north of the railroad. Glen Ellyn's many antique shops make the town popular with collectors and weekend browsers.

What to See and Do

Stacy's Tavern Museum. (1846) Old country inn was once a popular stagecoach stop for travelers going from Chicago to the Fox River Valley. Restored with period furnishings. (Mar-Dec, Wed, Sun, afternoons; closed hols) 557 Geneva Rd, at Main St. Phone 630/858-8696. **FREE**

Special Event

Taste of Glen Ellyn. Mid-May. Phone 630/469-0907.

Motel/Motor Lodge

★ ★ **HOLIDAY INN.** *1250 Roosevelt Rd (60137). 630/629-6000; fax 630/629-0025; toll-free 800/465-4329. www.holiday-inn.com.* 120 rms, 4 story. S, D $110; under 18 free. Crib free. Pet accepted, $25, some restrictions. TV; cable (premium). Heated pool. Complimentary coffee in lobby, rms. Restaurant 6:30 am-2 pm, 5-10 pm. Rm serv. Bar. Ck-out 1 pm. Coin lndry. Valet serv. Meeting rms. Business servs avail. In-rm modem link. Health club privileges. Exercise equipt. Cr cds: A, C, D, DS, JCB, MC, V.

[D] [🐾] [≈] [🏋] [≥] [🐾] [SC]

Restaurant

★ ★ **GREEK ISLANDS WEST.** *300 E 22nd St, Lombard (60148). 630/932-4545.* Hrs: 11 am-11 pm; Fri, Sat to midnight. Res accepted. Greek menu. Bar. A la carte entrees: lunch, dinner $4.75-$21.95. Child's menu. Specializes in seafood, authentic Greek cuisine. Own pastries. Greek, Mediterranean decor. Cr cds: A, D, DS, MC, V.

[D] [≥]

Glenview

See also Northbrook, Skokie, Wheeling, Wilmette

Pop 41,847 **Elev** 635 ft **Area code** 847 **Zip** 60025

Information Chamber of Commerce, 2320 Glenview Rd; 847/724-0900

Web glenviewchamber.com

What to See and Do

The Grove National Historic Landmark. This 124-acre nature preserve includes miles of hiking trails and three structures: the restored 1856 Kennicott House (tours Sun, Feb-Sept); the Interpretative Center (daily), a nature center museum; and the Redfield Center (now a banquet facility that is not open to the public), a house designed by George G. Elmslie, who studied under and worked with Louis Sullivan. During the 1930s, this stone house was lived in by author Donald Culross Peattie, who wrote *A Prairie Grove* about his experiences at the Grove. (See SPECIAL EVENTS) Park (daily; closed Jan 1, Dec 25). 1421 N Milwaukee Ave, just S of Lake Ave. Phone 847/299-6096. **FREE**

Hartung's Automotive Museum. Display of more than 100 antique autos, trucks, tractors, and motorcycles; many unrestored. License plate collection; 75 antique bicycles; promotional model cars; antique auto hub caps, radiator emblems, and auto mascots. Also includes some Model T Fords (1909-1926), a 1926 Hertz touring car, a 1932 Essex Terraplane, and other rare, classic automobiles. (Daily, hrs vary) 3623 W Lake St. Phone 847/724-4354. ¢¢

Special Events

Summer Festival. Glenview Rd. Entertainment, vendors, and food. Last Sat June. Phone 847/724-0900.

Civil War Living History Days. The Grove National Historic Landmark. Features realistic battle reenactment with hospital tent and camps of the period; participants in authentic clothing and uniforms. Exhibits, lectures, house tours. Last wkend July. Phone 847/299-6096.

Grovefest. The Grove National Historic Landmark. Crafts, music, activities, and food; costumed volunteers gather to re-create a typical afternoon of the mid-1800s. First Sun Oct. Phone 847/299-6096.

Motels/Motor Lodges

★★ **BAYMONT INN.** *1625 Milwaukee Ave (60025). 847/635-8300; fax 847/635-8166; toll-free 800/301-0200. www.baymontinns.com.* 150 rms, 3 story. S, D $69-$79; each addl $7; under 18 free. Crib free. Pet accepted, some restrictions. TV; cable (premium); VCR avail. Complimentary bkfst. Coffee in rms. Restaurant opp open 24 hrs. Ck-out noon. Coin lndry. Meeting rm. Business servs avail. In-rm modem link. Valet serv. Some refrigerators, microwaves. Cr cds: A, C, D, DS, MC, V.
D ⬚ ⬚ ⬚ SC

★★ **COURTYARD BY MARRIOTT.** *1801 Milwaukee Ave (60025). 847/803-2500; fax 847/803-2520. www.courtyard.com.* 149 rms, 12 suites, 3 story. S, D $99; suites $119; wkend rates. Crib free. TV; cable (premium). Indoor pool; whirlpool. Complimentary coffee in rms, lobby. Restaurant 6:30-10:30 am; Sat, Sun 7-11 am. Bar 4-11 pm. Ck-out noon. Coin lndry. Meeting rms. Business servs avail. In-rm modem link. Valet serv. Exercise equipt. Microwaves avail; refrigerator in suites. Balconies. Cr cds: A, C, D, DS, JCB, MC, V.
D ⬚ ⬚ ⬚ SC ⬚

★★ **FAIRFIELD INN.** *4514 W Lake Ave (60025). 847/299-1600; fax 847/803-9943; res 800/228-2800. www.fairfieldinn.com.* 138 rms, 3 story. Apr-Oct: S, D $74; each addl $4; under 18 free; lower rates rest of yr. Crib free. TV; cable (premium). Heated pool. Complimentary continental bkfst. Restaurant opp 11-2 am. Ck-out noon. Meeting rm. Business servs avail. In-rm modem link. Valet serv. Health club privileges. Cr cds: A, C, D, DS, MC, V.
D ⬚ ⬚ SC ⬚

All Suite

★★★ **DOUBLETREE GUEST SUITES.** *1400 Milwaukee Ave (60025). 847/803-9800; fax 847/803-0380. www.doubletree.com.* 252 suites, 7 story. S $160-$269; D $180-$289; each addl $10; under 17 free; wkend rates. Crib free. TV; cable (premium). Indoor pool; whirlpool. Restaurant 11 am-11 pm. Rm serv. Bar to 1 am. Coffee in rms. Ck-out noon. Coin lndry. Valet servs. Meeting rms. Business servs avail. In-rm modem link. Gift shop. Airport transportation. Exercise equipt; sauna. Health club privileges. Refrigerators, microwaves, wet bars. Cr cds: A, C, D, DS, ER, JCB, MC, V.
D ⬚ ⬚ ⬚ ⬚ ⬚ SC

Restaurants

★ **DAPPER'S.** *4520 W Lake Ave (60025). 847/699-0020.* Hrs: 5:30-1 am. Serv bar. Bkfst $2.70-$9.15, lunch $5.40-$7.95, dinner $7.40-$15.10. Complete meals: dinner $7.15-$15.35. Child's menu. Specializes in steak, Grecian chicken, fish. Own cheesecake, pastries. Cr cds: A, D, DS, MC, V.
D ⬚

★★ **DRAGON INN NORTH.** *1650 Waukegan Rd (IL 43) (60025). 847/729-8383.* Hrs: 11:30 am-9:30 pm; Fri to 10:30 pm; Sat 5-10:30 pm; Sun noon-9:30 pm. Closed July 4, Thanksgiving. Res accepted. Mandarin, Szechwan, Hunan menu. Bar. Lunch $4.95-$6.75, dinner $8.95-$16.95. Specialties: moo shu pork, orange beef, shrimp saute Hunan. Parking. Chinese decor. Cr cds: A, MC, V.
⬚

★ **MYKONOS.** *8660 Golf Rd, Niles (60714). 847/296-6777.* Hrs: 11 am-11 pm; Fri, Sat to midnight; Sun noon-11 pm. Res accepted. Greek menu. Bar. A la carte entrees: lunch from $4.50, dinner $7-$20. Specialties: whole sea bass, red snapper, octopus vinaigrette. Own pastries. Valet parking. Outdoor garden dining. Cr cds: A, DS, V.
D ⬚

★ **PERIYALI GREEK TAVERN.** *9860 Milwaukee Ave, Des Plaines (60016). 847/296-2232.* Hrs: 11 am-11 pm; Fri, Sat to midnight. Closed Thanksgiving. Res accepted. Greek menu. Bar. Lunch, dinner $6.25-$18.95. Specializes in fresh fish, wood-roasted chicken, lamb dishes. Parking. Out-

door dining. Greek village atmosphere. Cr cds: A, DS, MC, V.

D 🏴

★ **WILLOW ON WAGNER.** *1519
Wagner Rd (60025). 847/724-5100.*
Hrs: 11:30 am-2:30 pm, 5-9 pm; Fri,
Sat to 10:30 pm; Sun 4-9 pm. Closed
Dec 25. Res accepted. Lunch $4.95-
$8.50, dinner $7.95-$15.95. Child's
menu. Specializes in prime rib,
chicken, seafood. Parking. Overlooks
garden. Cr cds: A, C, D, DS, MC, V.

D

Grayslake

See also Gurnee, Libertyville, Waukegan

Pop 18,506 **Elev** 790 ft **Area code** 847
Zip 60030
Information Chamber of Commerce,
10 Seymour Ave; 847/223-6888

Special Event

Lake County Fair. Fairgrounds.
Rodeo, exhibits, contests, midway;
horse show, tractor and horse pulls.
Phone 847/223-2204. Late July.

Restaurant

★ ★ ★ **COUNTRY SQUIRE.** *19133
W IL 120 (60030). 847/223-0121.
www.csquire.com.* Hrs: 11 am-10 pm;
Sat to 11 pm; Sun 10 am-9 pm; Sun
brunch to 2 pm. Closed Mon. Res
accepted. Continental menu. Bar.
Lunch $7-$13, dinner $9.95-$21. Sun
brunch $7.95-$14.95. Child's menu.
Specialties: roast duckling, shrimp de
jonghe, veal Oscar. Entertainment
Fri-Sun. Parking. Restored Georgian
mansion (1938), once owned by
Wesley Sears; extensive gardens,
fountain. Cr cds: A, D, DS, MC, V.

D

Greenville

(F-4) *See also Vandalia*

Settled 1815 **Pop** 6,955 **Elev** 619 ft
Area code 618 **Zip** 62246
Information Chamber of Commerce,
405 S Third St; 618/664-9272
Web www.greenvilleillinois.com

This rural community, nestled in the
center of Bond County, is within
easy commuting distance of downtown St. Louis, Missouri. The community is host to a number of
manufacturing companies and the
home of Greenville College.

What to See and Do

Richard W. Bock Museum. Inside the
original Almira College house (1855)
is a collection of works by sculptor
Richard W. Bock (1865-1949), who,
between 1895-1915, executed a number of works for Frank Lloyd Wright-
designed buildings. Also on display
are Wright-designed prototypes of
leaded-glass windows and lamps for
Wright's Dana House in Springfield.
(Mon-Fri; limited hrs Sat; closed during summer, call for appt) Greenville
College, College Ave. Phone
618/664-2800 or 618/664-6724.
FREE

Motel/Motor Lodge

★ ★ **BEST WESTERN COUNTRY
VIEW INN.** *I-70 and IL 127 (62246).
618/664-3030; fax 618/664-3030; res
800/780-7234.* 83 rms, 2 story. May-
Sept: S $45.95-$53.95; D $51.95-
$61.95; each addl $4; under 17 free;
lower rates rest of yr. Crib $5. Pet
accepted, some restrictions; $2. TV;
cable. Heated pool. Complimentary
continental bkfst. Coffee in lobby.
Restaurant adj 6 am-10 pm. Ck-out
11 am. Meeting rm. Microwaves
avail. Exercise equipt. Cr cds: A, C,
D, DS, MC, V.

🖼️ 🐾 🧍 🏴 🐾 SC

Gurnee

See also Libertyville, Waukegan

Pop 28,834 **Elev** 700 ft **Area code** 847 **Zip** 60031
Information Lake County Chamber of Commerce, 5221 W Grand Ave, 60031-1818; 847/249-3800
Web www.lakecounty-il.org

What to See and Do

Gurnee Mills Mall. More than 250 stores can be found in this indoor mall; food courts. (Daily) I-94 at IL 132. Phone 847/263-7500 or 800/937-7467.

Six Flags Great America. This 200-acre entertainment center features rides, shows, shops, and restaurants. Among the rides and attractions are Deja Vu, the world's tallest and fastest suspending, looping boomerang coaster; The Giant Drop, a seated, vertical, high-speed drop; *Batman,* The Ride, a suspended looping thrill ride; Iron Wolf, a stand-up looping steel roller coaster; Shock-Wave, a steel roller coaster; American Eagle, a double-racing wooden roller coaster; Condor, a spinning thrill ride; water rides; and a children's area. Theaters feature live stage shows daily. (Fourth wk May-last wk Aug, daily; late Apr-fourth wk May and Sept-mid-Oct, wkends) Admission includes all rides and shows. On Grand Ave, off I-94, exit IL 132. Phone 847/249-1776. ¢¢¢¢¢

Motels/Motor Lodges

★★ **BAYMONT INN.** *5688 N Ridge Rd (60031). 847/662-7600; fax 847/662-5300; res 877/229-6668. www.baymontinns.com.* 106 rms, 4 story. Memorial Day-Labor Day: S, D $84-$104; suites $124; under 18 free; lower rates rest of yr. Crib free. Pet accepted. TV; cable (premium). Complimentary continental bkfst. Indoor pool; whirlpool. Complimentary coffee in rms. Restaurant adj 7 am-10 pm. Ck-out noon. Business servs avail. In-rm modem link. Coin lndry.

Meeting rm. Refrigerator, microwave in suites. Cr cds: A, C, D, DS, MC, V.

★★ **COMFORT INN.** *6080 Gurnee Mills Circle E (60031). 847/855-8866; fax 847/855-8866. www.comfortinn. com.* 63 rms, 3 story. June-Sept: S, D $69; each addl $5; suites $74.95; under 18 free; lower rates rest of yr. Crib free. TV; cable (premium), VCR avail (movies). Heated indoor pool; whirlpool. Complimentary continental bkfst. Restaurant opp 6 am-midnight. Ck-out 11 am. Meeting rm. Refrigerator, microwave in suites. Health club privileges. Cr cds: A, D, DS, MC, V.

★★ **FAIRFIELD INN.** *6090 Gurnee Mills Blvd (60031). 847/855-8868; fax 847/855-8868. www.fairfieldinn.com.* 63 rms, 3 story. Apr-Dec: S, D $89.95-$129.95; suites $114.95-$149.95; under 18 free; higher rates some hols; lower rates rest of yr. Crib free. TV; cable (premium). Indoor pool; whirlpool. Complimentary continental bkfst. Restaurant nearby. Ck-out noon. Meeting rm. Valet serv. Business servs avail. Refrigerator, microwave in suites. Health club privileges. Cr cds: A, C, D, DS, MC, V.

★★ **HAMPTON INN.** *5550 Grand Ave (60031). 847/662-1100; fax 847/662-2556; toll-free 800/426-7866. www.hamptoninn.com.* 134 rms, 5 story. Mid-May-mid-Sept: S, D $69; under 18 free; lower rates rest of yr. Crib free. TV; cable (premium), VCR avail. Heated pool. Complimentary continental bkfst. Restaurant nearby. Coffee in rms. Metting rms. Business servs avail. In-rm modem link. Sundries. Game rm. Coin lndry. Valet serv. Health club privileges. Refrigerators avail. Balconies. Six Flags Great America 2 blks. Cr cds: A, C, D, DS, ER, JCB, MC, V.

★★ **HOLIDAY INN.** *6161 W Grand Ave (60031). 847/336-6300; fax 847/336-6303; toll-free 800/465-4329. www.holiday-inn.com.* 223 rms, 4 story. S, D $99.99; suites $159; under 18 free. Crib free. TV; cable (premium). Heated indoor pool; whirlpool. Restaurant 6:30 am-10 pm. Rm serv. Bar 4 pm-1 am. Coffee, tea in rms. Ck-out noon. Coin lndry. Meeting rms. Business servs avail. In-rm modem link. Valet serv. Exercise equipt. Health club privileges. Game rm. Great America 1 mi. Cr cds: A, C, D, DS, JCB, MC, V.

B&B/Small Inn

★★ **SWEET BASIL HILL BED & BREAKFAST.** *15937 W Washington St (60031). 847/244-3333; fax 847/263-6693. www.sweetbasilhill. com.* 3 suites, 2 story, 1 cottage. S, D $95; cottage $175; wkly rates. TV; VCR. Complimentary full bkfst; evening snacks. Business servs avail. X-country ski on site. Hiking trails. Converted farmhouse on 7½ acres; sheep, llamas. Herb garden. Near Great America, Gurnee Mills Mall. Cr cds: A, C, D, DS, MC, V.

Havana

(D-4) *See also Petersburg*

Settled 1824 **Pop** 3,577 **Elev** 470 ft
Area code 309 **Zip** 62644
Information Chamber of Commerce, PO Box 116; 309/543-3528

Once a bustling steamboat and fishing port at the confluence of the Spoon and Illinois Rivers, Havana is now a quiet river town, important as a grain center with a few light industries. One of the famous Lincoln-Douglas debates took place in what is now Rockwell Park.

What to See and Do

Dickson Mounds State Museum. Exhibits include multimedia programs relating to Native American inhabitants over 12,000-yr time span. Also agricultural plot and remains of excavated houses. Picnic area. (Daily; closed hols) 5 mi NW via IL 78/97, on hill above Spoon and Illinois rivers. Phone 309/547-3721. **FREE**

Illinois River National Wildlife and Fish Refuges. These 4,488 acres are used as a resting, breeding, and feed-ing area for waterfowl. Concentrations of shorebirds (Aug-Sept). Eagles are seen here (Nov-Feb). Sportfishing (daily) and waterfowl hunting (fall) permitted in specified areas. Designated public-use areas open all yr. Interpretive nature trail; wheelchair access. 9 mi NE on Manito Rd. Contact Refuge Manager, US Fish and Wildlife Service, Illinois River National Wildlife and Fish Refuges, Rural Rte 2, PO Box 61B. Phone 309/535-2290. **FREE**

Special Event

Spoon River Scenic Drive Fall Festival. 5 mi NW on IL 78/97 to Dickson Mounds, then marked, circular route through Fulton County. Autumn drive through small towns and rolling, wooded countryside noted for fall color (complete drive 140 mi); 19th- and early 20th-century crafts, exhibits, demonstrations; antiques, collectibles; produce; food. First and second wkend Oct. Phone 309/647-8980.

Highland Park

(A-6) *See also Chicago, Highwood, Northbrook*

Settled 1834 **Pop** 31,365 **Elev** 690 ft
Area code 847 **Zip** 60035
Information Chamber of Commerce, 508 Central Ave, Suite 206; 847/432-0284
Web www.highland-park.com

What to See and Do

Francis Stupey Log Cabin. (1847) Oldest structure in town; restored with period furnishings. (May-Oct, Sat, Sun; also by appt) 1750 St. Johns Ave. Phone 847/432-7090. **FREE**

Highland Park Historical Society. Restored Victorian house (1871) has several period rooms; changing exhibits of local artifacts. On grounds is the Walt Durbahn Tool Museum with household items and primitive implements used in lumbering and local trades. (Daily; closed Mon, hols) Headquarters in Jean Butz

James Museum, 326 Central Ave. Phone 847/432-7090. **FREE**

Special Event

Ravinia Festival. On Green Bay Rd at Lake Cook Rd. Concerts by the Chicago Symphony Orchestra, guest soloists; chamber music, pop, jazz, and New Perspectives series; also dance and ballet. Pavilion and outdoor seating. Phone 847/266-5100. June-early Sept. On Green Bay Rd at Lake Cook Rd.

Motel/Motor Lodge

★ ★ **COURTYARD BY MARRIOTT.** *1505 Lake Cook Rd (60035). 847/831-3338; fax 847/831-0782. www. courtyard.com.* 149 units, 3 story. S, D $79; suites $109; under 18 free. Crib free. TV; cable (premium). Indoor pool; whirlpool. Complimentary coffee in rms. Restaurant 7 am-10 pm; Sat, Sun 6:30 am-11 pm. Rm serv. Bar 5-10 pm. Ck-out noon. Coin lndry. Meeting rms. Business servs avail. In-rm modem link. Valet serv. Sundries. Exercise equipt. Health club privileges. Refrigerator, microwave in suites. Some wet bars. Private patios, balconies. Cr cds: A, C, D, DS, JCB, MC, V.

D 🗭 🏊 🏃 🖼 🔥

Restaurants

★ **CAFE CENTRAL.** *455 Central Ave (60035). 847/266-7878.* Hrs: 11:30 am-9 pm; Fri, Sat to 10:30 pm; Sun 5-8 pm. Closed Mon; Jan 1, July 4, Dec 25. Res accepted (dinner). French menu. Bar. Lunch $6-$9, dinner $14-$18.50. Child's menu. Specialties: lamb shank, roasted duckling, bouillabaisse. Outdoor dining. Casual café dining. Totally nonsmoking. Cr cds: A, D, DS, MC, V.

D

★ ★ ★ ★ **CARLOS'.** *429 Temple Ave (60035). 847/432-0770. www.carlos-restaurant.com.* Even Chicago's most sophisticated diners travel to this north suburban outpost for a taste of the contemporary French cuisine. A vintage brick storefront is the unassuming home to renowned a la carte and multicourse degustation menus, as well as a 17,000-bottle wine cellar. Owners Debbie and Carlos Nieto, who opened the restaurant in 1981,

are impressively professional with no signs of pretense. Specializes in fresh seafood, game, fowl. Own pastries. Hrs: 5:30-9:30 pm. Closed Tues; hols. Res accepted. Serv bar. Wine cellar. A la carte entrees: dinner $25-$36.50. Degustation menu: dinner $70 and $100. Valet parking. Jacket. Cr cds: A, C, D, DS, MC, V.

★ **LITTLE SZECHWAN.** *1900 1st St (60035). 847/433-7007.* Hrs: 5-9:30 pm; Fri, Sat to 10:30 pm; Sun to 9 pm. Closed Thanksgiving. Res accepted. Szechwan, Mandarin menu. A la carte entrees: dinner $12.50-$15. Specialties: kung pao chicken, crispy duck, Taiwanese chicken rolls. Outdoor dining. Chinese decor; masks, costumes, murals. Totally nonsmoking. Cr cds: A, C, D, MC, V.

D

★ **PANDA PANDA SZECHWAN.** *1825 2nd St (60035). 847/432-9470.* Hrs: 11:30 am-9:30 pm; Fri, Sat to 10:30 pm. Closed Thanksgiving. Res accepted. Chinese menu. Bar. Lunch $5.50-$6.50, dinner $7.95-$24. Specialties: orange beef, smoked tea duck, pot stickers. Chinese decor; panda murals. Cr cds: A, MC, V.

🍴

★ ★ **TIMBERS CHARHOUSE.** *295 Skokie Valley Rd (60035). 847/831-1400.* Hrs: 11:30 am-10 pm; Fri to 10:30 pm; Sat noon-4 pm, 5-10:30 pm; Sun 4:30-8:30 pm. Closed most hols. Res accepted. Bar. Lunch $4.25-$11.95, dinner $7.95-$22.95. Child's menu. Specializes in chicken, barbecued ribs, steak. Own desserts. Parking. Cr cds: A, D, DS, MC, V.

D 🍴

Highwood

See also Highland Park

Pop 4,143 **Elev** 685 ft **Area code** 847 **Zip** 60040

B&B/Small Inn

★ ★ **DEER PATH INN.** *255 E Illinois Rd, Lake Forest (60045). 847/234-2280; fax 847/234-3352; toll-free 800/788-9480. www.dpihotel.com.* 54 rms, 3 story, 32 suites. S, D $155-

$205; each addl $10; suites $290-
$350. Crib $10. TV; cable (premium),
VCR avail. Complimentary full bkfst
buffet. Restaurant (see also ENGLISH
ROOM). Rm serv. Ck-out noon, ck-in
3 pm. Business center. In-rm modem
link. Luggage handling. Health club
privileges; $200. Some refrigerators,
microwaves, whirlpools. Built in
1929. Cr cds: A, C, D, DS, MC, V.

Restaurants

★★ **DEL RIO.** *228 Green Bay Rd
(60040). 847/432-4608.* Hrs: 5-10 pm;
Fri, Sat to 11 pm. Closed hols. Northern Italian menu. Bar. Dinner
$11.75-$24.50. Specializes in homemade pasta, seafood, veal. Parking.
Italian cafe decor. Cr cds: A, D, DS,
MC, V.

★ **EGG HARBOR CAFE.** *512 N
Western Ave, Lake Forest (60045).
847/295-3449. www.eggharborcafe.
com.* Hrs: 6:30 am-2 pm. Closed
Thanksgiving, Dec 25. Bkfst $3.95-
$7.95, lunch $4.95-$7.95. Child's
menu. Specializes in eggs, gourmet
pancakes, sandwiches. Country
decor; chicken and egg theme.
Totally nonsmoking. Cr cds: A, DS,
MC, V.

★★★ **ENGLISH ROOM.** *255 E Illinois St, Lake Forest (60045). 847/234-
2280.* Hrs: 6:30 am-2:30 pm, 5-9 pm;
Fri, Sat to 10 pm; Sun 11 am-2:30 pm
(brunch), 5-9 pm. Res accepted. Continental menu. Bar. Bkfst buffet $15.
Lunch $7.50-$18. A la carte entrees:
dinner $12-$37. Sun brunch $37.
Child's menu. Own desserts. Parking.
Outdoor dining. English manor
house decor; wall prints, antiques.
Jacket. Totally nonsmoking. Cr cds:
A, D, MC, V.

★★★ **FROGGY'S.** *306 Green Bay Rd
(60040). 847/433-7080.* Hrs: 11:30
am-2 pm, 5-10 pm; Fri to 11 pm; Sat
5-11 pm. Closed Sun; hols. French
menu. Bar. Wine list. Lunch $8.95-
$15.95, dinner $12.95-$17.95. Com-
plete meals: lunch $22.95, dinner
$28.95. Own pastries. Cr cds: C, D,
DS, MC, V.

★★★ **GABRIEL'S.** *310 Green Bay Rd
(60040). 847/433-0031.* Hrs: 5-10
pm. Closed Sun, Mon; hols. Res

accepted. French, Italian menu. Bar.
Wine cellar. A la carte entrees: din-
ner $24-$35. Complete meals: din-
ner $45. Specialties: rack of lamb,
Chilean sea bass, risotto. Own
desserts. Parking. Outdoor dining.
European bistro atmosphere. Cr cds:
A, C, D, DS, MC, V.

★★ **SOUTH GATE CAFE.** *655 Forest
Ave, Lake Forest (60045). 847/234-
8800. www.southgatecafe.com.* Hrs: 11
am-9 pm; Fri, Sat to 10 pm; Sun to 8
pm. Closed hols. Res accepted. Bar. A
la carte entrees: lunch $5.50-$12.95,
dinner $9.95-$22.00. Specializes in
fresh seafood, pasta, pizza. Own baking. In former fire station; overlooking town square. Cr cds: A, C, D, DS,
MC, V.

Hillside

See also Elmhurst, Hinsdale, La Grange

Pop 8,155 **Elev** 659 ft **Area code** 708
Zip 60162

Motel/Motor Lodge

★★ **HOLIDAY INN.** *4400 Frontage
Rd (60162). 708/544-9300; fax
708/544-9310; toll-free 800/465-4329.
www.holiday-inn.com.* 248 rms, 3
story. S, D $109; under 18 free;
wkend rates. Crib free. Pet accepted.
TV; cable (premium). Heated pool.
Restaurant 6 am-2 pm, 5-10 pm. Rm
serv. Bar 11 am-midnight, Fri, Sat to
2 am. Coffee, tea in rms. Ck-out
noon. Coin lndry. Meeting rms.
Business servs avail. In-rm modem
link. Valet serv. Golf privileges. Exercise equipt. Game rm. Health club
privileges. Cr cds: A, C, D, DS, JCB,
MC, V.

Hinsdale

See also Brookfield, Downers Grove, La Grange, Oak Brook

Pop 16,029 **Elev** 725 ft **Area code** 630
Zip 60521
Information Chamber of Commerce, 22 E First St; 630/323-3952

Named for a pioneer railroad director, Hinsdale includes what was once the town of Fullersburg. It is a quiet and secluded commuter community with a quaint shopping district.

What to See and Do

Robert Crown Center for Health Education. Programs to learn about the body's physical and emotional health. Displays include Valeda, a talking Plexiglas model. (Sept-June, Mon-Fri; closed hols) Res required. 21 Salt Creek Ln. Phone 630/325-1900. ¢¢

Motels/Motor Lodges

★★ **BAYMONT INN & SUITES.** *855 79th St, Willowbrook (60527). 630/654-0077; fax 630/654-0181. www.baymontinns.com.* 137 rms, 3 story. S, D $74-$94; under 18 free. Crib free. Pet accepted, some restrictions. TV; cable (premium). Complimentary bkfst. Restaurant nearby. Coffee in rms. Ck-out noon. Meeting rm. Business servs avail. Some refrigerators, microwaves. Cr cds: A, C, D, DS, MC, V.
🄳 🐾 ✈ ⊠ 🔥

★★ **FAIRFIELD INN.** *820 W 79th St, Willowbrook (60521). 630/789-6300; fax 630/789-6300. www.fairfieldinn. com.* 129 rms, 3 story. Mid-May-mid-Oct: S, D $69-$79; each addl $7; under 18 free; lower rates rest of yr. Crib free. TV; cable (premium). Heated pool. Complimentary continental bkfst. Restaurant nearby. Valet serv. Ck-out noon. Business servs avail. Health club privileges. Cr cds: A, C, D, DS, MC, V.
🄳 ⤫ ⊠ 🔥 SC

★★★ **HOLIDAY INN.** *7800 Kingery Hwy, Willowbrook (60521). 630/325-*

6400; fax 630/325-2362; toll-free 800/465-4329. www.holiday-inn.com. 220 rms, 3 story. S, D $119-$129; suites $150; studio rms $85; each addl $6; under 19 free; wkend rates. Crib free. TV; cable (premium), VCR (movies). Heated pool; lifeguard. Restaurant 6:30 am-2 pm, 5-10 pm. Rm serv. Bar 11-1 am; Fri, Sat to 2 am. Coffee, tea in rms. Ck-out noon. Meeting rms. Business servs avail. In-rm modem link. Coin lndry. Valet serv. Concierge. Gift shop. Free airport transportation. Exercise equipt; sauna. Refrigerators. Luxury level. Cr cds: A, C, D, DS, JCB, MC, V.
🄳 ⤫ 🕇 ✈ ⊠ 🔥

★★ **THE INN OF BURR RIDGE.** *300 S Frontage Rd, Burr Ridge (60527). 630/325-2900; fax 630/325-8907. www.innofburrridge.com.* 124 rms, 3 story. S $69-$89; each addl $5; suites $175; under 18 free. Crib free. TV; cable (premium) VCR (movies). Pool. Restaurant 6:30 am-2 pm, 5-10 pm. Rm serv. Bar. Ck-out noon. Coin lndry. Meeting rms. Valet serv. Airport transportation. Cr cds: A, C, D, DS, MC, V.
⤫ ⊠ 🔥 SC

★ **RED ROOF INN.** *7535 Kingery Hwy (Rte 83), Willowbrook (60521). 630/323-8811; fax 630/323-2714; toll-free 800/733-7663. www.redroof.com.* 109 rms, 3 story. S $59.99-$73.99; D $67.99-$79.99; under 18 free. Crib free. Pet accepted, some restrictions. TV; cable (premium). Complimentary coffee in lobby. Restaurant adj 8 am-10 pm. Ck-out noon. Business servs avail. In-rm modem link. Cr cds: A, C, D, DS, MC, V.
🄳 🐾 ⊠ 🔥 SC

Restaurant

★ **EGG HARBOR CAFE.** *777 N York Rd (60521). 630/920-1344.* Hrs: 6:30 am-2 pm. Closed Thanksgiving, Dec 25. Bkfst $2.95-$7.95, lunch $4.95-$7.95. Child's menu. Specialties: frittatas, egg white omelettes, California club sandwiches. Contemporary country American decor. Totally nonsmoking. Cr cds: A, DS, MC, V.
🄳

Homewood

Pop 19,543 **Elev** 650 ft **Area code** 708 **Zip** 60430

Located 24 miles south of Chicago's Loop, Homewood boasts two city blocks of fascinating art; New York muralist Richard Haas refurbished older business buildings with trompe l'oeil artwork on the backs of the structures.

What to See and Do

Midwest Carvers Museum. Housed in historic farmhouses, museum features hundreds of examples of carver's art, including ornate doll carriage, realistically carved bald eagle. Woodcarving classes; gift shop. (Mon-Sat; closed hols) NE via Thornton/Blue Island Rd to 16236 Vincennes Ave in South Holland. Phone 708/331-6011. **DONATION**

Motels/Motor Lodges

★★ **BEST WESTERN.** 17400 S Halsted St (60430). 708/957-1600; fax 708/957-1963. www.bestwestern.com. 188 rms, 5 story. S $68-$90; D $72-$95; each addl $5; suites $150-$400; under 18 free. Crib free. TV; cable (premium), VCR avail. Indoor/outdoor pool. Complimentary full bkfst. Restaurant 6 am-9 pm. Bar 11-1 am, Fri and Sat to 2 am. Ck-out 11 am. Meeting rms. Business servs avail. Bellhops. Valet serv. Sundries. Gift shop. Barber, beauty shop. Exercise equipt. Refrigerator in suites. Cr cds: A, C, D, DS, ER, JCB, MC, V.
D ⇌ 大 ⇖ ⚘

★ **ECONO LODGE.** 17225 Halsted St, South Holland (60473). 708/596-8700; fax 708/596-9978; toll-free 800/553-2666. www.econolodge.com. 102 rms, 2 story. S $49.95; D $58.95; each addl $7; under 18 free. Crib free. Pet accepted. TV, cable (premium). Complimentary continental bkfst. Restaurant adj open 24 hrs. Ck-out noon. Business servs avail. In-rm modem link. Valet serv. Cr cds: A, C, D, DS, MC, V.
D ⇒ ⇖ ⚘ SC

Restaurants

★ **AURELIO'S PIZZA.** 18162 Harwood Ave (60430). 708/798-8050. www.aureliospizza.com. Hrs: 11:30 am-10:30 pm; Fri to midnight; Sat 4 pm-midnight; Sun 4-10:30 pm. Closed hols. Italian menu. Bar. A la carte entrees: lunch, dinner $6-$12. Child's menu. Specializes in thin and thick-crust pizza, pasta. In former shipping warehouse. Outdoor patio. Family-owned. Cr cds: A, DS, MC, V.
D ⇥

★★ **DRAGON INN.** 18431 S Halsted St, Glenwood (60425). 708/756-3344. Hrs: 11:30 am-9:30 pm; Fri to 10:30 pm; Sat 4-10:30 pm; Sun noon-9:30 pm; lunch buffet to 2 pm. Closed Mon; Thanksgiving. Res accepted. Mandarin Chinese, American menu. Bar. Buffet: lunch $6.50. Lunch, dinner $12-$16. Specializes in Szechwan and Hunan dishes. Cr cds: A, D, MC, V.
⇥

Illinois Beach State Park

See also Gurnee, Waukegan

(3 mi N of Waukegan, E of IL 131; off Sheridan Rd in Zion).

This six-and-a-half-mile sand beach on Lake Michigan is a summer playground for more than two-and-a-half million visitors annually. The 4,160-acre park has facilities for beach swimming (no lifeguard) and beach houses available. Other activities include fishing and hiking. There is a boat marina in the park and a boat launch. Cross-country skiing is popular in winter. The park has picnic shelters, a playground, a concession area, and a lodge. Camping is permitted (standard fees). There is an interpretive center on the grounds. Contact Site Superintendent, Zion 60099; phone 847/662-4811 or 847/662-4828. **FREE**

Motel/Motor Lodge

★★ **ILLINOIS BEACH RESORT AND CONFRENCE CENTER.** *1 Lakefront Dr, Zion (60099). 847/625-7300; fax 847/625-0665. www.ilresorts.com.* 92 rms, 5 with shower only, 3 story. May-early Sept: S, D $79-$109; suites $160-$180; under 16 free; wkend rates; package plans; lower rates rest of yr. Crib free. TV; cable (premium). Heated indoor pool; whirlpool. Complimentary coffee in rms. Restaurant 7 am-10 pm. Rm serv. Bar. Ck-out 11 am. Meeting rms. Business servs avail. In-rm modem link. Shopping arcade. Exercise rm; sauna. Playground. Gift shop. Game rm. Hiking and biking trails. In-rm whirlpool in suites. Some balconies. Picnic tables, grills. On beach. Cr cds: A, C, D, DS, MC, V.

Itasca

See also Chicago, Chicago O'Hare Airport Area, Elmhurst, Schaumburg

Pop 8,302 **Elev** 686 ft **Area code** 630
Zip 60143

Hotel

★★ **WYNDHAM NORTHWEST CHICAGO.** *400 Park Blvd (60143). 630/773-4000; fax 630/773-4088. www.wyndham.com.* 408 rms, 12 story. S, D $169-$189; each addl $20; suites from $175; under 18 free; wkend rates. Crib free. TV; cable (premium). Indoor pool; whirlpool. Complimentary coffee in rms. Restaurant 6:30-11 pm. Bar 11:30 am-midnight. Ck-out noon. Convention facilities. Business center. In-rm modem link. Concierge. Shopping arcade. Barber, beauty shop. Coin lndry. Valet serv. Valet parking. Driving range. Airport transportation. Lighted tennis. Exercise rm; sauna, steam rms. Massage. Bathrm phone in suites. Cr cds: A, D, DS, MC, V.

Resorts

★★ **DORAL ENGLEWOOD CONFERENCE RESORT AND SPA.** *1401 Nordic Rd (60143). 630/773-1400; fax 630/773-1709; toll-free 800/487-1969. www.doralenglewood.com.* 295 rms, 9 story. S, D $109-$185; under 12 free; wkend rates. Crib free. TV; cable. 1 heated indoor pool; whirlpool. Dining rms 6:30 am-10 pm; wkends to 11 pm. Rm serv. Bar 11:30-1 am, Sat to 2 am; entertainment. Ck-out noon, ck-in 4 pm. Meeting rms. Business servs avail. Lighted tennis. 18-hole golf, greens fee $47-$52, pro, putting green. X-country ski on site. Game rm. Bowling. Exercise equipt; sauna. Refrigerator in suites. Balconies. Spacious grounds. Totally nonsmoking. Cr cds: A, C, D, DS, ER, JCB, MC, V.

★★★ **INDIAN LAKES RESORT.** *250 W Schick Rd, Bloomingdale (60108). 630/529-0200; fax 630/529-9271; toll-free 800/334-3417. www.indianlakesresort.com.* 310 rms, 6 story. S, D $99-$179; each addl $20; under 18 free; wkend rates; package plans. Crib free. TV; cable (premium). 2 pools, 1 indoor; whirlpool, poolside serv. Dining rm 6:30 am-10 pm. Rm serv. Bar 5 pm-midnight. Ck-out noon, ck-in 4 pm. Convention facilities. Business servs avail. In-rm modem link. Bellhops. Shopping arcade. Beauty shop. Rec dir. Lighted tennis. 36-hole golf, greens fee $50-$54, pro, putting green. Miniature golf. Exercise rm; sauna. Massage. Game rm. Some balconies. Cr cds: A, DS, MC, V.

Jacksonville

(D-3) *See also Springfield*

Founded 1825 **Pop** 18,940 **Elev** 613 ft
Area code 217 **Zip** 62650
Information Jacksonville Area Visitors & Conventions Bureau, 155 W Morton; 800/593-5678
Web www.jacksonvilleil.org

Although settled by Southerners, the town was largely developed by New

Englanders and became an important station on the Underground Railroad. A center of education, culture, and statesmanship, Jacksonville was named in honor of Andrew Jackson and nurtured the careers of Stephen A. Douglas and William Jennings Bryan. Lincoln often spoke here in the 1850s. Illinois College (1829), the oldest college west of the Alleghenies, and MacMurray College (1846) have played an important part in the city's history. This is also the home of the Illinois School for the Visually Impaired (1849), the Illinois School for the Deaf (1839), and Jacksonville Developmental Center (1846). Several national manufacturing companies are located here.

What to See and Do

Lake Jacksonville. Swimming (fee), fishing, boating (dock); camping (mid-Apr-mid-Oct; fee). 4½ mi SE off US 67.

Restaurant

★ ★ **LONZEROTTI'S.** *600 E State St (62650). 217/243-7151.* Hrs: 11 am-2 pm, 5-9 pm; Fri, Sat to 10 pm. Closed Sun; hols. Res accepted. Italian, American menu. Bar. Lunch $3.25-$6.25, dinner $6.95-$15.50. Child's menu. Specialties: lasagne, prime rib, chicken piccata. Own baking. Outdoor dining. In restored Chicago and Alton Railroad depot (1909). Cr cds: A, DS, MC, V.

D SC →

Joliet

(B-6) *See also Aurora, Lockport, Morris*

Settled 1831 **Pop** 106,221 **Elev** 564 ft **Area code** 815

Information Heritage Corridor Convention and Visitors Bureau, 81 N Chicago St, 60432; 815/727-2323 or 800/926-2262

Web www.heritagecorridorcvb.com

The Des Plaines River, the Chicago Sanitary and Ship Canal, and railroad freight lines triggered Joliet's growth as a center of commerce and industry. The canal's Brandon Road Locks, to the south of Joliet, are among the largest in the world, and the canal continues to carry many millions of tons of barge traffic annually through the city. Joliet once supplied limestone (Joliet/Lemont) to much of the nation and was once a major center for steel production. Although Joliet was named in honor of Louis Jolliet, the French-Canadian explorer who visited the area in 1673, it was incorporated in 1837 as Juliet, companion to the nearby town of Romeo (now renamed Romeoville).

What to See and Do

Bicentennial Park Theater/Band Shell Complex. Joliet Drama Guild and other productions (fee). Also outdoor concerts in band shell (June-Aug, Thurs eves). Historic walks. (See SPECIAL EVENTS) 201 W Jefferson St. Phone 815/724-3760. **FREE**

Empress **Casino Joliet.** (Daily) I-55 exit 248, left 3 mi to Empress Ln. Phone 888/436-7737.

Harrah's Joliet Casino. (Daily) Near I-55 and I-80. Downtown, at 150 N Joliet St. **FREE**

Pilcher Park. Walking, driving, and bicycle trails; nature center (daily), greenhouse, picnicking, playground. Off US 30, on Gougar Rd. Phone 815/741-7277.

Rialto Square Theatre. (1926) Performing arts center, designed by the Rapp brothers, is considered one of the most elaborate and beautiful of old 1920s movie palaces. Tours (Tues and by appt). 102 N Chicago St. Phone 815/726-6600. Tours ¢¢

Special Events

Festival of the Gnomes. Bicentennial Park. Celebration includes stage performances of gnome legends, gnome-related arts and crafts, refreshments. Costumed gnomes. Sat early Dec. Phone 815/740-2216.

Route 66 Raceway. 3200 S Chicago St. Facility includes two-mi road course, off-road and motorcross track. Late May-Sept. Phone 815/722-5500.

Waterway Daze. Bicentennial Park, along the waterway wall. Features parade of decorated, lighted water-craft; food, entertainment. Three days early Aug. Phone 815/724-3760.

Motels/Motor Lodges

★★ **COMFORT INN NORTH.** *3235 Norman Ave (60435). 815/436-5141; fax 815/436-5141. www.comfortinn. com.* 64 rms, 3 story. May-Sept: S $64-$94; D $74-$104; each addl $6; under 18 free; higher rates special events; lower rates rest of yr. Crib free. Pet accepted, some restrictions. TV; cable (premium). Indoor pool; whirlpool. Complimentary continental bkfst. Restaurant nearby. Ck-out 11 am. Refrigerators avail. Health club privileges. Cr cds: A, D, DS, MC, V.

★★ **COMFORT INN SOUTH.** *135 S Larkin Ave (60436). 815/744-1770; fax 815/744-1770; toll-free 800/228-5150. www.comfortinn.com.* 65 rms, 2 story. S $54.95-$89.95; D $64.95-$89.95; each addl $6; under 18 free. Crib free. TV; cable (premium). Indoor pool. Complimentary continental bkfst. Restaurant nearby. Ck-out 11 am. Meeting rm. Business servs avail. Health club privileges. Some refrigerators, microwaves. Cr cds: A, C, D, DS, MC, V.

★ **MANOR MOTEL.** *23926 W Eames St, Channahon (60410). 815/467-5385; fax 815/467-1617. www.manor-motel.com.* 100 rms, 1-2 story. S, D $35-$45; each addl $6; under 12 free; wkly. Crib $6.30. Pet accepted. TV; cable (premium). Pool. Complimentary coffee in lobby. Restaurant nearby. Ck-out 11 am. Business servs avail. Cr cds: A, C, D, DS, MC, V.

★ **MOTEL 6 SOUTH.** *1850 McDonough St (60436). 815/729-2800; fax 815/729-9528; toll-free 800/466-8356. www.motel6.com.* 129 rms, 2 story. S $35.99; D $41.99; each addl $6; under 17 free. Play pens. Pet accepted, some restrictions. TV; cable (premium). Complimentary coffee in lobby. Restaurant opp 6 am-10 pm. Ck-out noon. Business servs avail. Coin lndry. Cr cds: A, MC, V.

★ **SUPER 8 MOTEL.** *1730 McDonough St (60436). 815/725-8855; fax 815/725-2975; toll-free 800/800-8000. www.super8.com.* 64 rms, 2 story. S $48-$60; D $53-$66; each addl $6; under 17 free. TV; cable (premium). Complimentary continental bkfst. Coffee in rms. Restaurant nearby. Ck-out 11 am. Meeting rm. Business servs avail. Golf privileges. Cr cds: A, C, D, DS, MC, V.

Restaurants

★★ **SECRETS RIBS & MORE.** *2222 W Jefferson St (60435). 815/744-3745.* Hrs: 3:30-10 pm; Fri, Sat to 11 pm; Sun 11:30 am-10 pm. Closed Mon; July 4, Dec 25. Res accepted. Bar to 2 am. Dinner $7.50-$16.95. Child's menu. Specializes in ribs, steak, fresh seafood. Entertainment Wed-Sat. Cr cds: A, D, DS, MC, V.

★ **WHITE FENCE FARM.** *Joliet Rd, Romeoville (60439). 630/739-1720.* Hrs: 5-9 pm; Sat 4-9 pm; Sun noon-8 pm. Closed Mon; Thanksgiving, Dec 24, 25; also Jan-Feb. Serv bar. Dinner $10.65-$14.95. Child's menu. Specializes in chicken, aged steaks. Antiques; car museum. Children's zoo adj. Family-owned. Cr cds: A, D, DS, MC, V.

Kankakee (C-6)

Founded 1855 **Pop** 27,491 **Elev** 663 ft
Area code 815 **Zip** 60901

Information Kankakee River Valley Chamber of Commerce, PO Box 905; 815/933-7721

Web www.visitkankakee.com

Kankakee was originally a part of the old French settlement of Bourbonnais but was incorporated as a separate community around the Illinois Central rail lines and the river in the 1850s. The region retains early French characteristics in its old buildings and in its culture. Limestone quarried from the riverbed was used to erect many area walls.

What to See and Do

Antique shopping. There are over 600 antique dealers in the area, including the **Kankakee Antique Mall** at 147 S Schuyler Ave, the largest in Illinois with over 50,000 sq ft and 225 dealers. Contact the Convention & Visitors Bureau for a complete list of shops. Daily; closed hols. Phone 815/937-4957.

Gladiolus fields. More than 150,000 flowers are harvested here, from early summer to the first frost. E on IL 17 to Momence.

Kankakee County Historical Society Museum. History of Kankakee County. George Gray Barnard sculptures; also Native American artifacts, Civil War relics, toys, costumes, dishes; historical library. Adj is the 1855 house in which Governor Len Small was born; many original furnishings, temp exhibits. Also on property is restored, one-rm Taylor School (1904-1954). Gift shop. (Mon-Thurs; Sat and Sun afternoons; closed hols) Water St and 8th Ave, in Small Memorial Park. Phone 815/932-5279. **DONATION**

Kankakee River State Park. Approx 4,000 acres. Woodlands on both banks of the Kankakee River and canyon of Rock Creek. Fishing, boating (canoe rentals; ramp); hunting, hiking, x-country skiing, snowmobiling, picnicking, game and playground facilities, concession, camping. Interpretive program. 8 mi NW on IL 102. Phone 815/933-1383. **FREE**

Olivet Nazarene University. (1907) 3,400 students. On 200-acre campus are 29 major buildings including the Strickler Planetarium and Science Museum, Benner Library, Larsen Fine Arts Center; Snowbarger Athletic Park; Parrott Convocation and Athletic Center & Weber Center. Tours. 3 mi N on US 45/52 at IL 102 in Bourbonnais. Phone 815/939-5011.

River excursions. Canoe trips on the Kankakee river ranging from two hrs-full day. Canoes, kayaks, paddles, life jackets, and transportation provided. (Apr-mid-Oct, daily) Res suggested. Contact Reed's Canoe Trips, 907 N Indiana Ave. Phone 815/932-2663. ¢¢¢¢

Special Events

Kankakee River Valley Bicycle Classic. Late June. Phone 309/852-2141.

Kankakee River Fishing Derby. Ten days late June.

Kankakee County Fair. Fairgrounds. First wk Aug. Phone 815/932-6714.

Gladiolus Festival. Gladiolus fields in Momence. Thousands of visitors gather for celebration that includes parades, flower shows, antique car show. Second wkend Aug. Phone 815/472-6353.

Kankakee River Valley Regatta. Features the National OPC championships for power boats; raft races, carnival, entertainment. Labor Day wkend.

Kewanee

(B-4) *See also Bishop Hill*

Pop 12,944 **Elev** 820 ft **Area code** 309 **Zip** 61443
Information Chamber of Commerce, 113 E 2nd St; 309/852-2175
Web www.kewanee-il.com

What to See and Do

Historic Francis Park. Within this 40-acre park is Woodland Palace, a unique house built by Fred Francis, inventor, mechanical engineer, artist, and poet. Francis began the house in 1889, incorporating many early forms of modern conveniences, including an air-cooling system, water-purification system, automatically opening and closing doors, and circulating air. Also here is miniature log cabin built by Francis as a memorial to his parents. Hiking, picnicking, playground, camping. (See SPECIAL EVENTS) (Mid-Apr-Oct, daily) 4 mi E on US 34. Phone 309/852-0511. Tours of Woodland Palace ¢

Johnson Sauk Trail State Park. A focal point of this 1,361-acre park is Ryan's Round Barn, a massive cattle barn that contains interpretive exhibits; also 58-acre artificial lake. Fishing, boating (rentals); hiking, ice-skating, snowmobiling, x-country skiing, picnicking, camping (electric hookups, dump station). Standard fees. (See SPECIAL EVENTS) (Daily) 5 mi N on IL 78. Phone 309/853-5589. **FREE**

Special Events

Sauk Trail Heritage Days. Francis Park and Johnson Sauk Trail State Park. Four-day celebration including powwow, Native American crafts and storytelling. Railroad display and demonstrations. Tours. Food. Children's activities. Fireworks. Wkend of July 4. Phone 309/853-8307.

Hog Capital of the World Festival. Midway, entertainment, arts and crafts, variety of pork dishes. Labor Day wkend. Phone 309/852-2175.

Motel/Motor Lodge

★ **KEWANEE MOTOR LODGE.** *400 S Main St (61443). 309/853-4000; fax 309/853-4000.* 29 rms, 2 story. S $40-$45; D $47.50-$52.50; each addl $5. Crib $5. Pet accepted. TV; cable (premium). Complimentary coffee in lobby. Restaurant adj 6:30 am-11 pm; Fri, Sat 24hrs. Ck-out 11 am. Business servs avail. Some refrigerators, microwaves. Cr cds: D, DS, MC, V.

D 🔻 ⊠ 🐾 SC

Restaurants

★ **ANDRIS WAUNEE FARM.** *S on US 34/IL 78, Kewaunee (61443). 309/852-2481.* Hrs: 5-11 pm; Fri, Sat to midnight. Closed Sun; hols. Res accepted. Polynesian, American menu. Bar. Dinner $4.50-$13.95. Child's menu. Specializes in steak, prime rib, haddock. Salad bar. 3 dining rms, one with Polynesian theme. Entertainment Sat. Family-owned. Cr cds: DS, MC, V.

D SC ⊣

★★ **CELLAR.** *137 S State St, Geneseo (61254). 309/944-2177.* Hrs: 5-9 pm; Fri, Sat to 10 pm; Sun 11:30 am-8 pm. Closed Mon; Dec 24, 25. Res accepted. Bar 4 pm-midnight. Dinner $9.95-$27.95. Child's menu. Specializes in charcoal-broiled shrimp, steak, ribs. Casual dining in basement of downtown commercial building; original artwork. Cr cds: A, DS, MC, V.

D ⊣

La Grange

See also Brookfield, Cicero, Elmhurst, Hinsdale, Oak Brook

Pop 15,608 **Elev** 650 ft **Area code** 708 **Zip** 60525
Information West Suburban Chamber of Commerce, 47 S 6th Ave; 708/352-0494
Web www.westsuburbanchamber.org

What to See and Do

Historic District. Bordered by 47th St on the south, Brainard Ave on the west, and 8th Ave on the east, the area is split by the Burlington Northern Railroad tracks; an area north of the tracks, roughly bordered by Stone and Madison Aves, is also part of the Historic District. Here are a number of historically and culturally significant homes dating from the late 19th and early 20th centuries; included are houses designed by such prominent architects as Frank Lloyd Wright, J. C. Llewelyn, E. H. Turnock, and John S. Van Bergen.

Special Event

Pet Parade. First begun in 1946, this parade attracts thousands of visitors each yr. First Sat June. Phone 708/352-0494.

Motels/Motor Lodges

★★ **COUNTRYSIDE INN.** *5631 S LaGrange Rd (60525). 708/352-2480; fax 708/354-0998.* 47 rms, 1-2 story. June-Nov: S $56-$66; D $71-$76; each addl $5; under 12 free; lower rates rest of yr. Crib free. TV; cable (premium). Heated pool. Complimentary continental bkfst, beverages in lobby. Restaurant nearby. Ck-out noon. Some refrigerators, microwaves. Cr cds: A, D, DS, MC, V.

D ⊠ ⊠ 🐾

★★ **HAMPTON INN COUNTRYSIDE.** *6251 Joliet Rd, Countryside (60525). 708/354-5200; fax 708/354-1329; toll-free 800/426-7866. www.hamptoninn.com.* 108 rms, 6 story. S $90; D $95; under 18 free. Crib free. TV; cable (premium). Pool privileges. Complimentary continental bkfst. Ck-out noon. Business servs avail. In-

A foggy Illinois sunrise

rm modem link. Cr cds: A, D, DS, MC, V.

★★ **HOLIDAY INN COUNTRYSIDE - LAGRANGE.** *6201 Joliet Rd, Countryside (60525). 708/354-4200; fax 708/354-4241; toll-free 800/441-6041. www.holiday-inn.com.* 305 rms, 7 story. S, D $99; suites $154-$237; under 18 free; package plans. Crib free. TV; cable (premium). Indoor pool; wading pool, whirlpool, poolside serv. Complimentary coffee. Complimentary bkfst. Restaurant 6 am-10 pm. Rm serv. Bar 4 pm-1 am. Ck-out noon. Meeting rm. Business servs avail. In-rm modem link. Sundries. Exercise equipt; sauna. Game rm. Rec rm. Cr cds: A, C, MC, V.

Libertyville

See also Grayslake, Gurnee

Founded 1836 **Pop** 20,742 **Elev** 700 ft **Area code** 847 **Zip** 60048
Information Chamber of Commerce, 731 N Milwaukee Ave; 847/680-0750

Marlon Brando, Helen Hayes, and Adlai Stevenson are a few of the famous personalities who have lived in Libertyville. The St. Mary of the Lake Theological Seminary (Roman Catholic) borders the town; there are four lakes near the village limits.

What to See and Do

Cuneo Museum & Gardens. Opulent Venetian-style mansion featuring great hall with arcade balconies, chapel with stained glass and fresco ceiling, ship's room with hidden bookshelves. Collection of master paintings, 17th-century tapestries, Oriental rugs, Capo di Monte porcelain. 75-acre grounds includes fountains, gardens, conservatory. (Tues-Sun) N on IL 21, then W on IL 60 in Vernon Hills at 1350 N Milwaukee. Phone 847/362-2025. ¢¢¢

David Adler Cultural Center. The summer residence of the distinguished neoclassical architect David Adler. Folk concerts and children's events (fee for all). Exhibits and tours. 1700 N Milwaukee Ave. Phone 847/367-0707. **FREE**

Lambs Farm. Includes children's farmyard, small animal nursery, miniature golf (fees), thrift shop, country store, bakery, restaurant. Hay rides, bounce house, discovery center, pet shop, miniature train rides (fee). Gift shops. Nonprofit residential and vocational community benefitting mentally retarded adults. (Daily; closed hols) Jct I-94 and IL 176 exit. Phone 847/362-0098. **FREE**

Motels/Motor Lodges

★★ **BEST WESTERN HITCH INN POST.** *1765 N Milwaukee Ave (60048). 847/362-8700; fax 847/362-8725; toll-free 800/780-7234. www.bestwestern. com.* 128 rms, 1-2 story. S $59-$69; D $79-$99; suites from $99; under 12 free. Crib $3. TV; cable (premium). VCR avail. Indoor pool; whirlpool. Complimentary continental bkfst. Ck-out noon. Coin lndry. Business servs avail. In-rm modem link. Valet serv. Gift shop. Exercise equipt. Game rm. Some refrigerators, microwaves. Automobile museum on site. Cr cds: A, C, D, DS, MC, V.

★★ **DAYS INN.** *1809 N Milwaukee Ave (60048). 847/816-8006; fax 847/816-9771; toll-free 800/329-7466. www.daysinn.com.* 91 rms, 3 story. Mid-June-mid-Sept: S, D $55-$70; each addl $5; under 18 free. Crib free. Pet accepted. TV; cable (premium). Heated pool. Complimentary continental bkfst. Restaurant nearby. Ck-out noon. Some refrigerators. Cr cds: A, D, DS, MC, V.

Restaurants

★★ **GALE STREET INN.** *906 Diamond Lake Rd, Mundelein (60060). 847/566-1090.* Hrs: 11 am-10 pm; Fri, Sat to midnight. Closed Mon; Thanksgiving, Dec 25. Res accepted. Bar. Lunch $3.95-$6.95, dinner $7.95-$22.95. Specializes in barbecued baby-back ribs, prime rib, steak. Salad bar. Entertainment Tues-Sat. Patio dining. Multi-level dining overlooking Diamond Lake. Nautical decor. Cr cds: A, C, D, DS, MC, V.

★ **THE LAMBS FARM COUNTRY INN.** *At jct I-94 and IL 176 (60048). 847/362-5050.* Hrs: 11 am-8 pm; Sun to 7 pm; Sun brunch 10:30 am-2:30 pm. Closed hols. Res accepted; required Fri-Sun (summer). Serv bar. Lunch $5-$8, dinner $7-$14. Sun brunch $12.95. Child's menu. Specialties: fried chicken, prime rib, barbecued ribs. Salad bar. Own baking. Country inn atmosphere. Petting zoo adj. Cr cds: A, D, DS, MC, V.

★★★ **TAVERN IN THE TOWN.** *519 N Milwaukee Ave (IL 21) (60048). 847/367-5755.* Hrs: 11:30 am-2 pm, 6-9 pm; Fri, Sat from 6 pm. Closed Sun; hols. Res accepted. Continental menu. Bar. Wine cellar. Lunch $6.95-$11.95, dinner $12.95-$25. Specializes in grilled fish, seasonal game, roasted beef tenderloin. Cr cds: A, D, DS, MC, V.

Lincoln (D-4)

See also Bloomington, Decatur, Springfield

Founded 1853 **Pop** 15,369 **Elev** 591 ft
Area code 217 **Zip** 62656
Information Abraham Lincoln Tourism Bureau of Logan County, 303 S Kickapoo St; 217/732-8687
Web www.logancountytourism.org

Of all the cities named for Abraham Lincoln, this is the only one named with his knowledge and consent and before he was elected president. Lincoln participated in the legal work involved in the organization of the town site and its incorporation as the seat of Logan County. Later he acquired a lot here as compensation for a note he had endorsed.

What to See and Do

Mount Pulaski Courthouse State Historic Site. (1848) This restored Greek Revival building served as county courthouse until 1855. It is one of two surviving Eighth Circuit courthouses in Illinois visited by Lincoln. Interpretive program. (Tues-Sat afternoons; closed hols) 12 mi SE on IL 121, in Mount Pulaski. Phone 217/792-3919. **DONATION**

Postville Court House State Historic Site. Replica on site of original courthouse that Henry Ford acquired and restored for his Greenfield Village museum (see DEARBORN, MI). Lincoln practiced law in the original courthouse twice a yr while Postville was the county seat (1840-1848). Interpretive program. (See SPECIAL EVENTS) (Fri and Sat afternoons; closed hols) 914 5th St, I-55 Business on the W side of town. Phone 217/732-8930. **DONATION**

Special Events

Logan County Fair. Fairgrounds. Tractor pulls, agricultural and farm machinery exhibits; horse races; livestock shows. Early Aug. Phone 217/732-3311.

1800s Craft Fair. Postville Court House. Artisans demonstrate skills from 1800s, including blacksmithing, quilting, wood carving, and broom making. Traditional music. Late Aug. Phone 217/732-8930.

Abraham Lincoln National Railsplitter Contest & Crafts Festival. Fairgrounds. Contests, entertainment, flea market. Mid-Sept. Phone 217/732-7146.

Motels/Motor Lodges

★ **BUDGET INN.** *2011 N Kickapoo St (62656). 217/735-1202; fax 217/735-1202.* 60 rms. S, D $39-$60; each addl $5; under 12 free. Crib free. Pet accepted, some restrictions; $10/day. TV; cable (premium). Indoor pool. Restaurant nearby. Ck-out noon. Business servs avail. Sundries. Cr cds: A, C, D, DS, MC, V.

D 🐾 ≋ 🔥 SC

★ ★ **COMFORT INN.** *2811 Woodlawn Rd (62656). 217/735-3960; fax 217/735-3960; toll-free 800/221-2222. www.comfortinn.com.* 52 rms, 2 story, 6 suites. S $46.95-$62.95; D $49.95-$62.95; each addl $5; suites $54.95-$64.95; under 18 free. Crib free. Pet accepted. TV; cable (premium), VCR avail. Indoor pool; whirlpool. Complimentary continental bkfst. Restaurant adj 5:30 am-11 pm. Ck-out 11 am. Meeting rms. Business servs avail. Health club privileges. Game rm. Refrigerator, microwave in suites. Cr cds: A, C, D, DS, MC, V.

D 🐾 ≋ 🔀 🔥 SC

Lincoln's New Salem State Historic Site

2 mi S on IL 97.

The wooded, 700-acre park incorporates a complete reconstruction, based on original maps and family archives, of New Salem as the village appeared when Lincoln lived there (1831-1837). Authentic reconstruction began in the early 1930's, with much of the work carried out by the New Deal's Civilian Conservation Corps (CCC). Today, New Salem con-

sists of 12 timber houses; a school; and ten shops, stores, and industries, including the Denton Offutt store (where Lincoln first worked), the Lincoln-Berry store, the Rutledge tavern, and the saw and gristmill. The only original building is the Onstot cooper shop, which was discovered in Petersburg and returned to its original foundation in 1922. Interior furnishings are, for the most part, authentic to the 1830's period of Lincoln's residency. A variety of programs are offered throughout the yr: self-guided tours; historical demonstrations; interpreters in period clothing; scheduled special events (see Petersburg's SPECIAL EVENTS); rides in horse-drawn wagon. Visitor center offers 180-min orientation film; exhibits. Picnicking, concession. Gift shop. Camping, tent and trailer sites (standard fees). (Daily; closed hols)

What to See and Do

Kelso Hollow Outdoor Theatre. Performances nightly (early June-late Aug, Thurs-Sun). Phone 800/710-9290. ¢¢¢

***Talisman* Riverboat.** Replica of *Talisman,* small riverboat that went up the Sangamon River in Lincoln's day, offers hrly trips in season. (May-Labor Day, Tues-Sun; after Labor Day-Oct, Sat and Sun only) Dock near gristmill, across IL 97 from park. Phone 217/632-7681. ¢¢

Lockport

See also Joliet

Founded 1836 **Pop** 15,191 **Elev** 604 ft
Area code 815 **Zip** 60441
Information Chamber of Commerce, 132 E 9th; 815/838-3357
Web www.lockport.org

Lockport was founded as headquarters of the Illinois and Michigan Canal. In its heyday, the town boasted five different locks (four remain). Shipbuilding was once an important industry. The Old Canal Town National Historic District preserves several buildings from this bygone era.

What to See and Do

Illinois and Michigan Canal Museum. (1837) Includes artifacts, pictures, and documents relating to the construction and operation of the canal. Guided tours by costumed docents. (Daily, afternoons; closed hols, also wks of Thanksgiving and Dec 25) Canal Commissioner's office, 803 S State St. Phone 815/838-5080. **FREE** Also here are

Gaylord Building. (1838) Includes the Lockport Gallery, a branch site of the Illinois State Museum, which features art of various media by the state's past and present artists (Tues-Sun). Also in the building is the I & M Canal Visitor Center with interpreters and theater productions that highlight the area (Wed-Sun), and restaurant with views of the canal (Tues-Sun). 200 W 8th St. Phone 815/838-7400.

Old Stone Annex Building. Depicts early banking history and other exhibits. (Mid-Apr-Oct, daily) **FREE** Adj is the

Pioneer Settlement. Log cabins, village jail, root cellar, tinsmith and blacksmith shops, workshop, one-room schoolhouse, mid-19th century farmhouse, smokehouse, privy, and railroad station. (Mid-Apr-Oct, afternoons) **FREE**

Special Events

Old Canal Days. Pioneer craft demonstrations, horse-drawn wagon tours, I & M Canal walking tours, Lockport prairie tours, museum open house, races, games, carnival, entertainment, food. Third wkend June. Phone 815/838-4744.

Advil Western Open Golf Tournament. Approx 8 mi N via Archer Ave, at Cog Hill Golf Course in Lemont. Early July. Phone 630/257-5872.

Restaurants

★★ **PUBLIC LANDING.** *200 W 8th St (60441). 815/838-6500.* Hrs: 11:30 am-2 pm, 5-9 pm; Fri, Sat to 10 pm; Sun 1-7 pm. Closed Mon. Bar. A la carte entrees: lunch $5.95-$8.95. Dinner $12.95-$22.95. Child's menu.

Specializes in seafood, chicken, prime rib. Own pastries. Built 1838; an Illinois Historic Landmark. Overlooks Illinois and Michigan Canal. Regional museum, art gallery adj. Cr cds: MC, V.

[D] [≈]

★★★ **TALLGRASS.** *1006 S State (60441). 815/838-5566.* Hrs: 6-9 pm. Closed Mon, Tues; hols. Res required. French menu. Bar. Wine cellar. Prix fixe: dinner $45, $55. Specialties: lobster souffle, tower of Belgian chocolate. Own baking. Cr cds: MC, V.

[D]

Macomb

(C-3) *See also Galesburg, Monmouth*

Founded 1830 **Pop** 18,558 **Elev** 700 ft
Area code 309 **Zip** 61455
Information Macomb Area Convention and Visitors Bureau, 201 S Lafayette St; 309/833-1315
Web www.macomb.com

Originally known as Washington, the town was renamed to honor General Alexander Macomb, an officer in the War of 1812. Macomb is best known as the home of Western Illinois University.

What to See and Do

Argyle Lake State Park. The park has 1,700 acres with a 95-acre lake. Fishing, boating (ramp, rentals; motors, ten-hp limit); hunting, hiking, x-country skiing, snowmobiling, picnicking, playground, concession, shelter house, camping (showers). Standard fees. (Daily) 7 mi W on US 136, then 1½ mi N. Phone 309/776-3422. **FREE**

Spring Lake Park. On 300 acres. Fishing; picnicking, camping (fee). 3 mi N on US 67, then 2 mi W, then 1 mi N. Phone 309/833-2052. **FREE**

Western Illinois University. (1899) 12,000 students. The 1,050-acre campus includes an art gallery (Mon-Fri, free); 600,000 volume library; Illinois/National Business Hall of Fame in Stipes Hall; agricultural experiment station at north edge of campus; Geology Museum, first floor Tillman Hall; and a nine-hole public golf course, Tower Rd (Apr-Oct, daily; fee). One University Circle, NW edge of city. Phone 309/298-1993. Also on campus are

Biological Sciences Greenhouse. Gardens and nature area; includes tropical and temperate plants, native aquatic, prairie, and woodland plants and herbs. (Mon-Fri) S of Waggoner Hall. Phone 309/298-1004. **FREE**

WIU Museum. Houses antique farm equipment, early 1900s store and medical exhibits, trapping equipment; various artifacts of the region. Extensive Civil War collection (Tues-Sat) 201 S Lafayette. Phone 309/833-1315. **FREE**

Motel/Motor Lodge

★★ **DAYS INN.** *1400 N Lafayette St (61455). 309/833-5511; fax 309/836-2926. www.daysinn.com.* 144 rms, 2 story. S, D $50-$95; each addl $6; suites $95-$125; higher rates: Labor Day, special events. Crib free. TV; cable (premium); VCR avail. Pool. Playground. Restaurant. Bar 4 pm-1 am. Ck-out 11 am. Coin lndry. Meeting rms. Business servs avail. In-rm modem link. Some refrigerators, microwaves. Cr cds: A, D, DS, MC, V.

⛱ ✈ 🛏 🎿 🐾

Marion

(G-5) *See also Benton, Carbondale*

Founded 1839 **Pop** 16,035 **Elev** 448 ft
Area code 618 **Zip** 62959
Information Greater Marion Area Chamber of Commerce, 2305 W Main St, PO Box 307; 618/997-6311
Web www.cc.marion.il.us

A regional trade center serving 90,000 people, Marion is the seat of Williamson County.

What to See and Do

⭐ **Crab Orchard National Wildlife Refuge.** Refuge for wintering Canada geese includes 7,000-acre Crab Orchard Lake, west of headquarters; Little Grassy Lake, eight mi south;

and Devil's Kitchen Lake, just east of Little Grassy. Swimming, fishing, boat ramps and rentals; hunting, trapping, nature trails, picnicking; camping at Crab Orchard, Little Grassy, and Devil's Kitchen (fees; restrooms, showers at all campgrounds). Pets on leash only. Headquarters (Mon-Fri; closed hols). Area (all yr, daily). Headquarters, 5 mi W on IL 13, then 2½ mi S on IL 148. Phone 618/997-3344. ¢¢

Lake of Egypt. Activities on 2,300-acre stocked lake include waterskiing, fishing, boating (rentals, launching); camping. (Daily) 8 mi S via I-57, IL 37. Contact Pyramid Acres Campground and Marina. Phone 618/964-1184.

⭐ **Shawnee National Forest.** Approx 278,000 acres, bordered on east by Ohio River, on west by Mississippi River; unusual rock formations, varied wildlife. Swimming, fishing, boating; hunting, hiking and bridle trails, picnicking, camping on first-come basis. Fees may be charged at recreation sites. Via I-57, I-24. Contact Forest Supervisor, 901 S Commercial St, Harrisburg 62946. Phone 618/253-7114. ¢¢

Special Event

Williamson County Fair. June. Phone 618/997-6311.

Motels/Motor Lodges

★ **BEST INN.** *2700 W DeYoung St (62959). 618/997-9421; fax 618/997-1581. www.bestinn.com.* 104 rms, 2 story. S $37-$45; D $46.88-$60.88; under 18 free. Crib free. TV; cable. Pool. Complimentary continental bkfst. Restaurant nearby. Ck-out 1 pm. Cr cds: A, C, D, DS, MC, V.

Ⓓ 🐾 ✚ ⛱ ✈ 🛏 🎿

★★ **BEST WESTERN AIRPORT INN.** *150 Express Dr (62959). 618/993-3222; fax 618/993-8868. www.bestwestern.com.* 34 rms, 2 story, 10 suites. S $39-$49; D $44-$54; each addl $5; suites $52-$72; under 12 free; higher rates SIU special events. Crib free. Pet accepted. TV. Pool. Complimentary continental bkfst. Restaurant nearby. Ck-out 11 am. Meeting rms. Business servs avail. Free airport transportation.

Refrigerator, wet bar in suites. Cr cds: A, MC, V.

★★ **COMFORT INN.** *2600 W Main St (62959).* 618/993-6221; fax 618/993-8964. www.comfortinn.com. 122 rms, 2 story, 34 suites. S $53; D $59; each addl $5; suites $61; under 18 free. Crib free. TV; cable. Heated pool. Complimentary continental bkfst. Restaurant adj 6 am-10 pm. Ck-out noon. Meeting rm. Free airport transportation. Exercise equipt. Refrigerator, microwave, minibar in suites. Cr cds: A, MC, V.

Restaurant

★★ **TONY'S STEAK HOUSE.** *105 S Market St (62959).* 618/993-2220. Hrs: 4-10:30 pm. Closed Sun; hols. Res accepted. Bar to midnight. Complete meals: dinner $6.95-$19.95. Specializes in fresh-cut steak, prime rib. Cr cds: A, C, D, DS, MC, V.

Marshall

(E-6) *See also Terre Haute, IN*

Founded 1835 **Pop** 3,771 **Elev** 641 ft
Area code 217 **Zip** 62441
Information Chamber of Commerce, 708 Archer Ave, PO Box 263; 217/826-2034

The site on which Marshall is now located was purchased from the federal government in 1833 by Colonel William Archer and Joseph Duncan, sixth governor of Illinois. They named the town after John Marshall, fourth Chief Justice of the United States Supreme Court. Seat of Clark County, Marshall serves as a business center for the surrounding agricultural community.

What to See and Do

Lincoln Trail State Park. The Lincoln family passed through here en route from Indiana in 1830. This 1,022-acre park has fishing in an artificial lake, boating (ramp, rentals; motors, ten-hp limit); hiking, picnicking, concession, camping. Standard fees.

(Daily) 3 mi S off IL 1 and 1 mile W. Phone 217/826-2222. **FREE**

Mill Creek Park. Swimming, fishing, boating; camping, cabins, bridle and ATV trails (weather permitted). (Daily, end mar-Oct) 7 mi NW on Lincoln Heritage Trail (20482 North Park Entrance Rd). Phone 217/889-3901. **FREE**

Special Event

Autumn Fest. Town Sq. Third wkend Sept. Phone 217/826-5645.

Mattoon

(E-5) *See also Arcola, Charleston, Effingham*

Founded 1854 **Pop** 18,291 **Elev** 726 ft
Area code 217 **Zip** 61938
Information Mattoon Chamber of Commerce, 1701 Wabash Ave; 217/235-5661 or -5666
Web www.mattoonchamber.com

Named for a railroad official who built the Big Four Railroad from St. Louis to Indianapolis, Mattoon is an industrial town and a retail and market center for the surrounding farm area. Products vary from heavy road machinery to bagels and magazines. In 1861, General Ulysses S. Grant mustered the 25th Illinois Infantry into service in Mattoon.

What to See and Do

Lake Mattoon. Fishing, boating, launching facilities; picnicking, camping. 6 mi S on US 45, I-57, then 3 mi W.

Special Event

Bagelfest. World's biggest bagel bkfst. Bagelfest Queen Pageant, Beautiful Bagel Baby Contest. Parade, talent show, music. Last Sat July. Phone 217/235-5661.

Motel/Motor Lodge

★★ **RAMADA INN HOTEL & CONFERENCE CENTER.** *300 Broadway Ave E (61938).* 217/235-0313; fax 217/235-6005. www.ramada.com. 124 rms, 2 story. S $51-$90; D $59-$90; each addl $5; suites $76-$95; under

20 free. Crib $10. Pet accepted. TV; cable (premium). 2 pools, 1 indoor; whirlpool. Sauna. Complimentary coffee. Restaurant 6 am-10 pm. Bar 11:30-1 am. Ck-out noon. Coin lndry. Meeting rms. Business servs avail. Health club privileges. Atrium. Game rm. Rec rm. Cr cds: A, C, D, DS, JCB, V.

McHenry

(A-5) *See also Gurnee, Woodstock*

Pop 21,501 **Elev** 761 ft **Area code** 815 **Zip** 60050
Information Chamber of Commerce, 1257 N Green St; 815/385-4300

What to See and Do

Moraine Hills State Park. Three small lakes on 1,690 acres. Fishing, boating (rentals); bike and hiking trails (11 mi), x-country skiing (rentals), picnicking, concession. Nature center. (Daily; closed Dec 25) Standard fees. On S River Rd. Phone 815/385-1624. **FREE**

Volo Auto Museum and Village. Display of more than 300 antique and collector cars. Largest display of TV and movie cars including the "Batmobile" and the "General Lee" from The Dukes of Hazard. Gift, antique, and craft shops. Autos displayed and sold. Restaurant. (Daily; closed hols) ½ mile W of Rt 12 on IL 120 in Volo. Phone 815/385-3644. ¢¢

Motels/Motor Lodges

★ **DAYS INN.** *11200 US 12, Richmond (60071). 815/678-4711; fax 815/678-4623; toll-free 800/329-7466. www.daysinn.com.* 60 rms, 2 story. May-Sept: S $69; D $75; family rates; package plans; higher rates special events; lower rates rest of yr. Crib free. Pet accepted, some restrictions. TV. Pool. Complimentary continental bkfst. Restaurant nearby. Ck-out 11 am. Downhill/x-country ski 12 mi. Cr cds: A, C, D, DS, JCB, MC, V.

★★ **HOLIDAY INN.** *IL 31 and Three Oaks Rd, Crystal Lake (60014).* 815/477-7000; fax 815/477-7027; toll-free 800/465-4329. www.holiday-inn. com. 196 rms, 6 story. S $78-$99; D $78-$109; each addl $10; suites $159; under 18 free. Crib free. TV; cable (premium). Indoor pool; whirlpool. Complimentary coffee in lobby. Restaurant 6:30 am-10 pm; Fri, Sat to 11 pm. Rm serv. Bar from 11 am. Ck-out noon. Meeting rms. Bellhops. Gift shop. Free railroad station, bus depot transportation. Exercise equipt; sauna. Cr cds: A, D, DS, MC, V.

★★ **RAMADA INN.** *4100 Shamrock Ln (60173). 815/344-5500; fax 815/344-5527. www.ramada.com.* 58 rms, 2-3 story. S $70-$88; D $80-$98; each addl $10; suites $175-$225. Crib free. TV; cable (premium). Indoor pool; whirlpool. Complimentary coffee in lobby. Restaurant 7 am-2 pm, 5-10 pm. Rm serv. Bar; entertainment wkends. Ck-out noon. Meeting rms. Business servs avail. X-country ski 13 mi. Health club privileges. Whirlpool in suites. Picnic tables. In Chain O'Lakes region. Cr cds: A, MC, V.

Restaurants

★ **JENNY'S.** *2500 N Chapel Hill Rd (60050). 815/385-0333.* Hrs: 4:30-9 pm; Fri, Sat to 10 pm; Sun 3-8 pm; Sun brunch 10 am-2 pm. Closed Mon, Tues; Dec 25. Res accepted. Bar. Dinner $6.95-$18.95. Sun brunch $7.95. Child's menu. Specialties: prime rib, filet mignon. Salad bar. Own pastries. Entertainment wkends. View of club grounds. Cr cds: A, DS, MC, V.

★★★ **LE VICHYSSOIS.** *220 W IL 120, Lakemoor (60050). 815/385-8221. www.levichyssois.com.* Hrs: 5:30 pm-closing; Sun from 4:30 pm. Closed Mon, Tues; hols. Res accepted. French menu. Serv bar. Wine list. Dinner $15-$25. Prix fixe: dinner $21.50. Specialties: Dover sole, salmon en croute, rack of lamb. Own pastries, ice cream. French provincial decor; country inn atmosphere. Cr cds: D, MC, V.

Moline

(B-3) *See also Rock Island*

Founded 1848 **Pop** 43,768 **Elev** 580 ft
Area code 309 **Zip** 61265
Information Quad Cities Convention
& Visitors Bureau, 2021 River Dr;
309/788-7800 or 800/747-7800
Web www.visitquadcities.com

Settled by a significant number of
Belgians, Moline takes its name from
the French *moulin* (mill), in reference
to the many mills that were built
along the Mississippi to take advantage of the limitless supply of water
power. Today the city produces goods
varying from farm implements to
elevators. Moline and Rock Island,
along with Bettendorf and Davenport, Iowa (across the Mississippi
River), constitute the Quad Cities
metropolitan area.

What to See and Do

Center for Belgian Culture. Houses
Belgian memorabilia. (Wed and Sat
afternoons) 712 18th Ave. Phone
309/762-0167. **FREE**

⭐ **Deere & Company.** World headquarters for manufacturers of farm,
industrial, lawn, and garden equipt.
Administrative Center (1964),
designed by Eero Saarinen, who also
designed the arch in St. Louis, is considered a masterpiece of modern
architecture. On 1,000 acres overlooking Rock River Valley, the center
consists of a main office building
with display floor, 400-seat auditorium, and the newer West Office
Building. Main office building was
constructed of corrosion-resistant
unpainted steel and is set across the
floor of a wooded ravine; display
floor includes three-dimensional
mural, designed by Alexander Girard,
composed of more than 2,000 items
dating from 1837-1918 that relate to
agriculture and life in mid-America
during that period. West Office
Building (1978), designed by Roche
and Dinkeloo with a skylighted interior garden court, has been cited for
its harmonious relation to the original buildings. Grounds include two
large pools with many fountains and
an island with a Henry Moore sculpture. Tours of Administrative Center
(Mon-Fri; closed hols). Factory tours
(children over 11 yrs only). Main
building (daily). Phone 309/765-
8000. John Deere Rd. Phone
765/420-7309. **FREE**

John Deere Commons. On the banks
of the Mississippi River, this complex
is home to the **John Deere Pavilion**,
a visitor center with interactive displays about agriculture and vintage
and modern John Deere equipment.
Also here are a John Deere Store; a
restaurant; a hotel; **The MARK** of the
Quad Cities, a 12,000-seat arena
hosting high-profile events; and **Centre Station,** the transportation hub
and Information Center for the Quad
Cities. (Daily) 1400 River Dr. Phone
309/765-1001. **FREE**

Niabi Zoo. Miniature railroad (fee);
children's zoo; picnicking, snack bar.
(Daily; closed Jan 1 and Dec 25) Free
admission Tues. 10 mi SE on US 6, in
Coal Valley. Phone 309/799-5107. **¢¢**

Motels/Motor Lodges

★★ **BEST WESTERN AIRPORT
INN.** *2550 52nd Ave (61265).
309/762-9191; fax 309/762-9191; toll-
free 800/780-7234. www.bestwestern.
com.* 50 rms, 2 story. May-Sept: S, D
$58-$89; each addl $5; under 12 free;
lower rates rest of yr. Crib $3. TV;
cable (premium). Indoor pool; whirlpool. Complimentary continental
bkfst. Restaurant opp open 24 hrs.
Ck-out 11 am. Business servs avail.
Downhill/x-country ski 15 mi. Some
refrigerators, microwaves. Near Quad
City Airport. Cr cds: A, C, D, DS,
MC, V.

⬛ ⬛ ⬛ ⬛ ⬛ ⬛

★★ **HAMPTON INN.** *6920 27th St
(61265). 309/762-1711; fax 309/762-
1788. www.hamptoninn.com.* 138 rms,
2 story. Apr-Sept: S $69-$85; D $79-
$85; suites $99-$175; under 18 free;
lower rates rest of yr. Crib free. Pet
accepted. TV; cable (premium).
Heated pool. Complimentary continental bkfst. Ck-out noon. Business
servs avail. Valet serv. Free airport
transportation. Health club privileges. Cr cds: A, D, DS, MC, V.

⬛ ⬛ ⬛ ⬛ ⬛ ⬛ ⬛

★ ★ **LA QUINTA INN.** *5450 27th St (61265). 309/762-9008; fax 309/762-2455. www.laquinta.com.* 125 rms, 2 story. May-Sept: S $49.99-$59.99; D $59.99-$66.99; each addl $7; under 18 free; lower rates rest of yr. Crib free. Pet accepted, some restrictions. TV; cable (premium). Heated pool. Complimentary continental bkfst. Restaurant. Ck-out noon. Coin lndry. Meeting rm. Business servs avail. In-rm modem link. Airport transportation. Downhill ski 15 mi. Some refrigerators. Cr cds: A, MC, V.

Restaurant

★ ★ **C'EST MICHELE.** *1405 5th Ave (61265). 309/762-0585.* Hrs: 5:30-9 pm. Closed Sun, Mon; Thanksgiving, Dec 24, 25. Res accepted. French menu. Bar. A la carte entrees: dinner $13.75-$19.75. Complete meals: dinner $30. Specialties: magret de canard, roti d'agneau, veau Oscar moriel. Elegant decor. Cr cds: A, C, D, MC, V.

Monmouth

(C-3) *See also Galesburg*

Founded 1831 **Pop** 9,489 **Elev** 770 ft
Area code 309 **Zip** 61462
Information Monmouth Area Chamber of Commerce, 68 Public Sq; 309/734-3181

Monmouth was named to commemorate the Revolutionary War battle of Monmouth, New Jersey, and was the birthplace of Wyatt Earp. There is a memorial to Earp in Monmouth Park. The town is located on the prairie in a region famous for the production of corn, soybeans, hogs, and cattle.

What to See and Do

Buchanan Center for the Arts. Art and cultural exhibits in a modern gallery. (Mon-Sat) 64 Public Sq. Phone 309/734-3033. **FREE**
Pioneer Cemetery. Relatives of Wyatt Earp are buried here. E Archer Ave near 5th St. Phone 309/734-3181.
Wyatt Earp Birthplace. The US Deputy Marshal's first family home from his birth in 1848 until 1850, when the family left for the California gold rush. (Memorial Day-Labor Day, Sun afternoons; also by appt) 406 S Third St. Phone 309/734-3181. **DONATION**

Special Events

Maple City Summerfest. Downtown. Flea market, games, entertainment, bike run. Mid-July. Phone 309/734-3181.
Warren County Prime Beef Festival. Beef and hog shows and auctions. Displays, events, entertainment, carnival, parade. Four days beginning Wed after Labor Day. Phone 309/734-3181.

Motel/Motor Lodge

★ ★ **MELINGS.** *1129 N Main St (61462). 309/734-2196; fax 309/734-2127.* 34 rms, 1-2 story. S $38; D $47; each addl $5. Crib free. Pet accepted. TV; cable. Restaurant 5:30 am-9:30 pm; dining rm 11 am-1:30 pm, 5-8 pm; Sun 7 am-3 pm. Bar, closed Sun. Ck-out 11 am. Lndry facilities. Meeting rm. Business servs avail. Sundries. Free RR station, bus depot transportation. Cr cds: A, D, DS, MC, V.

Morris

(B-5) *See also Joliet, Ottawa*

Founded 1842 **Pop** 11,928 **Elev** 519 ft
Area code 815 **Zip** 60450
Information Grundy County Chamber of Commerce & Industry, 112 E Washington St; 815/942-0113

What to See and Do

Gebhard Woods State Park. The I & M Canal flows along the southern edge of this 30-acre park, which offers fishing and canoeing in small ponds, Nettle Creek, and the canal; hiking, biking, snowmobiling, picnicking, primitive camping. Standard fees. (Daily) W edge of town. Phone 815/942-0796. **FREE**

Illinois and Michigan Canal State Trail. The I & M Canal, completed in 1848 at a cost of $6.5 million, stretched 61 mi, linking Lake Michigan and Chicago with the Illinois River at La Salle. Four state parks have been established on the 60-mi trail, among them Buffalo Rock (see OTTAWA). (Daily) Phone 815/942-0796.

Special Event

Grundy County Corn Festival. Music, horse show, parade. Last wk Sept. Phone 815/942-0113.

Motel/Motor Lodge

★ ★ **HOLIDAY INN.** *200 Gore Rd (60450). 815/942-6600; fax 815/942-8255; toll-free 800/465-4329. www.holiday-inn.com.* 120 rms, 2 story. S $68; D $74; each addl $6; under 18 free. Crib free. Pet accepted, some restrictions. TV; cable (premium). Heated pool; whirlpool. Restaurant 6 am-2 pm, 5-10 pm. Rm serv. Bar 4 pm-midnight; closed Sun. Ck-out noon. Meeting rms. Business servs avail. In-rm modem link. Valet serv. Sundries. Health club privileges. Some refrigerators, microwaves. Cr cds: A, C, D, DS, JCB, MC, V.

D ⚄ ≈ ⊠ ⚒

Restaurants

★ **ROCKWELL INN.** *2400 W US 6 (60450). 815/942-6224.* Hrs: 11 am-10 pm; Sun brunch 11 am-3 pm. Closed Dec 25. Res accepted. Bar. Lunch $4.75-$11.75, dinner $8.75-$19.75. Sun brunch $12.50. Child's menu. Specialties: prime rib, chicken picatta. Own breads. Salad bar. Entertainment Fri, Sat evenings. Norman Rockwell prints; bar from 1893 Columbian Exposition. Cr cds: A, D, DS, MC, V.

D ⊟

★ **R-PLACE FAMILY EATERY.** *21 Romines Dr (60450). 815/942-3690.* Open 24 hrs. Bkfst $2.95-$5.50, lunch $4.95-$9.95, dinner $5.10-$9.95. Child's menu. Specializes in hamburgers, seasonal dishes. Own baking. Salad bar. Truck stop with Victorian-era decor; chandeliers, Tiffany-style lamps; extensive collec-

tion of Americana, antique toys, mechanical puppets, gas station memorabilia. Family-owned. Cr cds: MC, V.

D ⊟

Mount Vernon

(F-5) *See also Benton, Centralia, Du Quoin, Salem*

Pop 16,269 **Elev** 500 ft **Area code** 618 **Zip** 62864

Information Convention and Visitors Bureau, 200 Potomac Blvd; 618/242-3151 or 800/252-5464

Web www.southernillinois.com

What to See and Do

Cedarhurst. An 85-acre estate that includes **Mitchell Museum**, a nature walk and bird sanctuary; **Sculpture Park**, an outdoor art center with visual and performing arts programs; **Art Center** provides yr-round classes and workshops (fee); **Chamber Music** offers a series of concerts. (Tues-Sat, also Sun afternoons; closed hols) Richview Rd. **FREE**

Special Events

Sweetcorn-Watermelon Festival. Entertainment, flea market, parade. Free sweetcorn and watermelon served. Third wk Aug. Phone 618/242-3151.

Cedarhurst Craft Fair. Richview Rd. Entertainment, food, juried art and craft show. Sat and Sun after Labor Day. Phone 618/242-1236.

Motels/Motor Lodges

★ **BEST INNS.** *222 S 44th St (62864). 618/244-4343; fax 618/244-4343; toll-free 800/237-8466. www.bestinns.com.* 153 rms, 2 story. Mid-May-Oct S $37.99; D $45.99; each addl $7; under 18 free; golf plan; lower rates rest of yr. Crib free. Pet accepted, some restrictions. TV; cable (premium). Pool. Complimentary continental bkfst. Ck-out 1 pm. Cr cds: A, C, D, DS, MC, V.

D ⚄ ≈ ⊠ ⚒ SC

★ ★ **DRURY INN.** *145 N 44th St (62864). 618/244-4550; fax 618/244-*

4550; toll-free 800/325-8300. www.
druryinn.com. 82 rms, 3 story. S $57;
D $64-$70; each addl $7; under 18
free. Crib free. Pet accepted. TV;
cable. Pool. Complimentary continental bkfst. Restaurant adj open 24
hrs. Ck-out noon. Meeting rms. Sundries. Some refrigerators, microwaves.
Cr cds: A, C, D, DS, MC, V.

★★ **HOLIDAY INN.** 222 Potomac
Blvd (62864). 618/244-7100; fax
618/242-8876; toll-free 800/243-7171.
www.holiday-inn.com. 223 rms, 5
story. S, D $68-$76; suites $90-$125;
under 18 free; golf plan. Crib free.
Pet accepted, some restrictions. TV;
cable. Indoor pool; whirlpool.
Restaurants 6 am-10 pm. Rm serv.
Bar 4 pm-1 am. Ck-out 1 pm. Meeting rms. Valet serv. Sundries. Free airport transportation. Saunas. Cr cds:
A, C, D, DS, JCB, MC, V.

★★ **VILLAGE PREMIER.** 405 S 44th
St (62864). 618/244-3670; fax
618/244-6904; toll-free 800/328-7829.
www.villager.com. 188 rms, 4 story. S,
D $45; each addl $6; under 18 free.
Crib free. Pet accepted. TV, cable
(premium). Indoor pool; whirlpool.
Complimentary continental bkfst.
Restaurant 6 am-2 pm, 5-10 pm. Rm
serv. Bar 11-1 am; Fri, Sat to 2 am;
Sun noon-10 pm; entertainment
Tues-Sat. Ck-out noon. Meeting rms.
Business center. In-rm modem link.
Bellhops. Valet serv. Free airport, bus
depot transportation. Exercise equipt;
sauna. Health club privileges. Game
rm. Rec rm. Cr cds: A, C, D, DS, JCB,
MC, V.

Restaurant

★ **EL RANCHERITO.** 4303 Broadway
Ave (62864). 618/244-6121. Hrs: 11
am-10 pm; Fri, Sat to 11 pm. Closed
Thanksgiving. Res accepted. Mexican
menu. Bar. Lunch $2.99-$4.99, dinner $2.99-$10. Child's menu. Specializes in fajitas, chimichangas.
Two-level dining with Mexican
decor. Cr cds: A, DS, MC, V.

Naperville

*See also Aurora, Downers Grove,
Wheaton*

Settled 1831 **Pop** 128,358 **Elev** 700 ft
Area code 630
Information Visitors Bureau, 131 W
Jefferson Ave, 60540; 630/355-4141
Web www.napervilleil.com

Naperville, oldest town in Du Page
County, was settled by Captain
Joseph Naper. Soon after, in the late
1830s, settlers of German ancestry
came from Pennsylvania to trans-
form the prairie into farmland.
Although today's city is at the center
of a "research and high technology
corridor" and has been cited as one
of the fastest-growing suburbs in the
nation, Naperville retains something
of the atmosphere of a small town
with its core of large Victorian
houses and beautiful historic district.
The downtown shopping district features over 100 shops and restaurants
in historic buildings; it adjoins the
Riverwalk, a three-and-a-half mile
winding brick pathway along the
DuPage River.

What to See and Do

Naper Settlement. A 13-acre living
history museum of 25 buildings in a
village setting depicts a 19th-century
northern Illinois town (ca 1830-
1900). Tours by costumed guides
includes four residences of the
period; Martin-Mitchell mansion,
with period furnishings; several public buildings and working businesses
such as a printshop, smithy, and
stonecutter's shop. Also Les Schrader
Art Gallery with a 42-painting
exhibit depicting the growth and
development of a Midwest town, and
museum shop. Special events
throughout yr (fee). (Apr-Oct, Tues-
Sun; rest of yr, Tues-Fri) (See SPECIAL
EVENT) Aurora Ave and Webster St.
Phone 630/420-6010. ¢¢

Special Event

Christmas in the Village. Naper Settlement. Nineteenth-century festivi-

ties; decorations of period. Dec.
Phone 630/305-7701.

Motels/Motor Lodges

★★ **COURTYARD BY MARRIOTT
NAPERVILLE.** *1155 E Diehl Rd
(60563). 630/505-0550; fax 630/505-
8337; toll-free 800/321-2211. www.
courtyard.com.* 147 rms, 3 story. S, D
$114-$129; suites $149; under 12
free; wkly rates. Crib free. TV; cable
(premium), VCR avail. Indoor pool;
whirlpool. Restaurant 6:30-10 am;
wkends 7-11 am. Ck-out noon. Coin
lndry. Meeting rms. Business servs
avail. In-rm modem link. Valet serv.
Exercise equipt. Some refrigerators;
microwaves avail. Private patios, balconies. Cr cds: A, C, D, DS, JCB,
MC, V.
🄳 🖐 🏊 🛪

★ **EXEL INN.** *1585 Naperville/
Wheaton Rd (60563). 630/357-0022;
fax 630/357-9817; toll-free 800/367-
3935. www.exelinns.com.* 123 rms, 3
story. S $49; D $51.95; each addl $5;
under 18 free. Crib free. TV; cable
(premium). Complimentary continental bkfst. Restaurant nearby. Ck-
out noon. Coin lndry. Business servs
avail. In-rm modem link. Microwaves
avail. Cr cds: A, D, DS, MC, V.
🄳 🛦 🖐

★★ **HAMPTON INN.** *1087 E Diehl
Rd (60563). 630/505-1400; fax
630/505-1416. www.hamptoninn.com.*
128 rms, 4 story. S, D $69-$104;
under 18 free. Crib free. TV; cable
(premium). Heated pool. Complimentary continental bkfst. Ck-out
noon. Meeting rms. Business center.
In-rm modem link. Exercise equipt.
Health club privileges. Cr cds: A, D,
DS, JCB, MC, V.
🄳 🏊 🛪 🛦 🖐 🆂🅲 🛪

★ **RED ROOF INN.** *1698 W Diehl Rd
(60563). 630/369-2500; fax 630/369-
9987; toll-free 800/733-7663. www.
redroof.com.* 119 rms, 3 story. May-
Sept: S $59.99; D $67.99; under 18
free; lower rates rest of yr. Crib free.
Pet accepted. TV; cable (premium).
Complimentary coffee in lobby.
Restaurant opp. Ck-out noon. Business servs avail. In-rm modem link.
Cr cds: A, C, D, DS, MC, V.
🄳 🐾 🛦 🖐

★★ **WYNDHAM GARDEN HOTEL.**
*1837 Centre Point Cir (60563).
630/505-3353; fax 630/505-0176; toll-
free 800/822-4200. www.wyndham.
com.* 143 rms, 4 story, 40 suites. S
$99-$119; D $99-$129; suites $119;
wkend rates. Crib free. TV; cable (premium). Indoor pool; whirlpool.
Complimentary coffee in rm. Restaurant 6:30 am-10 pm. Rm serv from 5
pm. Bar 5 pm-midnight. Ck-out
noon. Meeting rms. Business servs
avail. In-rm modem link. Exercise
equipt. Some refrigerators; microwaves avail. Cr cds: A, C, D, DS, JCB,
MC, V.
🄳 🏊 🛪 🛦 🖐 🆂🅲

Hotels

★★★ **HILTON.** *3003 Corporate West
Dr, Lisle (60532). 630/505-0900; fax
630/505-8948. www.hilton.com.* 309
rms, 8 story. Apr-Nov: S $145-$180;
D $165-$200; each addl $20; suites
$325; lower rates rest of yr. Crib free.
TV; cable (premium). Indoor pool;
whirlpool. Complimentary coffee in
rms. Restaurant 6:30 am-10 pm. Ck-
out noon. Meeting rms. Business
servs avail. Exercise equipt. Health
club privileges. Gift shop. Some
refrigerators. Cr cds: A, C, D, DS,
JCB, MC, V.
🄳 🏊 🛪 🛦 🖐

★★ **HOLIDAY INN SELECT.** *1801
N Naper Blvd (60563). 630/505-4900;
fax 630/505-8239. www.hiselect.com/
napervilleil.* 426 rms, 7 story. S, D
$109-$129; suites $250; under 19
free; wkend rates. Crib free. TV; cable
(premium). Indoor pool. Restaurant
6 am-11 pm. Rm serv from
11:30 am, wkends 11-1 am. Ck-out
noon. Business center. In-rm modem
link. Exercise equipt; sauna. Health
club privileges. Cr cds: A, D, DS, JCB,
MC, V.
🄳 🏊 🛪 🛦 🖐 🛪

★★★ **HYATT.** *1400 Corporetum Dr,
Lisle (60532). 630/852-1234; fax
630/852-1260; toll-free 800/233-1234.
www.hyatt.com.* 312 rms, 14 story. S
$103-$125; D $128-$140; each addl
$25; wkend rates. Crib free. TV; cable
(premium), VCR avail. Indoor pool;
whirlpool. Coffee in rms. Restaurant
6 am-2 pm, 5-10 pm. Bar 11 am-
midnight, Fri, Sat to 2 am. Ck-out
noon. Convention facilities. Business

servs avail. In-rm modem link. Exercise equipt; sauna. Refrigerators avail. Cr cds: A, D, DS, MC, V.

⊡ ☲ 九 ☷ ☵

★★★ **WYNDHAM.** *3000 Warrenville Rd, Lisle (60532). 630/505-1000; fax 630/505-1165. www.wyndham.com.* 242 rms, 8 story. S, D $129-$250; each addl $10; suites from $119; under 18 free; wkend rates. Crib free. Pet accepted. TV; cable (premium). Indoor pool; whirlpool. Restaurant 6 am-10 pm. Bar 4 pm-1 am; wkends to 2 am. Ck-out noon. Convention facilities. Business servs avail. In-rm modem link. Concierge. Gift shop. Exercise rm; sauna. Massage. Game rm. Microwaves avail. Luxury level. Cr cds: A, C, D, DS, MC, V.

⊡ ☏ ☲ 九 ☷ ☵

Restaurants

★★★ **MESON SABIKA.** *1025 Aurora Ave (60540). 630/983-3000. www. mesonsabika.com.* Hrs: 11:30 am-10 pm; Fri to 11 pm; Sat 5-11 pm; Sun 4-9 pm. Sun brunch 11 am-2 pm. Closed hols. Res accepted. Spanish menu. Bar. Wine list. Lunch $6-$12, dinner $15-$30. Sun brunch $16.95. Specialties: scalloped shrimp and salmon, patatas con alioli, queso de cabra al horno. Own pastries. Flamenco entertainment Fri. Patio dining. In Victorian mansion (ca 1847). Cr cds: A, C, D, MC, V.

⊡ ☲

★★★ **MONTPARNASSE.** *200 E 5th Ave (60563). 630/961-8203. www.city search.com.* Hrs: 11:30 am-2:30 pm, 6-9 pm. Closed Sun; hols. Res accepted. French menu. Setups. Entrees: lunch $8-$15, dinner $18-$29. Complete meals $45. Specialties: creme brulee, carre d'agneau, grilled pheasant. Own baking. Entertainment Sat. In converted furniture factory. Cr cds: A, C, D, DS, MC, V.

⊡

★★★ **SAMBA.** *22 E Chicago Ave (60540). 630/753-0985.* Specializes in grilled Chilean sea bass, roast pork tenderloin, beef tenderloin. Hrs: 11:30 am-11 pm; Fri, Sat to midnight; Sun to 10 pm. Closed hols. Res accepted. Wine, beer. Lunch $6.50-$11; dinner $12-$23. Open

kitchen viewing. Cr cds: A, C, D, DS, MC, V.

⊡ ☲

Nauvoo

(C-2) *See also Macomb*

Settled 1839 **Pop** 1,063 **Elev** 659 ft
Area code 217 **Zip** 62354
Information Tourist Center, 1295 Mulholland (IL 96), PO Box 41; 217/453-6648

Once the largest city in Illinois, Nauvoo has a colorful history. When the Mormon prophet Joseph Smith was driven out of Missouri, he came with his Latter-day Saints to the tiny village called Commerce, on a promontory overlooking the Mississippi River, and established what was virtually an autonomous state. A city of 8,000 houses was created, and in 1841 construction began on a great temple. A schism in the church and the threat of Mormon political power led to riots and persecution of the Mormons. Joseph Smith and his brother were arrested and murdered by a mob while in the Carthage jail. Brigham Young became leader of the Nauvoo Mormons. When the city charter was repealed and armed clashes broke out anew, Young led much of the population westward in 1846 to its final settlement in Utah. Nauvoo became a ghost city, and the almost-completed temple was set on fire by an arsonist. In 1849, the Icarians, a band of French communalists, migrated to Nauvoo from Texas and established their short-lived experiment in communal living. They attempted to rebuild the temple, but a storm swept the building back into ruin. The Icarians failed to prosper and in 1856 moved on. The city was gradually resettled by a more conventional group of Germans, who developed the wine culture begun by the French group.

What to See and Do

Baxter's Vineyards. Established 1857. Tours, wine tasting. (Daily; closed Jan

1, Thanksgiving, Dec 25) 2010 E Parley St. Phone 217/453-2528. **FREE**

Joseph Smith Historic Center. A 50-min tour begins in visitor center and includes an 18-min video. Book/gift shop. (Daily; closed Jan 1, Thanksgiving, Dec 24, 25, 31) 149 Water St, 1 blk W of IL 96. Phone 217/453-2246. **FREE** Tour includes

> **Grave of Joseph Smith.** Also burial place of Smith's wife Emma and brother Hyrum; the location of these graves, originally kept secret, was eventually lost; they were found in 1928 after an extensive search. Phone 217/453-2246.
>
> **Joseph Smith Homestead.** (1803) Log cabin the prophet occupied upon coming to Nauvoo in 1839 and town's oldest structure; period furnishings. Phone 217/453-2246.
>
> **Smith's Mansion.** (1843) Refined, Federal-style frame house occupied by Smith from 1843-1844; period furnishings. Phone 217/453-2246.
>
> **Smith's Red Brick Store.** (1842) Reconstructed building. Gift shops. Merchandise on shelves reflects items sold in 1842-1844. Phone 217/453-2246.

⭐ **Nauvoo Restoration, Inc, Visitor Center.** Center has a 20-min movie on Nauvoo history; exhibits; pamphlet with suggested tour and info on points of interest. (Daily). Also here are Seventy Hall, an 1840s meetinghouse, Lyon Drug Store, the Nauvoo Temple site, Montrose Crossing Monument, Sarah Kimball Home, William Weeks Home, Noble-Smith Home, Pendleton log house, Webb blacksmith and wagon shop, Stoddard tin shop, Riser Cobbler shop, 1840 theater, brick kiln, Clark store, Old Post Office and Merryweather Mercantile, Family Living Center with barrel-, candle-, and pottery-making, Jonathan Browning Gunshop, Scovil Bakery, and other significant structures. Young and N Main Sts. Phone 217/453-2237. **FREE** Guide service in the following buildings:

> **Brigham Young Home.** Restored house of Joseph Smith's successor. Kimball and Granger Sts. Phone 217/453-6413.
>
> **Heber C. Kimball Home.** Restored house of one of Joseph Smith's 12 apostles. Munson and Partridge Sts.

> **Print Shop.** Restored offices of Mormon newspaper and post office. Kimball and Main Sts.
>
> **Wilford Woodruff Home.** Restored house of apostle and missionary. Durphy and Hotchkiss Sts. **FREE**

Nauvoo State Park. On 148 acres. Restored house with wine cellar and century-old vineyard adjoining; museum (May-Sept). Fishing, boating (ramp, electric motors only); hiking, picnic area (shelter), playgrounds, camping. (See SPECIAL EVENTS) Standard fees. (Daily) S on IL 96. Phone 217/453-2512. **FREE**

Old Carthage Jail. (1839-1841) Restored jail where Joseph Smith and his brother were killed; 10-min tour; visitor center has 18-min film presentation, pamphlets, exhibits. (Daily) 307 Walnut St in Carthage; 12 mi S on IL 96, then 14 mi E on US 136. Phone 217/357-2989. **FREE**

Special Events

City of Joseph Pageant. Main and Young Sts. Wkends late July. Phone 217/453-2237.

Grape Festival. Nauvoo State Park. Includes classic French ceremony Wedding of the Wine and Cheese. Labor Day wkend. Phone 217/453-2512.

Motels/Motor Lodges

★ **MOTEL NAUVOO.** *1610 Mulholland St (Hwy 96) (62354). 217/453-2219; fax 217/453-6100. www.hotelnavoo.com.* 11 rms, 8 with shower only. S $44-$64; D $54-$64; each addl $5; under 12 free. Crib avail $5. TV; cable (premium). Restaurant nearby. Ck-out 11 am. Picnic tables. Totally nonsmoking. Cr cds: A, DS, MC, V.
🚫 🔥

★★ **NAUVOO FAMILY MOTEL.** *1875 Mulholland St (62354). 217/453-6527; fax 217/453-6601; res 800/416-4470. www.nauvoonet.com.* 104 rms, 2 story, 26 suites. S, D $74-$89; suites $110-$190; under 12 free; lower rates rest of yr. Crib free. Pet accepted, some restrictions. TV; cable (premium). Indoor pool. Restaurant nearby. Ck-out 11 am. Meeting rms. Cr cds: A, D, DS, MC, V.
D 🔧 ⚡ 🏊 ✈ 🚫 🔥

B&Bs/Small Inns

★ ★ **HOTEL NAUVOO.** *1290 Mulholland St (62354). 217/453-2211; fax 217/453-6100. www.hotelnauvoo.com.* 8 rms. S, D $44-$54.50; each addl $5; suites $64.50-$94.50. Closed mid-Nov-mid-Mar. TV; cable (premium). Dining rm (see HOTEL NAUVOO). Bar. Ck-out 11 am, ck-in 4 pm. Restored historic inn (1840), originally a private residence. Totally nonsmoking. Cr cds: A, DS, MC, V.
⊠ ⓐ

★ ★ **MISSISSIPPI MEMORIES BED & BREAKFAST.** *1 Riverview Ter (62354). 217/453-2771.* 4 rms, 3 story. S, D $69-$99. Closed wk of Dec 25. TV avail. Complimentary full bkfst. Ck-out 10 am. Two fireplaces. In wooded area overlooking Mississippi River. Piano in sitting rm. Totally nonsmoking. Cr cds: MC, V.
D ⓣ ⊠ ⓐ

Restaurant

★ ★ ★ **HOTEL NAUVOO.** *1290 Mulholland St (IL 96) (62354). 217/453-2211. www.hotelnauvoo.com.* Hrs: 5-8:30 pm; Fri, Sat to 9 pm; Sun brunch 11 am-3 pm. Closed Mon; also mid-Nov-mid-Mar. Res accepted. Bar. Dinner $5.50-$14.95. Buffet: dinner $10.45. Sun brunch $10.45. Serv charge 12%. Specializes in catfish, chicken, ham. Salad bar. Own breads. Restored 1840 Mormon residence. Family-owned.
D

Unrated Dining Spot

GRANDPA JOHN'S. *1255 Mulholland St (IL 96) (62354). 217/453-2310.* Hrs: 7:15 am-5 pm. Closed Jan-Feb. Bkfst $1.50-$5, lunch $1.75-$6. Lunch buffet $5.95. Child's menu. Specializes in chicken, steak, homemade bakery goods. Own ice cream. Soda fountain. Original artwork; antiques. Established 1912. Totally nonsmoking.
D

Normal

(see Bloomington)

Northbrook

See also Glenview, Highland Park, Wheeling

Pop 33,435 **Elev** 650 ft **Area code** 847 **Zip** 60062
Information Chamber of Commerce, 2002 Walters Ave; 847/498-5555

The earliest European settlers in the Northbrook area were German immigrants who arrived after the construction of the Erie Canal in 1825. In 1901 the town was incorporated as Shermerville, in honor of one of the founding families. Brickyards played a major role in the prosperity and growth of the community. After the Chicago fire of 1871, brick manufacturing surpassed farming as a leading industry; 300,000 bricks per day were produced between 1915-1920. In 1923, Shermerville was renamed Northbrook in reference to the middle forks of the north branches of the Chicago River, which run through the town. Today Northbrook, located in the heart of Chicago's North Shore, is the headquarters of a number of major corporations.

What to See and Do

⊠ **Chicago Botanic Garden.** Managed by the Chicago Horticultural Society, this garden includes 300 acres of formal plantings, lakes, lagoons, and wooded naturalistic areas. Specialty gardens include bulb, aquatic, perennial, and herb landscaped demonstration gardens; Japanese garden; English walled garden; prairie and nature trail; fruit and vegetable garden; heritage garden; rose garden; waterfall garden; sensory garden for the visually impaired; and learning garden for the disabled. The Education Center consists of an auditorium, floral arts museum, exhibit hall, shop, greenhouses, concession. Narrated tram ride. (Daily; closed Dec 25) ½ mi E of I-94 (US 41), Lake Cook Rd exit, on Lake Cook Rd in Glencoe. Phone 847/835-5440. Per vehicle ¢¢

River Trail Nature Center. A 300-acre nature preserve within the Forest Preserve District of Cook County. Nature trails; interpretive museum (Mon-Thurs, Sat, Sun); special activities (see SPECIAL EVENT); naturalist. (Daily; closed Jan 1, Thanksgiving, Dec 25) 3120 N Milwaukee Ave, ½ mi S of Willow Rd. Phone 847/824-8360. **FREE**

Special Event

Maple Sugar Festival. River Trail Nature Center. Native American, pioneer, and modern methods of maple sugaring demonstrated by staff naturalist. Last Sun Mar. Phone 847/824-8360.

Motel/Motor Lodge

★★ **COURTYARD BY MARRIOTT.** *800 Lake Cook Rd, Deerfield (60015). 847/940-8222; fax 847/940-7741; toll-free 800/321-2211.* 131 rms, 2 story, 17 suites. Apr-Oct: S $129; D $139; suites $139; wkend rates; lower rates rest of yr. Crib free. TV; cable (premium). Indoor pool; whirlpool. Complimentary coffee in rms. Restaurant 6:30-10 am; Sat, Sun 7-11 am. Bar 4:30-10:30 pm. Ck-out noon. Coin lndry. Meeting rms. Business servs avail. In-rm modem link. Valet serv. Exercise equipt. Refrigerators, microwaves avail. Private patios, balconies. Cr cds: A, C, D, DS, MC, V.

Hotels

★★ **ADAM'S MARK.** *2875 N Milwaukee Ave (60062). 847/298-2525; fax 847/298-5592; res 800/444-2326. www.adamsmark.com.* 318 rms, 7 story, 19 suites. S, D $85-$199; each addl $10; suites $135-$225; under 18 free; lower rates rest of yr. Crib free. TV; cable (premium), VCR avail (movies). Heated pool; whirlpool. Complimentary coffee. Restaurant 6 am-10 pm. Rm serv 24 hrs. Bar 4 pm-midnight. Ck-out noon. Convention facilities. Business center. In-rm modem link. Gift shop. Airport transportation. Exercise equipt. Cr cds: A, D, DS, MC, V.

★★★ **HILTON NORTHBROOK.** *2855 N Milwaukee Ave (60062). 847/480-7500; fax 847/480-0827; res 800/445-8667. www.hilton.com.* 246 rms, 10 story. S, D $79-$179; suites $350-$600; under 18 free; wkend rates. Crib free. TV; cable (premium), VCR avail. Indoor pool; whirlpool. Restaurant 6 am-11 pm. Bar 11-2:30 am. Ck-out noon. Meeting rms. Business center. Concierge. Airport transportation. Exercise equipt; sauna. Health club privileges. Gift shop. Bathrm phones, refrigerators, minibars; microwaves. Adj to forest preserve. Luxury level. Cr cds: A, D, DS, MC, V.

★★★ **HYATT DEERFIELD.** *1750 Lake Cook Rd, Deerfield (60015). 847/945-3400; fax 847/945-3563; toll-free 800/233-1234. www.hyatt.com.* 301 rms, 6 story. S, D $69-$215; each addl $25; under 18 free. Crib free. TV; cable (premium). Indoor pool; whirlpool. Complimentary coffee in rms. Restaurant 6 am-9 pm. Bar 11:30 am-midnight. Rm serv 6 am-11 pm. Ck-out noon. Convention facilities. Business servs avail. In-rm modem link. Exercise equipt; sauna. Refrigerators. Cr cds: A, D, DS, JCB, MC, V.

★★★ **RENAISSANCE CHICAGO NORTH SHORE HOTEL.** *933 Skokie Blvd (60062). 847/498-6500; fax 847/498-9558. www.marriott.com.* 386 rms, 10 story. S, D $109-$199; each addl $10; suites from $225; under 18 free; wkend rates. TV; cable (premium). Indoor pool. Complimentary coffee in rms. Restaurant 6:30 am-10 pm. Bar 4 pm-midnight; Sat to 1 am. Ck-out noon. Coin lndry. Convention facilities. Business center. Gift shop. Exercise equipt. Health club privileges. Refrigerators avail. Luxury level. Cr cds: A, C, D, DS, JCB, MC, V.

All Suites

★★★ **EMBASSY SUITES.** *1445 Lake Cook Rd, Deerfield (60015). 847/945-4500; fax 847/945-8189; toll-free*

*800/362-2779. www.embassy
suites.com.* 237 suites, 7 story. S $89-
$249; D $99-$269; each addl $20;
under 18 free. Crib free. TV; cable
(premium). Indoor pool; whirlpool.
Complimentary full bkfst, coffee in
rms. Restaurant 11 am-10 pm; Fri,
Sat to 11 pm. Bar 11:30 am-midnight; Sun from noon. Ck-out noon.
Coin lndry. Meeting rms. Business
servs avail. In-rm modem link. Gift
shop. Exercise equipt; sauna. Refrigerators, wet bars, microwaves. Cr cds:
A, D, DS, JCB, MC, V.

★★ **MARRIOTT SUITES.** *2 Pkwy N,
Deerfield (60015). 847/405-9666; fax
847/405-0354. www.marriott.com.* 248
suites, 7 story. S, D $109-$140; under
18 free; family rates; package plans.
Crib free. TV; cable (premium). 2
pools, 1 indoor; whirlpool, poolside
serv. Complimentary coffee in rms.
Restaurant. Bar. Ck-out 1 pm. Coin
lndry. Convention facilities. Business
center. In-rm modem link. Gift shop.
Exercise equipt; sauna. Health club
privileges. Refrigerators, microwaves.
Picnic tables. Cr cds: A, C, D, DS, ER,
JCB, MC, V.

Extended Stay

★★ **RESIDENCE INN BY MAR-
RIOTT.** *530 Lake Cook Rd, Deerfield
(60015). 847/940-4644; fax 847/940-
7639; toll-free 800/331-3131. www.
residenceinn.com.* 128 kit. suites, 2
story. Kit. suites $129-$179; wkend
rates. Crib free. Pet accepted, fee. TV;
cable (premium). Heated pool; whirlpool. Complimentary bkfst buffet.
Coffee in rms. Restaurant nearby. Ck-
out noon. Coin lndry. Meeting rm.
Business servs avail. In-rm modem
link. Valet serv Mon-Fri. Sundries.
Exercise equipt. Microwaves; many
fireplaces. Balconies. Picnic tables. Cr
cds: A, C, D, DS, JCB, MC, V.

Restaurants

★★ **CEILING ZERO.** *500 Anthony
Trl (60062). 847/272-8111.* Hrs: 11:30
am-2 pm, 5:30-9 pm; Fri to 10 pm;
Sat 5:30-10 pm; Sun 5:30-9 pm.
Closed hols. Res accepted. Continen-
tal menu. Bar. Lunch $6-$12, dinner

$11-$24. Specializes in fresh seafood,
lamb, duck. Own pastries. Parking.
Cr cds: A, C, D, DS, MC, V.

★★ **FRANCESCA'S NORTH.** *1145
Church St (60062). 847/559-0260.
www.francescasnorth.com.* Hrs: 11:30
am-2 pm, 5-9 pm; Wed, Thurs to 10
pm; Fri to 10:30 pm; Sat 5-10:30 pm;
Sun 5-9 pm. Res accepted (lunch).
Italian menu. Bar. Lunch $5.95-
$8.95, dinner $8.95-$19.95. Child's
menu. Specializes in veal, chicken,
fish. Contemporary Italian decor
with extensive black-and-white
photo collection. Cr cds: A, MC, V.

★ **FRANCESCO'S HOLE IN THE
WALL.** *254 Skokie Blvd (60062).
847/272-0155.* Hrs: 11:30 am-2:15
pm, 5-9:15 pm; Fri to 10:15 pm; Sat
5-10:15 pm; Sun 4-8:45 pm. Closed
Tues; hols; also Jan. Italian menu.
Wine, beer. A la carte entrees: lunch
$3.50-$10, dinner $10-$19.95. Specializes in veal, chicken, spinach
bread. Own pasta. Totally nonsmoking.

★ **TONELLI'S.** *1038 Waukegan Rd (IL
43) (60062). 847/272-4730.* Hrs: 11
am-10:30 pm; Mon to 10 pm; Fri to
11:30 pm; Sat 4-11:30 pm; Sun 4-10
pm. Closed hols. Italian, American
menu. Bar. Lunch $4-$6.95, dinner
$6.50-$13.25. Child's menu. Specialties: Lake Superior whitefish, veal
piccante, mussels with linguine.
Parking. Cr cds: A, D, MC, V.

Oak Brook

*See also Brookfield, Downers Grove,
Elmhurst, Hinsdale, La Grange*

Pop 2,300 **Elev** 675 ft
Information Village of Oak Brook,
1200 Oak Brook Rd; 630/990-3000

Known as Fullersburg in the mid-
1800s, Oak Brook is the home of Butler National Golf Club. Sports and
recreation have long been important
in this carefully planned village; it
has established and maintains 12
miles of biking and hiking paths and

over 450 acres of parks and recreation land. Today, Oak Brook is identified as both a mecca for international polo players and the headquarters of many major corporations.

What to See and Do

Fullersburg Woods Environmental Center. Observation of wildlife in natural setting (all yr); environmental center and theater, native marsh ecology exhibit; four nature trails. (Daily) 3609 Spring Rd. Phone 630/850-8110. **FREE**

Graue Mill and Museum. Restored mill built in 1852; the only operating water-powered gristmill in the state; station of the Underground Railroad. Miller demonstrates grinding of corn on buhrstones. Exhibits include farm and home implements of the period; rms in Victorian and earlier periods; demonstrations of spinning and weaving. (Mid-Apr-mid-Nov, daily) York and Spring Rds. Phone 630/655-2090. ¢¢

Special Event

Sunday Polo. Mid-June-mid-Sept. Phone 630/990-2394.

Motels/Motor Lodges

★★ **CLUBHOUSE INN.** 630 *Pasquinelli Dr, Westmont (60559). 630/920-2200; fax 630/920-2766. www.clubhouseinn.com.* 137 rms, 2 story, 19 suites. S, D $79-$109; each addl $10; suites $94-$124; under 18 free; wkend rates. Crib free. TV; cable (premium). Indoor pool; whirlpool. Complimentary full bkfst. Restaurant opp 9 am-10:30 pm. Ck-out noon. Coin lndry. Meeting rms. Business servs avail. In-rm modem link. Health club privileges. Some refrigerators, microwaves. Cr cds: A, C, D, DS, MC, V.
🅳 ⇔ ≋ 🐾 🔥

★★ **COMFORT SUITES.** 17 W 445 *Roosevelt Rd, Oakbrook Ter (60181). 630/916-1000; fax 630/916-1068; toll-free 800/228-5150. www.comfortinn. com.* 104 suites, 3 story. S $109; D $119; each addl $10; under 18 free. Crib free. TV; cable (premium), VCR avail (movies). Indoor pool. Complimentary full bkfst, coffee in rms. Restaurant nearby. Ck-out noon. Coin lndry. Meeting rms. Business

servs avail. In-rm modem link. Valet serv. Exercise equipt; sauna. Refrigerators, microwaves. Cr cds: A, C, D, DS, JCB, MC, V.
🅳 🐾 ≋ 🔥 🆂🅲 ⇔

★★ **COURTYARD BY MARRIOTT.** 6 *Transam Plz Dr, Oakbrook Ter (60181). 630/691-1500; fax 630/691-1518; toll-free 800/321-2211. www. courtyard.com.* 147 rms, 3 story. S, D $114-$134; suites $149; under 18 free; wkend rates. Crib free. TV; cable (premium). Indoor pool; whirlpool. Coffee in rms. Restaurant 6:30-10 am. Rm serv. Bar 5-10 pm. Ck-out noon. Coin lndry. Meeting rms. Business servs avail. In-rm modem link. Valet serv. Exercise equipt. Refrigerator in suites. Balconies. Cr cds: A, C, D, DS, MC, V.
🅳 ⇔ 🐾 ≋ 🔥 🆂🅲

★★★ **FOUR POINTS BY SHERATON BARCELO HOTEL.** 17 W 350 *22nd St, Oakbrook Ter (60181). 630/833-3600; fax 630/833-7037. www.fourpoints.com.* 228 rms, 7 story. S $139; D $149; suites $206; under 12 free. Crib free. TV; cable (premium). Indoor pool; whirlpool. Complimentary full bkfst. Coffee in rms. Restaurant 6:30 am-10 pm. Bar to midnight. Ck-out noon. Meeting rms. Business servs avail. Sundries. Golf privileges. Exercise equipt. Some refrigerators, microwaves. Cr cds: A, D, DS, MC, V.
🅳 ⇔ 🐾 🔥 ≋

★★ **HAMPTON INN.** 222 E 22nd St, *Lombard (60148). 630/916-9000; fax 630/916-8016. www.hamptoninn.com.* 128 rms, 4 story. S, D $99; under 18 free. Crib free. TV; cable (premium). Complimentary continental bkfst. Restaurant nearby. Ck-out noon. Meeting rms. Business servs avail. In-rm modem link. Exercise equipt. Cr cds: A, D, DS, MC, V.
🅳 🐾 ≋ 🔥 🆂🅲

★★ **HAMPTON INN.** 2222 Enter-*prise Dr, Westchester (60154). 708/409-1000; fax 708/409-1055; toll-free 800/426-7866. www.hamptoninn. com.* 112 rms, 4 story. S, D $119-$129; under 18 free; wkend rates. Crib free. TV; cable (premium). Complimentary bkfst. Restaurant opp 11 am-10 pm. Ck-out noon. Meeting rms. Business servs avail.

Exercise equipt. Cr cds: A, C, D, DS, JCB, MC, V.

D ⬚ ⬚ ⬚ SC

★★ **LA QUINTA INN.** *1 S 666 Midwest Rd, Oakbrook Ter (60181). 630/495-4600; fax 630/495-2558; toll-free 800/531-5900. www.laquinta.com.* 151 rms, 3 story. S $79-$89; D $79-$93; each addl $10; under 18 free. Crib free. Pet accepted, some restrictions. TV; cable (premium). Heated pool. Complimentary continental bkfst. Coffee in rms. Restaurant adj open 24 hrs. Ck-out noon. Meeting rms. Business servs avail. In-rm modem link. Health club privileges. Cr cds: A, C, D, DS, MC, V.

D ⬚ ⬚ ⬚ ⬚ SC

Hotels

★★★ **HYATT REGENCY OAK BROOK.** *1909 Spring Rd (60523). 630/573-1234; fax 630/573-1133; toll-free 800/233-1234. www.hyatt.com.* 423 rms, 7 story. S $149-$245; D $174-$270; each addl $25; suites $350-$700; parlor $250-$350; under 18 free; wkend rates. Crib free. TV; cable (premium). Indoor pool; whirlpool. Restaurants 6:30 am-10:30 pm. Rm serv. Bar 11:30-1 am. Ck-out noon. Convention facilities. Business center. Sundries. Gift shop. Barber shop. Exercise equipt. Refrigerators, microwaves avail. 7-story circular, tiered lobby. Shopping center adj. Luxury level. Cr cds: A, C, D, DS, JCB, MC, V.

D ⬚ ⬚ ⬚ ⬚ SC ⬚

★★★ **MARRIOTT OAK BROOK CHICAGO.** *1401 W 22nd St (60523). 630/573-8555; fax 630/573-1026; toll-free 800/228-9290. www.marriott.com.* 347 rms, 12 story. S $169-$199; D $179-$209; each addl $10; suites $194-$204; under 18 free; wkend rates. Crib free. TV; cable (premium), VCR avail. Heated pool; whirlpool, poolside serv. Coffee in rms. Restaurant 6:30 am-10 pm. Bar noon-midnight, Fri-Sat to 1 am. Ck-out 1 pm. Coin lndry. Meeting rms. Business center. In-rm modem link. Gift shop. Exercise equipt. Some bathrm phones; refrigerators, microwaves avail. Luxury levels. Cr cds: A, C, D, DS, JCB, MC, V.

D ⬚ ⬚ ⬚ ⬚ SC ⬚

★★★ **RENAISSANCE OAK BROOK HOTEL.** *2100 Spring Rd (60523). 630/573-2800; fax 630/573-7134. www.renaissancehotels.com.* 166 rms, 10 story. S $159; D $174; each addl $15; suites $300; under 18 free; wkend package plans. Crib free. TV; cable (premium), VCR avail (free movies). Heated rooftop pool; wading pool, poolside serv. Complimentary coffee. Restaurant 6:30 am-10:30 pm. Rm serv 24 hrs. Bar 11:15-1 am. Ck-out 1 pm. Meeting rms. Business center. Concierge. Exercise equipt; sauna. Minibars. Cr cds: A, D, DS, MC, V.

D ⬚ ⬚ ⬚ ⬚ SC ⬚

★★★ **WYNDHAM DRAKE HOTEL.** *2301 York Rd (60523). 630/574-5700; fax 630/574-0830; toll-free 800/996-3426. www.wyndham.com.* 160 rms, 2-4 story. S, D $89-$179; each addl $10; under 18 free; wkend packages. Crib free. TV; cable (premium), VCR avail. 2 pools, 1 indoor; whirlpool, poolside serv. Restaurant 6:30 am-10 pm. Rm serv. Bar 11-1 am. Ck-out noon. Meeting rms. Business center. In-rm modem link. Bellhops. Valet serv. 18-hole golf course opp. Exercise equipt. Refrigerator upon request; minibar in some suites. Cr cds: A, C, D, DS, JCB, MC, V.

⬚ ⬚ ⬚ ⬚ ⬚ ⬚

Resort

★★★ **OAK BROOK HILLS HOTEL & RESORT.** *3500 Midwest Rd (60523). 630/850-5555; fax 630/850-5569; toll-free 800/445-3315. www.dolce.com.* 384 rms, 11 story, 38 suites. S $89-$189; D $99-$199; each addl $24; suites $350-$650; under 16 free. Crib free. TV; cable (premium), VCR avail (movies). 2 pools, 1 indoor; whirlpools, poolside serv. Restaurants 6:30 am-10:30 pm. Rm serv 24 hrs. Bars 11-1 am; wkends to 2 am; entertainment. Ck-out 1 pm. Convention facilities. Business center. In-rm modem link. Concierge. Shopping arcade. Barber, beauty shops. Lighted tennis. 18-hole golf, greens fee $65-$75, pro, putting green. X-country ski on site. Exercise rm; saunas. Lawn games. Minibars, bathrm phones. Balconies. Luxury level. Cr cds: A, C, D, DS, JCB, MC, V.

D ⬚ ⬚ ⬚ ⬚ ⬚ ⬚ ⬚

All Suite

★★★ **HILTON SUITES.** *10 Drury Ln, Oakbrook Ter (60181). 630/941-0100; fax 630/941-0299; toll-free 800/445-8667. www.hilton.com.* 212 suites, 10 story. S, D $109-$189; under 18 free. Crib free. TV; cable (premium), VCR. Indoor pool; whirlpool. Complimentary full bkfst, coffee in rms. Restaurant 11:30 am-1:30 pm, 5-10 pm. Rm serv from 5 pm. Bar 4 pm- midnight. Ck-out noon, ck-in 3 pm. Meeting rms. Business center. In-rm modem link. Gift shop. Exercise equipt; sauna. Health club privileges. Microwaves. Drury Lane Theater adj. Cr cds: A, C, D, DS, ER, JCB, MC, V.

Restaurants

★★ **BRAXTON SEAFOOD GRILL.** *3 Oak Brook Center Mall (60523). 630/574-2155.* Hrs: 11:30 am-10 pm; Fri, Sat to 11 pm; Sun 11:30 am-9 pm. Closed hols. Res accepted. Bar. Lunch $6.95-$12.95, dinner $8.95-$19.95. Child's menu. Specializes in seafood, steak. Own pastries. Dixieland jazz Fri, Sat. Nautical decor. Cr cds: A, C, D, DS, MC, V.

★★ **FOND DE LA TOUR.** *40 N Tower Rd (60521). 630/620-1500.* Hrs: 11:30 am-2:30 pm, 5:30-10 pm. Closed Sun; hols. Res accepted. French menu. Bar to 1 am. Wine list. Lunch $9.95-$15.95, dinner $20.95-$28.95. Specializes in veal, lobster, rack of lamb. Own pastries. Pianist (wkends). Valet parking. French outdoor café decor. Cr cds: A, C, D, DS, MC, V.

★ **MELTING POT.** *17 W 633 Roosevelt Rd, Oakbrook Terrace (60181). 630/495-5778. www.meltingpot.net.* Hrs: 5-11 pm; Fri, Sat to midnight; Sun to 10 pm. Closed hols. Res accepted. Bar. Dinner $11.99-$21.99. Specializes in fondues, combination platters. Parking. Traditional fondue dining experience. Cr cds: A, D, DS, MC, V.

★ **MORTON'S OF CHICAGO.** *1 Westbrook Corporate Ctr, Westchester (60153). 708/562-7000. www.mortons.*
com. Hrs: 11:30 am-2:30 pm, 5:30-11 pm; Sat from 5 pm; Sun 5-10 pm. Closed hols. Res accepted. Bar. Wine list. A la carte entrees: lunch $7.95-$18.95, dinner $16.95-$29.95. Specializes in steak, lobster, prime rib. Valet parking. Cr cds: A, D, MC, V.

★★ **PEPPER MILL.** *18 S 066 22nd St, Oakbrook Ter (60181). 630/620-5656. www.pepper-mill.com.* Hrs: 6 am-midnight; Fri, Sat to 2 am. Closed Thanksgiving, Dec 25. Res accepted. Continental menu. Serv bar. Bkfst $3.50-$6.50, lunch $4.95-$8, dinner $7.95-$15. Child's menu. Specializes in pasta, steaks, fresh seafood. Salad bar. Patio dining. Casual atmosphere. Cr cds: A, C, D, DS, MC, V.

Oak Lawn

Pop 55,245 **Elev** 615 ft **Area code** 708
Information Chamber of Commerce, 5314 W 95th St, 60453; 708/424-8300

In 1856, Oak Lawn was a settlement known as Black Oaks Grove. When the Wabash Railroad began to lay tracks through the community in 1879, an agreement was made with the railroad builder to create a permanent village. As a result of this agreement, the new town of Oak Lawn was officially established in 1882.

Motels/Motor Lodges

★★ **BAYMONT INN.** *12801 S Cicero, Alsip (60803). 708/597-3900; fax 708/597-3979. www.baymontinn. com.* 102 rms, 3 story. S, D $85-$160; suites $69.95-$109.95. Crib free. Pet accepted. TV; cable (premium), VCR avail (movies). Complimentary continental bkfst. Coffee in rms. Restaurant nearby. Ck-out noon. Meeting rm. Business servs avail. Some refrigerators. Cr cds: A, MC, V.

★★ **EXEL INN.** *9625 S 76th Ave, Bridgeview (60455). 708/430-1818; fax 708/430-1894; toll-free 800/356-*

8013. *www.exelinns.com*. 113 rms, 3 story. S $46-$90; D $53-$130; under 18 free. Crib free. Pet accepted, some restrictions. TV; cable (premium). Complimentary continental bkfst. Coffee in rms. Restaurant nearby. Ck-out noon. Coin lndry. Business servs avail. Game rm. Exercise equipt. Microwaves avail. Cr cds: A, C, D, DS, MC, V.

★★ **HAMPTON INN.** *13330 S Cicero Ave, Crestwood (60445). 708/597-3330; fax 708/597-3691; toll-free 800/426-7866. www.hamptoninn.com.* 123 rms, 4 story. S $72-$92; D $78-$94; under 18 free; higher rates New Years Eve. Crib free. Pet accepted, some restrictions. TV; cable (premium), VCR avail. Indoor pool. Complimentary continental bkfst. Restaurant nearby. Ck-out noon. Meeting rms. Business servs avail. In-rm modem link. Free airport transportation. Exercise equipt. Cr cds: A, C, D, DS, JCB, MC, V.

★★ **HOLIDAY INN.** *4140 W 95th St (60453). 708/425-7900; fax 708/425-7918; toll-free 800/362-5529. www.holiday-inn.com.* 140 rms, 5 story. S $89-$109; D $99-$119; each addl $10; under 19 free. Crib free. TV; cable (premium). Heated pool. Complimentary coffee in lobby. Restaurant 6:30 am-10:30 pm; wkends from 7 am. Bar 11-2 am. Ck-out noon. Meeting rms. Business servs avail. In-rm modem link. Valet serv. Sundries. Free airport transportation. Luxury level. Cr cds: A, MC, V.

Hotels

★★★ **HILTON OAK LAWN.** *9333 S Cicero Ave (60453). 708/425-7800; fax 708/425-1665. www.hilton.com.* 173 rms, 12 story. S $143; D $153; each addl $10; suites $329-$629; family rates; package plans. Crib free. TV; cable (premium), VCR avail. Indoor pool; whirlpool. Complimentary continental bkfst, coffee in rms. Restaurant (see WHITNEY'S BAR AND GRILL). Bar 11-2 am, Sun from noon; entertainment Tues-Sat. Ck-out noon. Meeting rms. Business servs avail. In-rm modem link. Gift shop. Free Midway Airport transportation. Exercise equipt; sauna. Luxury level. Cr cds: A, C, D, DS, MC, V.

★★★ **RADISSON HOTEL.** *5000 W 127th St, Alsip (60803). 708/371-7300; fax 708/371-9949. www.radisson.com.* 193 rms, 5 story. S, D $99-$119; each addl $10; suites $199; under 19 free; wkend rates. Crib free. TV; cable (premium). Indoor pool. Restaurant 6 am-10 pm. Rm serv. Bar 11 am-midnight; wkends to 2 am. Ck-out noon. Coin lndry. Meeting rms. Business servs avail. In-rm modem link. Bellhops. Sundries. Free airport transportation. Exercise equipt. Game rm. Microwaves avail. Cr cds: A, C, D, DS, MC, V.

Restaurants

★★ **OLD BARN.** *8100 S Central Ave, Burbank (60459). 708/422-5400.* Hrs: 11:30 am-3 pm, 4-9 pm; Fri, Sat 5-10 pm; early-bird dinner Mon-Thur 4-6 pm. Closed hols. Res accepted. Bar. Lunch $5-$8, dinner $8.95-$20. Child's menu. Specialties: prime rib, roast duck, barbecue ribs. Valet parking. Original building (1933) was speak-easy during Prohibition; original door buzzer. Family-owned. Cr cds: A, D, DS, MC, V.

★★ **WHITNEY'S BAR AND GRILL.** *9333 S Cicero Ave (60453). 708/229-8888. www.oaklawn.hilton.com.* Hrs: 6:30 am-10:30 pm; Fri to 11:30 pm; Sat 7 am-11:30 pm; Sun 7 am-10 pm; early-bird dinner Mon-Thurs 5-6 pm; Sun brunch 8 am-1:45 pm. Res accepted. Continental menu. Bar; Fri, Sat to 2 am. Bkfst $2.75-$10.75, lunch $7.95-$9.95, dinner $12.95-$21.95. Sun brunch $8.95. Child's menu. Specialties: strip steak, halibut, grilled pork chops. Pianist Tues-Sat. Contemporary decor. Cr cds: A, C, D, DS, MC, V.

Frank Lloyd Wright Home, Oak Park

Oak Park

See also Cicero

Settled 1837 **Pop** 52,524 **Elev** 620 ft
Area code 708
Information Oak Park Chamber of
Commerce, 1110 North Blvd, 60301;
708/848-8151
Web www.ci.river-forest.il.us

Oak Park, one of Chicago's oldest
suburbs, is a village of well-kept
houses and magnificent trees. The
town is internationally famous as the
birthplace of Ernest Hemingway and
for its concentration of Prairie School
houses by Frank Lloyd Wright and
other modern architects of the early
20th century. Wright both lived in
the town and practiced architecture
from his Oak Park studio between
1889-1909.

What to See and Do

Ernest Hemingway Museum.
Restored 1890's Victorian home.
Exhibits include rare photos, artifacts, and letters. Four video presentations. Walking tours of Hemingway
sites, including birthplace. (Sat, also
Fri and Sun afternoons; closed hols)
200 N Oak Park Ave, in Arts Center.
Phone 708/848-2222. ¢¢

**Frank Lloyd Wright Home and Stu-
dio.** Wright built this house in 1889,
when he was 22 yrs old. He remodeled the inside on an average of
every 18 months, testing his new
design ideas while creating the
Prairie School of architecture in the
process. Guided tours (daily, inquire
for schedule; closed Jan 1, Thanksgiving, Dec 25). National Trust for
Historic Preservation property. 951
Chicago Ave. Phone 708/848-1976.
¢¢¢

⭐ **Oak Park Visitors Center.** Information guidebooks; orientation program on Frank Lloyd Wright Prairie
School of Architecture National Historic District; recorded walking tour;
admission tickets for tours of
Wright's home and studio; other
walking tours. (Daily) 158 N Forest
Ave, at Lake St. Phone 708/848-
1976. ¢¢¢

Pleasant Home Mansion. Opulent 30-
room mansion designed by prominent Prairie School architect George
W. Maher in 1897. Second floor is
home to the Oak Park/River Forest
Historical Society and Museum.
(Thurs-Sun afternoons, guided tours
on the hr) 217 S Home Ave. Phone
708/383-2654. ¢¢

Unity Temple. (Unitarian Universalist
Church) National landmark was
designed by Frank Lloyd Wright in
1906. The church is noted as his first

monolithic concrete structure and his first public building. Self-guided tour (Mon-Fri, afternoons; wkend tours avail). 875 Lake St. Phone 708/848-6225. ¢¢

Olney (F-6)

Pop 8,631 **Elev** 482 ft **Area code** 618 **Zip** 62450

Information Chamber of Commerce, 309 E Main St, PO Box 575; 618/392-2241

Olney is locally famous as the "home of the white squirrels." Local legend has it that the white squirrels first appeared here in 1902 when a hunter captured a male and female albino and put them on display. An outraged citizen, learning of their capture, ordered their release into the woods. Although the male was killed shortly thereafter, baby white squirrels were seen in the woods weeks later. The population has since increased to approximately 800 of these unusual albino squirrels. Olney is serious about its albino colony and has passed laws for their protection, including right-of-way for the white squirrels on any street in town.

What to See and Do

Bird Haven-Robert Ridgway Memorial. Arboretum and bird sanctuary on 18 acres. Established on land purchased in 1906 by Robert Ridgway, noted naturalist, scientist, artist, and author. The sanctuary contains dozens of varieties of trees, shrubs, and vines, many of which are still being identified; nature trails; replica of the original porch of the Ridgway cottage; Ridgway's grave. (Daily) N on East St to Miller's Grove. **FREE**

Special Events

Richland County Fair. Fairgrounds on IL 130. Livestock shows and exhibits, car races, horse show, entertainment, food. Wk mid-July. Phone 618/392-2241.

Fall Festival of Arts & Crafts. Juried fine arts and crafts show. Last Sat Sept. Phone 618/395-4444.

Oregon

(A-4) *See also De Kalb, Dixon, Rockford*

Settled 1833 **Pop** 4,060 **Elev** 702 ft **Area code** 815 **Zip** 61061

Information Chamber of Commerce, 201 N 3rd St, Suite 14; 815/732-2100

Generations of artists have found inspiration in the scenic beauty of the region surrounding Oregon. In 1898, sculptor Lorado Taft and others founded a colony for artists and writers. Located on Rock River, Oregon is the home of Lorado Taft Field Campus, Northern Illinois University.

What to See and Do

Castle Rock State Park. On 2,000 acres. Fishing, boating (motors, launching ramp); hiking and ski trails, tobogganing, picnicking. Nature preserve. Canoe camping only (May-Oct; fee). Approx 3 mi SW on IL 2. Phone 815/732-7329. **FREE**

Ogle County Historical Society Museum. (1878) Restored frame house was home of Chester Nash, inventor of the cultivator. Displays local historical exhibits. (May-Oct, Thurs and Sun, limited hrs; also by appt) 111 N 6th St. Phone 815/732-6876. **FREE**

Oregon Public Library Art Gallery. Displays work of the original Lorado Taft Eagle's Nest art group. (Mon-Sat; closed hols) 300 Jefferson St. Phone 815/732-2724. **FREE**

Pride of Oregon. Lunch and dinner excursions aboard turn-of-the-century paddlewheeler along Rock River (2 1/2 hrs). (Apr-Nov, daily) Departs from Maxson Manor, 1469 Illinois St (IL 2 N). Phone 815/732-6761. ¢¢¢¢

Scenic drive. N on IL 2, along the Rock River. Two mi N of town is

Lowden Memorial State Park. Park established on 207 acres in memory of former Illinois Governor Frank O. Lowden, who lived nearby. Fishing, boating (ramp); hiking, picnicking, concession, camping. Standard fees. (Mid-May-mid-Oct) Phone 815/732-6828. **FREE** On the bluffs above Rock River is

Monument to the Native American. Rising 48 ft above brush-covered bluffs, this monumental work by Lorado Taft was constructed in 1911 of poured Portland cement. The statue is usually referred to as **Blackhawk** and is regarded as a monument to him.

Soldiers Memorial. War memorial by Beaux Arts sculptor Lorado Taft, completed in 1916, consists of two life-size soliders on either side of an allegorical figure symbolizing peace. On courthouse sq, downtown. Phone 800/369-2955.

Stronghold Castle. Replica of old English castle built in 1929 by newspaper publisher Walter Strong; now owned by the Presbytery of Blackhawk, Presbyterian Church. Grounds (daily). Tours avail; group of 15 min, by appt only (Mon-Fri). (See SPECIAL EVENT) Phone 815/732-6111. Tours ¢ Farther N on IL 2 and on the E side of the Rock River is

White Pines Forest State Park. On 385 acres. Contains the northernmost large stand of virgin white pine in Illinois. Fishing; hiking, x-country skiing, picnicking, concession, lodge, dining facilities, camping. Standard fees. 8 mi W on Pines Rd, near Mt Morris. Phone 815/946-3717. **FREE**

Special Event

Autumn on Parade. Farmers market, entertainment, parade, demonstrations; tours of Stronghold Castle. First wkend Oct. Phone 815/732-2100.

Ottawa

(B-5) *See also Morris, Peru*

Founded 1829 **Pop** 18,307 **Elev** 480 ft
Area code 815 **Zip** 61350
Information Ottawa Area Chamber of Commerce & Industry, 100 W Lafayette St, PO Box 888; 815/433-0084
Web www.ottawa.il.us

Founded by the commissioners of the Illinois and Michigan Canal, Ottawa took root only after the Black Hawk War. The first of the Lincoln-Douglas debates took place in the town's public square; a monument in Washington Park marks the site. Located at the confluence of the Fox and Illinois rivers, many industries are now located in this "Town of Two Rivers."

What to See and Do

Buffalo Rock State Park. Part of the I & M Canal State Trail on 243 acres. Live buffalo. Hiking, picnicking (shelters), playground. 5 mi W off US 6 on Dee Bennett Rd. Phone 815/433-2220 or 815/942-0796. **FREE** Adj is

Effigy Tumuli Sculpture. The largest earth sculptures since Mt Rushmore were formed as part of a reclamation project on the site of a former strip mine. Fashioned with the use of earthmoving equipt, the five enormous figures—a snake, turtle, catfish, frog, and water strider—were deliberately designed and formed to recall similar earth sculptures done by pre-Columbian Native Americans as ceremonial or burial mounds called *tumuli*. (Daily) 1100 Canal St. Phone 815/433-2220. **FREE**

Skydive Chicago, Inc. Largest skydiving center in Midwest. (Daily) Ottawa Airport, off I-80. Phone 815/433-0000. ¢¢¢¢

Starved Rock State Park. (see). 10 mi W on IL 71.

William Reddick Mansion (1855). Italianate, antebellum mansion has 22 rooms, ornate walnut woodwork, and ornamental plasterwork; period room contains many original furnishings. House served as public library from 1889-early 1970s. Mansion (Mon-Fri); guided tours (by appt). 100 W Lafayette St.

Special Event

Ottawa's Riverfest Celebration. Parade, fireworks, carnival, family activities, Gospel concert, and Polkafest. Ten days late July-early Aug. Phone 815/433-0161.

Motel/Motor Lodge

★★ **OTTAWA INN SUITES.** *3000 Columbus St (61350).* 815/434-3400; fax 815/434-3904. 120 rms, 2 story. S D $39.95-$44.95; each addl $6; suites

$58-$76; under 13 free. Crib free. Pet accepted, some restrictions. TV; cable. Indoor pool; whirlpool. Restaurant 7 am-1 pm, 5-9:15 pm; Sun 7 am-noon. Bar 11 am-midnight; Fri, Sat to 1 am. Ck-out 11 am. Meeting rms. Business servs avail. Game rm. Exercise equipt. Some refrigerators, microwaves. Cr cds: A, C, D, DS, MC, V.

Restaurants

★ **CAPTAIN'S COVE BAR AND GRILL.** *Starved Rock Marina (61350).* *815/434-0881.* Hrs: 11 am-9 pm; Sun 9 am-8 pm. Closed Mon; Jan-Feb. Res accepted. Bar. Lunch, dinner $4.95-$13.95. Specializes in steak, seafood, pasta. Own baking. Entertainment wkends (in season). Outdoor dining. Screened deck overlooks Illinois River, Starved Rock Canyon Basin. Cr cds: MC, V.

★ **MONTE'S RIVERSIDE INN.** *903 E Norris Dr (61350).* *815/434-5000.* Hrs: 11 am-9 pm; Sat 4-10 pm. Closed Dec 25. Res accepted. Lunch $4.95-$7.95, dinner $7.95-$18.95. Specializes in prime rib, pasta, chicken. Adj boat docking at Fox River. Cr cds: A, MC, V.

Peoria

(C-4) *See also Bloomington*

Settled 1691 **Pop** 112,936 **Elev** 510 ft **Area code** 309

Information Peoria Area Convention & Visitors Bureau, 456 Fulton St, Suite 300, 61602; 309/676-0303 or 800/747-0302

Web www.peoria.org

In the heart of a rich agricultural basin on the Illinois River, Peoria is the oldest settlement in the state. Louis Jolliet and Pere Marquette, along with a French party, discovered the area in 1673. La Salle established Fort Créve Coeur on the eastern shore of Peoria Lake (a wide stretch in the Illinois River) in 1680. In 1691-1692, Tonti and LaForest established Fort St. Louis II on a site within the city. The settlement that grew around the fort has, except for a brief period during the Fox Wars, been continuously occupied since. The British flag flew over Peoria from 1763-1778, and for a short time in 1781, the Spanish held Peoria. The city is named for the Native Americans who occupied the area when the French arrived.

Peoria is the international headquarters of Caterpillar, Inc., makers of earthmoving equipment used worldwide. The city is also known for steel; information/high-tech firms; and agricultural-based companies, including stockyards and a commodity market. Peoria is the home of Bradley University (1897) and the University of Illinois-Peoria College of Medicine.

What to See and Do

Eureka College. (1855) 500 students. Liberal arts and sciences. One of the first coeducational colleges in the country. The school's most famous graduate is Ronald Reagan. The ground's Peace Garden honors Ronald Reagan's famous 1982 speech regarding the end of the Cold War. There is a bronze bust of the president and a piece of the Berlin Wall. Also of interest are the historic Burrus Dickinson Hall (1857) and the Chapel (1869). Also here is 18 mi E on US 24 in Eureka. Phone 309/467-6318.

Forest Park Nature Center. More than 800 acres of hardwood forest with reconstructed prairie (1½ acres); nature trails (five mi); natural science museum. (Daily) 5809 Forest Park Dr, ½ mi off IL 29. Phone 309/686-3360. **FREE**

Glen Oak Park & Zoo. Park on heavily wooded bluffs includes zoo with more than 250 species; amphitheater (concerts in summer); Queen Anne/Victorian pavilion, tennis courts, playground, fishing lagoon, concession. Free on Tues. (Daily) Prospect Rd and McClure Ave. ¢¢ Also here is

   George L. Luthy Memorial Botanical Garden. All-season gardens, rose garden, herb garden, perennial garden on 4½ acres. Conservatory includes floral display areas, tropical plants; orchid, Easter lily display; also mum display (Nov), poinsettia display (Dec). Conservatory (daily; closed Dec 25, Jan 1; special schedule for displays). Gardens (daily). Phone 309/686-3362. **Donation**

Jubilee College State Historic Site. Historic site, on 90 acres, preserved Jubilee College campus, one of the first educational institutions in Illinois (1840-1862). Original Gothic Revival building and chapel are restored. Hiking, picnicking. (Daily; closed Jan 1, Thanksgiving, Dec 25) 15 mi NW on US 150, in Brimfield. Phone 309/243-9489. 3 mi NW on US 150 is

Jubilee College State Park. More than 3,000-acre park with hiking, bridle, x-country, and snowmobile trails; picnicking, camping. Standard fees. Phone 309/446-3758. **FREE**

Lakeview Museum of Arts and Sciences. Contains permanent and changing exhibits in the arts and sciences; 300-seat auditorium for concerts, lectures, movies; natural science history area; Children's Discovery Center; special exhibits. Gift shop. Sculpture garden and picnic area. (Tues-Sun; closed hols) 1125 W Lake Ave, at University St N. Phone 309/686-7000. ¢¢ Also here is the

Planetarium. Multimedia shows and constellation programs (schedule varies). Largest scale model of our solar system. Phone 309/686-NOVA. ¢¢

Metamora Courthouse State Historic Site. One of the two remaining courthouse structures on the old Eighth Judicial Circuit, in which Lincoln practiced law for 12 yrs. The building (1845), constructed of native materials, is a fine example of Classical Revival architecture. On the first floor is a museum containing collection of pioneer artifacts and an exhibit pertaining to the old Eighth Judicial Circuit; on the second floor is the restored courtroom. Guide service. (Tues-Sat; closed Jan 1, Thanksgiving, Dec 25) 10 mi NE on IL 116, at 113 E Partridge in Metamora. Phone 309/367-4470. **FREE**

Peoria Historical Society Buildings.

Flanagan House. Oldest standing house in Peoria (ca 1837), Federal in style, contains pre-Civil War furniture, primitive kitchen, children's room with antique toys, carpenter's shop with large collection of antique tools. Location on bluffs above Illinois River affords beautiful view of entire river valley. (Wed-Sun or by appt) 942 NE Glen Oak Ave. Phone 309/674-0322. ¢¢

Pettengill-Morron House. (1868) Italianate/Second Empire mansion, built by Moses Pettengill, was purchased by Jean Morron in 1953 to replace her ancestral house, which was being destroyed to make way for a freeway. She moved a two-century accumulation of household furnishings and family heirlooms, as well as such architectural pieces as the old house's cast-iron fence, chandeliers, marble mantles, and brass rails from the porch. (By appt) (See SPECIAL EVENTS) 1212 W Moss Ave. Phone 309/674-4745. ¢¢

Spirit of Peoria. Replica of turn-of-the-century sternwheeler offers cruises along Illinois River. Ninety-min sightseeing cruise; Starved Rock State Park cruise, with overnight stay; Peoria to Pere Marquette State Park cruise, with two-night stay. Departs from The Landing at foot of Main St. Phone 309/636-6169 or 800/676-8988.

Theater.

Corn Stock Theater. Theater-in-the-round summer stock under circus-type big top; dramas, comedies, musicals. (June-Aug) Call for schedule and pricing. Bradley Park, near Park Rd and Nebraska Ave. Phone 309/676-2196.

Peoria Players. Dramas, comedies, musicals. (Early Sept-early May, Thurs-Sun; closed hols) Call for schedule and pricing. 4300 N University St. Phone 309/688-4473.

Wheels O' Time Museum. Many antique autos, old tractors, and farm implements; fire engines; antique clocks; musical instruments; tools; model railroads and railroad memorabilia; kitchen equipt; early radios. Hands-on exhibits; outdoor display of steam-era train; changing exhibits; many items relating to Peoria history. (May-Oct, Wed-Sun, also Memorial Day, July 4, Labor Day) 8 mi N on IL 40, at 11923 N Knoxville Ave, PO Box 9636. Phone 309/243-9020. ¢¢

⚅ **Wildlife Prairie Park.** Wildlife and nature preserve with animals native to Illinois in natural habitats along wood-chipped trails: bears, cougars, bobcats, wolves, red foxes, and more. Pioneer homestead has working farm from late 1800s with authentic log cabin and one-room schoolhouse. Walking trails, playground, picnicking, food service; informational slide show (free); lectures and special events throughout summer; 24-inch scale railroad runs along park perimeter. Gift shop, country store. Park (daily); buildings, train, activities (Mar-mid-Dec, daily). No pets permitted. 10 mi W via I-74, Edwards exit 82, then 3 mi S on Taylor Rd. Phone 309/676-0998. ¢¢

Special Events

Steamboat Festival. Riverboat races, boat parade; band concerts, carnival; entertainment, pageant. Three days at Father's Day wkend. Phone 309/681-0696.

Spoon River Valley Scenic Drive. 19 mi W on IL 116 at Farmington, then marked, circular route through Fulton County. Autumn drive through small towns and rolling, wooded countryside noted for fall color (complete drive 140 mi); 19th- and early 20th-century crafts, exhibits, demonstrations; antiques, collectibles; produce, food. Usually first two full wkends Oct. Phone 309/547-3234.

Candlelight Christmas. Victorian Christmas setting at Pettengill-Morron House. Carolers and costumed volunteers in Christmas setting of Victorian period. Early-mid-Dec. Phone 309/674-4745.

Motels/Motor Lodges

★★★ **COMFORT SUITES.** *4021 N War Memorial Dr (61614). 309/688-3800; fax 309/688-3800; toll-free 800/228-5150. www.comfortsuites.com.* 66 suites, 2 story. S, D $79; each addl $5; under 18 free. Crib free. Pet accepted. TV, cable (premium). Indoor pool; whirlpool. Complimentary continental bkfst. Restaurant nearby. Ck-out 11 am. Meeting rm. Business servs avail. In-rm modem link. Health club privileges. Cr cds: A, C, D, DS, ER, JCB, MC, V.

🅓 🐾 ⛱ ⚊ 🐾 **SC**

★★ **FAIRFIELD INN.** *4203 N War Memorial Dr (61614). 309/686-7600; fax 309/686-0686. www.fairfieldinn.com.* 135 rms, 3 story. S, D $59-$69; under 18 free. Crib free. TV; cable (premium), VCR avail. Heated pool. Complimentary continental bkfst. Restaurant nearby. Ck-out noon. Business servs avail. In-rm modem link. Health club privileges. Cr cds: A, D, DS, MC, V.

🅓 ⛱ ⚊ 🐾

★★ **HAMPTON INN.** *11 Winners Way, East Peoria (61611). 309/694-0711; fax 309/694-0711. www.hamptoninn.com.* 154 rms, 5 story. S, D $89; suites $125; under 18 free. Crib free. TV; cable (premium). Indoor pool; whirlpool. Complimentary continental bkfst. Coffee in rms. Restaurant nearby. Ck-out noon. Meeting rms. Business servs avail. In-rm modem link. Bellhops. Free airport, bus depot transportation. Exercise equipt. Health club privileges. Refrigerator in suites. Cr cds: A, C, D, DS, MC, V.

🅓 ⚊ 🏋 ⚊ 🐾 **SC**

★ **MARK TWAIN HOTEL.** *401 N Main St, East Peoria (61611). 309/699-7231; fax 309/698-7833; toll-free 800/325-6088. www.marktwain hotels.com.* 116 rms, 2 story. S, D $49-$79; each addl $8; under 12 free. Crib $15. TV; cable (premium). Indoor pool; whirlpool. Complimentary full bkfst. Restaurant adj 11-1 am. Bar 11-1 am. Ck-out 11 am. Coin lndry. Meeting rms. Business servs avail. Free airport, bus depot transportation. Exercise equipt; sauna. Health club privileges. Cr cds: A, C, D, DS, MC, V.

🅓 ⚊ 🏋 ⚊ 🐾

★ **RED ROOF INN.** *4031 N War Memorial Dr (61614). 309/685-3911; fax 309/685-3941. www.redroof.com.* 108 rms, 2 story. S $41.99-$47.99; D $47.99-$59.99; under 18 free. Crib free. Pet accepted. TV; cable (premium), VCR avail. Complimentary coffee in lobby. Ck-out noon. Business servs avail. Cr cds: A, C, D, DS, MC, V.

🅓 🐾 ⚊ 🐾

★ ★ **SIGNATURE INN.** *4112 N Brandywine Dr (61614). 309/685-2556; fax 309/685-2556. www. signature-inns.com.* 124 rms, 3 story. S, D $69; each addl $7; under 17 free. Crib free. TV; cable (premium), VCR avail. Pool. Complimentary continental bkfst. Coffee in rms. Restaurant nearby. Ck-out noon. Meeting rms. Business center. In-rm modem link. Exercise equipt. Health club privileges. Some refrigerators, microwaves. Cr cds: A, D, DS, MC, V.
🄳 ⌁ 🏋 ✈ 🗟 🔥 🏃

Hotels

★ ★ **HOLIDAY INN CITY CENTRE.** *500 Hamilton Blvd (61602). 309/674-2500; fax 309/674-8705; toll-free 800/474-2501. www.holiday-inn.com.* 327 rms, 9 story. S $79-$89; D $89-$99; each addl $10; suites $105-$350; under 12 free. Crib free. Pet accepted. TV; cable. Pool. Coffee in rms. Restaurant 6 am-10 pm. Bar 11-2 am. Ck-out noon. Convention facilities. Business center. In-rm modem link. Gift shop. Barber. Free airport, bus depot transportation. Exercise equipt. Luxury level. Cr cds: A, MC, V.
🄳 ⌁ ⌁ 🏋 🗟 🔥 SC 🏃

★ ★ **HOTEL PÈRE MARQUETTE.** *501 Main St (61602). 309/637-6500; fax 309/637-6500; res 800/447-1676. www.hotelperemarquette.com.* 288 rms, 12 story. S $79-$105; D $79-$115; each addl $15; suites, kit. units $200-$500; studio rms $175; under 18 free; package plans. Crib free. Pet accepted. TV; cable (premium). Restaurant 6 am-2 pm, 5-10 pm. Bar. Ck-out noon. Convention facilities. Business servs avail. In-rm modem link. Gift shop. Free covered parking. Free airport transportation. Exercise equipt. Health club privileges. Refrigerator in suites. Restored 1920s hotel. Cr cds: A, D, DS, MC, V.
🄳 ⌁ 🏋 ✈ 🗟 🔥 SC

★ ★ ★ **JUMER'S CASTLE LODGE.** *117 N Western Ave (61604). 309/673-8040; fax 309/673-9782; toll-free 800/285-8637. www.jumers.com.* 175 rms, 4 story. S $79-$126; D $88-$135; each addl $10; under 18 free. Crib free. Pet accepted, some restrictions. TV; cable (premium), VCR avail. Pool; whirlpool. Complimentary coffee in lobby. Restaurant (see JUMER'S

CASTLE). Bar 11-1 am; entertainment exc Sun. Ck-out noon. Meeting rms. Business servs avail. In-rm modem link. Valet parking. Free airport transportation. Health club privileges. Some fireplaces. Bavarian decor. Cr cds: A, C, D, DS, MC, V.
🄳 ⌁ ⌁ 🗟 🔥 SC

Restaurants

★ ★ ★ **JUMER'S CASTLE.** *117 N Western Ave (61604). 309/673-8040. www.jumers.com.* Hrs: 6:30 am-10 pm; Fri to 11 pm; Sat 7 am-11 pm; Sun 7 am-10 pm; hols 7 am-8 pm; early-bird dinner 4:30-6 pm. Res accepted. German, American menu. Bar. Bkfst $1.95-$7.50, lunch $4.75-$6.95, dinner $7.50-$14.95. Child's menu. Specialties: Wiener schnitzel, pork roast, prime rib of beef. Own baking. Entertainment exc Sun. Bavarian decor; antiques. Family-owned. Cr cds: A, D, DS, MC, V.
🄳 ⌐

★ ★ **PAPARAZZI.** *4315 W Voss St, Peoria Heights (61614). 309/682-5205.* Hrs: 5:30-10:30 pm. Closed Sun, Mon; hols. Res accepted. Continental menu. Wine, beer. A la carte entrees: dinner $6-$12. Specializes in pasta, veal. Cozy, comfortable atmosphere. Totally nonsmoking. Cr cds: A, D, DS, MC, V.

Père Marquette State Park

See also Alton, Cahokia

(5 mi W of Grafton on IL 100)

This is Illinois's largest state park, with 8,000 acres at the confluence of the Illinois and Mississippi rivers. It is named after Pére Jacques Marquette, who passed the site with Louis Jolliet in 1673. They were the first white men to enter the present state of Illinois.

Fishing, hunting, boating (ramp, motors); hiking and bridle paths (horses may be rented), picnic areas, playground, concession, lodge, restaurant, campgrounds (standard fees). Interpretive center. Schedule of free guided trips is posted in the visitor center. For information contact the Park Superintendent, PO Box 158, Grafton 62037; 618/786-3323 or 618/786-2331 (lodge).

Peru

(B-5) *See also Ottawa*

Settled 1830 **Pop** 9,835 **Elev** 500 ft
Information Illinois Valley Area Chamber of Commerce and Economic Development, 300 Bucklin St, PO Box 446, La Salle 61301; 815/223-0227
Web www.ivaced.org

What to See and Do

Illinois Waterway Visitor Center. Located at the Starved Rock Lock and Dam; site offers excellent view across river to Starved Rock. The history of the Illinois River from the time of the Native American, the French explorers, the construction of canals, to the modern Illinois Waterway, is portrayed in a series of exhibits. The role of river transport in the nation's economy is also highlighted, with actual riverboat pilot house on display. Featured is a three-screen, 12-min slide presentation, "The Connecting Link," tracing humans' use of the Illinois River for more than 6,000 yrs. (Daily) E on Dee Bennett Rd, S of Utica. Phone 815/667-4054. **FREE**

Lake de Pue. Waterskiing, fishing, boating (ramp); picnicking. 6 mi W on IL 29.

La Salle County Historical Museum. (1848) Exhibits include pioneer furnishings, Native American artifacts, and agricultural displays; Lincoln carriage; historical library, local memorabilia. Prairie grass area; blacksmith shop, turn-of-the-century barn, and one-room schoolhouse. (Wed-Sun; closed hols) 5 mi E on I-80, 1½ mi S on IL 178, at Canal and Mill Sts in Utica. Phone 815/667-4861. ¢

Matthiessen State Park. This 1,938-acre park is particularly interesting for its geological formations, which can be explored via seven mi of hiking trails. Hikers should remain on marked trails because of steep cliffs and the depth of the canyon. The upper area and bluff tops are generally dry and easily hiked, but trails into the interiors of the two dells can be difficult, especially in spring and early summer. The dells feature scenic waterfalls. Also here is a replica of a small fort stockade of the type built by the French in the Midwest during the late 1600s and early 1700s. Model airplane field; archery range with sight-in area and eight separate fields; x-country skiing,

St. Louis Canyon, Starved Rock S.P.

horseback riding (wkends), bridle trails, picnicking, playground, vending area, park office (in dells area). Observation platform. (Daily) 9 mi SE via I-80 E, IL 178 S in Utica. Contact Site Superintendent, PO Box 381, Utica 61373. Phone 815/667-4868. **FREE**

Starved Rock State Park. (see). 6 mi E on I-80 to Utica exit, then S on IL 178.

Special Events

Winter Wilderness Weekend. Departs from Starved Rock Visitor Center. Guided hikes to see the spectacular ice falls of Starved Rock (see).

X-country skiing (rentals, instruction). Jan. Phone 815/667-4906.

Cross-Country Ski Weekend. Guided ski hikes to Matthiessen State Park; ski rentals, instruction. Feb. Phone 815/667-4868.

Wildflower Pilgrimage. Starved Rock Visitor Center. Guided hikes to Starved Rock (see). May. Phone 815/667-4906.

Montreal Canoe Weekends. Begins at Point Shelter at east end of Starved Rock. Ride a replica of the 34-ft "voyageur canoe" that the French used to explore North America. June. Phone 815/667-4906.

National Championship Boat Races. Lake de Pue. Seventeen classes of powerboats compete for national title; beer gardens and live entertainment. Late July. Phone 217/632-7681.

National Sweet Corn Festival. Approx 15 mi N via US 51 in Mendota. Music, parades, Sweet Corn Queen competition, carnival, six-mi race. Second wkend Aug. Phone 815/539-6507.

Motels/Motor Lodges

★★ **COMFORT INN.** 5240 Trompeter Rd (61354). 815/223-8585; fax 815/223-9292. www.comfortinn.com. 50 rms, 3 story. S, D $61-$66; each addl $5; suites $80-$84; under 18 free. Crib free. TV; cable (premium). Pool. Complimentary continental bkfst. Restaurant nearby. Ck-out 11 am. Coin lndry. Meeting rm. Business servs avail. Some refrigerators, microwaves. Cr cds: A, D, DS, MC, V.
[D] [≈] [⊠] [🐾]

★★ **ECONO LODGE.** 1840 May Rd (61354). 815/224-2500; fax 815/224-3693. www.econolodge.com. 104 rms, 2 story. S, D $54.95; each addl $5; under 18 free. Crib free. Pet accepted $10, some restrictions. TV. Pool. Complimentary continental bkfst. Restaurant. Ck-out noon. Coin lndry. Meeting rms. Business servs avail. Cr cds: A, C, D, DS, ER, JCB, MC, V.
[D] [🐾] [≈] [⊠] [🐾] [SC]

★ **SUPER 8 MOTEL.** 1851 May Rd (61354). 815/223-1848; fax 815/223-1848; toll-free 800/800-8000. www.super8.com. 60 rms, 3 story. June-Sept: S $36.88; D $47.88; each addl $5; under 12 free; higher rates special

events; lower rates rest of yr. Crib free. Pet accepted, some restrictions. TV; cable (premium). Complimentary coffee in lobby. Restaurant nearby. Ck-out 11 am. Coin lndry. Cr cds: A, C, D, DS, JCB, MC, V.
[D] [🐾] [⊠] [🐾] [SC]

B&Bs/Small Inns

★★ **BRIGHTWOOD INN.** 2407 IL 178N, Oglesby (61348). 815/667-4600; fax 815/667-4727; res 888/667-0600. www.starved-rock-inn.com. 8 rms, 2-3 story, 1 suite. No elvtr. D $100-$200; each addl $25; suite $235; golf plans; wkends (3-day min). Crib free. TV; VCR (movies). Complimentary full bkfst. Restaurant from 5:30 pm. Ck-out 11 am, ck-in 3-6 pm. Business servs avail. In-rm modem link. Luggage handling. X-country ski 2 mi. Fireplaces; many in-rm whirlpools; refrigerator, microwave in suite. Some balconies. Picnic table. Contemporary decor; adj to a prarie. Totally nonsmoking. Cr cds: A, DS, MC, V.
[D] [⊠] [⊠] [🐾]

★ **YESTERDAY'S MEMORIES BED AND BREAKFAST.** 303 E Peru St, Princeton (54548). 815/872-7753. 4 rms, 3 share bath, 2 story. S $60; D $65; each addl $10; under 3 free. Crib free. TV; VCR avail (movies). Complimentary full bkfst. Restaurant nearby. Ck-out 11 am, ck-in 2 pm. X-country ski 5 mi. Built in 1852; antiques. Totally nonsmoking. Cr cds: A, MC, V.
[⊠] [⊠] [🐾]

Restaurants

★ **THE MAPLES.** 1401 Shooting Park Rd (61354). 815/223-1938. Hrs: 11 am-2 pm, 5-10 pm; Sun to 5 pm (buffet only); Mon to 2 pm. Closed July 4. Res accepted. Bar. Dinner $4.95-$11. Buffet: lunch $5.95, dinner $7.95. Buffet (Sun): lunch, dinner $7.95. Child's menu. Own breads. Salad bar. Family-owned. Cr cds: MC, V.
[D] [SC] [⊠]

★★ **RED DOOR INN.** 1701 Water St (61354). 815/223-2500. Hrs: 11 am-2 pm, 5-11 pm; Sat 4 pm-midnight; Sun 4-10 pm; Sun brunch 10:30 am-2 pm. Closed hols. Res accepted. Bar.

Complete meals: lunch $4.75-$12.75, dinner $10-$25. Buffet: dinner (Fri) $19. Sun brunch $13.75. Specialties: steak Diane, chateaubriand, fresh seafood. Salad bar. Own baking. In historic 1850 riverhouse. Cr cds: A, DS, MC, V.

[D] [⊒]

★★ **UPTOWN GRILL.** *601 1st St, LaSalle (61301). 815/224-4545. www. uptowngrill.com.* Hrs: 11 am-11 pm; Sun noon-10 pm. Closed Thanksgiving, Dec 25. Res accepted. Bar. Lunch $7-$9, dinner $15-$20. Child's menu. Specializes in steak, pasta, seafood. Casual atmosphere. Seasonal outdoor dining. Cr cds: A, C, D, DS, MC, V.

[D] [⊒]

Petersburg

(D-4) *See also Havana, Springfield*

Founded 1833 **Pop** 2,299 **Elev** 524 ft
Area code 217 **Zip** 62675
Information Chamber of Commerce, 125 S 7th St, PO Box 452; 217/632-7363
Web www.petersburgil.com

Surveyed by Abraham Lincoln in 1836, Petersburg was made the seat of Menard County in 1839. Most of the residents of nearby New Salem then moved to Petersburg, and the village where Lincoln spent six years and began his political career eventually sank into ruin. Ironically, it was a later generation of Petersburg residents who were responsible for the rebirth of New Salem.

What to See and Do

Edgar Lee Masters Memorial Home. Boyhood residence of the poet. Living room restored to 1870-1875 period. Rest of house is museum of family history. (Memorial Day-Labor Day, Tues, Thurs-Sat, limited hrs) Contact the Chamber of Commerce. Jackson and 8th Sts. Phone 217/632-7363. **FREE**

Lincoln's New Salem State Historic Site. (see). 2 Erie Blvd. Phone 518/673-2314. **FREE**

Oakland Cemetery. Graves of Ann Rutledge, who some believe to have been Lincoln's first love, and poet Edgar Lee Masters, Petersburg native who wrote *Spoon River Anthology.* Oakland Ave. Phone 217/632-7363.

Special Events

Summer Festival at New Salem. Lincoln's New Salem State Historic Site. Reenactment of a summer day in early 1830s New Salem; crafts; interpretive activities. Wkend mid-July. Phone 217/632-4000.

"Prairie Tales" at New Salem. Lincoln's New Salem State Historic Site. Two-day festival of nationally acclaimed storytellers. Early Aug. Phone 217/632-4000.

Traditional Music Festival. Lincoln's New Salem State Historic Site. Early-Sept. Phone 217/632-4000.

Candlelight Tour of New Salem. Lincoln's New Salem State Historic Site. Early Oct. Phone 217/632-4000.

B&B/Small Inn

★★ **THE OAKS.** *510 W Sheridan (62675). 217/632-5444; res 888/724-6257.* 5 rms, 2 with shower only, 3 story, 2 suites. No rm phones. S, D $75-$90; each addl $10; suites $135; under 13 free. TV in some rms. Complimentary full bkfst; afternoon refreshments. Ck-out 11 am, ck-in 3-6 pm. Luggage handling. Valet serv. Whirlpool in suites. Many fireplaces. 19th century mansion; scenic views; antiques. Cr cds: DS, MC, V.

[⊠] [🐾] [SC]

Quincy (D-2)

Settled 1822 **Pop** 40,366 **Elev** 601 ft
Area code 217 **Zip** 62301
Information Quincy Area Chamber of Commerce, 300 Civic Center Plaza, Suite 245, 62301-4169; 217/222-7980
Web www.quincychamber.org

Quincy, seat of Adams County, was named for President John Quincy Adams. Located on the east bank of the Mississippi River, the town was the site of the sixth Lincoln-Douglas debate, October 13, 1858; a bronze bas-relief in Washington Park marks the spot. Quincy was, in the mid-19th century, the second largest city in Illinois and an industrial, agricultural, and river transportation center. Today Quincy, which remains a center of industry, is known for its historical business district and fine Victorian residences.

What to See and Do

John Wood Mansion. (1835) This two-story, Greek Revival mansion was the residence of the founder of Quincy and a former governor of Illinois. Moved to its present location in about 1864, the house was cut in half and moved across a special bridge. Restored; original furnishings of the period include the first piano in Quincy, three-story Victorian doll house; artifacts of the area; traveling exhibits; museum. (Daily, June-Aug; Apr-Oct, Sat and Sun; also by appt) 425 S 12th St. Phone 217/222-1835. ¢

Quincy Museum. Located in the Newcomb-Stillwell mansion, a Richardson Romanesque-style building. Rotating exhibits and a children's discovery room. (Tues-Sun afternoons) 1601 Maine St. Phone 217/224-7669. ¢

Motel/Motor Lodge

★ **TRAVELODGE.** *200 S 3rd St (62301). 217/222-5620; fax 217/224-2582; toll-free 800/578-7878. www. travelodge.com.* 68 rms, 2 story. S $49; D $59-$79; each addl $5; under 12 free. Crib free. Pet accepted, some restrictions; $10. TV; cable (premium). Pool. Complimentary continental bkfst, coffee in rms. Restaurant 11 am-11 pm. Rm serv. Bar. Ck-out noon. Business servs avail. Coin lndry. Some refrigerators, microwaves. Some balconies. Picnic table. Cr cds: A, C, D, DS, MC, V.

D 🐾 🏊 🐾 **SC**

Rockford

(A-5) *See also De Kalb, Freeport, Oregon*

Founded 1834 **Pop** 150,115 **Elev** 721 ft **Area code** 815
Information Rockford Area Convention & Visitors Bureau, Memorial Hall, 211 N Main St, 61101; 815/963-8111 or 800/521-0849
Web www.gorockford.com

The state's second largest city grew up on both sides of the Rock River and took its name from the ford that was used by the Galena-Chicago Stagecoach Line. The early settlers of Rockford were primarily from New England. Today, much of its population is of Swedish and Italian descent. A commercial center for a vast area, it is the largest manufacturer of screw products and fasteners in the United States and one of the most important machine tool producers in the world.

What to See and Do

Anderson Japanese Gardens. Formal nine-acre gardens with waterfall, ponds, bridges, tea house, guest house, and footpaths. (May-Oct, daily) Spring Creek and Parkview. Phone 815/229-9390. ¢¢

Burpee Museum of Natural History. New 40,000-sq-ft addition. New exhibits, including full-size skeletal cast of a T-Rex; 85-ft-long, two-story-high handpainted mural of prehistoric life; Olson viewing lab; Native American exhibit "First People", state-of-the-art "Geo-Science" exhibit. (Daily) 737 N Main. Phone 815/965-3433. ¢¢

Discovery Center Museum. Hands-on learning museum with more than 120 exhibits illustrating scientific and perceptual principles; visitors can leave their shadow hanging on a wall, create a bubble window, see a planetarium show, learn how a house is built, star in a TV show, or visit a carboniserous coal forest. Adj **Rock River Discovery Park** features weather station, earth and water exhibits. (Tues-Sun, also some Mon hols) 711 N Main St, in Riverfront Museum Park. Phone 815/963-6769. ¢¢

Erlander Home Museum. (1871) Rockford's Swedish heritage is reflected in this two-story brick house built for John Erlander, an early Swedish settler. Restored Victorian interior; display of numerous pioneer artifacts. (Wed-Fri afternoons; Sun, limited hrs; also by appt; closed hols) 404 S 3rd St. Phone 815/963-5559. ¢¢

Magic Waters. This 35-acre water theme park includes five 5-story water slides, wave pool, children's wading pool, island tree house, sand beach, tubing river, playground, concession, picnicking. (Memorial Day-Labor Day, daily) US 20 and US 51 in Cherry Valley. Phone 815/332-3260 or 800/373-1679.

Midway Village & Museum Center. Museum contains permanent and changing exhibits of area history; aviation gallery. Village features blacksmith shop, general store, bank, schoolhouse, church, police station, town hall, law office, residences, hospital, plumbing shop, and hotel. (Memorial Day-Labor Day, daily; Apr-May, Sept-Oct, Thurs-Sun) 6799 Guilford Rd. Phone 815/397-9112. ¢¢

Rock Cut State Park. A 3,092-acre park with two artificial lakes. Swimming beach (Memorial Day-Labor Day), fishing, ice fishing, boating (ramp, rentals; motors, ten-hp limit); ice boating, horseback trail, x-country skiing, snowmobiling, picnicking, concession, camping (fee). (Daily) NE via IL 251, W on IL 173. Phone 815/885-3311. **FREE**

Rockford Art Museum. Permanent collection of 19th- and 20th-century American and European paintings. Also sculpture, graphics, photographs, decorative arts; changing exhibits. (Tues-Sun; closed hols) (See SPECIAL EVENTS) 711 N Main St. Phone 815/968-2787. **FREE**

Sightseeing.

Forest City Queen. Narrated tours; dinner cruises. (June-early Sept, Tues-Sun; closed July 4) Phone 815/987-8894. ¢¢

Rockford Trolley. Scenic ride along the Rock River and Sinnissippi Park aboard replica of a turn-of-the-century trolley car; narrated. (June-

early Sept, Tues, Thurs, Sat, and Sun) Phone 815/987-8894. ¢¢

Sinnissippi Gardens. Sunken gardens, 30-ft-wide floral clock, greenhouse with aviary, lagoon; recreational trail. (Daily; closed Dec 25) 1300-1900 N 2nd St. Phone 815/987-8858. **FREE**

Tinker Swiss Cottage Museum. Built 1865 by a local industrialist to duplicate a Swiss chalet. The 20-room house contains Victorian furniture, art, textiles, porcelain, and handcrafted treasures from the Tinker family. The house features elaborate parquet floors, fine woodwork, and intricately painted ceiling and wall murals; walnut spiral staircase. Tours. (Tues-Sun; closed hols) 411 Kent St. Phone 815/964-2424. ¢¢

Trailside Equestrian Center at Lockwood Park. Pony- and horse-drawn wagon rides; petting corral, riding stable, horsemanship classes; special events. (Apr-Nov, daily) Fee for activities. 5209 Safford Rd, in Lockwood Park. Phone 815/987-8809.

Special Events

Illinois Snow Sculpting Competition. Teams from throughout Illinois compete to represent the state at national and international competitions. Jan. Phone 815/987-8800.

Rockford Speedway. 5 mi N, 9500 Forest Hills Rd. Stock car racing; special auto events. Apr-Oct. Phone 815/633-1500.

Winnebago County Fair. 500 W First St, in Pecatonica. Aug. Phone 815/239-1641.

New American Theater. 118 N Main St. Professional theater; six mainstage shows each season. Sept-June. Phone 815/964-6282.

Greenwich Village Art Fair. Rockford Art Museum. Wkend mid-Sept. Phone 815/968-2787.

Motels/Motor Lodges

★★ **BEST WESTERN COLONIAL INN.** *4850 E State St (61108). 815/398-5050; fax 815/398-8180; toll-free 800/613-1234. www.bestwestern. com.* 84 rms, 2-3 story. S $65-$79; D $89-$99; suites $99-$159; under 12 free. Crib free. Pet accepted. TV; cable, VCR avail (movies). Indoor pool; whirlpool. Complimentary continental bkfst, coffee in rms. Restaurant adj 11 am-11:30 pm. Bar noon-2 am. Ck-out 11 am. Meeting rm. Business servs avail. Coin lndry. Exercise equipt. Refrigerator in suites. Rockford College adj. Cr cds: A, D, DS, MC, V.

[D] [icons] SC [icon]

★★ **COMFORT INN.** *7392 Argus Dr (61107). 815/398-7061; fax 815/398-7061. www.comfortinn.com.* 64 rms, 3 story. May-Oct: S $66.95; D $72.95; each addl $5; under 18 free; lower rates rest of yr. Crib free. TV; cable (premium). Indoor pool; whirlpool. Complimentary continental bkfst. Restaurant nearby. Ck-out 11 am. Business servs avail. Health club privileges. Some refrigerators, microwaves. Cr cds: A, C, D, DS, MC, V.

[D icons] SC [icon]

★★ **COURTYARD BY MARRIOTT.** *7676 E State St (61108). 815/397-6222; fax 815/397-6254. www.courtyard.com.* 148 rms, 2-3 story. S, D $54-$99; suites $90-$139; under 18 free; wkend rates. Crib free. TV; cable (premium). Indoor pool; whirlpool. Complimentary coffee in rms. Restaurant 6:30-9:30 am; Sat, Sun 7-10:30 am. Bar. Ck-out noon. Coin lndry. Meeting rms. Business servs avail. In-rm modem link. Valet serv. Exercise equipt. Business center. Refrigerators, microwaves. Balconies. Cr cds: A, D, DS, MC, V.

[icons] SC [icons]

★ **EXEL INN.** *220 S Lyford Rd (61108). 815/332-4915; fax 815/332-4843. www.exelinns.com.* 100 rms, 2 story. S $39.99-$47.99; D $45.99-$52.99; each addl $5; under 18 free. Crib free. Pet accepted, some restrictions. TV; cable (premium). Complimentary continental bkfst. Restaurant opp. Ck-out noon. Coin lndry. In-rm modem link. Exercise equipt. Health club privileges. Cr cds: A, D, DS, MC, V.

[D icons]

★★ **FAIRFIELD INN.** *7712 Potawatomi Trl (61107). 815/397-8000; fax 815/397-8183. www.fairfield inn.com.* 135 rms, 3 story. S, D $59-$89; under 18 free. Crib free. TV; cable (premium). Pool. Complimentary continental bkfst. Restaurant adj 6 am-10 pm. Ck-out noon. Business

servs avail. In-rm modem link. Cr cds: A, C, D, DS, MC, V.

[D icons]

★★ **HAMPTON INN.** *615 Clark Dr (61107). 815/229-0404; fax 815/229-0175. www.hamptoninn.com.* 122 rms, 4 story. May-Oct: S, D $79-$89; under 18 free; lower rates rest of yr. Crib free. TV; cable (premium). Indoor pool; whirlpool. Complimentary continental bkfst. Restaurant adj 10 am-10 pm. Ck-out noon. Meeting rm. Business servs avail. In-rm modem link. X-country ski 15 mi. Exercise equipt. Cr cds: A, D, DS, MC, V.

[D icons]

★★ **HOLIDAY INN.** *7550 E State St (61108). 815/398-2200; fax 815/229-3122; toll-free 800/383-7829. www.holiday-inn.com.* 202 rms, 7 story. S, D $82-$140; each addl $7; suites $150-$195; under 19 free; higher rates New Years Eve. Crib free. TV; cable (premium). Indoor pool; whirlpool. Restaurant 7 am-9 pm. Rm serv. Bar 11-2 am. Ck-out noon. Meeting rms. Business servs avail. In-rm modem link. Gift shop. Barber, beauty shop. Free airport transportation. Exercise equipt. Game rm. Car rental. Cr cds: A, D, DS, JCB, MC, V.

[D icons]

★ **HOWARD JOHNSON.** *3909 11th St (61109). 815/397-9000; fax 815/397-4669. www.hojo.com.* 146 rms, 2 story. S $49-$70; D $59-$75; each addl $5; under 18 free; wkend rates; package plans. Crib free. TV; cable (premium). Indoor pool; whirlpool. Playground. Coffee in rms. Restaurant 7 am-2 pm, 5 pm-midnight. Bar from 11 am. Ck-out 11 am. Coin lndry. Meeting rms. Business servs avail. In-rm modem link. Free airport transportation. Tennis. Exercise equipt; sauna. Game rm. Private patios, balconies. Cr cds: A, C, D, DS, MC, V.

[D icons]

★ **RED ROOF INN.** *7434 E State St (61108). 815/398-9750; fax 815/398-9761; toll-free 800/843-7663.* 108 rms, 2 story. S $39.99-$60.99; D $44.99-$70.99; each addl $9; under 18 free. Crib free. TV; cable (premium). Complimentary coffee in lobby. Ck-out noon. Business servs avail. Cr cds: A, C, D, DS, MC, V.

[D] ⌨ ⟞

★★ **SWEDEN HOUSE LODGE.** *4605 E State St (61108). 815/398-4130; fax 815/398-9203; toll-free 800/886-4138. www.swedenhouse-lodge.com.* 107 rms, 2-3 story. S $50-$55; D $60-$70; suites $80-$90; each addl $10; under 18 free. Crib free. Pet accepted, some restrictions. TV; cable (premium). Complimentary continental bkfst. Indoor pool; whirlpool. Ck-out noon. Meeting rms. Business servs avail. Sundries. Exercise equipt. Game rm. Cr cds: A, C, D, DS, MC, V.

⟞ ⌨ 🏋 ⟞ ⟞ SC

Hotel

★★ **BEST WESTERN CLOCK-TOWER RESORT.** *7801 E State St (61125). 815/398-6000; fax 815/398-0443; res 800/358-7666. www.clocktowerresort.com.* 243 rms, 2 story. S $99-$159; D $105-$184; suites $119-$159; under 18 free; wkend packages. Crib free. TV; cable (premium). 3 pools, 1 indoor; 2 wading pools, whirlpools, poolside serv, lifeguard. Playground. Complimentary coffee in rms. Restaurants 6 am-11 pm. Rm serv. Bar 11-2 am; Sun 12:30-11 pm. Ck-out noon. Coin lndry. Convention facilities. Business center. In-rm modem link. Valet serv. Shopping arcade. Airport transportation. Indoor/outdoor tennis. Exercise rm; sauna. Game rm. Some refrigerators. Many private patios, balconies. Picnic tables. Cr cds: A, D, DS, MC, V.

[D] ⌨ ⟞ ⟞ 🏋 🎿 🏋

Extended Stay

★★ **RESIDENCE INN BY MAR-RIOTT.** *7542 Colosseum Dr (61107). 815/227-0013; fax 815/227-0013; toll-free 800/331-3131. www.residence inn.com.* 94 kit. units, 3 story. S, D $99-$154. Crib free. Pet accepted; $100 and $5/day. TV; cable (premium). Indoor pool; whirlpool. Complimentary continental bkfst, coffee in rms. Restaurant nearby. Ck-out noon. Coin lndry. Meeting rm. Business servs avail. In-rm modem

link. Exercise equipt. Cr cds: A, C, D, DS, JCB, MC, V.

[D] 🍴 ⟞ 🏋 ⟞ SC

Restaurants

★ **CAFE PATOU.** *3929 Broadway (61108). 815/227-4100.* Hrs: 11:30 am-2 pm, 5:30-10 pm; Mon, Sat from 5:30 pm. Closed Sun; hols. Res accepted. Continental menu. Bar. A la carte entrees: lunch $5.95-$12.50, dinner $9-$23. Child's menu. Specialties: flat breads, roasted lobster, Alaskan caribou tenderloin. Entertainment Fri, Sat. Casual country atmosphere. Own baking. Cr cds: A, DS, MC, V.

[D] ⟞

★★★ **GIOVANNI'S.** *610 N Bell School Rd (61107). 815/398-6411. www.giodine.com.* Hrs: 11:30 am-2 pm, 5:30-10 pm; Sat from 5:30 pm. Closed Sun; hols. Res accepted. Bar. Extensive cognac list. A la carte entrees: lunch $5.95-$9.50, dinner $14.95-$24.95. Child's menu. Specializes in seafood, steak, veal. Own baking. Cr cds: A, D, DS, MC, V.

[D] ⟞

★★ **GREAT WALL.** *4228 E State (61108). 815/226-0982.* Hrs: 11:30 am-2 pm, 4:30-10 pm; Fri, Sat to 11 pm; Sun to 9 pm; Sun brunch 11:30 am-2:30 pm. Closed hols. Res accepted. Mandarin, Szechwan menu. Bar. A la carte entrees: lunch $3.95-$5.25, dinner $5.95-$12. Complete meals: dinner $9.50-$11.50. Sun brunch buffet $7.50. Specialties: moo shu pork, Great Wall steak, black bean chicken. Mandarin decor. Cr cds: DS, MC, V.

[D] ⟞

Rock Island

(B-3) *See also Moline*

Settled 1828 **Pop** 39,684 **Elev** 560 ft **Zip** 61201

Information Quad Cities Convention & Visitors Bureau, 2021 River Dr, Moline, 61265; 309/788-7800 or 800/747-7800

Web www.rigov.org

One of the cities of the Quad-City metropolitan area (along with Moline, Illinois, and Bettendorf and Davenport, Iowa), Rock Island is rich in Native American, steamboat, and Civil War lore. Here Lincoln was sworn into the Illinois Militia under Zachary Taylor, and here Black Hawk and his warriors were defeated. The great steamboat era brought nearly 2,000 ships annually to Rock Island, and the first railway bridge across the Mississippi was opened here in 1855. One of the most important and notorious Union military prisons of the Civil War was on the 1,000-acre island in the river. Rock Island Arsenal, one of the largest manufacturing arsenals in the world, was established in 1862. Augustana College (1860), which has an art gallery, geology museum, and planetarium, is located here.

What to See and Do

Black Hawk State Historic Site. These wooded, steeply rolling hills provided the site on which the westernmost battle of the Revolutionary War was fought. The area was occupied for nearly a century by the capitol villages of the Sauk and Fox nations. The Watch Tower, on a promontory 150 ft above the Rock River, provides a view of the river valley and surrounding countryside. Hauberg Indian Museum contains an outstanding collection of Native American artifacts, paintings, and relics; dioramas of Sauk and Fox daily life, prehistoric display; also changing displays. Fishing; hiking, picnicking. (Daily) On S edge of town. **DONATION**

Quad City Botanical Center. Sun garden conservatory features over 100 tropical plants and trees, 14-ft waterfall over reflecting pools; horticulture resource center; gift shop. (Daily) 2525 4th Ave. Phone 309/794-0991. ¢¢

Rock Island Arsenal and US Army Armament, Munitions and Chemical Command. On Arsenal Island, between Rock Island, IL, and Davenport, IA, is the Rock Island Arsenal Museum, which contains an extensive firearms collection and Court of Patriots memorial (daily; closed hols; free; phone 309/782-5021); a replica of Fort Armstrong blockhouse;

Colonel Davenport house (Sat-Sun, free; phone 309/786-7336); Confederate soldiers cemetery; the Rock Island National Cemetery, at the center of the island, which has approx 1,300 interments. Site of the first railroad bridge to span the Mississippi, lock and dam with visitor center (daily; phone before visiting for site restrictions). Bicycle trail (seven mi) around island. Phone 309/782-6001.

Special Event

Genesius Guild. Lincoln Park, 40th St and 11th Ave. Free open-air presentations of opera, Shakespeare, and Greek classics. Sat and Sun eves. Mid-June-mid-Aug. Phone 309/788-7113.

Rosemont

(see Chicago O'Hare Airport Area)

St. Charles

(F-3) *See also Aurora, Elgin, Geneva*

Settled 1838 **Pop** 27,896 **Elev** 697 ft **Area code** 630

Information Greater St. Charles Convention & Visitors Bureau, 311 N 2nd St, PO Box 11, 60174; 630/377-6161 or 800/777-4373

Web www.visitstcharles.com

Located on the Fox River just one hour west of Chicago, St. Charles is a residential and light industry town. The downtown areas on both sides of the river contain antique and specialty shops housed in historic buildings.

What to See and Do

Kane County Flea Market. One of the nation's largest flea and antique markets. (First Sun and preceding Sat of month) Kane County Fairgrounds, on Randall Rd S of IL 64. Phone 630/377-2252. ¢¢

The Piano Factory. Outlet mall housed in a former piano factory built in 1901; contains over two dozen outlet stores and an antique store. (Daily) 410 S 1st St. Phone 630/584-2099.

Pottwatomie Park. One mi of frontage on the Fox River with swimming pools (first wkend June-Labor Day; fee); 9-hole golf (Mar-Oct; fee), tennis, 18-hole miniature golf (fee), playgrounds, ball fields. Also access to the Fox River Trail, used for biking, jogging, and x-country skiing. Picnic area, snack bars. (Daily) On 2nd Ave, ½ mi N of Main St (IL 64). Phone 630/584-1028. ¢¢ Also here are

St. Charles Belle II *and* **Fox River Queen.** These 132-passenger paddle-wheel boats offer afternoon sightseeing trips (45 min) along the Fox River. Boats depart from the park and follow the river trail of the Pottawamie. (June-Aug, daily; May and Sept-mid-Oct, Sat and Sun) Phone 630/584-2334.

St. Charles History Museum. Museum of local history, built in a unique Tudor-style filling station from the 1920s. (Tues-Sun). Call for pricing. 215 E Main St. Phone 630/584-6967.

Special Events

Pride of the Fox RiverFest. Four-day event features river events, food, entertainment, craft show. Second wkend June. Phone 630/377-6161.

Scarecrow Festival. Downtown, Lincoln Park. Display of up to 100 scarecrows; entertainment, food, crafts. Second full wkend Oct. Phone 630/377-6161.

Motels/Motor Lodges

★ ★ **BEST WESTERN INN.** *1635 E Main St (60174). 630/584-4550; fax 630/584-5221; toll-free 800/780-7234. www.bestwestern.com.* 54 rms, 2 story. June-Sept: S, D $79-$89; under 16 free; lower rates rest of yr. Crib free. TV; cable. Heated pool; outdoor. Complimentary continental bkfst. Restaurant adj 5:30 am-11 pm. Ck-out 11 am. Coin lndry. Business servs avail. Sundries. Exercise equipt. Cr cds: A, C, D, DS, ER, JCB, MC, V.
🄳 ⊠ 🏋 ✈ 🔅 ⬛

Restaurant

★ **FILLING STATION ANTIQUE EATERY.** *300 W Main St (60174). 630/584-4414.* Hrs: 11 am-9 pm; Fri, Sat to 10 pm; Sun to 8 pm. Closed Jan 1, Easter, Memorial Day, Thanksgiving. Bar. Lunch $4.50-$6.95, dinner $6.95-$10.95. Child's menu. Specialties: Texas barbecue beef, fajitas, oversized sandwiches. Entertainment Fri-Sun. Outdoor dining. Casual dining in renovated 1930s filling station; antiques. Cr cds: A, D, DS, MC, V.
🄳 ⊠

Salem

(F-5) *See also Centralia, Mount Vernon*

Pop 7,909 **Elev** 544 ft **Area code** 618 **Zip** 62881

Information Greater Salem Chamber of Commerce, 615 W Main St; 618/548-3010

Web www.ci.salem.il.us

Salem is located 75 miles east of St. Louis. It is the birthplace of William Jennings Bryan, whose statue by Gutzon Borglum stands in Bryan Memorial Park.

What to See and Do

Halfway Tavern. Tavern received name for being halfway between St. Louis, MO, and Vincennes, IN. Present structure is reconstructed; original was built in 1818 and served as a stagecoach stop until 1861. Located on trail used by George Rogers Clark when he crossed Illinois in 1799, the tavern was frequently used by Abraham Lincoln as a stopover. Interior not open to public. 7 mi E on US 50.

Ingram's Log Cabin Village. On 74 acres with 17 authentic log buildings dating from 1818-1860; 13 authentically furnished and open to the public. Picnicking. (Mid-Apr-mid-Nov, daily) 12 mi N via IL 37 in Kinmundy. Phone 618/547-3241. ¢

One-Room Schoolhouse. Restored schoolhouse contains artifacts, old photos; traces the history of every one-room school district in Marion

County. (Apr-Aug, Sat, limited hrs; other times by appt) N on IL 37, located on campus of Salem Community High School. Phone 618/548-2499 or 618/532-9026. **FREE**

Stephen A. Forbes State Park.
Approx 3,100 acres. Swimming, waterskiing, fishing, boating (ramp, rentals, motors); hunting, hiking, bridle trails, picnicking, concession, camping, horse campground. Standard fees. 8 mi E on US 50, then 7 mi N on Omega Rd, in Kinmundy. Phone 618/547-3381.

William Jennings Bryan Birthplace/Museum. (1852) Restored house contains personal artifacts and memorabilia of the famous orator, who was born here in 1860. (Mon-Wed and Fri-Sun, afternoons; closed hols) 408 S Broadway. Phone 618/548-7791. **FREE**

Special Events

Marion County Fair. Fairgrounds. Late July-Aug. Phone 618/548-3010.

Bluegrass and Chowder Festival. Bryan Memorial Park. Second wkend Sept. Phone 618/548-2222.

Days Fest. Main St. Celebration of television show *Days of Our Lives.* Souvenirs, celebrities, contests, and crafts. Late Apr. Phone 618/548-6400.

Schaumburg

See also Arlington Heights, Chicago O'Hare Airport Area, Itasca

Pop 75,386 **Elev** 799 ft **Area code** 847

Information Greater Woodfield Convention & Visitors Bureau, 1430 Meacham Rd, 60173; 847/490-1010

Web www.ci.schaumburg.il.us

What to See and Do

Chicago Athenaeum—The Museum of Architecture and Design. Museum honors the history of design in all apsects of civilization, from fashion to urban development. (Wed-Sun) 10090 S Roselle Rd. Phone 847/895-3950. ¢¢

Motels/Motor Lodges

★★ **HAMPTON INN.** *1300 E Higgins Rd (60173). 847/619-1000; fax 847/619-1019. www.hamptoninn.com.* 128 rms, 4 story. S $79-$109; D $79-$119; under 18 free; wkend rates. Crib free. TV; cable (premium). Complimentary continental bkfst. Restaurants nearby. Ck-out noon. Meeting rms. Business servs avail. Exercise equipt. Cr cds: A, C, D, DS, JCB, MC, V.
D 🏋 ⊠ 🔥 SC

★★★ **HOLIDAY INN** . *1550 N Roselle Rd (60195). 847/310-0500; fax 847/310-0579; toll-free 877/289-8443. www.holidayinnschaumburg.com.* 143 rms, 6 story. S, D $99-$149; suites $199-$209; wkend rates. Crib free. TV; cable (premium). Complimentary continental bkfst, coffee in lobby. Restaurant 6:30-1 am. Ck-out noon. Meeting rm. Business servs avail. In-rm modem link. Pool. Refrigerators avail. Whirlpool in suites. Cr cds: A, D, DS, JCB, MC, V.
D ⊠ ⊠ 🔥 SC

★★ **LA QUINTA INN.** *1730 E Higgins Rd (60173). 847/517-8484; fax 847/517-4477. www.laquinta.com.* 130 rms, 3 story. S, D $69-$89; under 18 free; wkend rates. Crib free. Pet accepted, some restrictions. TV; cable (premium). Heated pool. Complimentary continental bkfst. Restaurant adj open 24 hrs. Ck-out noon. Meeting rms. Business servs avail. In-rm modem link. Health club privileges. Some refrigerators; microwaves avail. Cr cds: A, C, D, DS, MC, V.
D 🐾 ⊠ ⊠ 🔥

★ **RED ROOF INN.** *2500 Hassell Rd, Hoffman Estates (60195). 847/885-7877; fax 847/885-8616. www.redroof. com.* 119 rms, 3 story. S $46-$64; D $50-$70; each addl $7. Crib avail. Pet accepted. TV; cable (premium). Coin lndry. Complimentary coffee in lobby. Restaurant opp 6 am-11 pm. Ck-out noon. Business servs avail. Cr cds: A, C, D, DS, MC, V.
D 🐾 ⊠ 🔥

★★ **WYNDHAM GARDEN.** *800 National Pkwy (60173). 847/605-9222; fax 847/605-9240; toll-free 800/WYNDHAM. www.wyndham.com.* 188 rms, 6 story. S, D $100-$165; under 18 free; wkend rates. Crib free.

TV; cable (premium). Indoor pool; whirlpool. Complimentary coffee in rms. Restaurant 6:30-10 am. Bar 5-10 pm. Ck-out noon. Meeting rms. Business servs avail. In-rm modem link. Exercise equipt; sauna. Health club privileges. Cr cds: A, D, DS, JCB, MC, V.

🏊 🕴 🔥 🖫

Hotels

★★★ **EMBASSY SUITES SCHAUMBURG.** *1939 N Meacham Rd (60173). 847/397-1313; fax 847/397-9007. www.embassy.com.* 209 suites, 7 story. S $169-$179; D $185-$199; each addl $10; under 18 free; wkend rates. Crib free. TV; cable (premium). Indoor pool; whirlpool. Complimentary full bkfst, coffee in rms. Restaurant 11 am-10 pm. Rm serv. Bar 11:30 am-midnight. Ck-out noon. Coin lndry. Meeting rms. Business servs avail. In-rm modem link. Gift shop. Exercise equipt; saunas. Health club privileges. Refrigerators, microwaves. Cr cds: A, D, DS, JCB, MC, V.

D 🏊 🕴 🖫 🔥 SC

★★ **HOMEWOOD SUITES BY HILTON.** *815 E American Ln (60173). 847/605-0400; fax 847/619-0990. www.homewoodsuites.com.* 108 kit. suites, 3 story. S, D $149; under 18 free. Crib free. Pet accepted, some restrictions; $75 refundable. TV; cable (premium), VCR (movies $4). Pool; whirlpool. Complimentary continental bkfst; evening refreshments. Complimentary coffee in rms. Restaurant nearby. Ck-out noon. Meeting rms. Business center. In-rm modem link. Valet serv. Gift shop. Coin lndry. Exercise equipt. Health club privileges. Microwaves. Picnic tables, grills. Cr cds: A, C, D, DS, MC, V.

D 🐾 🏊 🕴 🖫 🔥 🕴

★★★ **HYATT REGENCY WOOD-FIELD.** *1800 E Golf Rd (60173). 847/605-1234; fax 847/605-0328; toll-free 800/233-1234. www.hyatt.com.* 470 rms, 5 story. S, D $185-$210; each addl $25; suites $250-$515; under 18 free; wkend rates. Crib free. TV; cable (premium). 2 pools, 1 indoor; whirlpool. Restaurants 6:30 am-11 pm. Bar 11:30-2 am. Ck-out

noon. Convention facilities. Business servs avail. In-rm modem link. Concierge. Gift shop. Barber. Exercise equipt; sauna. Refrigerators avail. Some private patios, balconies. Cr cds: A, D, DS, MC, V.

D 🏊 🕴 🖫 🔥

★★★ **MARRIOTT.** *50 N Martingale Rd (60173). 847/240-0100; fax 847/240-2388; toll-free 800/228-9290. www.marriott.com.* 398 rms, 14 story. S, D $129-$189; suites $450; family, wkend rates. Crib free. Pet accepted, some restrictions. TV; cable (premium). Indoor/outdoor pool; whirlpool, poolside serv. Complimentary coffee in rms. Restaurant 6:30 am-11 pm. Bar 11-1 am. Ck-out 1 pm. Coin lndry. Convention facilities. Business center. In-rm modem link. Gift shop. Exercise equipt; sauna. Some private patios. Luxury level. Cr cds: A, C, D, DS, ER, JCB, MC, V.

D 🐾 🏊 🕴 🖫 🔥 🕴

Restaurants

★★ **BARRINGTON COUNTRY BISTRO.** *700 W Northwest Hwy, Barrington (60010). 847/842-1300. www.barringtonbistro.com.* Hrs: 11:30 am-2 pm, 5-8:30 pm; Fri, Sat 5-9:30 pm; Sun from 5 pm. Closed hols. Res accepted. French menu. Bar. Lunch $9-$14, dinner $14-$18. Specialties: pork tenderloin, escargot, salmon. Outdoor dining. Country French decor. Cr cds: A, D, DS, MC, V.

D 🖫

★★ **MILLROSE.** *45 S Barrington Rd, South Barrington (60010). 847/382-7673.* Hrs: 11-2 am; Sat from 10 am; Sun 10 am-10 pm; Sun brunch to 1:30 pm. Res accepted. Bar. Lunch $5.95-$9.95, dinner $9.95-$25.95. Sun brunch $11.95. Child's menu. Specializes in ribs, steak, chops. Outdoor dining. Tri-level dining; brewery, gift shop; on 14 acres. Cr cds: A, D, DS, MC, V.

D 🖫

Schiller Park

(see Chicago O'Hare Airport Area)

Skokie

See also Evanston, Wilmette

Pop 63,348 **Elev** 623 ft **Area code** 847
Information Chamber of Commerce, 5002 Oakton St, PO Box 53; 847/673-0240
Web www.skokiechamber.org

Originally called Niles Center, it was not until 1940 that the village changed its name to Skokie. In its early history, farmers of the area produced food for the growing city of Chicago; market trails carved by farm wagons later became paved roads, which accounts for the odd curves of Lincoln Avenue. Today, Skokie is the location of many major corporate headquarters.

What to See and Do

North Shore Center for the Performing Arts. Houses two individual theaters that offer many types of performances. 9501 Skokie Blvd. Phone 847/679-9501.

Motels/Motor Lodges

★★ **HOLIDAY INN.** *5300 W Touhy Ave (60077). 847/679-8900; fax 847/679-7447; toll-free 800/843-7663. www.holiday-inn.com/chi-skokie.* 244 rms, 2-4 story. S, D $145-$179; each addl $10; under 19 free; higher rates: Dec 31, Northwestern Univ graduation. Crib free. Pet accepted. TV; cable (premium). Indoor pool; whirlpool. Restaurant 6:30 am-2 pm, 5-10 pm; Fri, Sat to 11 pm. Rm serv. Bar 3:30 pm-1 am. Ck-out noon. Coin lndry. Business servs avail. Meeting rms. In-rm modem link. Valet serv. Gift shop. Exercise equipt; sauna. Game rm. Microwaves avail. Cr cds: A, C, D, DS, ER, JCB, MC, V.
D ⚑ ⚏ 🛦 🐾 SC

★★ **HOWARD JOHNSON HOTEL.** *9333 Skokie Blvd (60077). 847/679-4200; fax 847/679-4218. www.hojo skokie.com.* 134 rms, 2-5 story. S $105; D $127; each addl $10; under 18 free. Crib free. Pet accepted. TV; cable (premium), VCR avail. Indoor pool; whirlpool. Complimentary bkfst buffet. Restaurant adj 11:30 am-11 pm. Bar 11:30 am-midnight. Ck-out 1 pm. Meeting rms. Businss servs avail. In-rm modem link. Valet serv. Exercise equipt; sauna. Microwaves avail. Private patios, balconies. Cr cds: A, C, D, DS, MC, V.
D ⚑ ⚏ 🛦 ⚏ 🐾

Hotel

★★★ **DOUBLETREE.** *9599 Skokie Blvd (60077). 847/679-7000; fax 847/679-9841; toll-free 800/222-8733. www.doubletree.com.* 367 rms, 11 story. S, D $99-$199; each addl $10; suites $275; under 17 free; wkend rates. Crib free. TV; cable (premium). Indoor/outdoor pool; poolside serv. Restaurant 6 am-11 pm. Rm serv 24 hrs. Bar 4 pm-midnight. Ck-out noon. Convention facilities. Business center. In-rm modem link. Concierge. Gift shop. Exercise equipt. Luxury level. Cr cds: A, C, D, DS, JCB, MC, V.
D ⚏ 🛦 ⚏ 🐾 SC 🛦

Restaurants

★★ **DON'S FISHMARKET.** *9335 Skokie Blvd (60077). 847/677-3424.* Hrs: 11:30 am-2:30 pm, 5-10 pm; Fri, Sat to 11 pm; Sun 4-9 pm. Early-bird dinner 5-6 pm. Closed Jan 1, Thanksgiving, Dec 25. Res accepted. Bar. Lunch $4.75-$9.95, dinner $12.95-$23.95. Specializes in fresh seafood, chicken, steak. Nautical decor. Cr cds: A, D, DS, MC, V.
D

★★ **L. WOODS TAP & PINE LODGE.** *7110 N Lincoln Ave, Lincolnwood (60712). 847/677-3350.* American menu. Specializes in BBQ ribs, seafood, chicken. Hrs: 11:15 am-10 pm; Fri to 10:30 pm; Sat noon-10:30 pm; Sun noon-10:30 pm. Res accepted. Bar. Lunch, dinner a la carte entrees: $5.95-$14.95. Pine lodge decor. Cr cds: A, D, DS, MC, V.

★★ **MYRON & PHIL'S.** *3900 W Devon Ave, Lincolnwood (60712). 847/677-6663.* Hrs: 11:30 am-11 pm; Sat 5 pm-midnight; Sun 3:30-10 pm. Closed Thanksgiving, Dec 25. Res accepted. Bar. Lunch $7.95-$9.95, dinner $13.95-$28.95. Specializes in seafood, steak, ribs. Piano bar Fri, Sat

State Capitol, Springfield

Valet parking. Family-owned. Cr cds: A, D, DS, MC, V.

[D] [↦]

Springfield

(D-4) *See also Jacksonville, Lincoln, Petersburg*

Settled 1819 **Pop** 111,454 **Elev** 600 ft **Area code** 217

Information Convention & Visitors Bureau, 109 N 7th, 62701; 217/789-2360 or 800/545-7300

Web www.visit-springfieldillinois.com

Near the geographical center of the state, Springfield, the capitol of Illinois, is surrounded by rich farmland underlaid with veins of coal which were, at one time, intensively mined. The city has the grace of a Southern capital; the economic stability of an educational, professional, and service-oriented center; and the fame of having been Abraham Lincoln's home for a quarter of a century.

Illinois had already become a state when Elisha Kelly came to the area from North Carolina. Impressed by fertile land and plentiful game, he later returned and settled with his father and four brothers. A small community formed around the Kelly cabin. When Sangamon County was created in 1821, Springfield was selected as the seat and named for a nearby spring located on Kelly land. On February 25, 1837, as a result of a campaign led by Lincoln, Springfield—then a town of 1,500—was proclaimed the state capitol. In April of that year, Lincoln moved to Springfield from New Salem. He practiced law, married, and raised his family in the new capitol. On February 11, 1861, Lincoln made his famous farewell address when he left to become president. In May of 1865, Lincoln's body was returned to Springfield to be buried in the city's Oak Ridge Cemetery.

What to See and Do

Dana-Thomas House State Historic Site. (1902-1904) Designed by Frank Lloyd Wright for Springfield socialite Susan Lawrence Dana, this house is the best-preserved and most complete of the architect's Prairie period. The fully restored, highly unified interior boasts terra-cotta sculptures, more than 100 pieces of original furniture, 35 rooms and doors, 250 art-glass windows, and 200 art-glass light fixtures and light panels. This house was one of the largest and most elaborate of Wright's career. (Wed-Sun; closed hols) 301 E Lawrence Ave, at 4th St, two blks S of Governor's Mansion. Phone 217/782-6776. **DONATION**

Daughters of Union Veterans of the Civil War Museum. Civil War relics, documents. (Mon-Fri; also by appt) 503 S Walnut St. Phone 217/544-0616. **FREE**

Edwards Place. (1833) Built by Benjamin Edwards (brother of Ninian Edwards, early Illinois governor married to Mary Todd Lincoln's older sister), this Italianate mansion was Springfield's social and political center in yrs before Civil War; Lincoln addressed public from front gallery. Well-preserved house is furnished with original pieces and period antiques. (By appt only) 700 N 4th St. Phone 217/523-2631.

DONATION Adj is

> **Springfield Art Association.** Working studios, library, exhibition galleries. (Mon-Sat; closed hols) Phone 217/523-2631. **DONATION**

Executive Mansion. Red-brick Italianate mansion has been residence of Illinois governors since 1855; Georgian detailing dates from 1970s remodeling. Half-hr tours through 14 rooms. (Tues, Thurs, and Sat mornings; closed hols) On Jackson St between 4th and 5th Sts. Phone 217/782-6450. **FREE**

Henson Robinson Zoo. A 14-acre zoo with exotic and domestic animals; penguin exhibit; contact area; picnic area. (Daily) 1100 E Lake Dr, 4 mi SE on Lake Springfield. Phone 217/753-6217. **¢¢**

Lincoln Memorial Garden & Nature Center. An 80-acre garden of trees, shrubs, and flowers native to Illinois designed in naturalistic style by landscape architect Jens Jensen. Extensive display of spring wildflowers late Apr-early May; fall foliage mid-Oct. Nature trails (5 mi). X-country skiing in winter. Nature Center contains exhibits and shop (Tues-Sun; closed Dec 24-Jan 1). Garden (daily). (See SPECIAL EVENTS) 2301 E Lake Dr, 8 mi S, on E bank of Lake Springfield. Phone 217/529-1111. **FREE**

Lincoln shrines.

> ★ **Lincoln Depot.** Restored depot where Lincoln delivered his farewell address before departing

for Washington on Feb 11, 1861. Exhibits; DVD presentation. (Apr-Aug, daily) Monroe St between 9th and 10th Sts. Phone 217/544-8695 or 217/788-1356. **FREE**

Lincoln-Herndon Law Office Building. Restored building from which Lincoln practiced law. (Daily; closed hols) 6th and Adams Sts, opp Old State Capitol. Phone 217/785-7289. **DONATION**

Lincoln Home National Historic Site. Site features the only home Abraham Lincoln ever owned. In 1844, Abraham and Mary Lincoln purchased their 1½-story cottage and enlarged it several times to a full two-story house. The Lincoln family lived there until their February 1861 departure for Washington D.C. The home has been restored with Lincoln family furnishings, period artifacts, reproduced wallpapers and window hangings. The Lincoln Home stands in the midst of a four-block historic neighborhood, which the National Park Service is restoring, so that the neighborhood, like the house, will appear much as Lincoln would have remembered it. Exhibits are available for viewing in the neighboring Dean and Arnold Houses. Visitor Center includes exhibits, film, and museum shop. Tickets required to tour house (obtain at visitor center; free). (Daily; closed Jan 1, Thanksgiving, Dec 25) Parking (fee). Visitor center at 426 S 7th St, approx 5 blks S and E of Old State Capitol. Phone 217/492-4241. **FREE**

Lincoln Tomb State Historic Site. Under 117-ft granite obelisk, a belvedere, accessible via exterior staircases, offers views of ten-ft statue of Lincoln and four heroic groupings representing Civil War armed forces. Tomb interior follows circular route lined with statues commemorating periods of Lincoln's life. In center of domed burial chamber is monumental sarcophagus. However, Lincoln is actually buried ten ft below (grave robbers made attempts upon the remains). Mary Todd Lincoln and three of four Lincoln sons are interred within the wall opposite. Self-guided tours; interpretive program. (Daily; closed hols) (See SPE-

CIAL EVENTS) Oak Ridge Cemetery. Approx 16 blks N of Old State Capitol, via 2nd St to N Grand, then W to Monument Ave. Phone 217/782-2717. **FREE**

Old State Capitol State Historic Site. Restored Greek Revival sandstone structure was first state house in Springfield (state's fifth). Although first occupied in 1839, it was not fully completed until 1853; it became the Sangamon County courthouse after being vacated by the state in 1876. Called the most historic structure west of the Alleghenies, it was here that Lincoln made his famous "House Divided" speech. Restored between 1966-1969, interior features intersecting double staircases; reconstructed house, senate, and supreme court chambers; state offices. Living history program (Fri and Sat; no programs May). (Daily; closed hols) Downtown Mall, between Adams, Washington, 5th, and 6th Sts. Phone 217/785-7961. **Donation**

Oliver P. Parks Telephone Museum. Contains more than 100 antique telephones dating from 1882; film, exhibits, and displays relating to the telephone. (Mon-Fri; closed hols) 529 S 7th St. **FREE**

Springfield Children's Museum. Exhibits and programs featuring art, architecture, health, nature, and science. Children can discover weather phenomena, dig for a fossil, or put on a puppet show. (Mon, Wed-Sun; closed hols) 619 E Washington St. Phone 217/789-0679. ¢¢

State Capitol. One of the tallest buildings in central Illinois, the capitol dome, 405 ft high, can be seen for miles across the prairie. Built between 1868-1888, the state house is a Victorian combination of Renaissance Revival and Second Empire. Marble, granite, bronze, black walnut, encaustic tiles, stained and etched glass, and stencil work were employed throughout the structure; heroically scaled murals depict state history. Free guide service, first floor information desk (every 30 min, daily; closed hols). 2nd St and Capitol Ave. Phone 217/782-2099. **FREE** Nearby are

Capitol Complex Visitors Center. Displays, brochures, information. Picnic shelters. (Mon-Sat; closed hols) Capitol Ave, between Edwards and Monroe Sts. Phone 217/524-6620.

Illinois State Museum. Contains natural history, geology, anthropology, and art exhibits with life-size dioramas of wildlife and early inhabitants of Illinois; displays depict the state's botanical, zoological, ecological, and Native American heritage; art galleries of photography, fine and decorative arts with works by 19th- and 20th-century Illinois artists. Special hands-on discovery room for children. Audio tours (fee); special programs, films, lectures, tours. (Mon-Sat, also Sun afternoons; closed hols) Spring and Edwards Sts. Phone 217/782-7386. **FREE**

Thomas Rees Memorial Carillon. A 132-ft tower with three observation decks and 66-bell carillon. Bell museum. Concerts (June-Aug, Tues-Sun; Apr-May, Sept-Nov, wkends only). Ten-min film. Washington Park, Fayette Ave and Chatham Rd. Phone 217/753-6219. ¢

Special Events

Maple Syrup Time. Lincoln Memorial Garden & Nature Center. Watch maple syrup being made, from tapping trees to boiling the sap. Sat and Sun afternoons, mid-Feb-early Mar. Phone 217/529-1111.

114th Infantry Flag Retreat Ceremony. Lincoln Tomb State Historic Site. Illinois Volunteer Infantry, in authentic period uniforms, demonstrates drill movements and musket firings as part of a retreat ceremony. Tues eves, June-Aug. Phone 217/782-2717.

Municipal Band Concerts. Douglas Park. A 50-piece concert band performs a wide variety of music. Tues and Thurs eves. June and July. Phone 217/525-8586.

Springfield Muni Opera. 815 E Lake Dr. Broadway musicals presented in outdoor theater. June-Aug. Phone 217/793-6864.

International Carillon Festival. Thomas Rees Memorial Carillon, Washington Park. Eve concerts by visiting international carillonneurs. Entertainment. Early July. Phone 217/753-6219.

Springfield Air Rendezvous. Capitol Airport. Mid-Oct. Phone 217/789-4400.

Summer Festival. New Salem Village. July. Phone 217/632-4000.

Illinois State Fair. Contact PO Box 19427, 62794. Mid-Aug. Phone 217/782-6661.

LPGA State Farm Classic. Rail Golf Club. Women's professional 54-hole golf tournament. Late Aug. Phone 217/528-5742.

Ethnic Festival. State Fairgrounds. Ethnic foods, cultural exhibits; entertainment. Labor Day wkend. Phone 217/529-8189.

Motels/Motor Lodges

★★ **BEST INNS OF AMERICA.** *500 N 1st St (62702). 217/522-1100; fax 217/753-8589; toll-free 800/237-8466. www.bestinn.com.* 90 rms, 2 story. S $48-$54; D $53-$61; each addl $5-$10; under 18 free. Crib free. Pet accepted, some restrictions. TV; cable (premium). Pool. Complimentary continental bkfst. Restaurant adj 7 am-10 pm. Ck-out 11 am. Coin lndry. In-rm modem link. Cr cds: A, D, DS, MC, V.
🅳 🐾 ➳ 🔌 🔥 SC

★★ **COMFORT INN.** *3442 Freedom Dr (62704). 217/787-2250; fax 217/787-2250; toll-free 800/228-5150. www.comfortinn.com.* 67 rms, 2 story. S, D $82.99-$97.99; each addl $5; under 18 free. Crib free. Pet accepted; $25. TV; cable (premium). Indoor pool; whirlpool. Complimentary continental bkfst. Ck-out 11 am. In-rm modem link. Some refrigerators, microwaves. Cr cds: A, D, DS, MC, V.
🅳 🐾 ➳ 🔌 🔥 SC

★★ **COURTYARD BY MARRIOTT.** *3462 Freedom Dr (62704). 217/793-5300; fax 217/793-5300; toll-free 800/321-2211. www.courtyard.com.* 78 rms, 3 story. S, D $75-$95; suites $100-$120; under 16 free; wkly, wkend, hol rates. Crib free. TV; cable (premium). Indoor pool; whirlpool. Complimentary coffee in rms. Restaurant adj 6:30 am-9:30 pm. Bar 5-10 pm. Ck-out noon. Coin lndry. Meeting rms. Business servs avail. In-rm modem link. Valet serv. Exercise

equipt. Refrigerator in suites; microwaves avail. Cr cds: A, D, DS, MC, V.
🅳 ➳ 🔼 🔌 🔥 SC

★ **DAYS INN.** *3000 Stevenson Dr (62703). 217/529-0171; fax 217/529-9431; toll-free 800/329-7466. www.daysinn.com.* 155 rms, 2 story. S $55; D $65; each addl $5; under 12 free; higher rates special events. Crib $5. Pet accepted. TV; cable (premium). Pool. Complimentary continental bkfst. Ck-out noon. Meeting rms. Business servs avail. Free airport transportation. Microwaves avail. Picnic tables. Cr cds: A, C, D, DS, MC, V.
🅳 🐾 ➳ 🔌 🔥

★★ **HAMPTON INN.** *3185 S Dirksen Pkwy (62703). 217/529-1100; fax 217/529-1105; toll-free 800/426-7866. www.hamptoninn.com.* 124 rms, 4 story. S $72-$79; D $82-$99; suites $144; under 18 free. Crib free. TV; cable (premium). Indoor pool; whirlpool. Complimentary continental bkfst. Restaurants nearby. Ck-out noon. Meeting rms. Business servs avail. Valet serv (wkdays). Exercise equipt. Refrigerator in suite. Cr cds: A, C, D, DS, MC, V.
🅳 ➳ 🔼 🔌 🔥

★★ **RAMADA INN.** *625 E St. Joseph St (62703). 217/529-7131; fax 217/529-7160; toll-free 877/529-7131. www.ramada.com.* 116 rms, 2 story. S $56; D $62; each addl $6; suites $100-$150; under 18 free. Crib free. Pet accepted, some restrictions. TV; cable (premium). Pool. Restaurant 6:30 am-2 pm, 5-9 pm. Rm serv. Ck-out noon. Coin lndry. Meeting rms. Business servs avail. Some refrigerators, microwaves. Cr cds: A, C, D, DS, MC, V.
🅳 🐾 ➳ 🔌 🔥

★★ **RAMADA LIMITED.** *3281 Northfield Dr (62702). 217/523-4000; fax 217/523-4080; toll-free 800/272-6232. www.ramada.com.* 97 rms, 2 story. S $61; D $67; each addl $6; suites $90-$125; under 18 free. Crib free. TV; cable (premium). Indoor pool. Complimentary continental bkfst, coffee in rms. Restaurant nearby. Ck-out noon. Coin lndry. Meeting rms. Business servs avail. Valet serv. Free airport transportation. Exercise equipt. Refrigerator in suites; microwaves avail. Cr cds: A, C, D, DS, JCB, MC, V.

★ **RED ROOF INN.** *3200 Singer Ave (62703). 217/753-4302; fax 217/753-4391; toll-free 800/843-7663. www.redroof.com.* 108 rms, 2 story. S $32-$70; D $40-$80; under 18 free. Crib free. Pet accepted. TV; cable (premium). Complimentary coffee in lobby. Restaurants nearby. Ck-out noon. Business servs avail. In-rm modem link. Cr cds: A, C, D, DS, MC, V.

★ **SUPER 8 MOTEL.** *3675 S 6th St (62703). 217/529-8898; fax 217/529-4354; toll-free 800/800-8000. www.super8.com.* 122 rms, 3 story. S $32.99-$60.88; D $32.99-$90; each addl $5; suites $45.88-$99.88; under 12 free; higher rates special events; lower rates winter months. Crib free. Pet accepted, some restrictions. TV; cable. Complimentary continental bkfst. Restaurants nearby. Ck-out 11 am. Coin lndry. Meeting rms. Business servs avail. Some refrigerators, microwaves. Some balconies. Cr cds: A, C, D, DS, MC, V.

Hotels

★★★ **HILTON.** *700 E Adams (62701). 217/789-1530; fax 217/789-0709; toll-free 800/445-8667. www.hilton.com.* 367 rms, 30 story. S, D $79-$149; each addl $10; suites $119-$600; under 18 free; wkend rates. Crib free. Pet accepted, some restrictions. TV; cable (premium). Indoor pool. Restaurants 6:30 am-10 pm. Bar 2 pm-2 am; entertainment. Ck-out noon. Convention facilities. Business center. Shopping arcade. Barber, beauty shop. Free airport, RR station transportation. Exercise equipt. Luxury level. Cr cds: A, C, D, DS, ER, JCB, MC, V.

★★★ **RENAISSANCE SPRINGFIELD.** *701 E Adams (62701). 217/544-8800; fax 217/544-9607; toll-free 800/228-9898. www.marriott.com.* 316 rms, 12 story. S $103-$115; D $115-$127; suites $206-$395; under 18 free; wkend rates. Crib free. Covered parking $5, valet $6. TV; cable (premium). Indoor pool; whirlpool. Coffee in rms. Restaurant 6:30 am-11 pm. Bar. Ck-out noon, ck-in 3 pm. Convention facilities. Business center. In-rm modem link. Concierge. Gift shop. Free airport, RR station transportation. Exercise equipt; sauna. Game rm. Bathrm phones. Luxury level. Cr cds: A, C, D, DS, ER, JCB, MC, V.

Restaurants

★★ **CHESAPEAKE SEAFOOD HOUSE.** *3045 Clear Lake Ave (62702). 217/522-5220.* Hrs: 4-10 pm; Fri, Sat to 11 pm. Closed Sun; Dec 25. Res accepted. Bar. Dinner $10-$20. Child's menu. Specializes in steak, seafood, barbecue ribs. In mansion (1860); nautical decor. Cr cds: A, C, D, DS, MC, V.

★★ **MALDANER'S.** *222 S 6th St (62701). 217/522-4313.* Hrs: 11 am-2:30 pm, 5-10 pm. Closed Sun; also Jan 1, July 4, Dec 25. Res accepted. Continental menu. Bar. Lunch $2-$7, dinner $4.50-$20. Specialties: pistachio-crusted salmon, braised pork shank, chicken with truffles. Own baking. Restored 19th-century bar. Features late 1930s art. Cr cds: A, MC, V.

Abraham Lincoln Home, Springfield

Unrated Dining Spot

HERITAGE HOUSE. *3851 S 6th St (62703). 217/529-5571.* Hrs: 11 am-8:30 pm; Fri and Sat to 9 pm. Closed Dec 25. Res accepted. Smorgasbord: lunch $5.25, dinner $7.25. Specializes in catfish, fried shrimp, roast beef. Salad bar. Cr cds: MC, V.

D ⬛

Starved Rock State Park

See also Ottawa, Peru

(2 mi S of La Salle on IL 351, then 4 mi E on IL 71)

Illinois's second-oldest state park (1911) occupies 2,630 acres on the Illinois River between La Salle and Ottawa. Starved Rock, a sandstone butte that rises 125 feet from the river, was the site of Fort St. Louis, built by La Salle in 1682 and abandoned in 1702. The name is derived from a Native American legend that a band of Illiniwek, isolated by their enemies, starved to death on the rock.

The park has scenic trails, sandstone bluffs, and canyons formed by the surging rivers of melting glaciers. In spring there are often waterfalls in the canyons. While there are no true caves, erosion has created overhangs, undercuts, and cavelike depressions in the sandstone. There are 15 miles of well-marked hiking trails through a very wide variety of plant life that provides food and shelter to an abundant wildlife population. Spring wildflowers are prolific; more than 200 types can be found. Park activities include fishing and boating (ramp, rentals); hiking and bridle trails, picnic grounds, concessions, campgrounds, and horse campgrounds are available (standard fees). The visitor center has exhibits on park history, and an interpretive program is offered. Within the park are a lodge and cafe. Contact Site Superintendent, PO Box 509, Utica 61373; phone 815/667-4726 or 815/667-4906 (visitor center).

Resort

★★ **STARVED ROCK LODGE AND CONFERENCE CENTER.** *Rtes 71 and 178, Utica (61373). 815/667-4211; fax 815/667-4455; toll-free 800/868-7625. www.starvedrocklodge. com.* 72 lodge rms, 2-3 story, 21 units in log cabins. S, D $75-$95; each addl $9; under 10 free. Crib $3. TV; cable, DVD avail (movies). Indoor pool; wading pool, whirlpool. Dining rm 8 am-9 pm. Snack bar. Bar 11 am-11 pm. Ck-out 11 am, ck-in 3 pm. Meeting rms. Business servs avail. Gift shop. Canoeing. X-country ski on site. Tobogganing. Hiking. Saunas. Large lobbies, stone fireplace, Native American mementos. Rolling, wooded country. Cr cds: A, C, D, DS, MC, V.

D 🛠 ⚡ 🏊 🏊 🗻 🔥 SC

Union

(F-2) *See also Elgin*

Pop 576 **Elev** 842 ft **Area code** 815 **Zip** 60180

What to See and Do

Donley's Wild West Town. Large displays, including antique phonographs, movies, music boxes, toys, telephones; general store. Outdoor Western village features Wild West gunfights, pony rides, train rides, panning for gold pyrite, gift shops. (Memorial Day-Labor Day, daily; Apr-May and Sept-Oct, wkends) US 20 and S Union Rd. Phone 815/923-2214. ¢¢

Illinois Railway Museum. Outdoor displays, on 56 acres, of historic and antique railroad cars, steam engines, coaches, and trolleys; rides (3½-mi). Picnicking. (Memorial Day-Labor Day, daily; May and Sept, Sat and Sun; Apr and Oct, Sun only) Special events throughout the yr. Admission includes unlimited rides. Olson Rd. Phone 815/923-4000. ¢¢

McHenry County Historical Museum. Contains artifacts dating from first settlement in the 1830s to the present; also local history research library (by appt). On the grounds are rural schoolhouse (1895) and original log cabin (1847), authentically furnished and used for pioneer demonstrations. (May-Oct, Tues-Fri afternoons, also Sun afternoons) 6422 Main St. Phone 815/923-2267. ¢¢

Urbana

(see Champaign/Urbana)

Vandalia

See also Altamont, Greenville

Founded 1819 **Pop** 6,975 **Elev** 515 ft **Area code** 618 **Zip** 62471
Information Tourism Committee, Chamber of Commerce, 1408 N 5th St, PO Box 238; 618/283-2728
Web www.vandalia.net

The Illinois State Legislature chose the wilderness in the Kaskaskia River Valley as the site for the state's second capitol, laid out the city, and sold lots. Vandalia housed the state legislature from 1819-1839, when Abraham Lincoln led a successful campaign to transfer the capitol to Springfield.

What to See and Do

Little Brick House Museum. Simple Italianate architecture with six restored rooms furnished primarily in the 1820-1839 period; antique wallpapers, china, wooden utensils, dolls, doll carriages, pipes, parasols, powder horn, oil portraits, and engravings. Berry-Hall Room contains memorabilia of James Berry, artist, and James Hall, writer. Pays tribute to members of the Tenth General Assembly of Illinois. Outbuildings and period garden with original brick pathways around house. (Days open vary; by appt) 621 St. Clair St. Phone 618/283-0024. ¢¢

Ramsey Lake State Park. Approx 1,960 acres with 47-acre lake stocked with bass, bluegill, and red ear sunfish. Fishing, boating (ramp, rentals, electric motors only); hunting, hiking, horseback riding, picnicking (shelters), concession, camping (stan-

dard fees). 13 mi N on US 51, then W on 2900N. Phone 618/423-2215. **FREE**

⭐ **Vandalia Statehouse State Historic Site.** Lincoln and Stephen Douglas served in the House of Representatives in this two-story, Classical Revival building built by townspeople in 1836 in an effort to keep the capitol in Vandalia. Many antiques and period furnishings. Guide service. (Daily) (See SPECIAL EVENT) 315 W Gallatin St. Phone 618/283-1161. **FREE**

Special Event

Grande Levée. Vandalia Statehouse State Historic Site. Capitol Days (1820-1839) are celebrated with period crafts, music, and food. Candlelight tour of the building. Father's Day wkend. Phone 618/283-1161.

Motels/Motor Lodges

⭐ **DAYS INN.** *1920 N Kennedy Blvd (62471).* 618/283-4400; fax 618/283-4240; toll-free 800/329-7466. *www. daysinn.com.* 95 rms, 2 story. Late May-early Sept: S $49-$58; D $56-$69; each addl $6; under 13 free; wkly rates; higher rates special events; lower rates rest of yr. Crib free. Pet accepted; $10 deposit. TV; cable (premium). Playground. Complimentary continental bkfst. Ck-out noon, ck-in 2 pm. Game rm. Cr cds: A, D, DS, MC, V.
D ➡️ 🖅 🐾 SC

⭐ **JAY'S INN.** *720 W Gochenour St, Vandalia (62471).* 618/283-1200; fax 618/283-4588. 21 rms, 2 story. S $36-$40; D $46-$57. Crib free. Pet accepted. TV; cable (premium). Coffee in rms. Restaurant 6 am-10 pm. Bar 4 pm-midnight. Ck-out noon. Sundries. Cr cds: A, DS, MC, V.
➡️ ✈️ 🖅 🐾 SC

⭐⭐ **RAMADA LIMITED VANDALIA.** *2707 Veterans Ave (62471).* 618/283-1400; fax 618/283-3465. *www. ramada.com.* 61 rms, 2 story. S, D $50-$65; each addl $8; suites $70-$85; under 12 free. Crib free. Pet accepted; $10 deposit. TV; cable (premium), VCR avail. Pool. Complimentary bkfst. Restaurant adj 7 am-9 pm; Fri, Sat to 10 pm. Ck-out noon. Meeting rms. Business servs avail. Exercise equipt. Refrigerator, microwave in suites. Cr cds: A, D, DS, MC, V.

★ **TRAVELODGE.** *1500 N 6th St (62471). 618/283-2363; fax 618/283-2363. www.travelodge.com.* 44 rms, 2 story. S $40; D $46-$48; each addl $5. Crib free. Pet accepted. TV; cable (premium). Pool. Playground. Complimentary coffee in rms. Restaurant adj 6 am-10 pm. Bar 4 pm-midnight. Ck-out noon. Sun deck. Cr cds: A, D, DS, MC, V.

Waukegan

(A-6) *See also Gurnee*

Settled 1835 **Pop** 87,901 **Elev** 644 ft
Area code 847
Information Lake County Chamber of Commerce, 5221 W Grand Ave, Gurnee, 60031; 847/249-3800
Web www.lakecounty-il.org

On the site of what was once a Native American village and a French trading post, Waukegan was first incorporated as Little Fort because of a French stockade there. It was barred to settlement by treaty for many years, but after the establishment of a general store by a Chicago merchant, it became a US port of entry and thrived. On April 2, 1860, Lincoln delivered his "unfinished speech" here—he was interrupted by a fire. Waukegan is the most industrialized of all lakeshore communities north of Chicago. Waukegan Port, on Lake Michigan, provides dockage for lake-going vessels that serve local industry. Waukegan was the birthplace of comedian Jack Benny and author Ray Bradbury, who has used the town as a background in many of his works.

What to See and Do

Illinois Beach State Park. (see). Phone 716/694-3600.

Motels/Motor Lodges

★ **BEST INNS.** *31 N Green Bay Rd (60085). 847/336-9000; fax 847/336-9000. www.bestinn.com.* 88 rms, 2 story. S, D $49.99-$88.99; each addl $7; under 18 free. TV; cable (premium). Heated pool. Complimentary continental bkfst. Restaurant nearby. Ck-out 11 am. In-rm modem link. Six Flags Great America, naval training center nearby. Cr cds: A, D, DS, MC, V.

★★ **COMFORT INN NAVAL TRAINING CENTER.** *3031 Belvidere Rd (60085). 847/623-1400; fax 847/623-0686; toll-free 800/416-1327. www.comfortinnhotel.com/il407.* 64 rms, 2 story. Apr-Nov: S, D $79-$99; each addl $6; under 12 free. Crib free. TV; cable (premium). Complimentary continental bkfst. Restaurant adj 11 am-10 pm. Ck-out 11 am. Business servs avail. Sundries. Six Flags Great America, Great Lakes Naval Training Center nearby. Cr cds: A, C, D, DS, ER, JCB, MC, V.

★★ **COURTYARD BY MARRIOTT WAUKEGAN.** *800 Lakehurst Rd (60085). 847/689-8000; fax 847/689-0135; toll-free 800/321-2211. www.courtyard.com.* 149 rms, 3 story. S, D $89-$129; suites $129-$149; under 17 free; lower rates rest of yr. Crib free. TV; cable (premium). Indoor pool; whirlpool. Complimentary coffee in rms. Restaurant 6:30-11 am. Bar 5-10 pm. Ck-out 1 pm. Coin lndry. Meeting rms. Business servs avail. In-rm modem link. Valet serv. Exercise equipt. Health club privileges. Some refrigerators. Private patios, balconies. Six Flags Great America nearby. Cr cds: A, D, DS, MC, V.

★★ **HOLIDAY INN EXPRESS.** *619 S Green Bay Rd (60085). 847/662-3200; fax 847/662-7275. www.hiexpress.com.* 84 rms, 2 story. June-Aug: S, D $99.95; suites $109.95; each addl $7; lower rates rest of yr. Crib free. TV; cable, VCR avail (movies). Complimentary continental bkfst. Restaurant opp open 24 hrs. Ck-out noon.

Business servs avail. In-rm modem link. Airport transportation. Health club privileges. Some refrigerators. Cr cds: A, D, DS, JCB, MC, V.

★★ **RAMADA INN.** *200 N Green Bay Rd (60085). 847/244-2400; fax 847/249-9716; toll-free 800/272-6232. www.ramadainnwaukegan.com.* 185 rms, 2 story. June-Aug: S $75-$90; D $85-$105; each addl $5; under 18 free; lower rates rest of yr. Crib free. TV; cable (premium). Indoor pool; whirlpool. Restaurant 6:30 am-10 pm. Rm serv. Bar 11-1 am. Ck-out noon. Meeting rms. Business servs avail. Bellhops. Gift shop. Exercise equipt; sauna. Game rm. Some refrigerators, microwaves. Cr cds: A, C, D, DS, ER, JCB, MC, V.

★ **SUPER 8 MOTEL.** *630 N Green Bay Rd (60085). 847/249-2388; fax 847/249-0975. www.super8.com.* 61 rms, 3 story. June-Oct: S $74.99; D $86.99; each addl $6; under 12 free; lower rates rest of yr. Crib $10. Pet accepted; $25. TV; cable (premium). Complimentary coffee in lobby. Restaurant nearby. Ck-out 11 am. Business servs avail. Cr cds: A, D, DS, MC, V.

Restaurant

★★ **MATHON'S.** *6 E Clayton St (60085). 847/662-3610.* Hrs: 11 am-9 pm; Fri, Sat to 10 pm; Sun from 3 pm. Closed Mon; Jan 1, Thanksgiving, Dec 25. Res accepted. Bar. Complete meals: lunch $4.95-$9.95, dinner $7.95-$19.95. Child's menu. Specializes in fresh fish, steaks, chops. Nautical decor. Cr cds: A, DS, MC, V.

Wheaton

(B-6) *See also Geneva, Glen Ellyn, Naperville*

Pop 55,416 **Elev** 753 ft **Area code** 630
Zip 60187

Information Wheaton Chamber of Commerce, 108 E Wesley St, 60187; 630/668-6464

Web www.wheatonchamber.org

Wheaton, the seat of Du Page county, is primarily a residential community with 39 churches and the headquarters of approximately two dozen religious publishers and organizations. The town's most famous citizens are football great Red Grange, Elbert Gary, who created the Indiana steel city that bears his name, and evangelist Billy Graham.

What to See and Do

Cantigny. This is the 500-acre estate of the late Robert R. McCormick, editor and publisher of the *Chicago Tribune.* Picnic area, woodland trails; ten acres of formal gardens. (Daily) On Winfield Rd, S of IL 38. Phone 630/668-5161. Per vehicle ¢¢ On grounds are

First Division Museum. Narrated displays dramatize story of First Infantry Division in action in WWI, WWII, and Vietnam. (Mar-Dec, Tues-Sun; Feb, Fri-Sun; closed Thanksgiving, Dec 25, also Jan) Phone 630/668-5185. Per vehicle ¢¢

Robert R. McCormick Museum. Georgian residence begun by Joseph Medill (1896), enlarged by his grandson, Robert McCormick, in the 1930s. Original furnishings; unique Chinese mural in dining room; personal artifacts, photographs, paintings. Chamber music presentation (summer, Sun, limited hrs; rest of yr, first Sun of month); res required. Guided tours (Mar-Dec, Tues-Sun; Feb, Fri-Sun; closed Thanksgiving, Dec 25, also Jan). Phone 630/668-5161. Per vehicle ¢¢

Cosley Animal Farm & Museum. Children's petting zoo; antique farm equipment display; railroad caboose and equipment; aviary; herb garden; outdoor education center. (Daily; closed Jan 1, Thanksgiving, Dec 25) 1356 N Gary Ave. Phone 630/665-5534. **FREE**

Du Page County Historical Museum. Historic Romanesque limestone building (1891) houses changing exhibitions on county history; costume gallery; period rooms. Extensive HO-scale model railroad display. Research library. (Mon, Wed, Fri-Sun; closed hols) 102 E Wesley St. Phone 630/682-7343. **FREE**

Wheaton College. (1860) 2,400 students. Liberal arts, conservatory of music, graduate school. Tours. 501 College Ave. Phone 630/752-5000. On campus are art exhibits, the Perry Mastodon exhibit, and

Billy Graham Center Museum. Museum features exhibits on the history of evangelism in America and the ministries of the Billy Graham Evangelistic Association; also Rotunda of Witnesses, Gospel theme area. (Mon-Sat, also Sun afternoons; call for hol hrs) Phone 630/752-5909.

Marion E. Wade Center. Collection of books and papers of seven British authors: Owen Barfield, G. K. Chesterton, C. S. Lewis, George MacDonald, Dorothy L. Sayers, J.R.R. Tolkien, and Charles Williams. (Mon-Sat; closed hols) Lincoln and Washington Sts. Phone 630/752-5908.

Special Events

Cream of Wheaton. Downtown. First wkend after Memorial Day. Phone 630/668-6464.

Du Page County Fair. Fairgrounds, 2015 W Manchester Rd. Late July. Phone 630/668-6636.

Autumn Fest. Memorial Park. Second wkend after Labor Day. Phone 630/668-6464.

Wheeling

See also Arlington Heights, Glenview, Northbrook

Pop 34,496 **Elev** 650 ft **Area code** 847
Zip 60090

Information Wheeling/Prospect Heights Area Chamber of Commerce and Industry, 395 E Dundee Rd; 847/541-0170

Web www.wheeling.com

The Wheeling area was first occupied by the Potawatomi. Settlers arrived in 1833 and began farming the fertile prairie soil. In 1836, a stagecoach route was established along Milwaukee Avenue, which was the main northbound route out of Chicago. The first commercial enterprise was a tavern-hotel (1837), followed by the establishment of a brewery (1850) on the Des Plaines River.

Motels/Motor Lodges

★ ★ **COURTYARD BY MARRIOTT.** *505 Milwaukee Ave, Lincolnshire (60069). 847/634-9555; fax 847/634-8320; toll-free 800/321-2211. www. courtyard.com.* 146 rms, 3 story. S, D $89-$129; each addl $10; suites $109-$139; wkend rates. Crib free. TV; cable (premium). Indoor pool. Complimentary coffee in rms. Restaurant 6:30-10 am. Bar 6-11 pm. Ck-out 1 pm. Coin lndry. Meeting rms. Business servs avail. In-rm modem link. Exercise equipt. Some refrigerators. Private patios, balconies. Cr cds: A, C, D, DS, MC, V.

▢ ≈ 🏋 ⊠ 🔥 SC

★ ★ **EXEL INN.** *540 N Milwaukee Ave, Prospect Heights (60070). 847/459-0545; fax 847/459-8639; res 800/367-3935. www.exelinns.com.* 123 rms, 3 story. S $40-$60; D $55-$76; suites $90-$130; under 18 free; wkly rates. Crib free. Pet accepted, some restrictions. TV. Complimentary continental bkfst, coffee in rms. Restaurant nearby. Ck-out noon. Coin lndry. Business servs avail. In-rm modem link. Health club privileges. Some refrigerators; microwaves avail. Cr cds: A, C, D, DS, MC, V.

▢ 🐾 🏋 ⊠ 🔥 SC

★ ★ **HAWTHORN SUITES.** *10 Westminster Way Rd, Lincolnshire (60069). 847/945-9300; fax 847/945-0013; toll-free 800/527-1133. www.hawthorn. com.* 125 kit. suites, 3 story. May-Oct: Suites $119-$170; wkend rates; lower rates rest of yr. Crib free. TV; cable (premium), VCR. Indoor pool; whirlpool. Complimentary full bkfst, coffee in rms. Ck-out noon. Coin lndry. Meeting rms. Business servs avail. In-rm modem link. Valet serv. Sundries. Exercise equipt. Microwaves. Cr cds: A, C, D, DS, MC, V.

▢ ≈ 🏋 ⊠ 🔥

Resort

★★★ **MARRIOTT'S LINCOLNSHIRE RESORT.** *10 Marriott Dr, Lincolnshire (60069).* *847/634-0100; fax 847/634-1278; toll-free 800/228-9290. www.marriott.com.* 390 rms, 3 story. S, D $149-$199; suites $325; under 18 free; wkend rates; package plans. Crib free. Pet accepted, some restrictions; $25. TV; cable (premium). 2 pools, 1 indoor; wading pool, whirlpool, poolside serv. Playground. Restaurants 6:30 am-11 pm. Rm serv. Bars 11-1 am. Ck-out noon, ck-in 3 pm. Coin lndry. Convention facilities. Business center. Valet serv. Concierge. Gift shop. Sports dir. Indoor tennis, pro. 18-hole golf, greens fee $68, pro, putting green. Entertainment Thurs-Sat. 900-seat theater-in-the-round featuring musical comedies. Game rm. Exercise rm. Massage. Some private patios. Picnic tables. Luxury level. Cr cds: A, C, D, DS, ER, JCB, MC, V.

Restaurants

★★ **94TH AERO SQUADRON.** *1070 S Milwaukee Ave (IL 21) (60090).* *847/459-3700.* Hrs: 11:30 am-2:30 pm, 4-11 pm; Sun from 4 pm; Sun brunch 9 am-2 pm. Res accepted. Bar Fri, Sat to 1:30 am. Lunch $5.95-$10.95, dinner $9.95-$24.95. Sun brunch $16.95. Child's menu. Specializes in prime rib, pasta, seafood. Own baking. Parking. Outdoor dining. Country French farmhouse decor, fireplace, WWI memorabilia throughout. Interior, grounds simulate farmhouse under siege; sandbags, checkpoint at bridge, airplanes, military apparatus. Cr cds: A, DS, MC, V.

★★ **BOB CHINN'S CRAB HOUSE.** *393 S Milwaukee Ave (IL 21) (60090).* *847/520-3633. www.bobchinns.com.* Hrs: 11 am-2:30 pm, 4:30-10:30 pm; Fri to 11:30 pm; Sat 11:30 am-11:30 pm; Sun 3-10 pm. Closed Thanksgiving, Dec 25. Bar. Lunch $4.95-$10.95, dinner $10.95-$25.95. Child's meals (dinner). Specialties: garlic Dungeness crab, softshell and stone crab, 12 varieties of fresh fish daily. Salad bar. Raw seafood bar. Own baking. Parking. Valet serv. Cr cds: A, D, DS, MC, V.

★ **BUCA DI BEPPO.** *604 N Milwaukee Ave (60090). 847/808-9898.* Italian menu. Specializes in pasta, chicken cacciatore, tiramisu. Hrs: 5-10 pm; Fri to 11 pm; Sat, Sun from 4 pm. Closed Thanksgiving, Dec 24, 25. Res accepted. Bar. Dinner a la carte entrees: $7.95-$19.95. Eclectic decor. Cr cds: A, D, DS, MC, V.

★ **CRAWDADDY BAYOU.** *412 N Milwaukee Ave (60090). 847/520-4800. www.crawdaddybayou.com.* Hrs: 11:30 am-2:30 pm, 5-10 pm; Fri, Sat to 11 pm; Sun to 9 pm. Closed Mon. Cajun/Creole menu. Bar. Lunch $6.95-$13.95, dinner $8.95-$18.95. Child's menu. Specialties: boiled crawfish, chicken and smoked sausage gumbo, étoufé. Own desserts. Zydeco music. Valet parking. Outdoor dining. Authentic Louisiana bayou decor. Cr cds: A, D, DS, MC, V.

★★ **DON ROTH'S.** *61 N Milwaukee Ave (IL 21) (60090). 847/537-5800. www.donroths.com.* Hrs: 11:30 am-2:30 pm, 5:30-9:30 pm; Fri 5:30-10 pm; Sat 5-10:30 pm; Sun 4-8:30 pm. Closed Dec 25. Res accepted. Bar. Lunch $5.95-$12.95, dinner $15.95-$26.95. Specializes in prime rib, fresh fish. Parking. Outdoor dining. In converted farmhouse. Family-owned. Cr cds: A, D, DS, MC, V.

★★ **GILARDI'S.** *23397 US 45N, Vernon Hills (60061). 847/634-1811.* Hrs: 11 am-10 pm; Fri to 11 pm; Sat 4-11 pm; Sun 4-9 pm. Closed hols. Res accepted Sun-Thurs. Italian, American menu. Bar. Lunch $5.95-$8.95, dinner $10.95-$24.95. Specialties: veal Vesuvio, 8-finger cavatelli. Valet parking (dinner). Entertainment Fri, Sat. In turn-of-the-century mansion; Art Deco decor. Cr cds: A, D, DS, MC, V.

★★★★ **LE FRANCAIS.** *269 S Milwaukee Ave (60090). 847/541-7470.* Don't let the suburban location fool you. The elegant, country French dining room is filled with blond wood, calm, neutral colors and an

energetic, open kitchen that serves exquisite food. Hrs: 6-8 pm; Fri, Sat to 9 pm. Res required. Wine list. Dinner $28.50-$36.50. Entertainment. Cr cds: A, D, DS, MC, V.
D

★ ★ **WEBER GRILL.** *920 N Milwaukee Ave (IL 21) (60090). 847/215-0996.* Hrs: 11:30 am-2:30 pm, 4:30-10 pm; Fri to 11 pm; Sat noon-2:30 pm, 4:30-11 pm; Sun 3-9 pm. Closed hols. Res accepted. Bar. Lunch $4.95-$14.75, dinner $9.99-$26.50. Child's menu. Specializes in Weber kettle-grill cooking, steak, ribs. Own pastries. Parking. Outdoor dining. Cr cds: A, D, DS, MC, V.
D

Wilmette

See also Evanston, Glenview, Skokie

Settled 1829 **Pop** 27,651 **Elev** 610 ft
Area code 847 **Zip** 60091
Information Chamber of Commerce, 1150 Wilmette Ave; 847/251-3800
Web www.wilmettechamber.org

This community was once owned by a Native American woman who received the land under a government treaty. The town carries the name of her French-Canadian husband, Antoine Ouilmette.

What to See and Do

Baha'i House of Worship. Spiritual center of the Baha'i faith in the US, a remarkable nine-sided structure given lightness and grace by the use of glass and tracery. It is 191-ft high and overlooks Lake Michigan. Surrounded by nine gardens and fountains. Exhibits and slide programs in visitor center on lower level. (Daily) Sheridan Rd and Linden Ave. Phone 847/853-2300. **FREE**

Gillson Park. Contains Wilmette Beach with 1,000 ft of sandy shoreline, lifeguards, and beach house (June-Labor Day, daily; fee), sailing (lessons), fishing pier; tennis, x-country skiing, ice skating, picnic facilities, playground, concession. Sunfish and Hobie 16 catamaran rentals. Park (daily). Washington and

Michigan Aves. Phone 847/256-9656. ¢¢

Kohl Children's Museum. Science, interactive music and construction exhibit, and arts participatory exhibits designed for children ages up to eight; miniature food store; make-up area; special activities. (Daily; closed hols) 165 Green Bay Rd. Phone 847/256-6056. ¢¢

Wilmette Historical Museum. Local history; costumes; rotating exhibits; archives, reference library. (Sept-June, Tues-Thurs, Sat and Sun afternoons; closed hols and wk of Dec 25) 609 Ridge Rd. Phone 847/853-7666. **FREE**

Restaurants

★ **BETISE.** *1515 N Sheridan Rd (60091). 847/853-1711.* Hrs: 11:30 am-2 pm, 5:30-9 pm; Fri, Sat to 10 pm; Sun 5:30-9 pm; Sun brunch 11 am-2 pm. Closed hols. Res accepted. French bistro menu. Serv bar. Lunch $8-$14, dinner $22-$26. Sun brunch $8-$12. Specialties: roasted chicken, loin of lamb. Own desserts. Art displays. Cr cds: A, D, DS, MC, V.
D ⊶

★ ★ **TANGLEWOOD.** *566 Chestnut St, Winnetka (60093). 847/441-4600.* Hrs: 11:30 am-9 pm; Fri, Sat to 10 pm. Closed Sun; hols. Res accepted. Continental menu. Serv bar. Lunch $5-$9, dinner $8-$18. Child's menu. Specialties: salmon with wild mushrooms, curried lamb shank, grilled shrimp fettuccine. Outdoor dining. Fireplace, skylights. Cr cds: A, MC, V.
D

Unrated Dining Spots

CONVITO ITALIANO. *1515 N Sheridan Rd (60091). 847/251-3654.* Hrs: 11:30 am-8:30 pm; Fri, Sat to 10 pm; Sun to 8 pm. Closed hols. Italian menu. Wine, beer. Lunch $4.75-$12, dinner $7-$15. Specializes in pasta, fresh salads. Authentic regional Italian restaurant and market. Cr cds: A, D, DS, MC, V.
D

WALKER BROTHERS ORIGINAL PANCAKE HOUSE. *153 Green Bay Rd (60091). 847/251-6000.* Hrs: 7 am-10:30 pm; Fri, Sat to 11 pm. Closed Thanksgiving, Dec 25. A la carte entrees: bkfst, lunch, dinner $2.50-

$6.25. Child's menu. Specialties: apple pancakes, German pancakes, egg-white omelettes. Stained-glass collection, many antiques. Cr cds: D, DS, MC, V.

D

Woodstock

(A-5) *See also Gurnee, McHenry*

Pop 20,151 **Elev** 942 ft **Area code** 815 **Zip** 60098

Information Chamber of Commerce, 136 Cass St; 815/338-2436

Web www.woodstockil.com

Orson Welles, who went to school and performed his first Shake-spearean role here, once described Woodstock as the "grand capitol of mid-Victorianism in the Midwest." The Victorian charm has been care-fully retained, especially in the town square with its ornate gazebo, wooded park, cobblestone streets, and many historic houses and build-ings that now contain antique shops.

What to See and Do

Chester Gould-Dick Tracy Museum. Exhibits include permanent collec-tion of original art of Tracy; also Gould family memorabilia, Chester Gould's original drawing board, and various changing exhibits. Gift shop. (Thurs-Sat, also Sun afternoons) In Old Courthouse Arts Center on Woodstock Sq, 101 N Johnson St. Phone 815/338-8281. **FREE**

Woodstock Opera House. (1889) Restored; built in a style described as "Steamboat Gothic" in reference to the exterior's resemblance to a cathe-dral and the interior's similarity to the salon of a Mississippi River steamboat. Especially worth noting is the stencilled auditorium ceiling. (Daily) 121 Van Buren St. Phone 815/338-5300. **FREE**

Special Event

Mozart Festival. Woodstock Opera House (see). Performances by Wood-stock Festival Orchestra and renowned soloists. Late July-early Aug. Phone 815/338-5300.

Motel/Motor Lodge

★ **DAYS INN.** *990 Lake Ave (60098). 815/338-0629; fax 815/338-0895. www.daysinn.com.* 44 rms, 3 story. S $50; D $55-$110; each addl $5; under 12 free. Crib free. TV; cable (premium), VCR avail (movies). Indoor pool. Complimentary conti-nental bkfst. Restaurant adj open 24 hrs. Ck-out noon. Meeting rm. Busi-ness servs avail. Game rm. Some refrigerators. Cr cds: A, C, D, DS, MC, V.

D ⛵ 🚭 🐾

INDIANA

At the crossroads of the nation, Indiana is one of the most typically American states in the country. Against a still-visible background of Native American history and determined pioneer struggle for survival, it stands out today as a region that has come of age. It is a manufacturing state with widely distributed industrial centers surrounded by fertile farmlands and magnificent forests.

In the wooded hill country north of the Ohio River are pioneer villages where time seems to have stood still. Central Indiana is one of the richest agricultural regions in the United States. The Calumet District in the northwest has a large industrial area. Miles of sand dunes and beaches have made Lake Michigan's south shore the state's summer playground. In the northeastern section are hundreds of secluded lakes, an angler's paradise. Trails at state parks and recreation areas are marked for hiking and horseback riding. In the winter, skiing, ice-skating, and tobogganing are popular sports.

Population: 5,942,901
Area: 35,936 square miles
Elevation: 320-1,257 feet
Peak: Near Bethel (Wayne County)
Entered Union: December 11, 1816 (19th state)
Capital: Indianapolis
Motto: The Crossroads of America
Nickname: The Hoosier State
Flower: Peony
Bird: Cardinal
Tree: Tulip Tree
Fair: Mid-August, 2003, in Indianapolis
Time Zone: Eastern and Central
Web Site: www.indy.org

Indiana's highways and roads are lined with reminders of its colorful history. A pre-Columbian race of mound builders developed a highly ceremonial culture here. Their earth structures can still be seen in many parts of the state. In 1673 two Frenchmen, Pére Marquette and Louis Jolliet, wandered across northern Indiana and preached to the Native Americans. Between 1679-1685 Indiana was thoroughly explored by Robert de La Salle and became a part of the French provinces of Canada and Louisiana. After the French and Indian War, most of Indiana came under British control (1763), which was violently opposed by a Native American confederation led by Chief Pontiac. In 1779 General George Rogers Clark occupied southern Indiana with French assistance and claimed it for the state of Virginia. Virginia was as unable to control the region as the British, and Indiana became public domain in 1784 and remained chiefly Native American territory during the next 15 years.

Continuing pressure by the federal government in Washington and by white settlers on Native American land led the great Shawnee chief Tecumseh to form an unsuccessful confederation of Indian Nations, extending from the Great Lakes to the Gulf of Mexico. The Battle of Tippecanoe in 1811, brought about by General William Henry Harrison while Tecumseh was in the South, dealt a fatal blow to the Native American organization. In 1812, Native Americans, their towns and granaries burned by federal troops and militia, made a last furious attempt to defend their land. But Tecumseh's death in the Battle of the Thames in 1813 marked the end of the Native American era. In 1816 Indiana became the 19th state of the Union. Abraham Lincoln was seven years old when his family moved to southern Indiana in 1816. He lived here for 14 years.

Today, Indiana's industries manufacture transportation equipment, electrical supplies, heavy industrial machinery, and food products. More than 60 percent of the building limestone used in the United States is supplied by quarries in the Hoosier State. Soft coal deposits, mainly found in southwest Indiana, are the most abundant natural resource. Indiana's principal farm products are soybeans, tomatoes, corn, spearmint, peppermint, livestock, poultry, and wheat and dairy products.

Several explanations have been offered as to why Indianans are called "Hoosiers." The most logical is that in 1826, a contractor on the Ohio Falls Canal at Louisville, Samuel Hoosier, gave employment preference to men living on the Indiana side of the river. The men in his work gangs were called "Hoosier's men," then "Hoosiers."

When to Go/Climate

Hot, humid summers and cold, snowy winters are the norm in Indiana. The flat terrain provides no buffer against wind and storms, and tornadoes are not uncommon in spring and summer.

AVERAGE HIGH/LOW TEMPERATURES (°F)

INDIANAPOLIS

Jan 34/17	**May** 74/52	**Sept** 78/56
Feb 38/21	**June** 83/61	**Oct** 66/44
Mar 51/32	**July** 86/65	**Nov** 52/34
Apr 63/42	**Aug** 84/63	**Dec** 39/23

FORT WAYNE

Jan 30/15	**May** 71/49	**Sept** 76/54
Feb 34/18	**June** 81/59	**Oct** 63/43
Mar 46/29	**July** 85/63	**Nov** 49/34
Apr 60/39	**Aug** 82/61	**Dec** 36/22

Parks and Recreation Finder

Directions to and information about the parks and recreation areas below are given under their respective town/city sections. Please refer to those sections for details.

NATIONAL PARK AND RECREATION AREAS

Key to abbreviations. I.H.S. = International Historic Site; I.P.M. = International Peace Memorial; N.B. = National Battlefield; N.B.P. = National Battlefield Park; N.B.C. = National Battlefield and Cemetery; N.C.A. = National Conservation Area; N.E.M. = National Expansion Memorial; N.F. = National Forest; N.G. = National Grassland; N.H.P. = National Historical Park; N.H.C. = National Heritage Corridor; N.H.S. = National Historic Site; N.L. = National Lakeshore; N.M. = National Monument; N.M.P. = National Military Park; N.Mem. = National Memorial; N.P. = National Park; N.Pres. = National Preserve; N.R.A. = National Recreation Area; N.R.R. = National Recreational River; N.Riv. = National River; N.S. = National Seashore; N.S.R. = National Scenic Riverway; N.S.T. = National Scenic Trail; N.Sc. = National Scientific Reserve; N.V.M. = National Volcanic Monument.

Place Name	Listed Under
George Rogers Clark N.H.P.	VINCENNES
Hoosier N.F.	BEDFORD
Indiana Dunes N.L.	same
Lincoln Boyhood N.Mem.	same

STATE PARK AND RECREATION AREAS

Key to abbreviations. I.P. = Interstate Park; S.A.P. = State Archaeological Park; S.B. = State Beach; S.C.A. = State Conservation Area; S.C.P. = State Conservation Park; S.Cp. = State Campground; S.F. = State Forest; S.G. = State Garden; S.H.A. = State Historic Area; S.H.P. = State Historic Park; S.H.S. = State Historic

Site; S.M.P. = State Marine Park; S.N.A. = State Natural Area; S.P. = State Park; S.P.C. = State Public Campground; S.R. = State Reserve; S.R.A. = State Recreation Area; S.Res. = State Reservoir; S.Res.P. = State Resort Park; S.R.P. = State Rustic Park.

CALENDAR HIGHLIGHTS

APRIL

Little 500 Bicycle Race (Bloomington). Indiana University campus. Bicycle and tricycle races, golf jamboree, entertainment. Phone 812/855-9152.

MAY

"500" Festival (Indianapolis). Month-long celebration precedes the Indianapolis 500, held Memorial Day weekend. Numerous events include the 500 Ball, Mechanic's Recognition Party, Delco Electronics 500 Festival Parade, Mini-Marathon, Memorial Service. Phone 317/636-4556 or 800/638-4296.

Indianapolis 500 (Indianapolis). A full schedule of activities, including mini-marathon, mayor's breakfast, and hot-air balloon race, lead up to the big race. Phone 317/484-6780.

Little 500 (Anderson). Anderson Speedway. Auto races. Phone 765/642-0206.

JULY

Three Rivers Festival (Fort Wayne). More than 280 events, including parades, balloon races, arts and crafts, music, ethnic dancing, sports, and fireworks at various locations in Fort Wayne. Phone 219/426-5556.

AUGUST

Amish Acres Arts and Crafts Festival (Nappanee). Amish Acres. Entries from many states; paintings, ceramics, jewelry; entertainment, dancing, feasts. Phone Amish Acres Visitor Center, 219/773-4188 or 800/800-4942.

Indiana State Fair (Indianapolis). Fairgrounds. Grand circuit horse racing, livestock exhibitions, entertainment, and special agricultural exhibits. Phone 317/927-7500 or 317/923-3431 (evenings).

SEPTEMBER

Fairmount Museum Days/Remembering James Dean (Fairmount/Marion). James Dean/Fairmount Historical Museum. Large car show, including 2,500 classic and custom autos; James Dean look-alike contest, '50s dance contest, parade, downtown street fair. Phone 765/948-4555.

OCTOBER

Parke County Covered Bridge Festival (Rockville). Celebration of Parke County's 32 historic covered bridges. Five self-guided tours are available. Arts and crafts, craft demonstrations, food, animals, and rides at living museum. Phone 765/569-5226.

Place Name	Listed Under
Angel Mounds S.H.S.	EVANSVILLE
Brookville Lake S.Res.	CONNERSVILLE
Brown County S.P.	same
Clifty Falls S.P.	MADISON
Corydon Capitol S.H.S.	CORYDON

Culbertson Mansion S.H.S.	NEW ALBANY
Harmonie S.P.	NEW HARMONY
Indiana Dunes S.P.	same
Lake Monroe (Paynetown S.R.A.)	BLOOMINGTON
Levi Coffin House S.H.S.	RICHMOND
Lieber S.R.A.	GREENCASTLE
Limberlost S.H.S.	GENEVA
Lincoln S.P.	LINCOLN BOYHOOD NATIONAL MEMORIAL & LINCOLN STATE PARK
McCormick's Creek S.P.	BLOOMINGTON
Mounds S.P.	ANDERSON
Pokagon S.P.	ANGOLA
Potato Creek S.P.	SOUTH BEND
Raccoon Lake S.R.A.	ROCKVILLE
Salamonie Reservoir, Dam & Forest	WABASH
Shades S.P.	CRAWFORDSVILLE
Shakamak S.P.	same
Spring Mill S.P.	same
Summit Lake S.P.	NEW CASTLE
T. C. Steele S.H.S.	NASHVILLE
Tippecanoe River S.P.	same
Turkey Run S.P.	same
Whitewater Canal S.H.S.	BATESVILLE
Whitewater Memorial S.P.	CONNERSVILLE
Yellowwood S.F.	NASHVILLE

Water-related activities, hiking, biking, various other sports, picnicking, and visitor centers, as well as camping, are available in many of these areas. Standard admission fees to state parks are: $4/carload (out-of-state, $5/carload); $22/yr permit; use of horses, fee varies. Camping, limited to two weeks, is on a first-come basis at most parks: $8-$21/night/site/family; winter, half price. Campsite reservations are accepted for all parks except at Harmonie, Shades, Summit Lake, and Tippecanoe. Several parks have housekeeping cabins. Six parks have inns, open all year. Pools and beaches are open from Memorial Day-late August (varies at each park); swimming permitted only when lifeguards are on duty. Pets on leash only. For detailed information contact the Indiana Department of Natural Resources, Division of State Parks and Reservoirs, 402 W Washington, W-298, Indianapolis 46204, phone 317/232-4124.

SKI AREAS

Place Name	**Listed Under**
Bendix Woods Ski Area	SOUTH BEND
Paoli Peaks Ski Area	FRENCH LICK
Ski World Ski Area	NASHVILLE

FISHING AND HUNTING

Nonresident licenses are available for hunting, five-day hunting, deer hunting, fishing (one-, three-, and seven-day; annual), and trapping; trout/salmon, game bird, and waterfowl stamps. Resident licenses are available for hunting, deer hunting, one-day fishing, trapping, and turkey hunting. Youth hunting license allows children under 18 to hunt all game. Residents ages 17-65 and all nonresidents must obtain fishing license. For additional information, including exceptions, bag limits, and license fees, contact Division of Fish and Wildlife, Department of Natural Resources, 402 W Washington St, Rm W273, Indianapolis 46204, phone 317/232-4080. A free quarterly newsletter, *Focus,* is available to keep sportspersons up to date on division activities. Write to *Focus* at the same address.

Driving Information

Safety belts are mandatory for all persons in front seat of vehicle. Children under five years must be in an approved passenger restraint anywhere in vehicle: ages three and four may use a regulation safety belt; age two and under must use an approved safety seat. Phone 317/232-1295.

INTERSTATE HIGHWAY SYSTEM

The following alphabetical listing of Indiana towns in *Mobil Travel Guide* shows that these cities are within ten miles of the indicated Interstate highways. A highway map, however, should be checked for the nearest exit.

Highway Number	Cities/Towns within ten miles
Interstate 64	Corydon, Jeffersonville, New Albany, Wyandotte.
Interstate 65	Columbus, Indianapolis, Jeffersonville, Lafayette, New Albany, Remington.
Interstate 69	Anderson, Angola, Fort Wayne, Huntington, Indianapolis, Marion, Muncie, Noblesville.
Interstate 70	Brazil, Greencastle, Greenfield, Indianapolis, New Castle, Richmond, Terre Haute.
Interstate 74	Batesville, Crawfordsville, Indianapolis.
Interstate 94	Hammond, Michigan City.

Additional Visitor Information

Six-issue subscriptions to *Outdoor Indiana* may be obtained by contacting Department of Natural Resources, 402 W Washington, Rm W-160, Indianapolis 46204, phone 317/232-4200. This official publication of the Department of Natural Resources is $10 for one year or $18 for two years.

Brochures on attractions, calendar of events, information about historic sites, and other subjects are available from the Indiana Department of Commerce, Tourism & Film Development Division, 1 N Capitol St, Suite 700, Indianapolis 46204, phone 800/289-6646.

There are Welcome Centers on highways entering southern Indiana as well as travel information centers located at highway rest areas throughout Indiana. Those who stop by will find information and brochures most helpful in planning stops at points of interest. All are open daily, 24 hours.

DUNE COUNTRY

Just as Californians head for the sand and surf of Malibu and Easterners flock to sandy expanses of the Jersey shore, Midwesterners journey to the rolling sand dunes and hidden beaches of northwestern Indiana. A popular way to "do the dunes" is to travel along US 12, known colloquially as "the Dunes Highway." Roughly paralleling the lakefront between Gary and Michigan City, the route passes through vast protected areas of lake shore, tunneling through shady avenues of trees. Large expanses of "dune country" are protected by 2,182-acre Indiana Dunes State Park and Indiana Dunes National Lakeshore, a federally administered preserve containing about 15,000 acres. Together, these areas contain some of the most diverse flora and fauna in the Midwest. They also provide a wide range of highly popular interpretive programs.

Begin at West Beach, part of the National Lakeshore north of US 12 and east of County Line Road. It offers four miles of open beach, a modern bathhouse, nature-study activities, picnic area, duneland grass prairie, a lake, and three miles of hiking trails. A boardwalk provides panoramic views from elevations of up to 110 feet. Continue east on US 12 and take IN 49 north to Indiana Dunes State Park. Diverse park interpretive programs range from naturalist hikes to explore the semiarid, desertlike dune environment to a video presentation about edible wild foods. Other kid-friendly, fun programs include beach-blanket bingo and scavenger hunts that teach participants about the unique habitats found in and around the dunes. The park offers three miles of beach, flanked by one of the nation's finest examples of a preserved natural dune ecosystem. More than 16 miles of trails offer a variety of challenges, including the opportunity to scale Mount Tom, the tallest dune at 192 feet.

Heading north on IN 49 to I-94, find excellent lodgings and a pampering health-and-beauty spa at Indian Oak Resort & Spa that offers lakeside rooms with fireplaces and whirlpool tubs and a variety of body treatments and massages. It's a tranquil spot, nestled around a private lake on 100 acres of wooded trails that thread through towering oaks. Nearby on IN 49 is the Yellow Brick Road Gift Shop and Fantasy Museum, full of memorabilia related to the classic movie, *The Wizard of Oz,* and the work of its creator, L. Frank Baum. Return to the Dunes Highway and continue east to Kemil Road. **(APPROX 26 MI)**

Anderson

(D-5) *See also Indianapolis, Muncie*

Founded 1823 **Pop** 59,459 **Elev** 883 ft
Area code 765
Information Anderson/Madison
County Visitors and Convention
Bureau, 6335 S Scatterfield Rd,
46013; 765/643-5633 or 800/533-
6569
Web www.madtourism.com

Originally, this was the site of a
Delaware village in the hills south of
the White River. The city was named
for Kikthawenund, also called Captain Anderson, a well-known chief of
the Delawares. The discovery of natural gas pockets underneath the city
in 1886 sparked a ten-year boom,
which gave the city the title "Queen
of the Gas Belt." One hundred
Newport-style gaslights have been
added to what is now known as Historic 8th Street. Restored Victorian
homes reflect the area's fashionable
past.

Anderson is the seat of grain and
livestock production in Madison
County and an important manufacturing center. Two subsidiaries of
General Motors, Delco-Remy America and Delphi Interior Lighting Systems, manufacture automotive
equipment. Other industrial products
include castings, glass, cabinets, corrugated boxes, recreation equipment,
and packaging machinery. The international headquarters of the nonsec-
tarian Church of God is in Anderson.

What to See and Do

Anderson University. (1917) 2,000
students. School of Theology (Sept-
June) has collection of Holy Land
artifacts. Also on campus are the
Jessie Wilson Art Galleries, Boehm
Bird Collection, and 2,250-seat Rear-
don Auditorium. The Indianapolis
Colts hold summer training camp
here (mid-July-mid-Aug). Tours (by
appt). E 5th St and College Dr. Phone
765/649-9071. **FREE**

Gruenewald Historic House. (1873)
Twelve-rm, Second Empire town
house of successful German saloon-
keeper, decorated in style of 1890s.
(Apr-mid-Dec) Living history tours
(by appt). One-hr house tours (Tues-

Fri). 626 Main St. Phone 765/648-
6875. ¢¢

Historical Military Armor Museum.
Large collection of lightweight tanks
from WWI to the present; com-
pletely restored and operational.
(Tues, Thurs, Sat; closed hols) 2330
Crystal St, I-69 exit 26. ¢¢

Historic West 8th Street. Eleven blks
of restored Victorian homes lined
with Newport-style gaslights re-create
the 1890s. Phone 765/643-5633.
FREE

Mounds State Park. Within this
290-acre park of rolling woodlands
are several well-preserved earth formations constructed many centuries
ago by a prehistoric race of Adena-
Hopewell mound builders. On bluffs
overlooking the White River are
earth structures that were once an
important center of an ancient civilization of which very little is
known. The largest earth structure is
nine ft high and nearly ¼ mi in circumference. Smaller structures
nearby incl conical mounds and a
fiddle-shaped earthwork. 2 mi E on
IN 232. Phone 765/642-6627. ¢¢

Park facilities. Incl swimming pool,
fishing on White River; hiking
trails, picnicking, playground, concession, camping. Nature center;
naturalist service. Standard fees.
(Daily) Phone 765/642-6627.

**Paramount Theatre and Centre Ball-
room.** Restored 1929 atmospheric
theatre designed to appear as a Spanish courtyard. Tours (by appt; closed
hols) 1124 Meridian Plaza. Phone
765/642-1234. ¢¢

Special Event

"Little 500". Anderson Speedway,
1311 Pendleton Ave. Auto races. Res
necessary. Phone 765/642-0206.
Wkend of Indianapolis 500.

Motels/Motor Lodges

★ **BEST INNS OF AMERICA.** *5706 S
Scatterfield Rd (46013). 765/644-2000;
toll-free 800/237-8466. www.bestinn.
com.* 93 rms, 2 story. S $43.88-
$50.88; D $46.88-$53.88; each addl
$7; under 18 free. Crib free. Pet
accepted. TV; cable. Complimentary
continental bkfst. Restaurant nearby.

Ck-out 1 pm. Cr cds: A, C, D, DS, MC, V.

⊞ 🐾 ⊠ 🔥 SC

★ ★ **COMFORT INN.** *2205 E 59th St (46013). 765/644-4422; toll-free 800/228-5150. www.comfortinn.com.* 56 rms, 2 story, 14 suites. Mar-July: S, D $55-$65; each addl $5; suites $65-$75; under 18 free; wkend rates; lower rates rest of yr. Crib free. Pet accepted, some restrictions. TV; cable. Indoor pool; whirlpool. Complimentary continental bkfst. Ck-out 11 am. Game rm. Refrigerator, microwave in suites. Cr cds: A, C, D, DS, ER, JCB, MC, V.

⊞ 🐾 ⊠ ⊠ 🔥 SC

★ ★ **HOLIDAY INN.** *5920 Scatterfield Rd (46013). 765/644-2581; fax 765/642-8545; toll-free 800/465-4329. www.holiday-inn.con.* 158 rms, 2 story. S, D $79; under 18 free; special rates for Indianapolis 500. Crib free. TV; cable (premium). 2 pools, 1 indoor; whirlpool, poolside serv. Coffee in rms. Restaurants 6 am-10 pm. Bar 11-1 am, Sun noon-midnight. Ck-out 11 am. Coin lndry. Meeting rms. Business servs avail. In-rm modem link. Bellhops. Valet serv. Gift shop. Free airport transportation. Cr cds: A, C, D, DS, JCB, MC, V.

⊞ ⊠ ⊠ 🔥

★ **LEES INN.** *2114 E 59th St (46013). 765/649-2500; fax 765/643-0349.* 72 rms, 2 story. S, D $69-$145; each addl $10; under 15 free. Crib free. TV; cable. Complimentary continental bkfst. Restaurant adj 7 am-10 pm. Ck-out noon. Cr cds: A, D, DS, MC, V.

⊞ ⊠ 🔥

Angola

(A-5) *See also Auburn*

Pop 5,824 **Elev** 1,055 ft
Area code 219 **Zip** 46703
Information Steuben County Tourism Bureau, 207 S Wayne St; 800/525-3101
Web www.lakes101.org

This is a tranquil town in the northeastern corner of Indiana's resort area. The wooded hills surrounding Angola provide more than 100 lakes for swimming, boating, and fishing in the summer and ice-skating in the winter.

What to See and Do

Pokagon State Park. A 1,203-acre park on the shores of Lake James and Snow Lake in the heart of the northern Indiana lake country. Swimming beach, bathhouse, waterskiing, fishing, boating (rentals); hiking trails, saddle barn, skiing, ice skating, tobogganing, ice fishing, picnicking, concession, camping. Nature center; wildlife exhibit; naturalist service. Standard fees. (Daily) IN 80/90 toll-road & I-69, exit 154. Phone 219/833-2012.

Resort

★ ★ ★ **POTAWATOMI INN.** *6 Ln 100A Lake James (46703). 260/833-1077; fax 260/833-4087; toll-free 877/768-2928.* 126 rms in 2-story inn, 16 cabin-style rms, 3 suites. S, D $48-$89; suites $109-$119. Crib $3. TV. Indoor pool; whirlpools. Dining rm 7 am-8 pm. Ck-out noon, ck-in 4 pm. Meeting rms. Business servs avail. Gift shop. Grocery in summer. Guest lndry. X-country ski on site. Exercise equipt; sauna. Health club privileges. Hayrides. Private beach; lifeguard in summer. Dock, boats. Tobogganing. Game rm. Lawn games. Fireplace. On Lake James. Built in 1926 in the Pokagon State Park, land acquired from the Potawatomi Indians. Cr cds: A, DS, MC, V.

⊞ 🎿 🏄 ⊠ 🎿 ⊠ 🔥

Restaurant

★ ★ ★ **HATCHERY.** *118 S Elizabeth St (46703). 219/665-9957. www.the hatcheryrestaurant.com.* Hrs: 5-9 pm; Fri, Sat to 10 pm. Closed Sun; hols. Res accepted; required in summer. Bar 4 pm-midnight. Wine cellar. A la carte entrees: dinner $15-$28. Specializes in fresh seafood, lamb, steak. Patio dining. Entertainment Sat. Cr cds: A, C, D, DS, MC, V.

⊞ ⊠

Lake Michigan at sunset

Auburn

(B-5) *See also Angola, Fort Wayne*

Pop 9,379 **Elev** 870 ft **Area code** 219
Zip 46706
Information Chamber of Commerce,
208 S Jackson St; 219/925-2100 or
DeKalb County Visitors Bureau, 204
N Jackson; 219/927-1499 or 877/833-
DCVB
Web www.dekalbcvb.org

What to See and Do

Auburn-Cord-Duesenberg Museum.
More than 140 examples of these
and other well-known antique, clas-
sic, and special-interest cars are dis-
played in the original showrm of the
Auburn Automobile Company; col-
lections of automotive literature.
(Daily; closed Jan 1, Thanksgiving,
Dec 25) (See SPECIAL EVENT) 1600 S
Wayne St. Phone 219/925-1444. ¢¢¢

Gene Stratton Porter Historic Site.
Home of well-known Indiana
author/naturalist/photographer. Built
on Sylvan Lake in a forested area
with a great variety of wildflowers
and wildlife; designed by Mrs. Porter
and completed in 1914. Two-story
log cabin furnished with many original pieces, photographs, memorabilia. Special events. Tours of cabin
(Apr-mid Dec, Tues-Sun; closed
Easter, Thanksgiving, Dec 25). 25 mi
NW via I-69, US 6, IN 9, near Rome
City. Phone 219/854-3790. **Donation**

**National Automotive and Truck
Museum.** More than 100 cars and
trucks on display with a focus on
post-WWI automobiles; also auto-
related exhibits. (Daily; closed Jan
1, Thanksgiving, Dec 25) 1000 Gordon M. Buerig Pl. Phone 219/925-
9100. ¢¢

Special Event

Auburn-Cord-Duesenberg Festival.
Auto auction, classic car show,
parades, many events. Phone
219/925-3600. Late Aug.

Motels/Motor Lodges

★★ **AUBURN INN.** *225 Touring Dr
(46706)*. 219/925-6363. 53 rms, 2
story. Apr-Oct: S $60-$150; D $68-
$150; each addl $8; suites $125;
under 16 free; wkend rates. Crib
free. TV; cable. Heated pool. Complimentary bkfst buffet. Ck-out
noon. Meeting rms. Business servs
avail. Health club privileges. Cr cds:
A, D, DS, MC, V.
D 🏊 ⬜ 🔥 **SC**

★ **COUNTRY HEARTH INN.** *1115
W 7th St (46706)*. 219/925-1316; fax

219/927-8012. *www.countryhearth. com*. 78 rms, 2 story. S $61-$67; D $63-$69; each addl $6; suites, kit. units $70-$78; under 18 free. Crib free. TV; cable (premium). Pool. Complimentary continental bkfst. Ck-out noon. Meeting rm. Business servs avail. Cr cds: A, C, D, DS, JCB, MC, V.

★★ **HOLIDAY INN EXPRESS.** *404 Touring Dr (46706). 219/925-1900; fax 219/927-1138; 800/465-4329. www. holiday-inn.com.* 70 rms, 3 story. S $74-$80; D $80-$85; suites $90-$95; under 18 free; higher rates special events. Pet accepted. TV; cable (premium). Complimentary continental bkfst. Coffee in rms. Restaurant 6 am-10 pm. Ck-out noon. Meeting rm. Business servs avail. In-rm modem link. Coin lndry. Indoor pool; whirlpool. Some refrigerators, microwaves. Cr cds: A, D, DS, MC, V.

Aurora (A-1)

Founded 1819 **Pop** 3,825 **Elev** 501 ft
Area code 812 **Zip** 47001
Information Office of the Mayor, PO Box 158; 812/926-1777

What to See and Do

Hillforest. (ca 1855) Fully restored Italian Renaissance villa on ten acres. Architecture and period furnishings incorporate characteristics of steamboat era. (Apr-mid-Dec, Tues-Sun; closed hols) (See SPECIAL EVENTS) 213 5th St. Phone 812/926-0087. ¢¢

Special Events

Aurora Farmers Fair. Three-day fair featuring rides, games, parade; entertainment. First wkend Oct. Phone 812/926-2176.

Victorian Christmas. Hillforest. Recreation of a Victorian Christmas. First two wkends Dec. Phone 812/926-0087.

Resort

★★ **GRAND VICTORIA CASINO & RESORT BY HYATT.** *600 Grand Victoria Dr, Rising Sun (47040). 812/438-1234; fax 812/438-5155; toll-free 800/472-6311. www.hyatt.com.* 201 rms, 3 story. S, D $110-$250; each addl $15; under 17 free. Crib avail. Indoor pool; whirlpool. TV; cable (premium), VCR avail. Restaurant 6 am-midnight. Ck-out 11 am. Meeting rms. Business center. Gift shop. Exercise rm. Some refrigerators, minibars. Cr cds: A, C, D, DS, MC, V.

Restaurant

★ **WHISKY'S.** *334 Front St, Lawrenceburg (47025). 812/537-4239.* Hrs: 11:30 am-10 pm; Sat 4-11 pm. Closed Sun; Easter, July 4, Dec 25. Res accepted Mon-Fri. Bar. Lunch, dinner $4.95-$16.50. Children's meals. Specialties: pork ribs. Dining in two restored buildings (circa 1850 and 1835) joined together. Cr cds: A, DS, MC, V.

Batesville (E-5)

Pop 4,720 **Elev** 983 ft **Area code** 812
Zip 47006
Information Chamber of Commerce, 132 S Main; 812/934-3101

What to See and Do

Whitewater Canal State Historic Site. Incl part of a restored 14-mi section of the Whitewater Canal, which provided transportation between Hagerstown and the Ohio River at Lawrenceburg from 1836-1860. *Ben Franklin III* canal boat offers horse-drawn boat cruise (25 min) through the Duck Creek aqueduct (1848) to the canal's only remaining operating lock (May-Oct, Tues-Sun; other times by appt). Working gristmill in Metamora (Tues-Sun; free). Fishing, canoeing; hiking, picnicking permitted along the canal. 14 mi N on US 52 in Metamora. Phone 812/647-6512. ¢

B&B/Small Inn

★★ **SHERMAN HOUSE.** *35 S Main St (47006). 812/934-1000; fax 812/934-1230; toll-free 800/445-4939. www.sherman-house.com.* 23 rms, 2 story. S $44-$55; D $51-$55; suites $84; under 12 free. Crib free. TV; cable (premium). Restaurant (see SHERMAN HOUSE). Bar 11 am-midnight. Ck-out 11 am, ck-in 1 pm. Meeting rms. Business servs avail. Gift shop. Exercise equipt. Inn since 1852. Cr cds: A, C, D, MC, V.
🅳 🏋 ☒ 🔥 SC

Restaurant

★★ **SHERMAN HOUSE.** *35 S Main St (IN 229) (47006). 812/934-2407. www.sherman-house.com.* Hrs: 6:30 am-9 pm; Fri, Sat to 10 pm; Sun to 8 pm. Closed Jan 1, Dec 25. Res accepted. German, Amer menu. Bar. Bkfst $2.50-$4, lunch $2.95-$6.25, dinner $8.95-$15.95. Child's menu. Specialties: châteaubriand, veal. Salad bar. Lobster tank. Old World atmosphere. Established in 1852. Cr cds: A, D, MC, V.
🅳 ☒

Bedford

(F-4) *See also Bloomington, French Lick*

Founded 1825 **Pop** 13,817 **Elev** 699 ft
Area code 812 **Zip** 47421
Information Lawrence County Tourism Commission, 1116 16th St, PO Box 1193; 812/275-4493 or 800/798-0769
Web www.kiva.net/~bedford/

Bedford is the center of Indiana limestone quarrying, one of the state's foremost industries. Limestone quarried here was used in the construction of the World War Memorial in Indianapolis, the Empire State Building in New York, and the Federal Triangle in Washington, D.C.

This is an agricultural area producing livestock, grain, and fruit. Headquarters of Hoosier National Forest and Wayne National Forest (see IRONTON, OH) are here. Williams Dam, 11 miles southwest on IN 450, offers fishing on the White River.

What to See and Do

Antique Auto & Race Car Museum. Over 100 race and antique cars. (Apr-Dec, daily) US 50 and IN 450 exit off IN 37, in Stone City Mall. Phone 812/275-0556. ¢¢

Bluespring Caverns. One of the world's largest cavern systems; more than 20 mi of explored passageways and 15 mi of underground streams join to form the large river upon which tour boats travel. Electric lighting reveals many unusual sights, incl eyeless blindfish and blind crawfish. Picnicking. Gift shop. (Apr-Oct) 6 mi SW via US 50. Phone 812/279-9471. ¢¢¢

Hoosier National Forest. Approx 189,000 acres spread through nine counties. Swimming, boating, fishing; picnicking, hiking, horseback trails, hunting, nature study; historic sites. Campsites at Hardin Ridge (Monroe County), German Ridge, Celina Lake, Tipson Lake, Indian Lake (Perry County), and Springs Valley (Orange County) recreation areas. Campsites on first-come basis. Both north and south of Bedford: to reach the north portion, NE on IN 58 (or E on US 50 then N on IN 446); to reach the south portion, SW on US 50 (or S on IN 37 and W on IN 60). Contact Forest Supervisor, US Forest Service, 811 Constitution Ave. Phone 812/275-5987. In portion of the forest south of Bedford is

Pioneer Mothers Memorial Forest. An 88-acre forest of virgin timber that incl white oak and black walnut trees of giant dimensions. From Paoli, S on IN 37, in Orange County.

Lawrence County Historical Museum. Display of Indiana limestone, Native American artifacts, Civil War items, pioneer relics, WWI and WWII items; genealogical library. (Mon-Fri; closed hols) County Courthouse basement, rm 12. Phone 812/275-4141. **FREE**

Osborne Spring Park. Approx 30 acres. Restored log cabin (1817). Picnicking, camping (fee). (Daily) 17 mi NW via IN 58 to Owensburg, then 3 mi NW on Osborne Spring Rd. ¢¢

Spring Mill State Park. (see) 1300 Elmwood Ave. Phone 716/878-6011 or 716/878-4000.

Motels/Motor Lodges

★ **MARK III.** *1709 M St (47421). 812/275-5935; res 888/884-5814.* 21 rms, 2 story. S $30; D $35; each addl $3; under 12 free. Crib free. Pet accepted, some restrictions. TV; cable (premium). Complimentary coffee in rms. Restaurant adj 11 am-midnight. Ck-out 11 am. Grill. Cr cds: A, DS, MC, V.

⬛⬛⬛

★★ **STONEHENGE LODGE.** *911 Constitution Ave (47421). 812/279-8111; fax 812/279-2974; toll-free 800/274-2974. www.stonehengelodge.com.* 97 rms, 3 story. S $60-$125; D $66-$135; each addl $4; under 16 free. Crib $6. TV; cable (premium). Pool. Restaurant 6 am-9 pm; Fri to 10 pm; Sat 5-10 pm. Bar 4-10 pm; closed Sun. Ck-out noon. Meeting rms. Business servs avail. Health club privileges. Cr cds: A, C, D, DS, JCB, V.

⬛⬛⬛⬛⬛⬛

Bloomington

(E-3) *See also Bedford, Nashville*

Settled 1818 **Pop** 60,633 **Elev** 745 ft **Area code** 812

Information Bloomington/Monroe County Convention and Visitors Bureau, 2855 N Walnut St, 47404; 812/334-8900 or 800/800-0037

Web www.visitbloomington.com

Bloomington is an industrial and college town, the seat of Monroe County. Limestone quarries and mills in the vicinity contributed to its early industrial growth. The electronics industry and tourism play an important part in the city's economy today.

What to See and Do

Bloomington Antique Mall. Largest antique mall in southern Indiana. Over 100 dealers under one roof. (Daily) 311 W 7th St. Phone 812/332-2290.

Brown County State Park. (see) 17 mi E on IN 46.

Butler Winery. Wines made in vineyard; cheeses and preserves; tastings. (Daily; closed Jan 1, Dec 25) 1022 N College Ave. Phone 812/339-7233. **FREE**

Indiana University. (1820) 34,863 students. One of the outstanding state universities in the country. Notable are the Lilly Library of Rare Books (Mon-Sat); Dailey Family Collection of Hoosier Art and Thomas Hart Benton murals in auditorium (Mon-Sat; special tours, phone 812/855-9528); Art Museum (Tues-Sun); Glenn Black Laboratory of Archaeology (daily); Hoagy Carmichael Room (by appt); William H. Mathers Museum (Tues-Sun; summer hrs vary); Musical Arts Center (tours by appt, phone 812/855-9055). All buildings closed university hols. 5 blks E of public square. Incl

Jordan Hall and Greenhouse. Displays re-creations of flora from different environments, incl desert and rainforest. (Daily) 1001 E 3rd St. Phone 812/855-7717. **FREE**

Lake Monroe. Joint project of Indiana Department of Natural Resources and US Army Corps of Engineers. A 10,000-acre lake with approx 150-mi shoreline. Waterskiing, swimming at Hardin Ridge, Fairfax, and Paynetown areas (Memorial Day-Labor Day); fishing (all yr); boating (ramps); picnicking, tent and trailer sites (standard fees; no camping at Fairfax). Paynetown State Recreation Area (standard fees). Hardin Ridge Federal Recreation Area in Hoosier National Forest (see BEDFORD). 7 mi SE via IN 46 to IN 446. Contact Monroe Reservoir, Department of Natural Resources, 4850 S State Rd 446, 47401. Phone 812/837-9546. ¢¢

McCormick's Creek State Park. The creek plunges headlong through a limestone canyon in this 1,833-acre park to join the White River at its border. Trails, bridle paths, and roads lead through beech and pine forests, ravines, and gullies. Wolf Cave and the stone bridge over McCormick's Creek are unusual features. Swimming pool, creek fishing; tennis, picnicking, playground, camping, cabins, inn. Nature center; nature trails, naturalist service. Standard fees. 12 mi NW on IN 46. Phone 812/829-2235. ¢¢

Monroe County Historical Society Museum. Displays depicting history of county and limestone industry. (Tues-Sat, also Sun afternoons; closed hols) 6th and Washington Sts. Phone 812/332-2517. **FREE**

Oliver Winery. Tastings, food and gift items. Tours (wkends). (Mon-Sat, also Sun afternoons; closed hols) 7 mi N on IN 37. Phone 812/876-5800. **FREE**

Special Events

Indiana Heritage Quilt Show. Quilts from all over the country. Also classes and quilt style show. Monroe County Convention Center, 302 S College Ave. Phone 800/800-0037. Early Mar.

Little 500 Bicycle Race. Indiana University campus. Bicycle and tricycle races, golf jamboree, entertainment. Phone 812/855-9152. Apr.

Monroe County Fair. Monroe County Fairgrounds. Rodeo; midway; exhibits. Late July-early Aug. Phone 812/825-7439.

Fourth Street Art Fair. Downtown. Pottery, jewelry, paintings, glass art. Labor Day wkend. Phone 812/334-8900.

Lotus World Music and Arts Festival. Downtown. Musicians from around the globe perform in five venues. Late Sept. Phone 812/336-6599.

Madrigal Feasts. Indiana University Campus. Dec. Phone 812/855-0463.

Motels/Motor Lodges

★★ **COURTYARD BY MARRIOTT.** *310 S College Ave (47403). 812/335-8000; fax 812/336-9997; toll-free 800/321-2211. www.marriott.com.* 117 rms, 5 story. S, D $86-$129; suites $140; under 18 free; higher rates special events. Crib free. TV; cable (premium). Complimentary coffee in rms. Restaurant nearby. Ck-out noon. Business servs avail. In-rm modem link. Coin lndry. Downhill ski 10 mi. Exercise equipt. Health club privileges. Indoor pool; whirlpool. Refrigerator, microwave, wet bar in suites. Cr cds: A, C, D, DS, MC, V.

⌨ 🏊 ⛷ 🗺 🔥

★★ **HAMPTON INN.** *2100 N Walnut (47404). 812/334-2100; fax 812/334-8433; toll-free 800/426-7866. www.hamptoninn.com.* 131 rms, 4 story. S $63; D $71; under 18 free. Crib free. Pet accepted, some restrictions. TV; cable (premium), VCR avail. Pool. Complimentary continental bkfst. Restaurant adj open 24 hrs. Ck-out noon. Meeting rms. Business servs avail. In-rm modem link. Valet serv. Downhill/x-country ski 12 mi. Some in-rm whirlpools. Cr cds: A, C, DS, MC, V.

🐾 🏊 🗺 🔥

★★ **HOLIDAY INN.** *1710 N Kinser Pike (47404). 812/334-3252; fax 812/333-1702; toll-free 800/465-4329. www.holiday-inn.com.* 189 rms, 4 story. S, D $59-$89; each addl $6; under 18 free. Crib free. TV; cable (premium). Indoor pool; whirlpool. Coffee in rms. Restaurant 6:30 am-10 pm. Bar 2 pm-3 am; Sun to midnight. Ck-out noon. Meeting rms. Business servs avail. In-rm modem link. Free airport transportation. Sundries. Downhill ski 10 mi; x-country ski 15 mi. Sauna. Game rm. Microwaves avail. University stadium 2 blks. Cr cds: A, C, D, DS, JCB, MC, V.

🄳 🏊 🗺 🔥 🆂🅲 ⛷

Resort

★★ **CLARION FOURWINDS RESORT.** *9301 Fairfax Rd (47401). 812/824-9904; fax 812/824-9816.* 126 rms, 3 story. May-Oct: S, D $126-$140; suites $225-$400; lower rates rest of yr. TV; cable (premium), VCR avail. Indoor/outdoor pool; whirlpool. Playground. Supervised children's activities (Memorial Day-Labor Day). Dining rm 7 am-2 pm, 6-9 pm; Fri, Sat to 10:30 pm. Snack bar. Deli. Box lunches. Picnics. Bar; entertainment. Ck-out noon, ck-in 4 pm. Meeting rms. Business servs avail. Grocery. Package store. Airport transportation. Golf privileges, pro. Miniature golf. Public beach. Boat rental, marina. Lawn games. Soc dir; entertainment, movies. Shared patios, balconies. Picnic tables. Landscaped grounds. Overlooks Lake Monroe Reservoir. Cr cds: A, C, D, DS, JCB, MC, V.

🔥 🏊 ⛷ 🎿

Restaurants

★ **COLORADO STEAKHOUSE.**
1800 N College Ave (47404). 812/339-9979. Hrs: 11 am-10 pm; Sat to 11 pm. Closed Dec 25. Res accepted. Bar to midnight. Lunch $5-$8, dinner $9.95-$18.95. Child's menu. Specializes in BBQ ribs, salmon, shrimp. Atrium dining area. Cr cds: A, C, D, DS, MC, V.
D SC ⊐

★ **GRISANTI'S.** *850 Auto Mall Rd (IN 46) (47401). 812/339-9391.* Hrs: 11 am-10 pm; Fri, Sat to 11 pm; Sun to 9 pm. Closed Thanksgiving, Dec 25. Italian menu. Bar. Lunch $4.75-$7, dinner $8-$14. Specializes in chicken, seafood, lasagne. Own pasta. Italian country atmosphere. Cr cds: A, D, DS, MC, V.
D ⊐

★ **LE PETIT CAFE.** *308 W 6th St (47404). 812/334-9747.* Hrs: 11 am-2 pm, 5:30-9 pm; Sat, Sun to 10 pm. Closed Mon; hols. Res accepted. Continental menu. Wine, beer. Lunch $5-$10, dinner $13-$20. Specializes in steak, fish, crepes. Own pasta. Casual dining. Family-owned. Cr cds: MC, V.
D ⊐

Brazil

(E-3) *See also Greencastle, Terre Haute*

Pop 7,640 **Elev** 659 ft **Area code** 812 **Zip** 47834
Information Clay County Chamber of Commerce, PO Box 23; 812/448-8457

A former mining center, Brazil was also widely known for its manufacture of building brick, tile, and block coal. Bituminous coal is taken extensively from huge open strip mines. Farmers in surrounding Clay County grow corn, wheat, soybeans, and raise livestock. Brazil was named for the South American country.

What to See and Do

Clay County Historical Museum. Post office is now museum offering exhibits of past and present. (Mar-Dec; closed hols) 100 E National Ave. Phone 812/446-4036. **FREE**

Forest Park. Outdoor auditorium and stadium; 18-hole golf adj (fee); swimming pool, wading pool (Memorial Day-Labor Day; fee); playground, ball fields, picnic areas (shelters); Sun evening band concerts in summer. Log cabins preserved from pioneer days, with a display of relics. The Chafariz dos Contas, a granite fountain presented to the city by the Republic of Brazil, is located here. S on IN 59. Phone 812/442-5681. **FREE**

Special Event

Christmas in the Park. Forest Park. Incl parade, holiday fireworks display, musical events, and decorated homes and businesses. Phone 812/448-8457. Day after Thanksgiving-Dec 26.

Brown County State Park

See also Columbus, Nashville

(S and E of Nashville on IN 46)

There are 15,800 acres of hilly woodland here, with two lakes, streams, a covered bridge, and miles of drives and trails. Among the wildlife commonly seen here are white-tailed deer, raccoon, gray squirrel, and various birds, including the robin, white-breasted nuthatch, blue jay, cardinal, and junco.

This is the largest of Indiana's parks. Swimming (Memorial Day-Labor Day), fishing; hiking, bridle trails, saddle barn (April-November), picnicking, concession (April-November), camping. Nature center, naturalist service; 80-foot observation tower with view of Weed Patch Hill. (Daily) Standard fees. Contact Superintendent, PO Box 608, Nashville 47448; 812/988-6406.

Columbus

(E-4) *See also Bloomington, Nashville*

Settled 1820 **Pop** 31,802 **Elev** 656 ft
Area code 812
Information Visitors Center, 506 5th
St, 47201; 812/378-2622 or 800/468-
6564
Web www.columbus.in.us

The architectural designs of many
modern buildings in Columbus have
attracted international attention. In
the heart of the prairie, the project
was launched in the late 1930s with
the commissioning of Eliel Saarinen
to design a church. Since then, more
than 50 public and private buildings
have been designed by architects
such as Saarinen, John Carl War-
necke, Harry Weese, I. M. Pei, Kevin
Roche, Eliot Noyes, and J. M.
Johansen.

What to See and Do

Columbus Area Visitors Center.
Video presentation and gift shop are
also here. Architectural tours of the
town are given; res advised. (Daily)
506 5th St. Phone 800/468-6564.

The Commons. Downtown common
area; features shopping mall, recreational facilities, museums, and
Chaos I, a sculpture by noted artist
Jean Tinguely. Third & Fourth and
Washington Sts. Phone 812/372-
4541.

**Indianapolis Museum of Art-
Columbus.** Displays changing
exhibits from the Indianapolis
Museum of Art (see INDIANAPOLIS)
collection. Special exhibitions. (Tues-
Sun; closed hols) 390 The Commons.
Phone 812/376-2597. **FREE**

Otter Creek Golf Course. Bent grass
tees; 90 sand bunkers; rolling hills;
Robert Trent Jones design. Golf packages. (Mar-Nov) 4 mi E on 25th.
Phone 812/579-5227. ¢¢¢¢

Special Event

Columbus Bluegrass & Craft Show.
Downtown. Free festival features
bluegrass performances. Food and
crafts. Phone 812/376-2535. Second
wkend Mar.

Motels/Motor Lodges

★ ★ **HOLIDAY INN.** *2480 W
Jonathan Moore Pike (47201). 812/372-
1541; fax 812/378-9049; res 800/465-
4989. www.holiday-inn.com.* 253 rms,
2-7 story. S $59-$89; D $69-$108;
each addl $10; suites $150-$175;
under 18 free. Crib free. Pet accepted.
TV; cable (premium). Indoor pool;
whirlpool. Restaurant 6 am-10 pm.
Bars 11-1 am; entertainment. Ck-out
11 am. Convention facilities. Business servs avail. In-rm modem link.
Bellhops. Gift shop. Barber, beauty
shop. Exercise equipt; sauna. Health
club privileges. Game rms. Atrium.
Many antiques. Turn-of-the-century
atmosphere. Cr cds: A, MC, V.

🄳 🔧 🛠 🏊 🐾

★ ★ **RAMADA INN & PLAZA
HOTEL.** *2485 Jonathan Moore Pike
(47201). 812/376-3051; fax 812/376-
0949; toll-free 888/298-2054. www.
ramada.com.* 166 rms, 3 story. S $65-
$95; D $75-$125; each addl $10;
suites $85-$250; under 18 free. Crib
free. TV; cable (premium). 2 pools, 1
indoor; whirlpool. Restaurant 6 am-
10 pm. Bar. Ck-out noon. Meeting
rms. Business servs avail. In-rm
modem link. Valet serv. Sundries.
Lighted tennis. Exercise equipt. Paddle boats. Refrigerators, microwaves
avail. On 10-acre lake. Cr cds: A, C,
D, DS, ER, JCB, MC, V.

🄳 🛠 🎿 🏊 🏊 ✈ 🔧 🐾 **SC**

Connersville

(D-5) *See also Batesville*

Founded 1813 **Pop** 15,550 **Elev** 835 ft
Area code 765 **Zip** 47331
Information Chamber of Commerce,
504 Central Ave; 765/825-2561
Web www.connersvillein.com/
chamber

John Connor, who established a fur-
trading post here in 1808, later
founded the town. Connor was kid-
napped from his parents as a child
and raised by Native Americans. He
served as a Native American guide
for General William H. Harrison in
1812, took a Native American wife,
and became a wealthy landowner
and businessman.

Auburn, Cord, McFarlan, and Lexington automobiles were once manufactured here. Today, the most important industrial products are dishwashers, automobile components, and building supplies.

What to See and Do

Brookville Lake State Reservoir. US government flood control project, now a state recreation area. Approx 16,500 acres. Swimming, waterskiing, fishing, boating (ramps, rentals); hiking, hunting, picnicking, camping. Standard fees. (Summer, daily; winter Mon-Fri) 12 mi E on IN 44 to Liberty, then 5 mi S on IN 101. Phone 765/647-2657. ¢¢

Mary Gray Bird Sanctuary of the Indiana Audubon Society. Has 686 wooded acres with marked trails and picnicking facilities. Museum and library (by appt). (Daily) 3½ mi S on IN 121, then 3½ mi W on County Rd 350 S. Contact Sanctuary Manager, 3497 S Bird Sanctuary Rd. Phone 765/827-0908. **Donation**

Whitewater Memorial State Park. More than 1,700 acres, with lake. Swimming beach, bathhouse, fishing, boating (electric motors only; ramps, dock, rentals); hiking and bridle trails, picnicking (shelters), concession, campground, family cabins. Visitor center. Park (daily). Standard fees. 12 mi E on IN 44 to Liberty, then 1 mi S on IN 101. Phone 765/458-5565. ¢¢

Whitewater Valley Railroad. Round-trip excursions on vintage railroad cars. (May-Sept, Sat, Sun, hols; Oct, Thurs, Fri) 1 mi S on IN 121. Contact PO Box 406. Phone 765/825-2054. ¢¢¢¢

Special Events

Veterans Armed Forces Celebration. Vintage and modern military aircraft exhibits; marching bands with military flyovers. Second Sat May. Phone 765/825-7538.

Fayette County Free Fair. Park Rd. Agricultural and industrial displays; midway, entertainment, horse racing. Last wkend July-early Aug. Phone 765/825-1351.

Fall Festival, Car Show, and 5-K Pumpkin Run/Walk. Phone 765/825-2561. Fourth wkend Sept.

Corydon

(G-4) *See also New Albany, Wyandotte*

Founded 1808 **Pop** 2,661 **Elev** 549 ft **Area code** 812 **Zip** 47112

Information Chamber of Commerce of Harrison County, 310 N Elm St; 812/738-2137 or 888/738-2137

Corydon was the scene of the only battle fought on Indiana soil during the Civil War. A Confederate raiding party under General John Hunt Morgan occupied the town briefly on July 9, 1863, holding the home guard captive.

What to See and Do

Battle of Corydon Memorial Park. Approx 5⅓ acres, with period cabin, authentic Civil War cannon, and nature trail. Park marks the site of one of the few Civil War battles fought on Northern soil, July 9, 1863. (Daily) S on IN 135 Business. Phone 812/738-8236. **FREE**

Buffalo Trace Park. Approx 150 acres with sports facilities, camping (fee), picnicking. Thirty-acre lake with swimming, fishing, boating; petting zoo; bumper boats. (May-Oct, daily) Some fees. Approx 10 mi N on IN 135, then ½ mi E on US 150, near Palmyra. Phone 812/364-6112. ¢

Corydon Capitol State Historic Site. Corydon was the seat of the Indiana Territorial government (1813-1816) when the first constitutional convention assembled here. Following Indiana's admission to the Union in 1816, this building was the state capitol, housing the first sessions of the state legislature and supreme court, until 1825. Construction of the blue limestone building started in 1814 and was completed in 1816. Nearby is Governor Hendricks' headquarters, home of Indiana's second governor; restored. (Tues-Sun; closed Jan 1, Thanksgiving, Dec 25) Capitol Ave. Phone 812/738-4890. **Donation** Nearby is

> **Constitution Elm Monument.** Indiana's first constitution was drawn up here in June, 1816, in the shade of this large elm tree. High St.

Governor Hendricks' Headquarters. (1817) Governor's headquarters from 1822-1824. A restoration project by the State of Indiana portrays Indiana home life in three distinct time periods between 1820 and 1880. (Early Apr-early Dec; Tues-Sun; closed Jan 1, Thanksgiving, Dec 25) 202 E Walnut St. Phone 812/738-4890. **Donation**

Industrial tour. Zimmerman Art Glass. Glass sculpturing, paperweights and hand-blown objects. (Tues-Sat) 395 Valley Rd. Phone 812/738-2206. **FREE**

Marengo Cave Park. Dripstone Trail tour (one mi) of underground cave features huge corridors with colorful formations. Crystal Palace Tour (⅓ mi) features underground palace. (Daily; closed Thanksgiving, Dec 25) Also picnic area (shelters), nature trail, camping (Apr-Oct) Approx 10 mi N of I-64 via IN 66 exit 92, on IN 64 at Marengo. Phone 812/365-2705. ¢¢¢

Squire Boone Caverns and Village. Caverns discovered in 1790 by Daniel Boone's brother, Squire, while hiding from Native Americans. Travertine formations, stalactites, stalagmites, underground streams and waterfalls. Above-ground village incl restored working gristmill, craft shops, demonstrations. Hayrides; 110 acres of forest with nature trails and picnic areas. One-hr cavern tours. (Memorial Day wkend-Labor Day wkend, daily) Admission incl all activities and facilities. 10 mi S on IN 135. Phone 812/732-4381. ¢¢¢

Special Events

Old Capitol Day. Early July. Phone 812/738-4890.

Harrison County Fair. Livestock, poultry, farm, and 4-H Club exhibits; harness racing. Held annually since 1860. Late July-early Aug. Phone 812/738-2137.

Christmas on the Square. Sat after Thanksgiving. Phone 812/738-4890.

Motel/Motor Lodge

★★ **BEST WESTERN OLD CAPITOL INN.** I-64 and IN 135 (47112). 812/738-4192; 800/780-7234. 77 rms, 2 story. S $46-$60; D $56-$68; each addl $8; higher rates Kentucky Derby.

Crib free. TV; cable. Pool. Complimentary coffee in lobby. Ck-out noon. Meeting rms. Business servs avail. Sundries. Cr cds: A, MC, V. 🔥

B&B/Small Inn

★★ **KINTNER HOUSE INN.** 101 S Capitol Ave (47112). 812/738-2020; fax 812/738-7430. 15 rms, 3 story. July-Oct: S, D $49-$99; under 12 free; higher rates wkends; lower rates rest of yr. TV; cable (premium), VCR avail. Complimentary full bkfst. Ck-out 11 am, ck-in 1 pm. Business servs avail. Lighted tennis privileges, pro. 18-hole golf privileges, greens fee $15-$20, pro. Brick Victorian house (1873); antique furnishings. Totally nonsmoking. Cr cds: A, DS, MC, V.
D ⛄ 🔥 🎣 🎿

Restaurant

★ **MAGDALENA'S.** 103 E Chestnut St (47112). 812/738-8075. Hrs: 10:30 am-9:30 pm; Fri, Sat to 10:30 pm; Sun from 11 am. Closed hols. Res accepted. Wine. A la carte entrees: lunch $3-$5.99, dinner $7-$14.99. Specializes in soup, steak, chicken. Street parking. Casual dining. Cr cds: A, DS, MC, V.
D ⛄

Crawfordsville

(D-3)

Settled 1822 **Pop** 13,584 **Elev** 769 ft
Area code 765 **Zip** 47933

Information Montgomery County Visitors & Convention Bureau, 218 E Pike St; 765/362-5200 or 800/866-3973

Web www.crawfordsville.org

Crawfordsville, "Athens of the Hoosier State," has long been a literary center. It has been the home of nearly a dozen authors and playwrights, among them General Lew Wallace, who wrote *Ben Hur* here; Maurice Thompson, author of *Alice of Old Vincennes;* and Meredith Nicholson, author of *House of a*

Thousand Candles. Wabash College is located here.

Printing, steel, and the production of travel trailers, fencing, nails, and plastics are some of the local industries. Montgomery County, of which Crawfordsville is the seat, is a rich corn and hog region.

What to See and Do

Ben Hur Museum. The study of General Lew Wallace, author of *Ben Hur;* he was also a soldier, diplomat, and painter. Memorabilia from the movie *Ben Hur* along with war relics, art objects, and personal items. (June-Aug, Tues-Sun; early Apr-May, Sept-Oct, Tues-Sun afternoons) E Pike St and Wallace Ave. Phone 765/362-5769. ¢¢

Clements Canoes. Canoe livery with more than 500 units avail. Canoe on Sugar Creek, designated by the DNR as the state's most scenic waterway. Various length trips avail; also guided or self-guided rafting avail. (Apr-Oct, daily) 613 Old Lafayette Rd. Phone 765/362-2781. ¢¢¢¢

Lake Waveland. A 360-acre lake with canoeing, boating (rentals; fee), swimming, waterslide, fishing; tennis courts. Also 248-acre park with camping (fee), tent and trailer sites (fee), showers, picnic area. (Apr-Oct) 13 mi S via IN 47 in Waveland. Phone 765/435-2073. ¢¢¢¢

Lane Place. Greek Revival residence of Henry S. Lane (1811-1881), Indiana governor and US senator. Collection of Colonial, Federal, and Victorian furnishings, dolls, and china; Civil War memorabilia; furnished log cabin (by appt). (Apr-Oct, Tues-Fri, Sun; closed hols) (See SPECIAL EVENTS) 212 S Water St. Phone 765/362-3416. ¢¢

Old Jail Museum. Completed in 1882, the building's unique feature is a two-story cylindrical cellblock; the cells rotate while the bars remain stationary. Sheriff's residence has changing exhibits. (June-Aug, daily; Apr-May, Sept-Oct, Wed-Sun, afternoons) (See SPECIAL EVENTS) 225 N Washington St. Phone 765/362-5222. **FREE**

Shades State Park. Approx 3,000 acres of woods. Deep ravines, high sandstone cliffs, overlooks. Fishing in Sugar Creek; hiking trails, picnicking, playground, campsites (no electric hookups). Backpack and canoe camps. Naturalist service (May-Aug). (Daily) Standard fees. 9 mi SW on IN 47, then 5 mi W on IN 234. Phone 765/435-2810. ¢¢

Turkey Run State Park. (see). 23 mi SW on IN 47.

Special Events

Sugar Creek Canoe Race. Elston Park South. Late Apr. Phone 765/362-3875.

Strawberry Festival. Lane Place. Sport tournaments, parade, arts and crafts, food, entertainment. Second wknd in June. Phone 800/866-3973.

Old Jail Museum Breakout. Old Jail Museum. Craft booths, refreshments; entertainment. Phone 765/362-5222. Labor Day.

Motel/Motor Lodge

★ ★ **HOLIDAY INN.** *2500 N Lafayette Rd (47933).* 765/362-8700; toll-free 800/465-4329. www.holiday-inn.com. 150 rms, 2 story. S, D $67-$77; each addl $6; under 19 free; higher rates Indianapolis 500; (2-day min). Crib free. Pet accepted. TV; cable (premium), VCR avail. Heated pool. Restaurant 6 am-2 pm, 5-9 pm. Bar 11 am-midnight, Fri, Sat noon-2 am, Sun from 3 pm. Ck-out noon. Coin lndry. Meeting rms. Business servs avail. In-rm modem link. Exercise equipt. Valet serv. Sundries. Game rm. Some microwaves. Cr cds: A, C, D, DS, JCB, MC, V.

D ⧉ ⇌ ⚷ ⊠ ⚒

Restaurant

★ **BUNGALOW.** *210 E Pike St (47933).* 765/362-2596. Hrs: 11 am-2 pm, 4:30 pm-midnight; Tues to 2 pm; Fri to 2 am; Sat 5 pm-2 am. Closed Sun; hols. Res accepted. Italian, American menu. Bar. Lunch $4.95-$7.95, dinner $8.95-$16.95. Specializes in steak, chicken Alfredo. Cr cds: A, D, MC, V.

D ⧉

Elkhart

(A-4) *See also Goshen, Mishawaka, Nap-panee, South Bend*

Founded 1832 **Pop** 43,627 **Elev** 748 ft
Area code 219
Information Elkhart County Convention and Visitor Bureau, 219 Caravan Dr, 46514; 800/262-8161
Web www.elkhart.org

Located at the confluence of the St. Joseph and Elkhart rivers and on Christiana Creek, Elkhart is a community of bridges. Originally a crossroads of Native American trails, the town was named for a small island in the St. Joseph River that Native Americans said was shaped like an elk's heart.

A 19th-century grocer (cornetist in the town band) suffered an injured upper lip in a brawl and devised a soft rubber mouthpiece for cornets. He received so many requests for mouthpieces that in 1875 he rented a one-room building and started the manufacture of brass cornets. This led to Elkhart's becoming the band instrument center of the country. Approximately 50 percent of the nation's band instruments are manufactured here by 15 firms.

Elkhart also has many industrial plants, producing diverse items such as pharmaceuticals, mobile homes, recreational vehicles, electronic components, construction machinery, and plastic machinery.

What to See and Do

Elkhart County Historical Museum. Furnished cottage; Victorian home, country store, schoolrm, barn; rm depicting a 1930s house; uniforms from Civil War through Vietnam; research library; Native American artifacts; railroad rm; special programs. (Tues-Fri, Sun; closed hols; also mid-Dec-Feb) 304 W Vistula St, 8 mi E via IN 120 (Vistula St), in Bristol. Phone 219/848-4322. **Donation**

Midwest Museum of American Art. Permanent collection of 19th- and 20th-century artists, incl Rockwell, Wood, Avery, and Grandma Moses; traveling exhibits; lectures; tours. (Tues-Sun; closed hols) 429 S Main St. Phone 219/293-6660. ¢¢

National New York Central Railroad Museum. Large collection of memorabilia from NYC railroad stations and rail cars, along with videos of NYC trains in action. Housed in a late 1880s freight house, the museum also boasts three restored locomotives: a 3001 L-3A "Mohawk" steam locomotive (the only one of its kind in existence), the E-8 diesel locomotive, and the GG-1 electric locomotive. (Tues-Sun, limited hrs; closed hols) 721 S Main St. Phone 219/294-3001. ¢¢

Ruthmere. (ca 1910) Restored mansion features elaborate handcrafted ceilings, walls, and woodwork; murals, silk wall coverings, period furnishings; landscaped grounds. Guided tours (Apr-mid-Jan, Tues-Sun; closed hols). 302 E Beardsley Ave. Phone 219/264-0330. ¢¢¢

S. Ray Miller Antique Auto Museum. More than 35 antique and classic cars on display; dozens restored to showrm quality. Incl 1930 Duesenberg "J" Murphy convertible, 1928 Rolls-Royce Phantom I Town Car, 1931 Stutz, and 1954 Corvette. Also extensive collection of radiator auto emblems; artifacts of early auto industry; vintage clothing. (Daily; closed hols) 2130 Middlebury St. Phone 219/522-0539. ¢¢

Woodlawn Nature Center. A ten-acre trail system provides a forest in its natural state for exploring and a center with displays and nature library. In the center, a working beehive, a Native American artifacts rm, and a rare collection of bird eggs gathered in 1896 can be found. (Tues-Sat; closed hols) 604 Woodlawn Ave. Phone 219/264-0525. ¢

Motels/Motor Lodges

★ **ECONO LODGE.** *3440 Cassopolis St (46514). 219/262-0540; toll-free 800/424-4777. www.econolodge.com.* 35 rms, 2 story. May-Oct: S $34-$45; D $39-$59; each addl $6; suites $65-$85; under 16 free; family rates; package plans; higher rates special events; lower rates rest of yr. Crib $6. Pet accepted, some restrictions. TV; cable (premium), VCR avail. Complimentary continental bkfst. Restaurant opp 6 am-midnight. Ck-out 11 am. Coin lndry. Business servs avail. Golf privileges. Cr cds: A, C, D, DS, ER, MC, V.

D ➤ ⚓ 🍴 ≋ 🔥 SC

★ **KNIGHTS INN.** *3252 Cassopolis St (46514). 219/264-4262; toll-free 800/843-5644. www.knightsinn.com.* 118 rms, 10 kit. units. S $32.95-$70; D $35.95-$70; each addl $5; kit. units $39.95-$70; under 18 free. Crib free. Pet accepted; deposit. TV; cable (premium). Pool. Complimentary coffee in lobby. Restaurant opp open 24 hrs. Ck-out 11 am. Meeting rm. Business servs avail. In-rm modem link. Some refrigerators, microwaves. Cr cds: A, C, D, DS, MC, V.

🄳 🔧 🏊 🖼 🔥

★★ **QUALITY INN AND SUITES.** *3321 Plaza Ct (46514). 219/264-0404; toll-free 800/228-5151. www.quality inn.com.* 54 rms, 2 story. S $53; D $61; each addl $8; suites $95; under 18 free. Crib free. Pet accepted, some restrictions. TV; cable (premium). Pool. Complimentary continental bkfst. Restaurant adj 4-10 pm. Ck-out 11 am. Business servs avail. Whirl-pool in suites. Cr cds: A, C, D, DS, ER, JCB, MC, V.

🄳 🔧 🏊 🖼 🖼

★★ **RAMADA INN.** *3011 Belvedere Rd (46514). 219/262-1581; fax 219/262-1590; toll-free 888/298-2054. www.ramada.com.* 145 rms, 2 story. Apr-Sept: S $79-$84; D $84-$89; each addl $8; suites, kit. units $91-$98; under 18 free; lower rates rest of yr. Crib free. Pet accepted, some restrictions. TV; cable (premium), VCR avail. 2 pools, 1 indoor; whirlpool, poolside serv. Complimentary continental bkfst. Restaurant 6:30 am-2 pm, 5-9 pm. Bar 5-10 pm; Fri, Sat to 2 am. Ck-out noon. Meeting rms. Business center. In-rm modem link. Game rm. Putting green. Downhill ski 10 mi; x-country 5 mi. Sauna. Health club privileges. Some refrigerators. Cr cds: A, C, D, DS, ER, JCB, MC, V.

🄳 🔧 🏊 🏊 SC

★ **RED ROOF INN.** *2902 Cassopolis St (46514). 219/262-3691; fax 219/262-3695; toll-free 800/733-7663. www.redroof.com.* 80 rms, 2 story. S $40.99-$65.99; D $40.99-$79.99; under 19 free; 2-day min football wkends; higher rates special events. Crib free. Pet accepted. TV; cable (premium). Complimentary coffee in lobby. Restaurant adj open 24 hrs. Ck-out noon. Business servs avail.

Downhill ski 20 mi. Cr cds: A, C, D, DS, MC, V.

🄳 🔧 🏊 🖼 🔥

★★ **SIGNATURE INN.** *3010 Brittany Ct (46514). 219/264-7222; toll-free 800/822-5252. www.signatureinns.com.* 125 rms, 2 story. S $65-$68; D $72-$75; under 18 free. Crib free. TV; cable (premium), VCR avail. Pool. Complimentary continental bkfst. Coffee in rms. Restaurant nearby. Ck-out noon. Meeting rms. Business center. In-rm modem link. Health club privileges. Cr cds: A, MC, V.

🏊 ✈ 🖼 🎿

★★ **WESTON PLAZA HOTEL.** *2725 Cassopolis St (46514). 219/264-7502; fax 219/264-0042.* 202 rms, 2 story. S, D $60-$85; studio rms $60-$75; under 8 free. Crib free. TV; cable. Indoor pool; whirlpool, pool-side serv. Complimentary coffee in lobby. Restaurant 6 am-2 pm, 5-9:30 pm; wkend hrs vary. Bar 4 pm-1 am; entertainment. Ck-out noon. Coin lndry. Meeting rms. Valet serv. Sundries. Putting green. Downhill/x-country ski 10 mi. Rec rm. Game rm. Sauna. Massage. Health club privileges. Refrigerators. Cr cds: A, D, DS, MC, V.

🄳 🏊 🖼 🔥 🏊

Restaurant

★★ **MATTERHORN.** *2041 Cassopolis St (IN 19) (46514). 219/262-1509.* Hrs: 11 am-2 pm, 5-10 pm; Sat from 5 pm; Sun brunch 10 am-2 pm. Closed Dec 25. Res accepted. Bar 10:30 am-11 pm. Lunch $3.95-$7.95, dinner $8.95-$17.95. Buffet: lunch (Mon-Fri) $5.95, dinner (Fri) $17.95. Sun brunch $8.95. Child's menu. Specializes in prime rib, steak, seafood. Cr cds: A, D, DS, MC, V.

🄳 ⬛

Evansville

(G-2) *See also New Harmony*

Founded 1819 **Pop** 126,272 **Elev** 394 ft **Area code** 812

Information Evansville Convention & Visitors Bureau, 401 SE Riverside Dr, 47713; 800/433-3025
Web www.evansvillecvb.org

Separated from Kentucky by the Ohio River, Evansville has retained some of the atmosphere of the busy river town of the days when steamboats plied the waters of the Ohio and Mississippi rivers. The largest city in southern Indiana, Evansville combines the pleasant and leisurely ways of the South with the industrious activity of the North.

Evansville is the principal transportation, trade, and industrial center of southwestern Indiana. A modern river/rail/highway terminal facilitates simultaneous exchange of cargo between trucks, freight trains, and riverboats. Local industry manufactures refrigerators, agricultural equipment, aluminum ingots and sheets, furniture, textiles, nutritional and pharmaceutical products, and plastics.

The Ohio River offers many recreational opportunities for boating, swimming, waterskiing, and fishing.

What to See and Do

⭐ **Angel Mounds State Historic Site.** Largest and best-preserved group of prehistoric mounds (1100-1450) in Indiana. Approx 100 acres. Interpretive center has film, exhibits, and artifacts; reconstructed dwellings on grounds. (Mid-Mar-Dec, Tues-Sun; closed hols) 7 mi E on IN 662 at 8215 Pollack Ave. Phone 812/853-3956. **Donation**

Burdette Park. County park, approx 160 acres. Fishing, pool and waterslides (summer); picnicking (shelters), cabins, miniature golf (Apr-Oct), tennis courts. Some fees. 5301 Nurrenbern Rd, 47712. Phone 812/435-5602.

Evansville Museum of Arts, History and Science. Permanent art, history, and science exhibits; sculpture garden, Koch Planetarium (fee). Rivertown USA, re-creation of turn-of-the-century village. Tours. (Tues-Sun; closed hols) 411 SE Riverside Dr, on Ohio River. Phone 812/425-2406. **Donation**

Mesker Park Zoo. Zoo has more than 700 animals; bird collection; children's petting zoo. Also the Discovery Center Education Building. Tour train and paddleboats (Apr-Oct). (Daily) NW edge of town in Mesker Park, 2421 Bement Ave. Phone 812/428-0715. ¢¢

Reitz Home Museum. (1871) French Second Empire mansion of pioneer lumber baron John Augustus Reitz; gold leaf cornices, family furniture. (Tues-Sun; closed hols, first two wks Jan) 224 SE First St, in Historic Riverfront District. Phone 812/426-1871. ¢¢

University of Southern Indiana. (1965) 9,362 students. On 300-acre campus is the Bent Twig Outdoor Education Center, 25 acres with foot trails, log lodges, and a lake (daily). 5 mi W on IN 62 (Lloyd Expy). Phone 812/464-8600.

Wesselman Park. Approx 400 acres; picnicking, tennis, handball, softball, basketball, bike trails, jogging trail, playground, 18-hole golf course (fee). Half of park is devoted to nature preserve (free, phone 812/479-0771). Hartkey swimming pool and Swonder ice rink (fees) adj (phone 812/479-0989). 5 mi E at N Boeke Rd and Iowa St. Phone 812/424-6921.
FREE Also here is

Roberts Municipal Stadium. Ice shows, circuses, rodeos, musicals, concerts, basketball tournaments. 2600 Division St, Lloyd Expy exit Vann St. Phone 812/476-1383.

Special Events

Evansville Freedom Festival. Citywide. Parade, fireworks, food. Hydroplane racing. Phone 812/433-4069. June.

Germania Maennerchor Volkfest. German food, beer, and music. Phone 812/422-1915. Aug.

Evansville Philharmonic Orchestra. Phone 812/425-5050. May-Sept.

Motels/Motor Lodges

★★ **COMFORT INN.** *5006 E Morgan Ave (47715). 812/477-2211; toll-free 800/228-5150. www.comfortinns.com.* 52 rms, 3 story, 11 suites. S, D $59.95-$64.95; each addl $7; suites $64.95-$71.25; under 18 free. Crib free. Pet accepted. TV; cable. Indoor pool; whirlpool. Complimentary continental bkfst. Ck-out 11 am.

Business servs avail. Game rm. Cr cds: A, D, DS, MC, V.

★ **DAYS INN.** *5701 US 41N (47711). 812/464-1010; fax 812/464-2742; toll-free 800/325-2525. www.daysinn.com.* 120 rms, 3 story. S $54-$59; D $59-$65; each addl $5; suites $80-$125; under 18 free. Crib free. TV; cable (premium). Indoor pool; whirlpool. Complimentary continental bkfst. Restaurant 6:30 am-1:30 pm, 5-10 pm. Bar 5-11 pm; Fri, Sat to 2:30 am; closed Sun. Ck-out noon. Meeting rms. Business servs avail. In-rm modem link. Valet serv. Free airport transportation. Sauna. Refrigerators, microwaves avail. Cr cds: A, C, D, DS, JCB, MC, V.

★★ **DRURY INN.** *3901 US 41N (47711). 812/423-5818; toll-free 800/378-7946. www.drury-inn.com.* 151 rms, 4 story. S $63-$79; D $73-$89; each addl $8; under 18 free. Crib free. Pet accepted. TV; cable. Indoor pool; whirlpool. Complimentary continental bkfst. Restaurant adj open 24 hrs. Ck-out noon. Coin lndry. Business servs avail. In-rm modem link. Valet serv. Exercise equipt. Cr cds: A, C, DS, MC, V.

★★ **FAIRFIELD INN.** *5400 Weston Rd (47712). 812/429-0900; fax 812/429-0900; toll-free 800/228-2800. www.fairfieldinn.com.* 110 rms, 4 story. S, D $57-$60; each addl $7; under 18 free. Crib free. TV; cable (premium). Complimentary continental bkfst. Restaurant nearby. Ck-out noon. Meeting rm. Business servs avail. In-rm modem link. Exercise equipt. Indoor pool. Cr cds: A, MC, V.

★★ **FAIRFIELD INN EAST.** *7879 Eagle Crest Blvd (47715). 812/471-7000; fax 812/471-7007; toll-free 800/228-2800. www.fairfieldinn.com.* 118 rms, 3 story. S, D $55.50-$65.50; each addl $7; under 18 free. Crib free. TV; cable (premium). Complimentary continental bkfst. Restaurant nearby. Ck-out noon. Business servs avail. In-rm modem link. Valet

serv. Exercise equipt. Indoor pool. Cr cds: A, MC, V.

★★ **HAMPTON INN.** *8000 Eagle Crest Blvd (47715). 812/473-5000; fax 812/479-1664; toll-free 800/426-7866. www.hampton-inn.com.* 143 rms, 5 story. S $63; D $72; under 19 free. Crib free. TV; cable (premium), VCR avail. Indoor pool. Complimentary continental bkfst. Restaurant adj 6 am-10 pm. Ck-out noon. Meeting rms. Business servs avail. Valet serv. Exercise equipt. Cr cds: A, C, D, DS, MC, V.

★★ **HOLIDAY INN.** *4101 US 41N (47711). 812/424-6400; fax 812/424-6409; toll-free 800/465-4329. www. holiday-inn.com.* 198 rms, 1-2 story. S, D $79; each addl $10; suites $89; under 19 free; wknd rates. Crib free. TV; cable (premium), VCR avail. Indoor pool; wading pool, whirlpool. Playground. Restaurant 6 am-10 pm; Sun 7 am-9 pm. Bar from noon. Ck-out 11 am. Guest lndry. Meeting rms. Business center. In-rm modem link. Sundries. Free airport transportation. Exercise equipt; sauna. Solardome pavilion. Game rm. Cr cds: A, D, DS, MC, V.

★★ **HOLIDAY INN EXPRESS.** *100 S Green River Rd (47715). 812/473-0171; fax 812/473-5021; 800/465-4329. www.holiday-inn.com.* 109 rms, 2 story. S, D $62; under 19 free. Crib free. TV; cable (premium). Pool. Ck-out noon. Business servs avail. In-rm modem link. Sundries. Cr cds: A, D, DS, JCB, MC, V.

★ **SIGNATURE INN.** *1101 N Green River Rd (47715). 812/476-9626; toll-free 800/822-5252. www.signatureinn. com.* 125 rms, 2 story. S, D $67-$74; under 18 free. Crib free. TV; cable (premium). Pool. Complimentary continental bkfst. Restaurant nearby. Ck-out noon. Meeting rms. Business servs avail. In-rm modem link. Health club privileges. Cr cds: A, D, DS, MC, V.

★ **STUDIO PLUS.** *301 Eagle Crest Dr (47715). 812/479-0103; fax 812/469-7172; toll-free 888/788-3467. www.*

extendedstay.com. 71 kit. units, 3 story. S $59-$69; D $89; package plans. Crib free. TV; cable (premium). Complimentary coffee in rms. Restaurant nearby. Ck-out noon. Business servs avail. In-rm modem link. Coin lndry. Exercise equipt. Pool. Microwaves. Cr cds: A, C, D, DS, ER, MC, V.

Hotel

★ ★ ★ **MARRIOTT EVANSVILLE AIRPORT.** *7101 Hwy 41 N (47725). 812/867-7999; fax 812/867-0241; toll-free 888/236-2427. www.marriott.com.* 199 rms, 5 story. S, D $129; suites $250-$350; wkend rates. Crib free. TV; cable (premium). Indoor pool; whirlpool. Restaurant 6 am-2 pm, 5-11 pm. Bar 4 pm-2 am. Ck-out 11 am. Meeting rms. Business servs avail. Concierge. Free airport transportation. Exercise equipt. Game rm. Balconies. Cr cds: A, C, D, DS, ER, JCB, MC, V.

Fort Wayne

(B-5) *See also Auburn*

Settled ca 1690 **Pop** 173,072 **Elev** 767 ft **Area code** 260

Information Fort Wayne/Allen County Convention & Visitors Bureau, 1021 S Calhoun St, 46802; 260/424-3700 or 800/767-7752

Web www.fwcvb.org

The Fort Wayne area is one of the most historically significant in Indiana. The point where the St. Joseph and St. Mary's rivers meet to form the Maumee was, for many years before and after the first European explorers ventured into eastern Indiana, the headquarters of the Miami Native Americans. Among the first settlers were French fur traders; a French fort was established about 1690. The settlement became known as Miami Town and Frenchtown. In 1760, English troops occupied the French fort, but were driven out three years later by warriors led by

Chief Pontiac. During the next 30 years Miami Town became one of the most important trading centers in the West. President Washington sent out two armies in 1790-1791 to establish a fort for the United States at the river junction, but both armies were defeated by the Miami under the leadership of the famous Miami chief, Little Turtle. A third American army, under General "Mad Anthony" Wayne, succeeded in defeating Little Turtle and set up a post, Fort Wayne, across the river from Miami Town. From this humble beginning Fort Wayne has grown steadily. Today it is the second-largest city in Indiana and a commercial center.

Establishment of the first railroad connections with Chicago and Pittsburgh in the 1850s laid the foundation for the city's development. Today its widely diversified companies include General Electric, Phelps Dodge, ITT, Lincoln National Corporation, North American Van Lines, Central Soya, Essex Group, General Motors, Magnavox, Uniroyal, Goodrich Tire Company, and many others. Most of the world's wire die tools come from here.

Fort Wayne is home to Indiana University-Purdue University at Fort Wayne (1964), St. Francis College (1890) and the Indiana Institute of Technology (1930).

What to See and Do

Allen County-Fort Wayne Historical Society Museum. Exhibits on six themes: earliest times to the Civil War; 19th-century industrialization (1860s-1894); culture and society (1894-1920); 20th-century technology and industry (1920-present); old city jail and law enforcement (1820-1970); ethnic heritage. Special temporary exhibits. (Tues-Sun; closed hols) 302 E Berry St, in Old City Hall. Phone 260/426-2882. ¢¢

Cathedral of the Immaculate Conception and Museum. Bavarian stained-glass windows. Features Gothic wood carvings at the main altar; statues and furnishings; wood-carved reredos in the sanctuary. Museum at southwest corner of Cathedral Square (Wed-Fri, second and fourth Sun of month; also by appt). Cathedral (daily; closed hols).

1100 S Calhoun St. Phone 260/424-1485. **FREE**

Embassy Theatre. Entertainment and cultural center hosts musicals, concerts, ballet companies; distinctive architecture; Grand Page pipe organ. Tours (Mon-Fri, by appt). 125 W Jefferson St. Phone 260/424-5665. ¢

Foellinger-Freimann Botanical Conservatory. Showcase House with seasonally changing displays of colorful flowers; Tropical House with exotic plants; Arid House with cacti and other desert flora native to Sonoran desert. Cascading waterfall. (Daily; closed Dec 25) 1100 S Calhoun St. Phone 260/427-6440. ¢

Fort Wayne Children's Zoo. Especially designed for children. Exotic animals, pony rides, train ride, contact area; 22-acre African Veldt area allows animals to roam free while visitors travel by miniature safari cars; tropical rain forest; also five-acre Australian Outback area with dugout canoe ride; kangaroos, Tasmanian devils. (Late Apr-mid-Oct, daily) 3411 Sherman Blvd, in Franke Park. Phone 260/427-6800. ¢¢¢

Fort Wayne Museum of Art. A 1,300-piece permanent collection; changing exhibitions. Art classes, interactive programs, and lectures. (Tues-Sun; closed hols) 311 E Main St. Phone 260/422-6467. ¢¢

Lakeside Rose Garden. Approx 2,000 plants of about 225 varieties; display rose garden (June-mid-Oct). Garden (all yr, daily). 1401 Lake Ave. Phone 260/427-6000. **FREE**

The New Lincoln Museum. Museum dedicated to Abraham Lincoln. 30,000-sq-ft facility; interactive exhibits; 11 galleries; theatres; gift shop. (Tues-Sun) 200 E Berry St. Phone 260/455-3864. ¢¢

Special Events

Foellinger Theatre. Sherman St, in Franke Park. Concerts and special attractions. Covered open-air theater. Programs vary. Phone 260/427-6715 June-Sept.

Germanfest. Celebration of city's German heritage; ethnic food, music, exhibits. Phone 260/436-4064. Eight days mid-June.

Three Rivers Festival. More than 280 events, incl parades, balloon races, arts and crafts, music, ethnic dancing, sports, and fireworks at various locations in Fort Wayne. Phone 260/426-5556. Ten days mid-July.

Johnny Appleseed Festival. Johnny Appleseed Park. Pioneer village; period crafts; contests, entertainment, Living History Hill, farmers market. Phone 260/420-2020. Third wkend Sept.

Motels/Motor Lodges

★ ★ **BEST WESTERN AIRPORT PLAZA.** *3939 W Ferguson Rd (46809). 260/747-9171; fax 260/747-1848; toll-free 888/492-7142. www.bestwestern. com.* 147 rms, 2 story. S, D $65; suites $150; family, wkend rates. Crib free. TV; cable. Heated pool. Restaurant 6 am-2 pm, 5:30-10 pm. Bar 4 pm-midnight, Fri, Sat to 2 am. Ck-out 11 am. Meeting rms. Business servs avail. Bellhops. Valet serv. Free airport transportation. Golf privileges. Exercise equipt; sauna. Cr cds: A, C, D, DS, MC, V.

D ≈ 🖈 ✈ ➘ 🔥

★ ★ **COURTYARD BY MARRIOTT.** *1619 W Washington Center Rd (46818). 260/489-1500; fax 260/489-3273; toll-free 800/321-2211. www. courtyard.com.* 142 rms, 19 suites, 2 story. S, D $69-$89; suites $89-$229; under 18 free. Crib free. TV; cable (premium). Indoor/outdoor pool; whirlpool. Ck-out noon. Meeting rms. Business servs avail. In-rm modem link. Valet serv. Sundries. Exercise equipt. Refrigerator in some suites. Cr cds: A, D, DS, MC, V.

D ≈ 🖈 ➘ 🔥

★ ★ **DON HALL'S GUESTHOUSE.** *1313 W Washington Center Rd (46825). 260/489-2524; fax 260/489-7067; toll-free 800/348-1999. www. donhalls.com.* 130 rms, 2 story. S $79; D $89; suites $90; wkend rates. Crib free. TV; cable (premium). 2 pools, 1 indoor; whirlpool. Complimentary continental bkfst. Complimentary coffee in rms. Restaurant 6 am-11 pm; Sun to 9 pm. Bar 11-1 am, Sun to 10 pm; entertainment Tues-Sat. Ck-out noon. Meeting rms. In-rm modem link. Sundries. Free airport transportation. Exercise equipt. Cr cds: A, C, D, DS.

≈ ✈ 🖈 ➘ 🔥 SC

★ ★ ★ **HOLIDAY INN.** *300 E Washington Blvd (46802).* 260/422-5511; *fax* 260/424-1511. *www.holiday-inn.com.* 208 rms, 14 story, 28 suites. S $84-$94; D $89-$99; each addl $8; suites $125-$190; under 18 free; wkend rates. Crib free. TV; cable. Indoor pool; whirlpool. Coffee in rms. Restaurant 6 am-2 pm, 5-10 pm. Bar 3 pm-midnight; entertainment. Ck-out noon. Coin lndry. Meeting rms. Business servs avail. In-rm modem link. Free airport, bus depot transportation. Exercise equipt. Game rm. Luxury level. Cr cds: A, MC, V.

🔲 ➿ 🏋 ✈ 🔥

★ **SIGNATURE INN.** *1734 W Washington Center (46818).* 260/489-5554; *toll-free* 800/822-5252. *www.signature inn.com.* 102 rms, 2 story. S $62; D $77; under 17 free; wkend rates. Crib free. TV; cable (premium), VCR avail. Pool. Complimentary continental bkfst. Ck-out noon. Meeting rms. Business servs avail. In-rm modem link. Sundries. Cr cds: A, C, D, DS, MC, V.

🔲 ➿ 🔜 🔥 SC

Hotels

★ ★ ★ **HILTON.** *1020 S Calhoun St (46802).* 260/420-1100; *fax* 260/424-7775; *toll-free* 800/744-1500. *www.hilton.com.* 250 rms, 9 story. S $99; D $109; each addl $10; suites $190-$350; under 18 free. Crib free. TV; cable. Indoor pool; whirlpool. Restaurants 6 am-11 pm. Bar. Ck-out 11 am. Convention facilities. Business servs avail. In-rm modem link. Free airport transportation. Concierge. Gift shop. Exercise equipt. Garden lounge in lobby. Adj Grand Wayne Convention Center. Luxury level. Cr cds: A, C, D, DS, MC, V.

🔲 ➿ 🏋 ✈ 🔜 🔥

★ ★ ★ **MARRIOTT FORT WAYNE.** *305 E Washington Center Rd (46825).* 260/484-0411; *fax* 260/483-2892; *toll-free* 800/228-9290. *www.marriott.com.* 222 rms, 3 suites, 2-6 story. S $130; D $140; each addl $10; suites $235-$350; under 18 free; wkend rates. Crib free. Pet accepted. TV; cable (premium). Indoor/outdoor pool; whirlpool, poolside serv. Restaurant 6 am-10 pm; Fri, Sat to 11 pm. Bar 11-2:30 am. Ck-out noon. Coin lndry. Meeting rms. Business servs avail. In-rm modem link. Bellhops. Valet serv. Sundries. Gift shop. Free airport transportation. Putting green. Exercise equipt. Game rm. Lawn games. Some refrigerators. Picnic tables. Cr cds: A, MC, V.

🔹 ➿ 🏋 ✈ 🔥

Extended Stay

★ ★ **RESIDENCE INN BY MARRIOTT.** *4919 Lima Rd, Ft Wayne (46808).* 260/484-4700; *fax* 260/484-9772; *toll-free* 800/331-3131. *www.residenceinn.com.* 80 kit. units, 2 story. S, D $75-$129; higher rates special events. Crib free. Pet accepted; $100. TV; cable (premium), VCR avail (movies). Complimentary continental bkfst. Coffee in rms. Restaurant nearby. Ck-out noon. Health club privileges. Heated pool. Playground. Microwaves; many fireplaces. Cr cds: A, MC, V.

🔹 🔥 ➿

Restaurants

★ ★ ★ **CAFE JOHNELL.** *2529 S Calhoun St (46856).* 260/456-1939. Hrs: 6-9 pm; Sat 5-10 pm. Closed Sun, Mon; hols. Res accepted. French, continental menu. Bar. Wine cellar. Dinner $17-$30. Complete meals: dinner $20. Specialties: caneton a l'orange flambe, tournedos de boeuf Rossini, sole amandine de Dover. Own pastries. Victorian atmosphere. Collection of original 17th-to-20th-century art. Family-owned. Cr cds: A, DS, MC, V.

★ **DON HALL'S-THE FACTORY.** *5811 Coldwater Rd (US 27) (46825).* 260/484-8693. *www.donhalls.com.* Hrs: 11 am-11 pm; Fri, Sat to midnight; Sun to 8 pm. Closed hols, except Labor Day. Res accepted Sun-Thurs. Bar. Lunch $3-$8.50, dinner $7.50-$18. Child's menu. Specialties: Greek salad, prime rib. Family-owned. Cr cds: A, D, DS, MC, V.

🔲 🔜

★ ★ **FLANAGAN'S.** *6525 Covington Rd (46804).* 260/432-6666. Hrs: 11-1 am; Fri, Sat to 2 am; Sun to 11 pm. Closed Thanksgiving, Dec 25. Res accepted. Bar. Lunch $4-$7, dinner $6-$16. Child's menu. Specializes in baby back ribs, pasta, seafood. Victorian decor; garden gazebo, carousel. Antiques on display. Cr cds: A, DS, MC, V.

D

French Lick

(F-3) *See also Bedford*

Founded 1811 **Pop** 2,087 **Elev** 511 ft
Area code 812 **Zip** 47432
Information French Lick-West Baden Chamber of Commerce, PO Box 347; 812/936-2405

In the early 18th century this was the site of a French trading post. The post, plus the existence of a nearby salt lick, influenced the pioneer founders of the later settlement to name it French Lick.

Today this small community is a well-known health and vacation resort centered around the French Lick springs, situated on 1,600 acres of woodland. Near it is an artesian spring, Pluto, covered by an edifice of marble and tile. The water contains a high concentration of minerals.

What to See and Do

Diesel Locomotive Excursion. French Lick, West Baden, and Southern Railway operates a diesel locomotive that makes 20-mi round-trip through wooded limestone country and a 2,200-ft tunnel. Train departs from the Monon Railroad station in French Lick (Apr-Nov, Sat, Sun, hols). Museum (Mon-Fri, free). On IN 56. Contact Indiana Railway Museum, Inc, PO Box 150. Phone 812/936-2405. ¢¢

Skiing. Paoli Peaks Ski Area. Quad, one double, three triple chairlifts, three surface tows; snowmaking, rentals, school, patrol; cafeteria. Longest run 3,300 ft; vertical drop 300 ft. (Dec-Mar, daily; open 24 hrs on wkends) N via IN 56, then E on US 150; 1½ mi W of Paoli off US 150. Phone 812/723-4696. ¢¢¢¢

Special Event

Orange County Pumpkin Festival. Parades, arts and crafts displays,

entertainment. First wk Oct. Phone 812/936-2405.

Motel/Motor Lodge

★ **LANE MOTEL.** *8483 W Hwy 56 (47432).* 812/936-9919; fax 812/936-7857. 43 rms. S, D $40; each addl $6. Crib $6. Pet accepted. TV; cable (premium). Pool. Restaurant nearby. Ck-out 11 am. Picnic tables. Grill. Cr cds: MC, V.

D 🐾 ⇌ 🔥

Resort

★ ★ ★ **FRENCH LICK SPRINGS RESORT.** *8670 IN 56 W (47432).* 812/936-9300; fax 812/936-2100; toll-free 800/457-4042. www.frenchlick. com. 500 rms, 6 story. MAP: S $89-$99; D $99-$109; each addl $40; suites $157-$450; EP: S, D $89-$99; package plans. TV; cable (premium). 2 pools, 1 indoor; whirlpool. Supervised children's activities (mid-Apr-mid-Nov), ages 5 and over. Dining rms 6 am-10 pm. Bar 11-1 am; entertainment. Ck-out noon, ck-in 4 pm. Convention facilities. Business servs avail. In-rm modem link. Sundries. Barber, beauty shop. Indoor/outdoor lighted tennis, pro. Two 18-hole golf courses, greens fee $18-$48, driving range. Downhill ski 9 mi; x-country ski on site. Stables. Indoor/outdoor games. Soc dir. Rec rm. Bowling, billiards. Exercise rm; sauna, steam rm. Mineral baths, massage. Country estate setting on 2,600 acres; landscaped grounds, gardens, woodland trails. Cr cds: A, C, D, DS, MC, V.

D 🐾 ➳ 🎿 🎱 ⛷ ⇌ 🏃 ✈ ⛵ 🔥

B&B/Small Inn

★ **BRAXTAN HOUSE INN BED & BREAKFAST.** *210 N Gospel St, Paoli (47454).* 812/723-4677; fax 812/723-2112; toll-free 800/627-2982. www. kiva.net/~braxtan. 6 rms, 5 with shower only, 3 story. No rm phones. S $40; D $60. Crib free. TV in guest area. Complimentary full bkfst. Restaurant nearby. Ck-out 11 am, ck-in 3 pm. Downhill ski 3 mi. Queen Anne Victorian built in 1893. Cr cds: A, DS, MC, V.

🎿 ⇌ 🔥

Cottage Colony

★ **PINES AT PATOKA LAKE VIL-
LAGE.** *7900 W 1025 S (47432).
812/936-9854; fax 812/936-9855; toll-
free 888/324-5350.* 12 log cabins. No
rm phones. S, D $89; each addl (after
2nd person) $10; 6-12, $5; under 6
free; wkly rates. Crib free. Pet
accepted. TV. Playground. Ck-out 11
am. Coin lndry. Meeting rms. Microwaves. Picnic tables, grills. Surrounded by woods; near lake. Cr cds:
A, DS, MC, V.

Geneva (Adams County)

(C-6) *See also Fort Wayne*

Pop 1,280 **Elev** 846 ft **Area code** 219
Zip 46740

This town in eastern Indiana, near
the Ohio border, is surrounded by
the "Limberlost Country," which
Gene Stratton Porter used as background for her romantic stories of
life in the swamplands. Geneva is
near the headwaters of the Wabash
River and includes a large settlement
of Old Order Amish families.

What to See and Do

Amishville. Amish house (tour);
farm, barn, animals; working gristmill; buggy rides. Swimming, fishing;
picnicking, camping (Apr-Oct); activities; restaurant. (Apr-mid-Dec, daily;
closed Thanksgiving) 3 mi E via local
road. Phone 219/589-3536. ¢¢
Bearcreek Farms. Entertainment
complex: restaurants, theater, shops,
miniature golf course, general store.
Fishing. 4 mi SE near Bryant. Phone
219/997-6822.
Limberlost State Historic Site. A 14-
rm cedar log cabin, for 18 yrs the
residence of Gene Stratton Porter,
author/naturalist/photographer, and
her family. Furniture, books, and
photographs. Gift shop. (Apr-mid-
Dec, Wed-Sun, also Sun afternoons;
closed hols) E of US 27 at S edge of
town. Phone 219/368-7428. **FREE**

George Rogers Clark National Historical Park

Downtown off US 50 and US 41.

Memorial building (daily) commemorates the George Rogers Clark
campaign during the American Revolution. Incl the site of Fort Sackville,
captured from the British by Clark's
force in 1779. Visitor center with
museum, exhibits (daily; closed Jan
1, Thanksgiving, Dec 25); film shown
every ½-hr.

Goshen

(A-4) *See also Elkhart, Mishawaka, Nappanee*

Settled 1830 **Pop** 23,797 **Elev** 799 ft
Area code 219 **Zip** 46526
Information Chamber of Commerce,
232 S Main St; 219/533-2102 or
800/307-4204.
Web www.goshen.org

What to See and Do

Mennonite Historical Library.
Anabaptist, Mennonite, and Amish
research collection; genealogical
resources. (Mon-Fri; closed hols)
Goshen College campus, 1700 S
Main St. Phone 219/535-7418. **FREE**
The Old Bag Factory. Restored fac-
tory (1890) houses various types of
crafters as well as 18 shops. (Mon-
Sat; closed hols) 1100 Chicago Ave.
Phone 219/534-2502. **FREE**

> **Bonneyville Mill.** Restored gristmill
> (May-Oct, daily). Park (daily). 9 mi
> N on IN 15 to Bristol, then 2½ mi
> E on IN 120, ½ mi S on County
> 131. Phone 219/825-1324. **FREE**
> **Ox Bow.** Canoeing; sports fields,
> archery. (Daily) 5 mi NE off US 33.
> Per vehicle (Apr-Oct) ¢

Parks. Fishing; picnicking, nature
trails, winter sports. Contact the
Elkhart County Park Department,
211 W Lincoln Ave. Phone 219/535-
6458.

Motels/Motor Lodges

★ ★ **BEST WESTERN INN.** *900 Lincolnway E (46526). 219/533-0408; toll-free 800/780-7234. www.best western.com.* 77 rms, 2 story. S $60; D $62; each addl $3; under 12 free. Crib free. Pet accepted. TV; cable (premium), VCR avail. Complimentary continental bkfst. Restaurant opp 7 am-10 pm. Ck-out 11 am. Business servs avail. In-rm modem link. Valet serv Mon-Fri. Exercise equipt. Cr cds: A, C, D, DS, MC, V.

[icons]

★ ★ **COURTYARD BY MARRIOTT.** *1930 Lincolnway E (US 33) (46526). 574/534-3133; fax 574/534-6929; toll-free 800/321-2211. www. courtyard.com.* 91 rms, 13 suites, 2 story. S, D $59-$79; suites $79-$179; under 16 free; higher rates football wkends. Crib free. TV; cable (premium). Indoor/outdoor pool. Complimentary full bkfst. Restaurant nearby. Ck-out noon. Meeting rms. Business servs avail. In-rm modem link. Exercise equipt. Cr cds: A, D, DS, MC, V.

[icons]

★ ★ **GOSHEN INN & CONFERENCE CENTER.** *1375 Lincolnway E (46526). 574/533-9551; fax 574/533-2840; toll-free 888/246-7436. www. gosheninn.com.* 211 rms, 2 story. Late May-Sept: S, D $76; under 18 free; higher rates football wkends; lower rates rest of yr. Crib free. TV; cable (premium). Indoor pool. Complimentary full bkfst. Restaurant 6 am-2 pm, 5-9 pm. Bar. Ck-out 11 am. Coin lndry. Meeting rms. Business servs avail. Putting green. Exercise equipt. Game rm. Cr cds: A, C, D, DS, MC, V.

[icons]

B&Bs/Small Inns

★ ★ **THE CHECKERBERRY INN.** *62644 Country Rd 37 (46528). 219/642-4445. www.checkerberryinn. com.* 14 rms, 3 story, 3 suites. S $90; D $155; each addl $30; suites $160-$325; wkly, wkend rates. TV; VCR avail. Pool. Complimentary continental bkfst. Coffee in rms. Restaurant (see CHECKERBERRY). Ck-out 11 am, ck-in 1 pm. Business servs

avail. In-rm modem link. Tennis. Putting green. Lawn games. Refrigerators; microwaves avail. In scenic rural Amish area; contemporary French, American decor. Totally nonsmoking. Cr cds: A, MC, V.

[icons]

★ ★ **ESSENHAUS COUNTRY INN.** *240 US 20, Middlebury (46540). 574/825-9471; fax 574/825-0455; toll-free 800/455-9471. www.essenhaus. com.* 40 rms, 2 story. S $55-$72; D $87-$92; each addl $10; suites $99-$130; under 12 free. Crib $4. TV; cable. Complimentary coffee in lobby. Dining rm 6 am-8 pm; Fri, Sat to 9 pm. Ck-out 11 am, ck-in 3 pm. Meeting rm. Business servs avail. Whirlpool in suites. Amish country setting; handcrafted furnishings, antiques. Totally nonsmoking. Cr cds: A, DS, MC, V.

[icons]

★ ★ **INDIAN CREEK BED & BREAKFAST.** *20300 County Rd 18 (46528). 574/875-6606; fax 574/875-3968. www.bestinns.net/usa/in/ indiancreek.html.* 5 rms, 4 with shower only, 3 story, 1 suite. S $69; D $79; each addl $10; suites $99; under 4 free. Crib free. TV; VCR avail (movies). Complimentary full bkfst. Ck-out 10:30 am, ck-in 4-6 pm. Business servs avail. Luggage handling. 18-hole golf privileges, greens fee $15-$22, putting green, driving range. Picnic tables, grills. Country Victorian decor; family antiques. Totally nonsmoking. Cr cds: A, DS, MC, V.

[icons]

★ ★ **VARNS GUEST HOUSE.** *205 S Main St, Middlebury (46540). 219/825-9666; toll-free 800/398-5424. www. varnsb-b.com.* 5 rms, 2 story. 1 rm phone. S, D $75-$85; each addl $10. TV in sitting rm; cable. Complimentary full bkfst. Restaurant nearby. Ck-out 11 am, ck-in 3 pm. Built 1898; wrap-around porch. Totally nonsmoking. Cr cds: MC, V.

[icons]

Restaurants

★ ★ **BUGGY WHEEL BUFFET.** *160 Morton St, Shipshewana (46565).*

219/768-4444. Hrs: 11 am-7 pm; Tues, Wed from 7 am. Closed Sun; hols. Res accepted Fri, Sat. Buffet: bkfst $6.99, lunch, dinner $3.99-$9.99. Child's menu. Specialties: broasted chicken, meat loaf, casseroles. Salad bar. Own desserts. Oak woodwork crafted by Amish carpenter.
D

★★ **CHECKERBERRY.** *62644 Country Rd 37 (46526). 219/642-4445. www.checkerberryinn.com.* Hrs: 6-9 pm. Closed Sun, Mon; Jan 1. Res required. Dinner $28-$42. Specialties: seasonal wild game, crispy salmon, chicken breast. Own pasta, desserts. Country French decor on 100 acres of farmland. Cr cds: A, MC, V.
D

Greencastle

(D-3) *See also Brazil, Terre Haute*

Founded 1823 **Pop** 8,984 **Elev** 849 ft **Area code** 765 **Zip** 46135
Information Chamber of Commerce, 2 S Jackson St, PO Box 389; 765/653-4517
Web www.greencastle.com

Greencastle is within 15 miles of two man-made lakes—Raccoon Lake Reservoir and Cataract Lake—with boating and camping facilities.

What to See and Do

DePauw University. (1837) 2,100 students. Liberal arts; School of Music; founded by Methodist Church. State's oldest Methodist church is on campus as well as nation's first Greek letter sorority, Kappa Alpha Theta. Restored 19th-century classrm building. Tours (by appt). Phone 765/658-4800.

Lieber State Recreation Area. Approx 775 acres on Cataract Lake (1,500 acres). Swimming, lifeguard, bathhouse, waterskiing, fishing, boating (dock, rentals); picnicking, concession, camping. Activity center (Memorial Day-Labor Day). Adj are 342 acres of state forest and 7,300 acres of federal land, part of Cagles Mill Flood Control Reservoir Project. Standard fees. 8 mi S via US 231,

then 4 mi SW on IN 42. Phone 765/795-4576. ¢¢

B&B/Small Inn

★★★ **WALDEN INN.** *2 W Seminary St (46135). 765/653-2761; fax 765/653-4833; toll-free 800/225-8655. www.waldeninn.com.* 55 rms, 2 story. S $70; D $80; each addl $8; suites $120-$130; under 12 free; wkend rates; higher rates Indianapolis 500. Crib $8. TV. Restaurant (see DIFFERENT DRUMMER). Ck-out 1 pm, ck-in 4 pm. Meeting rms. Business servs avail. Tennis privileges. Amish furniture. Cr cds: A, D, DS, MC, V.
D 🐾 ⌐ ⚓

Restaurant

★★★ **DIFFERENT DRUMMER.** *2 Seminary Sq (46135). 765/653-2761. www.waldeninn.com.* Hrs: 6 am-2 pm, 5-9 pm; Fri, Sat until 10 pm. Closed Dec 25. Res accepted. Bar 11-2 am; Sun noon-midnight. Wine list. A la carte entrees: bkfst $2.50-$6, lunch $4.95-$7.95, dinner $14.50-$24.50. Specialties: filet mignon, Atlantic salmon, lamb. Own breads. Classical American decor; some Amish furnishings. Cr cds: A, C, D, DS, MC, V.
D

Greenfield

(D-4) *See also Indianapolis*

Pop 11,657 **Elev** 888 ft **Area code** 317 **Zip** 46140
Information Greater Greenfield Chamber of Commerce, 1 Courthouse Plaza; 317/477-4188
Web www.greenfieldcc.org

This town is the birthplace of poet James Whitcomb Riley.

What to See and Do

James Whitcomb Riley Home. (1850) Boyhood home of the poet from 1850-1869. Riley wrote "When the Frost Is on the Punkin" and many other verses in Hoosier dialect. Tours. Museum adj. (Apr-late Dec, Mon-Sat, also Sun afternoons) 250 W Main St. Phone 317/462-8539. ¢

Old Log Jail and Chapel-in-the-Park Museums. Historical displays incl arrowheads, clothing, china; local memorabilia. (Apr-Nov, Sat and Sun) Corner of E Main and N Apple Sts. Phone 317/462-7780. ¢

Special Event

James Whitcomb Riley Festival. Parade, carnival, entertainment, arts and crafts. Held wkend closest to Riley's birthday, Oct 7. Phone 317/462-2141.

Motel/Motor Lodge

★ **LEES INN.** *2270 N State St (46140). 317/462-7112; fax 317/462-9801; toll-free 800/733-5337. www. leesinn.com.* 100 rms, 2 story. S, D $59-$67; each addl $7; suites $89-$119; under 15 free; higher rates Indianapolis 500. Crib avail. Pet accepted. TV; cable. Complimentary continental bkfst. Ck-out noon. Meeting rms. Valet serv. Cr cds: A, D, DS, MC, V.

Hammond (A-2)

Pop 84,236 **Elev** 591 ft **Area code** 219
Information Chamber of Commerce, 7034 Indianapolis Blvd, 46324; 219/931-1000
Web www.hammondchamber.org

Hammond is one of the highly industrialized cities of the Calumet area on the southwest shore of Lake Michigan. The Indiana-Illinois state line is two blocks away from Hammond's business district and separates it from its sister community, Calumet City, IL. Hammond is also adjacent to Chicago. Industrial products manufactured here include railway supplies and equipment, cold-drawn steel, car wheels, forgings, printing, and hospital and surgical supplies.

What to See and Do

Little Red Schoolhouse. (1869) Oldest one-rm schoolhouse in Lake County. Used as presidential campaign headquarters by William Jennings Bryan. Original desks, tower bell, books, desk, and tools. (See SPECIAL EVENT) (By appt) 7205 Kennedy Ave. Phone 219/844-5666. **FREE**

Wicker Memorial Park. Eighteen-hole golf, driving range, pro shop. Tennis; x-country skiing; picnicking; playground; restaurant. Park (daily). Some fees. S on US 41 at jct US 6, in Highland. Phone 219/838-3420. **FREE**

Special Event

Hammond Fest. Carnival, food, entertainment. Phone 219/853-6378. Wkend July or Aug.

Motels/Motor Lodges

★★ **HOLIDAY INN.** *3830 179th St (46323). 219/844-2140; fax 219/845-7760; toll-free 800/465-4329. www. holiday-inn.com.* 154 rms, 4 story. S, D $86; under 18 free. Crib free. Pet accepted, some restrictions. TV; cable (premium). Heated pool; poolside serv. Restaurant 6:30-9:30 am, 6-9 pm. Rm serv. Bar 4 pm-1 am; Sat to 2 am. Ck-out noon. Coin lndry. Meeting rms. Business servs avail. In-rm modem link. Bellhops. Valet serv. Sundries. Exercise equipt. Luxury level. Cr cds: A, C, D, DS, ER, JCB, MC, V.

★★ **RAMADA INN & CONFERENCE CENTER.** *4141 Calumet Ave (46320). 219/933-0500; fax 219/933-0506; res 800/562-5987. www.ramada. com.* 100 rms, 2 story, 16 suites. S $72-$77; D $82-$87; each addl $10; suites $95-$105; under 12 free. Crib free. TV; cable. Complimentary continental bkfst, coffee in rms. Restaurant nearby. Ck-out 11 am. Meeting rms. Business servs avail. In-rm modem link. Coin lndry. Exercise equipt. Some in-rm whirlpools, refrigerators, microwaves, fireplaces. Cr cds: A, D, DS, MC, V.

Restaurant

★★ **PHIL SMIDT'S.** *1205 N Calumet Ave (46320). 219/659-0025. www. philsmidts.com.* Hrs: 11:15 am-9 pm; Fri, Sat to 10 pm; Sun 2:30-7 pm. Closed Sun Jan-Apr; hols. Res accepted. Bar. Lunch $6.95-$13, dinner $9.95-$24.50. Child's menu. Specializes in lake perch, frogs' legs, seafood. Cr cds: A, C, D, MC, V.
D SC ⊸

Huntington

(B-5) *See also Fort Wayne, Wabash*

Founded 1831 **Pop** 16,389 **Elev** 739 ft
Area code 219 **Zip** 46750
Information Huntington County Visitor & Convention Bureau, 407 N Jefferson, PO Box 212; 219/359-8687 or 800/848-4282
Web www.visithuntington.org

Originally called Wepecheange, the town was later named for Samuel Huntington, a member of the first Continental Congress. Huntington lies in a farming and industrial area and is home to Huntington College (1897).

What to See and Do

The Dan Quayle Center, Home of the United States Vice-Presidential Museum. Only vice presidential museum in the country has exhibits and educational programs about our nation's past vice presidents. Special focus on the five Indiana natives who have held the position. (Tues-Sat, also Sun afternoons; closed hols) 815 Warren St. Phone 219/356-6356.
Donation

Forks of the Wabash. Treaty grounds of Miami Native Americans. Tours of Miami Chief Richardville Home & Log House. Hiking trails, picnic area. 2 mi W on US 24. Phone 219/356-1903.

Huntington Reservoir. A 900-acre lake. Swimming at Little Turtle Area (Memorial Day-Labor Day, daily); primitive campsites (all yr; fee). Fishing, boating (launch); hunting; archery range, shooting range; picnicking, hiking trails, interpretive

programs. Office (May-Labor Day, daily; rest of yr, Mon-Fri; closed hols exc Memorial Day, July 4, Labor Day). 2 mi S on IN 5. Phone 219/468-2165. ¢¢

Special Events

Huntington County Heritage Days. Parade, bed race, ducky run; arts and crafts, food, entertainment. Three days mid-June. Phone 219/356-5300.
Forks of the Wabash Pioneer Festival. Pioneer food, pioneer arts and crafts demonstrations, Civil War encampment, antique show, banjo and fiddle contest. Last wkend Sept. Phone 219/356-1903. ¢¢

Indiana Dunes National Lakeshore

See also Hammond, Michigan City

(Along southern shore of Lake Michigan, between Gary and Michigan City.)

In 1966, 8,000 acres surrounding Indiana Dunes State Park (see) were established as Indiana Dunes National Lakeshore. Another 7,139 acres have since been acquired, and development continues.

The lakeshore contains a number of distinct environments: clean, sandy beaches; huge sand dunes, many covered with trees and shrubs; several bogs and marshes; and the various plants and animals peculiar to each. To preserve these environments, dune buggies and off-road vehicles are prohibited.

The visitor center is located at the junction of Kemil Road and US 12, three miles east of IN 49 (daily; closed Jan 1, Thanksgiving, December 25). Facilities include a hard-surfaced nature trail for the disabled. Day-use facilities include West Beach, north of US 12 between Gary and Ogden Dunes, which has swimming (lifeguard), bathhouse, visitor information center, picnic area, and marked nature trails; Bailly Homestead and Chellberg Farm area, between US 12 and 20, feature restored homestead, turn-of-the-century Swedish farm, hiking trails, cultural events, and a visitor information center. Other lifeguarded beaches are located on State Park/Kemil Road, off US 12. The Horse Trail, north of US 20, has a picnic area, parking facilities, and marked hiking, cross-country skiing, and riding trails. On US 12, near Michigan City, is Mount Baldy, largest dune in the Lakeshore, with hiking trails and a beach. Camping is available just off the intersection of IN 12 and Broadway, near Beverly Shores (tent and trailer sites; rest rms). Contact Superintendent, 1100 N Mineral Springs Rd, Porter 46304; phone 219/926-7561.

Indiana Dunes State Park

See also Hammond, Michigan City

(Approximately 15 mi E of Gary via US 12; 4 mi N of Chesterton on IN 49)

This beautiful and unique 2,182-acre state park extends three miles along Lake Michigan's south shore, with white sand dunes and beaches that can accommodate thousands of bathers. Approximately 1,800 acres are densely forested hills with a wide variety of rare flowers and ferns, cre-

ating an almost tropical appearance in summer. Many of the sand dunes continue to shift, creating hills such as 192-foot Mount Tom. There are 17 miles of marked hiking trails through forest and dune country. Swimming. Cross-country skiing in winter. Picnic facilities, snack bar, store. Campgrounds. Nature center, naturalist service. Entrance fees. Phone 219/926-4520 or 219/926-1952.

Indianapolis

(D-4) *See also Anderson, Greenfield*

Founded 1820 **Pop** 731,327 **Elev** 717 ft **Area code** 317

Information Convention & Visitors Association, 1 RCA Dome, Suite 100, 46225; 317/639-4282 or 800/323-INDY

Web www.indy.org

The present site of Indianapolis was an area of rolling woodland when it was selected by a group of ten commissioners as the location of the new Indiana state capital on June 7, 1820. It was chosen because it was close to the geographical center of the state. Only scattered Native American villages and two white settler families were located in the region at the

The white sand dunes of Indiana Dunes State Park

time. The city was laid out in the wheel pattern of Washington, D.C. In January, 1825, the capital of Indiana was moved here from Corydon.

In its early days the city grew mainly because of its importance as seat of the state government. By the turn of the century Indianapolis had emerged as an important manufacturing center in the Midwest and the commercial center of the rich agricultural region surrounding it.

It is the largest city in Indiana, one of the leading US distribution hubs, and an important business and financial center. The annual 500-mile automobile race at the Indianapolis Motor Speedway, an outstanding race course, has brought international fame to the city. Indianapolis is also referred to as the nation's amateur sports capital. Indianapolis has hosted more than 400 national and international amateur sporting events. Among the city's industrial products are pharmaceuticals, airplane and automobile parts, television sets, electronic equipment, and medical diagnostic equipment.

Additional Visitor Information

This is Indianapolis magazine, available locally, has up-to-date information on events and articles of interest to visitors.

The Indianapolis City Center, 201 S Capitol Ave, Pan Am Plaza, Suite 200, 46225, phone 800/323-INDY, has general information brochures, maps, and tourist guidebooks (daily). Information is also available through the Convention & Visitors Assoc, 1 RCA Dome, Suite 100, 46225, phone 317/639-4282.

Transportation

Car Rental Agencies. See IMPORTANT TOLL-FREE NUMBERS.

Public Transportation. Buses (Indy G.), phone 317/635-3344.

Rail Passenger Service. Amtrak 800/872-7245.

Airport Information

Indianapolis International Airport. Information 317/487-9594; lost and found, 317/487-5084; weather, 317/635-5959; cash

machines, adj Delta and USAir ticket offices.

What to See and Do

Butler University. (1855) 4,264 students. The 290-acre campus is located seven mi N of downtown Indianapolis. 4600 Sunset Ave. Phone 317/940-8000. On campus are

   Clowes Memorial Hall. Performing arts center. Programs (all yr). Phone 317/940-9697.

   Hinkle Fieldhouse and Butler Bowl. 15,000 seats; home of Butler basketball and one of the first university fieldhouses in the country. Home football games are played in the Butler Bowl, which seats 20,000. Phone 317/940-9375.

   Holcomb Observatory & Planetarium. Features the largest telescope in Indiana, a 38-inch Cassegrain reflector. Planetarium shows (call for schedule). Phone 317/940-9333. ¢

   Starlight Theatre. Covered outdoor theater. Programs (May-Aug). Phone 317/940-6444.

Children's Museum. The largest of its kind; ten major galleries; exhibits cover science, social cultures, space, history, and exploration. SpaceQuest Planetarium (fee), Welcome Center, 30-ft-high Water Clock, Playscape gallery for preschoolers, Computer Discovery Center, hands-on science exhibits, simulated limestone cave, carousel rides (fee), performing arts theater, special exhibits. The largest gallery, Center for Exploration, is designed for ages 12 and up. Fee for special programs and exhibits. (Mar-Labor Day, daily; rest of yr, Tues-Sun; closed Easter, Thanksgiving, Dec 25) 3000 N Meridian St. Phone 317/334-3322. ¢¢

City Market. Renovated marketplace was constructed in 1886. This building and two adj areas feature smoked meat, dairy, specialty bakery and fruit stands and ethnic foods. (Mon-Sat; closed hols) 222 E Market St. Phone 317/634-9266. **FREE**

Colonel Eli Lilly Civil War Museum. Exhibits present Hoosier involvement and perspective of the Civil War. Incl photos, letters, and diaries of Indiana soldiers. (Wed-Sun; closed hols) Phone 317/233-2124. **FREE**

Conner Prairie. A 250-acre nationally acclaimed living history museum. Costumed interpreters depict life and times of early settlement in this 1836 village; contains 39 buildings, incl Federal-style brick mansion (1823) built by fur trader William Conner (self-guided tours). Working blacksmith, weaving, and pottery shops; woodworkers complex; self-guided tours. Visitor center with changing exhibits. Hands-on activities at Pioneer Adventure Area; games, toys. Picnic area, restaurant, gift shop. (Tues-Sun; closed hols) Special events throughout yr. 13400 Allisonville Rd, approx 6 mi N of Expy 465, in Fishers. Phone 317/776-6000. ¢¢¢

Crispus Attucks Museum. Four galleries established to recognize, honor, and celebrate the contributions made by African-Americans. (Mon-Fri; closed hols) 1140 Dr. Martin Luther King Jr. St. Phone 317/226-4613. **FREE**

Crown Hill Cemetery. Third-largest cemetery in nation. President Benjamin Harrison, poet James Whitcomb Riley, novelist Booth Tarkington, and gangster John Dillinger are among the notables buried here. 700 W 38th St. Phone 317/925-8231.

Eagle Creek Park. Approx 3,800 acres of wooded terrain with 1,300-acre reservoir. Fishing, boat ramps, rentals, swimming beach (Memorial Day-Labor Day), bathhouse, water sports center; shelters, golf course, x-country skiing, hiking trails, playgrounds, picnicking. (Daily; some facilities closed in winter) Some fees.

7840 W 56th St, just W of I-465. Phone 317/327-7110. ¢¢

Easley's Winery. Sales rm; wine tasting (21 yrs and over). Tours by appt. (Daily; closed hols) 205 N College Ave. Phone 317/636-4516. **FREE**

Eiteljorg Museum of American Indian and Western Art. Collections of Native American and American Western art. Considered one of the finest collections of its kind. (Memorial Day-Labor Day, Mon-Sat, also Sun afternoons; rest of yr, Tues-Sat, also Sun afternoons; closed Easter, Thanksgiving, Dec 25) 500 W Washington St. Phone 317/636-9378. ¢¢¢

Garfield Park and Conservatory. This 128-acre park features restored pagoda, conservatory (daily; closed hols; fee), sunken gardens, and illuminated fountains. Conservatory shows (fee): bulb (spring); chrysanthemum (late Nov); poinsettia (Dec). Picnic area; swimming pool (late May-Labor Day, daily; fee); tennis and horseshoe courts, other sports facilities. (Daily; facilities closed hols) Musical programs in amphitheater (early June-late Aug, Thurs-Sun; free). 2505 Conservatory Dr. Phone 317/327-7184. **FREE**

⭐ **Historic Lockerbie Square.** Late 19th-century private houses have been restored in this six-blk area. Cobblestone streets, brick sidewalks, and fine architecture make this an interesting area for sightseeing. Bounded by New York, College, Michigan, and East Sts. Walking tour ¢¢ Here is

> **James Whitcomb Riley Home.** Maintained in same condition as when the "Hoosier Poet" lived here (1893-1916). Tours (Tues-Sun; closed hols). 528 Lockerbie St. Phone 317/631-5885. ¢¢

Hook's American Drug Store Museum. Celebrates the 400-yr history of drug stores in America. Incl ornate 1852 furnishings, drugstore and medical antiques; operating soda fountain. (Daily; closed hols; also Mon in winter) Phone 317/924-1503. **FREE**

Indiana Convention Center & RCA Dome. Features seven exhibition halls, four ballrms, 48 meeting rms, and various offices. The 60,500-seat RCA Dome is one of only a few air-supported domed stadiums in the US. The Dome is the home of the Indianapolis Colts football team, conventions, auto shows, trade shows, and more. 100 S Capitol. Phone 317/262-3410. Tours ¢¢

⭐ **Indianapolis Motor Speedway and Hall of Fame Museum.** Site of the famous 500-mi automobile classic held each yr the Sun before Memorial Day (see SPECIAL EVENTS). Many innovations in modern cars have been tested at races here. The oval track is 2½ mi long, lined by grandstands, paddocks, and bleachers. Hall of Fame Museum (fee) has exhibit of antique and classic passenger cars, many built in Indiana; more than 30 Indianapolis-winning race cars. (Daily; closed Dec 25) 4790 W 16th St, 7 mi NW. Phone 317/484-6747. ¢¢

⭐ **Indianapolis Museum of Art.** Extensive collections with many special exhibits (fee). Tours (Tues-Sun; closed Jan 1, Thanksgiving, Dec 25) 1200 W 38th St. Phone 317/923-1331. **Donation** Incl

> **Clowes Pavilion.** Medieval and Renaissance art; J.M.W. Turner watercolors; lecture hall with special programs; courtyard garden. Phone 317/940-6444.

> **Krannert Pavilion.** Collection features American, Asian, and pre-Columbian art; 20th-century art and textiles. Outdoor concert terrace, sculpture court. Phone 317/920-2660.

> **Lilly Pavilion of Decorative Arts.** French chateau showcases two centuries of English, Continental, and American furniture, silver, and ceramics. Also examples of 18th-century German porcelain. Tours. Phone 317/920-2660.

> **Mary Fendrich Hulman Pavilion.** Collection features Baroque through Neo-Impressionist works and the Eiteljorg Gallery of African and South Pacific Art. Allen Whitehill Clowes Special Exhibition Gallery. Phone 317/920-2660.

Indianapolis Sightseeing. Contact Indianapolis Sight Seeing, Inc, 9075 N Meridian, 46260. Phone 317/573-0404.

Indianapolis Zoo. This 64-acre facility incl state's largest aquarium, enclosed whale and dolphin pavilion, and more than 3,000 animals from around the world. Sea lions, penguins, sharks, polar bears; daily whale and dolphin shows; camels and reptiles of the deserts; lions, giraffes, and elephants in the Plains; tigers, bears, and snow monkeys in the Forests. Encounters features domesticated animals from around the world, and a 600-seat outside arena offers daily programs and demonstrations. Living Deserts of the World is a conservatory covered by an 80-ft diameter transparent dome. New White River Gardens is a conservatory and gardens. Commons Plaza incl restaurant and snack bar; additional animal exhibits; amphitheater for shows and concerts. Horse-drawn streetcar, elephant, camel, carousel, and miniature train rides. Stroller and locker rentals. (Daily) 1200 W Washington St (US 40), Downtown. Phone 317/630-2010. ¢¢¢

Indiana State Museum. Depicts Indiana's history, art, science, and popular culture with five floors of displays. Exhibits incl the Indiana Museum of Sports, Indiana radio, forests of 200 yrs ago, a small-town community at the turn of the century, paintings by Indiana artists. Changing exhibits. (Daily; closed hols) 202 N Alabama St, at Ohio St. Phone 317/232-1637. **FREE**

Indiana University—Purdue University Indianapolis. (organized 1969) 27,036 students. More than 200 areas of study offered in 19 schools. Home of Indiana University Medical Center, one of the foremost research and treatment centers in the world and a primary international center for sports medicine, fitness, heart research, cancer treatment, and kidney transplants. Incl five teaching hospitals and 90 clinics. IUPUI hosts many national and international athletic competitions. Home of the RCA Tennis Championships (see SPECIAL EVENTS). Main site on W Michigan St, one mi W of downtown. Phone 317/274-5555.

Indiana World War Memorial Plaza. A five-blk area dedicated to Indiana citizens who gave their lives in the two World Wars and the Korean and Vietnam conflicts. The World War Memorial in middle of plaza is a massive edifice of Indiana limestone and granite. The Shrine Room (upper level) is dedicated to the American flag; Military Museum (lower level). (Wed-Sun; closed hols) Outside in the center of the south stairway stands a bronze statue, *Pro Patria*. The four-story building in northeast corner of plaza is national headquarters of the American Legion. Landscaped parks are located north and south of the building; Veterans Memorial Plaza has flags of 50 states. (Wed-Sun) 431 N Meridian St, bounded by New York, St. Clair, Meridian, and Pennsylvania Sts. Phone 317/232-7615. **FREE**

Madame Walker Theatre Center. The Walker Theatre, erected and embellished in an African and Egyptian motif, was built in 1927 as a tribute to Madame C. J. Walker, America's first self-made female millionaire. The renovated theater now has theatrical productions, concerts, and other cultural events. The center serves as an educational and cultural center for the city's black community. Tours (Mon-Fri). 617 Indiana Ave. Phone 317/236-2099. ¢

Morris-Butler House. (1865) A museum of Victorian lifestyles from 1850-1886. Belter & Meeks furniture, paintings, silver, and other decorative arts. Special events. (Wed-Sun; closed hols) 1204 N Park Ave. Phone 317/636-5409. ¢¢

★ **NCAA Hall of Champions.** The center celebrates intercollegiate athletics through photographs, video presentations, and displays covering 22 men's and women's sports and all NCAA championships. The 25,000-sq-ft area contains two levels of interactive displays and multimedia presentations. Three theaters present videos about the Final Four and coaching, for example, while the Hall of Honor contains a salute to individuals who have been honored with an NCAA award. (Memorial Day-Labor Day, Mon; rest of yr, Tue-Sun; closed Jan 1, Thanksgiving, Dec 25) 700 W Washington St in the White River State Park. Phone 800/735-6222. ¢¢¢

President Benjamin Harrison Home. (1874) Residence of 23rd president of the US. Sixteen rms with original furniture, paintings, and family's personal effects. Herb garden. Guided tours (every 30 min). (Daily; closed hols, also 500 Race Day) 1230 N Delaware St. Phone 317/631-1898. ¢¢

Professional sports.

Indiana Fever (WNBA). Conseco Fieldhouse, 125 S Pennsylvania St. Phone 317/917-2500.

Indiana Pacers (NBA). Conseco Fieldhouse, 125 S Pennsylvania St. Phone 317/917-2500.

Indianapolis Colts (NFL). RCA Dome, 100 S Capitol Ave. Phone 317/297-2658.

Scottish Rite Cathedral. Structure of Tudor/Gothic design, built in 1929. The 212-ft tower has a carillon of 54 bells; auditorium has a 7,500-pipe organ. Interior is elaborately decorated. Tours. (Mon-Fri; closed wkends and hols) 650 N Meridian St. Phone 317/262-3100. **FREE**

State Capitol. (1878-1888) Structure of Indiana limestone with copper dome. (Mon-Fri; closed hols) Tours by appt. Between Washington and Ohio Sts and Capitol and Senate Aves. Phone 317/233-5293. **FREE**

Special Events

Indiana Flower & Patio Show. State Fairgrounds. More than 25 full-size gardens display fine flowers and landscaping techniques. Phone 317/576-9933. Second wkend Mar. Phone 317/927-7500.

500 Festival. Month-long celebration precedes the Indianapolis 500, held Memorial Day wkend. Numerous events incl the 500 Ball, Mechanic's Recognition Party, Delco Electronics 500 Festival Parade, Mini-Marathon, Memorial Service. Phone 317/636-4556 or 800/638-4296. May.

Indianapolis 500. For ticket information, contact the Indianapolis Motor Speedway. Phone 317/484-6780. Sun before Memorial Day.

Indiana Black Expo. Consumer exhibits, health fair. Phone 317/262-3452. July.

Indiana State Fair. Fairgrounds. E 38th St between College Ave and Fall Creek Pkwy. Grand circuit horse racing, livestock exhibitions, entertainment, and special agricultural exhibits. Phone 317/927-7500. Mid-Aug.

RCA Championships (tennis). Indianapolis Tennis Center, 815 W New York St. 10,000-seat stadium. World-

class players compete in wk-long event. Contact 815 W New York St, 46202. Phone 317/632-4100 or 800/622-LOVE. Mid-Aug.

Penrod Arts Fair. State's largest art fair. Phone 317/252-9895. Sept.

Entertainment. Indianapolis Civic Theater, 1200 W 38th St, 46208, 317/924-6770; Hilbert Circle Theatre (Indianapolis Symphony Orchestra and a variety of other shows), 45 Monument Cir, 46204, 317/262-1100. Dance Kaleidoscope (Oct-Nov, Mar and June), 4600 Sunset Ave, 317/940-6555; Indiana Repertory Theater (Sept-May), 140 W Washington St, 46204, 317/635-5277; Ballet Internationale (July-Apr), 502 N Capitol, Suite B, 46204, 317/637-8979; Butler University, Edyrvean Repertory Theatre, 100 W 42nd St, 317/783-4000; Beef & Boards Dinner Theatre, 9301 N Michigan Ave, 317/876-0504; Madame Walker Theatre Center, 617 Indiana Ave, 317/236-2099; and Marian College offer a variety of productions throughout the yr; contact the individual venues for details.

Motels/Motor Lodges

★ ★ **AMERISUITES.** *9104 Keystone Crossing (46240). 317/843-0064; fax 317/843-1851; toll-free 800/833-1516. www.amerisuites.com.* 126 suites, 6 story. S, D $99-$119; each addl $10. Crib free. TV; cable (premium), VCR (movies). Complimentary continental bkfst. Ck-out noon. Meeting rms. Business center. In-rm modem link. Coin lndry. Exercise equipt. Health club privileges. Heated pool. Refrigerators, microwaves, wet bars. Cr cds: A, C, D, DS, MC, V.

D ⌖ 🏋 ➘🔥 🏃

★ ★ **CASTLETON BY MARRIOTT COURTYARD.** *8670 Allisonville Rd (46250). 317/576-9559; fax 317/576-0695; toll-free 800/321-2211. www.courtyard.com.* 146 rms, 3 story. S, D $92; suites $107-$117; wkend rates. Crib free. TV; cable (premium). Indoor pool; whirlpool. Continental bkfst. Complimentary coffee in rms. Bar. Ck-out noon. Coin lndry. Meeting rms. Business servs avail. In-rm modem link. Valet serv. Sundries. Exercise equipt. Refrigerator in suites. Balconies. Cr cds: A, D, DS, MC, V.

D ⌖ ➘ 🏋 🏃

★★ **COMFORT INN WEST.** *5855 Rockville Rd (46224). 317/487-9800; fax 317/487-1125; toll-free 800/323-2086. www.comfortinn.com.* 94 rms, 4 story, 24 suites. S $79-$180; D $84-$185; each addl $5; suites $91-$185; under 18 free. Crib free. TV; cable. Complimentary continental bkfst. Coffee in rms. Ck-out noon. Meeting rms. Business servs avail. In-rm modem link. Bellhops. Valet serv. Sundries. Coin lndry. Free airport transportation. Exercise equipt. Indoor pool; whirlpool. Playground. Game rm. Some refrigerators, microwaves, wet bars; in-rm whirlpool in suites. Cr cds: A, MC, V.

★ **COUNTRY HEARTH INN.** *3851 Shore Dr (46254). 317/297-1848; fax 317/297-2096; toll-free 800/217-9182. www.countryhearth.com.* 83 rms, 2 story, 12 suites. S $53-$65; D $59-$71; each addl $6; suites, kits. $74-$86; under 18 free. Crib free. TV; cable (premium). Pool. Complimentary continental bkfst. Restaurant adj 6 am-10 pm. Ck-out noon. Meeting rms. Business servs avail. Health club privileges. Cr cds: A, C, D, DS, MC, V.

★★ **COURTYARD BY MARRIOTT.** *10290 N Meridian St (46290). 317/571-1110; fax 317/571-0416; toll-free 800/321-2211. www.courtyard. com.* 149 rms, 12 suites, 4 story. S, D $92-$108; each addl $10; suites $125-$145; under 18 free; higher rates special events. Crib free. TV; cable (premium). Complimentary coffee in rms. Bar 4-11 pm. Ck-out 1 pm. Meeting rms. Business servs avail. In-rm modem link. Sundries. Coin lndry. Exercise equipt. Indoor pool; whirlpool. Refrigerator in suites. Cr cds: A, D, DS, MC, V.

★★ **COURTYARD BY MARRIOTT.** *5525 Fortune Cir E (46241). 317/248-0300; fax 317/248-1834; toll-free 800/321-2211. www.courtyard.com.* 151 rms, 10 suites, 4 story. S $95; D $105; each addl $10; suites $130; higher rates special events. Crib free. TV; cable (premium), VCR avail. Indoor pool; whirlpool. Continental bkfst. Complimentary coffee in rms. Restaurant nearby. Bar 5-11 pm;

closed Sun. Ck-out noon. Meeting rms. Business servs avail. Sundries. Free airport transportation. Exercise equipt. Balconies. Cr cds: A, MC, V.

★★ **DRURY INN.** *9320 N Michigan Rd (46268). 317/876-9777; toll-free 800/378-7946. www.druryinn.com.* 110 rms, 4 story. S $65; D $75; each addl $10; under 18 free; some wkend rates. Crib free. Pet accepted, some restrictions. TV; cable (premium). Pool. Complimentary bkfst. Restaurant nearby. Ck-out noon. Meeting rms. Business servs avail. In-rm modem link. Sundries. Cr cds: A, C, D, DS, MC, V.

★★ **FAIRFIELD INN.** *8325 Bash Rd (46250). 317/577-0455; toll-free 800/228-2800. www.fairfieldinn.com.* 132 rms, 3 story. S, D $49-$69; each addl $8; under 18 free. Crib free. TV; cable (premium). Heated pool. Complimentary continental bkfst. Restaurant nearby. Ck-out noon. Business servs avail. In-rm modem link. Cr cds: A, C, D, DS, MC, V.

★★ **HAMPTON INN.** *105 S Meridian St (46225). 317/261-1200; fax 317/261-1030; toll-free 800/426-7866. www.hamptoninn.com.* 180 rms, 9 story, 22 suites. S $94-$114; D $104-$114; suites $159-$179; under 18 free; higher rates special events. Crib free. Valet parking $8. TV; cable (premium). Complimentary continental bkfst. Restaurant 11 am-midnight. Bar. Ck-out noon. Meeting rms. Business servs avail. In-rm modem link. Bellhops. Valet serv. Exercise equipt. Some in-rm whirlpools, refrigerators, wet bars. Cr cds: A, D, DS, MC, V.

★★ **HAMPTON INN EAST.** *2311 N Shadeland Ave (46219). 317/359-9900; fax 317/359-1376; toll-free 800/426-7866. www.hamptoninn.com.* 125 rms, 4 story. S $72-$77; D $77-$79; under 18 free. Crib free. Pet accepted, some restrictions. TV; cable (premium). Indoor pool; whirlpool. Complimentary continental bkfst. Restaurant nearby. Ck-out noon. Meeting rm. Business servs avail. In-rm modem link. Cr cds: A, C, D, DS, MC, V.

★★ **HAMPTON INN NW.** *7220 Woodland Dr (46278). 317/290-1212; fax 317/291-1579; toll-free 800/426-7866. www.hamptoninn.com.* 124 rms, 4 story. S, D $79-$84; under 18 free; special events rates. Crib free. Pet accepted, some restrictions. TV; cable (premium). Indoor pool; whirlpool. Complimentary continental bkfst. Restaurant adj 24 hrs. Ck-out noon. Meeting rms. Business servs avail. In-rm modem link. Valet serv. Exercise equipt. Cr cds: A, C, D, DS, MC, V.

★★ **HOLIDAY INN EAST.** *6990 E 21st St (46219). 317/359-5341; fax 317/351-1666; toll-free 800/465-4329. www.holiday-inn.com.* 184 rms, 6 story. S, D $89; higher rates special events. Crib free. Pet accepted. TV; cable (premium). Complimentary full bkfst (Mon-Fri). Coffee in rms. Restaurant 6 am-11 pm; Fri-Sun to midnight. Bar. Ck-out noon. Meeting rms. In-rm modem link. Bellhops. Valet serv. Sundries. Coin lndry. Exercise equipt. Indoor pool; whirlpool. Game rm. Cr cds: A, C, D, DS, MC, V.

★★ **HOLIDAY INN SELECT.** *3850 DePauw Blvd (46268). 317/872-9790; fax 317/871-5608; toll-free 800/465-4329. www.holiday-inn.com.* 349 rms, 5 story. S, D $125; suites $170; under 18 free; wkend rates. Crib free. TV; cable (premium). Indoor pool; whirlpool. Coffee in rms. Restaurant 6 am-10 pm. Bar 11-2 am. Ck-out 11 am. Coin lndry. Convention facilities. Business servs avail. In-rm modem link. Bellhops. Valet serv. Gift shop. Sundries. Putting green. Exercise equipt; sauna. Private patios; balconies. Cr cds: A, C, D, DS, JCB, MC, V.

★★ **HOMEWOOD SUITES.** *2501 E 86th St (46240). 317/253-1919; fax 317/255-8223; toll-free 800/225-5466. www.homewoodsuites.com.* 116 suites, 3 story. S, D $99-$109; higher rates special events. Crib free. Pet accepted; $50. TV; cable (premium), VCR. Complimentary continental bkfst. Coffee in rms. Ck-out noon. Meeting rms. Business center. In-rm modem link. Valet serv. Coin lndry. Exercise equipt; sauna. Heated pool; whirlpool. Refrigerators, microwaves. Cr cds: A, C, D, DS, MC, V.

★★ **LA QUINTA INN.** *7304 E 21st St (46219). 317/359-1021; fax 317/359-0578; toll-free 800/531-5900. www.laquinta.com.* 122 rms, 2 story. S, D $59-$69; each addl $7; under 18 free. Crib free. Pet accepted. TV; cable (premium). Heated pool. Continental bkfst. Coffee in rms. Ck-out

The mighty towers of Indianapolis

noon. Coin lndry. Valet serv. Cr cds: A, C, D, DS, MC, V.

★★ **MARTEN HOUSE HOTEL AND LILLY CONFERENCE CENTER.** *1801 W 86th St (46260). 317/872-4111; fax 317/415-5245; toll-free 800/736-5634. martenhouse.com.* 176 rms, 2 story. S $99-$129; D $109-$139; each addl $10; suites $135-$250; under 18 free. Crib free. TV; cable. Indoor pool. Restaurant 6:30 am-2 pm, 5:30-10 pm. Bar 5 pm-midnight. Ck-out noon. Coin lndry. Meeting rms. Business servs avail. In-rm modem link. Bellhops. Valet serv. Exercise equipt; sauna. Some refrigerators. St. Vincent's Hospital adj. Cr cds: A, C, D, DS, MC, V.

★★ **RAMADA.** *505 S State Rd 39, Lebanon (46052). 765/482-0500; fax 765/482-0311; toll-free 800/499-3339. www.ramada.com.* 209 rms, 2 story. S, D $79-$99; each addl $8; suites $154; under 19 free; higher rates special events. Crib free. TV; cable, VCR. Complimentary coffee in rms. Restaurant 7 am-10 pm; Fri, Sat to 11 pm. Bar from noon; Fri, Sat to midnight. Ck-out 11 am. Meeting rms. Business center. In-rm modem link. Bellhops. Valet serv. Sundries. Coin lndry. 18-hole golf privileges. Exercise equipt. Indoor pool; whirlpool. Playground. Game rm. Some refrigerators, microwaves, wet bars. Cr cds: A, C, D, DS, JCB, MC, V.

★★ **RAMADA INN INDIANAPOLIS AIRPORT.** *2500 S High School Rd (46251). 317/244-3361; fax 317/241-9202; toll-free 800/297-4639. www.ramada.com.* 288 rms, 6 story. S $89-$250; D $99-$275; each addl $10; suites $195-$275; under 18 free; higher rates special events. Crib $10. TV; cable (premium). Indoor pool. Restaurant 6-11 am, 5-10 pm. Bar 11-1 am. Ck-out noon. Meeting rms. Business servs avail. In-rm modem link. Bellhops. Sundries. Gift shop. Free airport transportation. Cr cds: A, C, D, DS, MC, V.

★ **SIGNATURE INN SOUTH.** *4402 E Creek View Dr (46237). 317/784-7006; toll-free 800/822-5252.* 101 rms, 2 story. S, D $65-$72; under 18 free; wkend rates. Crib free. TV; cable (premium). Pool. Complimentary continental bkfst. Restaurant adj 6 am-10 pm. Ck-out noon. Meeting rms. Business servs avail. In-rm modem link. Valet serv. Sundries. Health club privileges. Microwaves avail. Cr cds: A, D, DS, MC, V.

★★ **WYNDHAM GARDEN.** *251 E Pennsylvania Pkwy (46280). 317/574-4600; fax 317/574-4633; toll-free 800/996-3426. www.wyndham.com.* 171 rms, 6 story. S, D $89-$109; suites $109-$129. Crib free. TV; cable, VCR avail. Indoor pool; whirlpool. Complimentary coffee in rms. Restaurant 6:30 am-10 pm. Rm serv from 5 pm. Bar 11 am-midnight. Ck-out noon. Meeting rms. Business servs avail. Sundries. Exercise equipt. Cr cds: A, C, D, DS, JCB, MC, V.

Hotels

★★★ **CANTERBURY HOTEL.** *123 S Illinois St (46225). 317/634-3000; fax 317/685-2519; toll-free 800/538-8186. www.canterburyhotel.com.* 99 rms, 12 story. S, D $190-$215; each addl $25; suites $525-$1,400; lower rates wkends. Crib $25. Garage $14/day. TV; cable, VCR avail. Complimentary continental bkfst. Restaurant (see RESTAURANT AT THE CANTERBURY). Afternoon tea 4-5:30 pm. Ck-out noon. Meeting rms. Business servs avail. In-rm modem link. Concierge. Bathrm phones, minibars. 2-story atrium lobby. Formal decor; 4-poster beds, Chippendale-style furniture. Historic landmark; built 1928. Cr cds: A, C, D, DS, ER, JCB, MC, V.

★★★ **CROWNE PLAZA HOTEL UNION STATION.** *123 W Louisiana (46225). 317/631-2221; fax 317/236-7474. www.crowneplaza.com.* 275 rms, 3 story, 2 suites. S, D $169; suites $219-$250; under 18 free; wkend rates; higher rates Dec 31. Crib free. Valet parking $10. TV; cable. Indoor pool; whirlpool. Restaurant 6 am-midnight; closed Sat, Sun. Bar 4 pm-midnight. Ck-out noon. Convention facilities. Business servs avail. In-rm modem link. Concierge. Exercise equipt. Rec rm. First US union railway depot (1853); Pullman sleeper cars from the 1920's. Cr cds: A, C, D, DS, JCB, MC, V.

⬛ ≈ 👤 🚭 🔥 SC

★★★ **DOUBLETREE GUEST SUITES HOTEL.** *11355 N Meridian St, Carmel (46032). 317/844-7994; fax 317/844-2118; toll-free 800/222-8733. www.doubletree.com.* 137 suites, 3 story. S, D $99-$355; each addl $15; under 18 free. Crib free. TV; cable. Indoor/outdoor pool; whirlpool, poolside serv. Complimentary coffee in rms. Restaurant 6:30 am-11 pm. Rm serv. Bar from 5 pm. Ck-out noon. Meeting rms. Business servs avail. Exercise equipt. Refrigerators, microwaves. Private patios. Cr cds: A, C, D, DS, MC, V.

⬛ ≈ 👤 🚭 🔥 SC

★★★ **HYATT REGENCY.** *1 S Capitol Ave (46204). 317/632-1234; fax 317/616-6299; toll-free 800/233-1234. www.hyatt.com.* 500 rms, 21 story. S $175; D $200; each addl $25; suites $350-$1,000; parlor $175-$700; under 18 free; some wkend rates. Valet, garage parking $12. Crib free. TV. Indoor pool. Restaurants 6 am-midnight. Bars 11-2 am. Ck-out noon. Convention facilities. Business center. In-rm modem link. Concierge. Barber, beauty shop. Exercise equipt. Massage. Atrium. Revolving restaurant. Cr cds: A, C, D, DS, ER, JCB, MC, V.

⬛ ≈ 👤 🚭 🔥 👤

★★★ **INDIANAPOLIS MARRIOTT NORTH.** *3645 River Crossing Pkwy (46240). 317/705-0000; toll-free 800/228-9290.* 315 rms, 11 story. S, D $125-$195; each addl $15; under 17 free. Crib avail. Indoor pool. TV; cable (premium), VCR avail. Complimentary coffee, newspaper in rms. Restaurant 6 am-10 pm. Ck-out noon. Meeting rms. Business center. Gift shop. Exercise rm. Some refrigerators, minibars. Cr cds: A, C, D, DS, MC, V.

≈ 🏌 👤 🔥

★★★ **MARRIOTT DOWNTOWN INDIANAPOLIS.** *350 W Maryland St (46225). 317/822-3500; toll-free 800/228-9290. www.marriott.com.* 615 rms, 19 story. S, D $150-$295; each addl $20; under 17 free. Crib avail. Indoor pool. TV; cable (premium),

VCR avail. Complimentary coffee in rms. Restaurant 6 am-10 pm. Ck-out noon. Meeting rms. Business center. Gift shop. Exercise rm. Some refrigerators, minibars. Cr cds: A, C, D, DS, MC, V.

≈ 🏌 👤 🔥

★★★ **MARRIOTT INDIANAPOLIS.** *7202 E 21st St (46219). 317/352-1231; fax 317/352-9775; toll-free 800/228-9290. www.marriott.com.* 252 rms, 3-5 story. S, D, studio rms $124-$134; suites $300; under 18 free; wkend rates; higher rates Memorial Day wkend. Crib free. Pet accepted, some restrictions. TV; cable, VCR avail. Indoor/outdoor pool; wading pool, whirlpool, poolside serv. Restaurant 6:30 am-10 pm. Bar 11-1 am, Sun to midnight. Ck-out noon. Coin lndry. Meeting rms. Business center. In-rm modem link. Bellhops. Valet serv. Sundries. Gift shop. Tennis privileges. Putting green. Exercise equipt. Rec rm. Some private patios. Luxury level. Cr cds: A, MC, V.

🐾 🏌 ≈ 👤 🔥 🏌

★★★ **OMNI INDIANAPOLIS NORTH HOTEL.** *8181 N Shadeland Ave (46250). 317/849-6668; fax 317/849-4936; toll-free 800/843-6664. www.omnihotels.com.* 215 rms, 6 story. S, D $99-$125; suites $175-$250; wkend rates. Crib free. TV; cable (premium). Indoor pool. Complimentary coffee in rms. Restaurant 7 am-10 pm; wkend hrs vary. Rm serv to midnight. Bar 11:30 am-midnight. Ck-out noon. Coin lndry. Meeting rms. In-rm modem link. Gift shop. Exercise equipt; sauna. Game rm. Many refrigerators. Cr cds: A, C, D, DS, ER, MC, V.

⬛ ≈ 👤 🚭 🔥 SC

★★★ **OMNI SEVERIN HOTEL.** *40 W Jackson Pl (46225). 317/634-6664; fax 317/687-3612; toll-free 800/843-6664. www.omnihotels.com.* 424 rms, 13 story. S, D $129-$189; each addl $20; suites $225-$675; under 18 free. Crib free. Garage parking $6. TV; cable, VCR avail. Indoor pool; poolside serv. Coffee in rms. Restaurant 6 am-11 pm. Bar 11-1 am. Ck-out noon. Convention facilities. Business center. In-rm modem link. Concierge. Gift shop. Exercise equipt. Some refrigerators. Built in

WANDERING AROUND WHITE RIVER STATE PARK

Indiana's first urban state park, 250-acre White River State Park is within easy walking distance of Indy's downtown core. In this parklike setting, visitors can watch professional baseball, enjoy a dolphin show, ride a restored carousel, visit a number of unique museums, or simply stroll alongside a restored canal (or glide a pedal boat on it).

Begin at Pumphouse Visitor Center. Built in 1870, just five years after the Civil War ended, this is where the first water for drinking and fire protection was pumped throughout Indianapolis. Walk west (or left) to the bridge over the White River. In 1831, the *Robert Hanna* journeyed to Indianapolis in an effort to win a prize offered to the first steamboat able to travel from the Ohio River up the White River. However, the steamboat ran aground on the return trip, discounting the river as a major trade route.

At the far end of the bridge, to the right, is the Indianapolis Zoo. This 64-acre complex is a cageless zoo emphasizing global ecosystems. It is arranged in "biomes," or collections of habitats: Waters, Deserts, Plains, and Forests, plus Encounters (domestic animals from around the world). The zoo has nearly 3,000 animals and 1,700 species of plants and is the only facility in the country accredited as a zoological park, botanical garden, and aquarium. Opened in 1999 adjacent to the zoo, 3.3-acre White River Gardens is a year-round botanical showcase. It provides a secluded haven for more than 1,000 varieties of plants and has a towering conservatory that stages many special floral shows. River Promenade, a ½ mile walkway lined with flowering trees and evergreens, is constructed of more than 1,200 blocks of Indiana limestone. Fourteen of the stones feature carved renderings of famous buildings constructed of Indiana limestone.

Walk left off the bridge toward the NCAA Hall of Champions. From track and field, football, and basketball to water polo and field hockey, the hall covers all 22 sports and 81 national championships administered by the NCAA. Interactive displays recapture great moments in collegiate sports and draw visitors into the action. From here, stroll alongside a new version of historic Central Canal, originally built in 1836 to boost trade. Cross the footbridge and follow the canal to the Congressional Medal of Honor Memorial, the nation's first memorial dedicated to recipients of its highest award for military valor. The one-acre memorial has 27 curved walls of glass, each between seven and ten feet high, representing specific conflicts in which medals were awarded. The glass walls feature names of 3,410 medal recipients. The memorial includes recorded stories of honorees and the conflicts in which they fought. Continuing on, the Eiteljorg Museum is one of only two museums east of the Mississippi with both Native American objects and Western paintings and bronzes. Built with honey-colored stone, it has a distinctive Southwestern look. The museum houses the work of such icons as Remington, Russell, and Georgia O'Keeffe. If time allows, take in a ball game at 15,500-seat Victory Field, named best minor league ballpark in America by *Baseball America* magazine. Try to sit behind home plate for stunning skyline views. The park is home to the Triple-A Indianapolis Indians, top farm team of the Milwaukee Brewers.

1913. Across from Union Station. Cr cds: A, MC, V.

★★★ **RADISSON HOTEL CITY CENTRE.** *31 W Ohio St (46204). 317/635-2000; fax 317/638-0782; toll-free 800/333-3333. www.radisson.com.* 374 rms, 21 story. S $129-$179; D $144-$199; each addl $15; suites $149-$229; under 18 free. Crib free. Garage $8. TV; cable, VCR avail. Pool; poolside serv. Restaurant 6:30 am-midnight. Bar 11-1 am. Ck-out noon. Convention facilities. Business center. Health club privileges. Luxury level. Cr cds: A, MC, V.

★ ★ ★ **RENAISSANCE TOWER.** *230 E 9th St (46204). 317/261-1652; fax 317/262-8648; res 800/676-7786. www.rentowerinn.com.* 80 kit. units, 6 story. S $85-$225; D $95-$235; higher rates special events. TV; cable. Complimentary coffee in rms. Ck-out noon. Business servs avail. In-rm modem link. Valet serv. Coin lndry. Microwaves. Cr cds: A, D, DS, MC, V.

★ ★ ★ **SHERATON INDIANAPOLIS HOTEL & SUITES.** *8787 Keystone Crossing (46240). 317/846-2700; toll-free 800/325-3535.* 560 rms, 15 story. S, D $175-$350; each addl $25; under 17 free. Crib avail. Indoor pool. TV; cable (premium), VCR avail. Complimentary coffee, newspaper in rms. Restaurant 6 am-10 pm. Ck-out noon. Meeting rms. Business center. Gift shop. Exercise rm. Some refrigerators, minibars. Cr cds: A, C, D, DS, MC, V.

★ ★ ★ **UNIVERSITY PLACE.** *850 W Michigan St (46202). 317/269-9000; fax 317/231-5178; toll-free 800/627-2700.* 278 rms, 10 story. Mar-May, Sept-Nov: S, D $184; suites $250-$600; lower rates rest of yr. Crib avail. Garage parking $6. TV; cable (premium). Coffee in rms. Restaurant 6 am-midnight. Bar from 11 am. Ck-out noon. Convention facilities. Business center. In-rm modem link. Gift shop. Barber. Health club privileges. Refrigerators. Cr cds: A, C, D, DS, MC, V.

★ ★ ★ **WESTIN INDIANAPOLIS.** *50 S Capitol Ave (46204). 317/262-8100; fax 317/231-3997; toll-free 800/228-3000. www.westin.com.* 573 rms, 15 story. S $211; D $240; each addl $30; suites $225-$1,000; under 13 free. Crib free. Valet, garage parking $13. TV; cable, VCR avail. Indoor pool; whirlpool. Restaurant 6:30 am-11 pm. Rm serv 24 hrs. Bar 11-2 am, Sun to midnight. Ck-out noon. Convention facilities. Business center. In-rm modem link. Concierge. Exercise equipt. Health club privileges. Some bathrm phones, minibars. Luxury level. Cr cds: A, MC, V.

All Suites

★ ★ ★ **EMBASSY SUITES.** *110 W Washington St (46204). 317/236-1800; fax 317/236-1816; 800/362-2779. www.embassysuites.com.* 360 suites, 18 story. S $159-$179; D $179-$229; under 18 free. Crib free. Parking in/out $5. TV; cable, VCR avail. Indoor pool; whirlpool. Complimentary full bkfst. Complimentary coffee in rms. Restaurant 11 am-10 pm; Sat, Sun from 5 pm. Bar to 1 am. Ck-out noon. Convention facilities. Business servs avail. In-rm modem link. Shopping arcade. Exercise equipt. Refrigerators, microwaves. Cr cds: A, D, DS, MC, V.

★ ★ ★ **EMBASSY SUITES.** *3912 Vincennes Rd (46268). 317/872-7700; fax 317/872-2974; toll-free 800/362-2779. www.embassy-suites.com.* 221 suites, 8 story. S $109-$159; D $109-$174; under 12 free; wkend rates. Crib avail. TV; cable (premium). Indoor pool; whirlpool. Complimentary full bkfst; afternoon refreshments. Complimentary coffee in rms. Restaurant 11 am-2 pm, 5-11 pm. Bar from 4 pm. Ck-out noon. Meeting rms. Business servs avail. In-rm modem link. Gift shop. Exercise equipt; sauna. Game rm. Refrigerators, microwaves. Cr cds: A, C, D, DS, JCB, MC, V.

Restaurants

★ **ARISTOCRAT PUB.** *5212 N College Ave (46220). 317/283-7388. www.indyfood.com.* Hrs: 11 am-11 pm; Wed, Thurs to midnight; Fri, Sat to 1 am; Sun from 10 am; Sun brunch to 3 pm. Closed hols. Bar. Lunch, dinner $4.95-$14.95. Sun brunch $4.95-$7. Child's menu. Specializes in pasta. Parking. Outdoor dining. Casual atmosphere. Cr cds: A, D, DS, MC, V.

★ ★ **DADDY JACK'S.** *9419 N Meridian St (46260). 317/843-1609.* Hrs: 11 am-10 pm; Sat 5-11 pm. Closed Sun; hols. Res accepted. Bar. Lunch $5-$10.95, dinner $12.95-$29.95. Specializes in seafood, sushi. Parking.

Outdoor dining. Nautical decor. Cr cds: A, D, DS, MC, V.

⊡ ⊟

★★ **GLASS CHIMNEY.** *12901 Old Meridian St, Carmel (46032). 317/844-0921.* Hrs: 5-10 pm; Fri, Sat to 11 pm. Closed Sun; Thanksgiving, Dec 25. Res accepted. Continental menu. Bar. Dinner $15-$38. Specializes in veal, seafood, steak. Outdoor dining. Elegant European decor. Cr cds: A, C, D, DS, MC, V.

★★ **HOLLYHOCK HILL.** *8110 N College Ave (46240). 317/251-2294.* Hrs: 5-8 pm; Sun noon-7:30 pm. Closed Mon; July 4, Dec 24, 25. Res accepted. Serv bar. Complete meals: dinner $12.95-$17.50. Child's menu. Specializes in chicken, seafood, steak. Tea room atmosphere. Family-owned. Cr cds: A, MC, V.

⊡

★★ **MAJESTIC OYSTER.** *47 S Pennsylvania (46204). 317/636-5418. www. indymenu.com.* Hrs: 11 am-2 pm, 5-8:30 pm; Fri, Sat 5-9 pm. Closed Sun; hols. Res accepted. Continental menu. Bar. Lunch $6-$17.95, dinner $12.95-$38.95. Child's menu. Specializes in seafood, steak, chicken. Own pasta, pastries. Old building with beveled, leaded glass, Tiffany fixtures, handcarved bar. Cr cds: A, C, D, DS, MC, V.

⊡ ⊟

★★★ **PETER'S.** *8505 Keystone Crossing Blvd (46240). 317/465-1155.* Hrs: 5-10 pm; Fri, Sat to 10:30 pm. Closed Sun; hols. Res accepted. Bar. A la carte entrees: dinner $12.95-$23.95. Specializes in Indiana duckling, fresh fish, desserts. Parking. Cr cds: A, D, MC, V.

⊡ ⊟

★★★ **RESTAURANT AT THE CANTERBURY.** *123 S Illinois (46255). 317/634-3000. www.canterburyhotel. com.* Hrs: 7-10:30 am, 11:30 am-2 pm, 5:30-10 pm; Fri, Sat to 11 pm; Sun brunch 10:30 am-2 pm. Res accepted. Continental menu. Bar. Wine list. A la carte entrees: bkfst $4.50-$14.95, lunch $6.95-$14.95, dinner $16.50-$29.50. Sun brunch $6.95-$13.95. Specializes in seafood, veal. Own baking. Valet parking.

International decor; artwork. Jacket (dinner). Cr cds: A, C, D, DS, MC, V.

⊡ ⊟

★★ **ST. ELMO STEAK HOUSE.** *127 S Illinois (46225). 317/637-1811.* Hrs: 4-10:30 pm; Sun 5-9:30 pm. Closed hols. Res accepted. Bar. Dinner $19.95-$37.95. Specializes in steak, fresh seafood. Turn-of-the-century decor, historic photographs. Cr cds: A, D, DS, MC, V.

⊡ ⊟

Jasper (F-3)

Pop 10,030 **Elev** 472 ft **Area code** 812 **Zip** 47546

Information Dubois County Tourism Commission, 610 Main St, 2nd Fl; 812/482-9115 or 800/968-4578

Web www.duboiscounty.org

What to See and Do

Monastery of the Immaculate Conception. (1867) Historic monastery, home to the Sisters of St. Benedict, is located on 190 acres. The church, one of the most famous examples of Romanesque architecture in the country, features brilliant stained-glass windows, handsome wood panels and pews hand-carved in Oberammergau, and an interior dome rising 87 ft from the marble floor. An information office at the main entrance has historical display, a scale model of the entire complex and a video about the monastery. Guided tours (by appt). Monastery (daily). S on IN 162, in Ferdinand at 802 E 10th St. Phone 812/367-1411.

Motels/Motor Lodges

★★ **BEST WESTERN DUTCHMAN INN.** *406 E 22nd St, Huntingburg (47542). 812/683-2334; fax 812/683-8474; toll-free 800/926-2334. www. bestwestern.com.* 89 rms, 2 story. S, D $49-$89; under 18 free. Crib free. TV; cable (premium). Pool; wading pool. Restaurant 6 am-2 pm. Bar 4-11 pm. Ck-out 11 am, ck-in 2 pm. Meeting rms. Business servs avail. Valet serv.

Refrigerators, microwaves avail. Cr cds: A, C, D, DS, MC, V.

D ⚊ ⊠ 🖐 SC

★ **DAYS INN.** *IN 162 & IN 164 (47546). 812/482-6000; fax 812/482-7207; toll-free 800/325-2525. www. daysinn.com.* 84 rms, 2 story. S $56-$77; D $67-$77; each addl $6; under 18 free. Crib free. Pet accepted, some restrictions; $5. TV; cable (premium), VCR avail. Pool. Complimentary continental bkfst. Restaurant adj. Ck-out noon. Meeting rms. Business servs avail. Valet serv. Sundries. Some refrigerators. Cr cds: A, D, DS, MC, V.

D 🐾 ⚊ ⊠ 🖐

★ ★ **HOLIDAY INN.** *951 Wernsing Rd (47547). 812/482-5555; fax 812/482-7908; toll-free 800/872-3176. www.holiday-inn.com.* 200 rms, 2 story. May-Aug: S, D $99-$125; under 19 free; lower rates rest of yr. Crib free. TV; cable (premium). Indoor pool; wading pool, whirlpool. Restaurant 6 am-2 pm, 5-9 pm. Bar 3 pm-1:30 am, closed Sun. Ck-out noon. Coin lndry. Convention facilities. Business servs avail. In-rm modem link. Game rm. Rec rm. Exercise equipt; sauna. Cr cds: A, C, D, DS, JCB, MC, V.

D ⚊ 🏋 ⊠ 🖐 SC

Restaurant

★ ★ **SCHNITZELBANK.** *393 Third Ave (47546). 812/482-2640.* Hrs: 8 am-10 pm. Closed Sun; hols. German, American menu. Bar to 11 pm. Bkfst, lunch $3-$6.95, dinner $5.50-$19.95. Specializes in steak, seafood. Salad bar. Bavarian decor. Cr cds: DS, MC, V.

D SC ⫟

Jeffersonville

(G-5) *See also New Albany*

Founded 1802 **Pop** 21,841 **Elev** 448 ft
Area code 812 **Zip** 47130
Information Southern Indiana Convention and Tourism Bureau, 315 Southern Indiana Ave; 812/282-6654 or 800/552-3842
Web www.sunnysideoflouisville.org

Jeffersonville, on the north bank of the Ohio River and opposite Louisville, KY, has a proud history as a shipbuilding center. One of the oldest towns in Indiana, it was built according to plans by Thomas Jefferson. The city is an industrial manufacturing center and a terminal for the American Commercial Line, Inc, a large river transportation company. Grain, tobacco, strawberries, and dairy goods are the main farm products in surrounding Clark County.

What to See and Do

Colgate Clock. Said to be the second-largest clock in the world (40 ft in diameter). Atop the Clarksville Colgate-Palmolive plant.

Howard Steamboat Museum. Housed in 22-rm mansion featuring stained- and leaded-glass windows, hand-carved panels, brass chandeliers, a grand stairway, Victorian furniture (1893); steamboat models, shipyard artifacts and tools, pictures, and other memorabilia (1834-1941). Tours (Tues-Sun; closed hols). 1101 E Market St. Phone 812/283-3728. ¢¢

Special Events

Victorian Chautauqua. Howard Steamboat Museum. Victorian-style cafe, speakers, children's activities. Phone 812/283-3728. Mid-May.

Steamboat Days Festival. On the riverfront, downtown. Parade, entertainment, 5K run. Phone 812/282-6654. Early or mid-Sept.

Motels/Motor Lodges

★ ★ **BEST WESTERN GREEN TREE INN.** *1425 Broadway, Clarksville (47129). 812/288-9281; toll-free 800/950-9281. www.bestwestern.com.* 107 rms. S $59; D $69; each addl $5. Crib free. Pet accepted, some restrictions. TV; cable (premium). Pool. Restaurant adj open 24 hrs. Ck-out noon. Business servs avail. In-rm modem link. Health club privileges. Bathrm phones. Cr cds: A, C, D, DS, MC, V.

D 🐾 ⚊ ⊠ 🖐

★ ★ **HOLIDAY INN LAKEVIEW.** *505 Marriott Dr, Clarksville (47129). 812/283-4411; fax 812/288-8976; toll-free 800/544-7075. www.holiday-inn. com.* 356 rms, 3-10 story. S $72; D

$78; each addl $6; suites $90-$200; under 18 free; wkend rates. Crib free. TV; cable. 2 pools, 1 indoor; poolside serv. Playground. Coffee in rms. Restaurant 6:30 am-2 pm, 5-10 pm. Bar 11-1 am; entertainment. Ck-out noon. Coin lndry. Convention facilities. Business servs avail. Gift shop. Barber, beauty shop. Free airport transportation. Tennis. Miniature golf. Exercise equipt. Refrigerator in suites. Private patios, balconies. Picnic tables. Heliport. Scenic grounds with lake view. Cr cds: A, MC, V.

★★ **RAMADA INN.** *700 W Riverside Dr (47130). 812/284-6711; fax 812/283-3686; toll-free 888/298-2054. www.ramada.com.* 187 units, 10 story, 20 suites. S $72; D $82; each addl $10; suites $95-$145; under 18 free. Crib free. Pet accepted, some restrictions. TV; cable (premium). Pool. Restaurant 6:30 am-2 pm, 5-10 pm. Bar 5 pm-2 am. Ck-out noon. Meeting rms. Business servs avail. Free airport transportation. Game rm. On Ohio River. Cr cds: A, C, D, DS, ER, JCB, MC, V.

Kokomo

(C-4) *See also Logansport, Peru*

Founded 1842 **Pop** 44,962 **Elev** 810 ft
Area code 765
Information Kokomo Indiana Visitors Bureau, 1504 N Reed Rd, 46901; 765/457-6802 or 800/837-0971
Web www.kokomo-in.org

This is a lively manufacturing center where the first clutch-driven automobile with electric ignition was invented by Elwood Haynes. Since then Kokomo manufacturers have invented several more useful items, from the first pneumatic rubber tire to canned tomato juice. The automobile industry is represented by Delphi-Delco Electronics and Chrysler plants, which manufacture automotive entertainment systems, semiconductor devices, transmissions, and aluminum die castings. Indiana University has a branch

here, and Grissom Air Reserve Base is located 14 miles north of town.

What to See and Do

Elwood Haynes Museum. Home of Elwood Haynes; memorabilia, items relating to early development of the automobile; 1905 and 1924 Haynes cars on display; industrial exhibits; also Haynes Stellite (alloy used in space ships). (Tues-Sun; closed hols) 1915 S Webster St. Phone 765/456-7500. **FREE**

Haynes Memorial. Pumpkinvine Pike is site of the first successful road test of Haynes' car. 3 mi E, off US 31 Bypass. Phone 765/456-7500.

Highland Park. County's last covered bridge was moved here from Vermont. Recreational facilities. (Daily) 1402 W Defenbaugh St. Phone 765/456-7275. **FREE** Also in park are

"Old Ben". An enormous, stuffed Hereford steer that weighed 4,720 pounds, was 16 ft, 8 inches long and 6 ft, 4 inches high. His life ended in 1910, at the height of his fame, when he slipped and fell on ice.

Sycamore stump. The original tree died in the early 1900s, leaving a stump that measures 51 ft in circumference. The interior of the stump has held 24 people and once served as a telephone booth. Phone 765/456-7275.

Seiberling Mansion. (1891) This late-Victorian mansion houses exhibits of historical and educational interest; county history; manufacturing artifacts. (Tues-Sun, afternoons; closed hols; also Jan) 1200 W Sycamore St. Phone 765/452-4314. ¢

Special Events

Greentown Glass Festival. E on I-35, in downtown Greentown. Commemorates the production of Greentown Glass. Carnival, beauty pageant, antique show, many events. Second wkend June. Phone 765/628-6206.

Haynes Apperson Festival. Entertainment, crafts, parade, carnival. July 4 wkend. Phone 800/456-1106.

Howard County Fair. Greentown fairgrounds. Last wk July. Phone 765/628-3247.

Motels/Motor Lodges

★★ **FAIRFIELD INN.** *1717 E Lincoln (46902). 765/453-8822; fax 765/453-8822; toll-free 800/228-2800. www.fairfieldinn.com.* 61 rms, 3 story, 20 suites. S $65-$70; D $69-$76; each addl $5; suites $79; under 18 free; higher rates special events. TV; cable (premium). Complimentary continental bkfst. Ck-out noon. Meeting rm. Business servs avail. In-rm modem link. Indoor pool; whirlpool. Health club privileges. Game rm. Some refrigerators, microwaves. Cr cds: A, D, DS, MC, V.
D ⌫ ⊠ ⊕ SC

★★ **HAMPTON INN AND SUITES.** *2920 S Reed Rd (46902). 765/455-2900; fax 765/455-2800; toll-free 800/426-7866. www.hampton-inn.com.* 105 rms, 5 story, 31 kit. suites. S $73; D $80; suites $115; under 18 free; higher rates special events. Crib free. Pet accepted. TV; cable (premium), VCR avail (movies). Complimentary continental bkfst. Complimentary coffee in rms. Meeting rms. Business servs avail. In-rm modem link. Valet serv. Sundries. Gift shop. Grocery store. Coin lndry. Exercise equipt. Health club privileges. Indoor pool. Cr cds: A, C, D, DS, JCB, MC, V.
D ⊕ ⊠ ⊕ SC ⌫ 大

★★ **HOLIDAY INN EXPRESS.** *511 Albany Dr (46904). 765/453-2222; fax 765/453-4398; toll-free 800/465-4329. www.holiday-inn.com.* 79 rms, 3 story. S, D $79-$86; suites $105-$160; under 19 free; higher rates special events. Crib free. TV; cable (premium). Complimentary continental bkfst. Coffee in rms. Restaurant opp 11 am-11 pm. Ck-out 11 am, ck-in 3 pm. Meeting rms. Business servs avail. In-rm modem link. Coin lndry. Exercise equipt. Indoor pool. Bathrm phones, refrigerators, microwaves, wet bars; some in-rm whirlpools, fireplaces. Cr cds: A, MC, V.
D ⌫ 大 ⊠ ⊕ SC

★ **MOTEL 6.** *2808 S Reed Rd (46902). 765/457-8211; fax 765/454-9774; toll-free 800/466-8356. www.motel6.com.* 93 rms, 2 story. S $39-$45; D $45-$51; each addl $3; under 18 free; higher rates Indianapolis 500; wkend (2-day min). Crib free. Pet accepted, some restrictions. TV; cable. Complimentary coffee. Restaurant adj 6 am-11 pm. Ck-out noon. Cr cds: A, D, DS, MC, V.
D ⊕ ⊠ ⊕

★★ **RAMADA INN.** *1709 E Lincoln Rd (46902). 765/459-8001; fax 765/457-6636; toll-free 800/228-2828. www.ramada.com.* 132 rms, 3 story. S $55-$89; D $60-$95; each addl $10; under 18 free; wkend rates; higher rates Indianapolis 500; wkend (2-day min). Crib free. TV; cable. Indoor pool. Restaurant 6 am-2 pm, 5-10 pm; Sat, Sun from 7 am. Bar 4 pm-1 am, Thurs-Sat to 2 am, Sun to midnight; entertainment. Ck-out noon. Meeting rms. Business servs avail. Free airport transportation. Exercise equipt; sauna. Health club privileges. Picnic tables. Cr cds: A, C, D, DS, MC, V.
D ⌫ 大 ⊠ ⊕

★ **SIGNATURE INN.** *4021 S LaFountain St (46902). 765/455-1000; fax 765/455-1000; toll-free 800/822-5252. www.signatureinn.com.* 101 rms, 2 story. S, D $79-$88; under 17 free; wkend rates; higher rates: Indy 500. Crib free. Indoor pool; whirlpool. Complimentary continental bkfst. Ck-out noon. Meeting rms. Cr cds: A, D, DS, MC, V.
D ⌫ ⊠ ⊕

Restaurant

★★ **SYCAMORE GRILLE.** *115 W Sycamore (46901). 765/457-2220.* Hrs: 11 am-9 pm; Fri, Sat to 10 pm. Closed Sun; hols. Res accepted. Bar. Lunch $5-$10, dinner $8-$20. Child's menu. Specializes in seafood, pasta, beef. Street parking. Turn-of-the-century decor. Cr cds: A, D, MC, V.
D ⊠

Lafayette (C-3)

Founded 1825 **Pop** 43,764 **Elev** 560 ft
Area code 765

Information Convention and Visitors Bureau, 301 Frontage Rd, 47905-4564; 765/447-9999 or 800/872-6648

Web www.lafayette-in.com

Lafayette, on the east bank of the Wabash River, was named for the Marquis de Lafayette, who served as a general under George Washington in the Revolutionary War.

The city is surrounded by an extensive farm area, including cattle and dairy farms. A large number of diversified industries in the area manufacture automotive gears and supplies, electrical equipment, and pharmaceuticals. On the west bank of the river in West Lafayette is Purdue University. Established as an agricultural college in 1869, Purdue is also noted for many other programs, especially engineering.

What to See and Do

Clegg Botanical Garden. Approx 15 acres of rugged terrain with glacier-made ridges, native trees and wildflowers, ravines; nature trails, lookout point. (Daily) E on IN 25 to County Rd 300N, then 1 mi E to County Rd 400E, then 1¼ mi S. Phone 765/423-1325. **FREE**

Columbian Park. Zoo (daily; closed Thanksgiving, Dec 25). Amusement park; outdoor theater; water slide, swimming pool; tennis courts; concession, picnicking. Facilities (Memorial Day-Labor Day, Tues-Sun). Park (daily). Some fees. 5 mi SW via I-65, to IN 26 Lafayette exit. Phone 765/771-2220. **FREE**

Fort Ouiatenon. (1717) A 30-acre park; replica blockhouse with 18th-century French trading post. Museum depicts history of French, Native American, British, and American struggles to control Wabash Valley. (Seasonal) (See SPECIAL EVENTS) Picnicking, boating. Park (daily). 4 mi SW of West Lafayette on S River Rd. Phone 765/743-3921. **FREE**

Greater Lafayette Museum of Art. Maintains permanent collection of 19th- and 20th-century American art; East and Weil Galleries present contemporary and historical exhibits. Rental gallery, library, gift shop, children's activity area. Art classes, lectures, and workshops. (Tues-Sun afternoons; closed hols, Aug) 101 S 9th St. Phone 765/742-1128. **FREE**

Purdue University. (1869) 38,208 students. More than 140 major buildings on 1,579 acres with private airport. In West Lafayette via I-65, IN 26. Contact Visitor Information Center; 765/494-4636.

Tippecanoe Battlefield Museum and Park. Site of 1811 battle in which soldiers and local militia led by General William H. Harrison, territorial governor of Indiana, defeated a confederation of Native Americans headed by The Prophet, brother of Tecumseh. Wabash Heritage Trail begins here. (See SPECIAL EVENTS) (Daily) I-65 at IN 43 exit, in Battle Ground. Phone 765/567-2147. ¢

Tippecanoe County Historical Museum. Collection of Americana, period rms, topic exhibits, housed in an English Gothic-style mansion (1852). (Tues-Sun; closed hols, Jan) 909 South St. Phone 765/476-8411. ¢¢

Wolf Park. Education/research facility, home to several packs of wolves, a small herd of bison, some coyotes, and foxes. See wolves close at hand as they eat and socialize. (May-Nov, Tue-Sun afternoons; closed hols) Also "wolf howl" (all yr, Sat evenings; inquire for hrs). 10 mi NE via I-65, exit 178 or IN 43. Phone 765/567-2265. ¢¢

Special Events

Fiddlers' Gathering. Tippecanoe Battlefield. Old-time folk and country musicians from across the country. Late June. Phone 765/742-1419.

Feast of the Hunters' Moon. Fort Ouiatenon. Reenactment of life 250 yrs ago. Features French, English, and Native American lifestyles. Phone 765/476-8402. Early Oct.

Motels/Motor Lodges

★ ★ **FAIRFIELD INN.** *4000 IN 26 E (47905).* 765/449-0083; toll-free 888/236-2427. www.fairfieldinn.com. 79 rms, 3 story, 11 suites. S $65-$75; D $70-$85; each addl $10; suites $75-$85; under 18 free; higher rates special events. Crib free. TV; cable (premium). Complimentary continental bkfst. Restaurant adj 6 am-11 pm. Ck-out noon. Meeting rms. Business servs avail. In-rm modem link. Health club privileges. Indoor pool; whirlpool. Game rm. Refrigerator, microwave in suites. Cr cds: A, D, DS, MC, V.

D ⊠ ⇘ ᴺ 🐾

★★ **HOLIDAY INN.** *I-65 & IN 43 N, West Lafayette (47906). 765/567-2131; fax 765/567-2511. www.holiday-inn. com.* 150 rms, 4 story. S $58-$78; D $62-$80; each addl $6; under 18 free; higher rates: special events. Crib free. Pet accepted. TV. Indoor pool. Restaurant 6 am-10 pm. Bar 4 pm-1 am. Ck-out 11 am, ck-in 3 pm. Free guest lndry. Meeting rms. Valet serv. Golf privileges. Sauna. Health club privileges. Game rm. Cr cds: MC, V.

★★ **HOMEWOOD SUITES BY HILTON.** *3939 IN 26 E (47905). 765/448-9700; fax 765/449-1297; toll-free 800/225-5466. www.homewood-suites.com.* 84 kit. suites, 3 story. S, D $95; under 18 free; higher rates: university events, Indy 500. Crib free. Pet accepted, some restrictions. TV; cable, VCR (movies). Heated pool; whirlpool. Complimentary continental bkfst. Complimentary coffee in rms. Restaurant nearby. Ck-out noon. Coin lndry. Meeting rms. Business center. In-rm modem link. Sundries. Gift shop. Free airport, RR station, bus depot transportation. Exercise equipt; sauna. Health club privileges. Lawn games. Microwaves. Cr cds: A, C, D, DS, ER, JCB, MC, V.

★★ **LEES INN.** *4701 Meijer Ct (47905). 765/447-3434; fax 765/448-6105; toll-free 800/733-5337. www.leesinn.com.* 81 rms, 3 story. S $74-$119; D $89-$139; each addl $10; suites $99-$250; under 16 free; higher rates Indy 500. Crib free. TV; cable (premium). Complimentary continental bkfst. Restaurant opp 6 am-10 pm. Ck-out noon. Meeting rms. Business servs avail. In-rm modem link. Indoor pool; whirlpool. Refrigerators, wet bars. Cr cds: A, D, DS, MC, V.

★★ **RAMADA INN.** *4221 IN 26 E (47905). 765/447-9460; fax 765/447-4905; toll-free 800/272-6232. www.ramada.com.* 143 rms, 4 story. S $73-$99; D $77-$99; each addl $7; suites $95-$155; under 18 free; wkend rates; higher rates special events. Crib free. Pet accepted, some restrictions. TV; cable, VCR avail (movies). Complimentary continental bkfst. Complimentary coffee in rms. Restaurant 11 am-midnight. Bar. Ck-out noon. Meeting rms. Business servs avail. In-rm modem link. Valet serv. Coin lndry. Exercise equipt. Pool. Lawn games. Cr cds: A, C, D, DS, JCB, MC, V.

★ **SIGNATURE INN.** *4320 IN 26E (47905). 765/447-4142; toll-free 800/822-5252. www.signatureinn.com.* 150 rms, 2 story. S $75; D $85; under 18 free; higher rates: Indy 500; football wkends. Crib free. TV; cable. Pool. Complimentary continental bkfst. Restaurant nearby. Ck-out noon. Meeting rms. Business servs avail. Cr cds: A, D, DS, MC, V.

★★★ **UNIVERSITY INN & CONFERENCE CENTER.** *3001 Northwestern Ave, West Lafayette (47906). 765/463-5511; fax 765/497-3850; toll-free 800/777-9808.* 149 rms, 3 story. S, D $68-$70; each addl $5; suites $100-$200; under 18 free; higher rates: motor races, football wkends (2-day min), university events. Crib free. TV; cable. Indoor pool; whirlpool. Restaurant 5:30-9:30 pm; Fri, Sat to 11 pm. Bar 4-11 pm. Ck-out 11 am. Meeting rms. Business servs avail. Free airport transportation. Exercise equipt. Microwave in suites. Garden atrium. Cr cds: A, D, DS, MC, V.

Hotel

★★★ **RADISSON INN.** *4343 IN 26 E (47905). 765/447-0575; fax 765/447-0901; toll-free 800/333-3333. www.radisson.com.* 124 rms, 6 story. S, D $59-$189; each addl $10; suites $154; under 18 free; higher rates: Indianapolis 500; university events (2-day min). Crib free. Pet accepted, some restrictions. TV; cable (premium). Indoor pool; whirlpool. Complimentary coffee in rms. Restaurant 6:30 am-2 pm, 5-9:30 pm. Rm serv. Bar 4 pm-midnight; pianist Fri, Sat. Ck-out noon. Coin lndry. Meeting rms. In-rm modem link. Valet serv. Sauna. Refrigerators. Cr cds: A, D, DS, JCB, MC, V.

B&B/Small Inn

★★ **LOEB HOUSE B & B.** *708 Cincinnati St (47901). 765/420-7737; fax 765/420-7805. www.loebhouseinn. com.* 5 rms, 3 story, 1 suite. No elvtr. S, D, suites $85-$175. Pet accepted. TV. Complimentary full bkfst. Ck-out 11 am, ck-in 4 pm. Business servs avail. In-rm modem link. Health club privileges. Some in-rm whirlpools, fireplaces. Built in 1882; antiques. Totally nonsmoking. Cr cds: A, MC, V.

La Porte

(A-3) *See also Michigan City, South Bend*

Founded 1832 **Pop** 21,507 **Elev** 807 ft
Area code 219 **Zip** 46350
Information Greater La Porte Chamber of Commerce, 414 Lincolnway, PO Box 486; 219/362-3178
Web www.lpchamber.com

This is a busy manufacturing center and a popular resort area in both winter and summer. City lakes offer fishing, ice fishing, snowmobiling, and other recreational activities. Seven lakes with fishing and boating facilities border the town on the north and west. Chief industrial products are industrial fans, coil coating, corrugated and plastic containers, rubber products, and iron and metal castings.

What to See and Do

Door Prairie Museum. Collection covers over 100 yrs of automobiles, incl models by Citroen, Ford, Mercedes Benz, Rolls Royce, Tucker. (Apr-Dec, Tues-Sun) 2405 Indiana Ave, 1 mi S on US 35. Phone 219/326-1337. ¢¢

Kingsbury Fish and Wildlife Area. Approx 8,000 acres of state hunting and fishing areas with access to Kankakee River and Tamarack Lake. Area incl boating, canoeing; nature trails, archery range, shooting range, hunting, picnicking, bird-watching. Mixsawbah State Fish Hatchery adj. (Daily) 5 mi SE via US 35, exit County 500 S. Phone 219/393-3612.

La Porte County Historical Society Museum. Period rms, archives, antique gun collection. (Tues-Sat; closed hols) County Complex. 809 State St. Phone 219/326-6808. **FREE**

Special Event

La Porte County Fair. Fairgrounds. Exhibits, livestock judging, harness races, shows, food, rides. Phone 219/362-2647. July.

Motel/Motor Lodge

★★ **RAMADA INN.** *444 Pine Lake Ave (46350). 219/362-4585; fax 219/324-6993. www.ramada.com.* 146 rms, 2-4 story. S $59-$99; D $69-$99; each addl $10; under 18 free; higher rates special events. Crib free. Pet accepted; $25. TV; cable (premium). Indoor/outdoor pool; whirlpool, poolside serv. Complimentary continental bkfst. Restaurant 7 am-2 pm, 5-9 pm. Bar 5 am-midnight; wkend hrs vary. Ck-out noon. Meeting rms. Business servs avail. In-rm modem link. Gift shop. Beauty shop. Downhill ski 12 mi; x-country ski 5 mi. Exercise equipt; sauna. Rec rm. Game rm. Cr cds: A, C, D, DS, MC, V.

B&B/Small Inn

★★★ **ARBOR HILL.** *263 W Johnson Rd (46350). 219/362-9200; fax 219/326-1778. www.arborhillinn.com.* 7 rms, 3 with shower only, 3 story, 4 suites. S, D $71-$119; suites $139-$229; higher rates special events. Crib free. TV; cable (premium). Complimentary full bkfst. Ck-out 11 am, ck-in 4 pm. Business servs avail. In-rm modem link. Luggage handling. Downhill ski 10 mi; x-country ski 1 mi. Refrigerators. In-rm whirlpool, fireplace in suites. Some balconies. Built in 1910; Greek Revival, turn-of-the-century design. Cr cds: A, DS, MC, V.

Restaurant

★ **REED'S STATE STREET PUB.** *502 State St (46350). 219/326-8339.*

Hrs: 11 am-2 pm, 5-9 pm; Fri, Sat to 10 pm. Closed Sun; Jan 1, Dec 25. Res accepted. Bar. Lunch $4.95-$10, dinner $6.95-$18.95. Child's menu. Specializes in prime rib, steak, pasta. Historic art prints, stained-glass church windows. Cr cds: A, DS, MC, V.

D

Lincoln Boyhood National Memorial & Lincoln State Park

See also Santa Claus

(4 mi W of Santa Claus on IN 162)

Lincoln spent his boyhood years (1816-1830) in this area, reading books, clerking at James Gentry's store, and helping his father with farm work. When Lincoln was 21, his family moved to Illinois, where his political career began. The 200-acre wooded and landscaped park includes the grave of Nancy Hanks Lincoln, mother of Abraham Lincoln. She was 35 years old, and Abraham was 9, when she died on October 5, 1818.

The Memorial Visitor Center has information available on the park, including the Cabin Site Memorial, the park's two miles of walking trails, and the gravesite. A film is shown at the visitor center every hour depicting Lincoln's Indiana years. Nearby, on the original Thomas Lincoln tract, is the Lincoln Living Historical Farm, with a furnished log cabin similar to the one the Lincolns lived in, log buildings, animals, and crops of a pioneer farm. Costumed pioneers carry out family living and farming activities typical of an early 19th-century farm. Farm (May-September). (Daily; closed January 1, Thanksgiving, December 25) Phone 812/937-4541. Per person ¢; Per family ¢¢

The park includes approximately 1,700 acres with a 58-acre lake. Swimming, bathhouse, fishing, boating (no motors; rentals); hiking trails, picnic areas, concessions, primitive and improved camping, cabins, group camp. Naturalist service (June-August). Standard fees. Phone 812/937-4710 or 812/937-4541.

The Lincoln Amphitheatre has an outdoor musical/theatrical production about the life of Lincoln when he lived in Indiana between the ages of 7 and 21. Drama is in a covered amphitheater near the site of Lincoln's home. (Mid-June-mid-August, Tuesday-Sunday) Phone 800/264-4-ABE.

Logansport

(B-4) *See also Kokomo, Peru*

Founded 1828 **Pop** 16,812 **Elev** 620 ft
Area code 219 **Zip** 46947
Information Logansport/Cass County Chamber of Commerce, 300 E Broadway, Suite 103; 219/753-6388
Web www.logan-casschamber.com

Located at the confluence of the Wabash and Eel rivers, Logansport is situated in the agricultural heartland. An active trading center for more than a century, batteries, auto-related components, and cement are among the commodities produced here. The rivers and many nearby lakes offer fishing and hunting.

The town was named in honor of James Logan, nephew of the famous Shawnee chief, Tecumseh. Captain Logan was fatally wounded by British-led Native Americans after having served with distinction as leader of a company of Native American scouts fighting for the United States in the War of 1812.

What to See and Do

Cass County Historical Museum (Jerolaman-Long House). Antique china collection; Native American artifacts; paintings, local memorabilia. (Tues-Sat and first Sun of month; closed hols) 1004 E Market St. Phone 219/753-3866. **FREE**

France Park. A 500-acre park with waterfall; 100-yr-old log cabin at entrance. Swimming beach (Memorial Day-Labor Day), scuba diving, fishing; nature trail, miniature golf (fee), rockhounding, x-country skiing (fee), snowmobiling, ice fishing, ice skating. Picnicking (shelters). Primitive and improved camping, camp store. (Daily) 4 mi W via US 24. Phone 219/753-2928. ¢

Indiana Beach. Rides, games, arcades; beach, swimming; shops. Cottages and camping. Amusement area (mid-May-Labor Day, daily; early May and early Sept, wkends only). 306 Indiana Beach Dr, approx 20 mi W via US 24, in Monticello. Phone 219/583-4141. ¢

Motel/Motor Lodge

★ ★ **HOLIDAY INN.** 3550 E Market St (46947). 574/753-6351; fax 219/722-1568. www.holiday-inn.com. 95 rms, 2 story. S $60-$86; D $66-$100; each addl $6; suites $125; under 18 free; higher rates Indianapolis 500. Crib free. Pet accepted. TV; cable. Heated pool. Restaurant 6 am-10 pm. Bar 4 pm-midnight. Ck-out noon. Meeting rms. Sundries. Free airport transportation. Cr cds: A, MC, V.

Madison (F-5)

Settled 1809 **Pop** 12,006 **Elev** 497 ft
Area code 812 **Zip** 47250
Information Madison Area Convention and Visitors Bureau, 301 E Main St; 812/265-2956 or 800/559-2956
Web www.visitmadison.org

Between the Ohio River and Crooked Creek, the settlement of Madison grew rapidly during the river transport days of the 1850s and was briefly the largest city in Indiana, with a population of 5,000. Many of the fine homes reflect the architecture of pre-Civil War days in the South. The 555-acre campus of Hanover College (1827) overlooks the river.

What to See and Do

Clifty Falls State Park. From a high, wooded plateau, this 1,360-acre park offers a view of the Ohio River and its traffic, as well as hills on the Kentucky shore. It also contains waterfalls of Clifty Creek and Little Clifty Creek, bedrock exposures, numerous fossil beds, and a deep boulder-strewn canyon reached by the sun at high noon only; variety of wildlife, regional winter vulture roost. Swimming pool (Memorial Day-Labor Day; fee); tennis, picnicking (shelters, fireplaces), playground, concession. Inn in park has lodgings all yr (for res contact PO Box 387; 812/265-4135). Primitive and developed camping (fee). Naturalist service; nature center. 1 mi W on IN 56. Phone 812/265-1331. ¢¢

Dr. William Hutchings Hospital Museum. A 19th-century Greek Revival building, which served as office and hospital of a "horse-and-buggy" doctor in the late 1800s. Furnishings, surgical tools, and medical library. (Mid-Apr-Oct, daily) 120 W 3rd St. Phone 812/265-2967. ¢¢

Jeremiah Sullivan House. (1818) Federal-style furnished home; pioneer kitchen, smokehouse, bake oven. (Mid-Apr-Oct, daily) 304 W 2nd St. Phone 812/265-2967. ¢¢ Nearby is

Talbot-Hyatt Pioneer Garden. Frontier garden incl many regional plants and flowers. Some plants brought from Virginia. (Daily) **FREE**

Lanier State Historic Site. Greek Revival mansion completed in 1844 for James F. D. Lanier, a financier who loaned the state of Indiana a total of $1,040,000 when its treasury was in need during the Civil War. Some original possessions. (Tues-Sun; closed hols) 511 W 1st St, between Elm and Vine. Phone 812/265-3526. **Donation**

Madison Train Station Museum. Eight-sided railroad station from the late 19th century; features two-story waiting rm. Incl various train memorabilia. (Daily) 615 W First St. Phone 812/265-2335. ¢¢

Schofield House. (1809-1814) Two-story, handmade, sun-dried brick tavern-house; early Federal style.

(Apr-Oct, Mon, Tues, Thurs-Sun; candlelight tours by appt) 217 W 2nd St. Phone 812/265-4759. ¢¢

Special Events

Madison In Bloom. Visit several private courtyard gardens throughout the historic downtown during peak spring color. Last wkend Apr and first wkend May. Phone 812/265-2335.

Regatta and Governor's Cup Race. Hydroplanes compete on the Ohio River. Phone 812/265-5000. Late June-early July.

Restaurant

★ ★ **KEY WEST SHRIMP HOUSE.** *117 Ferry St (IN 56) (47250). 812/265-2831.* Hrs: 11 am-2 pm, 5-9 pm; Sun noon-8 pm. Closed Mon. Lunch $4.25-$7.25, dinner $10.45-$20.95. Child's menu. Specializes in seafood, steak. Salad bar. Own desserts. Century-old building; fireplace. Cr cds: A, DS, MC, V.

D ➥

Marion

(C-5) *See also Peru, Wabash*

Settled 1826 **Pop** 32,618
Area code 765
Information Marion/Grant County Convention & Visitors Bureau, 217 S Adams St, 46952; 765/668-5435 or 800/662-9474
Web www.jamesdeancountry.com

An industrial center and farm trading town, Marion lies on the Mississinewa River. Its principal industrial products are automotive parts, video displays and components, plastics, glass, and paper and wire products. Indiana Wesleyan University (1920) is located here.

What to See and Do

Fairmount, Hometown of James Dean. (1950s screen idol) S via I-69, exit 55 then W on IN 26. Phone 765/948-4555. In Fairmount is

James Dean/Fairmount Historical Museum. Contains the most complete collection of articles of James Dean. Also here are exhibits by Jim Davis, creator of the cartoon cat Garfield. (Mar-Nov, Mon-Sat, also Sun afternoons; rest of yr, by appt) 203 E Washington St. Phone 765/948-4555. ¢

The James Dean Memorial Gallery. Extensive collection of memorabilia and archives dealing with the career of James Dean. Exhibit incl clothing from his films, high school yearbooks, original movie posters from around the world. (Daily; closed Jan 1, Thanksgiving, Dec 25) 425 N Main St. Phone 765/948-3326. ¢¢

Matthews Covered Bridge. Cumberland Covered Bridge (1876-1877), 175-ft long, spans the Mississinewa River. 5 mi E via IN 18, S via I-69 then E on IN 26, in Matthews. Phone 765/998-2928.

Miami Indian Historical Site. Large Native American cemetery with memorials; hiking trails, fishing, hunting. (Daily) 7 mi NW via IN 15, then W on 600 N St. Phone 765/668-5435. **FREE**

Mississinewa Lake. 15 mi NW, off IN 15 (see PERU). Phone 765/473-5946.

Special Events

Marion Easter Pageant. Marion Coliseum between Washington and Branson Sts. 2,000 in cast. Eve of Good Friday and Easter Sunday morning. Phone 765/664-3947.

Fairmount Museum Days/Remembering James Dean. James Dean/Fairmount Historical Museum. Large car show, James Dean look-alike contest, parade, downtown street fair. Last full wkend Sept. Phone 765/948-4555.

Mississinewa 1812. Battle re-enactment with period food, crafts, and storytelling. Phone 800/822-1812. Mid-Oct.

Motels/Motor Lodges

★ ★ **COMFORT SUITES.** *1345 N Baldwin Ave (46952). 765/651-1006; fax 765/651-0145; toll-free 800/445-1210. www.comfortsuites.com.* 62 suites. S $74-$99; D $79-$99; each addl $5; under 18 free; higher rates special events. Crib avail. TV; cable (premium). Complimentary continental bkfst. Coffee in rms. Ck-out noon, ck-in 3 pm. Meeting rms. Business servs avail. In-rm modem link. Valet serv. Coin lndry. Exercise equipt; sauna. Indoor pool; whirlpool. Refrigerators, microwaves; some bathrm phones, in-rm whirlpools. Cr cds: A, MC, V.

★★ **HOLIDAY INN MARION.** *501 E 4th St (46952). 765/668-8801; fax 765/662-6827; toll-free 800/465-4329. www.holiday-inn.com.* 121 rms, 5 story. S, D $65-$89; under 19 free. Crib free. TV; cable (premium). Pool. Coffee in rms. Restaurant 6 am-3 pm, 5-10 pm; Sat from 7 am; Sun 7 am-3 pm, 5-9 pm. Bar 4 pm-midnight, closed Sun. Ck-out noon. Meeting rms. Sundries. Cr cds: A, MC, V.

Merrillville (A-2)

Pop 27,257 **Elev** 661 ft **Area code** 219 **Zip** 46410

Information Chamber of Commerce, 255 W 80th Pl; 219/769-8180.

Web www.merrillvillecoc.org

Once a thriving stop-off point for the many wagon trains headed west, Merrillville has left its rural beginnings to become a regional center of commerce; it has also established its identity as a leader in commercial-industrial development. Area parks and nearby agricultural lands provide pleasant surroundings.

What to See and Do

Lemon Lake County Park. Approx 290 acres of recreation facilities adj to Cedar Lake. Park offers fishing, paddleboats; basketball and tennis courts, volleyball, softball fields, hiking/fitness/jogging trails, picnicking (shelters). Arboretum. (Daily) 1 mi E via US 30, then S on IN 55, SW of Crown Point. Phone 219/769-7275. ¢¢

Star Plaza Theatre. 3,400-seat theater hosts top-name performers. Bill changes weekly and offers a variety of entertainers from comedians to rock and roll, jazz, country, and pop artists. (See RADISSON HOTEL) I-65

and US 30. Phone 219/769-6600. ¢¢¢¢

Motels/Motor Lodges

★★ **FAIRFIELD INN.** *8275 Georgia St (46410). 219/736-0500; fax 219/736-5116; toll-free 800/228-2800. www.fairfieldinn.com.* 132 rms, 3 story. S $64; D $69; each addl $3; under 18 free; higher rates wkends. Crib free. TV; cable (premium), VCR avail. Heated pool. Complimentary continental bkfst. Restaurant nearby. Ck-out noon, ck-in 3 pm. Business servs avail. In-rm modem link. Health club privileges. Cr cds: A, MC, V.

★ **RED ROOF INN.** *8290 Georgia St (46410). 219/738-2430; fax 219/738-2436.* 108 rms, 2 story. S $39-$45; D $45-$51; each addl $6; under 18 free. Crib free. TV; cable (premium). Complimentary coffee. Ck-out noon. Business servs avail. In-rm modem link. Cr cds: A, C, D, DS, MC, V.

Hotel

★★★ **RADISSON HOTEL AT STAR PLAZA.** *800 E 81st Ave (46410). 219/769-6311; fax 219/793-9025; toll-free 800/333-3333. www.radisson.com.* 347 rms, 4 story. S $89-$135; D $99-$145; each addl $10; suites $225-$800; under 18 free; package plans. Crib free. Pet accepted. TV; cable (premium), VCR avail (movies). 2 pools, 1 indoor; poolside serv. Playground. Complimentary coffee in rms. Restaurant 6:30 am-10 pm. Bar 11:30-2 am; Sun 5 pm-midnight; entertainment. Ck-out 11 am. Coin lndry. Convention facilities. Business servs avail. In-rm modem link. Shopping arcade. Barber, beauty shop. Valet parking. Exercise equipt. Game rm. Bathrm phones; some refrigerators, in-rm whirlpools, saunas; microwaves avail. Health club privileges. Private patios, balconies. Cr cds: A, D, DS, MC, V.

Restaurant

★★★ **LOUIS' BON APPETIT.** *302 S Main St, Crown Point (46307). 219/663-6363. www.219.com/louis.*

Hrs: 5:30-9:30 pm. Closed Sun, Mon; Dec 24, 25. Res accepted. French menu. Serv bar. Wine list. Dinner $12-$26. Specialties: filet of duck, loin of lamb, pork tenderloin. Own baking. Outdoor dining. In 19th-century mansion; antiques. Cr cds: A, D, DS, MC, V.

D

Michigan City

(A-3) *See also La Porte*

Founded 1833 **Pop** 33,822 **Elev** 600 ft
Area code 219 **Zip** 46360
Information La Porte County Convention & Visitors Bureau, 1503 S Meer Rd; 800/634-2650. There is a visitor center directly off I-94, exit 40B
Web www.harborcountry-in.org

This is Indiana's summer playground on the southeast shore of Lake Michigan. In the center of the famous Indiana sand dunes region, Michigan City offers miles of fine beaches. For fishermen, the lake offers coho salmon (late Mar-Nov), chinook salmon, lake trout, and perch.

What to See and Do

Barker Mansion. (1900) A 38-rm mansion modeled after an English manor house; marble fireplaces; Tiffany glass; Italian sunken garden. Tours (June-Oct, daily; rest of yr, Mon-Fri). 631 Washington St. Phone 219/873-1520. ¢¢

Indiana Dunes National Lakeshore. (see) 1 Seymour H. Knox III Plaza. Phone 716/855-4444.

John G. Blank Center for the Arts. Painting, sculpture, graphic art exhibits of regional, national, and international origin. (Mon-Sat; closed hols) 312 E 8th St. Phone 219/874-4900. **Donation**

Lighthouse Place Outlet Center. More than 135 outlet stores. (Daily) Sixth and Wabash Sts. Phone 219/879-6506.

Washington Park. Swimming beach, yacht basin, marina, fishing; picnic facilities, concession, tennis courts, observation tower. Zoo (daily). Recreational facilities (daily).

Amphitheater (Thurs eve and wkend band concerts in summer). Senior citizens center (Mon-Fri). N end of Franklin St. Phone 219/873-1506. ¢¢ Also here is

Old Lighthouse Museum. (1858) Marine exhibits, Fresnel lens, ship-building tools, local history displays. Site of launching of first submarine on Great Lakes in 1845. (Mar-Dec, Tues-Sun; closed hols) Phone 219/872-6133. ¢

Special Events

Michigan City Summer Festival. City-wide. Parades, concerts, fireworks. Early July. Phone 219/874-9775.

Lakefront Music Fest. Washington Park. Mid-July. Phone 317/327-7177.

Motels/Motor Lodges

★ **AL & SALLY'S.** *3221 W Dunes Hwy (46360). 219/872-9131.* 16 rms. May-late Sept: S $45-$55; D $65-$75; each addl $5; lower rates rest of yr. Crib $5. TV; cable (premium). Heated pool. Playground. Complimentary coffee in rms. Restaurant nearby. Ck-out 11 am. Lighted tennis. Downhill ski 15 mi; x-country ski 3 mi. Lawn games. Refrigerators. Picnic tables. Located in Indiana Dunes National Lakeshore. Cr cds: A, MC, V.

🐾 ⬇ 📼 ⛱ 🔥

★ **BLACKHAWK MOTEL.** *3651 W Dunes Hwy (46360). 219/872-8656; fax 219/872-5427.* 20 rms, showers only. May-Sept: S, D $35-$55; family, wkly, wkend rates; ski plans; lower rates rest of yr. Pet accepted; $20 deposit. TV; cable (premium). Heated pool. Complimentary coffee in lobby. Ck-out 11 am. Downhill/x-country ski 8 mi. Refrigerators. Picnic tables. Cr cds: A, MC, V.

🐾 ⬇ ⛱ 🛏 🔥 SC

★★ **HOLIDAY INN EXECUTIVE CONFERENCE CENTER.** *5820 S Franklin St (46360). 219/879-0311; fax 219/879-2536; toll-free 800/465-4329. www.holiday-inn.com.* 164 rms, 2-3 story. S, D $99-$125; suites $150; under 18 free. Crib free. TV; cable (premium). Indoor pool. Complimentary coffee in lobby. Restaurant 6:30 am-10 pm. Rm serv. Bar 3 pm-1 am; Sun to midnight. Ck-out 11 am. Meeting rms. Business servs avail. Exercise equipt. X-country ski 5 mi.

Health club privileges. Some refrigerators. Balconies. Cr cds: A, C, D, DS, JCB, MC, V.

★ **KNIGHTS INN.** *201 W Kieffer Rd (46360). 219/874-9500; fax 219/874-5122.* 103 rms. Mid-June-mid-Sept: S, kit. units $58-$99; D $68-$99; under 16 free; higher rates special events; lower rates rest of yr. Crib free. Pet accepted, some restrictions. TV; cable (premium). Pool. Complimentary coffee in lobby. Ck-out 11 am. Meeting rm. Some refrigerators. Cr cds: A, C, D, DS, MC, V.

★ **RED ROOF INN.** *110 W Kieffer Rd (46360). 219/874-5251; fax 219/874-5287.* 79 rms, 2 story. S $35-$42; D $41-$48; under 18 free. Crib free. Pet accepted. TV; cable (premium). Complimentary coffee in lobby. Ck-out noon. Business servs avail. In-rm modem link. Sundries. Cr cds: A, C, D, DS, MC, V.

Hotel

★★ **BLUE CHIP HOTEL AND CASINO.** *2 Easy St (46360). 219/879-7711; fax 219/879-6631; toll-free 888/879-7711. www.bluechip-casino. com.* 188 rms, 7 story. S, D $99-$225; each addl $15; under 17 free. Crib avail. TV; cable (premium), VCR avail. Indoor pool. Restaurant open 24 hrs. Ck-out noon. Meeting rms. Business center. Gift shop. Exercise rm. Some refrigerators, minibars. Cr cds: A, C, D, DS, MC, V.

B&Bs/Small Inns

★★★ **CREEKWOOD INN.** *5727 N 600 W (46360). 219/872-8357; toll-free 800/400-1981. www.creekwoodinn. com.* 13 rms, 2 story. S $140-$165; D $150-$175; each addl $16; suite $200. Crib $8. Closed early Jan. TV; VCR avail (movies). Whirlpool. Complimentary continental bkfst. Ck-out noon, ck-in 4 pm. Business servs avail. Downhill ski 20 mi; x-country ski on site. Lawn games. Exercise equipt. Refrigerators; some fireplaces. Some private patios. Reconstructed from remains of early 1800s trading post way station. On 33 wooded acres; hiking trails; near Lake Michigan. Cr cds: A, D, MC, V.

★★ **DUNE LAND BEACH INN.** *3311 Pottawattomie Tr (46360). 219/874-7729; fax 219/874-0053; res 800/423-7729.* 10 rms, 5 with shower only, 2 story. May-Oct: S, D $79-$119; lower rates rest of yr. TV. Complimentary full bkfst. Complimentary coffee in rms. Ck-out 11 am, ck-in 3 pm. Business servs avail. X-country ski 5 mi. Many in-rm whirlpools. On beach. Turn-of-the-century inn built in 1892; country atmosphere. Totally nonsmoking. Cr cds: MC, V.

Restaurant

★★ **BASIL'S LE FRANKLIN RESTAURANT.** *521 Franklin Sq (46360). 219/872-4500. www.basils bistro.com.* Hrs: 11 am-2 pm, 4:30-10 pm; Sat 5:30-10:30 pm. Closed Thanksgiving, Dec 25. Bar. Dinner $13-$24. Specializes in chops, seafood, steak. Entertainment wkends. Paintings by local artists. Family-owned. Cr cds: A, D, DS, MC, V.

Mishawaka

(A-4) See also Elkhart, Goshen, South Bend

Founded 1832 **Pop** 42,608 **Elev** 720 ft
Area code 219

Information South Bend-Mishawaka Convention & Visitors Bureau, 401 E Colfax Ave, Suite 310, PO Box 1677, South Bend 46634-1677; 219/234-0051 or 800/828-7881

Web www.livethelegends.org

Directly east of South Bend, Mishawaka is mainly an industrial city. Divided by the St. Joseph River, it was named for a beautiful daughter of Chief Elkhart of the Shawnee, who lived in this region before 1800.

In the southwestern part of the city is a Belgian quarter populated by some 6,000 Flemish-Dutch speaking citizens, most of whom came to Mishawaka following World War I.

What to See and Do

Hannah Lindahl Children's Museum. Hands-on exhibits with Native American and historical items. Also re-created here is a brick street of stores from the 1800s, a traditional Japanese house, and a Survive Alive House that teaches fire prevention. (Sept-May, Tues-Fri; June, Tues-Thurs; closed July-Aug) 1402 S Main St. Phone 219/254-4540. ¢

Merrifield Park. This 31-acre park features Shiojiri Niwa Friendship Gardens, a 1½-acre Japanese garden. Also swimming, water slide, fishing, boating (launch); ice-skating, playground, picnic area. (Daily) 1000 E Mishawaka Ave. Phone 219/258-1664. ¢¢

100 Center Complex. 35 retail shops; also restaurants, movie theater; lodging, entertainment; arts and crafts festival second wk July. (Daily) 700 Lincoln Way W. Phone 219/259-7861. **FREE**

Special Event

Summerfest. Merrifield Park. Food, arts and crafts, entertainment. Phone 219/258-1664. Fourth Sat June.

Restaurants

★★ **DOC PIERCE'S.** *120 N Main St (46544).* *219/255-7737.* Hrs: 11 am-2 pm, 5-10 pm; Fri, Sat to 11 pm. Closed Sun; hols. Res accepted. Bar. Lunch $3.95-$6.25, dinner $6.25-$14.95. Specializes in aged steak, shrimp. 1920s decor. Cr cds: A, DS, MC, V.
🖪

★ **PAT'S COLONIAL PUB.** *901 W 4th St (46544).* *219/259-8282.* Hrs: 11 am-11 pm; Mon to 9 pm; Sat from 4 pm. Closed Sun; hols. Res accepted. Bar. A la carte entrees: lunch $3.50-$6.75. Complete meals: lunch $5.95-$8.95, dinner $7.95-$19.95. Specializes in steak, lake perch, seafood. Casual dining. Cr cds: A, MC, V.
🅳 🖪

Muncie

(C-5) *See also Anderson, New Castle*

Founded 1818 **Pop** 71,035 **Elev** 950 ft **Area code** 765

Information Muncie-Delaware County Convention & Visitors Bureau, 425 N High St, 47305; 765/284-2700 or 800/568-6862

Web www.muncievisitorsbureau.org

This area was once the home of the Munsee tribe of the Delaware. The town became an agricultural trading center during the first half of the 19th century; with the construction of railroads and the discovery of natural gas it developed into an industrial city. Many industrial plants are located here.

Ball Corporation, which for years produced the famous Ball jars, maintains its international headquarters in Muncie. The five Ball brothers took an active part in the city's life and in many philanthropic undertakings. They also supported a number of other industrial enterprises and contributed substantially to Ball State University.

Muncie became nationally famous in the 1930s as the subject of sociological studies of a "typical" small city by Robert and Helen Lynd, *Middletown* and *Middletown in Transition.*

What to See and Do

Appeal to the Great Spirit. Copy of Cyrus Dallin's famous statue, which stands in front of Boston Museum of Fine Arts. N bank of White River at Walnut St and Granville Ave. Phone 765/747-4845.

Ball Corporation Museum. Extensive collection of rare Ball glass food preserving jars and current company products. (Mon-Fri; closed hols) 345 S High St. Phone 765/747-6100. **FREE**

Ball State University. (1918) 20,300 students. Purchased by the Ball family and presented to the state of Indiana. Campus has a state-of-the-art telecommunication production facility (phone 765/285-1481); planetarium and observatory (phone 765/285-8871 or 765/285-8862; free). Tours. (Mon-Fri) 2000 University

Ave. Phone 765/285-5683. Also on campus are

Christy Woods. A 17-acre biology department laboratory with arboretum, gardens, and greenhouses. Extensive assemblage incl the Wheeler Orchid Collection. Tours (by appt). Phone 765/285-8839. **FREE**

Museum of Art. Collections of 18th- and 19th-century paintings, prints, and drawings; contemporary works; changing exhibits. (Tues-Sun) Fine Arts Building. Phone 765/285-5242. **FREE**

Minnetrista Cultural Center. A 70,000-sq-ft facility exhibiting the history, art, and industry of east central Indiana. Changing exhibits feature Native American history, the family, technology, and art. Nationally touring science exhibits offered each spring and fall. Floral gardens, landscaped lawns, and a historic apple orchard surround the center. (Daily; closed Dec 25) 1200 N Minnetrista Pkwy. Phone 765/282-4848. ¢¢

Muncie Children's Museum. Exhibits allow visitors to explore the world around them in this completely hands-on museum. Outdoor learning center. Changing exhibits. Gift shop. (Tues-Sun; closed hols) 515 S High St. Phone 765/286-1660. ¢¢

Oakhurst Gardens. Six-acre gardens house many naturalized plants. Renovated home (1895) of George, Frances, and Elizabeth Ball has exhibits on gardens and natural history. One-hr guided tours. (Tues-Sun) 1200 N Minnetrista Pkwy. Phone 765/282-4848. ¢¢

Prairie Creek Reservoir. A 2,333-acre park with 1,252-acre lake. Boating (70 mph limit), fishing, swimming (Memorial Day-Labor Day); picnicking, concession, playground, camping. Some fees. 6 mi SE on Burlington Dr. Phone 765/747-4776.

Special Events

Muncie Dragway. 5 mi NE on IN 67 near Albany. Drag racing Sat. Phone 765/789-8470. Apr-Oct.

Delaware County Fair. Fairgrounds, Wheeling Ave. Nine days mid-late July. Phone 765/284-2700.

Motels/Motor Lodges

★ **DAYS INN.** *3509 N Everbrook Ln (47304). 765/288-2311; fax 765/288-0485; toll-free 800/325-2525. www. daysinn.com.* 62 rms, 2 story. S $45-$50; D $50-$65; each addl $5; under 12 free; higher rates: Indianapolis 500, university events. Crib free. Pet accepted; $20 deposit. TV. Complimentary continental bkfst. Restaurant nearby. Ck-out 11 am. Health club privileges. Cr cds: A, C, D, DS, MC, V.
⊡ 🐾 🐾 ✈

★ **LEES INN.** *3302 N Everbrook Ln (47304). 765/282-7557; fax 765/282-0345. www.leesinn.com.* 92 rms, 2 story. S $59; D $67; each addl $8; suites $69-$159; under 16 free; higher rates Indianapolis 500. Crib avail. Pet accepted. Complimentary continental bkfst. Restaurant nearby. Ck-out noon. Meeting rms. Valet serv. Health club privileges. Cr cds: A, D, DS, JCB, MC, V.
⊡ 🐾 ⊠ 🔥

★★ **RAMADA INN.** *3400 S Madison St (47302). 765/288-1911; fax 765/282-9458; toll-free 800/272-6232. www.ramada.com.* 148 rms, 2 story. S, D $65-$109; under 18 free. Crib avail. Pet accepted, some restrictions. TV; cable (premium), VCR avail. Pool. Complimentary continental bkfst. Restaurant 6:30 am-2 pm, 5-10 pm; Sun 7 am-2 pm. Bar 2 pm-1 am; entertainment. Ck-out noon. Coin lndry. Meeting rms. Business servs avail. Valet serv. Cr cds: A, C, D, DS, MC, V.
⊡ 🐾 ⊠ ⊠ 🔥 **SC**

★ **SIGNATURE INN.** *3400 N Chadam Ln (47304). 765/284-4200; toll-free 800/822-5252. www.signature-inns.com.* 101 rms, 2 story. S, D $74-$95; under 17 free; higher rates: James Dean wkend, Indianapolis 500. Crib free. TV; cable. Pool. Complimentary continental bkfst. Restaurant nearby. Ck-out noon. Meeting rms. Sundries. Health club privileges. Cr cds: A, MC, V.
⊠ ✈ ⊠ 🔥 **SC**

Hotel

★ ★ ★ **RADISSON HOTEL ROBERTS.** *420 S High St (47305). 765/741-7777; fax 765/747-0067; toll-free 800/333-3333. www.radisson.com.* 130 rms, 7 story, 28 suites. S, D $78-$90; suites $95-$299; under 17 free; wkend rates. Crib free. Pet accepted. TV; cable (premium). Indoor pool; whirlpool. Restaurant 6:30 am-10 pm. Rm serv 24 hrs. Bar noon-midnight; wkends to 1 am; entertainment. Ck-out noon. Meeting rms. Business servs avail. Health club privileges. Microwaves avail. Cr cds: A, D, DS, MC, V.

D 🐾 ⇔ ✈ 🛏 🔥

Nappanee

(A-4) *See also Elkhart, Goshen, Warsaw*

Founded 1874 **Pop** 5,510 **Elev** 878 ft
Area code 219 **Zip** 46550
Information Amish Acres Visitor Center, 1600 W Market St; 219/773-4188 or 800/800-4942
Web www.amishacres.com

Many Amish-run farms dot the countryside surrounding Nappanee. Rich, productive soil makes agricultural crops a major part of the economy; local industry manufactures kitchen cabinets, mobile homes, recreational vehicles, vitreous steel products, and furniture.

What to See and Do

⭐ **Amish Acres.** Restored Amish homestead and farm. Guided tours, horse-drawn rides, music theater (fees); bakery, restaurant (see), inns, shops. (Daily) (see SPECIAL EVENT) 1 mi W on US 6. Phone 219/773-4188. **FREE**

Special Event

Amish Acres Arts & Crafts Festival. Amish Acres. Entries from many states; paintings, ceramics, jewelry; entertainment, dancing, feasts. Mid-Aug. Phone 800/800-4942.

Motels/Motor Lodges

★ ★ **THE INN AT AMISH ACRES.** *1234 W Market St (46550). 574/773-2011; fax 574/773-2078; toll-free 800/800-4942. www.amishacres.com.* 64 rms, 2 story, 16 suites. June-Labor Day: S $69-$89; D $74-$94; each addl $10; suites $110-$115; under 18 free; higher rates: Village Art Festival, Notre Dame football wkends; lower rates rest of yr. Crib free. TV; cable (premium). Pool. Complimentary continental bkfst. Restaurant nearby. Ck-out noon. Meeting rms. Business servs avail. Some refrigerators, microwaves. Cr cds: A, D, DS, MC, V.

D ⇔ 🛏 🔥 SC

★ ★ **THE NAPPANEE INN.** *2004 W Market St (46550). 574/773-5999; fax 574/773-5988; toll-free 800/800-4942. www.amishacres.com.* 66 rms, 2 story. June-Oct: S $59-$79; D $64-$89; each addl $10; under 18 free; higher rates special events; lower rates rest of yr. Crib free. TV; cable (premium), VCR avail. Heated pool. Complimentary continental bkfst. Restaurant nearby. Ck-out noon. Business servs avail. The inn takes its name from the Nappanee House, the town's first hotel, which opened in 1875. Part of a restored 80-acre farm. Cr cds: A, MC, V.

D ⇔ 🛏 🔥 SC

★ ★ **OAKWOOD INN & CONFERENCE CENTER.** *702 E Lake View Rd, Syracuse (46567). 219/457-5600; fax 219/457-3104. www.oakwoodpark.org.* 78 rms, 3 story, 10 suites. June-Aug: S, D $85-$105; suites $105-$160; lower rates rest of yr. Crib free. TV; cable (premium), VCR (movies). Complimentary continental bkfst. Complimentary coffee in rms. Restaurant 11 am-2 pm, 5:30-7 pm. Ck-out 11 am. Business servs avail. In-rm modem link. Bellhops. Gift shop. Coin lndry. 18-hole golf privileges, putting green, driving range. Exercise equipt. Playground. Some in-rm whirlpools; refrigerators, microwaves avail. Picnic tables. On lake. Totally nonsmoking. Cr cds: A, DS, MC, V.

D 🐾 🏋 ✈ 🛏 🔥 SC

Restaurant

★ ★ ★ **AMISH ACRES.** *1600 W Market St (46550). 219/773-4188. www.*

amishacres.com. Hrs: 11 am-7 pm; Sun, hols to 6 pm. Closed Jan-Feb. Complete meals: lunch $5.95-$8.95, dinner $8.95-$13.95. Child's menu. Specialties: cider-baked ham, roast turkey. Own baking. Early American decor. Located in historic farm; combination tour tickets incl dinner $23. Theater May-late Dec. Family-owned. Cr cds: D, DS, MC, V.

D

Nashville

(E-4) *See also Bloomington, Columbus*

Pop 873 **Elev** 629 ft **Area code** 812 **Zip** 47448
Information Brown County Convention & Visitors Bureau, Main and Van Buren Sts, PO Box 840; 812/988-7303 or 800/753-3255
Web www.browncounty.com

The heart of Brown County, Nashville has been called "log cabin country" because of its many log cabins. This area is also known for art, antiques and collectibles.

What to See and Do

Bill Monroe Bluegrass Hall of Fame. Museum of memorabilia from bluegrass and country western performers; log cabin. Special events throughout the summer. (June-Oct, Tues-Sun) 5 mi N via IN 135, in Bean Blossom. Phone 812/988-6422. ¢¢

Brown County Art Gallery. Permanent and changing exhibits of Indiana art. (Daily; closed Jan 1, Dec 25) 1 Artist Dr. Phone 812/988-4609. **FREE**

Brown County Art Guild. Changing exhibits; Goth estate collection. (Mar-Dec, daily; rest of yr, by appt only) Van Buren St. Phone 812/988-6185. **Donation**

Brown County State Park. (see) 2 mi SE of town on IN 46.

County Museum. Weaving and spinning rm; antiques; log cabin (ca 1845); county doctor's office and furnishings; blacksmith shop, Old Log Jail (fee). (Sat-Sun; daily by appt) 1 blk E of courthouse. Phone 812/988-8547. ¢¢

Hoosier National Forest. (see BEDFORD) South of town. Phone 812/275-5987.

Skiing. Ski World. Two chairlifts, four rope tows; patrol, school, rentals, snowmaking; cafeteria and lounge. Longest run 3,400 ft; vertical drop 325 ft. Dry toboggan slide; summer amusement area. (Apr-Oct, mid-Dec-early Mar, daily) 4 mi W via IN 46. Phone 812/988-6638. ¢¢

T. C. Steele State Historic Site. Home and studio of American Impressionist artist Theodore C. Steele (1847-1926). Site incl 15 acres of gardens, four hiking trails, and exhibits of more than 60 Steele canvases. (Mid-Mar-Dec, Tues-Sun; closed hols) 8 mi W on IN 46 to Belmont, then 1½ mi S on T. C. Steele Rd. Phone 812/988-2785.

Yellowwood State Forest. A 23,326-acre forest with three lakes. Fishing, boating (ramp, rentals); hiking trails, picnicking (shelter), playground, primitive camping; horseback riders' camp. Standard fees. 7 mi W on IN 46. Phone 812/988-7945. **FREE**

Special Events

Brown County Playhouse. Presents four theater productions. Phone 812/855-1103. June-Aug, Wed-Sun; Sept-Oct, Fri-Sun.

Log Cabin Tour. Unescorted tours of five log homes in Brown County. Contact the Convention & Visitors Bureau. Early June. Phone 812/988-7303.

Motels/Motor Lodges

★ ★ ★ **BROWN COUNTY INN.** *IN 46 (47448). 812/988-2291; fax 812/988-8312; toll-free 800/772-5249. www.browncountyinn.com.* 99 rms, 2 story. Apr-Oct: S, D $65-$106; each addl $6; under 18 free; lower rates rest of yr. Crib free. TV; cable. Indoor/outdoor pool. Playground. Restaurant (see HARVEST DINING ROOM). Bar 11:30 am-11 pm, Sat to 1 am; entertainment Fri, Sat. Ck-out noon. Meeting rms. Tennis. Downhill ski 5 mi; x-country ski 2 mi. Miniature golf. Game rm. Lawn games. Rustic; many antiques. Cr cds: A, D, DS, MC, V.

D 🦶 🏊 🎿 🎱 ⛷

★ **SALT CREEK INN.** *551 E IN 46 (47448).* 812/988-1149. 66 rms, 2 story, 20 kit. units (no equipt). S $40-$75; D $48-$83; each addl $5; suites $85-$110; kit. units $53-$85; under 16 free. Pet accepted, some restrictions; $5. TV; cable. Complimentary coffee in lobby. Restaurant nearby. Ck-out 11 am. Downhill ski 5 mi. Cr cds: A, DS, MC, V.

🄳 🏊 🕾 🔜 🐾 SC

★★ **THE SEASONS LODGE.** *560 IN 46 E (47448).* 812/988-2284; toll-free 800/365-7327. *www.seasons lodge.com.* 80 rms, 2 story. S, D $60-$115; each addl $5; under 18 free. TV; cable, VCR avail (movies). Indoor/outdoor pool. Playground. Restaurant 7 am-9 pm. Bar noon-10 pm; Sat, Sun to 1 am; entertainment Fri, Sat. Ck-out noon. Meeting rms. Business servs avail. Sundries. Golf 2 mi. Downhill ski 4 mi; x-country ski 1 mi. Game rm. Lawn games. Some fireplaces. Private patios, balconies. Adj to Brown County State Park. Cr cds: A, MC, V.

🄳 🕼 🔜 🔜 🔥 SC 🗡

B&Bs/Small Inns

★ **ALLISON HOUSE INN.** *90 S Jefferson St (47448).* 812/988-0814. 5 rms, 2 story. No rm phones. S, D $95; 2-day min. Complimentary full bkfst. Restaurant nearby. Ck-out 11 am, ck-in 2 pm. Downhill ski 5 mi; x-country ski 3 mi. Built in 1883; walking distance to Arts and Crafts colony. Totally nonsmoking. Cr cds: A, DS, MC, V.

🔜 🕼 🔜 🐾

★★ **CORNERSTONE INN.** *54 E Franklin St (47448).* 812/988-0300; fax 812/988-0200; toll-free 888/383-0300. *www.cornerstoneinn.com.* 20 rms, 3 story. June-Dec: S, D $100-$175; suites $145; under 12 free; package plans; lower rates rest of yr. TV; VCR avail. Complimentary full bkfst; afternoon refreshments. Restaurant nearby. Ck-out 11 am, ck-in 3 pm. In-rm whirlpool in suites. Totally nonsmoking. Cr cds: A, DS, MC, V.

🄳 🔜 🔥

Restaurants

★★ **HARVEST DINING ROOM.** *IN 135 and IN 46 (47448).* 812/988-2291. Hrs: 7 am-2 pm, 4:30-8:30 pm; Fri, Sat to 9 pm; Sun 7 am-8:30 pm, brunch to 11:30 am. Res accepted. Bar 11:30-1 am. Bkfst $4.25-$6.95, lunch $4.95-$6.95, dinner $8.95-$16.95. Sun brunch $6.95. Child's menu. Specializes in prime rib, chicken. Salad bar. Entertainment Fri, Sat. Outdoor dining. Cr cds: A, C, D, DS, MC, V.

🄳

★ **NASHVILLE HOUSE.** *Main St at Van Buren (47448).* 812/988-4554. Hrs: 11:30 am-8 pm; Fri, Sat to 9 pm. Closed Tues in Oct; also late Dec-early Jan. Res accepted. Lunch $6.95-$11.95, dinner $10.45-$18.95. Child's menu. Specialties: baked ham, fried chicken, fried biscuits and apple butter. Limited menu. Bake shop. Rustic country atmosphere; fireplace. Family-owned. Cr cds: DS, MC, V.

🄳

★ **THE ORDINARY.** *Van Buren St (47448).* 812/988-6166. Hrs: 11:30 am-8 pm; Fri, Sat to 10 pm. Closed Mon (exc Oct), Jan 1, Thanksgiving, Dec 24, 25, 31. Res accepted. Bar. Lunch $3.75-$8.50, dinner $11.50-$18.95. Child's menu. Specializes in sandwiches, wild game, ribs. Entertainment Fri, Sat. Rustic country tavern. Cr cds: DS, MC, V.

🄳

New Albany

See also Corydon, Jeffersonville

Founded 1813 **Pop** 36,322 **Elev** 450 ft
Area code 812 **Zip** 47150

Information Southern Indiana Convention and Tourism Bureau, 315 Southern Indiana Ave, Jeffersonville 47130; 812/282-6654 or 800/552-3842

Web www.sunnysideoflouisville.org

Opposite Louisville, KY, on the Ohio River, New Albany has the first public high school in Indiana, established 1853. In the last century this city was famous for its shipyards. Two of the best-known Mississippi and Ohio River steamers, the *Robert E. Lee* and the *Eclipse,* were built here. Today it is a plywood center; other principal products are furniture, machine tools, electronic equipment, frozen food, and fertilizer.

What to See and Do

Blue River Canoe Trips. Canoe trips (7-58 mi), some incl camping (two-four days). (Apr-Oct) Contact Cave Country Canoes, PO Box 145, Milltown 47145. Approx 20 mi W via IN 64 in Milltown, at bridge and dam. Phone 812/365-2705. ¢¢¢¢

Carnegie Center for Art and History. History and heritage of the area; changing exhibits. Hand-carved animated diorama. Art gallery has works by local and regional artists; lectures, demonstrations, workshops. (Tues-Sat; closed hols) 201 E Spring St. Phone 812/944-7336. **FREE**

Culbertson Mansion State Historic Site. A 25-rm, Second Empire/Victorian residence built in 1869. Period furnishings; cantilevered three-story staircase, hand-painted frescoed ceilings. Serpentine stone walks. Guided tours. (Mar-Dec, Tues-Sun; closed hols) 914 E Main St. Phone 812/944-9600. ¢¢

Special Event

Harvest Homecoming. Wk-long festivities incl open house on Mansion Row, parade, hot air balloon race, music. Early Oct. Phone 812/944-8572.

B&B/Small Inn

★★ **HONEYMOON MANSION BED & BREAKFAST.** *1014 E Main St (47150). 812/945-0312; toll-free 800/759-7270. www.bbonline.com/in/ honeymoon.* 6 rms, 3 story. No rm phones. S, D $69.95-$149.95; wkend, hol plans. Children over 12 yrs only. TV; cable (premium), VCR. Complimentary full bkfst. Ck-out noon, ck-in 2 pm. Concierge serv. Luggage handling. Business servs avail. Many in-rm whirlpools. Restored 1850 mansion; Victorian chapel. Totally nonsmoking. Cr cds: A, DS, MC, V.

D 🖼 🐾

New Castle

See also Muncie, Richmond

Founded 1819 **Pop** 17,753 **Elev** 1,055 ft **Area code** 765 **Zip** 47362

Information Chamber of Commerce, 100 S Main St, Suite 108, PO Box 485; 765/529-5210

Web www.nchcchamber.com

New Castle is a productive city; numerous plants manufacture hundreds of diversified products.

What to See and Do

Henry County Historical Society Museum. (1870) Residence of Civil War general William Grose; houses pioneer and war relics, Wilbur Wright memorabilia, collection of WWI items; genealogical records. (Mon-Sat, limited hrs; closed hols) 606 S 14th St. Phone 765/529-4028. ¢

Henry County Memorial Park. More than 300 acres; lake; picnic facilities, playground, 18-hole golf (fee), ball fields, concession; open-air theater; boats (fee); fishing; ice-skating; auditorium. (Daily) 1½ mi N on IN 3. Phone 765/529-1004. **FREE**

The Indiana Basketball Hall of Fame. "The home of Hoosier hysteria," a 14,000-sq-ft brick and glass museum, honors the spirit of basketball as well as the game's historical significance and outstanding individuals. An auditorium, library, interactive exhibits, and video inventory of game films and interviews all help explore what basketball means to Indiana's culture, history, and personality. (Tues-Sun; closed Jan 1, Thanksgiving, Dec 25) 1 Hall of Fame Ct. Phone 765/529-1891. ¢¢

Summit Lake State Park. Approx 2,550 acres, incl 800-acre lake. Swimming, boating; hiking, camping. Naturalist service (summer). (All yr) Standard fees. 9 mi NE on IN 3 to IN 36. Phone 765/766-5873. ¢¢

New Harmony

See also Evansville

Founded 1814 **Pop** 846 **Elev** 384 ft
Area code 812 **Zip** 47631

During the first half of the 19th century, this was the site of two social experiments in communal living. New Harmony was founded by members of the Harmony Society, under the leadership of George Rapp, who had come with many of his followers from Wüttemberg, Germany, and settled at Harmony, Pennsylvania. In 1814 the society came to Indiana. The deeply religious members believed in equality, mutual protection and common ownership of property, practiced celibacy, and prepared for the imminent return of Christ. In a ten-year period they succeeded in transforming 30,000 acres of dense forest and swampland into farms and a town that was the envy of the surrounding region. In 1825 it was sold to Robert Owen, a Scottish industrialist, social reformer, and communal idealist. Rapp and his followers returned to Pennsylvania.

Owen, supported by his four sons and William Maclure, attempted to organize a new social order, eliminating financial exploitation, poverty, and competition. He tried to establish a model society in New Harmony, with equal opportunities for all, full cooperative effort, and advanced educational facilities to develop the highest type of human beings. Within a short time, many of the world's most distinguished scientists, educators, scholars, and writers came to New Harmony, which became one of the scientific centers of America. Owen's original experiment was doomed to early failure, mainly because of his absence from the community and rivalry among his followers. But the scientists and educators stayed on. The first US Geological Survey was done here, and the Smithsonian Institution has its origins in this community.

The town is in a rural area surrounded by rich farmland. Historic New Harmony and the New Harmony State Historic Sites are dedicated to the efforts and contributions made to Indiana's development by the founders and settlers of this community. Many of the buildings and old homes still dominate New Harmony today.

What to See and Do

⭐ **The Atheneum Visitors' Center.**
Documentary film. Orientation area in building designed by Richard Meier. All tours begin here; tickets must be purchased here to view sites. (Apr-Oct, daily; Mar, Nov-Dec, call for hrs; closed Jan-Feb) North and Arthur Sts. Phone 812/682-4488. Area incl

1830 Owen House. Example of English architectural style. Phone 800/231-2168.

1850 Doctor's Office. Collection of medical equipment and apothecary workshop from mid- to late 1800s. Phone 800/231-2168.

David Lenz House. (1820) Harmonist frame residence furnished with Harmonist artifacts. 324 North St. Phone 800/231-2168.

Early West Street Log Structures. Reconstructed buildings establish the character of early Harmonist streetscape (1814-1819). Phone 800/231-2168.

George Keppler House. (1820) Harmonist frame residence contains David Dale Owen geological collection. Phone 800/231-2168.

Harmonist Cemetery. 230 members of the Harmony Society are buried here in unmarked graves dating from 1814-1824. Site incl several prehistoric Woodland mounds and an apple orchard. Phone 800/231-2168.

The Labyrinth. Circular maze of shrubbery created to symbolize the twists and choices along life's pathway. Phone 800/231-2168.

Lichtenberger Building/Maximilian-Bodmer Exhibit. Exhibit of Maximilian-Bodmer expedition (1832-1834) of upper Missouri region incl original lithographs of field sketches and original prints of life among the Mandan. Phone 800/231-2168.

Robert Henry Fauntleroy House. (1822-1840) Harmonist family residence. Enlarged and restyled by Robert and Jane Owen Fauntleroy. House museum contains period furniture. Phone 800/231-2168.

Salomon Wolf House. (1823) Building houses electronic scale model of New Harmony in 1824. Audiovisual program. Phone 800/231-2168.

Scholle House. Former Harmonist residence now houses changing exhibits. Phone 812/682-4523.

Thrall's Opera House. Originally Harmonist Dormitory Number 4 and later converted to a concert hall by Owen descendants. Phone 812/682-4503.

Tillich Park. (1963) Burial place of German theologian Paul Johannes Tillich. Engraved stones contain selections of Dr. Tillich's writing. Phone 800/231-2168.

Community House Number 2. (1822) An example of Harmonist brick institutional architecture. Houses exhibits on education and printing in old New Harmony. Phone 800/231-2168.

Harmonie State Park. Approx 3,500 acres of open fields and woods on banks of Wabash River. Swimming pool, boating (launch, ramp), fishing; nature and hiking trails, picnicking (shelters), playground, camping (tent and trailer sites, electrical hookups; cabins). Interpretive, cultural arts programs (summer). (Daily) Standard fees. 4 mi S on IN 69, then 1 mi W on Harmonie Pkwy. Phone 812/682-4821.

Murphy Auditorium. (1913) Facility is used for performing arts, lectures, theater, and local events. Professional summer theatre under direction of University of Southern Indiana. Phone 812/465-1635.

Roofless Church. (1959) Interdenominational church, designed by Philip Johnson, commemorates New Harmony's religious heritage. Jacques Lipchitz's sculpture, *Descent of the Holy Spirit,* is in center. Phone 800/231-2168. **FREE**

Workingmen's Institute. (1894) One of America's first free public libraries, begun in 1838. Archives of early New Harmony manuscript collections, art gallery, museum, public library. (Tues-Sun; closed hols) 407 W Tavern St. Phone 812/682-4806. ¢

Motel/Motor Lodge

★★★ **NEW HARMONY INN.** *504 North St (47631). 812/682-4491; fax 812/682-3423; res 800/782-8605. redg.com.* 90 rms, 3 story. Apr-Oct: S $65-$75; D $75-$85; each addl $10; under 12 free; lower rates rest of yr. Crib free. TV; cable, VCR avail. Indoor pool; whirlpool. Restaurant (see RED GERANIUM). Bar. Ck-out noon. Meeting rms. Business servs avail. Tennis. Exercise equipt; sauna. Rec rm. Some refrigerators, fireplaces. Balconies. Pastoral landscape. Chapel. Cr cds: A, C, D, DS, MC, V.

Restaurant

★★ **RED GERANIUM.** *504 North St (47631). 812/682-4431. www.redg. com.* Hrs: 11 am-10 pm; Fri, Sat to 11 pm; Sun to 8 pm. Closed Mon; Jan 1, Dec 25. Bar to 11 pm. Lunch $4.95-$10.75, dinner $14.95-$23.95. Specialties: charcoal-broiled prime rib, old-fashioned Shaker lemon pie. Garden rm with painted orchard ceiling. Cr cds: A, DS, MC, V.

Peru

(B-4) *See also Kokomo, Logansport, Marion, Wabash*

Founded 1826 **Pop** 12,843 **Elev** 650 ft **Area code** 765 **Zip** 46970

Information Peru/Miami County Chamber of Commerce, 13 E Main; 765/472-1923

Web www.miamicochamber.com

Peru is an industrial and agricultural trading community on the banks of the Wabash, near the confluence of the Mississinewa and Wabash rivers. The surroundings are filled with historic landmarks and memories of the times when the Miami made their home here, and the great Tecumseh tried to unite the various Native American tribes into one nation. Peru was once the largest circus winter quarters in the world, home of the famous Hagenbeck-Wallace circus. Peru was also the home town of composer Cole Porter; his birthplace was a large frame house that is now a duplex apartment at the northeast corner of Huntington and East 3rd Street.

What to See and Do

Circus Museum. Vast collection of circus memorabilia and relics, historical items from professional circuses and the Peru Amateur Circus. (Daily; closed hols) (See SPECIAL EVENTS) 154 N Broadway. Phone 765/472-3918. **Donation**

Miami County Museum. Exhibits on the circus, pioneers, Miami tribe, Victorian rms and stores, Cole Porter archive; Art Room. (Tues-Sat; closed hols) 51 N Broadway. Phone 765/473-9183. **Donation**

Special Events

Circus City Festival. Circus Museum. Amateur circus, museum, displays, performances, rides, booths; parade (last Sat). Phone 765/472-3918. Mid-July.

Heritage Days. Miami County Courthouse Sq. Celebrates the county's pioneer heritage. Phone 765/473-9183. Late Aug.

Plymouth

(B-4) *See also South Bend*

Founded 1834 **Pop** 8,303 **Elev** 799 ft **Area code** 574 **Zip** 46563
Information Marshall County Convention and Visitors Bureau, 220 N Center St; 574/936-9000 or 800/626-5353
Web www.blueberrycountry.org

Plymouth is a farming and industrial center. Southwest of the town was the site of the last Potawatomi village in this area. In 1838 their chief, Menominee, refused to turn his village over. The surviving men, women, and children were dispossessed and evacuated by the government to Kansas. So many members of the tribe died of malaria that fresh graves were left at every campsite during their long and tragic journey.

What to See and Do

Chief Menominee Monument. A granite memorial with a statue of Menominee at the site of his original village. SW of town at Twin Lakes. Phone 800/626-5353.

Marshall County Historical Museum. Relics pertaining to local history; Native American artifacts; genealogical materials. (Tues-Sat; closed hols) 123 N Michigan St. Phone 574/936-2306. **FREE**

Special Event

Marshall County Blueberry Festival. Centennial Park. Parade, exhibits, tractor pull, "Blueberry Stomp" road race, canoe and bike races, balloon race, circus, fireworks. Labor Day wkend. Phone 574/936-5020.

Motels/Motor Lodges

★★ **CULVER COVE RESORT & CONFERENCE CENTER.** *319 E Jefferson St, Culver (46511). 574/842-2683; fax 574/842-2821. www.culvercove.com.* 80 kit. units, 2 story. May-Aug: S, D $105-$152; suites $152-$184; wkly, wkend rates; higher rates special events; lower rates rest of yr. Crib free. TV; cable (premium), VCR avail. Complimentary continental bkfst. Complimentary coffee in rms. Restaurant 11 am-2 pm, 5-8 pm; Fri, Sat to 9 pm. Bar 4 pm-midnight. Ck-out 11 am, ck-in 3 pm. Meeting rms. Business servs avail. In-rm modem link. Valet serv. Barber, beauty shop. Coin lndry. Tennis. Exercise equipt; sauna. Massage. Rec rm. Indoor pool; whirlpool. On beach. Microwaves, fireplaces; many in-rm whirlpools. Balconies. Picnic tables. On lake. Cr cds: A, D, DS, MC, V.
🄳 ⛷ ⛐ 🕴 ⬦ 🔥

★★ **RAMADA INN.** *2550 N Michigan St (46563). 574/936-4013; fax 574/936-4553; toll-free 800/272-6232. www.ramada.com.* 108 rms, 2 story. S, D $73; each addl $5; under 19 free; higher rates special events. Crib free. Pet accepted. TV; cable (premium). Pool. Restaurant 6:30 am-9 pm; Fri, Sat to 10 pm; Sun 7 am-9 pm. Bar 11-1 am; wkend hrs vary. Ck-out noon. Coin lndry. Meeting rms. Business servs avail. In-rm modem link. Sundries. 18-hole golf course adj.

Health club privileges. Cr cds: A, C, D, DS, MC, V.

Richmond

(D-6) *See also New Castle*

Settled 1806 **Pop** 38,705 **Elev** 980 ft **Area code** 765 **Zip** 47374
Information Richmond/Wayne County Tourism Bureau, 5701 National Rd E; 765/935-8687 or 800/828-8414
Web www.visitrichmond.org

Established by Quakers, this city on the Whitewater River is one of Indiana's leading industrial communities; it is the trade and distribution center for agriculturally rich Wayne County.

What to See and Do

Antique Alley. Over 900 dealers display their treasures within a 33-mi loop. Contact Tourism Bureau for complete listing. Phone 765/935-8687.

Cardinal Greenway Rail Trail. Asphalt trail connects Richmond to Muncie. When completed in 2003, the trail will be 60 miles long and run all the way to Marion. Open to walkers, joggers, skaters, horseback riders. (Daily) Phone 765/287-0399.

Earlham College. (1847) 1,200 students. Liberal arts. Owns and operates Conner Prairie. W of Whitewater River on US 40. Phone 765/983-1200. On campus are Lilly Library, Stout Memorial Meetinghouse, Runyan Student Center, and

Joseph Moore Museum of Natural Science. Birds and mammals in natural settings, fossils, mastodon and allosaurus skeletons. (Academic yr, Mon, Wed, Fri, Sun; rest of yr, Sun only) Phone 765/983-1303. **FREE**

Glen Miller Park. A 194-acre park; E. G. Hill Memorial Rose Garden, ninehole golf (fee), natural springs, picnic shelters, concessions, fishing, paddleboats, playground, tennis courts, and outdoor amphitheatre (summer concerts). 2514 E Main St (US 40). Phone 765/983-7285. **FREE** Also in the park is

The German Friendship Garden. Features 200 German hybridized roses sent by the German city of Zweibrücken from its own rose garden. In bloom May-Oct. 2500 National Rd E. **FREE**

Hayes Regional Arboretum. A 355-acre site with trees, shrubs, and vines native to this region; 40-acre beech-maple forest; auto tour (3½ mi) of site. Fern garden; spring house. Hiking trails; bird sanctuary; nature center with exhibits; gift shop. (Tues-Sun; closed hols) 801 Elks Rd, 2 mi W of jct US 40 and I-70. Phone 765/962-3745. **FREE**

Huddleston Farmhouse Inn Museum. Restored 1840s farmhouse/inn complex with outbuildings once served National Road travelers. (May-Aug, Tues-Sat, also Sun afternoons; rest of yr, Tues-Sat only; closed hols; also Jan) 1 mi W on US 40, at W edge of town, in Cambridge City. Phone 765/478-3172. ¢

Indiana Football Hall of Fame. History of football in Indiana; photos, plaques, memorabilia of more than 300 inductees. High schools, colleges, and universities are represented. (Mon-Fri, also by appt; closed hols) N 9th and A Sts. Phone 765/966-2235. ¢

Levi Coffin House State Historic Site. (1839) Federal-style brick home of Quaker abolitionist who helped 2,000 fugitive slaves escape to Canada; period furnishings. Tours (Tues-Sat, afternoons; closed July 4). 113 US 27N, in Fountain City. Phone 765/847-2432. ¢

Madonna of the Trails. One of 12 monuments erected along Old National Rd (US 40) in honor of pioneer women. Phone 765/983-7200.

Middlefork Reservoir. A 405-acre park with 175-acre stream and spring-fed lake. Fishing, boating (dock rental), bait and tackle supplies; hiking trails, picnicking, playground. Sylvan Nook Dr, 2 mi N on IN 27, just S of I-70. Phone 765/983-7293. **FREE**

Wayne County Historical Museum. Pioneer rms incl general store; bakery, cobbler, print, bicycle, blacksmith, and apothecary shops; log cabin (1823), loom house; agricultural hall; decorative arts gallery; antique cars and old carriages; Egyptian mummy; collections of the Mediterranean world. (Feb-Dec, Tues-Sun; closed hols) (See SPECIAL EVENT) 1150 N A St, at 12th St. Phone 765/962-5756. ¢¢

Special Event

Pioneer Day Festival. Wayne Country Historical Museum. Pioneer crafts, food. Wkend after Labor Day. Phone 765/962-5756.

Motels/Motor Lodges

★ ★ **BEST WESTERN.** 3020 E Main St (47374). 765/966-1505; fax 765/935-1426. www.bestwestern.com. 44 rms, 2 story. S, D $29-$52; each addl $5; kit. units $10 addl; under 12 free; higher rates rest for special events. Crib $2. TV; cable. Heated pool. Complimentary continental bkfst. Restaurant nearby. Ck-out noon. Some microwaves, refrigerators. Cr cds: A, C, D, DS, MC, V.
🄳 🗖 🗟 🐾

★ ★ **COMFORT INN.** 912 Mendelson Dr (47374). 765/935-4766; toll-free 800/228-5150. www.comfortinn.com. 52 rms, 2 story. S, D $54.95-$59.95; each addl $5; suites $61.95-$69.95; under 18 free. Crib free. Pet accepted. Indoor pool; whirlpool. Restaurant adj 6 am-8 pm. Ck-out 11 am. Game rm. Refrigerator, microwave in suites. Cr cds: A, D, DS, MC, V.
🄳 🐾 🗖 🗟 🐾

★ **KNIGHTS INN.** 419 Commerce Dr (47374). 765/966-6682; fax 765/962-7717; toll-free 800/843-5644. 103 rms, 10 kits. S, D $37.95-$49.95; each addl $5; kit. units $41.95-$49.95; under 18 free; higher rates special events. Crib free. Pet accepted. TV; cable (premium), VCR avail. Pool. Complimentary coffee in lobby. Restaurant adj 6 am-10 pm; Fri, Sat open 24 hrs. Ck-out noon. Meeting rm. Some refrigerators. Cr cds: A, C, D, DS, MC, V.
🐾 🗖 🗟 🐾 SC

★ ★ **LEES INN.** 6030 National Rd E (47374). 765/966-6559; fax 765/966-7732; toll-free 800/733-5337. www.leesinn.com. 91 rms, 2 story, 12 suites. S $65-$85; D $75-$95; each

addl $10; suites $73-$162; under 16 free. Crib free. Pet accepted. TV; cable (premium), VCR avail. Complimentary continental bkfst. Restaurant adj 6 am-10 pm. Ck-out noon. Meeting rms. Business servs avail. Health club privileges. Some in-rm whirlpools, microwaves. Cr cds: A, C, D, DS, MC, V.
🄳 🐾 🗖 🐾 SC

★ ★ **RAMADA INN.** 4700 National Rd E (47374). 765/962-5551; fax 765/966-6250. www.ramada.com. 158 rms, 2 story. S, D $68-$98; each addl $10; under 18 free. Crib free. Pet accepted, some restrictions. TV; cable. Heated pool. Restaurant 11 am-11 pm. Bar. Ck-out noon. Meeting rms. Business servs avail. Valet serv. Sundries. Game rm. Health club privileges. Cr cds: A, D, DS, MC, V.
🄳 🐾 🗖 🗟 🐾

Restaurants

★ ★ **OLDE RICHMOND INN.** 138 S 5th St (47374). 765/962-2247. Hrs: 11 am-9 pm; Fri, Sat to 10 pm; Sun to 8 pm. Closed Jan 1, Labor Day, Dec 25. Res accepted. Continental menu. Bar. Lunch $5-$11, dinner $9-$27. Child's menu. Specializes in fresh seafood, steak. Outdoor dining. Restored mansion built 1892. Cr cds: MC, V.
🄳 🗖

★ **TASTE OF THE TOWN.** 1616 E Main St (47374). 765/935-5464. Hrs: 11 am-10 pm; Sat from 4 pm. Closed Sun; hols. Res accepted. Italian, American menu. Bar. Complete meals: lunch $4.50-$5.95, dinner $7.50-$15.95. Child's menu. Specializes in homemade soup, steak, seafood. Casual dining. Cr cds: A, D, DS, MC, V.
🄳 🗖

Rockville

See also Terre Haute

Pop 2,706 **Elev** 711 ft **Area code** 765 **Zip** 47872

Information Convention & Visitors Bureau, PO Box 165; 765/569-5226

Web www.coveredbridgescountry.com

What to See and Do

⬛ **Historic Billie Creek Village.** Re-created turn-of-the-century village and working farmstead with three covered bridges; more than 30 buildings, incl one-rm schoolhouse, country store, blacksmith shop, burr mill, livery; governor's house, log cabin; nature preserve; special events (see SPECIAL EVENTS). Weaving, candle dipping, and many other old-time craft demonstrations (Memorial Day-Halloween, wkends). Self-guided tours (Jan-late Dec, Mon-Fri; free admission). 1 mi E on US 36. Phone 765/569-3430. ¢¢

Raccoon Lake State Recreation Area. Approx 4,000 acres on reservoir. Swimming, waterskiing, fishing, boating (rentals); campground. Standard fees. 9 mi E on US 36. Phone 765/344-1412. ¢¢

Shades State Park. (see)

Turkey Run State Park. (see) 10 mi NE via US 41, IN 47.

Special Events

Parke County Maple Fair. 4-H Fairground. Celebration of maple sugar harvest. Bus and self-guided tours to six maple camps. Arts and crafts. Last wkend Feb and first wkend Mar. Phone 765/569-5226.

Civil War Days. Historic Billie Creek Village. State's largest reenactment of Civil War battle; costumes, battlefield; ladies tea; dance. Mid-June. Phone 765/569-3430.

Sorghum & Cider Fair. Historic Billie Creek Village. Cider made in copper kettles; sorghum cane squeezed by horse-powered press. Early Oct. Phone 765/569-3430.

Parke County Covered Bridge Festival. Arts and crafts, craft demonstrations; food; animals and rides at living museum. Activities countywide. Mid-Oct. Phone 765/569-5226.

Old Fashioned Arts and Crafts Christmas. Historic Billie Creek Village. Christmas celebration at village. Early Dec. Phone 765/569-3430.

Santa Claus

Founded 1846 **Pop** 927 **Elev** 519 ft
Area code 812 **Zip** 47579

This is a small, one-street town with a first-class post office. Its name has made it particularly significant to millions of Americans at Christmas time. At the start of the season several hundred thousand parcels and a million other pieces of mail arrive at the post office from all over the country, to be remailed with the Santa Claus postmark.

What to See and Do

Holiday World & Splashin' Safari. Holiday World theme park incl more than 60 rides, games, shows, exhibits, and attractions themed around Christmas, July 4th, and Halloween. Live music; high-dive shows; Lincoln-era exhibit; wax museum; antique toy and doll museums; craftspersons at work; petting zoo; and Santa himself! Sidewalk and indoor restaurants. (Mid-May-Aug, daily; early May and Sept-early Oct, wkends) Jct IN 162, 245. ¢¢¢¢ Admission incl rides, shows, exhibits, and

Splashin' Safari Water Park. Offers adult and children's water slides, an action river, children's activity pool, and a sandy beach area. (Memorial Day wkend-Labor Day) Phone 812/937-4401.

Motel/Motor Lodge

★★ **SANTA'S LODGE.** 91 W Christmas Blvd (47579). 812/937-1902. 87 rms, 2 story. S, D $79.99-$149.99; each addl $10; under 17 free. Crib avail. Indoor pool. TV; cable (premium), VCR avail. Complimentary coffee in rms. Ck-out 11 am. Meeting rms. Gift shop. Exercise rm. Some refrigerators, minibars. Cr cds: A, C, D, DS, MC, V.
🏊 🏃 🔥

Shakamak State Park

See also Terre Haute

(2 mi W of Jasonville on IN 48)

More than 1,766 acres with three artificial lakes stocked with game fish. Swimming pool, lifeguard, bathhouse; boating (rentals, no gasoline motors). Picnicking, playground, hiking, camping, trailer facilities; cabins. Naturalist service (May-Aug); nature center. Standard fees. Phone 812/665-2158. Per vehicle ¢¢

South Bend

(A-4) *See also Elkhart, La Porte, Mishawaka*

Founded 1823 **Pop** 105,511 **Elev** 710 ft **Area code** 574

Information South Bend-Mishawaka Convention and Visitors Bureau, 401 E Colfax Ave, Suite 310, PO Box 1677, 46617; 574/234-0051 or 800/828-7881

Web www.livethelegends.com

South Bend is probably most famous, at least in the eyes of football fans, as the home of the "Fighting Irish" of the University of Notre Dame. A visit to the campus, distinguished by the massive golden dome of the Administration Building, is worth the trip. Indiana University also has a branch here.

Two Frenchmen, Pére Marquette and Louis Jolliet, who traveled through northern Indiana between 1673-1675, were the first Europeans to enter the South Bend area. In December, 1679, the famous French writer René Robert Cavelier and explorer Sieur de la Salle proceeded from here with 32 men to the Mississippi River. During a second trip in 1681, la Salle negotiated a peace treaty between the Miami and Illinois Confederations under an oak tree known as the Council Oak. The first permanent settlers arrived in 1820, when Pierre Freischuetz Navarre set up a trading post for the American Fur Company.

South Bend was founded in 1823 by Alexis Coquillard, who, with his partner Francis Comparet, bought the fur trading agency from John Jacob Astor. Joined by Lathrop Taylor, another trading post agent, Coquillard was instrumental in promoting European settlement of the area and in the construction of ferries, dams, and mills, which began the industrial development of the town.

Industries formerly based in South Bend and contributing to its growth were the Studebaker auto plant and the Oliver Corporation. The St. Joseph River runs at its southernmost bend through the center of the city, which was officially named South Bend by the US Post Office Department in 1830.

What to See and Do

Century Center. Multipurpose facility, designed by Philip Johnson and John Burgee, housing a convention center, performing arts and art centers, museum, and park area. General building (daily; closed hols). 120 S St. Joseph St. Phone 574/235-9711. **FREE** Within the center is

South Bend Regional Museum of Art. Permanent collection, changing exhibitions. Classes, lecture series. Museum shop. (Tues-Fri, also Sat and Sun afternoons) Phone 574/235-9102. **Donation**

College Football Hall of Fame. Sports shrine and museum dedicated to the preservation of college football. The educational and interpretive exhibits bring to life the history, color, and pageantry of the game. (Daily; closed Jan 1, Thanksgiving and Dec 25). 111 S St. Joseph St. Phone 574/235-9999. ¢¢

East Race Waterway. Only man-made whitewater raceway in North America. Recreational, instructional, and competitive canoeing, kayaking, rafting. Lighted sidewalks, foot bridges, seating areas. (June-Aug, Wed, Thurs, Sat, Sun; closed for races) E side of St. Joseph River at

South Bend Dam, downtown. Phone 574/299-4768. ¢¢

Northern Indiana Center for History. Incl permanent, temporary, and interactive exhibition galleries; research library. Permanent exhibits depict history of the St. Joseph River Valley Region of Northern Indiana and Southern Michigan. (Tues-Sun) 808 W Washington, located in the West Washington National Historic District. Phone 574/235-9664. On the grounds is

Copshaholm. Built in 1895-1896 by the Oliver family, this 38-rm mansion is complete with original furnishings. The grounds incl 2-½ acres of historic gardens, tea house, sunken Italianate gardens, fountain, and more. The mansion, gardens, and carriage house are on the National Register of Historic Places. Guided tours. (Tues-Sun) Phone 574/235-9664. ¢¢

Parks.

Bendix Woods. Nature center. Hiking, picnicking, exercise trail, x-country skiing. (Daily) 12 mi W on IN 2. Phone 574/654-3155. ¢¢

City Greenhouses and Conservatory. Spring and fall flower shows. (Daily; closed hols) 2105 Mishawaka Ave. Phone 574/235-9442. ¢

Leeper Park Tennis. Lighted tennis (daily, fee); fragrance garden for the visually impaired; Pierre Navarre Cabin (1820), was the home and fur-trading post of South Bend's first settler. Michigan St, on US 31. Phone 574/235-9405. ¢¢

Pinhook. Historical park has lagoon, picnic area; fishing and small boating. 2901 N Riverside Dr, 1 mi W. Phone 574/235-9417. **FREE**

Potawatomi Zoo. Zoo (daily); conservatories; tropical gardens; concerts; picnic area (fee); swimming (mid-June-late Aug, daily; fee). 500 Greenlawn. Phone 574/235-9800. ¢¢

Rum Village. Nature center, picnic area, hiking and nature trails on 160 acres of woodland. Also contains Safetyville, miniature village teaching youngsters pedestrian, bike, and auto safety. W Ewing St at Gertrude St. Phone 574/235-9455. **FREE**

St. Patrick's Park. Canoeing, boat launch; hiking, picnicking, x-country skiing. (Daily) (See SPECIAL EVENTS) 7 mi N near US 31, on the St. Joseph River. Phone 574/277-4828. ¢¢

Potato Creek State Park. Approx 3,800 acres. Swimming beach (lifeguard), fishing on Lake Worster, boating, canoeing, paddleboats (rentals); hiking, paved bike trails (rentals), x-country skiing, picnicking (shelter rentals), camping, horse camping (tie-rail at site), cabins. Nature center, naturalist service (all yr). Standard fees. (Daily) 7 mi S on US 31, then 4 mi W on IN 4. Phone 574/656-8186.

St. Mary's College. (1844) 1,400 women. Music, theatrical, and art events throughout the yr. Campus tours (by appt). 2 mi N on US 33 at IN Toll Rd exit 77. Phone 574/284-4626.

The Studebaker National Museum. Houses and displays the Studebaker vehicle collection and artifacts. Exhibits depict evolution of the industry in the US from 1852-1966, the 150-yr span of the company. Shows more than 80 Studebaker wagons, carriages, and motorized vehicles, incl carriages of four US presidents. (Daily; closed hols). 525 S Main St. Phone 574/235-9714. ¢¢¢

★ **University of Notre Dame.** (1842) 10,126 students. One of leading universities in the US; noted for its biotechnology and vector biology research, and studies focusing on radiation, aerodynamics, and social ministry. The school is a major center for constitutional law studies. N on US 31, 33, and I-80/90. Phone 574/631-5000. On campus are

Administrative Building. (1879) The "Golden Dome" houses Columbus murals by Luigi Gregori, a former director of the university's art department and portrait painter at the Vatican Museum in the late 1860s. Phone 574/631-5000.

The Basilica of the Sacred Heart. (1871) Contains French stained-glass windows and a baroque altar in Our Lady Chapel. Its spire houses the oldest carillon in North America. Contains works by famed Croatian sculptor Ivan Mestrovic. Phone 574/631-7329.

Eck Visitors Center. Offers guided tours of the 1,250-acre campus. (Academic yr, Mon-Fri; summer, by appt) Phone 574/631-5726.

Grotto of Our Lady of Lourdes. Replica of original in the French Pyrenees. Phone 574/631-5000.

Guided tours. Tours of the 1,250-acre campus can be arranged at the Eck Visitor Center. (Summer, Mon-Fri; academic yr, by appt; closed hols) Phone 574/631-5726. **FREE**

Hesburgh Library. (1963) South wall of two-million volume library has ten-story granite mural, "The Word of Life." Phone 574/631-6258.

Joyce Center. (1968) A 10½-acre complex under twin domes for athletic, cultural, and civic events. Incl Sports Heritage Hall, with memorabilia from Notre Dame sports history.

Notre Dame Stadium. Home to Notre Dame Fighting Irish football games. Look for the "Touchdown Jesus" mosaic across the way. Phone 574/631-5000.

Snite Museum of Art. Contains more than 19,000 works of art representing ancient to contemporary periods. Incl are works of Chagall, Picasso, Rodin, and Boucher, as well as 18th- and 19th-century European art. (Tues-Sun; closed hols) Phone 574/631-5466. **FREE**

Special Events

Minor League Baseball. Stanley Coveleski Regional Baseball Stadium. 501 W South St. 5,000 seat baseball stadium. Home of the South Bend Silver Hawks. Apr-Aug. Phone 574/235-9988.

South Bend Summer in the City Festival. Parade, performances. Arts and crafts. June. Phone 574/299-4768.

Firefly Festival of the Performing Arts. St. Patrick's Park. Plays, music, concerts in outdoor amphitheater. Mid-June-early Aug, wkends. Phone 574/288-3472.

Enshrinement Festival. At the College Football Hall of Fame. Some of college football's all-time greats are

inducted into the Hall. Incl entertainment, food, events. Aug. Phone 574/235-9999.

Leeper Park Art Fair. In Leeper Park. Voted one of the 50 best art fairs in the country by renowned trade magazines. June. Phone 574/272-8598.

Motels/Motor Lodges

★★ **BEST INNS OF AMERICA.** *425 Dixie Hwy N (46637). 574/277-7700. www.bestinn.com.* 93 rms, 2 story. May-Nov: S, D $45.88-$56.88; each addl $6; under 18 free; lower rates rest of yr. Crib free. TV; cable. Complimentary continental bkfst. Restaurant nearby. Ck-out 1 pm. Meeting rm. Cr cds: A, D, DS, MC, V.

[icons]

★ **DAYS INN.** *52727 SR 933 (46637). 574/277-0510; fax 574/277-9316; toll-free 800/329-7466. www.daysinn.com.* 180 rms, 3 story. S $39-$60; D $49-$70; each addl $5; under 8 free; higher rates special events. Crib free. Pet accepted. TV; cable (premium). Pool. Playground. Complimentary continental bkfst. Ck-out noon. Meeting rm. Business servs avail. In-rm modem link. Cr cds: A, C, D, DS, MC, V.

[icons]

★★ **HOLIDAY INN.** *515 Dixie Hwy N (46637). 574/272-6600; fax 574/272-5553; toll-free 800/465-4329. www.holiday-inn.com.* 220 rms, 2 story. S, D $99-$109; each addl $10; under 18 free; wkend, hol rates. Crib free. Pet accepted, some restrictions. TV; cable (premium). 2 pools, 1 indoor; wading pool, whirlpool. Complimentary continental bkfst. Coffee in rms. Restaurant 7-10 am, 5:30-9:30 pm. Bar 11 am-midnight; Fri, Sat to 1 am. Ck-out 11 am. Coin lndry. Meeting rms. Business servs avail. Bellhops. Free airport transportation. Exercise equipt; sauna. Game rm. Rec rm. Balconies. Picnic tables. Cr cds: A, C, D, DS, JCB, MC, V.

[icons]

★★ **HOLIDAY INN CITY CENTER.** *213 W Washington St (46601). 574/232-3941; fax 574/284-3715; toll-free 800/465-4329. www.holiday-inn. com.* 165 rms, 25 story. S, D $99-$239; each addl $10; suites $105-$150; under 19 free; higher rates special events. Crib free. TV; cable (premium). Indoor pool. Complimentary coffee in lobby. Restaurant 6:30 am-2 pm, 5-10 pm. Rm serv 6:30 am-9:30 pm. Bar 11:30-1 am; Sun noon-midnight. Ck-out noon. Meeting rms. Business servs avail. Free airport transportation. Exercise equipt. X-country ski 9 mi. Massage. Health club privileges. Cr cds: A, D, DS, MC, V.

★★ **INN AT ST. MARYS.** *53993 US 31/33 N (46637). 574/232-4000; fax 574/289-0986; toll-free 800/947-8627.* 150 rms, 3 story, 80 suites. S $91; D $101; suites $109-$169; under 18 free; higher rates special events. Crib free. TV; cable (premium), VCR. Complimentary continental bkfst. Restaurant nearby. Bar. Ck-out noon. Coin lndry. Meeting rms. Business center. In-rm modem link. Gift shop. Free airport, RR station, bus depot transportation. Exercise equipt. Refrigerator, microwave in suites. Cr cds: A, D, DS, MC, V.

★ **KNIGHTS INN.** *236 Dixie Hwy N (46637). 574/277-2960; fax 574/277-0203.* 108 rms. S $34.95-$49.95; D $38.95-$54.95; each addl $6; kit. units $42.95-$64.95; under 18 free; higher rates special events. Crib free. TV; cable (premium). Pool. Complimentary continental bkfst. Restaurant nearby. Ck-out noon. Business servs avail. X-country ski 15 mi. Cr cds: A, C, D, DS, MC, V.

★★ **THE MORRIS INN.** *Notre Dame Ave, Notre Dame (46556). 574/631-2000; fax 574/631-2017. www.morrisinn.com.* 92 rms, 3 story. S $94; D $112; under 12 free. Crib free. TV; cable. Complimentary coffee in lobby. Restaurant (see MORRIS INN). Rm serv. Bar. Ck-out noon. Meeting rms. Business servs avail. Bellhops. Sundries. Gift shop. Tennis. 9-hole golf, greens fee $10. Downhill ski 1 mi; x-country ski 20 mi. Exercise equipt. Health club privileges. Some refrigerators. Picnic tables. Cr cds: A, C, D, DS, MC, V.

★★ **SIGNATURE INN.** *215 Dixie Hwy S (46637). 574/277-3211; toll-free*

800/822-5252. www.signatureinns.com. 123 rms, 2 story. S $70-$72; D $77-$79; each addl $7; under 17 free; higher rates special events. Crib free. TV; cable (premium). Pool, whirlpool. Complimentary continental bkfst. Restaurant opp open 24 hrs. Ck-out noon. Meeting rms. Business servs avail. In-rm modem link. Exercise equipt. Cr cds: A, D, DS, MC, V.

★ **SUPER 8.** *52825 US 31-33 N (46637). 574/272-9000; fax 574/273-0035; toll-free 800/800-8000.* 111 rms, 2 story. S $43; D $53; each addl $4; under 17 free; higher rates special events. TV; cable (premium). Complimentary continental bkfst. Ck-out 11 am. X-country ski 10 mi. Some refrigerators, microwaves, in-rm whirlpools. Cr cds: A, D, DS, MC, V.

Hotel

★★★ **MARRIOTT.** *123 N St. Joseph St (46601). 574/234-2000; fax 574/234-2252; toll-free 800/328-7349. www.marriott.com.* 300 rms, 9 story. S $89-$150; D $99-$170; suites $295-$425; under 18 free; wknd packages; higher rates special events. Crib free. Garage. TV; cable (premium), VCR avail (movies). Indoor pool; whirlpool, poolside serv. Restaurant 6:30 am-10 pm; Sun from 7 am; wknd hrs vary. Bar 3 pm-1:30 am. Ck-out noon. Convention facilities. Business center. In-rm modem link. Gift shop. Garage. X-country ski 9 mi. Exercise equipt; sauna. Game rm. Atrium. Connected to Century Center. Cr cds: A, C, D, DS, MC, V.

B&Bs/Small Inns

★★ **BOOK INN BED & BREAKFAST.** *508 W Washington St (46601). 574/288-1990; fax 574/234-2338; toll-free 877/288-1990. www.book-inn.com.* 5 rms, 1 with shower only, 2 story, 2 suites. S, D, suites $75-$120; higher rates special events. TV; VCR avail (movies). Complimentary full bkfst. Restaurant adj 11:30 am-10 pm. Business servs avail. X-country ski 4 mi. Built in 1872; contains used bookstore. Totally nonsmoking. Cr cds: A, MC, V.

★ ★ **OLIVER INN BED & BREAK-FAST.** *630 W Washington St (46601). 574/232-4545; fax 574/288-9788; res 888/697-4466. www.oliverinn.com.* 9 rms, 2 share bath, 3 story. S $115; D $145; higher rates special events. Pet accepted, some restrictions. TV; cable (premium). Complimentary continental bkfst; afternoon refreshments. Restaurant adj 11:30 am-2 pm, 5-10 pm; Fri to 11 pm; Sat 4:30-11 pm; Sun 4-9 pm; Sun brunch 9 am-2 pm. Ck-out 11 am, ck-in 4-6 pm. Business servs avail. Luggage handling. Airport transportation. 18-hole golf privileges, pro, putting green. Downhill/x-country ski 20 mi. Lawn games. Some fireplaces. Picnic tables. Built in 1886; Victorian decor. Totally nonsmoking. Cr cds: A, DS, MC, V.

★ ★ **QUEEN ANNE INN.** *420 W Washington St (46601). 574/234-5959; res 800/582-2379.* 6 rms, 3 story, 1 suite. S $65-$100; D $70-$105; each addl $15; suite $105; special package plans. TV; VCR avail (movies). Complimentary full bkfst. Restaurant nearby. Ck-out 11 am, ck-in 4 pm. Business servs avail. Free airport transportation. X-country ski 4 mi. Health club privileges. Some fireplaces. Built in 1893; Victorian decor. Totally nonsmoking. Cr cds: A, DS, MC, V.

Extended Stay

★ ★ **RESIDENCE INN BY MAR-RIOTT.** *716 N Niles Ave (46617). 574/289-5555; fax 574/288-4531; toll-free 800/331-3131. www.marriott.com.* 80 kit. suites, 2 story. July-Nov: S, D $99-$129; higher rates graduation; lower rates rest of yr. Crib free. Pet accepted; $100. TV; cable (premium), VCR avail (movies). Heated pool; whirlpool. Playground. Complimentary continental bkfst. Coffee in rms. Restaurant nearby. Ck-out noon. Coin lndry. Meeting rms. Business servs avail. Exercise equipt. Microwaves. Balconies. Cr cds: A, C, D, DS, MC, V.

Restaurants

★ ★ ★ **THE CARRIAGE HOUSE DINING ROOM.** *24460 Adams Rd (46628). 574/272-9220.* Hrs: 5-9:30 pm. Closed Sun, Mon; hols; also early Jan. Res accepted. Continental menu. Bar. Complete meals: dinner $16-$28. Specialties: chicken Chardonnay, beef Wellington, roast rack of lamb. Own baking. Outdoor dining. Restored church (ca 1850); European-style dining. Cr cds: A, D, MC, V.

★ ★ **DAMON'S THE PLACE FOR RIBS.** *52885 US 31 (Business) (46637). 574/272-5478.* Hrs: 11 am-11 pm; Fri, Sat to midnight; Sun to 10 pm. Closed Thanksgiving, Dec 25. Res accepted. Bar. Lunch $4.95-$15.95, dinner $5.95-$15.95. Child's menu. Specializes in onion loaf, barbecued ribs, barbecued chicken. Cr cds: A, MC, V.

★ ★ **LA SALLE GRILL.** *115 W Colfax (46601). 574/288-1155. www.lasalle grill.com.* Hrs: 5-10 pm; Fri, Sat to 11 pm. Closed Sun; hols. Res accepted. Bar. Dinner $14.25-$28.95. Specialties: prime steak, grilled salmon. Own baking. Mix of contemporary and traditional decor. Cr cds: A, C, D, MC, V.

★ ★ **MORRIS INN.** *University of Notre Dame, Notre Dame (46556). 574/631-2000.* Hrs: 7-10:30 am, 11:30 am-2 pm, 5:30-8:30 pm; Sun brunch 11:30 am-2 pm. Closed mid-Dec-early Jan. Res accepted; required lunch. Bar. Bkfst $3-$6, lunch $4.75-$5.50, dinner $9.95-$24.95. Sun brunch $7.95-$14.95. Child's menu. Specializes in fresh fish, chicken dishes, prime rib. Own ice cream. Traditional American fine dining; contemporary decor with some original art. Totally nonsmoking. Cr cds: A, D, DS, V.

★ ★ **TIPPECANOE PLACE.** *620 W Washington (46601). 574/234-9077. www.tippe.com.* Hrs: 11:30 am-2 pm, 5-10 pm; Fri to 10:30 pm; Sat 4:30-10:30 pm; Sun 4-9 pm; Sun brunch 9 am-2 pm. Res accepted. Bar to 11:30 pm, wkends to midnight. Wine list. Lunch $6-$10, dinner $14-$19. Sun brunch $10.95. Specializes in seafood, prime rib, steaks. Own pas-

tries. Parking. Former Studebaker mansion (1886-1889); many antiques. Cr cds: A, D, DS, MC, V.
D

Spring Mill State Park

See also Bedford, Bloomington

(3 mi E of Mitchell on IN 60)

In this 1,319-acre park an abandoned pioneer village has been restored in a small valley among wooded hills. Built around a gristmill, which dates to 1817, are the log shops and homes of a pioneer trading post. The village's main street is flanked by a tavern, distillery, post office, and an apothecary shop. A small stream flowing through the valley turns an overshot waterwheel at the gristmill and furnishes power for a sawmill. The homes of the pioneers have been furnished with household articles from a century ago.

The Virgil I. Grissom Memorial, dedicated to the Indiana astronaut who was the second American in space, is located here. In the building are space exhibits, a slide show, and a visitor center.

In the surrounding forest, which includes 60 acres of woods, are some of the largest oak and tulip trees in Indiana. Some of the many caverns in the park have underground streams with blind fish. In Twin Caves, boat trips may be taken on an underground stream (April-October). Park facilities include swimming pool, lifeguard, fishing, boating (rentals, no motors) on a 30-acre artificial lake; hiking trails, tennis, picnicking, camping. Inn has accommodations (phone 812/849-4081). Standard fees. Phone 812/849-4129.

Terre Haute

(E-2) *See also Brazil, Greencastle, Rockville*

Founded 1816 **Pop** 57,483 **Elev** 507 ft
Area code 812
Information Terre Haute Convention & Visitors Bureau, 643 Wabash Ave, 47807; 812/234-5555 or 800/366-3043
Web www.terrehaute.com

Terre Haute was founded as a river town on the lower Wabash River and has become an important industrial, financial, agricultural, educational, and cultural center.

The plateau on which the city is built (27 square miles) was named *Terre Haute* (high land) by the French, who governed this area until 1763. The dividing line that separated the French provinces of Canada and Louisiana runs through this section. American settlers arrived with the establishment of Fort Harrison in 1811. In later years, it became a terminal for river trade on the Wabash, Ohio, and Mississippi rivers to New Orleans. Many wagon trains with westbound settlers passed through here. The advance of the railroads made large-scale coal operations possible; Terre Haute became a railroad and coal mining center and developed a highly diversified industrial and manufacturing complex.

Novelist Theodore Dreiser, author of *Sister Carrie* and *An American Tragedy,* and his brother, Paul Dresser, composer of Indiana's state song, "On the Banks of the Wabash," lived here. Eugene V. Debs founded the American Railway Union, first industrial union in America, in Terre Haute. The city is also the home of Rose-Hulman Institute of Technology (1874).

What to See and Do

Children's Science & Technology Museum. Hands-on museum exhibits allow visitors, both young and old, to experience science, to explore the world around them, and to understand today's ever-changing technology. (Tues-Sat; closed Jan 1,

Thanksgiving, Dec 25) 523 Wabash Ave. Phone 812/235-5548. ¢¢

Deming Park. 177 acres of wooded hills; swimming pool (June-Labor Day, fee), fishing; x-country skiing (rentals), tennis, picnicking, concession; miniature train rides (wkends and hols, fee); water slide (fee), 18-hole Frisbee disc course. E end of Ohio Blvd at Fruitridge Ave. Phone 812/232-2727. **FREE**

Dobbs Park & Nature Center. Approx 105 acres. A 25-acre state nature preserve; 2½-acre lake, fishing; three-acre wetlands area, four mi of nature trails, interpretive nature center; butterfly and hummingbird garden (June-Sept). Tree nursery. Picnicking (shelters). (Daily) 4 mi E via IN 42 at jct IN 46. Phone 812/877-1095. **FREE** Also here is

    Native American Museum. Exhibits incl dwellings, clothing, weapons, and music of Eastern Woodland Native American cultures. Hands-on activities. Phone 812/877-6007. **FREE**

Eugene V. Debs Home. Restored home of the labor and Socialist leader; memorabilia. (Wed-Sun afternoons; also by appt; closed hols) 451 N 8th St. Phone 812/232-2163. **FREE**

Farrington's Grove Historical District. More than 800 residential dwellings in a 70-sq-blk area; homes dating from 1849.

Fowler Park Pioneer Village. An 1840s pioneer village with 12 log cabins, a general store, schoolhouse, and gristmill. (Summer wkends; also by appt) 3000 E Oregon Church Rd. Phone 812/462-3391. **FREE**

Indiana State University. (1865) 11,000 students. Turman Gallery and the University Gallery in the Center for Performing and Fine Arts have paintings, sculpture, ceramics, jewelry (Tues-Fri, Sun; free). Cunningham Memorial Library houses the Cordell Collection of rare and early English language dictionaries. Historic Condit House (1860), office of the university president, is an example of Italianate architecture. Campus tours. Bounded by 3rd (US 41), 9th, Cherry, and Tippecanoe Sts. Phone 812/237-3773.

Paul Dresser Birthplace State Shrine and Memorial. Restoration of mid-19th-century workingman's home; birthplace of Dresser, author of state song, and composer of other popular songs. (May-Sept, Sun; also by appt) 1st and Farrington Sts in Fairbanks Park. Phone 812/235-9717. **FREE**

St. Mary-of-the-Woods College. (1840) 1,286 students. On beautiful 67-acre campus. Nation's oldest Catholic liberal arts college for women. Tours by appt. 4½ mi NW on US 150. Phone 812/535-5212.

Sheldon Swope Art Museum. The museum's permanent collections of nineteenth- and twentieth-century American art. Special exhibits, films, lectures, classes, and performing arts events. (Daily; closed hols) 25 S 7th St. Phone 812/238-1676. **FREE**

Vigo County Historical Museum. Local exhibits in 15 rms of 1868 house; one-rm school, country store, military rm, dressmaker's shop. (Tues-Sun; closed hols) 1411 S 6th St, at Washington Ave. Phone 812/235-9717.

Special Events

Maple Sugarin' Days. Prairie Creek Park. Demonstrations of syrup-making process at syrup camp. Actual syrup-making takes place in hand-hewn log house (1852). Phone 812/462-3391 or 812/898-2279 (wkends). Early Feb-early Mar.

Wabash Valley Festival. Fairbanks Park. Flea market, carnival, entertainment. Phone 812/232-2727. Last wk May.

Frontier Day. Wabash Valley Fairgrounds, 2 mi S on US 41. Horse show, events. July 4. Phone 217/275-3443.

Buffalo Chip Throwing Contest. Native American Museum. Phone 812/877-6007. Late Sept.

Pioneer Days. 7 mi S via US 41. Old fashioned crafts demonstrated; pioneer exhibits. Phone 812/462-3392. First wkend Oct.

Motels/Motor Lodges

★ **DAYS INN.** *555 S 3rd St (47807). 812/235-3333; fax 812/232-9563; toll-free 800/262-0033. www.daysinn.com.* 95 rms, 4 story. S $58-$65; D $75-$85; suites $107; under 18 free; higher rates special events. Crib free. TV; cable (premium). Pool. Restaurants 6:30 am-9 pm. Bar 11-2 am; entertainment Fri, Sat. Ck-out noon.

Meeting rms. Business servs avail. Bellhops. Sundries. Gift shop. Free airport transportation. Health club privileges. Refrigerator avail. Cr cds: A, C, D, DS, JCB, MC, V.

★★ **DRURY INN.** 3040 S US 41 (47802). 812/238-1206; toll-free 800/325-8300. www.druryinn.com. 153 rms, 7 story. S $58.95; D $68.95; each addl $10; suites $125; under 18 free; higher rates special events. Crib free. TV; cable. Indoor pool. Continental bkfst. Complimentary coffee in rms. Restaurant adj 6 am-10 pm. Ck-out noon. Meeting rms. Business servs avail. Bellhops. Sundries. Cr cds: A, D, DS, MC, V.

★★ **FAIRFIELD INN.** 475 E Margaret Ave (47802). 812/235-2444; toll-free 800/228-2800. www.fairfieldinn.com. 62 rms, 3 story. S, D $53.99-$59.99; each addl $6; suites $85.95-$95.95; under 18 free; higher rates Indy 500. Crib free. TV; cable (premium). Complimentary continental bkfst. Restaurant opp 6 am-10 pm. Ck-out noon. Business servs avail. In-rm modem link. Indoor pool; whirlpool. Some refrigerators, microwaves. Cr cds: A, D, DS, MC, V.

★★ **HOLIDAY INN.** 3300 US 41 S (47802). 812/232-6081; fax 812/238-9934; toll-free 800/465-4329. www. holiday-inn.com. 230 rms, 2-5 story. S, D $89-$99; suites $115-$175; under 20 free; higher rates special events. Crib free. Pet accepted. TV; cable (premium). Indoor pool; whirlpool. Complimentary coffee in rms. Restaurant 6:30 am-2 pm, 5-10:30 pm. Rm serv. Bar 11-1 am. Ck-out noon. Guest lndry. Meeting rms. Business servs avail. In-rm modem link. Bellhops. Valet serv. Exercise equipt. Cr cds: A, C, D, DS, JCB, MC, V.

★ **PEAR TREE INN.** 3050 S US 41 (47802). 812/234-4268; toll-free 800/282-8733. 64 rms, 4 story. S $55.95; D $65.95; each addl $10; under 18 free. Crib free. Pet accepted. TV; cable (premium). Ck-out noon. Business serv avail. Sundries. Health club privileges. Cr cds: A, C, D, DS, MC, V.

★★ **SIGNATURE INN.** 3053 US 41 S (47802). 812/238-1461; toll-free 800/822-5252. www.signatureinns.com. 157 rms, 3 story. S, D $63; each addl $7; under 18 free; wkend rates; higher rates special events. Crib free. TV; cable (premium). Pool. Continental bkfst. Ck-out noon. Meeting rms. Business servs avail. In-rm modem link. Exercise equipt. Cr cds: A, C, D, DS, MC, V.

Tippecanoe River State Park

See also Plymouth

(5 mi N of Winamac on US 35)

One of Indiana's larger state parks, its 2,761 acres stretch for more than seven miles along the Tippecanoe River, on the east side of US 35. (The area west of the highway is operated by the Division of Fish and Wildlife as Winamac State Fish and Wildlife Area.)

Tippecanoe is ideal for outdoor enthusiasts, with its oak forests, pine plantations, fields, winding roads, marshes, and an occasional sand dune. Fishing, boating (launch); hiking, bridle trails, x-country skiing, picnicking (shelter), playground; camping (electrical hookups) and horseback camping, group camping. Naturalist service (May-Aug). View from fire tower. Standard fees. (Daily) Phone 574/946-3213. Per vehicle ¢¢

Turkey Run State Park

(2 mi N of Marshall on IN 47)

This is a 2,382-acre wooded area. Within the park are deep, rock-

Wetlands at Tippecanoe River State Park

walled prehistoric canyons and winding streams that twist through solid rock. Canoeing and fishing in Sugar Creek for bluegill, crappie, and rock bass. Hiking trails (13½ mi) lead through canyons, along cliffs, and into forests. A historic house, built by one of the area's first settlers, is open for tours (seasonal).

Facilities include swimming pool; hiking, saddle barn, tennis, picnicking, concession (summer), trailer and tent camping. Nature Center (daily; winter, wkends only); bird observation room. Planetarium. Naturalist service. Standard fees. (Daily) Phone 765/597-2635. Per vehicle ¢¢

Motel/Motor Lodge

★ **TURKEY RUN INN.** *RR 1 Box 444, Marshall (47859).* 765/597-2211; fax 765/597-2660; toll-free 877/500-6151. 82 rms, 3 story. S $64.90; D $75.90; suites $97.90; higher rates wkends. TV; VCR avail. Indoor pool. Playground. Supervised children's activities. Restaurant 7 am-8 pm. Ck-out noon. Meeting rms. Business servs avail. Gift shop. Lighted tennis. Game rm. Picnic tables, grills in park. Hiking trails; nature center. 2 lakes and Sugar Creek nearby. Cr cds: A, DS, MC, V.

Valparaiso

(A-3) *See also Hammond, La Porte*

Founded 1865 **Pop** 24,414 **Elev** 738 ft
Area code 219 **Zip** 46383
Information Chamber of Commerce, 150 Lincolnway, Suite 1005, PO Box 330, 46384; 219/462-1105
Web www.valparaiso.com

Special Events

Porter County Fair. Porter County Expo Center. Phone 219/464-0133. Late July.

Popcorn Festival. Downtown. Parade, five-mi Fun Run; arts and crafts, entertainment, hot air balloon show. Phone 219/464-8332. First Sat after Labor Day.

Motels/Motor Lodges

★★ **COURTYARD BY MARRIOTT.** *2301 E Morthland Dr (46383).* 219/465-1700; fax 219/477-2430; toll-free 800/321-2211. www.marriott.com. 111 rms, 2 story. S, D $72-$99; suites $79-$129. Crib free. TV; cable (premium). Indoor/outdoor pool. Ck-out noon. Meeting rm. Business servs avail. In-rm modem link. Valet serv.

Sundries. Exercise equipt. Cr cds: A, D, DS, MC, V.

★ ★ **HOLIDAY INN EXPRESS.** *760 Morthland Dr (46385). 219/464-8555; fax 219/477-2492; toll-free 800/953-6287. www.holiday-inn.com.* 54 rms, 4 story. S, D $79-$89; higher rates university related events. Crib free. TV; cable (premium). Complimentary continental bkfst. Restaurant nearby. Ck-out noon. Business servs avail. Exercise equipt. Cr cds: A, C, D, DS, MC, V.

Resort

★ ★ ★ **INDIAN OAK RESORT & SPA.** *528 Boundary Rd (46304). 219/926-2200.* 95 rms, 2 story. S, D $125-$275; each addl $25. Crib avail. TV; cable (premium), VCR avail. Complimentary continental bkfst. Restaurant 6 am-10 pm. Ck-out 11 am. Meeting rms. Business center. Exercise rm. Spa. Some refrigerators, minibars. Cr cds: A, D, DS, MC, V.

Vincennes (F-2)

Founded 1732 **Pop** 19,859 **Elev** 429 ft
Area code 812 **Zip** 47591
Information Vincennes Area Chamber of Commerce, 102 N 3rd St, PO Box 553; 812/882-6440 or 888/895-6622
Web www.accessknoxcounty.com

This city on the banks of the Wabash River is the oldest town in Indiana. French fur traders roamed through the region as early as 1683, established a trading post, and were soon followed by settlers. Fort Vincennes was built by French troops under Francis Morgamme de Vincennes in 1732. It was turned over to British control in 1763, but many of the French settlers (who frequently intermarried with Native Americans) remained in the area. In 1778, the State of Virginia furnished $12,000 and seven companies of militia to 25-year-old George Rogers Clark and directed him to secure all land north-

west of the Ohio River for Virginia. Clark's troops seized Fort Sackville in the summer of 1778, but it fell back into British hands several months later. The second and final capture of Vincennes by Clark the following year opened up the entire Northwest Territory. In 1784 the territory was ceded by Virginia to the United States and became a public domain. Vincennes was, from 1800-1813, the capital of the Indiana Territory; between 1808-1811 several meetings and negotiations took place here between Governor William H. Harrison and the famous Shawnee Chief Tecumseh and his brother, The Prophet. During the 18th century the town was almost entirely populated by descendants of the French founders. After 1800 a large number of Easterners and German families settled in Vincennes and advanced farming, local business, and industry. The first newspaper in the Indiana Territory, the *Indiana Gazette,* was published here in 1804.

Today Vincennes is a Midwest shipping and trading center and the seat of Knox County—notable for its melons and livestock raising. For recreation, the Wabash River offers fishing and boating.

What to See and Do

Fort Knox II. Military post built and garrisoned by new American nation during early 1800s to protect western frontier prior to Battle of Tippecanoe. As tensions on the frontier increased, additional troops were gathered here, the fort having been hurriedly enlarged and strengthened by Captain Zachary Taylor in 1810. The outline of the fort is marked for self-guided tours. (Daily) 3 mi N via Fort Knox Rd. **FREE**

George Rogers Clark National Historical Park. (see) Phone 716/831-9376.

Indiana Military Museum. Extensive and varied collection of military memorabilia. Military vehicles, artillery, uniforms, insignia, equipt, and related artifacts spanning the Civil War to Desert Storm. Museum (May-Sept, Mon-Fri, afternoons; winter and wkends by appt; closed Jan 1, Thanksgiving, Dec 25); outdoor display (summer, daily). 2074 N Bruceville Rd. Phone 812/882-8668. ¢

Indiana Territory Site. From this two-story capitol building, an area consisting of the present states of Indiana, Illinois, Michigan, Wisconsin, and a part of Minnesota was governed in 1811. A replica of the first newspaper printing shop in Indiana is also here, where Elihu Stout first issued the *Indiana Gazette* in 1804. Nearby is the **Maurice Thompson Birthplace**, restored 1840 home of author of *Alice of Old Vincennes*. Tours (Apr-Dec, Wed-Sun). First and Harrison Sts. Phone 812/882-7422. ¢

Kimmell Park. Boating (ramp), fishing; picnicking. (May-Oct) Oliphant Dr. Phone 812/882-1140.

Log Cabin Visitors Center. (Apr-Dec, Wed-Sun) Phone 812/882-7422. **FREE**

Michel Brouillet Old French House. (ca 1806) French Creole house; period furniture. (May-Sept, Thurs-Sun) 509 First St. Phone 812/882-7886. ¢

The Old Cathedral Minor Basilica. (1826) (Daily) 2nd and Church Sts. Phone 812/882-5638. **Donation** Behind the cathedral is St. Rose Chapel and

  Old Cathedral Library and Museum. (1794) Indiana's oldest library; more than 12,000 documents, books, artworks—some dating from 1400s. (June-Aug, Mon-Fri) Phone 812/882-5638. **Donation**

  The Old French Cemetery. William Clark, Judge of the Indiana Territory, was buried here in 1802; also local Frenchmen who served in George Rogers Clark's army (1778-1779). Phone 812/882-5638.

Old State Bank, Indiana State Memorial. (1838) Operated as a bank until 1877; one of the oldest bank buildings in Indiana. Guided tours (Mid-Mar-mid-Dec, Wed-Sun; closed hols) Busseron and 2nd Sts. Phone 812/882-7422. ¢

Ouabache Trails Park. Two picnicking areas (six shelters), camping (tent and trailer sites, hookups, dump station); interpretive center. Nature and hiking trails. Sand volleyball court, horseshoe pits. Approx 250 acres of wooded area bordered on west by Wabash River. Contact Knox County Parks and Recreation Department, Rural Rte 6, Box 227H. Phone 812/882-4316.

Vincennes University. (1801) 7,000 students. A junior college established as Jefferson Academy; first land-grant college in the Indiana Territory. Tours. 1st and College Sts. Phone 812/888-8888.

William Henry Harrison Mansion (Grouseland). (1803-1804) Residence of the ninth President of the US while he was governor of the Indiana Territory; first brick building constructed in Indiana; 1803-1812 period furnishings. (Daily; closed hols) 3 W Scott St, opp Indiana Territorial Capitol. Phone 812/882-2096. ¢¢

Special Events

Spirit of Vincennes Rendezvous. Old French Commons, at Willow St and River Rd. 1700-1840 era encampment and battle reenactment. Phone 812/882-6440. Memorial Day wkend.

Indiana State Chili Cook-off. Patrick Henry Dr, downtown. Chili cooking contest, sanctioned by International Chili Society. Winner advances to national cook-off. Phone 812/882-6440. One-day event. Sept.

Wabash

(B-4) *See also Huntington, Marion, Peru*

Founded 1834 **Pop** 12,127 **Elev** 700 ft
Area code 260 **Zip** 46992
Information Wabash County Convention & Visitors Bureau, 111 S Wabash, PO Box 746; 260/563-7171 or 800/563-1169
Web www.wabashcountycvb.com

On March 31, 1880, the Wabash Courthouse was illuminated by four electric carbon lamps. Wabash thus became the first electrically illuminated city in the world. This is the home town of Mark C. Honeywell, founder of the Honeywell Corporation, and country singer Crystal Gayle.

The hill from which the town overlooks the Wabash River was, in

1826, the site of the signing of the
Paradise Spring Treaty, by which
Chief Pierish of the Potawatomi
ceded the land between the Wabash
and Eel rivers to the US government
for cultivation by white settlers.

In 1835, a section of the Wabash
and Erie Canal was dug through this
area. Much of the work was done by
immigrant Irish laborers who
brought with them long-smoldering
differences from the old country. On
July 12, about 300 men from County
Cork and a roughly equal number
from the north of Ireland decided to
settle old scores by fighting a battle
near the present site of Wabash. The
first shots had been fired when the
state militia arrived and separated
the two groups by force.

What to See and Do

Honeywell Center. Historic Art Deco
building is a community center with
cultural and recreational facilities;
gallery; special events, concerts. Fee
for some activities. (Daily; closed
hols) 275 W Market St. Phone
800/626-6345. **FREE**

**Salamonie Reservoir, Dam, and For-
est.** Observation mound and nature
center at Army Corps of Engineers
project (daily; phone 260/782-2181).
Several state recreation areas provide
camping on 2,860-acre lake; also
fishing, waterskiing, swimming, boating, launching sites (fee) and ramps
(Memorial Day-Labor Day); picnicking, hunting, hiking trails. 7 mi NE
on US 24 to Lagro, then 5 mi SE on
IN 524. Contact office at Lost Bridge
West State Recreation Area, 10 mi NE
via US 24, then 8 mi S on IN 105
(daily); phone 260/468-2125. The
state forest offers picnicking, camping, and fishing in Hominy Ridge,
11-acre lake; phone 260/782-2349.
Fishing below the Salamonie Reservoir Dam; phone 260/782-2181 or
260/468-2125. 7 mi NE on US 24 to
Lagro, then 5 mi SE on IN 524.

Wabash County Historical Museum.
Items incl records and artifacts from
the periods of Native American occu-
pation, pioneer settlement, and the
Civil War; research materials incl
local newspapers dating from 1846.
(Tues-Sat; closed hols) One Market St.
Phone 219/563-0661. **FREE**

Warsaw

(B-4) *See also Nappanee*

Pop 10,968 **Area code** 219 **Zip** 46580
Information Kosciusko County Convention & Visitors Bureau, 313 S Buffalo St; 219/269-6090 or
800/800-6090
Web www.wkchamber.com

Warsaw is in the heart of the Indiana
lake region and primarily a vacation
resort. Many fine lakes in surrounding Kosciusko County have excellent
swimming and boating facilities; fish
are plentiful.

Local industry manufactures surgical supplies and movie projection
screens; located here is one of the
largest rotogravure printing plants in
the United States. Kosciusko County
is also home to the world's largest
duck producer, Maple Leaf Farms.
One mile southeast, in Winona Lake,
is Grace College (1948) and Seminary
(1937).

What to See and Do

Tippecanoe Lake. Secluded four-mi-
long lake with recreational facilities.
This is Indiana's deepest natural lake.
6 mi N on IN 15, then 4 mi E.

Special Event

Back to the Days of Kosciuszko. Reenactment of the Revolutionary War
era. Food of the period, crafts,
demonstrations. Participants in
period clothing. Phone 219/269-
6090. Late Sept.

Motel/Motor Lodge

★ ★ **RAMADA PLAZA.** *2519 E Center St (46580). 219/269-2323; fax
219/269-2432; toll-free 800/272-
6232. www.ramada.com.* 156 rms, 4
story. S $89; D $95; each addl $10;
suites $95-$115; under 12 free;
higher rates summer wkends. Crib
free. Pet accepted. TV; cable, VCR
avail. Complimentary coffee in rms.
Restaurant 7-10:30 am, 11 am-2 pm,
5-10 pm. Bar. Ck-out noon. Meeting
rms. Business servs avail. In-rm
modem link. Valet serv. Sundries.
Coin lndry. 18-hole golf privileges,

pro. Exercise equipt; sauna. Indoor/outdoor pool; whirlpool, poolside serv. Game rm. Rec rm. Microwaves avail. Cr cds: A, D, DS, MC.

◧ ◆ ⬖ ⚡ ⚖ ➳ ⚔ ✈ ⬄ ⬙

Wyandotte

See also Corydon, New Albany

Pop 50 **Elev** 760 ft **Area code** 812
Zip 47179

What to See and Do

Little Wyandotte Cave. Large variety of cave life and formations. Impressively illuminated. Guided tours (30-45-min). (Memorial Day-Labor Day, daily; rest of yr, Tues-Sun; closed hols) On IN 62, 2 mi S of I-64 via IN 66 or IN 135. Phone 812/738-2782.

✦ **Wyandotte Caves.** Approx seven mi of mapped passages. Features incl Garden of Helictites, a large collection of gravity-defying formations; Rothrock's Cathedral, an underground mountain 105 ft high, 140 ft wide, 360 ft long; and Pillar of the Constitution, a stalagmite approx 35 ft high and 71 ft in circumference. The cave was used by prehistoric Native Americans for mining aragonite and is known to have been the source of saltpeter and Epsom salts around 1812. Jacket recommended, cave temperature 52°F. One-hr guided tours (Memorial Day-Labor Day, daily). Two-hr guided tours (Memorial Day-Labor Day, daily; rest of yr, Tues-Sun; closed hols). Two-, three-, five-, and eight-hr tours (Sat and Sun, by res only). On IN 62, 2 mi S of I-64 via either IN 66 or IN 135. Phone 812/738-2782.

MICHIGAN

Michigan has a mighty industrial heritage and is well known as the birthplace of the automobile industry, but rivaling the machines, mines, and mills is the more than $9 billion a year tourist industry. The two great Michigan peninsulas, surrounded by four of the five Great Lakes, unfold a tapestry of lakeshore beaches, trout-filled streams, more than 11,000 inland lakes, nearly seven million acres of public hunting grounds—and the cultural attractions of Dearborn, Detroit, Ann Arbor, Grand Rapids, and other cities.

Michigan has a geographically split personality linked by a single—but magnificent—five-mile-long bridge. The Upper Peninsula faces Lake Superior on one side and Lake Michigan on the other. It revels in its north-country beauty and ruggedness. The Lower Peninsula has shores on Lakes Michigan, Huron, and Erie. Its highly productive Midwestern-style farmland is dotted with diversified cities.

Population: 9,295,297
Area: 56,954 square miles
Elevation: 570-1,980 feet
Peak: Mount Arvon (Baraga County)
Entered Union: January 26, 1837 (26th state)
Capital: Lansing
Motto: If you seek a pleasant peninsula, look around you
Nickname: Wolverine State
Flower: Apple Blossom
Bird: Robin
Tree: White Pine
Fair: Late August-early September, 2003, in Detroit
Time Zone: Eastern and Central (Menominee, Dickinson, Iron, and Gogebic counties)
Web Site: www.michigan.org

Michigan is a four-season vacationland, with the tempering winds off the Great Lakes taming what might otherwise be a climate of extremes. In a land of cherry blossoms, tulips, ski slopes, and sugar-sand beaches, you can fish through the ice, hunt deer with a bow and arrow, follow the trail of a bobcat, rough it on an uncluttered island, trace Native American paths, or hunt for copper, iron ore, and Lake Superior agates or Petoskey stones. One of the country's finest art museums is in Detroit, and Dearborn's Henry Ford Museum and historic Greenfield Village attract visitors from all over the world. Michigan has an increasing array of challenging resort golf courses as well as more than 750 public courses. Ann Arbor, Detroit, and East Lansing offer outstanding universities.

A world center for automobile manufacture, Michigan leads in the production of automobiles and light trucks. More than two-thirds of the nation's tart red cherries are harvested here; so are more than 90 percent of the dry edible beans. This state is also one of the nation's leading producers of blueberries. Wheat, hay, corn, oats, turkey, cattle, and hogs are produced in vast quantities. The Soo Locks at Sault Ste. Marie boast the two longest locks in the world that can accommodate superfreighters 1,000 feet long.

French explorers were the first known Europeans to penetrate the lakes, rivers, and streams of Michigan. In their wake came armies of trappers eager to barter with the natives and platoons of soldiers to guard the newly acquired territory. Frenchmen and Native Americans teamed to unsuccessfully fight the British, who in turn were forced to retreat into Canada after the American colonies successfully revolted. The British briefly forged into Michigan again during the War of 1812, retreating finally to become Michigan's good neighbors in Canada.

There has been a wavelike pattern to Michigan's economic development. First there were the trees that created a great lumber industry. These were rapidly depleted. The copper and iron-ore mines followed. They also are now mostly inactive, although the discovery of new copper deposits is leading to renewed activity. Finally, the automobile industry, diversified industries, and tourism have become successful. Today, the St. Lawrence Seaway makes the cities of Michigan international ports and the state's future a prosperous one.

When to Go/Climate

Long, hard winters and hot, humid summers are common on Michigan's Upper Peninsula. The Lower Peninsula benefits from the moderating influence of the Great Lakes. Summers are warm; and brilliant fall foliage spreads southward from the Upper Peninsula beginning in September.

AVERAGE HIGH/LOW TEMPERATURES (°F)

DETROIT

Jan 30/16	May 70/47	Sept 74/63
Feb 33/18	June 79/56	Oct 62/41
Mar 44/27	July 83/61	Nov 48/32
Apr 58/37	Aug 81/60	Dec 35/21

GRAND RAPIDS

Jan 29/15	May 79/55	Sept 72/50
Feb 43/25	June 83/60	Oct 60/39
Mar 57/35	July 81/58	Nov 46/30
Apr 69/46	Aug 81/58	Dec 34/21

SAULT STE. MARIE

Jan 21/5	May 63/38	Sept 66/44
Feb 23/5	June 71/46	Oct 54/36
Mar 33/15	July 76/51	Nov 40/26
Apr 48/28	Aug 74/51	Dec 26/12

Parks and Recreation Finder

Directions to and information about the parks and recreation areas below are given under their respective town/city sections. Please refer to those sections for details.

NATIONAL PARK AND RECREATION AREAS

Key to abbreviations. I.H.S. = International Historic Site; I.P.M. = International Peace Memorial; N.B. = National Battlefield; N.B.P. = National Battlefield Park; N.B.C. = National Battlefield and Cemetery; N.C.A. = National Conservation Area; N.E.M. = National Expansion Memorial; N.F. = National Forest; N.G. = National Grassland; N.H.P. = National Historical Park; N.H.C. = National Heritage Corridor; N.H.S. = National Historic Site; N.L. = National Lakeshore; N.M. = National Monument; N.M.P. = National Military Park; N.Mem. = National Memorial; N.P. = National Park; N.Pres. = National Preserve; N.R.A. = National Recreational Area; N.R.R. = National Recreational River; N.Riv. = National River; N.S. = National Seashore; N.S.R. = National Scenic Riverway; N.S.T. = National Scenic Trail; N.Sc. = National Scientific Reserve; N.V.M. = National Volcanic Monument.

Place Name	Listed Under
Hiawatha N.F.	ESCANABA
Huron-Manistee N.F.	MANISTEE, OSCODA
Isle Royale N.P.	same
Keweenaw N.H.P.	CALUMET
Ottawa N.F.	IRONWOOD
Pictured Rocks N.L.	MUNISING
Sleeping Bear Dunes N.L.	same

CALENDAR HIGHLIGHTS

JANUARY

Ice Sculpture Spectacular (Plymouth). Hundreds of ice sculptures line the streets and fill Kellogg Park, as professional and student chefs compete with each other carving huge blocks of ice. Sculptures are lighted at night. Phone 734/453-1540.

MAY

Tulip Time Festival (Holland). A celebration of Dutch heritage: 1,800 klompen dancers, three parades, street scrubbing, Dutch markets, entertainment, and millions of tulips. Phone 616/396-4221 or 800/822-2770.

JUNE

Cereal City Festival (Battle Creek). On Michigan Avenue. Children's Parade, Queen's Pageant, arts and crafts exhibits; also the world's longest breakfast table. Phone 616/962-2240.

Bavarian Festival (Frankenmuth). Heritage Park. Celebration of German heritage. Music, dancing, parades, and other entertainment; food; art demonstrations and agricultural displays. Phone 800/BAVARIA.

International Freedom Festival (Detroit and Windsor, ON). Joint celebration with Detroit and Windsor; nearly 100 events, including fireworks. Phone 313/923-7400.

JULY

Street Art Fairs (Ann Arbor). Nearly 1,000 artists and craftspeople display and sell works. Contact Convention and Visitors Bureau, 800/888-9487.

Sailing Races (Mackinac Island). Port Huron-to-Mackinac and Chicago-to-Mackinac. Phone 810/985-7101 for Port Huron race; 312/861-7777 for Chicago race.

AUGUST

Michigan State Fair (Detroit). Michigan Exposition and Fairgrounds. Phone 313/369-8428.

SEPTEMBER

Mackinac Bridge Walk (Mackinaw City and St. Ignace). 70,000 participants take a recreational walk across Mackinac Bridge (some lanes open to motor vehicles). Phone 231/436-5574 or 800/666-0160.

Historic Home Tour (Marshall). Informal tours of nine 19th-century homes, including Honolulu House, Governor's Mansion, and Capitol Hill School. Phone 616/781-5163 or 800/877-5163.

DECEMBER

Dickens Christmas (Holly). Re-creates the Dickensian period with carolers, town crier, strolling characters, skits, bell choirs, street hawkers, carriage rides. Thanksgiving weekend-weekend before December 25.

STATE PARK AND RECREATION AREAS

Key to abbreviations. I.P. = Interstate Park; S.A.P. = State Archaeological Park; S.B. = State Beach; S.C.A. = State Conservation Area; S.C.P. = State Conservation Park; S.Cp. = State Campground; S.F. = State Forest; S.G. = State Garden; S.H.A. = State Historic Area; S.H.P. = State Historic Park; S.H.S. = State Historic Site; S.M.P. = State Marine Park; S.N.A. = State Natural Area; S.P. = State Park; S.P.C. = State Public Campground; S.R. = State Reserve; S.R.A. = State Recreation

Area; S.Res. = State Reservoir; S.Res.P. = State Resort Park; S.R.P. = State Rustic Park.

Place Name	Listed Under
Albert E. Sleeper S.P.	PORT AUSTIN
Aloha S.P.	CHEBOYGAN
Bay City S.R.A.	BAY CITY
Burt Lake S.P.	INDIAN RIVER
Cheboygan S.P.	CHEBOYGAN
Fayette S.P.	MANISTIQUE
Fort Custer S.R.A.	BATTLE CREEK
Fort Wilkins S.P.	COPPER HARBOR
Grand Haven S.P.	GRAND HAVEN
Hartwick Pines S.P.	GRAYLING
Highland S.R.A.	PONTIAC
Holland S.P.	HOLLAND
Indian Lake S.P.	MANISTIQUE
Interlochen S.P.	TRAVERSE CITY
J.W. Wells S.P.	MENOMINEE
Lakeport S.P.	PORT HURON
Ludington S.P.	LUDINGTON
Muskegon S.P.	MUSKEGON
Orchard Beach S.P.	MANISTEE
Otsego Lake S.P.	GAYLORD
Palms Book S.P.	MANISTIQUE
Petoskey S.P.	PETOSKEY
P. J. Hoffmaster S.P.	MUSKEGON
Pontiac Lake S.R.A.	PONTIAC
Porcupine Mountains Wilderness S.P.	ONTONAGON
Sterling S.P.	MONROE
Tahquamenon Falls S.P.	NEWBERRY
Van Buren S.P.	SOUTH HAVEN
Van Riper S.P.	ISHPEMING
Warren Dunes S.P.	ST. JOSEPH
Waterloo S.R.A.	JACKSON
Wilderness S.P.	MACKINAW CITY
William Mitchell S.P.	CADILLAC
Wilson S.P.	HARRISON

Water-related activities, hiking, riding, various other sports, picnicking, and visitor centers, as well as camping, are available in many of these areas. Motor vehicle permits are required to enter parks: $4/day (except Warren Dunes, $5/day for nonresidents); annual sticker: $20. From May through September, about 80 percent of the campsites in each park are available by reservation for stays of 1-15 nights. The fee is $9-$23/night. Pets on leash only. For reservations phone 800/44-PARKS. For reservation applications and further information about state parks, contact Department of Natural Resources, Parks and Recreation Division, PO Box 30257, Lansing 48909-7757, phone 517/373-9900. For information on state forests, contact Department of Natural Resources, Forest Management Division, PO Box 30452, Lansing 48909, phone 517/373-1275.

SKI AREAS

Place Name	Listed Under
Alpine Valley Ski Resort	PONTIAC
Big Powderhorn Mountain Ski Area	IRONWOOD
Bittersweet Ski Area	KALAMAZOO

Blackjack Ski Area	IRONWOOOD
Boyne Highlands Ski Area	HARBOR SPRINGS
Boyne Mountain Ski Area	BOYNE CITY
Caberfae Peaks Ski Resort	CADILLAC
Cannonsburg Ski Area	GRAND RAPIDS
Chalet Cross-Country Ski Area	CLARE
Crystal Mountain Resort	BEULAH
Hickory Hills Ski	TRAVERSE CITY
Indianhead Mountain-Bear Creek Ski Resort	WAKEFIELD
Maasto Hiihto Ski Trail	HANCOCK
Marquette Mountain Ski Area	MARQUETTE
Mount Ripley Ski Area	HOUGHTON
Mount Holly Ski Area	HOLLY
Mount Zion Ski Area	IRONWOOD
Nub's Nob Ski Area	HARBOR SPRINGS
Pando Ski Area	GRAND RAPIDS
Pine Mountain Lodge	IRON MOUNTAIN
Porcupine Mountains Wilderness State Park	ONTONAGON
Shanty Creek Resort	BELLAIRE
Ski Brule	IRON RIVER
Skyline Ski Area	GRAYLING
Snowsnake Mountain	HARRISON
Sugar Loaf Resort	TRAVERSE CITY
Swiss Valley Ski Area	THREE RIVERS
Timber Ridge Ski Area	KALAMAZOO
Treetops Sylvan Resort	GAYLORD

FISHING AND HUNTING

In the 1960s coho and chinook salmon were transplanted from the Pacific Northwest into the streams feeding into Lake Michigan and subsequently into Lakes Huron and Superior. The success of the program was immediate and today salmon fishing, especially for chinook, is a major sport. Chinook fishing is good throughout the summer in the Great Lakes and through the early fall during the spawning season in the rivers; the fish may weigh as much as 45 pounds. Information on charter boat fishing can be obtained from Travel Michigan, Michigan Jobs Commission, PO Box 3393, Livonia 48151, phone 888/78-GREAT.

Nonresident restricted fishing licenses: annual $26; all-species fishing includes spike, salmon, and brook, brown, rainbow, and lake trout: $41. A fishing license for all waters is required for everyone 17 years of age and older. Resident and nonresident 24-hour fishing license $7.

Nonresident hunting licenses: small game $65; deer $129; bear $150; archery (deer only) $129. For further information on hunting and fishing, write Department of Natural Resources, Retail Sales Section, PO Box 30181, Lansing 48909, phone 517/373-1204.

Driving Information

Safety belts are mandatory for all persons in front seat of vehicle. Children ages 4-16 must be in an approved passenger restraint anywhere in vehicle. Children ages 1-4 may use a regulation safety belt in back seat, but must use an approved safety seat in front seat of vehicle. Children under age one must use an approved safety seat anywhere in vehicle. For further information phone Office of Highway Safety Planning, 517/336-6477.

INTERSTATE HIGHWAY SYSTEM

The following alphabetical listing of Michigan towns in *Mobil Travel Guide* shows that these cities are within ten miles of the indicated Interstate highways. A highway map, however, should be checked for the nearest exit.

Highway Number	Cities/Towns within ten miles
Interstate 69	Coldwater, Flint, Lansing, Marshall, Owosso, Port Huron.
Interstate 75	Bay City, Birmingham, Bloomfield Hills, Cheboygan, Dearborn, Detroit, Flint, Frankenmuth, Gaylord, Grayling, Holly, Mackinaw City, Monroe, Pontiac, Saginaw, St. Ignace, Sault Ste. Marie, Warren.
Interstate 94	Ann Arbor, Battle Creek, Dearborn, Detroit, Jackson, Kalamazoo, Marshall, Mount Clemens, Port Huron, St. Clair, St. Joseph, Warren, Ypsilanti.
Interstate 96	Detroit, Grand Haven, Grand Rapids, Lansing, Muskegon.

Additional Visitor Information

Travel Michigan, Michigan Jobs Commission, PO Box 30226, Lansing 48909, phone 888/78-GREAT, distributes publications including an annual travel planner, seasonal travel guides, and calendars of events, and directories of lodgings, campgrounds, golf courses, and charter boat and canoe companies. Travel counselors are available (daily) to assist in planning a Michigan getaway.

There are 13 Welcome Centers in Michigan, open daily; visitors who stop will find information, brochures, and an extensive database of lodging facilities and attractions most helpful in planning stops at points of interest. Their locations are as follows: Clare, off US 27; Coldwater, off I-69; Dundee, off US 23; Iron Mountain, off US 2; Ironwood, off US 2; Mackinaw City, off I-75; Marquette, off US 41; Menominee, off US 41/MI 35; Monroe, off I-75; New Buffalo, off I-94; Port Huron, off I-94; St. Ignace, off I-75; and Sault Ste. Marie, off I-75.

THE KEWEENAW PENINSULA

The drive up the Keweenaw Peninsula is Michigan's most popular road trip—and with good reason. This route offers everything you could ever want in a driving tour: awe-inspiring waterfalls, amazing coastal scenery, colorful history, sunny beaches, and picturesque towns. Surrounded on three sides by spectacular Lake Superior, the Keweenaw Peninsula also offers visitors the rare treat of watching the sun rise and set over the same body of water.

No visit to the Keweenaw, often referred to as "Copper Country," would be complete without exploring the history of its days as a copper-mining boomtown. Quincy Mine, located in the town of Hancock, offers guided copper-mine tours, as well as a passenger cog rail tram. The nearby town of Houghton was runner-up in the *Chicago Tribune*'s "Best Little Town in the Midwest" contest and is well worth a visit. Houghton also offers seasonal ferry service to Isle Royale National Park, the United States' most isolated national park and an amazing wilderness experience that outdoor enthusiasts won't want to miss. Advance reservations are required. Isle Royale can also be accessed by seaplane. Eleven miles north of Hancock/Houghton is Calumet, an almost perfectly preserved mining town, replete with flagstone streets and entire districts of restored dwellings. Keweenaw National Historic Park, located here, features a self-guided walking tour commemorating the history of copper mining in the area. From Calumet, head north on Route 26 to Eagle River, pausing at Eagle River Falls for a look at the beautiful scenery and a photograph or two. Route 26 between Eagle Harbor and Copper Harbor is Brockway Mountain Drive, believed to be the most beautiful road in the state. This nine-mile drive is the highest above-sea-level road between the Rockies and Alleghenies—the views are superlative from this commanding height! Fall paints this route with an amazing palate of colors; spring brings the migration of hawks and eagles. Whatever the season, Brockway Mountain is an ideal place to watch the sunset over Lake Superior—the perfect end to a perfect day in the Keweenaw Peninsula.

If you have more than one day—and we hope you do because there is so much yet to see—spend tomorrow exploring attractions in and around Copper Harbor. Take the 20-minute boat ride out to Copper Harbor Lighthouse for a guided tour of one of the oldest lighthouses on Lake Superior. Visit Delaware Mine for a copper mine tour that will take you 110 feet down a mine shaft. Stop at Estivant Pines, located a few miles south of Copper Harbor, to see some of the oldest trees in Michigan. Take the ferry out to Isle Royale for a wilderness experience you won't soon forget. Scuba dive at the Keweenaw Preserve to explore the 18 shipwrecks submerged there (note: it is illegal to remove anything from the wrecks). Whatever you choose to see and do, you are sure to enjoy your time in the Keweenaw Peninsula!
(APPROX 45 MI)

Alma

(F-5) *See also Mount Pleasant*

Pop 9,034 **Elev** 736 ft **Area code** 989
Zip 48801
Information Gratiot Area Chamber of
Commerce, 110 W Superior St, PO
Box 516; 989/463-5525
Web www.gratoit.org

What to See and Do

Alma College. (1886) 1,400 students.
On 87-acre campus. Campus tours.
190,000-volume library. Frank Knox
Memorial Room in Reid-Knox building has mementos of former secretary of the Navy (by appt). 614 W
Superior St. Phone 989/463-7111.

Special Event

Highland Festival & Games. Bahlke
Field at Alma College. Piping, drumming, fiddling, Ceilidh, dancing;
caber toss, sheaf toss, hammer throw
competitions; art fair, parade. Memorial Day wkend. Phone 989/463-
8979.

Motels/Motor Lodges

★★ **COMFORT INN.** *3110 W Monroe Rd (48801). 989/463-4400; fax
989/463-2970; res 800/228-5150. www.
comfortinn.com.* 87 rms, 2 story. S, D
$53-$89; each addl $5; under 18 free.
Crib free. TV; cable (premium), VCR
avail (movies). Indoor pool; whirlpool. Complimentary continental
bkfst. Restaurant 4:30-10 pm; closed
Sun, Mon. Bar. Ck-out 11 am. Meeting rms. Business servs avail. Valet
serv. Some bathrm phones. Cr cds: A,
D, DS, MC, V.

★ **PETTICOAT INN.** *2454 W Monroe
Rd (48801). 989/681-5728.* 11 rms. S
$36-$40; D $45-$52; each addl $3;
higher rates special events. Pet
accepted. TV; cable (premium).
Restaurant adj open 24 hrs. Ck-out
11 am. Country setting. Cr cds: A,
DS, MC, V.

Alpena (D-6)

Pop 11,354 **Elev** 593 ft **Area code** 989
Zip 49707
Information Convention and Visitors
Bureau, 235 W Chisholm St, PO Box
65; 989/354-4181 or 800/4-ALPENA
Web www.oweb.com/upnorth/cvb/

Located at the head of Thunder Bay,
Alpena is a center for industry as
well as recreation. Approximately 80
shipwrecks have occurred in this
area, making it an excellent diving
location.

What to See and Do

Dinosaur Gardens Prehistorical Zoo.
Authentic reproductions of prehistoric birds and animals. (Mid-May-
mid-Oct, daily) 11168 US 23, 10 mi S
in Ossineke. Phone 989/471-5477. ¢¢

**Island Park and Alpena Wildfowl
Sanctuary.** Intown wildfowl sanctuary and self-guided nature trails,
fishing platforms, and picnic area.
US 23 N.

Jesse Besser Museum. Historical
exhibits feature agricultural, lumber,
and early industrial era; reconstructed avenue of 1890 shops and
businesses; restored cabins, Maltz
Exchange Bank (1872), Green School
(1895). Jesse Besser exhibit. Science
exhibits incl geology, natural history,
and archaeological displays. Also
planetarium, shows (Sun; fee).
Museum (daily; closed hols). 491
Johnson St, 2 blks E off US 23. Phone
989/356-2202. ¢

**Old Presque Isle Lighthouse and
Museum.** Nautical instruments,
marine artifacts, and other antiques
housed in lighthouse and keeper's
cottage (1840). Antiques from mid-
1800s. (May-mid-Oct, daily) 23 mi N
via US 23 on Presque Isle. Phone
989/595-2787. ¢

Special Events

**"Art on the Bay"—Thunder Bay Art
Show.** Bay View Park. Third wkend
July. Phone 989/356-6678.

Brown Trout Festival. Phone
989/354-4181. Third full wk July.

Alpena County Fair. Alpena County Fairgrounds. Phone 517/356-1174. First wk Aug.

Motels/Motor Lodges

★ ★ **BEST WESTERN OF ALPENA.** *1286 MI 32 W (49707). 989/356-9087; fax 989/354-0543; res 800/780-7234. www.bestwestern.com.* 36 rms, 1-2 story. Late May-Oct: S $45-$55; $59-$70; each addl $6; under 12 free; lower rates rest of yr. Crib $4. TV; cable (premium). Indoor pool; whirlpool. Complimentary continental bkfst. Restaurant adj 7 am-9 pm. Bar. Ck-out 11 am. Sundries. Game rm. Cr cds: A, C, D, DS, MC, V.

D ⇌ ⇟ ☼ SC

★ **FLETCHER.** *1001 US 23 N (49707). 989/354-4191; fax 989/354-4056; toll-free 800/334-5920.* 96 rms, 2 story. June-Oct: S $58; D $64; each addl $6; suites $115; kit. units $85; under 16 free; wkly rates; lower rates rest of yr. Crib $6. Pet accepted. TV; cable. Indoor pool; whirlpool, sauna. Restaurant 7 am-9 pm. Bar 11-2 am; Sun from noon. Ck-out 11 am. Meeting rms. Bellhops. Free airport, bus depot transportation. Tennis. Nature trail. Refrigerators; some in-rm whirlpools. Some balconies. Grills. Overlooks wooded acres. Cr cds: A, DS, MC, V.

D ➤ ♨ ✗ ⇌ ✈ ⇟ ☼

★ ★ **HOLIDAY INN.** *1000 US 23 N (49707). 989/356-2151; fax 989/356-2151; toll-free 800/465-4329. www.holiday-inn.com.* 148 rms, 2 story. S $69-$99; D $79-$109; each addl $10; studio rms $99; under 19 free. Crib free. Pet accepted. TV; cable. Indoor pool; whirlpool, poolside serv. Restaurant 6:30 am-2 pm, 5-10 pm. Bar 4 pm-2 am; entertainment. Ck-out noon. Coin lndry. Meeting rms. Business servs avail. Bellhops. Valet serv. Sundries. Gift shop. Free airport, bus depot transportation. Putting green. X-country ski 8 mi. Exercise equipt; sauna. Game rm. Cr cds: A, MC, V.

D ➤ ♨ ☙ ⇌ ♀ ✈ ☼

Ann Arbor

(H-6) *See also Dearborn, Detroit, Jackson, Ypsilanti*

Settled 1823 **Pop** 109,592 **Elev** 840 ft **Area code** 734

Information Convention & Visitors Bureau, 120 W Huron, 48104; 734/995-7281 or 800/888-9487

Web www.annarbor.org

Most famous as the home of the University of Michigan, Ann Arbor has a college-town atmosphere enjoyed by both students and residents. The community's economy is diversified, with more than 100 research and high-technology firms.

There are two interesting theories about the origin of the town's unusual name. One explanation is that two of the pioneer settlers had wives named Ann who liked to sit together under a wild grape arbor—hence, "Ann Arbor." The other theory, recognized by many historians, claims that the latter part of the name came from the many openings, or, in those days, "arbors," which appeared in the thick forests covering the nearby hills. The "arbors" were said to have resulted from agricultural methods of the Native Americans.

What to See and Do

Huron-Clinton Metroparks. A regional park system with 13 recreation areas located along the Huron and Clinton rivers in southeast Michigan. A motor vehicle entry permit, which is good at all metroparks, is required (free on Tues). (Also see FARMINGTON, MOUNT CLEMENS, TROY) Phone 800/477-3191.

Delhi. On this 50-acre site are the Delhi Rapids. Fishing, canoeing, rentals (May-Sept); hiking trails, x-country skiing, picnicking, playground. 5½ mi NW on Delhi Rd, near Huron River Dr. Phone 734/426-8211.

Dexter-Huron. Fishing, canoeing; hiking trails, x-country skiing, picnicking, playground. 7½ mi NW along Huron River Dr. Phone 734/426-8211.

Hudson Mills. More than 1,600-acre recreation area; fishing, boating, canoe rentals; hiking, bicycle trail (rentals), 18-hole golf, x-country skiing (winter), picnicking, playground, camping, activity center. 12 mi NW on N Territorial Rd. Phone 734/426-8211.

Kempf House Center for Local History. (1853) Unusual example of Greek Revival architecture, restored structure owned and maintained by the city of Ann Arbor. Antique Victorian furnishings; displays of local historical artifacts. Tours (Sun afternoons; closed Jan and Aug). 312 S Division. Phone 734/994-4898. ¢

★ **University of Michigan.** (1817) 36,000 students. Established here in 1837, after having moved from Detroit where it was founded. One of the largest universities in the country, it makes significant contributions in teaching and research. Phone 734/764-INFO. Points of particular interest are

Exhibit Museum of Natural History. Anthropology, Michigan wildlife, geology, and prehistoric life exhibits. (Daily; closed hols) Planetarium shows (Sat and Sun; fee). 1109 Geddes Ave. Phone 734/764-0478. **Donation**

Gerald R. Ford Presidential Library. Research library that houses Ford's presidential, vice-presidential, and congressional documents. (Mon-Fri; closed hols) N campus, 1000 Beal Ave. Phone 734/741-2218. **FREE**

Kelsey Museum of Ancient and Medieval Archaeology. (Tues-Sun) 434 S State St. Phone 734/764-9304. **FREE**

Law Quadrangle. Quadrangle incl four beautiful Gothic-style buildings. The law library, with an underground addition, has one of the nation's most extensive collections. S State St and S University Ave. Phone 734/764-9322.

Matthaei Botanical Gardens. Approx 250 acres incl greenhouses (daily; closed hols). Seasonal exhibits. Grounds (daily). 1800 N Dixboro Rd, 3 mi NE of campus. Phone 734/998-7060. ¢¢

Museum of Art. (Tues-Sun) S State St and S University Ave. Phone 734/764-0395. **Donation**

Nichols Arboretum. Approx 125 acres. (Daily) Geddes Ave. Phone 734/998-9540. **FREE**

North Campus. Contains research areas; School of Music designed by Eero Saarinen; School of Art and Architecture with public art gallery (Mon-Sat); School of Engineering. 2 mi NE of central campus.

Power Center for the Performing Arts. A 1,414-seat theater houses performances of drama, opera, music, and dance. 121 S Fletcher. Phone 734/763-3333.

Special Events

Ann Arbor Summer Festival. Power Center, University of Michigan. A performing arts festival of mime, dance, theater, and music; also lectures, films, and exhibits. Phone 734/647-2278. June-early July.

Street Art Fair. S University Ave, Main St, State St, Liberty St. Nearly 1,000 artists and craftspeople display and sell works. Phone 734/994-5260. Four days mid-July.

Motels/Motor Lodges

★★ **COURTYARD BY MARRIOTT.** *3205 Boardwalk (48108). 734/995-5900; fax 734/995-2937; 800/321-2211. www.marriott.com.* 160 rms, 4 story, 40 suites. S $89-$159; D $89-$169; each addl $10; suites $99-$179; under 18 free. Crib free. TV; cable (premium). Indoor pool; whirlpool. Restaurant 6:30 am-1 pm. Bar 4:30 pm-midnight. Ck-out noon. Meeting rms. Valet serv. X-country ski 3 mi. Exercise equipt. Many refrigerators. Cr cds: A, D, DS, MC, V.
🏊 ⚓ 🏋 🎿 🔥

★★ **FAIRFIELD INN.** *3285 Boardwalk Dr (48108). 734/995-5200; fax 734/995-5394; toll-free 800/228-2800. www.fairfieldinn.com.* 110 rms, 4 story. S, D $59-$129; each addl $6; under 18 free; higher rates: football wkends, some university events. Crib free. TV; cable (premium). Indoor pool; whirlpool. Complimentary continental bkfst. Restaurant adj 6:30 am-1 pm. Ck-out noon. Valet serv. X-country ski 3 mi. Refrigerators. Cr cds: A, D, DS, JCB, MC, V.

★ ★ **HAMPTON INN.** *925 Victors Way (48108). 734/665-5000; fax 734/665-8452; res 800/426-7866. www.hamptoninn.com.* 150 rms, 4 story. June-Nov: S $65-$75; D $80-$95; under 18 free; higher rates special events (2-day min); lower rates rest of yr. Crib free. TV; cable (premium). Indoor pool; whirlpool. Complimentary continental bkfst. Complimentary coffee in lobby. Restaurant nearby. Ck-out noon. Coin lndry. Meeting rms. Business servs avail. Valet serv Mon-Fri. Exercise equipt. Refrigerators. Cr cds: A, D, DS, MC, V.

★ ★ **HAMPTON INN NORTH.** *2300 Green Rd (48105). 734/996-4444; fax 734/996-0196; res 800/426-7866. www.hamptoninn.com.* 130 rms, 4 story. S $59-$85; D $66-$95; under 18 free. Crib free. Pet accepted, some restrictions. TV; cable (premium). Indoor pool; whirlpool. Complimentary continental bkfst. Restaurant nearby. Ck-out noon. Meeting rms. Business servs avail. Exercise equipt. Valet serv. X-country ski 3 mi. Cr cds: A, MC, V.

★ ★ **HOLIDAY INN.** *3600 Plymouth Rd (48105). 734/769-9800; fax 734/761-1290; toll-free 800/800-5560. www.holiday-inn.com.* 223 rms, 2-5 story. S $77-$99; D $109-$139; under 18 free; wkend rates. Crib free. Pet accepted, some restrictions; $50 refundable. TV; cable. Indoor/outdoor pool; whirlpool. Restaurant 6:30 am-10 pm; Fri, Sat to 11 pm; Sun 7:30 am-9 pm. Bar. Ck-out 11 am. Meeting rms. Business servs avail. Valet serv. Tennis. X-country ski 2½ mi. Exercise equipt, sauna. Game rm. Picnic tables. Cr cds: A, C, D, DS, MC, V.

★ **LAMP POST INN.** *2424 E Stadium Blvd (48104). 734/971-8000; fax 734/971-7483. www.lamppostinn.com.* 54 rms, 16 kit. units, 27 with shower only, 2 story. S, D $44.95-$89.95; family, wkly rates; higher rates special events. Crib free. Pet accepted,

some restrictions. TV; cable, VCR avail. Pool. Complimentary continental bkfst. Ck-out 11 am. Downhill ski 20 mi; x-country ski 1½ mi. Health club privileges. Microwaves, refrigerators. Cr cds: A, D, DS, MC, V.

★ **RED ROOF INN - NORTH.** *3621 Plymouth Rd (48105). 734/996-5800; fax 734/996-5707; res 800/843-7663. www.redroof.com.* 108 rms, 2 story. S $39.99-$61.99; D $48.99-$71.99; 3 or more persons $51.99-$64.99; under 18 free; higher rates special events. Crib free. Pet accepted. TV; cable (premium). Restaurant adj 6 am-midnight. Ck-out noon. Cr cds: A, D, DS, MC, V.

★ ★ ★ **WEBER'S INN.** *3050 Jackson Ave (48103). 734/769-2500; fax 734/769-4743; toll-free 800/443-3050. www.webersinn.com.* 160 rms, 4 story. S, D $95-$135; each addl $10; suites $199-$275; under 18 free. Crib free. TV; cable (premium), VCR avail (movies). Indoor pool; whirlpool, poolside serv. Complimentary continental bkfst. Restaurant 6:30 am-10:30 pm; Mon to 9:30 pm; Fri to midnight; Sat 8 am-midnight; Sun 8 am-9:30 pm. Bar 11-1:30 am; entertainment. Ck-out noon. Meeting rms. Business center. In-rm modem link. Valet serv. Sundries. Tennis privileges. X-country ski 5 mi. Exercise equipt; sauna. Some refrigerators. Some rms with spiral staircase to pool. Cr cds: A, C, D, DS, JCB, MC, V.

Hotels

★ ★ **BELL TOWER HOTEL.** *300 S Thayer St (48104). 734/769-3010; fax 734/769-4339; toll-free 800/562-3559. www.belltowerhotel.com.* 66 rms, 3-4 story, 10 suites. S $125; D $140; each addl $15; suites $154-$238; under 3 free. Crib free. TV; cable, VCR avail. Complimentary continental bkfst. Restaurant 6-10 pm; closed Sun. Ck-out noon. Meeting rms. Business servs avail. In-rm modem link. Free valet parking. X-country ski 2 mi. Health club privileges. Refrigerator, minibar in suites. European-style decor, ambience. Cr cds: A, C, D, ER, MC, V.

[icons]

★ ★ ★ **CROWNE PLAZA.** *610 Hilton Blvd (48108). 734/761-7800; fax 734/995-1085; toll-free 800/465-4329. www.crowneplazaaa.com.* 200 rms, 3 story. S, D $125-$164; suites $200-$300; family, wkend rates. Crib free. TV; cable (premium). Indoor pool; whirlpool. Complimentary coffee. Restaurant 6 am-11 pm; Sun from 7 am. Bar 5 pm-midnight. Ck-out 11 am. Meeting rms. Concierge. Bellhops. Valet serv. Sundries. Gift shop. X-country ski 10 mi. Exercise equipt; sauna. Cr cds: A, D, DS, JCB, MC, V.

[icons]

★ ★ ★ **THE DAHLMANN CAMPUS INN.** *615 E Huron St (48104). 734/769-2200; fax 734/769-6222; toll-free 800/666-8693. www.campusinn.com.* 208 rms, 15 story. S $138-$150; D $153-$200; each addl $15; suites $175-$350; under 2 free; higher rates special events (2-day min). Crib avail. TV; cable, VCR avail. Pool. Complimentary coffee. Restaurant 7 am-2 pm, 5-9 pm; Fri, Sat to 10 pm. Bar from 5 pm. Ck-out 11 am. Meeting rms. Business servs avail. In-rm modem link. Concierge. Gift shop. X-country ski 3 mi. Exercise equipt; sauna. Cr cds: A, C, D, DS, MC, V.

[icons]

★ ★ **SHERATON INN ANN HARBOR.** *3200 Boardwalk (48108). 734/996-0600; fax 734/996-8136; toll-free 800/848-2770. www.sheraton.com.* 197 rms, 6 story. S, D, studio rms $79-$135; each addl $10; suites $109-$175; under 18 free; wkend rates. Crib free. TV; cable (premium). Indoor/outdoor pool; whirlpool, poolside serv. Restaurant 6:30 am-10:30 pm; Fri, Sat to 11:30 pm. Bar noon-1 am. Ck-out noon. Meeting rms. Business center. In-rm modem link. Bellhops. Sundries. X-country ski 10 mi. Exercise equipt; sauna. Health club privileges. Some refrigerators, microwaves. Cr cds: A, MC, V.

[icons]

Extended Stay

★ ★ **RESIDENCE INN BY MARRIOTT.** *800 Victors Way (48108).* 734/996-5666; fax 734/996-1919. www.residenceinn.com. 114 kit. suites, 2-3 story. S $109-$139; D $169. Crib free. Pet accepted; fee. TV; cable (premium). Heated pool; whirlpool. Complimentary continental bkfst. Restaurant opp 6 am-11 pm. Ck-out noon. Coin lndry. Meeting rm. Valet serv. Balconies. Picnic tables, grills. Cr cds: A, D, DS, MC, V.

[icons]

Restaurants

★ **BELLA CIAO.** *118 W Liberty St (48104). 734/995-2107. www.bellaciao. com.* Hrs: 5:30-10 pm. Closed Sun; hols. Res accepted. Italian menu. Serv bar. A la carte entrees: dinner $16-$24. Specializes in veal, pasta, seafood. Outdoor dining. Cr cds: A, D, DS, MC, V.

★ ★ **DANIELS ON LIBERTY AND THE MOVEABLE FEAST.** *326 W Liberty (48103). 734/663-3278. www. danielsonliberty.com.* Hrs: 5:30-10 pm. Closed Sun; hols. Res accepted. Serv bar. A la carte entrees: dinner $19-$29. Complete meals: dinner $30-$50. Specializes in duck, seafood, veal. Parking. Outdoor dining. Historic Victorian house (1870). Cr cds: A, D, DS, MC, V.

[icon]

★ ★ **EARLE.** *121 W Washington (48104). 734/994-0211. www.theearle. com.* Hrs: 5:30-10 pm; Fri to midnight; Sat 6 pm-midnight; Sun 5-9 pm. Closed hols; Sun June-Aug. Res accepted. French, Italian provincial menu. Bar. Dinner $10-$25. Own sorbet. Pianist wkdays, jazz trio wkends. Outdoor dining. In historic brick building (1885). Cr cds: A, D, DS, MC, V.

[icon]

★ ★ ★ **ESCOFFIER.** *300 S Thayer St (48104). 734/995-3800.* Hrs: 5:30-9:30 pm. Closed Sun; hols. Res accepted. French menu. Bar. Wine list. A la carte entrees: dinner $20-$35. Complete meals: dinner $30. Own pastries. Pianist. Valet parking. Cr cds: A, D, MC, V.

[icons]

★ ★ **GANDY DANCER.** *401 Depot St (48104). 734/769-0592. www. muer.com.* Hrs: 11:30 am-4 pm, 5-10

pm; Sat from 5 pm; Sun 3:30-9 pm; early-bird dinner Mon-Sat 4:30-5:30 pm; Sun brunch 10 am-2 pm. Closed Jan 1, Dec 25. Res accepted. Bar. Lunch $5.50-$14, dinner $16-$35. Sun brunch $18.95. Child's menu. Specializes in fresh seafood, rack of lamb, pasta. Own pasta. Valet parking. Historic converted railroad station. Cr cds: A, D, DS, MC, V.
D

★ ★ **KERRYTOWN BISTRO.** *415 N 5th Ave (48104). 734/994-6424. www. kerrytownbistro.com.* Hrs: 11:30 am-2 pm, 5:30-10 pm; Sun 10:30 am-2 pm; Mon 5-9 pm; Sat, Sun brunch 10:30 am-2 pm. Closed hols. Res accepted. French menu. Bar. A la carte entrees: lunch $7-$14, dinner $17-$25. Sat, Sun brunch $7-$14. Specialty: lamb shanks Provençale. French country atmosphere. Cr cds: A, D, DS, MC, V.
D ⬈

★ **PAESANO'S.** *3411 Washtenaw Ave (48104). 734/971-0484.* Hrs: 11 am-11 pm; Fri to midnight; Sat noon-midnight; Sun noon-10 pm. Closed Jan 1, Thanksgiving, Dec 25. Res accepted. Italian menu. Bar. Lunch $5.50-$9, dinner $7.50-$17.95. Child's menu. Specializes in pasta, fresh seafood. Strolling mandolinists Fri. Parking. Outdoor dining. Cr cds: A, DS, MC, V.
D

Unrated Dining Spot

ZINGERMAN'S DELICATESSEN. *422 Detroit St (48104). 734/663-3354. www.zingermans.com.* Specializes in rueben, corned beef hash, vegetarian hash. Hrs: 7 am-10 pm. Closed hols. Lunch, dinner $7.50-$12.99. Child's menu. Cr cds: A, MC, V.
D

Battle Creek

(G-5) *See also Kalamazoo, Marshall*

Settled 1831 **Pop** 53,540 **Elev** 830 ft
Area code 616
Information Greater Battle Creek/Calhoun County Visitor and Convention Bureau, 77 E Michigan, Suite

100, 49017; 616/962-2240 or 800/397-2240
Web www.battlecreek.org

Battle Creek's fame was built by two cereal tycoons, W.K. Kellogg and C.W. Post. The Kellogg and Post cereal plants are the largest of their type anywhere. The city has a variety of other food-packing industries plus many heavy industries. Post and Kellogg have influenced more than the economy; signs, streets, parks, and many public institutions also bear their names. The city takes its name from a "battle" that took place on the banks of the creek in 1825 between a native and a land surveyor.

What to See and Do

Binder Park Zoo. Exotic, endangered, and domestic animals in natural exhibits. Fifty-acre Wild Africa exhibit incl giraffes, zebras, antelope, African wild dogs; trading village, ranger station, research camp, and working diamond mine alongside a panoramic African savanna. Ride the Wilderness Tram and the Z.O. & O. Railroad (fee). Miller Children's Zoo. (Mid-Apr-mid-Oct, daily) Special events during Halloween and Christmas. 7400 Division Dr. Phone 616/979-1351. ¢¢

Fort Custer State Recreation Area. Swimming beach, fishing, boating (launch); nature, bridle, and bicycle trails, picnic areas, hunting. Improved campgrounds (res required). X-country skiing, snowmobiling. (Daily) Standard fees. 8 mi W via MI 96, 5163 W Fort Custer Dr in Augusta. Phone 616/731-4200. ¢

Kellogg's Cereal City USA. Themed family attraction celebrating the cereal industry in an educational, historical, and entertaining manner. Visit the re-created cereal production line, a historical timeline focusing on Battle Creek; also Cereal City, a nutrition and health-interactive playland. View three themed theater presentations. Restaurant, gift shop. (Daily, closed hols) 171 W Michigan Ave. Phone 616/962-6230. ¢¢

Kimball House Museum. (1886). Restored and refurnished Victorian home; displays trace development of use of appliances, tools, medical instruments; herb garden; country store. (Fri afternoons; closed Jan-Mar) 196 Capital Ave NE. Phone 616/966-2496. ¢

Leila Arboretum. A 72-acre park containing native trees and shrubs. W Michigan Ave at 20th St. Phone 616/969-0270. On grounds is

> **Kingman Museum of Natural History.** Exhibits incl Journey Through the Crust of the Earth, Walk in the Footsteps of the Dinosaurs, Mammals of the Ice Age, Window to the Universe, Planetarium, Wonder of Life, Discovery Room, and others. (Wed-Sun afternoons; closed hols) Phone 616/965-5117. ¢

Sojourner Truth Grave. On the cemetery's Fifth St is the plain square monument marking the resting place of this remarkable fighter for freedom. Born a slave in the 1790s, Truth gained her freedom in the 1820s and crusaded against slavery until her death in 1883. Although uneducated, she had a brilliant mind as well as unquenchable devotion to her cause. Oak Hill Cemetery, South Ave and Oak Hill Dr.

Willard Beach. Lavishly landscaped; has a wide bathing beach. Supervised swimming; picnicking, pavilion. (Memorial Day-Labor Day, daily) 2 mi S, on shores of Goguac Lake. ¢

W. K. Kellogg Bird Sanctuary of Michigan State University. Experimental farm and forest nearby. Seven kinds of swans and more than 20 species of ducks and geese inhabit the ponds and Wintergreen Lake. One of the finest bird of prey collections in the Midwest, along with free-roaming upland game birds. Colorful viewing all seasons of the yr. Observation deck and educational displays. Grounds and reception center (daily). 13 mi NW off MI 89, 12685 E C Ave. Phone 616/671-2510.

Special Event

Cereal City Festival. On Michigan Ave. Children's Parade, Queen's Pageant, arts and crafts exhibits; also the world's longest breakfast table. Second Sat June. Phone 616/962-2240.

Motels/Motor Lodges

★ ★ **BATTLE CREEK INN.** *5050 Beckley Rd (49015). 616/979-1100; fax 616/979-1899; toll-free 800/232-3405. www.battlecreekinn.com.* 211 rms, 2 story. S $60-$70; D $73-$77; each addl $8; family rates; golf plans. Crib free. Pet accepted. TV; cable (premium). Indoor heated pool; poolside serv. Coffee in rms. Complimentary continental bkfst. Restaurant 6:30 am-2 pm, 5-10 pm. Bar 4 pm-midnight. Ck-out noon. Coin lndry. Meeting rms. Business servs avail. Valet serv. Putting green. Exercise equipt. Health club privileges. Game rm. Refrigerators avail. Cr cds: A, DS, MC, V.

D 🐾 ➳ 🖎 🖎 SC 🏋

★ **DAYS INN.** *4786 Beckley Rd (49017). 616/979-3561; fax 616/979-1400; res 800/329-7466. www.daysinn.com.* 88 rms, 9 kit. units. S $40.75-$44.75; D $42.75-$62.75; each addl $4; kit. units $51.25-$63.75; under 18 free; wkly rates; golf plans; higher rates Balloon Festival. Crib free. Pet accepted. TV; cable (premium). Coffee in rms. Complimentary continental bkfst. Restaurant opp open 24 hrs. Ck-out noon, ck-in 4 pm. Meeting rm. Business servs avail. Tennis privileges. X-country ski 4 mi. Health club privileges. Some in-rm whirlpools. Cr cds: A, C, D, DS, MC, V.

D 🐾 🖎 🖎 ➳ 🖎 🖎

★ **SUPER 8 MOTEL.** *5395 Beckley Rd (49015). 616/979-1828; toll-free 800/800-8000. www.super8.com.* 62 rms, 3 story. No elvtr. S, D $37-$72; each addl $5; suites $51-$100; under 12 free; higher rates special events. Crib free. TV; cable (premium). Complimentary coffee. Restaurant 6 am-midnight. Ck-out 11 am, ck-in 2 pm. Business servs avail. X-country ski 4 mi. Cr cds: A, C, D, DS, MC, V.

D ➳ 🖎 🖎 SC

Hotel

★ ★ ★ **MCCAMLY PLAZA.** *50 SW Capital Ave (49017). 616/963-7050; fax 616/963-3880; toll-free 888/622-2659. www.mccamlyplazahotel.com.* 242 rms, 16 story. S $149; D $159; each addl $20; suites $200-$300; under 17 free; wkly, wkend rates. Crib free. TV; cable, VCR avail (movies). Indoor pool; whirlpool, poolside serv. Coffee in rms. Restaurant 6:30 am-1:30 pm; 5:30-10 pm. Bar 4 pm-1 am; entertainment Mon-Sat. Ck-out 1 pm. Meeting rms. Business servs avail. Shopping arcade. Free RR station, bus depot transportation. X-country ski 3 mi. Exercise equipt; sauna. Refrigerators, minibars. Cr cds: A, C, D, DS, JCB, MC, V.

D ⛊ ⬌ ⇟ ⊠ ⬙ **SC**

B&B/Small Inn

★ ★ **GREENCREST MANOR.** *6174 Halbert Rd E (49017). 616/962-8633; fax 616/962-7254. www.greencrest manor.com.* 8 rms, 2 share bath, 3 story. S, D $95-$175. TV; cable (premium). Complimentary continental bkfst. Restaurant nearby. Ck-out 11 am, ck-in 4:30 pm. Business servs avail. 18-hole golf privileges. X-country ski 5 mi. Some in-rm whirlpools. Marble fireplaces, expansive lawns. Totally nonsmoking. Cr cds: A, D, MC, V.

⬙ ⛊ ⇟ ⊠ ⬙

Bay City

(F-6) *See also Midland, Saginaw*

Settled 1831 **Pop** 38,936 **Elev** 595 ft **Area code** 989

Information Bay Area Convention & Visitors Bureau, 901 Saginaw St, 48708; 989/893-1222 or 888/BAY-TOWN

Web www.tourbaycitymi.org

Bay City is a historic port community located on Saginaw Bay, which services Great Lakes freighters as well as seagoing vessels in the handling of millions of tons of products annually. The city, which is the county seat, is noted for tree-shaded streets and residential areas with new homes and Victorian and Georgian mansions built by the 19th-century lumber barons. Industries include shipbuilding, automobile parts, petrochemicals, and electronics. Sugar beet production and potato and melon crops are important to its economy.

Retail, service, specialty dining, and entertainment businesses can be found in the Historic Midland Street area on the west side of Bay City.

What to See and Do

Bay City State Recreation Area. Approx 200 acres. Swimming, bathhouse, fishing, boating; hiking, picnicking, concession, camping. Standard fees. 5 mi N on MI 247, along Saginaw Bay. Phone 989/684-3020.

Jennison Nature Center. Displays on the history, geology, wildlife, and general ecology of the area. Hiking trails. (Tues-Sun; closed hols) Phone 989/667-0717. **FREE**

Tobico Marsh. 1,700 acres of wetland, the largest remaining wildlife refuge on Saginaw Bay's western shore. Two 32-ft towers allow panoramic viewing of deer, beaver, mink, and hundreds of species of waterfowl and song, shore, and marsh birds. Visitor Center (Tues-Sun). Killarney Beach Rd. Phone 989/684-3020. **FREE**

Bay County Historical Museum. Preserving and displaying the heritage of Bay County. Exhibits interpret life of Native Americans; depict fur trading, lumbering, shipbuilding, industrial development; life of pioneering women; changing exhibits. (Mon-Sat; closed hols) 321 Washington Ave. Phone 989/893-5733. **Donation**

City Hall and Bell Tower. (ca 1895) Meticulously restored Romanesque structure; council chamber has 31-ft-long woven tapestry depicting history of Bay City. View of city and its waterway from bell tower. (Mon-Fri; closed hols) 301 Washington Ave. Phone 989/893-1222. **FREE**

Deer Acres. Storybook theme park with petting zoo. Train rides (fee), antique cars, more. (Mid-May-Labor Day, daily; after Labor Day-mid-Oct, Sat and Sun) 17 mi N on MI 13, in Pinconning. Phone 989/879-2849. ¢¢¢

Scottish Rite Cathedral. The only Scottish Rite Cathedral in the state; contains Lord Cornwallis's surrender chair. (Mon-Fri) 614 Center Ave. Phone 989/893-3700. **FREE**

Special Events

St. Stanislaus Polish Festival. Lincoln Ave, S end of Bay City. Late June. Phone 989/893-1749.

Munger Potato Festival. SE on MI 15, then E on MI 138 in Munger. Four days late July. Phone 989/659-3270.

Motels/Motor Lodges

★★ **BEST WESTERN CREEKSIDE INN.** *6285 Westside Saginaw Rd (48706). 989/686-0840; toll-free 800/528-1234. www.bestwestern.com.* 70 rms, 2 story. S $55-$60; D $55-$65; each addl $5; under 12 free. Crib free. TV; cable (premium). Heated pool; whirlpool, sauna. Restaurant adj 6 am-9 pm. Ck-out 11 am. Meeting rms. Business servs avail. Game rm. Some refrigerators. Private patios, balconies. Cr cds: A, C, D, DS, MC, V.

⌨ ☒ 🐾 SC

★ **EUCLID.** *809 N Euclid Ave (48706). 989/684-9455; fax 989/686-6440.* 36 rms. S $36; D $46; each addl $4. Crib $5. TV; cable (premium). Heated pool. Playground. Restaurant nearby. Ck-out 11 am. Some refrigerators. Picnic tables, grill. Cr cds: A, C, D, DS, MC, V.

🐕 📺 ☒ ☒ 🐾

★★ **HOLIDAY INN.** *501 Saginaw St (48708). 989/892-3501; fax 989/892-9342; res 800/465-4329. www.holiday-inn.com.* 100 rms, 4 story. S, D $84; each addl $7; under 18 free. Crib free. Pet accepted. TV; cable. Indoor pool; whirlpool, sauna. Restaurant 6:30 am-10 pm; Sat, Sun from 7 am. Bar from noon. Ck-out noon. Coin lndry. Meeting rms. Business servs avail. Valet serv. Sundries. Cr cds: A, C, D, DS, JCB, MC, V.

D 🐾 🐕 ☒ 🐾

Resort

★★ **BAY VALLEY HOTEL & RESORT.** *2470 Old Bridge Rd (48706). 989/686-3500; fax 989/686-6950; toll-free 800/241-4653. www.bayvalley.com.* 150 rms, 3 story. Mid-Apr-Oct: S, D $55-$95; each addl $10; suites $150; under 12 free; package plans; lower rates rest of yr. Crib free. Pet accepted. TV; cable (premium), VCR avail. Heated indoor/outdoor pool; whirlpool, poolside serv. Playground.

Restaurant 7 am-10 pm; Fri, Sat to 11 pm. Bar 11-1:30 am; Sun from noon; entertainment. Ck-out noon. Meeting rms. Business servs avail. In-rm modem link. Free airport transportation. Concierge. Bellhops. Gift shop. Valet serv. Sundries. 18-hole golf, greens fee $39-$54, pro, putting green, driving range, golf cart. X-country ski on site, instruction. Exercise rm; sauna. Free airport transportation. Game rm. Lawn games. Private patios, balconies. Picnic tables, grills. Cr cds: A, C, D, DS, MC, V.

🐾 ☒ 🏊 ☒ 🐕 ✈ ☒ 🔥 🏃

Bellaire (D-4)

Pop 1,104 **Elev** 616 ft **Area code** 231 **Zip** 49615

Information Bellaire Chamber of Commerce, PO Box 205; 231/533-6023

Web www.bellairemichigan.com/chamber

What to See and Do

Skiing. Shanty Creek Resort. Two separate mountains: five quad, two double chairlifts, four surface lifts; patrol, school, rentals; snowmaking; nursery; night skiing; lodge (see RESORT), restaurant, snack bar, entertainment; indoor/outdoor pool, two whirlpools; health club. Thirty trails on two mountains; longest run approx one mi; vertical drop 450 ft. X-country trails (25 mi). (Thanksgiving-Mar, daily) Shanty Creek Rd, 2 mi SE off MI 88. Phone 231/533-8621. ¢¢¢¢

Resort

★★★ **SHANTY CREEK RESORT.** *1 Shanty Creek Rd (49615). 231/533-8621; fax 231/533-7001; toll-free 800/678-4111. www.shantycreek.com.* 600 rms, 1-3 story, 259 kit. units (some equipt). June-Aug, winter wkends (2-day min), Christmas wk (4-day min): S, D $86-$148; each addl $10; kit. units, chalets $145-$325; under 18 free; package plans; lower rates rest of yr. Crib $10. TV; cable (premium), VCR avail. 5 pools, 2 indoor; whirlpool, poolside serv.

Playground. Supervised children's activities (seasonal). Dining rm 7 am-9 pm. Rm serv. Box lunches. Bars 11-2 am; Sun from noon. Coffee in lobby. Ck-out noon, ck-in 6 pm. Grocery. Package store. Meeting rms. Business center. Concierge. Gift shop. Airport transportation. Sports dir. Tennis $20/hr, pro. Four 18-hole golf courses, pro, putting greens, pro shop, driving ranges, carts avail. Downhill/x-country ski on site. Ice-skating. Sleighing. Lawn games. Exercise course, hiking trails. Entertainment, movies. Rec rm. Game rm. Exercise rm; sauna, steam rm. Massage. Spa. Some fireplaces. Private patios, balconies. Refrigerators in suites. Picnic tables, grills. Extensive grounds. Mountain bike trails (rentals). Private sand beach nearby. Cr cds: A, C, D, DS, MC, V.

🄳 ⛵ 🏊 🎿 ⛷ 🏌 🛷 ⛸ 🔥 SC

Benton Harbor

(H-3)

(see St. Joseph)

Beulah

(D-4) *See also Frankfort, Traverse City*

Pop 421 **Elev** 595 ft **Area code** 231 **Zip** 49617

Information Benzie County Chamber of Commerce, PO Box 204, Benzonia 49616; 231/882-5801 or 800/882-5801

Web www.benzie.org

This resort town is at the east end of Crystal Lake, which offers excellent fishing for salmon, trout, perch, bass, and smelt. Skiing, ice fishing, golf, and boating are also popular in the area.

What to See and Do

Benzie Area Historical Museum. Exhibits and artifacts depict area's lumbering, shipping, farming, transportation, homelife; display on Civil War author Bruce Catton. (June-Sept,

Tues-Sat; Apr-May and Oct-Nov, Fri and Sat only; special tours by appt) 3 mi S on US 31 in Benzonia, 6941 Traverse Ave. Phone 231/882-5539. ¢

Gwen Frostic Prints. Original block prints designed by artist and poet Gwen Frostic are featured at this wildlife sanctuary and printing shop. Display rm lets visitors observe the printing presses in operation. (Early May-Oct, daily; rest of yr, Mon-Sat; closed hols) 3 mi S on US 31, 2 mi W, in Benzonia at 5140 River Rd. Phone 231/882-5505. **FREE**

Platte River State Anadromous Fish Hatchery. Michigan's largest hatchery annually produces about nine million anadromous salmon (salmon that live in oceans or lakes and return to the rivers to spawn). This is the birthplace of the coho salmon in the Great Lakes; also produces chinook salmon. Self-guided tours (daily). 15120 US 31, 10 mi E via US 31. Phone 231/325-4611. **FREE**

Skiing. Crystal Mountain Resort. High-speed lift, five chairlifts, two rope tows; night skiing; patrol, school, rentals; snowmaking; nursery; lodge, condominiums, restaurant, cafeteria, bar. Thirty-four trails; longest run ½ mi; vertical drop 375 ft. (Thanksgiving-early Apr, daily) Groomed, track-set x-country trails (14 mi), lighted night trail; rentals, instruction (Dec-Mar, daily). Snowboard half-pipe. Also two golf courses; indoor pool, fitness center; hiking, mountain bike trails; tennis courts. 3 mi S on US 31, then 7 mi SE on MI 115 at 12500 Crystal Mountain Dr, in Thompsonville. Phone 231/378-2000. ¢¢¢¢

Restaurants

★ ★ **BROOKSIDE INN.** *115 US 31 (49617). 231/882-9688. www.brookside inn.com.* Hrs: 8 am-9:30 pm; Fri, Sat to 11 pm; summer to midnight. Res accepted. Serv bar. Bkfst $2.75-$6.95, lunch $3.95, dinner $6.75-$30. Child's menu. Specializes in steak, seafood, desserts. Tableside stone cooking. Outdoor dining. Began as an ice cream shop; country decor, antiques. Guest rms avail. Cr cds: A, DS, MC, V.

🄳 ➡

★ **CHERRY HUT.** *211 N Michigan Ave (US 31) (49617). 231/882-4431. www.cherryhutproducts.com.* Hrs: 11 am-9 pm; mid-June-Labor Day 10 am-10 pm. Closed late Oct-Memorial Day. Lunch $3.65-$7.95, dinner $11.95-$13.95. Child's menu. Specialties: cherry chicken salad, cherry pie. Outdoor dining. Cr cds: DS, MC, V.

D

★ **SAIL INN.** *US 31 (49616). 231/882-4971.* Hrs: 9 am-10 pm; Fri, Sat to 11 pm; Sun brunch 11 am-2 pm. Bar. Bkfst, lunch $7.95-$10.95, dinner $11.95-$19.95. Sun brunch $8.95. Child's menu. Specializes in seafood, steak. Salad bar. Family-owned. Totally nonsmoking. Cr cds: A, DS, MC, V.

D

Big Rapids (F-4)

Settled 1854 **Pop** 12,603 **Elev** 920 ft
Area code 231 **Zip** 49307
Information Mecosta County Convention & Visitors Bureau, 246 N State St; 231/796-7640 or 800/833-6697
Web www.bigrapids.org

What to See and Do

Mecosta County Parks. Parks open May-Oct. No pets permitted in Brower and School Section Lake parks. Phone 616/832-3246. Permit for all county parks ¢¢¢ Camping ¢¢¢ Parks incl

Brower. Swimming, fishing, boating (launch); playgrounds, tennis courts, softball diamond, camping. 6 mi S on US 131 to Stanwood, then 1 mi W to Old State Rd, then 3 mi S on Polk Rd. Phone 231/823-2561.

Merrill Lake. Swimming (two beaches), fishing, boating (launch, ramps); picnicking (shelters), playgrounds, camping. E on MI 20 to MI 66, then N, 3 mi N of Barryton. Phone 517/382-7158.

Paris. Fishing, canoeing (ramp); wildlife area, picnicking (shelter), camping. 6 mi N on MI 131, in Paris. Phone 231/796-3420.

School Section Lake. Swimming beach, boating (launch); picnicking (shelters), concessions, playgrounds, camping. Approx 23 mi E via MI 20. Phone 231/972-7450.

Special Event

Labor Day Arts Fair. Hemlock Park on Muskegon River. More than 150 exhibitors of various arts and crafts; concessions. Labor Day. Phone 231/796-7649.

Motel/Motor Lodge

★★ **HOLIDAY INN.** *1005 Perry Ave (49307). 616/796-4400; fax 616/796-0220; toll-free 800/465-4329. www.holiday-inn.com.* 118 rms, 4 story. S $68-$77; D $78-$87; each addl $10; suites $150; under 18 free; golf plans. Crib free. TV; cable (premium). Indoor pool; whirlpool, sauna. Restaurant 6:30 am-10 pm; Fri, Sat 7 am-11 pm; Sun 7 am-8 pm. Bar 11 am-11 pm; Fri, Sat to midnight; Sun noon-9 pm. Ck-out noon. Meeting rms. Business servs avail. In-rm modem link. Valet serv. Gift shop. Tennis privileges, pro. 18-hole golf, greens fee, pro, putting green, driving range. Cr cds: A, C, D, DS, ER, JCB, MC, V.

D ★ ★ ★ ★ ★ ★ SC

Birmingham

(G-7) *See also Bloomfield Hills, Detroit, Southfield*

Pop 19,997 **Elev** 781 ft **Area code** 248
Information Birmingham-Bloomfield Chamber of Commerce, 124 W Maple, 48009; 248/644-1700
Web www.bbcc.com

Motel/Motor Lodge

★★ **HOLIDAY INN EXPRESS.** *34952 Woodward Ave (48009). 248/646-7300; fax 248/646-4501; res 800/521-3509. www.hiexpress birmingham.com.* 126 rms, 2-5 story. S, D $109-$169; suites $125-$250; under 18 free; wkend rates. Crib free. TV; cable (premium). Complimentary

continental bkfst. Coffee in rms. Restaurant nearby. Business servs avail. In-rm modem link. Ck-out noon. Valet serv. Health club privileges. Refrigerators. Cr cds: A, C, D, DS, ER, JCB, MC, V.
D ⊠ ⊛ SC

Hotel

★★★★ **THE TOWNSEND HOTEL.** *100 Townsend St (48009). 248/642-7900; fax 248/645-9061; toll-free 800/548-4172. www.townsendhotel. com.* Located near metropolitan Detroit's business locations, this The two-hour ritual of afternoon tea is a tradition here, with live piano music in the elegant lobby. The fine Continental cuisine of the Rugby Grille draws hotel guests and outside visitors alike. 150 rooms, 4 story, 51 suites. S, D $275-$290; each addl $20; suites $229-$700; under 12 free. Crib free. TV; cable (premium), VCR (movies). Restaurant (see also RUGBY GRILLE). Afternoon tea Tues-Sat by res; pianist. Rm serv 24 hrs. Bar to 2 am. Ck-out noon. Meeting rms. Business center. In-rm modem link. Concierge. Gift shop. Covered parking. Valet parking $17. Tennis privileges. Downhill ski 20 mi; x-country ski 5 mi. Exercise bicycle brought to rm on request. Health club privileges. Bathrm phones; many minibars. Balconies. Located opp park. Cr cds: A, D, DS, MC, V.
D ⊁ ≒ ⊠ ⊛ 🏃

Restaurants

★★★ **FORTE'.** *201 S Old Woodward Ave (48009). 248/594-7300. www. forterestaurant.com.* Specializes in short ribs, seared yellowfin tuna, penne pasta. Hrs: 11:30 am-2 pm. 5-10 pm; Thurs-Sat to 11 pm. Closed Sun; hols. Res accepted. Wine, beer. Lunch $7-$14, dinner $15-$29. Entertainment Thurs. Open kitchen viewing. Cr cds: A, D, DS, MC, V.
D

★★★ **RUGBY GRILLE.** *100 Townsend St (48009). 248/642-5999. www.townsendhotel.com.* Hrs: 6:30 am-midnight; Fri, Sat 7-1 am. Res accepted. Bar. Wine cellar. Prix fixe: bkfst $7.95-$19.95. A la carte entrees: lunch $9.95-$18.95, dinner $20-$40.

Specialties: steak tartare, Caesar salad, black Angus beef, Dover sole. Own baking. Valet parking. Intimate dining rm with cherry woodwork, marble-top tables, French doors. Cr cds: A, D, DS, MC, V.
D ⊟

Bloomfield Hills

(G-7) *See also Birmingham, Detroit, Pontiac, Southfield, Troy, Warren*

Settled 1819 **Pop** 4,288 **Elev** 830 ft
Area code 248
Information Birmingham-Bloomfield Chamber of Commerce, 124 W Maple, Birmingham 48009; 248/644-1700
Web www.bbcc.com

Amasa Bagley followed a Native American trail and cleared land on what is today the business section of this small residential city. It was known as Bagley's Corners, later as Bloomfield Center, and then as Bloomfield Hills. In 1904, Ellen Scripps Booth and George G. Booth, president of the *Detroit News,* bought 300 acres of farmland here, naming it Cranbrook after the English village in which Mr. Booth's father was born. Since then, they have turned the estate into a vast cultural and educational complex.

What to See and Do

Cranbrook Educational Community. This famous campus is the site of the renowned center for the arts, education, science, and culture. Located on more than 300 acres, Cranbrook is noted for its exceptional architecture, gardens, and sculpture. 1221 N Woodward Ave. Phone 248/645-3000. Cranbrook is composed of

Cranbrook Academy of Art and Museum. 150 students. Graduate school for design, architecture, and the fine arts. Museum has international arts exhibits and collections.

(Wed-Sun afternoons; closed hols) Phone 248/645-3312. ¢¢

Cranbrook Gardens. Forty acres of formal and informal gardens; trails, fountains, outdoor Greek theater. (May-Aug, daily; Sept, afternoons only; Oct, Sat and Sun afternoons) Phone 248/645-3149. ¢¢

Cranbrook House. (1908) Tudor-style structure designed by Albert Kahn. Contains exceptional examples of decorative and fine art from the late 19th and early 20th centuries. 380 Lone Pine Rd. Phone 248/645-3149. ¢¢

Cranbrook Institute of Science. Natural history and science museum with exhibits, observatory, nature center; planetarium and laser demonstrations. (Mon-Sat, also Sun afternoons; closed hols) Phone 248/645-3200. ¢¢

Motel/Motor Lodge

★ ★ ★ **KINGSLEY.** *39475 Woodward Ave (48304). 248/644-1400; fax 248/644-5449; toll-free 800/544-6835. www.whghotels.com/kingsley/.* 160 rms, 3 story. S, D $139-$169; each addl $10; suites $125-$398; under 18 free; wkend rates. Crib free. TV; cable. Indoor pool; whirlpool. Restaurant 6-1 am. Rm serv 7 am-11 pm; Sun to 10 pm. Bar from 11 am; Sun noon-midnight; entertainment Tues-Sat. Ck-out noon. Meeting rms. Business servs avail. Bellhops. Barber, beauty shop. Downhill ski 20 mi. Exercise equipt. Some refrigerators. Some balconies. Cr cds: A, D, DS, JCB, MC, V.

🄳 ⊠ 🛏 🏃 ⊠ 🔥

Restaurant

★ ★ ★ ★ **THE LARK.** *6430 Farmington Rd, West Bloomfield (48322). 248/661-4466. www.thelark.com.* A pleasant destination during any season, this European country-style restaurant offers chef Marcus Haight's classic French and internationally flavored dishes. In winter, two fireplaces warm the cozy interior of terra-cotta and Portuguese-tiled walls. In summer, outdoor dining rests beside a walled garden, a grape trellis, and a quiet fountain. The name refers to the obvious as well as to owners Jim and Mary Lark. French

menu. Specializes in rack of lamb, monthly theme dinners. Hrs: 6-10:30 pm (last sitting 9 pm); Fri, Sat to 9 pm (last sitting). Closed Sun, Mon; hols; also 1st wk Jan and 1st wk Aug. Res required. Bar. Wine cellar. Complete meals: dinner $70-$75. Totally nonsmoking. Cr cds: A, D, MC, V.

🄳

Boyne City

(D-5) *See also Charlevoix, Petoskey*

Pop 3,400 **Elev** 600 ft **Area code** 231 **Zip** 49712
Information Chamber of Commerce, 28 S Lake St; 231/582-6222
Web www.boynecity.com

What to See and Do

Skiing. Boyne Mountain. Triple, six-passenger, three quad, three double chairlifts; rope tow; patrol, school, rentals; snowmaking; lodge (see RESORT), cafeteria, restaurant, bar, nursery. Longest run one mi; vertical drop 500 ft. X-country trails (35 mi), rentals. (Trail ticket; fee) (Late Nov-mid-Apr, daily) SE via MI 75 to Boyne Falls, off US 131. Phone 231/549-6000. ¢¢¢¢

Motel/Motor Lodge

★ ★ **WATER STREET INN.** *240 Front St (49712). 231/582-3000; fax 616/582-3001.* 27 kit. units, 3 story. Late June-early Sept: S, D $145-$165; each addl $10; under 13 free; higher rates hol wks; wkly rates; ski plans; lower rates rest of yr. Crib $10. TV; cable (premium). Restaurant adj 4-10 pm; Fri, Sat to 11 pm; Sun noon-9 pm; hrs vary late June-early Sept. Ck-out 11 am. Business servs avail. Downhill ski 6 mi; x-country ski 1½ mi. In-rm whirlpools. Private patios, balconies. On Lake Charlevoix. Private swimming beach. Cr cds: A, D, MC, V.

🄳 🛁 🛗 ⊠ ⊠ 🔥

Resort

★ ★ **BOYNE MOUNTAIN.** *1 Boyne Mountain Rd, Boyne Falls (49713).*

*231/549-6000; fax 616/549-6094.
www.boynemountain.com.* 265 units in lodges, villas, condos, 1-3 story, 109 kits. Dec-mid-Mar, mid-June-Aug: S, D $72-$105; 1-3 bedrm kit. apts $135-$325; AP; package plans; lower rates rest of yr. Crib free. TV; cable, VCR avail (movies). 2 pools, heated; whirlpool. Dining rm 7 am-10 pm. Box lunches. Bar noon-2 am. Ck-out 1 pm, ck-in 5 pm. Meeting rms. Business servs avail. Tennis, pro. 9-hole and two 18-hole golf courses, greens fee $70-$80, pro. Private beach. Paddleboats. Downhill/x-country ski on site. Ice rink; rentals. Lawn games. Bicycles. Entertainment. Exercise equipt; sauna. 5,000-ft paved, lighted airstrip. Many minibars. Some balconies. Alpine-style decor; fireplace in lobby. Cr cds: A, C, D, DS, MC, V.

🄳 🕴 🛏 🏊 🎿 🔄 🔥

Restaurants

★ **PIPPINS.** *5 W Main St (49712). 231/582-3311. www.pippins.com.* Hrs: 8 am-9 pm; Sun to 2 pm. Closed Oct-Dec 25; also mid-March-May. Bar. Bkfst $2.25-$5.50, lunch $5-$8, dinner $7.95-$15. Child's menu. Specializes in homemade soups and desserts, broiled fresh whitefish. Cr cds: DS, MC, V.

🄳

Cadillac (E-4)

Settled 1871 **Pop** 10,104 **Elev** 1,328 ft
Area code 231 **Zip** 49601
Information Cadillac Area Visitor Bureau, 222 Lake St; 231/775-0657 or 800/22-LAKES
Web www.cadillacmichigan.com

On the shores of lakes Cadillac and Mitchell, Cadillac was founded as a lumber camp and was once the major lumber center of the area. The city today prospers on diversified industry and tourism. Named for Antoine de la Mothe Cadillac, founder of Detroit, it is also headquarters for the Huron-Manistee National Forest (see MANISTEE and OSCODA). A Ranger District office of the forests is also located here.

What to See and Do

Adventure Island. Park incl mountain miniature golf, go-karts, batting cages, bumper boats, water slides, concessions, arcade, hydro-tube water slide. (Daily May-Oct) Phone 231/775-2527. ¢¢¢¢

Johnny's Game and Fish Park. Wild and tame animals; 75-ft-long elevated goat walk; fishing for rainbow trout (no license, no limit; fee). (Mid-May-Labor Day, daily) 5 mi SW on MI 115, follow signs. Phone 231/775-3700. ¢¢¢

Skiing. Caberfae Peaks Ski Resort. Quad, triple, three double chairlifts, two T-bars, two rope tows; patrol, school, rentals; snowmaking; bar, cafeteria, lodge, motel, nursery, restaurant; snowboard, x-country, and snowmobile trails. (Late Nov-Mar, daily) 12 mi W on MI 55. Phone 231/862-3300. ¢¢¢¢

William Mitchell State Park. Approx 260 acres between Cadillac and Mitchell lakes. Swimming beach, bathhouse, fishing, boating (launching, rentals); interpretive hiking trail, picnicking, playground, camping (tent and trailer facilities). Visitor center. Nature study area. Standard fees. 2½ mi W via MI 55 and 115. Phone 231/775-7911.

Motels/Motor Lodges

★★ **BEST WESTERN.** *5676 MI 55 E (49601). 231/775-2458; fax 231/775-8383; toll-free 800/654-8375. www.bestwestern.com.* 66 rms. May-mid-Oct, Dec 26-mid-Mar: D $72-$87; each addl $5; lower rates rest of yr. Crib $3. TV; cable (premium). Indoor pool; whirlpool, sauna. Playground. Restaurant 7 am-10 pm. Ck-out 11 am. Business servs avail. Tennis. Golf privileges. Downhill ski 12 mi; x-country ski ½ mi. Bowling. Game rm. Lawn games. Cr cds: A, C, D, DS, MC, V.

🄳 🐾 🎿 🏊 🕴 🔄 🔥

★★ **CADILLAC SANDS RESORT.** *6319 E MI 115 (49601). 231/775-2407; fax 231/775-6422; toll-free 800/647-2637. www.cadillacsands.com.* 55 rms, 2 story. June-Sept: S, D $69.95-$125; each addl $5; under 12 free. Crib $2. Pet accepted. TV; cable (premium). Indoor pool. Complimentary continental bkfst. Restaurant 5-10:30 pm; also Sat, Sun 8-11 am (in season). Bar 4 pm-2:30 am; entertainment. Ck-out 11 am. Meeting rm. Business servs avail. Free airport transportation. Golf privileges, putting green. Downhill ski 13 mi; x-country ski 3½ mi. Lawn games. Some private patios, balconies. Boat rentals, paddleboats. Private beach; dockage. Cr cds: A, D, DS, MC, V.

★ **DAYS INN.** *6001 E Mills 115 (49601). 231/775-4414; fax 231/779-0370; toll-free 800/329-7466. www. daysinn.com.* 60 rms, 2 story. June-Sept, Dec-Feb: S, D $68-$121; family, mid-wk rates; lower rates rest of yr. Crib free. TV; cable (premium), VCR avail (movies). Indoor pool; whirlpool. Complimentary continental bkfst. Restaurant nearby. Ck-out 11 am. Meeting rm. Business servs avail. Valet serv. Downhill ski 12 mi; x-country ski 2 mi. Volleyball. Some refrigerators. Lake ¼ mi; swimming beach. Cr cds: A, C, D, DS, JCB, MC, V.

★★ **HAMPTON INN.** *1650 S Mitchell (49601). 231/779-2900; fax 231/779-0846; res 800/426-7866. www.hamptoninn.com.* 120 rms, 4 story. Memorial Day-Labor Day: S $79; D $99; family rates; under 18 free; lower rates rest of yr. Crib free. TV; cable (premium). Indoor pool; whirlpool. Complimentary continental bkfst. Coffee in rms. Restaurant nearby. Ck-out 11 am. Meeting rms. Business servs avail. Valet serv. Downhill ski 20 mi; x-country ski 1 mi. Cr cds: A, C, D, DS, ER, JCB, MC, V.

★★★ **MCGUIRE'S RESORT & CONFERENCE CENTER.** *7880 Mackinaw Tr (49601). 231/775-9947; fax 231/775-9621; toll-free 800/632-7302. www. mcguiresresort.com.* 122 rms, 1-3 story. May-Sept: S, D $69-$124; each addl $10; suites $109-$189; under 18 free; ski, golf plans; higher rates Dec

26-Jan 1. Cribs $15. Pet accepted; $15. TV; cable. Indoor pool; whirlpool, sauna. Restaurant 7 am-10 pm; off-season to 9 pm. Bar 11:30-1:30 am; entertainment. Coffee in rms. Ck-out 11 am. Meeting rm. Business servs avail. In-rm modem link. Valet serv. Gift shop. Free airport, bus depot transportation. Tennis. 27-hole golf, greens fee $45-$62, putting green, driving range. Downhill ski 15 mi; x-country ski on site. Health club privileges. Game rm. Lawn games. Refrigerators. Some, Fireplaces, private patios. Panoramic view of countryside. Cr cds: A, C, D, DS, MC, V.

★ **SUN-N-SNOW MOTEL.** *301 S Lake Mitchell Dr (49601). 231/775-9961; res 800/477-9961. www. cadillacmichigan.com.* 29 rms. June-Labor Day, winter wkends, Christmas wk: S $39-$59; D $49-$69; suites $90-$115; lower rates rest of yr. Crib free. Pet accepted. TV; cable. Restaurant nearby. Ck-out 11 am. Business servs avail. Downhill ski 15 mi; x-country ski ¼ mi. Golf privileges. Lawn games. Private beach. On Lake Mitchell. Park opp. Cr cds: A, DS, MC, V.

★ **SUPER 8.** *211 W MI 55 (49601). 231/775-8561; fax 231/775-9392; res 800/800-8000. www.super8.com.* 27 rms, 2 story. Jan-Feb, June-Aug: S $46; D $65; each addl $5; under 12 free; lower rates rest of yr. Crib free. TV. Indoor pool; whirlpool. Complimentary continental bkfst. Restaurant opp 8 am-3 pm. Ck-out 11 am. Downhill ski 15 mi; x-country ski ¼

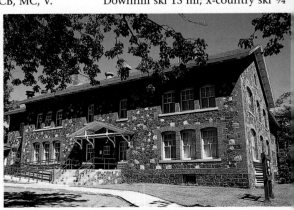

Keweenaw National Historical Park

mi. Health club privileges. Some refrigerators. Cr cds: A, C, D, DS, MC, V.

🔧 ⚡ 🐾 🏊 🔌 🔥

Restaurants

★ ★ **HERMANN'S EUROPEAN CAFE.** *214 N Mitchell (49601). 231/775-9563. www.chefhermann.com.* Hrs: 11 am-9:30 pm; Fri, Sat to 10 pm. Closed Sun; hols. Bar. Wine list. Continental menu. Lunch $5.50-$12, dinner $9.50-$25.95. Child's menu. Specialties: Austrian apple strudel, Wiener schnitzel. Own baking. Guest rms avail. Cr cds: A, D, DS, MC, V.

▤

★ ★ **LAKESIDE CHARLIE'S.** *301 S Lake Mitchell (49601). 231/775-5332.* Hrs: 11:30 am-10 pm; Fri, Sat to 11 pm; Sun 11 am-8 pm; early-bird dinner 4-6 pm. Closed Mon; Thanksgiving, Dec 25. Res accepted. Bar to midnight; Fri, Sat to 1:30 am. Lunch $5-$7, dinner $6.95-$18.25. Child's menu. Specializes in fresh seafood, prime beef. Entertainment Fri, Sat. Patio overlooking lake. Cr cds: A, D, DS, MC, V.

D SC ▤

Calumet

(A-1) *See also Copper Harbor, Hancock, Houghton*

Pop 818 **Elev** 1,208 ft **Area code** 906 **Zip** 49913
Information Keweenaw Peninsula Chamber of Commerce, 326 Shelden, Houghton 49931; 906/482-5240 or 800/338-7982
Web www.keweenaw.org

What to See and Do

⭐ **Calumet Theatre.** (1899) Built with boom town wealth and continually being restored, this ornate theater was host to such great stars as Lillian Russell, Sarah Bernhardt, Lon Chaney, Otis Skinner, James O'Neil, Douglas Fairbanks, and John Philip Sousa. Guided tours (mid-June-Sept, daily). Live performances throughout the yr. 340 6th St. Phone 906/337-2610. ¢¢

Keweenaw National Historical Park. Established in Oct, 1992, to commemorate the heritage of copper mining on the Keweenaw Peninsula-its mines, machinery, and people. Self-guided walking tour brochures of the historic business and residential districts are avail. Fees for cooperating sites incl mine tours, museums. Calumet Unit and Quincy Unit. Phone 906/337-3168. **FREE**

Upper Peninsula Firefighters Memorial Museum. Housed in the historic Red Jacket Fire Station, this museum features memorabilia and exhibits spanning almost a century of firefighting history. (Mon-Sat) 327 6th St. Phone 906/296-2561. ¢

Charlevoix (C-4)

Pop 3,116 **Elev** 599 ft **Area code** 231 **Zip** 49720
Information Charlevoix Area Chamber of Commerce, 408 Bridge St; 231/547-2101
Web www.charlevoix.org

What to See and Do

Beaver Island Boat Company. A 2¼-hr trip to Beaver Island, the largest island of the Beaver Archipelago. (June-Sept, daily; mid-Apr-May and Oct-mid-Dec, limited schedule) Advance car res necessary. City Dock, 103 Bridge Park Dr. Phone 231/547-2311. ¢¢¢¢

Swimming, picnicking. Depot and Ferry Ave beaches; charter fishing, boat rentals (power and sail), launching ramp; tennis courts; municipal nine-hole golf course (June-Labor Day). Lake Michigan and Lake Charlevoix beaches.

Special Events

Venetian Festival. Midway, street, and boat parades, fireworks. Fourth full wkend July. Phone 231/547-2101.

Waterfront Art Fair. East Park. Second Sat Aug. Phone 231/547-2675.

Apple Festival. Second wkend Oct. Phone 231/547-2101.

Motels/Motor Lodges

★ **ARCHWAY MOTEL.** *1440 Bridge St (49720).* 231/547-2096. 14 rms. Mid-June-mid-Aug: S, D $48-$99; higher rates: hols, special events; lower rates rest of yr. TV; cable (premium). Heated pool. Playground. Restaurant adj 5:30 am-3 pm. Ck-out 10 am. Free airport, ferry transportation. Downhill/x-country ski 2 mi. Picnic tables. Cr cds: DS, MC, V.
🏊 🛏 🎿 🔥

★ **LODGE.** *120 Michigan Ave (49720).* 231/547-6565; fax 231/547-0741. www.thelodge-charlevoix.com. 40 rms, 2 story. July-mid-Aug, hol wkends, Christmas hols: S, D $80-$115; each addl $5; suites $155-$165; under 12 free; lower rates rest of yr. Crib free. Pet accepted. TV; cable (premium). Pool. Complimentary coffee. Restaurant nearby. Ck-out 11 am. Business servs avail. Downhill/x-country ski 1 mi. Some private patios, balconies. Overlooks harbor. Cr cds: A, MC, V.
🅳 🔌 🐾 🎿 🏊 🛏 🔥

★★ **WEATHERVANE TERRACE HOTEL.** *111 Pine River Ln (49720).* 231/547-9955; fax 231/547-0070; toll-free 800/552-0025. 68 rms, 2-3 story. Late June-early Sept: S, D $90-$115; suites $150-$180; under 12 free; wkly rates; ski plans; higher rates: Venetian Festival, Art Fair, Dec 29-31; lower rates rest of yr. TV; cable (premium), VCR avail (movies). Heated pool; whirlpool. Complimentary continental bkfst. Restaurant adj 11 am-11 pm in season. Ck-out 11 am. Meeting rms. Business servs avail. Downhill/x-country ski 1 mi. Refrigerators, wet bars; some fireplaces, in-rm whirlpools. Many balconies. Sun deck overlooks 2 lakes, river. Cr cds: A, D, DS, MC, V.
🏊 🛏 🔥

All Suite

★★★ **EDGEWATER INN.** *100 Michigan Ave (49720).* 231/547-6044; fax 231/547-0038; toll-free 800/748-0424. www.edgewater-charlevoix.com. 60 kit. suites, 3 story. June-late Aug: 1 bedrm (up to 4) $178-$242; 2 bedrm (up to 6) $235-$325; each addl (after 4) $5; under 17 free; wkly rates; higher rates: Christmas hols, special events (2-day min); lower rates rest of yr. Crib free. TV; cable; VCR, DVD. 2 pools; 1 heated indoor; whirlpool. Restaurant 7 am-10 pm. Serv bar. Coffee in rms. Ck-out 11 am. Coin lndry. Meeting rm. Massage (by appt). Beauty shop. Downhill/x-country ski 1 mi. Exercise equipt; sauna. Some in-rm whirlpools. Refrigerators, fireplaces, private patios, balconies. Picnic tables. On lake; boat slips. Cr cds: A, MC, V.
🅳 🔌 🎿 🏊 🛏 🍴 🔥

Restaurants

★★★ **MAHOGANY'S.** *9600 Clubhouse Dr (49720).* 231/547-3555. Hrs: noon-2:30 pm, 6-10 pm. Closed Dec 24, 25. Res accepted. Continental menu. Bar to midnight. Wine list. Lunch $5.50-$9, dinner $15-$26. Child's menu. Specializes in veal, seafood. Entertainment Fri, Sat. Victorian country cottage. Cr cds: A, MC, V.
🅳

★★★ **ROWE INN.** *6303 County 48, Ellsworth (49729).* 231/588-7351. www.roweinn.com. Hrs: 6-10 pm. Closed Thanksgiving, Dec 25. Res required. Serv bar. Wine cellar. Complete meals: dinner $19.50-$36.50. Specializes in seasonal cuisine. Own baking. Family-owned. Cr cds: A, DS, MC, V.
🅳

★★ **STAFFORD'S WEATHERVANE.** *106 Pine River Ln (49720).* 231/547-4311. www.staffords.com. Hrs: 11:30 am-11 pm; Sun to 10 pm; early-bird dinner 5-6 pm. Closed Dec 25. Res accepted. Bar. Lunch $6.95-$9.95, dinner $6.95-$28.50. Child's menu. Specializes in fresh whitefish, prime rib. Overlooks Pine River Channel to Lake Michigan. Cr cds: A, DS, MC, V.
🅳

★★★★ **TAPAWINGO.** *9502 Lake St, Ellsworth (49729).* 231/588-7971. www.tapawingo.net. This restaurant's name, a Chippewa word meaning tranquility, is a hint to the environment chef Harlan (Pete) Peterson has created at his Michigan cherry-country destination. The internationally inspired dishes change daily and are full of local ingredients. Visitors have come from miles around for the nationally recognized cuisine, humble service, and calm of the St. Clair Lake view. Hrs: 6-9:30 pm; days vary Sept-mid-Nov, mid-Dec-June. Closed; also mid-Nov-mid-Dec. Res required. Bar. Wine cellar. Prix fixe: dinner $44-$55. Specializes in regional dishes. Menu changes seasonally. Own baking. Country atmosphere. Landscaped setting on small lake. Fieldstone fireplace. Totally non-smoking. Cr cds: A, MC, V.

D

Cheboygan

(C-5) *See also Indian River, Mackinaw City*

Founded 1871 **Pop** 4,999 **Elev** 600 ft
Area code 231 **Zip** 49721
Information Cheboygan Area Chamber of Commerce, 124 N Main St, PO Box 69; 231/627-7183 or 800/968-3302
Web www.cheboygan.com

Surrounded by two Great Lakes and large inland lakes, the city has long been famous as a premier boating area. Cheboygan was once a busy lumber port, but now has a wide variety of industry.

What to See and Do

Cheboygan Opera House. (1877) Renovated 580-seat auditorium featuring events ranging from bluegrass to ballet. Contact Box Office for show schedule. Huron and Backus Sts. Phone 231/627-5841.

Fishing. Locks here lift boats to Cheboygan River leading to inland waterway which incl Mullett and Burt lakes, famous for muskie, walleye, salmon, and bass. Cheboygan County is the only place in the state where sturgeon spearing is legal each winter (Feb). Along the route, marinas supply cruise needs; swimming,

boating. Contact the Chamber of Commerce.

State parks.

Aloha. Approx 95 acres with swimming, sand beach, fishing, boating (launch); picnicking, camping (dump station). Standard fees. (Daily) 9 mi S on MI 33, then W on MI 212, on Mullett Lake. Phone 231/625-2522. ¢¢

Cheboygan. More than 1,200 acres with swimming, fishing, boating; hunting, hiking, x-country skiing, picnicking, camping. Nature study. Standard fees. (Daily) 3 mi NE off US 23, on Lake Huron. Phone 231/627-2811. ¢¢

The US Coast Guard Cutter *Mackinaw*. One of the world's largest icebreakers, with a complement of 80 officers and crew. When in port, the *Mackinaw* is moored at the turning basin on the east side of the Cheboygan River.

Special Event

Cheboygan County Fair. Fairgrounds. Early Aug. Phone 231/627-7183.

Motels/Motor Lodges

★★ **BEST WESTERN RIVER TERRACE.** *847 S Main St (49721). 231/627-5688; fax 616/627-2472; toll-free 877/627-9552. www.bestwestern. com.* 53 rms, 2 story. Late June-early Sept: S $58-$93; D $67-$127; each addl $10; lower rates rest of yr. Crib $5. TV; cable (premium). Indoor pool; whirlpool. Restaurant adj 6 am-midnight; winter to 11 pm. Ck-out 11 am. Business servs avail. X-country ski 5 mi. Exercise equipt. Some in-rm whirlpools. Spacious grounds; excellent view of river. Cr cds: A, C, D, DS, MC, V.

D ♦ ➤ ➤ ✕ ▣ ▨

★ **DAYS INN.** *889 S Main St (49721). 231/627-3126; fax 616/627-2889; res 800/329-7466. www.daysinn.com.* 42 rms, 2 story. Mid-June-mid-Sept: S $58-$110; D $68-$125; suites $85-$175; under 16 free; higher rates Labor Day wknd; lower rates rest of yr. Crib free. TV; cable (premium). Complimentary continental bkfst. Restaurant adj 6 am-11 pm. Ck-out 11 am. Free airport, bus depot transportation. X-country ski 3 mi. Refrigerators. Balconies. On river; dockage. Cr cds: A, C, D, DS, MC, V.

Restaurant

★ ★ **HACK-MA-TACK INN.** *8131 Beebe Rd (49721). 231/625-2919. www.hack-ma-tack.com.* Hrs: 5 pm-closing; May-Oct from noon. Closed mid-Oct-mid-Apr. No A/C. Bar. Dinner $18.95-$29.95. Specializes in whitefish, prime rib. Early Amer decor; fireplace. Set in wooded area. Overlooks Cheboygan River, 400-ft dock. Guest rms avail. Cr cds: A, D, DS, MC, V.

Clare

(E-5) *See also Harrison, Midland, Mount Pleasant*

Pop 3,021 **Elev** 841 ft **Area code** 989 **Zip** 48617
Information Chamber of Commerce, 429 McEwan St; 989/386-2442 or 888/282-5273
Web www.claremichigan.com

What to See and Do

Chalet Cross-Country. Groomed x-country trails (approx 8½ mi) graded to skier's experience; patrol, school, rentals; store. (Dec-Mar, daily; closed Dec 25) 5931 Clare Ave, 6 mi N via Old US 27. Phone 989/386-9697. ¢¢

Special Event

Irish Festival. Mid-Mar. Phone 989/386-2442.

Motel/Motor Lodge

★ **DOHERTY HOTEL.** *604 N Mc-Ewan St (48617). 517/386-3441; fax 517/386-4231; toll-free 800/525-4115. www.dohertyhotel.com.* 92 rms, 3 story. S $39-$65; D $49-$90; each addl $5; suites $102-$115; wkly rates; golf plans. Crib $5. Pet accepted. Indoor pool; whirlpool, poolside serv. Complimentary full bkfst. Restaurant (see DOHERTY). Bar 11-2 am; entertainment Wed-Sat. Ck-out

noon. Meeting rms. Business servs avail. Bellhops. Valet serv. Free airport transportation. Golf privileges. Downhill ski 5 mi; x-country ski 7 mi. Game rm. Balconies. Cr cds: A, D, DS, MC, V.

Restaurant

★ **DOHERTY.** *604 McEwan St (US 27 Business) (48617). 989/386-3441. www.dohertyhotel.com.* Hrs: 6 am-2 pm, 5-10 pm; Fri, Sat to 11 pm; Sun to 9 pm. Res accepted. Bar 11-2 am. Bkfst $4.75-$9.25, lunch $4.95-$10.25, dinner $10-$27. Child's menu. Specializes in prime rib, fresh whitefish, homemade desserts. Salad bar. Entertainment Fri, Sat. Established 1924. Family-owned. Cr cds: A, D, DS, MC, V.

Coldwater

(H-5) *See also Marshall*

Pop 9,607 **Elev** 969 ft **Area code** 517 **Zip** 49036
Information Coldwater/Branch County Chamber of Commerce, 20 Division St; 517/278-5985 or 800/968-9333
Web www.branch-county.com

What to See and Do

Tibbits Opera House. (1882) Renovated 19th-century Victorian opera house. Presently home to professional summer theater series (see SPECIAL EVENTS), art exhibits, a winter concert series, children's programs, and community events. Originally owned and operated by businessman Barton S. Tibbits, the house attracted such performers as John Phillip Sousa, Ethel Barrymore, P. T. Barnum, John Sullivan, and William Gillette. Tours (Mon-Fri). 14 S Hanchett St. Phone 517/278-6029. **FREE**

Wing House Museum. (1875) Historical house museum exhibiting Second Empire architectural style. Incl original kitchen and dining rm in basement, collection of Oriental rugs, oil paintings, three generations of glassware, Regina music box; furniture from Empire to Eastlake styles. (Wed-Sun, afternoons; also by appt) 27 S Jefferson St. Phone 517/278-2871. ¢

Special Events

Quincy Chain of Lakes Tip-Up Festival. 5 mi E via US 12 on Tip-Up Island in Quincy. Parade, fishing and woodcutting contests; torchlight snowmobile ride; dancing, polar bear splash, pancake breakfast, fish fry. Second wkend Feb. Phone 800/968-9333.

Car Show Swap Meet. Antique and class car show, arts and crafts, vendors; trophies. Early May.

Tibbits Professional Summer Theatre Series. Tibbits Opera House. Resident professional company produces comedies, musicals. Phone 517/278-6029. Late June-Aug.

Bronson Polish Festival Days. SW on US 12 in Bronson. Heritage fest; games, vendors, concessions, dancing. Third wk July. Phone 800/968-9333.

Branch County 4-H Fair. 4-H Fairgrounds. Exhibits, animal showing, carnival booths, rides, horse show, tractor pulling. Second wk Aug. Phone 517/279-4313.

Motel/Motor Lodge

★★ **QUALITY INN AND CONVENTION CENTER.** *1000 Orleans Blvd (49036). 517/278-2017; fax 517/279-7214; toll-free 800/806-8226. www.qualityinn.com.* 122 rms, 2 story, 24 kits. May-Oct: S $60-$65; D $67-$72; each addl $7; suites, kit. units $72-$77; under 18 free; higher rates race wkends; lower rates rest of yr. Crib free. Pet accepted. TV; cable (premium). Indoor pool; whirlpool. Complimentary continental bkfst. Restaurant 11 am-2 pm, 5-8 pm; wkend hrs vary. Bar 5 pm-midnight; Fri, Sat to 2 am; closed Sun; entertainment Thurs-Sat. Ck-out 11 am. Meeting rms. Business servs avail. Valet serv. X-country ski 2 mi. Game rm. Cr cds: A, D, DS, MC, V.

B&B/Small Inn

★★ **CHICAGO PIKE.** *215 E Chicago St (49036). 517/279-8744; fax 517/278-8597; toll-free 800/471-0501. www.chicagopikeinn.com.* 8 rms, 2 story. 2 A/C. S $100; D $108-$178; each addl $20; suites $210. Closed Thanksgiving, Dec 24, 25. Children over 12 yrs only. TV; cable (premium), VCR avail (free movies). Complimentary full bkfst; afternoon refreshments. Restaurant nearby. Ck-out noon, ck-in 3 pm. Free airport

Fort Wilkins State Park

transportation. Golf privileges. X-country ski 20 mi. Bicycles. Horse and carriage rental. Picnic tables, grills. Victorian residence (1903); antiques; period furnishings; fireplace in sitting rm. Cr cds: A, DS, MC, V.

Copper Harbor

(A-2) *See also Calumet*

Pop 55 **Elev** 621 ft **Area code** 906 **Zip** 49918
Information Keweenaw Peninsula Chamber of Commerce, 325 Shelden, Houghton 49931; 906/482-5240 or 800/338-7982
Web www.copperharbor.org

Lumps of pure copper studded the lakeshore and attracted the first explorers to this area, but deposits proved thin and unfruitful. A later lumbering boom also ended. Today this northernmost village in the state is a small but beautiful resort. Streams and inland lakes provide excellent trout, walleye, bass, and northern pike fishing. Lake Superior yields trout, salmon, and other species.

What to See and Do

Astor House Antique Doll & Indian Artifact Museum. Early mining boom-days items and hundreds of antique dolls. (June-Oct, daily) Corner of US 41 and MI 26. Phone 906/289-4449. ¢

Brockway Mountain Drive. 10 mi; begins ¼ mi W of jct US 41 and MI 26; lookouts; views of Lake Superior and forests.

Copper Harbor Lighthouse Tour. Twenty-min boat ride to one of the oldest lighthouses on Lake Superior; incl guided tour of lighthouse. Trips depart hrly. (Memorial Day-mid-Oct, daily, weather permitting) Copper Harbor Marina. Phone 906/289-4410. ¢¢¢

Delaware Mine Tour. Underground guided tour of copper mine dating back to 1850s. (Mid-May-mid-Oct, daily) 11 mi W on US 41. Phone 906/289-4688. ¢¢¢

Ferry service to Isle Royale National Park. (see) Four ferries and a float plane provide transportation (June-Sept, daily; some trips in May). For fees and schedule contact Park Superintendent. Phone 906/482-0984.

Fort Wilkins State Park. Approx 200 acres. A historic army post (1844) on Lake Fanny Hooe. The stockade has been restored and the buildings have been preserved to maintain the frontier post atmosphere. Costumed guides demonstrate old army lifestyle. Fishing, boating (launch); x-country ski trails, picnicking, playground, concession, camping. Museum with relics of early mining days and various exhibits depicting army life in the 1870s. Standard fees. (Daily) 1 mi E on US 41. Phone 906/289-4215.

Isle Royale Queen III **Evening Cruises.** Narrated 1½-hr cruise on Lake Superior. Res advised. (July 4-Labor Day, eves) Phone 906/289-4437.

Snowmobiling. There is a series of interconnecting trails totaling several hundred miles; some overlook Lake Superior from high bluffs. Also 17 mi of x-country trails. (Dec-Mar) Phone 906/482-2388.

Special Events

Brockway Mountain Challenge. 15-km x-country ski race. Phone 906/337-4579. Feb.

Art in the Park. Community Center grounds. Juried art show featuring local and regional artists; food; live entertainment. Phone 906/337-4579. Mid-Aug.

Motels/Motor Lodges

★ **ASTOR HOUSE-MINNETONKA RESORT.** *560 Gratiot (49918). 906/289-4449; fax 906/289-4326; toll-free 800/433-2770. www.exploringthenorth.com.* 13 motel rms, 12 cottages, 8 kits. No A/C. Early May-late Oct: S $48-$50; D $50-$53; cottages for 2-10, $46-$95; $300-$525/wk. Closed rest of yr. Crib $5. Pet accepted; $5. TV; cable (premium). Restaurant opp 8 am-10 pm. Ck-out 10:30 am. Gift shop. Saunas. Picnic tables, grill. Pine-paneled cottages, many overlooking harbor, lake. Astor House Museum on premises. 8 rms across street. Cr cds: DS, MC, V.

★ **BELLA VISTA MOTEL.** *160 6th St (49918). 906/289-4213. www.bellavista motel.com.* 22 rms, 1-2 story, 8 kit. cottages. No A/C. Late June-mid-Oct: S, D $45-$55; each addl $4; cottages for 2-5, $39-$60; lower rates May-mid-June. Closed rest of yr. Crib avail. TV; cable (premium). Restaurant nearby. Ck-out 10 am. Some balconies. Picnic tables. Most rms overlook harbor. On Lake Superior; dock. Cr cds: DS, MC, V.

Restaurant

★ **TAMARACK INN.** *512 Gratiot St (49918). 906/289-4522.* Hrs: 8 am-9 pm. Closed 1st wk June, 2nd wk Oct. Res accepted. Bkfst $2-$6, lunch $3.75-$6, dinner $6.95-$16. Salad bar. Overlooking lake. Cr cds: DS, MC, V.

Dearborn

(G-7) See also Detroit, Ypsilanti

Settled 1763 **Pop** 89,286 **Elev** 605 ft
Area code 313

Information Chamber of Commerce, 15544 Michigan Ave, 48126; 313/584-6100
Web www.dearborn.org

Dearborn is the home of the Ford Motor Company Rouge Assembly Plant, Ford World Headquarters, the Henry Ford Museum, and Greenfield Village. Although Dearborn has a long and colorful history, its modern eminence is due to Henry Ford, who was born here in 1863.

What to See and Do

★ **Henry Ford Estate-Fair Lane.** (1913-1915) Built by automotive pioneer Henry Ford in 1915, the mansion cost in excess of $2 million and stands on 72 acres of property. The mansion, designed by William Van Tine, reflects Ford's penchant for simplicity and functionalism; its systems for heating, water, electricity, and refrigeration were entirely self-sufficient at that time. The powerhouse, boathouse, and gardens have been restored, and some original furniture and children's playhouse have been returned to the premises. (Apr-Dec, daily; rest of yr, Sun; closed Jan 1, Dec 25) 4901 Evergreen Rd (follow signs), on the University of Michigan-Dearborn Campus. Phone 313/593-5590. ¢¢¢

Henry Ford Museum

⭐ **Henry Ford Museum and Green-field Village.** On a 254-acre setting, this is an indoor-outdoor complex that preserves a panorama of American life of the past—an unequaled collection of American historical artifacts. Built by Henry Ford as a tribute to the culture, resourcefulness, and technology of the United States, the museum and village stand as monuments to America's achievements. Dedicated in 1929 to Thomas Edison, they attract visitors each year from around the world. (Daily; closed Thanksgiving, Dec 25) 20900 Oakwood Blvd, ½ mi S of US 12, 1½ mi W of Southfield Rd. Phone 313/271-1620.

Greenfield Village. Comprised of more than eighty 18th- and 19th-century buildings moved here from all over the country. Historic homes, shops, schools, mills, stores, and laboratories that figured in the lives of such historic figures as Lincoln, Webster, Burbank, McGuffey, Carver, the Wright brothers, Firestone, Edison, and Ford. Among the most interesting are the courthouse where Abraham Lincoln practiced law, the Wright brothers' cycle shop, Henry Ford's birthplace, Edison's Menlo Park laboratory, homes of Noah Webster and Luther Burbank, 19th-century farmstead of Harvey Firestone; steam-operated industries, crafts workers, demonstrations, home activites. (Daily; closed Thanksgiving, Dec 25; interiors also closed Jan-mid-Mar) Also winter sleigh tours. Phone 313/271-1620. ¢¢¢¢

Henry Ford Museum. Occupies 12 acres, incl major collections in transportation, power and machinery, agriculture, lighting, communications, household furnishings and appliances, ceramics, glass, silver, and pewter. Special exhibits, demonstrations, and hands-on activities. (Daily; closed Thanksgiving, Dec 25) Phone 313/271-1620.

Suwanee Park. Turn-of-the-century amusement center with antique merry-go-round, steamboat, train ride; restaurant, soda fountain. (Mid-May-Sept) Some fees. In addition, visitors can take narrated rides in a horse-drawn carriage (fee), on a steam train (fee), or on a riverboat; 1931 Ford bus rides are also avail (mid-May-Sept). Varied activities are scheduled throughout the yr (see SPECIAL EVENTS). Meals and refreshments are avail. Combination ticket for Henry Ford Museum and Greenfield Village. ¢¢¢¢

Special Events

Old Car Festival. Greenfield Village. Two days Sept. Phone 313/271-1620.
Fall Harvest Days. Greenfield Village. Celebrates turn-of-the-century farm chores, rural home life, and entertainment. Three days early Oct. Phone 313/271-1620.

Motels/Motor Lodges

★ ★ **BEST WESTERN GREENFIELD INN.** 3000 Enterprise Dr (48101). 313/271-1600; res 800/342-5802. www.bestwestern.com. 210 rms, 3 story. S $75-$95; D $85-$105; each addl $10; suites $99-$129; under 20 free. Crib $10. TV; cable (premium), VCR (movies). Indoor pool; whirlpool, poolside serv. Restaurant 6 am-10 pm. Bar 11 am-midnight. Ck-out noon. Coin lndry. Meeting rms. Business servs avail. In-rm modem link. Bellhops. Valet serv. Sundries. Free airport, RR station, bus depot, transportation. Downhill ski 14 mi; x-country ski 4 mi. Exercise equipt; sauna. Bathrm phones, refrigerators; some in-rm whirlpools. Cr cds: A, C, D, DS, ER, JCB, MC, V.
🄳 ⬇ ⇔ 🐾 🔼 ⌨ 🐾 SC

★ ★ **COURTYARD BY MARRIOTT.** 5200 Mercury Dr (48126). 313/271-1400; fax 313/271-1184; toll-free 800/321-2211. www.marriott.com. 147 rms, 14 suites, 2-3 story. S, D $89-$105; suites $105-$114; under 12 free; wkend rates. Crib free. TV; cable (premium). Indoor pool; whirlpool. Coffee in rms. Bkfst avail. Bar Sun-Thurs 5:30-9:30 pm. Ck-out noon. Coin lndry. Meeting rms. Business servs avail. In-rm modem link. Valet serv (Mon-Fri). Exercise equipt. Some refrigerators. Private patios, balconies. Cr cds: A, MC, V.
🄳 ⇔ 🐾 🔼 ⌨ 🐾 SC

★ ★ **HAMPTON INN.** 20061 Michigan Ave (48124). 313/436-9600; fax 313/436-8345; res 800/426-7866. www.hamptoninn.com. 119 rms, 4 story. S, D $83-$93; suites $122-$132;

under 18 free. Crib free. TV; cable (premium). Indoor pool. Complimentary continental bkfst. Complimentary coffee in rms. Restaurant nearby. Ck-out noon. Coin lndry. Meeting rm. Business servs avail. In-rm modem link. Valet serv. Exercise equipt. Refrigerator, wet bar in suites. Overlooks Henry Ford Museum and Greenfield Village. Cr cds: A, MC, V.

🅓 ⊠ 🛉 ⊠ 🔥 SC

★★ **QUALITY INN.** *21430 Michigan Ave (48124). 313/565-0800; fax 313/ 565-2813; toll-free 800/221-2222. www. qualityinn.com.* 100 rms, 2 story. S, D $89-$119; each addl $5; under 18 free; family, wkend rates. Crib free. TV; cable (premium). Heated pool. Complimentary continental bkfst. Ck-out noon. Meeting rms. Business servs avail. In-rm modem link. Refrigerators. Near Henry Ford Museum and Greenfield Village. Cr cds: A, C, D, DS, ER, JCB, MC, V.

🅓 ⊠ ⊠ 🔥 SC

★ **RED ROOF INN.** *24130 Michigan Ave (48124). 313/278-9732; fax 313/ 278-9741; res 800/843-7663. www. redroof.com.* 112 rms, 2 story. June-Aug: S $39.99-$59.99; D $49.99-$69.99; 1-2 addl $59.99-$69.99; under 18 free; lower rates rest of yr. Crib free. Pet accepted, some restrictions. TV; cable (premium). Complimentary coffee in lobby. Restaurant adj 6:30 am-5:30 pm; cafe opp to 11 pm. Ck-out noon. Business servs avail. Cr cds: A, C, D, DS, MC, V.

🅓 🐾 ⊠ 🔥

Hotels

★★★ **HYATT REGENCY DEARBORN.** *Fairlane Town Center (48126). 313/593-1234; fax 313/593-3366; res 800/233-1234. www.hyatt.com.* 772 rms, 16 story. S, D $160-$185; each addl $25; suites $350-$720; under 18 free; wkend rates. Crib free. Valet parking $10. TV; cable (premium). Indoor pool; whirlpool. Restaurants 6:30 am-midnight. Bars, 1 revolving. Ck-out noon. Convention facilities. Business center. In-rm modem link. Exercise equipt; sauna. Health club privileges. 16-story atrium, glass elevators. Near Henry Ford Museum

and Greenfield Village. Cr cds: A, MC, V.

🅓 ⊠ 🛉 ⊠ 🔥 SC 🏃

★★★ **MARRIOTT HOTEL, THE DEARBORN INN.** *20301 Oakwood Blvd (48124). 313/271-2700; fax 313/271-7464; res 800/228-9290. www.marriotthotels.com/dtwdi.* 222 rms, 2-4 story, 22 suites. S $149-$179; D $159-$189; suites $200-$275; under 18 free; wkend rates; package plans. Crib free. Pet accepted, some restrictions. TV; cable (premium), VCR avail. Heated pool; wading pool, poolside serv. Coffee in rms. Restaurant 6:30 am-11 pm. Bar 11-1 am; entertainment. Ck-out noon. Meeting rms. In-rm modem link. Concierge. Tennis. Exercise equipt. Health club privileges. Lawn games. Some refrigerators. Consists of Georgian-style inn built by Henry Ford (1931), two Colonial-style lodges and five Colonial-style houses; Early American decor and furnishings. On 23 acres; gardens. Luxury level. Cr cds: A, C, D, DS, ER, JCB, MC, V.

🅓 🎣 ⊠ 🛉 ⊠ 🔥

★★★ **THE RITZ-CARLTON, DEARBORN.** *300 Town Center Dr (48126). 313/441-2000; fax 313/253-2051; toll-free 800/241-3333. www.ritzcarlton. com.* 308 rms, 11 story. S, D $195-$225; suites $375-$1,500; under 18 free; wkend rates. Crib free. Valet/garage parking $15. TV; cable (premium). Indoor pool; whirlpool, poolside serv. Restaurant (see THE GRILLE ROOM). Rm serv 24 hrs. Bar 11-1 am; entertainment. Ck-out noon. Convention facilities. Business center. In-rm modem link. Concierge. Gift shop. Tennis privileges. Golf privileges. Exercise equipt; sauna. Massage. Health club privileges. Bathrm phones, minibars; some wet bars. Ballroom. Luxury level. Cr cds: A, D, DS, MC, V.

🋏 🎣 ⊠ ⊠ 🔥 🛉 ⊠ 🅓 🏃

Restaurants

★★★ **THE GRILLE ROOM.** *300 Town Center Dr (48126). 313/441-2000. www.ritz-carlton.com.* Hrs: 6:30 am-2:30 pm, 6-9:30 pm; Fri, Sat 6-11 pm; Sun brunch 11 am-2:30 pm. Res accepted. American-continental menu. Bar 11-1 am; Sun to midnight. A la carte entrees: bkfst $6.50-$14.50, lunch $12-$26, dinner $18-$50. Buffet: lunch $25.50. Sun brunch $39. Own baking, desserts. Pianist. Valet parking. Clublike setting; brass chandeliers, 18th- and 19th-century oil paintings. Cr cds: A, DS, MC, V.

D

★ ★ **KIERNAN'S STEAK HOUSE.** *21931 Michigan Ave (US 12) (48124). 313/565-4260.* Hrs: 11 am-11 pm; Sat from 5 pm; Sun 4-9 pm. Closed hols. Res accepted. Bar to midnight. Lunch $7-$35, dinner $9.95-$35. Specializes in steak, seafood, veal. Valet parking. Intimate atmosphere. Cr cds: A, DS, MC, V.

D

★ ★ ★ **MORO'S.** *6535 Allen Rd, Allen Park (48101). 313/382-7152.* Hrs: 11 am-10 pm; Sat 4-10 pm; Sun 2-8 pm. Closed hols; also Sun June-Aug. Italian menu. Wine list. Lunch $5-$15, dinner $10-$25. Specializes in veal, steak. Casual, Italian decor. Cr cds: A, MC, V.

D

Detroit (G-7)

Founded 1701 **Pop** 1,027,974
Elev 600 ft **Area code** 313
Information Metropolitan Detroit Convention and Visitors Bureau, 211 W Fort St, Suite 1000, 48226; 800/DETROIT
Web www.visitdetroit.com

Suburbs Ann Arbor, Birmingham, Bloomfield Hills, Dearborn, Farmington, Mount Clemens, Plymouth, Pontiac, St. Clair, Southfield, Troy, Warren, Ypsilanti.

Detroit, a high-speed city geared to the tempo of the production line, is the symbol throughout the world of America's productive might. Its name is almost synonymous with the word "automobile." The city that put the world on wheels, Detroit is the birthplace of mass production and the producer of nearly 25 percent of the nation's automobiles, trucks, and tractors. Every year a new generation

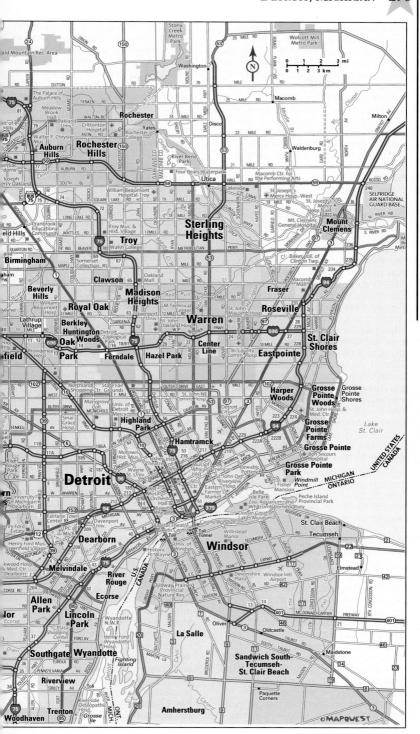

of vehicles is hammered out in its factories. This is the city of Ford, Chrysler, Dodge, the Fishers, and the UAW. Detroit is a major producer of space propulsion units, automation equipment, plane parts, hardware, rubber tires, office equipment, machine tools, fabricated metal, iron and steel forging, and auto stampings and accessories. Being a port and border city, Detroit puts the Michigan Customs District among the nation's top five customs districts.

Founded by Antoine de la Mothe Cadillac in the name of Louis XIV of France at *le place du détroit*—"the place of the strait"—this strategic frontier trading post was 75 years old when the Revolution began. During the War of Independence, Detroit was ruled by Henry Hamilton, the British governor hated throughout the colonies as "the hair buyer of Detroit." He encouraged Native Americans to take rebel scalps rather than prisoners. At the end of the war, the British ignored treaty obligations and refused to abandon Detroit. As long as Detroit remained in British hands, it was both a strategic threat and a barrier to westward expansion; however, the settlement was finally wrested away by Major General Anthony Wayne at the Battle of Fallen Timbers. On July 11, 1796, the Stars and Stripes flew over Detroit for the first time.

During the War of 1812, the fortress at Detroit fell mysteriously into British hands again, without a shot fired. It was recaptured by the Americans the following year. In 1815, when the city was incorporated, Detroit was still just a trading post; by 1837, it was a city of 10,000 people. Then, the development of more efficient transportation opened the floodgates of immigration, and the city was on its way as an industrial and shipping hub. Between 1830-1860, population doubled with every decade. At the turn of the century, the auto industry took hold. Today, Detroit is a leader in the fields of automation and space exploration equipment. Yet it is a city that acknowledges its traditions as a French fort and frontier trading post. It looks to the future as well as the past.

Detroit was a quiet city before the automobile—brewing beer and hammering together carriages and stoves. Most people owned their own homes—they called it "the most beautiful city in America." All this swiftly changed when the automobile age burst upon it. Growth became the important concern; production stood as the summit of achievement. The automobile lines produced a new civic personality—there was little time for culture at the end of a day on the line. The city rocketed out beyond its river-hugging confines, developing nearly 100 suburbs. Today growing pains have eased, the automobile worker has more leisure time, and a new Detroit personality is emerging. Civic planning is remodeling the face of the community, particularly downtown and along the riverfront. Five minutes from downtown, twenty separate institutions form Detroit's Cultural Center—all within easy walking distance of one another.

Detroit is one of the few cities in the United States where you can look due south into Canada. The city stretches out along the Detroit River between lakes Erie and St. Clair, opposite the Canadian city of Windsor, Ontario. Detroit is 143 square miles in size and almost completely flat. The buildings of the Renaissance Center and Civic Center are grouped about the shoreline, and a network of major highways and expressways radiate from this point like the spokes of a wheel. The original city was laid out on the lines of the L'Enfant plan for Washington, D.C., with a few major streets radiating from a series of circles. As the city grew, a gridiron pattern was superimposed to handle the maze of subdivisions that had developed into Detroit's 200 neighborhoods.

These main thoroughfares all originate near the Civic Center: Fort Street (MI 3); Michigan Avenue (US 12); Grand River Avenue (I-96); John Lodge Freeway (US 10); Woodward Ave (MI 1); Gratiot Avenue (MI 3); and Fisher and Chrysler freeways (I-75). Intersecting these and almost parallel with the shoreline are the Edsel Ford Freeway (I-94) and Jefferson Avenue (US 25).

Additional Visitor Information

For additional accommodations, see DETROIT WAYNE COUNTY AIRPORT AREA, which follows DETROIT.

The Metropolitan Detroit Convention and Visitors Bureau (211 Fort St, Suite 1000, 48226; phone 800/ DETROIT) publishes the *Visitor's Guide to Greater Detroit,* a helpful booklet describing the area. Information is also available from the City of Detroit, Department of Public Information, 608 Coleman A. Young Municipal Center, 48226; phone 313/224-3755. In addition, there are Detroit Visitor and Information Centers located at 100 Renaissance Center, first floor, and at Henry Ford Museum and Greenfield Village in Dearborn (see) that provide booklets and brochures on the city. To receive an information packet on Detroit or to inquire about lodging phone the "Whats Line," 800/DETROIT.

Transportation

Airport. See DETROIT WAYNE COUNTY AIRPORT AREA.

Car Rental Agencies. See IMPORTANT TOLL-FREE NUMBERS.

Public Transportation. Buses (Suburban Mobility Authority for Regional Transportation), phone 313/962-5515 (Detroit Department of Transportation). Elevated train downtown (the People Mover), phone 800/541-RAIL.

Rail Passenger Service. Amtrak 800/872-7245.

What to See and Do

⭐ **Belle Isle.** Between US and Canada, in sight of downtown Detroit, this 1,000-acre island park offers nine-hole golf, a nature center, guided nature walks, swimming, fishing (piers, docks). Picnicking, ball fields, tennis and lighted handball courts. An island park in middle of Detroit River, reached by MacArthur Bridge. **FREE** Also here are

Aquarium. One of the largest and oldest freshwater collections in the country. (Daily) Phone 313/852-4141. ¢

Belle Isle Zoo. Animals in natural habitat. (May-Oct, daily) Phone 313/852-4083. ¢¢

Dossin Great Lakes Museum. Scale models of Great Lakes ships; restored "Gothic salon" from Great Lakes liner; marine paintings, reconstructed ship's bridge, and full-scale racing boat, *Miss Pepsi.* (Wed-Sun) Phone 313/852-4051. **Donation**

Detroit skyline

Whitcomb Conservatory. Exhibits of ferns, cacti, palms, orchids; special exhibits. (Wed-Sun) Phone 313/852-4064. ¢

Canada. Windsor, Ontario (see), is only a five-min drive through the Detroit-Windsor tunnel or via the Ambassador Bridge. Tunnel and bridge tolls. Buses run every 12 min (fee). For Border Crossing Regulations, see MAKING THE MOST OF YOUR TRIP.

Children's Museum. Exhibits incl "America Discovered," Inuit culture, children's art, folk crafts, birds and mammals of Michigan, holiday themes. Participatory activities relate to exhibits. Special workshops and programs and planetarium demonstrations on Sat and during vacations. (Mon-Sat; closed hols) 67 E Kirby Ave. Phone 313/873-8100. **FREE**

Civic Center. Dramatic group of buildings in a 95-acre downtown riverfront setting. Woodward and Jefferson aves. Incl in this group are

Cobo Hall-Cobo Arena. Designed to be the world's finest convention-exposition-recreation building; features an 11,561-seat arena and 720,000 sq ft of exhibit area and related facilities. (Daily) W Jefferson Ave and Washington Blvd. Phone 313/877-8111.

Coleman A. Young Municipal Center. A $27-million, 13-story white marble office building and 19-story tower housing more than 36 government departments and courtrms. At front entrance is massive bronze sculpture *Spirit of Detroit.* Building (Mon-Fri; closed hols). 2 Woodward Ave. Phone 313/224-5585. **FREE**

Hart Plaza and Dodge Fountain. A $2 million water display designed by sculptor Isamu Noguchi. Jefferson Ave. Phone 313/877-8077.

Mariners' Church. Oldest stone church in the city, completed in 1849, was moved 800 ft to present site as part of Civic Center plan. Since that time it has been extensively restored and a belltower with carillon has been added. Tours (by appt). 170 E Jefferson Ave. Phone 313/259-2206. **FREE**

Michigan Consolidated Gas Company Building. Glass-walled sky-scraper designed by Minoru Yamasaki. 1 Woodward Ave.

Veterans' Memorial Building. Rises on site where Cadillac and first French settlers landed in 1701. This $5.75 million monument to the Detroit area war dead was the first unit of the $180-million Civic Center to be completed. The massive sculptured-marble eagle on the front of the building is by Marshall Fredericks, who also sculpted *Spirit of Detroit* at City-County Building. 151 W Jefferson Ave.

Detroit Historical Museum. Presents a walk through history along reconstructed streets of Old Detroit, period alcoves, costumes; changing exhibits portray city life. The museum now showcases a new automotive exhibition, celebrating over 100 yrs of the automotive industry. (Tues-Sun; closed hols) 5401 Woodward Ave. Phone 313/833-1805. ¢¢

Detroit Institute of Arts. (1885) One of the great art museums of the world, tells history of humankind through artistic creations. Every significant art-producing culture is represented. Exhibits incl *The Detroit Industry* murals by Diego Rivera, Van Eyck's *St. Jerome,* Bruegel's *Wedding Dance,* and Van Gogh's *Self-Portrait;* African, American, Indian, Dutch, French, Flemish, and Italian collections; medieval arms and armor; an 18th-century American country house reconstructed with period furnishings. Frequent special exhibitions (fee); lectures, films. (Wed-Sun; closed hols) 5200 Woodward Ave, between Farnsworth Ave and Kirby St. Phone 313/833-7900. ¢¢

Detroit Public Library. Murals by Coppin, Sheets, Melchers, and Blashfield; special collections incl National Automotive History, Burton Historical (Old Northwest Territory), Hackley (African Americans in performing arts), Labor, Maps, Rare Books, US Patents Collection from 1790 to present. (Tues-Sat; closed hols) 5201 Woodward Ave. Phone 313/833-1000. **FREE**

Detroit Symphony Orchestra Hall. (1919) Restored public concert hall features classical programs. The Detroit Symphony Orchestra performs here. 3711 Woodward Ave, at Parsons. Phone 313/576-5100.

Detroit Zoo. One of the world's outstanding zoos, with 40 exhibits of more than 1,200 animals in natural habitats. Outstanding chimpanzee, reptile, bear, penguin, and bird exhibits. (Daily; closed Jan 1, Thanksgiving, Dec 25) 10 mi N via Woodward Ave, at I-696 in Royal Oak. Phone 248/398-0900. ¢¢

Eastern Market. (1892) Built originally on the site of an early hay and wood market, this and the Chene-Ferry Market are the two remaining produce/wholesale markets. Today the Eastern Market encompasses produce and meat-packing houses, fish markets, and storefronts offering items ranging from spices to paper. It is also recognized as the world's largest bedding flower market. (Mon-Sat; closed hols) 2934 Russell, via I-75 at Gratiot. Phone 313/833-1560. **FREE**

Fisher Building. (1928) Designed by architect Albert Kahn, this building was recognized in 1928 as the most beautiful commercial building erected and given a silver medal by the Architectural League of New York. The building consists of a 28-story central tower and two 11-story wings. Housed here are the Fisher Theater, shops, restaurants, art galleries, and offices. Underground pedestrian walkways and skywalk bridges connect to parking deck and 11 separate structures, incl General Motors World Headquarters and New Center One. W Grand and Second blvds. Phone 313/874-4444.

Gray Line bus tours. Contact 1301 E Warren Ave, 48207. Phone 313/870-5012.

Historic Trinity Lutheran Church. (1931) Third church of congregation founded in 1850; 16th-century-style pier-and-clerestory, neo-Gothic small cathedral. Luther tower is a copy of the tower at a monastery in Erfurt, Germany. Much statuary and stained glass. Bell tower. (Tours by appt) 1345 Gratiot Ave. Phone 313/567-3100. **Donation**

Huron-Clinton Metroparks. A system of 13 recreation areas in the surrounding suburbs of Detroit (see ANN ARBOR, FARMINGTON, MOUNT CLEMENS, and TROY). Phone 810/463-4581.

International Institute of Metropolitan Detroit. Hall of Nations has cultural exhibits from five continents (Mon-Fri; closed hols). Cultural programs and ethnic festivals throughout the yr. 111 E Kirby Ave. Phone 313/871-8600. **FREE**

Motown Museum. "Hitsville USA," the house where legends like Diana Ross and the Supremes, Stevie Wonder, Marvin Gaye, the Jackson Five, and the Temptations recorded their first hits. Motown's original recording Studio A; artifacts, photographs, gold and platinum records, memorabilia. Guided tours. (Daily) 2648 W Grand Blvd. Phone 313/875-2264. ¢¢¢

Museum of African-American History. Exhibits trace the history and achievements of black people in the Americas. (Tues-Sun; closed hols) 315 E Warren Ave. In the University Cultural Center. Phone 313/494-5800. ¢¢¢

Professional sports.

> **Detroit Lions (NFL).** Ford Field. Phone 248/335-4131.
>
> **Detroit Pistons (NBA).** 2 Championship Dr (MI 24), Auburn Hills (see PONTIAC). Phone 248/377-0100.
>
> **Detroit Red Wings (NHL).** Joe Louis Arena, 600 Civic Center Dr. Phone 810/645-6666.
>
> **Detroit Shock (WNBA).** The Palace of Auburn Hills, 2 Championship Dr. Auburn Hills. Phone 248/377-0100.
>
> **Detroit Tigers (MLB).** Comerica Park, Woodward Ave and I-75. Phone 313/962-4000.

Renaissance Center. Seven-tower complex on the riverfront; incl 73-story hotel (see HOTELS), offices, restaurants, bars, movie theaters, retail shops, and business services. Jefferson Ave at Beaubien. Phone 313/568-5600.

⭐ **Washington Boulevard Trolley Car.** Antique electric trolley cars provide a unique transit service to downtown hotels, the Civic Center, and the Renaissance Center. From late May-Labor Day Detroit operates the only open-top double-decker trolley car in the world. (Daily) Phone 313/933-1300. ¢

Wayne State University. (1868) 34,950 students. Has 13 professional schools and colleges. The campus has almost 100 buildings, some of the most notable being the award-winning McGregor Memorial Conference Center designed by Minoru Yamasaki and its sculpture court; the Walter P. Reuther Library of Labor and Urban Affairs; and the Yamasaki-designed College of Education. Wayne has a medical campus of 16 acres adj in the Detroit Medical Center. Three theaters present performances. 656 W Kirby. Phone 313/577-2972.

Special Events

International Auto Show. Cobo Hall. Jan. Phone 248/643-0250.

Riverfront Festivals. Hart Plaza, downtown riverfront. Wkend festivals featuring entertainment, costumes, history, artifacts, and handicrafts of Detroit's diverse ethnic populations. Different country featured most wkends. May-Sept. Phone 313/877-8077.

Detroit Grand Prix. Belle Isle. Indy car race. Fri is Free Prix Day. Phone 800/498-RACE. June.

Michigan State Fair. Michigan Exposition & Fairgrounds. Phone 313/366-3300. Late Aug-early Sept.

Ford International Detroit Jazz Festival. Five days of free jazz concerts. Late Aug. Phone 313/963-7622.

The Theatre Company-University of Detroit Mercy. 8200 W Outer Dr. Dramas, comedies in university theater. Phone 313/993-1130. Sept-May.

Horse racing.

    Hazel Park. 1650 E Ten Mile Rd. Phone 248/398-1000. Harness racing. Mon, Tues, Thurs-Sat. Apr-mid-Oct.

    Northville Downs. 301 S Center St in Northville. Harness racing. Over 12 yrs only. Phone 248/349-1000. Mon, Tues, Thurs, Sat. Jan, Oct-Mar.

Meadow Brook Music Festival. (see PONTIAC). Phone 248/377-0100.

Meadow Brook Theatre. (see PONTIAC). Phone 248/377-3300.

Motels/Motor Lodges

★★ **BEST WESTERN.** 16999 S Laurel Park Dr, Livonia (48154). 734/464-0050; fax 734/464-5869; res 800/780-7234. www.bestwestern.com. 123 rms, 2 story. S, D $74-$120; under 18 free. Crib free. TV; cable (premium). Heated pool. Complimentary continental bkfst. Ck-out noon. Meeting rms. Business servs avail. In-rm modem link. X-country ski 5 mi. Exercise equipt. Refrigerators; some in-rm whirlpools, minibars. Cr cds: A, D, DS, MC, V.

★★ **COURTYARD BY MARRIOTT DETROIT DOWNTOWN.** 333 E Jefferson St (48226). 313/222-7700; fax 313/222-8517; res 800/321-2211. www.courtyard.com. 255 rms, 21 story. S $180-$250; D $190-$250; each addl $20; suites $250-$1,000; under 18 free; wkend rates. Valet parking $9. Crib free. TV; cable. Indoor pool; whirlpool, poolside serv. Coffee in rms. Restaurant 6:30 am-10 pm; Fri, Sat to 11 pm. Bar 11-2 am. Meeting rms. Business center. In-rm modem link. Shopping arcade. Barber, beauty shop. Tennis. Racquetball. Exercise rm; sauna. Bathrm phone and TV, refrigerator in suites. Opp river. Cr cds: A, MC, V.

★★ **COURTYARD BY MARRIOTT DETROIT LIVONIA.** 17200 N Laurel Park Dr, Livonia (48152). 734/462-2000; fax 734/462-5907; res 800/321-2211. www.marriott.com. 149 rms, 3 story. S, D $96-$106; suites $125-$135; wkend rates. Crib free. TV; cable (premium). Indoor pool; whirlpool. Restaurant 6:30-10 am; Sat 7-11 am; Sun 7 am-1 pm. Bar 4-11 pm; closed Sat, Sun. Ck-out noon. Coin lndry. Meeting rms. Business servs avail. In-rm modem link. Valet serv. Downhill/x-country ski 20 mi. Exercise equipt. Refrigerator in suites. Private patios, balconies. Cr cds: A, C, D, DS, JCB, MC, V.

★★ **HOLIDAY INN.** 5801 Southfield Service Dr (48228). 313/336-3340; fax 313/336-7037; res 800/465-4329. www.holiday-inn.com. 347 rms, 6 story. S, D $99; suites $250; under 18 free; wkend rates. Crib free. TV; cable (premium). 2 pools, 1 indoor; whirlpool. Coffee in rms. Restaurant 6 am-2 pm, 5-10 pm; Sat, Sun from 7 am. \Bar 11 am-midnight. Ck-out noon. Convention facilities. Business center. Bellhops. Gift shop. Exercise equipt;

sauna. Game rm. Cr cds: A, D, DS, MC, V.

★★ **PARKCREST INN.** *20000 Harper Ave, Harper Woods (48225). 313/884-8800; fax 313/884-7087.* 49 rms, 2 story. S $59; D $67-$72; kit. units $84; family rates. Crib free. Pet accepted. TV; cable (premium). Heated pool. Restaurant 6:30-2:30 am; Sun 7:30 am-10 pm. Bar to 2 am. Ck-out 11 am. Valet serv. X-country ski 15 mi. Cr cds: A, C, D, DS, MC, V.

★ **THE SHORECREST MOTOR INN.** *1316 E Jefferson Ave (48207).*

Dutch Village

313/568-3000; fax 313/568-3002; toll-free 800/992-9616. www.shorecrestmi. com. 54 rms, 2 story. S $69-$89; D $89-$99; family, wkly, wkend rates. Crib free. TV; cable (premium). Restaurant from 6 am; wkends from 7 am. Ck-out noon. Business servs avail. Valet serv. Health club privileges. Refrigerators. Cr cds: A, C, D, DS, MC, V.

Hotels

★★★ **MARRIOTT DETROIT METRO AIRPORT.** *Detroit Metropolitan Airport (48242). 734/941-9400; res 800/228-9290. www.marriott.com.* 160 rms, 5 story. S, D $145-$225; each addl $20; under 17 free. Crib avail. Pet accepted. TV; cable (premium), VCR avail. Complimentary continental bkfst. Ck-out noon. Meeting rms. Business center. Gift shop. Some refrigerators, minibars. Cr cds: A, C, D, DS, MC, V.

★★★ **MARRIOTT LIVONIA DETROIT.** *17100 Laurel Park Dr N, Livonia (48152). 734/462-3100; fax 734/462-2815; toll-free 800/321-2211. www. marriott.com.* 224 rms, 6 story. S, D $129-$149; suites $225; family, wkend rates. Crib free. TV; cable (premium), VCR avail. Indoor pool; whirlpool, poolside serv. Restaurant 6:30 am-10 pm. Bar noon-midnight. Ck-out noon. Meeting rms. Business center. In-rm modem link. Gift shop. Free garage parking. Downhill/x-country ski 20 mi. Exercise equipt; sauna. Health club privileges. Connected to Laurel Park Mall. Luxury level. Cr cds: A, C, D, DS, JCB, MC, V.

★★ **MARRIOTT RENAISSANCE CENTER.** *Renaissance Center (48243). 313/568-8000; fax 313/568-8146; toll-free 800/352-0831. www.marriott.com.* 1,306 rms, 50 story. S $175-$195; D $190-$210; each addl $15; suites $330-$1,200; under 18 free; wkend rates. Crib free. Pet accepted. TV; cable, VCR avail (movies). Indoor pool. Restaurants 6 am-11 pm. Rm serv 24 hrs. Bar 11:30-1:30 am. Ck-out 1 pm. Convention facilities. Business center. In-rm modem link. Shopping arcade. Barber, beauty shop. Exercise rm; sauna. Many minibars. Luxury level. Cr cds: A, C, D, DS, ER, JCB, MC, V.

⬚⬚⬚⬚⬚⬚⬚⬚

★ ★ ★ **OMNI DETROIT HOTEL AT RIVER PLACE.** *1000 River Place Dr (48207). 313/259-9500; fax 313/259-3744; res 800/843-6664. www.omni hotels.com.* 108 rms, 5 story, 18 suites. S $115-$185; D $135-$205; each addl $20; suites $165-$500; under 12 free; hol rates; higher rates some special events. Crib free. Valet parking $6. Pet accepted. TV; cable (premium), VCR avail. Indoor pool; whirlpool. Restaurant (see BARON'S STEAKHOUSE). Bar 11 am-11 pm; Fri, Sat to 1 am. Ck-out noon. Meeting rms. Business servs avail. In-rm modem link. Tennis privileges. Exercise rm; sauna. Massage. Croquet court. On Detroit River. Cr cds: A, C, D, DS, MC, V.

⬚⬚⬚⬚⬚⬚⬚

B&B/Small Inn

★ **BOTSFORD INN.** *28000 Grand River Ave, Plymouth (48336). 248/474-4800.* 65 rms. S $65-$75; D $70-$85; each addl $5; suites $75-$95; under 12 free; monthly rates. Crib $5. TV; cable (premium). Complimentary full bkfst. Coffee in rms. Dining rm 7 am-10 pm. Bar 11 am-midnight. Ck-out 1 pm, ck-in 3 pm. Guest lndry. Meeting rms. Tennis. Early American, Victorian furnishings; many antiques. Built in 1836; restored by Henry Ford. Cr cds: A, C, D, DS, MC, V.

⬚⬚⬚⬚⬚

All Suites

★ ★ ★ **THE ATHENEUM SUITE HOTEL.** *1000 Brush St (48226). 313/962-2323; fax 313/962-2424; toll-free 800/772-2323. www.atheneumsuites. com.* 174 suites, 10 story. Suites $195; each addl $20; family, wkly rates. Crib free. Valet parking $12. TV; cable (premium), VCR avail. Coffee in rms. Restaurant adj 8 am-midnight. Rm serv 24 hrs. Bar. Ck-out noon. Meeting rms. Business servs avail. In-rm modem link. Concierge. Exercise equipt. Health club privileges. Minibars; some bathrm

phones. Neoclassical structure adj International Center. Cr cds: A, D, DS, MC.

⬚⬚⬚⬚

★ ★ ★ **EMBASSY SUITES HOTEL.** *19525 Victor Pkwy, Livonia (48512). 734/462-6000; fax 734/462-6003. www.embassysuites.com.* 239 suites, 5 story. S $129-$149; D $139-$159; each addl $10; under 18 free (max 2); wkend rates; higher rates special events. Crib free. TV; cable (premium). Indoor pool; whirlpool. Complimentary full bkfst. Complimentary coffee in rms. Restaurant 6-9 am, 11 am-4 pm, 5-10 pm; hrs vary Fri-Sun. Bar 5 pm-midnight; closed Sun. Ck-out noon. Coin lndry. Meeting rms. Business servs avail. In-rm modem link. Gift shop. Exercise equipt; sauna. Refrigerators, microwaves. Balconies. Five-story atrium. Cr cds: A, C, D, DS, JCB, MC, V.

⬚⬚⬚⬚⬚

Restaurants

★ ★ ★ **BARON'S STEAKHOUSE.** *1000 River Place Dr (48207). 313/259-4855. www.omnihotels.com.* Hrs: 7 am-10 pm; Fri, Sat to 11 pm; Sun 7 am-2 pm. Closed Dec 25. Res accepted. Bar to 11 pm. Bkfst $4.95-$11.95, lunch $4.95-$16.95, dinner $13.95-$28.95. Child's menu. Specializes in beef, chicken, seafood. Outdoor dining. Overlooks Detroit River. Cr cds: A, DS, MC, V.

⬚⬚

★ ★ ★ **CAUCUS CLUB.** *150 W Congress St (48226). 313/965-4970.* Hrs: 11:30 am-8:30 pm; Fri to 10 pm; Sat 5 pm-10 pm; summer hrs vary. Closed Sun; hols. Res accepted. Continental menu. Lunch $7.75-$17.25, dinner $15-$24. Child's menu. Specialties: fresh fish, steak, ribs. Entertainment Fri, Sat. Cr cds: A, D, DS, MC, V.

⬚⬚

★ **EL ZOCALO.** *3400 Bagley (48216). 313/841-3700.* Hrs: 11-1 am; Fri, Sat to 2:30 am. Closed some major hols. Res accepted Sun-Thurs. Mexican menu. Bar. Lunch $5.95-$8.95, dinner $6.35-$9.95. Specialties: chiles rellenos, queso flameado, chimichangas. Parking. Mayan and Aztec art. Cr cds: A, D, DS, MC, V.

D ⌨

★★ **FISHBONE'S RHYTHM KITCHEN CAFE.** *400 Monroe St (48226).* 313/965-4600. Hrs: 6:30 am-midnight; Fri, Sat to 1:45 am; Sun brunch 10:30 am-2:30 pm; dinner 2 pm-midnight. Closed Dec 25. Southern Louisiana, Creole, Cajun menu. Bar. Lunch $5.95-$12.95, dinner $5.95-$19.95. Sun brunch $18.95. Specialties: smoked whiskey ribs, jambalaya, crawfish étoufeé. Valet parking. Bourbon Street bistro atmosphere; tin ceilings, antique lamps. Cr cds: A, D, DS, MC, V.

D ⌨

★★★ **INTERMEZZO.** *1435 Randolph St (48226).* 313/961-0707. *www. intermezzodetroit.com.* Hrs: 11 am-10 pm; Fri, Sat to 11 pm. Closed Sun, Mon; hols. Res accepted. Italian menu. Bar. Lunch $6-$22, dinner $12-$28. Specializes in veal, pasta. Entertainment Fri, Sat. Outdoor dining. Contemporary decor. Cr cds: A, D, DS, MC, V.

D ⌨

★★★ **OPUS ONE.** *565 E Larned (48226).* 313/961-7766. *www.opus-one. com.* Hrs: 11:30 am-10 pm; Fri to 11 pm; Sat 5-11 pm. Closed Sun; hols. Res accepted. Bar. Wine cellar. Continental, American menu. Lunch $8.95-$24.95, dinner $24.95-$38.95. Child's menu. Specializes in seafood, aged beef. Own baking, ice cream. Pianist Tues-Sat (dinner). Valet parking. In building designed by Albert Kahn; etched glass, original artwork. Cr cds: A, D, DS, MC, V.

D

★★ **PEGASUS TAVERNA.** *558 Monroe St (48226).* 313/964-6800. Hrs: 11-1 am; Fri, Sat to 2 am; Sun to midnight. Greek, American menu. Bar. A la carte entrees: lunch $4.95-$7.95, dinner $5.95-$17.95. Child's menu. Specializes in lamb chops, seafood, spinach cheese pie. Parking. Lattice-worked ceiling; hanging grape vines. Cr cds: A, D, DS, MC, V.

D ⌨

★★★ **RATTLESNAKE CLUB.** *300 Stroh River Pl (48207).* 313/567-4400. Hrs: 11:30 am-10 pm; Fri to mid-night; Sat 5:30-midnight. Closed Sun; hols. Res accepted. Bar. Lunch $11.95-$32.95, dinner $12.95-$34.95. Specializes in seasonal dishes. Valet parking. Outdoor dining. Modern decor; two dining areas overlook Detroit River. Cr cds: A, D, DS, MC, V.

D ⌨

★★★ **THE WHITNEY.** *4421 Woodward Ave (48201).* 313/832-5700. *www.thewhitney.com.* Hrs: 11 am-2 pm, 6-9:00 pm; Wed, Thurs 5-9 pm; Fri, Sat 5-10 pm; Sun 5-8 pm; Sun brunch 11 am-2 pm. Closed hols. Res accepted. Bar 5 pm-2 am; closed Sun and Mon. Wine cellar. A la carte entrees: lunch $6.95-$16.95, dinner $18-$35. Menu changes monthly. Prix fixe: dinner $48-$60. Sun brunch $26.95. Specializes in veal, beef, seafood. Own baking. Entertainment. Complimentary valet parking. Amer cuisine. Cr cds: A, D, DS, MC, V.

D

Unrated Dining Spot

TRAFFIC JAM & SNUG. *511 W Canfield St (48201).* 313/831-9470. *www. traffic-jam.com.* Hrs: 11 am-10:30 pm; Fri to midnight; Sat noon-midnight. Closed Sun; hols. Serv bar. Lunch $7-$10, dinner $9-$15. Child's menu. Own pastries, desserts, ice cream, cheese. Microbrewery and dairy on premises. Parking. Rustic decor; many antiques. Cr cds: A, DS, MC, V.

D

Detroit Wayne County Airport Area

(G-7) *See also Dearborn, Detroit, Ypsilanti*

Services and Information

Information. 313/942-3550.

Airlines. Air Canada, America West, American, Asiana, British Airways, Continental, Delta, Great Lakes, KLM, Midwest Express, Northwest,

Southwest, Spirit, TWA, United, USAir.

Motels/Motor Lodges

★★ **AIRPORT PLAZA INN.** *8270 Wickham, Romulus (48174). 734/729-6300; fax 734/722-8740.* 243 rms, 4 story. S, D $79-$89; each addl $10; suites from $150; family, wkend rates; package plans. Crib free. TV; cable (premium). Indoor pool. Playground. Restaurant 6 am-10 pm. Bar 11-2 am; Sun from noon; entertainment. Ck-out noon. Meeting rms. Business servs avail. Bellhops. Valet serv. Sundries. Free airport transportation. X-country ski 4 mi. Exercise equipt; sauna. Cr cds: A, C, D, DS, MC, V.

🅳 ⛵ ≈ 🏋 ✈ ≈ 🔥

★★ **COURTYARD BY MARRIOTT.** *30653 Flynn Dr, Romulus (48174). 734/721-3200; fax 734/721-1304; res 800/321-2211. www.marriott.com.* 146 rms, 3 story. S, D $93; each addl $10; suites $110; under 16 free; wkend rates. Crib free. TV; cable (premium). Indoor pool; whirlpool. Complimentary coffee in rms. Restaurant 6:30 am-2 pm, 5-10 pm; Sat 7 am-1 pm, 5-10 pm; Sun 7 am-1 pm. Bar. Ck-out noon. Coin lndry. Meeting rms. Business servs avail. In-rm modem link. Valet serv. Free airport transportation. Exercise equipt. Refrigerator in suites. Balconies. Cr cds: A, D, DS, MC, V.

🅳 ≈ 🏋 ✈ ≈ 🔥

★★ **HAMPTON INN.** *30847 Flynn Dr, Romulus (48174). 734/721-1100; fax 734/721-9915; res 800/426-7866. www.hamptoninn.com.* 136 rms, 3 story. S, D $69.95-$89.95; under 17 free. Crib $5. TV; cable (premium). Pool. Complimentary continental bkfst. Restaurant adj 6 am-10 pm; Fri, Sat to 11:30 pm. Ck-out noon. Meeting rms. Business center. In-rm modem link. Valet serv. Free airport transportation. Cr cds: A, C, D, DS, MC, V.

🅳 ≈ ✈ ≈ 🔥 SC 🏋

★★ **QUALITY INN.** *7600 Merriman Rd, Romulus (48174). 734/728-2430; fax 734/728-3756; toll-free 800/937-0005. www.choicehotels.com.* 140 rms. S, D $74-$79; each addl $5; under 12

free; wkly rates. Crib free. TV; cable (premium). Complimentary continental bkfst. Restaurant adj 11-1 am. Bar. Ck-out noon. Coin lndry. Meeting rms. Business servs avail. In-rm modem link. Free airport transportation. Cr cds: A, C, D, DS, MC, V.

🅳 ✈ ≈ 🔥

Hotels

★★★ **CROWNE PLAZA DETROIT METRO.** *8000 Merriman Rd, Romulus (48174). 734/729-2600; fax 734/729-9414; toll-free 800/227-6963. www.crowneplaza.com.* 365 rms, 11 story. S, D $149; each addl $10; suites $179-$229; family, wkend rates. Crib free. TV; cable (premium), VCR avail. Indoor pool; whirlpool. Coffee in rms. Restaurant 6 am-10 pm. Bar noon-1 am. Ck-out noon. Convention facilities. Business center. In-rm modem link. Gift shop. Free airport transportation. Exercise equipt. Game rm. Some balconies. Luxury level. Cr cds: A, C, D, DS, MC, V.

🅳 ≈ 🏋 ✈ ≈ 🔥 🏃

★★★ **MARRIOTT ROMULUS DETROIT.** *30559 Flynn Dr, Romulus (48174). 734/729-7555; fax 734/729-8634; toll-free 800/228-9290.* 245 rms, 4 story. S $134-$144; D $144-$154; suites $350; family, wkend rates. Crib free. TV; cable (premium). Indoor pool; whirlpool. Restaurant 6:30 am-10 pm. Bar from 11 am. Ck-out noon. Meeting rms. Business servs avail. In-rm modem link. Gift shop. Free airport transportation. Downhill ski 15 mi. Exercise equipt. Some bathrm phones. Refrigerator, minibar in suites. Luxury level. Cr cds: A, C, D, DS, ER, JCB, MC, V.

🅳 ⛵ ≈ 🏋 ✈ ≈ 🔥

All Suite

★★★ **HILTON SUITES DETROIT METRO AIRPORT.** *8600 Wickham Rd, Romulus. 734/728-9200; fax 734/728-9278; res 800/774-1500. www.detroitmetroairport.hilton.com.* 151 suites, 3 story. S $89-$169; D $99-$179; each addl $10; family, wkend rates. Crib free. TV; cable (premium), VCR (movies $6). Indoor/outdoor pool; whirlpool, poolside serv. Complimentary full bkfst. Complimentary coffee in rms. Restaurant 6 am-11 pm. Bar. Ck-out noon. Coin lndry. Meeting rms. Business center. In-rm modem link. Bellhops. Valet serv. Sundries. Free airport transportation. Downhill ski 10 mi. Exercise equipt. Game rm. Refrigerators. Some balconies. Cr cds: A, C, D, DS, ER, JCB, MC, V.

East Lansing (G-5)

(see Lansing and East Lansing)

Escanaba (C-3)

Settled 1830 **Pop** 13,659 **Elev** 598 ft
Area code 906 **Zip** 49829
Information Delta County Area Chamber of Commerce, 230 Ludington St; 906/786-2192 or 888/335-8264
Web www.deltami.org

The first European settlers in this area were lured by the pine timber, which they were quick to log; however, a second growth provides solid forest cover once again. Escanaba is the only ore-shipping port on Lake Michigan. Manufacture of paper is another important industry. Sports enthusiasts are attracted by the open water and huge tracts of undeveloped countryside. Fishing is excellent. Escanaba is the headquarters for the Hiawatha National Forest.

What to See and Do

Hiawatha National Forest. This 893,000-acre forest offers scenic drives, hunting, camping, picnicking, hiking, horseback riding, x-country skiing, snowmobiling, winter sports; lake and stream fishing, swimming, sailing, motorboating, and canoeing. It has shoreline on three Great Lakes—Huron, Michigan, and Superior. The eastern section of the forest is close to Sault Ste. Marie, St. Ignace, and the northern foot of the Mackinac Bridge. Fees charged at developed campground sites. (Daily) For further information contact the Supervisor, 2727 N Lincoln Rd. Phone 906/786-4062. **FREE**

Ludington Park. Fishing, boating (launch, marina; fee), swimming, bath house; tennis courts, playground, volleyball court, ball fields, picnic area, tables, stoves, scenic bike path, pavilion, bandshell. (Apr-Nov, daily) On MI 35, overlooks Little Bay de Noc. Phone 906/786-4141. **FREE** In the park is

Eagle Harbor Lighthouse

Delta County Historical Museum and Sand Point Lighthouse. Local historical artifacts; lumber, railroad, and maritime industry exhibits; 1867 restored lighthouse (fee). (June-Labor Day, daily) Phone 906/786-3763. ¢

Pioneer Trail Park and Campground. A 74-acre park on the Escanaba River. Shoreline fishing; picnicking, nature trails, playground, camping (fee). (May-Sept, daily) 3 mi N on US 2/41, MI 35. Phone 906/786-1020. ¢

Special Event

Upper Peninsula State Fair. Agricultural and 4-H exhibits, midway, entertainment. Six days mid-Aug. Phone 906/786-4011.

Motels/Motor Lodges

★ **BAYVIEW.** 7110 US 2/41 (MI 35), Gladstone (49837). 906/786-2843; fax 906/786-6218; toll-free 800/547-1201. baydenoc.com/bayview. 22 rms, 1-2 story. June-mid-Sept: S $35-$45; D $45-$60; family rates; some lower rates rest of yr. Crib free. Pet accepted; $8. TV; cable (premium). Indoor pool. Playground. Complimentary coffee in rms. Restaurant adj 7 am-8 pm. Ck-out 11 am. Business servs avail. Sauna. Some refrigerators. Picnic tables, barbecue area. Cr cds: A, MC, V.

D 🔧 🏊 🛏 🔥

★★ **BEST WESTERN PIONEER INN.** 2635 Ludington St (49829). 906/786-0602; fax 906/786-3938; toll-free 800/528-1234. www.bestwestern.com. 72 rms, 2 story. S $45-$91; D $55-$101; each addl $5. Crib $5. TV; cable (premium). Indoor pool. Restaurant 7 am-2 pm, 5-10 pm. Bar 5 pm-2 am. Ck-out 11 am. Meeting rms. Business servs avail. Sundries. Downhill/x-country ski 7 mi. Many balconies. Cr cds: A, C, D, DS, MC, V.

D 🏊 🛏 🔥 SC

★ **DAYS INN.** 2603 N Lincoln Rd (49829). 906/789-1200; fax 906/789-0128; toll-free 800/548-2822. www.daysinn.com. 123 rms, 4 story. Mid-Jun-mid Sept: S, D $65-$83; each addl $6; under 12 free; lower rates rest of yr. Crib free. TV; cable. Indoor pool; whirlpool. Restaurant adj 6 am-10 pm. Bar 11:30 am-midnight; Fri, Sat to 2 am. Ck-out noon. Meeting

rms. Free airport transportation. Downhill/x-country ski 7 mi. Cr cds: A, D, DS, MC, V.

D 🏊 🛏 🔥

★★ **TERRACE BLUFF BAY INN.** 7146 P Rd (49829). 906/786-7554; fax 906/786-7597; toll-free 800/283-4678. 71 rms, 1-2 story. Mid-June-Aug: S $52; D $72-$79 each addl $5; under 16 free; package plans; lower rates rest of yr. Crib $2. TV; cable, VCR avail. Indoor pool; whirlpool. Restaurant 5-9 pm; June-Aug 7-11 am, 5-10 pm. Bar 5-11 pm. Ck-out 11 am. Meeting rms. Business servs avail. Sundries. Tennis. Golf, driving range. Downhill ski 5 mi; x-country ski 7 mi. Exercise equipt; sauna. Game rm. Fish cleaning, storage. Boat launch. Private patios, balconies. Overlooks Little Bay de Noc. Cr cds: A, DS, MC, V.

D 🔧 🏊 🎣 🛏 🏊 SC

★ **VALUE HOST MOTOR INN.** 921 N Lincoln Rd (49829). 906/789-1066; fax 906/789-9202; toll-free 800/929-5997. 50 rms, 2 story. June-Sept: S $44.99; D $50.99; each addl $6; under 12 free; higher rates Upper Peninsula State Fair; lower rates rest of yr. TV; cable (premium). Whirlpool. Complimentary continental bkfst. Restaurant nearby. Ck-out 11 am. Meeting rm. Downhill/x-country ski 7 mi. Exercise equipt; sauna. Cr cds: DS, MC, V.

D 🏊 🛏 🔥 SC

Restaurants

★★ **LOG CABIN SUPPER CLUB.** 7531 US 2, Gladstone (49837). 906/786-5621. www.logcabinbythebay.com. Hrs: 11 am-10 pm; Sun from 4 pm. Closed most Bar to midnight. Lunch $4-$6, dinner $10.95-$22.95. Complete meals: dinner $10.95-$22.95. Child's menu. Specializes in steak, fresh fish. Salad bar. Rustic decor. Overlooks Little Bay de Noc. Cr cds: MC, V.

D 🛏

★★ **STONEHOUSE.** 2223 Ludington St (49829). 906/786-5003. Hrs: 11 am-2 pm, 5-9:30 pm; Sat from 5 pm. Closed Sun; hols. Res accepted. Bar to midnight. Lunch $4-$10, dinner $4-$30. Child's menu. Specializes in prime rib, seafood, veal. Collection of antique car models. Cr cds: A, D, DS, MC, V.

Farmington

(G-6) *See also Birmingham, Detroit, Southfield*

Pop 10,132 **Elev** 750 ft **Area code** 248
Information Chamber of Commerce, 30903-B Ten Mile Rd, 48336; 248/474-3440
Web www.ffhchamber.com

What to See and Do

Kensington Metropark. More than 4,000 acres on Kent Lake. Two swimming beaches (Memorial Day-Labor Day, daily), boating (rentals), ice fishing; biking/hiking trail, tobogganing, skating, picnicking, concessions, 18-hole golf (fee). Forty-five-min boat cruises on the *Island Queen* (summer, daily; fee). Nature trails; farm center, nature center. Park (daily). Free admission Tues. 14 mi NW on I-96, Kent Lake Rd or Kensington Rd exits. Phone 248/685-1561.

Special Event

Farmington Founders Festival. Ethnic food, arts and crafts, sidewalk sales, carnival, rides, concert, fireworks. Mid-July. Phone 248/474-3440.

Motels/Motor Lodges

★★ **COMFORT INN.** *30715 W Twelve Mile Rd, Farmington Hills (48334). 248/471-9220; fax 248/471-2053; toll-free 800/228-5150. www. comfortinn.com.* 135 rms, 4 story. S, D $69-$84; each addl $6; suites $109; under 18 free; wkend rates. Crib free. TV; cable (premium). Complimentary continental bkfst. Restaurant nearby. Ck-out noon. Meeting rms. Valet serv. Health club privileges. Refrigerator in suites. Balconies. Cr cds: A, C, D, DS, JCB, MC, V.

★★ **HAMPTON INN.** *20600 Haggerty Rd, Northville (48167). 734/462-1119; fax 734/462-6270; res 800/426-7866. www.hamptoninn.com.* 125 rms, 4 story. S, D $75-$89; under 18 free; wkend rates. Crib free. TV; cable (premium). Heated pool. Complimentary continental bkfst. Ck-out noon. Meeting rms. Business servs avail. In-rm modem link. Valet serv. Downhill ski 20 mi. Exercise equipt; sauna. Cr cds: A, C, D, DS, MC, V.

★★★ **THE HOTEL BARONETTE.** *27790 Novi Rd, Novi (48377). 248/349-7800; fax 248/349-7467.* 150 rms, 3 story. S $116; D $126; each addl $10; suites $140-$225; under 6 free; wkend rates. Crib free. TV; cable, VCR (movies). Indoor pool; whirlpool. Complimentary full bkfst. Complimentary coffee in rms. Restaurant 6:30 am-9:30 pm; wkends 7:30 am-10:30 pm. Bar 5 pm-midnight. Ck-out noon. Meeting rms. Valet serv. Putting green. Exercise equipt; sauna. Bathrm phones, minibars; some wet bars. Some balconies. Cr cds: A, C, D, DS, ER, JCB, MC, V.

★★ **RAMADA LIMITED OF NOVI.** *21100 Haggerty Rd, Northville (48167). 248/349-7400; fax 248/349-7454; res 800/228-2828. www.ramada.com.* 125 rms, 2 story. S, D $48-$55; each addl $6; under 18 free; wkly rates; higher rates Dec 31. Crib free. TV; cable (premium). Complimentary continental bkfst. Complimentary coffee in rms. Restaurant adj 7 am-3 pm. Ck-out noon. Meeting rms. Business servs avail. Valet serv. Some refrigerators. Cr cds: A, D, DS, MC, V.

★ **RED ROOF INN.** *24300 Sinacola Ct NE (48335). 248/478-8640; fax 248/478-4842; toll-free 800/843-7663. www.redroof.com.* 108 rms. S $31.99-$33.99; D $37.99-$39.99; 3 or more $47.99; under 18 free. Crib free. Pet accepted. TV; cable. Restaurant adj open 24 hrs. Ck-out noon. Cr cds: A, C, D, DS, MC, V.

★★ **WYNDHAM GARDEN HOTEL.** *42100 Crescent Blvd, Novi (48375). 248/344-8800; fax 248/344-8535; toll-free 800/822-4200. www.wyndham.*

com. 148 rms, 2 story, 22 suites. S $118; D $128; each addl $10; suites $94-$104; under 18 free; wkend rates. Crib free. TV; cable. Indoor pool; whirlpool, sauna. Complimentary coffee in rms. Restaurant 6:30 am-2 pm, 5-10 pm; Sat, Sun from 7 am. Rm serv (dinner). Bar. Ck-out noon. Meeting rms. Valet serv. Health club privileges. Refrigerators avail. Cr cds: A, C, D, DS, JCB, MC, V.

[D] [⇌] [⇓] [⊛]

Hotels

★ ★ ★ **DOUBLETREE.** *2700 Sheraton Dr, Novi (48377). 248/348-5000; fax 248/348-2315; res 800/713-3513. www.doubletree.com.* 217 rms, 3 story. S $88-$140; D $93-$150; each addl $10; suites $175-$275; under 18 free; wkend rates. Crib free. TV; cable (premium). 2 pools, 1 indoor; whirlpool. Restaurant 6:30 am-10:30 pm. Bar 11-1 am; entertainment. Ck-out noon. Meeting rms. Business servs avail. Bellhops. Valet serv. Exercise equipt; sauna. Health club privileges. Cr cds: A, MC, V.

[D] [⇌] [X] [⇓] [⊛] [SC]

★ ★ ★ **HILTON NOVI.** *21111 Haggerty Rd, Novi (48375). 248/349-4000; fax 248/349-4066; res 800/445-8667. www.hilton.com.* 239 rms, 7 story. S $115-$175; D $130-$190; each addl $15; suites $275-$525; family, wkend rates. Crib free. TV; cable (premium). Pool; whirlpool. Restaurant 6:30 am-11 pm. Rm serv 24 hrs. Bar 11-2 am. Ck-out noon. Meeting rms. Business servs avail. In-rm modem link. Downhill ski 10 mi; x-country ski 2 mi. Exercise equipt; sauna. Refrigerator in suites. Cr cds: A, MC, V.

[D] [⇝] [⇌] [X] [⇓] [⊛] [SC]

★ ★ ★ **RADISSON HOTEL.** *37529 Grand River Ave, Farmington Hills (48335). 248/477-7800; fax 248/477-6512; toll-free 800/333-3333. www. radisson.com.* 137 suites, 4 story. S, D $114; wkend rates. Crib free. TV; cable (premium), VCR avail. Indoor pool; whirlpool. Complimentary continental bkfst. Coffee in rms. Restaurant 6:30 am-2 pm, 5-10 pm. Rm serv. Bar 5 pm-midnight. Ck-out noon. Meeting rms. Business servs avail. Valet serv. Downhill ski 20 mi. Exercise equipt; sauna. Health club

privileges. Refrigerators. Cr cds: A, C, D, DS, ER, JCB, MC, V.

[D] [⇝] [⇌] [X] [⇓] [⊛] [SC]

Restaurants

★ ★ **AH-WOK.** *41563 W Ten Mile Rd, Novi (48375). 248/349-9260.* Hrs: 11 am-9:30 pm; Fri to 11:30 pm; Sat 4 pm-11:30 pm; Sun noon-9:30 pm. Res accepted wkends. Chinese menu. Serv bar. Lunch $5.25-$7.95, dinner $7.50-$35. Specialties: Peking duck, seafood casserole, double butterfly shrimp, hot and sour soup. Parking. Cr cds: A, D, DS, MC, V.

[D] [⇓]

★ ★ **FIVE LAKES GRILL.** *424 N Main St, Milford (48381). 248/684-7455.* Hrs: 4-10 pm; Fri, Sat to 11 pm. Closed Sun; hols. Res accepted. Bar. Dinner $11.50-$30. Child's menu. Specializes in contemporary American cooking. Modern bistro decor. Cr cds: A, MC, V.

[D] [⇓]

★ ★ **LITTLE ITALY.** *227 Hutton St, Northville (48167). 248/348-0575. www.littleitalynorthville.com.* Hrs: 5 pm-10 pm; Fri, Sat to 11 pm; Sun 4-9 pm; closed hols. Res accepted. Italian menu. Bar. Lunch $6.95-$18.95, dinner $10.95-$28.95. Specializes in veal, seafood. Parking. Converted residence; small, intimate dining areas; antiques, original art. Cr cds: A, D, DS, MC, V.

[D]

★ ★ **MACKINNON'S.** *126 E Main St, Northville (48167). 248/348-1991.* Hrs: 11:30 am-10 pm; Fri, Sat to 11 pm. Closed Sun. Res accepted. Continental menu. Bar to 11 pm. Lunch $4.95-$10.95, dinner $13.95-$25.95. Specialties: charcoal duck, rack of lamb. Lobster tank. Outdoor dining. Victorian atmosphere; stained-glass windows. Cr cds: A, D, DS, MC, V.

[D]

★ **ROCKY'S OF NORTHVILLE.** *41122 W Seven Mile Rd, Northville (48167). 248/349-4434.* Hrs: 11:30 am-10 pm; Fri, Sat to 11 pm; Sun 1-9 pm. Closed Jan 1, Dec 25. Bar. Lunch $4.95-$10.95, dinner $8.95-$15.50. Child's menu. Specializes in seafood, pasta, steak. Parking. Cr cds: A, D, DS, MC, V.

[D] [⇓]

★ ★ ★ **TOO CHEZ.** *27155 Sheraton Dr, Novi (48377).* 248/348-5555. *www.toochez.com.* Hrs: 11:30 am-2:30 pm, 5:30-10 pm; Fri, Sat to 11 pm; Sun 10 am-2 pm. Closed Dec 25. Continental menu. Res accepted. Bar. Wine list. A la carte entrees: lunch $5-$9, dinner $8-$30. Sun brunch $14.95. Child's menu. Own baking. Parking. Outdoor dining. Cr cds: A, D, DS, MC, V.

D **□**

★ ★ ★ **TRIBUTE.** *9502 Lake St, Farmington Hills (48334).* 248/848-9393. *www.tribute-restaurant.com.* Hrs: 5:30-9:30 pm. Closed Sun, Mon; also hols. Res accepted. A la carte entrees: $18-$38. Degustation menu $88. Vegetable degustation menu $65. Wine pairings avail $35-$45. Extensive wine cellar. Valet parking only. Cr cds: A, D, DS, MC, V.

D

Flint

(F-6) *See also Holly, Owosso, Saginaw*

Settled 1819 **Pop** 140,761 **Elev** 750 ft
Area code 810

Information Flint Area Convention and Visitors Bureau, 519 S Saginaw St, 48502; 810/232-8900 or 800/25-FLINT

Web www.visitflint.org

Once a small, wagon-producing town, Flint is now an important automobile manufacturer. The fur trade brought Flint its first prestige; lumbering opened the way to carriage manufacturing, which prepared the city for the advent of the automobile. General Motors, the city's major employer, has Buick plants here. One of the largest cities in the state, it also has many other industrial firms.

What to See and Do

County recreation areas.

Genesee-C. S. Mott Lake. Approx 650 acres. Swimming, fishing, boating (launches, fee); snowmobiling. Picnicking with view of Stepping Stone Falls. Riverboat cruises (fee).

Holloway Reservoir. Approx 2,000 acres. Swimming, water sports, fishing, boating (launches, fee); snowmobiling, picnicking, camping (fee). (Daily) 12 mi E on MI 21, then 8 mi NE via MI 15, Stanley Rd. Phone 810/653-4062. **FREE**

★ **Crossroads Village/Huckleberry Railroad.** Restored living community of the 1860-1880 period; 28 buildings and sites incl a railroad depot, carousel, Ferris wheel, general store, schoolhouse, and several homes; working sawmill, gristmill, cidermill, blacksmith shop; eight-mi steam train ride; entertainment. Paddlewheel riverboat cruises (fee). Special events most wkends. (Memorial Day-Labor Day, daily; Sept, wkends; also special Halloween programs, Dec holiday lighting spectacular) G-6140 Bray Rd, 6 mi NE via I-475, at exit 13. Phone 810/736-7100. ¢¢¢

Flint College and Cultural Corporation. A complex that incl the University of Michigan-Flint (5,700 students), Mott Community College, Whiting Auditorium, Flint Institute of Music, Bower Theater. 817 E Kearsley St. Phone 810/237-7330. Also here are

Flint Institute of Arts. Permanent collections incl Renaissance decorative arts, Oriental Gallery, 19th- and 20th-century paintings and sculpture, paperweights; changing exhibits. (Tues-Sun; closed hols) In the Cultural Center, 1120 E Kearsley St. Phone 810/234-1695. **FREE**

Robert T. Longway Planetarium. Ultraviolet, fluorescent murals; Spitz projector. Exhibits. Programs. (Phone for schedule) 1310 E Kearsly St. Phone 810/760-1181. ¢¢

Sloan Museum. Collection of antique autos and carriages, most manufactured in Flint; exhibitions of Michigan history; health and science exhibits. (Daily; closed hols) 1221 E Kearsley St. Phone 810/237-3450. ¢¢

For-Mar Nature Preserve and Arboretum. Approx 380 acres. Nature trails, indoor and outdoor exhibits, two interpretive buildings.

Guided hikes avail for groups of ten or more (fee). 2142 N Genesee Rd. Phone 810/789-8567. ¢

Motels/Motor Lodges

★ ★ **HOLIDAY INN.** *5353 Gateway Centre (48507). 810/232-5300; fax 810/232-9806; toll-free 888/570-1770. www.holiday-inn.com.* 171 rms, 4 story. S $99-$129; D $99-$149; each addl $10; suites $114-$229; family, wkly rates. Crib free. TV; cable. Indoor pool; whirlpool. Restaurant 6:30 am-10 pm; Fri, Sat 7 am-11 pm. Bar 11:30 am-midnight; Fri, Sat to 2 am. Ck-out noon. Coin lndry. Meeting rms. Business servs avail. In-rm modem link. Bellhops. Valet serv. Concierge. Free airport, RR station, bus depot transportation. Game rm. Exercise equipt; sauna. Health club privileges. Some refrigerators, wet bars. Picnic tables. Cr cds: A, MC, V.

⊡ ≈ 🐾 ✈ ⊠ 🖎 SC

★ ★ **HOLIDAY INN EXPRESS.** *1150 Longway Blvd (48503). 810/238-7744; fax 810/233-7444; toll-free 800/278-1810. www.holiday-inn.com.* 124 rms, 5 story. S, D $79-$89; under 18 free. Crib free. TV; cable (premium). Complimentary continental bkfst. Ck-out noon. Meeting rm. Business center. In-rm modem link. Valet serv. Free airport transportation. Downhill ski 20 mi. Health club privileges. Some in-rm whirlpools. Cr cds: A, D, DS, MC, V.

⊡ ≈ ✈ ⊠ 🖎 SC

★ **RED ROOF INN.** *G3219 Miller Rd (48507). 810/733-1660; fax 810/733-6310; toll-free 800/843-7663. www.redroof.com.* 107 rms, 2 story. June-mid-Sept: S $34.99-$42; D $42-$49; 3 or more $52-$56; under 18 free; lower rates rest of yr. Crib free. TV; cable (premium). Restaurant adj 6:30 am-11 pm. Business servs avail. Ck-out noon. Cr cds: A, C, D, DS, MC, V.

⊡ ⊠ 🖎

★ **SUPER 8 MOTEL.** *3033 Claude Ave (48507). 810/230-7888; toll-free 800/800-8000. www.super8.com.* 61 rms, 3 story. No elvtr. S $38.98; D $44.98; each addl $6; under 12 free; higher rates Buick Open. Pet accepted. TV; cable. Complimentary coffee in lobby. Restaurant nearby.

Ck-out 11 am. Cr cds: A, C, D, DS, JCB, MC, V.

⊡ 🐾 ⊠ 🖎 SC

Hotel

★ ★ **CHARACTER INN.** *1 W Riverfront Center (48502). 810/239-1234; fax 810/239-5843.* 369 rms, 16 story. S, D $89; suites $99-$295; under 18 free. Crib free. TV; cable. Indoor pool; whirlpool. Restaurant 6:30 am-11 pm; Fri, Sat to 1 am. Bar. Ck-out noon. Meeting rms. Business center. Free garage parking. Free airport transportation. Concierge. Exercise equipt. Some refrigerators. On river. Cr cds: A, DS, MC, V.

⊡ 🏃 ≈ ⊠ 🖎 🏃

B&B/Small Inn

★ ★ **BONNYMILL.** *710 Broad St, Chesaning (48616). 517/845-7780; fax 517/845-5165. www.bonnymillin.com.* 29 rms, 3 story, 11 suites. S, D $65; each addl $10; suites $135-$145; under 11 free; winter rates. Crib free. TV; cable (premium), VCR avail (movies). Complimentary full bkfst; afternoon refreshments. Complimentary coffee in rms. Dining rm 7:30-9 am; Sat, Sun 8-9:30 am. Ck-out 11 am, ck-in 3 pm. Business servs avail. Valet serv. Airport transportation. Golf privileges. X-country ski 7 mi. Health club privileges. Balconies. Picnic tables. Rebuilt from 1920 farmer's grain mill. Antique winding oak staircase. Cr cds: A, MC, V.

⊡ 🐾 ≈ 🍴 ✈ 🖎

Restaurants

★ ★ ★ **CHESANING HERITAGE HOUSE.** *605 Broad St, Chesaning (48616). 989/845-7700. www.bonnymillinn.com.* Hrs: 11 am-8 pm; Fri, Sat to 9 pm; Sun 9:30 am-8 pm. Closed Dec 24, 25. Res accepted. Bar to 10 pm; Fri, Sat to midnight. Lunch $5-$15, dinner $12-$22. Child's menu. Specializes in stuffed pork tenderloin, prime rib, seafood. Outdoor dining. Victorian decor; crystal chandelier, fireplace. Georgian Revival mansion (1908) converted into nine dining areas. Cr cds: A, DS, MC, V.

⊡

★ ★ ★ **MAKUCH'S RED ROOSTER.** *3302 Davison Rd (48506). 810/742-*

9310. Hrs: 11 am-9 pm; Fri to 9:30 pm; Sat 5-9:30 pm. Closed Sun; hols. Res accepted. Bar. Lunch $4.50-$12.95; dinner $18.95-$32.95. Child's menu. Specializes in Caesar salad, fresh seafood, steak. Own baking. Tableside preparation. Family-owned. Cr cds: MC, V.

Frankenmuth

(F-6) *See also Bay City, Flint, Saginaw*

Settled 1845 **Pop** 4,408 **Elev** 645 ft
Area code 989 **Zip** 48734
Information Convention & Visitors Bureau, 635 S Main St; 989/652-6106, 800/386-8696 or 800/386-3378
Web www.frankenmuth.org

This city was settled by 15 immigrants from Franconia, Germany, who came here as Lutheran missionaries to spread the faith to the Chippewas. Today, Frankenmuth boasts authentic Bavarian architecture, flower beds, and warm German hospitality.

What to See and Do

⭐ **Bronner's Christmas Wonderland.** Thought to be the world's largest Christmas store: more than 50,000 trims and gifts from around the world. Multi-image presentation "World of Bronner's" (18 min); outdoor Christmas lighting display along Christmas Lane (dusk-midnight). (Daily; closed hols). 25 Christmas Ln.

Factory Outlet Stores. More than 175 outlet stores can be found at The Outlets at Birch Run. (Daily) Approx 5 mi S on I-75, exit 136. Phone 989/624-7467.

Frankenmuth Historical Museum. Local historical exhibits, hands-on displays, audio recordings, and cast-form life figures. Gift shop features folk art. (Mon-Sat, also Sun afternoons; closed hols) 613 S Main St. Phone 989/652-9701. ¢

Frankenmuth Riverboat Tours. Narrated tours (45 min) along Cass River. (May-Oct, daily, weather permitting) Board at dock behind Riverview Cafe, 445 S Main St. Phone 989/652-8844. ¢¢

Glockenspiel. Tops the Bavarian Inn (see RESTAURANTS); 35-bell carillon with carved wooden figures moving on a track acting out the story of the Pied Piper of Hamelin. 713 S Main St. Phone 989/652-9941.

Michigan's Own Military & Space Museum. Features uniforms, decorations, and photos of men and women from Michigan who served the nation in war and peace; also displays on Medal of Honor recipients, astronauts, former governors. (Mar-Dec, daily; closed Easter, Dec 25) 1250 S Weiss St. Phone 989/652-8005. ¢¢

Special Events

Bavarian Festival. Heritage Park. Celebration of German heritage. Music, dancing, parades and other entertainment; food; art demonstrations and agricultural displays. Phone 989/652-8155. Four days early June.

Frankenmuth Oktoberfest. Serving authentic Munich Oktoberfest and American beer. German food, music, and entertainment. Third wkend Sept. Phone 989/652-6106.

Motels/Motor Lodges

★★★ **FRANKENMUTH BAVARIAN INN LODGE.** *1 Covered Bridge Ln (48734). 989/652-7200; fax 989/652-6711; res 888/775-6343. www.bavarianinn.com.* 354 units, 4 story. June-Oct: S, D $89-$135; suites $145-$210; lower rates rest of yr. Crib $5. TV; cable, VCR avail. 3 indoor pools; whirlpools. Restaurant 7 am-9 pm. Bar to 12:30 am; entertainment. Ck-out 11 am. Convention facilities. Business servs avail. Airport transportation. Gift shops. Tennis. Exercise equipt. Game rms. Lawn games. Balconies. View of Cass River. Cr cds: A, DS, MC, V.

★★★ **ZENDER'S BAVARIAN HAUS.** *730 S Main St (48734). 989/652-0400; fax 989/652-9777; toll-free 800/863-7999.* 137 rms, 2 story. Early June-late Oct: D $85-$125; suites $165-$200; lower rates rest of yr. Crib free. TV; cable (premium). Indoor/outdoor pool; whirlpool. Restaurant

7:30-10:30 am. Ck-out 11 am. Business servs avail. 18-hole golf privileges. Exercise equipt; sauna. Game rm. Private balconies. Cr cds: DS, MC, V.

🄳 ⟨icons⟩

Restaurants

★★ **FRANKENMUTH BAVARIAN INN.** 713 S Main St (MI 83) (48734). 989/652-9941. www.bavarianinn.com. Hrs: 11 am-9:30 pm. Closed Dec 24 eve; also 1st wk Jan. Res accepted. German, American menu. Bar. Lunch $7.50-$12.95, dinner $12.95-$26. Child's menu. Specializes in Bavarian dinner, family-style chicken dinner. Bavarian atmosphere; 35-bell carillon with moving figurines. Bakery. Established 1888. Family-owned. Cr cds: A, DS, MC, V.

🄳 ⟨icon⟩

★★ **ZEHNDER'S.** 730 S Main St (MI 83) (48734). 989/652-0400. www.zehnders.com. Hrs: 8 am-9:30 pm. Closed Dec 24. Bar. Lunch $5.95-$8.95, dinner $13.75-$18.95. Child's menu. Specializes in all-you-can-eat family-style chicken dinner, steak, seafood. Early American decor. Bakery. Gift shop. Family-owned. Cr cds: DS, MC, V.

🄳 ⟨icon⟩

Frankfort

(D-3) See also Beulah

Pop 1,546 **Elev** 585 ft **Area code** 231
Zip 49635
Information Benzie County Chamber of Commerce, PO Box 204, Benzonia 49616; 231/882-5801 or 800/882-5801
Web www.benzie.org

An important harbor on Lake Michigan, Frankfort is a popular resort area. Fishing for coho and chinook salmon is excellent here. Frankfort is the burial site of Father Marquette. Nearby is Sleeping Bear Dunes National Lakeshore (see). Development of the lakeshore is complete with 40-slip marina, gas, sewage pumpout, electricity, and bathing facilities.

Motels/Motor Lodges

★ **BAY VALLEY INN.** 1561 Scenic Hwy (49635). 231/352-7113; fax 231/352-7114. 20 rms. Memorial Day-Labor Day: S $45-$55; D $65-$75; suite $90; family, wkly rates; lower rates rest of yr. Crib free. Pet accepted. TV; cable, VCR avail (free movies). Playground. Complimentary continental bkfst. Ck-out 11 am. Free lndry. Meeting rms. Business servs avail. Downhill/x-country ski 18 mi. Rec rm. Refrigerators. Picnic tables, grills. Cr cds: A, DS, MC, V.

🄳 ⟨icons⟩ SC

★★ **HARBOR LIGHTS MOTEL & CONDOS.** 15 2nd St (49635). 231/352-9614; fax 231/352-6580. 57 rms, 33 A/C, 2 story, 45 condominiums. July, Aug: D $85-$95; kit. units $80-$120; condo units $110-$225; wkly rates; ski, golf plans; lower rates rest of yr. Crib free. TV; cable (premium). Indoor pool; whirlpool. Ck-out 11 am. Meeting rm. Business servs avail. Downhill ski 18 mi; x-country ski 3 mi. Lawn games. Some in-rm whirlpools. Balconies. Park, beach opp. Some rms with lake view. Cr cds: C, DS, MC, V.

🄳 ⟨icons⟩

Resort

★★ **CHIMNEY CORNERS RESORT.** 1602 Crystal Dr (49635). 231/352-7522; fax 231/352-7252. www.benzie.com. 8 rms in lodge, 2 share bath, 1-2 story, 7 kit. apts (1-2 bedrm), 13 kit. cottages for 1-20. No A/C. May-Nov: lodge rms for 2, $55-$60 (maid serv avail); kit. apts for 2-6 $825-$875/wk; kit. cottages $1,175-$1,500/wk. Closed rest of yr. Crib free. Pet accepted, some restrictions. TV in lobby; cable. Playground. Dining rm in season 8-10:30 am, noon-2 pm. Ck-out 10 am, ck-in 3 pm. Grocery, coin lndry, package store 7 mi. Tennis. Private beach; rowboats, hoists; paddleboats. Sailboats. Fireplaces. Many private patios. Picnic tables, grills. 1,000-ft beach on Crystal Lake, 300 acres of wooded hills. Cr cds: A, MC, V.

⟨icons⟩

Restaurants

★ **HOTEL FRANKFORT.** *231 Main St (49635). 231/352-4303. www.hotelfrank fort.com.* Hrs: 8 am-9 pm; Fri, Sat to 10 pm; June-Aug to 10 pm. Res accepted. Bar. Bkfst $2.05-$6.95, lunch $2.95-$7, dinner $7.95-$19.95. Child's menu. Specializes in prime rib, Icelandic scrod, desserts. Pianist. Victorian decor; gingerbread wood-work on exterior. Guest rms avail. Cr cds: A, D, DS, MC, V.

⊡ ⊟

★ **MANITOU.** *4349 Scenic Hwy (MI 22) (49635). 231/882-4761.* Hrs: 4:30-10 pm; early-bird dinner to 6 pm. Closed Jan-Apr. Res accepted. Dinner $13.95-$29.95. Specialties: fresh broiled whitefish, sauteed perch, rack of lamb. Extensive wine list. Outdoor dining. Wildlife theme. Cr cds: MC, V.

⊡

★★ **RHONDA'S WHARFSIDE.** *300 Main St (49635). 231/352-5300.* Hrs: vary seasonally. Closed Sun, Mon; Dec 25. Continental menu. Serv bar. Lunch $4.50-$10.95, dinner $14.25-$20.2. Child's menu. Specializes in California cuisine. Overlooks Betsy Bay. Totally nonsmoking. Cr cds: A, DS, MC, V.

⊡

Gaylord

(D-5) *See also Boyne City, Grayling*

Settled 1873 **Pop** 3,256 **Elev** 1,349 ft
Area code 989 **Zip** 49735
Information Gaylord Area Convention & Tourism Bureau, 101 W Main, PO Box 3069; 989/732-4000 or 800/345-8621
Web www.gaylordmichigan.net

What to See and Do

Otsego Lake State Park. Approx 60 acres. Swimming beach, bathhouse, waterskiing, boating (rentals, launch); fishing for pike, bass, and perch; picnicking, playground, concession, camping. (Mid-Apr-mid-Oct) Standard fees. 7 mi S off I-75 on Old US 27. Phone 517/732-5485. ¢¢

Skiing. Treetops Sylvan Resort. Double, two triple chairlifts, four rope tows; patrol, school, rentals; cafeteria, bar. Nineteen runs; longest run ½ mi; vertical drop 225 ft. (Dec-mid-Mar, daily) 10 mi of x-country trails; 3½ mi of lighted trails. 5 mi E via MI 32 to Wilkinson Rd. Phone 989/732-6711. ¢¢¢¢

Special Events

Winterfest. Ski racing and slalom, x-country events, snowmobile events, activities for children, snow sculpting, downhill tubing. Early Feb. Phone 800/345-8621.

Alpenfest. Participants dressed in costumes of Switzerland; carnival, pageant, grand parade; "world's largest coffee break." Third wkend July. Phone 989/732-6333.

Otsego County Fair. Mid-Aug. Phone 989/732-4119.

Motels/Motor Lodges

★★ **BEST WESTERN ROYAL CREST.** *803 S Otsego Ave (49735). 989/732-6451; fax 989/732-7634; toll-free 800/876-9252. www.bestwestern.com.* 44 rms, 1-2 story. Mid-May-Oct, Christmas wk, ski wkends: S $59-$99; D $69-$99; each addl $6; under 16 free; lower rates rest of yr. Crib free. Pet accepted. TV; cable. Indoor pool. Complimentary continental bkfst. Complimentary coffee in rms. Ck-out 11 am. Downhill/x-country ski 3 mi. Exercise equipt; sauna. Whirl-pool. Cr cds: A, C, D, DS, MC, V.

⊡ 🐕 ⊠ ⊠ 🏋 ⊠ 🔥 SC

★ **DAYS INN.** *1201 W Main St (49735). 989/732-2200; fax 989/732-0300; toll-free 800/952-9584. www. daysinn.com.* 95 rms, 2 story. Mid-June-early Sept: S $57-$84; D $67-$94; each addl $5; family rates; ski, golf plans; higher rates late Dec-Jan 1; lower rates rest of yr. Crib free. TV; cable (premium). Indoor pool; whirl-pool. Complimentary continental bkfst. Restaurant adj 6 am-10 pm. Ck-out 11 am. Coin lndry. Meeting rm. Business servs avail. Downhill ski 4 mi; x-country ski 1½ mi. Exercise equipt; sauna. Game rm. Refrigerators. Cr cds: A, D, DS, MC, V.

⊡ ⊠ ⊠ 🏋 ⊠ 🔥

★ ★ **HOLIDAY INN.** *833 W Main St (49735). 989/732-2431; fax 989/732-9640; toll-free 800/684-2233. www. holiday-inn.com.* 137 rms, 2 story. Mid-June-Sept, ski wkends, Christmas wk: S, D $85-$91; each addl $6; under 19 free; golf plans; lower rates rest of yr. Crib free. Pet accepted. TV; cable, VCR avail (movies). Indoor pool; whirlpool. Restaurant 6 am-10 pm. Bar 3 pm-midnight. Ck-out 11 am. Coin lndry. Meeting rms. Business servs avail. Valet serv. Sundries. Downhill/x-country ski 4 mi. Exercise equipt; sauna. Game rm. Cr cds: A, D, DS, MC, V.

D ⬦ ⬦ ⬦ ⬦ ⬦ ⬦ ⬦ ⬦ ⬦ ⬦

★ ★ **QUALITY INN.** *137 W Main St (49735). 989/732-7541; fax 989/732-0930; toll-free 800/228-5151. www. qualityinn.com.* 117 rms, 2 story. Memorial Day-Labor Day, ski wkends, Christmas wk: S, D $89-$103; each addl $5; golf plans; lower rates rest of yr. Crib free. TV; cable (premium). Indoor pool; whirlpool. Restaurant 7 am-10 pm; Sun to 9 pm. Ck-out 11 am. Business servs avail. Downhill/x-country ski ½ mi. Exercise equipt. Cr cds: A, MC, V.

⬦ ⬦ ⬦ ⬦ ⬦ ⬦

Resorts

★ **EL RANCHO STEVENS.** *2332 E Dixon Lake Rd (49735). 989/732-5090; fax 989/732-5059. www.elrancho stevens.com.* 32 rms in 2 lodges, 2-3 story. No A/C. Memorial Day-Sept (2-day min), MAP: S $110-$150; D $83-$115/person. Closed rest of yr. Crib free. Heated pool. Free supervised children's activities. Teen club. Dining rm 6-9 pm. Snacks; barbecues. Bar noon-midnight. Ck-out 11 am, ck-in 3 pm. Grocery, coin lndry, package store 3 mi. Meeting rms. Free airport transportation. Sports dir; instructors. Tennis. Sand beach; water sports, paddleboats, boats. Waterskiing avail. Hayrides. Nature hike. Lawn games. Soc dir; entertainment. Game rm. Rec rm. Picnic tables. 1,000 acres on Lake Dixon. Cr cds: DS, MC, V.

⬦ ⬦ ⬦ ⬦ ⬦ ⬦

★ ★ ★ **GARLAND RESORT & GOLF COURSE.** *4700 N Red Oak, Lewiston (49756). 989/786-2211; fax 989/786-2254. www.garlandusa.com.* 58 rms in main bldg, 60 cottages. May-Oct, MAP: S, D $79-$179; cottages $159; family, wkly, wkend, hol rates; golf, ski plans; lower rates rest of yr. Closed wk of Thanksgiving, mid-Mar-Apr. Crib free. TV; cable, VCR avail. 2 pools, 1 indoor; whirlpool, poolside serv. Restaurant 6 am-11 pm; winter hrs vary. Box lunches. Bar 6-2 am; entertainment. Ck-out 11 am, ck-in 4 pm. Grocery, coin lndry 5 mi. Bellhops. Valet serv. Concierge. Meeting rms. Business servs avail. Airport transportation. Sports dir. Lighted tennis. 72-hole golf course, pro, greens fee $75, putting green, driving range. Downhill ski 12 mi; x-country ski on site. Sleighing. Hiking. Bicycles. Lawn games. Soc dir. Exercise equipt; sauna, steam rm. Massage. Refrigerators. Balconies. Picnic tables. Cr cds: A, DS, MC, V.

D ⬦ ⬦ ⬦ ⬦ ⬦ ⬦ ⬦ ⬦ SC

★ ★ **MARSH RIDGE RESORT.** *4815 Old 27 S (49735). 989/705-3900; fax 989/732-2134; toll-free 800/743-7529. www.marshridge.com.* 50 rms, 1-2 story, 4 kit. units. Mid-May-late Oct, late Dec-late Mar: S, D $135-$139; each addl $10; kit. units up to 4 $129-$165; under 16 free; ski, golf plans; wkend rates; lower rates rest of yr. Crib free. TV; cable (premium); VCR avail (fee). Heated pool; whirlpool, sauna. Restaurant 7 am-10 pm; 5-9 pm off season. Coffee in lobby. Complimentary continental bkfst. Ck-out 11 am. Meeting rms. Valet serv. 18-hole golf, greens fee (incl cart) $55, putting green, lighted driving range. Downhill ski 5 mi; lighted x-country ski on site. Rec rm. Lawn games. Some fireplaces. Refrigerators, private patios, balconies. Picnic tables. Cr cds: A, MC, V.

D ⬦ ⬦ ⬦ ⬦ ⬦ ⬦

★ ★ ★ **TREETOPS RESORT.** *3962 Wilkinson Rd (49735). 989/732-6711; fax 989/732-6595. www.treetops.com.* 260 rms in main bldgs, 2-3 story, 30 rms in chalets, 2 story, 8 kits. May-Sept, Dec 25-Feb: S, D $115-$358; each addl $6; chalet rms, kit. units $300-$380; under 18 free; MAP avail; ski, golf plans; Christmas wk (4-day min); winter wkends (2-day min); lower rates rest of yr. Crib $5. TV; cable (premium), VCR avail. 4 pools, 2 heated indoor; children's pool; whirlpools, poolside serv. Playground. Supervised children's activities, ages 1-12 yrs. Coffee in rms. Dining rm (public by res) 8 am-10 pm; Fri, Sat to 10:30 pm. Snack bar; box lunches; picnics. Rm serv 4 pm-midnight. Bar to 2 am. Ck-out noon, ck-in 4 pm. Meeting rms. Business servs avail. Lighted tennis. 81-hole golf, greens fee $36-$99, pro, putting green, 2 driving ranges, golf cart. Downhill/x-country ski on site; rentals. Exercise equipt; sauna. Concierge. Lawn games. Hiking trails. Soc dir. Game rm. Volleyball. Massage. Barber/beauty shop. Ice skating. Arcade shops. Free airport transportation. Many refrigerators. Private patios, balconies. Picnic tables, grills. 4,000-acre hilltop complex on the crest of Pigeon River Valley. Cr cds: A, D, MC, V.

⬛ 🏊 🧖 🛏 ⛷ 🚶 ✈ 🔜 🔥

Restaurants

★ **SCHLANG'S BAVARIAN INN.** *Old US 27 S (49735). 989/732-9288.* Hrs: 5-10 pm; Closed Sun; hols. German, American menu. Bar. Dinner $12.95-$23. Specialties: pork chops, ribeye steak. Authentic Bavarian atmosphere; fireplace. Family-owned. Cr cds: MC, V.

⬛ 🔜

★★ **SUGAR BOWL.** *216 W Main St (MI 32) (49734). 989/732-5524.* Hrs: 7 am-11 pm; Sun to 10 pm. Closed Easter, Thanksgiving, Dec 25; also last wk Mar and 1st wk Apr. Res accepted. Greek, American menu. Bar. Bkfst $2.99-$6.25, lunch $6.95-$8.95, dinner $6.95-$25. Child's menu. Specializes in fresh Lake Superior whitefish, prime rib. Greek gourmet table. Salad bar. Fireplace. Family-owned. Cr cds: A, DS, MC, V.

⬛ 🔜

Glen Arbor

(D-4) *See also Leland, Traverse City*

Settled 1848 **Pop** 250 **Elev** 591 ft
Area code 231 **Zip** 49636

Information Sleeping Bear Area Chamber of Commerce, PO Box 217; 231/334-3238

Web www.sleepingbeararea.com

This community, situated on Lake Michigan, lies just north of Sleeping Bear Dunes National Lakeshore (see).

Resort

★★★ **THE HOMESTEAD.** *Wood Ridge Rd (49636). 231/334-5000; fax 616/334-5246; res 616/334-5100. www.thehomesteadresort.com.* 130 condos, 2-3 story, 94 lodge rms. No A/C in condos. July-Labor Day: condos (2-day min) $140-$740; lodge rms $76-$311; suite $165-$445; MAP avail; lower rates May-June, early Sept-Oct. Closed mid-Mar-Apr, Nov-late-Dec. TV; cable; VCR avail. 4 heated pools, children's pool, lifeguard, whirlpool, poolside serv in season. Playground. Supervised children's activities (July-Sept, to age 10; $32-$75). Restaurant 8 am-10 pm. Coffee in rms. Ck-out 11 am, ck-in 5 pm. Grocery, package store on site. Meeting rms. Business servs avail. In-rm modem link. Sports dir. Tennis, pro (July-Sept). 9-hole par-3 golf, greens fee $34-$76, pro, driving range, putting green, carts avail. Private beach. Sailboats, canoes. Charter fishing. Downhill/x-country ski on site. Skating. Bicycles. Exercise equipt; sauna. Massage (by appt). Entertainment. Many fireplaces. Patios, balconies. On Lake Michigan shoreline. Cr cds: DS, MC, V.

⬛ 🎿 🧖 🛏 🔜 🚶 🔜 🐾 SC

Restaurants

★★ **LA BECASSE.** *9001 S Dunn's Farm Rd, Maple City (49664). 231/334-3944.* Hrs: 5:45-9:15 pm. Closed Mon; Tues May-mid-June; also mid-Feb-early May. Res accepted. French menu. Serv bar. Dinner $19-$32. Specializes in profitéroles, veal, wild game dishes. Outdoor dining. European-style cafe. Cr cds: A, DS, MC, V.

⬛

★ **WESTERN AVENUE GRILL.** *6410 Western Ave (49636). 231/334-3362.* Hrs: 11 am-9 pm. Serv bar. Lunch $4.95-$9.95, dinner $8.95-$22.95. Child's menu. Specializes in seafood, pasta, ribs. Modern rustic decor. Cr cds: MC, V.

⬛ 🔜

Pictured Rocks National Lakeshore

Grand Haven

(G-4) *See also Grand Rapids, Holland, Muskegon*

Settled 1834 **Pop** 11,951 **Elev** 590 ft
Area code 616 **Zip** 49417

Information Grand Haven/Spring Lake Area Visitors Bureau, One S Harbor Dr; 616/842-4910 or 800/303-4092

Web www.grandhavenchamber.org

Through this port city at the mouth of the Grand River flows a stream of produce for all the Midwest. The port has the largest charter fishing fleet on Lake Michigan and is also used for sportfishing, recreational boating, and as a Coast Guard base. Connecting the pier to downtown shops are a boardwalk and park.

What to See and Do

Grand Haven State Park. Almost 50 acres on Lake Michigan beach. Swimming, bathhouse, fishing; picnicking (shelter), playground, concession, camping. Standard fees. (Daily) 1 mi SW. Phone 616/798-3711. ¢¢

Harbor Trolleys. Two different routes: Grand Haven trolley operates between downtown and state park; second trolley goes to Spring Lake. (Memorial Day-Labor Day, daily) Transfer point at Chinook Pier. Phone 616/842-3200. ¢

Municipal Marina. Contains 57 transient slips; fish-cleaning station; stores and restaurants; trolley stop. At foot of Washington St, Downtown. Phone 616/847-3478. Also docked here is the

> **Harbor Steamer.** Stern-wheel paddleboat cruises to Spring Lake; scenic views, narrated by captain. (Mid-May-Sept, daily) 301 N Harbor. Phone 616/842-8950.

Musical Fountain. Said to be the world's largest electronically controlled musical fountain; water, lights, and music are synchronized. Programs (Memorial Day-Labor Day, eves; May and rest of Sept, Fri and Sat only). Special Christmas nativity scene in Dec covering all of Dewey Hill. Dewey Hill. Phone 616/842-2550.

Special Events

Polar Ice Cap Golf Tournament. Spring Lake. 18-hole, par-three golf game on ice. Late Jan. Phone 800/303-4097.

Winterfest. Music, dance, parade, children's activities. Late Jan. Phone 616/842-4499.

Great Lakes Kite Festival. Grand Haven State Park. Phone 616/846-7501. May.

On the Waterfront Big Band Concert Series. Wed eves. July-Aug. Phone 616/842-2550.

Coast Guard Festival. Incl a parade, carnival, craft exhibit, ship tours, pageant and variety shows, fireworks. Late July-early Aug. Phone 888/207-2434.

Motels/Motor Lodges

★★ **BEST WESTERN.** *1525 S Beacon Blvd (49417). 616/842-4720; fax 616/847-7821; toll-free 800/780-7234. www.bestwestern.com.* 101 rms. May-Sept: S $52-$60; D $62-$130; each addl $4; under 12 free; higher rates special events; lower rates rest of yr. Crib $2. TV; cable (premium). Heated pool. Restaurant adj 6 am-11 pm. Ck-out 11 am. Free airport, bus depot transportation. X-country ski 8 mi. Some in-rm whirlpools, refrigerators. Picnic tables. Cr cds: A, C, D, DS, MC, V.

🄳 ⚡ 🏊 ⛵ ➷ 🔥

★ **DAYS INN.** *1500 S Beacon Blvd (49417). 616/842-1999; fax 616/842-3892; toll-free 800/547-1855. www.daysinn.com.* 100 rms, 2 story. May-early Sept: S, D $69-$110; each addl $6; lower rates rest of yr. Crib free. TV; cable. Indoor pool; whirlpool. Restaurant 8 am-10 pm; Sun 10:30 am-2 pm. Bar noon-midnight. Ck-out noon. Coin lndry. Meeting rms. Business servs avail. Downhill ski 2 mi; x-country ski 6 mi. Health club privileges. Game rm. Cr cds: A, C, D, DS, JCB, MC, V.

🄳 ⚡ 🏊 ⛵ ➷ 🔥

★ **FOUNTAIN INN.** *1010 S Beacon Blvd (49417). 616/846-1800; fax 616/846-9287; toll-free 800/745-8660.* 47 rms, 2 story. Mid-May-Labor Day: S, D $49.95-$89.95; each addl $5; higher rates special events; lower rates rest of yr. TV; cable. Complimentary continental bkfst. Restaurant nearby. Ck-out 11 am. Meeting rms. X-country ski 3 mi. Cr cds: A, DS, MC, V.

🄳 🏊 ➷ 🔥

B&Bs/Small Inns

★★ **HARBOR HOUSE INN.** *114 S Harbor Dr (49417). 616/846-0610; fax 616/846-0530.* 17 rms, 3 story. Memorial Day-Labor Day: S, D $120-$140; each addl $25; suite $140-$180; higher rates wkends (2-day min); lower rates rest of yr. Closed Dec 24, 25. TV in sitting rm; cable. Complimentary continental bkfst. Restaurant nearby. Ck-out 11 am, ck-in 2 pm. Business servs avail. Downhill ski 2 blks; x-country ski 15 mi. Health club privileges. Game rm. Some balconies. Early American decor. Totally nonsmoking. Cr cds: A, MC, V.

🄳 ⚡ 🏊 ➷ 🔥

★★ **HIDEAWAY ACRES.** *1870 Pontaluna Rd, Spring Lake (49456). 231/798-7271; fax 231/798-3352; res 800/865-3545. www.bbonline.com/mi/pontaluna.* 5 rms, 2 story. No rm phones. May-Sept: S, D $119-$169; each addl $25; lower rates rest of yr. TV; cable (premium), VCR (movies). Indoor pool; whirlpool, sauna. Complimentary continental bkfst. Restaurant nearby. Ck-out 11 am, ck-in 4 pm. Lighted tennis. Rec rm. X-country ski on site. Totally nonsmoking. Cr cds: A, MC, V.

🏊 🎿 ➷ 🧍 ✈

Restaurant

★ **ARBOREAL INN.** *18191 174th Ave, Spring Lake (49417). 616/842-3800.* Hrs: 5-10 pm. Closed Sun; hols. Res accepted. Bar. A la carte entrees: dinner $16.95-$32.95. Specialties: tournedos Oscar, whitefish jardiniere. Early Amer decor. Cr cds: A, DS, MC, V.

🄳 ➶

Grand Marais (B-4)

Pop 350 **Elev** 640 ft **Area code** 906 **Zip** 49839

Information Chamber of Commerce, PO Box 139; 906/494-2447

Web www.grandmaraismichigan.com

On the shore of Lake Superior, Grand Marais has a harbor with marina and is surrounded by cool, clear lakes, trout streams, and agate beaches. In the winter, there is snowmobiling and cross-country skiing.

What to See and Do

Pictured Rocks National Lakeshore.
This scenic stretch of shoreline
begins at the western edge of Grand
Marais and continues west to Munising (see). Swimming, fishing; hiking,
hunting, rock climbing, x-country
skiing, snowmobiling. Phone
906/387-3700.

Special Events

500-Miler Snowmobile Run. Mid-Jan.
Phone 906/494-2447.

Music and Arts Festival. Second
wkend Aug. Phone 906/494-2447.

Motel/Motor Lodge

★ ★ **WELKER'S LODGE.** *Canal St
(49839). 906/494-2361; fax 906/494-
2371.* 41 rms, 1-2 story, 9 kit. cottages. Some A/C. Some rm phones. S
$35-$47; D $48-$57; each addl $5;
kit. cottages $235-$325/wk. Crib $5.
Pet accepted. TV; cable (premium),
VCR avail (movies $5). Indoor pool;
whirlpool. Sauna. Playground.
Restaurant 7:30 am-8:30 pm. Bar. Ck-
out 11 am, cottages 10 am. Coin
lndry. Meeting rm. Business servs
avail. Tennis. Sauna. Lawn games.
On Lake Superior; private beach. Cr
cds: A, DS, MC, V.

Grand Rapids

(G-4) *See also Grand Haven, Holland,
Muskegon*

Settled 1826 **Pop** 189,126 **Elev** 657 ft
Area code 616
Information Grand Rapids/Kent
County Convention & Visitors
Bureau, 140 Monroe Center NW,
Suite 300, 49503; 616/459-8287 or
800/678-9859
Web www.grcvb.org

Grand Rapids, a widely known furniture center and convention city, is
located on the site where Louis Cam-
pau established a Native American
trading post in 1826. The city derives
its name from the rapids in the
Grand River, which flows through

the heart of the city. There are 50
parks here, totalling 1,270 acres.
Calvin College and Calvin Seminary
(1876) are located here; several other
colleges are in the area.

Thirty-eighth president Gerald R.
Ford was raised in Grand Rapids and
represented the Fifth Congressional
District in Michigan from 1948-1973,
when he became the nation's vice
president.

What to See and Do

Berlin Raceway. Late model stock car,
sportsman stock car, and super stock
car racing. (May-Sept, Fri-Sun) Phone
616/677-1140.

Blandford Nature Center. More than
140 acres of woods, fields, and ponds
with self-guiding trails; guided tours
(fee); interpretive center has exhibits,
live animals; furnished pioneer garden; one-rm schoolhouse. (Mon-Fri,
also Sat and Sun afternoons; closed
hols) 1715 Hillburn Ave NW. Phone
616/453-6192. **FREE**

Fish Ladder. A unique fish ladder for
watching salmon leap the rapids of
the Grand River during spawning
season. Sixth St Dam.

⊠ **Frederik Meijer Gardens and
Sculpture Park.** Botanic garden and
sculpture park incl 15,000-sq-ft glass
conservatory, desert garden, exotic
indoor and outdoor gardens, more
than 60 bronze works in sculpture
park. Also outdoor nature trails and
tram tour. Gift shop, restaurant.
(Daily; closed Jan 1, Dec 25) 3411
Bradford NE. Phone 616/957-1580.
¢¢¢

⊠ **Gerald R. Ford Museum.** Exhibits
tracing the life and public service of
the 38th president of the US. A 28-
min introductory film on Ford;
reproduction of the White House
Oval Office; educational exhibits on
the US House of Representatives and
the presidency; original burglar tools
used in the Watergate break-in.
(Daily; closed Jan 1, Thanksgiving,
Dec 25) 303 Pearl St NW. Phone
616/451-9263. ¢¢

Grand Rapids Art Museum. Collections incl Renaissance, German
Expressionist, French, and American
paintings; graphics and a children's
gallery augmented by special traveling exhibitions. (Tues-Sun; closed

hols) 155 Division St N. Phone 616/831-1000. ¢¢

John Ball Zoo. Located in 100-acre park, zoo features more than 700 animals, Living Shores Aquarium, African Forest exhibit, and children's zoo. (Daily; closed Dec 25) 1300 W Fulton St. Phone 616/336-4300. ¢¢

La Grande Vitesse. This 42-ton stabile was created by Alexander Calder. County Building, downtown.

Meyer May House. (1908) Frank Lloyd Wright house from the late prairie period. Authentically restored with all architect-designed furniture, leaded-glass windows, lighting fixtures, rugs, and textiles. Tours begin at visitor center, 442 Madison St SE. (Tues, Thurs, Sun; schedule varies) 450 Madison St SE. Phone 616/246-4821. **FREE**

The Public Museum of Grand Rapids. Located in the Van Andel Museum Center; exhibits of interactive history and natural science, incl mammals, birds, furniture, Native American artifacts, re-creation of 1890s Grand Rapids street scene and 1928 carousel. Chaffee Planetarium offers sky shows and laser light shows (fee). (Daily; closed Jan 1, Easter, Dec 25) 272 Pearl St NW. Phone 456/399-7616. ¢¢

Skiing.

Cannonsburg. Quad, triple, double chairlift, two T-bars, eight rope tows. Longest run approx ⅓ mi; vertical drop 250 ft. Patrol, school, rentals, snowmaking; nursery, cafeteria, bar. (Thanksgiving-mid-Mar, daily) 6800 Cannonsburg Rd, 10 mi NE via US 131, W River Dr. Phone 616/874-6711. ¢¢¢¢

Pando. Six rope tows, seven lighted runs; patrol, school, rentals, grooming equipment, snowmaking; cafeteria. Vertical drop 125 ft. (Dec-Mar, daily) Seven mi of x-country trails; three mi of lighted trails, track-setting equipt; rentals. Night skiing. 8076 Belding Rd NE, 12 mi NE on MI 44, in Rockford. Phone 616/874-8343. ¢¢¢

Special Events

Community Circle Theater. John Ball Park Pavilion. Mid-May-Sept. Phone 616/456-6656.

Festival. Calder Plaza. Arts and crafts shows, entertainment, international foods. First full wkend June. Phone 616/459-2787.

Motels/Motor Lodges

★ ★ **AMERIHOST INN.** *2171 Holton Ct, Walker (49544). 616/791-8500; fax 616/791-8630.* 60 rms, 2 story. June-Aug: S $58-$73; D $63-$78; each addl $8; suites $99-$129; under 17 free; lower rates rest of yr. Crib free. TV; cable (premium). Indoor pool; whirlpool. Complimentary continental bkfst. Restaurant adj 5:30 am-11 pm. Ck-out noon. Meeting rm. Business servs avail. Valet serv. Downhill/x-country ski 15 mi. Exercise equipt; sauna. Some refrigerators. Cr cds: A, MC, V.

[D] [✈] [≈] [⅄] [≈] [🔥] [SC]

★ ★ **BEST WESTERN GRANDVILLAGE INN.** *3425 Fairlane Ave, Grandville (49418). 616/532-3222; fax 616/532-4959; toll-free 800/237-8737. www.bestwestern.com.* 82 units, 2 story. S $62-$120; D $69-$120; each addl $5; suites $94-$120; under 12 free. Crib $5. TV; cable (premium). Indoor pool. Complimentary continental bkfst. Coffee in rms. Ck-out 11 am. Coin lndry. Meeting rm. Business servs avail. Downhill ski 20 mi; x-country ski 10 mi. Game rm. Adj to Grand Village Mall. Cr cds: A, C, D, DS, MC, V.

[D] [✈] [≈] [≈] [🔥]

★ ★ **BEST WESTERN MIDWAY HOTEL.** *4101 SE 28th St (49512). 616/942-2550; fax 616/942-2446; toll-free 888/280-0081. www.bestwestern. com.* 146 rms, 3 story. S $85; D $95; each addl $10; under 18 free; wkend, hol rates. Crib free. TV; cable (premium). Indoor pool; whirlpool, poolside serv. Complimentary full bkfst. Complimentary coffee in rms. Restaurant 7 am-2 pm, 5-10 pm; Sun 6:30 am-2 pm, 5-9 pm. Bar noon-midnight; Fri, Sat to 2 am. Ck-out noon. Meeting rms. Business servs avail. Bellhops. Valet serv. Free airport transportation. Downhill ski 14 mi; x-country ski 4 mi. Exercise equipt; sauna. Health club privileges. Game rm. Rec rm. Some refrigerators.

Picnic tables. Cr cds: A, C, D, DS, MC, V.

★★ **COMFORT INN.** *4155 SE 28th St (49512). 616/957-2080; fax 616/957-9712; toll-free 800/638-7949. www.comfortinn.com.* 109 rms, 3 story. S, D $89; suites $73; under 18 free; wkend rates. Crib free. TV; cable (premium). Complimentary continental bkfst. Restaurant adj 6 am-10 pm. Ck-out noon. Meeting rm. Business servs avail. Valet serv. Downhill ski 15 mi; x-country ski 4 mi. Some balconies. Cr cds: A, C, D, DS, JCB, MC.

★ **DAYS INN.** *310 NW Pearl St (49504). 616/235-7611; fax 616/235-1995; toll-free 800/329-7466. www.daysinn.com.* 175 units, 8 story. S, D $49-$96; each addl $7; suites $74-$96; under 16 free; ski plans; higher rates special events. Crib free. TV; cable (premium), VCR avail. Indoor pool; whirlpool. Restaurant 6 am-10 pm; wkend hrs vary. Bar 11-1 am; Sun to 10 pm. Ck-out 11 am. Meeting rms. Business servs avail. Bellhops. Valet serv. Downhill/x-country ski 12 mi. Exercise equipt. Refrigerator in suites. Cr cds: A, C, D, DS, ER, JCB, MC, V.

★ **EXEL INN.** *4855 28th St SE (49512). 616/957-3000; fax 616/957-0194; toll-free 800/367-3935. www.exel inns.com.* 110 rms, 2 story. S $36.99-$38.99; D $41.99-$47.99; each addl $4; under 18 free. Crib free. Pet accepted. TV. Complimentary continental bkfst. Ck-out noon. Downhill ski 15 mi; x-country ski 4 mi. Cr cds: A, MC, V.

★★ **HAMPTON INN.** *4981 S 28th St (49512). 616/956-9304; fax 616/956-6617; toll-free 800/426-7866. www.hamptoninn.com.* 120 rms, 2 story. S $72; D $79; each addl $7; under 18 free. Crib free. Pet accepted. TV; cable (premium). Heated pool. Complimentary continental bkfst. Coffee in rms. Restaurant adj 11 am-10 pm. Ck-out noon. Meeting rm. Business servs avail. Valet serv. Downhill ski 15 mi; x-country ski 4 mi. Exercise equipt. Cr cds: A, D, DS, MC, V.

★★ **HAWTHORN SUITES.** *2985 SE Kraft Ave (49512). 616/940-1777; fax 616/940-9809.* 40 suites, 2 story. S, D $85. Crib free. Pet accepted. TV; cable (premium), VCR (free movies). Complimentary bkfst. Complimentary coffee in rms. Restaurant nearby. Ck-out noon. Business servs avail. Valet serv. Refrigerators. Cr cds: A, C, D, DS, MC, V.

★★ **HOLIDAY INN.** *255 SW 28th St (49548). 616/241-6444; fax 616/241-1807; toll-free 800/465-4329. www.holiday-inn.com.* 156 rms, 5 story. S, D $75; under 19 free. Crib free. TV; cable (premium), VCR avail. 2 pools, 1 indoor; whirlpool, poolside serv. Coffee in rms. Restaurant 6:30 am-11 pm. Bar 11 am-midnight. Ck-out noon. Meeting rms. Business servs avail. In-rm modem link. Bellhops. Valet serv. Downhill ski 12 mi; x-country ski 3 mi. Exercise equipt; sauna. Health club privileges. Game rm. Rec rm. Cr cds: A, C, D, DS, JCB, MC, V.

★★ **HOLIDAY INN.** *3333 SE 28th St (49512). 616/949-9222; fax 616/949-3841; res 800/465-4329. www.holiday-inn.com.* 200 rms, 5 story. S, D $85; family, wkend rates. Crib free. TV; cable (premium). Indoor pool; whirlpool, sauna, poolside serv. Restaurant 6:30 am-10 pm; Fri to 11 pm; Sat 7 am-11 pm; Sun 7 am-10 pm. Bar 4 pm-midnight. Ck-out noon. Meeting rms. Business servs avail. Bellhops. Valet serv. Free airport transportation. Downhill ski 15 mi; x-country ski 3 mi. Rec rm. Putting green. Cr cds: A, C, D, DS, ER, JCB, MC, V.

★★ **LEXINGTON HOTEL SUITES.** *5401 SE 28th Ct (49546). 616/940-8100; fax 616/940-0914; toll-free 800/441-9628. www.lexingtonsuites.com.* 121 suites, 3 story. S $79-$99; D $87-$107; each addl $8; under 18 free; higher rates special events. Crib free. TV; cable (premium). Indoor pool; whirlpool. Complimentary continental bkfst; afternoon refreshments. Complimentary coffee in rms. Restaurant nearby. Ck-out noon. Coin lndry. Meeting rms. Business servs avail. Valet serv. Free airport transportation. Downhill ski 15 mi;

x-country ski 5 mi. Exercise equipt. Refrigerators. Cr cds: A, MC, V.

🖵 ➤ 🏊 ⚓ 🐾 **SC**

★★ **QUALITY INN TERRACE CLUB.** *4495 SE 28th St, Kentwood (49512). 616/956-8080; fax 616/956-0619; res 800/228-5151. www.quality inn.com.* 126 rms, 3 story. S $69-$99; D $79-$109; each addl $10; suites $109-$139; under 18 free; wkly, wkend rates; ski, golf plans. Crib free. TV; cable (premium). Indoor pool; whirlpool. Complimentary full bkfst. Complimentary coffee in rms. Restaurant nearby. Ck-out noon. Coin lndry. Meeting rms. Business servs avail. In-rm modem link. Free airport transportation. Downhill ski 15 mi; x-country ski 3 mi. Exercise equipt. Health club privileges. Refrigerator, minibar in suites. Cr cds: A, C, D, DS, ER, JCB, MC, V.

🖵 **D** 🏊 🎿 ✈ ⚓ 🐾

★ **RED ROOF INN.** *5131 SE 28th St (49512). 616/942-0800; fax 616/942-8341; toll-free 800/843-7663. www. redroof.com.* 107 rms, 2 story. S $40.99-$47.99; D $46.99-$54.99; 1st addl $6; under 18 free. Crib free. Pet accepted. TV; cable (premium). Complimentary coffee in lobby. Restaurant adj 6 am-11 pm; Fri, Sat open 24 hrs; Sun to 10 pm. Ck-out noon. Business servs avail. Downhill ski 15 mi; x-country ski 5 mi. Cr cds: A, C, D, DS, MC, V.

🖵 ➤ 🐕 ⚓ 🐾

★ **SWAN INN.** *5182 NW Alpine Ave, Comstock Park (49321). 616/784-1224; fax 616/784-6565; toll-free 800/ 875-7926.* 38 rms, 1-2 story, 4 kits. S $40-$50; D, kit. units $48-$65; each addl $2; under 12 free; wkly rates. Crib free. TV; cable (premium). Heated pool. Restaurant 6 am-10 pm; Sun to 4 pm. Ck-out 11:30 am. Coin lndry. Meeting rms. Business servs avail. Downhill/x-country ski 12 mi. Cr cds: A, MC, V.

✈ 🏊 🏊 🐾

Hotels

★★★★ **AMWAY GRAND PLAZA HOTEL.** *187 Monroe Ave NW (49503). 616/774-2000; fax 616/776-6489; toll-free 800/253-3590. www.amway grand.com.* This hotel and convention facility is located downtown and

offers 682 guest rooms in either the 29-story tower, with Grand River and city views, or the more historic Pantlind building. A popular group destination, the property has 40,000 square feet of meeting space and is connected to Grand Center, the city's convention and exhibition hall, with 119,000 square feet of additional space. 682 rms, 29 story. S, D $115-$215 ; each addl $15; suites $315-$465; under 12 free; wkend rates. Crib free. Garage parking $9, valet $13. TV; cable (premium), VCR avail. Indoor pool; whirlpool, poolside serv. 7 restaurants. Rm serv 24 hrs. Bars 11:30-2 am; Sun from noon; entertainment Mon-Sat. Ck-out noon. Meeting rms. Business center. Concierge. Shopping arcade. Barber, beauty shop. Gift shop. Airport transportation $10. Tennis. Downhill ski 15 mi; x-country ski 10 mi. Exercise rm; sauna. Massage. Bathrm phone, balconies in suites. Some refrigerators. On Grand River. Luxury level. Cr cds: A, C, D, DS, MC, V.

🖵 ➤ 🐕 🏊 ⚓ ✈ ⚓ 🐾 🏃

★★★ **CROWNE PLAZA.** *5700 28th St SE (49546). 616/957-1770; fax 616/ 957-0629; toll-free 800/957-9575. www. crowneplaza.com/grr-airport.* 320 rms, 5 story. S, D $87-$163; suites $250; under 18 free; wkend packages. Free self and valet parking. Crib free. TV; cable (premium), VCR avail (movies). 2 pools, 1 heated indoor; whirlpool, poolside serv. Restaurant 6:30 am-10 pm. Bar 11-2 am; Sun noon-midnight. Coffee in rms. Ck-out noon. Coin lndry. Meeting rms. Business center. In-rm modem link. Concierge. Bellhops. Valet serv. Gift shop. Free airport transportation. Tennis privileges. 18-hole golf privileges, greens fee $33, pro, putting green. Downhill ski 14 mi; x-country ski 5 mi. Exercise equipt; sauna. Free airport transportation. Refrigerators in suites. Some private patios, balconies. Cr cds: A, C, D, DS, ER, JCB, MC, V.

🖵 🏌 🏃 🐕 🏊 ➤ ⚓ 🐾 **SC** 🏌 🏃

★★★ **HILTON GRAND RAPIDS AIRPORT.** *4747 SE 28th St SE (49512). 616/957-0100; fax 616/957-2977; toll-free 877/944-5866. www. hilton.com.* 224 rms, 4 story. S, D $72-$152; each addl $10; suites $165-$375; family, ski, wkend rates. Crib free. TV; cable (premium). Heated indoor pool; whirlpool; poolside serv. Restaurant 6:30 am-11 pm; Sat, Sun from 7 am. Bar 11-2 am; entertainment Tues-Sat. Coffee in rms. Ck-out noon. Meeting rms. Business servs avail. In-rm modem link. Bellhops. Valet serv. Free 24-hr airport transportation. Downhill ski 14 mi; x-country ski 4 mi. Exercise equipt; sauna. Health club privileges. Game rm. Some refrigerators. Cr cds: A, D, DS, JCB, MC, V.

⊡ ⊠ ⊠ ⊼ ⊠ ⊠

★★ **HOLIDAY INN NORTH.** *270 Ann St NW (49504). 616/363-9001; fax 616/363-0670; res 800/465-4329. www.holiday-inn.com/grr-north.* 164 rms, 7 story. S $74, D $82; each addl $8; under 20 free; ski plan; wkend, hol rates. Crib free. Pet accepted, some restrictions. TV; cable (premium), VCR avail. Indoor pool; whirlpool, sauna, poolside serv. Restaurant 6:30 am-10 pm; Fri, Sat 7 am-11 pm. Bar 11-1 am; entertainment. Ck-out noon. Coin lndry. Meeting rms. Business servs avail. Downhill/x-country ski 14 mi. Game rm. Picnic tables. On Grand River. Cr cds: A, MC, V.

⊡ ⊠ ⊠ ⊠ ⊠ ⊠

Extended Stay

★★ **RESIDENCE INN BY MARRIOTT.** *2701 E Beltline Ave SE (49546). 616/957-8111; fax 616/957-3699; res 800/331-3131. www.residenceinn.com/grrgr.* 96 kit. suites, 2 story. Suites $102-$135; under 12 free. Crib free. Pet accepted, some restrictions; $60 and $6/day. TV; cable (premium), VCR avail. Heated pool; whirlpool. Complimentary continental bkfst. Restaurant adj 11-2 am. Ck-out noon. Coin lndry. Meeting rm. Business servs avail. Valet serv. Free airport transportation. Downhill ski 15 mi; x-country ski 5 mi. Exercise equipt. Health club privileges. Private patios; some balconies. Picnic tables, grills. Cr cds: A, C, D, DS, MC, V.

⊠ ⊠ ⊠ ⊼ ⊠ ⊠ ⊠

Restaurants

★★ **ARNIE'S.** *3561 SE 28th St (49512). 616/956-7901.* Hrs: 7 am-

10:30 pm; Sat from 8 am; Sun 9 am-3 pm. Closed hols. Bkfst $3-$6, lunch $5-$7, dinner $6-$10.50. Child's menu. Specializes in desserts, sandwiches, fresh seafood. Pianist. Retail bakery. Cr cds: A, MC, V.

★★ **DUBA'S.** *420 E Beltline NE (49506). 616/949-1011.* Hrs: 11 am-10 pm; Fri, Sat to 11 pm. Closed Sun; hols. Res accepted. Bar. Lunch $5.95-$10, dinner $22-$26. Child's menu. Specializes in prime rib, fish. Parking. Family-owned. Cr cds: A, MC, V.

⊡

★★★ **GIBSON'S.** *1033 Lake Dr (49506). 616/774-8535.* Hrs: 11:30 am-11 pm; Sat from 5 pm. Closed Jan 1, July 4, Dec 25; also Sun June-Aug. Res accepted. Continental menu. Bar 11:30-1 am. Wine list. Lunch $5-$11.50, dinner $18.75-$29.95. Specializes in aged beef, lamb, fowl. Own baking, ice cream. Parking. Patio dining. In former Franciscan friary (1860s). Cr cds: A, D, DS, MC, V.

⊡ ⊠

★ **JOHN BRANN'S STEAKHOUSE.** *5510 SE 28th St (49512). 616/285-7800.* Hrs: 11 am-10 pm; Fri, Sat to 11 pm; Sun 10 am-9 pm; early-bird dinner Sun-Thurs 4-8 pm; Sun brunch to 2:30 pm. Closed Thanksgiving, Dec 25. Res accepted. Bar to 2 am. Lunch $5.99-$8.99, dinner $7.99-$15.99. Sun brunch $8.99. Child's menu. Specializes in steak, prime rib. Salad bar. Family-owned. Cr cds: A, D, DS, MC, V.

⊡ ⊠

★★ **PIETRO'S BACK DOOR PIZZERIA.** *2780 SE Birchcrest St (49506). 616/452-3228. www.rcfc.com.* Hrs: 11:30 am-10 pm; Fri to 11 pm; Sat 3-11 pm; Sun noon-10 pm. Closed Thanksgiving, Dec 25. Northern Italian, American menu. Bar. Lunch $6-$7, dinner $7-$11. Child's menu. Specializes in fresh pasta, chicken, veal dishes. Parking. Outdoor dining. Cr cds: A, D, DS, MC, V.

⊡ ⊠

★★ **SAYFEE'S.** *3555 SE Lake Eastbrook Blvd (49546). 616/949-5750.* Hrs: 11 am-11 pm. Closed Sun exc Mother's Day, Easter; hols. Continental menu. Bar. Lunch 25.95-$11.50, dinner $9.95-$24.95. Child's menu.

Specializes in steak, seafood. Band Wed-Sat. Cr cds: A, D, DS, MC, V.

D ⬛

★★ **SCHNITZELBANK.** *342 SE Jefferson Ave (49503). 616/459-9527. www.schnitzel.kvi.net.* Hrs: 11 am-8 pm; Fri to 9 pm; Sat 4:30-9 pm. Closed Sun; hols. Res accepted. German, American menu. Bar. Lunch $4.50-$9.95, dinner $8.95-$19.95. Child's menu. Specialties: sauerbraten, roast chicken, Wiener schnitzel. Parking. Bavarian atmosphere. Family-owned. Totally nonsmoking. Cr cds: A, DS, MC, V.

D

★★ **WYOMING CATTLE CO.** *1820 44th St SW, Wyoming (49509). 616/534-0704. www.michiganmenu.com.* Hrs: 11 am-10 pm; Fri, Sat to 11 pm. Closed Thanksgiving, Dec 24, 25. Bar to 11 pm. Lunch $4.50-$8.95, dinner $8.75-$21.95. Child's menu. Specializes in steak. Outdoor dining. Western decor. Cr cds: A, DS, MC, V.

D

Grayling

(D-5) *See also Gaylord, Houghton Lake*

Pop 1,944 **Elev** 1,137 ft
Area code 517 **Zip** 49738
Information Grayling Area Visitors Council, PO Box 406; 800/937-8837
Web www.grayling-mi.com

What to See and Do

Canoe trips. There are many canoe liveries in the area, with trip itineraries for the Manistee and Au Sable rivers. Contact Grayling Area Visitors Council for details.

Hartwick Pines State Park. Approx 9,700 acres. Fishing for trout, perch, and largemouth bass; hunting, marked x-country ski trails, picnicking, playground, concession, camping. Three-dimensional exhibits in interpretive center tell the story of the white pine. Log memorial building, lumberman's museum near virgin pine forest; "Chapel in the Pines." Naturalist. Standard fees. (Daily) 7 mi NE on MI 93. Phone 517/348-7068. ¢¢

Skiing. Skyline Ski Area. Double chairlift, five rope tows; patrol, school, rentals; cafeteria, ski shop. Longest run approx ½ mi; vertical drop 210 ft. (Mid-Dec-Mar, daily) 2 mi S off I-75, exit 251. Phone 517/275-5445. ¢¢¢¢

Special Events

Winter Wolf Festival. Early Feb. Phone 800/937-8837.

Au Sable River Festival. Arts and crafts, parade, car show. Last full wkend July. Phone 800/937-8837.

Motels/Motor Lodges

★★ **HOLIDAY INN.** *2650 I-75 Business Loop (49738). 517/348-7611; fax 517/348-7984; res 800/465-4329. www.holiday-inn.com.* 151 rms, 2 story. July-Aug: S, D $69-$119; each addl $6; suites $150-$175; under 19 free; lower rates rest of yr. Pet accepted. TV; cable (premium), VCR avail. Indoor pool; wading pool, whirlpool, poolside serv. Playground. Restaurant 6 am-2 pm, 5-10 pm; Sun 6 am-9 pm. Bar 11-2 am; entertainment. Ck-out 11 am. Meeting rms. Business servs avail. Bellhops. Valet serv. Sundries. Airport, bus depot transportation. Downhill ski 5 mi; x-country ski on site. Game rm. Lawn games. Exercise equipt; sauna. Picnic tables. On wooded property. Some refrigerators. Cr cds: A, C, D, DS, JCB, MC, V.

D 🐾 ⬛ ⬛ ⬛ 🏃 ✈ ⬛ ⬛ SC

★ **HOSPITALITY HOUSE.** *1232 I-75 Business Loop (49738). 517/348-8900; fax 517/348-6509; toll-free 800/722-4151.* 80 rms, 1-2 story. Memorial Day-Labor Day, wkends: S, D $65-$92; each addl $5; suites $125-$175; under 16 free; lower rates rest of yr. Crib free. TV; cable (premium), VCR avail (movies $4). Indoor pool; whirlpool. Restaurant 6:30 am-2 pm, 5-9 pm. Ck-out 11 am. Business servs avail. Valet serv. Free airport, bus depot transportation. Downhill/x-country ski 3 mi. Game rm. Refrigerators, microwaves. Cr cds: A, C, D, DS, MC, V.

D ⬛ ⬛ ⬛ ⬛ ⬛ ⬛

★ **NORTH COUNTRY LODGE.** *615 I-75 Business Loop (49738). 517/348-8471; fax 517/348-6114; toll-free 800/*

475-6300. *www.grayling-mi.com/
northcountrylodge.* 24 rms, 8 kits. Mid-
June-Labor Day, winter wkends,
Christmas wk: S $40-$50; D $45-$60;
each addl $5; kit. units $55-$70;
suite $140-$160; family, wkly rates;
lower rates rest of yr. Crib free. Pet
accepted. TV; cable. Restaurant
nearby. Ck-out 11 am. Free airport,
bus depot transportation. Downhill/
x-country ski 3 mi. Cr cds: A, C, D,
DS, MC, V.

★ **POINTE NORTH OF GRAYLING
MOTEL.** *1024 S I-75 Business Loop N
(49738).* 517/348-5950. 21 rms. Mid-
June-Labor Day, Christmas wk, winter wkends: S $40-$50; D $45-$65;
each addl $5; kit. unit $65-$85; lower
rates rest of yr. TV; cable (premium).
Ck-out 10 am. Downhill ski 3 mi; x-
country ski 2 mi. Refrigerators,
microwaves. Picnic table, grill. Cr
cds: A, C, D, DS, MC, V.

★ **SUPER 8.** *5828 Nelson A Miles
Pkwy (49738).* 517/348-8888; fax 517/
348-2030; res 800/800-8000. *www.
super8.com.* 61 rms, 2 story. Apr-Sept:
S $46.69; D $55.88-$67.88; each addl
$4; under 12 free; lower rates rest of
yr. TV; cable (premuim). Pet accepted.
Complimentary continental bkfst.
Restaurant adj open 24 hrs. Ck-out
11 am. Meeting rm. Coin lndry.
Downhill ski 1 mi; x-country ski 6
mi. Lawn games. Cr cds: A, D, DS,
MC, V.

Cottage Colony

★ **PENRODS AUSABLE RIVER
RESORT.** *100 Maple (49738).* 517/
348-2910; toll-free 888/467-4837. 11
cabins, 7 kits. Cabins for 2-3, $45-
$60; kit. cabins for 2-3, $55-$60; kit.
cabins for 4-6, $80-$90; wkly rates.
TV. Playground. Restaurant nearby.
Ck-out 11 am, ck-in 2 pm. Grocery,
package store 3 blks. Bi-wkly maid
serv. Free airport, bus depot transportation. Canoe trips, rentals. Inner
tubes. Lawn games. Picnic tables,
grills. Rustic log cabins; some with
screened porches. 6½ acres on Au
Sable River. Cr cds: A, MC, V.

Hancock

(A-1) *See also Copper Harbor, Houghton*

Pop 4,547 **Elev** 686 ft **Area code** 906
Zip 49930
Information Keweenaw Peninsula
Chamber of Commerce, 326 Shelden
Ave, PO Box 336, Houghton 49931;
906/482-5240 or 800/338-7982
Web www.portup.com/snow

Named for John Hancock, the town
is the home of Suomi College (1896),
the only Finnish college in the
United States.

What to See and Do

Finnish-American Heritage Center.
Center houses the Finnish-American
Historical Archives, a museum, the-
ater, art gallery, and the Finnish-
American Family History Center.
(Mon-Fri; closed hols) Special events
eves and wkends. Located on the
campus of Suomi College, 601 Quincy
St. Phone 906/487-7367. **FREE**

Maasto Hiihto Ski Trail. A 9½-mi
public x-country ski trail with begin-
ner-to-expert trails groomed daily.
(Dec-Apr, daily) ½ mi N via US 41,
then 2 mi N on side road. Phone
906/482-2388. **FREE**

**Quincy Steam Hoist, Shaft House,
Tram Rides, and Underground Mine
Tours.** This 790-ton hoist was used at
the Quincy Copper Mine between
1920 and 1931; it could raise 10 tons
of ore at a speed of 3,200 ft per
minute from an inclined depth of
more than 9,000 ft. Also guided tour
of mine shafts (45 min). (Mid-May-
mid-Oct, daily) 1 mi N on US 41.
Phone 906/482-3101. ¢¢

Special Event

Houghton County Fair. Fairgrounds.
Phone 906/482-6200. Late Aug.

Motel/Motor Lodge

★★ **BEST WESTERN COPPER
CROWN.** *235 Hancock Ave (49930).*
906/482-6111; fax 906/482-0185; toll-
free 800/528-1234. *www.bestwestern.
com.* 47 rms, 2 story. S $45-$55; D

$50-$60; each addl $3; under 12 free; higher rates special events. TV; cable (premium). Indoor pool; whirlpool, saunas. Restaurant adj 6 am-6 pm. Ck-out 11 am. Meeting rm. Business servs avail. Sundries. Downhill/x-country ski 1 mi. Some carports. Cr cds: A, D, DS, MC, V.

Harbor Springs

(C-5) See also Petoskey

Settled 1827 **Pop** 1,540 **Elev** 600 ft
Area code 231 **Zip** 49740
Information Chamber of Commerce, 205 State St; 231/526-7999
Web www.harbor
springs-mi.com

Known as a year-round vacation spot, Harbor Springs is a picturesque town on Little Traverse Bay.

What to See and Do

Andrew J. Blackbird Museum.
Museum of the Ottawa; artifacts. (Memorial Day-Labor Day, daily; Sept-Oct, wkends) Special exhibits (fee). 368 E Main St. Phone 231/526-7731. ¢

Shore Drive. One of the most scenic drives in the state. Passes through Devil's Elbow and Springs area, said to be haunted by an evil spirit. Along MI 119.

Skiing.

Boyne Highlands. Four triple, four quad chairlifts, rope tow; patrol, school, rentals, snowmaking; cafeteria, restaurant, bar, nursery, lodge (see RESORT). (Thanksgiving wkend-mid-Apr, daily) Wkend plan. X-country trails (4 mi); rentals. 4½ mi NE off MI 119. Phone 231/526-2171. ¢¢¢¢

Nub's Nob. Two double, three quad, three triple chairlifts; patrol, school, rentals, snowmaking; cafeteria, bar. Longest run one mi; vertical drop 427 ft. (Thanksgiving-Easter, daily) Half-day rates. X-country trails (same seasons, hrs as downhill skiing); night skiing (five nights/wk). 500 Nub's Nob Rd, 5 mi NE. Phone 526/213-1800. ¢¢¢¢

Motels/Motor Lodges

★ **BIRCHWOOD INN.** 7077 S Lake Shore Dr (49740). 231/526-2151; fax 231/526-2108; toll-free 800/530-9955. 48 rms, 1-2 story, 2 suites in lodge. Mid-June-mid-Oct: S, D, suites $55-$99; each addl $10; kit. units $105-$215; lower rates rest of yr. Crib $10. TV; cable. Heated pool. Playground. Complimentary continental bkfst. Restaurant adj 5:30-10 pm. Ck-out 11 am. Meeting rms. Business servs avail. Tennis. Downhill ski 8 mi; x-country ski 1 mi. Refrigerators avail. Private patios, balconies. Cr cds: MC, V.

★★ **COLONIAL INN.** 210 Artesian Ave (49740). 231/526-2111; fax 231/526-5458. www.harborsprings.com. 45 rms, 2 story, 8 kits. Late June-early Sept: S, D $108-$158; kit. units $138-$188; some wkend rates; lower rates May-late June, early Sept-Oct. Closed rest of yr. TV; cable. Heated pool; whirlpool. Complimentary continental bkfst (July-Aug). Restaurant

Replica Dutch House

nearby 11 am-10 pm. Bar 5-11 pm. Ck-out 11 am. Meeting rm. Some fireplaces; refrigerators avail. Porches, balconies. Built 1894; landscaped grounds. Lake 1 blk. Cr cds: MC, V.

★ **HARBOR SPRINGS COTTAGE INN.** *145 Zoll St, Harbor Spring (49740). 231/526-5431; fax 231/526-8094.* 21 rms, 2 A/C, 4 kits. Mid-June-Labor Day: S $58-$90; D $68-$100; kit. units $100; under 14 free; lower rates rest of yr. Crib $5. Pet accepted. TV; cable. Complimentary continental bkfst. Ck-out 11 am. Downhill/x-country ski 5 mi. Guest bicycles, sailboats. Little Traverse Bay opp. Cr cds: A, D, DS, MC, V.

Resort

★★ **BOYNE HIGHLANDS RESORT.** *600 Highlands Dr (49740). 231/526-3000; fax 231/526-3100; toll-free 800/462-6963. www.boyne.com.* 228 rms, 3 story, 195 condo units. June-Sept, Dec-Mar: D $119-$187; condo units $187; ski, golf plans; lower rates rest of yr. Crib free. TV; cable. 4 heated pools; wading pool, whirlpool, poolside serv. Children's activities, 4-10 yrs, summer. Dining rm 7:30 am-10:30 pm. Bar 4 pm-2 am. Ck-out 1 pm, ck-in 5 pm. Coin lndry. Meeting rms. Business center. Grocery 2 mi; package store 1 mi. Tennis. May-late-Oct: 18-hole golf, greens fee $39-$129, 2 driving ranges, 2 putting greens, 2 pro shops. Downhill/x-country ski on site. Ice skating. Lawn games. Hiking. Game rm. Gift shop. Entertainment. Exercise equipt; sauna, steam rm. Massage (by appt). Refrigerators. Some private patios, balconies. European atmosphere. On 6,000 acres. Cr cds: A, D, DS, MC, V.

B&B/Small Inn

★★★ **KIMBERLY COUNTRY ESTATE.** *2287 Bester Rd (49740). 231/526-7646; fax 231/526-8054. www.kimberlycountryestate.com.* 6 rms, 2 story. S, D $155-$195; suites $235-$275; hols (3-day min); package plans. Children over 12 yrs only. TV, VCR in library. Heated pool. Complimentary full bkfst; afternoon refresh-

ments. Restaurant nearby. Ck-out 11 am, ck-in 2-6 pm. Luggage handling. Downhill/x-country ski 5 mi. Airport transportation. Rec rm. Lawn games. Some fireplaces, whirlpools. Totally nonsmoking. Cr cds: A, MC, V.

Restaurants

★★ **LEGS INN.** *6425 S Lake Shore Dr, Cross Village (49740). 231/526-2281. www.legsinn.com.* Hrs: noon-9 pm; July-Labor Day noon-10 pm. Closed late Oct-late May. No A/C. Polish, American menu. Bar. Lunch $4-$9, dinner $11-$18. Child's menu. Specialties: pierogi, stuffed cabbage, goulash. Entertainment Fri-Sun. Fieldstone exterior with roofline railing composed of inverted stove legs; collection of wooden sculptures and curios; warm, cheerful atmosphere. Cr cds: DS, MC, V.

★ **THE NEW YORK.** *101 State St (49740). 231/526-1904. www.thenewyork.com.* Hrs: 5-10 pm; Fri, Sat to 11 pm. Closed Thanksgiving, Dec 25; also Apr, 2 wks Nov. Res accepted. Continental menu. A la carte entrees: dinner $14.50-$24. Child's menu. Specializes in veal, rack of lamb. Victorian-style former hotel building. Cr cds: A, MC, V.

★★ **STAFFORD'S PIER.** *102 Bay St (49740). 231/526-6201. www.staffords. com.* Hrs: 11:30 am-11 pm; Sun to 10 pm. Closed Dec 25. Res accepted. Bar. Lunch $6.95-$10.95, dinner $9.50-$28. Child's menu. Specializes in whitefish, perch, rack of lamb. Outdoor dining. Overlooks harbor. Family-owned. Cr cds: A, DS, MC, V.

Harrison

(E-5) *See also Clare, Houghton Lake*

Pop 1,835 **Elev** 1,186 ft
Area code 989 **Zip** 48625

Information Chamber of Commerce, 809 N 1st St, PO Box 682; 989/539-6011

Web www.harrisonchamber.com

What to See and Do

Skiing. Snowsnake Mountain. Triple chairlift, five rope tows; patrol, school, rentals, snowmaking; snack bar. Longest run ½ mi; vertical drop 210 ft. Night skiing. (Mid-Dec-mid-Mar, daily) X-country trails. 3407 Mannsiding Rd, 5 mi S on US 27. Phone 989/539-6583. ¢¢¢¢

Wilson State Park. Approx 35 acres on the shore of Budd Lake. Swimming; fishing for largemouth bass, bluegill, perch; picnicking, playground, camping. Standard fees. 1 mi N on Old US 27. Phone 989/539-3021. ¢¢

Special Events

Frostbite Open. Winter golf tournament. Feb. Phone 989/539-6011.

Clare County Fair. Clare County Fairgrounds. Late July-early Aug. Phone 989/539-9011.

Holland

(G-4) *See also Grand Haven, Saugatuck*

Founded 1847 **Pop** 30,745 **Elev** 610 ft **Area code** 616
Information Holland Area Chamber of Commerce, 272 E 8th St, PO Box 1888, 49422-1888; 616/392-2389 or Holland Convention and Visitors Bureau, 76 E 8th St; 616/394-0000 or 800/506-1299
Web www.holland.org

In 1847, a group of Dutch seeking religious freedom left the Netherlands and settled in this area because its sand dunes and fertile land reminded them of their homeland. Today much of the population is of Dutch descent. The town prides itself on being the center of Dutch culture in the United States. The city is located at the mouth of the Black River, on the shores of Lake Macatawa, and has developed a resort colony along the shores of lakes Macatawa and Michigan.

What to See and Do

Cappon House. (1874) Italianate house of first mayor of Holland. Original furnishings, millwork. (May-Sept, Fri and Sat afternoons or by appt) Washington Blvd and W 9th St. Phone 616/392-6740. ¢¢

Dutch Village. Buildings of Dutch architecture; canals, windmills, tulips, street organs, Dutch dancing; animals, movies, rides; wooden shoe carving and other crafts; museum, tours; restaurant. (Mid-Apr-late Oct, daily) 1 mi NE on US 31. Phone 616/396-1475. ¢¢

Holland Museum. Features decorative arts from the Netherlands Collection, the Volendam Room. Permanent and changing exhibits pertaining to local history. Gift shop. (Mon, Wed-Sun; closed hols) 31 W 10th St. Phone 616/392-9084. ¢¢

Holland State Park. This 143-acre park incl a ¼-mi beach on Lake Michigan. Swimming, bathhouse, boating (launch), fishing; picnicking, playground, concessions, camping. Standard fees. 7 mi W off US 31. Phone 616/399-9390. ¢¢

Hope College. (1866) 2,550 students. Liberal arts. Tours of campus. Theater series (July-Aug, fee; phone 616/395-7000). Between College and Columbia aves. Phone 616/392-5111.

Veldheer's Tulip Gardens and Deklomp Wooden Shoe & Delftware Factory. The only Delftware factory in the US; factory tours (free). Visitors can try on wooden shoes and talk to the artisans who made them. (Daily) Phone 616/399-1900.

★ **Windmill Island.** The 225-yr-old windmill, "De Zwaan" (the swan), is the only operating imported Dutch windmill in the US. It was relocated here by special permission of the Dutch government, as the remaining windmills in the Netherlands are considered historic monuments. It is still used today to grind flour. The imported carousel, "Draaimolen," offers free rides. (May-Aug, daily; Labor Day-Oct, limited hrs) 7th St and Lincoln. Phone 616/836-1490. ¢¢ Incl

Little Netherlands. A miniature reproduction of old Holland; 20-min film on Dutch windmills in the posthouse; klompen dancing in summer; exhibits, tulips. Phone 616/355-1030.

Wooden Shoe Factory. Factory operations can be viewed by public (Mon-Sat). Also gift shop (daily; hrs may be limited off-season). 447 US 31 at 16th St. Phone 616/396-6513. ¢

Special Event

Tulip Time Festival. A celebration of Dutch heritage: 1,800 klompen dancers, three parades, street scrubbing, Dutch markets, musical and professional entertainment, and millions of tulips. Phone 800/822-2770. Eight days mid-May.

Motels/Motor Lodges

★★ **COUNTRY INN BY CARLSON.** *12260 James St (49424). 616/396-6677; fax 616/396-1197.* 116 rms, 2 story. July-Aug: S $79-$89; D $89-$99; each addl $5; under 18 free; lower rates rest of yr. Crib free. TV; cable, VCR avail. Complimentary continental bkfst. Coffee in rms. Restaurant nearby. Ck-out noon. Meeting rms. Business servs avail. Valet serv. X-country ski 5 mi. Bathrm phones. Country-style decor. Cr cds: A, D, DS, MC, V.
D 🏊 ⛖ 🐾

★★ **HOLIDAY INN.** *650 E 24th St (49423). 616/394-0111; fax 616/394-4832; res 800/279-5286. www.holiday-inn.com.* 168 units, 4 story. May-Nov: S, D $109-$129; under 17 free; lower rates rest of yr. TV; cable (premium). Indoor pool. Coffee in rms. Restaurant 6 am-10 pm. Bar 4 pm-2 am; entertainment Mon-Sat. Ck-out noon. Meeting rms. Business servs avail. In-rm modem link. Bellhops. Free airport, RR station, bus depot transportation. X-country ski 3 mi. Exercise equipt; sauna. Game rm. Rec rm. Refrigerator in suites. Patios, balconies. Cr cds: A, DS, MC, V.
D 🏊 ⛖ 🏋 ✈ ⛖ 🐾 SC

★ **SUPER 8 MOTEL.** *680 E 24th St (49423). 616/396-8822; fax 616/396-2050; toll-free 800/800-8000. www.super8.com.* 68 rms, 3 story, 6 suites. May-Labor Day: S $52.88; D $57.88; each addl $6; suites $85; under 12 free; wknd rates; lower rates rest of yr. Crib free. TV; cable (premium). Complimentary coffee in lobby. Restaurant nearby. Ck-out 11 am. Coin lndry. Business servs avail. In-rm modem link. Valet serv. X-country ski 3 mi. Cr cds: A, C, D, DS, MC, V.
D 🏊 ⛖ 🐾 SC

B&B/Small Inn

★★ **DUTCH COLONIAL INN.** *560 Central Ave (49423). 616/396-3664; fax 616/396-0461. www.dutchcolonialinn.com.* 4 rms, 1 with shower only, 1-3 story. S $100; D $110; each addl $20; hols (3-day min). TV; cable, VCR avail (free movies). Complimentary full bkfst. Ck-out 11 am, ck-in 3 pm. In-rm modem link. X-country ski 3 mi. In-rm whirlpools; some fireplaces. Built 1928; many antiques. Totally nonsmoking. Cr cds: A, DS, MC, V.
🏊 ⛖ 🐾

Restaurants

★ **84 EAST PASTA ETC.** *84 E 8th St (49423). 616/396-8484.* Hrs: 11 am-11 pm. Closed Sun; hols. Italian, American menu. Bar. A la carte entrees: lunch $5-$7, dinner $6-$9. Child's menu. Specializes in pasta. Casual decor. Cr cds: A, DS, MC, V.
D

★★★ **ALPENROSE.** *4 E 8th St (49423). 616/393-2111. www.alpenroserestaurant.com.* Hrs: 7:30 am-9 pm; Sun brunch 10 am-2 pm; summer hrs vary. Closed Dec 25. Res accepted. Austrian, continental menu. Serv bar. Extensive wine list. Lunch $5.95-$9.95, dinner $8.95-$18.95. Sun brunch $16.95. Child's menu. Specialties: chicken shortcake, Wiener schnitzel. Outdoor dining. Authentic Austrian-style dining. Totally nonsmoking. Cr cds: A, D, DS, MC, V.
D

★ **PEREDDIE'S.** *447 Washington Sq (49423). 616/394-3061. www.pereddies.net.* Hrs: 10 am-9 pm; Fri, Sat to 10 pm. Closed Sun; hols. Res accepted; required Fri, Sat. Italian menu. Serv bar. Lunch $5-$10, dinner $12-$25. Specializes in pasta. European-style cafe with deli and Italian galleria. Cr cds: A, DS, MC, V.
D

★★★ **PIPER.** *2225 South Shore Dr, Macatawa (49434). 616/335-5866. www.piperrestaurant.com.* Hrs: 5-9:30 pm. Closed hols; also Sun in winter.

Bar. Wine list. A la carte entrees: dinner $123-$21. Child's menu. Specializes in seafood. Parking. Overlooks Lake Macatawa. Cr cds: A, DS, MC, V. **D**

★★ **TILL MIDNIGHT.** *208 College Ave (49423). 616/392-6883. www.tillmidnight.com.* Hrs: 11 am-2:30 pm, 5 pm-midnight. Closed Sun; hols. Res accepted. Eclectic menu. Bar. A la carte entrees: lunch $6-$8, dinner $18-$25. Child's menu. Specializes in breads, desserts. Modern art by local artist adorns the walls. Totally nonsmoking. Cr cds: A, DS, MC, V. **D**

Holly

(G-6) *See also Detroit, Flint, Pontiac*

Pop 5,595 **Elev** 937 ft **Area code** 248 **Zip** 48442

Information Chamber of Commerce, 120 S Saginaw St, PO Box 214; 248/634-1900

Web www.hollymi.com

What to See and Do

Davisburg Candle Factory. Located in 125-yr-old building; produces unique and beautiful handcrafted candles. Unusual taper production line. Showrm and gift shop. Demonstrations by appt (wkdays). (Daily) 634 Broadway; 2 mi S, then 3 mi E on Davisburg Rd. Phone 248/634-4214. **FREE**

🚩 **Historic Battle Alley.** Once known for its taverns and brawls, Battle Alley is now a restored 19th-century street featuring antiques, boutiques, specialty shops, crafters; dining at the Historic Holly Hotel (see RESTAURANT). On the Alley is a mosaic of the bicentennial logo made from 1,000 red, white, and blue bricks. (Daily; closed hols) Downtown, State and National Historic District. Phone 248/634-5208. **FREE**

Skiing. Mount Holly Ski Area. Three quad, three triple, double chairlift, six rope tows; patrol, school, rentals, snowmaking; two cafeterias, two bars. Vertical drop 350 ft. Night skiing. (Dec-Mar, daily; closed Dec 24 eve) 13536 S Dixie Hwy, 7 mi NE off I-75. Phone 248/634-8260.

Special Events

Michigan Renaissance Festival. One mi N of Mt Holly on Dixie Hwy. Festivities incl jousting tournaments, entertainment, food, and crafts in Renaissance-style village. Phone 248/634-5552. Eight wkends Aug-Sept.

Carry Nation Festival. Re-creation of Carry Nation's 1908 visit to Holly. The "temperance crusader" charged down Battle Alley with her famed umbrella, smashing bottles and a few heads along the way. Pageant, parade, antique car show, race, games, arts and crafts show, model railroad. Wkend after Labor Day. Phone 248/634-1055.

Dickens Festival. Re-creates the Dickensian period with carolers, town crier, strolling characters, skits, bell choirs, street hawkers, carriage rides. Thanksgiving-wkend before Dec 25. Phone 248/634-1900.

Restaurant

★★ **HISTORIC HOLLY HOTEL.** *110 Battle Alley (48442). 248/634-5208. www.hollyhotel.com.* Hrs: 11 am-3 pm, 5-10 pm; Fri, Sat to 11 pm; Sun noon-8 pm; Sun brunch 11 am-3 pm. Closed hols. Res accepted. Bar. Lunch $3.50-$18, dinner $23-$40. Sun brunch $19. Specialties: beef Wellington, medallions of beef. Own baking. Comedy theater Fri-Sat; pianist Sat. In restored hotel (1891); Victorian decor. Cr cds: A, MC, V. **⊡**

Houghton

(A-1) *See also Calumet, Hancock*

Settled 1843 **Pop** 7,498 **Elev** 607 ft **Area code** 906 **Zip** 49931

Information Keweenaw Peninsula Chamber of Commerce, 326 Shelden

Ave, PO Box 336; 906/482-5240 or 800/338-7982

Web www.cityofhoughton.com

Houghton and its sister city, Hancock (see), face each other across the narrowest part of Portage Lake. This is the area of America's first mining capital, the scene of the first great mineral strike in the Western Hemisphere. The copper-bearing geological formations are believed to be the oldest rock formations in the world. The great mining rush of 1843 and the years following brought people from all over Europe. Two main ethnic groups are identifiable today: Cornishmen, who came from England; and Finns, who have made this their cultural center in the United States.

What to See and Do

Ferry service to Isle Royale National Park. (see) Four ferries and a float plane provide transportation (June-Sept, daily; some trips in May). For fees and schedule contact Park Superintendent. Phone 906/482-0984.

Michigan Technological University. (1885) 6,200 students. Campus tours leave from University Career Center in Administration Building. (See SPECIAL EVENTS) 1400 Townsend Dr. Phone 906/487-1885. On campus is

A. E. Seaman Mineralogical Museum. Exhibits one of the nation's best mineral collections. (May-Oct, Mon-Sat; rest of yr, Mon-Fri; closed hols) In Electrical Energy Resources Center. Phone 906/487-2572.

Mont Ripley Ski Area. Double chairlift, T-bar; patrol, school, rentals, snowmaking; cafeteria. (Early Dec-late Mar, daily; closed Dec 25) ½ mi E on MI 26. Phone 906/487-2340. ¢¢¢¢

Special Events

Winter Carnival. Michigan Technological University. Snow sculptures and statues; dogsled and snowshoe racing, broomball, skiing, skating; skit contests; Queen Coronation and Snoball Dance. Phone 906/487-2818. Late Jan-early Feb.

Bridgefest. On the Houghton and Hancock waterfronts. Parade, arts and crafts show, entertainment,

powerboat races, fireworks. Phone 906/482-2388. Father's Day wkend. Mid-June.

Motels/Motor Lodges

★★ **BEST WESTERN INN FRANKLIN SQUARE.** *820 Shelden Ave (49931). 906/487-1700; fax 906/487-9432; toll-free 888/487-1700. www.bestwestern.com.* 105 rms, 7 story. June-Oct: S $65-$75; D $72-$82; each addl $6; suites $95-$110; under 12 free; higher rates special events; lower rates rest of yr. Crib $4. TV; cable (premium). Indoor pool; whirlpool, sauna. Restaurant 6:30 am-10 pm. Bar 2 pm-2 am. Ck-out 11 am. Meeting rms. Business servs avail. Downhill ski 3 mi; x-country ski 5 mi. Refrigerator avail. Cr cds: A, C, D, DS, JCB, MC, V.

🄳 ⏏ 🏊 ⇌ 🔌 🐾

★★ **BEST WESTERN KING'S INN.** *215 Shelden Ave (49931). 906/482-5000; fax 906/482-9795; res 888/482-5005. www.bestwestern.com.* 68 rms, 4 story. July-Sept: S $53-$69; D $63-$79; each addl $6; under 17 free; lower rates rest of yr. Crib free. Pet accepted. TV; cable (premium), VCR avail (movies). Indoor pool; whirlpool, sauna. Complimentary continental bkfst. Restaurant adj 11 am-midnight. Ck-out 11 am. Meeting rm. Valet serv. Downhill ski 2 mi; x-country ski 3 mi. Cr cds: A, C, D, DS, MC, V.

🄳 🐾 ⏏ 🏊 ⇌ ✈ 🔌 🐾 SC

★ **CHIPPEWA MOTEL.** *217 Willson Memorial Dr, Chassell (49916). 906/523-4611.* 15 rms, 7 kit. units. June-mid-Oct: S $36; D $44-$46; kit. units for 2-6, $50-$70; lower rates rest of yr. Crib $2. TV; cable. Coffee in rms. Restaurant adj 7 am-8 pm; Sun 8 am-7 pm. Ck-out 10 am. Meeting rms. Downhill ski 9 mi; x-country ski 1 blk. Picnic tables. Some rms overlook bay of Portage Lake. City park with beach, playground, picnic area and boat launch adj. Cr cds: C, D, DS, MC, V.

⏏ 🏊 🔌 🐾

★ **L'ANSE MOTEL AND SUITES.** *Rte 2 and US 41 Box 606, L'Anse (49946). 906/524-7820; fax 906/524-7247; toll-free 800/800-6198.* 21 rms, 2 with shower only. S $31; D $40; each addl $2. Crib $5. TV; cable (premium).

Complimentary coffee in lobby. Ck-out 11 am. X-country ski 2 mi. Cr cds: A, C, D, DS, MC, V.

★ **SUPER 8.** *790 Michigan Ave, Baraga (49908). 906/353-6680; fax 906/353-7246; res 800/800-8000. www. super8.com.* 40 rms, 2 story. S $41.88; D $49.88; each addl $4; under 12 free. Crib $2. Pet accepted. TV; cable. Complimentary continental bkfst. Restaurant opp. Ck-out 11 am. Meeting rm. Business servs avail. X-country ski 8 mi. Cr cds: A, C, D, DS, MC, V.

★ **SUPER 8 MOTEL.** *1200 E Lakeshore Dr (49931). 906/482-2240; fax 906/482-0686; res 800/800-8000. www. super8.com.* 86 rms, 2 story. S $48-$53; D $53-$58; each addl $3; suites $75; under 12 free. Crib $3. TV; cable (premium). Indoor pool; whirlpool, sauna. Complimentary continental bkfst. Restaurant nearby. Ck-out 11 am. Meeting rm. Downhill ski 1 mi; x-country ski ½ mi. Cr cds: A, C, MC, V.

★ **VACATIONLAND MOTEL.** *US 41 Box 93 (49931). 906/482-5351; toll-free 800/822-3279.* 24 rms, 1-2 story. July-Labor Day: S $34-$58; D $44-$58; family rates; lower rates rest of yr. Crib $2. TV; cable (premium). Heated pool. Complimentary continental bkfst. Restaurant nearby. Ck-out 11 am. Sundries. Downhill ski 5 mi; x-country ski 3 mi. Picnic tables. 18-hole golf adj. Cr cds: A, C, D, DS, MC, V.

Houghton Lake

(E-5) *See also Grayling, Harrison*

Pop 3,353 **Elev** 1,162 ft
Area code 989 **Zip** 48629
Information Chamber of Commerce, 1625 W Houghton Lake Dr; 989/366-5644 or 800/248-5253
Web www.houghtonlakechamber.org

The Houghton Lake area is the gateway to a popular north country resort area including three of the largest inland lakes in the state and 200,000 acres of state forests.

What to See and Do

Higgins Lake. One of the most beautiful in America, Higgins Lake covers 10,317 acres and has 25 mi of sandy shoreline. Between US 27 and I-75.

Houghton Lake. Largest inland lake in Michigan. The source of the Muskegon River. This lake has a 32-mi shoreline and 22,000 acres of water. Also 200 mi of groomed and marked snowmobile trails. A variety of resorts are in the area. Between US 27 and I-75.

St. Helen Lake. This pine-bordered lake has 12 mi of shoreline. E on MI 55, then N on MI 76.

Special Event

Tip-Up-Town USA Ice Festival. Ice-fishing contests, games, food, parade, carnival. Third and fourth wkend Jan. Phone 989/366-5644.

Motels/Motor Lodges

★★ **VAL HALLA MOTEL.** *9869 W Houghton Lake Dr (48629). 989/422-5137.* 12 rms, 2 kits. Memorial Day-Labor Day: S $38-$48, D $45-$62; each addl $5; 2-bedrm kit. apts $525/wk; some lower rates rest of yr. Crib $1. Pet accepted. TV. Heated pool. Restaurant nearby. Ck-out 11 am. Free airport transportation. Putting green. Downhill ski 17 mi; x-country ski 2 mi. Lawn games. Private patios. Picnic table, grills. Cr cds: A, DS, JCB, MC, V.

★ **VENTURE INN MOTEL.** *8939 W Houghton Lake Dr (48629). 989/422-5591.* 12 rms. Mid-June-Labor Day: S $40-$45; D $50; each addl $5; higher rates hols; lower rates rest of yr. Crib $2. TV. Heated pool. Complimentary coffee in rms. Restaurant opp open 24 hrs. Ck-out 11 am. Downhill ski 20 mi; x-country ski 10 mi. Cr cds: MC, V.

Cottage Colonies

★ **MORRIS' NORTHERNAIRE RESORT.** *11544 Westshore Dr*

(48629). 989/422-6644. www.morris resort.com. 6 cottages for 3-8, 5 with shower only. June-Labor Day: S, D $75; wkly rates; lower rates rest of yr. Crib free. TV; cable. Playground. Restaurant nearby. Ck-out 10 am. Grocery 3 mi. Coin lndry 1 mi. Lawn games. Picinic tables. On beach. Cr cds: MC, V.

★★ **WOODBINE VILLA.** *12122 Westshore Dr (48629). 517/422-5349.* 9 kit. cottages. No A/C. Wkly: 2-4, $525; 4-6, $575-$625; daily rates Apr-mid-June, Labor Day-late Nov; higher rates special events. Crib free. TV; cable. Playground. Restaurant nearby. Ck-out 10 am, ck-in 4 pm. Grocery, package store 2 mi, coin lndry 3 blks. Sand beach, dock; motorboats, rowboats. Downhill ski 15 mi; x-country ski 5 mi. Sauna. Game rm. Lawn games. Picnic table, grill. Fish-cleaning house. Screened porches. Rustic setting with private beach on Houghton Lake. Cr cds: MC, V.

Hulbert

(B-5) *See also Newberry, Soo Junction*

Pop 250 **Elev** 750 ft **Area code** 906 **Zip** 49748

North of Hulbert is a particularly wild portion of the Upper Peninsula with much wildlife. Popular activities are fishing for northern pike, bass, perch, and trout on Hulbert Lake; canoeing; and other outdoor sports.

What to See and Do

Tahquamenon Falls State Park. (see NEWBERRY) E on MI 28, then approx 15 mi N on MI 123. Phone 906/492-3415.

Indian River

(C-5) *See also Cheboygan, Petoskey*

Pop 2,500 **Elev** 616 ft **Area code** 231 **Zip** 49749

Information Chamber of Commerce, 3435 S Straits Hwy, PO Box 57; 231/238-9325 or 800/394-8310

Web www.irmi.org

What to See and Do

Burt Lake State Park. Approx 400 acres. Beach, beachhouse, waterski-ing, fishing for walleyed pike and perch, boating (ramp, rentals); pic-nicking, playground, concession, camping. Standard fees. (May-Oct, daily) ½ mi S off I-75, exit 310. Phone 231/238-9392. ¢¢

Canoeing. Trips on Sturgeon and/or Pigeon rivers; difficulty varies with streams. Various trips offered. Res advised. Phone 231/238-9092.

> **Sturgeon & Pigeon River Outfit-ters.** Canoeing, tubing, kayaking. (May-mid-Sept) Contact 4271 S Straits Hwy. Phone 231/238-8181.

> **Tomahawk Trails Canoe Livery.** (May-Oct, daily) Contact PO Box 814. Phone 231/238-8703.

Cross in the Woods. Wooden crucifix 55 ft tall. Outdoor shrines. (Mar-Nov, daily) 1 mi W of I-75 exit 310, on MI 68. Phone 231/238-8973. **FREE**

Motel/Motor Lodge

★ **NOR-GATE.** *4846 Straits Hwy (49749). 231/238-7788.* 12 rms, 3 kits. S $34; D $44; each addl $3; kit. units $40-$69; wkly rates. Crib $5. TV; cable (premium). Complimentary coffee in lobby. Restaurant nearby. Ck-out 11 am. Picnic tables. State park ½ mi. Cr cds: A, DS, MC, V.

Iron Mountain

(C-2) *See also Iron River, Ishpeming*

Settled 1878 **Pop** 8,525 **Elev** 1,138 ft **Area code** 906 **Zip** 49801

Information Tourism Association of the Dickinson County Area, 600 S Stephenson Ave, PO Box 672; 906/774-2002 or 800/236-2447

Web www.dickinsonchamber.com

After more than a half-century of production, the underground shaft mines of high-grade ore deposits here have closed. Logging, tourism, and wood products are the main economic factors now, and Iron Mountain is the distribution point for the entire Menominee Range area. A nearby bluff heavily striped with iron ore gave the city its name. Abandoned mines, cave-ins, and a huge Cornish mine pump, preserved as tourist attractions, are reminders of mining days.

What to See and Do

Iron Mountain Iron Mine. Mine train tours 2,600 ft of underground drifts and tunnels 400 ft below surface. Working machinery, museum. Tours (June-mid-Oct, daily). 8 mi E on US 2 in Vulcan. Phone 906/563-8077. ¢¢

Lake Antoine Park. Swimming, boating, waterskiing; nature trail, picnicking, concession, improved county campgrounds (fee); band concerts. (Memorial Day-Labor Day, daily) 2 mi NE. Phone 906/774-8875. ¢¢¢

Menominee Range Historical Museum. More than 100 exhibits depict life on the Menominee Iron Range in the 1880s and early 1900s; one-rm school, Victorian parlor, trapper's cabin, country store. (Mid-May-Sept, daily; rest of yr, by appt) 300 E Ludington St, in Carnegie Public Library. Phone 906/774-4276. Combination ticket ¢¢¢ incl

Cornish Pumping Engine & Mining Museum. Features largest steam-driven pumping engine built in US, with 40-ft-diameter flywheel in engine and weighing 160 tons; also display of underground mining equipment used in Michigan; WWII glider display. (Mid-May-Sept, daily; rest of yr, by appt) Kent St. Phone 906/774-1086. ¢¢

Skiing. Pine Mountain Lodge. Triple, two double chairlifts, rope tow; snowmaking, patrol, school, rentals; nine-hole golf; two tennis courts; indoor/outdoor pools; restaurant, cafeteria, bar; lodge, condos. Longest run ¾ mi; vertical drop 500 ft. (Late Nov-early Apr, daily) X-country trails. N3332 Pine Mountain Rd, 2½ mi N off US 2/141. Phone 906/774-2747.

Special Events

Pine Mountain Ski Jumping Tournament. Pine Mtn Lodge. Jan. Phone 906/774-2747.

Festival of the Arts. Crafts demonstrations, antique car show, concerts, square and folk dancing, community theater, international foods. Mid-June-mid-Aug. Phone 906/774-2945.

Wood-Bee Carvers Show. Premiere Center. Wood carvers competition and show. Phone 906/774-2945. Oct.

Motels/Motor Lodges

★★ **BEST WESTERN EXECUTIVE INN.** *1518 S Stephenson Ave (Us 2) (49801).* 906/774-2040; fax 906/774-0238; toll-free 800/528-1234. *www. bestwestern.com.* 57 rms, 2 story. June-Sept: S $56; D $63; each addl $6; lower rates rest of yr. Crib free. Pet accepted. TV; cable (premium), VCR avail (movies $2.50). Indoor pool. Complimentary continental bkfst. Ck-out 11 am. Downhill/x-country ski 3 mi. Cr cds: A, C, D, DS, MC, V.
🔲 🐾 ⛷ 🏊 ⚃ 🔥 SC

★★ **COMFORT INN.** *1555 N Stephenson Ave (49801).* 906/774-5505; fax 906/774-2631; toll-free 800/638-7949. *www.comfortinn.com.* 48 rms, 2 story. S $52; D $59; each addl $6; under 18 free. Crib free. TV; cable (premium), VCR avail. Complimentary continental bkfst. Restaurant nearby. Ck-out 11 am. Meeting rm. Business servs avail. Valet serv. Coin lndry. Downhill/x-country ski 2 mi. Exercise equipt. Some refrigerators. Cr cds: A, C, D, DS, ER, JCB, MC, V.
⛷ ⚃ 🔥 🏋

★ **SUPER 8.** *2702 N Stephenson Ave (49801).* 906/774-3400; fax 906/774-9903; toll-free 888/711-8090. *www. super8.com.* 90 rms, 2 story. S $44.88; D $56.88; each addl $6; suites from $64.88; under 12 free. Crib free. TV; cable (premium), VCR avail. Pool; whirlpool, sauna. Complimentary continental bkfst. Restaurant nearby. Ck-out 11 am. Coin lndry. Meeting rm. Business servs avail. Downhill/x-country ski 4 mi. Some refrigerators. Picnic tables. Cr cds: A, D, DS, MC, V.
🔲 ⛷ 🏊 ⚃ 🔥 SC

★ **TIMBERS MOTOR LODGE.** *200 S Stephenson Ave (49801).* 906/774-

7600; fax 906/774-6222; toll-free 800/433-8533. www.thetimbers.com. 53 rms, 2 story. S $40; D $50; each addl $5; suites $54. Crib $4. TV; cable (premium). Indoor pool; whirlpool. Restaurant nearby. Ck-out noon. Meeting rms. Business servs avail. In-rm modem link. Downhill/x-country ski 1½ mi. Exercise equipt; sauna. Cr cds: A, C, D, DS, MC, V.

D ⚲ ⚳ 🕴 ⚲ 🏂

Iron River

(C-2) *See also Iron Mountain*

Pop 2,095 **Elev** 1,510 ft
Area code 906 **Zip** 49935
Information Iron County Chamber of Commerce, 50 E Genesee St; 906/265-3822 or 888/879-IRON
Web www.iron.org

Just north of the Wisconsin-Michigan state line, Iron River was one of the last of the large mining towns to spring up on the Menominee Range. Lumbering has also played a prominent part in the town's past. Ottawa National Forest (see IRONWOOD) lies a few miles to the west, and a Ranger District office is located here.

What to See and Do

Iron County Museum. Indoor/outdoor museum of 22 buildings. Miniature logging exhibit with more than 2,000 pieces; iron mining dioramas; more than 100 major exhibits; log homestead; 1896 one-rm schoolhouse; logging camp, home of composer Carrie Jacobs-Bond; Lee LeBlanc Wildlife Art Gallery. Annual ethnic festivals (Scandinavian, Polish, Italian, Yugoslavian; inquire for schedule). (Mid-May-Oct, daily; rest of yr, by appt) 2 mi S on County 424 in Caspian. Phone 906/265-2617. ¢

Skiing, Ski Brule. Four chairlifts, two T-bars, pony lift, rope tow; patrol, school, rentals, snowmaking; chalet and condo lodging, restaurant, cafeteria, bar, nursery. Seventeen runs, longest run one mi; vertical drop 500 ft. (Nov-Apr, daily) X-country trails. 119 Big Bear Rd, 3 mi SW off MI 189. Phone 906/265-4957. ¢¢¢¢

Special Events

Bass Festival. Canoe races on the Paint River, softball game, barbecue, music, and events at Runkle Park and Runkle Lake. First wkend July. Phone 906/265-3822.

Ferrous Frolics. Iron County Museum. Arts, crafts, demonstrations, band concert, flea market. Third wkend July. Phone 906/265-2617.

Upper Peninsula Championship Rodeo. Fairgrounds. Late July. Phone 906/265-3822.

Iron County Fair. Fairgrounds. Four days late Aug. Phone 888/879-4766.

Ironwood

(B-7) *See also Wakefield; also see Hurley, WI*

Settled 1885 **Pop** 6,849 **Elev** 1,503 ft
Area code 906 **Zip** 49938
Information Ironwood Area Chamber of Commerce, 150 N Lowell; 906/932-1122
Web www.ironwoodmi.org

Ironwood, the first part of Gogebic County to be settled, is a center for summer and winter recreation. The town was linked at first with fur trading. It quickly blossomed into a mining town when a deposit of iron was found in what is now the eastern section of the city. John R. Wood, one of the first mining captains, was known as "Iron" because of his interest in ore—thus, the name Ironwood.

What to See and Do

Black River Harbor. Deep-sea fishing boats for rent, boat rides, Lake Superior cruises; picnicking, playground, camping. 4 mi E, then 15 mi N on County 513. Phone 906/932-7250.

Copper Peak Ski Flying. The only ski flying facility in North America, and one of six in the world, where athletes test their skill in an event that requires more athletic ability than ski jumping; skiers reach speeds of more than 60 mi per hour and fly farther than 500 ft. International tournament held every winter. In summer, chairlift and elevator rides take visitors 240 ft above the crest of Copper

Peak for view of three states, Lake Superior, and Canada. (Mid-June-Labor Day, daily; Sept-Oct, wkends) 12 mi N on County 513. Phone 906/932-3500. ¢¢

Hiawatha—World's Tallest Indian. Statue of famous Iroquois stands 52 ft high and looks north to the legendary "shining big-sea-water"—Gitchee Gumee, also known as Lake Superior. Houk St.

Little Girl's Point Park. Notable for the agate pebbles on the beaches. Picnic tables (fee), campsites (fee); Native American burial grounds. (May-Sept) County 505 N, 18 mi N, off US 2; on Lake Superior. Phone 906/932-1420.

Ottawa National Forest. Wooded hills, picturesque lakes and streams, waterfalls, J. W. Toumey Nursery, Black River Harbor, North Country National Scenic Trail, Watersmeet Visitor Center and Sylvania, Sturgeon River Gorge, and McCormick Wildernesses are all part of this 953,600-acre forest. Fishing for trout, muskie, northern pike, walleye, bass, and panfish; swimming, canoeing, boat landing; hunting for big and small game, hiking, x-country and downhill skiing, picnicking, camping. Some fees. (Daily) E via US 2, MI 28. Contact Supervisor, 2100 E Cloverland Dr. Phone 906/932-1330. **FREE**

Skiing.

Big Powderhorn Mountain. Nine double chairlifts; patrol, school, rentals; three restaurants, cafeteria, three bars, nursery. Twenty-five runs; longest run one mi; vertical drop 600 ft. (Thanksgiving-early Apr, daily) N11375 Powderhorn Rd. Phone 906/932-4838.

Blackjack. Four double chairlifts, two rope tows; patrol, school, rentals; cafeteria, restaurant, bar, nursery, lodging. Longest run one mi; vertical drop 465 ft. (Nov-Mar, daily) 12 mi E of MI 51 via US 2, Blackjack exit. Phone 906/229-5115. ¢¢¢¢

Mount Zion. One of the highest points on the Gogebic Range, with 1,750-ft altitude, 1,150 ft above Lake Superior. Double chairlift, two rope tows; patrol, school, rentals; snack bar. Longest run ¾ mi; vertical drop 300 ft. (Mid-Dec-Mar, Tues-Sun; closed Dec 25) Two mi

of x-country trails, rentals. ¾ mi N of US 2 at E4946 Jackson Rd. Phone 906/932-3718.

Special Event

Gogebic County Fair. Fairgrounds. Phone 906/932-1420. Second wkend Aug.

Motels/Motor Lodges

★ **BLACK RIVER LODGE.** *N12390 Black River Rd (49938). 906/932-3857; fax 906/932-6601.* 25 rms, 12 A/C, 2 story, 4 townhouses (no A/C), some kits. Dec-Mar: S $30-$45; D $35-$65; Suites $35-$98; kit. units $45-$100; townhouses $80-$180; wkly rates; ski plans; AP, MAP avail; lower rates rest of yr. Crib free. TV; cable (premium), VCR avail. Indoor pool; whirlpool. Playground. Restaurant (hrs vary). Bar 6 pm-2 am. Ck-out 11 am. Meeting rms. Downhill ski 1½ mi; x-country ski on site. Lawn games. Game rm. Hiking. Fishing/hunting guides. Some refrigerators. Picnic tables, grill. Cr cds: DS, MC, V.
⬛🐾🏊🛏🎿🔥

★★ **COMFORT INN.** *210 E Cloverland Dr (49938). 906/932-2224; fax 906/932-9929; res 800/572-9412. www.comfortinn.com.* 63 rms, 2 story. S $52-$100; D $59-$125; each addl $6; under 18 free. Crib free. TV; cable (premium), VCR avail (movies). Indoor pool; whirlpool. Complimentary continental bkfst. Restaurant opp open 24 hrs. Ck-out 11 am. Meeting rm. Business servs avail. Downhill/x-country ski 6 mi. Some refrigerators, wet bars. Cr cds: A, D, DS, MC, V.
⬛🏊🛏🎿🔥

Ishpeming

(B-2) *See also Iron Mountain, Marquette*

Founded 1844 **Pop** 7,200
Area code 906 **Zip** 49849
Information Ishpeming-Negaunee Area Chamber of Commerce, 661 Palms Ave; 906/486-4841
Web www.marquette.org

Iron mines gave birth to this city and still sustain it. Skiing is the basis of its recreation and tourism business. In 1887, three Norwegians formed a ski club in Ishpeming, which is a Native American word for "high grounds." That ski club eventually became a national ski association.

What to See and Do

⭐ **National Ski Hall of Fame and Ski Museum.** Affiliated with the US Ski Association. Houses national trophies and displays of old skis and ski equipment, incl a replica of the oldest-known ski and ski pole in the world. Roland Palmedo National Ski Library, collection of ski publications for researchers in-house only. (Daily; closed hols) Between 2nd and 3rd Sts, on US 41. Phone 906/485-6323. ¢¢

Suicide Bowl. Incl five ski-jumping hills from mini-hill to 70-m hill. There are also four x-country trails; one is lighted for eve use. On Cliffs Dr at E end of city. Phone 906/485-4242. ¢¢

Van Riper State Park. Approx 1,000 acres on Lake Michigamme. Swimming, waterskiing, bathhouse, fishing, boating (ramp, rentals); hunting, hiking, picnic grounds, concession, playground, camping. Standard fees. (Daily) 17 mi W on US 41. Phone 906/339-4461. ¢¢

Special Event

Annual Ski Jumping Championships. Paul Bietila Memorial. Also cross-country ski race. Feb. Phone 906/485-6323.

Motel/Motor Lodge

★ ★ **BEST WESTERN COUNTRY INN.** 850 US 41 W (49849). 906/485-6345; fax 906/485-6348; toll-free 800/780-7234. www.bestwestern.com. 60 rms, 2 story. Mid-June-Oct: S $70; D $75; each addl $5; family rates; ski plans; lower rates rest of yr. Crib free. Pet accepted. TV; cable (premium). Indoor pool; whirlpool. Complimentary continental bkfst. Complimentary coffee in lobby. Restaurant adj 6 am-10 pm; Fri, Sat to 11 pm. Ck-out noon. Business servs avail. Downhill ski 15 mi; x-country ski 2 mi. Health club privileges. Game rm. Cr cds: A, C, D, DS, MC, V.

D ◀ ⊱ ⇌ ⊠ ⋒ SC

Isle Royale National Park

(N of Upper Peninsula, on island in Lake Superior)

This unique wilderness area, covering 571,790 acres, is the largest island in Lake Superior, 15 miles from Canada (the nearest mainland), 18 miles from Minnesota, and 45 miles from Michigan. There are no roads, and no automobiles are allowed. The main island, 45 miles long and 8½ miles across at its widest point, is surrounded by more than 400 smaller islands. Isle Royale may be reached by boat from Houghton or Copper Harbor (see) in Michigan, from Grand Portage in Minnesota, or by seaplane from Houghton. Schedules vary; inquire each year around January 1. Contact Superintendent, Isle Royale National Park, 800 E Lakeshore Dr, Houghton 49931; phone 906/482-0984.

The only wildlife here are those animals able to fly, swim, drift across the water, or travel on ice. Moose, wolf, fox, and beaver are the dominant mammals; however, before 1900 no moose existed on the island. The current population of 700 evolved from a few moose that swam to the island around 1912. In the winter of 1949 wolves came across on the ice and stayed. More than 200 species of birds have been observed, including loons, bald eagles, and ospreys.

Prehistoric peoples discovered copper on the island 4,000 years ago. Later, white men tried to mine in a number of places. The remains of these mining operations may still be seen; some of the ancient mining pits date back 3,800 years.

There are more than 165 miles of foot trails leading to beautiful inland lakes, more than 20 of which have game fish, including pike, perch, walleye, and, in a few, whitefish cisco. There are trout in many streams and lakes. Fishing is under National Park Service and Michigan regulations (see FISHING AND HUNTING in state text). Boat rental and charter fishing are available at Rock Harbor Lodge (see). Basic supplies are available on the island in limited quantities. Nights are usually cold; bring warm clothing and be prepared to rough it. Group camping is available for parties of seven to ten people; inquire for group information; group campsites must be reserved. The park is open from approximately May to October.

Rock Harbor Lodge is at the east end of the island, about 3½ miles east of Mott Island, which is the Park Service headquarters during the summer. The lodge offers rooms, cabins, restaurant, and a camp store. Room reservations should be made at least three months in advance; lodge open June through Labor Day. For lodge information write National Park Concessions, Inc., PO Box 605, Houghton 49931, phone 906/337-4993 (summer); or National Park Concessions, Inc., PO Box 27, Mammoth Cave, KY 42259, phone 270/773-2191 (winter).

Jackson

(H-5) *See also Ann Arbor, Battle Creek, Lansing*

Founded 1829 **Pop** 37,446 **Elev** 960 ft **Area code** 517

Information Convention & Tourist Bureau, 6007 Ann Arbor Rd, 49201; 517/764-4440 or 800/245-5282

Web www.jackson-mich.org

Four major highways and heavy rail traffic make this a transportation center. Industries are the foundation of the city's economy. In Jackson on July 6, 1854, the Republican Party was officially born at a convention held "under the green spreading oaks," as there was no hall large enough to accommodate the delegates. Each year, the city attracts thousands of tourists, who use it as a base to explore more than 200 natural lakes in Jackson County.

What to See and Do

Cascades Falls Park. Approx 465 acres. Fishing ponds and pier, paddle-boating (rentals); picnicking, playground; 18-hole miniature golf, driving range; fitness and jogging trail; basketball, tennis, and horseshoe courts; restaurant. Some fees. Brown St, via I-94 to exit 138. Phone 517/788-4320. Also here are

Sparks Illuminated Cascades Waterfalls. Approx 500 ft of water cascading over 16 waterfalls and six fountains in continually changing patterns of light, color, and music. (Memorial Day-Labor Day, nightly) Phone 517/788-4320. ¢¢ Fee incl

Cascades-Sparks Museum. Depicts early history of falls and its builder, Captain William Sparks; original drawings, models, audiovisual displays. (Memorial Day-Labor Day, nightly) Phone 517/788-4320.

Dahlem Environmental Education Center. Nature center with five mi of trails through forests, fields, marshes; ½-mi "special needs" trail for the disabled; visitor center with exhibits, gift shop. (Tues-Sun) 7117 S Jackson Rd. Phone 517/782-3453. **FREE**

Ella Sharp Park. Approx 530 acres with 18-hole golf course, tennis courts, ballfields, swimming pool, miniature golf, picnic facilities, formal gardens. (Daily) 3225 4th St, at S edge of city. Phone 517/788-4040. **FREE** In park is

Ella Sharp Museum. Complex incl Victorian farmhouse, historic farm lane, one-rm schoolhouse, log cabin, galleries with rotating art and historic exhibits; studios; planetarium; visitor center. (Tues-Sun; closed hols) Phone 517/787-2320. ¢¢

★ **Michigan Space Center.** US space artifacts and memorabilia displayed in geodesic dome, incl Gemini trainer, Apollo 9 Command Module, replica of space shuttle, *Challenger* memorial, space food, space suits, lunar rover, moon rock, satellites, orbiters, landers, giant rocket engines; films and special presentations. Picnicking and children's play areas. Gift shop. (May-Labor Day, daily; Jan-Apr, Tues-Sun) Phone 517/787-4425. ¢¢

Republican Party founding site.
Marked with a tablet dedicated by
President William Howard Taft. W
Franklin and 2nd Sts.

Waterloo Farm Museum. Tours of
furnished pioneer farmhouse (1855-
1885), bakehouse, windmill, farm
workshop, barn, milk cellar, log
house, granary. (June-Aug, Tues-Sun
afternoons; Sept, Sat and Sun; Pioneer Festival second Sun Oct) 10 mi
E via I-94 to exit 150, N on Mt Hope
Rd, E on Waterloo-Munith Rd, at
9998 Waterloo-Munith Rd, near
Waterloo. Phone 517/596-2254. ¢¢

Waterloo State Recreation Area.
This is the state's largest recreation
area, with 20,072 acres. Swimming,
beach, bathhouse, waterskiing, fishing, boating (ramp, rentals) on
numerous lakes; horseback riding,
nature trails, hunting, picnicking,
concession, cabins, tent and trailer
sites; geology center. Standard fees.
15 mi E on I-94, then N on unnumbered road.

Special Events

Harness racing. Jackson Harness
Raceway, Jackson County Fairgrounds. Pari-mutuel betting. Phone
517/788-4500. Spring and fall races.

Rose Festival. Ella Sharp Park.
Parade, pageant, garden tours, enter-
tainment. Phone 517/787-2065. Mid-
May-mid-June.

Michigan Speedway. SE on MI 50 to
US 12, then 1 mi W. NASCAR, ARCA,
IROC and Indy Car races on a 2-mi
oval track. Contact 12626 US 12,
Brooklyn 49230; 800/354-1010. Mid-
June-mid-Aug.

Hot-Air Balloon Jubilee. Jackson
County Airport. Competitive balloon
events; skydivers; arts and crafts.
Phone 517/782-1515. Mid-July.

Jackson County Fair. Stage shows;
displays of produce, handicrafts,
farm animals; midway shows; rides.
Phone 517/788-4405. Second wk Aug.

**Civil War Muster & Battle Reenact-
ment.** Cascade Falls Park. Thousands
of participants re-create a different
Civil War battle each yr; living history demonstrations, parades, food,
entertainment. Third wkend Aug.
Phone 517/788-4320.

Motels/Motor Lodges

★ ★ **BAYMONT INN.** *2035 N Service
Dr (49202). 517/789-6000; fax 517/
782-6836; toll-free 800/428-3438.
www.baymontinns.com.* 67 rms, 2
story. S $39.95-$52.95; D $46.95-
$59.95; family rates. Crib free. Pet
accepted. TV, cable (premium). Complimentary continental bkfst. Complimentary coffee in rms. Restaurant
adj 6:30 am-10 pm. Ck-out noon.
Meeting rm. Business servs avail.
Valet serv. Some refrigerators. Cr cds:
A, C, D, DS, MC, V.
D 🐾 ⊠ 🔥 SC

★ ★ **COUNTRY HEARTH INN.** *1111
Boardman Rd (49202). 517/783-6404;
fax 517/783-6529; toll-free 800/267-
5023.* 73 rms, 2 story. S $53-$67; D
$59-$73; each addl $6; kit. units $67-
$73; under 18 free; higher rates auto
races. Crib free. TV; cable. Complimentary continental bkfst. Restaurant nearby. Ck-out noon. Business
servs avail. Health club privileges.
Country inn decor. Cr cds: A, C, D,
DS, MC, V.
D ⊠ 🔥 SC

★ ★ **HOLIDAY INN.** *2000 Holiday
Inn Dr (49202). 517/783-2681; fax
517/783-5744; res 800/465-4329.
www.holiday-inn.com.* 184 rms, 2
story. S, D $79-$89; under 19 free.
Crib free. Pet accepted; $15. TV;
cable, VCR avail. Heated pool; whirlpool, sauna. Restaurant 6:30 am-2
pm, 5-10 pm. Bar 4 pm-midnight;
Sun 5-10 pm. Ck-out 11 am. Coin
lndry. Meeting rms. Business servs
avail. Bellhops. Putting green; miniature golf. X-country ski 10 mi. Game
rm. Cr cds: A, MC, V.
D 🐾 ⊁ ⊷ ⊠ 🔥 SC

Restaurants

★ ★ **GILBERT'S STEAK HOUSE.**
*2323 Shirley Dr (49202). 517/782-
7135. www.gilbertsteakhouse.com.* Hrs:
11 am-10 pm; Fri, Sat to 11 pm; Sun
noon-7 pm. Closed hols. Res
accepted. Bar. Lunch $4.95-$8.50,
dinner $9.95-$19.95. Child's menu.
Specializes in steak, prime rib,
seafood. Victorian atmosphere. Cr
cds: A, D, DS, MC, V.
D ⊠

★ ★ **KNIGHT'S STEAKHOUSE &
GRILL.** *2125 Horton Rd (49203).*

517/783-2777. Hrs: 11 am-10 pm; Fri, Sat to 11 pm; early-bird dinner Mon-Fri 4-6 pm. Closed Sun; hols. Res accepted. Bar. Dinner $5-$25. Child's menu. Specializes in steak. Modern contemporary decor; Tiffany-style lighting. Cr cds: A, MC, V.

Kalamazoo

(G-4) *See also Battle Creek, Paw Paw, Three Rivers*

Settled 1829 **Pop** 80,277 **Elev** 780 ft **Area code** 616

Information Kalamazoo County Convention and Visitors Bureau, 346 W Michigan Ave, 49007; 616/381-4003 or 800/222-6363

Web www.kazoofun.com

Yes, there really is a Kalamazoo—a unique name, immortalized in song and verse. The name is derived from the Native American name for the Kalamazoo River, which means "where the water boils in the pot." The concept is noted not only in the community's name but also in its cultural, industrial, and recreational makeup. Diversified industry from bedding plants to pharmaceuticals thrive here. Many recreational activities complete the picture.

What to See and Do

Bronson Park. A bronze tablet marks the spot where Abraham Lincoln made an antislavery speech in 1856. Extending for two blks on South St.

Crane Park. Formal floral gardens, tennis courts. Park St, at the crest of Westnedge Hill overlooking city.

Echo Valley. 60-mph tobogganing (toboggans furnished), ice-skating (rentals). (Dec-Mar, Fri-Sun; closed Dec 25) 8495 E H Ave. Phone 616/349-3291. ¢¢¢

Gilmore-CCCA Museum. More than 120 antique autos tracing the significant technical developments in automotive transportation; on 90 acres of landscaped grounds. (Mid-May-mid-Oct, daily) 6865 Hickory Rd, 15 mi NE via MI 43 in Hickory Corners. Phone 616/671-5089. ¢¢¢

 Kalamazoo Air Zoo. (Kalamazoo Aviation History Museum) Home to more than 70 beautiful historic and restored aircraft of the WWII period, many in flying condition; exhibits, video theater, flight simulator, observation deck. Tours of Restoration Center (May-Sept). Flight of the Day (May-Sept, afternoons). (Daily; closed major hols) 3101 E Milham Rd, on the grounds of Kalamazoo/Battle Creek Airport. Phone 616/382-6555. ¢¢¢

Kalamazoo College. (1833) 1,300 students. Private, liberal arts college. Red-brick streets and Georgian architecture characterize this school, one of the 100 oldest colleges in the nation. A 3,023-pipe organ is in Stetson Chapel; Bach Festival (Mar); Festival Playhouse (June-July). 1200 Academy St. Phone 616/337-7000.

Kalamazoo Institute of Arts. Galleries, school, shop, library, and auditorium. Collection of 20th-century American art; circulating exhibits. (Tues-Sun; closed hols; also Aug) 314 S Park St. Phone 616/349-7775. **Donation**

Kalamazoo Nature Center. Interpretive Center; restored 1860s pioneer homestead; nature trails (tours by appt); barnyard (May-Labor Day); Public Orientation Room programs, slides, movies, live animals. (Daily; closed hols) 7000 N Westnedge Ave, 5 mi N. Phone 616/381-1574. ¢¢

Kalamazoo Valley Museum. Incl Mary Jane Stryker Interactive Learning Hall with an interactive theater, science gallery, Challenger Learning Center, Egyptian artifacts, and Universe Theater and Planetarium. (Mon-Sat, Sun afternoons) 230 N Rose St. Phone 616/373-7990. ¢

Skiing.

Bittersweet Ski Area. Quad, four triple chairlifts, double chairlift, five rope tows; school, rentals; lodge, cafeteria, bar. Sixteen trails; longest run 2,300 ft; vertical drop 300 ft. Night skiing. (Dec-Mar, daily) 600 River Rd, 18 mi N via US 131, MI 89 W to Jefferson Rd exit. Phone 616/694-2820. ¢¢¢¢¢

Timber Ridge Ski Area. Four chairlifts, Pomalift, three rope tows; patrol, school, snowmaking; snack bar, cafeteria, two bars. Store, repairs, rentals. Fifteen trails; longest run ⅔ mi; vertical drop 250 ft. (Late Nov-mid-Mar, daily) 5 mi N on US 131, then W at D Ave exit. Phone 616/694-9449. ¢¢¢¢

Western Michigan University. (1903) 28,000 students. Contemporary plays, musical comedies, operas, and melodramas offered in Shaw and York theaters. Touring professional shows, dance programs, and entertainers in Miller Auditorium; dance and music performances are featured in the Irving S. Gilmore University Theatre Complex. Art exhibits in Sangren Hall and East Hall. Inquire for schedules. W Michigan Ave. Phone 616/387-1000.

Special Events

Kalamazoo County Flowerfest. July. Phone 616/381-3597.

Kalamazoo County Fair. Aug. Phone 616/381-4003.

Wine and Harvest Festival. Kalamazoo-Paw Paw. First wkend Sept. Phone 800/222-6363.

Motels/Motor Lodges

★★ **BEST WESTERN HOSPITALITY INN.** 3640 E Cork St (49001). 616/381-1900; fax 616/373-6136; res 800/528-1234. www.bestwestern.com. 124 rms, 3 story. S $59-$79; D $69-$89; each addl $8; under 14 free. Crib free. TV; cable. Indoor pool; whirlpool. Complimentary continental bkfst. Coffee in rms. Restaurant nearby. Ck-out noon. Exercise equipt; sauna. Meeting rms. Business servs avail. Valet serv. Downhill/x-country ski 15 mi. Cr cds: A, D, DS, ER, MC, V.
🄳 🏊 🌊 🏋 ✈ 🖎 🔥 SC

★ **DAYS INN.** 3522 Sprinkle Rd (49001). 616/381-7070; fax 616/381-4341; res 800/329-7466. www.daysinn.com. 146 rms, 2 story. S, studio rms $75; D $83; under 18 free. Crib free. Pet accepted. TV; cable (premium), VCR avail. 2 pools, 1 indoor; whirlpool, sauna, poolside serv. Restaurant 6:30 am-10 pm; Fri, Sat to 11 pm. Bar 11:30 am-midnight; closed Sun. Ck-out noon. Coin lndry. Meeting

rms. Business servs avail. Bellhops. Valet serv. Sundries. Free airport transportation. Downhill/x-country ski 15 mi. Adj to stadium. Cr cds: A, D, DS, MC, V.
🄳 🏊 🌊 ✈ 🖎 🔥

★★ **FAIRFIELD INN.** 3800 E Cork St (49001). 616/344-8300; fax 616/344-8300; res 800/228-2800. www.fairfieldinn.com. 133 rms, 3 story. Late May-mid-Sept: S $39.95; D $55.95; each addl $3; under 18 free; lower rates rest of yr. Crib free. TV; cable. Heated pool. Complimentary continental bkfst. Restaurant adj 6 am-midnight. Ck-out noon. Meeting rm. Business servs avail. Valet serv. Downhill/x-country ski 15 mi. Cr cds: A, D, DS, MC, V.
🄳 🌊 🖎 🔥

★★ **HOLIDAY INN.** 2747 S 11th St (49009). 616/375-6000; fax 616/375-1220; res 800/465-4329. www.holiday-inn.com. 186 rms, 4 story. S, D $79-$89; studio rms $79; under 19 free. Crib free. Pet accepted. TV. Indoor pool; whirlpool, poolside serv. Restaurant 6:30 am-10:30 pm; Fri, Sat to 11 pm. Bar 11:30 am-midnight; Fri, Sat to 1 am. Ck-out 11 am. Coin lndry. Meeting rm. Business servs avail. Bellhops. Valet serv. Putting green. Downhill ski 8 mi; x-country ski 3 mi. Exercise rm; sauna. Game rm. Cr cds: A, D, DS, MC, V.
🄳 🏊 🌊 🏋 🖎 🔥

★★ **LA QUINTA INN.** 3750 Easy St (49001). 616/388-3551; fax 616/342-9132; toll-free 800/687-6667. www.laquinta.com. 116 rms, 2 story. S $61; D $67; each addl $6; under 18 free. Crib free. Pet accepted. TV; cable (premium). Heated pool. Complimentary continental bkfst. Restaurant adj 6 am-11 pm. Ck-out noon. Meeting rms. Business servs avail. Valet serv. Free airport, RR station, bus depot transportation. Downhill/x-country ski 15 mi. Cr cds: A, C, D, DS, MC, V.
🄳 🏊 🌊 ✈ 🖎 🔥 SC

★ **RED ROOF INN.** 5425 W Michigan Ave (49009). 616/375-7400; fax 616/375-7533; res 800/843-7663. www.redroof.com. 108 rms, 2 story. S $36-$45; D $40-$52; 3 or more $50; under 18 free; higher rates special events. Crib free. Pet accepted. TV. Complimentary coffee. Restaurant nearby. Ck-out noon. Business servs avail. Downhill ski 8 mi; x-country ski 3 mi. Picnic tables, grill. Cr cds: A, C, D, DS, MC, V.

D 🏌 ⛷ 🏊 🔥

★ **SUPER 8 MOTEL.** *618 Maple Hill Dr (49009). 616/345-0146; res 800/800-8000. www.super8.com.* 62 rms, 3 story. No elvtr. Apr-Oct: S $43.99; D $48.99-$52.99; under 12 free; higher rates wkends; lower rates rest of yr. Crib free. Pet accepted. TV; cable (premium). Restaurant adj 7 am-10 pm. Ck-out 11 am. Downhill ski 11 mi. Some refrigerators, microwaves. Cr cds: A, C, D, DS, MC, V.

D 🏌 ⛷ 🏊 🔥 SC

Hotel

★★★ **RADISSON PLAZA.** *100 W Michigan Ave (49007). 616/343-3333; fax 616/381-1560; res 800/333-3333. www.radisson.com.* 281 rms, 9 story. S, D $149; each addl $10; suites $150-$275; family rates. Crib free. Garage $4; valet $6. TV; cable. Indoor pool; whirlpool. Coffee in rms. Restaurant (see WEBSTER'S). Bar 11-1:30 am. Ck-out noon. Convention facilities. Business servs avail. In-rm modem link. Concierge. Shopping arcade. Free airport, RR station, bus depot transportation. Exercise rm; sauna. Wet bar in some suites. Cr cds: A, C, D, DS, MC, V.

D 🏌 🏋 🏊 🏃 ✈ 🏊 🔥 SC

B&Bs/Small Inns

★★ **HALL HOUSE BED & BREAK-FAST.** *106 Thompson St (49006). 616/343-2500; fax 616/343-1374; toll-free 888/761-2525. www.hallhouse.com.* 6 rms, 3 story. S $79; D $99; some special events (2-day min). TV; cable, VCR. Complimentary bkfst. Georgian Colonial Revival building (1923). Original artwork. Some antiques. Cr cds: A, MC, V.

🏊 🔥

★★ **STUART AVENUE INN BED & BREAKFAST.** *229 Stuart Ave (49007). 616/342-0230; fax 616/385-3442; toll-free 800/461-0621. www.stuartaveinn. com.* 17 rms in 3 buildings, 2-3 story. 4 suites, 12 kit. units. S $85; D $95; each addl $10; suites $120-$150; kit.

units $150-$250/wk (4-wk min); wkly rates. Crib $10. TV; cable. Complimentary continental bkfst; afternoon refreshments. Restaurant nearby. Ck-out noon, ck-in 4 pm. Meeting rms. Downhill/x-country ski 15 mi. Some fireplaces. Totally non-smoking. Cr cds: A, D, DS, MC, V.

🏊 🔥

Extended Stay

★★ **RESIDENCE INN BY MAR-RIOTT.** *1500 E Kilgore Rd (49001). 616/349-0855; fax 616/373-5971; toll-free 800/331-3131. www.marriott.com.* 83 kit. suites, 2 story. S, D $105-$130; wkly rates. Crib free. Pet accepted, some restrictions; fee. TV; cable, VCR avail (movies). Heated pool; whirlpool. Complimentary continental bkfst. Complimentary coffee in rms. Restaurant nearby. Ck-out noon. Coin lndry. Meeting rm. Business servs avail. In-rm modem link. Valet serv. Free airport transportation. 9-hole golf privileges. Downhill/x-country ski 20 mi. Health club privileges. Some fireplaces. Picnic tables, grills. Cr cds: A, C, D, DS, JCB, MC, V.

D 🏌 🏊 🍴 🏊 ✈ 🏊 🔥 SC

Restaurants

★★★ **BLACK SWAN.** *3501 Greenleaf Blvd (49008). 616/375-2105. www. millenniumrestaurants.com.* Hrs: 11:30 am-2 pm, 5-10 pm; Sun 4-8 pm. Closed hols. Res accepted. Continental menu. Bar to midnight. Lunch $5.95-$15.95, dinner $14.95-$23.95. Sun brunch $11.95. Child's menu. Specializes in seafood, steak. Valet parking. Overlooks lake. Cr cds: A, D, DS, MC, V.

D

★★ **BRAVO.** *5402 Portage Rd (49002). 616/344-7700.* Hrs: 11:30 am-10 pm; Fri to 11 pm; Sat 5-11 pm; Sun 4-9 pm; Sun brunch 10:30 am-2 pm. Closed hols. Res accepted. Italian, American menu. Bar. Lunch $5-$12, dinner $10.95-$21.95. Sun brunch $14.95. Child's menu. Specialties: scampi with linguine, veal with morels. Wood-burning pizza

oven. Contemporary Italian decor. Cr
cds: A, DS, MC, V.

D

★ ★ ★ **WEBSTER'S.** *100 W Michigan
Ave (49007). 616/343-4444.* Hrs: 5-10
pm. Closed Sun; hols. Res accepted.
Contemporary Amer menu. Bar. Dinner $17-$28. Specialties: filet,
seafood. Entertainment Fri, Sat. Club
atmosphere. Cr cds: A, D, DS, MC, V.

D

Lansing (G-5)

Settled 1847 **Pop** 127,321 **Elev** 860 ft
Area code 517
Information Greater Lansing Con-
vention & Visitors Bureau, 1223
Turner St, Suite 200, 48906; 517/487-
6800 or 888/252-6746
Web www.lansing.org

When the capital of Michigan moved
here in 1847 for lack of agreement
on a better place, the "city" consisted
of one log house and a sawmill.
Today, in addition to state government, Lansing is the headquarters for
many trade and professional associa-
tions and has much heavy industry.
R. E. Olds, who built and marketed
one of America's earliest automobiles, started the city's industrial
growth. Lansing is the home of the
Lansing Automotive Division of General Motors and many allied industries. East Lansing, a neighboring
community, is the home of the
Michigan State University Spartans
and is part of the capital city in all
respects except government.

What to See and Do

BoarsHead Theater. A regional center
with a professional resident theater
company. Center for the Arts, 425 S
Grand Ave. Phone 517/484-7800.

**Brenke River Sculpture and Fish Lad-
der.** Located at North Lansing Dam
on the Riverfront Park scenic walk,
sculpture encompasses the ladder
designed by artist/sculptor Joseph E.
Kinnebrew and landscape architect
Robert O'Boyle. 2 mi N via Washington Ave.

Fenner Nature Center. Park features
a bald eagle, two waterfowl ponds,

replica of a pioneer cabin and garden, five miles of nature trails
through a variety of habitats; picnicking. Nature center with small
animal exhibits (Tues-Sun). Trails
(daily). 2020 E Mt Hope Ave, at Aure-
lius Rd. Phone 517/483-4224. **FREE**

Impression 5 Science Center. Center
has more than 200 interactive,
hands-on exhibits, incl computer lab,
chemistry experiments; restaurant.
(Mon-Sat; closed hols) 200 Museum
Dr. Phone 517/485-8116. ¢¢

The Ledges. Edging the Grand River,
the Ledges are quartz sandstone 300
million yrs old. They are considered
a good rock climbing area for the
experienced. (Daily) 10 mi W via MI
43 in Grand Ledge. Phone 517/627-
7351. ¢

Michigan Historical Museum. (Michigan Library & Historical Center)
Exhibits incl a copper mine, sawmill,
and 54-ft-high relief map of Michigan; audiovisual programs, hands-on
exhibits. (Daily; closed hols) 717 W
Allegan St. Phone 517/373-3559.
FREE

Michigan State University. (1855)
42,000 students. Founded as the
country's first agricultural college
and forerunner of the nationwide
land-grant university system, MSU,
located on a 5,300-acre landscaped
campus with 7,800 different species
and varieties of trees, shrubs, and
vines, is known for its research, Honors College, and many innovations
in education. Among the interesting
features of the campus are Abrams
Planetarium (shows: Fri-Sun, fee;
phone 517/355-4672); Horticultural
Gardens; W. J. Beal Botanical Garden;
Breslin Student Events Center (box
office, phone 517/432-5000); Whar-
ton Center for Performing Arts (box
office, phone 517/432-2000); Michigan State University Museum (Mon-
Sat, also Sun afternoons, closed
hols); and Kresge Art Museum (Daily;
closed hols). In East Lansing. Phone
517/353-1855.

Potter Park Zoo. Zoo on the Red
Cedar River; has more than 400 animals. Educational programs, camel
and pony rides, playground, concession, and picnic facilities. (Daily)
1301 S Pennsylvania Ave. Phone
517/483-4222. ¢¢

✪ **R. E. Olds Transportation Museum.**
Named after Ransom Eli Olds, the

museum houses Lansing-built vehicles incl Oldsmobile, REO, Star, and Durant autos; REO and Duplex trucks, bicycles, airplanes; period clothing, photographic display of Olds' Victorian home, and a "Wall of Wheels" from the Motor Wheel Corp. (Tues-Sat; closed Jan 1, Dec 25) 240 Museum Dr. Phone 517/372-0422.

State Capitol Building. Dedicated in 1879, this was one of the first state capitol buildings to emulate the dome and wings of the US Capitol in Washington, D.C. Interior walls and ceilings reflect the work of many skilled artisans, muralists, and portrait painters. Tours (daily). Capitol and Michigan aves. Phone 517/373-2353. **FREE**

Woldumar Nature Center. A 188-acre wildlife preserve; nature walks, interpretive center (Mon-Sat; closed hols). Trails open for hiking and skiing (daily, dawn-dusk). 5539 Lansing Rd. Phone 517/322-0030. **Donation**

Special Events

East Lansing Art Festival. Artists' work for sale, continuous performances, ethnic foods, children's activities. Phone 517/337-1731. Third wkend May.

Mint Festival. 18 mi N via US 27 in St. Johns. Queen contest, parade, mint farm tours, antiques, arts and crafts, flea market, entertainment. Second wkend Aug. Phone 517/224-7248.

Motels/Motor Lodges

★★ **BEST WESTERN MIDWAY HOTEL.** 7111 W Saginaw Hwy (48917). 517/627-8471; fax 517/627-8597; toll-free 877/772-6100. www. bestwestern.com. 149 rms, 2-3 story. Sept-May: S $78; D $88; each addl $5; under 12 free; lower rates rest of yr. Crib free. Pet accepted. TV; cable (premium). Indoor pool; whirlpool. Coffee in rms. Restaurant 6:30 am-10 pm; wkend hrs vary. Bar 11-2 am. Ck-out noon. Meeting rms. Business servs avail. Bellhops. Valet serv. Sundries. Free airport transportation. Exercise equipt; sauna. Game rm.

Refrigerators avail. Cr cds: A, C, D, DS, MC, V.

★★ **COMFORT INN & EXECUTIVE SUITES.** 2209 University Park Dr, Okemos (48864). 517/349-8700; fax 517/349-5638; res 800/349-8701. www. comfortinn.com. 160 rms, 2 story. S, D $59-$95; each addl $6; suites $85-$115; under 18 free; higher rates special events. Crib free. TV; cable. Indoor pool; whirlpool. Complimentary continental bkfst. Restaurant adj 6 am-midnight. Ck-out 11 am. Meeting rm. Business servs avail. X-country ski 5 mi. Exercise equipt; sauna, steam rm. Whirlpool in suites. Cr cds: A, D, DS, MC, V.

★★ **COURTYARD BY MARRIOTT.** 2710 Lake Lansing Rd (48912). 517/482-0500; fax 517/482-0557. www. marriott.com. 129 rms, 2 story, 17 suites. S $56; D $64; suites $70-$105; under 16 free. Crib free. TV; cable (premium), VCR avail. Indoor pool; whirlpool. Complimentary full bkfst. Ck-out noon. Coin lndry. Meeting rms. Business center. Valet serv. X-country ski 5 mi. Private patios, balconies. Picnic tables, grills. Cr cds: A, D, DS, MC, V.

★★ **FAIRFIELD INN.** 2335 Woodlake Dr, Okemos (48864). 517/347-1000; fax 517/347-5092; toll-free 800/568-4421. www.fairfieldinn.com. 79 rms, 2 story. S $59; D $64; each addl $5; suites $125; under 18 free. Crib free. TV; cable (premium). Indoor pool; whirlpool. Complimentary continental bkfst. Restaurant nearby. Ck-out noon. Valet serv. Some refrigerators. Cr cds: A, MC, V.

★★ **HAMPTON INN.** 525 N Canal Rd (48917). 517/627-8381; fax 517/627-5502; res 800/426-7866. www. hamptoninn.com. 109 rms, 3 story. S $71; D $79; suites $84; under 18 free. Crib free. TV; cable (premium). Complimentary continental bkfst. Restaurant adj 6 am-10 pm. Ck-out noon. Meeting rms. Business servs avail. Valet serv. Refrigerator in suites. Some balconies. Cr cds: A, C, D, DS, MC, V.

★ ★ ★ **HARELEY HOTEL.** *3600 Dunckel Dr (48910). 517/351-7600; fax 517/351-4640.* 150 rms, 2 story. S $71-$110; D $81-$112; each addl $10; suites $175; under 18 free; wkly rates. Crib free. TV; cable (premium). 2 pools, 1 indoor; whirlpool. Restaurant 6:30 am-11 pm; Sat, Sun from 7 am. Bar 11-1 am; entertainment Mon-Sat. Ck-out 11 am. Meeting rm. Business servs avail. Bellhops. Valet serv. Sundries. Free airport, RR station, bus depot transportation. Lighted tennis. Putting green. X-country ski 7 mi. Exercise equipt; sauna. Lawn games. Game rm. Private patios, balconies. Cr cds: A, D, DS, MC, V.

D 🍴 🏊 🏋 🎿 🏊 🚲

★ ★ **HOLIDAY INN.** *6820 S Cedar St (48911). 517/694-8123; fax 517/699-3753; toll-free 800/465-4329. www.holiday-inn.com.* 300 rms, 5 story. S $120; D $130; each addl $10; suites $200-$390; under 18 free; wkend rates. Crib free. TV; cable. Indoor pool; whirlpool. Coffee in rms. Restaurant 6:30 am-10 pm. Bar 4 pm-1 am. Ck-out noon. Convention facilities. Business servs avail. Airport, RR station, bus depot transportation. X-country ski 3 mi. Exercise equipt; sauna. Sun deck. Game rm. Refrigerators. Cr cds: A, C, D, DS, JCB, MC, V.

D 🏊 🏋 ✈ 🎿 🏊 🚲

★ ★ **QUALITY SUITES.** *901 Delta Commerce Dr (48917). 517/886-0600; fax 517/886-0103; res 800/228-5151. www.qualityinn.com.* 117 suites, 4 story. S $89; D $99; each addl $10; under 18 free; wkend rates. Crib free. TV; cable (premium), VCR avail (movies). Complimentary full bkfst. Restaurant nearby. Ck-out 11 am. Meeting rms. Business servs avail. Valet serv. Sundries. Free airport transportation. Exercise equipt; sauna. Refrigerators. Some balconies. Cr cds: A, C, D, DS, MC, V.

D 🏋 ✈ 🎿 🏊

★ **RED ROOF INN LANSING EAST.** *3615 Dunckel Rd (48910). 517/332-2575; fax 517/332-1459; toll-free 800/843-7663. www.redroof.com.* 80 rms, 2 story. S $41-$51; D $42-$54; each addl $6; under 18 free. Crib free. Pet accepted. TV. Restaurant opp 7 am-11 pm. Ck-out noon. Business servs avail. Cr cds: A, C, D, DS, MC, V.

D 🍴 🎿 🏊 SC

Hotels

★ ★ ★ **MARRIOTT AT UNIVERSITY PLACE EAST LANSING.** *300 M.A.C. Ave, East Lansing (48823). 517/337-4440; fax 517/337-5001; res 800/228-9290. www.marriott.com.* 180 rms, 7 story. S, D $119; wkend rates; higher rates: university football wkends, graduation. Crib free. TV; cable (premium). Indoor pool; whirlpool. Complimentary coffee in lobby. Restaurant 6:30 am-midnight; Sat from 7 am; Sun 7 am-10 pm. Bar 11 am-midnight; Sun to 10 pm. Ck-out noon. Coin lndry. Meeting rms. Business servs avail. Bellhops. Valet serv. Sundries. Free garage parking. Free airport transportation. Exercise equipt; sauna. Balconies. Cr cds: A, C, D, DS, V.

D 🏊 🏋 🎿 🏊

★ ★ ★ **RADISSON.** *111 N Grand Ave (48933). 517/482-0188; fax 517/487-6646; toll-free 800/333-3333. www.radisson.com.* 260 rms, 11 story. S, D $79-$139; suites $185-$199; under 19 free. Crib free. TV; cable (premium). Indoor pool; whirlpool. Coffee in rms. Restaurant 6 am-11 pm. Bar 11-1 am. Ck-out noon. Convention facilities. Business servs avail. Concierge. Gift shop. Free valet parking. Free airport, RR station, bus depot transportation. X-country ski 6 mi. Exercise equipt; sauna. Bathrm phone, refrigerator in suites. Cr cds: A, C, D, DS, ER, JCB, MC, V.

D 🏊 🏋 ✈ 🎿 🏊 SC 🚲

★ ★ ★ **SHERATON HOTEL.** *925 S Creyts Rd (48917). 517/323-7100; fax 517/323-2180; toll-free 800/325-3535. www.sheratonlansing.com.* 219 rms, 5 story. S $89-$119; D $99-$129; each addl $12; suites $225; under 18 free; wkend rates. Crib free. TV; cable (premium). Indoor pool. Coffee in rms. Restaurant 6:30 am-midnight. Bar 11-2 am. Ck-out noon. Meeting rms. Business servs avail. Bellhops. Gift shop. Free airport transportation. X-country ski 5 mi. Exercise equipt; sauna. Some refrigerators. Cr cds: A, C, D, DS, ER, MC, V.

D 🚲 🏊 🏋 ✈ 🎿 🏊

B&B/Small Inn

★★ **THE ENGLISH INN.** *677 S Michigan Rd, Eaton Rapids (48827). 517/663-2500; fax 517/663-2643; toll-free 800/858-0598. www.englishinn. com.* 10 rms, 3 story. S, D $130; each addl $15; suites $135-$155. Children over 12 yrs only. TV; cable (premium), VCR avail. Pool. Complimentary continental bkfst. Restaurant 11:30 am-1:30 pm, 5:30-8:30 pm. Ck-out 11 am, ck-in 3 pm. Business servs avail. 18-hole golf privileges. X-country ski on site. Built in 1927; antiques. Totally nonsmoking. Cr cds: A, DS, MC, V.

Extended Stay

★★ **RESIDENCE INN BY MARRIOTT EAST LANSING.** *1600 Grand River, East Lansing (48823). 517/332-7711; fax 517/332-7711; res 800/331-3131. www.marriott.com.* 60 kit. suites, 2 story. S $115; D $165; each addl $10; family rates. Crib free. TV; cable (premium), VCR avail (movies). Heated pool; whirlpool. Complimentary continental bkfst. Complimentary coffee in rms. Restaurants nearby. Ck-out noon. Coin lndry. Business servs avail. Valet serv. Health club privileges. Balconies. Picnic table, grill. Cr cds: A, MC, V.

Leland

(D-4) *See also Glen Arbor*

Pop 400 **Elev** 602 ft **Area code** 231 **Zip** 49654

What to See and Do

⭐ **Boat trips to Manitou Islands.** The *Mishe-mokwa* makes daily trips in summer, incl overnight camping excursions, to North and South Manitou islands (see SLEEPING BEAR DUNES NATIONAL LAKESHORE); also eve cocktail cruise. (June-Aug, daily; May, Sept-Oct, Mon, Wed, Fri-Sun) Leland Harbor. Phone 231/256-9061. ¢¢¢¢

Motel/Motor Lodge

★★ **LELAND LODGE.** *565 E Pearl St (49654). 616/256-9848; fax 616/256-8812.* 18 rms, 2 story, 4 kits. Mid-June-Labor Day: S, D $89-$149; each addl $10; kit. units $805-$995/wk; lower rates rest of yr. Crib free. TV; cable. Complimentary continental bkfst wkends (in season). Restaurant 11 am-10 pm; off-season to 9 pm. Bar 11 am-11 pm. Ck-out 11 am. Business servs avail. 18-hole golf privileges. Cr cds: A, DS, MC, V.

B&B/Small Inn

★★ **MANITOU MANOR BED & BREAKFAST.** *147 Manitou Trl W, Lake Leelanau (49654). 231/256-7712; fax 231/256-7941.* 5 rms. No A/C. Memorial Day-mid-Oct: S, D $125; each addl $15; family, wkly rates; lower rates rest of yr. TV in sitting rm; VCR. Complimentary full bkfst. Ck-out 11 am, ck-in 3 pm. Downhill ski 5 mi; x-country ski on site. Library. Historic (1873) farmhouse with 6 acres of cherry trees. Totally nonsmoking. Cr cds: DS, MC, V.

Restaurants

★★ **BLUE BIRD.** *102 River St (49654). 231/256-9081. www.leelanav. com/bluebird.* Hrs: 11:30 am-3 pm, 5-9 pm; Sun 5-9 pm; Late-Nov-Mar: Sun brunch 10 am-2 pm; Fri, Sat 5-9 pm. Closed first 3 wks Nov; also Mon Apr-mid-June, after Labor Day-Oct. Res accepted. Bar 11:30 am-midnight. Lunch $4-$8.50, dinner $8.95-$16.95. Child's menu. Specializes in prime rib, seafood, Great Lakes fish. Salad bar. Overlooks channel. Family-owned. Cr cds: DS, MC, V.

★★ **COVE.** *111 River St (49654). 231/256-9834.* Hrs: 11 am-10 pm. Closed mid-Oct-mid-May. Res accepted. Bar. Lunch $3.95-$8.95, dinner $9.95-$19.95. Child's menu. Specializes in seafood. Outdoor dining. On channel overlooking Lake Michigan. Cr cds: A, MC, V.

★ ★ LEELANAU COUNTRY INN.
149 E Harbor Hwy, Maple City (49664). 231/228-5060. Hrs: 5-9 pm; early-bird dinner 5-6 pm; hrs vary Nov-May. Closed Dec 24-26. Res accepted. Dinner $9.95-$18.95. Child's menu. Specializes in fresh seafood, prime rib, pasta. Own desserts. Converted house (1891); guest rms avail. Cr cds: MC, V.

D SC

Ludington

(E-3) *See also Manistee*

Settled 1880 **Pop** 8,507 **Elev** 610 ft
Area code 231 **Zip** 49431
Information Ludington Area Convention & Visitor Bureau, 5300 W US 10; 231/845-0324 or 877/420-6618
Web www.ludingtoncvb.com

A large passenger car ferry and freighters keep this important Lake Michigan port busy. First named Père Marquette, in honor of the missionary explorer who died here in 1675, the community later adopted the name of its more recent founder, James Ludington, a lumber baron. Ludington draws vacationers because of its long stretch of beach on Lake Michigan and miles of forests, lakes, streams, and dunes surrounding the town. The Père Marquette River has been stocked with chinook salmon; fishing boats may be chartered.

What to See and Do

Auto ferry service. (to Manitowoc, WI) Amenities incl museum, game rm, theater, staterms, food serv. (May-Oct, daily) End of US 10. Phone 231/845-5555. ¢¢¢¢
Ludington Pumped Storage Hydroelectric Plant. Scenic overlooks beside Lake Michigan and the plant's 840-acre reservoir. One of the world's largest facilities of this type. (Apr-Nov, daily) 6 mi S on S Lakeshore Dr. Phone 800/477-5050. **FREE** Footpaths connect to

> **Mason County Campground and Picnic Area.** Picnicking, playground, camping (hookups). (Memorial Day-Labor Day, daily) S

Old US 31 to Chauvez Rd, then 1½ mi S. Phone 231/845-7609. ¢¢
Ludington State Park. Approx 4,500 acres on lakes Michigan and Hamlin and the Sable River. Swimming, bathhouse, waterskiing, fishing, boating (ramp, rentals); hunting, x-country skiing, picnicking, playground, concession, camping. Visitor center (May-Sept). Standard fees. 8½ mi N on MI 116. Phone 231/843-8671. ¢¢
Pere Marquette Memorial Cross. Towers high into the skyline, overlooks the harbor and Lake Michigan.
Stearns Park. Half-mi swimming beach (lifeguard, June-Labor Day), fishing, boating, ramps, launch, 150-slip marina; picnicking, playground, miniature golf, shuffleboard. Fee for some activities.
White Pine Village. Historical buildings re-create small-town Michigan life in the late 1800s; general store, trapper's cabin, courthouse/jail, town hall, one-rm school, and others. (June-early Sept, Tues-Sun) 3 mi S via US 31 to Iris Rd, follow signs. Phone 231/843-4808. ¢¢

Motels/Motor Lodges

★ **FOUR SEASONS MOTEL.** *717 E Ludington Ave (49431).* 231/843-3448; fax 231/843-2635; toll-free 800/968-0180. www.fourseasonsmotel.com. 33 rms. Mid-June-mid-Oct: S, D $45-$99; higher rates: hols, festivals; lower rates rest of yr. Crib free. TV; cable (premium), VCR avail. Complimentary continental bkfst. Coffee in rms. Restaurant nearby. Ck-out 11 am. Free airport transportation. Golf privileges. X-country ski 6 mi. Cr cds: DS, MC, V.

D ⚓ ⊠ 🐾 SC

★ **LANDS INN.** *4079 W US 10 & Brye Rd (49431).* 231/845-7311; fax 231/843-8551; toll-free 800/707-7475. 116 rms, 4 story. Mid-May-early Sept: S $89; D $99; each addl $10; suites $125; under 16 free; wkly rates; golf plans; lower rates rest of yr. Crib free. TV; cable (premium). Indoor pool; whirlpool. Restaurant 6:30 am-10 pm. Bar 5 pm-midnight; entertainment Thurs-Sat. Ck-out 11 am. Coin lndry. Meeting rms. Business servs avail. Exercise equipt; sauna. Game rm. Cr cds: A, C, D, DS, MC, V.

D ⚓ 🕴 ⊠ 🐾 SC

★ **MARINA BAY MOTOR LODGE.**
*604 W Ludington Ave (49431). 231/
845-5124; fax 231/843-7929; toll-free
800/968-1440.* 24 rms, 1-2 story. Late
June-early Sept: S, D $60-$135; each
addl $5; higher rates special events;
lower rates rest of yr. Crib free. TV;
cable (premium), VCR avail (movies
$2). Complimentary coffee in lobby.
Restaurant nearby. Ck-out 11 am.
Business servs avail. Free airport
transportation. X-country ski 4 mi.
Some in-rm whirlpools. Cr cds: DS,
MC, V.
⬚⬚

★ **MILLERS LAKESIDE MOTEL.** *808
W Ludington Ave (49431). 231/843-
3458; fax 231/843-3450; toll-free 800/
843-2177.* 52 rms. Mid-May-mid-
Sept: S, D $65-$80; each addl $5;
suites $95; higher rates: hols, special

Mackinac Island transportation

events; wkly rates off-season; lower
rates rest of yr. Crib free. TV; cable
(premium), VCR avail. Heated pool.
Restaurant nearby. Ck-out 11 am.
Business servs avail. Free airport
transportation. X-country ski 5 mi.
Public beach, launching ramp, park,
miniature golf opp. Cr cds: A, DS,
MC, V.
⬚⬚⬚⬚⬚⬚

★★ **SNYDER'S SHORELINE INN.**
*903 W Ludington Ave (49431). 231/
845-1261; fax 231/843-4441.* 44 rms,
2 story, 8 suites. Mid-June-Oct: S
$69-$199; D $89-$249; each addl
$20; suites $159-$249; higher rates
special events; lower rates May-mid-
June. Closed rest of yr. TV; cable (pre-

mium), VCR avail (free movies).
Heated pool; whirlpool. Complimentary continental bkfst. Ck-out 11 am.
Business servs avail. Free airport
transportation. Many refrigerators;
some wet bars. Balconies. On lake;
swimming beach. Cr cds: A, MC, V.
⬚⬚⬚⬚⬚⬚

★★ **VIKING ARMS INN.** *930 E Ludington Ave (49431). 231/843-3441;
fax 231/845-7703; toll-free 800/748-
0173. www.vikingarmsinn.com.* 45
rms. Mid-May-mid-Oct: S $45-$110;
D $50-$150; each addl $5; family
rates; higher rates: hols, special
events; lower rates rest of yr. Crib
$2. TV; cable, VCR (movies $3).
Heated pool; whirlpool. Complimentary continental bkfst. Coffee in
rms. Restaurant nearby. Ck-out 11
am. Meeting rm. Business servs
avail. Free airport
transportation. X-
country ski 7 mi.
Some in-rm whirl-
pools, fireplaces. Cr
cds: MC, V.
⬚⬚⬚⬚⬚⬚

B&B/Small Inn

★★ **NICKERSON
INN.** *262 W Lowell,
Pentwater (48858).
231/869-6731; fax
231/869-6151.* 11
rms, 3 suites, 3 story.
No rm phones. June-
Oct: S, D $100-$225;
each addl $25; lower
rates rest of yr. Chil-
dren over 12 yrs only. Complimentary full bkfst. Restaurant (see
HISTORIC NICKERSON INN). Ck-out
11 am, ck-in 2 pm. Luggage handling. Whirlpool in suites. X-country
ski 2 mi. Built in 1914; antiques. Cr
cds: DS, MC, V.
⬚⬚⬚⬚⬚

Restaurants

★ **HISTORIC NICKERSON INN.**
*262 W Lowell St, Pentwater (49449).
231/869-6731. www.nickersoninn.com.*
Hrs: 6-9 pm; Sun 8 am-1 pm, 6-9
pm. Closed Dec 25; Jan-Mar. Res
accepted. Eclectic menu. Serv bar.
Dinner $14-$28. Child's menu. Specializes in rack of lamb, fresh

---

EXPLORING MACKINAC ISLAND

Mackinac is truly an island that time forgot: the clippety-clop of horse-drawn wagons echoes in the streets, period-garbed docents stroll among historical reconstructions, and quaint candy shops roll out fudge by the ton. And yet, many tourists manage to go there and only see the two or three square-blocks off the tour-boat docks and miss all the rest. Mackinac Island is the perfect approximation of living history, tacky tourism, sublime aesthetics, and lovely natural scenery—all contained on an island that can be circumnavigated in one very long but rewarding day hike.

The best option is to take the early-morning ferry. Spend some time lolling around the anachronistic downtown, and make a quick visit to historic Fort Mackinac. Then head a few miles to Arch Rock for stunning views of the sun rising steadily over the Great Lake. From there, head inland to the modest but occasionally daunting central rise of the island, bypassing an old fort and two cemeteries where original settlers and soldiers are buried. Next head south via British Landing Road for a look at the Governor's Residence before returning to the downtown. Or, if you are in marathon shape, you may want to hike from the cemeteries all the way to the northwest shoreline, where historic markers indicate the site of the British invasion that occurred over a century ago. If you stay along the main road to the south, you may be lucky enough to witness a most resplendent sunset as you waltz back into downtown.

---

seafood. Outdoor dining. Overlooks Lake Michigan. Totally nonsmoking. Cr cds: DS, MC, V.

⓪

★ ★ **SCOTTY'S.** *5910 E Ludington Ave (US 10) (49431).* 231/843-4033. Hrs: 11:30 am-2 pm, 5-10 pm; Sat from 5 pm; Sun 9 am-1 pm. Closed Thanksgiving, Dec 25. Res accepted. Bar. Lunch $3.50-$7.95, dinner $9.95-$26.95. Child's menu. Specializes in prime rib, steak, seafood. Family-owned. Cr cds: A, MC, V.

⓪ ⤴

Mackinac Island

(C-5) *See also Mackinaw City, St. Ignace*

(By ferry from St. Ignace and Mackinaw City. By air from Pellston, Detroit, and St. Ignace.)
Pop 469 **Elev** 600-925 ft
Area code 906 **Zip** 49757
Information Chamber of Commerce, PO Box 451; 906/847-3783 or 800/454-5227
Web www.mackinac.com

Labeled the "Bermuda of the North," Mackinac (MAK-i-naw) Island retains the atmosphere of the 19th century

and the imprint of history. In view of the Mackinac Bridge, it has been a famous resort for the last century. The island was called "great turtle" by Native Americans who believed that its towering heights and rock formations were shaped by supernatural forces. Later, because of its strategic position, the island became the key to the struggle between England and France for control of the rich fur trade of the great Northwest. Held by the French until 1760, it became English after Wolfe's victory at Québec, was turned over to the United States at the close of the American Revolution, reverted to the British during the War of 1812, and finally was restored to the United States.

With the decline of the fur trade in the 1830s, Mackinac Island began to develop its potential as a resort area. Southern planters and their families summered here prior to the Civil War; wealthy Chicagoans took their place in the years following. No automobiles are allowed on the island; transportation is by horse and carriage or bicycle. Horse and carriages and bicycles can be rented. Passenger ferries make regularly scheduled trips to the island from Mackinaw City and St. Ignace, or visitors can reach the island by air from St. Ignace, Pellston, or Detroit.

What to See and Do

Ferry services.

    Arnold Transit Company. Fifteen-min trip from St. Ignace or Mackinaw City. (May-Dec, daily) Phone 906/847-3351.

    Shepler's Mackinac Island Ferry. Departs 556 E Central Ave, Mackinaw City or from downtown St. Ignace. (Early May-early Nov) Phone 906/436-5023. ¢¢¢

    Star Line Ferry. "Hydro Jet" service from Mackinaw City and St. Ignace. (May-Oct) Phone 800/638-9892. ¢¢¢

Mackinac Island Carriage Tours, Inc. Narrated, historic, and scenic horse-drawn carriage tour (1¾ hrs) covering 20 sights. (Mid-May-mid-Oct, daily; some tours avail rest of yr) Main St. Phone 906/847-3307. ¢¢¢

⭐ **Mackinac Island State Park.** Comprises approx 80 percent of the island. Michigan's first state park has views of the Straits of Mackinac, prehistoric geological formations incl Arch Rock, shoreline and inland trails. Visitor center at Huron St has informative exhibits, slide presentation, and guidebooks (mid-May-mid-Oct, daily). British Landing Nature Center (May-Labor Day). (Daily) Phone 906/847-3328. **FREE** Here is

    Beaumont Memorial. Monument to Dr. William Beaumont, who charted observations of the human digestive system by viewing this action through an opening in the abdomen of a wounded French-Canadian. (Mid-June-Labor Day, daily)

    Benjamin Blacksmith Shop. A working forge in replica of blacksmith shop dating from 1880s. (Mid-June-Labor Day, daily) Market St.

    Fort Mackinac. (1780-1895) High on a bluff overlooking the Straits of Mackinac, this 18th-19th-century British and American military outpost is complete with massive limestone ramparts, cannon, guardhouse, blockhouses, barracks; costumed interpreters, reenactments, children's discovery rm, crafts demonstrations; rifle and cannon firings; audiovisual presentation. (Mid-May-mid-Oct, daily) Phone 906/847-3328. ¢¢¢

    Indian Dormitory. (1838) Built as a place for Native Americans to live during annual visits to the Mackinac Island office of the US Indian Agency; interpretive displays, craft demonstrations; murals depicting scenes from Longfellow's "Hiawatha." (Mid-June-Labor Day, daily)

    Other places. Incl in the admission price are Mission Church (1830), Biddle House (1780), and McGulpin House.

Marquette Park. Statue of Father Marquette, historic marker, and 66 varieties of lilacs dominate this park. Main St. Phone 906/228-0460.

Special Events

Lilac Festival. Second wk June.

Sailing races. Port Huron to Mackinac and Chicago to Mackinac. Mid-late July. Phone 906/847-3783.

Hotels

★ ★ ★ **IROQUOIS MOTEL.** *Main St (49757). 906/847-3321; fax 906/847-6274. www.iroquoishotel.com.* 47 rms, 3 story. No A/C. Mid-June-mid-Sept: S, D $115-$280; each addl $15; suites $360; spring, fall packages; lower rates mid-May-mid-June, mid-Sept-late Oct. Closed rest of yr. TV in some rms, sitting rm. Restaurant (see CARRIAGE HOUSE). Ck-out noon, ck-in 3 pm. Business servs avail. Luggage handling. Valet serv. 18-hole golf privileges. Overlooks water, private beach. Cr cds: A, MC, V.

✕ 🎿 ⛵ 📶

★ ★ ★ **ISLAND HOUSE.** *100 Main St (49757). 906/847-3347; fax 906/847-3819; toll-free 800/626-6304. www.theislandhouse.com.* 97 rms, 50 A/C, 4 story. Mid-June-Labor Day: S, D $145-$165; each addl $20; suites $400; under 13 free; MAP avail; lower rates mid-May-mid-June, after Labor Day-mid-Oct. Closed rest of yr. Crib free. Indoor pool; whirlpool, steam rm. Restaurant (see GOVNOR'S LOUNGE). No rm serv. Bar noon-2 am; entertainment Tues-Sun. Ck-out 11 am. Meeting rms. Business servs avail. Airport transportation. Tennis privileges. Golf privileges. One of first summer hotels on island

(1852); Victorian architecture. Lake opp. Cr cds: A, DS, MC.

⊡ ⬧ ⚡ ✕ ⌂ ☞ ⬇ ⟵ ⬠

★ ★ ★ **LAKE VIEW.** *1 Huron St (49757).* 906/847-3384; fax 906/847-6283. www.mackinac.com. 85 rms, some A/C, 4 story. May-Oct: S $99-$179; D $139-$275; each addl $20; under 16 free. Closed rest of yr. Crib free. Indoor pool; whirlpool, sauna. Restaurant 7:30 am-10 pm, off season to 8 pm. Ck-out 11 am. Meeting rms. Business servs avail. Lake opp. Cr cds: DS, MC, V.

⊡ ⬧ ⚡ ☞ ⬇ ⬠

★ ★ ★ **LILAC TREE HOTEL.** *Main St (49757).* 906/847-6575; fax 906/847-3501. 39 suites, 3 story. July-Aug: S, D $175-$250; family, hol rates; lower rates May-June, Sept-Oct. Closed rest of yr. Crib free. TV; cable (premium). Complimentary coffee in rms. Restaurant 11 am-2 pm. No rm serv. Ck-out 11 am. In-rm modem link. Shopping arcade. Refrigerators. Balconies. Each suite uniquely decorated; antique and reproduction furnishings. Cr cds: A, MC, V.

✕ ⬠

Resorts

★ ★ ★ **GRAND HOTEL.** *1 Grand Ave (49757).* 906/847-3331; fax 906/847-3259; res 800/334-7263. www.grand hotel.com. 387 rms, 6 story. Mid-May-Nov, MAP: S $275-$315; D $340-$360; each addl $99. Serv charge 18%. Closed rest of yr. Crib avail. TV; cable. Heated pool; whirlpool, sauna, lifeguard. Restaurant 8 am-8:45 pm. Afternoon tea. Box lunches. Bar to 2 am. Ck-out noon, ck-in 3 pm. Convention facilities. Tennis, pro. 18-hole golf, greens fee $75, putting green. Bicycles. Exercise equipt. Lawn games. Rec rm. Entertainment. Some balconies. Large veranda overlooks Straits of Mackinac, formal gardens. On 500 acres; 2,000-acre state park adj. Cr cds: A, DS, MC, V.

⊡ ⬧ ⚡ ✕ ☞ ⬇ ⮞ ⟵ ⬠

★ ★ ★ **MISSION POINT RESORT.** *One Lakeshore Dr (49757).* 906/847-3312; fax 906/847-3408. www.mission point.com. 236 air-cooled rms, 2-3 story, 90 suites. Late June-early Sept: S, D $189-$269; each addl $20; suites $210-$695; under 18 free; MAP avail; higher rates: July 4, yacht races (3-

day min); lower rates mid-May-late June, early Sept-mid-Oct. Closed rest of yr. Crib free. TV; cable (premium), VCR avail. Heated pool; whirlpool, poolside serv. Supervised children's activities; ages 4-12. Dining rm 7 am-11 pm. Snack bar. Box lunches. Picnics. Bar 11-2 am. Ck-out 11 am, ck-in 3 pm. Grocery, coin lndry, package store ½ mi. Meeting rms. Business center. Concierge. Gift shop. Tennis. Golf privileges. Sunset cruises Sat eves (in season). Sailing nearby. Bicycle rentals. Lawn games. Soc dir. Movies nightly. Game rm. Exercise equipt; sauna. 18 acres on lakefront. Cr cds: A, D, DS, MC, V.

⊡ ⬧ ⚡ ✕ ☞ ⬇ ⮞ ⟵ ⬠ ⚐

B&B/Small Inn

★ ★ **BAY VIEW AT MACKINAC.** *100 Huron St (49757).* 906/847-3295; fax 906/847-6219. www.mackinacbayview. com. 20 air-cooled rms, 10 with shower only, 3 story. No rm phones. Mid-June-mid-Sept: S, D $95-$285; wkly rates; wkends (2-day min); lower rates May-mid-June, mid-Sept-Oct. Closed rest of yr. Adults only. TV; VCR in suites. Complimentary continental bkfst. Restaurant opp 7 am-10 pm. Ck-out 11 am, ck-in 3 pm. Some balconies. Built 1891 in Grand Victorian style; on bay. Totally nonsmoking. Cr cds: MC, V.

⊡ ⬧ ⟵ ⬠

Restaurants

★ ★ **CARRIAGE HOUSE.** *298 Main St (49757).* 906/847-3321. www.iroquois hotel.com. Hrs: 8 am-10 pm. Closed mid-Oct-Memorial Day. Res accepted. No A/C. Bar. A la carte entrees: bkfst $4.25-$7.25. Lunch $8.95-$15.95, dinner $19.50-$28.50. Child's menu. Specializes in whitefish, prime rib, veal. Outdoor dining. Overlooks water. Family-owned. Cr cds: DS, MC, V.

★ ★ **GOVNOR'S LOUNGE.** *Main St (49757).* 906/847-3347. www.theisland house.com. Hrs: 7:30-10:30 am, 5:30-10 pm. Closed mid-Oct-mid-May. Bar noon-2 am. Buffet: bkfst $13.95. A la carte entrees: dinner $12.95-$26.95. Specializes in prime rib, pasta. Entertainment Tues-Sun. In Mackinac Island's oldest hotel (1852). Cr cds: A, DS, MC, V.

⊡

Mackinaw City

(C-5) *See also Cheboygan, Mackinac Island, St. Ignace*

Settled 1681 **Pop** 875 **Elev** 590 ft
Area code 231 **Zip** 49701
Information Greater Mackinaw Area Chamber of Commerce, 706 S Huron, PO Box 856, phone 231/436-5574; or the Mackinaw Area Tourist Bureau, 708 S Huron, PO Box 160, phone 800/666-0160
Web www.mackinawcity.com

The only place in America where one can see the sun rise on one Great Lake (Huron) and set on another (Michigan); Mackinaw City sits in the shadow of the Mackinac Bridge. The French trading post built here became Fort Michilimackinac about 1715. It was taken over by the British in 1761 and two years later was captured by Native Americans. The British reoccupied the fort in 1764. The fort was rebuilt on Mackinac Island (see) between 1780-1781.

What to See and Do

⭐ **Colonial Michilimackinac.** Reconstructed French and British outpost and fur-trading village of 1715-1781; costumed interpreters provide music and military demonstrations, pioneer cooking and crafts, children's program, and reenactments of French colonial wedding and arrival of the Voyageurs. Working artisans, musket and cannon firing (mid-June-Labor Day, daily). Murals, dioramas in restored barracks (mid-May-mid-Oct, daily). Re-created Native American encampment (mid-June-Labor Day). Archaeoligical tunnel "Treasures from the Sand"; visitors can view the longest ongoing archaeological dig in US (mid-June-Labor Day, daily). Visitor center, audiovisual presentation. At south end of Mackinac Bridge. Phone 231/436-5563. ¢¢¢

Mill Creek. Scenic 625-acre park features working water-powered sawmill (1790); nature trails, forest demonstration areas, maple sugar shack, active beaver colony, picnicking. Sawmill demonstrations; archaeological excavations (mid-

June-Labor Day, Mon-Fri). Visitor center, audiovisual presentation. (Mid-May-mid-Oct, daily) 3 mi SE via US 23. Phone 231/436-7301. ¢¢

Mackinac Bridge. This imposing structure has reduced crossing time to the Upper Peninsula over the Straits of Mackinac to ten min. Connecting Michigan's upper and lower peninsulas between St. Ignace (see) and Mackinaw City, the 8,344-ft distance between cable anchorages makes it one of the world's longest suspension bridges. (Total length of steel superstructure: 19,243 ft; height above water at midspan: 199 ft; clearance for ships: 155 ft) Fine view from the bridge. Auto toll ¢

Mackinac Bridge Museum. Displays on the construction and maintenance of the bridge. Features original pieces of equipt. (Daily) 231 E Central Ave. Phone 231/436-5534.

Mackinac Island ferries.

Shepler's Mackinac Island Ferry. (Early May-early Nov) 556 E Central. Phone 231/436-5023. ¢¢¢¢

Star Line Ferry. "Hydro-Jet" (May-Oct). 711 S Huron. Phone 231/436-5045. ¢¢¢¢

Wilderness State Park. Approx 8,200 acres. Beaches, waterskiing, fishing, boating (launch); hunting in season, snowmobiling, x-country skiing, picnic areas, playgrounds. Trailside cabins, camping. Standard fees. 11 mi W of I-75, on Lake Michigan and Straits of Mackinac. Phone 231/436-5381. ¢¢

Special Events

Winterfest. Late Jan. Phone 231/436-5574.

Mackinaw Mush Sled Dog Race. The biggest dog sled race in the contiguous US. First wk Feb. Phone 231/436-5574.

Colonial Michilimackinac Pageant. Pageant and reenactment of Chief Pontiac's capture of the frontier fort in 1763; parade, muzzle-loading contests. Three days Memorial Day wkend. Phone 231/436-5574.

Spring/Fall Bike Tours. Biannual bicycle rides, ranging from 25-100 mi. Mid-June-mid-Sept. Phone 231/436-5574.

Vesper Cruises. Arnold's Line Dock. Phone 231/436-5902. Sun eve. July-Sept.

Mackinac Bridge Walk. Recreational walk for all across Mackinac Bridge (some lanes open to motor vehicles). Labor Day morning. Phone 231/436-5574.

Motels/Motor Lodges

★ **BEACHCOMBER MOTEL ON THE WATER.** *1011 S Huron St (49701). 231/436-8451; toll-free 800/ 968-1383.* 22 rms. July-early Aug: S $30-$125; D $35-$125; each addl $3; cottage $550/wk; higher rates: July 4, antique car show, Labor Day wkend (2-day min); lower rates mid-Apr-June, early Sept-Oct. Closed rest of yr. Crib free. Pet accepted, some restrictions. TV; cable (premium). Restaurant nearby. Ck-out 10 am. Refrigerators avail. Picnic tables. On lake; private beach. Cr cds: A, DS, MC, V.

D 🐾 🏖 ≈ SC

★★ **BEST WESTERN INN.** *112 Old US 31 (49701). 231/436-5544; fax 231/436-7180; toll-free 800/528-1234. www.bestwestern.com.* 73 rms, 2 story. Late June-early Sept: S $46-$89; D $52-$95; each addl $5; higher rates: Labor Day wkend (2-day min), special events; lower rates mid-Apr-late June, early Sept-Oct. Closed rest of yr. Crib $4. TV; cable (premium), VCR avail. Indoor pool; whirlpool. Complimentary contintental bkfst. Restaurant nearby. Ck-out 11 am. Coin lndry. In-rm modem link. Refrigerators; some in-rm whirlpools. Cr cds: A, C, D, DS, MC, V.

≈ ≈ 🔥 SC

★★ **CHIPPEWA MOTOR LODGE.** *929 S Huron Ave (49701). 231/436-8661; toll-free 800/748-0124. www. largestbeach.com.* 39 rms, 1-3 story. July-late Aug: S, D $49-$85; each addl $3-$5; under 12 free; higher rates: wkends, auto shows, Labor Day wkend (3-day min), special events; lower rates May-June, late Aug-Oct. Closed rest of yr. Crib $4. TV; cable (premium). Indoor pool; whirlpool. Playground. Complimentary coffee. Restaurant opp 7 am-10 pm. Ck-out 10:30 am. Business servs avail. Lawn games. Game rm. Many refrigerators. Picnic tables, grill. Patio; sun deck.

Landscaped grounds. Private beach on Lake Huron. Cr cds: DS, MC, V.

D 🛶 🏖 ≈ 🔥

★★ **COMFORT INN.** *611 S Huron St (49701). 231/436-5057; fax 231/436-7385; toll-free 800/221-2222. www. comfortinn.com.* 60 rms, 3 story. No elvtr. Late June-early Sept: S, D $88-$130; each addl $6; under 18 free; higher rates: Labor Day wkend, antique auto show (3-day min); lower rates May-late June, early Sept-Oct. Closed rest of yr. Crib $6. TV; cable (premium). Indoor pool; whirlpool. Restaurant nearby. Ck-out 10 am. Refrigerators. Balconies. On lake, beach. Cr cds: A, C, D, DS, ER, JCB, MC, V.

D ≈ ≈ 🔥 SC

★ **DAYS INN.** *825 S Huron St (49701). 231/436-5557; fax 231/436-5703; toll-free 800/329-7466. www. daysinn.com.* 84 rms, 2 story. Late June-early Sept: S $64-$144; D $68-$148; each addl $6; under 18 free; higher rates: summer hols, antique car show, special events; Labor Day, antique car show (2-day min); lower rates Apr-late June, early Sept-Oct. Closed rest of yr. Crib avail. TV; cable, VCR avail. Indoor pool; whirlpool, sauna. Playground. Complimentary coffee. Restaurant 7 am-9 pm. Ck-out 11 am. Coin lndry. Meeting rm. Putting green. Game rm. Lawn games. Refrigerators avail. Balconies. Picnic table. On lake; ferry terminal adj. Cr cds: A, D, DS, MC, V.

D ≈ ≈ 🔥 SC

★★ **GRAND MACKINAW INN AND SUITES.** *907 S Huron (49701). 231/436-8831; toll-free 800/822-8314. www.grandmackinaw.com.* 40 rms, 1-2 story. Late June-early Sept: S, D $65-$95; each addl $5; family, wkly rates off-season; lower rates May-late June, early Sept-Oct. Closed rest of yr. Crib $5. Pet accepted, some restrictions; $5-$10. TV; cable (premium). Indoor pool; whirlpool. Playground. Complimentary coffee. Restaurant nearby. Ck-out 11 am. Business servs avail. Lawn games. Refrigerators. Balconies, patios. Grills. Private sand beach; overlooks Lake Huron. Cr cds: A, MC, V.

D 🛶 ≈ ≈ 🔥 SC

★★ **HOLIDAY INN EXPRESS.** *364 Lowingney (49701). 231/436-7100; fax*

231/436-7070; toll-free 800/465-4329. *www.holiday-inn.com.* 71 rms, 3 story. Mid-June-early Sept: S $75-$145; D $81-$145; each addl $6; family rates; higher rates special events; lower rates rest of yr. Crib free. TV; cable (premium), VCR (movies). Indoor pool; whirlpool. Complimentary continental bkfst. Restaurant opp 8 am-10 pm. Ck-out 11 am. Coin lndry. Business servs avail. X-country ski 7 mi. Exercise equipt; sauna. Game rm. Some refrigerators. Balconies. Lake, swimming beach 3 blks. Cr cds: A, C, D, DS, JCB, MC, V.

★ **HOWARD JOHNSON.** *150 Old US 31 (49701). 231/436-5733; fax 231/ 436-5733; res 888/436-7591. www.hojo. com.* 46 rms, 1-2 story. Late June-Aug: S $75; D $98; each addl $5; family rates; higher rates July 4; higher rates (2-day min): Labor Day, Antique Car Show; lower rates May-late June, Sept-Oct. Closed rest of yr. Crib free. TV; cable (premium). 2 pools, 1 indoor; whirlpool. Playground. Complimentary coffee in lobby. Restaurant nearby. Ck-out 11 am. Cr cds: A, C, D, DS, JCB, MC, V.

★ **KEWADIN.** *619 S Nicolet St (MI 108) (49701). 231/436-5332; fax 231/ 436-7726; toll-free 800/503-9699.* 76 rms, 2 story. Mid-June-early Sept: S $64.50-$84.50; D $69.50-$84.50; each addl $5; family rates; higher rates special events; lower rates May-mid-June, early Sept-mid-Oct. Closed rest of yr. Crib free. Pet accepted. TV; cable. Heated pool. Playground. Restaurant nearby. Ck-out 11 am. Refrigerators. Cr cds: A, C, D, DS, MC, V.

★★ **LIGHTHOUSE VIEW.** *699 N Huron St (49701). 231/436-5304.* 25 rms, 2 story. July-early Sept: S, D $45-$95; each addl $5; family, wkly rates; higher rates: antique auto show, hol wkends, Labor Day wkend (2-day min); lower rates May-June, early Sept-Oct. Closed rest of yr. Crib $4. Pet accepted, some restrictions. TV; cable. Indoor pool; whirlpool. Restaurant nearby. Ck-out 11 am. Some in-rm whirlpools, saunas,

refrigerators. Beach opp. Cr cds: A, C, D, DS, MC, V.

★ **MOTEL 6.** *206 N Nicolet St (49701). 231/436-8961; fax 231/436-7317; toll-free 800/466-8356. www. motel6.com.* 53 rms, 2 story. Mid-June-Labor Day: S, D $38.95-$88.95; each addl $6; higher rates: hol wkends, special events; Labor Day wkend (2-day min); lower rates rest of yr. Crib free. Pet accepted; $3. TV; cable (premium). Indoor pool; whirlpool. Restaurant adj 7 am-10 pm. Ck-out 11 am. X-country ski on site. Some refrigerators. Cr cds: A, C, D, DS, MC, V.

★★ **PARKSIDE.** *711 N Heron (49701). 231/436-8301; fax 231/436-8301.* 44 rms, 1-2 story. Late June-early Sept: S, D $48-$88; family rates; higher rates: antique auto show, hol wkends; lower rates May-late June, early Sept-late Oct. Closed rest of yr. Crib $3. Pet accepted, some restrictions. TV; cable (premium). Indoor pool; whirlpool. Restaurant adj 6 am-10 pm. Ck-out 10 am. Game rm. Refrigerators avail. Picnic tables, sun deck. Some rms overlook lake, bridge. Colonel Michilimackinac State Park opp. Cr cds: A, DS, MC, V.

★★ **QUALITY INN & SUITES BEACHFRONT.** *917 S Huron Ave (49701). 231/436-5051; fax 231/436-7221; toll-free 877/436-5051.* 60 rms, 1-2 story. Late June-early Sept: S $32-$119; D $35-$149; each addl $5; family rates; higher rates: hol wkends, antique auto show, Labor Day wkend (2-day min); lower rates mid-Apr-late June, early Sept-Oct. Closed rest of yr. Pet accepted, some restrictions. TV; cable (premium), VCR avail. Indoor pool; whirlpool, sauna. Playground. Coffee in rms. Restaurant nearby. Ck-out 10 am. Business servs avail. Lawn games. Many refrigerators. Many balconies. Picnic area, grills. Private beach on Lake Huron. Near ferry dock. Cr cds: A, C, D, DS, ER, JCB, MC, V.

★★ **RAMADA INN.** *450 S Nicolet St (49701). 231/436-5535; fax 231/436-5849. www.ramada.com.* 162 rms, 3 story. Mid-June-early Sept: S $60.50-$115; D $66.50-$115; each addl $8; under 18 free; lower rates rest of yr. Crib free. TV; cable (premium), VCR avail. Indoor pool; whirlpool, sauna. Complimentary coffee. Restaurant 6:30 am-11 pm; off season to 9 pm. Bar 3 pm-2 am. Ck-out 11 am. Coin lndry. Meeting rms. X-country ski 5 mi. Game rm. Refrigerators; some in-rm whirlpools. Cr cds: A, C, D, DS, MC, V.

⊠ D ⇌ ⊠ 🔥

★★ **RAMADA LIMITED WATER-FRONT.** *723 S Huron Ave (49721). 231/436-5055; fax 231/436-5921; toll-free 888/852-4165. www.ramada.com.* 42 rms, 3 story. Late June-early Sept: S, D $79-$159; each addl $5; suites $169; Labor Day wkend (3-day min), special events (2-day min); lower rates mid-Apr-late June, early Sept-Oct. Closed rest of yr. Crib free. TV; cable (premium), VCR avail. Indoor pool; whirlpools. Complimentary continental bkfst. Restaurant opp 7 am-10:30 pm. Ck-out 11 am. Business servs avail. Refrigerators. Balconies. On beach. Cr cds: A, C, D, DS, MC, V.

D 🛱 ⇌ ⊠ 🔥

★ **STARLITE BUDGET INN.** *116 Old US 31 (49701). 231/436-5959; fax 231/436-5988; toll-free 800/288-8190. www.mackinawcity.com/lodging/starlite.* 33 rms. Mid-June-late Aug: S $42-$89; D $42-$149; family, wkly rates; higher rates: July 4, Labor Day, auto show; lower rates May-mid-June, late Aug-Oct. Closed rest of yr. Crib free. Pet accepted, some restrictions; $5. TV; cable (premium). Heated pool. Playground. Complimentary coffee in rms. Restaurant nearby. Ck-out 10 am. Refrigerators. Cr cds: A, MC, V.

D 🛱 ⇌ ⊠ 🔥

★ **SUPER 8 MOTEL.** *601 N Huron Ave (49701). 231/436-5252; fax 231/436-7004; toll-free 800/800-8000. www.super8.com.* 50 rms, 2 story. July-mid-Oct: S $74-$135; D $79-$145; each addl $6; higher rates special events (2-day min); lower rates rest of yr. Crib $6. Pet accepted, some restrictions. TV; cable, VCR avail. Indoor pool; whirlpool, sauna. Complimentary coffee in lobby. Restaurant nearby. Ck-out 11 am. Coin lndry. Game rm. Refrigerators

avail. Some balconies. Cr cds: A, C, D, DS, MC, V.

D 🛱 ⇌ ⊠ 🔥 SC

★★ **WATERFRONT INN.** *1009 S Huron St (US 23) (49701). 231/436-5527; fax 231/436-8661. www.largest beach.com.* 69 rms. July-early Sept: S $63-$71.95; D $49-$96.95; each addl $5; kit. units (up to 6) $350-$775/wk; higher rates: Labor Day wkend, antique auto show (3-day min); lower rates rest of yr. TV; cable (premium). Pool; whirlpool. Playground. Coffee in rms. Restaurant nearby. Ck-out 11 am. Some refrigerators. Picnic table. Private beach on Lake Huron. Cr cds: A, DS, MC, V.

D 🛱 ⇌ ⊠ 🔥

Restaurants

★★ **DAM SITE INN.** *6705 Woodland Rd, Pellston (49769). 231/539-8851. www.damsiteinn.com.* Hrs: 5-9 pm; Sun 3-8 pm, Apr-Oct. Closed late Oct-late Apr; also Mon Sept-June. No A/C. Bar. Dinner $12.75-$37. Specializes in own noodles, buttermilk biscuits, whitefish. Family-style chicken dinner. Fireplace. Overlooks dam. Cr cds: MC, V.

D ⊟

★ **EMBERS.** *810 S Huron Ave (US 23) (49701). 231/436-5773.* Hrs: 7 am-9 pm. Closed Nov-early Apr. Bar 8-midnight. Bkfst $1.95-$8, lunch $3.95-$8.95, dinner $6.95-$16.99. Buffet: bkfst $5.99, lunch $6.49, dinner $10.95. Specializes in broasted chicken, soups, bread pudding. Cr cds: DS, MC, V.

SC ⊟

★★ **'NEATH THE BIRCHES.** *14277 Mackinaw Hwy (49701). 231/436-5401.* Hrs: 4-10 pm; early-bird dinner 4-6 pm. Closed late Oct-mid-May. Res accepted. Bar. Dinner $8.95-$32.95. Child's menu. Specializes in prime rib, whitefish. Salad bar. Family-owned. Cr cds: A, D, DS, MC, V.

⊟

★ **PANCAKE CHEF.** *327 Central (49701). 231/436-5578. www.pancake chef.com.* Hrs: 7 am-10 pm; off-season to 9 pm. Bkfst $2.95-$7.50, lunch $5.25-$8.95, dinner $10.95-$12.95. Buffet: bkfst $6.95, dinner $11.50. Specializes in variety of pancakes, steak, fish. Salad bar. Cr cds: A, D, DS, MC, V.

Manistee

(E-3) *See also Ludington*

Pop 6,734 **Elev** 600 ft **Area code** 231 **Zip** 49660
Information Manistee Area Chamber of Commerce, 11 Cypress St; 231/723-2575 or 800/288-2286
Web www.manistee.com

With Lake Michigan on the west and the Manistee National Forest on the east, this site was once the home of 1,000 Native Americans who called it Manistee—"spirit of the woods." In the mid-1800s this was a thriving lumber town, serving as headquarters for more than 100 companies. When the timber supply was exhausted, the early settlers found other sources of revenue. Manistee is rich in natural resources including salt, oil, and natural gas. A Ranger District office of the Huron-Manistee National Forest is located in Manistee.

What to See and Do

Huron-Manistee National Forest. This 520,968-acre forest is the Manistee section of the Huron-Manistee National Forest (for Huron section see OSCODA). The forest incl the Lake Michigan Recreation Area, which contains trails and panoramic views of the sand dunes and offers beaches; fishing in lakes and in the Pine, Manistee, Little Manistee, White, Little Muskegon, and Pere Marquette rivers; boating; hiking, bicycle, and vehicle trails; hunting for deer and small game, camping, and picnicking. Winter sports incl downhill and x-country skiing, snowmobiling, ice fishing, and ice sailing. Fees charged at recreation sites. (Daily) E and S of town, via US 31 and MI 55. Contact Forest Supervisor, 412 Red Apple Rd. Phone 800/821-6263. **FREE**

Manistee County Historical Museum. Fixtures and fittings of 1880 drugstore and early general store; Victorian period rms, historical photographs; Civil War, marine collections; antique dolls, costumes, housewares. (June-Sept, Mon-Sat; rest of yr, Tues-Sat; closed hols) Russell Memorial Building, 425 River St. Phone 231/723-5531. ¢

> **Old Waterworks Building.** Logging wheels, early lumbering, shipping, and railroad exhibits; Victorian parlor, barbershop, shoe shop, kitchen. (Late June-Aug, Tues-Sat) W 1st St. Phone 231/723-5531.
> **Donation**

Orchard Beach State Park. High on a bluff overlooking Lake Michigan; 201 acres. Swimming beach; hiking, picnicking, playground, stone pavilion, camping. 2 mi N on MI 110. Contact Park Manager, 2064 Lakeshore Rd. Phone 231/723-7422. ¢¢

Ramsdell Theatre and Hall. (1903) Constructed by T. J. Ramsdell, pioneer attorney, this opulent building is home to the Manistee Civic Players, who present professional and community productions throughout the yr; also art and museum exhibits. Tours (June-Aug, Wed and Sat; rest of yr, by appt). 101 Maple St at 1st St. Phone 231/723-9948. **Donation**

Special Events

Shoot Time in Manistee. Old Fort Rendezvous. Traditional shooting events, costumed participants. Phone 231/723-9006. Late June.

National Forest Festival. Boat show; car show; US Forestry Service forest tours; parades, athletic events, raft and canoe races, Venetian boat parade, fireworks. Sponsored by the Chamber of Commerce. Phone 231/723-2575. July 4 wk.

Victorian Port City Festival. Musical entertainment, street art fair, antique auto exhibit, food, schooner rides. Early Sept. Phone 231/723-2575.

Motels/Motor Lodges

★ ★ **BEST WESTERN INN.** *200 Arthur St (US 31 N) (49660). 231/723-9949; toll-free 800/296-6835. www.bestwestern.com.* 72 rms, 2 story. Late May-Oct: S $48-$90; D $54-$130;

each addl $6; lower rates rest of yr.
Crib $6. TV; cable (premium). Indoor
pool. Restaurant 6 am-10 pm. Bar 2
pm-2 am. Ck-out 11 am. Meeting
rms. Business servs avail. Sundries.
Free airport transportation. X-
country ski 3 mi. Exercise equipt.
Game rm. Sun deck. Manistee Lake
opp. Cr cds: A, D, DS, MC, V.

★ **DAYS INN-MANISTEE.** *1462 US
31S (49660). 231/723-8385; fax 231/
723-2154; toll-free 888/626-4783. www.
daysinn.com.* 90 rms, 2 story. July-
Sept: S, D $55-$120; each addl $6;
under 12 free; lower rates rest of yr.
Crib free. TV; cable, VCR avail
(movies). Indoor pool; whirlpool.
Continental bkfst. Restaurant opp 5
am-midnight. Ck-out 11 am. Coin
lndry. Meeting rms. Business servs
avail. Sundries. Free airport transportation. X-country ski 3 mi. Game
rm. Cr cds: A, C, D, DS, JCB, MC, V.

★ **MANISTEE INN & MARINA.** *378
River St (49660). 231/723-4000; fax
231/723-0007; toll-free 800/968-6277.
www.manisteeinn.com.* 25 rms, 2 story.
Mid-May-mid-Sept: S $59-$73; D
$64-$77; each addl $9; whirlpool rms
$91-$129; lower rates rest of yr. Crib
free. TV; cable, VCR (movies $2).
Complimentary continental bkfst.
Restaurant nearby. Ck-out 11 am.
Coin lndry. Meeting rm. Business
servs avail. X-country ski 10 mi. Cr
cds: A, D, DS, MC, V.

Manistique (C-3)

Pop 3,456 **Elev** 600 ft **Area code** 906
Zip 49854
Information Schoolcraft County
Chamber of Commerce, 1000 W
Lakeshore Dr; 906/341-5010
Web www.manistique.com

Manistique, the county seat of
Schoolcraft County, has a bridge in
town named "The Siphon Bridge"
that is partially supported by the
water that flows underneath it. The
roadway is approximately four feet

below the water level. Fishing for
salmon is good in the area. A Ranger
District office of the Hiawatha
National Forest (see ESCANABA) is
located here.

What to See and Do

State parks.

Fayette. Approx 700 acres. Fayette,
formerly an industrial town producing charcoal iron (1867-1891),
is now a ghost town; self-guided
tour of restored remains; interpretive center (May-Oct). Swimming,
fishing; picnicking, playground,
camping. 15 mi W on US 2, then
17 mi S on MI 183 to Fayette on
Big Bay de Noc. Phone 906/644-
2603. ¢¢

Indian Lake. Approx 550 acres.
Swimming, sand beach, bathhouse,
waterskiing, boating (rentals,
launch); fishing for pike, perch,
walleye, bass, and bluegill; hiking,
picnicking, camping. (Daily) 6 mi
W on US 2, then 3 mi N on MI
149, ½ mi E on County Rd 442.
Phone 906/341-2355. ¢¢

Palms Book. Approx 300 acres.
Here is Kitch-iti-ki-pi, the state's
largest spring, 200 ft wide, 40 ft
deep; 16,000 gallons of water per
min form a stream to Indian Lake.
Observation raft for viewing the
spring. Picnicking, concession. No
camping allowed. Standard fees.
Closed in winter. S on US 2 to
Thompson, then 12 mi NW on MI
149. Phone 906/341-2355. ¢¢

Thompson State Fish Hatchery. 7 mi
SW via US 2, MI 149. Phone
906/341-5587. **FREE**

Special Events

**Schoolcraft County Snowmobile
Poker Run.** Late Jan. Phone 906/341-
5010.

Folkfest. Mid-July. Phone 906/341-
5010.

Motels/Motor Lodges

★ ★ **BEST WESTERN BREAKERS.**
*1199 E Lakeshore Dr (49854).
906/341-2410; fax 906/341-2207; toll-
free 888/335-3674. www.bestwestern.
com.* 40 rms. Mid-June-early Sept: S
$49-$69; D $54-$74; each addl $5;
studio rms $89; under 13 free; lower
rates rest of yr. Crib free. TV; cable

(premium). Indoor/outdoor pool; whirlpool. Restaurant adj 7 am-9 pm. Ck-out 11 am. Overlooks Lake Michigan. Private beach opp. Cr cds: A, C, D, DS, MC, V.

★ **BUDGET HOST/MANISTIQUE MOTOR INN.** *RR 1, Box 1505 (49854). 906/341-2552; toll-free 800/ 283-4678. www.budgethost.com.* 26 rms, 13 A/C. Mid-June-Labor Day: S $44-$55; D $46-$58; each addl $5; suites $65-$100; lower rates rest of yr. Crib $3. TV; cable (premium). Heated pool. Restaurant adj 5 am-11 pm; bar. Ck-out 11 am. Business servs avail. Free airport, bus depot transportation. X-country ski 5 mi. Lawn games. Cr cds: A, C, D, DS, ER, MC, V.

★ **ECONO LODGE.** *US 2 E (49854). 906/341-6014; fax 906/341-2979; res 800/446-6900. www.econolodge.com.* 31 rms. July-Labor Day: S $49-$59; D $59-$66; each addl $5; under 18 free; lower rates rest of yr. TV; cable (premium). Complimentary continental bkfst. Restaurant nearby. Ck-out 11 am. X-country ski 10 mi. Lake Michigan boardwalk opp. Cr cds: A, C, D, DS, JCB, MC, V.

★ **HOLIDAY MOTEL.** *E US Hwy 2 (49854). 906/341-2710.* 20 rms. No A/C. June-Labor Day: D $48; lower rates rest of yr. Crib $5. Pet accepted. TV; cable (premium). Heated pool. Playground. Complimentary continental bkfst. Restaurant nearby. Ck-out 10 am. Lawn games. Picnic tables. Cr cds: A, DS, MC, V.

★ **NORTHSHORE MOTOR INN.** *Rte 1 Box 1967, US 2 E (49854). 906/341-2420; toll-free 800/297-7107.* 12 rms. July-Aug: S $28-$36; D $38-$52; each addl $4; under 12 free; lower rates rest of yr. Crib free. TV; cable (premium). Restaurant nearby. Ck-out 11 am. X-country ski 6 mi. Picnic tables. Opp lake. Cr cds: A, C, D, DS, MC, V.

B&B/Small Inn

★ **CELIBETH HOUSE.** *RR1 Box 58 A, Blaney Park (49836). 906/283-* 3409. *www.celibethhouse.com.* 7 air-cooled rms, 3 story. No rm phones. S, D $85; each addl $10; suite $98. Closed Dec-Apr. Complimentary continental bkfst. Restaurant nearby. Ck-out 11 am, ck-in 3 pm. X-country ski 11 mi. Picnic tables. Renovated house (1895) used as logging company's headquarters and then as part of resort. Antiques, sitting rm with fireplace. On 85 acres overlooking private lake. Totally nonsmoking. Cr cds: MC, V.

Marquette

(B-2) *See also Ishpeming*

Settled 1849 **Pop** 21,977 **Elev** 628 ft
Area code 906 **Zip** 49855
Information Marquette Area Chamber of Commerce, 501 S Front St; 906/226-6591
Web www.marquette.org

The largest city in the Upper Peninsula, Marquette is the regional center for retailing, government, medicine, and iron ore shipping. Miles of public beaches and picnic areas flank the dock areas on Lake Superior. Rocks rise by the water and bedrock runs just a few feet below the surface. The city is named for the missionary explorer Father Jacques Marquette, who made canoe trips along the shore here between 1669 and 1671. At the rear flank of the city is sand-plain blueberry country, as well as forests and mountains of granite and iron.

What to See and Do

Marquette County Historical Museum. Exhibits of regional historical interest; J. M. Longyear Research Library. (Mon-Fri; closed hols) 213 N Front St. Phone 906/226-3571. ¢

Mount Marquette Scenic Outlook Area. Provides lovely view. (May-mid-Oct, daily) 1 mi S via US 41.

Northern Michigan University. (1899) 8,900 students. The 300-acre campus incl the Superior Dome, the world's largest wooden dome (spans 5.1 acres); Lee Hall Gallery; and a five-acre technology and applied sciences center. Olson Library has Tyler Collection on Early American literature. The school has been designated an Olympic Education Center. Tours avail. Presque Isle Ave. Phone 906/227-1700.

Presque Isle Park. Picnic facilities (four picnic sites for the disabled), swimming, water slide (fees), boating (launch, fee); nature trails, x-country skiing, tennis courts, playground. Bog walk features 4,000-ft trail with plank walkways and observation decks; self-guided with interpretive sign boards at ten conservation points. (May-Oct, daily; rest of yr, open only for winter sports) On the lake in NE part of city. Phone 906/228-0460. **FREE** Near the park is

> **Upper Harbor ore dock.** Several million tons of ore are shipped annually from this site; the loading of ore freighters is a fascinating sight to watch. Adj parking lot for viewing and photography.

Skiing. Marquette Mountain Ski Area. Three double chairlifts, rope tow; patrol, school, rentals, snowmaking, night skiing, wkly NASTAR; cafeteria, bar, nursery. Longest run 1¼ mi; vertical drop 600 ft. (Late Nov-Apr, daily) X-country trails (three mi) nearby. 3 mi SW on County 553. Phone 906/115-5800.

Statue of Father Marquette. On top of a bluff overlooking the site of the first settlement. Marquette Park. Phone 906/228-0460.

Sugar Loaf Mountain. A 3,200-ft trail leads to summit for panoramic view of Lake Superior coastline and forestland. 7 mi N on County 550.

Tourist Park. Swimming, fishing; playground, tent and trailer sites (mid-May-mid-Oct, daily; fee). Entrance fee charged during Hiawatha Music Festival (see SPECIAL EVENTS). On County 550. Phone 906/225-1555. **FREE**

Upper Peninsula Children's Museum. All exhibits are products of kids' imaginations; regional youth planned their conceptual development. (Tues-Sun; closed hols) 123 W Baraga Ave. Phone 906/226-3911. ¢¢

Special Events

UP 200 Dog Sled Race. Dog sled race; features food, games, entertainment, dog-sledding exhibitions. Mid-late Feb. Phone 800/544-4321.

International Food Festival. Ellwood Mattson Lower Harbor Park. Ethnic foods, crafts, music. July 4 wkend. Phone 906/249-1595.

Hiawatha Music Festival. Tourist Park. Bluegrass, traditional music festival. Third wkend July. Phone 906/226-8575.

Art on the Rocks. Presque Isle Park. Nationwide art display and sale. Last full wkend July. Phone 906/228-4137.

Seafood Festival. Ellwood Mattson Lower Harbor Park. Wkend before Labor Day. Phone 906/226-6591.

Motels/Motor Lodges

★ **CEDAR MOTOR INN.** *2523 US Hwy 41 W (49855). 906/228-2280.* 44 rms, 1-2 story. Mid-June-mid-Oct: S, D $44-$58; each addl $3; lower rates rest of yr. Crib $5. TV; cable (premium). Indoor pool; whirlpool, sauna. Coffee in rms. Restaurant nearby. Ck-out 11 am. Meeting rm. Business servs avail. In-rm modem link. Downhill ski 5 mi; x-country ski 3 mi. Sun deck. Cr cds: A, D, DS, MC, V.

🄳 ⊠ ≈ ⊠ 🔥

★ **DAYS INN.** *2403 US 41 W (49855). 906/225-1393; fax 906/225-9845; res 800/329-7466. www.days inn.com.* 65 rms. July-Sept: S $55-$60, D $60-$65; each addl $6; family rates; lower rates rest of yr. Crib free. TV; cable (premium). Indoor pool; whirlpool, sauna. Complimentary continental bkfst. Restaurant nearby. Ck-out 11 am. Downhill ski 5 mi; x-country ski 3 mi. Some refrigerators. Cr cds: A, C, D, DS, MC, V.

🄳 ⊠ ≈ ⊠ 🄰 SC

★★ **HOLIDAY INN.** *1951 US 41 W (49855). 906/225-1351; fax 906/228-4329; toll-free 800/465-4329. www. holiday-inn.com.* 203 rms, 5 story. S, D $69-$104; each addl $4; family rates; ski plans. Crib free. Pet accepted. TV; cable (premium). Indoor pool; whirlpool. Restaurant 6 am-2 pm, 5-10 pm. Bar 3 pm-2 am; Sun to midnight. Ck-out noon. Meeting rm. Business servs avail. Bellhops. Valet serv. Sundries. Free airport transportation. Downhill ski 7 mi; x-country ski 3 mi. Sauna.

Health club privileges. Nature trails. Picnic tables. Cr cds: A, C, D, DS, MC, V.

D ⧖ ⛵ ⚓ ✈ 🏊 🔥

★ **IMPERIAL MOTEL.** *2493 US 41 W (49855). 906/228-7430; fax 906/228-3883; toll-free 800/424-9514. www. imperialmotel.com.* 43 rms, 2 story. June-Oct: S $38-$45; D $48-$57; each addl $4; lower rates rest of yr. Crib $7. TV; cable (premium). Indoor pool; sauna. Coffee in lobby. Restaurants nearby. Ck-out 11 am. Business servs avail. Downhill ski 5 mi; x-country ski 3 mi. Game rm. Cr cds: A, C, D, DS, MC, V.

D ⛵ ⚓ 🏊 🔥 **SC**

★★ **RAMADA INN.** *412 W Washington St (49855). 906/228-6000; fax 906/228-2963; toll-free 800/272-6232. www.ramada.com.* 113 rms, 2-7 story. S $84-$89; D $89-$94; each addl $5; under 18 free. Crib free. Pet accepted. TV; cable (premium). Indoor pool; whirlpool, sauna. Restaurant 6 am-10 pm; Fri, Sat to 11 pm. Bar 11-2 am. Ck-out noon. Coin lndry. Meeting rms. Business servs avail. Airport transportation. Downhill ski 3 mi; x-country ski ½ mi. Many poolside rms. Health club privileges. Cr cds: A, C, D, DS, JCB, MC, V.

D ⧖ ⛵ 🐾 ⚓ ✈ 🏊 🔥

★★ **TIROLER HOF INN.** *1880 US 41 S (49855). 906/226-7516; fax 906/226-0699; toll-free 800/892-9376.* 44 rms, 36 A/C, 2 story. Mid-May-mid-Oct: S $42; D $50-$52; each addl $5; suites $68; studio rms $50-$52; lower rates rest of yr. Crib avail. TV; cable (premium). Playground. Restaurant (in season) 7:30-10 am, 5:30-9 pm. Ck-out 11 am. Coin lndry. Meeting rm. Downhill/x-country ski 1½ mi. Rec rm. Sauna. Private patios, balconies. Picnic tables, grills. On 13 acres; pond. Overlooks Lake Superior. Cr cds: A, DS, MC, V.

⛵ 🏊 🔥

★ **VALUE HOST MOTOR INN.** *1101 US 41 W (49801). 906/225-5000; fax 906/225-5096; toll-free 800/929-5996.* 52 rms, 2 story. May-Oct: S $34.45-$37.45; D $38.45-$48.50; each addl $5; family rates; lower rates rest of yr. Crib free. TV; cable (premium). Complimentary continental bkfst. Restaurant nearby. Ck-out 11 am. Meeting

rm. Business servs avail. Downhill/x-country ski 4 mi. Sauna. Whirlpool. Some refrigerators. Picnic tables. Cr cds: A, MC, V.

D ⛵ 🏊 🔥 🔥

Restaurant

★★ **NORTHWOODS SUPPER CLUB.** *260 Northwoods Rd (49855). 906/228-4343.* Hrs: 11 am-11 pm; Sun 10 am-10 pm; Sun brunch 10 am-2 pm. Closed Dec 24-26. Res accepted. Bar. Lunch $4.95-$8, dinner $9-$21. Buffet (dinner): Tues $10.95. Sun brunch $8.95. Child's menu. Specializes in steak, seafood, fresh Lake Superior fish. Salad bar. Own baking. Entertainment Fri-Sun. Rustic atmosphere; 5 fireplaces. Family-owned. Cr cds: A, DS, MC, V.

D **SC** 🍽

Marshall (G-5)

Founded 1830 **Pop** 6,891 **Elev** 916 ft
Area code 616 **Zip** 49068

Information Chamber of Commerce, 424 E Michigan; 616/781-5163 or 800/877-5163

Web www.marshallmi.org

Marshall was, at one time, slated to be Michigan's capital—a grand governor's mansion was built, land was set aside for the capitol, and wealthy and influential people swarmed into the town. In 1847, Marshall lost its capital bid to Lansing. Today, many of the elaborate houses and buildings of the period remain, and more than 30 historical markers dot the city's streets.

What to See and Do

American Museum of Magic. Display of vintage magical equipt, rare posters, photographs, and personal effects of some of the well-known magicians of history. (By appt) 107 E Michigan Ave. Phone 616/781-7674. ¢¢

Honolulu House Museum. (1860) This exotic structure, blending traditional Italianate architecture with tropical motifs of island plantation houses, was built by first US Consul to the Sandwich Islands (now Hawaii); period furnishings, artifacts. Also headquarters of Marshall Historical Society, which provides free self-guided walking tour brochures listing town's many interesting 19th-century buildings and more than 30 historical markers. (May-Oct, daily; rest of yr, wkends) 107 N Kalamazoo Ave. Phone 616/781-8544. ¢¢

Special Events

Welcome to My Garden Tour. Tour of Marshall's most distinctive gardens. Phone 616/781-5434. Second wkend July.

Historic Home Tour. Informal tours of nine 19th-century homes, incl Honolulu House (see), Governor's Mansion, and Capitol Hill School. First wkend after Labor Day. Phone 800/877-5163.

B&Bs/Small Inns

★★ **MCCARTHY'S BEAR CREEK INN.** *15230 C Drive N (49068). 616/781-8255.* 14 rms, 2-3 story. No rm phones. S, D $65-$98; each addl $10. Crib free. Complimentary continental bkfst. Ck-out noon, ck-in 3 pm. X-country ski 12 mi. Some balconies. Picnic tables. Rms in renovated house and dairy barn (1948); country decor, antiques. On wooded knoll overlooking Bear Creek; handbuilt fieldstone fencing. Cr cds: A, MC, V.

★★ **NATIONAL HOUSE INN.** *102 S Parkview St (49068). 616/781-7374; fax 616/781-4510. www.national houseinn.com.* 16 rms, 2 story. S, D $69-$130; each addl $10; under 6 free. Closed Dec 24-25. Crib free. TV; cable (premium), VCR avail. Complimentary bkfst. Restaurant nearby. Ck-out noon, ck-in after 3 pm. Business servs avail. Airport transportation. X-country ski 10 mi. Oldest operating inn in state; authentically restored, antique furnishings. Established in 1835. Cr cds: A, MC, V.

Restaurant

★★ **SCHULER'S OF MARSHALL.** *115 S Eagle St (49068). 616/781-0600. www.schulersrestaurant.com.* Hrs: 11 am-10 pm; Sat to 11 pm; Sun to 9 pm; Sun brunch 10 am-2 pm; hols to 9 pm. Closed Dec 25. Res accepted. Bar; wkends to midnight. Lunch $5.75-$9.95, dinner $13.95-$24.95. Sun brunch $17.95. Child's menu. Specializes in prime rib, fresh fish. Own desserts. Menu changes seasonally. Patio dining. 3 dining rms with fireplaces. Bakery on premises. Family-owned. Cr cds: A, D, DS, MC, V.

Unrated Dining Spot

CORNWELL'S TURKEYVILLE. *18935 15-1/2 Mile Rd (49068). 616/781-4293. www.turkeyville.com.* Hrs: 11 am-8 pm. Closed late Dec-mid-Jan. Avg ck: lunch, dinner $4-$8. Child's menu. Specializes in various turkey meals. Dinner theater. Outdoor dining. Family-owned. Cr cds: DS, MC, V.

Menominee

(D-2) *Also see Marinette, WI*

Settled 1796 **Pop** 9,398 **Elev** 600 ft
Area code 906 **Zip** 49858
Information Menominee Area Chamber of Commerce, 1005 10th Ave, PO Box 427; 906/863-2679

Because of water transportation and water power, many manufacturing industries have located in Menominee. Green Bay and the Menominee River form two sides of the triangle-shaped city. Across the river is the sister city of Marinette, Wisconsin (see). Established as a fur-trading post, later a lumbering center, Menominee County is the largest dairy producer in the state of Michigan. Menominee is a Native American word for "wild rice," which once grew profusely on the riverbanks.

What to See and Do

First Street Historic District. Variety of specialty shops located in a setting of restored 19th-century buildings. Marina, parks, restaurants, galleries. From 10th Ave to 4th Ave.

Henes Park. Small zoo with deer yards, nature trails, bathing beach, and picnic area. (Memorial Day-mid Oct, daily) Henes Park Dr, NE of city off MI 35. Phone 906/863-2656. **FREE**

J. W. Wells State Park. Approx 700 acres, incl two mi along Green Bay and 1,400 ft along Big Cedar River. Swimming, bathhouse, waterskiing, fishing, boating (ramp); hunting, snowmobiling, x-country skiing, picnicking, playground, camping, cabins and shelters. Standard fees. 23 mi NE on MI 35, Cedar River. Phone 906/863-9747.

Menominee Marina. One of the best small-craft anchorages on the Great Lakes. Swimming beach, lifeguard. (May-Oct, daily) 1st St between 8th and 10th aves. Phone 906/863-8498.

Stephenson Island. Reached by bridge that also carries traffic between the sister cities on US 41 (see MARINETTE, WI). On island are picnic areas and a historical museum. In middle of Menominee River.

Special Event

Waterfront Festival. Entertainment, music, dancing, footraces, fireworks, food, parade. Four days, first wkend Aug. Phone 906/863-2679.

Midland

(F-5) *See also Bay City, Mount Pleasant, Saginaw*

Pop 38,053 **Elev** 629 ft **Area code** 989
Information Midland County Convention & Visitors Bureau, 300 Rodd St, Suite 101, 48640; 989/839-9522 or 888/4-MIDLAND
Web www.midlandcvb.org

Midland owed its prosperity to the lumber industry until Herbert Henry Dow founded The Dow Chemical Company in 1897.

What to See and Do

Architectural Tour. Self-guided driving tour of buildings designed by Alden B. Dow, son of Herbert H. Dow. The younger Dow studied under Frank Lloyd Wright at Taliesin.

He designed more than 45 buildings in Midland, incl the architect's house and studio, churches, Stein House (his Taliesin apprentice project), and the Whitman House, for which he won the 1937 Grand Prix for residential architecture. Many buildings are privately owned and not open to the public. Maps and audio cassettes are avail at the Midland Center for the Arts. Audio cassettes ¢¢

Chippewa Nature Center. On more than 1,000 acres; 14 mi of marked and mowed trails; wildflower walkway and pond boardwalk; Homestead Farm; reconstructed 1870s log cabin, barn, sugarhouse, one-rm schoolhouse; visitor center; museum depicting evolutionary natural history of the Saginaw Valley; auditorium, library; seasonal programs. (Daily; closed Thanksgiving, Dec 25) 400 S Badour Rd. Phone 989/631-0830. **FREE**

★ **Dow Gardens.** Gardens, originally grounds of the residence of Herbert H. Dow, founder of The Dow Chemical Company, incl more than 100 acres of trees, flowers, streams, waterfalls; greenhouse, conservatory. (Daily; closed hols) Tours by appt. Entrance at Eastman Rd and W St. Andrews. Phone 989/631-2677. ¢¢

Herbert H. Dow Historical Museum. Composed of replicated Evans Flour Mill and adj buildings that housed Dow's Midland Chemical Company, predecessor to the Dow Chemical Company. Interpretive galleries incl Joseph Dow's workshop, Herbert Dow's office, drillhouse with steam-powered brine pump, laboratory; audiovisual theater. (Wed-Sat, also Sun afternoons; closed hols) 3200 Cook Rd, 2 mi NW via W Main St. Phone 989/832-5319. ¢

Midland Center for the Arts. Designed by Alden B. Dow. Houses Hall of Ideas, a museum of science, technology, health, history, and art exhibits. Also concerts, plays. Architectural tour begins here. (Daily; closed hols) 1801 W St. Andrews. Phone 989/631-5930. ¢¢

Special Events

Maple Syrup Festival. Chippewa Nature Center. Third Sat Mar. Phone 989/631-0830.

Michigan Antique Festivals. Midland Center for the Arts. 1,000 vendors inside and outside. Mid-May-mid-June. Phone 989/687-9001.

Matrix: Midland Festival. County Fairgrounds. Celebration of the arts, sciences, humanities; classical and popular music, theater, dance; lectures by noted professionals. Phone 989/631-7980. Late June-Sept.

Fall Festival. Chippewa Nature Center. Second wkend Oct. Phone 989/631-0830.

Motels/Motor Lodges

★ ★ **BEST WESTERN VALLEY PLAZA RESORT.** *5221 Bay City Rd (48642). 989/496-2700; fax 989/496-9233; toll-free 800/825-2700. www. valleyplazaresort.com.* 162 rms, 2 story. S $67; D $77; suites $125-$175; under 18 free; higher rates wkends. Crib free. Pet accepted, some restrictions. TV; cable. Indoor pool; wading pool. Playground. Complimentary continental bkfst. Restaurant 6 am-9 pm; Sat from 7 am; Sun to noon. Bar noon-1 am. Ck-out noon. Meeting rms. In-rm modem link. Bellhops. Valet serv. Gift shop. Free airport transportation. Exercise rm. Game rm. Lawn games. Bowling. Movie theater. Small lake with beach. Cr cds: A, C, D, DS, JCB, MC, V.
🅳 ⬛ ⬛ ⬛ ⬛ ⬛ ⬛

★ ★ **HOLIDAY INN.** *1500 W Wackerly St (48640). 989/631-4220; fax 989/631-3776; res 800/377-6856. www.holiday-inn.com.* 235 rms, 2 story. S, D $85; under 18 free; wkend rates. Crib free. Pet accepted, some restrictions. TV; cable (premium). Indoor pool; whirlpool, poolside serv. Playground. Restaurant 6 am-3 pm, 5:30-10 pm. Bar 11:30 am-11 pm; entertainment. Ck-out 11 am. Meeting rms. Business center. In-rm modem link. Bellhops. Valet serv. Sundries. Free airport transportation. Tennis privileges. X-country ski 2 mi. Exercise equipt; sauna. Game rm. Cr cds: A, C, D, DS, JCB, MC, V.
🅳 ⬛ ⬛ ⬛ ⬛ ⬛ ⬛ ⬛ ⬛

★ **SUPER 8.** *4955 Garfield Rd, Auburn (68467). 989/662-7888; fax 989/662-7607; toll-free 800/800-8000. www. super8.com.* 60 rms, 3 story. S $44; D $52-$58; each addl $3; suites $66-$77; under 12 free; wkly rates. Crib

free. TV; cable (premium). Indoor pool. Complimentary continental bkfst. Complimentary coffee in lobby. Ck-out 11 am. Coin lndry. Airport transportation. Downhill ski 15 mi. Game rm. Some refrigerators. Cr cds: A, DS, MC, V.
🅳 ⬛ ⬛ ⬛ ⬛

Monroe

(H-6) *See also Detroit; also see Toledo, OH*

Settled 1780 **Pop** 22,902 **Elev** 599 ft
Area code 734 **Zip** 48161
Information Monroe County Chamber of Commerce, 106 W Front St, PO Box 1094; 734/457-1030
Web www.monroeinfo.com

Originally called Frenchtown because of the many French families that settled here, this city on Lake Erie was renamed in 1817 in honor of President James Monroe. The river that flows through the center of the city was named the River Aux Raisin because of the many grapes growing in the area. At one time, Monroe was briefly the home of General George Armstrong Custer of "Little Big Horn" fame.

What to See and Do

Monroe County Historical Museum. Exhibits of General George Custer, Woodland Native Americans, pioneers, War of 1812; trading post, country store museum. (Summer, daily; rest of yr, Wed-Sun; closed hols) 126 S Monroe St. Phone 734/243-7137. ¢

River Raisin Battlefield Visitor Center. Interprets fierce War of 1812 battle of River Raisin (Jan 1813). Nearly 1,000 US soldiers from Kentucky clashed with British, Native American, and Canadian forces on this site; only 33 Americans escaped death or capture. Exhibits of weapons and uniforms, dioramas, fiber optic audiovisual map program. (Memorial Day-Labor Day, daily; rest of yr, wkends; closed hols) 1402 Elm Ave, just off I-75 at Elm Ave exit. Phone 734/243-7136. **FREE**

Sterling State Park. On 1,001 acres. Swimming, waterskiing, fishing, boating (ramp); hiking, picnicking, playground, concession, camping. Standard fees. N of city, off I-75. Phone 734/289-2715. ¢¢

Special Event

Monroe County Fair. Monroe County Fairgrounds, jct MI 50 and Raisinville Rd. Rides, concessions, merchant buildings. Phone 734/241-5775. Late July-early Aug.

Motels/Motor Lodges

★ **DAYS INN.** *1440 N Dixie Hwy (48162). 734/289-4000; fax 734/289-4262; res 800/329-7466. www.days inn.com.* 115 rms, 2 story. S $50-$70; D $50-$85; each addl $10; under 12 free. Crib free. TV; cable (premium). Indoor pool; whirlpool, sauna. Restaurant 5 am-10 pm. Bar 11-2 am. Ck-out noon. Meeting rms. Business servs avail. In-rm modem link. Game rm. Private patios, balconies. Cr cds: A, DS, MC, V.

★★ **HOLIDAY INN EXPRESS HOTEL.** *1225 N Dixie Hwy (48162). 734/242-6000; fax 734/242-0555; toll-free 800/242-6008. www.holiday-inn.com.* 161 rms, 34 suites, 4 story. S $60; D $68; each addl $8; under 18 free; wkend rates off-season; golf plans. Crib free. Pet accepted. TV; cable (premium), VCR avail. Indoor pool; whirlpool, sauna, poolside serv. Restaurant 6 am-10 pm. Bar 11-2 am; Sun noon-midnight; entertainment Mon-Sat. Ck-out noon. Meeting rms. In-rm modem link. Bellhops. Valet serv. Sundries. Golf privileges. Game rm. Cr cds: A, MC, V.

Mount Clemens

Pop 18,405 **Elev** 614 ft **Area code** 586
Information Central Macomb County Chamber of Commerce, 58 S Gratiot, 48043; 586/493-7600

What to See and Do

Art Center. Exhibits and classes, sponsors tours. Sales gallery, gift shop. Holiday Fair (Dec). (Mon-Fri, limited hrs Sat; closed July and Aug) 125 Macomb Pl. Phone 586/469-8666. **FREE**

Crocker House. (1869) This Italianate building, home of the Macomb County Historical Society, was originally owned by the first two mayors of Mount Clemens; period rms, changing exhibits. (Mar-Dec, Tues-Thurs; also first Sun month) 15 Union St. Phone 586/465-2488. ¢

Metro Beach Metropark. Park features ¾-mi beach (late May-Sept, daily), pool (Memorial Day-Labor Day, daily; fee), bathhouse, boating, marinas, ramps, launch, dock (fee); 18-hole par-three golf course, miniature golf, shuffleboard, tennis, group rental activity center, playgrounds. Picnicking, concessions. Nature center. (Daily, hrs vary) No pets. Free admission Tues. 4 mi SE off I-94 on Lake St. Clair, exit 236. Phone 586/463-4581. ¢

Special Event

Farm City Festival. Late Aug. Phone 586/463-1528.

Motel/Motor Lodge

★★ **COMFORT INN OF UTICA.** *11401 Hall Rd, Utica (48317). 586/739-7111; fax 586/739-1041; res 800/228-5150. www.comfortinn.com.* 104 rms, 3 story. S $69-$84; D $69-$94; each addl $5; under 16 free. Crib free. TV; cable (premium), VCR avail (movies). Complimentary continental bkfst. Restaurant nearby. Ck-out noon. Coin lndry. Business servs avail. In-rm modem link. Valet serv. Airport transportation. Cr cds: A, MC, V.

Mount Pleasant

(E-5) *See also Alma, Clare, Midland*

Pop 23,285 **Elev** 770 ft **Area code** 989
Zip 48858

Information Convention & Visitors Bureau, 114 E Broadway; 800/772-4433

Web www.mt-pleasant.net

What to See and Do

Center for Cultural & Natural History. Incl 45 exhibits and dioramas on anthropology, history, and natural science. (Daily; closed hols) Rowe Hall. **FREE**

Central Michigan University. (1892) 16,300 students. Phone 989/774-4000. Here is

    Clarke Historical Library. Rare books, manuscripts; historical documents of Northwest Territory; children's library; changing exhibits. (School yr, Mon-Fri) Phone 989/774-3352. **FREE**

Soaring Eagle Casino. Incl 2,500-seat Bingo Hall, slot machines, blackjack, craps, and roulette. Saginaw Chippewa Campground is nearby. (Daily) 2395 S Leaton Rd. Phone 888/732-4537. **FREE**

Special Events

Maple Syrup Festival. Approx 5 mi S via US 27, in Shepherd. Last wkend Apr. Phone 989/828-6486.

Apple Fest. First wkend Oct. Phone 989/773-3028.

Motels/Motor Lodges

★★ **COMFORT INN.** 2424 S Mission St (48858). 989/772-4000; fax 989/773-6052; res 800/228-5150. www.comfortinn.com. 138 rms, 2 story, 12 suites. S, D $48.50-$119.50; each addl $5; suites $135; under 18 free; wkly, wkday rates; golf plans; higher rates: CMU football wkends, festivals. Crib free. Pet accepted. TV; cable (premium), VCR (movies). Indoor pool. Complimentary continental bkfst. Restaurant nearby. Ck-out noon. Coin lndry. Meeting rms. Business servs avail. In-rm modem link. Game rm. Cr cds: A, D, DS, MC, V.

D 🐾 ➳ 🏖 🐾

★★ **HOLIDAY INN.** 5665 E Pickard St (48858). 989/772-2905; fax 989/772-4952; toll-free 800/299-8891. www.holiday-inn.com. 184 rms, 2-3 story. S, D $58-$145; each addl $10; under 12 free; golf plan. Crib free.

Pet accepted. TV; cable (premium). 2 pools, 1 indoor; whirlpool. Playground. Coffee in rms. Restaurants 6:30 am-10 pm; Sun to 8 pm. Bar noon-2 am; Sun to 8 pm; entertainment Mon-Sat. Ck-out 11 am. Coin lndry. Meeting rms. Business servs avail. In-rm modem link. Bellhops. Valet serv. Sundries. Free airport, bus depot transportation. Lighted tennis. 36-hole golf, greens fee $35-$65, putting green, driving range. Exercise rm; sauna. Rec rm. Lawn games. In-rm whirlpools, refrigerators; some minibars. Balconies. Cr cds: A, MC, V.

D 🐾 🏂 🎣 ➳ 🏃 🛏 🐾 SC

★ **SUPER 8.** 2323 S Mission St (48858). 989/773-8888; fax 989/772-5371; toll-free 800/868-5252. www.super8.com. 143 rms, 3 story. Apr-Sept: S $59.88-$84; D $59.88-$89; each addl $5; under 16 free; lower rates rest of yr. Crib free. Pet accepted. TV; cable (premium), VCR avail (movies). Complimentary continental bkfst. Restaurant nearby. Ck-out noon. Meeting rm. Business servs avail. Valet serv. Tennis privileges. X-country ski 3 mi. Some in-rm whirlpools, refrigerators. Cr cds: A, C, D, DS, JCB, MC, V.

D 🐾 🎣 🛏 🐾 SC ➳

Resort

★★★ **SOARING EAGLE CASINO & RESORT.** 6800 Soaring Eagle Blvd (48858). 989/775-7777; fax 989/775-5383; toll-free 888/732-4537. www.soaringeaglecasino.com. 512 rms, 7 story, 20 suites. S, D $119-$179; suites $199-$350; children $10; lower rates rest of yr. Crib Free. Free valet parking avail. Heated indoor pool, children's pool, lifeguard, lap pool, whirlpool, poolside serv. TV; cable (premium). Complimentary coffee in rms, newspaper, toll-free calls. Restaurant 7 am-11 pm. 24-hr rm serv. Bar. Ck-out 11 am, ck-in 4 pm. Conference center, meeting rms. Business servs avail. Bellhops. Concierge. Valet serv. Gift shop. Full-service spa. Salon/barber. Exercise rm, sauna, steam rm. Golf. Supervised children's activities. Video games. Casino. Bingo. Refrigerators avail. Some fireplaces, balconies.

Native Americam theme. Cr cds: A, D, DS, MC, V.

[D] [X] [≈] [X] [✈] [≈] [♠] [SC]

Restaurants

★ ★ ★ **EMBERS.** *1217 S Mission St (US 27 Business) (48858). 989/773-5007.* Hrs: 5 pm-9 pm; Fri, Sat to 10 pm; Sun 10 am-7 pm; Sun brunch to 2 pm. Closed hols. Res accepted. Serv bar. Dinner $15.95-$25.95. Sun brunch $10.95. Child's menu. Specializes in pork chops, certified Angus beef. Smorgasbord 1st and 3rd Thurs. Own baking. Open charcoal grill. Family-owned. Cr cds: A, D, DS, MC, V.

[D] [≈]

★ ★ ★ **WATER LILY.** *6800 Soaring Eagle Blvd (48858). 989/775-5496.* American menu. Specializes in fricassee of Maine lobster, herb-roasted chicken, roasted muscovy duck breast. Hrs: 6:30 am-9:30 pm; Fri, Sat to 10 pm; Sun 10:30 am-2 pm, 5:30-9:30 pm. Res accepted. Bar. Bkfst, lunch, dinner a la carte entrees: $7.50-$32. 47-ft long water wall. Cr cds: A, D, DS, MC, V.

Munising (B-3)

Pop 2,783 **Elev** 620 ft **Area code** 906 **Zip** 49862

Information Alger Chamber of Commerce, 422 E Munising Ave, PO Box 405; 906/387-2138

Web www.algercounty.org

Colorful sandstone formations, waterfalls, sand dunes, agate beaches, hiking trails, and outdoor recreational facilities are part of the Hiawatha National Forest and the Pictured Rocks National Lakeshore, which stretches eastward from Munising along 42 miles of the south shore of Lake Superior. Camping areas are plentiful in the Lakeshore, Hiawatha National Forest, and on Lake Superior. A Ranger District office of the Hiawatha National Forest (see ESCANABA) is located in Munising.

What to See and Do

Pictured Rocks Boat Cruise. A 37-mi cruise on the *Miners Castle, Pictured Rocks, Grand Island,* or *Miss Superior.* (June-early Oct, daily) City Pier, Elm Ave. Phone 906/387-2379. ¢¢¢¢

★ **Pictured Rocks National Lakeshore.** Along a 15-mi section of the Lake Superior shoreline are multicolored sandstone cliffs rising to heights of 200 ft. Here the erosive action of the waves, rain, and ice has carved the cliffs to create caves, arches, columns, and promontories. Although many consider views from a boat superior, most sections are accessible by trails and roads that provide spectacular views of the cliffs and the lake (most roads closed in winter). The cliffs give way to 12 mi of sand beach followed by the Grand Sable Banks; five sq mi (3,200 acres) of sand dunes are perched atop the banks. Also here are waterfalls, inland lakes, ponds, streams, hardwood and coniferous forests, and numerous birds and animals. Phone 906/387-2379.

Visitor activities. Incl swimming, scuba diving, fishing, boating; hunting, sightseeing, hiking, photography, picnicking. Offered in summer are guided historical walks and campfire programs; in winter there is snowmobiling, x-country skiing on groomed and tracked ski trails, and snowshoeing. Also here are the Grand Marais Maritime Museum (summer) and Munising Falls Interpretive Center (summer, daily). There are three drive-in campgrounds (fee) and numerous hike-in backcountry campsites (permit required, free, obtain from any visitor station). Pets are not permitted in the backcountry; must be on leash in other areas. Visitors can obtain information at Pictured Rocks National Lakeshore-Hiawatha National Forest Visitor Information Station (daily); Munising Headquarters (Mon-Fri); or Grand Sable Visitor Center (summer). Contact the Superintendent, PO Box 40. Phone 906/387-3700. **FREE**

Special Event

Pictured Rocks Road Race. Course runs over wooded, hilly trails, roads passing waterfalls, streams, and Lake Superior. Late June.

Motels/Motor Lodges

★ **ALGER FALLS MOTEL.** *M28 E (49862). 906/387-3536; fax 906/387-5228.* 17 rms. July-Labor Day: S $39-$45; D $45-$50; kit. cottages $55-$65; lower rates rest of yr. Crib $4. Pet accepted. TV; cable. Restaurant nearby. Ck-out 11 am. X-country ski 3 mi. Rec rm. Picnic tables. Wooded area with trails. Cr cds: A, DS, MC, V.
🐾 🏊 🖼 🔥

★★ **BEST WESTERN.** *MI 28 E (49895). 906/387-4864; fax 906/387-2038; toll-free 800/528-1234. www. bestwestern.com.* 80 rms, 2 story. Late June-Aug: S, D $59-$64; each addl $5; suites $80-$95; lower rates rest of yr. Crib $5. Pet accepted. TV. Indoor pool; whirlpool, sauna. Restaurant 7 am-10 pm. Bar 11-1 am; Sun from noon. Ck-out 11 am. Meeting rm. Business servs avail. Picnic tables. Some refrigerators. Cr cds: A, D, DS, MC, V.
🅓 🐾 🖼 🔥 **SC**

★★ **COMFORT INN.** *MI 28 E (49862). 906/387-5292; fax 906/387-3753; res 800/228-5150. www.comfort inn.com.* 61 rms, 2 story. S $69-$98, D $74-$103. Crib free. Pet accepted. TV; cable (premium), VCR (movies). Indoor pool; whirlpool. Complimentary continental bkfst. Ck-out 11 am. Coin lndry. Meeting rms. Business servs avail. X-country ski 6 mi. Exercise equipt. Game rm. Cr cds: A, C, D, DS, JCB, MC, V.
🅓 🐾 🖼 🔥

★ **DAYS INN.** *MI 28 E (49862). 906/387-2493; fax 906/387-5214; toll-free 800/329-7466. www.daysinn.com.* 66 rms. July-Sept, late Dec: S, D $65-$85; kit. units $125; lower rates rest of yr. Crib free. TV; cable (premium), VCR (movies). Indoor pool; whirlpool, sauna. Restaurant adj 6 am-11 pm. Ck-out 11 am. Business servs avail. X-country ski 1 mi. Cr cds: A, MC, V.
🅓 🖼 ✈ 🔥

★ **SUNSET RESORT MOTEL.** *1315 Bay St (49862). 906/387-4574. www. exploringthenorth.com.* 16 units (1-3-rm), 6 kits. No A/C. June-Labor Day: S $38-$51; D $42-$55; kit. units $56-$60; lower rates rest of yr. Closed 3rd wk Oct-Apr. Crib $1. Pet accepted. TV; cable. Playground. Complimentary coffee. Restaurant nearby. Ck-out 11 am. Lawn games. Picnic tables, grills. On Lake Superior; dockage. Cr cds: DS, MC, V.
🐾 🖼

★ **SUPER 8.** *M 28 and US 13 (49862). 906/387-2466; fax 906/387-2355. www.super8.com.* 43 rms, 2 story. Mid-June-Labor Day, Dec-Mar: S $45.88; D $55.88-$65.88; each addl $5; suite $73.88; under 12 free; lower rates rest of yr. Crib free. TV; cable (premium). Complimentary continental bkfst. Restaurant nearby. Ck-out 11 am. X-country ski 3 mi. Whirlpool, sauna. Some refrigerators. Cr cds: A, DS, MC, V.
🅓 🛗 ⚡ 🖼 🔥

Restaurant

★ **SYDNEY'S.** *400 Cedar St (MI 28) (49862). 906/387-4067.* Hrs: 6 am-10 pm; Sun brunch 8 am-1 pm. Bar 3 pm-2 am. Bkfst $1.50-$4.50, lunch, dinner $5-$13.50. Sun brunch $6. Specializes in fresh lake trout, whitefish, steak. Salad bar. Cr cds: A, MC, V.
🅓 🔳

Muskegon

(F-3) *See also Grand Haven, Whitehall*

Settled 1810 **Pop** 40,283 **Elev** 625 ft
Area code 231

Information Muskegon County Convention & Visitors Bureau, 610 W Western Ave, 49440; 800/235-3866 or 800/250-WAVE

Web www.visitmuskegon.org

Muskegon County is located in the western part of the lower peninsula, along 26 miles of Lake Michigan shoreline. Muskegon Channel, which runs from Lake Michigan through the sand dunes to Muskegon Lake, opens the harbor to world trade. It has 80 miles of waterfront, including ten miles of public waterfront, and 3,000 acres of public parks—an acre for every 50 persons in the county. The downtown has been enclosed as a climate-controlled shopping and business mall.

Muskegon Lake, largest of 40 lakes in Muskegon County, is the focal point of the area comprised of Muskegon, Muskegon Heights, North Muskegon, Norton Shores, Roosevelt Park, and surrounding townships. Fishing for coho, chinook salmon, lake trout, perch, walleye, and other fish is good here; ice fishing is popular in the winter months. The first freshwater reef in North America, a natural fish attractant, is located in Lake Michigan, off Pére Marquette Park.

What to See and Do

Hackley and Hume Historic Site. Restored Queen Anne/Victorian mansions (1888-1889) built by two wealthy lumbermen; elaborately carved woodwork, stenciled walls, 15 Renaissance-style stained-glass windows, tiled fireplaces with carved mantels, period furniture. Tours (mid-May-Sept, Wed, Sat, Sun; also some wkends Dec). 472 and 484 W Webster. Phone 231/722-7578. ¢

Michigan's Adventure Amusement Park. More than 24 amusement rides, incl Wolverine Wildcat, largest wooden roller coaster in the state; Corkscrew roller coaster, Mammoth River water slide, log flume; games, arcade. Also water park with wave pool, lazy river, body flumes, tube slides. Family play areas. (Mid-May-early Sept, daily) 4750 Whitehall Rd, 8 mi N on US 31 via Russell Rd exit. Phone 231/766-3377. ¢¢¢

Muskegon Museum of Art. Permanent collection incl American and European paintings, an extensive print collection, Tiffany and contemporary glass, paintings by Hopper, Inness, Whistler, Homer, Wyeth, and others. (Tues-Sun; closed hols) 296 W Webster Ave. Phone 231/722-2600. **Donation**

Muskegon State Park. A 1,165-acre area with replica of frontier blockhouse on one of the park's highest sand dunes, observation point. Swimming, beaches, bathhouse, waterskiing, fishing, boating (ramp,

launch); 12 mi of hiking trails, x-country skiing, skating rink, luge run, picnicking, concession, playground, camping (electrical hookups). Standard fees. On MI 213. Phone 231/744-3480. ¢¢

Muskegon Trolley Company. Two routes cover north side, south side, and downtown; each trolley stops at 11 locations, incl Hackley and Hume Historic Site, USS *Silversides*, Muskegon State Park. (Memorial Day-Labor Day, daily; no trips during special events) Phone 231/724-6420. ¢

P. J. Hoffmaster State Park. More than 1,000 acres incl forest-covered dunes along 2½ mi of Lake Michigan shoreline. Swimming, sandy beach. Ten mi of trails, Dune Climb Stairway to top of one of highest dunes, observation deck. X-country ski trails (three mi), picnicking, concession, camping (electric hookups, dump station). Visitor center has displays, exhibits on dune formation (daily). Standard fees. S on Henry St to Pontaluna Rd, then W on Lake Harbor Rd. Phone 231/798-3711. Also here is

Gillette Visitor Center. Sand dune interpretive center. Multi-image slide presentations on the Great Lakes and dune habitats; dune ecology exhibit, hands-on classrm; seasonal animal exhibits. (Daily) 6585 Lake Harbor Rd. Phone 231/798-3573.

USS *Silversides* and Maritime Museum. Famous WWII submarine that served with Pacific Fleet along Japan's coasts. The *Silverside's* outstanding aggressive war record incl sinking 23 enemy ships, embarking on special minelaying and reconnaisance missions, and rescuing two American aviators downed in air strikes over Japan. Guided tours. (June-Aug, daily; Apr-May and Sept-Oct, Sat and Sun) No high heels, skirts. Bluff St at Muskegon Channel. Phone 231/755-1230.

Special Events

Luge Run. Muskegon Winter Sports Complex in Muskegon State Park. Jan-Mar. Phone 231/744-9629.

Muskegon Summer Celebration. Family music and entertainment parade, midway, food and beer tents,

Venetian boat parade. Phone 231/722-6520. June-July.

Muskegon Air Fair. More than 100 military and civilian aircraft; displays. Phone 231/798-4596. Mid-July.

Blueberry Festival. Fruitland Township Park. Phone 231/766-3208. Late July.

Muskegon Shoreline Spectacular. Pere Marquette Park. Concerts, sporting events, arts and crafts, hot-air balloon rides. Phone 231/737-5791. Labor Day wkend.

Motels/Motor Lodges

★ **BEL-AIRE MOTEL.** *4240 Airline Rd (49444). 321/733-2196; fax 321/733-2196.* 16 rms. June-Aug: S $48; D $58; each addl $5; higher rates special events; lower rates rest of yr. Crib $3. TV; cable (premium). Restaurant nearby. Ck-out 11 am. X-country ski 5 mi. Cr cds: A, DS, MC, V.
🏊 🖼 🎿 🔥 **SC**

★★ **BEST WESTERN PARK PLAZA.** *2967 Henry St (49441). 231/733-2651; fax 616/733-5202; res 800/780-7234. www.bestwestern.com.* 111 rms, 4 story. June-Aug: S, D $64-$80; each addl $6; suites $80-$100; under 18 free; lower rates rest of yr. Crib free. TV; cable. Indoor pool. Bar noon-2 am; entertainment Wed-Sat. Ck-out noon. Meeting rms. Business servs avail. Valet serv. Free airport, RR station, bus depot transportation. Sauna. Game rm. Rec rm. Cr cds: A, C, D, DS, JCB, MC, V.
🗔 🖼 🎿 🔥

★ **DAYS INN.** *3450 Hoyt St, Muskegon Heights (49444). 231/733-2601; res 800/326-7466. www.daysinn.com.* 106 rms, 2 story. S $50-$80; D $60-$85; each addl $5. Crib free. TV; cable (premium). Heated pool; whirlpool. Complimentary continental bkfst. Restaurant nearby. Ck-out 11 am. Coin lndry. Meeting rms. Business servs avail. Health club privileges. X-country ski 5 mi. Cr cds: A, C, D, DS, MC, V.
🗔 🐾 🥾 🎿 🏊 🖼 🔥

★★ **HOLIDAY INN.** *939 3rd St (49440). 231/720-7100; fax 231/722-5118; toll-free 800/846-5253. www.holiday-inn.com.* 200 rms, 8 story. S, D $99-$125; each addl $10; suites $220-$325; under 18 free. Crib free. TV; cable. Indoor pool; whirlpool. Restaurant 6:30 am-10 pm; wkends 7 am-11 pm. Bar 2 pm-midnight; Fri, Sat to 1 am. Ck-out 11 am. Meeting rms. Business servs avail. Bellhops. Valet serv. Gift shop. Free airport, bus depot transportation. Exercise equipt; steam rm, sauna. Cr cds: A, C, D, DS, MC, V.
🗔 🖼 🎿 🖼 🔥

★ **SUPER 8.** *3380 Hoyt St (49444). 231/733-0088; res 800/800-8000. www.super8.com.* 62 rms, 2 story. Apr-Sept: S, D $35-$70; each addl $5; under 12 free; lower rates rest of yr. TV; cable (premium), VCR avail (movies). Pet accepted. Restaurant nearby. Ck-out 11 am. Business servs avail. Cr cds: A, D, DS, MC, V.
🗔 🐾 🐾 🥾 🖼 🔥

Restaurants

★ **HOUSE OF CHAN.** *375 Gin Chan Ave (49444). 231/733-9624.* Hrs: 11:30 am-10 pm; Fri to 11 pm; Sat 4-11 pm; Sun 11 am-9 pm. Closed Mon; Jan 1, Thanksgiving, Dec 25. Res accepted. Wine. Chinese, American menu. Lunch $5-$7, dinner $8-$12. Buffet: lunch $5.75, dinner $11-$25. Sun brunch $8.95. Child's menu. Specialties: Beijing shrimp, crispy chicken, crispy fish. Pagoda in center of large dining rm. Cr cds: A, MC, V.
🗔 🖼

★★ **RAFFERTY'S DOCKSIDE.** *601 Terrace Point Blvd (49440). 231/722-4461. www.shorelineinn.com.* Hrs: 11:30 am-11 pm; Sun to 8 pm. Closed Jan 1, Dec 25. Res accepted. Bar. Lunch $5.95-$9.95, dinner $9.95-$33. Child's menu. Specializes in salads, steak, fresh fish. Outdoor dining. Overlooks marina. Cr cds: A, DS, MC, V.
🗔 🖼

★★ **TONY'S.** *785 W Broadway (49441). 231/739-7196.* Hrs: 11:30 am-10 pm; Fri to 11 pm; Sat 5-11 pm; early-bird dinner Mon-Sat 4:30-6:30 pm. Closed Sun; hols. Res accepted. Bar. Lunch $6.50-$10.50, dinner $11.99-$26.99. Child's menu. Specializes in prime rib, seafood, steak. Parking. Stained-glass windows depicting Mediterranean scenes. Family-owned since 1969. Cr cds: A, D, DS, MC, V.
🗔 🖼

Newberry

(B-4) *See also Hulbert, Soo Junction*

Pop 1,873 **Elev** 788 ft **Area code** 906
Zip 49868
Information Newberry Area Chamber of Commerce, PO Box 308; 906/293-5562 or 800/831-7292
Web www.exploringthenorth.com/newbchamb/main.html

What to See and Do

Luce County Historical Museum. (1894) Restored Queen Anne structure; the stone on the lower portion is Marquette or Jacobsville sandstone, some of the oldest rock in the country. Originally a sheriff's residence and jail, it was saved from razing and is now a museum. The staterm fireplace is original; many of the rms have been refurbished to hold records, books, and other artifacts; jail cells are still intact. (Tues-Thurs) 411 W Harrie St. Phone 906/293-5753. **FREE**

Seney National Wildlife Refuge. On 95,455 acres. Canada geese, bald eagles, sandhill cranes, loons, deer, beaver, otter; several species of ducks. Visitor center has exhibits, films and information on wildlife observation (mid-May-Sept, daily). Headquarters (Mon-Fri). Self-guided auto tour (mid-May-mid-Oct). Half-mi nature trail (daylight hrs). Fishing; picnicking, limited hunting. Pets on leash only. 3 mi S on MI 123, then 23 mi W on MI 28 to Seney, then 5 mi S on MI 77. Phone 906/586-9851. **FREE**

Tahquamenon Falls State Park. Approx 35,000 acres of scenic wilderness; incl Upper (40 ft) and Lower Falls (a series of several scenic falls of lesser height). Swimming, fishing, boating (rentals, launch); snowmobiling, x-country skiing, hunting in season, playground, picnicking, concession; camping near rapids and near shore of Whitefish Bay, Lake Superior. Standard fees. 30 mi NE on MI 123. Phone 906/492-3415. ¢¢

Special Events

Lumberjack Days. One mi N on MI 123, at Tahquamenon Logging Museum. Wood carvings, traditional music, logging contests, lumberjack breakfast. Wkend late Aug. Phone 800/831-7292.

Michigan Fiddlers' Jamboree. At American Legion. Wkend late Sept. Phone 906/293-8711.

Motels/Motor Lodges

★★ **COMFORT INN.** *Hwy M 28 & M 123 (49868). 906/293-3218; fax 906/293-9375; toll-free 800/228-5150. www.comfortinn.com.* 54 rms, 2 story. Early June-Oct, Dec-Mar: S, D $50-$84; each addl $10; under 18 free; lower rates rest of yr. Crib free. TV; cable. Complimentary continental bkfst. Restaurant opp 6 am-midnight. Ck-out 10 am. Coin lndry. Meeting rm. Business servs avail. Valet serv. X-country ski ¾ mi. Game rm. Some in-rm whirlpools. Cr cds: A, C, D, DS, ER, JCB, MC, V.
D ⌖ ⛅ ➷ 🐾 SC

★ **DAYS INN.** *Rte 1 Box 680 (60611). 906/293-4000; fax 906/293-4005; res 800/293-3297. www.daysinn.com.* 66 rms, 2 story. June-Aug, mid-Dec-Feb: S $60-$90; D $66-$105; each addl $6; under 12 free; lower rates rest of yr. Crib free. TV; cable (premium). Indoor pool; whirlpool, sauna. Complimentary continental bkfst. Restaurant nearby. Ck-out 11 am. Meeting rm. Business servs avail. Coin lndry. X-country ski 2 mi. Game rm. Some refrigerators. Cr cds: A, C, D, DS, ER, JCB, MC, V.
D ⌖ ≈ ➷ 🐾 SC

★ **GATEWAY MOTEL.** *MI 123 S (49868). 906/293-5651; toll-free 800/791-9485.* 11 rms, 1 story. No rm phones. July-Sept, late Dec-Apr: S $32-$52; D $42-$62; each addl $4; suite $66-$78; lower rates rest of yr. Crib free. TV; cable (premium). Restaurant nearby. Ck-out 10 am. X-country ski 4 mi. Refrigerator, microwave in suite. Cr cds: DS, MC, V.
⌖ ➷ 🐾

★ **MANOR MOTEL.** *M123 Newberry Ave (49868). 906/293-5000.* 12 rms. Mid-June-mid-Oct, Christmas wk: S $44-$54; D $52-$59; each addl $4; suites $54-$72; family rates; lower rates rest of yr. Crib free. Pet accepted. TV; cable (premium). Restaurant nearby. Ck-out 10 am.

Game rm. Lawn games. Cr cds: DS, MC, V.

★ **ZELLAR'S VILLAGE INN.** *MI 123 S (Newberry Ave) (49868).* 906/293-5114; fax 906/293-5116. 20 rms. S $40; D $50-$60; each addl $4. Crib $5. Pet accepted. TV; cable (premium). Restaurant 6 am-10 pm. Bar. Ck-out 11 am. Meeting rms. Business servs avail. In-rm modem link. Sundries. Game rm. Cr cds: A, D, DS, MC, V.

New Buffalo

(H-3) *See also Niles, St. Joseph*

Pop 2,317 **Elev** 630 ft **Area code** 616 **Zip** 49117
Information Harbor County Chamber of Commerce, 530 S Whittaker, Suite F; 616/469-5409
Web www.harborcountry.com

Because of its proximity to large midwestern cities, Lake Michigan, and beaches, New Buffalo and the Harbor County area have become a popular resort community for year-round vacationers.

What to See and Do

Red Arrow Highway. Many antique stores, inns, galleries, shops, and restaurants can be found along this road that travels from Union Pier to Sawyer, between Lake Michigan and the Interstate. I-94, exits 4B, 6, or 12.

Niles

(H-3) *See also New Buffalo, St. Joseph; also see Mishawaka and South Bend, IN*

Pop 12,458 **Elev** 658 ft **Area code** 616 **Zip** 49120
Information Four Flags Area Council on Tourism, 321 E Main, PO Box 1300; 616/684-7444
Web www.ci.niles.mi.us

Niles calls itself the "city of four flags" because the banners of France, England, Spain, and the United States each have flown over the area. Montgomery Ward and the Dodge brothers are native sons of the town.

What to See and Do

Fernwood Botanic Gardens. The scenic grounds comprise 100 acres of woodland trails, spring-fed ponds, a tall grass prairie and nearly 20 gardens, incl rock and fern gardens and Japanese garden. Nature center features hands-on educational exhibits and panoramic bird observation windows. (Tues-Sun; closed Thanksgiving, Dec 25) 13988 Range Line Rd, 5 mi NW via US 31/33, Walton Rd exit. Phone 616/695-6491. ¢¢

Fort St. Joseph Museum. Contains one of the top five Sioux art collections in the nation. Incl autobiographical pictographs by Sitting Bull and Rain-In-The-Face. Other collections are Fort St. Joseph (1691-1781) and Potawatomi artifacts, local history memorabilia. (Wed-Sat; closed hols) 508 E Main St. Phone 616/683-4702.

Special Events

Riverfest. Riverfront Park. Crafts, games, food, entertainment, raft race. Phone 616/684-5766 or 616/683-8888. Early Aug.

Four Flags Area Apple Festival. Phone 616/683-8870. Fourth wk Sept.

Ontonagon (A-7)

Pop 2,040 **Elev** 620 ft **Area code** 906 **Zip** 49953
Information Ontonagon County Chamber of Commerce, PO Box 266; 906/884-4735
Web www.ontonagonmi.com

A Ranger District office of the Ottawa National Forest (see IRONWOOD) is located here.

What to See and Do

Adventure Copper Mine. Guided tour 300 ft underground; walk through passages worked by miners

100 yrs ago. Also above ground walking tour encompasses the historical aspects of copper mining from the pre-historic period to the 1930s. (Memorial Day-mid-Oct, daily) 200 Adventure Rd, in Greenland. Phone 906/883-3371. ¢¢¢

Porcupine Mountains Wilderness State Park. This 63,000-acre forested, mountainous semiwilderness area harbors otters, bears, coyotes, bald eagles, and many other species. There are many streams and lakes with fishing for bass, perch, and trout; boating (launch); hunting in season for grouse, deer, and bear; downhill and x-country skiing, snowmobiling; hiking trails with overnight rustic cabins (res avail) and shelters; scenic overlooks, waterfalls, abandoned mine sites. Visitor center. Picnicking, playground, camping. Standard fees. (Daily) 20 mi W on MI 107, on shore of Lake Superior. Phone 906/885-5275. ¢¢ In the park is

   Ski area. Triple, double chairlifts, T-bar, rope tow; patrol, school, rentals; snack bar. Longest run one mi; vertical drop 641 ft. 25 mi of x-country trails. (Mid-Dec-Mar, daily; closed Dec 25) Phone 906/885-5275. ¢¢¢¢

Motels/Motor Lodges

★ ★ **BEST WESTERN PORCUPINE MOUNTAIN LODGE.** *120 Lincoln, Silver City (49953). 906/885-5311; fax 906/885-5847; res 800/780-7234. www. bestwestern.com.* 71 rms, 3 story. June-mid-Oct, late Dec-late Mar: S, D $75-$100; each addl $5; family rates; ski plan; lower rates rest of yr. Crib free. TV; cable (premium), VCR avail. Indoor pool; whirlpool. Complimentary continental bkfst. Restaurant 7 am-9:30 pm; off-season from 4:30 pm. Bar 1 pm-2 am. Ck-out 11 am. Meeting rms. Business servs avail. Gift shop. Airport transportation. Downhill/x-country ski 3 mi. Sauna. Game rm. Rec rm. Picnic tables. On lake; swimming beach. Cr cds: A, C, D, DS, MC, V.

🅳 ⛴ ➤ ⊠ ⇘ ▨

★ ★ **MOUNTAIN VIEW LODGES.** *237 MI 107 (49953). 906/885-5256. www.mtnviewlodges.com.* 11 (2-bedrm) kit. lodges. No A/C. S $79-$109; D $89-$109; each addl $11. TV; cable,

VCR (movies). Restaurant nearby. Ck-out 11 am. Downhill/x-country ski 1 mi. Fireplaces. Cr cds: A, DS, MC, V.

🅳 ⛴ ➤ ⊠ ▨

★ **PETERSON'S CHALET COTTAGES.** *287 Lakeshore Rd (49953). 906/884-4230; fax 906/884-2965. www.petersonschaletcottages.com.* 13 kit. cottages for 2-8 (1-2-bedrm), 2 vacation homes for 2-12 (3-bedrm). No A/C. S $60-$90; D $72-$110; each addl $10; vacation homes $225; under 18, $5. Crib avail. TV; cable (premium). Restaurant nearby. Ck-out 11 am. Gift shop. Free airport transportation. Downhill/x-country ski 15 mi. Many fireplaces. Picnic tables, grills. Private beach on Lake Superior. Cr cds: A, DS, MC, V.

⛴ ➤ ✈ ⊠ ▨

Oscoda

(E-6) *See also Tawas City*

Pop 1,061 **Elev** 590 ft **Area code** 989 **Zip** 48750

Information Oscoda-Au Sable Chamber of Commerce, 4440 N US 23; 989/739-7322 or 800/235-4625

Web www.oscoda.com

This is a resort community where the Au Sable River, a famous trout stream, empties into Lake Huron. In 1890, when it was a logging town, Oscoda reached a population of 23,600.

What to See and Do

Huron-Manistee National Forest. This 427,000-acre forest is the Huron section of the Huron-Manistee National Forest (for Manistee section see MANISTEE). A major attraction of the forest is the Lumberman's Monument overlooking the Au Sable River. A three-figure bronze memorial, depicting a timber cruiser, sawyer, and river driver, commemorates the loggers who cut the virgin timber in Michigan in the latter part of the 19th century. The visitor center at the monument offers interpretations of this colorful era (Memorial Day-Labor Day). Scenic drives; beaches, swimming, streams, lakes, trout fishing, canoe trips down the Au Sable

River; hunting for deer and small game, camping, picnicking, winter sports areas. (Daily) W of town on River Rd. Contact Huron Shores Ranger Station, US Forest Service, 5761 Skeel Ave. Phone 989/739-0728. **FREE**

Paddle-wheeler boat trips. Boat makes 19-mi (two-hr) round-trips on Au Sable River. (Memorial Day-mid-Oct, daily; schedule may vary, res advised) *Au Sable River Queen,* Foote Dam, 6 mi W on River Rd. Phone 989/739-7351. ¢¢¢

Special Events

Au Sable River International Canoe Marathon. This 120-mi marathon begins in Grayling (see) and ends in Oscoda. Last wkend July. Phone 989/739-7322.

Paul Bunyan Days. Lumberjack show, chainsaw carving competition, children's events. Third wkend Sept. Phone 989/739-7322.

Motels/Motor Lodges

★ **LAKE TRAIL.** *5400 US 23 N (48750). 989/739-2096; fax 989/739-2565; toll-free 800/843-6007.* 42 rms, 1-2 story, 20 suites, 2 kit. cottages. S $50-$55; D $50-$60; each addl $6; suites $72-$125; kit. cottages $85 ($525/wk in season); under 12 free. Crib free. TV; cable, VCR avail (movies $4). Complimentary continental bkfst. Ck-out 11 am. Airport transportation. Lighted tennis. Lawn games. Health club privileges. Some refrigerators. Balconies. Picnic tables, grills. On lake; paddleboats, waverunners avail; swimming beach. Cr cds: A, DS, MC, V.

★★ **REDWOOD MOTOR LODGE.** *3111 US 23 N (48750). 989/739-2021; fax 989/739-1121. www.redwoodmotor lodge.com.* 37 rms, 1-2 story, 9 kit. cottages. S, D $70-$80; each addl $5; under 5 free. Crib free. TV; cable (premium). Indoor pool; whirlpool. Playground. Complimentary continental bkfst. Bar 5 pm-midnight. Ck-out 11 am. Meeting rm. Sauna. Game rm. Lawn games. Picnic tables, grill. Private beach on Lake Huron opp. Cr cds: A, C, D, DS, MC, V.

Owosso

(G-6) *See also Flint, Lansing*

Settled 1836 **Pop** 16,322 **Elev** 730 ft **Area code** 989 **Zip** 48867
Information Owosso-Corunna Area Chamber of Commerce, 215 N Water St; 989/723-5149
Web www.shianet.org

Owosso's most famous sons were James Oliver Curwood, author of many wildlife novels about the Canadian wilderness, and Thomas E. Dewey, governor of New York and twice Republican presidential nominee. The city, rising on the banks of the Shiawassee River, has five parks and many industries.

What to See and Do

Curwood Castle. This replica of a Norman castle, thought to be architecturally unique in the state, was used as a studio by James Oliver Curwood, author and conservationist. It is maintained as a museum with Curwood memorabilia and local artifacts displayed. (Tues-Sun afternoons; closed hols) 224 Curwood Castle Dr. Phone 989/723-8844. **Donation**

Special Events

Curwood Festival. River raft, bed and canoe races, juried art show, pioneer displays and demonstrations, fun run, parade, entertainment. First full wkend June. Phone 989/723-2161.

Shiawassee County Fair. County Fairgrounds, 2900 E Hibbard in Corunna. Agricultural and home economics exhibits, rides. Phone 989/743-3611. First wk Aug.

Paw Paw

(H-4) *See also Kalamazoo*

Pop 3,169 **Elev** 740 ft **Area code** 616 **Zip** 49079

Information Chamber of Commerce, 804 S Kalamazo St; PO Box 105; 616/657-5395

Web www.pawpaw.net

The center of an important grape-growing area, this town takes its name from the Paw Paw River, so designated by Native Americans for the papaw trees that grew along its banks.

What to See and Do

Maple Lake. Created in 1908 when river waters were dammed for electric power. Boating and swimming on Maple Island; picnicking.

Winery tours.

St. Julian Wine Company. The oldest and largest winery in the state; wine tasting. Tours every ½ hour. (Mon-Sat, also Sun afternoons; closed hols) 716 S Kalamazoo St, 2 blks N of I-94 exit 60. Phone 616/657-5568.

Warner Vineyards. Produces wine, champagne, and juices. Tours and tasting. (Daily; closed hols) 706 S Kalamazoo St, 3 blks N of I-94. Phone 616/657-3165. **FREE**

Motel/Motor Lodge

★ **MROCZER INN.** *139 Ampey Rd (49079).* 616/657-2578. 43 rms, 2 story. S $45-$55; D $55-$65; 3-4 persons $44.95. Crib free. TV. Complimentary coffee in lobby. Restaurant nearby. Ck-out 11 am. Downhill ski 20 mi. Cr cds: A, DS, MC, V.

Petoskey

(C-5) *See also Boyne City, Charlevoix, Harbor Springs*

Settled 1852 **Pop** 6,056 **Elev** 786 ft
Area code 231 **Zip** 49770
Information Petoskey Regional Chamber of Commerce, 401 E Mitchell St; 231/347-4150
Web www.petoskey.com

A popular resort stretching along Little Traverse Bay, Petoskey is known for its historic Gaslight Shopping District. A diverse industrial base provides a viable year-round economy.

What to See and Do

Little Traverse Historical Museum. Housed in a former railroad depot, visitors can see historical exhibits from the area's Native American, pioneer, and Victorian past. (May-Nov, daily). Waterfront Park. Phone 231/347-2620.

Petoskey State Park. A 305-acre park with swimming beach, beach house, fishing; hiking, x-country skiing, picnicking, playground, camping (electrical hookups, dump station). Standard fees. 4 mi NE, on MI 119. Phone 231/347-2311.

St. Francis Solanus Indian Mission. (1859) Built of square hand-cut timbers, held together by dovetailed corners. Native American burial grounds (not open to public) adj the church. W Lake St.

Special Event

Art in the Park. 401 E Mitchell. Phone 231/347-4150. Third Sat July.

Motels/Motor Lodges

★★ **BAYWINDS INN.** *909 Spring St (49770).* 231/347-4193; fax 231/347-5927; toll-free 800/204-1748. 48 rms, 2 story. Mid-June-Labor Day, late Dec-Mar: S, D $89-$97; each addl $5; lower rates rest of yr. Crib $5. TV; cable (premium). Indoor pool; whirlpool. Complimentary continental bkfst. Ck-out 11 am. Downhill/x-country ski 10 mi. Exercise equipt. Game rm. Refrigerators; some in-rm whirlpools. Some balconies. Cr cds: A, D, DS, MC, V.

★ **ECONO LODGE.** *1858 US 131 (49770).* 231/348-3324; fax 616/348-3521; toll-free 800/748-0417. www.econolodge.com. 59 rms, 2 story. Mid-June-early Sept: S $46-$95; D $56-$120; family rates; package plans; lower rates rest of yr. Crib avail. Pet accepted; fee. TV; cable. Indoor pool; whirlpool. Complimentary continental bkfst. Restaurant nearby. Ck-out 11 am. Business servs avail. Downhill ski 15 mi; x-country ski 10 mi. Cr cds: A, D, DS, MC, V.

★★ **HOLIDAY INN.** *1444 S US 131 (49770). 231/347-6041; res 800/465-4329. www.holiday-inn.com.* 144 rms, 5 story. July-Aug: S, D $115; under 19 free; hol rates; ski, golf plans; higher rates wkends, Dec 20-Jan 2; lower rates rest of yr. Crib free. TV; cable (premium). Indoor pool; whirlpool. Playground. Complimentary coffee in rms. Restaurant 7 am-2 pm, 5-10 pm. Bar 4 pm-midnight; Fri, Sat to 2 am; entertainment Fri, Sat. Ck-out noon. Coin lndry. Meeting rms. Business servs avail. Bellhops. Valet serv. Gift shop. Downhill/x-country ski 15 mi. Health club privileges. Game rm. Balconies. Cr cds: A, C, D, DS, JCB, MC, V.

Hotel

★★ **STAFFORD'S PERRY HOTEL.** *Bay and Lewis Sts (49770). 231/347-4000; fax 231/347-0636; toll-free 800/737-1899. www.staffords.com.* 81 rms, 3 story. Late June-early Sept, wkends Sept-Feb, Christmas wk: S $80-$125; D $95-$185; suites $185; ski packages; lower rates rest of yr. Crib $5. TV; cable, VCR avail. Restaurant 7-10:30 am, 11:30 am-2:30 pm, 5:30-10 pm. Bar noon-11 pm. Ck-out 11 am. Meeting rms. Business servs avail. Downhill/x-country ski 8 mi. Exercise equipt. Whirlpool. Some private patios, balconies. Cr cds: A, DS, MC, V.

Resort

★★★ **THE INN AT BAY HARBOR.** *3600 Village Harbor Dr (49770). 231/439-4000; toll-free 800/362-6963. www.innatbayharbor.com.* 85 suites, 5 story. S, D $99-$334; suite $481-$1,808. Free valet parking. Crib avail. Heated pool; whirlpool, poolside serv. Supervised children's activities, ages 4-15 (summer). TV; cable (premium). Restaurant 6 am-10 pm. Comlimentary continental bkfst. Coffee in rms. Ck-out noon. Meeting rms. Business center. Bellhops. Concierge. Valet serv. Exercise rm. Spa. Gift shop. 27-hole golf; driving range; putting green; golf carts; pro; pro shop; greens fees. Outdoor chess board. Refrigerators, minibars. Some fireplaces, balconies, kitchenettes. Beach. On Lake Michigan. Cr cds: A, C, D, DS, JCB, MC, V.

B&B/Small Inn

★★★ **STAFFORD'S BAY VIEW INN.** *2011 Woodland Ave (49770). 231/347-2771; fax 201/347-3413; toll-free 800/258-1886. www.staffords.com.* 31 rms, 3 story, 10 suites. No rm phones. July-Aug, late-Dec, wkends: S, D $135-$260; each addl $18; suites $260; under 3 free; ski plan; lower rates rest of yr. Crib free. Pet accepted; $20. TV in library. Complimentary full bkfst. Coffee in library 24 hrs. Restaurant (see STAFFORD'S BAY VIEW INN). Ck-out 11 am, ck-in after 3 pm. Business servs avail. Valet serv. Gift shop. Tennis privileges. Downhill ski 6 mi; x-country ski on site. Sleigh rides. Bicycles. Lawn games. Picnic tables. Some fireplaces, balconies. Airport/local transportation. Victorian-style inn with green, mansard roof (1886); antiques, reproductions. Overlooks Little Traverse Bay. Cr cds: A, DS, MC, V.

Restaurants

★★ **ANDANTE.** *321 Bay St (49770). 231/348-3321.* Hrs: 5:30-9 pm. Closed Sun, Mon Oct-May; hols. Res accepted. Eclectic menu. Serv bar. Dinner $26-$39. Overlooks Little Traverse Bay. Totally nonsmoking. Cr cds: A, MC, V.

★★ **STAFFORD'S BAY VIEW INN.** *2011 Woodland Ave (49770). 231/347-2771. www.staffords.com.* Hrs: 8-10:30 am, noon-2:30 pm, 5:30-9 pm; Fri, Sat to 10 pm; Sun brunch 10 am-2 pm. Res accepted. Bkfst $5.50-$10.50, lunch $6-$9.50, dinner $15.50-$24. Sun brunch $16.95. Specializes in fresh lake fish. Own pasta. Family-owned. Views of bay. Cr cds: A, DS, MC, V.

Plymouth

Pop 9,560 **Elev** 730 ft **Area code** 734
Zip 48170
Information Chamber of Commerce,
386 S Main St; 734/453-1540
Web www.plymouthchamber.org

Plymouth is a quaint town with historical attractions and unique shopping areas.

Special Events

Ice Sculpture Spectacular. Hundreds of ice sculptures line the streets and fill Kellogg Park, as professional and student chefs compete with each other carving huge blocks of ice; the sculptures are lighted at night. Second wkend in Jan.

Fall Festival. Antique mart, music, ethnic food. First wkend after Labor Day. Phone 734/453-1540.

Motels/Motor Lodges

★★ **FAIRFIELD INN DETROIT WEST CANTON.** *5700 Haggerty, Canton (48187). 734/981-2440; res 800/228-2800. www.fairfieldinn.com.* 133 rms, 3 story. S, D $55-$75; each addl $7; under 18 free. Crib free. TV; cable (premium). Heated pool. Complimentary continental bkfst. Restaurant 6 am-10 pm. Ck-out noon. Business servs avail. Valet serv. Cr cds: A, MC, V.
🄳 ⊠ 🅽 🔥 🆂🅲

★★ **QUALITY INN.** *40455 E Ann Arbor Rd (48170). 734/455-8100; fax 734/455-5711; res 800/228-5151. www. qualityinn.com.* 123 rms, 2 story. S, D $75.95-$139.95; family, wkend rates. Crib free. TV; cable (premium). Pool. Coffee in rms. Complimentary continental bkfst. Restaurant adj 11-2 am. Ck-out noon. Meeting rms. Business servs avail. In-rm modem link. Valet serv. Health club privileges. Cr cds: A, C, D, DS, ER, JCB, MC, V.
🄳 ⊠ 🅽 🔥

★ **RED ROOF INN.** *39700 Ann Arbor Rd (48170). 734/459-3300; fax 734/459-3072; toll-free 800/843-7663. www.*

redroof.com. 109 rms, 2 story. S $33.99-$48.99; D $41.99-$50.99; under 18 free. Crib free. Pet accepted. TV; cable (premium). Restaurant opp open 24 hrs. Ck-out noon. In-rm modem link. Cr cds: A, C, D, DS, MC, V.
🄳 🐾 🅽 🔥

Restaurants

★★★ **CAFE BON HOMME.** *844 Penniman (48170). 734/453-6260.* Hrs: 11:30 am-3 pm, 5 pm-9 pm; Sat noon-3 pm, 5 pm-9 pm. Closed Sun; hols. Res accepted. Contemporary European menu. Bar. Lunch $7-$15, dinner $32-$38. Specialties: veal, rack of lamb, whitefish. Cr cds: A, D, DS, MC, V.
🄳

★★ **ERNESTO'S.** *41661 Plymouth Rd (48170). 734/453-2002.* Hrs: 11 am-3 pm, 5-10 pm; Fri, Sat 11 am-11 pm; Sun noon-9 pm. Closed Jan 1, Dec 25. Res accepted. Italian menu. Bar. Lunch $7.25-$12.95, dinner $13.95-$24.95. Specializes in lamb chops, veal, pasta. Pianist Fri-Sat, strolling minstrels Mon-Sat. Outdoor dining. Cr cds: A, D, DS, MC, V.
🄳

Pontiac

(G-6) See also Bloomfield Hills, Detroit, Southfield

Founded 1818 **Pop** 71,166 **Elev** 943 ft
Area code 248
Information Chamber of Commerce, 30 N Saginaw, Suite 404, 48342; 248/335-9600
Web www.pontiacchamber.com

What was once the summer home of Chief Pontiac of the Ottawas is now the home of the Pontiac division of General Motors. A group of Detroit businessmen established a village here that became a way station on the wagon trail to the West. The Pontiac Spring Wagon Works, in production by the middle 1880s, is the lineal ancestor of the present industry. Pontiac is surrounded by 11 state parks, and 400 lakes are within a short distance.

What to See and Do

Oakland University. (1959) 12,500 students. On the grounds of the former Meadow Brook Farms estate of Mr. and Mrs. Alfred G. Wilson. The Eye Research Institute is internationally recognized; Center for Robotics and Advanced Automation promotes education, research, and development in high technology and manufacturing methods. (See SPECIAL EVENT) 3 mi NE off I-75, in Rochester. Phone 248/370-2100. Also on campus are

> **Meadow Brook Art Gallery.** Series of contemporary, primitive, and Asian art exhibitions, incl permanent collection of African art; outdoor sculpture garden adj to music festival grounds. (Oct-May, Tues-Sun) Phone 248/370-3005. **FREE**

> **Meadow Brook Hall.** (1926-1929) English Tudor mansion (100 rms) with nearly all original furnishings and art objects; antique needlepoint draperies, 24 fireplaces; library has hand-carved paneling; dining rm has sculptured ceiling; ballrm has elaborate stone and woodwork. Serves as cultural and conference center of the university. (July-Aug, afternoons; rest of yr, Sun afternoons) Phone 248/370-3140. ¢¢¢

> **Meadow Brook Theatre.** Professional company. (Early Oct-mid-May, Tues-Sun; matinees Wed, Sat, Sun) Phone 248/377-3300.

Professional sports team. Detroit Pistons (NBA). The Palace of Auburn Hills, 3777 Lapeer Rd (MI 24), Auburn Hills. Phone 248/377-0100.

Skiing. Alpine Valley Ski Resort. Ten chairlifts, ten rope tows; patrol, school, rentals, snowmaking; bar, cafeteria. Longest run ⅓ mi; vertical drop 320 ft. (Nov-Mar, daily; closed Dec 24 afternoon and Dec 25 morning) 12 mi W of Telegraph Rd on MI 59 (Highland Rd), at 6775 E Highland, in White Lake. Phone 248/887-2180. ¢¢¢¢

State recreation areas.

> **Highland.** On 5,524 wooded acres. Swimming, bathhouse, fishing, boating (launch); hiking, horseback riding, hunting in season, x-country skiing, picnicking, playground, concession, camping. Standard fees. 17 mi W on MI 59. Phone 248/685-2433.

> **Pontiac Lake.** Approx 3,700 acres. Swimming, bathhouse, waterskiing, fishing, boating (launch); horseback riding, riding stable, hunting in season, archery and rifle ranges, winter sports, picnicking, playground, concession, camping. Standard fees. 7 mi W on MI 59. Contact Park Manager, 7800 Gale Rd, Rte 2, 48327. Phone 248/666-1020. ¢¢

Special Event

Meadow Brook Music Festival. Oakland University. Concerts featuring popular and classical artists. Dining and picnicking facilities. Phone 248/567-6000. Mid-June-Aug.

Motels/Motor Lodges

★★ **COURTYARD BY MARRIOTT.** *1296 N Opdyke Rd, Auburn Hills (48326). 248/373-4100; fax 248/373-1885; res 800/321-2211. www.marriott.com.* 148 rms, 2-3 story, 10 suites. Apr-July: S $92; D $102; each addl $10; suites $110-$120; under 14 free; wkly, wkend, hol rates; ski plans; higher rates sports wkends; lower rates rest of yr. Crib free. TV; cable (premium), VCR avail. Indoor pool; whirlpool. Complimentary coffee in rms. Bar 4-11 pm. Ck-out noon. Coin lndry. Meeting rms. Business center. In-rm modem link. Valet serv. Downhill ski 10 mi; x-country ski 2 mi. Exercise equipt. Some refrigerators, minibars. Balconies. Cr cds: A, D, DS, MC, V.

★★ **FAIRFIELD INN.** *1294 N Opdyke Rd, Auburn Hills (48326). 248/373-2228; res 800/28-2800. www.fairfield inn.com.* 134 rms, 3 story. S $36.95-$49.95; D $48.95-$59.95; under 18 free; higher rates: special events, wkends. Crib free. TV; cable (premium). Heated pool. Complimentary continental bkfst. Restaurant adj 6 am-11 pm. Ck-out noon. Valet serv (Mon-Fri). In-rm modem link. Downhill/x-country ski 10 mi. Near Palace,

Silverdome, Pine Knob Music Theatre. Cr cds: A, D, DS, MC, V.

★★ **HAMPTON INN.** *1461 N Opdyke Rd, Auburn Hills (48326). 248/ 370-0044; fax 248/370-9590; res 800/ 426-7866. www.hamptoninn.com.* 124 rms, 3 story. S $58-$65; D $65-$72; under 17 free. Crib free. TV; cable (premium), VCR avail (movies). Pool. Complimentary continental bkfst. Ck-out noon. Meeting rms. In-rm modem link. Valet serv. Downhill/x-country ski 10 mi. Exercise equipt. Cr cds: A, MC, V.

Hotel

★★★ **MARRIOTT PONTIAC AT CENTERPOINT DETROIT.** *3600 Centerpoint Pkwy (48341). 248/253-9800; res 800/228-9290. www.marriott. com.* 290 rms, 11 story. S, D $175-$255; each addl $25; under 17 free. Crib avail. Indoor pool. TV; cable (premium), VCR avail. Restaurant 6 am-10 pm. Ck-out noon. Meeting rms. Business center. Exercise rm. Gift shop. Some refrigerators, minibars. Cr cds: A, C, D, MC, V.

All Suite

★★★ **HILTON SUITES.** *2300 Featherstone Rd, Auburn Hills (48326). 248/ 334-2222; fax 248/322-2321; res 800/ 445-8667. www.hilton.com.* 224 suites, 5 story. S, D $89-$149; each addl $15; family, wkend rates; package plans. Crib free. Pet accepted, some restrictions. TV; cable (premium), VCR (movies $3). Indoor pool; whirlpool. Complimentary full bkfst. Complimentary coffee in rms. Restaurant 6-9:30 am, 11:30 am-1:30 pm, 5:30-10 pm; wkend hrs vary. Bar. Ck-out noon. Coin lndry. Meeting rms. Business center. In-rm modem link. Bellhops. Sundries. Valet serv. Gift shop. Golf privileges. Downhill/x-country ski 12 mi. Exercise equipt; sauna. Game rm. Refrigerators. Some balconies. Cr cds: A, D, DS, ER, MC, V.

Port Austin (E-7)

Pop 815 **Elev** 600 ft **Area code** 989 **Zip** 48467

Information Port Austin Chamber of Commerce, 2 W Spring St, PO Box 274; 989/738-7600

Web www.port-austin.com

What to See and Do

Albert E. Sleeper State Park. On 723 acres. Sand beach, bathhouse, fishing; hunting, hiking, x-country skiing, picnicking, playground, camping. Standard fees. (Daily) 13 mi S on MI 25, on Saginaw Bay, Lake Huron. Phone 989/856-4411. ¢¢

Huron City Museum. Nine preserved buildings from the 1850-1890 Victorian era, incl the LaGasse Log Cabin, Phelps Memorial Church, Point Aux Barques US Life Saving Station, Hubbard's General Store, Community House/Inn, Brick Museum, Carriage Shed, and Barn House of Seven Gables, former residence of Langdon Hubbard and later Dr. William Lyon Phelps (additional fee). Buildings house period furnishings and memorabilia. Tours (July-Labor Day, Thurs-Mon) 7930 Huron City Rd, 8 mi E on MI 25. Phone 989/428-4123. ¢¢¢

Port Huron

(F-7) *See also St. Clair*

Pop 33,694 **Elev** 600 ft **Area code** 810 **Zip** 48060

Information Greater Port Huron Area Chamber of Commerce, 920 Pine Grove Ave; 810/985-7101

Web www.porthuron-chamber.org

Fort Gratiot Lighthouse, oldest on the Great Lakes, marks the St. Clair Straits. The famous International Blue Water Bridge (toll), south of the lighthouse, crosses to Sarnia, Ontario (see). (For Border Crossing Regulations see MAKING THE MOST OF YOUR TRIP.)

What to See and Do

Lakeport State Park. 565 acres on Lake Huron. Beach, bathhouse, waterskiing, fishing for perch, boating (ramp); hiking, picnicking, concession, playground, camping (fee). (Daily) 10 mi N on MI 25. Phone 810/327-6765. ¢¢

Museum of Arts and History. Historical and fine arts exhibits; pioneer log home, Native American collections, Thomas Edison's boyhood home archaeological exhibit, marine lore, natural history exhibits, period furniture; also lectures. (Wed-Sun; closed hols) (See SPECIAL EVENTS) 1115 6th St. Phone 810/982-0891. **Donation** Also here is

> **Huron Lightship Museum.** Lightships were constructed as floating lighthouses, anchored in areas where lighthouse construction was not possible, using their powerful lights and fog horns to guide ships safely past points of danger. Built in 1920, the *Huron* was stationed at various shoals in Lake Michigan and Lake Huron until her retirement in 1971. (June-Sept, Wed-Sun afternoons or by appt)

Special Events

Feast of the Ste. Claire. Pine Grove Park. Reenactment of 18th-century crafts, lifestyles, battles; also foods, fife and drum corps. Memorial Day wkend. Phone 810/985-7101.

Mackinac Race. Mid-July. Phone 810/985-7101.

Motels/Motor Lodges

★ ★ **COMFORT INN.** *1700 Yeager St (48060). 810/982-5500; fax 810/982-7199; res 800/228-5150. www.comfort inn.com.* 80 rms, 2 story, 16 suites. June-Aug: S, D $69-$109; each addl $5; suites $89-$99; under 18 free; higher rates special events; lower rates rest of yr. Crib free. TV; cable (premium), VCR avail. Indoor pool; whirlpool. Complimentary continental bkfst. Complimentary coffee in lobby. Restaurant opp 6 am-10 pm. Ck-out 11 am. Coin lndry. Meeting rms. In-rm modem link. Valet serv. Exercise equipt. Game rm. Refrigerator in suites. Cr cds: A, C, D, DS, JCB, MC, V.

★ **KNIGHTS INN.** *2160 Water St (48060). 810/982-1022; fax 810/982-0927; toll-free 800/843-5644. www. knightsinn.com.* 104 units. Apr-Oct: S $51.95-$62.95; D $57.99-$67.95; each addl $5; kit. units $61.95-$77.95; under 18 free; lower rates rest of yr. Crib free. Pet accepted. TV; cable (premium), VCR avail. Pool. Coffee in rms. Restaurant nearby. Ck-out noon. Cr cds: A, C, D, DS, MC, V.

★ ★ ★ **THOMAS EDISON INN.** *500 Thomas Edison Pkwy (48060). 810/984-8000; fax 810/984-3230; toll-free 800/451-7991. www.thomasedison inn.com.* 149 rms, 3 story, 12 suites. S, D $85-$120, each addl $10; suites $150-$345. Crib free. TV; cable (premium), VCR avail. Indoor pool; whirlpool. Restaurant 7 am-11 pm; Sun 8 am-9 pm. Bar 11-2 am; entertainment (days vary). Ck-out noon. Meeting rms. Business center. Bellhops. Sundries. Gift shop. Tennis privileges. Golf privileges. Exercise rm; sauna. Bathrm phones. Balconies. Opp river. Cr cds: A, MC, V.

Restaurant

★ ★ **FOGCUTTER.** *511 Fort St (48060). 810/987-3300.* Hrs: 11 am-10 pm; Sat from noon; Sun noon-7 pm. Closed hols. Res accepted. Bar. Lunch $4.95-$8.95, dinner $9.85-$19.95. Child's menu. Specializes in Swiss onion soup, almond-fried jumbo shrimp, prime rib. Panoramic view. Cr cds: A, D, DS, MC, V.

Romulus (H-6)

(see Detroit Wayne County Airport Area)

Saginaw

(F-6) *See also Bay City, Midland*

Settled 1816 **Pop** 69,512 **Elev** 595 ft
Area code 989
Information Saginaw County Convention and Visitors Bureau, One Tuscola St, Suite 101, 48607; 989/752-7164 or 800/444-9979
Web www.saginawcvb.org

When this was the land of the Sauk, the trees grew so thick that it was always night in the swamps on both sides of the Saginaw River. When the loggers "brought daylight to the swamp," the city became the timber capital of the world. When the trees were depleted, Saginaw turned its attention to industry and agriculture. Today, it is the home of numerous General Motors plants and is a leading manufacturer of malleable castings, as well as marketer of sugar beets, beans, bran, and wheat.

What to See and Do

Andersen Water Park & Wave Pool. Park features pool with three-ft waves, wading pool, 350-ft double water slide, and other water activities. (Memorial Day wkend-Labor Day wkend, daily) Under ten with adult only; children must be four ft in height to ride water slide. Rust Ave (MI 46) and Fordney St. Phone 517/759-1386. ¢¢

Castle Museum of Saginaw County History. Housed in a replica of a French chateau; collections pertaining to the history of the Saginaw Valley and central Michigan. (Daily; closed hols) 500 Federal. Phone 989/752-2861. ¢

Children's Zoo. Small animals incl llamas, macaws, swans, snakes, and porcupines. Contact yard featuring goats; train and pony rides (fees); lectures; educational programs. (Mid-May-Labor Day, daily) S Washington Ave and Ezra Rust Dr, in Celebration Sq. Phone 989/759-1657. ¢

Japanese Cultural Center & Tea House. Unique showplace on Lake Linton, designed by Yataro Suzue;

gift from sister city of Tokushima, Japan. Tea service (fee); garden. (Tues-Sun) 527 Ezra Rust Dr. Phone 989/759-1648.

Kokomo's Family Fun Center. Go-karts, bumper boats, laser tag, batting cages, miniature golf, indoor driving range. More than 50 arcade games. (Daily) Fee for individual activities. 5200 Kokomo Dr. Phone 989/797-5656.

Marshall M. Fredericks Sculpture Gallery. Houses an extraordinary collection of more than 200 works by the world-renowned sculptor. (Tues-Sun) 2250 Pierce Rd, at Saginaw Valley State University. Phone 989/790-5667. **Donation**

Saginaw Art Museum. Permanent and changing exhibits of paintings, sculpture, fine art; children's gallery; historic formal garden. (Tues-Sun; closed hols) 1126 N Michigan Ave. Phone 989/754-2491. **Donation**

Special Events

Saginaw Harness Raceway. 2701 E Genesee Ave, N via I-75, Bridgeport exit. Over 12 yrs only. For schedule phone 989/755-3451. Racing season May-late Aug.

Saginaw County Fair. Late July. Phone 989/752-7164.

Great Lakes Rendezvous. Third wkend Aug. Phone 989/754-2928.

Motels/Motor Lodges

★★ **FOUR POINTS BY SHERATON.** *4960 Towne Centre Rd (48604). 517/790-5050; fax 517/790-1466; res 800/428-1470. www.fourpoints.com.* 156 rms, 6 story. S, D $69-$139; each addl $10; under 18 free; wkend plan. Crib free. Pet accepted, some restrictions; $20 refundable. TV; cable (premium), VCR avail. Indoor/outdoor pool; whirlpool. Restaurant 6:30 am-10 pm. Bar 11-2 am; entertainment. Ck-out noon. Meeting rms. Business servs avail. Bellhops. Valet serv. Free airport transportation. Exercise equipt; sauna. Health club privileges. Game rm. Country French decor. Cr cds: A, C, D, DS, ER, JCB, MC, V.
D ⭐ 🏊 ✈ 🔌 🐾 **SC**

★★ **HAMPTON INN.** *2222 Tittabawassee Rd (48604). 517/792-7666; fax 517/792-3213; res 800/426-7866.*

www.hamptoninn.com. 120 rms, 2 story. S $56-$60; D $63-$67; under 18 free. Crib free. TV; cable (premium), VCR avail. Heated pool. Complimentary continental bkfst. Restaurant nearby. Ck-out noon. Meeting rms. Valet serv. Downhill ski 10 mi. Game rm. Cr cds: A, C, D, DS, MC, V.

🄳 ⇌ ⊠ 🐾 ⊠

★ **SUPER 8 MOTEL.** *4848 Towne Center Rd (48603). 517/791-3003; res 800/800-8000. www.super8.com.* 62 rms, 3 story. Apr-Sept: S $37.88; D $43.88-$47.88; each addl $5; suite $53.88; under 12 free; lower rates rest of yr. Crib free. Pet accepted, some restrictions. TV; cable (premium). Restaurant nearby. Ck-out 11 am. Health club privileges. Cr cds: A, D, DS, MC, V.

🄳 🐾 ⊠ 🐾

B&B/Small Inn

★★ **MONTAGUE INN.** *1581 S Washington (48601). 517/752-3937; fax 517/752-3159. www.montagueinn. com.* 18 rms, 16 with bath, 2-3 story. S $55-$140; D $65-$150; each addl $10. Crib free. TV; cable. Complimentary continental bkfst. Dining rm (public by res) 11:30 am-2 pm, 6-10 pm; Mon from 6 pm; closed Sun. Ck-out noon, ck-in 3 pm. Health club privileges. Lawn games. On lake. Restored Georgian mansion (1929); antiques. Cr cds: A, MC, V.

🄳 ⊠ 🐾 SC

St. Clair

(G-7) *See also Detroit, Mount Clemens, Port Huron, Warren*

Pop 5,116 **Elev** 600 ft **Area code** 810 **Zip** 48079

Information St. Clair Chamber of Commerce, 505 N Riverside Ave; 810/329-2962

Web www.stclairchamber.com

Motels/Motor Lodges

★★★ **BLUE WATER INN.** *1337 N River Rd (48079). 810/329-2261; fax 810/329-6056; toll-free 800/468-3727. www.muer.com.* 21 rms. May-

Labor Day: S, D $92.50; each addl $5; under 16 free; lower rates rest of yr. Crib free. TV; cable (premium). Heated pool. Complimentary continental bkfst. Restaurant (see RIVER CRAB). Bar 4:30-11 pm; off-season hrs vary. Ck-out 11 am. Business servs avail. Refrigerators. All rms overlook river. Cr cds: A, D, DS, MC, V.

🐾 ⇌ 🐾

★★ **ST. CLAIR INN.** *500 N Riverside (48079). 810/329-2222; fax 810/329-2348; toll-free 800/482-8327. www. stclairinn.com.* 78 rms, 3 story. S, D $80-$145; each addl $10; suites $100-$300; family rates. Crib free. TV; cable. Indoor pool; whirlpool. Restaurant (see ST. CLAIR INN). Bar 11-2 am; entertainment Wed-Sat. Ck-out noon, ck-in 3 pm. Business servs avail. Bellhops. Valet serv. Tennis privileges. 18-hole golf privileges. Game rm. Some bathrm phones. Private patios, balconies. Overlooks St. Clair River. Cr cds: A, C, D, DS, MC, V.

🄳 🐾 🏌 ⇌ ⊠ 🐾 SC 🎿

Restaurants

★★ **RIVER CRAB.** *1337 N River Rd (MI 29) (48079). 810/329-2261. www. muer.com.* Hrs: 11:30 am-9 pm; Sat-Sun to 10 pm; early-bird dinner Mon-Fri 4-6 pm. Closed Dec 25. Res accepted. Bar. A la carte entrees: lunch $6-$15, dinner $9-$30. Sun brunch $16.95. Child's menu. Specializes in clam bakes, Maine lobster, Charley's chowder. Entertainment. Valet parking. Outdoor dining. Cr cds: A, D, DS, MC, V.

🄳 ⊟

★★ **ST. CLAIR INN.** *500 N Riverside (48079). 810/329-2222. www.stclairinn. com.* Hrs: 7-10:30 am, 11:30 am-4 pm, 5-10 pm; Fri, Sat to midnight; Sun 8 am-noon, 1-9 pm. Res accepted. Bar. Bkfst $4-$11, lunch $8-$14, dinner $15-$40. Child's menu. Specializes in prime rib, seafood, steak. Entertainment Tues-Sat. Valet parking Fri, Sat. Outdoor dining. River view. Cr cds: A, D, DS, MC, V.

🄳 ⊟

St. Ignace

(C-5) *See also Mackinac Island, Mackinaw City*

Pop 2,568 **Elev** 600 ft **Area code** 906 **Zip** 49781

Information St. Ignace Area Chamber of Commerce, 560 N State St; 906/643-8717 or 800/338-6660

Web www.stignace.com

Located at the north end of the Mackinac Bridge, across the Straits of Mackinac from Mackinaw City (see), St. Ignace was founded more than 300 years ago by the famous missionary/explorer, Père Marquette. St. Ignace is the gateway to Michigan's Upper Peninsula, which offers beautiful scenery and vast opportunities for outdoor recreation. A Ranger District office of the Hiawatha National Forest (see ESCANABA) is located in St. Ignace.

What to See and Do

Castle Rock. Climb the 170 steps to the top of this 200-ft-high rock to see excellent views of Mackinac Island and Lake Huron. Also features statue of Paul Bunyan and Babe, the blue ox. (Daily) I-75 exit 348, 5 mi N of Mackinac Bridge. Phone 906/643-8268.

Father Marquette National Memorial. This 52-acre memorial pays tribute to the life and work of the famed Jesuit explorer who came to area in the 1600s. Adj Mackinac Bridge Authority Plaza.

Mackinac Island ferries. Fifteen-min trips to the island.

  Arnold Transit Company. (May-Dec, daily) Phone 906/847-3351.

  Star Line Ferry. "Hydro Jet" service (May-Oct). Contact 590 N State St. Phone 906/643-7635.

Marquette Mission Park and Museum of Ojibwa Culture. Gravesite of Father Marquette. Museum interprets 17th-century Native American life and the coming of the French. (Memorial Day-Labor Day, daily; after Labor Day-rest of Sept, Tues-Sat) Phone 906/643-9161. ¢

Special Events

Down Memory Lane Parade and Straits Area Antique Auto Show. Last Sat June. Phone 906/643-9402.

Arts and Crafts Dockside and St. Ignace Powwow. Juried show held in conjunction with the Bridge Walk; traditional Native American powwow. Labor Day wkend. Phone 906/643-8717.

Mackinac Bridge Walk. The only day each yr when walking across the bridge is permitted (some lanes open to motor vehicles). Labor Day. Phone 906/643-8717.

Motels/Motor Lodges

★ ★ **AURORA BOREALIS MOTOR INN.** *635 W US 2 (49781). 906/643-7488; toll-free 800/462-6783.* 56 rms, 2 story. Late June-mid-Aug: S, D $50-$75; each addl $5; higher rates: Labor Day (2-day min), Auto Show (3-day min); lower rates May-late June, mid-Aug-Oct. Closed rest of yr. Crib $5. TV; cable (premium). Restaurant adj 7 am-10 pm. Ck-out 10 am. Cr cds: DS, MC, V.
🄳 ⬙ 🄽 🆂🅲

★ **BAY VIEW BEACHFRONT MOTEL.** *1133 N State St (49781). 906/643-9444.* 19 rms. Late June-Labor Day: S, D $42-$72; each addl $4; lower rates mid-May-late June, after Labor Day-late Oct. Closed rest of yr. Crib free. Pet accepted. TV; cable. Restaurant nearby. Ck-out 10 am. Free airport transportation. Picnic tables, grill. On Lake Huron; private beach. Cr cds: DS, MC, V.
🄳 ⬙ 🅻 ⬙ 🄽 🄵

★ ★ **BEST WESTERN GEORGIAN HOUSE LAKEFRONT.** *1131 N State St (49781). 906/643-8411; fax 906/643-8924; toll-free 800/322-8411. www.bestwestern.com.* 85 rms, 2-3 story. June-Labor Day: S, D $69-$129; each addl $5; under 12 free; wkday rates; higher rates (3-day min) Labor Day, auto show; lower rates rest of yr. Crib $10. TV; cable (premium). Indoor pool; whirlpool. Playground. Ck-out 11 am. Coin lndry. Business servs avail. Downhill ski 5 mi; x-country ski 2 mi. Miniature golf.

Game rm. On Lake Huron; sun deck. Cr cds: A, D, DS, MC, V.

★ **BUDGET HOST INN.** *700 N State St (49781). 906/643-9666; fax 906/643-9126; toll-free 800/872-7057. www.stignacebudgethost.com.* 56 rms, 2 story. Mid-June-Labor Day: S $64-$66; D $94-$98; each addl $4; higher rates special events, holidays, auto show (3-day min); Labor day (2-day min); lower rates rest of yr. Crib free. Pet accepted; $20 refundable. TV; cable (premium). Indoor pool; whirlpool. Guest lndry. Playground. Ck-out 11 am. Business servs avail. In-rm modem link. Downhill/x-country ski 5 mi. Some refrigerators, in-rm whirlpools. Sun deck. Overlooks Moran Bay. Ferry 1 blk. Cr cds: A, C, D, DS, MC, V.

★★ **COMFORT INN.** *927 N State St (49781). 906/643-7733; fax 906/643-6420; toll-free 800/228-5150. www.comfortinn.com.* 100 rms, 4 story. July-late Aug: S, D $68-$130; each addl $5; under 18 free; higher rates (2-day min) auto show, Labor Day; lower rates late Apr-June, Aug-Dec. Closed rest of yr. Crib $5. TV; cable (premium). Indoor pool; whirlpool. Playground. Complimentary continental bkfst. Ck-out 11 am. Meeting rm. Business servs avail. Exercise equipt. Game rm. Lawn games. Refrigerators. Balconies. On beach. Cr cds: A, C, D, DS, JCB, MC, V.

★ **DAYS INN.** *1067 N State St (49781). 906/643-8008; fax 906/643-9400; toll-free 800/732-9746. www.daysinn.com.* 119 rms, 2-3 story. Late June-early Sept: S $59-$99; D $64-$104; each addl $6; suites $96-$156; under 13 free; higher rates (3-day min) Labor Day, auto show; lower rates rest of yr. Crib free. TV; cable (premium). Indoor pool; whirlpools. Playground. Complimentary continental bkfst. Restaurant opp 7 am-10 pm. Ck-out 10 am. Coin lndry. Free airport, bus depot transportation. Game rm. Sauna. Refrigerators avail. Lakefront balconies. Cr cds: A, C, D, DS, JCB, MC, V.

★ **ECONO LODGE.** *1030 N State St (49781). 906/643-8060; fax 906/643-7251; toll-free 800/638-7949. www.econolodge.com.* 47 rms, 2 story. Late June-late Aug: S, D $62-$92; each addl $6; under 18 free; higher rates (2-day min) Labor Day, auto show; lower rates May-late June, late Aug-mid-Oct. Closed rest of yr. Crib free. TV; cable (premium). Indoor pool; whirlpool. Playground. Restaurant adj 7:30 am-9 pm. Ck-out 10 am. In-rm modem link. Some refrigerators. Cr cds: A, D, DS, MC, V.

★★ **HARBOUR POINTE MOTOR INN.** *797 N State St (49781). 906/643-9882; fax 906/643-6946; toll-free 800/642-3318.* 123 rms, 1-3 story. No elvtr. July-late Aug: S, D $69-$135; higher rates hols, auto show, boat show; Labor Day (2-day min); lower rates May-June, late Aug-Oct. Closed rest of yr. Crib $5. TV; cable (premium), VCR avail. 2 pools, 1 indoor; 3 whirlpools. Playground. Complimentary continental bkfst. Restaurant nearby. Ck-out 11 am. Coin lndry. Meeting rms. Business servs avail. Free airport, bus depot transportation. Game rm. Lawn games. Some refrigerators. Balconies. Picnic tables. On lake. Cr cds: A, C, D, DS, MC, V.

★ **HOWARD JOHNSON EXPRESS INN.** *913 Boulevard Dr (49781). 906/643-9700; fax 906/643-6762; toll-free 800/906-4656. www.hojo.com.* 57 rms, 2 story. Mid-June-mid-Sept: S $68-$76; D $73-$87; each addl $6; under 18 free; higher rates Labor Day (2-day min), auto show (3-day min); lower rates rest of yr. Crib free. Pet accepted; $6. Indoor pool; whirlpool. TV; cable, VCR avail. Complimentary continental bkfst. Complimentary coffee in lobby. Restaurant nearby. Ck-out noon. Coin lndry. Meeting rms. Sundries. X-country ski 7 mi. Game rm. Cr cds: A, MC, V.

★★ **KEWADIN INN.** *1140 N State St (49781). 906/643-9141; fax 906/643-9405; toll-free 800/345-9457.* 71 rms. S, D $59-$79; package plans; higher rates antique auto show, hols. Crib free. TV; cable (premium). Heated pool. Playground. Complimentary continental bkfst. Restaurant nearby. Ck-out 11 am. Free airport transportation. Lawn games. Picnic tables, grills. Nature trail. Cr cds: A, C, D, DS, MC, V.

⊡ 🏊 🛏 🐾 SC

★ ★ **K ROYALE MOTOR INN.** *1037 N State St (49781). 906/643-7737; fax 906/643-8556; toll-free 800/882-7122. www.stignace.com.* 95 rms, 3 story. S, D $38-$125; each addl $5; higher rates Labor Day (2-day min), auto show (3-day min), special events. Closed Nov-Mar. Crib avail. TV; cable (premium). Indoor pool; whirlpool. Playground. Complimentary continental bkfst. Restaurant opp 7:30 am-10 pm in season. Coin lndry. Ck-out 10 am. Free airport, bus depot transportation. Game rm. Refrigerators. Balconies. Picnic tables. Sun deck. Overlooks Lake Huron; private beach. Cr cds: A, MC, V.

✈ 🏊 🛏 🐾

★ **THUNDERBIRD MOTOR INN.** *10 South St (49781). 906/643-8900; fax 906/643-8596.* 34 rms, 2 story. Mid-June-Labor Day: S, D $70-$125; each addl $5; higher rates (3-day min) Labor Day, auto show; lower rates mid-May-mid-June, Labor Day-Oct. Closed rest of yr. Crib $4. TV; cable (premium). Restaurant nearby. Ck-out 11 am. Cr cds: A, MC, V.

🐾 🛠 🛏 🐾

★ **TRADEWINDS.** *1190 N State St (49781). 906/643-9388.* 25 rms. No rm phones. Late June-Labor Day: S, D $55; each addl $4; higher rates (3-day min) Labor Day, auto show; lower rates late May-late June, Labor Day-mid-Oct. Closed rest of yr. TV; cable (premium). Pool. Playground. Complimentary coffee in rms. Restaurant adj 7 am-11 pm. Ck-out 11 am. Picnic tables. Overlooks Lake Huron. Cr cds: DS, MC, V.

🐾 🛠 🏊 🛏 🐾

St. Joseph

(H-3) *See also New Buffalo, Niles*

Pop 9,214 **Elev** 630 ft **Area code** 616 **Zip** 49085

Information Cornerstone Chamber Services, 38 W Wall St, PO Box 428,

Benton Harbor 49023-0428; 616/925-6100

Web www.cstonealliance.org

This town is opposite Benton Harbor on the St. Joseph River.

What to See and Do

Curious Kids Museum. Interactive museum for children; kids can interact with such exhibits as balloon flying and apple picking and can even run their own TV station. (Wed-Sun) 415 Lake Blvd. Phone 616/983-2543. ¢¢

Deer Forest. Approx 30 acres; more than 500 animals and birds; Story Book Lane, "Santa's Summer Home," train, children's rides, stage events, picnicking. (Memorial Day-Labor Day, daily) Approx 12 mi NE via I-94, in Coloma. Phone 616/468-4961. ¢¢

Krasl Art Center. Three galleries house contemporary and traditional works, fine and folk arts, local and major museum collections; art reference library; lectures, tours, films; gift shop. (Daily; closed hols) 707 Lake Blvd. Phone 616/983-0271. **FREE**

Warren Dunes State Park. On 1,499 acres on Lake Michigan. Swimming, beach house; hiking, picnicking, playground, concession, camping, cabins. 200 acres of virgin forest in Warren Woods. Standard fees. (Daily) 14 mi S via MI 63 and I-94, in Sawyer. Phone 616/426-4013. ¢¢

Special Events

Blossomtime Festival. A spring salute to agriculture, industry, and recreation in southwest Michigan; Blessing of the Blossoms; Blossomtime Ball, Grand Floral Parade. Early May. Phone 616/926-7397.

Krasl Art Fair. Lake Bluff Park. One of the major art shows in the state. Second wkend July. Phone 616/983-0271.

Venetian Festival. Boat parades, fireworks, concerts, land and water contests, races, sand-castle sculptures, food booths, photography competition. Phone 616/983-7917. Mid-July.

Sailing Festival. Labor Day wkend. Phone 616/982-0032.

Motels/Motor Lodges

★★ **BENTON HOTEL SUITES.**
2860 M 139 S, Benton Harbor (54547).
616/925-3234; fax 616/925-6131. 150
rms, 2 story. June-Sept: S $63-$75; D
$68-$75; each addl $5; under 18 free;
golf plan; lower rates rest of yr. Crib
free. TV; cable (premium). Indoor/
outdoor pool; whirlpool. Restaurant
6:30 am-10 pm; Sat 7 am-11 pm; Sun
7 am-9 pm. Bar 4 pm-midnight. Ck-
out 11 am. Meeting rms. Business
servs avail. Bellhops. Gift shop. Free
RR station, bus depot transportation.
Exercise equipt; sauna. Game rm. Rec
rm. Cr cds: A, MC, V.

★★ **BEST WESTERN.** *2723 Niles*
Ave (49085). 616/983-6321; fax 616/
983-7630; res 800/780-7234. www.
bestwestern.com. 36 rms, 2 story, 2
kits. May-Sept: S $31-$38; D $49-$55;
each addl $4; suite $52-$55; kit.
units $38-$52; under 12 free; wkly
rates off-season; lower rates rest of yr.
Crib $4. TV; cable (premium). Heated
pool. Complimentary continental
bkfst. Restaurant adj open 24 hrs.
Ck-out noon. X-country ski 5 mi.
Many refrigerators. Cr cds: A, C, D,
DS, JCB, MC, V.

★★ **COMFORT INN.** *1598 Mall Dr,*
Benton Harbor (49022). 616/925-1880;
toll-free 800/228-5150. www.comfort
inn.com. 52 rms, 2 story. Mid-May-
mid-Sept: S $59.95; D $64.95; under
18 free; family rates; lower rates rest
of yr. Crib free. Pet accepted. TV;
cable (premium). Indoor pool; whirlpool. Complimentary continental
bkfst. Restaurant nearby. Ck-out 11
am. Business servs avail. Game rm.
Health club privileges. Some refrigerators. Cr cds: A, D, DS, MC, V.

★★ **COURTYARD BY MARRIOTT.**
1592 Mall Dr, Benton Harbor (49022).
616/925-3000; fax 616/925-8796; res
800/321-2211. www.marriott.com. 98
rms, 2 story. May-Sept: S, D $77-$96;
suites $129-$299; lower rates rest of
yr. Crib free. TV; cable. Indoor/out-
door pool. Complimentary coffee.
Restaurant nearby. Ck-out noon.
Meeting rms. Business servs avail. In-
rm modem link. Valet serv. X-country ski 5 mi. Exercise equipt. Picnic
tables. Cr cds: A, MC, V.

★ **DAYS INN.** *2699 US 31, Benton*
Harbor (49022). 616/925-7021; fax
616/925-7115; res 800/329-7466.
www.daysinn.com. 120 rms, 2 story.
May-Labor Day: S $47-$58; D $59-
$70; each addl $5; under 16 free;
higher rates festivals; lower rates rest
of yr. Crib free. TV, VCR avail
(movies). Indoor pool; whirlpool.
Complimentary continental bkfst.
Restaurant open 24 hrs. Rm serv 8
am-9 pm. Ck-out noon. Coin lndry.
Meeting rm. Business servs avail.
Sundries. X-country ski 20 mi. Exercise equipt; sauna. Health club privileges. Game rm. Some refrigerators.
Private patios, balconies. Cr cds: A,
D, DS, MC, V.

★ **SUPER 8 MOTEL.** *1950 E Napier*
Ave, Benton Harbor (49022). 616/926-
1371; toll-free 800/800-8000. www.
super8.com. 62 rms, 3 story. S $35.88-
$47.88; D $46.88-$60.88; under 12
free; higher rates: wkends, special
events. Crib free. Pet accepted. TV;
cable (premium). Complimentary
coffee in lobby. Restaurant nearby.
Ck-out 11 am. Business servs avail.
Cr cds: A, C, D, DS, MC, V.

Hotel

★★ **BOULEVARD INN.** *521 Lake*
Blvd (49085). 616/983-6600; fax
616/983-0520; toll-free 800/875-6600.
85 suites, 7 story. Suites $97-$128;
each addl $10; under 12 free; golf
plans; higher rates (2-day min):
Memorial Day wkend, Venetian Festival; lower rates rest of yr. Crib free.
TV; cable (premium), VCR avail.
Complimentary continental bkfst.
Coffee in rms. Restaurant 7 am-2 pm,
5:30-10 pm. Bar from 5 pm. Ck-out
noon. Meeting rms. Business center.
Health club privileges. Refrigerators,
wet bars. Cr cds: A, MC, V.

Restaurant

★★ **SCHULER'S OF**
STEVENSVILLE. *5000 Red Arrow*
Hwy (I-94), Stevensville (49127).
616/429-3273. www.schulersrest.com.

Hrs: 11 am-10 pm; Fri, Sat to 11 pm; Sun 11 am-9 pm; hols noon-8 pm. Closed Dec 25. Res accepted. Lunch $5.95-$9.50, dinner $6.95-$18.50. Child's menu. Specializes in prime rib, pork chop, fresh seafood. Old English theme; stone fireplace. Family-owned. Cr cds: A, D, DS, MC, V.

[D] [🖼]

Saugatuck

See also Holland, South Haven

Pop 954 **Elev** 600 ft **Area code** 616 **Zip** 49453

Information Saugatuck-Douglas Visitors & Convention Bureau, PO Box 28; 616/857-1701

Web www.saugatuck.com

Long one of the major art colonies in the Midwest, Saugatuck/Douglas is growing as a year-round resort area. It offers beautiful beaches for swimming and surfing on Lake Michigan, hiking and cross-country skiing in the dunes, canoeing and boating on the Kalamazoo River, yachting from marinas, and a charming shopping area. The northern end of the village covers an ancient Native American burial ground. During the summer months, arts and crafts shows are abundant.

What to See and Do

Fenn Valley Vineyards and Wine Cellar. Self-guided tour overlooking wine cellar; audiovisual program, wine tasting. (Daily; closed hols) 5 mi SE via I-196 exit 34, at 6130 122nd Ave in Fennville. Phone 616/561-2396. **FREE**

Keewatin Marine Museum. Tours of restored, turn-of-the-century, passenger steamship of the Canadian Pacific Railroad; maintained as "in-service" ship; features original, elegant furnishings, carved paneling, brass fixtures. Quadruple-expansion engine rm also open to tours. (Memorial Day-Labor Day, daily) Harbour Village, just S of the Saugatuck-Douglas Bridge. Phone 616/857-2107. ¢¢

Saugatuck Dune Rides. Buggy rides over the sand dunes near Lake Michigan. (May-Sept, daily; Oct, wkends only) ½ mi W of I-196, exit 41. Phone 616/857-2253. ¢¢¢

Sightseeing cruises.

City of Douglas. Scenic afternoon, buffet brunch luncheon, and dinner cruises to Lake Michigan via Kalamazoo River. (Memorial Day wkend-Labor Day, daily) Docked just S of the Douglas-Saugatuck Bridge. Phone 616/857-2107.

Star of Saugatuck. Stern-wheel paddleboat with narrated tours on the Kalamazoo River and Lake Michigan (weather permitting). (Early May-Sept, daily; Oct, wkends only) At the Fish Dock, 716 Water St. Phone 616/857-4261.

Special Events

Harbor Days. Venetian boat parade, family activities. Last wkend July. Phone 616/857-1701.

Taste of Saugatuck. Late Aug. Phone 616/857-1701.

Halloween Harvest Festival. Late Oct. Phone 616/857-1701.

Motels/Motor Lodges

★ ★ **LAKE SHORE RESORT.** *2885 Lakeshore Dr (49453). 616/857-7121. www.lakeshoreresortsaugatuck.com.* 30 rms. June-mid-Sept, hols: S $70-$130; D $80-$150; each addl $30; lower rates May, mid-Sept-Oct. Closed rest of yr. TV; cable. Heated pool. Continental bkfst. Restaurant nearby. Ck-out 11 am. Viewing decks overlook lake. Nature trails. Cr cds: MC, V.
[🐾] [🏊] [🎿] [🔥]

★ ★ **SHANGRA-LA MOTEL.** *6190 Blue Star Hwy (49453). 616/857-1453; fax 616/857-5905; toll-free 800/877-1453.* 20 rms. May-Labor Day: S $50-$110; D $50-$140; each addl $5; lower rates rest of yr. Closed Jan. Crib $5. TV; VCR (movies $3). Heated pool. Restaurant nearby. Ck-out 11 am. X-country ski 4 mi. Lawn games. Refrigerators avail. Picnic tables, grill. Cr cds: DS, MC, V.
[🏊] [🏊] [🎿] [🔥] [SC]

★ ★ **TIMBERLINE.** *3353 Blue Star Hwy (49453). 616/857-2147; res 800/257-2147. www.timberlinemotel.*

com. 28 rms. May-early Sept: S $55-$130; D $65-$150; each addl $5; lower rates rest of yr. Crib free. TV; cable (premium). Heated pool; whirlpool. Playground. Complimentary coffee. Restaurant nearby. Ck-out 11 am. Free airport, bus depot transportation. X-country ski 2½ mi. Game rm. Lawn games. Cr cds: A, DS, MC, V.

D ⚞ ⚟ ⚠ ♨

B&Bs/Small Inns

★★ **KINGSLEY HOUSE BED & BREAKFAST.** *626 W Main St, Fennville (49408). 616/561-6425; fax 616/561-2593. www.kingsleyhouse. com.* 8 rms, 4 with shower only, 3 story, 3 suites. No rm phones. Apr-Oct: S, D $120-$140; suites $150-$175; wkends (2-day min), hols (3-day min); lower rates rest of yr. Children over 12 yrs only. TV in suites; VCR avail. Complimentary full bkfst wkends. Restaurant nearby. Ck-out 11 am, ck-in 4 pm. Luggage handling. X-country ski 5 mi. Bicycles. Victorian house built 1886; antiques. Totally nonsmoking. Cr cds: A, DS, MC, V.

⚞ ⚠ ♨

★★ **MAPLEWOOD HOTEL.** *428 Butler (49453). 616/857-1771; fax 616/857-1773; toll-free 800/650-9790.* 15 rms, 11 with shower only, 2 story. May-Oct: S, D $115-$185; each addl $15; under 3 free; lower rates rest of yr. Crib free. TV; cable. Heated pool. Complimentary full bkfst. Restaurant nearby. Ck-out noon, ck-in 3-6 pm. 18-hole golf privileges. X-country ski 3 mi. Built in 1860; antiques. Totally nonsmoking. Cr cds: A, MC, V.

D ⚞ ⚸ ⚠ ⚟ ♨ SC

★★ **PARK HOUSE BED & BREAKFAST.** *888 Holland St (49453). 616/857-4535; fax 616/857-1065; toll-free 800/321-4535. www.parkhouseinn. com.* 9 rms, 2 story, 3 suites, 4 cottages. Some rm phones. S, D $95-$165; suites $165; cottage $125-$225; wkly rates; 2-day min wkends Sept-June, 3-day min wkends July-Aug. TV in parlor, suites, cottages; VCR avail (movies). Complimentary full bkfst. Restaurant adj (in season) 7 am-3 pm. Ck-out 11 am, ck-in 3 pm. Business servs avail. X-country ski 2 mi. Many fireplaces. Some balconies. Picnic tables, grill. White, clapboard

house built for lumberman (1857); oldest house in Saugatuck, once visited by Susan B. Anthony. Sitting rm; wide-planked pine floors, antiques. Cr cds: A, DS, MC, V.

⚞ ⚠ ♨

★★ **ROSEMONT INN RESORT.** *83 Lakeshore Dr (49453). 616/857-2637; toll-free 800/721-2637. www.rosemont inn.com.* 14 rms, 2 story. Mid-June-mid-Sept: S $95-$145; D $105-$145; hols (3-day min); lower rates rest of yr. Adults only. TV; cable. Heated pool; whirlpool. Complimentary full bkfst; afternoon refreshments. Restaurant nearby. Ck-out noon, ck-in 3 pm. Business servs avail. In-rm modem link. Golf privileges. X-country ski on site. Sauna. Rec rm. On Lake Michigan; swimming beach. Built 1901. Totally nonsmoking. Cr cds: A, DS, MC, V.

D ⚞ ⚸ ⚠ ⚟ ♨

★★ **SHERWOOD FOREST BED & BREAKFAST.** *938 Center St, Douglas (49406). 616/857-1246; fax 616/857-1996; toll-free 800/838-1246.* 5 rms, shower only, 2 story, 1 kit. cottage. No rm phones. Memorial Day-Labor Day: S, D $85-$165; cottage $850/wk; higher rates wkends (2-day min); lower rates rest of yr. TV in sitting rm; VCR (free movies). Heated pool; whirlpool. Complimentary continental bkfst. Ck-out noon, ck-in 3 pm. Bicycles. Picnic tables. Near Lake Michigan, beach. Victorian-style house built 1890s; many antiques. Totally nonsmoking. Cr cds: DS, MC, V.

⚠ ⚟ ♨

★ **TWIN GABLES INN.** *900 Lake St (49453). 616/857-4346; fax 616/857-3482; toll-free 800/231-2185. www. twingablesinn.com.* 14 rms, 2 story, 3 cottages (1-2 bedrm). No rm phones. May-Oct: S, D $75-$170; each addl $10-$15; cottages $495-$720/wk; under 3 free; wkly rates; lower rates rest of yr. TV in sitting rm. Heated pool; whirlpool. Complimentary bkfst buffet (inn). Ck-out 11 am, ck-in 3 pm. Free airport, RR station, bus depot transportation. X-country ski 3 mi. Some fireplaces. Picnic tables, grills. Fireplace in sitting rm, embossed tin ceilings and walls; antiques. Near lake. Cr cds: A, D, DS, MC, V.

D ⚞ ⚠ ⚟ ♨

★ ★ ★ **WICKWOOD INN.** *510 Butler St (49453). 616/857-1465; fax 616/857-1552.* 11 rms, 2 story, 2 suites. No rm phones. May-Nov: S, D $165-$175; suites $185-$195; lower rates rest of yr. Closed Dec 24, 25. Complimentary continental bkfst. Restaurant nearby. Setups. Ck-out noon, ck-in 3 pm. Business servs avail. X-country ski 5 mi. Inn (1940) designed after English country house; library, sitting rm, antiques. Screened gazebo. Cr cds: MC, V.

D ⌖ ♨

Restaurants

★ **CHEQUERS.** *220 Culver St (49453). 616/857-1868. www.chequers ofsaugatuck.com.* Hrs: 11:30 am-10 pm; Sat to 11 pm; Sun noon-10 pm; winter hrs vary. Closed Jan 1, Dec 25. English pub menu. Bar. Lunch $6-$10, dinner $10-$19. Specialties: shepherd's pie, fish and chips. English-style pub. Cr cds: A, MC, V.

D ⌁

★ ★ **TOULOUSE.** *248 Culver St (49453). 616/857-1561. www.restaurant toulouse.com.* Hrs: 5:30-10 pm; Wed, Thurs to 9 pm. Closed Jan 1, Dec 25; also Mar. Res accepted. French menu. Bar. Dinner $20-$30. Specializes in French country cuisine. Patio dining. French country atmosphere. Cr cds: A, MC, V.

D

Sault Ste. Marie

(B-5)

Settled 1668 **Pop** 14,689 **Elev** 613 ft
Area code 906 **Zip** 49783
Information Sault Convention and Visitors Bureau, 2581 I-75 Business Spur; 906/632-3301 or 800/MI-SAULT
Web www.ssmcoc.com

Sault Ste. Marie (SOO-Saint-Marie) is the home of one of the nation's great engineering marvels—the locks of St. Mary's River. Along the river the locks lower or raise lake and ocean vessels 21 feet between Lake Superior and Lake Huron in 6 to 15 minutes.

From April to December, about 100 vessels a day pass through with no toll charge. The cascades of the river, which made the locks necessary, give the city its name: the French word for a cascade is *sault* and the name of the patron saint was Mary; combined, the two made Sault de Sainte Marie or "Leap of the Saint Mary's."

The only entrance into Canada for almost 300 miles, the Sault Ste. Marie community began in 1668 when Father Jacques Marquette built the first mission church here. An international bridge spans the St. Mary's River to Sault Ste. Marie, Ontario (toll). (For Border Crossing Regulations see MAKING THE MOST OF YOUR TRIP.) A Ranger District office of the Hiawatha National Forest (see ESCANABA) is located in Sault Ste. Marie.

What to See and Do

Federal Building. Grounds occupy what was the site of Jesuit Fathers' mission and later the original site of Fort Brady (1822) before it was moved. Ground floor houses **River of History Museum,** an interpretive center depicting the history of the St. Mary's River. E Portage Ave.

Lake Superior State University. (1946) 3,000 students. This hillside campus was the second site of historic Fort Brady after it was moved from its original location; many old buildings, incl some that were part of the fort, still stand. Library's Marine Collection on Great Lakes Shipping open on request. Carillon concerts (June-Sept, twice daily; free). Headquarters of the famous Unicorn Hunters, official keepers of the Queen's English. Tours. 6550 W Easter Day. Phone 906/635-2315.

Museum Ship Valley Camp and Great Lakes Maritime Museum. Great Lakes Marine Hall of Fame. Ship's store, picnic area, and park. (Mid-May-mid-Oct, daily) 5 blks E of locks. Phone 906/632-3658. ¢¢¢

★ **"Soo" Locks.** The famous locks can be seen from both the upper and lower parks paralleling the locks. The upper park has three observation towers. There is a scale model of the locks at the east end of the MacArthur Lock and a working lock model, photos, and a movie in visitor building in upper park. (Mar-Feb, daily) 119 Park Pl. Phone 906/632-3311. **FREE**

Soo Locks Boat Tours. Two-hr narrated excursions travel through the Soo Locks, focusing on their history. Sunset dinner cruises (approx 2¾ hrs; res suggested). (Mid-May-mid-Oct, daily) Docks located at 515 and 1157 E Portage Ave. Phone 906/632-6301. ¢¢¢¢

Tower of History. A 21-story observation tower with 20-mi view of Canadian and American cities; show in lobby, displays. (Mid-May-mid-Oct, daily) 501 E Water St. Phone 906/632-3658. ¢¢

Twin Soo Tour. Guided tour (two to four hrs) of both Canadian and American cities of Sault Ste. Marie; provides view of Soo Locks; passengers may disembark in Canada. (June-Oct, daily) 315-317 W Portage Ave. Phone 906/635-5241. ¢¢ Also here is

> **The Haunted Depot.** Guided tours through depot's many unusual chambers; visitors can "fall uphill" in the mystery bedrm, walk through a "storm" in the cemetery, "lose their heads" at the guillotine. (June-Oct, daily) Phone 906/635-5912.

Motels/Motor Lodges

★★ **BEST WESTERN SAULT STE. MARIE.** *4281 I-75 Business Spur (49783). 906/632-2170; fax 906/632-7877; toll-free 800/297-2858. www. bestwestern.com.* 110 rms, 2 story. S, D $49-$109; family rates; package plans. Crib free. TV; cable (premium), VCR avail. Indoor pool. Complimentary continental bkfst. Restaurant nearby. Ck-out 11 am. Coin lndry. In-rm modem link. Sauna. Game rm. Refrigerators. Cr cds: A, C, D, DS, ER, JCB, MC, V.
🄳 ⇌ 🈯 🐾

★ **BUDGET HOST CRESTVIEW INN.** *1200 Ashmun St (49783). 906/635-5213; fax 906/635-9672; toll-free 800/955-5213. www.crestviewinn. com.* 44 rms. July-mid-Oct: S $54; D $64-$74; package plans; under 18 free; lower rates rest of yr. Crib free. Pet accepted. TV; cable (premium). Complimentary continental bkfst. Complimentary coffee in lobby. Restaurant nearby. Ck-out 11 am. In-

rm modem link. Health club privileges. Some refrigerators. Locks 1 mi. Cr cds: A, MC, V.
🐾 🈯 🐾 SC

★★ **COMFORT INN.** *4404 I-75 Business Spur (49783). 906/635-1118; fax 906/635-1119; toll-free 800/228-5150. www.comfortinn.com.* 86 rms, 2 story. May-Oct: S, D $59-$79; each addl $8; under 18 free; lower rates rest of yr. Crib free. TV; cable (premium). Heated pool; whirlpool. Complimentary continental bkfst. Restaurant adj. Ck-out 11 am. Exercise equipt. Cr cds: A, D, DS, JCB, MC, V.
🄳 🐾 ⇌ 🈯 🈯 🐾 SC

★ **DAYS INN.** *3651 I-75 Business Spur (49783). 906/635-5200; fax 906/635-9750; toll-free 800/329-7466. www.days inn.com.* 85 rms, 2 story. June-Oct: S, D $49-$89; each addl $6; under 12 free; higher rates special events, hols; lower rates rest of yr. Crib free. TV; cable (premium), VCR avail (movies). Indoor pool; whirlpool. Complimentary coffee in lobby. Restaurant adj 7 am-10 pm. Ck-out 11 am. Coin lndry. In-rm modem link. Valet serv. X-country ski 5 mi. Game rm. Refrigerator avail. Cr cds: A, DS, MC, V.
🄳 ⇌ ⇌ 🈯 🐾 SC

★ **DORAL MOTEL.** *518 E Portage Ave (49783). 906/632-6621; toll-free 800/998-6720.* 20 rms, 2 story. Mid-June-Oct: S $56; D $66; each addl $6; under 12 free; lower rates mid-Apr-mid-June. Closed rest of yr. Crib $2.50. TV; cable. Heated pool; whirlpool. Restaurant nearby. Ck-out 10 am. Sauna. Game rm. Lawn games. Picnic tables. Cr cds: DS, MC, V.
⇌ 🈯 🐾

★ **LAWSON MOTEL.** *2049 Ashmun St (49783). 906/632-3322; fax 906/632-4234.* 16 rms, 3 story. July-Oct: S $48; D $62; each addl $4; lower rates rest of yr. Crib avail. TV; cable (premium), VCR avail. Complimentary coffee in lobby. Restaurant nearby. Ck-out 11 am. Airport transportation. X-country ski ¼ mi. Some refrigerators. Cr cds: A, DS, MC, V.
🐾 🐾 🈯 🐾

★★ **QUALITY INN.** *3290 I-75 Business Spur (49783). 906/635-1523; fax 906/635-2941; toll-free 877/923-7887. www.qualityinn.com.* 130 rms, 2 story. Mid-June-mid-Oct: S, D

$70-$95; each addl $10; suites from $110; under 18 free; lower rates rest of yr. Crib free. TV; cable. Indoor pool; whirlpool. Playground. Restaurant 6 am-10 pm. Bar noon-2 am; entertainment Thurs-Sat. Ck-out noon. Meeting rms. Business servs avail. Valet serv. Sundries. X-country ski on site. Exercise equipt; sauna. Game rm. Cr cds: A, C, D, DS, MC, V.

★★ **RAMADA PLAZA HOTEL OJIBWAY.** *240 W Portage Ave (49783). 906/632-4100; fax 906/632-6050; toll-free 800/654-2929. www. ramada.com.* 71 rms, 6 story. June-mid-Oct: S, D $119; each addl $15; suites $210; under 18 free; package plans; lower rates rest of yr. Crib free. TV; cable (premium). Indoor pool; whirlpool. Coffee in rms. Restaurant (see FREIGHTERS). No rm serv. Bar 11:30-1 am. Ck-out 11 am. Meeting rms. Business servs avail. In-rm modem link. Sauna. Some in-rm whirlpools. Soo Locks adj. Cr cds: A, DS, MC, V.

★ **SUPER 8.** *3826 I-75 Business Spur (49783). 906/632-8882; fax 906/632-3766; toll-free 800/800-8000. www. super8.com.* 61 rms, 2 story. July-Aug: S $54.88-$70.88; D $60.88-$75.88; under 12 free; lower rates rest of yr. Crib free. Pet accepted, some restrictions; $50 deposit. TV; cable (premium). Complimentary continental bkfst. Restaurant nearby. Ck-out 11 am. Coin lndry. Cr cds: A, C, D, DS, MC, V.

Restaurants

★ **ANTLER'S.** *804 E Portage Ave (49783). 906/632-3571.* Hrs: 11 am-closing. Closed hols. Bar. Lunch, dinner $4.95-$22.95. Child's menu. Specializes in steak, seafood, barbecue ribs. Rustic atmosphere. Historic building (1800s). Same owner since 1948. Cr cds: MC, V.

★★ **FREIGHTERS.** *240 W Portage St (49783). 906/632-4211. www.ramada. com.* Hrs: 6 am-2 pm, 4 pm-9 pm; Sun brunch 10 am-2 pm. Closed Dec 25. Bar noon-2 am. Bkfst $5-$8, lunch $7-$12, dinner $14-$30. Sun brunch $12.95. Child's menu. Specializes in seafood, prime rib. Extensive beer selection. Bilevel dining on river, overlooking Soo Locks. Cr cds: A, D, DS, MC, V.

Sleeping Bear Dunes National Lakeshore

See also Glen Arbor, Leland, Traverse City

(On Lake Michigan shoreline between Frankfort and Leland)

In 1970, Congress designated the Manitou Islands and 35 miles of mainland Lake Michigan shoreline, in the vicinity of Empire, as Sleeping Bear Dunes National Lakeshore. An Ojibway legend tells of a mother bear, who with her two cubs tried to swim across Lake Michigan from Wisconsin to escape from a forest fire. Nearing the Michigan shore, the exhausted cubs fell behind. Mother bear climbed to the top of a bluff to watch and wait for her offspring. They never reached her. Today she can still be seen as the Sleeping Bear, a solitary dune higher than its surroundings. Her cubs are the Manitou Islands, which lie a few miles offshore.

The lakeshore's variety of landforms support a diversity of interrelated plant habitats. Sand dune deserts contrast sharply with hardwood forests. There are stands of pine, dense cedar swamps, and a few secluded bogs of sphagnum moss. Against this green background are stands of white birch. In addition, the park supports many kinds of animal life, including porcupine, deer, rabbit, squirrel, coyote, and raccoon. More than 200 species of birds may be seen. Fishing and hunting are state-regulated; a Michigan license is required. Bass, bluegill, perch, and pike are plentiful; salmon are numerous in the fall.

Dune Climb takes visitors up 150 feet on foot through the dunes for a panoramic view of Glen Lake and the surrounding countryside. Pierce Stocking Scenic Drive, a seven-mile loop, is a road with self-guiding brochure available that offers visitors an opportunity to view the high dunes and overlooks from their cars (May-October; park pass required).

Sleeping Bear Point Maritime Museum, one mile west of Glen Haven on MI 209, located in the restored US Coast Guard Station, contains exhibits on the activities of the US Life-Saving Service and the US Coast Guard and the general maritime activities these organizations have aided on the Great Lakes. A restored boat house contains original and replica surf boats and other related rescue equipment. (Memorial Day-Labor Day, daily).

South Manitou Island, an eight-square-mile, 5,260-acre island with 12 miles of shoreline, has a fascinating history. Formed from glacial moraines more than 10,000 years ago, the island slowly grew a covering of forest. European settlers and the US Lighthouse Service, attracted by the forest and the natural harbor, established permanent sites here as early as the 1830s. On the southwest corner is the Valley of the Giants, a grove of white cedar trees more than 500 years old. There are three developed campgrounds on the island, and ranger-guided tours of the 1873 lighthouse.

North Manitou Island, nearby, is a 28-square-mile wilderness with 20 miles of shoreline. There are no facilities for visitors. All travel is by foot and is dependent on weather. Camping is allowed under wilderness regulations; no ground fires are permitted. There is no safe harbor or anchorage on either of the Manitou islands; however, from May-October, the islands are accessible by commercial ferry service from Leland (see).

Camping is available at D. H. Day Campground (May-November; dump station; fee) and Platte River Campground (year-round); camping is limited to 14 days. Pets on leash only. Information may be obtained from Headquarters in Empire (daily; closed off-season holidays). The visitor center there has information on park passes, self-guided trails, hiking, cross-country skiing, evening campfire programs, maritime and natural history exhibits, and other park activities (daily; closed off-season holidays). For further information and fees contact Chief of Interpretation, 9922 Front St, Empire 49630; 231/326-5134.

Soo Junction

See also Hulbert, Newberry

Pop 100 **Elev** 840 ft **Area code** 906 **Zip** 49868

What to See and Do

Toonerville Trolley and Riverboat Trip to Tahquamenon Falls. Narrated 6½-hr, 53-mi round-trip through Tahquamenon region via narrow-gauge railroad and riverboat, with 1¼-hr stop at Upper Tahquamenon Falls. Trolley leaves Soo Junction (mid-June-early Oct, daily). Also 1¾-hr train tour (July-Aug, Tues-Sat). Contact Tahquamenon Boat Service, Inc, Rural Rte 2, Box 938, Newberry 49868. Phone 906/876-2311. ¢¢¢¢

Southfield

See also Birmingham, Bloomfield Hills, Detroit, Farmington, Pontiac

---

Pop 75,728 **Elev** 684 ft **Area code** 248

Information Chamber of Commerce, 17515 W 9 Mile Rd, Suite 750; 248/557-6661

Web www.southfieldchamber.com

Southfield, a northwestern suburb of Detroit, is the largest office center in the Detroit metro area. It is also home to the Lawrence Institute of Technology and has branch campuses of Wayne State University, Central Michigan University, and the University of Phoenix.

Motels/Motor Lodges

★★ **COURTYARD BY MARRIOTT.**
27027 Northwestern Hwy (MI 10)

(48034). 248/358-1222; fax 248/354-3820; res 800/321-2211. www.marriott.com. 147 rms, 2-3 story. S $119; D $129; suites $129-$149; under 18 free; wkend rates; higher rates special events. Crib free. TV; cable (premium). Indoor pool; whirlpool. Restaurant 6:30-10 am. Serv bar. Ck-out noon. Coin lndry. Meeting rms. Business servs avail. In-rm modem link. Valet serv. Exercise equipt. Health club privileges. Balconies. Cr cds: A, D, DS, MC, V.

⊡ ⇔ 𝕏 ⊠ 🔥

★★ **HAMPTON INN.** 27500 Northwestern Hwy (MI 10) (48034). 248/356-5500; fax 248/356-2083; res 800/426-7866. www.hamptoninn.com. 153 rms, 2 story. S $65-$75; D $75-$85; under 18 free; some wkly, wkend rates. Crib free. TV; cable. Indoor pool; whirlpool. Complimentary continental bkfst. Restaurant nearby. Ck-out noon. Coin lndry. Meeting rms. Business servs avail. In-rm modem link. Valet serv. Downhill/x-country ski 20 mi. Exercise equipt. Picnic tables. Cr cds: A, D, DS, MC, V.

⊡ ⇔ 𝕏 ⊠ 🔥

★★ **HOLIDAY INN.** 26555 Telegraph Rd (48034). 248/353-7700; fax 248/353-8377; toll-free 800/465-4329. www.holiday-inn.com. 417 rms, 2 suites, 16 story. S, D $109; each addl $8; suites $275-$350; under 19 free; wkend rates. Crib free. Pet accepted, some restrictions. TV; cable (premium). Indoor pool; whirlpool. Restaurant 6:30 am-2 pm, 5-10 pm; Sat, Sun from 7 am. Bar 11-1 am. Ck-out noon. Coin lndry. Convention facilities. Bellhops. Sundries. Gift shop. Barber, beauty shop. Downhill/x-country ski 20 mi. Exercise equipt. Game rm. Rec rm. Many rms in circular tower. Cr cds: A, C, D, DS, ER, JCB, MC, V.

⊡ 🐾 ⇔ 𝕏 ⊠ 🔥

★ **MARVIN'S GARDEN INN.** 27650 Northwestern Hwy (48034). 248/353-6777; fax 248/353-2944; toll-free 888/200-5200. 110 rms, 2 story. S, D $40-$45; family rates. Crib $6. TV; cable (premium). Complimentary continental bkfst. Complimentary coffee in rms. Restaurant nearby. Ck-out

noon. Meeting rms. Some refrigerators. Cr cds: A, C, D, DS, MC, V.

⊡ ⚡ ⊠ 🔥

Hotels

★★★ **HILTON INN SOUTHFIELD.** 26000 American Dr (48034). 248/357-1100; fax 248/799-7030; res 800/445-8667. www.hilton.com. 195 rms, 7 story. S, D $89; each addl $10; suites $175; under 12 free; wkend rates. Crib free. Pet accepted, some restrictions. TV; cable (premium). Indoor pool; whirlpool. Restaurant 6-10 am, 11 am-2 pm, 5-10 pm; wkend hrs vary. Bar 5 pm-midnight. Ck-out 1 pm. Meeting rms. Business center. In-rm modem link. Exercise equipt; sauna. Cr cds: A, C, D, DS, JCB, MC, V.

⊡ 🐾 ⇔ 𝕏 ⊠ 🔥 🏃

★★★ **MARRIOTT SOUTHFIELD DETROIT.** 27033 Northwestern Hwy (MI 10) (48034). 248/356-7400; fax 248/356-5501; res 800/228-9290. www.marriott.com. 226 rms, 6 story. S, D $109-$129; suites $250; under 16 free; wkend rates. Crib free. TV; cable, VCR avail. Indoor pool; whirlpool. Restaurant 6:30 am-11 pm. Bar 11-1 am. Ck-out noon. Meeting rms. In-rm modem link. Concierge. Gift shop. Exercise equipt; sauna. Health club privileges. Refrigerator. Luxury level. Cr cds: A, C, D, DS, JCB, MC, V.

⊡ ⇔ 𝕏 ⊠ 🔥

★★★ **THE WESTIN SOUTHFIELD-DETROIT.** 1500 Town Center (48075). 248/827-4000; fax 248/827-1364; res 800/937-8461. www.westin.com. 385 rms, 12 story. S $169-$199; D $179-$209; each addl $15; suites $180-$425; under 17 free. Crib free. Valet parking $6. TV; cable (premium), VCR avail. Indoor pool; whirlpool, poolside serv. Restaurant 6:30 am-10:30 pm. Rm serv 24 hrs. Bar 11-2 am; Sun noon-midnight; entertainment Tues-Sat. Ck-out noon. Convention facilities. Business servs avail. In-rm modem link. Concierge. Downhill/x-country ski 20 mi. Exercise equipt; sauna. Refrigerators avail. Luxury level. Cr cds: A, C, D, DS, JCB, MC, V.

⊡ ⇔ 𝕏 ⊠ 🔥 SC

Restaurants

★ ★ ★ **GOLDEN MUSHROOM.**
18100 W Ten Mile Rd (48075). 248/
559-4230. Hrs: 11:30 am-4 pm, 5-11
pm; Fri to midnight; Sat 5:30 pm-
midnight. Closed Sun; hols. Res
accepted. Continental menu. Bar
11:30 am-midnight. A la carte
entrees: lunch $9-$15, dinner
$20.50-$32.50. Specializes in wild
game dishes. Own baking. Valet
parking. Cr cds: D, MC, V.
⬛

★ ★ ★ **MORTON'S OF CHICAGO.** *1*
Towne Sq (48076). 248/354-6006.
www.mortons.com. Hrs: 5:30-11 pm;
Sun 5-10 pm. Closed major hols. Res
accepted. Bar. A la carte entrees: dinner $16.95-$59.90. Specializes in
fresh seafood, beef. Valet parking
(dinner). Menu recited. Semiformal
steak house atmosphere. Cr cds: A,
D, MC, V.
[D] ⬛

★ ★ **SWEET LORRAINE'S CAFE.**
29101 Greenfield Dr (48076). 248/559-
5985. www.sweetlorraines.com. Hrs: 11
am-10 pm; Fri, Sat to 11 pm; Sun to
9:30 pm; Sun brunch 11 am-4 pm.
Closed hols. Bar. A la carte entrees:
lunch $4.95-$9.95, dinner $9.45-
$16.95. Sun brunch $5.95-$8.95. Spe-
cialties: pecan chicken, Jamaican jerk
chicken, shrimp Creole, vegetarian
entrees. Modern-style bistro. Cr cds:
A, DS, MC, V.
[D] ⬛

★ ★ ★ **TOM'S OYSTER BAR.** *29106*
Franklin Rd (48034). 248/356-8881.
www.tomsoysterbar.com. Hrs: 11 am-
midnight. Closed Jan 1, Dec 25. Res
accepted. Bar. Lunch $5-$12, dinner
$10-$18. Child's menu. Specializes in
seafood. Outdoor dining. Contemporary decor. Cr cds: A, D, DS, MC, V.
[D] ⬛

South Haven

(G-4) *See also Saugatuck*

Pop 5,563 **Elev** 618 ft **Area code** 616
Zip 49090
Information South Haven/Van Buren
County Lakeshore Convention &

Visitors Bureau, 415 Phoenix St;
616/637-5252 or 800/SO-HAVEN
Web www.bythebigbluewater.com

A five-mile beach on Lake Michigan
and surrounding lakes make sport
fishing a popular summer pastime in
South Haven; numerous marinas and
charter boat services are available in
the area.

What to See and Do

**Liberty Hyde Bailey Birthsite
Museum.** The 19th-century house of
the famous botanist and horticultur-
ist; family memorabilia, period furnishings, Native American artifacts.
(Tues and Fri afternoons; closed hols)
903 S Bailey Ave. Phone 616/637-
3251. **Donation**

Michigan Maritime Museum. Exhibits
of Great Lakes maps, photographs,
maritime artifacts, historic boats;
public boardwalk and park. (All yr)
260 Dyckman Ave. Phone 616/637-
8078. ¢¢

Van Buren State Park. 326 acres incl
scenic wooded sand dunes. Swimming, bathhouse; hunting, picnicking, playground, concession, camping.
4 mi S off I-196. Phone 616/637-
2788. ¢¢

Special Events

Harborfest. Dragon boat races, arts
and crafts, musical entertainment,
children's activities. Third wkend
June. Phone 616/637-5252.

Blueberry Festival. Arts and crafts,
entertainment, children's parade, 5K
run. Second wkend Aug. Phone
616/637-0800.

Motels/Motor Lodges

★ **ECONO LODGE AND SUITES.**
09817 M-140 Hwy (49090). 616/637-
5141; fax 616/637-1109; toll-free 800/
955-1831. www.econolodge.com. 60
rms. May-Sept: S $70-$82; D $80-
$90; each addl $5; suites $100-$120;
under 18 free; higher rates: Tulip Festival, some hols; lower rates rest of
yr. Crib $5. Pet accepted. TV; cable
(premium), VCR avail (movies). Playground. Indoor pool. Complimentary
coffee in rms. Restaurant adj 6:30
am-8 pm; Fri, Sat to 10 pm. Bar. Ck-
out 11 am. Coin lndry. Valet serv.
Downhill ski 20 mi; x-country ski 5

mi. Exercise rm; sauna. Cr cds: A, MC, V.

⊡ ⊡ ⊡ ⊡ ⊡ ⊡ **SC**

★ **LAKE BLUFF.** *76648 11th Ave (49090). 616/637-8531; fax 616/637-8532; toll-free 800/686-1305. www.lake bluffmotel.com.* 49 rms, 17 kits. May-Sept: S $48-$74; D $65-$94; kit. units $69-$135; wkly rates; lower rates rest of yr. Crib free. TV. Heated pool; wading pool, whirlpool. Coffee in rms. Restaurant nearby. Ck-out 11 am. Business servs avail. Free bus depot transportation. X-country ski 2 mi. Sauna. Lawn games. Rec rm. Picnic tables, grills. On Lake Michigan. Cr cds: A, C, D, DS, MC, V.

D ⊡ ⊡ ⊡ ⊡ ⊡

B&B/Small Inn

★★ **YELTON MANOR BED & BREAKFAST.** *140 N Shore Dr (49090). 616/637-5220; fax 616/637-4957. www.yeltonmanor.com.* 17 rms, 3 story. No rm phones. July-Labor Day: S $90-$205; D $90-$270; lower rates rest of yr. TV; cable, VCR avail (movies). Complimentary full bkfst. Restaurant nearby. Ck-out 11 am, ck-in 3 pm. Luggage handling. Concierge serv. Business servs avail. 18-hole golf privileges. X-country ski 1 mi. Health club privileges. Built in 1890; antiques. Totally nonsmoking. Cr cds: A, MC, V.

⊡ ⊡ ⊡ ⊡ ⊡

Restaurants

★ **CLEMENTINE'S.** *500 Phoenix St (49090). 616/637-4755. www.ohmy darling.com.* Hrs: 11 am-10 pm; Fri, Sat to 11 pm; Sun noon-10 pm. Closed hols. Bar. Lunch $4-$7, dinner $4-$13. Child's menu. Specializes in pan-fried perch, sandwiches, onion rings. Built 1903; original tin ceiling. Brass chandeliers, old photographs. Cr cds: DS, MC, V.

D ⊡

★ **MAGNOLIA GRILLE/IDLER RIVERBOAT.** *515 Williams St, #10 (49090). 616/637-8435.* Hrs: 11 am-midnight. Closed Nov-mid-Apr. Res accepted. Continental menu. Bar. Lunch $3.50-$6.50, dinner $12.50-$18.95. Child's menu. Specializes in prime rib, seafood, Cajun dishes.

Outdoor dining. On historic riverboat (1897), overlooking Black River. Cr cds: A, D, DS, MC, V.

D ⊡

Tawas City (E-6)

Pop 2,009 **Elev** 587 ft **Area code** 989 **Zip** 48763

Information Tawas Area Chamber of Commerce, 402 Lake St, PO Box 608, 48764; 989/362-8643 or 800/55-TAWAS

Web www.tawas.com

A Ranger District office of the Huron-Manitee National Forest (see MANITEE and OSCODA) is located in East Tawas.

Special Events

Perchville USA. Perch fishing festival featuring parade, fishing contests, softball. First wkend Feb. Phone 989/362-8643.

Tawas Bay Waterfront Art Show. Tawas City Park. More than 200 professional and amateur artists display art and craftwork; juried show. First wkend Aug. Phone 989/362-8643.

Motels/Motor Lodges

★ **DALE MOTEL.** *1086 S US-23 (48763). 989/362-6153; fax 989/362-6154.* 16 rms. June-Nov: S $40-$60; D $50-$65; each addl $4; lower rates rest of yr. TV; cable (premium). Complimentary coffee in rms. Restaurant nearby. Ck-out 11 am. Bus depot transportation. X-country ski 7 mi. Refrigerators. Cr cds: A, MC, V.

⊡ ⊡ ⊡ ⊡ **SC**

★★ **TAWAS BAY HOLIDAY INN RESORT.** *300 E Bay St, East Tawas (48730). 989/362-8601; fax 989/362-5111; toll-free 800/336-8601. www. tawasholidayinn.com.* 103 rms, 2 story. July-Aug: S, D $59-$169; each addl $8; suites $184; under 18 free; ski, golf plans; higher rates: major hols, Perchville USA; lower rates rest of yr. Crib free. Pet accepted. TV; cable (premium). Indoor pool; whirlpool, poolside serv. Playground. Free supervised children's activities (July-Aug). Restaurant 6:30 am-10 pm. Bar 11 am-midnight; Fri, Sat 10-2 am; entertainment Mon-Sat. Ck-out 11 am. Coin lndry. Meeting rms. Business center. In-rm modem link. Valet serv. Sundries. Gift shop. Golf privileges. X-country ski 15 mi. Sauna. Health club privileges. Beach; jet ski, paddleboats, rafts. Game rm. Lawn games. Cr cds: A, C, D, DS, JCB, MC, V.

[icons]

★ **TAWAS MOTEL - RESORT.** *1124 US 23 (48763). 989/362-3822; toll-free 888/263-3260. www.tawasmotel.com.* 21 rms. June-Aug: S $40-$60; D $45-$65; each addl $5; lower rates rest of yr. Crib $5. TV; cable (premium). Pool; whirlpool. Playground. Complimentary coffee. Ck-out 11 am. X-country ski 15 mi. Sauna. Game rm. Lawn games. Refrigerators; some in-rm whirlpools. Cr cds: A, C, DS, MC, V.

[icons]

Restaurant

★ **GENII'S FINE FOODS.** *601 W Bay St, East Tawas (48730). 989/362-5913.* Hrs: 7 am-9 pm; wkends to 10 pm in season. Closed Dec 25. Res accepted. Bkfst $1.35-$8, lunch $3.75-$7, dinner $4.95-$15. Child's menu. Specializes in fish, steak, spaghetti, Chinese food. Salad bar. Own pies. Rustic decor; overlooks lake. Cr cds: A, DS, MC, V.

[icon]

Three Rivers

(H-4) *See also Kalamazoo*

Pop 7,413 **Elev** 810 ft **Area code** 616 **Zip** 49093

Information Three Rivers Area Chamber of Commerce, 103 Portage Ave; 616/278-8193

Web www.trchamber.com

What to See and Do

Skiing. Swiss Valley Ski Area. Two quad, triple chairlift, four rope tows; patrol, school, rentals, ski shop, snowmaking; NASTAR; restaurant, cafeteria, bar. Vertical drop 225 ft. Night skiing. (Dec-Mar, daily) 10 mi W on MI 60, then N on Patterson

Hill Rd, in Jones. Phone 616/244-5635. ¢¢¢¢

B&Bs/Small Inns

★★ **MENDON COUNTRY INN.** *440 W Main St, Mendon (49072). 616/496-8132; toll-free 800/304-3366. www. rivercountry.com/mci.* 18 rms, 2 story. No rm phones. S, D $69-$159; each addl $10. Children over 12 yrs only. TV in sitting rm. Complimentary continental bkfst. Restaurant nearby. Ck-out 11 am, ck-in 3 pm. Luggage handling. Concierge serv. Business servs avail. 18-hole golf privileges. X-country ski 15 mi. Some refrigerators. Built in 1843; antiques. Totally nonsmoking. Cr cds: A, MC, V.

[icons]

★★ **SANCTUARY AT WILDWOOD.** *58138 N M40, Jones (49061). 616/244-5910; toll-free 800/249-5910. www.sanctuaryatwildwood.com.* 11 rms, 2 story. No rm phones. Mid-May-Oct: S $159; D $199; each addl $10; lower rates rest of yr. TV. Pool. Complimentary continental bkfst. Restaurant nearby. Ck-out 11 am, ck-in 3 pm. X-country ski on site. Totally nonsmoking. Cr cds: A, D, DS, MC, V.

[icons]

Traverse City (D-4)

Settled 1847 **Pop** 15,155 **Elev** 600 ft **Area code** 231

Information Traverse City Convention and Visitors Bureau, 101 W Grandview Pkwy, 49684; 231/947-1120 or 800/TRAVERS

Web www.mytraversecity.com

What to See and Do

Clinch Park. Zoo and aquarium featuring animals native to Michigan (mid-Apr-Nov, daily). Con Foster Museum has exhibits on local history, Native American and pioneer life, and folklore (Memorial Day-Labor Day, daily). Steam train rides; marina (May-Oct). Grandview Pkwy and Cass St. Phone 231/922-4904. Docked in marina is

Schooner *Madeline*. Full-scale replica of 1850s Great Lakes sailing ship. Original *Madeline* served as first school in Grand Traverse region. Tours (early May-late Sept, Wed-Sun afternoons). Phone 231/946-2647.

Dennos Art Center. Three galleries; incl one of the largest collections of Inuit art in the Midwest. (Daily) On campus of Northwestern Michigan College. Phone 231/922-1055.

Interlochen Center for the Arts. The Interlochen Arts Academy, a fine arts boarding high school, is located here (Sept-May). Concerts by students, faculty, and internationally known guests; art exhibits, drama and dance productions (all yr). Approx 2,500 students assemble here every summer to study music, art, drama, and dance (see SPECIAL EVENTS). 13 mi SW via US 31, then 2 mi S on MI 137, in Interlochen. Phone 231/276-6230.

Interlochen State Park. A 187-acre park with sand beach on Green and Duck lakes. Swimming, bathhouse, fishing, boating (rentals, launch); picnicking, playground, concession, camping, pavilion. Standard fees. 15 mi SW via US 31, then S on MI 137, in Interlochen, adj to National Music Camp. Phone 231/276-9511. ¢¢

L. Mawby Vineyards/Winery. Wine tasting. Guided tours (May-Oct, Thurs-Sat; by appt only). 7 mi N via MI 22 toward Suttons Bay, then 1 mi W on Hilltop Rd, ¼ mi N on Elm Valley Rd. Phone 231/271-3522. **FREE**

Scenic drive. Extends length of Old Mission Peninsula. At tip is the midway point between the North Pole and the Equator (the 45th parallel). On it stands the Old Mission Lighthouse, one of the first built on the Great Lakes. N on MI 37.

Ski areas.

Hickory Hills. Five rope tows; snowmaking, patrol; snack bar. Vertical drop 250 ft. (Mid-Dec-mid-Mar, daily; closed Jan 1, Dec 25) Lighted x-country trails (fee). 2 mi W of Division St (US 31) on Randolph Rd. Phone 231/947-8566. ¢¢¢

Sugar Loaf Resort. Triple, five double chairlifts, three surface lifts; rentals, school, snowmaking; 20 slopes; snowboarding; 17 mi of groomed and tracked x-country trails. Night skiing. (Dec-Mar, daily) Three restaurants, two bars, entertainment. Vertical drop 500 ft. Kids Klub for children, nursery. 18-hole golf; mountain biking (rentals). 7 mi W on MI 72, then 11 mi NW on County 651, follow signs. Phone 231/228-5461. ¢¢¢¢

Tall Ship *Malabar*. Tours of the classic topsail schooner (Late May-early Oct, four times daily). Bed-and-breakfast lodging. 13390 S West-Bay Shore Dr. Phone 231/941-2000. ¢¢¢¢

Special Events

Mesick Mushroom Festival. Carnival, rodeo, baseball tournament, flea market, music, parade, mushroom contest, food wagons. Phone 231/885-2679. Second wkend May.

Interlochen Arts Camp. Interlochen Center for the Arts. A variety of performing arts events by students and visiting professionals. Mid-June-early Sept. Phone 231/276-6230.

National Cherry Festival. 108 W Grandview Pkwy. More than 150 activities, incl pageants, parades, concerts, fireworks, air show, Native American pow-wow and crafts, children's contests. Phone 231/947-1120. Early July.

Downtown Traverse City Art Fair. 100 blk of E Front St. Late Aug. Phone 231/264-8202.

Motels/Motor Lodges

★ ★ **BAYSHORE RESORT.** *833 E Front St (49686). 231/935-4400; fax 231/935-0262; toll-free 800/634-4401. www.bayshore-resort.com.* 120 rms, 4 story. Late June-late Aug S, D $110-$200; each addl $10; suites $265-$320; under 12 free; lower rates rest of yr. Crib free. TV; cable (premium). Indoor pool; whirlpool. Complimentary continental bkfst. Ck-out 11 am. Meeting rm. Business servs avail. Sundries. Coin lndry. Free airport transportation. Downhill/x-country ski 5 mi. Exercise equipt. Game rm. Cr cds: A, D, DS, MC, V.

🄳 🐾 🛟 🕺 ✈ 🛍 🖐

★ ★ **BEACH CONDOMINIUMS.** *1995 US 31 N (49686). 231/938-2228; fax 231/938-9774.* 30 kit. units, 3 story. Late June-early Sept S, D $119-

$239; package plans; lower rates rest of yr. Crib $10. TV; cable (premium). Heated pool; whirlpool. Ck-out 11 am. Business servs avail. Downhill ski 1½ mi; x-country ski 4½ mi. In-rm whirlpools. Private patios, balconies. On bay; sand beach, lake swimming. Cr cds: A, D, DS, MC, V.

★★ **BEST WESTERN FOUR SEASONS MOTEL.** *305 Munson Ave (49686). 231/946-8424; fax 231/946-1971; toll-free 800/528-1234. www. bestwestern.com.* 111 rms. June-Oct: S, D $101-$139; each addl $7; under 18 free; wkend rates; lower rates rest of yr. Crib $7. TV; cable (premium), VCR avail. 2 pools, 1 indoor; whirlpool. Restaurant nearby. Ck-out 11 am. Business servs avail. Downhill ski 3 mi; x-country ski 6 mi. Game rm. Some refrigerators, in-rm whirlpools. Cr cds: A, C, D, DS, MC, V.

★ **DAYS INN.** *420 Munson Ave (49686). 231/941-0208; fax 231/941-7521; toll-free 800/329-7466. www.days inn.com.* 182 rms, 2 story. Mid-June-Labor Day S, D $119-$135; each addl $2-$5; suites $139-$150; under 12 free; lower rates rest of yr. Crib free. TV; cable (premium), VCR avail. Indoor pool; whirlpool. Playground. Complimentary continental bkfst. Coffee in rms. Restaurant adj 7 am-10 pm. Ck-out 11 am. Coin lndry. Meeting rms. Business servs avail. Free airport transportation. Downhill ski 3 mi; x-country ski 6 mi. Some in-rm whirlpools. Cr cds: A, C, D, DS, ER, JCB, MC, V.

★★ **ELK RAPIDS BEACH RESORT.** *8975 N Bayshore Dr, Elk Rapids (49629). 231/264-6400; toll-free 800/784-0049. www.elkrapidsbeachresort. com.* 25 kit. condos, 3 story. No elvtr. Memorial Day wkend-Labor Day: S, D $89-$195; each addl $10; lower rates rest of yr. TV; cable. Heated pool. Complimentary coffee in rms. Ck-out 10:30 am. Coin lndry. Downhill/x-country ski 17 mi. Grills. Opp lake, beach. Cr cds: A, DS, MC, V.

★★ **GRAND BEACH RESORT HOTEL.** *1683 N US Hwy 31 N (49686). 231/938-4455; toll-free 800/968-1992. www.grandbeach.com.* 95 rms, 3 story. Mid-June-Labor Day S, D $130-$158; each addl $10; suites $198-$298; family rates; ski, golf plans; lower rates rest of yr. Crib $5. TV; cable (premium), VCR (movies $3). Indoor pool; whirlpool. Complimentary continental bkfst. Restaurant nearby. Ck-out 11 am. Coin lndry. Meeting rm. Business servs avail. Downhill/x-country ski 2 mi. Exercise equipt. Game rm. Refrigerators, wet bars. Balconies. On lake; swimming beach. Cr cds: A, C, D, DS, MC, V.

★★ **HAMPTON INN.** *247 N Division St (49686). 231/946-8900; fax 231/946-2817; toll-free 800/426-7866. www. hampton-inn.com.* 127 rms, 4 story. June-Sept: S $49-$129; D $69-$159; under 18 free; lower rates rest of yr. Crib free. TV; cable (premium). Indoor pool; whirlpool. Complimentary continental bkfst. Ck-out noon. Meeting rm. Business servs avail. In-rm modem link. Valet serv Mon-Fri. Golf privileges. Downhill/x-country ski 5 mi. Exercise equipt. Some refrigerators. Opp beach. Cr cds: A, D, DS, MC, V.

★★ **HERITAGE INN.** *417 Munson Ave (49686). 231/947-9520; fax 231/947-9523; toll-free 800/968-0105.* 39 rms, 2 story. Mid-June-early Sept: S, D $90-$140; each addl $4-$6; lower rates rest of yr. Crib $5. TV; cable (premium), VCR (movies $2). Heated pool. Continental bkfst. Restaurant opp 7 am-10 pm. Ck-out 11 am. Downhill ski 3 mi; x-country ski 6 mi. Exercise equipt. Game rm. Some in-rm whirlpools. Picnic tables. Cr cds: A, C, D, DS, MC, V.

★★ **HOLIDAY INN.** *615 E Front St (49686). 231/947-3700; fax 231/947-0361; res 800/888-8020. www. holiday-inn.com.* 179 rms, 4 story. June-Labor Day: S, D $149-$199; each addl $8; under 19 free; lower rates rest of yr. Crib free. Pet accepted. TV; cable (premium). Indoor pool; whirlpool. Restaurant 7-1 am. Ck-out 11 am. Meeting rm. Business servs avail. Bellhops. Sundries. Gift shop. Valet serv. Free airport, bus depot transportation. Downhill ski 5 mi; x-country ski 8 mi. Exercise equipt; sauna. Game rm. Lawn games. Some refrigerators. Cr cds: A, C, D, DS, MC, V.

🅳 🔌 ⌷ 🕴 ⌻ 🔥 ⌷

★ **MAIN STREET INN.** *618 E Front St (49686). 231/929-0410; fax 231/929-0489; toll-free 800/255-7180. www.mainstreetinnsusa.com.* 93 rms, 20 kit. units. June-Aug: S, D $59.95-$199.95; each addl $5; kit. units $99.95; under 18 free; lower rates rest of yr. Crib free. Pet accepted. TV; cable (premium), VCR avail (movies). Heated pool. Ck-out 11 am. Coin lndry. Meeting rm. Business servs avail. Downhill ski 5 mi; x-country ski 8 mi. Opp beach. Cr cds: A, C, D, DS, ER, MC, V.

🅳 🔌 ⌷ ⌻ 🔥 SC

★ ★ **NORTH SHORE INN.** *2305 US 31 N (49686). 231/938-2365; fax 231/938-2368; toll-free 800/968-2365. www.northshoreinn.com.* 26 rms, 9 with shower only, 3 story. June-Labor Day: S, D $69-$195; under 18 free; lower rates rest of yr. Crib free. TV; cable (premium), VCR avail. Heated pool. Restaurant nearby. Ck-out 11 am. Coin lndry. Downhill/x-country ski 1 mi. Some refrigerators. Totally nonsmoking. Cr cds: A, DS, MC, V.

⌷ ⌷ ⌻ 🔥 SC

★ ★ **PINECREST.** *360 Munson Ave (49686). 231/947-8900; fax 231/947-8900; toll-free 800/223-4433.* 35 rms, 2 story. July-Aug: S $90-$110; D $95-$110; lower rates rest of yr. Crib free. TV; cable (premium), VCR (movies). Heated pool; whirlpool. Complimentary continental bkfst. Restaurant adj 6 am-11 pm. Ck-out 11 am. X-country ski 6 mi. Refrigerators avail. Cr cds: A, C, D, DS, MC, V.

🔥 🕴 ⌷ ⌷ ⌻ 🔥

★ ★ **POINTES NORTH INN.** *2211 US 31 N (49686). 231/938-9191; fax 231/938-0070; toll-free 800/968-3422.* 52 rms, 3 story. Mid-June-Aug: S, D $135-$145; under 12 free; wkly rates; lower rates rest of yr. Crib free. TV; cable, VCR avail (movies $3). Heated pool. Complimentary continental bkfst. Restaurant adj 8 am-11 pm. Ck-out 11 am. Downhill/x-country ski 1½ mi. Refrigerators. Private patios, balconies. Private beach. Cr cds: A, MC, V.

🅳 ⌷ ⌷ ⌻ 🔥

★ ★ **SUGAR BEACH RESORT HOTEL.** *1773 US 31 N (49686). 231/938-0100; fax 231/938-0200; toll-free 800/509-1995.* 95 rms, 3 story. Mid-June-Labor Day: S $64-$193; D $64-$198; each addl $5-$10; lower rates rest of yr. Crib $5. TV; cable (premuim), VCR (movies). Indoor pool; whirlpool. Complimentary continental bkfst. Ck-out 11 am. Coin lndry. Meeting rm. Business servs avail. Downhill ski 3 mi; x-country ski 5 mi. Exercise equipt. Game rm. Refrigerators. Cr cds: A, C, D, DS, MC, V.

🅳 ⌷ ⌷ 🕴 ⌻ 🔥

★ ★ **TRAVERSE BAY INN.** *2300 US 31 N (49686). 231/938-2646; fax 231/938-5845; toll-free 800/968-2646. www.traversebayinn.com.* 24 rms, 2 story. July-late Aug: S, D: $69-$199; under 12 free; lower rates rest of yr. Crib free. Pet accepted. TV; cable (premium), VCR avail (movies). Pool; whirlpool. Playground. Restaurant nearby. Ck-out 11 am. Business servs avail. Gift shop. Valet serv. Coin lndry. Downhill/x-country ski 1 mi. Game rm. Refrigerators, microwaves. Beach opp. Cr cds: A, DS, MC, V.

🅳 🔌 ⌷ ⌷ ⌻ 🔥

Hotel

★ ★ **PARK PLACE.** *300 E State St (49684). 231/946-5000; fax 231/946-2772; toll-free 800/748-0133. www.park-place-hotel.com.* 140 rms, 10 story. June-Sept: S, D $109-$189; each addl $15; suites $289-$398; ski, golf plans; lower rates rest of yr. Crib $10. TV; cable (premium); VCR, DVD avail. Indoor pool; whirlpool. Restaurant 6:30 am-10 pm. Bar 11 am-midnight; Fri, Sat to 2 am. Coffee in rms. Ck-out 11 am. Meeting rms. Business servs avail. In-rm modem link. Gift shop. Free airport, bus depot transportation. Valet serv. Downhill ski 5 mi; x-country ski 1 mi. Exercise equipt; sauna. Bathrm phones, refrigerators. Some balconies. Restored to 1930s appearance; Victorian decor. Cr cds: A, D, DS, MC, V.

🅳 ⌷ 🕴 ⌻ 🔥 ⌷ 🕴

Resorts

★ ★ ★ **CRYSTAL MOUNTAIN RESORT.** *12500 Crystal Mtn Dr,*

Thompsonville (49683). 231/378-2000; fax 231/378-2998; toll-free 800/968-9686. www.crystalmountain.com. 230 rms, 2-3 story, 29 suites, 17 condos. A/C in motel, most condos/houses. Jan-Feb, mid-June-Aug S, D $80-$300; each addl $15; condos, houses $250-$600; wkends (2-day min); family, wkly rates; ski, golf plans; MAP avail; higher rates hols; lower rates rest of yr. Crib $5. TV; cable, VCR; some DVDs. 2 pools, 1 indoor; whirlpool, poolside serv. Playground. Supervised children's activities (seasonal; ages 6 and under). Dining rm 7 am-9 pm. Snack bar. Bar; hrs vary. Coffee in rms. Ck-out noon, ck-in 5 pm (6 pm in winter). Coin lndry. Grocery, package store 2 mi. Meeting rms. Business center. Bellhops. Concierge. Gift shop. Airport transportation. Sports dir. Tennis $7/hr, pro. 36-hole golf, greens fee $33-$82 (w/cart), 10-acre golf practice center, driving range, putting greens, pro shop. Downhill/x-country ski on site; rentals. Sleighing. Hiking. Bicycles (rentals). Lawn games. Chairlift rides (summer). Soc dir. Game rm. Exercise rm. Many refrigerators, wet bars. Balconies. Some fireplaces. Picnic tables, grills. Cr cds: A, DS, MC, V.

★ ★ ★ **GRAND TRAVERSE RESORT.** *100 Grand Traverse Village Blvd, Acme (49610). 231/938-2100; fax 231/938-5494; toll-free 800/748-0303. www.grandtraverseresort.com.* 660 rms, 17 story; 200 kit. condos (1-3 bedrm), 50 studio condos, 2-5 story. May-Oct S, D $150-$210; each addl $15; condos $130-$275; suites $420-$590; under 18 free; family rates; wkly, ski, golf plans; lower rates rest of yr. Crib free. TV; cable (premium), VCR. 4 pools, 2 indoor; 2 whirlpools, poolside serv, lifeguard. Supervised children's activities; to age 15. Dining rm 6:30 am-11 pm. Box lunches. Deli. Picnics. Rm serv 7 am-11 pm. Bar noon-2 am; entertainment. Ck-out noon, ck-in 11 am. Business center. In-rm modem link. Concierge. Valet serv. Grocery 1 blk. Coin lndry, package store 1 mi. Convention facilities. Airport, bus depot transportation on property shuttle. Sports dir. Indoor tennis $20, pro. 54-hole golf Apr-Nov, greens fee $35-$55 for 9 holes, $40-$140 for 18 holes, pro, putting green, driving range. Swimming

beach, snack bar, paddleboats, jet skis. Downhill ski 3 mi; x-country ski on site. Ski rentals; ice rink, rentals. Horse-drawn carriage rides (summer), horse-drawn sleigh rides (winter). Entertainment. Gift shop. Game rm. Exercise rm; sauna. Full-service spa. Massage. Fish store. Some refrigerators; fireplaces; VCRs/DVDs; private patios, balconies. Cr cds: A, C, D, DS, ER, JCB, MC, V.

★ ★ **SUGAR LOAF RESORT.** *4500 Sugar Loaf Mtn Rd, Cedar (49621). 231/228-5461; fax 231/228-6545; toll-free 800/952-6390.* 150 rms in 2-4 story lodge, 53 townhouses (2-4 bedrm), 2 story, 16 condo units. July-Aug S, D $69-$109; each addl $10; studio rms $120-$130; kit. units $145-$320; under 18 free; MAP avail; ski, golf plans; higher rates Christmas hols; lower rates rest of yr. Crib free. TV; cable. 3 pools, 1 indoor; whirlpool. Supervised children's activities (Dec-Mar, July-Aug). Dining rm 7-11 am, 5-10 pm; hrs vary off-season. Bar 4 pm-midnight. Ck-out 11 am, ck-in 5 pm. Meeting rms. Business servs avail. Gift shop. Tennis. 36-hole championship golf, greens fee $25-$80, pro, putting green, driving range. Lawn games. Downhill/x-country ski on site; instructor, rentals, ski shop. Entertainment. Game rm. Exercise equipt. Bike rentals. Some refrigerators. 3,500-ft paved airstrip. Cr cds: A, C, D, DS, MC, V.

Restaurants

★ **AUNTIE PASTA'S.** *2030 S Airport Rd (49684). 231/941-8147.* Hrs: 11 am-10 pm; Sun from noon. Closed Thanksgiving, Dec 24-25. Italian menu. Bar to 11 pm. Lunch $5.25-$9.95, dinner $8.50-$19.50. Child's menu. Specializes in fresh pasta. Own bread, sauces. Parking. Totally nonsmoking. Cr cds: A, DS, MC, V.

★ ★ ★ **BOWERS HARBOR INN.** *13512 Peninsula Dr (49686). 231/223-4222. www.michiganmenu.com.* Hrs: 5-10 pm; Fri, Sat to 11 pm; Nov-Apr hrs vary. Closed Thanksgiving, Dec 24-25. Res required. Bar. Dinner $18-$28. Child's menu. Specialty: fish in a bag. Parking. In historic mansion

(1880); Early American decor. Overlooks bay. Totally nonsmoking. Cr cds: A, DS, MC, V.

D

★ **LA SENORITA.** *1245 S Garfield St (49686). 231/947-8820.* Hrs: 11 am-10 pm; Fri, Sat to 11 pm; Sun noon-10 pm; summer to 11 pm, Fri, Sat to midnight. Closed Easter, Thanksgiving, Dec 25. Mexican, American menu. Bar 4 pm-midnight. Lunch $4-$6, dinner $5-$12. Child's menu. Specializes in fajitas. Parking. Mexican decor, artifacts. Cr cds: A, D, DS, MC, V.

D ⊸

★ ★ **REFLECTIONS.** *2061 US 31N (49686). 231/938-2321. www.waterfrontinntc.com.* Hrs: 7 am-2:30 pm, 5-9 pm. Closed Sun; Thanksgiving, Dec 24, 25. Res accepted. Bar to 11 pm. Bkfst $4.95-$7.95, lunch 6.95-$8.95, dinner $18-$24. Specializes in seafood. Overlooks Little Traverse Bay. Cr cds: A, C, D, DS, MC, V.

D

★ **SCHELDE'S.** *714 Munson Ave (49686). 231/946-0981.* Hrs: 11 am-10 pm; Fri, Sat to 11 pm. Closed Thanksgiving, Dec 25. Bar 11 am-midnight. Lunch $6.95-$10, dinner $10-$16. Child's menu. Specializes in prime rib. Salad bar. Parking. Cr cds: A, DS, MC, V.

D

★ ★ ★ **WINDOWS.** *7677 S West Bay Shore Dr (49684). 231/941-0100. www.windowstc.com.* Hrs: 5-10 pm. Closed Dec 25; also Mon Sept-May and Sun Nov-May. Res accepted. Bar. Dinner $29-$38. Specializes in fresh seafood, beef. Own chocolates, ice cream. Parking. Outdoor dining. View of bay. Totally nonsmoking. Cr cds: A, MC, V.

D SC

Troy

(G-7) *See also Detroit, Pontiac, Warren*

Settled 1820 **Pop** 72,884 **Elev** 670 ft
Area code 248

Information Chamber of Commerce, 4555 Investment Dr, Suite 300, 48098; 248/641-8151
Web www.troychamber.com

What to See and Do

Stony Creek Metropark. More than 4,000 acres. Swimming beaches with bathhouse, lifeguard (Memorial Day-Labor Day, daily), fishing, boating (ramp, rentals); bicycling (rentals, trails), winter sports, picnicking, playground, golf (fee). Nature center with trails, exhibits. Pets on leash only. Approx 6 mi N on MI 150 (Rochester Rd) to 26 Mile Rd. Phone 810/781-4242. ¢

Troy Museum and Historical Village. Village museum incl 1820 log cabin, 1832 Caswell House, 1877 Poppleton School, 1880 general store, 1890 blacksmith shop, and 1900 print shop; exhibits, displays. (Tues-Sun; closed hols) 60 W Wattles Rd, 1 mi NE of I-75, Big Beaver Rd exit. Phone 248/524-3570. **FREE**

Motels/Motor Lodges

★ ★ **COURTYARD BY MARRIOTT.** *1525 E Maple Rd (48083). 248/528-2800; fax 248/528-0963; res 800/321-2211. www.marriott.com.* 147 rms, 3 story, 14 suites. S $89; D $99; suites $109; under 16 free; wkly, wkend rates; higher rates special events. Crib free. TV; cable (premium), VCR avail. Indoor pool; whirlpool. Complimentary coffee in rms. Restaurant adj 11-1 am. Ck-out noon. Coin lndry. Meeting rms. Business center. In-rm modem link. Valet serv. Downhill ski 15 mi. Exercise equipt. Refrigerator in suites. Balconies. Cr cds: A, C, D, DS, JCB, MC, V.

D ⊷ 🏋 🐾 ☀ 🏃

★ ★ **DRURY INN.** *575 W Big Beaver Rd (48084). 248/528-3330; toll-free 800/325-8300. www.druryinn.com.* 153 rms, 4 story. S, D $66-$76; each addl $6; under 18 free; wkend rates. Crib free. Pet accepted, some restrictions. TV; cable (premium), VCR avail. Pool. Complimentary continental bkfst. Restaurant adj 6 am-midnight; Thurs-Sat open 24 hrs. Ck-out noon. Meeting rms. In-rm modem link. Valet serv. X-country ski 4 mi. Health club privileges. Cr cds: A, C, D, DS, MC, V.

[D] 🔧 ✈ 🛏 ≈ 🔥 SC

★★ **FAIRFIELD INN.** *32800 Stephenson Hwy, Madison Heights (48071). 248/588-3388; res 800/228-2800. www. fairfieldinn.com.* 134 rms, 3 story. S, D $55-$69; each addl $7; under 18 free; wkend rates. Crib free. TV; cable (premium). Pool. Complimentary continental bkfst. Restaurant adj 11-2 am. Ck-out noon. Valet serv. Health club privileges. Cr cds: A, MC, V.

[D] ≈ ≈ 🔥 SC

★★ **HAMPTON INN.** *32420 Stephenson Hwy, Madison Heights (48071). 248/585-8881; fax 248/585-9446; res 800/426-7866. www.hampton inn.com.* 124 rms, 4 story. S $53-$65; D $57-$70; under 18 free. Crib free. Pet accepted, some restrictions. TV; cable (premium). Complimentary continental bkfst. Restaurant nearby. Ck-out noon. Meeting rm. In-rm modem link. Valet serv. Exercise equipt; sauna. Cr cds: A, MC, V.

🔧 🏃 ≈

★★ **HOLIDAY INN.** *2537 Rochester Ct (48083). 248/689-7500; fax 248/689-9015; toll-free 800/465-4329. www. holiday-inn.com.* 150 rms, 4 story. S, D $99-$144; suites $119; under 18 free; wkend rates. Crib free. Pet accepted. TV; cable. Pool. Restaurant 6:30 am-noon, 5:30-10 pm; Sat, Sun from 7 am. Bar. Ck-out noon. Coin lndry. Meeting rms. In-rm modem link. Valet serv. X-country ski 5 mi. Exercise equipt; sauna. Cr cds: A, C, D, DS, JCB, MC, V.

[D] 🔧 ≈ 🏃 ≈ 🔥

★ **RED ROOF INN TROY.** *2350 Rochester Ct (48083). 248/689-4391; fax 248/689-4397; res 800/843-7663. www.redroof.com.* 109 rms, 2 story. S $53-$69; D $64-$76; under 18 free. Crib free. Pet accepted. TV; cable (premium). Restaurant nearby. Ck-out noon. In-rm modem link. X-country ski 10 mi. Cr cds: A, C, D, DS, MC, V.

🔧 ≈ 🔥 SC ✈

★★ **SOMERSET INN.** *2601 W Big Beaver Rd (48084). 248/643-7800; fax 248/643-2296; toll-free 800/228-8769. www.somersetinn.com.* 250 rms, 13 story. S $159; D $179; each addl $15; suites $290-$325; family, wkend

rates. Crib free. TV; cable. Heated pool. Restaurant 6 am-11 pm; Sat, Sun from 7 am. Bar 11-1 am. Ck-out noon. Meeting rms. Business center. In-rm modem link. Bellhops. Valet serv. Shopping arcade. Exercise equipt. Cr cds: A, D, DS, MC, V.

[D] ≈ 🏃 ≈ 🔥 🏃

Hotels

★★★ **HILTON NORTHFIELD.** *5500 Crooks Rd (48098). 248/879-2100; fax 248/879-6054; res 800/445-8667. www. hilton.com.* 191 rms, 3 story. S, D $159; each addl $10; suites $250-$350; under 18 free; family, wkend rates; package plans. Crib free. Pet accepted, some restrictions. TV; cable (premium). Indoor pool. Coffee in rms. Restaurant 6:30 am-11 pm; Sat, Sun from 7 am. Bar 10:30-2 am; entertainment. Ck-out noon. Meeting rms. Business center. In-rm modem link. Bellhops. Valet serv. Sundries. X-country ski 3 mi. Exercise equipt; sauna. Health club privileges. Game rm. Some refrigerators. Private patios, balconies. Cr cds: A, C, D, DS, MC, V.

[D] 🔧 ✈ ≈ 🏃 ≈ 🔥 SC 🏃

★★★ **MARRIOTT TROY.** *200 W Big Beaver Rd (48084). 248/680-9797; fax 248/680-9774; res 800/228-9290. www.marriott.com.* 350 rms, 17 story. S $164-$169; D $194-$199; each addl $30; suites $600; under 18 free; wkend rates. Crib free. Pet accepted. Valet parking $4/day, $8/overnight; free garage. TV; cable (premium), VCR avail. Indoor pool; whirlpool, poolside serv. Restaurant 7 am-11 pm. Bar 4 pm-1 am; entertainment Tues-Sat. Ck-out noon. Convention facilities. Business servs avail. In-rm modem link. Concierge. Gift shop. X-country ski 5 mi. Exercise equipt; sauna. Refrigerators avail. Luxury level. Cr cds: A, MC, V.

[D] 🔧 ✈ ≈ 🏃 ≈ 🔥 SC

All Suite

★★★ **EMBASSY SUITES.** *850 Tower Dr (48098). 248/879-7500; fax 248/879-9139; res 800/362-2779. www. embassysuites.com.* 251 suites, 8 story. S, D $85-$175; each addl $20; under 18 free; wkend rates. Crib free. TV; cable. Indoor pool; whirlpool, poolside serv. Coffee in rms. Restaurant

6:30 am-10 pm. Bar 11:30 am-midnight. Ck-out noon. Convention facilities. In-rm modem link. Gift shop. X-country ski 4 mi. Exercise equipt; sauna. Bathrm phones, refrigerators, minibars. Cr cds: A, MC, V.

D ⊠ ⊠ 🛉 ⊠ 🔥 SC

Extended Stay

★★ **RESIDENCE INN BY MAR-RIOTT.** *2600 Livernois Rd (48083). 248/689-6856; fax 248/689-3788; res 800/331-3131. www.residenceinn.com.* 152 kit. suites, 2 story. May-Sept S $109-$129; D $119-$179; family, wkly, wkend, hol rates; hols (2-day min); lower rates rest of yr. Crib free. Pet accepted, some restrictions; $6/day. TV; cable (premium), VCR avail. Heated pool; whirlpool. Complimentary coffee in rms. Complimentary continental bkfst. Restaurant opp 7 am-8 pm. Ck-out noon. Coin lndry. In-rm modem link. Valet serv. Downhill/x-country ski 20 mi. Health club privileges. Balconies. Picnic tables. Cr cds: A, D, DS, JCB, MC, V.

D ⭘ ⊠ ⊠ ⊠ 🔥

Restaurants

★★ **MON JIN LAU.** *1515 E Maple Rd (48083). 248/689-2332.* Hrs: 11-1 am; Fri to 2 am; Sat 4 pm-2 am; Sun 3 pm-midnight; hols 4 pm-2 am. Closed Thanksgiving, Dec 25. Res accepted. Asian, American menu. Bar. Lunch $7.50-$11.95, dinner $11.95-$22.95. Specialties: Mongolian rack of lamb, chili pepper squid, Chinese angel hair pasta. Asian atmosphere. Family-owned. Cr cds: A, MC, V.

D ⊐

★★ **PICANO'S.** *3775 Rochester Rd (48083). 248/689-8050.* Hrs: 11 am-10:30 pm; Fri, Sat to 11 pm; Sun noon-9:30 pm. Closed hols. Italian menu. Bar. Lunch $7-$10, dinner $8-$16. Specializes in veal, chicken, pasta. Own pasta. Valet parking. Modern Italian decor; mural. Cr cds: A, D, DS, MC, V.

D ⊐

Wakefield

(B-7) *See also Ironwood*

Pop 2,318 **Elev** 1,550 ft
Area code 906 **Zip** 49968

What to See and Do

Skiing. Indianhead Mountain-Bear Creek Ski Resort. Quad, triple, three double chairlifts; Pomalift, two T-bars; beginner's lift; patrol, school, rentals; NASTAR (daily); snowmaking; lodge (see RESORT), restaurants, cafeterias, bars, nursery. Longest run one mi; vertical drop 638 ft. (Nov-mid-Apr, daily) 500 Indianhead Rd, 1 mi W on US 2, then 1 mi N. Phone 906/229-5181. ¢¢¢¢

Motel/Motor Lodge

★ **REGAL COUNTRY INN.** *1602 US 2 E (49968). 906/229-5122; fax 906/229-5755. www.westernup.com/regal inn.* 18 rms, 2 story. July-Aug, mid-Nov-Easter: S $43-$80; D $55-$90; each addl $10; higher rates Christmas hols; lower rates rest of yr. Crib free. TV; cable. Complimentary continental bkfst. Restaurant nearby. Ck-out 11 am. Downhill ski 2 mi; x-country ski 6 mi. Sauna. 1950s ice cream parlor on premises. Cr cds: A, DS, MC, V.

⊠ ⊠ 🔥

Resort

★★ **INDIANHEAD MOUNTAIN RESORT.** *500 Indianhead Mountain Rd (49968). 906/229-5181; fax 906/229-5920; toll-free 800/346-3426. www. indianheadmtn.com.* 62 rms, 2-3 story, 51 chalets, 32 condo units. S, D $58-$160; under 12 free; mid-wk rates; ski plan. Closed mid-Apr-June, Oct-mid-Nov. Crib avail. Pet accepted. TV; cable, VCR avail (movies). Indoor pool; whirlpool. Playground. Supervised children's activities (Nov-mid-Apr). Complimentary continental bkfst. Dining rm 7:30 am-9 pm. Bar 8-2 am; Sun from noon; summer from 4 pm. Ck-out 11 am, ck-in 4 pm. Meeting rms. Business servs avail. Free bus depot transportation. Tennis. 9-hole, par 3 golf, greens fee $6-$10. Downhill ski on site. Hiking, mountain biking, nature trails. Game rm. Exercise rm; sauna. Cr cds: A, DS, MC, V.

Warren

(G-7) See also Detroit, St. Clair, Troy

Pop 144,864 **Elev** 615 ft
Area code 586
Information Chamber of Commerce, 30500 Van Dyke Ave, Suite 118, 48093; 586/751-3939
Web www.wcschamber.com

Motels/Motor Lodges

★★ **BEST WESTERN STERLING INN BANQUET & CONFERENCE CENTER.** 34911 Van Dyke Ave, Sterling Heights (48312). 586/979-1400; fax 586/979-7962; toll-free 800/953-1400. www.sterlinginn.com. 160 rms, 2-3 story. S, D $161-$171; each addl $6; suites $135-$275; under 18 free; wkend rates. Crib free. TV; cable. Indoor pool; whirlpool. Restaurant 6-11 pm; Fri to midnight; Sat 7 am-midnight; Sun 7 am-10 pm. Bar from 11 am; Sat to midnight; Sun noon-10 pm. Ck-out noon. Meeting rms. Business center. In-rm modem link. Valet serv. Exercise equipt; sauna. Refrigerators; some in-rm whirlpools, bathrm phones. Cr cds: A, C, D, DS, MC, V.

★★ **COURTYARD BY MARRIOTT.** 30190 Van Dyke Ave (48093). 810/751-5777; fax 586/751-4463; res 800/321-2211. www.marriott.com. 147 rms, 3 story, 14 suites, 113 kit. units. S $85; D $95; each addl $10; suites $95-$105; under 5 free; wkend rates. Crib free. TV; cable (premium), VCR avail. Indoor pool; whirlpool. Complimentary coffee in rms. Bkfst avail. Restaurant adj open 24 hrs. Ck-out 1 pm. Coin lndry. Meeting rms. In-rm modem link. Valet serv. Exercise equipt. Refrigerator in suites. Balconies. Cr cds: A, D, DS, MC, V.

★★ **FAIRFIELD INN.** 7454 Convention Blvd (48092). 586/939-1700; res 800/228-2800. www.fairfieldinn.com.

132 rms, 3 story. S, D $45-$59; each addl $7; under 18 free. Crib free. TV; cable (premium). Heated pool. Complimentary continental bkfst. Restaurant nearby. Ck-out noon. In-rm modem link. Valet serv. Cr cds: A, C, D, DS, MC, V.

★★ **GEORGIAN INN.** 31327 Gratiot Ave, Roseville (48066). 586/294-0400; fax 586/294-1020; toll-free 800/446-1866. 111 rms, 2 story. Mid-May-mid-Sept: S, D $60-$73; each addl $5; suites $135; kit. units $81; under 12 free; lower rates rest of yr. Crib free. Pet accepted, some restrictions. TV; cable. Heated pool; poolside serv. Restaurant 6 am-11 pm. Bar. Ck-out noon. Coin lndry. Meeting rms. Business servs avail. In-rm modem link. Valet serv. Exercise equipt. Game rm. Cr cds: A, D, DS, MC, V.

★★ **HAMPTON INN.** 7447 Convention Blvd (48092). 586/977-7270; fax 586/977-3889; toll-free 800/426-7866. www.hamptoninn.com. 124 rms, 3 story. S $52-$57; D $58-$63; suites $75-$81; under 18 free; wknd rates. Crib $6. TV; cable (premium). Complimentary continental bkfst. Restaurant nearby. Ck-out noon. Meeting rms. In-rm modem link. Valet serv. X-country ski 20 mi. Refrigerator, wet bar in suites. Cr cds: A, D, DS, MC, V.

★★ **HOLIDAY INN EXPRESS.** 11500 E 11 Mile Rd (48089). 586/754-9700; fax 586/754-0376; toll-free 800/465-4329. www.holiday-inn.com. 125 rms, 2 story. S, D $62; under 17 free; wkend rates. Crib free. TV; cable (premium). Pool. Complimentary continental bkfst. Restaurant adj 11 am-midnight. Ck-out noon. Meeting rms. In-rm modem link. Valet serv. Cr cds: A, C, D, DS, ER, JCB, MC, V.

★★ **HOMEWOOD SUITES.** 30180 N Civic Center Blvd (48093). 586/558-7870; fax 586/558-8072; toll-free 800/225-5466. www.homewoodsuites.com. 76 kit. suites, 3 story. S, D $114; suites $119-$139. Crib avail. Pet accepted, some restrictions; $100 refundable. TV; cable (premium), VCR. Pool; whirlpool. Complimentary continental bkfst. Complimentary coffee in rms. Restaurant nearby. Ck-out noon. Coin lndry. Meeting rms. Business center. In-rm modem link. Valet serv. Sundries. Gift shop. Downhill/x-country ski 20 mi. Exercise equipt. Health club privileges. Grills. Cr cds: A, D, DS, MC, V.

★ **RED ROOF INN.** *26300 Dequindre Rd (48091). 586/573-4300; fax 586/ 573-6157; res 800/843-7663. www. redroof.com.* 136 rms, 2 story. S $32.99-$42.99; D $46.99-$53.99; 3 or more $44.99-$60.99; under 18 free; higher rates special events. Crib free. Pet accepted, some restrictions. TV; cable (premium). Complimentary coffee. Restaurant nearby. Ck-out noon. Business servs avail. In-rm modem link. Cr cds: A, C, D, DS, MC, V.

Extended Stay

★★ **RESIDENCE INN BY MAR-RIOTT.** *30120 Civic Center Blvd (48093). 586/558-8050; fax 586/558-8214; res 800/331-3131. www.marriott. com.* 133 kit. suites, 3 story. Mid-May-mid-Sept: S, D $109; under 18 free; wkly, wkend rates; lower rates rest of yr. Crib free. Pet accepted; $50 deposit and $8/day. TV; cable (premium), VCR. Pool; whirlpool. Complimentary continental bkfst. Complimentary coffee in rms. Restaurant nearby. Ck-out noon. Coin lndry. In-rm modem link. Valet serv. Exercise equipt. Health club privileges. Some balconies. Picnic tables. Cr cds: A, MC, V.

Restaurant

★★ **ANDIAMO ITALIA.** *7096 E 14 Mile Rd (48092). 586/268-3200. www. andiamoitalia.com.* Hrs: 11 am-11 pm; Fri to midnight; Sat 4 pm-midnight; Sun 4-9 pm. Closed hols. Italian menu. Bar. Lunch $8-$14, dinner $9-$22. Specialties: gnocchi, bocconcini di vitello. Valet parking. Cr cds: A, MC, V.

Whitehall

(F-3) *See also Muskegon*

Pop 3,027 **Elev** 593 ft **Area code** 231 **Zip** 49461

Information White Lake Area Chamber of Commerce, 124 W Hanson St; 231/893-4585 or 800/879-9702

Web www.whitelake.org

What to See and Do

Montague City Museum. History of lumbering era, artifacts; displays on Montague resident Nancy Ann Fleming, who was Miss America 1961. (June-Aug, Sat and Sun) N on US 31 Business, at Church and Meade Sts in Montague. Phone 231/894-6813. **Donation**

White River Light Station Museum. In 1875 lighthouse made of Michigan limestone and brick; ship relics and artifacts incl binnacle, ship's helm, chronograph, compasses, sextant, charts, models, photographs, paintings. View of Lake Michigan's sand dunes along coastline. (Memorial Day-Labor Day, Tues-Sun; Sept, wkends) 6199 Murray Rd, S of the channel on White Lake. Phone 231/894-8265. ¢¢

World's Largest Weather Vane. This 48-ft-tall structure weighs 4,300 pounds and is topped with a model of the lumber schooner *Ella Ellenwood* that once traveled the Great Lakes. Trademark of Whitehall Products Ltd, the company that created it, the vane is mentioned in the *Guinness Book of Records*. Just S of town on US 31 Business, at edge of White Lake in Montague.

Special Events

White Lake Arts & Crafts Festival. Funnel Field. 150 exhibitors. Father's Day wkend. Phone 231/893-4585.

Summer concerts. White Lake Music Shell, Launch Ramp Rd, in Montague. Phone 231/893-4585. Every Tues mid-June-late Aug.

Ypsilanti

(H-6) *See also Ann Arbor*

Settled 1823 **Pop** 24,846 **Elev** 720 ft
Area code 734 **Zip** 48197
Information Ypsilanti Area Visitors
and Convention Bureau, 301 W
Michigan Ave, Suite 101; 734/482-
4920
Web www.ypsichamber.org

What to See and Do

Eastern Michigan University. (1849)
25,000 students. The university is
home to Quirk/Sponberg Dramatic
Arts Theaters, Pease Auditorium,
Bowen Field House, Rynearson Stadium, Olds Student Recreation Center; Ford Art Gallery with changing
exhibits (Mon-Fri; phone 734/487-
1268; free); Intermedia Art Gallery
(free). Tours (by appt) depart from
historic Starkweather Hall. (Daily)
Phone 734/487-1849.

Ford Lake Park. This park offers fishing, boating (launch; fee); volleyball,
tennis, and handball courts; horse-
shoes, softball field, four picnic shelters. (Daily; some fees May-Sept)
9075 S Huron River Dr. Phone
734/485-6880. ¢¢

Ypsilanti Historical Museum. Victorian house with 11 rms, incl a special
children's rm and craft rm; exhibits.
(Thurs, Sat, Sun) Ypsilanti Historical
Archives are located here and are
open for research pertaining to local
history and genealogy (Mon-Fri
mornings). 220 N Huron St. Phone
734/482-4990. **Donation**

**Ypsilanti Monument and Water
Tower.** Marble column with a bust of
Demetrius Ypsilanti, Greek patriot.
Century-old water tower. Cross and
Washtenaw Sts.

Special Event

Ypsilanti Heritage Festival. Riverside
Park. Classic cars, arts and crafts,
18th-century encampment, jazz competition, and continuous entertainment. Phone 734/483-4444. Third
full wkend Aug.

Hotel

★★★ **MARRIOTT AT EAGLE
CREST YPSILANTI.** *1275 S Huron St
(48197). 734/487-2000; fax 734/481-
0773; toll-free 800/228-9290. www.
marriott.com.* 236 rms, 8 story. May-
Oct: S, D $95-$135; under 12 free;
golf plan; wkend rates; lower rates
rest of yr. Crib free. TV; cable (premium), VCR avail. Indoor pool;
whirlpool. Restaurant 6:30 am-10
pm. Bar 11-2 am; Sun noon-midnight. Ck-out noon. Convention
facilities. Business servs avail. In-rm
modem link. Concierge. Gift shop.
18-hole golf, pro, putting green, driving range. Exercise equipt; sauna.
Health club privileges. Game rm.
Bathrm phones. Luxury level. Cr cds:
A, C, D, DS, ER, MC, V.
D 🏋 ⚓ 🏌 ⬇ 🐾 SC

Restaurant

★★ **HAAB'S.** *18 W Michigan Ave
(48197). 734/483-8200.* Hrs: 11 am-9
pm; Fri, Sat to 10 pm. Closed Dec 25.
Res accepted. Bar. Lunch $4-$8, dinner $8-$19. Child's menu. Specializes
in steak. Early American decor. Building dates from 19th century. Family-
owned. Cr cds: A, C, D, DS, MC, V.
SC ⬒

OHIO

Ohio is a combination of rich agricultural farmland and forests, as well as a center for technology, education, industry, and recreation. Its farmland is dotted with major industrial cities and crisscrossed by roads and railways that carry most of the traffic between the East and Midwest. Taking its name from the Iroquois word for "something great," the state has produced its share of great men, including Thomas Edison, astronauts John Glenn and Neil Armstrong, and eight of the nation's presidents—William Harrison, Grant, Hayes, Garfield, Benjamin Harrison, McKinley, Taft, and Harding.

The earliest inhabitants of the area were prehistoric people who built more than 10,000 mounds, many of them effigy mounds of great beauty. The first European to explore the Ohio area was probably the French explorer La Salle, in about 1669. Conflicting French and British claims of the area led to the French and Indian War, which ended in a treaty giving most of France's lands east of the Mississippi to Great Britain.

The Northwest Ordinance of 1787 set up the Northwest Territory, of which the future state of Ohio was a division. New Englanders of the Ohio Company bought land in the Muskingum River Valley and founded Marietta, the first permanent settlement. Other settlements soon sprang up along the Ohio River. The area grew as Revolutionary War veterans received land in payment for their services. Ohio became a state in 1803.

Though Ohioans had mixed feelings about the issue of slavery and the Civil War, about 345,000 men responded to Union calls for volunteers—more than twice the state's quota. Ohio also provided several Union commanders, including Ulysses S. Grant and William T. Sherman.

After the Civil War ended, Ohio's abundant natural resources and its strategic position between two of the country's principal waterways—Lake Erie on the north and the Ohio River on the south—paved the way for rapid industrialization and growth. Today, Ohio has many major metropolitan areas, but its citizens are equally proud of Ohio's excellent park system, its wealth of small, tree-shaded towns, and its "queen city," Cincinnati.

Population: 10,847,115
Area: 41,004 square miles
Elevation: 433-1,550 feet
Peak: Campbell Hill (Logan County)
Entered Union: March 1, 1803 (17th state)
Capital: Columbus
Motto: With God, all things are possible
Nickname: Buckeye State
Flower: Scarlet Carnation
Bird: Cardinal
Tree: Ohio Buckeye
Fair: Early August, 2003, in Columbus
Time Zone: Eastern
Web Site:
www.ohiotourism.com

When to Go/Climate

Ohio summers can be hot and humid, especially in the south. The Lake Erie shore areas often experience cooler summer temperatures than elsewhere in the state, but can be subject to harsh winter winds and sudden snowstorms.

AVERAGE HIGH/LOW TEMPERATURES (°F)

CLEVELAND

Jan 32/18	**May** 69/47	**Sept** 74/54
Feb 35/19	**June** 78/57	**Oct** 62/44
Mar 46/28	**July** 82/61	**Nov** 50/35
Apr 58/37	**Aug** 81/60	**Dec** 37/25

COLUMBUS

Jan 34/19	**May** 72/50	**Sept** 76/55
Feb 38/21	**June** 80/58	**Oct** 65/43
Mar 51/31	**July** 84/63	**Nov** 51/34
Apr 62/40	**Aug** 82/61	**Dec** 39/25

Parks and Recreation Finder

Directions to and information about the parks and recreation areas below are given under their respective town/city sections. Please refer to those sections for details.

NATIONAL PARK AND RECREATION AREAS

Key to abbreviations. I.H.S. = International Historic Site; I.P.M. = International Peace Memorial; N.B. = National Battlefield; N.B.P. = National Battlefield Park; N.B.C. = National Battlefield and Cemetery; N.C.A. = National Conservation Area; N.E.M. = National Expansion Memorial; N.F. = National Forest; N.G. = National Grassland; N.H.P. = National Historical Park; N.H.C. = National Heritage Corridor; N.H.S. = National Historic Site; N.L. = National Lakeshore; N.M. = National Monument; N.M.P. = National Military Park; N.Mem. = National Memorial; N.P. = National Park; N.Pres. = National Preserve; N.R.A. = National Recreational Area; N.R.R. = National Recreational River; N.Riv. = National River; N.S. = National Seashore; N.S.R. = National Scenic Riverway; N.S.T. = National Scenic Trail; N.Sc. = National Scientific Reserve; N.V.M. = National Volcanic Monument.

Place Name	Listed Under
Hopewell Culture N.H.	CHILLICOTHE
Lawnfield (James A. Garfield N.H.S.)	MENTOR
Perry's Victory and I.P.M.	PUT-IN-BAY
Wayne N.F.	IRONTON
William Howard Taft N.H.S.	CINCINNATI

STATE PARK AND RECREATION AREAS

Key to abbreviations. I.P. = Interstate Park; S.A.P. = State Archaeological Park; S.B. = State Beach; S.C.A. = State Conservation Area; S.C.P. = State Conservation Park; S.Cp. = State Campground; S.F. = State Forest; S.G. = State Garden; S.H.A. = State Historic Area; S.H.P. = State Historic Park; S.H.S. = State Historic Site; S.M.P. = State Marine Park; S.N.A. = State Natural Area; S.P. = State Park; S.P.C. = State Public Campground; S.R. = State Reserve; S.R.A. = State Recreation Area; S.Res. = State Reservoir; S.Res.P. = State Resort Park; S.R.P. = State Rustic Park.

Place Name	Listed Under
Alum Creek S.P.	DELAWARE
Beaver Creek S.P.	EAST LIVERPOOL
Blue Rock S.P.	ZANESVILLE
Buck Creek S.P.	SPRINGFIELD
Buckeye Lake S.P.	NEWARK
Burr Oak S.P.	ATHENS

CALENDAR HIGHLIGHTS

JULY

Pro Football Hall of Fame Festival (Canton). Pro Football Hall of Fame. Events include parade, induction ceremony, AFC-NFC Hall of Fame Pro Game. Phone 330/456-7253 or 800/533-4302.

All-American Soap Box Derby (Akron). Derby Downs, Municipal Airport. More than 200 boys and girls (9-16 years) from United States and abroad compete with homemade, gravity-powered cars for scholarships, prizes. Phone 330/733-8723.

AUGUST

Boat Regatta (Put-in-Bay and Vermilion). More than 200 sailboats race to Vermilion. Phone 440/967-6634.

Ohio State Fair (Columbus). Expositions Center. Agricultural and industrial exposition plus grandstand entertainment, pageants, and horse show. Phone 614/644-3247 or 800/BUCKEYE.

SEPTEMBER

Riverfest (Cincinnati). Celebration of Cincinnati's river heritage held along the city's waterfront parks. Festivities include fireworks, three stages of entertainment, food. Phone Convention and Visitors Bureau, 800/CINCY-USA.

OCTOBER

Bob Evans Farm Festival (Gallipolis). Bob Evans Farm. Bluegrass and country entertainment; food, 150 heritage craftspeople and demonstrations; Appalachian clogging, square dancing. Camping. Phone 740/245-5305 or 800/994-3276.

DECEMBER

Christmas Candle Lightings (Coshocton). Roscoe Village. Tree- and candle-lighting ceremonies; hot-mulled cider and ginger cookies. Phone 800/877-1830.

Christmas in Zoar (New Philadelphia). Tours of private houses, craft show, German food, strolling carolers, and tree-lighting ceremony. Phone 330/874-3011.

Caesar Creek S.P.	WILMINGTON
Catawba Island S.P.	PORT CLINTON
Cowan Lake S.P.	WILMINGTON
Crane Creek S.P.	TOLEDO
Delaware S.P.	DELAWARE
Dillon S.P.	ZANESVILLE
East Fork S.P.	CINCINNATI
East Harbor S.P.	PORT CLINTON
Geneva S.P.	GENEVA-ON-THE-LAKE
Grand Lake-St. Marys S.P.	CELINA
Headlands Beach S.P.	MENTOR
Hocking Hills S.P.	same

Hueston Woods S.P.	OXFORD
Independence Dam S.P.	DEFIANCE
Indian Lake S.P.	BELLEFONTAINE
John Bryan S.P.	SPRINGFIELD
Kelleys Island S.P.	KELLEYS ISLAND
Lake Erie Island S.P.	PUT-IN-BAY
Lake Hope S.P.	ATHENS
Little Miami Scenic S.P.	WILMINGTON
Malabar Farm S.P.	MANSFIELD
Mary Jane Thurston S.P.	BOWLING GREEN
Maumee Bay S.P.	TOLEDO
Mosquito Lake S.P.	WARREN
Mount Gilead S.P.	same
Paint Creek S.P.	CHILLICOTHE
Portage Lakes S.P.	AKRON
Punderson S.P.	CHARDON
Salt Fork S.P.	CAMBRIDGE
Shawnee S.F.	PORTSMOUTH
Shawnee S.P.	PORTSMOUTH
Strouds Run S.P.	ATHENS
West Branch S.P.	KENT

Water-related activities, hiking, riding, various other sports, picnicking, camping, and visitor centers are available in many of these areas. Camping is permitted all year in 57 parks: $9-$30/site/night, no reservations. Reservations taken by application beginning March 1 for Rent-A-Camp program (May-September) at many parks: $24-$38/site/night, including all equipment. Reservations taken up to one year in advance for housekeeping cabins at 16 parks (all year-round): $140-$350/night; June-August, by the week only, $285-$900/week. Resort lodges are also available at eight locations. Pets allowed in designated campsites only. For details contact Information Center, Ohio Department of Natural Resources, Division of Parks & Recreation, 1952 Belcher Dr, Building C-3, Columbus 43224-1386, phone 614/265-6561 or 800/AT-A-PARK (reservations only).

SKI AREAS

Place Name	Listed Under
Alpine Valley Ski Area	CLEVELAND
Boston Mills Ski Area	AKRON
Brandywine Ski Area	AKRON
Clear Fork Ski Area	MANSFIELD
Mad River Mountain Ski Resort	BELLEFONTAINE
Snow Trails Ski Area	MANSFIELD

FISHING AND HUNTING

Annual fishing license $15, nonresident $24; one-day permit $7; three-day permit $15. Hunting license $15 (resident youth $8), nonresident $91. Special deer and wild turkey permits $20. Fur-taker permit $11. Wetlands habitat stamp $11. Tourist small game permit $25. Hunting forbidden on Sunday except for coyote, fox, woodchuck, and waterfowl in season. For latest game and fishing regulations contact the Department of Natural Resources, Division of Wildlife, 1840 Belcher Dr, Columbus 43224-1329, phone 614/265-6300 or 800/WILDLIF.

Driving Information

Safety belts are mandatory for all persons in front seat of vehicle. Children under four years or under 40 pounds in weight must be in an approved safety seat anywhere in vehicle. For further information phone 614/466-2550.

INTERSTATE HIGHWAY SYSTEM

The following alphabetical listing of Ohio towns in *Mobil Travel Guide* shows that these cities are within ten miles of the indicated Interstate highways. A highway map should, however, be checked for the nearest exit.

Highway Number	Cities/Towns within ten miles
Interstate 70	Cambridge, Columbus, Dayton, Newark, St. Clairsville, Springfield, Vandalia, Zanesville.
Interstate 71	Akron, Cincinnati, Cleveland, Columbus, Delaware, Lebanon, Mansfield, Mason, Mount Gilead, Strongsville, Wilmington.
Interstate 75	Bowling Green, Cincinnati, Dayton, Findlay, Lebanon, Lima, Mason, Miamisburg, Middletown, Piqua, Sidney, Toledo, Vandalia, Wapakoneta.
Interstate 76	Akron, Kent, Youngstown.
Interstate 77	Akron, Brecksville, Cambridge, Canton, Cleveland, Gnadenhutten, Marietta, Massillon, New Philadelphia.
Interstate 90	Ashtabula, Chardon, Cleveland, Geneva-on-the-Lake, Mentor, Painesville.

Additional Visitor Information

For free travel information contact Ohio Division of Travel and Tourism, PO Box 1001, Columbus 43216, phone 800/BUCKEYE. The Ohio Historical Society is a good source for historical information; contact Director, 1982 Velma Ave, Columbus 43211, phone 614/297-2300 or 800/BUCKEYE.

Travel information centers are located on Interstate highways at key roadside rest areas. These centers offer free brochures containing information on Ohio's attractions and events; staff are also on hand to answer any questions.

THE BRIDGES OF ASHTABULA COUNTY

This tour explores Ashtabula County, also known as "Covered Bridge Capital of Ohio" and "Wine Capital of Ohio." Sixty-five percent of Ohio's grapes grow in this county, which is located along 27 miles of Lake Erie shoreline; a collection of family-owned wineries produce excellent award-winning domestic wines. Add 16 covered bridges set in quaint villages, and you have the recipe for a perfect romantic getaway.

This tour can take a few hours, or it can take all day; it all depends on how many of the bridges you plan on visiting, how much time you spend at each one, and how many side trips you make. Keep in mind that road conditions on the route between bridges may vary—a lot of gravel awaits you. Directional signs are up but one or two are missing, so be prepared to backtrack. You can pick up a map outlining several different tour routes from the Ashtabula County Chamber of Commerce.

Jefferson, ten miles south of Ashtabula, is our starting point for this tour, which includes 11 of the 16 covered bridges in the area. First on our route is **Netcher Road Bridge,** which crosses Mill Creek. Built in 1998, the Netcher Road Bridge is the newest in this area and features a neo-Victorian design. Head next to nearby **South Denmark Bridge,** also over Mill Creek. **Caine Road Bridge,** built to commemorate the 175th anniversary of Ashtabula County, is in Pierpont Township over Ashtabula River, just six miles away. Next stop is the **Graham Road Bridge,** which is no longer in use. You'll find it in a picturesque little park on the south side of the road. **Root Road Bridge** is just four miles away, spanning the Ashtabula River. **Middle Road Bridge, State Road Bridge,** and **Creek Road Bridge** (all within a few miles of one another) have the distinct honor of crossing Conneaut Creek, the longest river in eastern Ashtabula County. Middle Road Bridge, originally built in 1868, was rehabilitated in 1984 by a handful of volunteers. State Road Bridge was constructed of over 97,000 feet of southern pine and oak. Continue two miles to **Benetka Road Bridge,** then three more miles to **Olin Bridge,** which is the only Ashtabula County bridge named after a family. The Olin family and their descendants have lived in this area since the bridge was built in 1873. The last bridge on our route is the **Giddings Road Bridge,** 12 miles away over Mill Creek in Jefferson Township.

To round out your day of covered bridge travels, head north from Jefferson to the Lake Erie shoreline where you'll have your pick of wineries to visit. The largest concentration of these are in the town of Conneaut. If you're looking for a place to spend the night, look no further than the bed-and-breakfast at Buccia Vineyard. Ferrante Winery & Ristorante is a great place to sample award-winning wines alongside authentic Italian cuisine. Old Firehouse Winery, west of Conneaut in Geneva-on-the-Lake, is a great place to head if you are looking for a more casual eatery. Located in what was originally the village's first firehouse, this winery has the added bonus of a lakefront location. **(APPROX 80 MI)**

Akron

(B-6) *See also Aurora, Canton, Cleveland, Kent, Massillon*

Founded 1825 **Pop** 223,019
Elev 1,027 ft **Area code** 330
Information Akron/Summit Convention & Visitors Bureau, 77 E Mill St, 44308-1401; 330/374-7560 or 800/245-4254
Web www.visitakron-summit.org

The "rubber capital of the world" is 35 miles south of the St. Lawrence Seaway, on the highest point on the Ohio and Erie Canal, covering an area of approximately 54 square miles. Metropolitan Akron has many manufacturing plants as well as strong service, trade, and government sectors. Although best known for its rubber factories, housing corporate headquarters of four major rubber companies, Akron is also a center for polymer research.

Akron owes its start to the Ohio and Erie Canal, which was opened to traffic in 1827. General Simon Perkins, commissioner of the Ohio Canal Fund, seeing the trade possibilities, laid out the town two years earlier. The seat of Summit County was already thriving when Dr. Benjamin Franklin Goodrich organized the first rubber plant in 1870. This event aroused little interest and it took the "horseless carriage" to spark the future of Akron. By 1915 it was a boom town. The major rubber companies maintain large research laboratories and developmental departments. Other products range from fishing tackle to plastics and industrial machine products.

What to See and Do

Akron Art Museum. Regional, national, and international art, 1850 to present; also changing exhibits; sculpture garden. (Daily; closed major hols) 70 E Market St. Phone 330/376-9185. **FREE**

Akron Civic Theatre. (1929) Lavishly designed by Viennese architect John Eberson to resemble a night in a Moorish garden, complete with blinking stars and floating clouds. The theater is one of four atmospheric-type facilities of its size remaining in the country. (Daily) 182 S Main St. Phone 330/535-3179.

Akron Zoological Park. This 26-acre zoo features more than 300 birds, mammals, and reptiles from around the world. Exhibits incl the Ohio Farmyard where children can pet and feed the animals, Tiger Valley with tigers, lions, and bears, walk-through aviary, and underwater viewing window for observing the river otters. (Daily; closed hols). 500 Edgewood Ave. Phone 330/375-2525. ¢¢

Cuyahoga River Gorge Reservation. Part of park system. On north bank is the cave where Mary Campbell, first white child in the Western Reserve, was held prisoner by Native Americans. 3 mi N of Main and Market Sts. Phone 330/867-5511.

Cuyahoga Valley National Park. On 33,000 acres. Beautiful and varied area with extensive recreational facilities, many historic sites and entertainment facilities; 20-mi long, fully accessible Ohio and Erie Canal Towpath Trail. Artistic events, performances, campfire programs, nature walks. Three visitor centers (daily; closed hols). Park (daily). Fee for some activities. Located along 22 mi of the Cuyahoga River just north of Akron. Phone 330/650-4636. Also here is

   Dover Lake Waterpark. Swimming, beach, wave pool, water slides, tube slides; concessions, pavilions, chairlift ride, picnic grounds. (Mid-June-Mid-Aug, daily) Approx 13 mi N on OH 8, then 1 mi W on OH 82, then S on Brandywine Rd, then W on Highland (Vaughn) Rd. Phone 330/467-7946. ¢¢¢¢

Goodyear World of Rubber. Historic and product displays. A one-hr tour incl movies. The Goodyear Blimp. (Daily; closed hols) Fourth floor Goodyear Hall; 1201 E Market St, 1½ mi E of OH 8, on I-76, at jct Goodyear Blvd. Phone 330/796-7117. **FREE**

Hale Farm and Village. Authentic Western Reserve house (ca 1825), other authentic buildings in a village setting depict northeastern Ohio's rural life in the mid-1800s; pioneer implements; craft demonstrations, special events; farming; costumed guides. (May-Oct, Tues-Sat, Sun afternoons) Approx 10 mi N on unnumbered road at 2686 Oak Hill Rd in Bath (10 mi S of I-80 exit 11); in Cuyahoga Valley National Recreation Area. Phone 330/666-3711. ¢¢¢ Also here is

Cuyahoga Valley Scenic Railroad. Scenic railroad trips through the Cuyahoga Valley National Recreation Area between Cleveland and Akron aboard vintage railroad cars pulled by first generation ALCO diesels. Stations incl Independence (south of Cleveland), Hale Farm, Akron Valley Business District, NPS Canal Visitor Center, Howard St and Quaker Sq in Akron. Res required. Phone 330/657-2000. ¢¢¢¢

National Inventors Hall of Fame. Dedicated to the creative process; houses interactive exhibit area, national inventors hall of fame. (Tues-Sun) 221 S Broadway St. ¢¢

Naturealm Visitors Center. A 4,000-sq-ft "Gateway to Nature" underground exhibit area surrounded by many sights and sounds of nature. (Daily; closed hols) 1828 Smith Rd. Phone 330/865-8065. **FREE**

Portage Lakes State Park. Several reservoir lakes totaling 2,520 acres. Swimming, fishing, boating (launch); hunting, hiking, snowmobiling, picnicking (shelter), camping (campground located five mi from park headquarters), pet camping. Standard fees. 4 mi S off OH 93, 619. Phone 330/644-2220. **FREE**

Portage Princess Cruise. Cruise the glacier-made lakes on enclosed riverboat (May-Oct 13, daily). On OH 619, 4 mi W of I-77. Phone 330/499-6891. ¢¢

Quaker Square. Shopping, hotel, restaurants, and entertainment center in the original mills and silos of the Quaker Oats Company. Historical displays incl famous Quaker Oats advertising memorabilia. (Daily; closed hols) 135 S Broadway, in downtown area. Phone 330/253-5970. **FREE**

Skiing.

Boston Mills. Four triple, two double chairlifts, two handle tows; patrol, school, rentals, snowmaking; cafeteria, bar. Longest run 1,800 ft; vertical drop 240 ft. (Dec-mid-Mar, daily) 9 mi N on OH 8 to exit 12, then W on OH 303 to

7100 Riverview Rd, in Peninsula. Phone 330/657-2334. ¢¢¢¢

Brandywine. Triple, four quad chairlifts, three handle tows; patrol, school, rentals, snowmaking; cafeteria, bars. Longest run 1,800 ft; vertical drop 240 ft. (Early Dec-mid-Mar, daily) Approx 13 mi N on OH 8, then 4 mi W at 1146 W Highland Rd. Phone 330/657-2334. ¢¢¢¢

Stan Hywet Hall and Gardens. Tudor Revival manor house built by F. A. Seiberling, co-founder of Goodyear Tire & Rubber; contains 65 rms with antiques and art treasures dating from the 14th century. More than 70 acres of grounds and gardens. (Apr-Dec, daily; rest of yr, Tues-Sun; closed hols, also Jan) 714 N Portage Path, 1½ mi N of Jct OH 18. Phone 330/836-5533. ¢¢

Summit County Historical Society. 550 Copley Rd. Phone 330/535-1120. Museums incl

John Brown Home. Remodeled residence where the abolitionist lived 1844-1846. (Wed-Sun afternoons; closed hols) 514 Diagonal Rd at Copley Rd. ¢¢

Perkins Mansion. (1837) Greek Revival home built of Ohio sandstone by Simon Perkins, Jr., on ten landscaped acres. (Wed-Sun afternoons; closed hols) 550 Copley Rd at S Portage Path. ¢¢

The University of Akron. (1870) 24,300 students. Third-largest four-yr university in Ohio; known for its Colleges of Polymer Science, Polymer Engineering, Global Business, and Fine and Applied Arts. Its science and engineering program is ranked in the top five nationally. The E. J. Thomas Performing Arts Hall is home to the Ohio Ballet and Akron Symphony. Bierce Library houses many collections incl the Archives of the History of American Psychology. Campus tours arranged through Admissions. Just east of downtown. Phone 330/972-7100. Also here is

Hower House. (1871) A 28-rm Victorian mansion, Second Empire Italianate-style architecture, built by John Henry Hower; lavish furnishing from around the world. (Feb-Dec, Wed-Fri and Sun afternoons; closed hols) 60 Fir Hill. Phone 330/972-6909. ¢¢

The Winery at Wolf Creek. Tasting rm overlooks vineyard and lake. (Apr-Dec daily; Dec-Mar Thurs-Sun; closed hols) Approx 1½ mi N of I-76, at exit 14, 2637 S Cleveland-Massillon Rd in Norton. Phone 330/666-9285. **FREE**

Special Events

Ohio Ballet. E. J. Thomas Hall, University of Akron. Phone 330/375-2835. Performances in Feb, Apr, July, Aug, Sept, and Nov.

Blossom Music Center. 1145 W Steels Corners Rd, in Cuyahoga Falls, approx 8 mi N on OH 8, then W; Ohio Tpke exits 11, 12; in Cuyahoga National Recreation Area. Summer home of Cleveland Orchestra; symphony, jazz, pop, rock, country music concerts. Phone 330/920-8040. Mid-May-late Sept.

All-American Soap Box Derby. Derby Downs, Municipal Airport. More than 200 boys and girls (9-16 yrs) from US and abroad compete with homemade, gravity-powered cars for scholarships, prizes. Phone 330/733-8723. Late July.

Akron Symphony Orchestra. E. J. Thomas Hall, University of Akron. Phone 330/535-8131. Sept-May.

Yankee Peddler Festival. 10 mi S on OH 21 S, in Canal Fulton, at Clay's Park Resort. Arts, crafts, entertainment, costumes, food of pioneer period 1776-1825. Phone 800/535-5634. Three wkends Sept.

Harvest Festival. Hale Farm and Western Reserve Village. Celebrates end of the harvest season. Hands-on 19th-century rural activities incl cider pressing, hayrides, crafts; musical entertainment, food. Phone 330/666-3711 or 800/589-9703. Early Oct.

Wonderful World of Ohio Mart. Stan Hywet Hall. Renaissance Fair with handicrafts, food, entertainment. Phone 330/836-5533. Early Oct.

Motels/Motor Lodges

★★ **BEST WESTERN INN.** 2677 Gilchrist Rd (44305). 330/794-1050; fax 330/794-8495; toll-free 800/780-7234. www.bestwestern.com. 112 rms, 3 story. May-Sept: S $57-$65; D $63-$71; each addl $6; under 17 free; lower rates rest of yr. Crib free. TV; cable (premium), VCR avail. Heated pool. Restaurant 6 am-10 pm; Sat from 7 am; Sun 7 am-8 pm. Rm serv. Bar 11-2 exc Sun. Ck-out 11 am. Meeting rms. Business servs avail. Valet serv. Exercise equipt. Cr cds: A, C, D, DS, MC, V.

⊡ ⇌ 🏋 ⊠ 🔥

★★ **COMFORT INN WEST.** 130 Montrose West Ave (44321). 330/666-5050; fax 330/668-2550; toll-free 800/228-5150. www.comfortinn.com. 132 rms, 2 story. S $65-$139; D $65-$139; each addl $8; under 19 free; wkend rates. Crib free. TV; cable (premium), VCR avail (movies). Indoor pool. Complimentary continental bkfst. Restaurant nearby. Ck-out 11 am. Coin lndry. Meeting rm. Business servs avail. In-rm modem link. Valet serv. Health club privileges. Some in-rm whirlpools, refrigerators, wet bars. Cr cds: A, C, D, DS, MC, V.

⊡ ⊠ 🔥 SC ⇌

★★ **HOLIDAY INN.** 2940 Chenoweth Rd (44312). 330/644-7126; fax 330/644-1776; toll-free 800/465-4329. www.holiday-inn.com. 129 rms, 2 story. S, D $84-$129; each addl $6; suites $130-$185; under 18 free. Crib free. Pet accepted. TV; cable. Pool; poolside serv. Restaurant 6 am-10 pm; Sat, Sun from 7 am. Rm serv. Bar 11-2:30 am; entertainment Tues-Sat. Ck-out noon. Meeting rms. Business servs avail. Bellhops. Valet serv. Sundries. Airport transportation. Cr cds: A, C, D, DS, MC, V.

⊡ ⇥ ⇌ ✈ ⊠ 🔥 SC

★★ **HOLIDAY INN.** 4073 Medina Rd (44333). 330/666-4131; fax 330/666-7190; toll-free 800/465-4329. www.holiday-inn.com. 166 rms, 4 story. S, D $79-$109; each addl $8; under 19 free. Crib free. TV; cable (premium). Heated pool. Restaurant 6:30 am-10 pm; Fri, Sat to midnight. Rm serv. Ck-out noon. Coin lndry. Meeting rms. Business servs avail. In-rm modem link. Valet serv. Sundries. Exercise equipt. Health club privileges. Cr cds: A, C, D, DS, MC, V.

⊡ ⊠ 🔥 SC 🏋 ⇌

★ **RED ROOF INN.** 99 Rothrock Rd (44321). 330/666-0566; fax 330/666-6874; toll-free 800/733-7663. www.redroof.com. 108 rms, 2 story. S $53-

$62; D $58-$66; each addl $7; under 18 free. Crib free. Pet accepted. TV; cable (premium). Complimentary coffee. Restaurant adj 6 am-10 pm. Ck-out noon Business servs avail. Cr cds: A, C, D, DS, MC, V.

Hotels

★★★ **HILTON INN.** 3180 W Market St (44333). 330/867-5000; fax 330/867-1648; toll-free 800/445-8667. www.hilton.com. 204 rms, 4 story. S, D $109; each addl $10; suites $109-$159; studio rms $75; family rates. Crib free. TV; cable. 2 pools, 1 indoor; whirlpool, poolside serv. Restaurant 6:30 am-10 pm; Fri, Sat from 7:30 am. Rm serv. Bar 11:30-2 am; Sun 4 pm-midnight; entertainment Fri, Sat. Ck-out noon. Coin lndry. Meeting rms. Business center. In-rm modem link. Bellhops. Valet serv. Sundries. Gift shop. Airport transportation. Exercise equipt; sauna. Health club privileges. Some refrigerators. Cr cds: A, C, D, DS, JCB, MC, V.

★★★ **HILTON QUAKER SQUARE.** 135 S Broadway St (44308). 330/253-5970; fax 330/253-2574; res 800/445-8667. 196 rms, 8 story. S, D $89-$135; each addl $15; suites $220-$295; studio rms $110-$150; family rates; wkend rates. Crib free. TV; cable. Indoor pool. Restaurant 6:30 am-11 pm; Sun 7 am-10 pm. Bar 11-2:30 am; entertainment wkends. Ck-out noon. Meeting rms. Business center. Airport transportation. Exercise equipt. Balconies. Historic building; all rms are in grain silos, built in 1932 for Quaker Oats Co. Cr cds: A, C, D, DS, JCB, MC, V.

★★★ **RADISSON AKRON FAIR-LAWN.** 200 Montrose West Ave (44321). 330/666-9300; fax 330/668-2270; res 800/333-3333. www.radisson.com. 130 rms, 4 story. S, D $100-$130; each addl $10; suites $150; under 18 free; wkend rates; higher rates NEC World Series of Golf. Crib free. TV; cable. Indoor pool. Coffee in rms. Restaurant 6 am-2 pm, 5-10 pm. Rm serv. Bar to 10 pm. Ck-out noon. Meeting rms. Business servs avail. In-rm modem link. Valet serv. Sundries. Airport trans-

portation. Exercise equipt; sauna. Minibars; some refrigerators. Some balconies. Cr cds: A, MC, V.

Restaurants

★ **ART'S PLACE.** 2225 State Rd, Cuyahoga Falls (44223). 330/928-2188. Hrs: 11 am-10 pm; Fri to 11 pm; Sat 4-11 pm; Sun noon-7 pm. Res accepted. Bar to 1 am. Lunch $4.15-$6.75, dinner $5.50-$12.95. Child's menu. Specializes in prime rib, chicken, barbecued ribs. Parking. Cr cds: A, DS, MC, V.

★ **HOUSE OF HUNAN.** 2717 W Market St, Fairlawn (44333). 330/864-8215. Hrs: 11:30 am-10 pm; Fri to 11 pm; Sat noon-11 pm; Sun noon-10 pm; early-bird dinner 4-6 pm; Sun noon-4 pm. Res accepted. Chinese menu. Bar. A la carte entrees: lunch $4.50-$7.50, dinner $5.25-$12.95. Specializes in Hunan and Szechwan dishes. Parking. Asian decor. Cr cds: A, D, DS, MC, V.

★★★ **LANNING'S.** 826 N Cleveland-Massillon Rd (44333). 330/666-1159. www.lannings-restaurant.com. Hrs: 5:30-11 pm; Sat 5 pm-midnight. Closed Sun; major hols. Res accepted. Bar from 4 pm. Dinner $14-$27.50. Specializes in steak, fresh seafood. Pianist Sat. Valet parking. Mediterranean decor. View of stream. Family-owned. Jacket. Cr cds: A, D, DS, MC, V.

★★★ **TANGIER.** 532 W Market St (44303). 330/376-7171. Hrs: 11:30 am-11 pm; Sun to 3 pm. Closed most major hols. Res accepted. Continental menu. Bar to 2:30 am. Lunch $5.95-$8.95, dinner $8.95-$23. Child's menu. Specialties: rack of lamb Phoenicia, authentic Mediterranean feast. Own baking. Entertainment. Parking. Floor shows. Mediterranean-Middle Eastern decor. Cr cds: A, D, DS, MC, V.

★★ **TRIPLE CROWN.** 335 S Main, Munroe Falls (44262). 330/633-5325. Hrs: 11 am-10 pm; Sun 3-8 pm; early-bird dinner Tues-Fri 4-6 pm; Sun brunch 10 am-2:30 pm. Closed major hols. Res accepted. Bar. Lunch $4.85-$10.95, dinner from $7.95. Sun brunch $8.95. Child's menu. Specializes in fish, steak. Pianist. Parking. Horse racing memorabilia. Cr cds: A, DS, MC, V.

⬜ ⬜

Alliance

(C-6) *See also Akron, Canton, Kent, Massillon, Youngstown*

Settled 1805 **Pop** 23,376 **Elev** 1,174 ft
Area code 330 **Zip** 44601
Information Chamber of Commerce, 210 E Main St; 330/823-6260
Web www.chamber.alliance.oh.us

What to See and Do

Glamorgan Castle. Historic complex (1904) built by Colonel William H. Morgan. (Mon-Fri, afternoon tours; also by appt) 200 Glamorgan Ave. Phone 330/821-2100. ¢¢

Mabel Hartzell Museum. Furniture, clothes of 18th and 19th centuries, local historical items, early pewter, glass, china in century-old house. (afternoons during Carnation City festival; rest of yr by appt) 840 N Park Ave. Phone 330/167-7330.
Donation

Mount Union College. (1846) 2,100 students. Liberal arts college. On campus is Crandall Art Gallery (Sept-Apr, Mon-Fri; closed hols; free). Guided tours. 1972 Clark Ave. Phone 330/821-5320.

Special Event

Carnation Festival. Honoring state flower. Second wk Aug. Phone 330/823-6260.

Motel/Motor Lodge

★★ **COMFORT INN.** *2500 W State St (44601). 330/821-5555; fax 330/821-4919; toll-free 800/948-5555. www.comfortinn.com.* 113 rms, 5 story. S $80-$180; D $84-$180; each addl $5; suites $80-$115; under 18 free; golf packages. Crib free. Pet accepted, some restrictions; $10. TV; cable (premium), VCR avail (movies).

Indoor pool; whirlpool. Complimentary continental bkfst. Ck-out noon. Coin lndry. Meeting rms. Business servs avail. Bellhops. Exercise equipt. Cr cds: A, C, D, DS, MC, V.

⬜ ⬜ ⬜ ⬜ ⬜ ⬜ ⬜

Ashtabula

(A-7) *See also Geneva-on-the-Lake, Painesville*

Settled 1796 **Pop** 21,633 **Elev** 695 ft
Area code 440 **Zip** 44004
Information Ashtabula Area Chamber of Commerce, 4536 Main Ave, PO Box 96; 440/998-6998

This modern harbor at the mouth of the Ashtabula River is an important shipping center for coal and iron ore. Swimming, fishing, and boating are possible in Lake Erie.

What to See and Do

Conneaut Historical Railroad Museum. Museum in former New York Central depot; memorabilia of early railroading, model engines. Adj on siding are the *Old Iron Horse 755* (retired Nickel Plate Railroad locomotive) and a caboose, which may be boarded. (Memorial Day-Labor Day, daily) Children 11 yrs and under only with adult. 12 mi NE on US 20 to Conneaut, at 342 Depot St, just off Broad St. Phone 440/599-7878.
FREE

Great Lakes Marine and US Coast Guard Memorial Museum. In former lighthouse keeper's home built 1898. Incl working scale model of Hulett ore unloading machine, ship's pilot house, marine artifacts, paintings, photos, models, handmade miniature tools. Guides; tours (by appt, all yr). View of river, harbor, docks; picnicking. (Memorial Day-Oct, Fri-Sun and hols, afternoons) 1071-1073 Walnut Blvd. Phone 440/964-6847.
Donation

Special Events

Blessing of the Fleet. Boat parades on lake; tours, art shows, fireworks. First wkend June. Phone 440/998-6998.

Ashtabula County Fair. In Jefferson. Mid-Aug. Phone 440/576-7626.

Covered Bridge Festival. Fairgrounds. Second wkend Oct. Phone 440/576-3769.

Motels/Motor Lodges

★ **CEDARS MOTEL.** *2015 W Prospect Rd (44004). 440/992-5406.* 15 rms. S $50-$55; D $65; each addl $5. Pet accepted, some restrictions; $5. TV; cable (premium). Restaurant nearby. Ck-out 11 am. Business servs avail. Health club privileges. Cr cds: A, D, DS, MC, V.

★★ **COMFORT INN.** *1860 Austinburg Rd, Austinburg (44010). 440/275-2711; fax 440/275-7314; toll-free 800/228-5150. www.comfortinn.com.* 119 rms, 2 story. S, D $90-$135; D $95-$135; under 18 free. Crib free. TV; cable (premium), VCR avail. Heated pool. Coffee in rms. Restaurant 6 am-2 pm, 5-10 pm. Rm serv. Bar 5 pm-midnight. Ck-out noon. Coin lndry. Meeting rms. Business servs avail. In-rm modem link. Bellhops. Sundries. Cr cds: A, D, DS, MC, V.

Restaurant

★★ **EL GRANDE.** *2145 W Prospect St (44004). 440/998-2228.* Hrs: 11 am-9 pm; Fri to 10 pm; Sat 4-11 pm. Closed Sun, Mon; major hols. Italian, Amer menu. Lunch $3.95-$9.95, dinner $5.45-$13.45. Specializes in steak, pasta, seafood. Western decor. Cr cds: A, D, MC, V.

Athens (F-5)

Founded 1800 **Pop** 21,265 **Elev** 723 ft
Area code 740 **Zip** 45701
Information Athens County Convention & Visitors Bureau, 667 E State St; 740/592-1819 or 800/878-9767
Web www.athensohio.com

The establishment of Ohio University, oldest college in what was the Northwest Territory, created the town of Athens. It is also the seat of Athens County. A Ranger District office of the Wayne National Forest (see IRONTON) is located here.

What to See and Do

Ohio University. (1804) 19,000 students. First university in Northwest Territory. Information and self-guided tours of historic campus available at Visitor Center, Richland Ave. Athens Campus. Phone 740/593-2097. Also here is

Kennedy Museum of Art. Permanent collection, traveling exhibits from other institutions. Tours. (Tues-Sun, daily) Lin Hall. Phone 740/593-1304. **FREE**

State parks.

Burr Oak. More than 2,500 acres. Swimming, lifeguard, bathhouse (Memorial Day-Labor Day), fishing, boating (rentals, ramp); picnicking, hiking, nearby golf course, cabins, lodge, camping. Standard fees. 3 mi N on US 33, then 14 mi N on OH 13, borders on Wayne National Forest (see IRONTON). Phone 740/767-2112. **FREE**

Lake Hope. Over 3,220 acres. Swimming, bathhouse, fishing, boating (rentals); hiking, concession, picnicking, camping, pet camping; 66 cabins, lodge. Nature center with naturalist (May-Labor Day). Standard fees. 14 mi NW on OH 56, then 6 mi S on OH 278 in Zaleski State Forest. Phone 740/596-5253. **FREE**

Strouds Run. On 161-acre Dow Lake. Swimming (Memorial Day-Labor Day), fishing, boating (rentals); picnicking, hiking, camping, pet camping. Standard fees. (Daily) 5 mi E off US 50. Phone 740/592-2302. **FREE**

Wayne National Forest. (see IRONTON) Sections west, north, and east. Phone 740/592-6644.

Special Event

Ohio Valley Summer Theater. Elizabeth Baker Theater & Forum Theater, Ohio University. For schedule phone 740/593-4800. June-July.

Motels/Motor Lodges

★★ **AMERIHOST INN.** *20 Home St (45701). 740/594-3000; fax 740/594-5546. www.amerihostinn.com.* 102 rms, 2 story. S, D $76-$99; each addl $6; under 12 free; higher rates special events. Crib free. TV. Indoor pool; whirlpool. Complimentary continental bkfst. Restaurant adj 6 am-10 pm. Ck-out noon. Meeting rm. Exercise equipt; sauna. Cr cds: A, C, D, DS, MC, V.

D ⊷ ⊠ 🐾 🔥 🏋

★ **DAYS INN.** *330 Columbus Rd (45701). 740/592-4000; fax 740/593-7687; toll-free 800/329-7466. www.daysinn.com.* 60 rms, 2 story. S, D $62-$100; each addl $6; under 14 free; higher rates special events. Crib free. TV; cable (premium). Complimentary continental bkfst. Restaurant nearby. Ck-out noon. Business servs avail. Miniature golf, driving range adj. Cr cds: A, C, D, DS, MC, V.

D ⊠ 🐾

★★★ **THE OHIO UNIVERSITY INN AND CONFERENCE CENTER.** *331 Richland Ave (45701). 740/593-6661; fax 740/592-5139. www.ouinn.com.* 139 rms, 2-3 story. S, D $89-$139; suites $149-$169; under 12 free; higher rates special events. Crib free. TV; cable. Pool. Coffee in rms. Restaurant 6:30 am-2 pm, 5-10 pm; Sun, hols 7 am-9 pm. Rm serv. Bar. Ck-out noon. Meeting rms. In-rm modem link. Business servs avail. Valet serv exc Sun. Sundries. Health club privileges. Some private patios, balconies. Cr cds: A, C, D, DS, MC, V.

D ⊷ ⊠ 🐾 SC

Resort

★ **BURR OAK RESORT.** *Rte 2, Glouster (45732). 740/767-2112; fax 740/767-4878; res 800/282-7275.* 60 rms in 3-story lodge; 30 kit. cottages, 2-bedrm. May-Oct: S, D $69-$99; each addl $5; kit. cottages $125 ($595/wk); under 12 free; lower rates rest of yr. Crib free. TV; VCR avail (movies). Indoor pool. Playground. Dining rm 7 am-9 pm. Bar. Ck-out noon. Meeting rms. Business servs avail. Sundries. Gift shop. Lighted tennis. Game rm. Overlooks Burr Oak Lake; all state park facilities avail. Cr cds: A, D, MC, V.

🐾 🏹 ⊷ 🐾 SC

Restaurant

★★ **SEVEN SAUCES.** *66 N Court (45701). 740/592-5555.* Hrs: 5-9 pm; Fri, Sat to 10 pm; Sun to 8:30 pm. Closed major hols. Res accepted. Continental menu. Bar (Fri, Sat only). A la carte entrees: dinner $8.50-$15.95. Specializes in seafood, steak, vegetarian and international dishes. Cr cds: A, D, MC, V.

D

Aurora

(B-6) *See also Akron, Cleveland, Kent, Warren*

Pop 9,192 **Elev** 1,130 ft
Area code 330 **Zip** 44202
Information Aurora Chamber of Commerce, 173 S Chillicothe Rd; 330/562-3355
Web www.auroraohiochamber.com

What to See and Do

⊠ **Six Flags Worlds of Adventure.** A 120-acre lake with boardwalk; wave pool, water slides, swimming. Amusement park with rides incl ten roller coasters and historic carousel; Turtle Beach; live musical shows. Marine park incl sea lions, walruses, otters; interactive dolphin show. (Memorial Day-Labor Day, daily; May and Sept-Oct, wkends only) 5 mi N on OH 43. Phone 330/562-7131. ¢¢¢¢

Motel/Motor Lodge

★★★ **THE INN AT SIX FLAGS.** *800 N Aurora Rd (Rte 43) (44202). 330/562-9151; fax 330/562-5701; res 800/970-7666. www.sixflags.com.* 144 rms, 2 story. Mid-May-early Sept: S, D $170-$180; suites $275; under 18 free; lower rates rest of yr. Crib free. TV; cable (premium). Indoor pool; whirlpool, lifeguard. Restaurant 7 am-midnight. Rm serv. Ck-out 11 am. Coin lndry. Meeting rms. Business servs avail. Valet serv. Sundries.

Exercise equipt; sauna. Game rm. Cr cds: A, C, D, DS, MC, V.

Restaurant

★ ★ **WELSHFIELD INN.** *14001 Main Market, Burton (44021). 440/834-4164.* Hrs: 11:30 am-2:30 pm, 4:30-9 pm; Fri to 10 pm; Sat to 2:30 pm, 4:30-10 pm; Sun noon-8 pm. Closed Mon. Res accepted; required some hols. Serv bar. Lunch $2.50-$10.95, dinner $9.50-$21.95. Child's menu. Specialties: fresh salmon, baked chicken, prime rib. Cr cds: A, D, MC, V.

Beachwood

See also Brecksville, Cleveland

Pop 10,677 **Area code** 216 **Zip** 44122
Information Beachwood Chamber of Commerce, 24500 Chagrin Blvd, Suite 110; 216/831-0003

The suburb of Beachwood is located east of Cleveland.

What to See and Do

Nature Center at Shaker Lakes. This 300-acre tract has nature and hiking trails, bird observation area, two man-made lakes. Six natural habitats, Nature Center facilities include indoor and outdoor classrooms, community meeting rm, gift shop. (Mon-Sat, also Sun afternoons) N to OH 87, at 2600 S Park Blvd in Shaker Heights. Phone 216/321-5935. **FREE**

Thistledown Racing Club. Thoroughbred horse racing; pari-mutuel betting. (Mar-late Dec, Mon, Wed, Fri-Sun) At Northfield and Emery Rd, in North Randall. Phone 216/662-8600. ¢¢

Motels/Motor Lodges

★ ★ **HOLIDAY INN.** *3750 Orange Pl (44122). 216/831-3300; fax 216/831-0486; res 800/465-4329. www.holiday-inn.com.* 170 rms, 4 story. S, D $110-$139; under 19 free. Crib free. TV; cable (premium). Indoor/outdoor pool; lifeguard. Sauna. Restaurant 6:30 am-10 pm. Rm serv. Bar 11-1 am, Sun 1-10 pm. Ck-out 11 am. Coin lndry. Meeting rms. Business servs avail. In-rm modem link. Valet serv. Sundries. Cr cds: A, D, DS, MC, V.

★ **SUPER 8.** *3795 Orange Pl (44122). 216/831-7200; fax 216/831-0616; res 800/800-8000. www.super8.com.* 128 rms, 2 story. May-Sept: S $60-$81; D $66-$109; each addl $6; under 18 free; package plans; lower rates rest of yr. Crib free. TV; cable. Complimentary continental bkfst. Coffee in rms. Ck-out 11 am. Meeting rms. Business servs avail. Sundries. Airport transportation. Some refrigerators. Cr cds: A, D, DS, MC, V.

Hotels

★ ★ ★ **MARRIOTT EAST.** *3663 Park East Dr (44122). 216/464-5950; fax 216/464-6539; res 800/334-2118. www.marriotthotels.com/cleea.* 403 rms, 4-7 story. S, D $129-$169; suites $225-$500; under 18 free. Crib free. TV; cable (premium), VCR avail. Indoor/outdoor pool; whirlpool, lifeguard, poolside serv. Restaurant 6:30 am-11 pm; Sat, Sun from 7 am. Rm serv. Bar 11:30-2 am. Ck-out noon. Coin lndry. Convention facilities. Business center. Bellhops. Concierge. Gift shop. Downhill ski 15 mi; x-country ski 10 mi. Exercise equipt; sauna. Health club privileges. Game rm. Rec rm. Some refrigerators. Luxury level. Cr cds: A, C, D, DS, ER, JCB, MC, V.

★ ★ ★ **RADISSON HOTEL - BEACHWOOD.** *26300 Chagrin Blvd (44122). 216/831-5150; fax 216/765-1156; res 800/333-3333. www.radisson.com.* 196 rms, 2-4 story. May-Sept: S, D $105; each addl $10; suites $150-$185; under 18 free; lower rates rest of yr. Crib free. TV; cable (premium). Heated pool. Restaurants 6:30 am-10 pm. Rm serv 7 am-10 pm. Bar 11 am-midnight. Ck-out noon. Coin lndry. Meeting rms. Business servs avail. Gift shop. Valet serv. Barber. Downhill ski 12 mi; x-country ski 1½ mi. Exercise equipt. Some refrigerators. Cr cds: A, MC, V.

All Suite

★ ★ ★ **EMBASSY SUITES.** 3775 Park East Dr (44122). 216/765-8066; fax 216/765-0930; toll-free 800/362-2779. www.embassysuitesbeachwood.com. 216 suites, 4 story. S, D $139-$179; each addl $15; under 16 free; higher rates New Year's Eve. Crib free. TV; cable (premium), VCR avail. Indoor pool; whirlpool, lifeguard. Complimentary full bkfst; evening refreshments. Complimentary coffee in rms. Restaurant 11:30 am-10 pm; Fri, Sat to 11 pm. Bar. Ck-out 1 pm. Coin lndry. Meeting rms. Business servs avail. In-rm modem link. Gift shop. Downhill/x-country ski 12 mi. Exercise equipt; sauna. Game rm. Refrigerators. Cr cds: A, C, D, DS, JCB, MC, V.
[D] [⚡] [≈] [🕴] [⛷] [🔥] [SC]

Restaurants

★ ★ **CHARLEY'S CRAB.** 25765 Chagrin Blvd (44122). 216/831-8222. www.muer.com. Hrs: 11:30 am-10 pm; Sat to 11 pm; Sun 4-10 pm; early-bird dinner Mon-Sat 5-6 pm, Sun 4-10 pm. Closed major hols. Res accepted. Bar. Lunch $6.75-$18, dinner $11.50-$30. Child's menu. Specializes in fresh fish, pasta. Valet parking. Cr cds: A, D, DS, MC, V.
[D]

★ ★ **LION & LAMB.** 30519 Pine Tree Rd, Cleveland (44124). 216/831-1213. Hrs: 11:30 am-3 pm, 5-10 pm; Fri, Sat to 11 pm. Closed Sun; major hols. Res accepted. Italian, Amer menu. Bar 11-2:30 am. Lunch $4.95-$6.75, dinner $12.50-$26.95. Entertainment exc Sun. Family-owned. Cr cds: A, D, DS, MC, V.
[D] [🖼]

★ ★ ★ **RISTORANTE GIOVANNI.** 25550 Chagrin Blvd (44122). 216/831-8625. Hrs: 11:30 am-2:30 pm, 5:30-9:30 pm; Sat 5:30-10:30 pm. Closed Sun; major hols. Res required. Northern Italian menu. Bar. Wine list. Lunch $6.50-$14.95, dinner $18.50-$34. Specializes in fresh seafood, homemade pasta. Own baking. Valet parking. Jacket. Cr cds: A, D, DS, MC, V.
[D] [🖼]

★ ★ **SHUHEI.** 23360 Chagrin Blvd (44122). 216/464-1720. Hrs: 11:30 am-2:30 pm, 5:30-10 pm; Fri, Sat to 11 pm; Sun 5-9 pm. Closed most major hols. Res accepted. Japanese menu. Bar. Lunch $8.50-$14.50, dinner $15.95-$23.50. Specializes in seafood, poultry, sushi. Japanese decor. Jacket. Cr cds: A, D, DS, MC, V.
[D]

Bellefontaine

(D-3) See also Lima, Sidney

Settled 1806 **Pop** 12,142 **Elev** 1,251 ft **Area code** 937 **Zip** 43311

Information Greater Logan County Convention and Tourist Bureau, 100 S Main St; 937/599-5121

Web www.logancountyohio.com

The French name, which means "beautiful fountain," resulted from the natural springs at the site. An industrial town, this area was once a Shawnee village called Blue Jacket's Town, for a white man who was captured by the Shawnee, married the chief's daughter, and became chief of the tribe. The area is rich in Native American lore, Revolutionary history, and scenic and recreational attractions. At Campbell Hill, the elevation is 1,550 feet, the highest point in Ohio.

What to See and Do

Indian Lake State Park. Recreational area and summer resort. Land once belonged to Wyandot, Shawnee, and other tribes. More than 640 acres of land with a 5,800-acre water area. Swimming; fishing for bass, crappie, channel catfish and bluegill; boating (dock, launch, rentals); hiking trails, snowmobiling on frozen lake, picnicking, concession, camping. Standard fees. (Daily) 12 mi NW off US 33. Phone 937/843-2717. **FREE**

Ohio Caverns. Noted for the coloring and white crystal formations; illuminated. Picnicking. One-hr guided tours covering one mi. (Daily; closed Thanksgiving, Dec 25) 8 mi S on US 68 to West Liberty, then 3 mi SE on OH 245. Phone 937/465-4017. ¢¢¢

Piatt Castles. Castle Mac-A-Cheek (1864-1871) is the Norman-style home of Civil War General Abram Sanders Piatt; original furnishings, firearms, Native American artifacts, patent models, extensive library. **Mac-O-Chee** (1879-1881) is the Flemish-style home of social critic, writer, editor, and Civil War Colonel Donn Piatt; restored to 1880s style and format. Both castles (Apr-Oct, daily; Mar, wkends). Guided tours. 7 mi S on US 68 to West Liberty, then 1 mi E on OH 245. Phone 937/465-2821. ¢¢

Skiing. Mad River Mountain Ski Resort. Five chairlifts, T-bar, three rope tows; patrol, school, rentals, snowmaking; lodge, cafeteria, bar. Slopes (1,000-3,000 ft). (Dec-Mar, daily) 5 mi SE on US 33 at 1000 Snow Valley Rd. Phone 937/599-1015.

Zane Caverns. Illuminated stalactites, stalagmites; display of cave pearls; guided tour. Gift shop. (May-Sept, daily; rest of yr, Wed-Sun) 7092 OH 540. Phone 937/592-9592. ¢¢¢ Also here is

> **Southwind Park.** Swimming pond; hiking trails, picnicking, playground, cabins, camping (fee). Pets (on leash). Contact Zane Caverns. Phone 937/592-9592. ¢

Special Event

Logan County Fair. Harness racing. Mid-late July. Phone 937/599-4227.

Motel/Motor Lodge

★ **COMFORT INN.** *260 Northview Dr (43311). 937/599-5555; fax 937/599-2300; toll-free 800/589-3666. www. comfortinn.com.* 73 rms, 2 story. S, D $99-$125; each addl $5; suites $105-$130; under 18 free. Crib free. Pet accepted; $10. TV; cable (premium), VCR avail (movies). Heated pool. Complimentary continental bkfst. Restaurant nearby. Bar; entertainment. Ck-out noon. Coin lndry. Meeting rms. In-rm modem link. Sundries. Downhill ski 8 mi. Exercise equipt. Some refrigerators, microwaves. Cr cds: A, C, D, DS, MC, V.
🅳 🐾 🏊 🐾 🔥 👤 ✖

Bellevue

(B-4) *See also Fremont, Milan, Sandusky*

Settled 1815 **Pop** 8,146 **Elev** 751 ft
Area code 419 **Zip** 44811
Information Bellevue Area Tourism & Visitors Bureau, PO Box 63; 419/483-5359 or 800/562-6978
Web www.bellevuetourism.org

What to See and Do

Historic Lyme Village. The John Wright Victorian mansion is featured with several other buildings that have been moved here and restored to create village depicting 19th-century life. (June-Aug, Tues-Sun; May and Sept, wkends only) Several events throughout the yr. 2 mi E on OH 113. Phone 419/483-4949. ¢¢

Mad River and NKP Railroad Society Museum. Display of various old railroad cars, artifacts; gift shop. (Memorial Day-Labor Day, daily; May and Sept-Oct, wkends only) 253 S West St. Phone 419/483-2222. **Donation**

Seneca Caverns. One of Ohio's largest natural caverns, it is actually a unique "earth crack," created by undetermined geologic forces. Registered Natural Landmark. Eight rms on seven levels; Old Mist'ry River flows at lowest level (110 ft); electrically lighted. One-hr guided tours; constant temperature of 54°F. Pan for gemstones and minerals (fee). (Memorial Day-Labor Day, daily; May and Sept-mid-Oct, wkends only). 3 mi S on OH 269, then 2 mi W on Thompson Township Rd 178. Phone 419/483-6711. ¢¢¢

Motel/Motor Lodge

★ ★ **BEST WESTERN BELLEVUE RESORT INN.** *1120 E Main St (44811). 419/483-5740; fax 419/483-5566; toll-free 800/528-1234. www. bestwestern.com.* 83 rms, 1-2 story. Late June-early Sept: S, D $53-$109; each addl $4; suites $135-$250; higher rates wkends; lower rates rest of yr. Crib $10. TV; cable (premium). 2 pools, 1 indoor; whirlpool. Restaurant 6 am-9 pm. Bar. Ck-out 11 am. Coin lndry. Meeting rms. Sundries.

Sauna. Refrigerators; microwaves avail. Cr cds: A, C, D, DS, MC, V.

D ☒ ☒ SC ☒

Restaurant

★★ **MCCLAIN'S.** *137 E Main St (44811). 419/483-2727.* Hrs: 11 am-10 pm. Closed Sun; some major hols. Bar. Lunch, dinner $3.25-$13. Child's menu. Specializes in barbecued ribs, steak, seafood. Old-time decor. Family-owned since 1880. Cr cds: MC, V.

D ☒

Bowling Green

(B-3) *See also Findlay, Fremont, Toledo*

Founded 1834 **Pop** 28,176 **Elev** 705 ft
Area code 419 **Zip** 43402
Information Chamber of Commerce, 163 N Main St, PO Box 31; 419/353-7945 or 800/866-0046
Web www.visitbgohio.org

Surrounded by rich farmland, Bowling Green is an educational center with diversified industries. It is also the seat of Wood County.

What to See and Do

Bowling Green State University. (1910) 18,000 students. Attractive 1,300-acre campus. Undergraduate colleges of arts and sciences, education, health and human services, music, business administration, and technology; graduate college. A golf course and an all-yr ice-skating arena are open to the public (fees). E Wooster St, just W of I-75. Phone 419/372-2531. Located on campus is

   The Educational Memorabilia Center. (1875) Restored one-rm schoolhouse and memorabilia collection; more than 1,500 items reminiscent of education's past, such as desks, slates, inkwells, McGuffey's Readers, maps, globes; potbellied stove and 100-yr-old pump organ. (Sat and Sun afternoons; wkdays, by appt; closed hols and school breaks). 900 blk of E Wooster. Phone 419/372-7405. **FREE**

Mary Jane Thurston State Park. A 555-acre park. Fishing, boating (unlimited horsepower, dock, launch); hunting, hiking, sledding, picnicking (shelter), tent camping. Standard fees. 4 mi NW on OH 64, then 8 mi W on OH 65, near Napoleon. Phone 419/832-7662.

Special Events

Wood County Fair. County Fairgrounds. Agricultural and livestock shows, displays, rides and concessions. Early Aug. Phone 419/353-7945.

National Tractor Pulling Championship. World's largest outdoor pull held at Wood County Fairgrounds. Phone 419/354-1434. Mid-Aug.

Motel/Motor Lodge

★ **DAYS INN.** *1550 E Wooster St (43402). 419/352-5211; fax 419/354-8030; res 800/329-7466. www.daysinn. com.* 100 rms, 2 story. S $45-$53; D $54-$58; each addl $6; under 18 free; higher rates special events. Crib free. Pet accepted. TV; cable (premium). Complimentary continental bkfst. Complimentary coffee in rms. Ck-out 11 am. Some in-rm whirlpools; refrigerators, microwaves avail. Cr cds: A, C, D, DS, MC, V.

D ☒ ☒ ☒

Restaurants

★ **JUNCTION.** *110 N Main St (43402). 419/352-9222.* Hrs: 11 am-10 pm; Sat to 11 pm; Sun to 9 pm. Closed Easter, Thanksgiving, Dec 25. Res accepted. Mexican, Amer menu. Bar. Lunch $1.99-$6.45, dinner $1.99-$12.95. Child's menu. Specializes in appetizers, steak, vegetarian entrees. Cr cds: A, D, DS, MC, V.

D ☒

★★ **KAUFMAN'S.** *163 S Main St (43402). 419/352-2595.* Hrs: 11-12:30 am. Closed Sun; major hols. Res accepted. Bar to 1 am. Lunch $3-$7.50, dinner $5-$26.45. Buffet: dinner (Fri, Sat) $14.95. Child's menu. Specializes in steak, seafood, prime rib. Salad bar. Family-owned. Cr cds: A, D, MC, V.

D ☒

Brecksville

See also Beachwood, Cleveland

Pop 11,818 **Elev** 900 ft **Area code** 440
Zip 44141
Information Chamber of Commerce,
4450 Oakes Rd; 440/526-7350

The suburb Brecksville is located
approximately nine miles south of
Cleveland and is adjacent to the
Cuyahoga Valley National Recreation
Area.

Motels/Motor Lodges

★★ **COMFORT INN.** *6191 Quarry
Ln, Independence (44131). 216/328-
7777; fax toll-free 800/638-7949.
www.comfortinn.com.* 90 rms, 3 story.
June-Aug: S $60-$72; D $68-$80;
under 18 free; lower rates rest of yr.
TV; cable; VCR (movies $4). Pool.
Complimentary continental bkfst.
Restaurant adj 6 am-10 pm. Ck-out
noon. Meeting rms. Business servs
avail. Sundries. Health club privileges. Cr cds: A, C, D, DS, MC, V.
🄳 ➰ 🔄 🔥 SC

★★★ **FOUR POINTS BY SHERA-
TON.** *5300 Rockside Rd, Independence
(44131). 216/524-0700; fax 216/524-
6477; toll-free 800/325-3535. www.
sheraton.com.* 179 rms, 5 story. S, D
$69-$169; each addl $10; under 18
free. Crib free. TV; cable (premium),
VCR avail. Indoor/outdoor pool;
whirlpool. Restaurant 6:30 am-10
pm; Fri, Sat to 11 pm. Bar 11:30-1
am; Fri, Sat to 2 am; Sun 1-11 pm;
entertainment Sat. Ck-out 11 am.
Meeting rms. Business servs avail. In-
rm modem link. Lighted tennis. Free
airport transportation. Sauna. Health
club privileges. Luxury level. Cr cds:
A, C, D, DS, MC, V.
🄳 🏌 ➰ 🔄 🔥 SC

★★ **HOLIDAY INN.** *6001 Rockside
Rd, Independence (44131). 216/524-
8050; fax 216/524-9280; toll-free
800/465-4329. www.hiclevelandand
south-independence.com.* 364 rms, 5
story. S $99-$139; under 19 free. Crib
free. TV; cable (premium), VCR avail.
Indoor pool. Sauna. Coffee in rms.
Restaurant 6:30 am-10 pm. Rm serv.
Bar 11-2 am; entertainment exc Sun.
Ck-out noon. Coin lndry. Convention facilities. Business servs avail.

Bellhops. Valet serv. Gift shop. Free
airport transportation. Cr cds: A, C,
D, DS, MC, V.
🄳 ➰ ✈ 🔄 🔥

Hotel

★★★ **HILTON.** *6200 Quarry Ln,
Independence (44131). 216/447-0020;
fax 216/447-1300; toll-free 800/445-
8667.* 195 rms, 5 story. S $119-$149;
each addl $12; wkend, family rates.
Crib free. Pet accepted, some restrictions. TV; cable. Indoor/outdoor
pool; whirlpool, poolside serv (summer), lifeguard. Playground. Coffee
in rms. Restaurant 6 am-10 pm; Fri,
Sat to 11 pm. Rm serv. Entertainment. Ck-out noon. Meeting rms.
Business servs avail. In-rm modem
link. Bellhops. Gift shop. Free airport
transportation. Tennis. Exercise
equipt; sauna. Cr cds: A, DS, MC, V.
🄳 ➰ 🏌 ✈ 🔄 🔥 SC 🏌

Restaurant

★★ **MARCO POLO'S.** *8188
Brecksville Rd (44141). 440/526-6130.
www.marcopoloscleveland.com.* Hrs:
11:30 am-10 pm; Fri to midnight; Sat
4 pm-midnight; Sun 9:30 am-9 pm.
Closed Dec 25. Res accepted. Italian
menu. Bar to 2:30 am; Sun 1 pm-
midnight. Lunch $5.99-$8.95, dinner
$7.95-$19.95. Specializes in pasta.
Entertainment Fri, Sat. Former stagecoach stop, built 1800s. Beamed ceilings with large iron chandeliers. Cr
cds: A, C, D, DS, MC, V.
🄳 🔄

Cambridge

(D-6) *See also Gnadenhutten, Zanesville*

Founded 1806 **Pop** 11,748 **Elev** 886 ft
Area code 740 **Zip** 43725
Information Visitors & Convention
Bureau, 2146 Southgate Pkwy, PO
Box 427, 740/432-2022 or 800/933-
5480
Web www.visitguernseycounty.com

Cambridge, an important center for
the glassmaking industry, was named
by early settlers who came from the
English Isle of Guernsey. At one time
a center of mining and oil, it is

located at the crossroads of three major federal highways.

What to See and Do

The Cambridge Glass Museum. More than 5,000 pieces of Cambridge glass and pottery made between 1902-1954. (June-Oct, Mon-Sat; closed hols) 812 Jefferson Ave. Phone 740/432-3045. ¢

Degenhart Paperweight and Glass Museum. Large collection of Midwestern pattern glass, Cambridge glass, and Degenhart paperweights. Gift shop. (Apr-Dec, daily; rest of yr, Mon-Fri; closed major hols) 65323 Highland Hills Rd; E on US 22, to Highland Hills Rd at intersection of US 22 and I-77. Phone 740/432-2626. ¢

Industrial tours.

Boyd's Crystal Art Glass. Glass factory and showrm; glass from molten form to finished product. Tours of factory (Mon-Fri; closed hols) and showrm (Mon-Fri; closed hols). 1203 Morton Ave. Phone 740/439-2077. **FREE**

Mosser Glass. Glass-making tours; gift shop. (Mon-Fri; closed hols; also first two wks July, last wk Dec) US 22 E, ½ mi W via I-77 exit 47. Phone 740/439-1827. **FREE**

Muskingum Watershed Conservancy District. Seneca Lake Park. A 3,550-acre lake offers swimming, fishing, boating (299-hp limit), marina; playground, Class A tent and trailer sites at marina and park (daily; hookups). Pets on leash. 9 mi S on I-77, then 7 mi E on OH 313, then 2 mi S on OH 574 to park entrance. Phone 740/685-6013. ¢¢

Salt Fork State Park. A 20,181-acre park with swimming, fishing, boating (rentals, docks, marina); hiking trails, golf, picnicking (shelter), concession, tent and trailer sites, cabins (res accepted), lodge. Standard fees. 9 mi NE off US 22. Phone 740/439-2751.

Special Events

The Living Word Outdoor Drama. On S OH 209 W, at 6010 College Hill Rd. Ohio's Passion Play in outdoor amphitheater retells the life of Jesus Christ. Phone 740/439-2761. Mid-June-early Sept, Thurs-Sat.

Salt Fork Arts and Crafts Festival. City Park. Early Aug. Phone 740/439-6688.

Motels/Motor Lodges

★ ★ **BEST WESTERN.** *1945 Southgate Pkwy (43725). 740/439-3581; fax 740/439-1824; toll-free 800/528-1234. www.bestwestern.com.* 95 rms, 2 story. Mid-May-mid-Sept: S, D $69-$110; under 18 free; higher rates special events; lower rates rest of yr. Crib $1. Pet accepted. TV; cable, VCR avail (movies). Pool. Coffee in rms. Restaurant nearby. Bar 11-2 am. Ck-out 11 am. Business servs avail. In-rm modem link. Cr cds: A, C, D, DS, MC, V.

D ⤷ ≈ ⊠ 🔥

★ **DAYS INN.** *2328 Southgate Pkwy (43725). 740/432-5691; fax 740/432-3526; res 800/329-7466. www.daysinn.com.* 102 rms, 4 story. May-Nov: S, D $79-$110; each addl $6; under 12 free; lower rates rest of yr. Crib free. TV; cable (premium). Complimentary continental bkfst. Ck-out 11 am. Meeting rms. Business servs avail. Valet serv (Mon-Fri). Health club privileges. Outdoor pool. Some refrigerators, microwaves. Cr cds: A, C, D, DS, MC, V.

D ≈ ⊠ 🔥 SC

★ ★ **HOLIDAY INN.** *2248 Southgate Pkwy (43725). 740/432-7313; fax 740/432-2337; toll-free 800/465-4329. www.holiday-inn.com.* 108 rms, 2 story. May-Nov: S, D $62-$79; under 18 free; lower rates rest of yr. Crib free. Pet accepted. TV; cable. Pool. Restaurant 6 am-10 pm; Sat, Sun 7 am-11 pm. Rm serv. Bar 4 pm-midnight, Sun 5-10 pm. Ck-out noon. Coin lndry. Meeting rms. Business servs avail. In-rm modem link. Health club privileges. Cr cds: A, C, D, DS, JCB, MC, V.

D ⤷ ≈ ⊠ 🔥 SC

★ **TRAVELODGE.** *8777 Georgetown Rd (43725). 740/432-7375; fax 740/432-5808; toll-free 800/578-7878. www.travelodge.com.* 48 rms, 2 story. May-Oct: S, D $72-$77; each addl $5; under 18 free; lower rates rest of yr. Crib free. TV; cable. Heated pool; whirlpool. Sauna. Complimentary coffee in rms. Restaurant adj 6 am-10 pm. Ck-out noon. Business servs avail. Health club privileges. Some balconies. Cr cds: A, C, D, DS, MC, V.

D ⊠ 🐾 SC 🏊

Resort

★★ **SALT FORK RESORT & CONFERENCE CENTER.** *OH 22, 70 & 77 (43725). 740/439-2751; fax 740/432-6615; toll-free 800/282-7275. www. saltforkresort.com.* 148 rms in lodge, 3 story, 54 2-bedrm kit. cottages. No A/C, no rm phones in cottages. S, D $93-$118; each addl $5; cottages $120-$145 ($650-$850/wk); under 18 free; wkly rates; golf plans. Crib free. TV; cable; VCR avail (movies). 2 pools, 1 indoor; wading pool, poolside serv. Playground. Dining rm 7-11 am, noon-2 pm, 5-8 pm. Snack bar. Bar 5-9 pm. Ck-out noon (lodge), 10 am (cottages). Coin lndry. Meeting rooms. Business servs avail. Gift shop. Lighted tennis. 18-hole golf, greens fee $14-$17.50, pro. Exercise equipt; sauna. Marina; canoes, motorboats, rowboats, sailboats. Hiking trails. Game rm. Rec rm. Lawn games. Some refrigerators. Private patios, balconies. Picnic tables. Cr cds: A, D, DS, MC, V.

D 🛶 🎿 🎱 🎣 🏊 🏕 ⊠ 🔥

Restaurants

★ **THE FORUM.** *2205 Southgate Pkwy (43725). 740/439-2777. www. theobros.com.* Hrs: 11 am-10 pm; Fri, Sat to 11 pm. Closed major hols. Res accepted. Bar. Lunch $3.99-$6.95, dinner $5.95-$15.95. Child's menu. Specializes in pasta, steaks, pizza. Parking. Casual contemporary dining; some etched glass, marquee lights. Cr cds: A, D, MC, V.

D 🍴

★ **THEO'S.** *632 Wheeling Ave (43725). 740/432-3878.* Hrs: 9 am-9 pm. Closed Sun; major hols. Res accepted. Bar. Bkfst $1.95-$4.95, lunch $2.95-$5.95, dinner $4.25-$11.95. Specializes in home-cooked meals, pies. Street parking. Family, casual dining. Family-owned since 1932. Cr cds: A, D, DS, MC, V.

D 🍴

Canton

(C-6) *See also Akron, Alliance, Massillon, New Philadelphia, Wooster*

Settled 1805 **Pop** 84,161 **Elev** 1,060 ft **Area code** 330
Information Canton/Stark County Convention & Visitors Bureau, 229 Wells Ave NW, 44703-2642; 330/454-1439 or 800/533-4302
Web www.visitcantonohio.com

John Saxton, grandfather of Mrs. William McKinley, first published the still-circulating *Ohio Repository* (*The Repository* today) in 1815. In 1867 William McKinley opened a law office in the town, and in 1896 conducted his "front porch campaign" for the presidency. After his assassination, his body was brought back to Canton for burial. Because of his love for the red carnation, it was made the state flower.

This large steel-processing city, important a century ago for farm machinery, is in the middle of rich farmland, on the edge of "steel valley" where the three branches of Nimishillen Creek come together. It is one of the largest producers of specialty steels in the world.

What to See and Do

Canton Classic Car Museum. Collection of antique, classic cars; fire pumper; police bandit car; cars of '50s and '60s; restoration shop; memorabilia, period fashions, advertising, nostalgia, and popular culture. (Daily; closed Easter, Thanksgiving, Dec 25) Market Ave at 6th Ave SW. Phone 330/455-3603. ¢¢

The Canton Cultural Center for the Arts. Center is the hub of the arts in Canton, incl the Canton Ballet, Canton Museum of Art (Tues-Sun), Canton Civic Opera, Canton Symphony Orchestra, and Player's Guild of Canton. (Mon-Fri) Phone 330/627-4096.

Canton Garden Center. Tulips, daffodils, peonies, chrysanthemums; five senses garden; JFK memorial fountain with continuous flame (daily). Garden Center (Tues-Fri).

1615 Stadium Park NW, in Stadium Park. Phone 330/455-6172. **FREE**

Harry London Chocolate Factory. Tours (Mon-Sat). (Closed Sun, hols) 5353 Lauby Rd. Phone 330/494-0833. ¢

Hoover Historical Center. Hoover farmhouse restored to Victorian era; boyhood home of W. H. Hoover, founder of the Hoover Company. One of the most extensive antique vacuum cleaner collections in the world; memorabilia reflecting the growth and development of the company and the industry; changing exhibits; herb gardens. Tours. (Tues-Sun; closed hols) 1875 Easton St NW, in North Canton. Phone 330/499-0287. **FREE**

McKinley National Memorial. Tomb, statue of McKinley; panoramic view of city. McKinley Monument Dr NW. (Daily) Adj is

    McKinley Museum of History, Science and Industry. (1963) McKinley memorabilia; **Discover World**, an interactive science center; Historical Hall; Street of Shops. (Daily; planetarium shows Sat and Sun; closed hols) 800 McKinley Monument Dr NW. Phone 330/455-7043. ¢¢¢

⭐ **Pro Football Hall of Fame.** (1963) Museum, a five-building complex, dedicated to the game and its players; memorabilia; research library;

movie theater; museum store. (Daily; closed Dec 25) (See SPECIAL EVENT). 2121 George Halas Dr NW, N of Fawcett Stadium, adj to I-77. Phone 330/456-8207. ¢¢¢

Waterworks Park. Picnic facilities (tables, cooking stoves, shelter), playground. Between Tuscarawas St W and 7th St NW. Phone 330/489-3015.

Special Event

Pro Football Hall of Fame Festival. Pro Football Hall of Fame. Events incl parade, induction ceremony, AFC-NFC Hall of Fame Pro Game. Early Aug. Phone 330/456-8207.

Motels/Motor Lodges

★★ **COMFORT INN.** *5345 Broadmoor Cir NW (44709). 330/492-1331; fax 330/492-9093; toll-free 800/228-5150. www.comfortinn-canton.com.* 124 rms, 3 story. S $69-$106; D $79-$116; each addl $10; under 18 free; wkend rates; golf plans; higher rates Hall of Fame wk. Crib free. TV; cable (premium). Pool. Complimentary continental bkfst. Restaurant nearby. Ck-out noon. Meeting rms. Business servs avail. In-rm modem link. Valet serv. Health club privileges. Cr cds: A, C, D, DS, MC, V.

D ⊠ ⊠ 🔥

Pro Football Hall of Fame

★★★ **FOUR POINTS BY SHERATON.** *4375 Metro Cir NW (44720). 330/494-6494; fax 330/494-7129; toll-free 877/867-7666. www.fourpoints.com.* 152 rms, 6 story. S $85-$112; D $89-$122; each addl $10; suites $125-$250; under 18 free; higher rates Hall of Fame wkend. Crib free. TV; cable (premium). Indoor/outdoor pool; poolside serv. Restaurant 6:30 am-10 pm. Rm serv. Bar 1 pm-2 am; Sun noon-midnight. Ck-out noon. Meeting rms. Business center. Bellhops. Valet serv. Free airport transportation. Exercise equipt; sauna. Game rm. Some refrigerators. Cr cds: A, C, D, DS, MC, V.

⊡ ⊵ 🛉 ✕ ⊵ 🐾 SC 🛉

★★ **HAMPTON INN.** *5335 Broadmoor Cir NW (44709). 330/492-0151; fax 330/492-7523; res 800/426-7866. www.hamptoninn.com.* 107 rms, 4 story. S $71-$79; D $75-$85; under 18 free; golf packages; higher rates special events. Crib free. TV; cable. Complimentary continental bkfst. Restaurant nearby. Ck-out noon. Meeting rms. In-rm modem link. Valet serv. Health club privileges. Game rm. Cr cds: A, D, DS, MC, V.

⊡ ⊵ 🐾 SC

★★ **HOLIDAY INN CANTON.** *4520 Everhard Rd NW (44718). 330/494-2770; fax 330/494-6473; toll-free 800/465-4329. www.holiday-inn.com* 194 rms, 2-3 story. S, D $84-$91; each addl $8; suites $179; under 19 free; higher rates Hall of Fame wkend. Crib free. Pet accepted. TV. Pool; poolside serv. Restaurant 6:30 am-10 pm; Sun from 7 am. Rm serv. Bar 2 pm-2:30 am; entertainment. Ck-out noon. Meeting rms. Business servs avail. In-rm modem link. Free airport transportation. Exercise equipt. Health club privileges. Cr cds: A, MC, V.

⊡ 🐕 ⊵ 🐾 SC ⊷ 🛉

★ **RED ROOF INN.** *5353 Inn Circle Ct NW, North Canton (44720). 330/499-1970; fax 330/499-1975; toll-free 800/733-7663. www.redroof.com.* 108 rms, 2 story. S $53-$61; D $61-$67; each addl $7; under 18 free. Crib free. Pet accepted. TV. Restaurant adj 6 am-10 pm. Ck-out noon. Business servs avail. Cr cds: A, C, D, DS, MC, V.

⊡ 🐕 ⊵ 🐾

Hotel

★★★ **HILTON.** *320 S Market Ave (44702). 330/454-5000; fax 330/454-5090; toll-free 800/742-0379. www.hilton.com.* 170 rms, 8 story. S $85-$119; D $95-$129; suites $195-$295; under 18 free. Covered parking $3. TV; cable, VCR avail (movies). Indoor pool; whirlpool. Restaurant 6:30 am-10:30 pm; Sat, Sun from 7 am. Rm serv. Bar 11-2 am. Ck-out noon. Meeting rms. Business servs avail. Gift shop. Free airport transportation. Exercise equipt; sauna. Game rm. Cr cds: A, C, D, DS, MC, V.

⊡ ⊵ 🛉 ✕ ⊵ 🐾 SC

Restaurants

★ **JOHN'S.** *2749 Cleveland Ave (44709). 330/454-1259.* Hrs: 7 am-11 pm; Fri, Sat to midnight. Closed Sun; major hols. Bar. Bkfst $3.50-$5.50, lunch $5.50-$14.50, dinner $8.95-$14.95. Specializes in steak, seafood. Casual decor. Cr cds: A, D, DS, MC, V.

⊵

★★★ **LOLLI'S.** *4801 NW Dressler Rd (44178). 330/492-6846.* Hrs: 11:30 am-2 pm, 5-9 pm; Sat from 5 pm. Closed Sun, Mon; major hols. Res accepted. Italian menu. Bar. Wine list. Lunch, dinner $8.95-$16.95. Specializes in fresh pasta, fish, steaks. Own baking. Family-owned. Cr cds: A, D, MC, V.

⊡ ⊵

Celina

(C-1) See also Van Wert, Wapakoneta

Settled 1834 **Pop** 9,650 **Elev** 876 ft **Area code** 419 **Zip** 45822

Information Celina-Mercer County Chamber of Commerce, 226 N Main St; 419/586-2219

Web www.celinamercer.com

Celina is on Grand Lake, a 17,500-acre man-made lake lined with houses and resorts. The town is a home for metal products, dairying, and wood fabricating industries, and it also attracts anglers and vacationers.

What to See and Do

Grand Lake-St. Marys State Park.
Offers swimming, fishing for panfish
and bass, boating (marina, rentals,
ramps); snowmobiling, picnicking
(shelters), concession, camping. Standard fees. The lake is Ohio's largest
inland lake (15,000 acres). The park
is 7 mi E on OH 703, then follow
park signs. Phone 419/394-2774.

Mercer County Courthouse. Greek
architecture with great bronze doors
opening on halls of marble; dome of
colored glass has near-perfect
acoustics. (Mon-Fri) Main and Market Sts. Phone 419/586-3178. **FREE**

**Mercer County Historical Museum,
the Riley Home.** History of area
depicted by 18th- and 19th-century
artifacts incl Native American, medical, and farm; also pioneer home
furniture displays. (Wed-Fri, Sun) 130
E Market St. Phone 419/586-6065.
FREE

Special Event

Celina Lake Festival. At jct US 127
and OH 29. Antique car show,
parade, triathlon, arts and crafts
show, fireworks. Usually late July.
Phone 419/586-2219.

Motel/Motor Lodge

★★ **COMFORT INN.** *1421 SR 703 E
(45822). 419/586-4656; fax 419/586-
4152; toll-free 800/638-7949. www.
comfortinn.com.* 40 rms, 1-2 story. S
$59-$84; D $69-$84; each addl $6;
suite $85-$159; kit. units $57-$59;
under 18 free; higher rates special
events. Crib $5. TV; cable (premium).
Complimentary continental bkfst.
Restaurant adj 11 am-10 pm. Ck-out
11 am. Sundries. Microwaves avail.
Cr cds: A, C, D, DS, MC, V.
D ⊠ 🐾 SC

Chardon

(B-6) *See also Aurora, Cleveland, Mentor,
Painesville*

Pop 4,446 **Elev** 1,225 ft
Area code 440 **Zip** 44024

Information Chardon Area Chamber
of Commerce, 112 E Park St;
440/285-9050

What to See and Do

**Geauga County Historical Society-
Century Village.** Restored 19th-
century Western Reserve village with
homes, shops, school, country store.
All original with period furnishings
(1798-1875). (May-Oct, Tues-Sun;
Mar-Apr and Nov-Dec 24, Sat and
Sun; closed Easter, Thanksgiving)
Museum and country store (Mar-Dec
24). 8 mi S on OH 44 then 3 mi E on
OH 87, at 14653 E Park St in Burton.
Phone 440/834-1492. ¢¢

Materials Park Geodesic Dome. An
11-story latticework of aluminum
tubing designed by R. Buckminster
Fuller; world headquarters of ASM
International; mineral garden with
more than 75 ore specimens. (Daily)
10 mi S on OH 44, then 6 mi W on
OH 87. Phone 440/338-5151. **FREE**

Punderson State Park. A 990-acre
park with a 90-acre lake. Swimming,
fishing, boating (rentals); hiking,
golf, winter sports area, snowmobiling, camping, cabins, lodge (pool,
summer), snack bar. Standard fees.
(Daily) 10 mi S via OH 44, then W 1
mi on OH 87. Phone 440/564-2279.
FREE

Special Event

Geauga County Maple Festival.
Demonstrations of making syrup,
candy, cream, and other maple products; beard and ax-throwing contests;
entertainment. Phone 440/286-3007.
Wkend after Easter.

Restaurants

★★ **BASS LAKE TAVERN.** *426 South
St (44024). 440/285-3100.* Hrs: 11:30
am-2:30 pm, 5-10 pm; Sun 5-9 pm;
early-bird dinner Mon-Fri 5-6:30 pm.
Closed major hols. Res accepted. Bar.
Lunch $8-$15, dinner $15-$24. Specializes in chops and steaks, game,
seafood. Entertainment Fri, Sat. Outdoor dining. Casual country atmosphere. Cr cds: A, D, DS, MC, V.
D ⊟

★★ **THE INN AT FOWLER'S MILL.**
*10700 Mayfield Rd (44024). 440/286-
3111.* Hrs: 11:30 am-2:30 pm, 5:30-

9:30 pm; Fri, Sat 5:30-10:30 pm; Sun 10 am-2:30 pm. Closed Mon. Res accepted; required hols. Closed major hols. Continental menu. Bar to 4:30-11 pm; Fri, Sat to midnight. Lunch, dinner $4.95-15.95. Child's menu. Specializes in fresh seafood, steaks. Outdoor dining. Cr cds: A, D, DS, MC, V.

D ➘

Chillicothe (F-4)

Settled 1796 **Pop** 21,923 **Elev** 620 ft
Area code 740 **Zip** 45601
Information Ross-Chillicothe Convention & Visitors Bureau, 25 E Main St, PO Box 353, phone; 740/702-7677 or 800/413-4118
Web www.chillicotheohio.com/rccvb

Chillicothe, first capital of the Northwest Territory, became the first capital of Ohio in 1803. Among the early settlers from Virginia who were active in achieving statehood for Ohio were Edward Tiffin, first state governor, and Thomas Worthington, governor and US senator. The Greek Revival mansions which today give Paint Street its character were built for the pioneer statesmen.

On the west side of Scioto River Valley, 45 miles south of the present capital, Chillicothe is quite industrialized, though still fringed by wheat fields. Papermaking, begun in the early 1800s, is still an essential industry here. Just east of town is Mount Logan, which is pictured on the State Seal.

What to See and Do

Franklin House. This 1907 Prairie-style home houses museum devoted primarily to the women of Ross County; rotating exhibits of period costumes and accessories, coverlets, quilts and linens, decorative arts. 80 S Paint St. Phone 740/772-1936. ¢

Hopewell Culture National Historical Park. At this site are 23 prehistoric Hopewell burial mounds (200 B.C. to A.D. 500), concentrated within a 13-acre area surrounded by an earthwall. Self-guided trails; wayside exhibits. Visitor center with museum exhibits (daily; closed Jan 1, Thanks-giving, Dec 25). W bank of Scioto River, 4 mi N on OH 104. Phone 740/774-1125. ¢¢

James M. Thomas Telecommunication Museum. Collection of documents and equipt depicting evolution of modern phone sytem. (Mon-Fri) Phone 740/772-8200. **FREE**

Knoles Log Home. This simple two-story log home (1800-1825) features open-hearth cooking, kitchen garden, early household utensils and tools; also on-site demonstrations (seasonal). 39 W 5th St. Phone 740/772-1936. ¢ Also here is

Ross County Historical Society Museum. Housed in an 1838 Federal-style home, museum features two floors of exhibits, antiques, furnishings, pioneer crafts, and toys. Incl Ohio's first capital exhibit, Civil War Room, Indian Room, and Camp Sherman Room. Tours; inquire for schedule. (Apr-Aug, Tues-Sun afternoons; Sept-Dec, Sat and Sun afternoons) 45 W 5th St. Phone 740/772-1936. ¢¢

Paint Creek State Park. Large lake offers swimming, fishing, boating (ramp, rentals); hiking, bridle trails, x-country skiing, camping (tent rentals). Paint Creek Pioneer Farm; living history program, summer programs. Standard fees. 25 mi W off US 50 in Bainbridge. Phone 937/365-1401.

Seip Mound State Memorial. Prehistoric burial mound, 250 ft long and 30 ft high, surrounded by smaller mounds and earthworks. Exhibit pavilion; picnicking. (Daily) 14 mi SW on S side of US 50. This archaeological site is operated by the Ohio Historical Society. Phone 740/297-2630. **FREE**

Seven Caves. A natural attraction of seven caves centered on self-guided walk along trails winding up and down the sides of cliffs, into canyons and gorges; rock formations; wooded park. Picnic area, snack bar. (Daily) 15 mi E of Hillsboro on US 50. Phone 937/365-1283. ¢¢

Yoctangee Park. Swimming pool (fee), 12-acre lake. Six tennis courts, basketball and volleyball courts, softball diamonds, picnicking facilities, playground. Yoctangee Blvd and Riverside St. Phone 740/702-7677. **FREE**

Special Events

Feast of the Flowering Moon. Downtown. Native American, frontier, and early American feast featuring Native American demonstrations and encampment, crafts, and parade. Phone 740/702-7677. Memorial Day wkend.

Tecumseh! Sugarloaf Mtn Amphitheater, 5 mi NE off US 23, OH 159 N exit. Epic outdoor drama depicts the struggle of Tecumseh, the legendary Shawnee warrior who nearly united all the Native American nations. Museum, open-air restaurant, backstage tours. Phone 740/775-0700 (after Mar 1). Nightly Mon-Sat. Mid-June-early Sept.

Fall Festival of Leaves. 19 mi W on US 50, in Bainbridge. Arts and crafts demonstrations, entertainment; scenic self-guided tours. Phone 740/634-2085. Third wkend Oct.

Motels/Motor Lodges

★★ **COMFORT INN.** *20 N Plaza Blvd (45601). 740/775-3500; fax 740/775-3588; toll-free 800/542-7919. www.comfortinn.com.* 106 rms, 2 story. S, D $70-$75; each addl $5; suites $85-$90; under 18 free. Crib free. Pet accepted. TV; cable. Heated pool. Complimentary continental bkfst. Coffee in rms. Restaurant nearby. Bar; entertainment Fri, Sat. Ck-out noon. Meeting rms. Business servs avail. Valet serv. Health club privileges. Cr cds: A, C, D, DS, MC, V.
⊡ 🐾 ⊠ ⊠ 🔥

★ **COUNTRY HEARTH INN.** *1135 E Main St (45601). 740/775-2500; res 888/395-4289. www.countryhearth. com.* 58 rms. S, D $51-$99; each addl $6; under 18 free. TV. Pool. Coffee in rms. Restaurant opp 6 am-11 pm. Ck-out noon. Meeting rm. Business servs avail. Cr cds: A, C, D, DS, MC, V.
⊠ 🐾 SC

★ **DAYS INN.** *1250 N Bridge St (45601). 740/775-7000; fax 740/773-1622; toll-free 800/329-7466. www. daysinn.com.* 42 rms, 2 story. June-Sept: S, D $60-$70; under 19 free; lower rates rest of yr. Crib free. Pet accepted. TV; cable (premium). Heated pool; poolside serv. Complimentary full bkfst. Complimentary

coffee in rms. Restaurant 6 am-2 pm, 4-9 pm; Sun 7 am-2 pm; Sun brunch 10 am-2 pm. Rm serv. Bar 4 pm-2 am; closed Sun; entertainment Fri, Sat. Ck-out noon. Coin lndry. Meeting rms. Business servs avail. Valet serv. Cr cds: A, C, D, DS, MC, V.
⊡ 🐾 ⊠ 🔥 SC ⊠

★★★ **HAMPTON INN & SUITES.** *100 N Plaza Blvd (45601). 740/773-1616; fax 740/773-1770; toll-free 800/426-7866. www.christopherhotels. com.* 71 rms, 15 with shower only, 3 story, 22 suites. June-Sept: S, D $89; suites $95-$135; under 18 free; wkend rates; rodeo 2-day min; higher rates rodeo; lower rates rest of yr. Crib free. Pet accepted; $150 (nonrefundable). TV; cable (premium), VCR avail. Complimentary continental bkfst. Complimentary coffee in rms. Restaurant adj 11 am-10 pm. Ck-out noon. Meeting rms. Business center. In-rm modem link. Valet serv (Mon-Fri). Gift shop. Coin lndry. Exercise equipt; sauna. Indoor pool; whirlpool. Refrigerator, microwave in suites. Grills. Cr cds: A, C, D, DS, MC, V.
⊡ 🐾 ⊠ 🏋 ⊠ 🔥 SC 🏃

★★ **HOLIDAY INN EXPRESS.** *1003 East Main St (45601). 740/779-2424; fax 740/779-2425; toll-free 866/669-6668. www.holiday-inn.com.* 60 rms, 3 story. S $71-$91; D $77-$97; each addl $6; suites $128-$138; under 18 free; higher rates special events. Crib free. TV; cable (premium). Complimentary continental bkfst. Complimentary coffee in rms. Restaurant adj 6 am-10 pm. Ck-out noon. Meeting rms. Business servs avail. In-rm modem link. Valet serv. Coin lndry. Indoor pool. Cr cds: A, C, D, DS, MC, V.
⊡ ⊠ ⊠ 🔥

Restaurant

★ **DAMON'S.** *10 N Plaza Blvd (45601). 740/775-8383. www.damons. com.* Hrs: 11 am-10 pm; Fri, Sat to 11 pm; Sun to 9 pm. Closed major hols. Res accepted Sun-Thurs. Bar. Lunch $4.99-$6.99, dinner $6.99-$16.99. Child's menu. Specializes in ribs, steak, onion rings. Casual atmosphere. Cr cds: A, D, MC, V.
⊡ SC ⊡

Cincinnati

(F-1) *See also Hamilton, Mason*

Settled 1788 **Pop** 364,040 **Elev** 683 ft
Area code 513
Information Greater Cincinnati Convention & Visitors Bureau, 300 W 6th St, 45202; 800/CINCY-USA
Web www.cincyusa.com

Cincinnati was a bustling frontier riverboat town and one of the largest cities in the nation when poet Henry Wadsworth Longfellow immortalized it as the "queen city of the West." Although other cities farther west have since outstripped it in size, Cincinnati is still the Queen City to its inhabitants and to the many visitors who are rediscovering it. With a wealth of fine restaurants, a redeveloped downtown with Skywalk, its own *Montmartre* (Mount Adams), and the beautiful Ohio River flowing alongside, Cincinnati has a cosmopolitan flavor uniquely its own.

Early settlers chose the site because it was an important river crossroads used by Native Americans. During 1788-1789, three small settlements—Columbia, North Bend, and Losantiville—were founded. In 1790 Arthur St. Clair, governor of the Northwest Territory, changed the name of Losantiville to Cincinnati, in honor of the revolutionary officers' Society of the Cincinnati, and made it the seat of Hamilton County. Despite smallpox, insects, floods, and crop failures, approximately 15,000 settlers came in the next five years. They had the protection of General Anthony Wayne, who broke the resistance of the Ohio Native Americans. In the early 1800s a large influx of immigrants, mostly German, settled in the area.

In the 1840s and 1850s Cincinnati boomed as a supplier of produce and goods to the cotton-growing South and great fortunes were accumulated. During the Civil War, the city was generally loyal to the Union, although its location on the Mason-Dixon line and the interruption of its trade from the South caused mixed emotions. After the Civil War,

prosperity brought art, music, a new library, and a professional baseball team. A period of municipal corruption in the late 19th century was ended by a victory for reform elements and the establishment of a city manager form of government, which has earned Cincinnati the title of America's best-governed city.

Today, the city is the home of two universities and several other institutions of higher education and has its own symphony orchestra, opera, and ballet. Cincinnati has also nearly completed a glittering multimillion dollar redevelopment of its downtown area and renovation of its riverfront into an entertainment and recreation center. Major hotels, stores, office complexes, restaurants, entertainment centers, and the Cincinnati Convention Center are now connected by a skywalk system, making the city easily accessible to pedestrians. One can still echo the words of Charles Dickens, who described the city in 1842 as "a place that commends itself...favorably and pleasantly to a stranger."

Additional Visitor Information

The Greater Cincinnati Convention and Visitors Bureau, 300 W 6th St, 45202, phone 800/CINCY-USA, has interesting tourist guides and maps. Visitor information centers are located at 5th and Vine Sts at Fountain Square, and two others are located off southbound I-71 and I-75.

Transportation

Car Rental Agencies. See IMPORTANT TOLL-FREE NUMBERS.

Public Transportation. Bus (Queen City Metro), 513/621-4455.

Rail Passenger Service. Amtrak 800/872-7245.

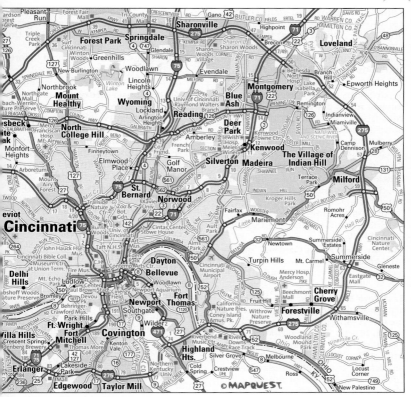

Airport Information

Cincinnati/Northern Kentucky Intl Airport. Information 859/767-3151; 859/767-3495 (lost and found); 513/241-1010 (weather); cash machines, Terminal D.

What to See and Do

Airport Playfield. Baseball fields, 18- and 9-hole golf courses, driving range, miniature golf, tennis courts, paved biking and hiking trails, bike rentals. Land of Make Believe playground with wheelchair-accessible play equipt; jet plane, stagecoach; "Spirit of '76" picnic area. Summer concerts. (May-Sept, daily) Some fees. Beechmont Levee and Wilmer Ave, 8 mi E. Phone 513/321-6500.

Bicentennial Commons at Sawyer Point. Overlooks with different views of the Ohio River; four-mi Riverwalk has geologic river timeline. Performance pavilion and amphitheater. Tennis pavilion with eight courts; skating pavilion; three sand volleyball courts; fitness area with exercise stations. Picnicking, playground. Dining area with umbrella tables. Some fees. On Pete Rose Way, E of The Crown, along Ohio River. Phone 513/352-4000.

Carew Tower. Cincinnati's tallest building (48 stories). Observation tower (Daily; closed hols). 5th and Vine Sts. Phone 513/241-3888. ¢

Cincinnati Fire Museum. Restored firehouse (1907) exhibits firefighting artifacts preserved since 1808; hands-on displays; emphasis on fire prevention. (Tues-Sun; closed hols) 315 W Court St. Phone 513/621-5553. ¢¢

Cincinnati Zoo and Botanical Garden. Features more than 750 species in a variety of naturalistic habitats, incl its world-famous gorillas and white Bengal tigers. Cat House features 16 species of cats; Insect World is a one-of-a-kind exhibit. Jungle Trails exhibit is an indoor/outdoor rain forest. Rare okapi, walrus,

Komodo Dragons, and giant eland are also on display. Participatory children's zoo. Animal shows (summer). Elephant and camel rides. Picnic areas, restaurant. (Daily) 3400 Vine St. Phone 513/281-4701. ¢¢¢¢

City Hall. (1888) Houses many departments of city government. The interior incl a grand marble stairway with historical stained-art glass windows at the landings and murals on the ceiling. (Mon-Fri) 801 Plum St, at 8th St. Phone 513/352-3000.

Civic Garden Center of Greater Cincinnati. Specimen trees; perennials, dwarf evergreens, herbs, raised vegetable gardens; greenhouse; gift shop; library. (Mon-Sat; closed hols) 2715 Reading Rd. Phone 513/221-0981. **FREE**

Contemporary Arts Center. Changing exhibits and performances of recent art. (Daily; closed hols) 115 E 5th St. Phone 513/721-0390. ¢¢

East Fork State Park. This 10,580-acre park incl rugged hills, open meadows, and reservoir. Swimming beach, fishing, boating; hiking (overnight hiking areas with permit from park office) and bridle trails, picnicking, camping. Standard fees. Off OH 125, 4 mi SE of Amelia. Phone 513/734-4323.

Eden Park. More than 185 acres initially called "the Garden of Eden." Ice-skating on Mirror Lake. The Murray Seasongood Pavilion features spring and summer band concerts and other events. Picnicking. Four overlooks with scenic views of Ohio River, city, and Kentucky hillsides. At Gilbert Ave between Elsinore and Morris. Cultural institutions within park incl

Cincinnati Art Museum. Houses paintings, sculpture, prints, photographs, costumes, decorative and tribal arts, and musical instruments, representing most major civilizations for the past 5,000 yrs. Also examples of Cincinnati decorative arts, such as art furniture and Rookwood pottery. Continuous schedule of temporary exhibits. Restaurant, gift shop. (Tues-Sun; closed hols) Tours for the visually impaired (call Education Department for appt). Phone 513/721-5204. ¢¢

Cincinnati Playhouse in the Park. Professional regional theater presenting classic and contemporary plays and musicals on two stages: the Robert S. Marx Theater and the Thompson Shelterhouse. (Sept-July, Tues-Sun) Dinner avail before each performance. 962 Mount Adams Cir. Phone 513/421-3888.

Krohn Conservatory. Floral conservatory of more than 5,000 species of exotic plants, incl a five-story tall indoor rain forest complete with 20-ft waterfall; major collection of unusual epiphytic plants. Individual horticultural houses contain palm, desert, orchid, and tropical collections. Themed flower and garden shows six times annually. Guided tours avail. Gift shop. (Daily; extended hrs for hol shows) Eden Park Dr, 1 mi E via Fort Washington Way and Martin St, or Gilbert Ave. Phone 513/421-5707. **FREE**

Fountain Square Plaza. Center of downtown activity whose focal point is the Tyler Davidson Fountain, cast in Munich, Germany, and erected in Cincinnati in 1871. The sculpture, whose highest point is the open-armed Genius of Water, symbolizes the many values of water. A bandstand pavilion enables lunch hour audiences to enjoy outdoor performances. Horsedrawn carriage tours of downtown also begin at the square.

Hamilton County Courthouse. Good example of adapted Greek Ionic architecture; contains one of America's most complete law libraries. (Mon-Fri; closed hols) 1000 Main St, between Court St and Central Pkwy. Phone 513/946-5879.

Harriet Beecher Stowe Memorial. Author of *Uncle Tom's Cabin* lived here from 1832-1836. Completely restored with some original furnishings. (Tues-Thurs) 2950 Gilbert Ave. Phone 513/632-5120. **Donation**

Hebrew Union College—Jewish Institute of Religion. (1875) 120 students. First institution of Jewish higher learning in the US. Graduate school offers a variety of programs. Klau Library incl Dalsheimer Rare Book Building with rare remnants of Chinese Jewry and collections of Spinoza and Americana. American Jewish Archives Building is dedicated to study and preservation of American Jewish historical records. Archaeological exhibits and Jewish ceremonial objects are in the Skirball Museum Cincinnati Branch. Guided tours (by appt). 3101 Clifton Ave, I-75 Hopple St exit. Phone 513/221-1875.

Heritage Village Museum. A 30-acre historic village recaptures life in southwestern Ohio prior to 1880. Eleven buildings (1804-1880), reconstructed and authentically restored and refurnished. Special exhibits and events; period craft demonstrations; guided tours. (May-Oct, Wed-Sun) N on I-75, E on I-275, exit at US 42 S, then 1 mi S; entrance to Sharon Woods Park on left. Phone 513/563-9484. ¢¢

Historic Loveland Castle. A one-fifth scale, medieval stone castle built by one man over a period of 50 yrs. (Apr-Sept, daily; rest of yr, Sat and Sun; closed Dec 25) 12025 Shore Dr. Phone 513/683-4686. ¢

John Hauck House Museum. Ornate 19th-century stonefront town house in historic district. Restored home contains period furnishings, memorabilia, antique children's toys, special displays. (Fri, last two Sun of month, by appt; also special Christmas hrs; closed hols) 812 Dayton St. Phone 513/721-3570. ¢

Meier's Wine Cellars. Country wine store, tasting rm. 45-min tours (June-Oct, Mon-Sat). 6955 Plainfield Pike, in Silverton; NE on US 22 or N on I-71 exit 10 (Stewart Rd), right on Stewart Rd and follow signs. Phone 513/891-2900. **FREE**

Mount Adams. Mount Adams is the *Montmartre* of Cincinnati: its narrow streets, intimate restaurants, boutiques, and art stores give the area a European flavor. Area directly southwest of Eden Park, on hill overlooking Cincinnati and the Ohio River.

Mount Airy Forest and Arboretum. First municipal reforestation project in the US. More than 1,450 acres incl 800 acres of conifers and hardwoods, 300 acres of native hardwoods, and 241 acres of grasslands. The 120-acre arboretum (guided tours by appt, phone 513/541-8176) incl specialty gardens, floral displays, and extensive plant collections. Area is used by students and amateur and professional gardeners as a testing area for observation of growth, habits, and tolerance of plants. Nature trails, picnic areas, lodges. (Daily) 5083 Col-

erain Ave, 8 mi NW on US 27, off I-75. Phone 513/352-4080. **FREE**

Paramount's Kings Island. (see MASON) 20 mi N on I-71. Phone 513/754-5800.

Professional sports.

  Cincinnati Bengals (NFL). One Paul Brown Stadium. Phone 513/621-3550.

  Cincinnati Reds (MLB). Cinergy Field, 100 Cinergy Field. Phone 513/421-4510.

Public Landing. Where first settlers touched the shore and first log cabin was built. Center of river trade; look for paddlewheelers, Cinergy Field, and six Ohio River bridges to northern Kentucky. Foot of Broadway.

River cruises.

  BB Riverboats. Variety of cruises incl sightseeing, lunch, and dinner cruises (res required), all-day. 1 mi SE via I-75 exit 192, foot of Madison, located at Covington (KY) Landing and Newport Dock on Riverboat Row. Phone 859/261-8500. ¢¢¢

  ***Delta Queen* and *Mississippi Queen*.** Each paddlewheeler, makes 3-8-night cruises on the Ohio, Mississippi, Cumberland, and Tennessee rivers. Phone 800/543-1949.

Scenic drives. On Columbia Pkwy to Ault Park, with views of Ohio River; and on Central Pkwy (US 27) along old Miami-Erie Canal to Mt Airy Forest.

Trailside Nature Center. Discovery center has displays on local birds, mammals, insects, and geology. Wkend nature walks and program (all yr). (Tues-Sat; also Sun afternoons) In Burnet Woods. Phone 513/751-3679. **FREE**

★ **Union Terminal.** (1933) Famous Art Deco landmark, noted for its mosaic murals, Verona marble walls, terrazzo floors, and large-domed rotunda. Cafe and museum shops. 1301 Western Ave. Also in terminal are

  Cincinnati History Museum. Permanent exhibit on the Public Landing of Cincinnati; also temporary exhibits. Library (Mon-Sat; free). (Daily; closed Thanksgiving, Dec 25) 1301 Western Ave. Phone 513/287-7000. ¢¢

Cinergy Children's Museum. More than 200 hands-on displays for preschoolers to preteens. Special performances, interactive and educational programs. (Daily) 1301 Western Ave. Phone 513/287-7000. ¢¢¢

Museum of Natural History & Science. Natural history of Ohio Valley. Wilderness Trail with Ohio flora and fauna and full-scale walk-through replica of a cavern with 32-ft waterfall; Children's Discovery Center. (Daily; closed Thanksgiving, Dec 25) 1301 Western Ave. Phone 513/287-7000. ¢¢

Omnimax Theater. A 260-degree domed screen five stories high and 72 ft wide. Films change every six months. (Daily; closed Thanksgiving, Dec 25) Phone 513/287-7000. ¢¢¢

University of Cincinnati. (1819) 37,000 students. Incl 18 colleges and divisions, of which Music, Law, Medicine, and Pharmacy are among the oldest west of the Alleghenies. Founded as Cincinnati College; chartered 1870 as municipal university; became a full state university July 1, 1977. The College-Conservatory of Music has an extensive schedule of performances, phone 513/556-4183. On campus is Tangeman University Center (Mon-Sat; closed hols). Bounded by Clifton and Jefferson aves, Calhoun St, and Martin Luther King Dr. Phone 513/556-6000.

William Howard Taft National Historic Site. Birthplace and boyhood home of the 27th president and Chief Justice of the United States. Four rms with period furnishings; other rms contain exhibits on Taft's life and careers. (Daily; closed Jan 1, Thanksgiving, Dec 25) 2038 Auburn Ave. Phone 513/684-3262. **FREE**

Xavier University. (1831) 6,800 students. Campus tours. 3800 Victory Pkwy. Phone 513/745-3000.

Special Events

River Downs Race Track. 6301 Kellogg Ave, 10 mi E on US 52. Thoroughbred racing. Phone 513/232-8000. Mon-Wed and Fri-Sun. Mid-Apr-Labor Day and mid-Oct-mid-Nov.

May Festival. Cincinnati Music Hall, 1241 Elm St. Oldest continuous choral festival in the nation; choral and operatic masterworks. Phone 513/381-3300 for schedule and information. Last two wkends May.

Cincinnati Opera. Music Hall. Nation's second-oldest opera company offers a summer season plus special performances throughout yr. Capsulized English translations projected above the stage complement all productions. Phone 513/241-ARIA. Mid-June-mid-July.

Cincinnati Symphony Orchestra. 1241 Elm St, in Music Hall. Nation's fifth oldest orchestra presents symphony and pops programs. Phone 513/381-3300. Sept-May.

Turfway Park Race Course. 10 mi SW off I-75 via exit 184, on Turfway Pike in Florence, KY. Phone 800/733-0200. Thoroughbred racing Wed-Sun. Early Sept-early Oct and late Nov-Mar.

Riverfest. Celebration in honor of Cincinnati's river heritage held along the city's waterfront parks. Festivities incl fireworks, three stages of entertainment, food. For details contact the Convention & Visitors Bureau. Labor Day wkend. Phone 513/621-9326.

Oktoberfest-Zinzinnati. Downtown Cincinnati becomes a German biergarten for this festive wkend. Nonstop German music, singing, dancing, food, and thousands of gallons of beer. Mid-Sept. Phone 513/579-3191.

Cincinnati Ballet. 1555 Central Pkwy. Performs five-series program at the Aronoff Center, both contemporary and classical works. For schedule, tickets phone 513/621-5219. Oct-May; also *Nutcracker* staged at Music Hall during Dec.

Motels/Motor Lodges

★ **AMERISUITES.** *11435 Reed Hartman Hwy, Blue Ash (45241). 513/489-3666; fax 513/489-4187; toll-free 800/833-1516. www.amerisuites.com.* 127 suites, 6 story. May-Sept: S, D $99-$149; each addl $10; under 18 free; lower rates rest of yr. Crib avail. Pet accepted. TV; cable (premium), VCR (movies). Heated pool. Complimentary continental bkfst. Restaurant nearby. Ck-out noon. Meeting rms. Business center. In-rm modem link. Valet serv. Coin lndry. Exercise equipt. Microwaves. Cr cds: A, C, D, DS, MC, V.

[D] [♠] [≈] [⋏] [⤓] [🔥] [SC] [⫓]

★ **BEST WESTERN INN SPRING-DALE.** *11911 Sheraton Ln, Springdale (45246). 513/671-6600; fax 513/671-0507; res 800/528-1234. www.best western.com.* 267 rms, 10 story. May-Aug: S, D $89-$129; each addl $10; suites $119-$149; under 18 free; package plans; lower rates rest of yr. Crib free. TV; cable (premium). Indoor pool; whirlpool. Coffee in rms. Restaurant 6:30 am-10 pm; Fri, Sat to 11 pm. Bar 5 pm-1 am. Ck-out noon. Coin lndry. Meeting rms. Business servs avail. In-rm modem link. Exercise equipt. Game rm. Some bathrm phones. Cr cds: A, C, D, DS, MC, V.

[D] [≈] [⋏] [⤓] [🔥]

★ ★ ★ **BEST WESTERN MARIEMONT INN.** *6880 Wooster Pike (45227). 513/271-2100; fax 513/271-1057; toll-free 800/528-1234. www.bestwestern.com.* 60 rms, 3 story. S $69-$71; D $76-$86; each addl $7; under 18 free; lower rates rest of yr. Crib free. TV; cable (premium). Complimentary coffee in lobby. Restaurant (see NATIONAL EXEMPLAR). Rm serv. Bar 11 am-midnight. Ck-out noon. Coin lndry. Business servs avail. In-rm modem link. Valet serv. Cr cds: A, C, D, DS, MC, V.

[⤓] [🔥] [SC]

★ **COMFORT INN NORTH EAST.** *9011 Fields Ertel Rd (45249). 513/683-9700; fax 513/683-1284; res 800/228-5150. www.comfortinn.com.* 115 rms, 3 story. May-Sept: S, D $79-$129; each addl $10; under 18 free; lower rates rest of yr. Crib free. TV; cable (premium). Pool. Complimentary continental bkfst. Restaurant adj open 24 hrs. Ck-out 11 am. Meeting rms. Business servs avail. Valet serv. Cr cds: A, C, D, DS, MC, V.

[D] [≈] [⤓] [🔥] [SC]

★ ★ **COMFORT SUITES.** *11349 Reed Hartman Hwy, Blue Ash (45241). 513/530-5999; fax 513/530-0179; toll-free 800/517-4000. www.comfortsuites. com.* 50 suites, 3 story. Mid-June-late Aug: S, D $99-$159; each addl $6; under 17 free; lower rates rest of yr. Crib free. TV; cable (premium), VCR avail (movies). Pool. Complimentary

continental bkfst. Coffee in rms. Bar 4:30-11 pm; closed Sat, Sun. Ck-out 11 am. Meeting rms. Business servs avail. Valet serv. Sundries. Exercise equipt; sauna. Refrigerators. Cr cds: A, C, D, DS, MC, V.

[D] [≈] [⋏] [⤓] [🔥] [SC]

★ ★ **COURTYARD BY MARRIOTT.** *4625 Lake Forest Dr, Blue Ash (45242). 513/733-4334; fax 513/733-5711; toll-free 800/321-2211. www.courtyard. com.* 149 rms, 2-3 story. May-Aug: S, D $119; suites $139; wkend rates; lower rates rest of yr. Crib free. TV; cable (premium). Indoor pool; whirlpool. Complimentary coffee in lobby. Restaurant 6:30-10:30 am; wkends 7-11:30 am. Ck-out noon. Coin lndry. Meeting rms. Business servs avail. In-rm modem link. Exercise equipt. Microwave, refrigerator in suites. Sun deck. Cr cds: A, D, DS, MC, V.

[D] [≈] [⋏] [⤓] [🔥] [SC]

★ **CROSS COUNTRY INN.** *330 Glensprings Dr, Springdale (45246). 513/671-0556; fax 513/671-4953; toll-free 800/621-1429. www.crosscountry inns.com.* 120 rms, 2 story. S $37.99-$49.99; D $49.99-$58.99; each addl $7; under 18 free. Crib free. TV; cable (premium). Heated pool. Complimentary coffee in lobby. Restaurant adj open 24 hrs. Ck-out noon. Meeting rm. Business servs avail. Cr cds: A, C, D, DS, MC, V.

[D] [≈] [⤓] [🔥] [SC]

★ **CROSS COUNTRY INN-CINCINNATI.** *4004 Williams Dr (45255). 513/528-7702; fax 513/528-1246. www.crosscountryinns.com.* 128 rms, 2 story. S $43-$50; D $50-$59; under 18 free. Crib free. TV; cable (premium). Pool. Complimentary coffee in lobby. Restaurant adj 6 am-11 pm. Ck-out noon. Business servs avail. Cr cds: A, C, D, DS, MC, V.

[≈] [⤓] [🔥] [SC]

★ ★ **FAIRFIELD INN.** *11171 Dowlin Rd, Sharonville (45241). 513/772-4114; toll-free 800/228-2800. www. fairfieldinn.com.* 135 rms, 3 story. May-Oct: S, D $62-$83; each addl $7; under 18 free; higher rates special events; lower rates rest of yr. Crib free. TV; cable (premium). Pool. Complimentary continental bkfst. Restaurant adj 6 am-midnight. Ck-out noon. Meeting rms. Business servs avail. In-rm modem link. Valet serv Mon-Fri. Cr cds: A, C, D, DS, MC, V.

🄳 ⇌ ⊠ 🔥 SC

★★ **HAMPTON INN.** *10900 Crowne Point Dr (45241). 513/771-6888; fax 513/771-5768; res 800/426-7866. www.hamptoninn.com.* 130 rms, 4 story. June-Aug: S, D $89-$95; under 18 free; higher rates special events; lower rates rest of yr. Crib free. TV; cable (premium). Pool. Complimentary continental bkfst. Restaurant nearby. Ck-out noon. Meeting rm. Business servs avail. Valet serv Mon-Fri. Cr cds: A, C, D, DS, MC, V.

🄳 ⇌ ⊠ 🔥 SC

★★ **HOLIDAY INN.** *800 W 8th St (45203). 513/241-8660; fax 513/241-9057; res 800/465-4329. www.holiday-inn.com.* 243 rms, 12 story. S, D $69-$119; suites $149; under 18 free. Crib free. Pet accepted. TV; cable (premium). Pool. Coffee in rms. Restaurant 6 am-9:30 pm. Bar 5 pm-10 pm. Ck-out noon. Coin lndry. Meeting rms. Business servs avail. In-rm modem link. Exercise equipt. Refrigerators avail. Cr cds: A, C, D, DS, MC, V.

🄳 🔌 ⇌ 🏊 ⊠ 🔥

★★ **QUALITY INN.** *4747 Montgomery Rd (45212). 513/351-6000; fax 513/351-0215; toll-free 800/292-2079. www.qualityhotelandsuites.com.* 148 units, 14 suites, 8 story. S, D $89-$130; each addl $5; under 18 free; wkend rates; higher rates special events. TV; cable (premium). Pool; poolside serv. Complimentary bkfst. Restaurant 6:30 am-10 pm. Rm serv. Bar 11 am-10 pm. Ck-out noon. Meeting rms. Business center. In-rm modem link. Bellhops. Some bathrm phones; refrigerator, microwave in suites. Some private patios, balconies. Picnic tables. Cr cds: A, C, D, DS, MC, V.

🄳 ⊠ 🔥 SC ⇌ 🏊

★ **RED ROOF INN.** *11345 Chester Rd, Sharonville (45246). 513/771-5141; fax 513/771-0812; res 800/843-7663. www.redroof.com.* 108 rms, 2 story. S $54.99-$59.99; D $64.99-$69.99; each addl $5; under 18 free; higher rates special events. Crib $5. Pet accepted. TV; cable (premium). Restaurant adj 11-2 am. Ck-out

noon. Business servs avail. Valet serv. Cr cds: A, D, DS, MC, V.

🄳 🔌 ⊠ 🔥

★★ **WOODFIELD SUITES.** *11029 Dowlin Dr (45241). 513/771-0300; fax 513/771-6411; res 800/338-0008. www.woodfieldsuites.com.* 103 rms, 48 suites, 8 story. May-Oct: S, D $94-$114; each addl $10; under 17 free; lower rates rest of yr. Crib free. Pet accepted, some restrictions; $10. TV; cable (premium), VCR avail. Indoor pool; whirlpool. Complimentary continental bkfst, afternoon refreshments. Coffee in rms. Restaurant nearby. Ck-out noon. Meeting rms. Business servs avail. In-rm modem link. Valet serv (Mon-Fri). Coin lndry. Exercise equipt. Rec rm. Refrigerators, microwaves; some wet bars, in-rm whirlpools. Cr cds: A, D, DS, MC, V.

🄳 🔌 ⇌ 🏋 ⊠ 🔥

Hotels

★★★★ **THE CINCINNATIAN HOTEL.** *601 Vine St (45202). 513/381-3000; fax 513/651-0256; toll-free 800/942-9000. www.cincinnatian hotel.com.* The grand walnut and marble staircase of this hotel's eight-story, skylit atrium makes a wonderful first impression. After experiencing the 146 rooms and suites, with their granite showers and European style, guests realize the stunning lobby is only the beginning of a wonderful stay. Relax with afternoon tea, listen to music in the lounge, or dine on regional American cuisine at The Palace restaurant. 146 rms, 8 story. S, D $225; suites $350-$1,500; under 12 free; wkend rates. Crib free. Covered parking $25. TV; cable (premium), VCR avail. Restaurant 6:30 am-11 pm (see also THE PALACE). Rm serv 24 hrs. Bar 11:30 am-11 pm; entertainment. Ck-out noon. Meeting rms. Business servs avail. Concierge. Exercise equipt; sauna. Bathrm phones, minibars; microwave avail. Restored landmark hotel (1882). Totally nonsmoking. Cr cds: A, C, D, DS, ER, JCB, MC, V.

🄳 🏋 ⊠ 🔥

★★★ **CROWNE PLAZA.** *15 W 6th St (45202). 513/381-4000; fax 513/381-5158; toll-free 888/279-8260. crowneplazacincinnati.com.* 321 rms, 20 story. S $129-$149; D $139-$159;

suites $200-$350; family rates. Crib free. Valet parking. TV; cable (premium). Coffee in rms. Restaurant 6 am-11 pm; Sun to 10 pm. Bar 11-2 am. Ck-out 11 am. Convention facilities. Business center. Concierge. Barber, beauty shop. Exercise equipt; sauna. Whirlpool. Refrigerators, minibars. Cr cds: A, C, D, DS, ER, JCB, MC, V.

D 🏂 ➡ 🏊 SC 🏃

★★★ **HOLIDAY INN EASTGATE.** *4501 Eastgate Blvd (45245). 513/752-4400; fax 513/753-3178; res 800/465-4329. www.holiday-inn.com.* 247 rms, 6 story. S, D $94-$109; each addl $10; suites $200-$275; under 18 free; wkend rates; higher rates special events. Crib free. TV; cable (premium). Complimentary coffee in rms. Restaurant 6:30 am-11 pm; Sun to 10 pm. Bar 11 am-midnight; Sun to 10 pm. Ck-out 11 am. Meeting rms. Business center. Gift shop. Exercise equipt. Indoor pool; whirlpool. Bathrm phone, in-rm whirlpool, refrigerator, microwave, wet bar in suites. Cr cds: A, MC, V.

D ➡ 🏂 ➡ 🔥 SC 🏃

★★★ **HYATT REGENCY CINCINNATI.** *151 W 5th St (45202). 513/579-1234; fax 513/579-0107; res 800/233-1234. www.cincinnati.hyatt.com.* 485 rms, 22 story. S, D $196-$224; each addl $25; suites $400-$750; under 18 free; wkend rates; higher rates special events. Crib free. TV; cable (premium). Indoor pool; whirlpool, poolside serv. Restaurant 6:30 am-midnight. Bar 11-2:30 am. Ck-out noon. Convention facilities. Business center. Concierge. Shopping arcade. Exercise equipt; sauna. Some bathrm phones; refrigerator in suites. Luxury level. Cr cds: A, C, DS, ER, JCB, MC, V.

D ➡ 🏂 SC 🏃

★★★ **MARRIOTT CINCINNATI AIRPORT.** *2395 Progress Dr, Hebron, KY (41048). 859/586-0166; fax 859/586-0266; res 800/228-9290. www.marriott.com.* 295 rms, 8 story. S, D $155-$225; each addl $25; under 17 free. Crib avail. Indoor pool. TV; cable (premium), VCR avail. Complimentary coffee, newspaper in rms. Restaurant 6 am-10 pm. Ck-out noon. Meeting rms. Business center. Gift shop. Exercise rm. Some refriger-

ators, minibars. Cr cds: A, C, D, DS, MC, V.

➡ 🏂 ➡ 🏃

★★★ **MARRIOTT NORTH CINCINNATI.** *6189 Muhlhauser Rd (45069). 513/874-7335; res 800/228-9290. www.marriott.com.* 295 rms, 8 story. S, D $145-$250; under 17 free. Crib avail. Indoor pool. TV; cable (premium), VCR avail. Complimentary coffee.Restaurant 6:30 am-10 pm. Ck-out noon. Meeting rms. Business center. Gift shop. Exercise rm. Some refrigerators. Cr cds: A, C, D, DS, JCB, MC, V.

D ➡ SC 🏃 🏃

★★ **MILLENNIUM HOTEL.** *141 W 6th St (45202). 513/352-2130; fax 513/352-2239. www.millenniumhotels.com.* 450 rms, 32 story. S, D $99-$189; each addl $10; suites $250-$900; under 18 free. Crib free. Garage $18. TV; cable (premium). Pool. Restaurants 6:30 am-11 pm; Sun to 10 pm (see also SEAFOOD 32). Bars 11-2:30 am; Sun from 1 pm. Ck-out noon. Convention facilities. Business center. In-rm modem link. Concierge. Shopping arcade. Barber. Exercise rm. Luxury level. Cr cds: A, C, D, DS, ER, JCB, MC, V.

D ➡ 🏂 ➡ 🔥 SC 🏃

★★★ **OMNI NETHERLAND PLAZA.** *35 W 5th St (45202). 513/421-9100; fax 513/421-4291; res 800/843-6664. www.omnihotels.com.* 619 rms, 29 story. S $185-$220; D $165-$225; suites $305-$1,680; under 18 free; wkly, wkend rates. Crib free. Valet parking. TV; cable (premium), VCR avail. Indoor pool. Restaurant see THE RESTAURANT AT THE PALM COURT). Bar 11-2 am; entertainment. Ck-out noon. Business center. Concierge. Shopping arcade. Exercise rm. Some private patios. Cr cds: A, C, D, DS, JCB, MC, V.

D ➡ ➡ 🔥 SC 🏃 🏃

★★ **THE VERNON MANOR HOTEL.** *400 Oak St (45219). 513/281-3300; fax 513/281-8933; toll-free 800/543-3999. www.vernon-manor.com.* 177 rms, 7 story. S, D $160-$185; each addl $15; suites $225-$700; studio rms $195; under 18 free. Crib free. TV; cable (premium). Complimentary coffee in lobby. Restaurant 6:30 am-10 pm; Sun brunch 10:30 am-2 pm. Bar 11-2 am; Sun 1 pm-midnight. Ck-out noon. Coin lndry. Meeting rms. Business center. In-rm modem link. Barber, beauty shop. Valet parking. Exercise equipt. Some refrigerators. Cr cds: A, C, D, DS, JCB, MC, V.

D K $\searrow$ W SC K

★★★ **WESTIN.** *21 E 5th St (45202). 513/621-7700; fax 513/852-5670; res 800/937-8461. www.westin.com.* 450 rms, 17 story. S $159-$250; each addl $20; suites $300-$1,200; under 18 free; wkend rates. Crib free. Valet parking $24. TV; cable (premium), VCR avail. Indoor pool; whirlpool, poolside serv. Complimentary coffee in rms. Restaurant 6:30 am-10 pm; Fri, Sat to midnight. Rm serv 24 hrs. Bar 11:30-2 am; Sun from noon. Ck-out noon. Convention facilities. Business center. In-rm modem link. Shopping. Exercise rm; steam rm. Some bathrm phones, refrigerators. Luxury level. Cr cds: A, C, D, DS, JCB, MC, V.

D $\searrow$ K $\searrow$ W SC K

All Suites

★★★ **EMBASSY SUITES CINCINNATI NORTHEAST.** *4554 Lake Forest Dr (45242). 513/733-8900; fax 513/733-3720; res 800/362-2779. www.embassysuites.com.* 235 suites, 5 story. S, D $99-$179; each addl $10; under 12 free; higher rates special events. Crib free. TV; cable (premium). Indoor pool; whirlpool. Complimentary full bkfst. Complimentary coffee in rms. Restaurant 11:30 am-10 pm. Bar 5 pm-midnight; closed Sun. Ck-out 1 pm. Coin lndry. Meeting rms. Business servs avail. In-rm modem link. Gift shop. Exercise equipt; sauna. Refrigerators, microwaves, wet bars. Balconies. Cr cds: A, C, D, DS, JCB, MC, V.

D $\searrow$ K $\searrow$ W SC

★★ **GARFIELD SUITES HOTEL.** *2 Garfield Pl (45202). 513/421-3355; fax 513/421-3729; toll-free 800/367-2155. www.garfieldsuiteshotel.com.* 152 kit. suites, 16 story. 1-bedrm $152-$172; 2-bedrm $172-$199; penthouse suites $435-$1,200; monthly rates. Crib free. Pet accepted; $100. Valet parking $17. TV; cable (premium), VCR avail. Complimentary coffee in rms. Restaurant 6:30 am-3 pm; wkends

from 7:30 pm. Rm serv 5-10 pm. Bar 5-10 pm. Ck-out noon. Coin lndry. Meeting rms. Business servs avail. In-rm modem link. Exercise equipt. Microwaves. Some balconies. Cr cds: A, C, D, DS, MC, V.

D $\searrow$ K $\searrow$ W

Extended Stay

★★ **RESIDENCE INN BY MARRIOTT.** *11689 Chester Rd, Sharonville (45246). 513/771-2525; fax 513/771-3444; res 800/331-3131. www.marriott.com.* 144 kit. suites, 1-2 story. 1 bedrm $99-$109; 2 bedrm $119-$129; higher rates July. Pet accepted; $100. TV; cable (premium). Pool; whirlpool. Complimentary bkfst. Ck-out noon. Coin lndry. Business servs avail. Valet serv. Microwaves. Picnic tables, grills. Cr cds: A, D, DS, JCB, MC, V.

D $\searrow$ $\searrow$ $\searrow$ W

Restaurants

★★ **BLACK FOREST.** *8675 Cincinnati-Columbus Rd, Pisgah (45069). 513/777-7600.* Hrs: 11:30 am-2 pm, 4:30-10 pm; Fri to 11 pm; Sat 4:30-11 pm; Sun 4:30-10 pm. Closed some major hols. Res accepted. German menu. Bar. Lunch $3.95-$9, dinner $8.50-$17. Buffet: lunch $5.95. Child's menu. Specialties: Wiener schnitzel, Oktoberfest chicken, sauerbraten. German band Fri, Sat. Parking. Old World German decor. Family-owned. Cr cds: A, C, DS, MC, V.

D $\square$

★★★ **THE CELESTIAL.** *1071 Celestial St (45202). 513/241-4455.* Hrs: 5:30-9 pm; Fri, Sat to 10 pm. Closed Sun; some major hols. Res accepted. Eclectic menu. Bar. Wine list. Dinner $18.95-$39. Specializes in game, fresh seafood. Own baking. Jazz Fri, Sat. Free valet parking. Panoramic view of city. Jacket. Cr cds: A, DS, MC, V.

D $\square$

★★ **CHATEAU POMIJE.** *2019 Madison Rd (45208). 513/871-8788. www.chateaupomije.com.* Hrs: 11 am-2:30 pm, 5:30-9:30 pm; Fri to 10:30 pm; Sat 5:30-10:30 pm. Closed Sun; major hols. Continental menu. Wine, beer. Lunch $6-$10, dinner

$10-$18. Specialties: cioppino, Chateau chicken, fresh salmon. Own desserts. Street parking. Outdoor dining. Casual, cafe dining; adj wine shop. Cr cds: D, MC, V.

D

★ **CHENG-I CUISINE.** *203 W McMillan St (45219). 513/723-1999.* Hrs: 11 am-10 pm; Fri to 10:30 pm; Sat noon-10:30 pm; Sun 4:30-10 pm. Closed Thanksgiving, Dec 25. Chinese menu. Serv bar. Lunch $4.25-$5.75, dinner $5.50-$12.95. Specialties: cashew chicken, pan-fried moo shu, sizzling shrimp and scallops. Cr cds: D, MC, V.

D ⊒

★★ **CHERRINGTON'S.** *950 Pavilion St (45202). 513/579-0131.* Hrs: 11 am-3 pm, 5-9 pm; Fri, Sat to 11 pm; Sat 8-11:30 am, 5-11 pm; Sun brunch 11 am-3 pm, 4-9 pm. Closed Mon; some major hols. Res accepted. Bar. Bkfst $2.95-$10.95, lunch $4.95-$8.95, dinner $8.95-$23.95. Specializes in fresh seafood. Outdoor dining. Blackboard menu. Guitarist Fri, Sat. Renovated residence (1880). Cr cds: A, D, DS, MC, V.

D ⊒

★★ **CHESTER'S ROAD HOUSE.** *9678 Montgomery Rd (45242). 513/793-8700. www.chesters.com.* Hrs: 11:30 am-2:30 pm, 5-10 pm; Fri to 10:30 pm; Sat to 11 pm; Sun 5-9 pm. Closed Jan 1, July 4, Dec 25; also Super Bowl Sun. Res accepted. Bar. Lunch $6.50-$9.95, dinner $11.95-$22.95. Specializes in fresh seafood, lamb, steak. Salad bar (dinner). Parking. Garden atmosphere; in converted brick farmhouse (1900). Family-owned. Cr cds: A, D, DS, MC, V.

D ⊒

★★ **CHINA GOURMET.** *3340 Erie Ave (45208). 513/871-6612. www.foodlinks.com.* Hrs: 11:30 am-10 pm; Fri to 11 pm; Sat noon-11 pm. Closed Sun; major

hols. Res accepted. Chinese menu. Bar. A la carte entrees: lunch $6-$9.95, dinner $9.95-$27.50. Specializes in fresh seafood. Parking. Cr cds: A, D, DS, MC, V.

D ⊒

★★ **DESHA'S.** *11320 Montgomery Rd (45249). 513/247-9933. www.deshas. com.* Hrs: 11 am-10 pm; Fri, Sat to 11 pm; Sun 10 am-9 pm; Sun brunch to 2 pm. Closed Jan 1, Dec 25. Res accepted. Bar. Lunch $8-$10, dinner $12-$20. Sun brunch $11.95. Child's menu. Specializes in steak, prime rib, seafood. Parking. Outdoor dining on patio. Casually elegant dining. Cr cds: A, D, DS, MC, V.

D

★ **THE DINER ON SYCAMORE.** *1203 Sycamore St (45210). 513/721-1212. www.foodlinks.com.* Hrs: 11 am-midnight; Fri, Sat to 1 am; Sun brunch 11 am-2:30 pm. Closed Dec 25. Bar. Lunch, dinner $6.25-$16.95. Sun brunch $4.95-$7.25. Child's menu. Specialties: Caribbean white crab chili, seafood Diablo, crab cakes. Parking. Outdoor dining. Nostalgic diner atmosphere. Cr cds: A, D, DS, MC, V.

D ⊒

★★ **FERRARI'S LITTLE ITALY.** *7677 Goff Ter (45243). 513/272-2220. www. gocincinnati/ferraris.com.* Hrs: 11:30 am-2:30 pm, 5-10 pm; Fri, Sat 5-11 pm; Sun 4-9 pm; early-bird dinner to 6 pm. Closed Jan 1, Easter, Dec 25. Res accepted. Northern and southern regional Italian menu. A la carte

A Hamilton County farm

entrees: lunch $4.95-$8.95, dinner $8.95-$17.95. Child's menu. Specialties: insalata Ferrari, lemon sole. Parking. Outdoor dining. Family-style. Cr cds: A, D, DS, MC, V.

[D] [⊷]

★ **FORE & AFT.** 7449 Forbes Rd (45233). 513/941-8400. Hrs: 11 am-10 pm; Fri to 11 pm; Sat 4-11 pm. Closed Jan 1, Dec 24, 25. Res accepted. Bar. Lunch $5.75-$14.95, dinner $8.75-$17.95. Child's menu. Specializes in hand-cut steak, prime rib, seafood. Parking. Outdoor dining. Floating barge on Ohio River; nautical memorabilia. Cr cds: A, MC, V.

[⊷]

★ **FOREST VIEW GARDENS.** 4508 North Bend Rd (45211). 513/661-6434. www.fvg.com. Hrs: Edelweiss Rm: 11 am-2 pm, 5-7:30 pm; Sat from 5 pm; Show Rm: Broadway music shows (sittings): Thurs 6 pm, Fri 7 pm, Sat 5 and 8 pm, Sun 5 pm. Closed Mon; Dec 24, 25; also 1st wk Jan. Res accepted; required for shows. German, Amer menu. Bar. Lunch $3.95-$7.95, dinner $12.95-$18.95. Child's menu. Specialties: Wiener schnitzel, sauerbraten, prime rib. Parking. Outdoor dining in beer garden. Bavarian Fest atmosphere. Banquet-style seating. Family-owned. Cr cds: A, D, MC, V.

[D] [⊷]

★★ **GERMANO'S.** 9415 Montgomery Rd (45242). 513/794-1155. www. cincinnati.com/germanos. Hrs: 11:30 am-2:30 pm, 5:30-9:30 pm; Fri to 10 pm; Sat 5-10 pm. Closed Sun; hols. Res accepted. Italian menu. Serv bar. Lunch $6.95-$13.95, dinner $13.95-$27.95. Specializes in pasta, seafood, veal. Own desserts. Tuscan decor with framed art, tapestries. Totally nonsmoking. Cr cds: A, D, MC, V.

[D]

★★★ **GRAND FINALE.** 3 E Sharon Ave (45246). 513/771-5925. Hrs: 11:15 am-10 pm; Fri, Sat to 11 pm; Sun 5-10 pm; Sun brunch 10:30 am-3 pm. Closed Mon; Dec 25. Continental menu. Bar. Lunch $5.95-$11.95, dinner $14.95-$19.95. Sun brunch $10.95. Child's menu. Specialties: steak salad Annie, chicken Ginger, rack of lamb. Own baking. Parking. Outdoor dining. Remodeled

turn-of-the-century saloon. Cr cds: A, D, DS, MC, V.

[D] [⊷]

★★★ **HERITAGE.** 7664 Wooster Pike (OH 50) (45227). 513/561-9300. www.theheritage.com. Hrs: 11:30 am-2:30 pm, 5-9 pm; Sat 5-10 pm; Sun 10:30 am-2 pm, 5-9 pm. Closed some major hols. Res accepted. Bar. Wine list. Lunch $5.95-$8.95, dinner $14.95-$21.95. Sun brunch $12.95. Child's menu. Specializes in regional Amer cuisine. Own baking. Valet parking. Outdoor dining. Restored 1827 farmhouse. Own herb garden. Family-owned. Cr cds: A, D, DS, MC, V.

[D] [⊷]

★ **HOUSE OF TAM.** 889 W Galbraith Rd (45231). 513/729-5566. Hrs: 11 am-9:30 pm; Fri to 10 pm; Sat 5-10:30 pm. Closed Sun; some major hols. Res accepted. Chinese menu. Bar. Lunch $4.50-$6.50, dinner $5.95-$16.95. Specialties: pine nuts chicken, sea emperor's feast, strawberry chicken. Parking. Totally nonsmoking. Cr cds: A, D, DS, MC, V.

[D]

★★ **IRON HORSE INN.** 40 Village Sq (45246). 513/771-4787. www.iron horseinn.net. Hrs: 11 am-2:30 pm, 5-10 pm; Fri to 11 pm; Sat 4:30-11 pm; Sun to 9 pm; Sun brunch 10 am-2:30 pm. Res accepted. Bar to midnight; Fri, Sat to 1 am; Sun to 11 pm. Lunch $5-$9, dinner $15-$20. Sun brunch $3-$8. Child's menu. Specialties: Iron Horse roasted sea bass, New Zealand lamb chops. Jazz Mon, Wed, Fri, Sat (night). Valet parking. Outdoor dining. Contemporary atmosphere. Totally nonsmoking. Cr cds: A, D, DS, MC, V.

[D]

★★ **LA NORMANDIE TAVERN & CHOPHOUSE.** 118 E 6th St (45202). 513/721-2761. www.maisonette.com. Hrs: 11:30 am-2:30 pm, 5-10 pm; Fri 5-11 pm; Sat from 5 pm. Closed Sun; major hols. Res accepted. Bar. Lunch $7.99-$13.50, dinner $14.50-$24.95. Specializes in aged beef, fresh fish. Valet parking. Four-sided fireplace. Family-owned. Cr cds: A, D, DS, MC, V.

[D] [⊷]

★ **LE BOX CAFE.** *819 Vine St (45202). 513/721-5638.* Hrs: 11:30 am-3 pm. Closed Sat, Sun; major hols. Contemporary Amer menu. Lunch $2.95-$5.75. Child's menu. Specializes in meatloaf, ribs, burgers. Casual decor. Cr cds: A, D, DS, MC, V.
[D] [⌨]

★ **LENHARDT'S.** *151 W McMillan St (45219). 513/281-3600.* Hrs: 11 am-9:30 pm; Sat from 4 pm. Closed Sun, Mon; July 4; also 1st 2 wks Aug, 2 wks at Christmas. Res accepted. German, Hungarian menu. Bar 7 pm-2 am; closed Sun. Lunch $3.95-$9.95, dinner $9.95-$15.95. Specialties: Wiener schnitzel, sauerbraten, Hungarian goulash. Free parking. Former Moerlin brewery mansion. Cr cds: A, D, DS, MC, V.
[⌨]

★★★★★ **MAISONETTE.** *114 E 6th St (45202). 513/721-2260. www. maisonette.com.* The setting of this Comisar family restaurant (one of four) is elegant and tranquil with art-filled walls, salmon and peach tones, and soft lighting. An extensive wine list with selections from around the world complements chef Bertrand Bouquin's continental cuisine, which features both French and northern Italian influences. Specializes in fresh, imported French fish dishes, seasonal offerings. Own pastries. Hrs: 11:30 am-2:30 pm, 6-11 pm; Sat 5:15-11 pm. Closed Sun; hols. Res accepted. Bar. Wine cellar. A la carte entrees: lunch $14.75-$25, dinner $25-$45. Valet parking (dinner). Jacket. Cr cds: A, D, DS, MC, V.
[D]

★ **MECKLENBURG GARDENS.** *302 E University (45219). 513/221-5353.* Hrs: 11 am-10 pm; Fri to 11 pm; Sat, Sun 5-10 pm. Closed major hols. Res accepted. German menu. Bar to 1 am. Lunch $5-$9, dinner $7-$17. Specialties: sauerbraten, potato pancakes, Mecklenburg pies. Own desserts. Entertainment Wed, Fri, Sat. Valet parking Fri, Sat. Outdoor dining. Casual dining; grapevine motif. Cr cds: A, D, DS, MC, V.
[D]

★★ **MONTGOMERY INN.** *9440 Montgomery Rd (45242). 513/791-3482. www.montgomeryinn.com.* Hrs: 11 am-10:30 pm; Fri to midnight; Sat 3 pm-midnight; Sun 3-9:30 pm. Closed major hols. Res accepted. Bar. A la carte entrees: lunch $4.50-$10.95, dinner $12.50-$21.95. Child's menu. Specializes in barbecued ribs, chicken. Parking. Family-owned. Cr cds: A, D, DS, MC, V.
[D] [⌨]

★★ **MONTGOMERY INN BOATHOUSE.** *925 Eastern Ave (45202). 513/721-7427. www. montgomeryinn.com.* Hrs: 11 am-10:30 pm; Fri to 11 pm; Sat 3-11 pm; Sun 3-10 pm. Closed major hols. Res accepted Sun-Fri. Bar. A la carte entrees: lunch $5.75-$18.95, dinner $12.95-$23.95. Child's menu. Specializes in barbecued ribs, seafood, chicken. Valet parking. Outdoor dining (in season). Unique circular building, located at the river; scenic view. Cr cds: A, D, DS, MC, V.
[D] [⌨]

★★ **NATIONAL EXEMPLAR.** *6880 Wooster Pike (45227). 513/271-2103.* Hrs: 7 am-2 pm, 5:30-10 pm; Fri, Sat to 10:30 pm; Sun 5-9 pm. Closed Dec 25. Res accepted. Bar. Bkfst $3.25-$7.50, lunch $4.50-$7.50, dinner $11.95-$19.95. Child's menu. Specializes in omelettes, steak, seafood. Casual Early American decor. Cr cds: A, D, DS, MC, V.
[D] [SC] [⌨]

★★ **NICOLA'S.** *1420 Sycamore St (45210). 513/721-6200.* Hrs: 11:30 am-2 pm, 5:30-10 pm; Fri to 11 pm; Sat 5:30-11 pm. Closed Sun; major hols. Res accepted. Northern Italian menu. Bar. Lunch $5.50-$9.95, dinner $9.95-$21.95. Specializes in regional Italian dishes, fresh fish. Own pasta, desserts. Valet parking. Outdoor dining. Contemporary decor; fine dining. Cr cds: A, D, DS, MC, V.
[D] [⌨]

★★ **PACIFIC MOON.** *8300 Market Place Ln (45242). 513/891-0091. www.pacificmooncafe.com.* Hrs: 11 am-10 pm; Fri, Sat to 11 pm; Sat, Sun brunch 10 am-3 pm. Closed Thanksgiving. Res accepted. Asian menu. Bar. Lunch $5.50-$9.50, dinner $12-$22. Specializes in pork, seafood, chicken. Entertainment Sat. Outdoor dining. Contemporary decor. Cr cds: A, D, DS, MC, V.

D ⊒

★★★ **THE PALACE.** *601 Vine St (45202). 513/381-6006. www. cincinnatianhotel.com.* Hrs: 6:30-10 pm; Sun to 9:30 pm. Res accepted. Bar 11-1 am; Fri, Sat to 2 am. Wine list. A la carte entrees: bkfst $5.75-$14.95, lunch $6.50-$18, dinner $21-$38. Specializes in seafood, rack of lamb, steak. Own baking. Pianist, jazz trio, harpist (dinner). Valet parking. Cr cds: A, D, DS, ER, JCB, MC, V.

D

★ **PETERSEN'S.** *1111 St. Gregory St (45202). 513/651-4777.* Hrs: 11:30 am-3 pm, 5-10 pm; Fri, Sat 5-11 pm. Closed Sun, Mon; major hols. Wine. A la carte entrees: lunch $4.75-$9.75, dinner $6.75-$15. Specializes in pasta, desserts. Jazz Mon-Sat. Cr cds: A, D, DS, MC, V.

D ⊒

★★★ **THE PHOENIX.** *812 Race St (45202). 513/721-8901. www.thephx. com.* Hrs: 5-9 pm; Sat 5:30-10 pm. Closed Sun, Mon; major hols. Res accepted. Wine cellar. A la carte entrees: dinner $12.95-$24.95. Specializes in seafood, pasta, lamb chops. Pianist Sat. Valet parking. Formal dining. Built in 1893; white marble staircase, 12 German stained-glass windows from the 1880s, hand-carved library breakfront built on site in 1905. Totally nonsmoking. Cr cds: A, D, DS, MC, V.

D

★★★ **PRECINCT.** *311 Delta Ave (45226). 513/321-5454. www.the precinctinc.com.* Hrs: 5-10 pm; Fri, Sat to 11:30 pm. Closed some major hols. Res accepted. Bar 5 pm-2:30 am. Wine list. Dinner $16.95-$28.50. Specializes in steak, veal, fresh seafood. Own pastries. Valet parking. In 1890s police station. Cr cds: A, DS, MC, V.

★★★ **PRIMAVISTA.** *810 Matson Pl (45204). 513/251-6467.* Hrs: 5:30-10 pm; Fri from 5 pm; Sat 5-11 pm; Sun 5-9 pm. Closed major hols. Res accepted. Italian menu. Bar. Dinner $13.95-$28.95. Specialties: Branzino con Aragosta, Costolette di Vitello.

Contemporary Italian decor, view of river. Cr cds: A, D, DS, MC, V.

D ⊒

★★ **THE RESTAURANT AT THE PALM COURT.** *35 W 5th St (45202). 513/421-9100.* Hrs: 11 am-2 pm, 5-10 pm; Sat 6-11 pm; Sun from 6 pm. Res accepted. Contemporary Amer menu. Bar to 2 am; Sun 1 pm-midnight. Wine list. A la carte entrees: lunch $10-$19.50, dinner $14-$58. Specializes in fresh seafood, veal, beef. Pianist; jazz Fri, Sat eves. Valet parking. Cr cds: A, D, DS, MC, V.

D SC

★ **ROOKWOOD POTTERY.** *1077 Celestial St (45202). 513/721-5456.* Hrs: 11:30 am-9:30 pm; Fri, Sat to 11:30 pm. Closed Memorial Day, Thanksgiving, Dec 25. Bar. Lunch $5-$10, dinner $9-$15. Child's menu. Specializes in gourmet burgers, seafood, salads. Free parking. Originally housed production of Rookwood Pottery; some seating in former pottery kilns. Collection of Rookwood Pottery. Cr cds: A, DS, MC, V.

D ⊒

★★ **SEAFOOD 32.** *150 W 5th St (45202). 513/352-2160.* Hrs: 5-11 pm; Fri, Sat to 11 pm. Closed Sun. Res accepted. Bar. Dinner $19.95-$27.50. Specialties: wild mushroom-crusted black bass, salmon, prime rib. Entertainment. Revolving restaurant overlooks the city. Cr cds: A, D, DS, ER, JCB, MC, V.

D

★ **TANDOOR'S.** *8702 Market Place Ln (45242). 513/793-7484.* Hrs: 11:30 am-2 pm, 5:30-9:30 pm; Fri, Sat to 10:30 pm. Closed Sun; Dec 25. Res accepted. Northern India menu. Bar. Buffet: lunch $6.50. Complete meals: lunch, dinner $4.95-$18.95. Specializes in tandoori cooking. Outdoor dining. Indian decor. Cr cds: A, DS, MC, V.

D

★ **TEAK.** *1049 St. Gregory St (45202). 513/665-9800.* Hrs: noon-3 pm, 5-9:30 pm; Fri to 10:30 pm; Sat 4-11 pm; Sun 4-9 pm. Closed major hols. Res accepted. Thai menu. Bar. Complete meals: lunch, dinner $6.50-$14.95. Specializes in noodle dishes, curry dishes. Outdoor dining. Contemporary decor with Thai art. Cr cds: A, D, DS, MC, V.

Unrated Dining Spot

AGLAMESIS BROS. *3046 Madison Rd (45209). 513/531-5196. www. aglamesis.com.* Hrs: 10 am-9:30 pm; Fri, Sat to 11 pm; Sun noon-10 pm. Closed Jan 1, Easter, Dec 25. Avg ck: $5.50. Specializes in homemade ice cream and candy. Old-time ice cream parlor; established 1908. Family-owned. Cr cds: MC, V.

Cleveland (B-5)

Founded 1796 **Pop** 505,616 **Elev** 680 ft **Area code** 216, 440

Information Convention & Visitors Bureau of Greater Cleveland, 3100 Terminal Tower, 50 Public Sq, 44113; 216/621-4110 or 800/321-1001

Web www.travelcleveland.com

Suburbs Beachwood, Brecksville, Mentor, Strongsville. (See individual alphabetical listings.)

Ohio's second-largest city extends 50 miles east and north along the shore of Lake Erie and 25 miles south inland. It is a combination of industrial flats, spacious suburbs, wide principal streets, and an informality due partially to its diverse population. Many nationalities have contributed to its growth—Poles, Italians, Croats, Slovenes, Serbs, Lithuanians, Germans, Irish, Romanians, Russians, and Greeks. Formerly the various national groups divided regionally, but this is less true today. Cleveland has more than 600 churches, 11 colleges, one metropolitan newspaper, and several suburban weeklies, as well as a progressive independent mayor-council form of government. A transportation crossroads and a big steel, electrical, and machine tool center, the city also serves as home to the famed Cleveland Clinic.

Cleveland's history has been peppered with industrial giants—John D. Rockefeller, the Mathers of iron and shipping, Mark Hanna of steel and political fame, the Van Sweringens, and others. The village, founded by

Gund Arena

Moses Cleaveland, profited from the combination of Great Lakes transportation and fertile country. At the time, northern Ohio was still almost entirely unoccupied; growth was slow. Not until 1827, when the Ohio Canal was opened to join Lake Erie with the Ohio River, did the town start to expand. Incoming supplies of coal and iron ore led to the manufacture of locomotives and iron castings. Before the Civil War, the city had surpassed Columbus in population to become the second largest in the state and was changing from a commercial to an industrial center. The boom era after World War I saw the birth of Shaker Heights, one of the more affluent suburbs, the Terminal Tower Group of buildings downtown, and the Group Plan, with civic buildings all surrounding the central mall.

The layout of the city is systematic. All the main avenues lead to the Public Square (Tower City Center), where the Terminal Tower is located. The east-west dividing line is Ontario Street, which runs north and south through the square. The north and south streets are numbered; the east and west thoroughfares are avenues, with a few roads and boulevards. Euclid Avenue is the main business street running through Cleveland and many of its suburbs. Many of the early buildings have been razed and replaced by planned urban architecture, while other buildings are being restored. "Millionaire's row" and the magnificent mansions on Euclid Avenue are all but gone. The Cuyahoga River Valley, where refineries, oil tanks, and steel mills once made many fortunes, now is known for its entertainment and dining area. The 39 city parks and 17,500 acres of metropolitan parks are still a tribute to what was once called "forest city." Cleveland is also home to many universities including Case Western Reserve, John Carroll, and Cleveland State.

Additional Visitor Information

Cleveland Magazine and *Northern Ohio Live,* at newsstands, have up-to-date information on cultural events and articles of interest to visitors.

Tourist information may be obtained from the Convention & Visitors Bureau of Greater Cleveland, 3100 Terminal Tower, 50 Public Square, 44113, phone 216/621-4110 or 800/321-1001. An information booth is located in the Terminal Tower Building on Public Square, Hopkins International Airport, and Powerhouse and Nautica Boardwalk in The Flats.

Transportation

Car Rental Agencies. See IMPORTANT TOLL-FREE NUMBERS.

Public Transportation. Buses and trains (RTA), phone 216/621-9500.

Rail Passenger Service. Amtrak 800/872-7245.

Airport Information

Cleveland Hopkins Intl Airport. Information 216/265-6030; 216/265-6030 (lost and found); 216/931-1212 (weather).

What to See and Do

Alpine Valley Ski Area. Area has quad, double chairlifts; J-bar, two rope tows; patrol, school, rentals, snowmaking; cafeteria, lounge. Longest run ⅓ mi; vertical drop 240 ft. (Early Dec-early Mar) 30 mi E on US 322, in Chesterland. Phone 440/285-2211. ¢¢¢¢

Beck Center for the Arts. (Sept-June; reduced schedule July-Aug) 17801 Detroit Ave, in Lakewood. Phone 216/521-2540.

Brookside Park. A 157-acre park with tennis courts; athletic fields. Picnic areas. Denison Ave and Fulton Pkwy, 4 mi SW of Public Sq (Downtown) on I-71. Phone 216/621-3300. Also here is

> **Cleveland Metroparks Zoo.**
> Seventh-oldest zoo in the country, with more than 3,300 animals occupying 165 acres. Incl mammals, land and water birds; animals displayed in naturalized settings. More than 600 animals and 7,000 plants are featured in the two-acre Rain Forest exhibit. (Daily; closed Jan 1, Dec 25) 3900 Wildlife Way. Phone 216/661-6500. ¢¢¢

The Cleveland Arcade. (1890) This five-story enclosed shopping mall, one of the world's first, features more than 80 shops and restaurants.

(Mon-Sat) 401 Euclid Ave, between Superior and Euclid at E 4th St, Downtown. Phone 216/776-4461.

Cleveland Hopkins International Airport. Municipally owned; 1,800 acres. Observation deck for ticketed passengers only. (May-Nov, weather permitting; free). 5300 Riverside Dr, 12 mi SW of Public Sq (Downtown). Adj is

> **NASA Lewis Visitor Center.** The display and exhibit area features the Space Shuttle, space station, aeronautics and propulsion, planets and space exploration; also Skylab 3, an Apollo capsule, and communications satellites. (Daily; closed hols) 21000 Brookpark Rd. Phone 216/433-2001. **FREE**

Cleveland Institute of Art. (1882) 460 students. Professional education in the visual arts. Professional and student exhibition gallery (Daily; closed hols). 11141 East Blvd and 11610 Euclid Ave in University Cir. Phone 216/421-7000.

Cleveland Institute of Music. (1920) A leading international conservatory that is distinguished by an exceptional degree of collaboration between students and teachers. This same stimulating environment extends to the Institute's community education programs, which help student's realize their musical potential. Students: conservatory, 370; preparatory, 1,700. Free public concerts and recitals. Tours. 11021 East Blvd. Phone 216/791-5000.

Cleveland Metroparks. Established in 1917, the system today consists of more than 20,000 acres of land in 14 reservations, their connecting parkways, and Cleveland Metroparks Zoo. Swimming, boating, and fishing; more than 100 mi of parkways provide scenic drives, picnic areas, and play fields; wildlife management areas and waterfowl sanctuaries; hiking and bridle trails, stables, golf courses; tobogganing, sledding, skating, and x-country skiing areas; eight outdoor education facilities offering nature exhibits and programs. Phone 216/351-6300.

⭐ **The Cleveland Museum of Art.** Extensive collections of approx 30,000 works of art represent a wide range of history and culture; incl are arts of the Islamic Near East, the pre-Columbian Americas, and European and Asian art; also African, Indian, American, ancient Roman, and Egyptian art. Concerts, lectures, special exhibitions, films; cafe. Museum entrance from East Blvd. (Tues-Sun; closed hols) Parking (fee). 11150 East Blvd at University Cir. Phone 216/421-7340. **FREE**

Cleveland Museum of Natural History. Dinosaurs, mammals, birds, geological specimens, gems; exhibits on prehistoric Ohio, North American native cultures, ecology; Woods Garden, live animals; library. (Daily; closed hols). Wade Oval at University Cir. Phone 216/231-4600. ¢¢ Also here is

> **Ralph Mueller Planetarium.** Shows (Daily). Observatory (Sept-May, Wed on cloudless nights; planetarium program on cloudy nights). Children's programs. Phone 216/231-4600. ¢

The Cleveland Orchestra. One of the world's finest orchestras. International soloists and guest conductors. (Mid-Sept-mid-May, Tues and Thurs-Sun) 1154 Steels Corner Rd. Phone 216/231-1111.

Cleveland Play House. America's oldest regional, professional Equity theater presents traditional American classics and premiere productions of new works in five performance spaces; organized in 1915. (Sept-June, Tues-Sun, also wkend matinees) 8500 Euclid Ave. Phone 216/795-7000.

Cleveland State University. (1964) 16,000 students. James J. Nance College of Business Administration, Fenn College of Engineering, Cleveland-Marshall College of Law, Maxine Goodman Levin College of Urban Affairs, Graduate Studies, Education, Arts and Sciences. Campus tours. Euclid Ave and E 24th St. Phone 216/687-2000.

Dittrick Museum of Medical History. Collection of objects relating to history of medicine, dentistry, pharmacy, nursing; doctor's offices of 1880 and 1930; exhibits on development of medical concepts in the Western Reserve to the present. Also history of the X-ray and microscopes. (Mon-Fri; closed hols, day after Thanksgiving) 11000 Euclid Ave, third floor of Allen Memorial

Medical Library, University Cir area. Phone 216/368-3648. **FREE**

Dunham Tavern Museum. Restoration of early stagecoach stop (1824) between Buffalo and Detroit; historic museum with changing exhibits; period furnishings. (Wed and Sun afternoons; closed hols) 6709 Euclid Ave, East Side. Phone 216/431-1060. ¢

Edgewater Park. A 119-acre park with swimming beach, fishing, boating (ramps, marina); biking; fitness course, picnic grounds (pavilions), playground, concessions. Scenic overlook. (Daily) West Blvd and Cleveland Memorial Shoreway; unit of Cleveland Lakefront State Park on Lake Erie. Phone 216/881-8141. **FREE**

Euclid Beach Park. A 51-acre park with swimming beach, fishing access; picnic grounds, concession. 16300 Lakeshore Blvd; unit of Cleveland Lakefront State Park on Lake Erie. Phone 216/881-8141. **FREE**

Gordon Park. A 117-acre park with fishing piers, boat ramp; picnic area, playground. (Daily) E 72nd St and Cleveland Memorial Shoreway; unit of Cleveland Lakefront State Park on Lake Erie. Phone 216/881-8141. **FREE**

Great Lakes Science Center. More than 350 hands-on exhibits explain scientific principles and topics specifically relating to the Great Lakes region. Also features an OmniMax domed theater. (Daily; closed hols) 601 Erieside Ave. Phone 216/694-2000. ¢¢¢

Hanna Fountain Mall. Rectangular section in downtown heart of city, with plaza, fountains, and memorial to WWII veterans. Surrounding the mall are the following governmental and municipal buildings:

City Hall. Lakeside Ave and E 6th St, overlooking Lake Erie.

County Court House and Administration Building. Justice Center. Ontario and Lakeside Ave.

Federal Buildings. Courts, customs, passport bureau. (Old) at Superior Ave and Public Square and (new) at E 6th St and Lakeside Ave.

Public Auditorium and Convention Center. Seats 10,000; incl ballroom, music hall, small theater, and 375,000 sq ft of usable space.

Space for 28 events at one time. St. Clair Ave, E 6th St and Lakeside Ave.

Public Library. Business and Science Building adjoining, separated by a reading garden; special exhibits. (Daily; closed hols) 325 Superior Ave, near Public Sq. Phone 216/623-2800.

Health Museum of Cleveland. More than 200 participatory exhibits and displays on the human body incl Juno, the transparent talking woman; and Wonder of New Life. Events and educational programs, including Corporate Wellness, Distance Learning, and school programs. (Daily; closed hols) 8911 Euclid Ave, East Side. Phone 216/231-5010. ¢¢

High-level bridges. Main Ave Bridge, Lorain Carnegie Bridge, Innerbelt Fwy Bridge, all spanning Cuyahoga River Valley.

John Carroll University. (1886) 4,500 students. Arts and sciences, business, and graduate schools in 21 Gothic-style buildings on 60-acre campus. Large collection of G. K. Chesterton works. Warrensville Center and Fairmount Blvd, in University Heights. Phone 216/397-1886.

Karamu House and Theater. Multicultural center for the arts. Classes/workshops in music, creative writing, dance, drama, and visual arts; dance, music, and theatrical performances (Sept-June); two theaters, art galleries. Fee for some activities. 2355 E 89th St at Quincy Ave. Phone 216/795-7070.

Lake Erie Nature and Science Center. Features animals, marine tanks, nature displays, wildlife/teaching garden; planetarium show (fee). Science Center (daily; closed hols). 28728 Wolf Rd, 14 mi W on US 6 or I-90 to Bay Village, in Metropark Huntington, West Side. Phone 440/871-2900. **FREE**

Lake View Cemetery. Graves of President James A. Garfield, Mark Hanna, John Hay, John D. Rockefeller. Garfield Monument (Apr-mid-Nov, daily). Cemetery (daily). 12316 Euclid Ave, at E 123rd St, East Side. Phone 216/421-2665.

Oldest Stone House Museum. (1838) Authentically restored and furnished with early 19th-century artifacts; herb garden. Guided tour by cos-

Rock and Roll Hall of Fame

tumed hostess. (Feb-Nov, Wed and Sun afternoons; closed hols) 5 mi W, 1 blk N of US 6 in Lakewood, at 14710 Lake Ave, West Side. Phone 216/221-7343. **Donation**

Playhouse Square Center. Five restored theaters form the nation's second-largest performing arts and entertainment center. Performances incl legitimate theater, Broadway productions, popular and classical music, ballet, opera, children's theater, and concerts. 1501 Euclid Ave. Phone 216/241-6000.

Professional sports.

Cleveland Browns (NFL). Cleveland Browns Stadium, 1085 W 3rd St. Phone 440/891-5001.

Cleveland Cavaliers (NBA). Gund Arena, 1 Center Ct. Phone 216/420-CAVS.

Cleveland Indians (MLB). Jacobs Field, 2404 Ontario St. Phone 216/420-4200.

Cleveland Rockers (WNBA). Gund Arena, 1 Center Ct. Phone 216/263-ROCK.

⭐ **Rock and Roll Hall of Fame and Museum.** A striking composition of geometric shapes, this building is now the permanent home of the Hall of Fame. More than 50,000 sq ft of exhibition areas explore rock's ongoing evolution and its impact on culture. Interactive database of rock and roll songs; videos; working studio with DJs conducting live broadcasts; exhibits on rhythm and blues, soul, country, folk, and blues music. (Daily; closed Jan 1, Thanksgiving, Dec 25) North Coast Harbor, E 9th St Pier. ¢¢¢¢

Rockefeller Park. Connects Wade Park and Gordon Park. A 296-acre park with lagoon area, playground, tennis courts, picnic facilities. Phone 216/881-8141. Also here are

Cultural Gardens. Chain of gardens combining landscape architecture and sculpture of 24 nationalities. Along East and Martin Luther King, Jr. blvds. (Daily) **FREE**

Rockefeller Greenhouse. Japanese, Latin American, and peace gardens; garden for the visually impaired; seasonal displays. (Daily) 750 E 88th St. Phone 216/664-3103. **FREE**

Sightseeing tours.

Cuyahoga Valley Line Steam Railroad. Scenic railroad trips between Independence (south of Cleveland) and Akron aboard vintage train. Phone 330/657-2000.

Goodtime III boat cruise. Two-hr sightseeing and dance cruises on Cuyahoga River, lake, and harbor. Leaves pier at E 9th St. (Mid-June-Sept, daily; limited schedule rest of yr) Phone 216/861-5110. ¢¢¢

Nautica Queen boat cruise. Lunch, brunch, and dinner cruises. For details, contact E 9th St Pier, North Coast Harbor, 44113. Phone 216/696-8888.

Trolley Tours of Cleveland. One- and two-hr tours leave from Powerhouse at Nautica Complex. Advanced res requested. Phone 216/771-4484. ¢¢¢

Steamship *William G. Mather* Museum. Former flagship of the Cleveland Cliffs Iron Company, this 618-ft steamship is now a floating discovery center. Built in 1925 to carry iron ore, coal, grain, and stone throughout the Great Lakes, she now houses exhibits and displays focusing on the heritage of the "Iron Boats." Her forward cargo hold is an exhibit hall and also houses a theater and gift shop. Guided and self-guided tours of the vessels are available (depending upon the time of yr); visitors will see the pilot house, crew and guest quarters, galley, guest and officers' dining rm, and the four-story engine rm. (June-Aug, daily; May and Sept-Oct, Fri-Sun) 1001 E 9th St Pier. Phone 216/574-6262. ¢¢

Temple Museum of Religious Art. Jewish ceremonial objects; antiquities of the Holy Land region. (Daily, by appt; closed Jewish hols) 1855 Ansel Rd, University Cir area. Phone 216/831-3233. **FREE**

Tower City Center. A former railroad station and terminal, built in the 1920s. "The Avenue," a three-level marble, glass, and brass complex of dining, entertainment, and retail establishments, has an 80-ft high skylight, a 55-ft glass dome, 26 escalators and elevators, and a 40-ft-long fountain. An underground walkway connects Tower City to the Gateway Complex containing Jacobs Field and Gund Arena. Terminal Tower (ca 1930) was reborn again in the 1990s as the nucleus of Tower City Center. On the 42nd floor of this 52-story building is an observation deck (Sat and Sun). Public Sq, Downtown. For further information check Terminal Tower Lobby. ¢

USS COD. World War II submarine credited with seven successful war patrols that sank more than 27,000 tons of Imperial Japanese shipping. Tours incl all major compartments of this completely restored *Gato* class submarine. (May-Sept, daily) Docked at N Marginal Rd, between E 9th St and Burke Lakefront Airport. Phone 216/566-8770.

Wade Park. More than 80 acres; lake; rose and herb gardens. Euclid Ave near 107th St at University Cir. Phone 216/621-4110. **FREE** Also here is

Cleveland Botanical Garden. Herb, rose, perennial, wildflower, Japanese, and reading gardens. (Grounds Apr-Oct, daily). 11030 East Blvd. Phone 216/721-1600. **FREE**

Western Reserve Historical Society Museum and Library. Changing exhibits; special programs; genealogy department; costume collection; American decorative arts. (Daily; closed hols) 10825 East Blvd in University Cir. Phone 216/721-5722. ¢¢ Also here and incl in admission is

Frederick C. Crawford Auto-Aviation Collection. Antique cars and planes; motorcycles and bicycles; National Air Racing exhibit; Main Street, Ohio, 1890. (Daily; closed hols)

Wildwood Park. An 80-acre park with fishing, boating (ramps); picnic grounds, playground, concession. Lakeshore Blvd and Neff Rd; unit of Cleveland Lakefront State Park on Lake Erie. Phone 216/881-8141. **FREE**

Special Events

Tri-City JazzFest. Phone 216/987-4400. Early Apr.

Cuyahoga County Fair. Fairgrounds, in Berea. One of largest in the state. Phone 440/243-0090. Early or mid-Aug.

Slavic Village Harvest Festival. Slavic Village (Fleet Ave at 55th St). Mid-Aug. Phone 216/429-1182.

Cleveland National Air Show. Burke Lakefront Airport. Phone 216/781-0747. Labor Day wkend.

Motels/Motor Lodges

★★ **CLARION HOTEL CLEVELAND WEST.** *17000 Bagley Rd,*

*Middleburg Heights (44130). 440/243-
5200; fax 440/243-5244; res 800/321-
2323. www.choicehotels.com.* 223 rms,
2 story. S, D $79-$112; suites $145-
$239; under 18 free; wkend rates.
Crib free. Pet accepted. TV; cable
(premium). 2 pools, 1 indoor; wading pool, lifeguard. Restaurant 6:30
am-10 pm; Fri, Sat to 11 pm. Rm
serv. Bar; entertainment Fri, Sat. Ck-
out 11 am. Coin lndry. Meeting rms.
In-rm modem link. Bellhops. Valet
serv. Sundries. Free airport transportation. Sauna. Cr cds: A, MC, V.
🐾 ➰ 🏊 ✕

★★ **COMFORT INN CLEVELAND
AIRPORT.** *17550 Rosbough Dr,
Middleburg Heights (44130). 440/234-
3131; fax 440/234-6111; res 800/228-
5150. www.comfortinn.com.* 136 rms,
3 story. S, D $89-$129; each addl
$10; under 18 free; wkend rates. Crib
free. Pet accepted, some restrictions.
TV; cable (premium). Pool. Complimentary continental bkfst. Coffee in
rms. Restaurants nearby. Ck-out
noon. Meeting rms. Business center.
Valet serv. Sundries. Free airport
transportation. Microwaves avail. Cr
cds: A, D, DS, MC, V.
D 🐾 ➰ 🏊 ✕ 🏊 🐾

★ **CROSS COUNTRY INN- CLEVE-
LAND SOUTH.** *7233 Engle Rd,
Middleburg Heights (44130). 440/243-
2277; fax 440/243-9852. www.cross
countryinns.com.* 112 rms, 2 story. S
$46.99; D $69.99; each addl $7;
under 18 free. Crib free. TV; cable
(premium). Heated pool. Complimentary coffee in lobby. Restaurant
adj open 24 hrs. Ck-out noon. Meeting rm. Downhill ski 18 mi; x-country ski 5 mi. Cr cds: A, C, D, DS,
MC, V.
D ➰ 🏊 ✕ 🐾 🚠

★★ **FAIRFIELD INN - CLEVELAND
AIRPORT.** *16644 Snow Rd, Brook Park
(44142). 216/676-5200; toll-free
800/228-2800. www.fairfieldinn.com.*
135 rms, 3 story. May-Aug: S, D $69;
each addl $7; lower rates rest of yr. Crib free. TV; cable
(premium). Pool. Complimentary
continental bkfst. Ck-out noon. Business servs avail. Cr cds: A, D, DS,
MC, V.
D ➰ 🏊 ✕ 🐾 SC

Hotels

★★★ **HYATT REGENCY CLEVE-
LAND.** *420 Superior (44114).
216/575-1234; res 800/233-1234.
www.hyatt.com.* 293 rms, 9 story. S, D
$150-$275; each addl $25; under 17
free. Crib avail. TV; cable (premium),
VCR avail. Complimentary coffee in
rms. Restaurant 6 am-10 pm. Ck-out
noon. Meeting rms. Business center.
Gift shop. Exercise rm. Some refrigerators, minibars. Cr cds: A, C, D, DS,
MC, V.
🏃 🧍 ✕ D

★★★ **INTER-CONTINENTAL
SUITE HOTEL.** *8800 Euclid Ave
(44106). 216/707-4300. www.
interconti.com.* 163 rms, 8 story. S, D
$195-$275; each addl $25; under 17
free. Crib avail. TV; cable (premium),
VCR avail. Complimentary coffee,
newspaper in rms. Restaurant 6 am-
10 pm. Ck-out noon. Meeting rms.
Business center. Gift shop. Exercise
rm. Some refrigerators, minibars. Cr
cds: A, C, D, DS, MC, V.
🏃 🧍 ✕ D

★★★ **MARRIOTT CLEVELAND
AIRPORT.** *4277 W 150th St (44135).
216/252-5333; fax 216/251-9404; res
800/228-9290. marriotthotels.com.* 371
rms, 4-9 story. S $139; D $159; suites
$175-$350; under 18 free; wkend
rates. Crib free. Pet accepted; $50.
TV; cable (premium), VCR avail.
Indoor pool; whirlpool, poolside
serv. Restaurant 6 am-11 pm. Bar
11:30-2 am. Ck-out noon. Coin
lndry. Convention facilities. Business
servs avail. In-rm modem link. Gift
shop. Free airport transportation.
Exercise equipt; sauna. Cr cds: A,
MC, V.
✕ D 🐾 🏊 🧍 ✈

★★★ **MARRIOTT DOWNTOWN
AT KEY CENTER.** *127 Public Sq
(44114). 216/696-9200; fax 216/696-
0966; res 800/228-9290. www.
marriott.com.* 400 rms, 25 story. S, D
$169-$189; suites $250-$750; under
18 free. Crib free. Garage $13. TV;
cable (premium), VCR avail. Indoor
pool; whirlpool. Restaurant 6 am-11
pm. Bar 11-2 am. Ck-out noon. Coin
lndry. Convention facilities. Business
center. In-rm modem link. Concierge.
Gift shop. Exercise equipt; sauna.

Minibars. Luxury level. Cr cds: A, C, D, DS, JCB, MC, V.

★ ★ ★ **RADISSON AIRPORT.** *25070 Country Club Blvd, North Olmsted (44070). 440/734-5060; fax 440/734-5471; res 800/333-3333. www. radisson.com.* 140 rms, 6 story. May-Oct: S, D $139-$149; each addl $10; suites $160; under 18 free; wkend, hol rates; higher rates conventions; lower rates rest of yr. Crib free. TV; cable (premium), VCR avail. Indoor pool; whirlpool. Complimentary coffee in rms. Restaurant 6:30 am-2 pm, 5-10 pm; Sat, Sun from 7 am. Bar 11 am-11 pm. Ck-out noon. Meeting rms. Business servs avail. In-rm modem link. Free airport transportation. Downhill ski 15 mi; x-country ski 10 mi. Exercise equipt; sauna. Some refrigerators; microwaves avail. Some balconies. Cr cds: A, C, D, DS, ER, JCB, MC, V.

★ ★ ★ **RENAISSANCE CLEVE-LAND.** *24 Public Sq (44113). 216/696-5600; fax 216/696-0432; toll-free 800/696-6898. www.renaissancehotels. com.* 491 rms, 14 story. S $139-$179; D $159-$299; each addl $20; suites $250-$1,500; under 18 free; wkend rates. Crib free. TV; cable (premium), VCR avail (movies). Indoor pool. Complimentary coffee. Restaurant (see SANS SOUCI). Bar 11-2 am; entertainment. Ck-out noon. Convention facilities. Business center. In-rm modem link. Concierge. Gift shop. Garage parking. Exercise rm; sauna. Health club privileges. Bathrm phones, refrigerators, minibars. 10-story indoor atrium. Luxury level. Cr cds: A, D, DS, MC, V.

★ ★ ★ ★ **THE RITZ-CARLTON, CLEVELAND.** *1515 W Third St (44113). 216/623-1300; fax 216/623-0515; toll-free 800/241-3333. www.ritz carlton.com.* Located in the center of the downtown business district adjacent to the upscale shops of The Avenue at Tower City Center, this 208-room, 27-suite property has the brand's characteristic luxurious interior, but with a comfortable feel. Century restaurant, filled with memorabilia reminiscent of The Twentieth Century Limited train, has a modern decor, a cool sushi bar, and

live, nightly entertainment. 208 rms, 7 story, 27 suites. S, D $175-$205; suites $249-$399; under 12 free; wkend rates. Pet accepted, fee. TV; cable, VCR avail (movies). Indoor pool; whirlpool, poolside serv. Restaurant (see also RIVERVIEW ROOM). Afternoon tea. Rm serv 24 hrs. Bar 11:30-1 am Mon-Sat; Sun to midnight; pianist. Ck-out noon. Meeting rms. Business center. In-rm modem link. Concierge. Exercise equipt; sauna. Massage. Health club privileges. Bathrm phones, minibars. Luxury level. Cr cds: A, C, D, DS, MC, V.

★ ★ ★ **SHERATON AIRPORT.** *5300 Riverside Dr (44135). 216/267-1500; res 800/325-3535.* 288 rms, 6 story. S, D $175-$250; each addl $25; under 17 free. Crib avail. Indoor pool. TV; cable (premium), VCR avail. Complimentary coffee in rms. Restaurant 6 am-10 pm. Ck-out noon. Meeting rms. Business center. Gift shop. Exercise rm. Some refrigerators, minibars. Cr cds: A, C, D, DS, MC, V.

★ ★ ★ **SHERATON CLEVELAND CITY CENTRE HOTEL.** *777 NE St. Clair Ave (44114). 216/771-7600; fax 216/566-0736; toll-free 800/321-1090.* 470 rms, 22 story. S, D $134-$154; each addl $15; suites $179-$850; under 18 free. Crib free. Garage $13. TV; cable (premium). Restaurant 6:30 am-11 pm. Bar from 11 am, Sun from 1 pm. Ck-out noon. Convention facilities. Business center. In-rm modem link. Gift shop. Airport transportation. Exercise equipt. Health club privileges. Many rms with view of lake. Luxury level. Cr cds: A, D, DS, MC, V.

★ ★ **WYNDHAM CLEVELAND HOTEL.** *1260 Euclid Ave (44115). 216/615-7500; fax 216/621-8659; toll-free 800/996-3426.* 205 rms, 14 story. S $149-$189; D $169-$209; each addl $20; suites $249; under 16 free. Crib avail. Valet parking $15. TV; cable. Indoor pool; whirlpool. Complimentary coffee in rms. Restaurant 6 am-10:30 pm. Bar to 2 am. Ck-out noon. Meeting rms. Business servs avail. Sundries. Valet serv. Exercise equipt;

sauna. Health club privileges. Cr cds: A, C, D, DS, MC, V.

[D] [≈] [🏋] [🐾] [SC]

B&B/Small Inn

★ ★ ★ **BARICELLI INN.** *2203 Cornell Rd (44106). 216/791-6500; fax 216/791-9131. baricelli.com.* 7 rms, 3 story. S, D $150. TV; cable. Complimentary continental bkfst. Dining rm (see BARICELLI INN). Ck-out 11 am, ck-in 2 pm. Business servs avail. Antiques, stained glass. Brownstone (1896) with individually decorated rms. Cr cds: A, D, MC, V.

[⊠]

All Suite

★ ★ ★ **EMBASSY SUITES-DOWNTOWN.** *1701 E 12th St (44114). 216/523-8000; fax 216/523-1698; res 800/362-2779. www.es-cleveland.com.* 268 suites, 13 story. S, D, Kit. units $119-$229; under 18 free; wkend rates. Crib free. Valet parking $14. TV; cable. Indoor pool. Complimentary coffee in rms. Restaurant 6:30 am-10:30 pm. Bar 11-1 am. Ck-out noon. Coin lndry. Meeting rms. In-rm modem link. Concierge. Lighted tennis. Exercise equipt; sauna. Refrigerators, microwaves. Balconies. Cr cds: A, MC, V.

[D] [🏃] [≈] [🏋] [⊠] [🔥]

Extended Stay

★ ★ **RESIDENCE INN BY MARRIOTT.** *17525 Rosbough Dr, Middleburg Heights (44130). 440/234-6688; fax 440/234-3459; toll-free 800/331-3131. www.marriott.com.* 158 kit. suites, 2 story. S, D $109-$169; package plans. Crib free. Pet accepted, some restrictions. TV; cable (premium), VCR avail (movies). Heated pool; whirlpool. Complimentary continental bkfst. Complimentary coffee in rms. Restaurant adj 6 am-midnight. Ck-out noon. Coin lndry. Business servs avail. Valet serv. Sundries. Airport transportation. Downhill ski 15 mi; x-country ski 5 mi. Lawn games. Exercise equipt. Microwaves; many fireplaces. Picnic tables, grills. Cr cds: A, C, D, DS, JCB, MC, V.

[D] [🐾] [🎿] [≈] [🏋] [⊠] [🔥] [SC]

Restaurants

★ ★ ★ **BARICELLI INN.** *2203 Cornell Rd (44106). 216/791-6500. www.baricelli.com.* Hrs: 5:30-11 pm. Closed Sun; most major hols. Res accepted. Continental menu. Wine, beer. Dinner $19.50-$39. Specialties: lobster and crab ravioli, beef tenderloin. Outdoor dining. Fireplaces, stained glass and paintings throughout room. Cr cds: A, DS, MC, V.

[D] [⊠]

★ **CABIN CLUB.** *30651 Detroit Rd, Westlake (44145). 440/899-7111.* Hrs: 11 am-10:30 pm; Fri, Sat to 11:30 pm; Sun 4-10:30 pm. Closed most major hols. Res accepted. Bar to 1 am. Lunch $8-$16, dinner $15-$30. Child's menu. Specializes in steak, seafood, chicken. Log cabin decor. Cr cds: A, D, DS, MC, V.

[⊠]

★ **CAFE SAUSALITO.** *1301 E 9th St (44114). 216/696-2233. www.savvy diner.com.* Hrs: 11:30 am-8 pm; Fri, Sat to 9 pm. Closed Sun; Thanksgiving, Dec 25. Res accepted. Lunch $5.50-$10.95, dinner $10.95-$19.95. Specializes in seafood, pasta. Pianist Fri, Sat (dinner). Valet parking. Dinner theater package. Cr cds: A, D, DS, MC, V.

[D] [⊠]

★ **CLUB ISABELLA.** *2025 University Hospital Dr (44106). 216/229-1177.* Hrs: 11:30 am-11 pm; Fri to 1 am; Sat 5:30 pm-1 am. Res accepted; required wkends. Bar. Lunch $4.95-$7.95, dinner $8.95-$17.95. Jazz nightly. Valet parking (dinner). Outdoor dining. Former stagecoach house. Cr cds: A, MC, V.

[⊠]

★ ★ **DON'S LIGHTHOUSE GRILLE.** *8905 Lake Ave (44102). 216/961-6700. www.donslighthouse.com.* Hrs: 11:30 am-10 pm; Fri to 11 pm; Sat 5 pm-11 pm; Sun 4:30-9 pm. Closed some major hols. Res accepted. Continental menu. Bar. Lunch $6.95-$9.95, dinner $10-$20. Specializes in fresh seafood, steaks. Valet parking. Contemporary decor. Cr cds: A, D, DS, MC, V.

[D] [⊠]

★ **GREAT LAKES BREWING CO.**
2516 Market Ave (44113). 216/771-4404. www.greatlakesbrewing.com. Hrs: 11:30 am-midnight; Fri, Sat to 1 am; Sun 1-10 pm. Closed major hols. Res accepted. Bar. Lunch, dinner $6-$16. Child's menu. Specializes in crab cakes, fresh pasta, seafood. Own beer. Outdoor dining. Microbrewery. Located in historic 1860s brewery; turn-of-the-century pub atmosphere. Cr cds: A, DS, MC, V.
D

★ **GUARINO'S.** *12309 Mayfield Rd (44106). 216/231-3100.* Hrs: 11:30 am-10:30 pm; Thurs to 11 pm; Fri, Sat to 11:30 pm; Sun 1-8 pm. Closed major hols. Res accepted; required Fri, Sat. Italian, Amer menu. Bar. A la carte entrees: lunch $7-$9.25, dinner $12-$16.75. Child's menus. Specializes in southern Italian cuisine. Valet parking. Outdoor dining. Oldest restaurant in Cleveland. In heart of Little Italy; antiques. Cr cds: A, D, DS, MC, V.
⊡

★★★ **JOHNNY'S BAR.** *3164 Fulton Rd (44109). 216/281-0055.* Hrs: 11:30 am-3 pm, 5-10 pm; Fri to 11 pm; Sat 5-11 pm. Closed Sun; most major hols. Res accepted; required Fri, Sat. Italian menu. Bar. Lunch $6-$13.95, dinner $14.50-$29.95. Specialties: Italian Feast; veal chops. Former neighborhood grocery. Family-owned. Cr cds: A, DS, MC, V.
D ⊡

★ **JOHN Q'S STEAKHOUSE.** *55 Public Sq (44113). 216/861-0900. www.johnq.savvydiner.com.* Hrs: 11:30 am-10 pm; Fri to 11 pm; Sat 4-11 pm; Sun 4-10 pm. Closed major hols. Res accepted. Bar. Lunch $5.25-$11.95, dinner $16.95-$29.95. Child's menu. Specialty: 16-oz pepper steak. Valet parking Sat. Outdoor dining. Traditional decor with dark wood floors and walls. Cr cds: A, D, DS, MC, V.
D ⊡

★ **LEMON GRASS.** *2179 Lee Rd, Cleveland Heights (44118). 216/321-0210.* Hrs: 11:30 am-2:30 pm, 5-10 pm; Fri to 11 pm; Sat 5-11 pm. Closed Sun; some major hols. Res accepted (dinner). Thai menu. Bar. Lunch $7-$10, dinner $11-$21. Specializes in seafood, curry dishes.

Blues, jazz Fri. Outdoor dining. Thai decor with two distinct dining areas: one formal, one informal. Cr cds: A, D, DS, MC, V.
D

★★★ **MORTON'S OF CHICAGO.** *1600 W 2nd (44113). 216/621-6200. www.mortons.com.* Hrs: 11:30 am-2:30 pm, 5-11 pm; Sat, Sun 5-10 pm. Closed most major hols. Res accepted. Bar. Wine list. A la carte entrees: lunch $14-$23, dinner $21-$36. Specializes in steak, prime beef. Club atmosphere. Cr cds: A, DS, MC, V.
D ⊡

★ **NEW YORK SPAGHETTI HOUSE.** *2173 E 9th St (44115). 216/696-6624.* Hrs: 11 am-9:30 pm; Fri, Sat to 10:30 pm; Sun 3-7 pm. Closed major hols. Res accepted. Italian, Amer menu. Bar. Lunch $6-$7, dinner $8-$24. Specializes in veal. Mural scenes of Italy. In former parsonage. Family-owned. Cr cds: A, D, DS, MC, V.
D ⊡

★★★ **PARKER'S.** *2801 Bridge Ave (44113). 216/771-7130.* French, Amer menu. Hrs: 5-10 pm; Fri, Sat to 11 pm; Sun 4-8 pm. Closed major hols. Res accepted. Bar. Wine cellar. A la carte entrees: dinner $18-$30. Valet parking. Tavern atmosphere. Totally nonsmoking. Cr cds: A, D, DS, MC, V.
D

★★ **PICCOLO MONDO.** *1352 W 6th St (44113). 216/241-1300.* Hrs: 11:30 am-11 pm; Fri, Sat to midnight. Closed Sun; most major hols. Res accepted. Italian menu. Bar. Lunch $9-$20, dinner $11-$32. Specialties: veal scallopine, brick-oven pizza. Italian villa decor. Cr cds: A, D, DS, MC, V.
D SC ⊡

★ **PLAYERS ON MADISON.** *14523 Madison Ave, Lakewood (44107). 216/226-5200. www.playersonmadison. com.* Hrs: 5-10 pm; Fri, Sat to 11 pm. Closed major hols. Italian menu. Bar. Dinner $14-$20. Specializes in pizza, pasta. Italian bistro decor. Cr cds: A, C, D, DS, ER, MC, V.
D ⊡

★★★ **RIVERVIEW ROOM.** *1515 W 3rd St (44113). 216/623-1300.* Hrs: 6:30 am-10 pm; Fri, Sat to 11 pm;

Sun brunch 10:30 am-2:30 pm. Res accepted; required brunch. Contemporary Amer menu. Bar. Wine cellar. Complete meals: bkfst $10.50-$15, lunch $15-$25, dinner $30-$40. Bkfst $8.50-$12, lunch $12.50-$17.50, dinner $24-$35. Bkfst buffet $8.50-$10.50. Sun brunch $32. Child's menu. Specialty: mushroom mystic. Own baking, pasta. Valet parking. Elegant restaurant with antiques and artwork throughout; large windows offer view of river and downtown. Cr cds: A, D, DS, MC, V.
D

★★★ **SANS SOUCI.** 24 Public Sq (44113). 216/696-5600. Hrs: 11:30 am-2:30 pm, 5:30-10 pm; Fri, Sat to 11 pm; Sun from 5:30 pm. Closed most major hols. Res accepted. Mediterranean menu. Bar to 2 am. Wine list. Lunch $5.75-$15, dinner $11.95-$19.50. Specializes in seafood. Mediterranean decor. Cr cds: A, D, DS, MC, V.
D

★ **THAT PLACE ON BELLFLOWER.** 11401 Bellflower Rd (44106). 216/231-4469. www.thatplace onbellflower.com. Hrs: 11:30 am-8:30 pm; Sun 5:30-8:30 pm; Mon to 3 pm. Closed major hols. Res accepted. Varied menu. Bar. Lunch $4.95-$6.95, dinner $9.95-$16.95. Child's menu. Specialties: beef Wellington, fresh salmon. Valet parking. Outdoor dining. Converted turn-of-the-century carriage house. Cr cds: A, DS, MC, V.

★ **WATERMARK.** 1250 Old River Rd (44113). 216/241-1600. www. watermark-flats.com. Hrs: 11:30 am-10 pm; Fri, Sat to 11 pm; Sun brunch 10:30 am-2:30 pm. Res accepted. Bar. Lunch, dinner $7.95-$22.95. Sun brunch $15.95. Seafood buffet (Fri) $17.95. Child's menu. Specializes in marinated and grilled seafood. Free valet parking. Outdoor dining. River cruises avail. Former ship provision warehouse on Cuyahoga River. Cr cds: A, D, DS, MC, V.
D

Unrated Dining Spot

ALVIE'S GATEWAY GRILLE. 2033 Ontario St (44115). 216/771-5322. Hrs: 6:30 am-4 pm; Sat 9 am-2 pm.

Closed Sun; major hols. Beer. Bkfst $2-$4, lunch $3-$8. Specializes in deli foods, salads. Own soups. Family-owned. Cr cds: A, D, MC, V.
D

Columbus

(D-4) *See also Delaware, Lancaster, Newark*

Founded 1812 **Pop** 632,910 **Elev** 780 ft **Area code** 614

Information Greater Columbus Convention & Visitors Bureau, 90 N High St, 43215-3014; 614/221-6623 or 800/345-4386

Web www.columbuscvb.org

Columbus was created and laid out to be the capital of Ohio; it is attractive, with broad, tree-lined streets, parks, Ohio State University, and a handsome Greek Revival capitol. Both Chillicothe and Zanesville had previously been capitals, but in 1812 two tracts were selected on the banks of the Scioto River, one for the capitol, the other for a state penitentiary, and construction began immediately. The legislature first met here in 1816.

By 1831 the new National Road reached Columbus and stagecoach travel stimulated its growth. The first railroad reached Columbus in 1850 and from then on the city grew rapidly. Floods in 1913 made it necessary to widen the channel of the Scioto River. Levees, fine arched bridges, and the Civic Center were built.

Transportation equipment, machinery, fabricated and primary metals, food, printing, and publishing are among the principal industries, but education and government are the most important functions of Columbus. Its people are civic-minded, sports-minded, and cultured. The city has more than 1,130 churches and congregations and 12 colleges and universities.

Additional Visitor Information

Tourist brochures and a quarterly calendar of events may be obtained at the Visitor Center/gift shop in the

Convention & Visitors Bureau, 90 N High St, or on the second level of Columbus City Center, S High St and S Third St at Rich St, phone 800/345-4FUN. A third visitor information center is located at the Columbus International Airport, I-670 E, I-270.

What to See and Do

Camp Chase Confederate Cemetery. Burial ground for Confederate soldiers who were prisoners in the camp. Sullivant Ave between Powell Ave and Binns Blvd.

City Hall. Occupies an entire block in the Civic Center. Greco-Roman style. Municipal departments and city council chamber. N Front, W Gay, W Broad Sts and Marconi Blvd.

Columbus Museum of Art. Collections focus on 19th- and 20th-century European and American paintings, sculpture, works on paper, and decorative arts; contemporary sculpture; also incl 16th- and 17th-century Dutch and Flemish Masters. Galleries arranged chronologically. Museum shop; indoor atrium; Sculpture Garden; cafe. (Tues-Sun; closed hols) 480 E Broad St at Washington Ave. Phone 614/221-6801. ¢¢¢

Columbus Symphony Orchestra. Performances at Ohio Theatre. 55 E State St. Phone 614/228-8600.

COSI Columbus, Ohio's Center of Science & Industry. Hands-on museum incl exhibits, programs, and demonstrations. Battelle Planetarium shows (daily). Coal Mine, Hi-Tech Showcase, Free Enterprise Area, Foucault pendulum, Solar Front Exhibit Area, Computer Experience, Street of Yesteryear, Weather Station, KIDSPACE, and FAMILIESPACE. (Daily) 280 E Broad St. Phone 614/228-2674. ¢¢¢

Federal Building. Federal offices. 200 N High St.

Fort Ancient State Memorial. (see).

German Village. Historic district restored as Old World village with shops, old homes, gardens; authentic foods. Bus tour avail; inquire. (Daily) S of Downtown, bounded by Livingston Ave, Blackberry Alley, Nursery Ln, Pearl Alley. 588 S 3rd St. Phone 614/221-8888. **FREE**

Hoover Reservoir Area. Fishing, boating; nature trails, picnicking.

(Daily) 12 mi NE on Sunbury Rd. Phone 614/645-1721. **FREE**

Martha Kinney Cooper Ohioana Library. Reference library of books on Ohio and by Ohioans. (Mon-Fri; closed hols) 274 E First Ave. Phone 614/466-3831. **FREE**

McKinley Memorial. Statue of President McKinley delivering his last address. West entrance to capitol grounds.

☒ **Ohio Historical Center.** (1970) Modern architectural design contrasts with the age-old themes of Ohio's prehistoric culture, natural history, and history. Exhibits incl an archaeology mall with computer interactive displays and life-size dioramas; a natural history mall with a mastodon skeleton and a demonstration laboratory; and a history mall with transportation, communication, and lifestyle exhibits. Ohio archives and historical library (Tues-Sat). Museum (daily; closed Jan 1, Thanksgiving, Dec 25). 17th Ave at I-71. Phone 614/297-2300. ¢¢¢ Also here, and incl in admission, is

> **Ohio Village.** (1974) Reconstruction of a rural, 1860s Ohio community with one-rm schoolhouse, town hall, general store, hotel, farmhouse, barn, doctor's house, and office. Costumed guides. (Memorial Day-Oct, Sat-Sun)

☒ **Ohio's Prehistoric Native American Mounds.** Driving tour of approx 244 mi for a visit to several of these areas. There are more than 10,000 Native American mounds in Ohio, many of which, like the famous Serpent Mound, were built in complex and fascinating forms, such as birds, snakes, and other animals. Ohio State University has been responsible for the excavation and exploration of Ohio's earliest history. The Ohio Historical Center, 17th Ave at I-71, is a good place to start; here the entire prehistory is made clear in exhibits. After taking in these exhibits, take US 23 approx 46 mi S to jct US 35, then head 1 mi W to OH 104/207, then turn right (N) and go 2 mi to

> **Hopewell Culture National Historical Park.** (see CHILLICOTHE) Thirteen acres of Hopewell mounds; pottery and relics in museum. Return S on OH 104, 4 mi to Chillicothe. Here drop in at the

Ross County Historical Society Museum. (see CHILLICOTHE) and see more exhibits on the lives of the earliest dwellers in Ohio. 45 W 5th St. Take US 50 approx 17 mi SW to

Seip Mound State Memorial. (see CHILLICOTHE)

Ohio State Capitol. Fine building that has at its northwest corner a group of bronze statues by Levi T. Scofield. The sculpture depicts Ohio soldiers and statesmen under Roman matron Cornelia. Her words, "These are my jewels," refer to Grant, Sherman, Sheridan, Stanton, Garfield, Hayes, and Chase, who stand below her. Rotunda. Observation window on 40th floor of State Office Tower Building, across from rotunda. (Daily) In a ten-acre park bounded by High, Broad, State, and 3rd Sts, on US 23, 40. Phone 614/728-2695. **FREE**

Ohio State University. (1870) 55,000 students. One of largest universities in the country with 19 colleges, a graduate school, and more than 100 departments; medical center. Libraries have more than four million volumes. Tours. N High St and 15th Ave. Phone 614/292-OHIO. Also on campus are

Chadwick Arboretum. (Apr-Oct) 2120 Fyffe Rd. **FREE**

Wexner Center for the Arts. Contemporary art. Film, video, performing arts, and education programs and exhibits. Gallery tours during exhibitions (free). (Tues-Sun; closed hols) 1871 N High St. Phone 614/292-0330.

O'Shaughnessy Reservoir. Waterskiing, fishing, boating, picnicking. 16 mi N on Riverside Dr, OH 257. **FREE** At reservoir dam is

Columbus Zoo. More than 11,000 birds, mammals, fish, and reptiles; children's zoo. Picnic areas. (Daily) 9990 Riverside Dr. Phone 614/645-3550.

Wyandot Lake Amusement & Water Park. Over 60 rides and attractions, incl a wooden roller coaster, a 55-ft-tall Ferris Wheel, water slides, wave pool, and a five-story aquatic treehouse. (Daily) 10101 Riverside Dr. Phone 614/889-9283. ¢¢¢¢

Park of Roses. Contains over 10,000 rose bushes representing 350 varieties. Picnic facilities. Rose festival (early June). Musical programs Sun eves in summer. (Daily) Acton and High Sts, 5½ mi N, in Whetstone Park. **FREE**

Professional sports.

Columbus Blue Jackets (NHL). Nationwide Arena, 200 W Nationwide Blvd. Phone 614/431-3600.

Columbus Crew (MLS). Columbus Crew Stadium. 2121 Velma Ave. Phone 614/221-CREW.

Santa Maria Replica. A full-scale, museum-quality replica of Christopher Columbus's flagship, the *Santa Maria*. Costumed guides offer tour of upper and lower decks. Visitors learn of life as a sailor on voyages in the late 1400s. (Apr-Jan, Tues-Sun; closed hols) Battelle Riverfront Park, Marconi Blvd and Broad St. Phone 614/645-8760.

Special Events

Thoroughbred racing. Beulah Park Jockey Club. Southwest Blvd, in Grove City. Phone 614/871-9600. Jan-May.

Harness racing. Scioto Downs. 6000 S High St, 3 mi S of I-270. Restaurants. Phone 614/491-2515. Nightly Mon-Sat. Early May-mid-Sept. Phone 614/491-7674.

Actors Theater. Schiller Park in German Village. Two Shakespearean productions, one American musical. Phone 614/444-6888. June-Aug.

Greater Columbus Arts Festival. Downtown riverfront area. Exhibits, music, dancing. Early June. Phone 800/345-4FUN.

Ohio State Fair. Expositions Center, I-71 and E 17th Ave. Agricultural and industrial exposition plus grandstand entertainment, pageants, and horse show. Phone 800/OHO-EXPO. Early-mid-Aug.

BalletMet. Ohio Theatre, 322 Mt Vernon Ave. For schedule phone 614/229-4848. Sept-mid-Apr.

Opera/Columbus. English translation projected onto screen above stage. Palace Theatre, 117 Naghten. Phone 614/461-0022. Oct-May.

Motels/Motor Lodges

★ ★ **AMERISUITES.** *7490 Vantage Dr (43235). 614/846-4355; fax 614/846-4493. www.amerisuites.com.* 126 suites, 6 story. S, D $104-$130; each addl $10; under 12 free. Crib free. TV; cable (premium), VCR avail (movies). Heated pool. Complimentary coffee in rms. Complimentary continental bkfst. Restaurant adj 6 am-11 pm. Ck-out noon. Meeting rms. Business center. Valet serv. Coin lndry. Free airport transportation. Exercise equipt. Microwaves, refrigerators in rms. Cr cds: A, C, D, DS, MC, V.

[D] [≈] [木] [⊠] [♨] [木]

★ **BEST WESTERN NORTH.** *888 E Dublin Granville Rd (43229). 614/888-8230; fax 614/888-8223; res 800/780-7234. www.bestwestern.com.* 180 rms, 2 story. S, D $70-$95; each addl $5; under 18 free; wkend rates. Crib free. Pet accepted. TV; cable (premium). 2 pools, 1 indoor. Restaurant 6:30 am-10 pm. Rm serv. Bar 5 pm-2 am. Ck-out noon. Coin lndry. Business servs avail. Valet serv. Exercise rm. Cr cds: A, C, D, DS, MC, V.

[D] [🐾] [⊠] [♨] [SC] [≈] [木]

★ ★ **BEST WESTERN SUITES.** *1133 Evans Way Ct (43228). 614/870-2378; fax 614/870-9919; res 888/870-2378. www.bestwestern.com.* 66 suites, 2 story. S, D $79.95-$99.95; under 18 free. Crib free. TV; cable (premium), VCR (movies). Complimentary continental bkfst. Complimentary coffee in rms. Restaurant adj 6 am-10 pm. Ck-out noon. Meeting rms. Business servs avail. In-rm modem link. Valet serv (Mon-Fri). Sundries. Guest lndry. Exercise equipt; sauna. Indoor pool; whirlpool. Refrigerators, microwaves; some in-rm whirlpools. Cr cds: A, C, D, DS, MC, V.

[≈] [SC] [木] [⊠]

★ ★ ★ **COMFORT SUITES-AIRPORT.** *4270 Sawyer Rd (43219). 614/237-5847; fax 614/231-5926; res 800/228-5150. www.comfortsuites.com.* 67 suites, 2 story. S, D $89-$120; under 18 free. Crib free. TV; cable (premium). Complimentary continental bkfst. Complimentary coffee in rms. Restaurant adj 6 am-11 pm. Ck-out noon. Meeting rms. Business servs avail. In-rm modem link. Valet serv (Mon-Fri). Free airport transportation. Pool. Refrigerators, microwaves. Cr cds: A, C, D, DS, MC, V.

[D] [≈] [⊠] [♨]

★ ★ **COURTYARD BY MARRIOTT.** *7411 Vantage Dr (43235). 614/436-7070; fax 614/436-4970; toll-free 800/321-2211. www.marriott.com.* 145 rms, 4 story. S, D $105-$115; each addl $10; suites $125-$135; under 18 free; wkend rates. Crib free. TV; cable (premium). Indoor pool; whirlpool. Complimentary coffee in rms. Restaurant 6:30-10 am. Bar 4:30-11 pm. Ck-out noon. Coin lndry. Meeting rms. Business servs avail. In-rm modem link. Valet serv (Mon-Fri). Exercise equipt. Refrigerator in suites. Balconies. Cr cds: A, C, DS, MC, V.

[D] [⊠] [♨] [SC] [≈] [木]

★ ★ **COURTYARD BY MARRIOTT.** *35 West Spring St (43215). 614/228-3200; fax 614/228-6752; res 800/321-2211. courtyard.com/cmhcy.* 149 rms, 5 story. S, D $134; suites $140-$150; under 18 free. Crib free. Valet parking $12.50. TV; cable, VCR avail. Indoor pool; whirlpool. Complimentary coffee in rms. Restaurant 6:30-10 am; Sat, Sun 7 am-noon. Bar 5-11 pm. Ck-out noon. Meeting rms. Business servs avail. In-rm modem link. Bellhops. Sundries. Valet serv. Coin lndry. Exercise equipt. Some refrigerators, microwaves. Cr cds: A, C, D, DS, JCB, MC, V.

[D] [≈] [木] [⊠] [♨]

★ **CROSS COUNTRY INN.** *4875 Sinclair Rd (43229). 614/431-3670; fax 614/431-7261. www.crosscountryinns.com.* 136 rms, 2 story. S $37.99-$41.99; D $60.99-$49.99; family rates. Crib free. TV; cable (premium). Heated pool. Restaurant adj 6 am-4 pm. Ck-out noon. Business servs avail. Cr cds: A, C, D, DS, MC, V.

[D] [≈] [⊠] [♨]

★ ★ **FAIRFIELD INN.** *887 Morse Rd (43229). 614/262-4000; toll-free 800/228-2800. www.fairfieldinn.com.* 135 rms, 3 story. Apr-Oct: S, D $51-$79; under 18 free; lower rates rest of yr. Crib free. TV; cable (premium). Pool. Complimentary continental bkfst. Restaurant nearby. Ck-out noon. Meeting rm. Business servs avail. In-rm modem link. Cr cds: A, C, D, DS, MC, V.

[D] [≈] [⊠] [♨] [SC]

★ ★ **HAMPTON INN.** *4280 International Gateway (43219). 614/235-0717; fax 614/231-0886; res 800/426-7866. www.hamptoninn.com.* 129 rms, 4 story. S, D $89-$98; each addl $10; suites $110-$130; under 18 free. Crib free. TV; cable (premium). Heated pool. Complimentary continental bkfst. Restaurant adj 6 am-midnight. Ck-out noon. Meeting rms. Business servs avail. In-rm modem link. Bellhops. Valet serv (Mon-Fri). Free airport transportation. In-rm whirlpool in suites. Cr cds: A, C, D, DS, MC, V.

D ⇌ ✕ ⊠ 🔥 🐾

★ **HOLIDAY INN CITY CENTER.** *175 E Town St (43215). 614/221-3281; fax 614/221-5266; toll-free 800/367-7870. www.holiday-inn.com.* 240 rms, 12 story. S, D $89-$139; under 18 free. Crib free. Pet accepted. TV; cable (premium). Pool. Complimentary coffee in rms. Restaurant 6:30 am-10 pm; Sat, Sun from 7 am. Bar 5 pm-midnight. Ck-out noon. Meeting rms. Business servs avail. Free airport transportation. Cr cds: A, C, D, DS, MC, V.

D 🐾 ⇌ ⊠ 🔥 SC

★ ★ **HOLIDAY INN WORTHINGTON.** *175 Hutchinson Ave (43235). 614/885-3334; fax 614/846-4353; res 800/465-4329. www.holiday-inn.com.* 306 rms, 6 story. S, D $79-$135; suites $205; under 17 free. Crib free. Pet accepted. TV; cable (premium), VCR avail. Indoor pool. Complimentary coffee in rms. Restaurant 6 am-11 pm. Rm serv. Bar. Ck-out noon. Coin lndry. Convention facilities. Business center. In-rm modem link. Bellhops. Gift shop. Exercise equipt. Refrigerator in suites. Cr cds: A, C, D, DS, MC, V.

D 🐾 ⊠ 🔥 SC ⇌ 🏃 🐾

★ ★ **HOMEWOOD SUITES.** *115 Hutchinson Ave (43235). 614/785-0001; fax 614/785-0143; toll-free 800/225-5466. www.homewoodsuites.com.* 99 kit. units, 3 story, 99 suites. S $79-$135; D $89-$145; wkend rates. Crib free. Pet accepted; from $10/day. TV; cable (premium), VCR (movies $6). Heated pool; whirlpool. Complimentary bkfst. Complimentary coffee in rms. Restaurant adj 6 am-midnight. Ck-out noon. Coin lndry. Meeting rms. Business

center. In-rm modem link. Sundries. Tennis. Exercise equipt. Lawn games. Microwaves. Grills. Cr cds: A, C, D, DS, MC, V.

D ⇌ 🏃 ⊠ 🐾 🏃 🐾 ⇌

★ **LENOX INN.** *2400 Reynoldsburg-Baltimore Rd, Reynoldsburg (43068). 614/861-7800; fax 614/759-9059; toll-free 800/821-0007. www.hotelroom.com/ohio/colenox.html.* 152 rms, 2 story. S, D $55-$77; each addl $6; suites $109-$134; under 18 free. Crib free. Pet accepted; $10. TV; cable (premium). Pool. Restaurant 6:30 am-2 pm. Rm serv. Bar. Ck-out 11 am. Meeting rms. Business servs avail. In-rm modem link. Valet serv. Sundries. Free airport transportation. Exercise rm. Cr cds: A, C, D, DS, MC, V.

D 🐾 ⇌ ⊠ 🐾 SC 🏃

★ ★ **RAMADA PLAZA HOTEL & CONFERENCE CENTER.** *4900 Sinclair Rd (43229). 614/846-0300; fax 614/847-1022; res 800/228-2828. www.ramda.com.* 266 rms, 5-6 story. S, D $69-$119; each addl $10; suites $125-$175; under 18 free; wkend rates. TV; cable (premium). VCR avail. 2 pools, 1 indoor; wading pool, whirlpool, poolside serv. Restaurant 6:30 am-2 pm, 5-11 pm. Bar 11-2 am; entertainment Thurs-Sat. Ck-out noon. Convention facilities. Business center. In-rm modem link. Gift shop. Free airport transportation. Exercise equipt. Game rm. Cr cds: A, C, D, DS, MC, V.

D ⇌ 🏃 ✕ ⊠ 🐾 SC 🏃

★ **RED ROOF INN COLUMBUS NORTH.** *750 Morse Rd (43229). 614/846-8520; fax 614/846-8526; toll-free 800/733-7663. www.redroof.com.* 107 rms, 2 story. S, D $47.99-$59.99; under 18 free. Crib free. Pet accepted. TV. Complimentary coffee in lobby. Restaurant adj 7 am-4 pm. Ck-out noon. Business servs avail. Cr cds: A, D, DS, MC, V.

D 🐾 ⊠ 🐾 SC

★ ★ **SIGNATURE INN.** *6767 Schrock Hill Court (43229). 614/890-8111. www.signatureinns.com.* 125 rms, 2 story. S, D $72-$99; under 17 free. Crib free. TV; cable (premium), VCR avail (movies). Pool. Complimentary continental bkfst. Restaurant adj 8 am-midnight. Ck-out noon. Meeting rms. Business center. Refrigerators, microwaves in rms. Cr cds: A, D, DS, MC, V.

⊡ 🏊 🍴 🔥 SC 🏃

★ ★ **UNIVERSITY PLAZA HOTEL.** *3110 Olentangy River Rd (43202). 614/267-7461; fax 614/267-3978; toll-free 877/677-5292. www.university plazaosu.com.* 243 rms, 5 story. S, D $95-$119; each addl $10; suites $139-$195; under 18 free. Pet accepted, $10. Crib free. TV; cable (premium), VCR avail. Pool; poolside serv. Complimentary coffee in rms. Restaurant 6:30 am-10 pm. Ck-out noon. Meeting rms. Business servs avail. Bellhops. Valet serv. Free airport transportation. Health club privileges. Refrigerator, minibar in suites. Cr cds: A, C, D, DS, MC, V.

⊡ 🐾 🏊 🍴 🔥 SC

Hotels

★ ★ **ADAM'S MARK.** *50 N 3rd St (43215). 614/228-5050; fax 614/228-2525; res 800/444-2326. www.adams mark.com.* 415 rms, 21 story. S, D $130-$150; each addl $20; suites $800; under 18 free; higher rates special events. Crib free. Valet parking $15. TV; cable (premium). Heated pool; whirlpool. Restaurant 6 am-11 pm. Rm serv. Bar 11-2 am; Sun to 11 pm. Ck-out noon. Convention facilities. Business servs avail. In-rm modem link. Gift shop. Coin lndry. Exercise equipt; sauna. Cr cds: A, D, DS, JCB, MC, V.

⊡ 🏊 🏃 🍴 🔥 SC

★ ★ ★ **CONCOURSE HOTEL.** *4300 International Gateway (43219). 614/237-2515; fax 614/237-6134. www.theconcoursehotel.com.* 147 rms, 2 story. S $116; D $124; each addl $10. Crib free. TV; cable (premium), VCR avail (movies). 2 pools, 1 indoor; whirlpool, poolside serv. Restaurants 6 am-11 pm. Bar 11-1 am. Ck-out noon. Meeting rms. Business servs avail. In-rm modem link. Free airport transportation. Valet serv. Exercise equipt; sauna, steam rm. Cr cds: A, D, DS, MC, V.

🏊 🏃 ✈ 🍴 🔥

★ ★ ★ **CROWNE PLAZA.** *33 Nationwide Blvd (43215). 614/461-4100; fax 614/224-1502. www.crowneplaza.com.* 378 rms, 12 story. S, D $129-$190; suites $350-$500; under 12 free;

wkend rates. Crib free. Garage $13.50. TV; cable. Indoor pool. Coffee in rms. Restaurant 6:30 am-11 pm. Bar from 11 am. Ck-out noon. Coin lndry. Convention facilities. Business servs avail. In-rm modem link. Exercise equipt; sauna. Connected to Convention Center. Luxury level. Cr cds: A, C, D, DS, JCB, MC, V.

⊡ 🏊 🏃 🍴 🔥 SC

★ ★ **HOLIDAY INN COLUMBUS EAST I-70.** *4560 Hilton Corp Dr (43232). 614/868-1380; fax 614/863-3210; res 800/465-4329. www.holiday-inn.com.* 278 rms, 21 story. S, D $99-$119; each addl $10; wkend plan. Crib free. TV; cable (premium). Indoor pool; poolside serv. Playground. Coffee in rms. Restaurant 6 am-midnight. Bar 11-2 am. Ck-out noon. Convention facilities. Business center. In-rm modem link. Free airport transportation. Exercise equipt; sauna. Cr cds: A, C, D, DS, ER, JCB, MC, V.

⊡ 🏊 🏃 ✈ 🔥 SC 🏃

★ ★ ★ **HYATT ON CAPITOL SQUARE.** *75 E State St (43215). 614/228-1234; fax 614/469-9664; res 800/233-1234. www.hyatt.com.* 400 rms, 21 story. S, D $219-$244; each addl $25; suites $450-$1350; under 18 free; wkend rates. TV; cable (premium). Restaurant 6:30 am-10 pm; wkends to 11 pm. Bar 11 am-midnight; wkends to 1 am; entertainment. Ck-out noon. Meeting rms. Business center. In-rm modem link. Concierge. Shopping arcade. Exercise equipt; sauna. Luxury level. Cr cds: A, C, D, DS, ER, JCB, MC, V.

⊡ 🏃 🍴 🔥 SC 🏃

★ ★ ★ **HYATT REGENCY.** *350 N High St (43215). 614/463-1234; fax 614/280-3034; res 800/233-1234. www.hyatt.com.* 631 rms, 20 story. S, D $185-$210; each addl $25; suites $625-$1,000; under 18 free. Crib free. Valet parking $21. TV; cable (premium). Indoor pool. Restaurant 6:30 am-2:30 pm, 5-11 pm; Thurs-Sat 5 pm-midnight; Sun 6:30 am-11 pm. Bar 11-1:30 am; entertainment. Ck-out noon. Business center. In-rm modem link. Concierge. Shopping arcade. Exercise equipt. Luxury level. Cr cds: A, C, D, DS, ER, JCB, MC, V.

⊡ 🏊 🏃 🍴 🔥 🏃

★★★ **LOFTS HOTEL & SUITES.** *55 E Nationwide Blvd (43215). 614/461-2663; fax 614/461-2630; res 800/735-6387. www.55lofts.com.* 44 rms, 4 story, 20 suites. S, D, suites $189-$289; under 12 free; higher rates special events. Crib free. Valet parking $19.50; garage parking $13.50. TV; cable (premium), VCR avail. Complimentary continental bkfst. Complimentary coffee in rms. Restaurant. Rm serv. Restaurant 6:30 am-11 pm. Bar 11 am-10 pm. Ck-out noon. Meeting rms. Business servs avail. Valet serv (Mon-Sat). Concierge. Exercise equipt; sauna. Indoor pool. Refrigeraotrs, minibars; some in-rm whirlpools, wet bars. Cr cds: A, C, D, DS, JCB, MC, V.

D ⇌ 🏋 🏊 🔥 SC

★★★ **MARRIOTT NORTH.** *6500 Doubletree Ave (43229). 614/885-1885; fax 614/885-7222; toll-free 800/228-9290. www.marriott.com.* 300 rms, 9 story. S, D $119-$149; suites $275; wkend rates. Crib free. TV; cable (premium). Indoor/outdoor pool; whirlpool, poolside serv. Restaurant 6:30 am-10 pm. Bar 11:30 am-midnight. Ck-out noon. Coin lndry. Convention facilities. Business center. In-rm modem link. Gift shop. Free airport transportation. Exercise equipt; sauna. Refrigerator avail. Cr cds: A, C, D, DS, ER, JCB, MC, V.

D ⇌ 🏋 🏊 🔥 SC 🏋

★★★ **MARRIOTT NORTHWEST COLUMBUS.** *5605 Paul G Blazer Memorial Pkwy, Dublin (43017). 614/791-1000; fax 614/336-4701; res 800/228-9290. www.marriottnorthwest.com.* 303 rms, 7 story. S, D $99-$149; each addl $15; suites $249-$269; under 18 free; wkend rates; higher rates special events. Crib free. TV; cable (premium). Complimentary coffee in rms. Restaurant 6 am-11 pm. Bar 3 pm-midnight. Ck-out noon. Meeting rms. Business center. In-rm modem link. Concierge. Gift shop. Coin lndry. Exercise equipt. Indoor pool. Bathrm phone, in-rm whirlpool, refrigerator, wet bar in suites. Luxury level. Cr cds: A, C, D, DS, ER, JCB, MC, V.

D ⇌ 🏋 🏊 🔥 🏋

★★★ **RADISSON AIRPORT HOTEL.** *1375 N Cassady Ave (43219). 614/475-7551; fax 614/476-1476; toll-free 800/333-3333. www.radisson airporthotel.com.* 247 units, 6 story. S, D $119-$139; each addl $10; suites $299; under 18 free; wkend, hol rates. TV; cable, VCR avail. Indoor pool; whirlpool. Coffee in rms. Restaurant 6 am-midnight. Bar 10-1 am, Sun noon-midnight. Ck-out noon. Coin lndry. Meeting rms. Business center. In-rm modem link. Gift shop. Free airport transportation. Exercise equipt; sauna. Some bathrm phones, refrigerators, in-rm whirlpools. Cr cds: A, MC, V.

D ⇌ SC 🏋 🏋

★★★ **SHERATON SUITES.** *201 Hutchinson Ave (43235). 614/436-0004; fax 614/436-0926; res 800/325-3535. www.sheraton.com.* 260 suites, 9 story. S $89-$169, D $109-$189; each addl $10; under 18 free; wkend, extended rates. Crib avail. TV; cable (premium), VCR avail. 2 pools, 1 indoor; whirlpool, poolside serv. Complimentary coffee in rms. Restaurant 6:30 am-10:30 pm; Sat from 7 am. Bar. Ck-out 1 pm. Meeting rms. Business servs avail. In-rm modem link. Gift shop. Exercise equipt. Refrigerators; microwaves avail. Cr cds: A, D, DS, MC, V.

D ⇌ 🏋 🏊 🔥 SC

★★★ **THE WESTIN GREAT SOUTHERN.** *310 S High St (43215). 614/228-3800; fax 614/228-7666; res 800/937-8461. www.greatsouthern hotel.com.* 196 rms, 6 story. S, D $205; each addl $15; suites $235-$800; family rates; wkend rates; higher rates special events. TV; cable (premium). Coffee in rms. Restaurant 6 am-11 pm. Rm serv 24 hrs. Bar 3 pm-2:30 am. Ck-out 1 pm. Meeting rms. Business servs avail. Exercise equipt. Health club privileges. Luxury level. Cr cds: A, C, D, DS, JCB, MC, V.

D 🏋 🏊 🔥 SC

★★ **WYNDHAM DUBLIN HOTEL.** *600 Metro Pl N, Dublin (43017). 614/764-2200; fax 614/764-1213; toll-free 800/996-3426. www.wyndham dublin.com.* 217 rms, 3 story. S, D $89-$159; under 18 free; wkend rates. Crib free. TV; cable (premium), VCR avail. Indoor pool. Coffee in rms. Restaurant 6:30 am-10 pm. Rm serv 24 hrs. Bar 4:30 pm-midnight; Sat from 11 am; closed Sun. Ck-out 1 pm. Meeting rms. Business servs avail. In-rm modem link. Sundries. Exercise equipt. Balconies. Cr cds: A, D, DS, JCB, MC, V.

🄳 ⇌ 🏋 🈁

B&B/Small Inn

★★★ **WORTHINGTON INN.** *649 High St, Worthington (43085). 614/885-2600; fax 614/885-1283.* 26 rms, 3 story. S, D $150-$175; suites $215-$275. TV; cable. Complimentary full bkfst. Dining rm (see SEVEN STARS DINING ROOM). Rm serv. Bar 5 pm-midnight. Ck-out noon, ck-in 3 pm. Business servs avail. In-rm modem link. Luggage handling. Concierge serv. Renovated Victorian inn. Cr cds: A, DS, MC, V.

🈁 🈂

All Suites

★★ **DOUBLETREE GUEST SUITES.** *50 S Front St (43215). 614/228-4600; fax 614/228-0297; res 800/222-8733. www.doubletree.com.* 194 suites, 10 story. S, D $185; each addl $20; suites $295; under 18 free; wkend rates; higher rates special events. Crib free. TV; cable (premium). Coffee in rms. Restaurant 6:30 am-10 pm; Sat 7 am-11 pm; Sun 7 am-10 pm. Bar 11 am-midnight, Sun from noon. Ck-out noon. In-rm modem link. Covered parking. Refrigerators; microwaves avail. Opp river. Cr cds: A, C, D, DS, ER, JCB, MC, V.

🄳 🆂🅲

★★★ **EMBASSY SUITES HOTEL.** *2700 Corporate Exchange Dr (43231). 614/890-8600; fax 614/890-8626; res 800/362-2779. www.embassysuites. com.* 221 kit. suites, 8 story. S, D $129-$149; each addl $10; under 18 free; wkend rates. Crib free. TV; cable (premium), VCR avail. Indoor/outdoor pool; whirlpool, poolside serv. Complimentary full bkfst. Restaurant 11 am-10 pm; wknds to 11 pm. Bar 11-1 am. Ck-out noon. Meeting rms. Business center. Concierge. Sundries. Free airport transportation. Exercise equipt; sauna. Game rm. Refrigerators, microwaves. Cr cds: A, C, D, DS, MC, V.

🄳 ⇌ 🏋 🈁 🈂 🆂🅲 🏋

★★★ **WOODFIN SUITE HOTEL.** *4130 Tuller Rd, Dublin (43017). 614/766-7762; fax 614/761-1906; toll-free 888/433-9408. www.woodfinsuite hotels.com.* 88 kit. suites, 2 story. 1 bedrm $160; 2 bedrm $199; each addl $10; under 12 free; lower rates wkends. Crib free. TV; cable (premium), VCR (free movies). Heated pool; whirlpool. Complimentary bkfst buffet. Complimentary coffee in rms. Restaurant nearby. Ck-out noon. Coin lndry. Meeting rms. Business center. In-rm modem link. Valet serv. Microwaves. Cr cds: A, C, D, DS, JCB, MC, V.

🄳 ⇌ 🈁 🈂 🏋

Restaurants

★★★ **ALEX'S BISTRO.** *4681 Reed Rd (43220). 614/457-8887.* Hrs: 11:30 am-2 pm, 5:30-10 pm. Closed Sun; major hols. Res accepted. French, Italian menu. Bar. Wine list. A la carte entrees: lunch $5.95-$8.95, dinner $9.50-18.50. Specializes in fresh seafood, wild game, pasta. Parking. Menu changes seasonally. French brasserie atmosphere. Cr cds: A, MC, V.

🈁

★★ **BEXLEY'S MONK.** *2232 E Main St (43209). 614/239-6665. www. bexleymonk.com.* Hrs: 11:30 am-2:30 pm, 5:30-10 pm; Fri, Sat to 11 pm; Sun from 5:30 pm. Closed major hols. Res accepted. Eclectic menu. Bar. A la carte entrees: lunch $6-$11, dinner $10-$20. Specializes in seafood, pasta. Entertainment. Contemporary decor. Cr cds: A, D, DS, MC, V.

🄳 🈁

★★ **BRAVO! ITALIAN KITCHEN.** *3000 Hayden Rd (43235). 614/791-1245. www.bestitalianusa.com.* Hrs: 11 am-10 pm; Fri to midnight; Sat 5 pm-midnight. Closed major hols. Res accepted. Italian menu. Bar. A la carte entrees: lunch $7-$9, dinner $10-$18. Specializes in northern Italian cuisine. Valet parking. Outdoor dining. Upscale bistro atmosphere. Cr cds: A, DS, MC, V.

🄳 🈁

★ **CAP CITY DINER-GRANDVIEW.** *1299 Olentangy River Rd (43212). 614/291-3663.* Hrs: 11 am-10 pm; Fri, Sat to midnight; Sun from 4 pm.

Closed major hols. Contemporary Amer menu. Bar. Lunch $4.95-$8.95, dinner $5.95-$16.95. Child's menu. Specialty: veal and mushroom meatloaf. Entertainment Sun, Tues. Outdoor dining. Upscale diner. Cr cds: A, D, DS, MC, V.
D ⊟

★ **CLARMONT.** *684 S High St (43215). 614/443-1125.* Hrs: 7 am-2:30 pm, 5-10 pm; Fri, Sat 7-11 pm; Sun 4-9 pm. Closed some major hols. Res accepted. Bar to 10 pm; Fri, Sat to midnight. Bkfst $2.95-$7.50, lunch $5.95-$10.95, dinner $12.95-$23.50. Specializes in steak, fresh seafood. Parking. Cr cds: A, D, DS, MC, V.
D SC ⊟

★ **COOKER.** *6193 Cleveland Ave (43231). 614/899-7000. www.the-cooker.com.* Hrs: 11 am-10:30 pm; Fri, Sat to 11:30 pm; Sun to 10 pm; Sun brunch 11 am-3 pm. Closed Thanksgiving, Dec 25. Bar. Lunch, dinner $6-$15. Sun brunch $6-$9.75. Child's menu. Specializes in prime rib, fresh fish, meatloaf. Own biscuits. Parking. Patio dining. Casual family-style dining. Cr cds: A, DS, MC, V.
D ⊟

★★ **ENGINE HOUSE NO. 5.** *121 Thurman Ave (43206). 614/443-4877.* Hrs: 11:30 am-10 pm; Fri, Sat 4-11 pm; Sun 4-9 pm; early-bird dinner 4-6 pm, Sun 4-9 pm. Closed some major hols. Res accepted. Bar. Lunch $6-$16, dinner $14-$30. Child's menu. Specializes in fresh seafood, homemade pasta. Pianist Fri, Sat. Old firehouse; firefighting equipment displayed. Parking. Cr cds: A, D, DS, MC, V.
D ⊟

★★★ **HANDKE'S CUISINE.** *520 S Front St (43215). 614/621-2500. www.chefhandke.com.* Hrs: 5:30-10 pm. Closed Sun; Dec 25. Res accepted. International menu. Bar. Extensive wine list. A la carte entrees: dinner $9.75-$23.75. Specializes in veal chop, duck, fresh seafood. Valet parking. Located in historic brewery building, the former Schlee Brewery; main dining rm on lower level. Cr cds: A, D, DS, MC, V.

★★ **HUNAN HOUSE.** *2350 E Dublin-Granville Rd (43229). 614/895-*

3330. Hrs: 11:30 am-10 pm; Fri, Sat to 10:30 pm. Closed Thanksgiving. Res accepted. Chinese menu. Bar. A la carte entrees: lunch $5-$8, dinner $8-$18. Specialties: Szechwan, Hunan and Mandarin delicacies. Parking. Cr cds: A, D, MC, V.
D

★★ **HUNAN LION.** *2038 Bethel Rd (43220). 614/459-3933.* Hrs: 11:30 am-10 pm; Fri, Sat to 10:30 pm. Res accepted. Chinese, Thai menu. Bar. Lunch $5.95-$8.95, dinner $8.95-$18. Specializes in Szechwan dishes. Parking. Modern decor with Oriental touches. Cr cds: A, D, DS, MC, V.
D ⊟

★ **K2U.** *641 N High St (43215). 614/461-4766.* Hrs: 11:30 am-midnight; Sat from 5:30 pm. Closed Sun; Memorial Day, Thanksgiving, Dec 25. Res accepted. Eclectic menu. Bar. Lunch $4-$12, dinner $4-$16. Specializes in soups, pasta, sandwiches. Entertainment Mon, Thurs, Fri. Outdoor dining. Casual European-style bistro. Cr cds: A, D, DS, MC, V.
D ⊟

★★★ **L'ANTIBES.** *772 N High St, #106 (43215). 614/291-1666.* Hrs: 5-9 pm; Fri, Sat to 11 pm. Closed Sun, Mon; Thanksgiving, Dec 25. Res accepted. French menu. A la carte entrees: dinner $18-$29. Specializes in fresh fish, veal, lamb. Parking. Modern decor. Owners' art collection displayed. Cr cds: A, C, D, DS, MC, V.
D ⊟

★★ **LINDEY'S.** *169 E Beck St (43206). 614/228-4343.* Hrs: 11:30 am-2:30 pm, 5:30-10 pm; Thurs-Sat to midnight. Closed most major hols. Res accepted. Bar. Lunch $9.95-$17.95, dinner $12.95-$24.95. Sun jazz brunch 11:30 am-2:30 pm. Specialties: angel hair pasta, grilled tournedos with Bearnaise sauce, gourmet pizza. Entertainment Thurs, Sun. Valet parking. Outdoor dining. Restored building (1888) in German Village. Cr cds: A, D, DS, MC, V.
D ⊟

★★★ **MORTON'S OF CHICAGO.** *2 Nationwide Plz (43215). 614/464-4442. www.mortons.com.* Hrs: 5:30-11 pm; Sun 5-10 pm. Closed major hols. Res accepted. Bar. A la carte entrees: dinner $18.95-$29.95. Specializes in prime aged beef, fresh seafood, dessert souffles. Valet parking. Contemporary decor; in downtown office complex. Cr cds: A, D, DS, MC, V.

[D] [⬛]

★ **OLD MOHAWK.** *821 Mohawk St (43206). 614/444-7204.* Hrs: 11 am-midnight; Tues, Wed to 1 am; Thur, Fri to 2:30 am; Sat 9-2:30 am; Sun from 9 am. Closed some major hols. Bar. Lunch, dinner $4.95-$9.95. Specialties: turtle soup, quesadillas. Building from 1800s was once a grocery and tavern; exposed brick walls. Cr cds: A, D, DS, MC, V.

[⬛]

★★★ **REFECTORY.** *1092 Bethel Rd (43220). 614/451-9774.* Hrs: 5-10:30 pm. Closed Sun; major hols. French menu. Bar 4:30 pm-midnight; Fri, Sat to 1 am. Res accepted. Wine cellar. A la carte entrees: dinner $19.95-$26.95. Specialties: cotelette de salmon, rosage d'agneau aux olives, filet de beouf a l'estragon. Own pastries. Parking. Outdoor dining. Former schoolhouse and sanctuary. Cr cds: A, D, DS, MC, V.

★★ **RIGSBY'S CUISINE VOLATILE.** *698 N High St (43215). 614/461-7888.* Hrs: 11 am-11 pm. Closed Sun. Res accepted. Mediterranean menu. Bar. A la carte entrees: lunch $8-$14, dinner $12-$24. Specializes in pasta, rack of lamb, seafood. Entertainment Wed, Thurs. Valet parking. Outdoor dining. Ultramodern decor. Cr cds: A, D, DS, MC, V.

[D]

★★ **RJ SNAPPERS.** *700 N High St (43215). 614/280-1070.* Hrs: 5-10 pm; Fri, Sat to 11 pm; Sun to 9 pm. Closed major hols. Res accepted. Seafood menu. Bar. dinner $15-$20. Child's menu. Specialties: Snapper's snapper, cioppino. Valet parking. Italian fishing village atmosphere and decor. Cr cds: A, D, DS, MC, V.

[D]

★ **SCHMIDT'S SAUSAGE HAUS.** *240 E Kossuth St (43204). 614/444-6808.* Hrs: 11 am-10 pm; Fri to 11 pm; Sat to midnight. Closed Easter, Thanksgiving, Dec 25. German, Amer menu. Bar. Lunch $5.25-$6.95, dinner $7.25-$12.95. Buffet: lunch $6.95, dinner $10.95. Child's menu. Specializes in homemade sausage, desserts. German music Thurs-Sat. Parking. Family-owned. Cr cds: A, DS, MC, V.

[D] [⬛]

★★★ **SEVEN STARS DINING ROOM.** *649 High St (43085). 614/885-2600.* Hrs: 7-10 am, 11 am-3 pm, 5:30-10 pm; Fri, Sat to 11 pm; Sun brunch 11:30 am-2:30 pm. Closed some major hols. Res accepted. Regional Amer menu. Bar. Wine list. Bkfst $5-$10, lunch $7.95-$15.95, dinner $15.95-$33.95. Sun brunch $17.95. Specializes in rack of lamb, fresh seafood, beef. Own baking. Entertainment Tues-Sat. Parking. Outdoor dining. Cr cds: A, DS, MC, V.

[⬛]

★★ **TAPATIO.** *491 N Park St (43215). 614/221-1085.* Hrs: 11:30 am-3:30 pm, 5-10 pm; Fri, Sat to 11 pm; Sun 5-10 pm. Closed Thanksgiving, Dec 25. Res accepted. Eclectic menu. Bar. Lunch $6-$9, dinner $8-$22. Specializes in seafood, beef tenderloin. Outdoor dining. Modern contemporary bistro. Cr cds: A, D, DS, MC, V.

[D] [⬛]

★★ **TONY'S.** *16 W Beck St (43215). 614/224-8669.* Hrs: 11:30 am-10 pm; Fri to 11 pm; Sat 5:30-11 pm. Closed Sun; major hols. Res accepted. Italian menu. Bar. Lunch $4-$8, dinner $8-$17. Specializes in veal, homemade pasta, classic Italian dishes. Pianist Sat evenings. Parking. Outdoor dining. Cr cds: A, D, DS, MC, V.

[D]

Unrated Dining Spot

KATZINGER'S. *475 S 3rd St (43215). 614/228-3354. www.katzingers.com.* Hrs: 8:30 am-8:30 pm; Sat, Sun from 9 am. Closed Easter, Thanksgiving, Dec 25. Continental menu. Beer. A la carte entrees: lunch, dinner $2.35-$10.50. Child's menu. Specializes in deli, ethnic foods. Outdoor dining. Delicatessen in German Village. Totally nonsmoking. Cr cds: A, D, DS, MC, V.

[D]

Conneaut (A-7)

(see Ashtabula)

Coshocton

(D-5) *See also Cambridge, Newark, Zanesville*

Founded 1802 **Pop** 12,193 **Elev** 775 ft
Information Coshocton County Convention & Visitors Bureau, PO Box 905; 740/622-4877 or 800/338-4724

This unusual name was derived from travelers' spellings of Native American words meaning either "river crossing" or "place of the black bear." The settlement was first known as Tuscarawa. Coshocton is on the banks of the Muskingum River at the junction of the Tuscarawas and Walhonding rivers; Johnny Appleseed planted some of his orchards here. Specialty advertising originated in Coshocton, which has a variety of other industries including leather goods, iron pipe, plastics, pottery, appliances, rubber products, stainless steel, and baskets.

What to See and Do

⭐ **Roscoe Village.** Visitor Center has information on canal era and historic attractions in the area; displays and continuous slide presentations. Roscoe Village creates a quaint living museum as an 1830s Ohio-Erie Canal town with pocket gardens, old-time shops, exhibits and crafts; also lodging and dining avail. Many special events throughout the yr. (Daily; closed Jan 1, Thanksgiving, Dec 25) NW edge of town on OH 16. Phone 800/877-1830. **FREE** Also in the village are

Boat trips. One-mi horse-drawn boat trips (35 min) on the Ohio-Erie Canal aboard *Monticello III.* (Memorial Day-Labor Day, daily; rest of May and after Labor Day-late Oct, wkends) Phone 740/622-7528. ¢¢

Johnson-Humrickhouse Museum. Houses four permanent galleries: Native American and Eskimo collection ranging from Stone Age to the present; Oriental Room with Chinese and Japanese collections; Early American gallery also has a pioneer room display; Decorative Arts has some European pieces. Museum also has traveling exhibits. (May-Oct, afternoons; rest of yr, afternoons Tues-Sun; closed hols) Phone 740/622-8710. ¢

Village Exhibit Tour. Exhibit buildings incl Township Hall (1880) with one-rm school exhibit; blacksmith's shop; 19th-century print shop; Craft and Learning Center with 1800s craft demonstrations; the Dr. Maro Johnson Home (1833), furnished with antiques (1690-1840); the Toll House, with model locks and canal artifacts; and the Craftsman's House, an 1825 workingman's house where the art of broom making is revived. Self-guided tour of exhibit buildings (daily; closed Jan 1, Thanksgiving, Dec 25); guided tours (Jan-Mar). Phone 740/622-9310. ¢¢

Special Events

Dulcimer Days. Roscoe Village. Displays, jam sessions, workshops. Third wkend May. Phone 800/877-1830.

Hot-Air Balloon Festival. Coshocton County fairground. Hot-air balloon launches, family entertainment. First wkend June. Phone 740/622-5411.

Olde Time Music Fest. Roscoe Village. Banjo and barbershop music. Mid-June. Phone 800/877-1830.

Coshocton Canal Festival. Roscoe Village. Celebrates arrival of first boat from Cleveland in 1830. Art exhibits, parades, old-time crafts, costume promenade, musical events, food. Third wkend Aug. Phone 800/877-1830.

Apple Butter Stirrin'. Roscoe Village. Third wkend Oct. Phone 800/877-1830.

Christmas Candle Lightings. Roscoe Village. Tree and candle lighting ceremonies; hot mulled cider and ginger cookies. First three Sat in Dec. Phone 800/877-1830.

Motel/Motor Lodge

★ ★ ★ **THE INN AT ROSCOE VIL-LAGE.** *200 N Whitewoman St (43812). 740/622-2222; fax 740/623-6568; toll-free 800/237-7397. www. roscoevillage.com.* 50 rms, 4 story. S, D $75-$99; family rates. Crib free. TV; cable. Restaurant 7 am-2 pm, 5-9 pm; wkend hrs vary. Bar noon-11 pm; entertainment Fri. Ck-out noon. Meeting rms. Business servs avail. 18-hole golf privileges. Cr cds: A, D, DS, MC, V.

D 🐾 SC 🎿

Restaurant

★ ★ **OLD WAREHOUSE.** *400 N Whitewoman St (43812). 740/622-4001. www.roscoevillage.com.* Hrs: 11 am-9 pm. Closed Mon; Jan 1, Dec 25. Lunch, dinner $3.50-$12.95. Child's menu. Specialties: bean soup, bran muffins. Own ice cream. In converted warehouse (1831) in Roscoe Village. Cr cds: A, DS, MC, V.

D

Dayton

(E-2) *See also Miamisburg, Middletown (Butler County), Springfield, Vandalia*

Founded 1796 **Pop** 182,044 **Elev** 757 ft **Area code** 937
Information Dayton/Montgomery County Convention & Visitors Bureau, Chamber Plaza, One Chamber Plaza, Suite A, 45402-2400; 937/226-8211 or 800/221-8235
Web www.daytoncvb.com

Dayton is situated at the fork of the Great Miami River. The river curves through the city from the northeast, uniting with the Stillwater River half a mile above Main Street Bridge. Mad River from the east and Wolf Creek from the west join the others four blocks from there. Dayton has 28 bridges crossing these rivers.

The first flood, in 1805, started a progression of higher levees. In 1913, the most disastrous flood took 361 lives and property worth $100 million and inspired a flood-control plan effective to date.

Here, between 1870-1910, James Ritty invented a "mechanical money drawer" (which only amused people at first); John Patterson, promoting this cash register, opened the first daylight factory with 80 percent glass walls; Barney Oldfield, in his "Old 999" pioneer racing car, won a local exhibition match; the Wright brothers experimented with kites, gliders, built a wind tunnel, and developed the aileron; and Charles Kettering sold a big order of automobile self-starters to the Cadillac Motor Company. During and after World War I the city added Frigidaire and Wright-Patterson Air Force Base to its economic base. Today Dayton is a well-planned, well-run industrial city with a council-manager form of government.

What to See and Do

Aullwood Audubon Center and Farm. A 350-acre environmental education center and working educational farm. Interpretive museum, nature trails, exhibits. Working farm has seasonal programs. (Daily; closed hols and hol wkends) 1000 Aullwood Rd, 10 mi NW on OH 48 to jct OH 40, at Englewood Dam. Phone 937/890-7360. ¢¢

Benjamin Wegerzyn Horticultural Center. Stillwater Gardens and wetland woods; horticultural library; Gift Gallery. Grounds (daily). 1301 E Siebenthaler. Phone 937/277-6545. **FREE**

Boonshoft Museum of Discovery. Houses natural history exhibits incl live animals common to Ohio; Philips Space Theater shows (daily). Bieser Discovery Center and the Dayton Science Center feature hands-on interactive exhibits and activities. (Daily) 2600 DeWeese Pkwy. Phone 937/275-7431. ¢¢¢

Carillon Park. Collections depict history of transportation and early pioneer life in the area; incl original early railroad depot, section of the Miami and Erie canal fitted with an original lock; Dayton-built motor vehicles; Wright brothers' 1905 plane; 1912 steam locomotive and tender. In 23 buildings and structures on 65 acres. (May-Oct, Tues-Sun, also Mon hols) Concerts (May-Oct, Sun; June-Aug, Sat). 1000 Carillon Blvd, 2 mi S via I-75 to exit 51. Phone 937/293-2841. ¢¢ Also in park is

Newcom Tavern. Oldest preserved house in the city; miraculously withstood the 1913 Dayton flood. Collection of pioneer, early Dayton relics. Phone 937/226-8211.

The Dayton Art Institute. European and American paintings and sculpture; Asian Gallery; pre-Columbian arts, prints, and decorative arts; changing exhibits; Experiencenter participatory gallery; reference library. Concerts. (Daily). Riverview and Forest aves. Phone 937/223-5277. **FREE**

Eastwood Lake. A 185-acre lake designed for most water sports: motor boating, fishing boats, and waterskiing (even calendar days); sailboards, personal water craft, sailing, fishing boats at idle speed (odd calendar days). Thirty-five mph speed limit and 40 power boat capacity. (Daily) OH 4 and Harshman Rd. **FREE**

Masonic Temple. Modern adaptation of Greek Ionic architecture; considered one of the most beautiful Masonic buildings in the country. (Daily) 525 W Riverview Ave at Belmonte Park N. Phone 937/224-9795. **FREE**

Paul Laurence Dunbar House State Memorial. The Dayton-born black poet and novelist lived here from 1903 until his death at age 34 in 1906. (Memorial Day-Labor Day, Wed-Sun; Sept-Oct, wkends; Nov-May, Mon-Fri) 219 Paul Laurence Dunbar St. Phone 937/224-7061. ¢¢

SunWatch Prehistoric Indian Village and Archaeological Park. Reconstructed village. Planting and harvesting of Native American gardens, house construction, demonstrations and hands-on activities avail throughout the yr. Visitor information center houses audiovisual program, exhibits and life-size dioramas. Tours. (Tues-Sun; closed Thanksgiving, Dec 25) S off I-75, 2301 W River Rd. Phone 937/268-8199. ¢¢

University of Dayton. (1850) 6,700 students. Engineering, liberal arts, arts and science, law, business, and education. On campus is Kennedy Union Art Gallery (academic yr, daily; free). Campus tours. 300 College Park Ave, southeast part of city. Phone 937/229-4114.

Woodland Cemetery and Arboretum. Graves of Orville and Wilbur Wright, Charles F. Kettering, Deeds, Cox, and Patterson. (Daily) 118 Woodland Ave. Maps avail. Phone 937/228-2581.

US Air Force Museum, Wright-Patterson AFB

Wright Brothers Memorial. A monolith dedicated to the "fathers" of aviation; overlooks Huffman Prairie where the Wrights practiced flying. E on OH 444 at jct old OH 4. Phone 937/226-8211.

Wright Cycle Shop. Replica of the shop where Wright brothers performed some of their experiments, turn-of-the-century bicycles. (Sat and Sun; also by appt) 22 S Williams St. **FREE**

Wright-Patterson Air Force Base. Center of research and aerospace logistics for US Air Force; also site of Air Force Institute of Technology. 10 mi NE on OH 444. Phone 937/257-7826. On grounds is

United States Air Force Museum. One of the world's most comprehensive military aviation museums; more than 200 major historic aircraft and missiles; exhibits span period from Wright brothers to space age. IMAX theater (fee). (Daily; closed major hols) Area B, Springfield and Harshman rds. Phone 937/255-3284. **FREE**

Wright State University. (1967) 15,000 students. Library contains one of the largest collections of Wright brothers memorabilia. Biological preserve with walking trails. The Creative Art Center is home to the Dayton Art Institute Museum of Contemporary Art. 8 mi E on Colonel Glenn Hwy (E 3rd St). Phone 937/775-5700.

Special Events

The Dayton Art Institute Concert Series. Summer concerts in cloistered garden. Phone 937/223-5277. June-mid-Aug. Thurs eves.

City Folk Festival. Phone 937/461-5149. Third wkend June.

Dayton Air Show. Dayton International Airport. Features approx 100 outdoor exhibits; flight teams. Phone 937/898-5901. Third wkend July.

Montgomery County Fair. Fairgrounds, 1043 S Main St. Phone 937/224-1619. Labor Day wkend.

Motels/Motor Lodges

★★ **COMFORT INN.** *7907 Brandt Pike, Huber Heights (45424). 937/237-7477; fax 937/237-5187; toll-free 800/228-5150. www.comfortinn.com.* 53 rms, 2 story, 6 suites. Apr-Oct: S, D $79.95; suites $95-$100; under 18 free; higher rates special events; lower rates rest of yr. Crib free. TV; cable (premium). Complimentary continental bkfst. Restaurant adj open 24 hrs. Ck-out 11 am. In-rm modem link. Exercise equipt. In-rm whirlpool, some refrigerators, microwave. Cr cds: A, D, DS, MC, V.
🅳 🏌 ⊠ 🐾 SC

★★ **CROSS COUNTRY INN.** *9325 N Main St (45415). 937/836-8339; fax 937/836-1772; toll-free 800/621-1429. www.crosscountryinns.com.* 120 rms, 2 story. S $38-$49; D $46-$54; each addl $7; under 18 free. Crib free. TV; cable (premium). Pool. Complimen-

tary coffee in lobby. Restaurant adj 6:30 am-midnight. Ck-out noon. Business servs avail. Cr cds: A, D, DS, MC, V.
⊠ ⊠ 🐾 SC

★ **DAYS INN.** *100 Parkview Dr, Brookville (45309). 937/833-4003; fax 937/833-4681; res 800/329-7466. www.daysinn.com.* 62 rms, 2 story. S $52; D $65; each addl $6; under 13 free; family rates; higher rates special events. Crib free. Pet accepted; $10/day. TV; cable. Complimentary continental bkfst. Restaurant adj open 24 hrs. Ck-out 11 am. Business servs avail. Pool. Cr cds: A, C, D, DS, MC, V.
🅳 🐾 ⊠ ⊠ 🐾

★★ **FAIRFIELD INN.** *6960 Miller Ln (45414). 937/898-1120; toll-free 800/228-2800. www.fairfieldinn.com.* 135 rms, 3 story. S, D $59-$89; under 18 free. Crib free. TV; cable. Pool. Complimentary continental bkfst. Restaurant nearby. Ck-out noon. Business servs avail. In-rm modem link. Cr cds: A, D, DS, MC, V.
🅳 ⊠ ⊠ 🐾

★★ **HAMPTON INN.** *2550 Paramount Pl, Fairborn (45324). 937/429-5505; fax 937/429-6828; res 800/426-7866. www.hamptoninn.com.* 63 rms, 3 story, 8 suites. S, D $79-$85; suites $87-$92; under 18 free; higher rates special events; lower rates winter. Crib free. TV; cable (premium). Indoor pool; whirlpool. Complimentary continental bkfst. Restaurant nearby. Ck-out 11 am. Business servs avail. In-rm modem link. Valet serv. Refrigerator, microwave in suites. Cr cds: A, C, D, DS, MC, V.
🅳 ⊠ ⊠ 🐾

★★ **HAMPTON INN DAYTON SOUTH.** *8099 Old Yankee St (45458). 937/436-3700; fax 937/436-2995; res 800/426-7866. www.hamptoninn.com.* 130 rms, 4 story. S, D $80-$90; under 18 free. Crib free. TV; cable (premium). Pool. Complimentary continental bkfst. Coffee in rms. Restaurant nearby. Ck-out noon. Meeting rm. Business servs avail. Exercise equipt. Health club privileges. Cr cds: A, D, DS, MC, V.
🅳 ⊠ 🏌 ⊠ 🐾 SC

★★ **HOLIDAY INN.** *2800 Presidential Dr, Fairborn (45324). 937/426-7800; fax 937/426-1284; res 800/465-4329. www.holiday-inn.com.* 204 rms, 6 story. S, D $89-$128; wkend rates. Crib free. TV; cable (premium), VCR avail. Indoor pool. Coffee in rms. Restaurant 6 am-10 pm. Rm serv. Bar 11-2 am; Sun to midnight. Ck-out noon. Meeting rms. Business servs avail. Valet serv. Exercise equipt. Many bathrm phones. Cr cds: A, D, DS, MC, V.

⧠ ⇌ 🕇 ⋈ 🔥

★★ **HOMEWOOD SUITES.** *2750 Presidential Dr, Fairborn (45324). 937/429-0600; fax 937/429-6311; toll-free 800/225-5466. www.homewood suites.com.* 128 suites, 3 story. S, D $85-$145; family, wkly, monthly rates. Crib free. Pet accepted. TV; cable (premium), VCR. Pool. Complimentary continental bkfst. Complimentary coffee in rms. Restaurant adj 6 am-11 pm. Ck-out noon. Coin lndry. Meeting rms. Business center. In-rm modem link. Sundries. Gift shop. Grocery store. Exercise equipt. Lawn games. Refrigerators, microwaves. Picnic tables, grills. Cr cds: A, D, DS, MC, V.

⧠ ⇦ ⇌ 🕇 ⋈ 🔥 🕇

★ **HOWARD JOHNSON.** *7575 Poe Ave (45414). 937/454-0550; fax 937/454-5566; toll-free 800/446-4656. www.hojo.com.* 121 rms, 2 story. S $54-$64; D $61-$69; each addl $7; under 18 free. Crib free. Pet accepted, some restrictions; $50 deposit. TV; cable (premium), VCR avail (movies). Pool. Complimentary continental bkfst. Bar 5 pm-midnight. Ck-out noon. Guest lndry. Meeting rms. Business servs avail. Valet serv. Free airport transportation. Health club privileges. Cr cds: A, C, D, DS, MC, V.

⧠ ⇦ ⋈ 🔥 SC

★★ **QUALITY INN.** *1944 Miamis-burg Centerville Rd (45459). 937/435-1550; fax 937/438-1878; toll-free 800/228-5151. www.qualityinn.com.* 72 rms, 2 story, 12 kit. units. S, D $69-$79; each addl $7; suites $65-$80; kit. units $65-$75; wkend rates; special events (2-day min). Crib free. TV; cable (premium), VCR avail. Pool. Complimentary continental bkfst. Coffee in rms. Restaurant adj

11-1 am. Ck-out 11 am. Business servs avail. Valet serv. Health club privileges. Some refrigerators. Cr cds: A, C, D, DS, MC, V.

⧠ ⇌ ⋈ 🔥 SC

★ **RED ROOF INN.** *7370 Miller Ln (45414). 937/898-1054; fax 937/898-1059; res 800/843-7663. www.redroof. com.* 109 rms, 2 story. S $47-$52; D $52-$69; each addl $5; under 18 free. Crib free. Pet accepted. TV; cable (premium). Complimentary coffee in lobby. Restaurant nearby. Ck-out noon. Business servs avail. Cr cds: A, D, DS, MC, V.

⧠ ⇦ ⋈ 🔥

Hotels

★★★ **CROWNE PLAZA.** *33 E 5th St; Fifth & Jefferson Sts (45402). 937/224-0800; fax 937/224-3913; toll-free 800/227-6963. www.crowneplaza. com.* 283 rms, 14 story. S, D $89-$150; each addl $15; suites $249-$394; under 12 free. Crib free. TV; cable (premium). Heated pool; poolside serv. Complimentary coffee in rms. Restaurant 6:30 am-11 pm. Rm serv 24 hrs. Bar; entertainment. Ck-out noon. Meeting rms. Business servs avail. Gift shop. Exercise equipt. Some refrigerators. Luxury level. Cr cds: A, C, D, DS, JCB, MC, V.

⧠ ⇌ 🕇 ⋈ 🔥 SC

★★ **MARRIOTT DAYTON.** *1414 S Patterson Blvd (45409). 937/223-1000; fax 937/223-7853; res 800/228-9290. www.marriott.com.* 399 rms, 6 story. S, D $89-$150; suites $200-$400; under 18 free; wkend rates. Crib free. Pet accepted, some restrictions; fee. TV; cable (premium), VCR avail. Indoor/outdoor pool; whirlpool, poolside serv. Restaurant 7 am-10 pm. Bar 11-1 am; entertainment. Ck-out noon. Coin lndry. Convention facilities. Business center. In-rm modem link. Gift shop. Exercise equipt; sauna. Balconies. Luxury level. Cr cds: A, C, D, DS, JCB, MC, V.

⇦ ⇌ 🕇 ⋈ 🔥 SC 🕇

All Suite

★★★ **DOUBLETREE GUEST SUITES.** *300 Prestige Pl (45342). 937/436-2400; fax 937/436-2886; res*

800/222-8733. www.doubletreehotels.com. 137 suites, 3 story. S, D $84-$174; under 18 free; wkend rates. Crib free. TV; cable (premium). Indoor/outdoor pool; whirlpool, poolside serv. Complimentary coffee in rms. Restaurant 6:30-9:30 am, 11:30 am-2 pm, 5-10 pm. Rm serv. Bar 11:30 am-11 pm. Ck-out noon. Coin lndry. Meeting rms. Business servs avail. Exercise equipt. Game rm. Refrigerators; microwaves avail. Some private patios, balconies. Cr cds: A, D, DS, JCB, MC, V.

D ⊠ ⼤ SC

Restaurants

★ **AMAR INDIA.** 2759 Miamisburg-Centerville Rd, Centerville (45459). 937/439-9005. Hrs: 11:30 am-2 pm, 5-10 pm; Sun noon-3 pm, 4:30-9 pm. Closed major hols. Northern Indian menu. Lunch $5-$8, dinner $8-$16. Specializes in vegetarian dishes, clay-oven bread dishes. Parking. Casual contemporary atmosphere. Cr cds: A, D, DS, MC, V.

D

★ **AMBER ROSE.** 1400 Valley St (45404). 937/228-2511. Hrs: 11 am-2 pm, 5-9 pm; Mon to 2 pm; Fri, Sat to 10 pm. Closed Sun; major hols. European, Amer menu. Bar. Lunch $4.95-$8.75, dinner $9.95-$15.25. Specialties: turtle soup, Lithuanian cabbage rolls, Mediterranean pasta. Parking. Victorian-style residence (1906); pressed tin ceilings, original wood flooring; stained-glass windows with rose motif. Cr cds: A, D, DS, MC, V.

D ⊣

★ **BARNSIDER.** 5202 N Main St (45415). 937/277-1332. Hrs: 5-10 pm; Fri, Sat 4-11 pm; Sun from noon; early-bird dinner to 6:30 pm Mon-Fri. Closed some major hols. Bar. Dinner $10-$20. Child's menu. Specializes in steak, chops, shrimp. Parking. Family-owned. Cr cds: A, MC, V.

D SC ⊣

★★ **BRAVO! ITALIAN KITCHEN.** 2148 Centerville Rd (45459). 937/439-1294. www.bestitalianusa.com. Hrs: 11 am-10 pm; Fri, Sat to 11 pm. Closed Thanksgiving, Dec 25. Italian menu. Bar. Lunch $7.50-$9.50, dinner $12.50-$16.50. Child's menu. Specializes in wood-fired pizza, lasagna.

Upscale family dining. Cr cds: A, DS, MC, V.

D ⊣

★★ **B R SCOTESE'S.** 1375 N Fairfield Rd, Beavercreek (45432). 937/431-1350. Hrs: 11 am-10 pm; Fri, Sat to 11 pm; Sat 4:30-11 pm. Closed Sun; major hols. Res accepted. Italian menu. Bar. Lunch $4.95-$7.95, dinner $9.95-$18.95. Child's menu. Specializes in chops, steaks. Accordionist Fri, Sat (night). Parking. Contemporary Italian decor. Cr cds: A, D, DS, MC, V.

D ⊣

★ **CHINA COTTAGE.** 6290 Far Hills Ave (OH 48) (45459). 937/434-2622. Hrs: 11 am-11 pm; Fri, Sat to midnight; Sun to 9 pm. Closed some major hols. Bar. Lunch $4-$6, dinner $6-$14. Specializes in chicken, Szechwan dishes, fresh fish. Parking. Cr cds: A, D, MC, V.

D ⊣

★★ **EL MESON.** 903 E Dixie Dr, West Carrolltown (45449). 937/859-8220. Hrs: 11 am-2 pm, 5-9 pm; Fri to 11 pm; Sat 5-11 pm. Closed Mon, Sun; major hols; also 1st 3 wks in Jan. Res required Thurs-Sat. Spanish, Latin Amer menu. Bar 4:30 pm-midnight; Fri, Sat to 1 am. Lunch $6-$8, dinner $15-$19. Specialties: el solomilla, tuna on clay, paella. Guitar, piano or folk dancers. Parking. Outdoor dining. Mexican hacienda; fountain. Cuisine of different countries on wkends. Family-owned since 1978. Totally nonsmoking. Cr cds: A, C, D, DS, ER, MC, V.

D

★★ **J ALEXANDER'S.** 7970 Washington Village Dr, Centerville (45459). 937/435-4441. www.jalexanders.com. Hrs: 11 am-11 pm; Fri, Sat to midnight; Sun to 10 pm. Closed Thanksgiving, Dec 25. Bar. Lunch $5.95-$8.95, dinner $6.50-$18.95. Child's menu. Specializes in prime rib, seafood, homemade desserts. Parking. Casual dining. Cr cds: A, D, DS, MC, V.

D ⊣

★★★ **JAY'S.** 225 E 6th St (45402). 937/222-2892. www.jays.com. Hrs: 5-10:30 pm; Fri, Sat to 11 pm; Sun to 9 pm. Closed major hols. Res accepted Sun-Fri. Bar. Wine cellar. Dinner

$12.95-$28.95. Child's menu. Specializes in fresh seafood, prime beef. Parking. Remodeled 1850s gristmill in Oregon Village. Cr cds: A, D, DS, MC, V.
🄳

★★★★ **L'AUBERGE.** *4120 Far Hills Ave, Kettering (45419). 937/299-5536. www.laubergedayton.com.* Josef Reif's French restaurant near Dayton presents refined meals in a bright, cozy setting. The charming white house is a relaxing haven, even though the surrounding area has become increasingly developed in recent years, and is filled with brightly colored china and interesting fabrics and artwork. The Bistro room offers a more casual atmosphere and less expensive menu. French menu. Specializes in pâte, imported fresh seafood, game. Own baking. Hrs: 11:30 am-2 pm, 5:30-10 pm. Closed Sun; hols. Res accepted. Bar. Wine cellar. Lunch $9.95-$18, dinner $26.50-$30. Pianist. Outdoor dining. Jacket and tie. Cr cds: A, D, MC, V.
🄳

★★ **LINCOLN PARK GRILLE.** *580 Lincoln Park Blvd (45429). 937/293-6293.* Hrs: 11 am-10 pm; Fri to 11 pm; Sat 5-11 pm; Sun (June-Aug) 5-11 pm. Closed Jan 1, Thanksgiving, Dec 25. Res accepted. Bar. Lunch $4.95-$7.95, dinner $8.95-$18.95. Parking. Patio dining. View of Lincoln Park Commons fountain and amphitheater. Cr cds: A, D, DS, MC, V.
🄳 🆂🄲 ➡

★★ **OAKWOOD CLUB.** *2414 Far Hills Ave, Oakwood (45419). 937/293-6973.* Hrs: 4:30 pm-midnight; Fri, Sat to 1 am. Closed Sun; major hols. Res accepted. Bar to 2:30 am. Dinner $13.95-$21.95. Specializes in steak, prime rib, fresh seafood. Own baking. Parking. Club atmosphere. Neiman originals on walls. Cr cds: A, D, MC, V.
🄳 ➡

★★ **PINE CLUB.** *1926 Brown St (45409). 937/228-7463.* Hrs: 5 pm-midnight. Fri, Sat to 1 am. Closed Sun; Jan 1, Thanksgiving, Dec 25. Bar 4 pm-2 am. Wine list. Dinner $9.95-$20.95. Child's menu. Specializes in steak, veal, pork. Parking. Casual atmosphere; collection of Toby mugs and beer steins. Braille menu.
🄳 ➡

★★ **STEVE KAO'S.** *8270 Springboro Pike (45342). 937/435-5261.* Hrs: 11:30 am-9:30 pm; Fri, Sat to 11 pm; Sun noon-10 pm; Sun brunch to 4 pm. Closed major hols. Res accepted. Chinese menu. Bar; entertainment. A la carte entrees: lunch $4.95-$7.25, dinner $7.95-$14.95. Sun brunch buffet: $6.95. Specializes in Peking duck, salmon, Szechwan dishes. Parking. Cr cds: A, D, DS, MC, V.
🄳 ➡

★★ **THOMATO'S.** *110 N Main St (45402). 937/228-3333.* Hrs: 11 am-2 pm, 5-10 pm; Fri, Sat 5-11 pm; Mon to 9 pm. Closed Sun; major hols. Res accepted. Bar from 11 am. Lunch $6.95-$8.25, dinner $14.95-$21.95. Specializes in pasta, salads, seafood. Pianist. Bistro decor. Cr cds: A, D, DS, MC, V.
🄳 ➡

★★ **WELTON'S.** *4614 Wilmington Pike (45440). 937/293-2233.* Hrs: 5-10 pm; Fri, Sat to 11 pm. Closed Sun; some major hols. Bar. Dinner $5.95-$18.95. Specializes in fresh fish, pizza, hand-cut steak. Cr cds: A, DS, MC, V.
🄳 ➡

Defiance (B-2)

Pop 16,768 **Elev** 691 ft **Area code** 419 **Zip** 43512

Information The Greater Defiance Area Tourism & Visitors Bureau, 415 Second St; 419/782-0864 or 800/686-4382

Web www.defiance-online.com

Defiance was named for Fort Defiance (1794), which was constructed during Major General "Mad Anthony" Wayne's vigorous campaign against the Native Americans. The fort was so named after Wayne said "I defy the English, the Indians, and all the devils in hell to take it." Defiance was also the site of a major Native American council in 1793 and is the birthplace of Chief Pontiac.

Johnny Appleseed lived in Defiance during 1811-1828 while growing his pioneer apple orchards.

What to See and Do

Au Glaize Village. Over 110 acres. Replicas and restored late 19th-century buildings incl Kieffer log cabin, Kinner log house; cider, sorghum, and saw mills; blacksmith shop; railroad station and rolling stock; church, school, post office, gas station, dental and doctor offices; four museum buildings, black powder range. (June-Sept, wkends) Special events throughout the season. 3 mi SW off US 24 on Krouse Rd. Phone 419/784-0107. ¢¢

Independence Dam State Park. A 604-acre park on the Maumee River. Fishing, boating (marina); hiking, picnicking (shelter), camping. Standard fees. 3 mi E on OH 424. Phone 419/784-3263.

Special Event

Fort Defiance Days. Riverboat cruises, hot-air balloon races. Early Aug. Phone 419/782-7946.

Motels/Motor Lodges

★★ **COMFORT INN.** *1068 Hotel Dr (43512). 419/784-4900; fax 419/784-5555; toll-free 800/228-5150. www.comfortinn.com.* 62 rms, 2 story, 10 suites. S $66-$80; D $66-$90; each addl $5; suites $75-$96; under 18 free. TV; cable (premium). Indoor pool; whirlpool. Complimentary continental bkfst. Restaurant opp 11-2 am. Ck-out 11 am. Coin lndry. Meeting rms. In-rm modem link. Sundries. Refrigerator in suites. Cr cds: A, C, D, DS, MC, V.
D ≥ ⓐ SC ≥

★ **DAYS INN.** *1835 N Clinton St (43512). 419/782-5555; fax 419/782-8085; toll-free 800/329-7466. www.daysinn.com.* 121 rms, 2 story. S $45-$54; D $54-$60; each addl $6; under 18 free. Crib free. TV; cable (premium), VCR avail. Indoor pool. Restaurant 6 am-2 pm; closed Sat, Sun. Rm serv. Bar. Ck-out noon. Meeting rms. Sundries. Cr cds: A, C, D, DS, MC, V.
D ≥ ⓐ SC ≥

★★ **QUALITY INN.** *2395 N Scott St, Napoleon (43545). 419/592-5010; fax 419/592-6618; res 800/827-8641. www.qualityinn.com.* 79 rms, 2 story. S, D $59-$69; each addl $6; suites $75-$80; under 18 free; wkend rates. Crib free. Pet accepted, some restrictions. TV; cable (premium). Complimentary coffee in lobby. Restaurant 6:30 am-10 pm. Rm serv. Bar 11-1:30 am. Ck-out noon. Meeting rms. Business servs avail. Sundries. Coin lndry. Pool. Microwaves avail. Cr cds: A, D, DS, MC, V.
D ⓐ ≥ ≥ ⓐ

Delaware

(D-3) *See also Columbus, Marion, Mount Gilead, Mount Vernon*

Founded 1808 **Pop** 20,030 **Elev** 880 ft **Area code** 740 **Zip** 43015

Information Delaware County Convention & Visitors Bureau, 44 E Winter St; 740/368-4748 or 888-335-6446

Web www.visitdelohio.com

Delaware, on the Olentangy River, derives its name and heritage from New England. Now a college town, trading center for farmers, and site of diversified industry, the area was chosen by Native Americans as a campsite because of its mineral springs. The Mansion House (a famous sulphur-spring resort built in 1833) is now Elliot Hall, the first building of Ohio Wesleyan University. There is a legend that President Rutherford B. Hayes (a native of Delaware) proposed to his bride-to-be, Lucy Webb (one of the school's first coeds), at the sulphur spring.

What to See and Do

Alum Creek State Park. On 8,600 acres. Versatile topography and character of lake provides for abundance of activities. Swimming, waterskiing, fishing, boating; hunting, hiking and bridle trails, snowmobiling, camping (rentals, fee). Nature programs. Standard fees. Daily. 6 mi E on OH 36, 37. Phone 740/548-4631. **FREE**

Delaware County Historical Society Museum. Relics tracing area's history from 1800. Genealogy library. (Mar-mid-Nov, Sun and Wed afternoons; also by appt; closed hols) 157 E William St. Phone 740/369-3831. **FREE**

Delaware State Park. 1,815-acre park with 1,330-acre lake. Swimming, bathhouse, fishing, boating (rentals, ramp); hiking, picnicking, concession, camping. Standard fees. Daily. Phone 740/369-2761. **FREE**

Ohio Wesleyan University. (1842) 2,000 students. Sandusky St passes through historic 200-acre campus. Liberal arts educational institution. Mayhew Gallery, Humphreys Art Hall (Sept-May, Mon-Sat). Gray Chapel houses one of three Klais organs in the US. Campus tours. Phone 740/369-4431.

Olentangy Indian Caverns and Ohio Frontierland. Natural limestone cave; 55-105 ft below ground on three levels are various rock strata and fossils; once refuge for the Wyandot. Tours (35 min) guided and self-guided (Apr-Oct). Also re-creation of Ohio frontierland and Native American village (Memorial Day-Labor Day). 1779 Home Rd, 7 mi S, off US 23. Phone 740/548-7917. ¢¢¢

Perkins Observatory. Operated by Ohio Wesleyan University. Thirty-two-inch reflecting telescope. (Mon-Fri; closed hols) Evening tour avail (Fri-Sat, limited hrs). 4 mi S on US 23. Phone 740/363-1257. **FREE**

Special Event

Delaware County Fair. Fairgrounds, 236 Pennsylvania Ave. Grand Circuit harness racing; Little Brown Jug harness race for pacers. Phone 740/362-3851. Usually third wk Sept.

Motels/Motor Lodges

★ **DAYS INN.** 16510 Square Dr, Marysville (43040). 937/644-8821; toll-free 877/644-8821. www.daysinn. com. 74 rms, 2 story, 12 kit. units. S, D $59-$69; each addl $5; suites $99; kit. units $69; under 19 free. Crib free. Pet accepted, $10 fee, some restrictions. TV; cable (premium), VCR avail. Complimentary bkfst. Restaurant adj 6 am-10 pm. Ck-out noon. Business center. In-rm modem link. Health club privileges. Whirl-

pool in some suites. Cr cds: A, C, D, DS, MC, V.
⊡ 🐾 ⊠ 🐾 **SC** 🏃

★ **TRAVELODGE.** 1001 US Hwy 23 N (43015). 740/369-4421; fax 740/362-9090; res 800/578-7878. www.travelodge.com. 31 rms, 1-2 story. S $42-$48; D $47-$65; each addl $6; under 18 free; higher rates: Little Brown Jug harness race, wkends during peak season. Crib $6. Pet accepted. TV; cable. Complimentary coffee in rms. Restaurant open 11 am-11 pm. Ck-out noon. Meeting rms. Business servs avail. Sundries. Cr cds: A, C, D, DS, MC, V.
🐾 ⊠ 🐾 **SC**

Restaurants

★ **BRANDING IRON.** 1400 Stratford Rd (43015). 740/363-1846. Hrs: 5-9:30 pm; Fri, Sat to 10:30 pm; Sun noon-8 pm. Closed Mon; Jan 1, Dec 24, 25; also first 2 wks Aug. Res accepted. Bar. Dinner $6.95-$14.95. Child's menu. Specializes in steak, barbecued ribs. Parking. Western decor. Family-owned. Cr cds: DS, MC, V.
⊡ ➡

★ **BUN'S OF DELAWARE.** 6 W Winter St (43015). 740/363-3731. Hrs: 7:30 am-8 pm; Sun 11 am- 7 pm. Closed Mon; major hols. Bar. Bkfst $2-$4.75, lunch $3.75-$6.75, dinner $5.35-$14.95. Child's menu. Cr cds: A, DS, MC, V.
➡

East Liverpool

(C-7) *See also Steubenville*

Settled 1798 **Pop** 13,654 **Elev** 689 ft
Area code 330 **Zip** 43920
Information East Liverpool Chamber of Commerce, 529 Market St; 330/385-0845
Web www.elchamber.com

Located where Ohio, Pennsylvania, and West Virginia meet on the Ohio River, East Liverpool was called Fawcett's Town (after its first settler) until 1860. Its clay deposits determined its destiny as a pottery center; everything from dinnerware to brick is produced here.

What to See and Do

Beaver Creek State Park. There are many streams in this 3,038-acre forested area that contains the ruins of the Sandy and Beaver Canal and one well-preserved lock. Gaston's Mill (ca 1837) has been restored. Fishing, canoeing; hunting, hiking, bridle trails, picnicking, primitive camping. Standard fees. (Daily) 8 mi NW off OH 7. Phone 330/385-3091. **FREE**

Museum of Ceramics. History museum contains collection of regional pottery and porcelain; bone china; life-size dioramas; multimedia presentation. (Mar-Apr, wknds; May-Nov, Wed-Sun; closed Thanksgiving) 400 E 5th St. Phone 330/386-6001. ¢¢

Pottery tours. Hall China Company. (Mon-Fri, mornings daily) Anna St. Phone 330/385-2900.

Special Event

Tri-State Pottery Festival. Pottery industry displays, plant tours, pottery olympics; art and antique show, rose show, rides. Third wkend June. Phone 330/385-0845.

Elyria

(B-5) *See also Cleveland, Lorain, Oberlin, Sandusky*

Settled 1817 **Pop** 56,746 **Elev** 730 ft
Area code 440 **Zip** 44035
Information Lorain County Visitors Bureau, 611 Broadway, Lorain 44052; 440/245-5282 or 800/334-1673
Web www.lcvb.org

This retailing and industrial city, at the junction of the east and west branches of the Black River, is the seat of Lorain County. The novelist Sherwood Anderson managed a paint factory here before his literary career began. Now the city has more than 130 industries manufacturing automotive parts, golf balls, air-conditioning and home-heating units, aircraft parts, and pumps and metal castings. Surrounding greenhouses and farms contribute poultry, fruits, vegetables, and dairy products to the city's economy.

What to See and Do

Cascade & Elywood parks. Picnic areas, playground; trails, sledding hill; waterfalls, views of rock cliffs. Washington Ave or Furnace St off W River St. Phone 440/322-0926.

The Hickories Museum. (1894) Shingle-style mansion of industrialist Arthur Lovett Garford. Changing exhibits on Lorain County. Hicks Memorial Research Library. 509 Washington Ave. Phone 440/322-3341. ¢¢

Special Event

Apple Festival. Third wkend Sept. Phone 440/245-5282.

Motels/Motor Lodges

★★ **COMFORT INN.** *739 Leona St (44035). 440/324-7676; fax 440/324-4046; res 800/228-5150. www.comfort inn.com.* 66 rms, 2 story, 9 suites. June-Aug: S, D $74-$99; each addl $6; suites $70-$125; under 18 free; lower rates rest of yr. Crib $6. Pet accepted; fee. TV; cable (premium). Complimentary continental bkfst. Restaurant nearby. Ck-out 11 am. Coin lndry. Meeting rm. Sundries. Refrigerator, microwave, in-rm whirlpool in suites. Cr cds: A, C, D, DS, MC, V.
🄳 🐾 🕭 🖾 🔥

★ **DAYS INN.** *621 Midway Blvd (44035). 440/324-4444; fax 440/324-2065; res 800/329-7466. www.daysinn. com.* 101 rms, 3 story, 30 suites. May-Sept: S $59-$96.95; D $59-$104.95; each addl $8; suites $69.95-$124.95; under 13 free; lower rates rest of yr. Crib free. TV; cable (premium). Indoor pool. Complimentary continental bkfst. Restaurant nearby. Ck-out noon. Coin lndry. Business servs avail. In-rm modem link. Game rm. Cr cds: A, C, D, DS, MC, V.
🄳 🏊 🖾 🔥

★★ **HOLIDAY INN ELYRIA.** *1825 Lorain Blvd (Rte 57) (44035). 440/324-5411; fax 440/324-2785; res 800/321-7333. www.holiday-inn.com.* 250 rms, 2-6 story. June-Aug: S, D $90-$129;

each addl $10; suites $139-$175; under 18 free. Crib free. TV; cable (premium). Heated pool; poolside serv. Restaurant 6 am-10 pm. Rm serv. Bar 11:30-2 am. Ck-out noon. Coin lndry. Meeting rms. Business servs avail. In-rm modem link. Valet serv. Sundries. Free airport transportation. Health club privileges. Cr cds: A, MC, V.

D ⚓ ⬚ 🖐 SC

Findlay

(C-3) *See also Bowling Green, Lima, Tiffin*

Founded 1821 **Pop** 35,703 **Elev** 780 ft **Area code** 419 **Zip** 45840
Information Hancock County Convention and Visitors Bureau, 123 East Main Cross St; 419/422-3315 or 800/424-3315
Web www.findlayhancockchamber.com

In 1860 the editor of the Findlay *Jeffersonian,* in letters signed "Petroleum V. Nasby," attacked slavery. In the previous decade the "grapevine telegraph" and Underground Railroad, piloting runaway slaves to safety, were active in Findlay. Named for Fort Findlay, one of the outposts of the War of 1812, it is the seat of Hancock County, 45 miles south of Toledo in the state's rich farm area. Congress designated Findlay as Flag City, USA in 1974.

Tell Taylor, educated in Findlay, was inspired to write "Down by the Old Mill Stream" while fishing along the Blanchard River. Marilyn Miller, Russell Crouse, Dr. Howard T. Ricketts, and Dr. Norman Vincent Peale also came from Findlay.

What to See and Do

Hancock Historical Museum. Exhibits depicting history of the county. Exhibits of glass, incl examples produced in Findlay during the great gas boom of the 1880s; Pendleton art glass collection. (Wed-Fri afternoons; tours, Sun afternoons by appt) 422 W Sandusky St. Phone 419/423-4433. **Donation**

Mazza Museum, International Art from Picture Books. Exhibited here is the Mazza Collection; original art created by illustrators of childrens' books. More than 2,000 works of distinguished illustrators are displayed, incl those of Ezra Jack Keats, Maurice Sendak, and other Caldecott Medal winners. (Wed-Fri, Sun afternoons; closed hols) 1000 N Main St, in the Virginia B. Gardner Fine Arts Pavilion on the campus of The University of Findlay. Phone 419/424-4777. **FREE**

Motels/Motor Lodges

★★ **COUNTRY HEARTH INN.** *1020 Interstate Ct (45840). 419/423-4303; fax 419/423-3459; toll-free 800/672-7935. www.countryhearth.com.* 72 rms, 8 suites, 10 kit. units. S $55-$62; D $62-$78; each addl $6; suites, kit. units $67-$73; under 18 free. Crib free. TV; cable (premium). Pool. Complimentary bkfst. Coffee in rms. Restaurant adj 6 am-10 pm. Ck-out noon. Meeting rms. Business servs avail. In-rm modem link. Valet serv. Microwaves avail. Cr cds: A, C, D, DS, MC, V.

D ⚓ ⬚ 🖐 SC

★★ **CROSS COUNTRY INN- FINDLAY.** *1951 Broad Ave (45840). 419/424-0466; fax 419/424-1043. www.crosscountryinns.com.* 120 rms. S $40.99; D $49.99; each addl $7; under 18 free. Crib free. TV. Heated pool. Complimentary coffee in lobby. Restaurant adj 7 am-11 pm. Ck-out noon. Cr cds: A, C, D, DS, MC, V.

⚓ ✈ ⬚ 🖐

★★ **FAIRFIELD INN.** *2000 Tiffin Ave (45839). 419/424-9940; res 800/228-2800. www.fairfieldinn.com.* 57 rms, 3 story, 13 suites. S, D $58-$110; each addl $6; suites $68-$120; under 18 free. TV; cable (premium). Indoor pool; whirlpool. Complimentary continental bkfst. Ck-out noon. Meeting rm. Business servs avail. Health club privileges. Sundries. Refrigerator in suites. Cr cds: A, MC, V.

D ⚓ ⬚ 🖐

★★★ **FINDLAY INN & CONFERENCE CENTER.** *200 E Main Cross St (45840). 419/422-5682; fax 419/422-*

5581; toll-free 800/825-1455. www.
findlayinn.com. 80 rms, 3 story, 12
suites. S $59-$95; D $63-$130; suites
$78-$130; wkend rates. Crib $6. TV;
cable. Indoor pool; whirlpool. Complimentary continental bkfst (Mon-
Fri). Restaurant 6:30 am-9 pm; Sat,
Sun from 7:30 am. Rm serv. Bar. Ck-
out noon. Meeting rms. Business
servs avail. Bellhops. Exercise equipt.
Health club privileges. Some refrigerators; microwaves avail. Cr cds: A, D,
DS, MC, V.

D ⊠ 🐾 ⚓ 🏃

Fort Ancient
State Memorial

See also Cincinnati, Dayton, Lebanon,
Middletown (Butler County)

(7 mi SE of Lebanon on OH 350)

Fort Ancient is one of the largest and
most impressive prehistoric earthworks of its kind in the United
States. The Fort Ancient earthworks
were built by the Hopewell people
between 100 B.C.-A.D. 500. This site
occupies an elevated plateau overlooking the Little Miami River Valley.
Its massive earthen walls, more than
23 feet high in places, enclose an
area of 100 acres; within this area are
earth mounds once used as a calendar of event markers and other
archaeological features. Relics from
the site and the nearby prehistoric
Native American village are displayed
in Fort Ancient Museum. Hiking
trails, picnic facilities. (Mar-Nov,
daily) Phone 513/932-4421. ¢¢

Fort Hill State
Memorial

See also Chillicothe

*(5 mi N of Sinking Spring off OH 41;
SW of Chillicothe via US 50, OH 41)*

This is the site of a prehistoric Native
American hilltop earth and stone
enclosure. The identity of its builders
has not been determined, but implements found in the vicinity point to

the Hopewell people. There is a
2,000-foot trail that leads to the
ancient earthworks. Picnic area and
shelterhouse. (Daily). Phone
937/588-3221 **FREE**

Fremont (B-3)

Founded 1820 **Pop** 17,648 **Elev** 601 ft
Area code 419 **Zip** 43420
Information Sandusky County Con-
vention & Visitors Bureau, 1510 E
State St, PO Box 643; 419/332-4470
or 800/255-8070
Web www.sanduskycounty.org

Wyandot settled here as early as
1650; scouts and settlers came in the
late 1700s. Fort Stephenson was built
and defended in the War of 1812.
Earlier known as Lower Sandusky,
the town became Fremont in 1849.
Rutherford B. Hayes, 19th US president, lived in Fremont and is buried
here. Seat of Sandusky County, 20
miles from Lake Erie on the Sandusky River, Fremont is an industrial
town known for cutlery, food processing, and tools and dyes. It is also
an agricultural area.

What to See and Do

**Hayes Presidential Center, Spiegel
Grove.** Rutherford B. Hayes Library,
Museum and home; period and community exhibits; Hayes memorabilia.
Graves of the President and Mrs.
Hayes. (Daily; closed Jan 1, Thanksgiving, Dec 25) Library (Mon-Sat;
closed hols). Tours of the residence
and museum (daily). Corner of Hayes
Ave & Buckland Ave. Phone 419/332-
2081. ¢¢¢

Library Park. Scene of 1813 Fort
Stephenson battle; "Old Betsy," only
cannon used to defend the fort; Soldiers Monument. (Mon-Sat) 423
Croghan St between Arch and High
sts. Phone 419/334-7101. **FREE**

Special Events

**Civil War Encampment & President
Hayes Birthday Reunion.** Phone
800/998-7737. First full wkend Oct.

Haunted Hydro. Phone 419/334-
2451. Late Oct.

Motel/Motor Lodge

★ **DAYS INN.** *3701 N OH 53 (43420). 419/334-9551; res 800/329-7466. www.daysinn.com.* 105 rms, 2 story. June-Aug: S, D $66-$115; each addl $8; suites $95-$150; under 12 free; higher rates special events; lower rates rest of yr. TV; cable (premium). Pool. Playground. Restaurant 6-11 am, 5-10 pm; Sun to 11 am. Rm serv. Bar. Ck-out noon. Coin lndry. Meeting rms. Valet serv. Game rm. Cr cds: A, C, D, DS, MC, V.

Gallipolis (F-5)

Settled 1790 **Pop** 4,831
Area code 740 **Zip** 45631
Information Ohio Valley Visitors Center, 45 State St; 740/446-6882 or 800/765-6482

Gallipolis, "the old French city" along the Ohio River, was the second permanent settlement in Ohio. The columnist O. O. McIntyre lived in Gallipolis, often wrote about it, and is buried here. The district library has an extensive collection of his work.

What to See and Do

Bob Evans Farm. A 1,100-acre farm. Canoeing (fee); hiking, horseback riding (fee), special wkend events (fee); Craftbarn and Farm Museum; craft demonstrations; domestic animals, farm crops. (Memorial Day wkend-Labor Day wkend, daily; Sept, wkends; call for schedule) 12 mi W; just off US 35, on OH 588 in Rio Grande. Phone 740/245-5305. **FREE**
French Art Colony. Monthly exhibits. (Tues-Sun; closed hols) 530 1st Ave. Phone 740/446-3834. **FREE**
Our House State Memorial. Built as a tavern in 1819; restored. Lafayette stayed here. (Memorial Day-Labor Day, Tues-Sun) 434 1st St. Phone 740/446-0586. ¢¢

Special Event

Bob Evans Farm Festival. Bob Evans Farm. Bluegrass and country entertainment; food, 150 heritage craftspeople and demonstrations; Appalachian clogging, square dancing. Camping. Phone 740/245-5305 or 800/994-3276. Mid-Oct.

Motel/Motor Lodge

★★ **HOLIDAY INN.** *577 OH 7 N (45631). 740/446-0090; res 800/465-4329. www.holiday-inn.com.* 100 rms, 3 suites, 2 story. S, D $62-$79; suites $69; under 19 free. Crib free. Pet accepted. TV; cable. Pool; wading pool. Restaurant 6 am-10 pm. Rm serv. Bar 4 pm-midnight. Ck-out noon. Coin lndry. Meeting rms. Business servs avail. Sundries. Cr cds: A, C, D, DS, MC, V.

Geneva-on-the-Lake

See also Ashtabula, Painesville

Founded 1869 **Pop** 1,626 **Elev** 605 ft
Area code 440 **Zip** 44041
Information Convention and Visitors Bureau, 5536 Lake Rd; 440/466-8600 or 800/862-9948
Web www.ncweb.com/gol

Geneva-on-the-Lake is Ohio's first summer resort. Its 129-year-old entertainment "strip" has a wide variety of nightlife, while Lake Erie offers boating, fishing, and beaches.

What to See and Do

Ashtabula County History Museum, Jennie Munger Gregory Memorial. (1823-1826) One of first frame houses built on Lake Erie's southern shore. Victorian furnishings, clothing, quilts, and artifacts. (June-Sept, Wed and Sun afternoons). Lake Rd (OH 534) between Putnam and Grandview drs. Phone 440/466-7337. **Donation**
Erieview Park. Amusement park with major and kiddie rides, water slides; train ride; arcade. Nightclub; lodging;

restaurant, picnicking. (May-Sept, daily; early and late season hrs vary) 5483 Lake Rd. Phone 440/466-8650. ¢¢¢

Geneva State Park. This 698-acre park offers swimming, fishing, boating, 383-slip marina with six-lane ramp; hunting, hiking, snowmobile and x-country ski trails, picnicking (shelter), concession, camping, pet camping, cabins. Standard fees. (Apr-Nov; daily) Off OH 534. Phone 440/466-8400. **FREE**

Special Event

Geneva Grape Jamboree. Downtown. Festival marks the grape harvesting season. Grape products, grape stomping; parades, entertainment, exhibits, contests, winery tours. Phone 440/466-5262. Last full wkend Sept.

Gnadenhutten

(D-6) *See also Cambridge, Coshocton, New Philadelphia*

Settled 1772 **Pop** 1,226 **Elev** 835 ft **Area code** 614 **Zip** 44629

Information Gnadenhutten Chamber of Commerce, PO Box 830; 614/254-4314

Gnadenhutten (ja-NA-den-hut-ten) is a rural center in Tuscarawas County in the Muskingum Conservancy District.

What to See and Do

Gnadenhutten Historical Park and Museum. Monument to 90 Christian Native Americans who were massacred here in 1782. Native American burial mound. Reconstructed log church and cooper's cabin. Museum. Oldest tombstone in Ohio. (Memorial Day-early Sept, daily; early Sept-Oct, wkends; rest of yr, by appt) 1 mi S. Phone 614/254-4756. **Donation**

Tappan Lake Park. Swimming, fishing, boating (ramp), marina; playground, tent and trailer sites (showers, flush toilets), cabins. Standard fees. Pets on leash. (Daily) 7 mi E on US 36, 15 mi SE on US 250, W on County 55, 3 mi to park entrance. Phone 614/922-3649. ¢¢

Clendening Lake Marina. Fishing, boating (ramp); lodgings, tent and trailer sites. Pets on leash. (Apr-Oct, daily; Mar and Nov, wkends) 7 mi E on US 36 to Dennison, then 12 mi S, off OH 800. Phone 614/658-3691.

Hamilton

(E-1) *See also Cincinnati, Mason, Middletown (Butler County), Oxford*

Founded 1791 **Pop** 61,368 **Elev** 580 ft **Area code** 513

Information Greater Hamilton Convention & Visitors Bureau, 201 Dayton St, 45011; 513/844-1500 or 800/311-5353

Web www.hamilton-ohio.com

Originally Fort Hamilton, an outpost of the Northwest Territory, the city became an industrial center in the 1850s with the completion of the Miami-Erie Canal. It continues as such today. Much of Hamilton's rich 19th-century heritage is preserved in the large number and variety of restored homes in several historic districts.

What to See and Do

Dayton Lane Historic Area Walking Tour. Many examples of restored Victorian and turn-of-the-century architecture, mostly homes. Allow an hr. From the railroad tracks on the W to OH 4 on the E; from Buckeye St on the N to High St on the S. Phone 800/311-5353.

German Village Walking Tour. Nine-blk area just north of the business district. German Village was part of the original city plan of 1796, with the first courts, school, newspaper, and many early businesses. Allow at least one hr; two mi. Phone 800/311-5353. Within the district are

Butler County Historical Museum (Benninghofen House). (1861) Historical museum housed in Victorian Italianate mansion. Period furnishings; antique clothing, toys; doll collection; 19th-century dentist's office; local memorabilia.

(Tues-Sun; closed hols) 327 N 2nd St. Phone 513/896-9930. ¢

Lane-Hooven House. (1863) Unusual octagonal home in the Gothic Revival style; octagonal turret, Tudor front door, cast iron balconies, jigsaw bargeboard-decorated eaves. Exterior and interior fully restored. Home of Hamilton Community Foundation. (Mon-Fri; closed hols) 319 N 3rd St. Phone 513/863-1389. **FREE**

Rossville Walking Tour. Eleven-block area on the west side of the Great Miami River. Until 1855 this was the separate town of Rossville, which was laid out in 1804 as a mercantile community. More buildings survived here, because it was less susceptible to flooding than the east bank. Wide range of styles from 1830-1920. Allow one hr; over two mi; level ground except for Millikin St. Phone 800/311-5353. Before crossing to Rossville, visit Monument Park with the 1804 Log Cabin and

> **Soldiers, Sailors and Pioneers Monument.** (1902) Permanent memorial to the pioneer settlers and those of the area who fought in conflicts from the Indian Wars to the Spanish-American War. Displays inside building. (Mon-Sat) High and Monument Sts. Phone 513/867-5823.

Special Events

Butler County Fair. Butler County Fairgrounds. Phone 513/892-1423. Last full wk July.

Antique Car Parade. Courthouse Sq. Three hundred cars in one of nation's oldest antique car parades. Fourth Sat July. Phone 513/844-8080.

Dam Fest. Two-day festival centered on the Great Miami River and Miami Campus; features world champion waterskiers in doubles and freestyle competition; booths, games, entertainment. Phone 513/867-2281. Wkend after Labor Day.

Hotel

★ ★ **HAMILTONIAN.** *1 Riverfront Plz (45011). 513/896-6200; fax 513/896-9463; toll-free 800/522-5570.* 120 rms, 6 story. S $65-$89; D $73-$89; each

addl $8; suites $149-$159; wkend rates. Crib free. Pet accepted. TV; cable (premium), VCR avail. Pool. Coffee in rms. Restaurant 7 am-9 pm. Bar 11-midnight; Fri, Sat to 1 am. Ck-out noon. Meeting rms. Business servs avail. In-rm modem link. Refrigerator avail. On river. Luxury level. Cr cds: A, C, D, DS, MC, V.

D ⬦ ≈ ⬦ ⬦ SC

Hocking Hills State Park

See also Athens, Chillicothe, Lancaster

(12 mi SW of Logan via OH 374, 664; or SE of Lancaster via US 33, SW on OH 664)

More than 2,000 acres divided into six scenic areas:

> **Ash Cave.** Natural rock shelter with 90-ft waterfall in spring and winter. Ashes from Native American campfires were found here. Picnicking, shelter, hiking; a ¼-mi wheelchair-accessible trail to Ash Cave. (Daily) Phone 614/385-6841. **FREE**

> **Old Man's Cave.** The most popular and highly developed area. Waterfalls, gorges, and caves. A hermit who lived in the main cave after the Civil War gave the cave its name. Fishing; hiking, picnicking, shelter, concession, restaurant, cabins, camping. Park naturalist in summer. Standard fees. (Daily) Phone 614/385-6841. **FREE**

> **Rock House.** Unusual "house" formation in the sandstone cliff. Picnicking, hiking. **FREE**

> **Cantwell Cliffs, Cedar Falls, Conkie's Hollow.** Feature cliffs, good trails, rare plants, and picnicking. (Daily) Phone 740/385-6841. **FREE**

Ironton

(G-4) *See also Gallipolis, Portsmouth*

Founded 1848 **Pop** 12,751 **Elev** 558 ft
Area code 740 **Zip** 45638

Old Man Upper Falls, Hocking Hills State Park

Information Greater Lawrence County Convention and Visitors Bureau, PO Box 488, South Point 45680; 740/377-4550 or 740/532-9991

Web www.lawrencecountyohio.org

Extensive ore pockets in the district once gave Ironton a thriving iron industry; the first charcoal furnace north of the Ohio River started producing pig iron here in 1826. The town was founded by one of the first ironmasters. Ironton was the southern terminus for the Detroit, Toledo, and Ironton. The Chesapeake and Ohio and the Norfolk and Southern railroads still serve the area.

Ironton is now an important industrial city and home to the large plants of many companies.

What to See and Do

Lawrence County Museum. Changing exhibits in Italian-style villa (1870). (Early Apr-mid-Dec, Fri-Sun afternoons) 506 S 6th St. Phone 740/532-1222. **Donation**

Wayne National Forest. Three sections make up this 202,967-acre area of southeast Ohio. Private lands are interspersed within the federal land. One section is the east side of Ohio, northeast of Marietta (see); the second is northeast of Athens (see); and the third section is in the southern tip of the state, southwest of Gallipolis. The forest lies in the foothills of the Appalachian Mtns. It is characterized by rugged hills covered with diverse stands of hardwoods, pine, and cedar; lakes, rivers, and streams; springs, rock shelters, covered bridges, trails, and campgrounds are located in the forest. A Ranger District office of the forest is also located here. (Daily) Contact the Supervisor, 13700 US Hwy 33, Nelsonville 45764. Phone 740/753-0101. **FREE** In the forest is

Lake Vesuvius. The stack of Vesuvius (1833), one of the earliest iron blast furnaces, still remains. Swimming, fishing, boating (dock; May-Sept); hiking, picnicking, camping. (Daily) 10 mi N off OH 93. Phone 740/534-6500. ¢¢

Special Events

Lawrence County Fair. E on US 52, at fairgrounds in Proctorville. Mid-July. Phone 740/532-9195.

Festival of the Hills. 1804 Liberty Ave. Celebrates cultural heritage of Lawrence County; musical entertainment, demonstrations, displays. Phone 740/532-5285. Mid-Sept.

Kelleys Island

See also Port Clinton, Put-in-Bay, Sandusky

Founded 1833 **Pop** 172 **Elev** 598 ft
Area code 419 **Zip** 43438

Information Chamber of Commerce, PO Box 783; 419/746-2360
Web www.kelleys island.com

Kelleys Island, one of the largest of 20 islands in Lake Erie, is five miles across at the widest point. This is a vacation spot with auto and passenger service available from Marblehead on Neuman Boat Line or Kelleys Island Ferry Boat Line. Island hopping cruises are available from Port Clinton and Sandusky (see).

What to See and Do

Glacial Grooves State Memorial. Limestone with unusually long, smooth grooves made by glacial action. The largest easily accessible such grooves in North America, they

Soldiers & Sailors Memorial

were scoured into solid limestone bedrock approx 30,000 yrs ago by glacier of the great ice sheet that covered part of North America. Outdoor exhibits. (Daily) Located on the northern side of Kelleys Island, west of dock, on western shore. Phone 419/797-4530. **FREE**

Inscription Rock State Memorial. Inscription Rock is marked with prehistoric Native American pictographs. The flat-topped limestone slab displays carvings of human figures smoking pipes and wearing headdresses as well as various animal forms. (Daily) Located on the southern shore, east of dock. Phone 419/797-4530. **FREE**

Kelleys Island State Park. This 661-acre park offers swimming, fishing, boating (launch); hunting, hiking, picnicking (shelter), camping. Standard fees. Northern shore. Phone 419/797-4530.

Kent

(B-6) *See also Akron, Alliance, Aurora, Canton, Cleveland*

Pop 28,835 **Elev** 1,097 ft
Area code 330 **Zip** 44240
Information Kent Area Chamber of Commerce, 155 E Main St; 330/673-9855
Web www.kentbiz.com

What to See and Do

Kent State University. (1910) 33,000 students. Twenty schools and colleges. Nonacademic campus tours arranged by University News and

Information Office. On campus are the Kent State University Museum, with more than 10,000 costumes and treasures (Wed-Sat, also Sun afternoons, donation); Gallery of the School of Art in the Art Building and the Student Center Gallery (academic yr, Mon-Fri); Planetarium (by appt); and the May 4th Memorial, next to Taylor Hall. E Main St, 8 mi S of OH Tpke on OH 43. Phone 330/672-2727.

West Branch State Park. An 8,002-acre park with swimming, fishing, boating (launch, rentals); hiking, bridle, and snowmobiling trails; picnicking (shelter), concession, camping. Standard fees. (Daily) 12 mi E on OH 5. Phone 330/296-3239. **FREE**

Motels/Motor Lodges

★ **DAYS INN.** *4422 Edson Rd (44240). 330/677-9400; fax 330/677-9456; res 800/329-7466. www.daysinn. com.* 67 rms, 2 story. June-early Sept: S, D $68-$85; each addl $6; under 12 free; lower rates rest of yr. Crib free. TV; cable. Heated pool. Complimentary continental bkfst. Restaurant nearby. Ck-out 11 am. Meeting rms. Business servs avail. Sundries. Cr cds: A, C, D, DS, MC, V.
🄳 ⊠ ⊠ 🐾

★ **INN OF KENT.** *303 E Main St (44240). 330/673-3411; fax 330/673-9878. www.go.to/the-inn.com.* 56 rms, 2 story, some kits. June-Labor Day: S $45-$55; D $45-$80; each addl $3; under 12 free; lower rates rest of yr. Crib free. Pet accepted, some restrictions. TV; cable. Indoor pool. Ck-out 11 am. Coin lndry. Cr cds: A, C, D, DS, MC, V.
🄳 🐾 ⊠ ⊠ 🐾

★ ★ **UNIVERSITY INN.** *540 S Water St (44240). 330/678-0123; fax 330/678-7356. www.kentuniversityinn. com.* 107 rms, 7 story. June-Sept: S, D $50-$85; lower rates rest of yr. Crib free. TV; cable (premium). Heated pool. Restaurant 6:30 am-2 pm. Ck-out 11 am. Coin lndry. Meeting rms. Business servs avail. Many refrigerators. Private patios, balconies. Cr cds: A, C, D, DS, MC, V.
⊠ ⊠ 🐾

Restaurant

★ ★ **PUFFERBELLY LTD.** *152 Franklin Ave (44240). 330/673-1771.* Hrs: 11 am-10 pm; Fri, Sat to 11 pm; Sun to 9 pm; Sun brunch 11 am-2:30 pm. Closed major hols. Continental menu. Bar to 1 am. Lunch $3.95-$7.95, dinner $3.95-$15.95. Sun brunch $8.95. Child's meals. Specializes in fresh seafood, steak. Historic railroad depot (1875); museum. Cr cds: DS, MC, V.
🄳 ⊰

Lancaster

(E-4) *See also Columbus, Newark*

Founded 1800 **Pop** 34,507 **Elev** 860 ft
Area code 740 **Zip** 43130
Information Fairfield County Visitors & Convention Bureau, One N Broad, PO Box 2450; 740/653-8251 or 800/626-1296
Web www.lancoc.org

What to See and Do

The Georgian. (1833) Two-story brick house reflects Federal and Regency styles. Headquarters of the Fairfield Heritage Association. (Apr-mid-Dec, Tues-Sun afternoons; closed hols) 105 E Wheeling St. Phone 740/654-9923.

Mount Pleasant. A 250-ft rock outcropping overlooking city; was a favorite Native American lookout. Trails wind to top. In Rising Park, N High St and Fair Ave.

Square 13. Here are 19 historic buildings; a free pamphlet describing these buildings may be obtained from the Fairfield County Visitors & Convention Bureau or from the Fairfield Heritage Association, 105 E Wheeling St; also inquire about walking tour tape rentals (free with refundable deposit). N High, Broad, Main, and Wheeling Sts. Phone 740/653-8251.

   Mumaugh Memorial. (1805-1824) First and second floors have restored rms. (By appt only) 162 E Main St. Phone 740/654-8451. **FREE**

   Sherman House Museum. (1811) Birthplace of General William

Tecumseh Sherman and Senator John Sherman (Sherman Anti-Trust Act). Civil War Museum. (Apr-mid-Dec, Tues-Sun afternoons; closed hols) 137 E Main St.

Stanbery-Rising. (1834) Educational building for First United Methodist Church. (Not open to the public) 131 N High St.

Special Events

Pilgrimage. Tours of mid-19th-century through modern houses and museums. Phone 740/837-4765. First wkend May.

Spring Old Car Club Spring Festival. Fairfield County Fairgrounds. Antique automobiles, steam engines, old farm equipment, car parts, and swap meet. Phone 740/862-8233. First wkend June.

Lancaster Festival. Throughout town. Features dance, musical, and theatrical performances; special art and museum exhibits; children's events. Phone 740/687-4808. Ten days mid-late July.

Zane Square Arts & Crafts Festival. Corner of Broad and Main Sts. More than 125 craftsmen display and sell handcrafted items; entertainment; street dancing. Phone 740/687-6651. Wkend mid-Aug.

Fairfield County Fair. Harness racing, exhibits, amusements. Phone 740/653-3041. Mid-Oct.

Christmas Candlelight Tour. Tour of downtown area churches; musical presentations. Tickets at The Georgian. Phone 740/654-9923. Second Sat Dec.

Motels/Motor Lodges

★ ★ **AMERIHOST INN.** *1721 River Valley Cir N (43130). 740/654-5111; fax 740/654-5108; res 800/434-5800. www.amerihostinn.com.* 60 rms, 2 story. S $55-$75; D $61-$109; each addl $6; under 12 free; wkly rates. Crib free. TV; cable. Indoor pool; whirlpool. Complimentary continental bkfst. Coffee in rms. Restaurant adj 7 am-midnight. Ck-out noon. Meeting rms. Business servs avail. Valet serv. Exercise equipt; sauna. Shopping center adj. Cr cds: A, C, D, DS, MC, V.

D 🔄 📶 🐾 🏋️

★ ★ **BEST WESTERN INN.** *1858 N Memorial Dr (43130). 740/653-3040; fax 740/653-1172; toll-free 800/780-7234. www.bestwestern.com.* 168 rms, 2 story. S, D $64-$79; each addl $7; under 19 free; higher rates special events. Crib free. Pet accepted. TV; cable. Pool. Complimentary coffee in rms. Restaurant 6 am-10 pm. Rm serv. Bar to 1 am. Ck-out noon. Meeting rms. Business servs avail. Valet serv. Coin lndry. Health club privileges. Some refrigerators. Cr cds: A, C, D, DS, MC, V.

D 🔄 📶 🐾 **SC** 🏊

★ **KNIGHTS INN.** *1327 River Valley Blvd (43130). 740/687-4823; toll-free 800/843-5644. www.knightsinn.com.* 60 units, 7 kits. S, D $53-$69; each addl $7; under 18 free. Crib free. Pet accepted. TV; VCR avail (movies). Complimentary coffee in lobby. Restaurant adj 7 am-10 pm. Ck-out noon. Business servs avail. Cr cds: A, C, D, DS, MC, V.

D 🔄 📶 🐾 **SC**

B&B/Small Inn

★ ★ ★ **GLENLAUREL.** *14940 Mount Olive Rd, Rockbridge (43149). 740/385-4070; fax 740/385-9669; res 800/809-7378. www.glenlaurelinn.com.* 10 rms, 1-2 story, 2 suites, 4 cottages. S, D, suites, cottages: $119-$249; each addl $20; wkends 2-day min. Children over 16 yrs only. Premium cable TV in common rm. Complimentary full bkfst. Dining rm: 7-10 pm (public by res). Ck-out noon, ck-in 3 pm. Business servs avail. Guest lndry. Lawn games. Refrigerators; many fireplaces; some in-rm whirlpools, microwaves, wet bars. Many balconies. Scottish country inn; private gorge. Totally non-smoking. Cr cds: A, D, DS, MC, V.

D 📶 🐾

Restaurant

★ ★ ★ **SHAW'S.** *123 N Broad St (43130). 740/654-1842.* Hrs: 7-10:30 am, 11:30 am-2:30 pm, 5-10 pm; Sun 7 am-9 pm. Closed Jan 1, 2; Dec 24, 25. Res accepted. Bar. Wine list. Bkfst $3.95-$8.95, lunch $5.95-$12.95, dinner $10.95-$24.95. Specializes in chicken, prime rib, fresh seafood.

Menu changes daily. Own baking. Outdoor dining. Cr cds: MC, V.

Lebanon

(E-2) *See also Cincinnati, Dayton, Mason, Middletown (Butler County), Wilmington*

Settled 1796 **Pop** 10,453 **Elev** 769 ft
Area code 513 **Zip** 45036
Information Chamber of Commerce, 25 W Mulberry, 513/932-1100

Some of the early settlers around Lebanon were Shakers who contributed much to the town's culture and economy. Though their community, Union Village, was sold over 50 years ago and is now a retirement home, local interest in the Shakers still thrives.

What to See and Do

Fort Ancient State Memorial. (see). 7 mi SE on OH 350.

Glendower State Memorial Museum. (1836) Period furnishings, relics of area in Greek Revival mansion. (June-Aug, Wed-Sun; Sept-Oct, Sat and Sun) 105 Cincinnati Ave, US 42. Phone 513/932-1817. ¢¢¢

Turtlecreek Valley Railway. Scenic train excursion. (May-Dec, Sat and Sun) Phone 513/398-8584. ¢¢¢

Valley Vineyards Winery. Tours of winery; wine tastings. (Daily; closed hols) 4 mi S on US 48 from I-71 then 3 mi NE on US 22. Phone 513/899-2485. **FREE**

Warren County Historical Society Museum. Historical museum portrays Warren County history from prehistoric times to present; incl exhibits of fossils and Native American artifacts; pioneer and period rooms; large indoor village green depicting 19th-century shops; extensive Shaker collection; library of historical, genealogical, and Shaker material. (Tues-Sun; closed hols) 105 S Broadway. Phone 513/932-1817. ¢¢

Special Events

Warren County Fair. Mid-July. Phone 513/932-1100.

Lebanon Raceway. Warren County Fairgrounds, OH 48 N. Night harness racing. For details phone 513/932-4936. Sept-May.

Applefest. Farmers' market; crafts; entertainment; food. Fourth Sat Sept. Phone 513/934-5252.

Motels/Motor Lodges

★ **HOUSTON MOTEL.** *4026 S Rte 42 (45036).* 513/398-7277; toll-free 800/732-4741. 42 rms, 6 suites. June-Labor Day: S $64.95-$67.95; D $66.95-$69.95; each addl $6; under 12 free; lower rates rest of yr. Crib free. TV; cable (premium). Pool. Restaurant adj 3:30-10 pm; Fri, Sat to 10:30 pm. Ck-out 11 am. Refrigerators avail. Cr cds: A, MC, V.
≈ ⊠ 🐾 SC

★ **KNIGHTS INN.** *725 E Main St (45036).* 513/932-3034; fax 513/932-3434; toll-free 800/843-5644. www.knightsinn.com. 58 rms. Apr-Sept: S $54-$65; D $67-$75; each addl $5; kits. $77-$88; under 18 free; lower rates rest of yr. Crib free. TV; cable (premium). Pool. Complimentary coffee in lobby. Restaurant adj 6 am-11 pm. Ck-out 11 am. Meeting rms. Business servs avail. Cr cds: A, C, D, DS, MC, V.
D ≈ ⊠ 🐾 SC

★ **SHAKER INN.** *600 Cincinnati Ave (45036).* 513/932-7575; toll-free 800/752-6151. 20 rms, 4 suites. Late May-early Sept: S $32-$58; D $43-$62; each addl $6; suites $75-$90; under 12 free; higher rates special events; lower rates rest of yr. Crib $4. TV; cable. Pool. Complimentary coffee in lobby. Ck-out 11 am. Refrigerators; microwaves avail. Cr cds: A, DS, MC, V.
≈ ⊠ 🐾

B&B/Small Inn

★ ★ **GOLDEN LAMB.** *27 S Broadway (45036).* 513/932-5065. 18 rms, 4 story. S $65-$90; D $75-$100; each addl $10; suite $120; higher rates wkends. TV; cable. Complimentary continental bkfst. Restaurant (see GOLDEN LAMB INN). Bar. Ck-out 11 am. Business servs avail. Built in

1803; antiques. Cr cds: A, C, D, DS, MC, V.
⊠ ⌨

Restaurant

★ ★ **GOLDEN LAMB INN.** *27 S Broadway (45036). 513/621-8373. www.goldenlamb.com.* Hrs: 8-10 am, 5-9 pm; Sun noon-8 pm; early-bird dinner Mon-Fri 5-6:30 pm. Closed Dec 25. Res accepted. Bar. Lunch $8-$12, dinner $10-$20. Child's menu. Specialties: roast leg of spring lamb, roast turkey, roast duck. Antique furnishings. Cr cds: A, D, DS, MC, V.
Ⓓ

Lima

(C-2) *See also Findlay, Van Wert, Wapakoneta*

Founded 1831 **Pop** 45,549 **Elev** 880 ft
Area code 419
Information Lima/Allen County Convention and Visitors Bureau, 147 N Main St, 45801; 419/222-6075 or 888/222-6075
Web www.allencvb.lima.oh.us

Lima is an industrial, agri-business, and retail center.

What to See and Do

Allen County Museum. Pioneer and Native American relics; displays of fossils and minerals; railroad and street railway history; separate children's museum. Scale model of George Washington's home, Mt Vernon, in separate room. (Tues-Sun; closed hols) 620 W Market St. Phone 419/222-9426. **FREE**

Lincoln Park Railway Exhibit. DT & I Railroad depot, last steam locomotive built by the Lima works of Baldwin-Lima Hamilton; 1883 private car and 1882 caboose. (All yr, lighted at night) Lincoln Park, E Elm and Shawnee Sts. Phone 419/222-9426. **FREE**

MacDonell House. Restored Victorian mansion, completely furnished in the style of the 1890s; listed in the National Register of Historical Places.

(Tues-Sun; closed hols) 632 W Market St. Phone 419/222-9426. ¢

Special Event

Allen County Fair. Rides, games, livestock shows, entertainment, grandstand shows, night harness racing, displays, and exhibits. Phone 419/228-7141. Late Aug.

Motel/Motor Lodge

★ ★ **HOLIDAY INN.** *1920 Roschman Ave (45804). 419/222-0004; fax 419/222-2176; toll-free 800/465-4329. www.holiday-inn.com.* 150 rms, 4 story. S, D $72-$110; under 18 free. Crib free. Pet accepted. TV. Indoor pool; whirlpool. Playground. Restaurant 6:30 am-10 pm; Sat to 11 pm. Rm serv. Bar; entertainment Fri, Sat. Ck-out noon. Meeting rms. In-rm modem link. Sundries. Exercise equipt; sauna. Game rm. Rec rm. Microwaves avail. Balconies. Cr cds: A, C, D, DS, ER, JCB, MC, V.
Ⓓ 🐾 ⊠ 🛉 ⊠ 🔥 SC

Restaurant

★ ★ **TUDOR'S.** *2383 Elida Rd (45805). 419/331-2220.* Hrs: 11 am-10:30 pm; wkends to 11:30 pm. Closed Memorial Day, Labor Day, Dec 25. Res accepted. Bar. Lunch $4.99-$7.99, dinner $5.99-$14.99. Child's menu. Specializes in seafood, steak, barbecued ribs. Salad bar. English pub atmosphere. Family-owned. Cr cds: A, D, DS, MC, V.
Ⓓ SC ⊠

Lorain

(B-5) *See also Cleveland, Elyria, Oberlin, Sandusky, Vermilion*

Settled 1807 **Pop** 71,245 **Elev** 608 ft
Area code 440
Information Lorain County Visitors Bureau, 611 Broadway, 44052; 440/245-5282 or 800/334-1673
Web http:www.lcvb.org

This industrial city, on Lake Erie's south shore at the mouth of the Black River, has a fine harbor and nine major public parks. Struck by a devastating tornado in 1924, the city was rebuilt. Lorain is the birthplace of Admiral Ernest J. King, of World War II fame.

What to See and Do

Lakeview Park. A 50-acre park along lake shore. Large beach, bathhouse; boardwalk. Colored-light fountain; garden with 3,000 roses of 40 varieties; tennis, baseball, basketball, volleyball, lawn bowling, ice-skating, picnicking, playground, concessions. (Daily) W Erie Ave at Lakeview Dr. Phone 440/244-9000. **FREE**

Lorain Harbor. Innovative ore transfer facility regularly brings giant ore vessels to port. Several excellent vantage points for viewing (Lake Erie shipping season only).

Municipal Pier. Pier fishing, boating (launch), supplies (fuel, bait); concession. Phone 440/204-2269.

Special Event

International Festival Week. Sheffield Shopping Center. Ten-day celebration of Lorain's ethnic diversity. Song, dance, crafts and foods of many nations; entertainers in ethnic costumes. Three days late June. Phone 440/245-5282.

Mansfield

(C-4) *See also Mount Gilead, Mount Vernon*

Founded 1808 **Pop** 50,627 **Elev** 1,230 ft **Area code** 419
Information Mansfield/Richland County Convention & Visitors Bureau, 124 N Main St, 44902; 419/525-1300 or 800/642-8282
Web www.mansfieldtourism.org

A pioneer log blockhouse, built as protection against the Native Americans in the War of 1812, still stands in South Park in the city's western section. Named for Jared Mansfield, United States Surveyor General, it is a diversified industrial center, 75 miles southwest of Cleveland. John Chapman, better known as Johnny Appleseed, lived and traveled in Richland County for many years.

Pulitzer Prize-winning novelist Louis Bromfield was born here and later returned to conduct agricultural research at his 1,000-acre Malabar Farm.

What to See and Do

Clear Fork Reservoir. Fishing, boating (docks); picnicking; camping (Mar-Nov, fee). (Daily) 7 mi S on US 42, then W on OH 97. Phone 419/884-0166. **FREE**

Kingwood Center and Gardens. Center has 47 acres of landscaped gardens, greenhouses, and wooded property. French Provincial mansion with horticultural library (Easter-Nov 1, Tues-Sat; also Sun afternoon; rest of yr, Tues-Sat; closed hols). Greenhouses and gardens (daily). Flower and art shows, special lectures, workshops throughout the yr. 900 Park Ave W. Phone 419/522-0211. **FREE**

Malabar Farm State Park. Louis Bromfield's farm and house are within this 917-acre park. Fishing; hiking, bridle trails, equestrian camp, picnicking. Tractor-drawn wagon tour of farm; house tour. (Memorial Day-Labor Day, daily; Nov-Apr, call for hrs; closed hols) (See SPECIAL EVENTS) 10 mi SE on OH 39, then S on OH 603 to Pleasant Valley Rd. Phone 419/892-2784. ¢¢

Muskingum Watershed Conservancy District. Charles Mill Lake Park. On 1,350-acre lake. Boating (10 hp limit). 9 mi E on OH 430. Phone 419/368-6885. ¢¢

Oak Hill Cottage. (1847) With seven gables, five double chimneys, and seven marble fireplaces, as well as all original period furnishings of the 1800s, this restored house is considered one of the most perfect Gothic houses in the nation. (Apr-Dec, Sun afternoons; closed hols) 310 Springmill St. Phone 419/524-1765. ¢¢

Ohio State Reformatory. Site was used as a prison in such films as *The Shawshank Redemption* and *Air Force One.* Tours (May-Oct, Sun; res necessary). Phone 419/522-2644. ¢¢¢

Richland Carrousel Park. Features a wooden, hand-carved, hand-painted, turn-of-the-century-style carousel with 52 animals and two chariots. (Daily; closed hols; may be closed for private functions) 75 N Main; corner of 4th and Main St. Phone 419/522-4223. ¢

Carrousel Magic!. Visitors can watch the carrousel figures get carved here. (Apr-Dec, Tues-Sat) Phone 419/526-4009. ¢¢

Richland County Museum. Remodeled schoolhouse (ca 1847), two period rms; local memorabilia, artifacts. (May-Oct, Sat and Sun) 7 mi SW on US 42, at 51 W Church St, in Lexington. Phone 419/884-2230.
Donation

Skiing.

Clear Fork Ski Area. Area has quad, triple, double chairlifts, J-bar, two handle bars; patrol, school, rentals; snowmaking; cafeteria, bar. Longest run 2,460 ft; vertical drop 300 ft. (Nov-Mar, daily) 12 mi S on OH 13, then 7 mi SE on OH 97, then N on OH 95, in Butler. Phone 419/883-2000. ¢¢¢¢

Snow Trails. Six chairlifts; patrol, school, rentals; snowmaking; cafeteria, bar. (Dec-mid-Mar, daily) X-country and night skiing. Possum Run Rd, 5 mi S near jct OH 13, I-71. Phone 419/522-7669. ¢¢¢¢¢

Special Events

Ohio Winter Ski Carnival. Snow Trails Ski Resort. Costumes, queen contest, races, dance. Late Feb. Phone 419/756-7768.

Auto racing. Mid-Ohio Sports Car Course. 6 mi S on US 42, then W on OH 97 to Steam Corners Rd. A 2¼-mi track. Phone 800/MID-OHIO or 419/884-4000. Usually June-Sept.

Richland County Fair. Fairgrounds, 750 N Home Rd. Flea market, circus; hardware and auto shows. Phone 419/747-3717. Early Aug.

Ohio Heritage Days. At Malabar Farm State Park. Celebration of the pioneer era with participants dressed in period clothing; apple butter-making, horse-drawn wagon rides, crafts displays, demonstrations; tour Bromfield house and farm. Phone 419/892-2784. Sept.

Motels/Motor Lodges

★ **BEST VALUE INN.** 880 Laver Rd (44905). 419/589-2200; fax 419/589-5624. www.bestvalueinn.com. 99 rms, 2 story. S $59-$79; D $69-$79; each

addl $6; under 18 free; higher rates: special events, summer wkends. Crib free. Pet accepted. TV; cable (premium). Pool. Restaurant 6-11 am, 5-9 pm. Rm serv. Bar 5 pm-2 am. Ck-out noon. Meeting rms. Business servs avail. Cr cds: A, C, D, DS, MC, V.

★★ **COMFORT INN.** 500 N Trimble Rd (44906). 419/529-1000; fax 419/529-2953; toll-free 800/918-9189. www.comfortinn.com. 114 rms, 2 story. 22 suites. S $58-$69; D $63-$79; each addl $5; suites $72-$89; under 18 free; higher rates auto racing wkends. Crib free. Pet accepted, some restrictions. TV; cable. Indoor pool. Complimentary continental bkfst. Restaurant adj 11 am-10 pm; Fri, Sat to 11 pm. Rm serv. Bar. Ck-out noon. Coin lndry. Meeting rms. Business servs avail. In-rm modem link. Sundries. Downhill/x-country ski 20 mi. Health club privileges. Refrigerator in suites. Cr cds: A, D, DS, MC, V.

★★ **HOLIDAY INN.** 116 Park Ave W (44902). 419/525-6000; fax 419/525-0197; toll-free 800/521-6744. www.holiday-inn.com. 149 rms, 7 story. S $64-$110; D $70-$110; each addl $6; suites $125-$225; under 18 free; ski plan; higher rates special events. Crib free. TV; cable (premium). Indoor pool; whirlpool. Coffee in rms. Restaurant 6:30 am-2 pm, 5-10 pm. Bar 11 am-midnight. Ck-out 11 am. Meeting rms. Business servs avail. In-rm modem link. Downhill ski 7 mi. Exercise equipt; sauna. Some refrigerators. Minibars. Cr cds: A, C, D, DS, ER, JCB, MC, V.

★ **KNIGHTS INN.** 555 North Trimble Rd, Masfield (44906). 419/529-2100; fax 419/529-6679; toll-free 800/843-5644. www.knightsinn.com. 89 rms. S, D $46-$61; kit. units $46-$66; under 16 free; higher rates auto races. Crib free. Pet accepted. TV; cable (premium). Pool. Complimentary continental bkfst. Restaurant adj 6 am-midnight. Ck-out noon. Business servs avail. Valet serv. Sundries. Health club privileges. Cr cds: A, C, D, DS, MC, V.

★ **TRAVELODGE.** *90 W Hanley Rd (44903). 419/756-7600; res 800/578-7878. www.travelodge.com.* 93 rms, 2 story. S $40-$47; D $42-$59; each addl $5; kit. units $52-$62; higher rates auto racing wkends; under 18 free. Crib free. Pet accepted. TV; cable. Pool. Coffee in rms. Restaurant open 24 hrs. Ck-out noon. Meeting rms. Business servs avail. Downhill/x-country ski 2 mi. Cr cds: A, D, DS, MC, V.

Marietta (E-6)

Founded 1788 **Pop** 15,026 **Elev** 616 ft
Area code 740 **Zip** 45750
Information Tourist and Convention Bureau, 316 3rd St; 740/373-5176 or 800/288-2577
Web www.marietta-ohio.com/chamber

General Rufus Putnam's New England flotilla, arriving at the junction of the Muskingum and Ohio rivers for western land-buying purposes, founded Marietta, the oldest settlement in Ohio. Its name is a tribute to Queen Marie Antoinette for French assistance to the American Revolution. Most of the landmarks are along the east side of the Muskingum River. Front Street is approximately the eastern boundary of the first stockade, which was called Picketed Point. Later the fortification called Campus Martius was erected and housed General Putnam, Governor St. Clair, and other public officials.

One of the most important Ohio River ports in steamboat days, Marietta today is a beautiful tree-filled town and the home of Marietta College and manufacturers producing oil, plastics, rubber, paints, glass, dolls, safes, and concrete. Information for Wayne National Forest (see IRONTON) may be obtained from the National Forest Service office in Marietta.

What to See and Do

Campus Martius, Museum of the Northwest Territory. Rufus Putnam home, which was part of the original Campus Martius Fort (1788); furnished with pioneer articles. On grounds is the Ohio Company Land Office (1788); restored and furnished. (Mar-Apr and Oct-Nov, Sat-Sun; May-Sept, Wed-Sun; closed Thanksgiving) 601 2nd St and Washington St. Phone 740/373-3750. ¢¢

Industrial tours.

  Fenton Art Glass Company. Handmade pressed and blown glassware. Free 30-min guided tours (Mon-Fri; closed hols, also first two wks July). Must wear shoes; no children under two. Gift shop and outlet on premises; also museum with film of tour (daily; closed hols). 420 Caroline Ave in Williamstown, WV, across Ohio River, off I-77 exit 185. Phone 304/375-7772.

  Rossi Pasta. Pasta makers for many fine stores offer opportunity (limited) to watch the process in factory. (Mon-Sat, also Sun afternoon; closed hols) Also retail outlet. 114 Greene St, at Front St. Phone 740/373-5155. **FREE**

Mound Cemetery. A 30-ft-high conical mound stands in the cemetery where 24 Revolutionary War officers are buried. 5th and Scammel Sts. Also here is

  Sacra Via Street. Built originally by Mound Builders as "sacred way" to Muskingum River. Extends from Muskingum River to Elevated Sq. Phone 740/373-5178.

Muskingum Park. Riverfront common where Arthur St. Clair was inaugurated first governor of the Northwest Territory in 1788; monument to westward migration sculpted by Gutzon Borglum. Between Front St and the Muskingum River, N of Putnam St. Phone 740/373-5178.

Ohio River Museum State Memorial. Exhibits on history and development of inland waterways (May-Sept, daily; Mar-Apr and Oct-Nov, Wed-Sun; closed Thanksgiving). Steamboat *W. P. Snyder, Jr.,* (1918) is moored on Muskingum River; guided tours (Apr-Oct). Front and St. Clair sts. Phone 740/373-3717. ¢¢

Trolley tours. One-hr narrated tours of Marietta aboard turn-of-the-century style trolley. (July-Aug, Tues-Sun; mid-late June, Wed-Sun; May-mid June Thurs-Sun and Sept-Oct, wkends) 127 Ohio St. Phone 740/374-2233. ¢¢¢

Valley Gem Sternwheeler. Excursions on the Ohio and Muskingum rivers aboard sternwheeler *Valley Gem*. Fall foliage trips in Oct. (June-Aug, Tues-Sun; May and Sept-Oct, wkends only) Phone 740/373-7862.

Special Events

Showboat *Becky Thatcher.* Rear of 237 Front St. Permanently docked stern-wheeler presents showboat melo-drama on its first deck. Restaurant and lounge occupy the second and third decks. Theater season may vary; phone 740/373-6033 for sched-ule. Late June-late Aug.

Ohio River Sternwheel Festival. Ohio Riverfront Park. Sternwheel races, fireworks, entertainment on river-front; several sternwheel boats from across the nation. Wkend after Labor Day. Phone 740/373-5178.

Autumn Leaves Craft Festival. Dis-plays and demonstrations of new and traditional crafts and artwork; musicians; food; children's activities. Phone 740/374-3708. Late Sept.

Motels/Motor Lodges

★★ **BEST WESTERN.** *279 Musk-ingum Dr (45750). 740/374-7211; toll-free 800/780-7234. www.bestwestern. com.* 47 rms, 1-2 story. S $44-$62; D $53-$69; each addl $5; under 12 free; higher rates wkends. Crib free. TV; cable. Complimentary continental bkfst. Restaurant nearby. Ck-out noon. Business servs avail. Sundries. Health club privileges. Refrigerators. Picnic tables, grill. On Muskingum River; free dockage. Cr cds: A, C, D, DS, MC.

[D] [🖫] [🗮] [🖎]

★★ **COMFORT INN.** *700 Pike St (45750). 740/374-8190; fax 740/374-3649; res 800/537-6858. www.comfort inn.com.* 120 rms, 4 story. Apr-Oct: S, D $69-$95; each addl $5; suites $75-$105; under 18 free; golf plans; higher rates Sternwheel festival; lower rates rest of yr. Crib $3. TV; cable (premium), VCR avail. Compli-mentary continental bkfst. Compli-

mentary coffee in rms. Restaurant 10:30 am-midnight. Bar. Ck-out 11 am. Meeting rms. Business servs avail. Valet serv. Free airport trans-portation. Exercise equipt. Indoor pool; poolside serv. Basketball court. Some refrigerators, microwaves. Cr cds: A, C, D, DS, MC, V.

[D] [🖫] [🗮] [🛉] [🖎] [🖎]

★ **ECONO LODGE.** *702 Pike St (45750). 740/374-8481; toll-free 800/553-2666. www.econolodge.com.* 48 rms, 2 story. S, D $50-$60; each addl $5. Crib free. TV; cable (pre-mium). Pool. Complimentary conti-nental bkfst. Restaurant nearby. Ck-out noon. Business servs avail. Cr cds: A, C, D, DS, MC, V.

[D] [🖎] [🖎] [SC] [🖎]

★★ **HOLIDAY INN.** *701 Pike St (45750). 740/374-9660; fax 740/373-1762; toll-free 800/465-4329. www. holiday-inn.com.* 109 rms, 2 story. S, D $56-$85; under 19 free. Crib free. TV; cable (premium), VCR avail. Pool; wading pool. Restaurant 6:30 am-2 pm, 5-10 pm; Sat, Sun from 7 am. Rm serv. Bar 4 pm-2 am; enter-tainment. Ck-out noon. Meeting rms. Business servs avail. In-rm modem link. Valet serv. Sundries. Cr cds: A, C, D, DS, MC, V.

[D] [🖎] [🖎] [🖎] [SC]

★ **KNIGHTS INN.** *506 Pike St (45750). 740/373-7373; fax 740/374-9466; toll-free 800/526-5947. www. knightsinn.com.* 97 rms, 15 kit. units. S $39.95-$52.95; D $45.95-$58.95; first addl $5; kit. units $48.95-$62.95; under 18 free. Crib free. Pet accepted; $5. TV; cable (premium), VCR avail (movies $6). Pool. Compli-mentary coffee. Restaurant adj 6 am-10 pm. Business servs avail. In-rm modem link. Cr cds: A, C, D, DS, MC, V.

[D] [🐾] [🖎] [🖎] [SC] [🖎]

Hotel

★★ **LAFAYETTE.** *101 Front St (45750). 740/373-5522; fax 740/373-4684; toll-free 800/331-9336. www. historiclafayette.com.* 78 rms, 5 story. S, D $60-$65; suites $70-$160. Crib free. TV; cable. Restaurant (see THE GUN ROOM). Bar 11-2 am. Ck-out noon. Meeting rms. Business servs avail. Gift shop. Free airport transportation. Health club privileges. Some balconies. On Ohio River. Cr cds: A, C, D, DS, MC, V.

D **t** **⊠** **🔥**

Restaurant

★ ★ ★ **THE GUN ROOM.** *101 Front St (45750). 740/373-5522. www. historiclafayette.com.* Hrs: 6:30 am-2 pm, 5-10 pm; Sun 6:30 am-9 pm; Sun brunch 8 am-2 pm; early-bird dinner 5-6 pm (Mon-Thurs). Closed Dec 25. Res accepted. Continental menu. Bar 11-2 am. Bkfst $4.95-$7.95, lunch $4.75-$6.95, dinner $9.95-$22.95. Lunch buffet $5.95. Sun brunch $7.95. Child's menu. Specializes in pasta, seafood, beef. Salad bar (lunch). Parking. 19th-century riverboat decor; gun display, artwork. Cr cds: A, D, DS, MC, V.

D **⊰**

Marion

(C-3) *See also Delaware, Mount Gilead*

Settled 1820 **Pop** 34,075 **Elev** 956 ft
Area code 740 **Zip** 43302
Information Marion Area Convention & Visitors Bureau, 1952 Marion-Mount Gilead Rd, Suite 121; 740/389-9770 or 800/371-6688
Web www.marion.net

Marion's beginnings are due to Jake Foos, a chainman on a party surveying the territory for a proposed road in 1808. Thirsty after a meal of salt bacon, he discovered a spring. From then on the area became a stopping place for travelers. Originally named Jacob's Well for this reason, it was renamed for General Francis Marion, the "Swamp Fox" of the Revolutionary War.

Both agricultural and industrial, Marion's growth was largely influenced by the Huber Manufacturing Company, which introduced the steam shovel (1874), and Marion Power Shovels, now known as Dresser Industries. Marion is also the center of a major popcorn-producing area in the United States. Its best-known citizen was Warren G. Harding, owner and publisher of the *Star.* Later he became a state senator, lieu-

tenant governor, and 29th President of the United States.

What to See and Do

Carousel Concepts. Working museum; view woodworkers carving carousel horses. (Daily) 2209 Marion-Waldo Rd. Phone 740/389-9755. ¢¢

Harding Memorial. A ten-acre area with rows of maple trees that create the shape of a Latin cross. The circular monument is made of white Georgia marble and contains the stone coffins of Harding and his wife. Grounds (daily). Delaware Ave and Vernon Heights Blvd. Phone 740/387-9630. **FREE**

President Harding's Home and Museum. Built during Harding's courtship with Florence Mabel Kling and where they were married in 1891. Harding administered much of his 1920 "front porch campaign" for presidency from the front of the house; the museum, at the rear of the house, was once used as the campaign's press headquarters. (Memorial Day wkend-Labor Day wkend, Wed-Sun; Apr-May, by appt; after Labor Day-Oct, Sat and Sun) 380 Mt Vernon Ave. Phone 740/387-9630. ¢¢

Stengel True Museum. Displays incl Native American artifacts; china and glassware; firearms; antique watches, clocks; toys; utensils. Under age 12 with adult only. (Sat and Sun afternoons; other times by appt; closed Easter, Dec 25) 504 S State St. Phone 740/387-6140. **FREE**

Special Events

Marion County Fair. Late June-early July. Phone 740/382-2558.

US Open Drum and Bugle Corps Competition. Harding High School Stadium. Phone 740/387-6736. Aug.

Popcorn Festival. Tours, food, entertainment. First wkend after Labor Day. Phone 740/387-FEST.

Motels/Motor Lodges

★ **COMFORT INN.** *256 Jamesway (43302). 740/389-5552; res 800/228-5150. www.comfortinn.com.* 56 rms, 2 story. May-Oct: S $64-$70; D $69-$75; suites $75-$85; under 18 free; higher rates special events; lower rates rest of yr. Crib $6. Pet accepted, some restrictions; $10. TV; cable (premium). Complimentary continental bkfst. Restaurant opp 5 am-11 pm. Ck-out 11 am. Business servs avail. Indoor pool; whirlpool. Refrigerator, microwave in suites. Cr cds: A, D, DS, MC, V.

★ **TRAVELODGE.** *1952 Marion Mount Gilead Rd (43302). 740/389-4671; res 800/578-7878. www. travelodge.com.* 46 rms, 2 story. S $45-$60; D $47-$65; each addl $6; suites $59-$79; under 18 free. Crib free. Pet accepted; $5. TV; cable (premium), VCR avail. Pool. Complimentary coffee in rms. Restaurant nearby. Ck-out noon. Meeting rms. Business servs avail. In-rm modem link. Valet serv. Health club privileges. Microwaves avail. Picnic tables. Cr cds: A, D, DS, MC, V.

Mason

(F-2) *See also Cincinnati, Dayton, Hamilton, Lebanon, Middletown (Butler County)*

Pop 11,452 **Elev** 800 ft **Area code** 513 **Zip** 45040
Information Mason Area Chamber of Commerce, 316 W Main St; 513/336-0125
Web www.mlkchamber.org

What to See and Do

The Beach Waterpark. Offers 30 water slides and attractions on 35 acres, incl The Aztec Adventure watercoaster, Thunder Beach, a 750,000-gallon wave pool, and Lazy Miami, a meandering river slowly winding through the park. Two sand volleyball courts. A children's activity area with pools, slides, and mini-waterfall. Picnic area; restaurants. (Memorial Day wkend-Labor Day, daily) 2590 Waterpark Dr, W of I-71 at Kings Mills Rd exit 25, opp Paramount's Kings Island. Phone 513/398-7946. ¢¢¢¢

Golf Center at Kings Island. Two golf courses designed by Jack Nicklaus and architect Desmond Muirhead (fee). Grizzly Course, features the famed 546-yard 18th hole. The 18-hole Bruin, a mid-length version of the Grizzly, features six par-4 holes. Also incl a tennis stadium that seats 10,500 for the Tennis Masters Championship. Restaurant, lounge, pro shop, driving range (fee) (Daily, weather permitting) 6042 Fairway Dr. Phone 513/398-7700.

★ **Paramount's Kings Island.** Premier seasonal family theme park. Three hundred fifty-acre facility with more than 100 rides and attractions. Incl "The Outer Limits" thrill ride and "Flight of Fear," an indoor roller coaster. (Late May-early Sept, daily; mid-Apr-late May, wkends; also selected wkends early Sept-Oct) I-71 to Kings Mills Rd exit. Phone 513/573-5700. ¢¢¢¢

Motels/Motor Lodges

★★ **COMFORT SUITES.** *5457 Kings Center Dr (45040). 513/336-9000; fax 513/336-9007; res 800/228-5150. www.comfortsuites.com.* 78 rms, 3 story. May-Oct: S, D $109-$200; under 18 free; Jazz fest 2-day min; lower rates rest of yr. Crib free. TV; cable (premium). Complimentary continental bkfst. Restaurant adj open 24 hrs. Ck-out 11 am. Meeting rms. Business servs avail. Valet serv (exc Sun). Coin lndry. Indoor pool. Refrigerators; some in-rm whirlpools. Cr cds: A, C, D, DS, MC, V.

★ **DAYS INN.** *9735 Mason-Montgomery Rd (45040). 513/398-3297; toll-free 800/329-7466. www.daysinn. com.* 124 rms, 2 story. S, D $53-$79; higher rates special events. Crib free. Pet accepted, some restrictions. TV; cable (premium). Pool. Playground. Complimentary continental bkfst. Restaurant adj. Ck-out 11 am. Meeting rms. Business servs avail. Game rm. Cr cds: A, C, D, DS, MC, V.

★★ **HANNAFORD INN & SUITES.** *9845 Escort Dr (45040). 513/398-8015; fax 513/398-0822.* 104 rms, 2 story. S, D $49-$79; under 12 free. Crib free. Pet accepted. TV; cable (premium). Pool. Ck-out noon. Meeting rms. Business servs avail. In-rm modem link. Cr cds: A, C, D, DS, MC, V.

⊡ ⬛ ⬛ ⬛ ⬛

★ ★ ★ **KINGS ISLAND RESORT & CONFERENCE CENTER.** *5691 Kings Island Dr, Kings Island (45034). 513/398-0115; fax 513/398-1095; toll-free 800/727-3050. www.kingsisland resort.com.* 288 rms, 2 story. Memorial Day-Labor Day: S, D $99-$184; under 12 free; lower rates rest of yr. Crib free. TV; cable (premium). 2 pools, 1 indoor; whirlpool. Playground. Coffee in rms. Restaurant 6:30 am-9 pm. Rm serv. Bar 3 pm-midnight, Sun from 3 pm. Ck-out 11 am. Meeting rms. Business servs avail. In-rm modem link. Bellhops. Valet serv. Sundries. Gift shop. Tennis. Game rm. Exercise rm. Many private patios, balconies. Cr cds: A, C, D, DS, MC, V.

⊡ ⬛ ⬛ ⬛ ⬛ ⬛ ⬛

★ **RED ROOF-KINGS ISLAND.** *9847 Bardes Rd (45040). 513/398-3633; res 800/543-7663. www.redroof.com.* 124 rms, 2 story. S, D $71-$150; under 12 free; higher rates special events. Crib free. TV; cable (premium). Pool. Complimentary coffee. Complimentary continental bkfst. Restaurant nearby. Ck-out 11 am. Business servs avail. Cr cds: A, C, D, DS, ER, JCB, MC, V.

⊡ ⬛ ⬛ ⬛

Hotel

★ ★ ★ **MARRIOTT NORTHEAST CINCINNATI.** *9664 Mason-Montgomery Rd (45040). 513/459-9800; fax 513/459-9808; toll-free 800/228-9290. marriotthotels.com/cvgne.* 302 rms, 6 story. S, D $135-$145; suites $225; under 12 free; higher rates special events. Crib avail. TV; cable (premium). Complimentary coffee in rms. Restaurant 6:30 am-10:30 pm. Bar 11:30-1 am. Ck-out noon. Convention facilities. Business center. In-rm modem link. Gift shop. Exercise equipt. 2 pools, 1 indoor; poolside serv. Bathrm phone, refrigerator in suites. Luxury level. Cr cds: A, C, D, DS, MC, V.

⊡ ⬛ ⬛ ⬛ ⬛ SC ⬛

Restaurant

★ ★ **HOUSTON INN.** *4026 US 42 (45040). 513/398-7377.* Hrs: 3:30-10 pm; Fri, Sat to 10:30 pm; Sun 11:30 am-8:30 pm. Closed Mon; some major hols. Bar. Dinner $10-$16 Specializes in seafood, steak. Salad bar. Antiques. Family-owned. Cr cds: A, C, D, DS, MC, V.

⊡ ⬛

Massillon

(C-6) *See also Akron, Canton, New Philadelphia, Wooster*

Founded 1826 **Pop** 31,007 **Elev** 1,015 ft **Area code** 330 **Zip** 44646

Information Chamber of Commerce, 137 Lincoln Way E; 330/833-3146

Web www.massillonchamber.com

Massillon is an industrial center on the Tuscarawas River in northeastern Ohio.

What to See and Do

Canal Fulton and Museum. *St. Helena III,* a replica of mule-drawn canal boat of the mid-19th century, takes 45-min trip on the Ohio-Erie Canal. Leaves Canal Fulton Park (June-Aug, daily; mid-May-late May and early Sept-mid-Sept, wkends only). 6 mi NW on OH 21, then 1 mi NE on OH 93. Phone 330/854-3808. ¢¢

Massillon Museum. Historical and art exhibits. (Tues-Sat; also Sun afternoons; closed hols) 121 Lincoln Way E. Phone 330/833-4061. **FREE**

Spring Hill. (1821) Historic 19th-century home incl basement kitchen and dining rm, secret stairway, original furnishings; on grounds are springhouse, smokehouse, woolhouse, and milkhouse; picnicking. (June-Aug, Wed-Sun; Apr-May and Sept-Oct, by appt) 1401 Spring Hill Ln NE, OH 241. Phone 330/833-6749. ¢

The Wilderness Center. Nature center on 573 acres incl six nature trails, 7½-acre lake, 23-ft observation platform; picnicking. Interpretive building (Tues-Sun; closed hols). Grounds (daily). 5 mi S on US 21, then 8 mi SW on US 62 to Wilmot, then 1 mi

NW on US 250. Phone 330/359-5235. **Donation**

Mentor

(A-6) *See also Chardon, Cleveland, Geneva-on-the-Lake, Painesville*

Founded 1797 **Pop** 47,358 **Elev** 690 ft **Area code** 440 **Zip** 44060

Information Mentor Area Chamber of Commerce, 7547 Mentor Ave, Rm 302; 440/946-2625; and City of Mentor, 8500 Civic Center Blvd; 440/225-1100

Web www.mentorchamber.org

Site of the first Lake County settlement, Mentor was once an agricultural center. James A. Garfield resided here before his election as US president. Mentor serves as a retail trade center.

What to See and Do

Headlands Beach State Park. A 125-acre park with one-mi-long beach on shore of Lake Erie. Swimming, lifeguard (Memorial Day-Labor Day, Fri-Sun), fishing; picnicking, concessions. OH 44 N, to Lake Erie. Phone 440/257-1330. ¢¢

🟥 **Lawnfield (James A. Garfield National Historic Site).** Garfield's last house before the White House. Two floors of original furnishings; memorial library contains Garfield's books, desk. On grounds are campaign office, carriage house, and picnic area. (Sat, Sun; closed hols) 8095 Mentor Ave, US 20. Phone 440/255-8722. ¢¢

Wildwood Cultural Center. English Tudor Revival manor house listed on National Register of Historic Places. (Mon-Fri; closed hols) 7645 Little Mountain Rd. Phone 440/974-5735. **FREE**

Motel/Motor Lodge

★★ **RAMADA INN AND CONFERENCE CENTER.** *6051 Som Center Rd, Willoughby (44094). 440/944-4300; fax 440/944-5344; toll-free 800/326-6232. www.ramada.com.* 147 rms, 2 story. S, D $112-$129; under 18 free;

wkend plans. Crib free. TV; cable (premium). 2 pools, 1 indoor; wading pool. Complimentary coffee. Restaurant 6:30 am-2:30 pm, 5-10 pm; Fri-Sun 7 am-11 pm. Bar 11:30-midnight; Fri, Sat to 1 am; Sun 1-9 pm. Ck-out 11 am. Coin lndry. Meeting rms. Business servs avail. In-rm modem link. Lighted tennis. Golf privileges ¼ mi. Downhill ski 18 mi; x-country ski 1 mi. Sauna. Health club privileges. Lawn games. Some refrigerators. Cr cds: A, D, DS, MC, V.

⊡ 🛠 🗾 🐾 SC 🛏 ➤ 🛠

Hotel

★★★ **RADISSON HOTEL & CONFERENCE CENTER CLEVELAND-EASTLAKE.** *35000 Curtis Blvd, Eastlake (44095). 440/953-8000; fax 440/953-1706; toll-free 800/228-5050. www.radisson.com.* 126 rms, 5 story. Apr-Oct: S, D $69-$129; each addl $10; suites $149-$179; under 18 free; package plans; lower rates rest of yr. Crib free. TV; cable (premium). Indoor pool. Restaurant 7 am-11 pm. Rm serv. Bar 2 pm-midnight. Ck-out noon. Meeting rms. Business center. Valet serv. Sundries. Exercise equipt; sauna. Health club privileges. Cr cds: A, C, D, DS, ER, JCB, MC, V.

⊡ 🛏 🛠 🗾 🔥 🛠

Restaurant

★★ **MOLINARI'S.** *8900 Mentor Ave (US 20) (44060). 440/974-2750. www.molinaris.com.* Hrs: 11:30 am-2 pm, 5:30-10 pm; Mon to 2 pm; Fri, Sat to 11 pm. Closed Sun; some major hols. Res accepted. Northern Italian, California menu. Bar. Lunch $6.95-$8.95, dinner $11.95-$19.95. Specializes in pasta, rack of lamb, steak. Open kitchen. Contemporary decor. Cr cds: A, D, DS, MC, V.

⊡ 🗾

Miamisburg

See also Dayton

Pop 17,834 **Elev** 690 ft **Area code** 937 **Zip** 45342

Information South Metro Chamber of Commerce, 1410 B Miamisburg Centerville Rd, Centerville, 45459; 937/433-2032

Web www.smcoc.org

Motels/Motor Lodges

★★ **COURTYARD BY MARRIOTT.** *100 Prestige Pl (45342). 937/433-3131; fax 937/433-0285; toll-free 800/321-2211. www.marriott.com.* 146 rms, 3 story, 12 suites. S, D $99-$125; suites $119-$129; under 18 free; wkend rates. Crib free. TV; cable (premium). Indoor pool; whirlpool. Complimentary coffee in rms. Restaurant 6:30-10:30 am; Sat, Sun 7-11 am. Bar Mon-Thurs 5-10 pm. Ck-out noon. Coin lndry. Meeting rms. Business servs avail. Valet serv. Sundries. Exercise equipt. Refrigerator in suites. Cr cds: A, D, DS, MC, V.

D ⇌ 🕇 ⊠ 🐾 SC

★ **HOLIDAY INN DAYTON MALL.** *31 Prestige Plz Dr (45342). 937/434-8030; fax 937/434-6452; toll-free 800/465-4329. www.holiday-inn.com.* 195 rms, 3 story. S $99; D $119; under 18 free; wkend rates; higher rates special events. Crib free. TV; cable (premium). 2 pools, 1 indoor; wading pool. Coffee in rms. Restaurant 6:30 am-10 pm. Rm serv 2 pm-11 pm. Bar 4 pm-midnight, wkend hrs vary; entertainment. Ck-out 11 am. Coin lndry. Meeting rms. Business servs avail. In-rm modem link. Bellhops. Sundries. Putting green. Exercise equipt; sauna. Game rm. Cr cds: A, C, D, DS, MC, V.

D ⇌ 🕇 ⊠ 🐾 SC

★ **RED ROOF INN.** *222 Byers Rd (45342). 937/866-0705; fax 937/866-0700; res 800/843-7663. www.redroof.com.* 107 rms, 2 story. S, D $44.99-$67.99; each addl $7; under 18 free. Crib free. Pet accepted, some restrictions. TV; cable (premium). Ck-out noon. Business servs avail. In-rm modem link. Cr cds: A, D, DS, MC, V.

D 🐾 ⊠ 🔥 SC

Extended Stay

★★ **RESIDENCE INN BY MARRIOTT.** *155 Prestige Pl (45342). 937/434-7881; fax 937/434-9308; toll-free 800/331-3131. www.marriott.com.* 96 suites, 2 story. 1-bedrm suites $114; 2-bedrm suites $135. Crib free. Pet accepted; fee. TV; cable (premium), VCR avail (movies). Heated pool; whirlpool. Complimentary continental bkfst. Restaurant nearby. Ck-out noon. Coin lndry. Business servs avail. Valet serv. Fireplaces. Balconies. Picnic tables, grills. Cr cds: A, C, D, DS, JCB, MC, V.

D 🐾 ⇌ ⊠ 🔥

Restaurants

★ **ALEX'S.** *125 Monarch Ln (45342). 937/866-2266.* Hrs: 5-10 pm; Fri, Sat to 11 pm; early-bird dinner Mon-Fri 5-7 pm. Closed Sun; major hols. Res accepted. Bar to midnight; wkends to 1 am. Dinner from $7.95. Child's menu. Specializes in prime rib, steak, fresh seafood. Piano bar wkends. Cr cds: A, C, D, MC, V.

D ⊒

★ **BULLWINKLE'S TOP HAT BISTRO.** *19 N Main St (45342). 937/859-7677.* Hrs: 11 am-11 pm; Fri to midnight; Sat noon-midnight. Closed Sun; major hols. Res accepted. Bar. Lunch $5.49-$6.95, dinner $8.59-$16.99. Child's menu. Specializes in baby back ribs, chicken, fish. Patrons may grill own entree. Cr cds: A, C, D, DS, MC, V.

D ⊒

★★★ **PEERLESS MILL INN.** *319 S 2nd St (45342). 937/866-5968. www.peerlessmill.com.* Hrs: 5-9 pm; Fri, Sat to 10 pm; Sun 1-7 pm; Sun brunch 10 am-1 pm. Closed Mon; Jan 1, July 4, Dec 25. Res accepted. Bar. Dinner $12.95-$18.95. Sun brunch $10.95. Child's menu. Specializes in fresh seafood, roast duckling, prime rib. Own baking. Pianist wkends. Converted flour mill (1828). Cr cds: D, MC, V.

D SC ⊒

Middletown (Butler County)

(E-2) *See also Cincinnati, Dayton, Lebanon, Mason, Oxford*

Pop 46,022 **Elev** 650 ft **Area code** 513 **Zip** 45042

Information Middletown Convention & Visitors Bureau, 1504 Central Ave; 513/422-3030 or 888/6-MIDDLE

Web www.visitmiddletown.org

What to See and Do

Americana Amusement Park. Over 100 rides, shows, and attractions, incl two roller coasters and log flume; also pony rides, petting zoo; swimming. (June-Aug, daily; Apr-May and Sept, wkends only) 5757 Middletown-Hamilton Rd. Phone 513/539-2193. ¢¢¢¢

Sorg Opera Company. Annually produces three major operas, fully staged with orchestra. 63 S Main St. Phone 513/425-0180. ¢¢¢¢

Special Event

MiddFest. Celebrates international arts, history, culture, sports, and food. Phone 513/425-7707. First wkend Oct.

Motels/Motor Lodges

★★ **FAIRFIELD INN.** *6750 Roosevelt Pkwy, Middletown (45044). 513/424-5444; toll-free 800/228-2800. www.fairfieldinn.com.* 57 rms, 3 story, 8 suites. S, D $79.95-$89.95; each addl $5; suites $80.95-$109; under 18 free; higher rates special events. Crib free. TV; cable (premium). Complimentary continental bkfst. Restaurant adj 6 am-10 pm. Ck-out noon. Business servs avail. Valet serv (Mon-Fri). Indoor pool; whirlpool. Refrigerator, microwave in suites. Cr cds: A, C, D, DS, MC, V.
D ⊠ ⊠ ⚒ SC

★★ **HOLIDAY INN EXPRESS.** *6575 Terhune Dr, Middletown (45044). 513/727-8440; res 800/465-4329. www.holiday-inn.com.* 64 rms, 3 story, 8 suites. S, D $79-$99; suites $89-$109; under 18 free; higher rates special events. Crib free. TV; cable (premium). Complimentary continental bkfst. Restaurant adj open 24 hrs. Ck-out 11 am. Meeting rm. Business servs avail. In-rm modem link. Valet serv (Mon-Fri). Indoor pool; whirlpool. Refrigerator, microwave in suites. Cr cds: A, D, DS, MC, V.
D ⊠ ⊠ ⚒ SC

★ **THE MANCHESTER INN AND CONFERENCE CENTER.** *1027 Manchester Ave, Middletown (45042). 513/422-5481; fax 513/422-4615; res 800/523-9126. www.manchesterinn. com.* 79 rms, some with shower only, 5 story, 16 suites. S, D $74-$92; each addl $8; suites $99-$108; under 18 free; hol rates. Crib free. Pet accepted; $8/day. TV; cable. Complimentary coffee in rms. Restaurant 6:30 am-10 pm; Sat 8 am-11 pm; Sun 8 am-9 pm. Rm serv. Bar; entertainment Fri, Sat. Ck-out noon. Meeting rms. Business servs avail. In-rm modem link. Bellhops. Valet serv (Mon-Fri). Refrigerator, microwave in suites. Microwaves avail. Cr cds: A, C, D, DS, MC, V.
D ⊠ ⊠ ⚒ SC

Restaurant

★ **DAMON'S.** *4750 Roosevelt Blvd, Middletown (45044). 513/423-8805.* Hrs: 11 am-11 pm; Fri, Sat to midnight; Sun to 10 pm. Closed major hols. Res accepted Sun-Thurs. Bar. Lunch $4.50-$6.50, dinner $8-$15. Child's menu. Specializes in ribs, seafood. Club decor with sports memorabilia. Cr cds: A, D, DS, MC, V.
D ⊠

Milan

(B-4) *See also Bellevue, Oberlin, Sandusky*

Founded 1817 **Pop** 1,464 **Elev** 602 ft **Area code** 419 **Zip** 44846

Information Chamber of Commerce, PO Box 544; 419/499-2001
Web www.milanohio.com

Milan was founded by settlers from Connecticut, and many homes here bear the mark of New England architecture. A canal connecting the town with Lake Erie was built in 1839, making Milan one of the largest shipping centers in the Midwest at that time.

What to See and Do

Galpin Wildlife and Bird Sanctuary. Woodland with many varieties of trees, wildflowers and birds; nature trail. (Daily) ½ mi SE on Edison Dr. Phone 419/499-4909. **FREE**

Milan Historical Museum. Seven-building complex incl House of Dr. Lehman Galpin, Edison family doctor. Contains nationally known glass collection; doll and toy houses; Native American artifacts; gun room, blacksmith shop, general store. (Apr-Oct, Tues-Sun) 10 Edison Dr. Phone 419/499-2968. ¢¢ Nearby are

> **Newton Memorial Arts Building.** Displays incl collections of antiques, fine arts, needlepoint and laces, netsukes (ornamental buttons or figures of ivory or wood, used to attach a purse or other article to a sash). 10 Edison Dr. Phone 419/499-2968.

> **Sayles House.** Restoration of mid-19th century home. 10 Edison Dr at Front St. Phone 419/499-2968.

Thomas A. Edison Birthplace Museum. Two-story red brick house where the inventor spent his first seven yrs; contains some original furnishings, inventions, and memorabilia. Guided tours. (June 2-Labor Day, Tues-Sat, also Sun afternoons; Feb-June 1, and after Labor Day-Nov, Tues-Sat afternoons; closed Thanksgiving) 9 Edison Dr, 3 mi S of OH Tpke exit 7. Phone 419/499-2135. ¢¢

Motels/Motor Lodges

★★ **COMFORT INN MILAN.** *11020 Milan Rd (44846). 419/499-4681; fax 419/499-3159; res 800/228-5150. www.comfortinn.com.* 102 rms, 2 story. May-Sept: S, D $79-$180; under 18 free; lower rates rest of yr. Crib $10. Pet accepted, some restrictions. TV; cable. 2 pools, 1 indoor; whirlpools. Continental bkfst. Complimentary coffee. Restaurant nearby. Ck-out noon. Coin lndry. Business servs avail. Sundries. Sauna. Cr cds: A, D, DS, MC, V.

★★ **RAMADA INN.** *11303 Milan Rd (44846). 419/499-4347; fax 419/499-4483; toll-free 888/298-2054. www.ramada.com.* 56 rms, 2 story. Late-May-Aug: S $101-$154; D $107-$174; each addl $10; under 18 free; lower rates rest of yr. Crib avail. TV; cable (premium). Complimentary continental bkfst. Restaurant adj 5-9:30 pm. Ck-out noon. Business servs avail. Sundries. Coin lndry. Sauna. Indoor pool; whirlpool. Cr cds: A, C, D, DS, MC, V.

Restaurant

★★ **HOMESTEAD INN.** *12018 US 250 N (44846). 419/499-4271.* Hrs: 7 am-9 pm; Fri, Sat to 10 pm; Sun to 8 pm. Closed some major hols. Res accepted Sun-Thurs. Bar; closed Sun. Bkfst $2.85-$4.50, lunch $5.75-$7.95, dinner $12.50-$16.50. Child's menu. Specializes in beef, salads, desserts.

Yoder Amish House, Millersburg

Salad bar. Victorian house (1883). Cr cds: A, D, DS, MC, V.

[D] [⤴]

Mount Gilead

See also Delaware, Mansfield, Marion, Mount Vernon

Pop 2,846 **Elev** 1,130 ft
Area code 419 **Zip** 43338
Information Morrow County Chamber of Commerce, 17 1/2 W High St; 419/946-2821
Web www.morrowcochamber.com

What to See and Do

Mount Gilead State Park. More than 170 acres. Fishing, boating (electric motors only); hiking, picnicking (shelter), camping. Standard fees. (Daily) 1 mi E on OH 95. Phone 419/946-1961.

Mount Vernon

(D-4) *See also Mansfield, Mount Gilead, Newark*

Founded 1805 **Pop** 14,550 **Elev** 990 ft
Area code 740 **Zip** 43050
Information Knox County Convention & Visitors Bureau, 236 S Main St; 740/392-6102 or 800/837-5282
Web www.knox.net/visitor

Descendants of the first settlers from Virginia, Maryland, New Jersey, and Pennsylvania still live in this manufacturing and trading center. Seat of Knox County, it is in a rich agricultural, sandstone, oil, and gas producing area. It is in the largest sheep-raising county east of the Mississippi.

Johnny Appleseed owned two lots in the original village plot at the south end of Main Street. Daniel Decatur Emmett, author and composer of "Dixie," was born here. The offices of the State Headquarters of the Ohio Conference of Seventh-Day Adventists are here. Colonial-style architecture has been used for many public buildings and residences.

Motel/Motor Lodge

★★ **HISTORIC CURTIS INN THE SQUARE.** *12 Public Sq, Mt. Vernon (43050). 740/397-4334; toll-free 800/934-6835.* 72 rms, 2 story. S, D $46-$52; each addl $5; under 13 free. Crib free. Pet accepted. TV; cable, VCR avail (movies). Complimentary coffee in rms. Restaurant 6:30 am-2 pm, 5-9 pm. Rm serv. Bar 11-1 am. Ck-out noon. Coin lndry. Business servs avail. Valet serv. Refrigerators; some minibars. Cr cds: A, C, D, DS, MC, V.
[🐾] [⤴] [♿]

B&B/Small Inn

★★★ **WHITE OAK INN.** *29683 Walhonding Rd, Danville (43014). 740/599-6107. www.whiteoakinn.com.* 10 rms, 1-2 story. Phones avail. S, D $75-$135; each addl $25. Children over 12 yrs only. Complimentary full bkfst. Ck-out 11 am, ck-in 3 pm. Business servs avail. Lawn games. Turn-of-the-century farmhouse with original white oak woodwork. Totally nonsmoking. Cr cds: A, DS, MC, V.
[♿] [⤴] [♿]

Newark

(D-4) *See also Columbus, Lancaster, Zanesville*

Founded 1802 **Pop** 44,389 **Elev** 829 ft
Area code 740 **Zip** 43055
Information Licking County Convention & Visitors Bureau, 50 W Locust St, PO Box 702; 740/345-8224 or 800/589-8224
Web www.lccvb.com

This industrial city on the Licking River attracts many visitors because of its large group of prehistoric mounds. Construction of the Ohio-Erie Canal was begun here on July 4, 1825, with Governor DeWitt Clinton of New York as the official groundbreaker and speaker. The Ohio Canal was then built north to Lake Erie and south to the Ohio River.

What to See and Do

Blackhand Gorge. On 970 wooden acres; bike trails, hiking, bird-watching, canoeing. 9 mi E of Newark, S of OH 146. Phone 740/763-4411. **FREE**

Buckeye Central Scenic Railroad. A 90-min scenic rail trip through Licking County. (Memorial Day wkend-Oct, wkends and hols) Also special holiday-theme trains avail (Oct and Dec). US 40. Phone 740/366-2029. ¢¢¢

Buckeye Lake State Park. Swimming, waterskiing, fishing, boating (ramp); picnicking (shelter). Standard fees. (Daily) 11 mi S on OH 79, on Buckeye Lake (3,300 acres water and 200 acres land). Phone 740/467-2690.

Dawes Arboretum. Over 2,000 species of woody plants on 355 acres; three-acre Japanese Garden; Cypress Swamp; All Seasons Garden; nature trails; picnic areas and shelter; special programs. (Daily; closed Jan 1, Thanksgiving, Dec 25) 7770 Jacksontown Rd SE. Phone 740/323-2355. **FREE**

Flint Ridge State Memorial. Prehistoric Native American flint quarry; trails for the disabled and the visually impaired; picnic area. Museum (Memorial Day-Labor Day, Wed-Sun; after Labor Day-Oct, wkends only). Park (Apr-Oct). 5 mi E on OH 16, then 5 mi S on County 668. Phone 740/787-2476. ¢¢

Gallery Shop. Bimonthly exhibits by regional and local artists. (Mon-Sat, daily; closed hols) 50 S 2nd St. Phone 740/349-8031. **FREE**

Licking County Historical Society Museum. Restored Sherwood-Davidson House (ca 1815) with period furnishings. Adj is restored Buckingham Meeting House (ca 1835). Guided tours (Apr-Dec, daily exc Mon). 6th St at W Main, Veterans Park. Phone 740/345-4898. **Donation** The Society also maintains

Robbins-Hunter Museum in the Avery Downer House. Outstanding Greek Revival house (1842). Period furnishings; decorative and fine arts. Guided tours. (Wed-Sun afternoons or by appt) 221 E Broadway in Granville. Phone 740/587-0430. **Donation**

Webb House Museum. Home (1908) of lumber executive incl family heirloom furnishings and wooden interior features. Guided tours. (Apr-Dec, Thurs, Fri, and Sun afternoons; also by appt) 303 Granville St. Phone 740/345-8540. **FREE**

National Heisey Glass Museum. Displays of Heiseyware manufactured in the area from 1896-1957. (Tues-Sat afternoons; closed hols) 169 W Church St, at 6th St. Phone 740/345-2932. ¢

⭐ **Newark Earthworks.** The group of earthworks here was originally one of the most extensive of its kind in the country, covering an area of more than four sq mi. The Hopewell used their geometric enclosures for social, religious, and ceremonial purposes. Remaining portions of the Newark group are Octagon Earthworks and Wright Earthworks, with many artifacts of pottery, beadwork, copper, bone, and shell exhibited at the nearby Moundbuilders Museum. Phone 800/600-7174.

Moundbuilders State Memorial. The Great Circle, 66 acres, has walls from 8 to 14 ft high with burial mounds in the center; picnic facilities. Museum containing Hopewell artifacts (Memorial Day-Labor Day, Wed-Sun; after Labor Day-Oct, wkends only). Park (Apr-Oct). SW on OH 79, at S 21st St and Cooper. Phone 800/600-7174. ¢¢

Octagon Earthworks. The octagon-shaped enclosure encircles 50 acres that incl small mounds, and is joined by parallel walls to a circular embankment enclosing 20 acres. N 30th St and Parkview. **FREE**

Wright Earthworks. One-acre area has a 100-ft wall remnant, an important part of original Newark group. ¼ mi NE of Great Circle at James and Waldo Sts. **FREE**

Ye Olde Mill. Museum of milling history; gift shop; ice cream parlor. Picnic areas. (May-Oct, daily) OH 13, 10 mi N of Newark. Phone 740/892-3921. **FREE**

Motel/Motor Lodge

★ ★ ★ **CHERRY VALLEY LODGE.** *2299 Cherry Valley Rd (43055). 740/788-1200; fax 740/788-8800; toll-free 800/788-8008. www.cherryvalley lodge.com.* 120 rms, 2 story. S $159-$169; D $169-179; each addl $10;

suites $175-$200; under 18 free; wkend rates; golf plan. Crib free. TV; cable, VCR (free movies). 2 pools, 1 indoor; whirlpool, poolside serv. Playground. Complimentary coffee in rms. Restaurant (see CHERRY VALLEY LODGE DINING ROOM). Rm serv. Bar 11-1 am. Ck-out noon. Meeting rms. Business servs avail. In-rm modem link. Gift shop. Valet serv Mon-Fri. Exercise equipt. Landscaped grounds with lake. Cr cds: A, C, D, DS, MC, V.

D ⚊ 🏋 ⬱ 🔥 SC 🛁

B&B/Small Inn

★ ★ ★ **BUXTON INN.** *313 E Broadway, Granville (43023). 740/587-0001; fax 740/587-1460.* 26 rms, 2 story. S $70-$80; D $80-$90; each addl $10; under 5 free. TV; cable. Complimentary continental bkfst. Coffee in rms. Restaurant (see BUXTON INN DINING ROOM). Ck-out noon, ck-in 2 pm. Business servs avail. 18-hole golf privileges. Refrigerators. Antiques, prints. Private patios. Rms in two houses (1812). Cr cds: A, MC, V.

🛁 ⬱

Restaurants

★ ★ ★ **BUXTON INN DINING ROOM.** *313 E Broadway, Granville (43023). 740/587-0001.* Hrs: 11:30 am-2 pm, 5:30-9 pm; Fri to 10 pm; Sat 8-11 am, 11:30 am-2 pm, 5:30-10 pm; Sun 8-10 am, 4-8 pm; Sun brunch 11 am-3 pm. Closed Jan 1, Dec 25. Res accepted. French, Amer menu. Bar 5 pm-midnight, closed Sun. Bkfst $4.95-$6.25, lunch $4.95-$7.95, dinner $12.95-$22.50. Sun brunch $4.95-$7.95. Specialties: Louisiana chicken, coquille of seafood, triple chocolate mousse cake. Greenhouse dining. New England-style inn (1812). Cr cds: A, C, DS, MC, V.

⬱

★ ★ **CHERRY VALLEY LODGE DINING ROOM.** *2299 Cherry Valley Rd (43055). 740/788-1336.* Hrs: 6:30-11 am, 11:30 am-2 pm, 5:30-10 pm; Fri to 11 pm; Sat (brunch) 9:30 am-2 pm, 5:30-11 pm; Sun (brunch) 9:30 am-2 pm, 5:30-9 pm. Res accepted. Contemporary Amer menu. Bar to 12:30 am; Fri, Sat to 1 am. Bkfst $3.95-$7.95, lunch $4.95-$10.95, dinner $11.95-$23.95. Sat, Sun brunch $3.95-$9.95. Child's menu. Specialties: paella, creme brulee. View of lake. Totally nonsmoking. Cr cds: A, D, DS, MC, V.

D

★ **DAMON'S.** *1486 Granville Rd (43055). 740/349-7427.* Hrs: 11 am-11 pm; Fri, Sat to midnight; Sun to 10 pm. Closed Dec 25. Res accepted. Bar. Lunch $4.99-$7.95, dinner $6.99-$15.95. Child's menu. Specializes in ribs, onion rings. Casual atmosphere. Cr cds: A, C, D, DS, MC, V.

D SC ⬱

★ **NATOMA.** *10 N Park (43055). 740/345-7260.* Hrs: 11 am-10 pm; Sat from 5 pm. Closed Sun; major hols. Res accepted Mon-Fri. Bar. A la carte entrees: lunch $4.50-$10.25, dinner $7.95-$17.95. Specialties: char-broiled chicken and ribs, baby beef filet mignon. Family-owned since 1922. Cr cds: A, DS, MC, V.

D ⬱

New Philadelphia

(C-6) *See also Canton, Coshocton, Gnadenhutten, Massillon*

Founded 1804 **Pop** 15,698 **Elev** 910 ft
Area code 330 **Zip** 44663
Information Tuscarawas County Convention & Visitors Bureau, 125 McDonald's Dr, SW; 330/339-5453 or 800/527-3387
Web www.neohiotravel.com

New Philadelphia, seat of Tuscarawas County, and its neighbor, Dover, still reflect the early influence of the German-Swiss who came from Pennsylvania. Some of the earliest town lots in New Philadelphia were set aside for German schools.

What to See and Do

Fort Laurens State Memorial. An 82-acre site of only American fort in Ohio during Revolutionary War. Named in honor of Henry Laurens,

Continental Congress president. Built in 1778 as a defense against the British and Native Americans. Picnicking; museum has artifacts and multimedia program on American Revolution. (Memorial Day-Labor Day, Wed-Sun; after Labor Day-Oct, wkends only) 14 mi N via OH 39, I-77, OH 212 to Bolivar, then ½ mi S. Phone 330/874-2059. ¢¢

Muskingum Watershed Conservancy District. A Muskingum River flood control and recreation project. The district maintains a total of ten lakes, five lake parks, ten marinas, and ten campgrounds. (Daily) Main office, 1319 Third St NW. Phone 330/343-6647. ¢¢

    Atwood Lake Park. A 1,540-acre lake with swimming, fishing, boating (25-hp limit), marinas; golf, tent and trailer sites (showers, flush toilets). Restaurant, cottages, resort. Standard fees. Pets on leash only. (Daily). 12 mi E on OH 39, then N off OH 212. Phone 330/343-6780. ¢¢

    Leesville Lake. Fishing and boating on 1,000-acre lake (10-hp limit); tent and trailer sites (Apr-Oct). 12 mi E on OH 39, then S off OH 212. **Southfork Marina**, on SW shore, off OH 212 (Apr-Nov, daily). Phone 740/269-5371.

Schoenbrunn Village State Memorial. Partial reconstruction of the first Ohio town built by Christian Native Americans under the leadership of Moravian missionaries; one of six villages constructed between 1772 and 1798. Picnicking; museum. (Memorial Day-Labor Day, daily; after Labor Day-Oct, wkends only) 3 mi SE off US 250 on OH 259. Phone 330/339-3636. ¢¢

Tuscora Park. Swimming (fee); tennis, shuffleboard, picnicking, concession; amusement rides (fee per ride), incl 100-yr-old carousel. (Late May-Labor Day, daily) Tuscora Ave, ½ mi N on OH 416. Phone 330/343-4644. **FREE**

Warther Museum. Collection of miniature locomotives by master carver Ernest Warther, carved of ebony, pearl, ivory, and walnut; largest model has 10,000 parts; collection of buttons in quilt patterns and arrow points. On landscaped grounds are telegraph station, operating hand car, and caboose. Tour of

cutlery shop. (Daily; closed hols) 331 Karl Ave, ½ mi E of I-77, in Dover. Phone 330/343-7513. ¢¢¢

Zoar State Memorial. A quaint village where the German religious Separatists found refuge from persecution (1817); an experiment in communal living that lasted for 80 yrs. Number One House on Main St houses the historical museum, and has Zoar Society pottery, and furniture. Zoar Garden, in the center of the village, follows the description of New Jerusalem in the Bible. Restoration incl the garden house, blacksmith shop, bakery, tinshop, wagon shop, kitchen, magazine shop, and dairy. (Memorial Day-Labor Day, Wed-Sat, also Sun and hol afternoons; Apr-May and after Labor Day-Oct, wkends) I-77 exit 93; 2½ mi SE on OH 212. Phone 330/874-3011. ¢¢

Special Events

Trumpet in the Land. Schoenbrunn Amphitheatre, off US 250 on University Dr. Outdoor musical drama by Paul Green takes you back to a time when Ohio was the western frontier of America, to witness the founding of Ohio's first settlement, Schoenbrunn, in 1772. Mon-Sat. Phone 330/339-1132. Mid-June-late Aug.

Zoar Harvest Festival. In Zoar. Antique show; 1850s craft demonstrations; music in 1853 church; museum tours, horse-drawn wagon rides. Phone 330/874-2646. Early Aug.

Swiss Festival. 8 mi W on OH 39, in Sugarcreek. Swiss cheese from more than 13 factories in the area. Swiss musicians, costumes, polka bands. Steinstossen (stone-throwing), Schwingfest (Swiss wrestling); parade each afternoon. Phone 330/852-4113. Fourth Fri and Sat after Labor Day.

Christmas in Zoar. Tours of private houses, craft show, German food, strolling carolers, and tree lighting ceremony. Phone 330/874-3011. Early Dec.

Motels/Motor Lodges

★ ★ **HOLIDAY INN.** *131 Bluebell Dr SW (44663). 330/339-7731; fax 330/339-1565; res 800/465-4329. www.holiday-inn.com.* 107 rms, 2 story. S, D $69-$79 wkdays, $89-$99 wkends; higher rates: Hall of Fame Week, Ohio Swiss Festival. Crib free.

Pet accepted. TV; cable, VCR avail. 2 pools, 1 indoor; whirlpool. Restaurant 6:30 am-10 pm. Bar 4 pm-1 am. Ck-out 11 am. Meeting rms. Business servs avail. Valet serv. Sundries. Exercise equipt; sauna. Cr cds: A, D, DS, MC, V.

🄳 🉐 🏊 🏋 🎿 🔥

Resort

★ ★ ★ **ATWOOD.** *2650 Lodge Rd, Delroy (46620). 330/735-2211; fax 330/735-2562.* 104 rms, 2 story, 17 kit. cottages (4-bedrm). Mid-June-Sept: S $98-$115; D $110-$125; each addl $10; cottages for 8-10, $790/wk; family rates; golf plans; lower rates rest of yr. TV; cable. 2 pools, 1 indoor; whirlpool. Playground. Free supervised children's activities (mid-June-Sept). Dining rm 7-11 am, noon-4 pm, 5-9 pm; Fri, Sat to 10 pm. Box lunches. Snack bar. Rm serv. Bar noon-2 am. Ck-out 1 pm, ck-in 4 pm. Meeting rms. Business servs avail. In-rm modem link. Gift shop. Airport, bus depot transportation. Lighted tennis, pro. 9-hole par-3 golf, 18-hole par-70 golf, pro, driving range, putting green. X-country ski on site; sledding. Exercise equipt; sauna. Motorboats, sailboats, canoes, rowboats. Bicycle rentals. Game rm. Lawn games. Picnic tables, grills at cottages. Glass walls open to patios in lodge. On hill overlooking lake; 1,540 acres. Private airstrip, heliport. A Muskingum Watershed Conservancy District facility. Cr cds: A, DS, MC, V.

🄳 🐾 🏌 🎿 ⛷ 🏊 🏋 🎿 🐎 🚣

Oberlin

(B-5) *See also Cleveland, Elyria, Lorain, Milan, Strongsville*

Founded 1833 **Pop** 8,191 **Elev** 800 ft
Area code 440 **Zip** 44074
Information Lorain County Visitors Bureau, 611 Broadway, Lorain 44052; 440/245-5282 or 800/334-1673
Web www.lcvb.org

Oberlin College and the town were founded together. Oberlin was the first college to offer equal degrees to men and women and the first in the United States to adopt a policy against discrimination because of race. The central portion of the campus forms a six-acre public square, called Tappan Square, in the center of the town.

Charles Martin Hall, a young Oberlin graduate, discovered the electrolytic process of making aluminum in Oberlin. The Federal Aviation Agency maintains an Air Traffic Control Center here.

What to See and Do

Oberlin College. (1833) 2,750 students. College of Arts and Sciences and Conservatory of Music (1867). Campus tours from admissions office, Carnegie Building. At jct OH 511, 58. Phone 440/775-8121. On campus are

> **Allen Memorial Art Museum.** Major collection of more than 14,000 works incl 17th-century Dutch paintings, 19th- and 20th-century European works, Japanese woodcuts, and contemporary works. (Tues-Sun; closed hols) 87 N Main. Phone 440/775-8665. **FREE**
>
> **Conservatory of Music.** Complex of buildings (1964) by architect Minoru Yamasaki; incl 667-seat Warner Concert Hall, a teaching and classroom building, rehearsal and library unit, and Robertson Hall, which houses practice facilities.
>
> **Hall Auditorium.** Dramatic arts center. Phone 440/775-8121.
>
> **Seeley G. Mudd Center.** Library with more than one million volumes; also houses archives, audiovisual center.

Tours. Oberlin Heritage Center tour incl James Monroe House (1866), Little Red School House (1836), and Jewett House (1884). Phone 440/774-1700. ¢¢

Motel/Motor Lodge

★ ★ **OBERLIN INN.** *7 N Main St (44074). 440/775-1111; fax 440/775-0676; toll-free 800/376-4173. www. oberlininn.com.* 76 rms, 2-3 story. S $72-$111; D $82-$131; each addl $10; suites $175; under 12 free. Crib free. TV; cable (premium). Coffee in rms. Restaurant 7 am-9 pm. Rm serv. Ck-out noon. Meeting rms. Business servs avail. Airport transportation. Health club privileges. Cr cds: A, C, D, DS, MC, V.

D ✈ ⊠ 🖐 SC

Oxford

See also Cincinnati, Hamilton, Mason, Middletown (Butler County)

Founded 1810 **Pop** 18,937 **Elev** 972 ft
Area code 513 **Zip** 45056
Information Visitors & Convention Bureau, 30 W Park; 513/523-8687
Web www.oxfordchamber.org

Situated in the rolling hills of southwestern Ohio, this small town has many brick streets and unique shops, and is home to Miami University.

What to See and Do

Hueston Woods State Park. A 3,596-acre park with swimming, bathhouse, boating (launch, rentals); nature, hiking, and bridle trails; 18-hole golf, picnicking, concession, lodge, camping, cabins. Nature center; naturalist. Standard fees. (Daily) 5 mi N on OH 732. Phone 513/523-6347. **FREE** At S entrance is

Pioneer Farm & House Museum. Farmhouse (1835) has period furniture, clothing, toys. Barn (ca 1850) has early farm implements, tools. Arts and crafts fair (first wkend June). Apple butter-making demonstrations (second wkend Oct). (Memorial Day-Oct, call for hrs) Doty and Brown rds. Phone 513/523-8005. ¢

Miami University. (1809) 16,000 students. On campus are the Miami University Art Museum (Tues-Sun) and two other art galleries; zoology, geology, and anthropology museums; entomological collections; Turrell Herbarium. Campus tours. 500 E High St. Phone 513/529-1809. Also on campus is

McGuffey Museum. Restored home of William Holmes McGuffey, who compiled the *McGuffey Eclectic Readers* while a member of the faculty here; memorabilia, collection of his books. (Call for schedule)

Spring and Oak Sts. Phone 513/529-2232. **FREE**

Special Events

Outdoor Summer Music Festival. Uptown Oxford at Martin Luther King Park. Every Thurs, June and July. Phone 513/523-8687.

Red Brick Rally Car Show. Uptown. Second Sun Oct. Phone 513/523-8687.

Motels/Motor Lodges

★ ★ **BEST WESTERN SYCAMORE INN.** *6 E Sycamore St (45056). 513/523-0000; fax 513/523-2093; res 800/528-1234. www.bestwestern.com.* 61 rms, 2 story. S $69-$89; D $79-$99; each addl $5; under 12 free; higher rates Miami Univ events. Crib avail. TV; cable (premium), VCR avail. Indoor pool; whirlpool. Complimentary continental bkfst. Complimentary coffee in rms. Ck-out noon. Meeting rm. Business servs avail. Exercise equipt; sauna. Cr cds: A, C, D, DS, MC, V.

≈ ⊠ 🖐 SC 🏌

★ ★ **HAMPTON INN.** *5056 College Corner Pike (45056). 513/524-0114; fax 513/524-1147; res 800/426-7866. www.hamptoninn.com.* 66 rms, 3 story. S, D $79-$99; suites $88-$115; under 18 free; higher rates special events. Crib free. TV; cable (premium), VCR avail. Complimentary continental bkfst. Restaurant adj 6 am-10 pm. Ck-out 11 am. Meeting rms. Business servs avail. In-rm modem link. Valet serv. Exercise equipt. Indoor pool; whirlpool. Some in-rm whirlpools, refrigerators. Cr cds: A, C, D, DS, MC, V.

D ≈ ⊠ 🖐 🏌

★ ★ ★ **HUESTON WOODS RESORT.** *5201 Lodge Rd, College Corner (45003). 513/523-6381; fax 513/523-1522; toll-free 800/282-7275. www.huestonwoodsresort.com.* 92 rms, 3 story. S, D $109-$129; suites $199-$219; under 16 free. Crib free. TV; cable (premium), VCR avail (movies). 2 pools, 1 indoor; wading pool. Playground. Free supervised children's activities (June-Aug). Complimentary coffee in rms. Restaurant. Bar evenings. Ck-out noon. Meeting rms. Business servs avail. Sundries. Lighted tennis. 18-hole golf.

X-country ski on site. Exercise equipt; sauna. Game rm. Rec rm. Lawn games. Microwaves in cabins. Private patios, balconies. Large fireplace in lobby. Indian motif. On bluff above lake; beach. All facilities of state park avail. Cr cds: A, D, DS, MC, V.

⊡ 🛶 ⚡ 🛥 🎿 🎣 🏊 🎿 ⛷ 🔥 SC

Painesville

(A-6) *See also Ashtabula, Cleveland, Geneva-on-the-Lake, Mentor*

Pop 15,699 **Elev** 677 ft **Area code** 440 **Zip** 44077

Information Lake County Visitors Bureau, 1610 Mentor Ave; 440/354-2424 or 800/368-5253

Web www.lakevisit.com

What to See and Do

Fairport Harbor Lighthouse and Marine Museum. Lighthouse, lightkeeper's dwelling (museum) with attached ship's pilothouse. (Memorial Day wkend-second wkend in Sept, Wed, Sat, and Sun, also hols) 2 mi N off OH 2 at 129 2nd St, in Fairport Harbor. Phone 440/354-4825. ¢

Special Event

Lake County Fair. Lake County Fairgrounds. Late Aug. Phone 440/354-3339.

Resort

★★★ **RENAISSANCE QUAIL HOLLOW.** *11080 Concord Hambden Rd, Concord (44077). 440/352-6201; fax 440/497-1111; toll-free 800/792-0258.* 169 rms, 2-4 story. Apr-Oct: S $116-$136; D $136-$156; each addl $15; under 18 free; wkend rates; ski, golf plans; lower rates rest of yr. Crib free. TV; cable, VCR avail. 2 pools, 1 indoor; whirlpool, poolside serv, lifeguard. Playground. Dining rm 6:30 am-10 pm; Fri, Sat 7 am-10 pm; Sun brunch 10:30 am-2:30 pm. Snack bar. Rm serv. Bar 11:30-2 am; entertainment Fri-Sat. Ck-out 11 am. Meeting rms. Business center. Valet serv. Gift shop. Tennis. Golf, greens fee $55-$75, pro, putting green, dri-

ving range. Downhill ski 12 mi; x-country ski nearby. Exercise equipt; sauna. Lawn games. Private patios, balconies. Cr cds: A, C, D, DS, JCB, MC, V.

⊡ 🛥 🎿 🏊 🎣 🎿 🔥 SC ⛷

B&B/Small Inn

★★ **RIDERS 1812.** *792 Mentor Ave (44077). 440/942-2742. www.ridersinn.com.* 10 rms, 2 story. S, D $75-$99; each addl $10. Crib free. Pet accepted. TV; cable, VCR avail (movies $2). Complimentary full bkfst in rm. Restaurant (see RIDER'S INN). Rm serv. Ck-out, ck-in flexible. Business servs avail. Bellhops. Concierge. Airport transportation. 18-hole golf privileges. Health club privileges. Original stagecoach stop (1812); historic stop on the underground railroad, some original antiques. Cr cds: A, DS, MC.

🔥 🛶 🎿 🎣 ⛷

Restaurants

★ **DINNER BELL DINER.** *1155 Bank St (44077). 440/354-3708.* Hrs: 8 am-9 pm; Sun to 8 pm. Closed July 4, Thanksgiving, Dec 25. Res accepted. Bkfst $2-$8.25, lunch $4-$9.95, dinner $5.75-$12.95. Specialties: prime rib, meat loaf, Greek steak tips over noodles. Parking. Eclectic decor. Photographs of celebrity guests. Cr cds: A, C, D, DS, MC, V.

⊡ SC ⛏

★★ **RIDER'S INN.** *792 Mentor Ave (44077). 440/942-2742. www.ridersinn.com.* Hrs: 9 am-9 pm; Fri, Sat to 10 pm; Sun 10 am-9pm. Closed Dec 25. Res accepted. Bar. Lunch $3.95-$8.95, dinner $8.95-$23. Sun brunch $10.95. Child's menu. Specialties: venison, duck, potato leek soup. Entertainment Fri, Sat. Outdoor dining. Features fare from original 19th-century recipes. Cr cds: A, C, DS, MC, V.

⊡ ⛏

Piqua

(D-2) *See also Dayton, Sidney, Vandalia*

Pop 20,612 **Elev** 869 ft **Area code** 937
Zip 45356
Information Piqua Area Chamber of
Commerce, 326 N Main, PO Box
1142; 937/773-2765

What to See and Do

⭐ **Piqua Historical Area.** More than
170 acres in Great Miami River valley, near crossroads used by prehistoric people, by French and English
fur traders, and by soldiers of General "Mad Anthony" Wayne. (Memorial Day-Labor Day, Wed-Sun; after
Labor Day-Oct, wkends only) 3½ mi
NW on OH 66. Phone 937/773-2522.
¢¢ Area and fee incl

Historic Indian Museum. Has artifacts from the 17th-19th centuries.
Phone 937/773-2522.

John Johnston Home. (1810)
Restored Dutch Colonial-style
farmhouse built by Ohio Indian
agent and businessman. Other
buildings incl double pen log barn,
springhouse, fruit kiln, and cider-
house; craft demonstrations.
Phone 937/773-2522.

Miami and Erie Canal. (1825-1845)
Rides on *Gen'l Harrison,* replica of a
mid-19th-century canal boat.

Special Event

Heritage Festival. Piqua heritage re-
created. Native American and square
dancing; demonstrations incl long
rifle, blacksmith, wood carving, dulcimer, soap making, weaving; contests; food; canal boat rides. Phone
937/773-2765. Labor Day wkend.

Motel/Motor Lodge

★ ★ **COMFORT INN.** *987 E Ash St &
Miami Valley Centre (45356). 937/778-
8100; fax 937/778-9573; res 800/228-
5150. www.comfortinn.com.* 124 rms,
5 story. S, D $78-$120; each addl $6;
under 18 free. Crib free. Pet accepted;
fee. TV; cable (premium). Indoor
pool; whirlpool. Complimentary
continental bkfst. Restaurant nearby.
Ck-out noon. Meeting rms. Business

servs avail. Valet serv. Exercise
equipt. Cr cds: A, D, DS, MC, V.

D 🐾 🖼 🎣 SC 🏊 🏌

Port Clinton

(B-4) *See also Fremont, Kelleys Island,
Put-in-Bay, Sandusky, Toledo*

Founded 1828 **Pop** 7,106 **Elev** 592 ft
Area code 419 **Zip** 43452
Information Chamber of Commerce,
304 Madison St, Suite C; 419/734-
5503; or the Ottawa County Visitors
Bureau, 109 Madison St, Suite E;
419/734-4386
Web www.portclintonchamber.com

What to See and Do

African Safari Wildlife Park. Visitors
may drive their own cars through
game preserve to lions, ostriches,
giraffes, zebras, and other animals
roaming free in natural setting.
Camel rides avail. (Mid-May-Labor
Day, daily; Sept, wkends if weather
permits) 4 mi E to Lightner Rd, off
US 2 Bypass. Phone 419/732-3606.
¢¢¢

Camp Perry Military Reservation.
Largest military camp on the Great
Lakes. (Daily) 5 mi W on OH 2.
Phone 888/889-7010. **FREE**

Catawba Island State Park. Fishing
(perch, catfish, bluegill, bass, crappie), boating on Lake Erie (ramps);
picnicking. (Daily) 4 mi E on OH
163, then N on OH 53. Phone
419/797-4530. **FREE**

East Harbor State Park. Swimming
beach, lifeguard, bathhouse (Memorial Day-Labor Day), fishing, boating,
marina, docks; hiking, snowmobiling, concession, camping. Standard
fees. (Daily) 7 mi E on OH 163, then
N on OH 269. Phone 419/734-4424.
FREE

Ottawa County Historical Museum.
Guns, dolls, Native American and
county relics; 1813 Battle of Lake
Erie exhibit. (Mon-Fri afternoons,
also by appt; closed hols) 126 W 3rd
St at Monroe St. Phone 419/732-
2237. **FREE**

**Perry's Victory and International
Peace Memorial.** 12 mi by ferry to
Put-in-Bay (see).

Special Event

National Matches. Camp Perry. Held since 1907. Hundreds of competitors each in outdoor pistol, small-bore, and highpower rifle championships. Small Arms Firing Schools. Early July-mid-Aug. Phone 419/635-0101.

Motels/Motor Lodges

★ **DAYS INN.** *2149 Gill Rd (43452). 419/734-4945; fax 419/734-0495; res 800/329-7466. www.daysinn.com.* 36 rms. May-Oct: S, D $68-$138; under 12 free; lower rates rest of yr. Closed Nov-March. Crib free. TV; cable. Complimentary continental bkfst. Ck-out noon. Coin lndry. Cr cds: A, C, D, DS, MC, V.

★★ **FAIRFIELD INN.** *3760 E State Rd (43452). 419/732-2434; toll-free 800/228-2800. www.fairfieldinn.com.* 64 rms, 2 story. Apr-Aug: S $68.95-$148; D $68.95-$180; under 18 free; lower rates rest of yr. Crib $10. TV; cable (premium). Complimentary continental bkfst. Ck-out noon. Business servs avail. Sundries. Coin lndry. Indoor pool. Game rm. Some in-rm whirlpools. Cr cds: A, C, D, DS, MC, V.

Restaurant

★★ **GARDEN AT THE LIGHTHOUSE.** *226 E Perry St (OH 163) (43452). 419/732-2151.* Hrs: 11 am-2 pm, 4-10 pm; early-bird dinner 4-6 pm. Closed some major hols; also Sun Sept-May. Res accepted. Continental menu. Bar. Lunch $4.50-$8.95, dinner $8.95-$21.95. Child's menu. Specializes in seafood. Patio dining. In former lighthouse keeper's building; glassed-in porch overlooking gardens. Cr cds: A, D, DS, MC, V.

Portsmouth

(G-4) *See also Ironton*

Founded 1803 **Pop** 22,676 **Elev** 533 ft
Area code 740 **Zip** 45662

Information Convention & Visitors Bureau, 324 Chillicothe St, PO Box 509; 740/353-1116
Web www.portsmouthcvb.org

Portsmouth is the leading firebrick and shoelace center of southern Ohio. At the confluence of the Ohio and Scioto rivers, 100 miles east of Cincinnati, it is connected to South Portsmouth, Kentucky, by bridge. The Boneyfiddle historic district in downtown Portsmouth includes many antique and specialty shops.

Portsmouth was the childhood home of cowboy movie star Roy Rogers and baseball's Branch Rickey.

What to See and Do

The 1810 House. Original homestead built by hand. Nine rms with period furniture. Guided tours. (May-Dec, Sat and Sun afternoons; wkdays by appt) 1926 Waller St. Phone 740/354-3760. **Donation**

Brewery Arcade. (1842) A former brewery, restored. 224 Second St, in the historic Boneyfiddle district.

Floodwall Murals Project. Thirty-four murals depicting area history completed by Robert Dafford. (Daily) Along Front St at Ohio River. Phone 740/353-1116. **FREE**

Shawnee State Forest. A 63,000-acre forest with six lakes. Hunting in season. Bridle trail. (Daily) (See SPECIAL EVENTS) 7 mi SW on US 52, then W on OH 125. Phone 740/858-6685. **FREE** In forest is

Shawnee State Park. Swimming, fishing, boating (ramps, dock) on 68-acre lake; 18-hole golf, picnicking (shelter), lodge, camping, teepees, cabins. Nature center. (Daily) Phone 740/858-4561. **FREE**

Southern Ohio Museum and Cultural Center. Changing exhibits in visual arts; performing arts; workshops; guided tours. (Tues-Sun; closed hols, also Jan and Aug) Free admission Fri. 825 Gallia St. Phone 740/354-5629. ¢

Special Events

Trout Derby. In Shawnee State Park. Phone 740/858-6652. Last wkend Apr.

Roy Rogers Festival. Downtown. Old-time Western stars, memorabilia, staged gunfights. First wkend June. Phone 740/353-0900.

Scioto County Fair. Fairgrounds. Second wk Aug. Phone 740/353-3698.

River Days Festival. Downtown. Labor Day wkend. Phone 740/355-6622.

Fall foliage hikes and tours. Shawnee State Park and Forest. Guided hikes, hoedowns, camp-outs, auto tours. Third wkend Oct. Phone 740/858-6621.

Motel/Motor Lodge

★ ★ **RAMADA INN.** *711 Second St (45662). 740/354-7711; fax 740/353-1539; toll-free 888/298-2054. www.ramada.com.* 119 rms, 5 story. S $49-$65; D $53-$80; each addl $7; under 18 free. Crib free. Pet accepted, some restrictions. TV; cable (premium). Indoor pool; wading pool, whirlpool, poolside serv. Complimentary continental bkfst. Restaurant 11 am-11 pm; Fri, Sat to midnight. Rm serv. Ck-out noon. Meeting rms. Business servs avail. Valet serv. Sundries. Exercise equipt. Health club privileges. Dockage. Some refrigerators. Cr cds: A, C, D, DS, MC, V.

D ⬛ ⬛ ⬛ SC ⬛ ⬛

Put-in-Bay

(B-4) See also Kelleys Island, Port Clinton, Sandusky

Settled 1811 **Pop** 141 **Elev** 570 ft
Area code 419 **Zip** 43456
Information Put-in-Bay Chamber of Commerce, PO Box 250; 419/285-2832
Web www.put-in-bay.com

On South Bass Island in Lake Erie, this village is an all-year resort which can be reached by ferry from Port Clinton (inquire as to time and seasons, phone 800/245-1538) and Catawba Point (inquire as to time and seasons, phone 419/285-2421) or by plane from Sandusky (phone 800/368-3743). The area claims the best smallmouth black bass fishing in America in spring; good walleye fishing in June, July, and August; and ice fishing for perch and walleye in winter. Boating, swimming, bicycling,

picnic grounds, yachting facilities, golf, and waterskiing are available. Wine is produced in the area.

What to See and Do

Crystal Cave. Unusual deposit of strontium sulphate crystals; the largest 18 inches long. Heineman Winery is located on the grounds; winery tour and tasting is incl in cave tour. (Mid-May-mid-Sept, daily) 978 Catawba Ave. Phone 419/285-2811. ¢¢

Lake Erie Island State Park. Incl South Bass Island, Kelleys Island, and Catawba parks. Waterskiing, fishing, boating (ramps); hiking trail, picnicking (shelter), camping (fee), cabins (fee). Standard fees. S shore. Phone 419/797-4530.

Perry's Cave. Commodore Perry is rumored to have stored supplies here before the Battle of Lake Erie in 1813; later prisoners were kept here for a short time. The cave is 52 ft below the surface and is 208 ft by 165 ft; the temperature is 50°F. It has an underground stream that rises and falls with the level of Lake Erie. Picnic area avail (no water). Mini-golf (fee), rock climbing (fee). Twenty-min guided tour. (June-Labor Day, daily; spring and fall, wkends; rest of yr, by appt) Catawba Ave. Phone 419/285-2405. ¢¢

Perry's Victory and International Peace Memorial. Greek Doric granite column (352 ft high) commemorates Commodore Oliver Hazard Perry's victory over the British Naval Squadron at the Battle of Lake Erie, near Put-in-Bay, in 1813. The US gained control of the lake, preventing a British invasion. Observation platform in monument (317 ft above lake) provides view of the battle site and neighboring islands on a clear day. The 3,986-mi US-Canadian boundary is the longest unfortified border in the world. Children over 16 only with adult. (May-late Oct, daily). 2 Bay View Ave. Phone 419/285-2184. ¢

Put-in-Bay Tour Train. Departs from downtown depot and Jet Express dock. A one-hr tour of the island (May-mid-Sept, daily). Phone 419/285-4855. ¢¢

Special Event

Boat Regatta. More than 200 sail-boats race to Vermilion (see). Early Aug. Phone 419/285-2832.

St. Clairsville

(D-6) *See also Steubenville*

Pop 5,162 **Elev** 1,284 ft
Area code 740 **Zip** 43950
Information St. Clairsville Area Chamber of Commerce, 116 W Main St; 740/695-9623
Web www.stclairsville.com

This charming tree-shaded town has been the seat of Belmont County since 1804.

Special Event

Jamboree in the Hills. 4 mi W off I-70 exit 208 or 213. A four-day coun-try music festival featuring more than 30 hrs of music; top country stars. Camping avail. Phone 800/624-5456. Third wkend July.

Motels/Motor Lodges

★ **DAYS INN.** *52601 Holiday Dr (43950). 740/695-0100; fax 740/695-4135; toll-free 800/551-0106. www. daysinn.com.* 137 rms, 2 story. S $50-$59; D $55-$64; each addl $5; under 18 free. Crib free. TV. Pool; poolside serv. Complimentary continental bkfst. Restaurant 11 am-10 pm; Fri, Sat to 11 pm. Rm serv. Bar. Ck-out noon. Meeting rms. Business servs avail. Refrigerators, microwaves avail. Cr cds: A, C, D, DS, MC, V.
🄳 ≋ 🐾 SC ≋

★ **KNIGHTS INN.** *51260 E National Rd (43950). 740/695-5038; fax 740/695-3014; toll-free 800/843-5644. www.knightsinn.com.* 104 rms, 16 kits. S $36.95-$44.95; D $38.95-$54.95; each addl $7; kit. units $44.95-$69.95; under 18 free. Crib free. Pet accepted, some restrictions. TV; cable (premium), VCR avail (movies). Pool. Complimentary coffee. Restaurant nearby. Ck-out noon. Business servs avail. In-rm modem link. Some in-rm

whirlpools; microwaves avail. Cr cds: A, C, D, DS, MC, V.
🄳 🐾 ≋ ⊠ 🐾

Sandusky

(B-4) *See also Bellevue, Milan, Port Clinton, Vermilion*

Settled 1816 **Pop** 29,764 **Elev** 600 ft
Area code 419 **Zip** 44870
Information Sandusky/Erie County Visitor & Convention Bureau, 4424 Milan Rd, Suite A; 419/625-2984 or 800/255-3743
Web www.buckeyenorth.com

On a flat slope facing 18-mile-long Sandusky Bay, this town stretches for more than six miles along the water-front. Originally explored by the French, named by the Wyandot "Sandouske," meaning "at the cold water," it is the second-largest coal-shipping port on the Great Lakes. It became a tourist center in 1882; automotive parts industry and man-ufacturing are also important to the economy.

What to See and Do

Battery Park. Piers, marina, sailing club; lighted tennis, picnicking (shel-ter), playground. Restaurant. At E end of Water St, overlooks Sandusky Bay. Phone 419/625-6142. **FREE**

Boat trips.

MV *City of Sandusky.* Three hundred-passenger excursion boat from downtown. (Memorial Day-Labor Day, daily; Sept, wkends) 226 W Shoreline Dr. Phone 419/627-0198.

MV *Pelee Islander.* (Res necessary for autos) Ferry transportation in summer to Leamington and Kingsville, Ontario (for Border Crossing Regulations see MAKING THE MOST OF YOUR TRIP). (Mid-June-Labor Day) Foot of Jackson St. Phone 519/724-2115.

Cedar Point. Swimming beach, marina; RV campground, resort hotels on Lake Erie. Amusement park has more than 50 rides, live shows, crafts area, restaurants, concessions. Also here is Challenge Park, incl Soak

City water park, Challenge Golf miniature golf course, and the Cedar Point Grand Prix go-kart race track (addl fee). (Early May-Labor Day, daily; after Labor Day-Oct, wkends only) Price incl unlimited rides and attractions exc Challenge Park. SE on US 6 to Causeway Dr, then N over Causeway (look for Cedar Point signs in town). Phone 419/627-2350. ¢¢¢¢

Merry-Go-Round Museum. Houses restored, working carousel, exhibits. Tours. (Memorial Day-Labor Day daily; Wed-Sun rest of yr; closed hols) W Washington and Jackson Sts. Phone 419/626-6111. ¢¢

Old Woman Creek National Estuar-ine Research Reserve. Old Woman Creek is protected as a National Estu-arine Research Reserve and State Nature Preserve. It is one of Ohio's best remaining examples of a natural estuary and serves as a field labora-tory for the study of estuarine ecol-ogy. Ohio Center for Coastal Wetlands Studies has a visitor center and reference library. Trails (daily). Visitor center (Apr-Dec, Wed-Sun afternoons; rest of yr, Mon-Fri; closed hols). Approx 12 mi E on US 6 (2 mi E of Huron). Phone 419/433-4601. **FREE**

Special Events

Erie County Fair. Fairgrounds. Live-stock show, rides, entertainment. Early Aug. Phone 419/626-1020.

Tour of homes. Tour historic homes decorated for the holidays. Early Dec. Phone 419/627-0640.

Motels/Motor Lodges

★★ **BEST WESTERN CEDAR POINT.** *1530 Cleveland Rd (44870). 419/625-9234; fax 419/625-9971; toll-free 800/780-7234. www.bestwestern. com.* 106 rms, 2 story. Early May-Labor Day: S $99-$175; D $99-$179; each addl $10; suites $150-$350; kit. units $200-$350; lower rates rest of yr; under 12 free. Crib $8. TV; cable (premium). Heated pool. Restaurant 7 am-midnight. Ck-out 11 am. Coin lndry. Sundries. Game rm. Micro-waves avail. Cr cds: A, C, D, DS, MC, V.

D ⟞ ⟝ ⟦ SC

★★ **CLARION INN RIVERS EDGE.** *132 N Main St, Huron (44839). 419/433-8000; fax 419/433-8552; toll-free 800/947-3400.* 65 rms, 3 story. May-Sept: S, D $50-$200; each addl $10; suites $84-$259; under 18 free; lower rates rest of yr. Crib free. TV; cable (premium). Indoor pool; whirl-

Serpent Mound State Memorial

pool, poolside serv. Complimentary continental bkfst. Complimentary coffee in rms. Restaurant 7 am-midnight; winter hrs vary. Rm serv. Bar 11-2:30 am; entertainment. Ck-out 11 am. Meeting rms. Business servs avail. Bellhops. Sundries. Coin lndry. Golf privileges. Exercise equipt. Health club privileges. Massage. Game rm. Some in-rm whirlpools; microwaves avail. Picnic tables. On beach. Cr cds: A, D, DS, MC, V.

★★ **FAIRFIELD INN.** *6220 Milan Rd (44870). 419/621-9500; res 800/228-2800. www.fairfieldinn.com.* 63 rms, 2 story. May-Aug: S, D $69-$189; each addl $6; under 18 free; lower rates rest of yr. Crib free. TV; cable (premium). Complimentary continental bkfst. Restaurant nearby. Business servs avail. Sundries. Coin lndry. Sauna. Indoor pool. Some in-rm whirlpools. Cr cds: A, C, D, DS, MC, V.

★★ **HOLIDAY INN.** *5513 Milan Rd (44870). 419/626-6671; fax 419/626-9780; toll-free 800/465-4329. www.holiday-inn.com.* 175 rms, 2 story, 15 suites. Late May-early Sept: S, D $130-$189; under 18 free; lower rates rest of yr. Crib free. TV; cable (premium). 2 pools, 1 indoor; whirl-pools. Restaurant 6 am-2 pm, 5-10 pm. Rm serv. Bar 11-2 am. Ck-out 11 am. Free guest lndry. Meeting rm. Business servs avail. In-rm modem link. Valet serv. Sundries. Miniature golf. Exercise equipt; sauna. Game rm. Rec rm. Tennis adj. Some in-rm whirlpools. Cr cds: A, C, D, DS, MC, V.

★ **SUPER 8 MOTEL.** *11313 Milan Rd (44846). 419/499-4671; res 800/800-8000. www.super8.com.* 69 rms, 2 story, 9 suites. Late May-Aug, wkends: S $53.88-$102.88; D $58.88-$128; each addl $6; suites $98.88-$174; under 12 free; lower rates rest of yr. Restaurant 5-9:30 pm; Fri, Sat to 10 pm; closed Sun night. TV; cable (premium). Pool. Complimentary continental bkfst. Ck-out noon. Coin lndry. Meeting rm. Sundries. Game

rm. Some refrigerators; microwaves avail. Cr cds: A, C, D, DS, MC, V.

Hotel

★★★ **RADISSON HARBOUR INN.** *2001 Cleveland Rd (44870). 419/627-2500; fax 419/627-0745; toll-free 800/333-3333. www.radisson.com.* 237 rms, 49 suites. May-mid-Sept: S, D $92-$209; suites $109-$359; under 18 free; lower rates rest of yr. Crib free. Pet accepted, some restrictions. TV; cable (premium), VCR avail. Indoor pool; whirlpool, pool-side serv. Supervised child's activities (May-mid-Sept); ages 4-13. Restaurant 6:30 am-11 pm. Rm serv. Bars 11-2 am; entertainment wkends. Ck-out noon. Coin lndry. Meeting rms. Business center. In-rm modem link. Bellhops. Valet serv. Gift shop. Airport, RR station, bus depot transportation. Exercise equipt. Health club privileges. Game rm. Rec rm. Some refrigerators. Private patios, balconies. Cr cds: A, D, DS, MC, V.

Resort

★★★ **SAWMILL CREEK RESORT.** *400 Sawmill (44839). 419/433-3800.* 240 rms, 4 story. S, D $150-$250; each addl $20; under 17 free. Crib avail. Indoor pool. TV; cable (premium), VCR avail. Complimentary coffee in rms. Restaurant 6 am-10 pm. Ck-out 11 am. Meeting rms. Business center. Gift shop. Exercise rm. Some refrigerators, minibars. Cr cds: A, C, D, DS, MC, V.

Restaurant

★★ **BAY HARBOR INN.** *1 Causeway Dr (44870). 419/625-6373.* Hrs: 5-10 pm. Closed major hols; also Sun Oct-Apr. Res accepted Sun-Thur (summer), Mon-Fri (rest of yr). Bar from 4 pm. Dinner $12.95-$42.50. Child's menu. Specializes in fresh seafood, prime rib. Own pasta. View of Sandusky Bay and marina. Cr cds: DS, MC, V.

Serpent Mound State Memorial

See also Chillicothe, Portsmouth

(4 mi NW of Locust Grove on OH 73)

The largest and most remarkable serpent effigy earthworks in North America. Built between 800 B.C.-A.D. 100 of stone and yellow clay, it curls like an enormous snake for 1,335 feet. An oval earthwall represents the serpent's open mouth. In the 61-acre area are an observation tower, a scenic gorge, a museum, and picnicking facilities. Site (all yr); museum (Apr-Oct, daily; Nov-Mar hrs vary, phone ahead). Phone 937/587-2796. Parking ¢¢

Sidney

(D-2) *See also Bellefontaine, Piqua, Wapakoneta*

Pop 18,710 **Elev** 956 ft **Area code** 937 **Zip** 45365

Information Sidney-Shelby County Chamber of Commerce, 100 S Main, Suite 201; 937/492-9122

Web www.accesswestohio.com

Special Event

Country Concert at Hickory Hill Lakes. Phone 937/295-3000. Mid-July.

Motels/Motor Lodges

★★ **HOLIDAY INN.** *400 Folkerth Ave (45365). 937/492-1131; fax 937/498-4655; res 800/465-4329. www.holiday-inn.com.* 134 rms, 2 story. S $65-$67; D $70-$77; each addl $5; suites $75-$77; under 19 free; package plans. Crib free. Pet accepted, some restrictions. TV; cable (premium), VCR avail. Pool. Playground. Restaurant 6:30 am-10 pm; Sat from 7 am; Sun to 8 pm. Rm serv. Bar 11 am-midnight, Fri, Sat to 1 am. Ck-out noon. Coin lndry. Meeting rms. Business servs avail. In-rm modem link. Valet serv. Sundries. Exercise equipt; sauna. Game rm. Microwave in suites. Cr cds: A, D, DS, MC, V.

D 🐾 🛏 🔥 🏃

Restaurant

★★ **FAIRINGTON.** *1103 Fairington Dr (45365). 937/492-6186.* Hrs: 11 am-2 pm, 4:30-10 pm; Sat from 5 pm. Closed Sun; most major hols. Res accepted. Bar. Lunch $4.99-$8.95, dinner $9.95-$17.95. Child's menu. Specializes in steak, seafood, pasta. Pianist Fri, Sat. Overlooks wooded area. Cr cds: A, D, DS, MC, V.

D 🔧

Springfield

(D-2) *See also Bellefontaine, Columbus, Dayton*

Founded 1801 **Pop** 70,487 **Elev** 980 ft **Area code** 937

Information Convention & Visitors Bureau, 333 N Limestone St, Suite 201, 45503; 937/325-7621

Web www.springfieldnet.com

Indian Scout Simon Kenton, an early settler, set up a gristmill and sawmill on the present site of the Navistar International plant. His wife gave the village its name. When the National Pike came in 1839, Springfield came to be known as the "town at the end of the National Pike."

Agricultural machinery gave Springfield its next boost. A farm journal, *Farm and Fireside,* published in the 1880s by P. J. Mast, a cultivator-manufacturer, was the start of the Crowell-Collier Publishing Company. The 4-H movement was started here in 1902 by A. B. Graham, and hybrid corn grown by George H. Shull had its beginning in Springfield. A center for some 200 diversified industries, Springfield is in the rich agricultural valley of west central Ohio.

What to See and Do

Antioch College. (1852) 800 students. Liberal arts and sciences. Horace Mann, first president, aimed to establish a school free of sectarianism. Known for the cooperative education plan under which students alternate periods of study and work. 9½ mi S on US 68, E Center College St in Yellow Springs. Phone 937/767-7331.

Buck Creek State Park. A 4,030-acre park with swimming, lifeguard, bathhouse (Memorial Day-Labor Day), fishing, boating (launch, ramp); hiking, snowmobile trails, picnicking, concession, camping, cabins. Standard fees. (Daily) 4 mi NE on OH 4; exit 62 off OH 70. Phone 937/322-5284. **FREE** On grounds is

> **David Crabill House.** (1826) Built by Clark County pioneer David Crabill; restored. Period rms; log barn; smokehouse. Maintained by Clark County Historical Society. (Tues-Fri) 818 N Fountain Ave. ¢

John Bryan State Park. A 750-acre park with fishing; hiking, picnic area, camping. Standard fees. (Daily) 9½ mi S of I-70 on US 68, then 3 mi SE via OH 343, 370, near Yellow Springs. Phone 937/767-1274. **FREE**

Pennsylvania House. (1824) Built as tavern and stagecoach stop on National Pike; period furnishings, pioneer artifacts; button, quilt, and doll collections. (First Sun afternoon of each month; also by appt; closed Easter and late Dec-Feb) 1311 W Main St. Phone 937/322-7668. ¢¢

Springfield Museum of Art. Loaned exhibits change monthly; permanent collection incl 19th- and 20th-century American and French art; fine arts school; library; docent tours. (Tues-Sun; closed hols, also wk of Dec 25) 107 Cliff Park Rd. Phone 937/325-4673. **FREE**

Wittenberg University. (1845) 2,000 students. Liberal arts and sciences. Private school affiliated with the Evangelical Lutheran Church in America. Ward St at N Wittenberg Ave. Phone 800/677-7558.

Special Events

Springfield Arts Festival. Veteran's Memorial Park amphitheater, area auditoriums. Six-wk series of free performances; music, dance, visual arts, drama. Phone 937/324-2712. June-mid-July.

Clark County Fair. Fairgrounds. Horse shows, rodeos, tractor pulls. Mid-July. Phone 937/325-7621.

Fair at New Boston. George Rogers Clark Park (OH 4), W of Springfield. Recreation of a 1790-1810 trade fair; period demonstrations, food, and displays. Late Aug. Phone 937/882-6000.

Motel/Motor Lodge

★ ★ **FAIRFIELD INN.** *1870 W 1st St (45504). 937/323-9554; toll-free 800/228-2800. www.fairfieldinn.com.* 63 rms, 3 story. Mar-Oct: S, D $67-$99; each addl $6; under 18 free; higher rates special events. Crib free. TV; cable (premium), VCR avail. Indoor pool; whirlpool. Complimentary continental bkfst. Restaurant adj 6 am-10 pm. Ck-out noon. Business servs avail. Health club privileges. Game rm. Some refrigerators. Microwave in suites. Cr cds: A, D, DS, MC, V.
🛌 **SC** 🔀

Hotel

★ ★ ★ **SPRINGFIELD INN.** *100 S Fountain Ave (45502). 937/322-3600; fax 937/322-0462. www.brilyn.com.* 124 rms, 6 story. S, D $78-$99; each addl $10; under 18 free; wkend rates. Crib free. TV; cable (premium), VCR avail. Complimentary coffee in rms. Restaurant 6 am-10 pm. Bar 11 am-midnight, wkends to 1 am. Ck-out noon. Meeting rms. Business servs avail. In-rm modem link. Refrigerators avail. Balconies. Luxury level. Cr cds: A, C, D, DS, MC, V.
D 🔀 ⚒

Restaurants

★ ★ **CASEY'S.** *2205 Park Rd (45504). 937/322-0397.* Hrs: 5-10 pm. Closed Sun; major hols. Res accepted. Bar. Dinner $9.95-$16.95. Specializes in steak, prime rib, fresh seafood. Own pasta, desserts. Cr cds: A, D, MC, V.
D 🔀

★ ★ **KLOSTERMAN'S DERR ROAD INN.** *4343 Derr Rd (45503). 937/399-0822.* Hrs: 11 am-2 pm, 4 pm-close; Fri 11 am-2 pm, 5 pm-close; Sat from 5 pm; Sun 4-8 pm. Closed major hols. Res accepted. Continental menu. Bar. Lunch $4.50-$6.95, dinner $10.95-$18.95. Child's menu. Specializes in steaks, prime rib, fresh seafood. Own desserts. 1860s manor house with large windows overlooking property. Cr cds: A, C, D, DS, MC, V.

[D] [⇥]

Steubenville

(D-7) *See also East Liverpool*

Settled 1797 **Pop** 22,125 **Elev** 715 ft
Area code 740 **Zip** 43952
Information Jefferson County Chamber of Commerce, 630 Market St, PO Box 278; 740/282-6226
Web www.jeffersoncountychamber. com

Although its early industries were pottery, coal, woolen cloth, glass, and shipbuilding, the rolling mills of Wheeling-Pittsburgh Steel and Weirton Steel started Steubenville's economic growth.

The town's location was selected by the government as a fort in 1786. Fort Steuben (destroyed by fire in 1790) and the town were named for the Prussian Baron Frederick William von Steuben, who aided the colonies in the Revolutionary War. It is the seat of Jefferson County.

What to See and Do

Creegan Company. Country's largest designer and manufacturer of animations, costume characters and decor offers guided tours (approx one hr) through its three-story factory and showroom. (Daily) 510 Washington St. Phone 740/283-3708. ¢

Jefferson County Courthouse. Contains first county deed record, signed by George Washington, and portraits of Steubenville personalities. Statue of Edwin Stanton, Lincoln's secretary of war, is on the lawn. (Mon-Fri; closed hols) 301 Market St. Phone 740/283-4111. **FREE**

Jefferson County Historical Association Museum and Genealogical Library. Tudor-style mansion with collection of historic memorabilia and genealogical materials; guided tours. (Mid-Apr-Dec, Tues-Sat; closed hols) 426 Franklin Ave. Phone 740/283-1133. ¢

Union Cemetery. Contains many Civil War graves, incl the "fighting McCook" plot, where members of a family that sent 13 men to fight in the Union Army are buried. (Daily) 1720 Sunset Blvd. Phone 740/283-3384.

Motel/Motor Lodge

★★ **HOLIDAY INN.** *1401 University Blvd (43952). 740/282-0901; fax 740/282-9540; res 800/465-4329. www.holiday-inn.com.* 120 rms, 2 story. No elvtr. S, D $69-$80; each addl $5; under 18 free. Crib avail. TV; cable (premium), VCR avail. Heated pool. Restaurant 6 am-midnight. Rm serv. Bar 7 am-10 pm. Ck-out noon. Coin lndry. Business servs avail. In-rm modem link. Bellhops. Valet serv. Cr cds: A, C, D, DS, MC, V.

[D] [≈] [⇥] [🔥]

Strongsville

(B-5) *See also Cleveland, Elyria*

Pop 35,308 **Elev** 932 ft **Area code** 440
Zip 44136
Information Chamber of Commerce, 18829 Royalton Rd; 440/238-3366
Web www.strongsvillecofc.com

First settled in 1816, Strongsville is the largest suburban community in Cuyahoga County.

What to See and Do

Gardenview Horticultural Park. English-style cottage gardens devoted to collecting uncommon and unusual plants. Sixteen acres incl six acres of gardens with seasonal plantings, and a ten-acre arboretum; 2,000 flowering crabapples bloom first two wks May. (Early Apr-mid-Oct, Sat and Sun afternoons) On US 42, 1½ mi S of US 82. Phone 440/238-6653. ¢¢

Tiffin

(B-3) *See also Bellevue, Findlay, Fremont*

Founded 1817 **Pop** 18,604 **Elev** 758 ft
Area code 419 **Zip** 44883
Information Seneca County Convention & Visitors Bureau, 114 S Washington; 419/447-5866 or
888/736-3221
Web www.senecacounty/visitor

Tiffin is a quiet, tree-shaded town on the Sandusky River; it has diversified industries that include pottery, glassware, electric motor, heavy machinery, and conveyor manufacturing.

What to See and Do

Glass Heritage Gallery. Museum houses a collection of glass made in Fostoria plants from 1887 to 1920; examples incl lamps, crystal bowls, mosaic art glass, novelty glass. (Tues-Sat; closed hols) 14 mi W via OH 18, at 109 N Main St in Fostoria. Phone 419/435-5077. **FREE**

Industrial tours.

Crystal Traditions. Glassblowing and glass engraving. Free factory tours. Showroom (Mon-Sat; closed hols). 145 Madison St. Phone 419/448-4286.

King's Glass Engraving. Demonstrations. (Mon-Sat; closed hols) 181 S Washington St. Phone 419/447-0232. **FREE**

Seneca County Museum. Historic house (ca 1853) museum contains extensive collection of Tiffin glass; drawing rm furnished with early Victorian pieces; porcelain collection; research library; kitchen with original built-in stove; second floor has music rm with a pianola and a 200-yr-old harp, and bedrms with a rope bed and trundle bed. The third floor has collection of Native American artifacts, and toy and doll collection. Tours (June-Aug, Tues-Thurs and Sun afternoons; rest of yr, Wed and Sun afternoons; also by appt). 28 Clay St. Phone 419/447-5955. **Donation**

Special Events

Glass Heritage Festival. Glass festival features glass shows, tours, entertainment, arts and crafts. Fostoria. Phone 419/435-0486. Third wkend July.

Tiffin-Seneca Heritage Festival. Entertainment, crafts, living history village; ethnic foods, parade. Phone 419/447-5866. Third wkend Sept.

Restaurant

★ **BLACK CAT.** *820 Sandusky St, Fostoria (44830). 419/435-2685.* Hrs: 11:30 am-10 pm; Sat from 4:30 pm; Sun 11:30 am-3 pm; early-bird dinner Mon-Fri 4:30-6:30 pm. Closed major hols; also mid-June-Labor Day Sun. Res accepted. Bar. Lunch $3.50-$4.50, dinner $7-$24.50. Child's menu. Specializes in steak, seafood. Over 575 black cat figurines on display. Cr cds: A, D, DS, MC, V.

Toledo

(A-3) *See also Bowling Green, Port Clinton*

Settled 1817 **Pop** 332,943 **Elev** 587 ft
Area code 419
Information Greater Toledo Convention & Visitors Bureau, 401 Jefferson, 43604; 419/321-6404 or 800/243-4667
Web www.toledocvb.com

The French first explored the Toledo area, situated at the mouth of the Maumee River on Lake Erie, in 1615. Probably named after Toledo, Spain, the present city began as a group of small villages along the river. During 1835-1836 it was claimed by both Michigan and Ohio in the Toledo War, which resulted in Toledo becoming part of Ohio and the Northern Peninsula going to Michigan.

Toledo's large, excellent natural harbor makes it an important port. Numerous railroads move coal and ore to the south, east, and north, grain from the southwest, steel from Cleveland and Pittsburgh, and automobile parts and accessories to and from Detroit.

Edward Libbey introduced the glass industry to Toledo in 1888 with high-grade crystal and lamp globes. Michael Owens, a glassblower, joined him and invented a machine that turned molten glass into bottles by the thousands. Today Owens-Illinois, Inc., Libbey-Owens-Ford Company, Owens-Corning Fiberglas Corporation, and Johns-Manville Fiber Glass, Inc. manufacture a variety of glass products. Metropolitan Toledo has more than 1,000 manufacturing plants producing Jeeps, spark plugs, chemicals, and other products.

What to See and Do

COSI Toledo. First-hand science learning is avail here through hands-on experiments, demonstrations, and eight Exhibition Worlds. These incl Kidspace, Babyspace, and an outdoors Science Park. Restaurant. (Mon-Sat, Sun afternoons; closed hols) 1 Discovery Way, corner of Summit and Adams Sts. ¢¢

Crane Creek State Park. A 79-acre park with swimming (lifeguard; Memorial Day-Labor Day), fishing, ice fishing; hiking, picnicking; trail for bird-watching. (Daily) 18 mi E off OH 2, SE of Bono. Phone 419/898-2495. **FREE**

Fort Meigs State Memorial. Reconstruction of fort built under supervision of William Henry Harrison in 1813; used during War of 1812. Blockhouses with exhibits; demonstrations of military life. (Memorial Day-Labor Day, Wed-Sun; after Labor Day-Oct, wkends and hols) Picnicking in area. Take I-475 to exit 2, turn N onto OH 65. Phone 419/874-4121. ¢¢

Maumee Bay State Park. The wet woods and marshes of this 1,860-acre shoreline park are havens to wildlife and are good for birdwatching. Beaches, fishing, boat rentals; hiking, 18-hole golf, camping (tent rentals avail), 24 cabins, lodge. Amphitheater. Nature center. Standard fees. (Daily) 8 mi E on OH 2, then N on Curtice Rd, in Oregon. Phone 419/836-7758. **FREE**

Parks.

Detwiler/Bay View Park. Pool (early May-Sept), boating (launch; fee), marina; picnicking, concessions, playgrounds on 219 acres, two golf courses (fee), tennis. Lighted ball field; view of port. (Daily) 4001 N Summit St at Manhattan Blvd. **FREE**

Ottawa Park. Picnicking on 305 acres, concessions, playgrounds, 18-hole golf course (fee), tennis, jogging and nature trails, x-country ski trails (fee). Nature center; artificial skating rink (fee). Bancroft at Parkside St.

Toledo Botanical Garden. Seasonal floral displays; herb, rhododendron, and azalea gardens, perennial garden, rose garden, fragrance garden for the visually and physically impaired. 1837 Pioneer Homestead; art galleries, glassblowing studios. Gift shops. Special musical and craft programs throughout yr. Arts festival (fee). (Daily) 5403 Elmer Dr, 6 mi W near I-475 W Central exit. Phone 419/936-2986. **FREE**

Port of Toledo. In total tonnage, this is one of the 25 largest ports in the US and one of the world's largest shippers of soft coal and grain. More than 1,000 vessels call at the port each yr. Lower 7 mi of Maumee River. Phone 419/243-8251.

SS *Willis B. Boyer* Museum Ship. This 600-ft freighter, launched in 1911, has been authentically restored and houses memoribilia, photos, and nautical artifacts. Tours (45 min-one hr). (May-Sept, daily; rest of yr, Tues-Sat) Moored across from Downtown, on the E side of the Maumee River at 26 Main St, in International Park. Phone 419/936-3070.

The Toledo Museum of Art. Considered to be one of the finest art museums in the country; collections range from ancient Egypt, Greece, and Rome through the Middle Ages and the Renaissance to European and American arts of the present; incl glass collections, paintings, sculpture, decorative and graphic arts; Egyptian mummy, medieval cloister, French chateau rm, African sculpture, Asian art, and Southeast Asian and Native American art. Art reference library; cafe; museum store. (Tues-Sun; closed hols) 2445 Monroe St at Scottwood, 1 blk off I-75. Phone 419/255-8000. **FREE**

The Toledo Symphony. Presents classics, pops, casual, chamber, and all-Mozart concerts. Performances at different locations. (Mid-Sept-May) Facilities for hearing and visually impaired. 1838 Parkwood Ave #310. Phone 419/241-1272.

The Toledo Zoo. On exhibit are nearly 2,000 specimens of 400 species. On its 30 acres are fresh and saltwater aquariums, large mammal collection, reptiles, birds, a Children's Zoo, botanical gardens and greenhouse, Museum of Science and the Diversity of Life hands-on exhibit; "Hippoquarium," offering filtered underwater viewing of hippopotamus. (Daily; closed Jan 1, Thanksgiving, Dec 25) 2700 Broadway, 3 mi S of downtown on US 25. Phone 419/385-5721. ¢¢

University of Toledo. (1872) 21,000 students. The 250-acre main campus has eight colleges, continuing education division, graduate school; several other campuses; 47-acre arboretum, Sylvania Ave and Corey Rd; Downtown at Jefferson Ave at Seagate Centre. Lake Erie Center is an environmental research facility. Campus tours. Planetarium presents several shows and educational programs (Oct-June). Savage Hall has frequent concerts and sports events. Music and theater departments have concerts and shows. Obtain free parking permit at transportation center. W Bancroft St, 4 mi W. Phone 419/530-INFO.

Wolcott Museum Complex. Museum complex incl early 19-century home, log house, Greek Revival village house, saltbox farmhouse, and depot furnished with period artifacts. (Apr-Dec, Wed-Sun; closed hols) 1031 River Rd, SW via I-75, I-475 Anthony Wayne Tr exit in Maumee. Phone 419/893-9602. ¢¢

Special Events

Horse racing. Toledo Raceway Park. 5700 Telegraph Rd, 5 mi N on US 24 or 2 mi W of I-75, exit Alexis Rd. Harness racing. Phone 419/476-7751. Wed and Fri-Sun. Mar-late Nov.

Crosby Festival of the Arts. At Toledo Botanical Garden. Fine arts and crafts, music, dance, and drama. Phone 419/936-2986. Last full wkend June.

Northwest Ohio Rib-Off. Promenade Park. Restaurants compete in rib-cooking contest and offer samples and full slabs at nominal prices; bands, children's events, special events. First wkend Aug. Phone 419/321-6404.

Motels/Motor Lodges

★★ **CLARION HOTEL.** *3536 Secor Rd (43606). 419/535-7070; fax 419/536-4836; res 800/252-7466. www.clarionhotel.com.* 305 rms, 3 story. S, D $99-$119; suites $99-$395; under 18 free. Crib free. TV; cable. Indoor pool; whirlpool. Restaurant 6:30 am-2 pm, 5-9 pm; Sat from 7 am; Sun 8 am-2 pm. Rm serv. Bar. Ck-out noon. Convention facilities. Business center. In-rm modem link. Valet serv. Exercise equipt. Game rm. Landscaped enclosed courtyard. Cr cds: A, C, D, DS, MC, V.

[D] [≈] [🏋] [↘] [♿] [SC] [🚶]

★★ **COMFORT INN.** *3560 Secor Rd (43606). 419/531-2666; fax 419/531-4757; toll-free 800/228-5150. www.comfortinn.com.* 70 rms, 2 story. S, D $65-$79. Crib free. TV; cable (premium). Complimentary continental bkfst. Restaurant nearby. Ck-out noon. Health club privileges. Picnic tables. Cr cds: A, C, D, DS, MC, V.

[D] [↘] [🔥] [SC]

★★ **COURTYARD BY MARRIOTT.** *1435 E Mall Dr, Holland (43528). 419/866-1001; fax 419/866-9869; rse 800/321-2211. www.marriott.com.* 149 units, 3 story, 12 suites. S $99; D $105; suites $115-$134; under 18 free; wkend rates. Crib free. TV; cable (premium). Indoor pool; whirlpool. Restaurant 6:30-10 am; wkend hrs vary. Bar 4-11 pm, closed Sun. Ck-out noon. Coin lndry. Meeting rms. In-rm modem link. Valet serv. Sundries. Free airport transportation. Exercise equipt. Refrigerator in suites. Private patios, balconies. Cr cds: A, D, DS, MC, V.

[D] [≈] [↘] [🔥] [🏋]

★ **CROWN INN.** *1727 W Alexis Rd (43613). 419/473-1485; fax 419/473-0364.* 40 rms. S, D $48.99-$53.99; each addl $6; suites $90.99-$113.99; kits. $55.99-$60.99; under 15 free. Crib $6. Pet accepted. TV; cable, VCR avail. Pool. Complimentary continental bkfst. Restaurant nearby. Ck-out noon. Sundries. Some refrigerators. Cr cds: A, C, D, DS, MC, V.

`D` `🦮` `⌦` `⊠` `🔥` `SC`

★ **DAYS INN.** *150 Dussel Dr, Maumee (43537). 419/893-9960; fax 419/893-9559; toll-free 800/431-2574. www.daysinn.com.* 120 units, 2 story. S $45-$85; D $49-$85; each addl $6; suites, kit. units $47-$85; under 18 free; wkly rates. Crib free. Pet accepted. TV; cable (premium). Pool. Complimentary continental bkfst. Restaurant adj 6 am-11 pm. Ck-out noon. Business servs avail. Valet serv. Health club privileges. Game rm. Some refrigerators; microwaves avail. Cr cds: A, D, DS, MC, V.

`D` `🦮` `⌦` `⊠` `🔥`

★★ **HAMPTON INN TOLEDO SOUTH/MAUMEE.** *1409 Reynolds Rd, Maumee (43537). 419/893-1004; fax 419/893-4613; res 800/426-7866. www.hamptoninn.com.* 129 rms, 4 story. S $68-$85; D $68-$90; under 18 free. Crib free. TV; cable (premium), VCR avail. Heated pool. Complimentary continental bkfst. Coffee in rms. Restaurant adj open 24 hrs. Ck-out noon. Meeting rms. Valet serv. Sundries. Free airport transportation. Exercise equipt. Cr cds: A, C, D, DS, MC, V.

`D` `⌦` `✈` `⊠` `🔥` `SC`

★★ **HOLIDAY INN.** *2340 S Reynolds Rd (43614). 419/865-1361; fax 419/865-6177; toll-free 800/465-4329. www.holiday-inn.com.* 218 rms, 11 story. S, D $99; each addl $10; suites $109-$119; under 18 free; family, wkend rates. Crib free. TV; cable (premium). Indoor pool. Restaurant 6:30 am-2 pm, 5-10 pm; Sat, Sun from 7 am. Rm serv. Bar 4:30 pm-midnight, Sat from 4 pm, closed Sun. Ck-out noon. Meeting rms. Business servs avail. In-rm modem link. Bellhops. Gift shop. Beauty shop. Free airport transportation. Exercise equipt. Cr cds: A, C, D, DS, MC, V.

`D` `⊠` `🔥` `SC` `⌦` `✈`

★★ **QUALITY INN & CONFERENCE CENTER.** *2429 S Reynolds Rd (43614). 419/381-8765; fax 419/381-0129; res 800/228-5151. www.qualityinn.com.* 264 rms, 6 story. S, D $59-$89; each addl $8; under 18 free; wkend rates. Crib free. Pet accepted, some restrictions. TV; cable (premium), VCR avail. Indoor pool; whirlpool, poolside serv. Playground. Restaurant 6 am-2 pm, 5-10 pm. Rm serv. Bar 11-2:30 am, Sun to 11 pm. Ck-out noon. Convention facilities. In-rm modem link. Bellhops. Valet serv. Sundries. Gift shop. Free airport transportation. Microwaves avail. Cr cds: A, C, D, DS, MC, V.

`D` `⌦` `⊠` `🔥` `✈` `🦮`

Hotels

★★★ **HILTON.** *3100 Glendale Ave (43614). 419/381-6800; fax 419/389-9716; toll-free 800/445-8667. hilton.com.* 213 rms, 6 story. S $59-$129; D $69-$139; each addl $10; family rates. Crib free. TV; cable (premium). Indoor pool; whirlpool. Complimentary coffee in rm. Restaurant 6:30 am-2 pm, 5-10 pm; Fri, Sat to 11 pm, Sun to 9 pm. Bar 4 pm-midnight. Ck-out noon. Meeting rms. Business servs avail. In-rm modem link. Free airport transportation. Lighted tennis. Exercise equipt; sauna. Health club privileges. Refrigerators avail. Cr cds: A, C, D, DS, MC, V.

`D` `🏃` `⌦` `✈` `✈` `⊠` `🔥`

★★ **WYNDHAM TOLEDO HOTEL.** *2 Summit St (43604). 419/241-1411; fax 419/241-8161; res 800/996-3426. www.wyndham.com.* 241 rms, 14 story. S, D $139; suites $149; under 18 free; wkend rates. Crib free. Pet accepted. Garage parking $10, valet. TV; cable (premium), VCR avail. Indoor pool; whirlpool. Restaurant 6:30 am-11 pm; Sat from 7 am. Bar from 11 am; Sun from 1 pm. Ck-out noon. Meeting rms. Business center. In-rm modem link. Gift shop. Exercise equipt; sauna. Health club privileges. Game rm. On river. Cr cds: A, MC, V.

`D` `🦮` `⌦` `✈` `⊠` `🔥` `SC` `🏃`

Restaurants

★★★ **FIFI'S.** *1423 Bernath Pkwy (43615). 419/866-6777.* Hrs: 5-11 pm; wkends to midnight. Closed Sun; major hols. Res accepted. French, continental menu. Bar. Wine cellar. Dinner $16.95-$24.95. Specializes in seafood, veal, tableside cooking. Pianist Fri, Sat. Cr cds: A, D, DS, MC, V.

`D` `⊠`

★★ **MANCY'S.** *953 Phillips Ave (43612). 419/476-4154. www.mancys. com.* Hrs: 11 am-2 pm, 5-9:30 pm; Fri to 10:30 pm; Sat 5-10:30 pm. Closed Sun; major hols. Res accepted. Bar. Lunch $4.95-$11.95, dinner $10.95-$22.95. Child's menu. Specializes in steak, fresh seafood. Tiffany lamps, antiques. Family-owned since 1921. Cr cds: A, D, DS, MC, V.

D ⌐⌐

★ **TONY PACKO'S CAFE.** *1902 Front St (43605). 419/691-6054. www. tonypacko.com.* Hrs: 11 am-10 pm; Sun noon-9 pm. Closed major hols. Res accepted. Hungarian menu. Bar. Lunch $4-$8, dinner $6.50-$10. Child's menu. Specialties: chili, stuffed cabbage, Hungarian hot dogs. Jazz band Fri, Sat evenings; Big Band last Tues of month. Family-owned. Cr cds: A, D, DS, MC, V.

D ⌐⌐

Vandalia

(E-2) *See also Dayton, Springfield*

Settled 1838 **Pop** 13,882 **Elev** 994 ft
Area code 937 **Zip** 45377
Information Chamber of Commerce, 76 Fordway Dr, PO Box 224; 937/898-5351
Web www.vandaliabutlerchamber. com

What to See and Do

Trapshooting Hall of Fame and Museum. Exhibits depict highlights of this sport. (Mon-Fri; closed hols) 601 W National Rd. Phone 937/898-1945. **FREE**

Special Events

Air Show Parade. Kick-off event for international Air Show. Involves over 150 parade units. Third Fri July. Phone 937/898-5901.

US Air & Trade Show. Dayton International Airport. Features approximately 100 outdoor exhibits; flight teams. Phone 937/898-5901. Late July.

Grand American World Trapshooting Championship of the Amateur Trap-shooting Association of America. Trapshooting Hall of Fame Museum (see). Grand American Shoot; membership and shooting fee. Phone 937/898-4638. Ten days mid-Aug.

Motel/Motor Lodge

★ **CROSS COUNTRY INN- DAYTON.** *550 E National Rd (45377). 937/898-7636; fax 937/898-0630. www.crosscountryinns.com.* 94 rms, 3 story. S $45.99; D $56.99. Crib free. TV; cable (premium). Pool. Complimentary coffee in lobby. Restaurant adj 6 am-11 pm. Ck-out noon. Meeting rm. Business servs avail. Cr cds: A, C, D, DS, MC, V.

⌐⌐ ⌐⌐

Van Wert

(C-1) *See also Celina, Lima, Wapakoneta*

Founded 1835 **Pop** 10,891 **Elev** 780 ft
Area code 419 **Zip** 45891
Information Van Wert County Chamber of Commerce, 118 W Main St; 419/238-4390
Web www.vanwert.com

What to See and Do

Van Wert County Historical Society Museum. Restored Victorian mansion (1890) houses the farm rm, fabric rm, children's rm; early town artifacts; research center. Annex built in 1985 houses war memorabilia; country store, cobbler's shop, and barbershop. One-rm school building and caboose also on grounds. (Sun afternoons; also by appt; closed hols and last wk Dec) 602 N Washington St at 3rd St. Phone 419/238-5297. **FREE**

Special Events

Peony Festival & Parade. Downtown. First wkend June. Phone 419/238-4390.

Van Wert County Fair. Fairgrounds, Fox Rd off S Washington St. Begins Wed before Labor Day. Phone 419/238-9270.

Vermilion

(B-4) *See also Elyria, Lorain, Milan, Oberlin, Sandusky*

Settled 1808 **Pop** 11,127 **Elev** 600 ft
Area code 440 **Zip** 44089
Information Chamber of Commerce, 5495 Liberty Ave; 440/967-4477
Web www.vermilionohio.com

What to See and Do

Inland Seas Maritime Museum. Maritime museum containing Great Lakes ship models, paintings, photographs, artifacts. Audiovisual displays. (Daily; closed Dec 25) 480 Main St (US 6), on lakeshore. Phone 440/967-3467. ¢¢

Special Events

Festival of the Fish. Entertainment, exhibits, sports events, parade, contests, crazy craft race, lighted boat parade. Father's Day wkend. Phone 440/967-4477.

Woolly Bear Festival. Races, children's games, crafts, entertainment. Phone 440/967-4477. Mid-Oct.

Restaurant

★ ★ ★ **CHEZ FRANCOIS.** *555 Main St (44089).* 440/967-0630. *www.chezfrancois.com.* Hrs: 5-9 pm; Fri, Sat to 10 pm; Sun 4-8 pm. Closed Mon; also Jan-mid-Mar. Res accepted. French menu. Wine list. Dinner $14.95-$28.95. Specialties: beef Wellington, lobster Thermadore. Outdoor dining. Overlooks Vermilion River. Jacket. Cr cds: A, V.

Wapakoneta

(C-2) *See also Bellefontaine, Celina, Lima*

Pop 9,214 **Elev** 895 ft **Area code** 419
Zip 45895
Information Wapakoneta Chamber of Commerce, 16 E Auglaize St, PO Box 208; 419/738-2911
Web www.wapakoneta.com

What to See and Do

Neil Armstrong Museum. A few aircraft, from early planes to spacecraft, showing aerospace accomplishments; audiovisual presentation, other exhibits. (Daily) 500 S Apollo Dr. Phone 419/738-8811. ¢¢

Motels/Motor Lodges

★ ★ **BEST WESTERN.** *1510 Saturn Dr (45895).* 419/738-8181; fax 419/738-6478; toll-free 877/738-8181. *www.bestwestern.com/wapakoneta.* 94 rms, 4 story. S, D $65; each addl $5; suites $75; under 18 free. Crib free. Pet accepted. TV; cable (premium), VCR avail. Pool. Complimentary continental bkfst. Complimentary coffee in rms. Restaurant 6 am-9 pm; Sat from 7 am; Sun 7 am-8 pm. Rm serv. Bar 11-1 am; Sat 5 pm-1 am. Ck-out noon. Coin lndry. Meeting rms. Business servs avail. In-rm modem link. Valet serv. Sundries. Exercise equipt. Neil Armstrong Museum adj. Cr cds: A, C, D, DS, MC, V.

🄳 🐾 ⊯ 🏌

★ **BUDGET HOST INN.** *505 E State St, Botkins (45306).* 937/693-6911; fax 937/693-8200; toll-free 800/283-4678. *www.budgethostinn.com.* 50 rms. S $32-$49; D $35-$65; each addl $3; kit. units $35-$65; under 12 free; wkly rates. Crib $6. TV; cable (premium). Complimentary continental bkfst. Restaurant 5-10 pm. Bar 5 pm-2:30 am. Ck-out 11 am. Meeting rms. Business servs avail. Coin lndry. Tennis. Pool. Cr cds: DS, MC, V.

🏊 🖎 🐾 🆂🅲 ⊯

Warren

(B-7) *See also Aurora, Kent, Youngstown*

Founded 1799 **Pop** 50,793 **Elev** 893 ft
Area code 330
Information Youngstown/Warren Regional Chamber, 160 E Market, Suite 225, 44481; 330/393-2565
Web www.regionalchamber.com

In 1800 Warren became the seat of the Western Reserve and then the seat of newly formed Trumbull County. At one of its stagecoach inns, the Austin House, Stephen Collins Foster is said to have begun writing "Jeannie with the Light Brown Hair," and, according to local history, while walking along the Mahoning River he found the inspiration for "My Old Kentucky Home."

What to See and Do

John Stark Edwards House. (1807) Oldest house in the Western Reserve, now maintained by Trumbull County Historical Society. (Sun afternoons, limited hrs; closed hols) Children must be accompanied by adult. 303 Monroe St NW. Phone 330/394-4653. ¢

Mosquito Lake State Park. A 11,811-acre park with 7,850-acre lake and 40 miles of lakeshore. Swimming, fishing, boating (launch, rentals); hunting, hiking, bridle trails, picnicking, snowmobiling, camping (showers; 218 sites with electric hookup). Standard fees. (Daily) 7 mi NE on OH 5, then 1 mi W on OH 305 to park entrance. Phone 330/637-2856. **FREE**

Motels/Motor Lodges

★ ★ ★ **AVALON INN & RESORT.** *9519 E Market St (44484). 330/856-1900; fax 330/856-2248; toll-free 800/828-2566. www.avaloninn.com.* 144 rms, 2 story. S $79; D $89-$95; each addl $10; suites $95-$150; under 16 free. Crib free. TV. Indoor pool; whirlpool, lifeguard. Restaurant 6:30 am-10 pm; Fri, Sat to 11 pm. Snack bar. Rm serv. Bar 10:30-2:30 am. Ck-out noon. Meeting rms. Bellhops. Indoor, outdoor lighted tennis. Two 18-hole golf courses, greens fee $27-$45, pro, putting green, driving range. Exercise equipt; saunas. Lawn games. Many refrigerators. Some patios. Cr cds: A, C, D, DS, MC, V.

★ ★ **BEST WESTERN.** *777 Mahoning Ave NW (44483). 330/392-2515; fax 330/392-7099; res 800/780-7234. www.bestwestern.com/downtown motorinn.* 73 rms, 2 story. S $51-$68; D $56-$70; each addl $3; under 16 free. Pet accepted. TV; cable (premium). Pool. Complimentary continental bkfst. Restaurant 3-11 pm. Bar to 2 am. Ck-out 11 am. Business servs avail. Valet serv. Health club

privileges. Some refrigerators. Cr cds: A, C, D, DS, MC, V.

Hotel

★ ★ **PARK HOTEL.** *136 N Park Ave (44483). 330/393-1200; fax 330/399-2875.* 55 rms, 4 story. 11 suites. S $60; D $70; each addl $10; suites $77; under 16 free. Crib free. Pet accepted. TV. Restaurant 6:30 am-10 pm. Bars. Ck-out noon. Meeting rms. Business servs avail. Airport transportation. Health club privileges. Restored brick hotel (1887). Cr cds: A, D, DS, MC, V.

Restaurant

★ ★ **ABRUZZI'S CAFE 422.** *4422 SE Youngstown Rd (44484). 330/369-2422. www.cafe422.com.* Hrs: 11 am-10 pm; Fri, Sat to 11 pm; Sun to 9 pm. Closed Dec 25. Res accepted. Bar. Lunch $5.50-$6.95, dinner $8.75-$20. Child's menu. Specializes in homemade Italian entrees, desserts. Family-owned. Cr cds: A, D, DS, MC, V.

Wauseon

(B-2) *See also Bowling Green, Toledo*

Pop 6,322 **Elev** 757 ft **Area code** 419 **Zip** 43567

Information Wauseon Chamber of Commerce, 115 N Fulton St, PO Box 217; 419/335-9966

Web www.wauseonchamber.com

What to See and Do

Sauder Farm & Craft Village. Three areas: farmstead has furnished turn-of-the-century farmhouse with summer kitchen and barnyard; pioneer village has craft demonstrations; museum building has antique implements and household items; costumed guides. Restaurant, lodging. Campground. (Late Apr-Oct, daily) 9 mi W via OH 2, near Archbold. Phone 419/446-2541. ¢¢¢

Motel/Motor Lodge

★★ **BEST WESTERN DEL MAR.**
8319 OH 108 (43567). 419/335-1565; fax 419/335-1828; toll-free 800/647-2260. www.bestwestern.com. 48 rms. June-Sept: S $60-$79; D $64-$84; each addl $10; suites $99-$139; under 18 free; lower rates rest of yr. Crib $6. Pet accepted. TV; cable (premium). Heated pool. Playground. Complimentary continental bkfst. Coffee in rms. Restaurant nearby. Ck-out 11 am. Refrigerators. Cr cds: A, C, D, DS, MC, V.

⌨ ⬛ ⬛ ⬛ SC ⬛

Wilmington

(E-2) *See also Dayton, Lebanon, Mason*

Pop 11,199 **Elev** 1,022 ft
Area code 937 **Zip** 45177
Information Wilmington-Clinton County Chamber of Commerce, 40 N South St; 937/382-2737
Web www.wcchamber.com

What to See and Do

Caesar Creek State Park. A 10,771-acre park. Crystal-blue lake waters have smallmouth and largemouth bass, crappie, catfish, bluegill and walleye. Swimming, fishing, boating (ramps); hiking, bridle trails, picnic areas. Campground has 287 sites (35 open in winter), 30-site horsemen's camp. Nature preserve, visitor center, and complex near dam. A focal point of the park is Pioneer Village with many restored examples of early log architecture. (Daily) 11 mi NW on OH 73. Phone 937/897-3055. **FREE**

Cowan Lake State Park. A 1,775-acre park with swimming, fishing, boating (launch, rentals) on 700-acre lake; hiking, picnicking, concession, camping, cabins. Standard fees. (Daily) 6 mi S via US 68, then W on OH 350. Phone 937/289-2105. **FREE**

Fort Ancient State Memorial. (see). 11 mi SW on US 22, then 5 mi W on OH 350.

Little Miami Scenic State Park. This 452-acre park offers 45 mi of hiking and bridle trails, 22 mi of paved bicycle trails. Canoeing, access points at Corwin, Morrow, and Loveland.

(Daily) 15 mi NW on OH 73. Phone 937/897-3055. **FREE**

Rombach Place—Museum of Clinton County Historical Society. Home of General James W. Denver, for whom Denver, CO, was named. Antique furniture, Quaker clothing, tools, implements, and kitchenware of pioneer days. Bronze animal sculptures and paintings by Eli Harvey, Quaker artist from Ohio. Photographs of Native American chieftains made in early 1900s by Karl Moon, a native of Wilmington. (Mar-Dec, Wed-Fri afternoons; closed hols) 149 E Locust St. Phone 937/382-4684.

Wilmington College. (1870) 1,000 students. Liberal arts school. On campus is the Simon Goodman Memorial Carillon. Campus tours. E on US 22. Phone 937/382-6661.

Special Event

Banana Split Festival. Commemorates the invention of the banana split. Second wkend June. Phone 937/382-1965.

Motels/Motor Lodges

★★ **AMERIHOST INN WILMINGTON.** *201 Carrie Dr (45177). 937/383-3950; fax 937/383-1693. www.amerihostinn.com.* 61 rms, 2 story. S $81; D $81-$89; each addl $5; suites $120-$145; under 18 free. Crib free. TV; cable (premium). Complimentary continental bkfst. Coffee in rms. Restaurant nearby. Ck-out noon. Meeting rms. Business servs avail. In-rm modem link. Valet serv (Mon-Fri). Exercise equipt; sauna. Indoor pool; whirlpool. In-rm whirlpool, refrigerator, microwave in suites. Cr cds: A, C, D, DS, MC, V.

⌨ ⬛ 🎿 ⬛ ⬛

★★ **HOLIDAY INN EXPRESS.** *155 Holiday Dr (45177). 937/382-5858; fax 937/382-0457; res 800/465-4329. www.holiday-inn.com.* 75 rms, 3 story, 12 suites. S, D $69-$75; suites $79-$89; under 18 free. Crib avail. Pet accepted. TV; cable (premium). Complimentary continental bkfst. Restaurant nearby. Ck-out noon. Meeting rms. Business servs avail. In-rm modem link. Valet serv (Mon-Fri). Coin lndry. Exercise equipt. Indoor pool; whirlpool. Some in-rm whirlpools, refrigerators, microwaves. Cr cds: A, C, D, DS, MC, V.

★ **WILMINGTON INN.** *909 Fife Ave (45177). 937/382-6000; fax 937/382-6655; toll-free 877/363-3614. www. wilmingtoninn.com.* 51 rms, 2 story. S $60-$125; D $65-$135; each addl $10; under 16 free. Crib $5. TV; cable (premium). Complimentary continental bkfst. Complimentary coffee in rms. Restaurant adj 6 am-10 pm. Ck-out 11 am. Meeting rms. Business servs avail. Cr cds: A, C, D, DS, MC, V.

Restaurant

★ **DAMON'S.** *1045 Eastside Dr (45177). 937/383-1400.* Hrs: 11 am-11 pm; Fri, Sat to midnight; Sun to 10 pm. Closed Thanksgiving, Dec 25. Res accepted. Bar. Lunch $5-$6, dinner $10-$13. Child's menu. Specializes in ribs, steak, seafood. Contemporary sports bar atmosphere. Cr cds: A, MC, V.

Wooster

(C-5) *See also Akron, Canton, Mansfield, Massillon*

Settled 1807 **Pop** 22,191 **Elev** 897 ft
Area code 330 **Zip** 44691
Information Wayne County Convention & Visitor Bureau, 428 W Liberty St; 330/264-1800 or 800/362-6474
Web www.wooster-wayne.com/wccvb

Wooster claims to have had one of the first Christmas trees in America, introduced in 1847 by August Imgard, a young German immigrant. Disappointed with American Christmas, he cut down and decorated a spruce tree, which so pleased his neighbors that the custom spread throughout Ohio and the nation.

The town is in very productive farm country with wheat, corn, potatoes, and many dairy farms. It also produces brass, paper, aluminum, roller bearings, brushes, rubber products, furniture, and other products.

What to See and Do

College of Wooster. (1866) 1,865 students. Liberal arts, sciences. Campus tours; art museum. Home of **Ohio Light Opera Company**, performing Gilbert & Sullivan and light opera classics with orchestra. (Mid-June-mid-Aug) E University St and Beall Ave, 1 mi N. Phone 330/263-2000.

Ohio Agricultural Research and Development Center. (1882) Research on livestock, fruits, vegetables, ornamentals, field crops, environmental and energy conservation, pesticides; greenhouses, orchards, Secrest Arboretum, rhododendron and rose gardens. (Mon-Fri; closed hols; grounds open daily, tours by appt) Ohio State University. 1 mi S on Madison Ave. Phone 330/263-3779. **FREE**

Wayne County Historical Society Museum. Pioneer relics, paintings, lusterware, Native American artifacts, mounted animals and birds; log cabin and country schoolhouse on grounds. Kister Building has carriage house, blacksmith and carpenter shops. (Tues-Sun, also by appt; closed hols) 546 E Bowman St. Phone 330/264-8856. ¢¢

Special Event

Wayne County Fair. Fairgrounds. W on US 30A. Five days, beginning wkend after Labor Day. Phone 330/262-8001.

Motels/Motor Lodges

★ ★ **BEST WESTERN INN.** *243 E Liberty St (44691). 330/264-7750; fax 330/262-5840; res 800/780-7234. www.bestwestern.com.* 100 rms, 3 story. S, D $62-$75; each addl $6; suites $100-$125; under 18 free. TV; cable (premium), VCR (movies). Pool. Restaurant 6 am-2 pm, 5-10 pm; Sun 7 am-2 pm, 5-9 pm. Rm serv. Bar 11-2 am. Ck-out noon. Meeting rms. Business servs avail. Valet serv. Beauty shop. Exercise equipt. Health club privileges. Cr cds: A, C, D, DS, MC, V.

★ **ECONO LODGE.** *2137 Lincoln Way E (44691). 330/264-8883; fax 330/263-0792; toll-free 800/553-2666. www.econolodge.com.* 98 rms, 2 story. S $54-$64; D $59-$69; each addl $4; under 18 free. Crib free. Pet accepted. TV; cable. Indoor pool; whirlpool. Continental bkfst. Complimentary coffee in lobby. Restaurant adj open 24 hrs. Ck-out 11 am. Coin lndry. Meeting rm. Business center. Sundries. Airport transportation. Picnic tables. Cr cds: A, D, DS, MC, V.

[icons]

B&Bs/Small Inns

★★ **INN AT HONEY RUN.** *6920 County Rd 203, Millersburg (44654). 330/674-0011; fax 330/674-2623; toll-free 800/468-6639. www.innat honeyrun.com.* 39 rms, 2-3 story. S, D $75-$280; each addl $15. Crib free. TV/VCR in rms. Hiking; shuffleboard. In-rm modem link. Ck-in 4:30 pm, Ck-out noon. Cr cds: A, DS, MC, V.

[icons]

★★★ **WOOSTER INN.** *801 E Wayne Ave (44691). 330/263-2660; fax 330/263-2661.* 16 rms, 2 story. S $85; D $100; each addl $15; suite $100-$135; 3-12 yrs, $5. Closed early Jan, Dec 25, 26. Crib free. Pet accepted, some restrictions. TV; cable. Restaurant (see also WOOSTER INN). Ck-out noon. Meeting rms. Business servs avail. Tennis privileges. 9-hole golf, greens fee $8-$9, putting green, driving range. Colonial decor. Owned and operated by College of Wooster; on campus. Cr cds: A, C, D, DS, MC, V.

[icons]

Restaurants

★★ **TJ'S.** *359 W Liberty St (44691). 330/264-6263.* Hrs: 11 am-10 pm; Fri to 10 pm; Sat 4:30-10 pm; early-bird dinner 4:30-6 pm. Closed Sun; major hols. Res accepted. Lunch $4.15-$7.50, dinner $6.95-$18.95. Child's menu. Specializes in prime rib, fresh seafood, cheesecake. Family-owned. Cr cds: A, D, DS, MC, V.

[icons]

★★★ **WOOSTER INN.** *801 E Wayne Ave (44691). 330/263-2660.*

www.wooster.edu. Hrs: 7 am-2 pm, 6-8:30 pm; Sun 7-11 am, 11:30 am-7 pm. Closed Jan 2-9, Dec 25, 26. Res accepted. Wine list. Bkfst $3-$8, lunch $6.50-$16, dinner $10-$21. Specializes in fresh seafood, local produce. Own baking. Totally nonsmoking. Cr cds: A, D, DS, MC, V.

[icons]

Youngstown

(B-7) *See also Warren*

Settled 1797 **Pop** 95,732 **Elev** 861 ft **Area code** 330
Information Youngstown/Mahoning County Convention & Visitors Bureau, 100 Federal Plaza E, Suite 101, 44503; 330/747-8200 or 800/447-8201
Web www.youngstowncvb.com

Youngstown, five miles from the Pennsylvania line, covers an area of 35 square miles in the eastern coal province, which has nine-tenths of the country's high-grade coal. It is the seat of Mahoning County.

Youngstown's steel history started in 1803 with a crude iron smelter; the first coal mine began operating in the valley in 1826; in 1892 the first valley steel plant opened, Union Iron and Steel Company. Youngstown industry has become more diversified in recent years, with products such as rubber goods, electric light bulbs, aluminum and paper goods, office equipment, clothes, rolling-mill equipment, vans, automobiles and parts, paint, electronic equipment, and plastics.

What to See and Do

The Arms Family Museum of Local History. Major arts and crafts house with original furnishings; local historical items; B. F. Wirt Collection of paintings, books and antiques; period costumes; pioneer and Native American artifacts. Guided tours. (Tues-Sun afternoons; closed hols) 648 Wick Ave. Phone 330/743-2589. ¢¢

The Butler Institute of American Art. Specializes in American art; collections incl works on Native Americans, clipper ships; antique glass bells. (Tues-Sun; closed hols) 524 Wick Ave. **FREE**

Mill Creek Park. Park has more than 3,200 acres of gorges, ravines, and rolling hills from the Mahoning River to S of US 224. A Western Reserve pioneer woolen mill (1821) is now the Pioneer Pavilion used for picnics and dancing. Lanternman's Mill (ca 1846), a working gristmill; tours. (May-Oct, Tues-Sun; Apr and Nov, wkends) Phone 330/740-7115. The Fellows Riverside Gardens has six acres of formal gardens incl rose, chrysanthemum, lily, tulip, and annual flower displays. Area incl Garden Center and a large stone terrace overlooking the city. The James L. Wick, Jr., Recreation Area has lighted tennis, horseshoe courts, and par-three golf course; supervised playground, ball diamonds, volleyball court, picnic facilities, ice-skating, and shelter house; on Old Furnace Rd is Ford Nature Education Center (daily; closed Jan 1, Thanksgiving, Dec 25; phone 330/740-7107). Walter Scholl Recreation Area and Volney Rogers Field have supervised playgrounds, picnic facilities, softball diamonds, tennis courts, shelter house. Two of the lakes provide fishing (May-Nov). Boat rides and rentals avail at Newport and Glacier lakes. Park (daily); facilities (in season, fees for some). Located in the SW part of city, bounded by Mahoning Ave, US 224, Lockwood, and Mill Creek Blvd. Phone 330/702-3000.

Stambaugh Auditorium. Seats 2,800. Local events, concerts, and Monday Musical Club. 1000 5th Ave. Phone 330/747-5175.

Youngstown Historical Center of Industry & Labor. Chronicles the rise and fall of the steel industry in Youngstown and its region; exhibit combines artifacts, videotaped interviews with steelworkers and executives, and full scale re-creation of the places the steelworkers lived and labored. (Wed-Sat, also Sun afternoon; closed Jan 1, Thanksgiving, Dec 25) 151 W Wood St. Phone 330/743-5934. ¢¢

Youngstown Playhouse. (Sept-June, wkends; addl summer productions)

Off 2000 blk of Glenwood Ave, 1½ mi S of I-680. Phone 330/788-8739.

Youngstown State University. (1908) 12,500 students. Planetarium on campus (by res only, phone 330/742-3616); also here is McDonough Museum of Art (phone 330/742-1400). Campus tours. 1 University Plaza. Phone 330/742-3000.

Youngstown Symphony Center. Seats 2,303. Presents concerts, symphony, ballet, and other cultural events. 260 Federal Plaza W. Phone 330/744-4269.

Motels/Motor Lodges

★★ **BEST WESTERN INN.** *870 N Canfield Niles Rd (44515). 330/544-2378; fax 330/544-7926; toll-free 800/780-7234. www.bestwestern.com.* 57 rms, 2 story. S $54-$69; D $68-$79; each addl $4; suites $85-$95; under 18 free. Crib free. Pet accepted. TV; cable. Pool. Complimentary continental bkfst. Restaurant 3-10 pm. Rm serv. Bar. Ck-out noon. Coin lndry. Meeting rm. Health club privileges. Cr cds: A, C, D, DS, MC, V.
🄳 🐾 ≈ 🏊 🔥 **SC**

★★ **COMFORT INN.** *4055 Belmont Ave (44505). 330/759-3180; fax 330/759-7713; res 800/228-5150. www.comfortinn.com.* 144 rms, 6 story. S $69; D $82; suites $125-$150; each addl $10; under 18 free. Crib free. TV; cable. Indoor pool. Complimentary continental bkfst. Restaurant 11:30 am-11 pm. Rm serv. Bar from 5 pm. Ck-out noon. Meeting rms. Business servs avail. In-rm modem link. Free airport transportation. Game rm. Some refrigerators. Private balconies. Cr cds: A, C, D, DS, MC, V.
🄳 ≈ 🏊 🔥

★ **MOTEL 6.** *5431 76 Dr, Austintown (44515). 330/793-9305; fax 330/793-2584; res 800/466-8356. www.motel6.com.* 79 rms, 10 kit. units. S $49.99; D $54.99; each addl $6; kit. units $49.95; under 18 free. Crib free. Pet accepted. TV; cable. Pool. Ck-out 11 am. Cr cds: A, C, D, DS, MC, V.
🄳 🐾 ≈ 🏊 🔥

Restaurant

★ ★ ★ **ALBERINI'S.** *1201 Youngstown-Warren Rd, Niles (44446). 330/652-5895.* Hrs: 11:30 am-11 pm. Closed Sun; most major hols. Res accepted. Italian menu. Bar. Wine cellar. Lunch $7-$10, dinner $13-$25. Child's menu. Specializes in classic and nouvelle Italian cuisine, fresh seafood. Formal dining. Oil murals. Family-owned. Cr cds: A, C, D, DS, MC, V.
D ⬛

Zanesville

(D-5) *See also Cambridge, Coshocton, Newark*

Settled 1797 **Pop** 26,778 **Elev** 705 ft
Area code 740 **Zip** 43701
Information Visitors and Convention Bureau, 205 N 5th St; 740/455-8282 or 800/743-2303
Web www.zanesville-ohio.com

Ebenezer Zane, surveyor of Zane's Trace through the dense Ohio forests and great-great-grandfather of Zane Grey, writer of Western novels, selected the Zanesville site because the valley was at the junction of the Muskingum and Licking rivers. First called Westbourne, it was the state capital from 1810-1812.

Today beautiful pottery is made here, as well as transformers, electrical steel sheets, and automobile components. The "Y" Bridge, which a person can cross and still remain on the same side of the river from which he started, divides the city into three parts.

What to See and Do

Blue Rock State Park. A 350-acre park with swimming, fishing, boating (launch, electric motors only); hiking, trails, picnicking, concession, camping. Standard fees. (Daily) 12 mi SE off OH 60, adj Blue Rock State Forest. Phone 740/674-4794. **FREE**

Dillon State Park. A 7,690-acre park with swimming, boating (ramps, rentals); picnicking (shelter), concession, camping, cabins (by res).

(Daily) 8 mi NW on OH 146. Phone 740/453-4377. **FREE**

⭐ **National Road-Zane Grey Museum.** A 136-ft diorama traces history of Old National Rd (Cumberland, MD, to Vandalia, IL); display of vehicles that once traveled the road; Zane Grey memorabilia, reconstructed craft shops, antique art pottery exhibit. (Mar-Apr and Oct-Nov, Wed-Sun; May-Sept, daily) On US 22/40, 10 mi E via I-70 exit 164, near Norwich. Phone 740/872-3143. ¢¢

Ohio Ceramic Center. Extensive displays of pottery housed in five buildings. Exhibits incl primitive stoneware; also area pottery. (Daily) Demonstrations of pottery making during pottery festival (wkend in mid-July). On OH 93, 12 mi S via US 22, near Roseville. Phone 740/697-7021. ¢

Robinson-Ransbottom Pottery Company. A 15-20-min self-guided tour of pottery factory; inquire for hrs. (Mon-Fri; closed hols) 12 mi S via US 22, OH 93, in Roseville. Phone 740/697-7355. **FREE**

Sternwheeler *The Lorena*. Named for the Civil War love song. One-hr trips on the Muskingum River. (May-Sept) Phone 740/455-8883.

The Wilds. A 9,154-acre conservation center dedicated to increasing the population of endangered species. (May-Oct, daily) 14000 International Rd, Cumberland, OH 43732. Phone 740/638-5030. ¢¢¢

Zane Grey Birthplace. The author's first story was written here. (Private residence) 705 Convers Ave.

Zanesville Art Center. American, European, and Asian art; children's art; early midwestern glass and ceramics; photographs; special programs; gallery tours. (Tues-Sun; closed hols) 620 Military Rd, 2 mi N on OH 60. Phone 740/452-0741. **FREE**

Special Events

Zane's Trace Commemoration. Commemorates Pioneer Heritage. Fine arts, crafts, parades, flea market. Three days mid-June.

Pottery Lovers Celebration. A wk of activities featuring collectible antiques and art pottery. Mid-July. Phone 740/697-0075.

Muskingum County Fair. Mid-Aug. Phone 740/872-3912.

Motels/Motor Lodges

★★ **AMERIHOST INN.** *230 Scenic Crest Dr (43701). 740/454-9332; fax 740/454-9342; res 800/434-5800. www.amerihostinn.com.* 60 rms, 2 story. June-Oct: S, D $71-$86; each addl $5; suites $110-$169; under 18 free; higher rates special events; lower rates rest of yr. Crib free. TV; cable (premium). Complimentary continental bkfst. Complimentary coffee in rms. Restaurant adj 6 am-10 pm. Ck-out noon. Meeting rms. Business servs avail. In-rm modem link. Exercise equipt; sauna. Indoor pool; whirlpool. In-rm whirlpool, refrigerator, microwave in suites. Cr cds: A, D, DS, MC, V.

D ⌖ ⌖ ⌖ ⌖

★★ **COMFORT INN.** *500 Monroe St (43701). 740/454-4144; res 800/228-5150. www.comfortinn.com.* 81 rms, 2 story. June-Aug: S, D $89-$154; under 18 free; lower rates rest of yr. Crib free. Pet accepted. TV; VCR avail (movies). Indoor pool; whirlpool. Complimentary continental bkfst. Restaurant adj 6 am-11 pm. Ck-out noon. Business servs avail. Coin lndry. Meeting rms. Valet serv. Exercise equipt; sauna. Cr cds: A, MC, V.

D ⌖ ⌖ ⌖ SC ⌖ ⌖

★ **DAYS INN.** *4925 East Pike (43701). 740/453-3400; fax 740/453-9715; toll-free 800/329-7466. www.daysinn.com.* 60 rms, 2 story. June-Sept: S, D $51-$100; under 12 free; lower rates rest of yr. Crib free. TV; cable (premium). Indoor pool. Complimentary continental bkfst. Restaurant nearby. Ck-out noon. Cr cds: A, C, D, DS, MC, V.

⌖ ⌖ ⌖ SC

★★ **FAIRFIELD INN.** *725 Zane St (43701). 740/453-8770; res 800/228-2800. www.fairfieldinn.com.* 63 rms, 3 story. June-Oct: S, D $75-$120; each addl $5; under 18 free; higher rates special events; lower rates rest of yr. Crib free. TV; cable (premium). Indoor pool. Complimentary continental bkfst. Restaurant nearby. Ck-out noon. Business servs avail. Valet serv. Health club privileges. Some refrigerators. Cr cds: A, D, DS, MC, V.

D ⌖ ⌖ ⌖ ⌖

★★ **HOLIDAY INN.** *4645 East Pike (43701). 740/453-0771; res 800/465-4329. www.holiday-inn.com.* 130 rms, 2 story. S, D $69-$109; each addl $5; under 19 free. Crib free. Pet accepted. TV; cable (premium). Indoor pool; whirlpool, poolside serv. Playground. Complimentary coffee in rms. Restaurant 6 am-2 pm, 5-9 pm; Sat, Sun 6:30 am-10 pm. Rm serv. Bars 2 pm-midnight. Ck-out noon. Coin lndry. Meeting rms. Business servs avail. In-rm modem link. Bellhops. Sundries. Exercise equipt; sauna. Refrigerators, microwaves avail. Cr cds: A, MC, V.

D ⌖ ⌖ ⌖ ⌖ ⌖ SC

Restaurants

★★ **MARIA ADORNETTO.** *953 Market St (43702). 740/453-0643.* Hrs: 11 am-10 pm, Fri to 11 pm; Sat 4-11 pm; early-bird dinner 4-6:30 pm. Closed Sun; major hols. Res accepted. Italian menu. Bar. A la carte entrees: lunch $5.50-$9.50, dinner $8.50-$18.95. Specializes in pasta, seafood, Italian dishes. Contemporary dining rm in converted home. Family-owned since 1937. Cr cds: A, D, DS, MC, V.

D SC ⌖

★★ **OLD MARKET HOUSE INN.** *424 Market St (43701). 740/454-2555. www.oldmarkethouseinn.com.* Hrs: 5-10 pm; Fri and Sat to 11 pm. Closed Sun; major hols. Italian, Amer menu. Bar. Dinner $7.50-$18.50. Specializes in shrimp, fresh fish, pasta. Old English decor. Cr cds: A, C, D, DS, MC, V.

D ⌖

WISCONSIN

Virgin forests blotted out the sky over Wisconsin when the first French voyageurs arrived more than three centuries ago. Rich in natural resources, modern conservation concepts took strong root here; Wisconsin's 15,000 lakes and 2,200 streams are teeming with fish, and millions of acres of its publicly owned forest are abundant with game.

People of many heritages have contributed to the state's colorful past, busy industries, and productive farms. Wisconsin is famous for the breweries of Milwaukee, great universities, forests, paper mills, dairy products, and diverse vacation attractions.

Wisconsin is the birthplace of the statewide primary election law, workmen's compensation law, unemployment compensation, and many other reforms that have since been widely adopted. It produced Senator Robert M. La Follette, one of the 20th century's foremost progressives, and many other honored citizens.

Population: 4,891,769
Area: 54,424 square miles
Elevation: 581-1,951 feet
Peak: Timms Hill (Price County)
Entered Union: May 29, 1848
(30th state)
Capital: Madison
Motto: Forward
Nickname: Badger State
Flower: Wood Violet
Bird: Robin
Tree: Sugar Maple
Fair: August, 2003, in Milwaukee
Time Zone: Central
Web Site:
www.tourism.state.wi.us

The Badger State acquired its nickname during the lead rush of 1827, when miners built their homes by digging into the hillsides like badgers. It is "America's dairyland," producing much of the nation's milk and over 30 percent of all cheese consumed in the United States. It is a leader in the production of hay, cranberries, and ginseng, and harvests huge crops of peas, beans, carrots, corn, and oats. It is the leading canner of fresh vegetables and an important source of cherries, apples, maple syrup, and wood pulp. A great part of the nation's paper products, agricultural implements, and nonferrous metal products and alloys are manufactured here.

The Wisconsin summer is balmy, and the winter offers an abundance of activities, making the state a year-round vacationland that lures millions of visitors annually. They find a land of many contrasts: rounded hills and narrow valleys to the southwest, a huge central plain, rolling prairie in the southeast, and the north, majestic with forests, marshes, and lakes.

Native Americans called this land *Ouisconsin* ("where the waters gather"). French explorer Jean Nicolet, seeking the Northwest Passage to the Orient, landed near Green Bay in 1634 and greeted what he thought were Asians. These Winnebago made a treaty of alliance with the French, and for the next 125 years a brisk trade in furs developed. The British won Wisconsin from the French in 1760 and lost it to the United States after the American Revolution.

Shortly before Wisconsin became a state it was a battleground in the Black Hawk War. After the campaign, word spread of the state's beauty and fertile land in the East, and opened the doors to a flood of settlers.

The rich lead mines brought another wave of settlers, and the forests attracted lumbermen—both groups remained to till the soil or work in the factories.

Diversified industry, enhanced recreational facilities, the trade opportunities opened by the St. Lawrence Seaway, and enlightened agricultural techniques promise continuing prosperity for Wisconsin.

When to Go/Climate

Cool forests and lake breezes make northern Wisconsin summers pleasant and comfortable, while the southern farmland is often hot. Temperatures from northern to southern Wisconsin can vary as much as 20°F. Winters are often snowy and harsh statewide. Fall is the best time to visit, with brilliant foliage, harvests, and festivals.

AVERAGE HIGH/LOW TEMPERATURES (°F)

GREEN BAY

Jan 23/6	**May** 67/44	**Sept** 69/49
Feb 27/10	**June** 76/54	**Oct** 57/39
Mar 39/21	**July** 81/59	**Nov** 42/27
Apr 54/34	**Aug** 78/57	**Dec** 28/13

MILWAUKEE

Jan 26/12	**May** 64/45	**Sept** 71/53
Feb 30/16	**June** 75/55	**Oct** 59/42
Mar 40/26	**July** 80/62	**Nov** 45/31
Apr 53/36	**Aug** 78/61	**Dec** 31/18

Parks and Recreation Finder

Directions to and information about the parks and recreation areas below are given under their respective town/city sections. Please refer to those sections for details.

NATIONAL PARK AND RECREATION AREAS

Key to abbreviations. I.H.S. = International Historic Site; I.P.M. = International Peace Memorial; N.B. = National Battlefield; N.B.P. = National Battlefield Park; N.B.C. = National Battlefield and Cemetery; N.C.A. = National Conservation Area; N.E.M. = National Expansion Memorial; N.F. = National Forest; N.G. = National Grassland; N.H.P. = National Historical Park; N.H.C. = National Heritage Corridor; N.H.S. = National Historic Site; N.L. = National Lakeshore; N.M. = National Monument; N.M.P. = National Military Park; N.Mem. = National Memorial; N.P. = National Park; N.Pres. = National Preserve; N.R.A. = National Recreational Area; N.R.R. = National Recreational River; N.Riv. = National River; N.S. = National Seashore; N.S.R. = National Scenic Riverway; N.S.T. = National Scenic Trail; N.Sc. = National Scientific Reserve; N.V.M. = National Volcanic Monument.

Place Name	Listed Under
Apostle Islands N.L.	BAYFIELD
Chequamegon N.F.	PARK FALLS
Ice Age N.Sc.	DEVIL'S LAKE STATE PARK
Nicolet N.F.	THREE LAKES
St. Croix N.S.R.	ST. CROIX FALLS

STATE PARK AND RECREATION AREAS

Key to abbreviations. I.P. = Interstate Park; S.A.P. = State Archaeological Park; S.B. = State Beach; S.C.A. = State Conservation Area; S.C.P. = State Conservation Park; S.Cp. = State Campground; S.F. = State Forest; S.G. = State Garden; S.H.A. = State Historic Area; S.H.P. = State Historic Park; S.H.S. = State Historic Site; S.M.P. = State Marine Park; S.N.A. = State Natural Area; S.P. = State Park; S.P.C. = State Public Campground; S.R. = State Reserve; S.R.A. = State Recreation Area; S.Res. = State Reservoir; S.Res.P. = State Resort Park; S.R.P. = State Rustic Park.

CALENDAR HIGHLIGHTS

JANUARY

World Championship Snowmobile Derby (Eagle River). More than 300 professional racers fight for the championship. Phone 800/359-6315.

FEBRUARY

Winter Festival (Cedarburg). Ice carving and snow sculpture contests, bed and barrel races across ice, winter softball and volleyball, Alaskan Malamute weight pull, snow goose egg hunt; torchlight parade, horse-drawn sleigh rides. Phone 262/377-9620 or 800/827-8020.

American Birkebeiner (Cable). Cross-country ski race. More than 6,000 participants from 40 states and 15 countries. Phone 800/872-2753.

MAY

Festival of Blossoms (Door County). Month-long celebration of spring, with a million daffodils and blooming cherry and apple trees. Phone 920/743-4456 or 800/527-3529.

Great Wisconsin Dells Balloon Rally (Wisconsin Dells). More than 90 hot-air balloons participate in contests and mass liftoffs. Phone 800/223-3557.

JUNE

Walleye Weekend Festival and Mercury Marine National Walleye Tournament (Fond du Lac). Lakeside Park. Fish fry, food, entertainment, sports competitions. Phone 800/937-9123.

Summerfest (Milwaukee). Eleven different music stages; food. Phone 800/273-3378.

JULY

Art Fair on the Square (Madison). Capitol Concourse. Exhibits by 500 artists and craftspersons; food, entertainment. Phone 608/257-0158.

AUGUST

EAA (Experimental Aircraft Association) International Fly-In Convention (Oshkosh). Wittman Regional Airport. One of the nation's largest aviation events. More than 500 educational forums, workshops, and seminars; daily air shows; exhibits; more than 12,000 aircraft. Phone 920/235-3007 for air show lodging information or 920/426-4800 for general information.

Wisconsin State Fair (Milwaukee). State Fair Park in West Allis. Entertainment, 12 stages, auto races, exhibits, contests, demonstrations, fireworks. Phone 414/266-7000.

Place Name	Listed Under
Amnicon Falls S.P.	SUPERIOR
Big Foot Beach S.P.	LAKE GENEVA
Black River Falls S.F.	BLACK RIVER FALLS
Blue Mound S.P.	MOUNT HOREB
Bong S.R.A.	KENOSHA
Brule River S.F.	SUPERIOR
Brunet Island S.P.	CHIPPEWA FALLS
Buckhorn S.P.	MAUSTON
Copper Falls S.P.	ASHLAND

Devil's Lake S.P.	ASHLAND
Flambeau River S.F.	LADYSMITH
Governor Dodge S.P.	DODGEVILLE
Governor Knowles S.F.	ST. CROIX FALLS
Hartman Creek S.P.	WAUPACA
Heritage Hill S.P.	GREEN BAY
High Cliff S.P.	NEENAH-MENASHA
Interstate S.P.	ST. CROIX FALLS
Kettle Moraine S.F. (North Unit)	FOND DU LAC
Kettle Moraine S.F. (South Unit)	WAUKESHA
Kohler-Andrae S.P.	SHEBOYGAN
Lake Kegonsa S.P.	MADISON
Lake Wissota S.P.	CHIPPEWA FALLS
Merrick S.P.	GALESVILLE
Mill Bluff S.P.	TOMAH
Mirror Lake S.P.	BARABOO
Nelson Dewey S.P.	PRAIRIE DU CHIEN
New Glarus Woods S.P.	NEW GLARUS
Newport S.P.	ELLISON BAY
Northern Highland-American Legion S.F.	BOULDER JUNCTION
Pattison S.P.	SUPERIOR
Peninsula S.P.	FISH CREEK
Perrot S.P.	GALESVILLE
Point Beach S.F.	TWO RIVERS
Potawatomi S.P.	STURGEON BAY
Rib Mountain S.P.	WAUSAU
Rock Island S.P.	WASHINGTON ISLAND
Tower Hill S.P.	SPRING GREEN
Wildcat Mountain S.P.	TOMAH
Willow River S.P.	HUDSON
Wyalusing S.P.	PRAIRIE DU CHIEN
Yellowstone Lake S.P.	MONROE

Water-related activities, hiking, bicycling, riding, various other sports, picnicking, and visitor centers, as well as camping, are available in many of these areas. From May-Oct, camping is limited to three weeks; fee is $9-$12/unit/night; electricity $3. Camps can be taken down or set up between 6 am and 11 pm. Motor vehicle sticker for nonresidents: daily $10; annual $30; residents: daily $5; annual $20. For additional information contact Wisconsin Department of Natural Resources, Bureau of Parks & Recreation, PO Box 7921, Madison 53707, phone 608/266-2181.

SKI AREAS

Place Name	Listed Under
Alpine Valley Ski Resort	ELKHORN
Cascade Mount Ski Area	PORTAGE
Christmas Mountain Village	WISCONSIN DELLS
Devil's Head Resort	BARABOO
Grand Geneva Resort	LAKE GENEVA
Hidden Valley Ski Area	MANITOWOC
Minocqua Winter Park Nordic Center	MINOCQUA
Mount Ashwabay Ski Area	BAYFIELD

Mount La Crosse Ski Area	LA CROSSE
Mount Telemark Ski Area	CABLE
Nordic Mountain Ski Area	WAUTOMA
Rib Mountain Ski Area	WAUSAU
Sky Line Ski Area	WISCONSIN DELLS
Trollhaugen Ski Resort	ST. CROIX FALLS
Whitecap Mountain Ski Area	HURLEY
Wilmot Mountain	LAKE GENEVA

FISHING AND HUNTING

Wisconsin, eager to have visitors share the abundance of fish in the lakes and streams, posts few barriers. The state is very conservation minded; regulations have been developed to ensure equally good fishing in the future. Fishing licenses: nonresident over 16, 4-day $15; 15-day $20; annual $34; family 15-day, $30; annual family $52; licenses expire March 31. Two-day Great Lakes, $10. A trout stamp must be purchased by all licensed anglers in order to fish for trout in inland waters, $7.25. A salmon and trout stamp is required, except those having a two-day license, to fish the Great Lakes, $7.25. For further information contact the Wisconsin Department of Natural Resources, Customer Service and Licensing, PO Box 7921, Madison 53707, phone 608/266-2621.

Wisconsin waters boast trout, muskellunge, northern pike, walleye, large and smallmouth bass, and panfish throughout the state; salmon are primarily found in the Lake Superior/Michigan area; lake sturgeon in Winnebago Waters/St. Croix/Wisconsin, Chippewa, Flambeau, and Menominee rivers; and catfish in Wolf, Mississippi, and Wisconsin rivers. Inquire for seasons and bag limits.

The Department of Natural Resources issues separate pamphlets on trapping big game, pheasant, and waterfowl hunting regulations. Hunting licenses: nonresident, furbearer $150; small game $75; archery $135; deer $135; five-day small game $43. Hunting migratory birds requires a special federal stamp ($15), obtainable at any post office, as well as a state stamp $7. A pheasant stamp ($7.25) is also required. Special hunting regulations apply to minors; contact Department of Natural Resources for further information. **Note:** License fees subject to change.

Driving Information

Safety belts are mandatory for all persons in designated seating spaces within the vehicle. Children under four years of age must be in an approved safety seat anywhere in vehicle. Children ages 4-8 years may use a regulation safety belt. Phone 608/266-3212.

INTERSTATE HIGHWAY SYSTEM

The following alphabetical listing of Wisconsin towns in the *Mobil Travel Guide* shows that these cities are within ten miles of the indicated Interstate highways. A highway map should, however, be checked for the nearest exit.

Highway Number	Cities/Towns within ten miles
Interstate 43	Cedarburg, Green Bay, Manitowoc, Milwaukee, Port Washington, Sheboygan.
Interstate 90	Baraboo, Beloit, Janesville, La Crosse, Madison, Mauston, Portage, Sparta, Tomah, Wisconsin Dells.
Interstate 94	Baraboo, Black River Falls, Eau Claire, Hudson, Kenosha, Madison, Milwaukee, Oconomowoc, Portage, Racine, Tomah, Watertown, Waukesha, Wauwatosa, Wisconsin Dells.

Additional Visitor Information

The Wisconsin Department of Tourism, PO Box 7976, Madison 53707, phone 608/266-2161, 800/372-2737 (northern IL, IA, MI, MN, WI only), or 800/432-TRIP (anywhere in US), produces and distributes a variety of publications covering sports, attractions, events, and recreation. When requesting information, ask for *Adventure Guide, Events/Recreation Guide, Heritage Guide, Where to Stay in Wisconsin, Guide to State Golf Courses, Campground Directory,* and/or state highway map.

There are several tourist information centers in Wisconsin. Visitors who stop will find helpful information and brochures. They are located in Beloit (I-90); Genoa City (US 12), (seasonal); Grant County (US 151/61), (seasonal); Hudson (I-94); Hurley (US 51); Kenosha (I-94); La Crosse (I-90); Madison (201 W Washington Ave); Prairie du Chien (211 Main St), (seasonal); Superior (305 E 2nd St), (seasonal). There is also an information center in Chicago, IL (140 S Dearborn St, Rm 104).

Wisconsin offers a fabulous system of bicycle routes. To order a free guide to bicycling in Wisconsin contact the Department of Tourism, PO Box 7976, Madison 53707, phone 608/266-2161 or 800/432-8747 or 800/372-2737.

THE CRANBERRY HIGHWAY

Cranberries are the big money crop around Wisconsin Rapids. In the fall, mechanical harvesters sweep across 13,000 acres of cranberry marshes, dislodging the bright red berries that then float to the surface creating a crimson sea of fruit. Although fall is an ideal time to visit, travel "The Cranberry Highway" year-round, stopping perhaps for a cranberry shake or cranberry muffin or to visit a cheese factory for "Cran-jack" cheese, studded with dried fruit. The full route runs approximately 40 miles and includes visits to numerous marsh areas, historic sites, museums, markets, shops, and restaurants. A south loop covers about 70 miles and is described below.

Begin in downtown Wisconsin Rapids at Paul Gross Jewelers (241 Oak Street), where you can pick up a gold cranberry rake necklace complete with ruby cranberry. Then stop at South Wood County Historical Museum (3rd Street between East Grand Avenue and Riverview Expressway) for a look at local history and changing displays, including a cranberry exhibit.

Continue on 3rd Street to WI 54, which traces the Wisconsin River through Port Edwards. Stop at Alexander House Art & History Center (1131 Wisconsin River Drive), a combination art gallery and historical museum that is located in a stately, colonial home along the banks of the river. Continue on WI 54 and take County D south. Along the way, visit Glacial Lake Cranberries for a thorough introduction to Wisconsin's cranberry industry, which produces about 150 million pounds of fruit annually. Operated by third-generation cranberry farmers, it offers Marsh Tours year-round. A gift shop carries fresh fruit in season and the Stone Cottage accommodates up to four guests. From here, continue south on County D, then east on WI 173 to County Z south. At the intersection of County Z and Wakely Road in Nekoosa find Historic Point Basse, an 1837 living history site that stages events throughout the year. It protects an endangered historic site placed on the National Register of Historic Places in 2001.

Golfers tired of shelling out outrageous greens fees enjoy the lower costs at the region's championship courses. Lake Arrowhead at Nekoosa (one mile off WI 13), with two challenging 18-hole courses, is ranked by *Golf Digest* as one of the nation's best golf values. A round of golf is only $62 (with cart). Another golfing bargain awaits at The Ridges (east on County Z), where greens fees are only $55 (with cart) for 18 holes with challenging elevations and plenty of water and woods—white birch, green willows, and towering pines. From the clubhouse restaurant watch golfers tee off for the back nine with a shot from an 80-foot-high ridge into a valley flanked by tall pines and a twisting creek.

A shopping find is Studio of Good Earth, located on 52nd Street, just a ½ mile north of Highway 53. Operated by William and Annette Gudim, the studio offers the work of more than 45 artists and crafters, ranging from paintings, calligraphy, and baskets to weavings, handmade paper, and stained glass. Included are Annette's pottery and William's woodwork. Find lots of bird feeders and bird baths among quality traditional and contemporary arts and crafts at prices based on the local economy—remarkably lower than those at well-traveled resorts. Take time to enjoy the Gudim's beautiful flower gardens.

For an aerial view of cranberry marshes, head for Wings Air Charter (at Alexander Field). Short flights cost $10 per person ($55 for a 30-minute flight for three persons). From Airport Avenue, head north on Lincoln Street to Grand Avenue to find luxury lodgings at the Hotel Mead and Conference Center (451 East Grand Avenue), where a $9-million expansion added an 89-room, four-story tower, bringing the total number of rooms and suites to 157. All new guest rooms have refrigerators, coffeemakers, hair dryers, and desks with work space and data ports. The Mead has an indoor swimming pool and sauna, a fitness center, two restaurants, and a lively bar with entertainment. Breakfast in the Grand Avenue Grill features cranberry French toast.

Local eateries in Wisconsin Rapids include Harriet's Kitchen Nook (9041 US 13 South) which, contrary to its blue-painted tables and cutesy motif, has true diner lineage. It's a good spot to find breakfast pancakes, eggs, and superb hash browns (this is also a potato-growing country). It is de rigueur to include a glass of cranberry juice with breakfast. Another local time-warp eatery is Herschleb's (640 16th Street North), where carhops serve burgers, homemade soups (try chicken with dumplings), and their own brand of ice cream (which in cranberry harvest season includes cranberry swirl flavor). This is an excellent spot for shakes, malts, and floats. Prices are retro, too. **(APPROX 40 MI)**

Algoma

See also Green Bay, Sturgeon Bay (Door County)

Settled 1818 **Pop** 3,353 **Elev** 600 ft
Area code 920 **Zip** 54201
Information Algoma Area Chamber of Commerce, 1226 Lake St; 920/487-2041 or 800/498-4888
Web www.algoma.org

What to See and Do

Ahnapee State Trail. More than 15 mi of hiking and biking along the Ahnapee River; snowmobiling. (Daily) Phone 920/487-2041. **FREE**

Kewaunee County Historical Museum. Century-old building; displays incl a letter written by George Washington, wood carvings, child's playroom with toys of 1890-1910 period, sheriff's office, ship models, old farm tools, and artifacts. (Memorial Day-Labor Day, daily; rest of yr, by appt) 10 mi S via WI 42. Court House Sq, 613 Dodge St in Kewaunee. Phone 920/388-4410. **DONATION**

Von Stiehl Winery. Housed in 140-yr-old brewery. Wine, cheese, and jelly tasting at end of tour. Under 21 only with adult (wine tasting); no smoking. Gift shop; candy shop features homemade fudge. (May-Oct, daily; rest of yr, Fri-Sun) 115 Navarino St. Phone 920/487-5208. ¢

Motel/Motor Lodge

★ **RIVER HILLS MOTEL.** *820 N Water St (54201). 920/487-3451; fax 920/487-2031; toll-free 800/236-3451.* 30 rms. D $45-$60. Crib $3. Pet accepted, some restrictions; $3. TV; cable (premium). Coffee in lobby. Ck-out 11 am. Business servs avail. Refrigerators avail. Boat dock, public ramps nearby. Cr cds: MC, V.
D 🐾 🐇 🏄

Restaurant

★ **CAPTAIN'S TABLE.** *133 N Water St (WI 42N) (54201). 920/487-5304.* Hrs: 5 am-9 pm; Nov-May hrs vary. Closed Thanksgiving, Dec 25. Res accepted. Bkfst $1.85-$5.95, lunch $1.55-$4.50, dinner $4.95-$9.95.

Child's menu. Specializes in fresh fish. Salad bar. Nautical motif.
D SC 🏄

Antigo

(C-5) *See also Wausau*

Settled 1876 **Pop** 8,276 **Elev** 1,498 ft
Area code 715 **Zip** 54409
Information Chamber of Commerce, 329 Superior St, PO Box 339; 715/623-4134 or 888/526-4523
Web www.newnorth.net/antigo.chamber

What to See and Do

F. A. Deleglise Cabin. (1878) First home of city's founder. (May-Sept, Wed-Mon) 7th and Superior Sts, on grounds of public library. Phone 715/627-4464. **DONATION**

Restaurant

★ **BLACKJACK STEAK HOUSE.** *800 S Superior St (54409). 715/623-2514. www.foodspot.com/blackjack.* Hrs: 11 am-2 pm, 5-11 pm; Sun buffet 11 am-3 pm. Closed Dec 24-25. Res accepted. Bar. Lunch $5-$10; dinner $5.50-$25. Friday fish fry $6.75-$8.75. Sun buffet $8.50. Child's menu. Specializes in seafood, prime rib. Salad bar. Family-owned. Cr cds: A, DS, MC, V.
D 🏄

Appleton

(D-6) *See also Green Bay, Neenah-Menasha, Oshkosh*

Settled 1848 **Pop** 65,695 **Elev** 780 ft
Area code 920
Information Fox Cities Convention & Visitors Bureau, 3433 W College Ave, 54914; 920/734-3358 or 800/236-6673
Web www.foxcities.org

Located astride the Fox River, Appleton's economy centers around the manufacture of paper and paper products, and insurance and service industries.

What to See and Do

◼ **Charles A. Grignon Mansion.** (1837) First deeded property in Wisconsin (1793); restored Greek Revival house of one of the area's early French-Canadian settlers; period furnishings, displays; summer events. Picnic area. Tours. (June-Aug, daily; rest of yr, by appt) 1313 Augustine St, 8 mi E off US 41 in Kaukauna. Phone 920/766-3122. ¢¢

Fox Cities Children's Museum. Hands-on exhibits; climb through a human heart, play in the New Happy Baby Garden, or visit Grandma's Attic. (Tues-Thurs 9 am-5 pm; Fri 9 am-8 pm; Sat 10 am-5 pm; Sun noon-5 pm; closed Mon) 100 College Ave, in Avenue Mall. Phone 920/734-3226. ¢¢¢¢

Lawrence University. (1847) 1,400 students. Merged in 1964 with Milwaukee-Downer College. Main Hall (1854), College Ave. 706 E College Ave at Lawe St. For campus tours contact Admissions Office. Phone 920/832-6500. On campus is

    Music-Drama Center. (1959) Quarters for Conservatory of Music, concert hall, practice rms, classrms; Cloak Theater, an experimental arena playhouse; Stansbury Theater. Concerts and plays (academic yr). Phone 920/832-6611.

    Wriston Art Center. Traveling exhibits, lectures, and art shows. (Sept-May, Tues-Sun; schedule may vary; closed hols) ½ blk S of College Ave on Lawe St. Phone 920/832-6621. **FREE**

Outagamie Museum. Features local technology and industrial accomplishments. Major exhibit themes incl electricity, papermaking, agriculture, transportation, communications. Also an extensive exhibit devoted to Appleton native Harry Houdini. (Sept-May, Tues-Sun; rest of yr, daily; closed hols) 330 E College Ave. Phone 920/735-9370. ¢¢

Motels/Motor Lodges

★ ★ **BEST WESTERN MIDWAY HOTEL.** *3033 W College Ave (54914). 920/731-4141; fax 920/731-6343; res 800/528-1234. www.bestwestern.com.* 105 rms, 2 story. S $72-$112; D $82-$130; each addl $10; under 18 free; wkend rates. Crib free. Pet accepted, some restrictions; $10. TV; cable. Indoor pool; whirlpool. Complimentary full bkfst (Mon-Fri). Coffee in rms. Restaurant 6:30 am-11 pm. Bar 11-1 am. Ck-out 11 am. Meeting rms. Business servs avail. In-rm modem link. Bellhops. Sundries. Free airport, bus depot transportation. Exercise equipt; sauna. Health club privileges. Rec rm. Cr cds: A, C, D, DS, MC, V.

D 🐾 ⤳ 🏋 🔌 🔥 SC

★ **EXEL INN.** *210 N Westhill Blvd (54914). 920/733-5551; fax 920/733-7199; res 800/367-3935. www.exelinns.com.* 104 rms, 2 story. S $42; D $52-$105; each addl $4; under 18 free. Crib free. Pet accepted, some restrictions. TV; cable (premium). Complimentary continental bkfst. Restaurant adj 6 am-11 pm. Ck-out noon. Business servs avail. In-rm modem link. Exercise equipt. Health club privileges. Some in-rm whirlpools. Refrigerators; microwaves avail. Cr cds: A, C, D, DS, MC, V.

D 🐾 🏋 🔌 🔥 SC

★ ★ **HOLIDAY INN.** *150 S Nicolet Rd (54914). 920/735-9955; fax 920/735-0309; res 800/465-4329. www.holiday-inn.com.* 228 units, 8 story. S $75-$99; D $79-$115; each addl $10; suites $139-$199.95; under 19 free; wkend rates; higher rates: Packer games, EAA Fly-In. Crib free. TV; cable (premium), VCR avail. Indoor pool; whirlpool, poolside serv. Complimentary coffee in rms. Restaurant 6 am-2 pm, 5-10 pm. Bar 3 pm-1 am; wkends 11-2 am. Ck-out noon. Coin lndry. Meeting rms. Business center. In-rm modem link. Gift shop. Free airport transportation. X-country ski 4 mi. Exercise rm; sauna. Massage. Refrigerator, microwave in suites. Cr cds: A, C, D, DS, JCB, MC, V.

D ⤳ 🏋 ✈ 🔌 🔥 🏃

★ **ROADSTAR INN.** *3623 W College Ave (54914). 920/731-5271; fax 920/731-0227; toll-free 800/445-4667.*

102 rms, 2 story. S $36-$40.95; D $42-$46.95; each addl $5; suites $44.95-$52; under 15 free; higher rates special events. Pet accepted. TV; cable (premium). Complimentary continental bkfst. Restaurant adj 7 am-9 pm. Ck-out noon. Guest lndry. Sundries. Cr cds: A, C, D, DS, MC, V.

★ ★ **WOODFIELD SUITES.** *3730 W College Ave (54914). 920/734-7777; fax 920/734-0049; res 800/338-0008. www.woodfieldsuites.com.* 98 rms, 2 story. S $105; D $110; each addl $10; under 19 free. Crib free. TV; cable (premium), VCR avail. Pet accepted; $10. 2 pools, 1 indoor; whirlpool. Complimentary continental bkfst. Coffee in rms. Restaurant adj 6 am-11 pm. Bar from 11 am. Ck-out noon. Meeting rm. Business servs avail. In-rm modem link. Valet serv. Sundries. Free airport transportation. Exercise equipt. Sauna. Bowling. Game rm. Rec rm. Lawn games. Refrigerators. Cr cds: A, C, D, DS, JCB, MC, V.

Restaurant

★ ★ **GEORGE'S STEAK HOUSE.** *2208 S Memorial Dr (54915). 920/733-4939. www.foodspot.com/georges.* Hrs: 11 am-2 pm, 5-10:30 pm; Sat from 5 pm. Closed Sun; hols. Res accepted. Bar to 1 am. Lunch $5-$10, dinner $9-$20. Child's menu. Specializes in steak, seafood. Piano bar. Cr cds: A, D, DS, MC, V.

Ashland

(A-3) *See also Bayfield*

Founded 1854 **Pop** 8,695 **Elev** 671 ft
Area code 715 **Zip** 54806
Information Ashland Area Chamber of Commerce, 320 4th Ave W, PO Box 746; 715/682-2500 or 800/284-9484
Web www.visitashland.com

Located on Chequamegon Bay, which legend says is the "shining big sea water" of Longfellow's *Hiawatha*, Ashland is a port for Great Lakes ships delivering coal for the Midwest. It is also a gateway to the Apostle Islands. Papermaking machinery, fabricated steel, and other industrial products provide a diversified economy.

What to See and Do

Copper Falls State Park. This 2,500-acre park has more than 8 mi of river; nature and hiking trails provide spectacular views of the river gorge and the falls. Swimming, fishing, canoeing; backpacking, x-country skiing, picnicking, playground, concession, primitive and improved camping (hookups, dump station). Standard fees. (Daily) S off WI 13, 169 in Mellen. Phone 715/274-5123. ¢¢¢

Fishing. In Chequamegon Bay and in 65 trout streams and inland lakes (license and stamp required). Ice fishing is a popular winter sport. Also spring smelting and deep sea trolling in Lake Superior. Public boat landing at Sunset Park; RV park adj to Sunset Park (hookups, dump station).

Northland College. (1892) 750 students. Founded to bring higher education to the people of the isolated logging camps and farm communities of northern Wisconsin. On campus are Sigurd Olson Environmental Institute, in an earth-sheltered, solar-heated building; and historic Wheeler Hall (1892), constructed of brownstone from the nearby Apostle Islands. Ellis Ave, on WI 13. Phone 715/682-1699.

Special Event

Bay Days Festival. Sailboat regatta, art fair, bicycle and foot races, ethnic food booths, entertainment, dancing. Third wkend July. Phone 800/284-9484.

Motels/Motor Lodges

★ ★ **BEST WESTERN HOLIDAY HOUSE.** *30600 US 2 (54806). 715/682-5235; fax 715/682-4730; toll-free 800/452-7749. www.bestwestern. com.* 65 rms, 2 story. Mid-May-early Oct: S $66-$103; D $71-$118; each addl $5; under 13 free; winter wkend packages; lower rates rest of yr. Crib free. TV; cable (premium). Sauna. Indoor pool; whirlpool. Game rm. Coffee in rms. Restaurants 7 am-1 pm, 4:30-10 pm. Bar. Ck-out 11 am. Downhill ski 15 mi; x-country ski opp. Many balconies. Overlooks Lake Superior. Cr cds: A, C, D, DS, MC, V.

★ **SUPER 8.** *1610 W Lake Shore Dr (54806). 715/682-9377; fax 715/682-9377. www.super8.com.* 70 rms, 2 story. Mid-June-Sept: S $78.88-$85.88; D $79.88-$94.88; each addl $5; under 12 free; lower rates rest of yr. Crib free. Pet accepted, some restrictions. TV; cable (premium), VCR avail. Indoor pool; whirlpool. Complimentary coffee in lobby. Ck-out 11 am. Coin lndry. Business servs avail. In-rm modem link. X-country ski 10 mi. Microwaves avail. Opp Lake Superior. Cr cds: A, C, D, DS, MC, V.

Hotel

★ ★ ★ **CHEQUAMEGON.** *101 W Lakeshore Dr (54806). 715/682-9095; fax 715/682-9410; toll-free 800/946-5555. www.hotelc.com.* 65 units, 3 story, 6 kit. units. June-mid-Oct: S, D $100-$120; each addl $10; suites $120-$165; kit. units $95; under 12 free; lower rates rest of yr. Crib free. TV; cable (premium). Sauna. Indoor pool; whirlpool. Restaurant 6 am-9 pm; dining rm 4:30-10 pm. Bar 11:30-1 am. Ck-out 11 am. Meeting rms. Business servs avail. Some refrigerators, in-rm whirlpools. On Lake Superior. Large veranda overlooks marina. Cr cds: A, DS, MC, V.

Baileys Harbor (Door County)

See also Door County

Settled 1851 **Pop** 780 **Elev** 595 ft
Area code 920 **Zip** 54202
Information Door County Chamber of Commerce, 1015 Green Bay Rd, PO Box 406, Sturgeon Bay 54235; 920/743-4456 or 800/527-3529
Web www.doorcountyvacations.com

Bailey's Harbor is the oldest village in Door County (see), with one of the best harbors on the east shore. Range lights, built in 1870 to guide ships into the harbor, still operate. Its waters feature charter fishing for trout and salmon.

What to See and Do

Bjorklunden. A 425-acre estate, owned by Lawrence University (Appleton), with a replica of a Norwegian wooden chapel (stavkirke). The chapel was handcrafted by the original owners, the Boynton family, during the summers of 1939-1947. Seminars in the humanities are held on the estate each summer. Tours of chapel. (Mid-June-Aug, Mon and Wed) WI 57, 1 mi S of Baileys Harbor Phone 920/839-2216. ¢¢

Kangaroo Lake. Swimming, fishing, boating; picnicking. S on WI 57.

Special Event

Baileys Harbor Brown Trout Tournament. Late Apr. Phone 920/743-4456.

Resort

★ ★ ★ **GORDON LODGE.** *1420 Pine Dr (54202). 920/839-2331; fax 920/839-2450; toll-free 800/830-6235. www.gordonlodge.com.* 20 rms, 11 villas (1-2 bedrm). Late June-mid-Oct: S, D $100-$212; each addl $29; suites $212; villas $231-$345; cottages $117-$257; 3-day min wkends July-Labor Day, Columbus Day; lower rates mid-May-mid-June. Closed rest of yr. TV; cable (premium). Heated pool, whirlpool. Complimentary full bkfst (in season). Complimentary coffee in rms. Dining rm (hrs vary). Box lunches. Bar noon-midnight; entertainment. Ck-out noon, ck-in 4 pm. Business servs avail. Lighted tennis. Putting green. Private sand beach. Row boats. Bicycles. Exercise equipt. Refrigerators; some microwaves, fireplaces. Some private patios. Spacious grounds; scenic lake view. Cr cds: A, DS, MC, V.

Restaurants

★★ **COMMON HOUSE.** *8041 WI 57 (54202). 920/839-2708.* Hrs: 5:30-10 pm. Res accepted. No A/C. Bar. Dinner $10-$26.95. Child's menu. Own desserts. Old-fashioned wood stove in dining rm. Cr cds: DS, MC, V.

D ➟

★★ **FLORIAN II.** *Hwy 57 (54202). 920/839-2361.* Hrs: 5-9 pm; Sat, Sun 8 am-2:30 pm, 5-9 pm. Closed Nov-Mar. Res accepted. Bar. Buffet: bkfst $5.95. Dinner $9.95-$19.95. Child's menu. Specializes in prime rib, roast duck, barbecued ribs. Salad bar. Entertainment Fri, Sat. Solarium dining; overlooks Lake Michigan. Dock. Family-owned. Cr cds: MC, V.

D SC ➟

★ **SANDPIPER.** *8166 WI 57 (54202). 920/839-2528.* Hrs: 7 am-9 pm; hrs vary off-season. Closed Nov-Mar. Wine, beer. Bkfst $3.95-$5.95, lunch $1.75-$6.95, dinner $6.95-$12.95. Fish boil mid-May-Oct Mon-Sat: $10.50. Child's menu. Specializes in chicken, fish. Own soups. Outdoor dining. Cr cds: MC, V.

D ➟

Baraboo

(F-4) *See also Portage, Prairie du Sac, Reedsburg, Wisconsin Dells*

Founded 1830 **Pop** 9,203 **Elev** 894 ft
Area code 608 **Zip** 53913
Information Chamber of Commerce, PO Box 442; 608/356-8333 or 800/BARABOO
Web www.baraboo.com/chamber

A center for the distribution of dairy products, Baraboo is a neatly ordered town of lawns, gardens, parks, homes, and factories. The city is the original home of the Ringling Brothers and Gollmar circuses and still holds memories of its circus-town days. It was founded by Jean Baribeau as a trading post for the Hudson's Bay Company. Beautiful spring-fed Devil's Lake is three miles south of town.

What to See and Do

★ **Circus World Museum.** Has 50 acres and eight buildings of circus lore; original winter quarters of Ringling Brothers Circus. Live circus acts under "Big Top," daily circus parade, display of circus parade wagons, steam calliope concerts, P. T. Barnum sideshow, wild animal menagerie; carousel, band organ. Unloading circus train with Percheron horses; picnic facilities. (Early May-mid-Sept, daily) Exhibit Hall open year-round. 550 Water St. Phone 608/356-8341.
¢¢¢

Devil's Lake State Park. (see) 1 Bills Dr. Orchard Park, NY 14127. Phone 716/648-1800.

Ho-Chunk Casino & Bingo. Gaming casino featuring 48 blackjack tables, 1,200 slot machines, video poker, and keno. (Daily, 24 hrs) S3214A US 12. Phone 800/746-2486.

International Crane Foundation. A nonprofit organization promoting the study and preservation of cranes. Features cranes and their chicks from all over the world. Movies, displays, nature trails. (May-Oct, daily) Guided tours (Memorial Day-Labor Day, daily; Sept-Oct, wkends) E11376 Shady Lane Rd. Phone 608/356-9462.
¢¢¢

Mid-Continent Railway Museum. Restored 1894 depot, complete 1900 rail environment; steam locomotives, coaches, steam wrecker, snowplows; artifacts and historical exhibits. Picnic area, gift shop. (Mid-May-Labor Day, daily; after Labor Day-mid-Oct, wkends only) One-hr steam train round-trip on a branch of C & NW Railroad line, which once served early iron mines and rock quarries. Leaves North Freedom (same dates as museum; four departures daily). 5 mi W via WI 136, then 2 mi S to North Freedom. Phone 608/522-4261. ¢¢¢

Mirror Lake State Park. A 2,050-acre park with swimming, fishing, boating, canoeing; hiking, x-country skiing, picnicking, playground, camping (fee; electric hookups, dump station). Standard fees. (Daily) 2 mi W off US 12. Phone 608/254-2333. ¢¢

Sauk County Historical Museum. Houses 19th-century household goods, textiles, toys, china, military items, pioneer collection, Native

American artifacts, circus memorabilia, natural history display, photos; research library. (May-Oct, Tues-Sun) 531 4th Ave. Phone 608/356-1001. ¢

Skiing. Devil's Head Resort. Area has triple, six double, three quad chairlifts; four rope tows; patrol, school, rentals, snowmaking; lodge, restaurants, cafeteria, bars. Longest run 1¾ mi; vertical drop 500 ft. (Dec-Mar, daily) Night skiing; x-country trails. Golf, 18 holes. Swimming pool, whirlpool. Tennis courts. Mountain biking. 12 mi SE via WI 113, 78 at S-6330 Bluff Rd, in Merrimac. Phone 608/493-2251. ¢¢¢¢

Motels/Motor Lodges

★ **SPINNING WHEEL MOTEL.** *809 8th St (53913). 608/356-3933.* 25 rms. S $33-$53; D $35-$63; each addl $6; under 12 free. Crib $6. Pet accepted. TV; cable (premium). Restaurant nearby. Downhill ski 10 mi; x-country ski 5 mi. Cr cds: A, DS, MC, V.

D ➤ ☀ ⊠ ✦ SC

Bayfield

See also Ashland

Pop 686 **Elev** 700 ft **Area code** 715 **Zip** 54814

Information Chamber of Commerce, 42 S Broad St, PO Box 138; 715/779-3335 or 800/447-4094

Web www.bayfield.org

What to See and Do

Apostle Islands National Lakeshore. Eleven mi of mainland shoreline and 21 islands of varying size. The lakeshore area features hiking, boating, fishing; primitive campsites on 18 islands. Two visitor centers, in Bayfield (all yr) and at Little Sand Bay (Memorial Day-Sept), 13 mi NW of Bayfield. National Lakeshore Headquarters/Visitor Center (daily; free). N and E off Bayfield Peninsula. Phone 715/779-3397. Boat trips provided by

> **Apostle Islands Cruise Service.** Lake Superior cruises to Apostle Islands on the *Island Princess* (May-early Oct, departures daily); also

Stockton Island shuttle with Raspberry Island Lighthouse Adventure: two-hr layover and naturalist hike. City Dock. Res advised, inquire for schedule. Phone 715/779-3925. ¢¢¢¢

Lake Superior Big Top Chautauqua. Outdoor theater; features folk and bluegrass performances; musicals and theater pieces. (June-Labor Day, Wed-Sat eves; some Tues, Sun, and matinee performances) 3 mi S on WI 13, then W on Ski Hill Rd. Phone 715/373-5552 or 888/244-8368. ¢¢¢¢ ¢¢¢¢

Madeline Island. Part of island group but not under federal jurisdiction. 14 mi long, has 45 mi of roads; off the dock at La Pointe is

> **Madeline Island Ferry Line.** The *Island Queen, Nichevo II,* and the *Madeline Bayfield* make frequent trips. (Apr-Jan, daily) Phone 715/747-2051. ¢¢
>
> **Madeline Island Historical Museum.** Located near the site of an American fur company post and housed in a single building combining four pioneer log structures. (Late May-early Oct, daily; fee) There are motels, housekeeping cottages, and restaurants on the island. Guided bus tours. Marina; camping in two parks, x-country skiing. Phone 715/747-2415.

Skiing. Mount Ashwabay Ski Area. T-bar, four rope tows; patrol, school, rentals; snow-making machine; restaurant, cafeteria, concession, bar. Longest run 1,500 ft; vertical drop 317 ft. (Dec-Mar, Wed, Sat-Sun; Christmas wk, daily) Half-day rates; night skiing (Wed and Sat); x-country skiing (Tues-Sun), 24 mi of trails. 3 mi S on WI 13. Phone 715/779-3227.

Special Events

Run on Water. First Sat Feb. Phone 800/447-4094.

Sailboat Race Week. First wk July. Phone 800/447-4094.

Bayfield Festival of Arts. Last full wkend July. Phone 800/447-4094.

Great Schooner Race. Last wkend Sept. Phone 800/447-4094.

Sand Island Lighthouse, Apostle Islands National Lakeshore

Apple Festival. First full wkend Oct. Phone 800/447-4094.

Motels/Motor Lodges

★ **BAYFIELD INN.** *20 Rittenhouse Ave (54814). 715/779-3363; fax 715/779-9810. toll-free 800/382-0995; www.bayfieldinn.com.* 21 rms, 2 story. No A/C. Mid-May-mid-June: S, D $95-$110; each addl $10; wkends 2-day min (July-Aug); higher rates Apple Festival; lower rates rest of yr. TV; cable, VCR avail (movies). Complimentary continental bkfst. Restaurant 11:30 am-9 pm. Ck-out 11 am. Business servs avail. Downhill ski 5 mi; x-country ski on-site. Sauna. Health club privileges. Game rm. On lake. Cr cds: AMEX, DS, MC, V.
⬛🖐🐾

★ **SUPER 8.** *Harbor View Dr, Washburn (54891). 715/373-5671; fax 715/373-5674; res 800/800-8000; www.super8.com.* 35 rms, 2 story. July-Sept: S $69.98-$75.98; D $79.98-$89.98; each addl $5; suite $89.98-$139; under 12 free; wkly and hol rates; higher rates Apple Fest; lower

rates rest of yr. Crib free. Pet accepted, some restrictions; $25. TV; cable. Complimentary continental bkfst. Restaurant adj 4-10 pm. Ck-out 11 am. Business servs avail. Downhill/x-country ski 8 mi. Sauna. Whirlpool. Game rm. On lake. Cr cds: A, C, D, DS, MC, V.
⬛🖐🐾🐾🖐🔥

★ **WINFIELD INN.** *225 E Lynde Ave (54814). 715/779-3252; fax 715/779-5180. www.winfieldinn.com.* 31 rms, 26 A/C, 1-2 story, 6 kit. apts (1-2 bedrm). June-Oct: S, D $79; kit. apts $110-$150; lower rates rest of yr. Crib free. Pet accepted. TV; cable. Complimentary coffee in rms. Restaurant nearby. Ck-out 11 am. Downhill/x-country ski 8 mi. Some balconies. Sun deck. 4 wooded acres on shore of Lake Superior. Cr cds: A, MC, V.
🐾🖐🔥

B&B/Small Inn

★★★ **OLD RITTENHOUSE INN.** *301 Rittenhouse Ave (54814). 715/779-5111; fax 715/779-5887; toll-free*

800/779-2129. *www.rittenhouseinn. com.* 21 units in 4 guest houses, 2-3 story. No rm phones. D $99; each addl $15; suites $159-$249; winter wkend plans. Crib avail. Complimentary continental bkfst in main house. Restaurant (see also OLD RITTEN-HOUSE). Ck-out noon, ck-in 3:30 pm. Downhill ski 3 mi; x-country ski 1 mi. Some in-rm whirlpools. Fireplaces. Individually decorated rms in 4 restored Victorian houses; antique furnishings. Totally nonsmoking. Cr cds: MC, V.

D ⤢ ⊠ ♨

Restaurant

★★★ **OLD RITTENHOUSE.** *301 Rittenhouse Ave (54814). 715/779-5111. www.rittenhouseinn.com.* Hrs: 7:30-9:30 am, 11:00 am-2:30 pm, 5-9 pm. Res required. Wine. Complete meals: bkfst $10. dinner $45. Sun brunch $17.50. Serv charge 18 percent. Child's menu. Specializes in fresh Lake Superior whitefish and trout, regional dishes. Own baking. Cr cds: MC, V.

D

Beaver Dam

(F-5) *See also Watertown, Waupun*

Settled 1841 **Pop** 14,196 **Elev** 879 ft
Area code 920 **Zip** 53916
Information Chamber of Commerce, 127 S Spring St; 920/887-8879
Web www.beaverdamchamber.com

What to See and Do

Beaver Dam Lake. Fourteen mi long. Fishing for bullhead, perch, crappie, walleye, and northern pike; ice fishing, boating (docks, ramps), waterskiing; waterfowl hunting. (Daily) West edge of town. Phone 920/885-6766. **FREE**

Dodge County Historical Museum. In 1890 Romanesque building; Chinese and Native American artifacts, spinning wheels, dolls. (Tues-Sat, afternoons; closed hols) 105 Park Ave. Phone 920/887-1266. **FREE**

Special Events

Swan City Car Show. Swan City Park. Phone 920/887-7000. Father's Day.

Dodge County Fair. Fairgrounds, 3 mi E on WI 33. Phone 920/885-3586. Five days mid-late Aug.

Motels/Motor Lodges

★★ **BEST WESTERN CAMPUS INN.** *815 Park Ave (53916). 920/887-7171; toll-free 800/572-4891. www.bestwestern.com.* 94 rms, 4 story. S, D $68-$82; each addl $5; suites $89-$125; under 12 free. Crib $4. TV; cable (premium), VCR avail. Indoor pool; whirlpool. Coffee in rms. Restaurant 6 am-11 pm. Bar 4 pm-2 am. Ck-out 11 am. Coin lndry. Meeting rms. In-rm modem link. Valet serv. Sundries. Putting green. Game rm. Some in-rm whirlpools. Cr cds: A, C, D, DS, MC, V.

D ⤢ ⊠ ♨ SC

★ **GRAND VIEW.** *1510 N Center St (53916). 920/885-9208; fax 920/887-8706.* 22 rms. S $30.94; D $40.89-$46.41; each addl $4. Crib $3. Pet accepted, some restrictions. TV; cable (premium). Ck-out 11 am. Cr cds: A, C, DS, MC, V.

🐾 ♨

★ **MAYVILLE INN.** *701 S Mountain Dr, Mayville (53050). 920/387-1234. www.mayvilleinn.com.* 29 rms, 2 story. S, D $46-$90; each addl $7; under 12 free. Crib free. TV; cable. Complimentary continental bkfst. Restaurant nearby. Bar. Ck-out 11 am. Meeting rm. Business servs avail. In-rm modem link. Gift shop. X-country ski 5 mi. Whirlpool. Some refrigerators, wet bars. Cr cds: A, DS, MC, V.

D ⤢ ⊠ ♨

Beloit

(G-5) *See also Delavan, Janesville, also see Rockford, IL*

Settled 1836 **Pop** 35,573 **Elev** 750 ft
Area code 608 **Zip** 53511
Information Convention and Visitors Bureau, 1003 Pleasant St; 608/365-4838 or 800/4-BELOIT
Web www.visitbeloit.com

In 1837, the town of Colebrook, New Hampshire, moved almost en masse to this point at the confluence of Turtle Creek and Rock River. The community, successively known as Turtle, Blodgett's Settlement, and New Albany, was finally named Beloit in 1857. The New Englanders, determined to sustain standards of Eastern culture and education, founded Beloit Seminary soon after settling; this small coeducational school became Beloit College. Today the city's economy centers around the college, food processing, and the production of heavy machinery.

What to See and Do

Angel Museum. Collection of 11,000 angels made from everything from leather to china. Oprah Winfrey has donated over 500 angels from her private collection. (Mon-Sat 10 am-5 pm; Sun afternoons; closed hols) 656 Pleasant St. Phone 608/362-9099. ¢¢

Beloit College. (1846) 1,100 students. Noted for Theodore Lyman Wright Museum of Art (academic yr, daily). Logan Museum of Anthropology has changing displays of Native American and Stone Age artifacts. Campus contains prehistoric mounds. Campus tours (by appt). On US 51. Phone 608/363-2000.

Hanchett-Bartlett Homestead. (1857) Restored historic limestone homestead on 15 acres is built in the transitional Greek Revival style, with Italianate details; restored in period colors. House contains furnishings of the mid-19th century; limestone barn houses collection of farm implements. On the grounds is a one-rm schoolhouse (1880); picnic area. (June-Sept, Wed-Sun afternoons; also by appt) 2149 St. Lawrence Ave. Phone 608/365-7835. ¢

Special Event

Riverfest. Riverside Dr, Riverside Park. Music festival with top-name performers; more than 50 bands feature variety of music. Food, carnival rides, children's entertainment. Phone 608/365-4838. Mid-July.

Motels/Motor Lodges

★ ★ **COMFORT INN.** 2786 Milwaukee Rd (53511). 608/362-2666. www.comfortinn.com. 56 rms, 2 story, 16 suites. June-Sept: S $55-$75; D $60-$80; each addl $5; suites $75-$100; under 18 free; wkly rates; higher rates special events; lower rates rest of yr. Crib free. Pet accepted; $10/day. TV; cable (premium), VCR avail (movies). Indoor pool; whirlpool. Complimentary continental bkfst. Restaurant nearby. Ck-out 11 am. Business servs avail. Game rm. Refrigerator in suites. Cr cds: A, D, DS, MC, V.

[icons]

★ ★ **HOLIDAY INN EXPRESS.** 2790 Milwaukee Rd (53511). 608/365-6000; fax 608/365-1974; res 800/465-4329. www.holiday-inn.com. 73 rms, 2 story. S $59-$75; D $70-$90; each addl $6; under 18 free. Crib free. TV; cable (premium). Indoor pool; whirlpool. Exercise equipt. Complimentary bkfst. Coffee in rms. Ck-out noon. Meeting rm. Business servs avail. Valet serv. Cr cds: A, C, D, DS, JCB, MC, V.

[icons]

Restaurant

★ ★ **BUTTERFLY CLUB.** 5246 E County Rd X (53511). 608/362-8577. Hrs: 5-9:30 pm; Sun noon-8 pm. Closed Mon; Jan 1, Dec 24-25. Res accepted Tues-Thurs, Sat-Sun. Bar. Dinner $7-$35. Child's menu. Specializes in prime rib, chicken, fish. Own baking. Entertainment Fri, Sat. Outdoor dining. Cr cds: A, D, DS, MC, V.

[icons]

Black River Falls

See also Sparta, Tomah

Pop 3,490 **Elev** 796 ft **Area code** 715
Zip 54615
Information Black River Area Chamber of Commerce, 120 N Water St; 715/284-4658 or 800/404-4008
Web www.blackrivercountry.com

In 1819, when the Black River countryside was a wilderness of pine, one of the first sawmills in Wisconsin was built here. Among the early settlers were a group of Mormons from Nauvoo, Illinois (see). Conflict developed with local landowners, and the Mormons soon returned to Nauvoo. The seat of Jackson County, Black River Falls is situated on the Black River, which offers boating and canoeing. The area is also noted for deer hunting and winter sports.

What to See and Do

Black River Falls State Forest. A 66,000-acre forest. Swimming, fishing, boating, canoeing; hiking, x-country skiing, snowmobiling, bridle trail, picnicking, playground, camping (fee). Lookout tower; abundant wildlife. Self-guided auto trail. All motor vehicles must have parking sticker. (Daily) Standard fees. 6 mi E on WI 54. Phone 715/284-1400. ¢¢

Thunderbird Museum. Exhibits incl Native American artifacts dating back to paleolithic man, weapons, minerals, dolls, coins, stamps, art. (May-Sept, wkends or by appt) In Hatfield, 10 mi NE via US 12, County K exit at Merrillan. Phone 715/333-5841. ¢¢

Special Event

Winnebago Pow-Wow. 3 mi NE via WI 54, at Red Cloud Memorial Pow-Wow Grounds. Dancing. Held twice annually: Sun and Mon, Memorial Day and Labor Day wkends. Phone 715/284-4658.

Motels/Motor Lodges

★ ★ **BEST WESTERN ARROW-HEAD LODGE.** *600 Oasis Rd (54615). 715/284-9471; fax 715/284-9664; toll-free 800/284-9471. www.bestwestern.com.* 143 rms, 3 story, 30 suites. S $59-$75; D $65-$85; each addl $5; suites $89.95-$184.95; under 12 free. Crib $3. Pet accepted. TV; cable. Sauna. Indoor pool; whirlpool. Playground. Complimentary continental bkfst. Restaurant 6:30 am-2 pm, 5-10 pm. Bar; entertainment Sat. Ck-out noon. Coffee in rms. Meeting rms. Business servs avail. In-rm modem link. Sundries. Snowmobile trails. Nature/fitness trail. On lake; docks, swimming beach. Cr cds: A, C, D, DS, MC, V.

⊡ 🐾 🦵 🏊 🛟 🔥

★ **DAYS INN-BLACK RIVER FALLS.** *919 Hwy 54 E, Black River (54615). 715/284-4333; fax 715/284-9068; toll-free 800/329-7466. www.daysinn.com.* 84 rms, 2 story. S $54.99-$67.99; D $61.99-$79.99; suites $75-$110; under 12 free. Crib free. Pet accepted. TV; cable, VCR avail. Sauna. Indoor pool; whirlpool. Complimentary continental bkfst. Coffee in rms. Restaurant adj 6 am-11 pm. Ck-out noon. Coin lndry. Meeting rm. Business servs avail. In-rm modem link. Downhill ski 15 mi; x-country ski 1 mi. Health club privileges. Game rm. Cr cds: A, C, D, DS, MC, V.

⊡ 🐾 🦵 🏊 🛟 🔥 **SC**

Boulder Junction

See also Eagle River, Land O' Lakes, Manitowish Waters, Minocqua, Sayner, Woodruff

Pop 1,000 **Elev** 1,640 ft
Area code 715 **Zip** 54512

Information Chamber of Commerce, PO Box 286; 715/385-2400 or 800/466-8759

Web www.boulderjet.org

This secluded little village within the Northern Highland-American Legion State Forest is the gateway to a vast recreational area with woodlands, scenic drives, streams, and several hundred lakes where fishing for muskellunge is excellent. Indeed, "Musky Capital of the World" is its registered trademark. Boulder Junction also offers various winter activities, including snowmobiling, cross-country skiing, and ice fishing. In nearby state nurseries, millions of young pine trees are raised and shipped all over the state for forest planting.

What to See and Do

Northern Highland-American Legion State Forest. A 225,000-acre forest with swimming beaches, waterskiing, fishing, boating, canoeing; hiking, x-country skiing, snowmobiling, picnicking, improved and primitive camping (896 sites on lakes; dump station; fee), sites also along water trails. Standard fees. (Daily) Phone 715/385-3521. ¢¢

Special Event

Musky Jamboree/Arts and Crafts Fair. Second Sun. Phone 715/385-2400.

Cottage Colonies

★★ **WHITE BIRCH VILLAGE.** *8764 Hwy K E (54512). 715/385-2182; fax 715/385-2537. www.whitebirchvillage. com.* 11 kit. cottages (1-4 bedrm), 1-2 story. Early July-mid-Aug: S, D $791-$1254/wk; lower rates mid-May-early July, mid-Aug-mid-Oct. Closed rest of yr. Crib free. Pet accepted. TV in sitting rm. Playground. Ck-out 9 am, ck-in 3 pm. Grocery. Coin lndry. Package store 8 mi. Business servs avail. Sand beach; dock, launching ramp, boats, canoes, sailboats, paddleboats. Lawn games. Tandem bicycles. Rec rm. Fishing guides, clean and store area. Library. Fireplaces. Private decks. Grills. Woodland setting on White Birch Lake. No cr cds accepted.

[D] [≈] [⚓] [🐾]

★ **ZASTROWS LYNX LAKE LODGE.** *PO Box 277L (54512). 715/686-2249; fax 715/686-2257; toll-free 800/882-5969. www.zastrows lynxlakelodge.com.* 11 cottages (1-4 bedrm), 7 with kit. No A/C. MAP, May-Oct: $295/wk/person; family rates; EP off-season; 3-day min some wkends; lower rates Dec-Feb. Closed Mar-Apr and late Oct-Dec 26. Crib avail. Pet accepted. TV; cable. Playground. Dining rm 8-9:30 am, 5-9:30 pm. Box lunches. Bar 4:30 pm-2 am. Ck-out 10 am, ck-in 2 pm. Business servs avail. Grocery 4 mi. Coin lndry 8 mi. Package store. Gift shop. Free airport, bus depot transportation. Private beach, swimming; boats, rowboats, canoes, paddleboats, pontoon boats, motors. X-country ski on site. Snowmobiles. Bicycles. Lawn games. Movies. Rec rm. Fish/game clean and store area. Some fireplaces. Cr cds: DS, MC, V.

[D] [⚓] [🐾] [≈] [✈] [🏂]

Restaurant

★★ **GUIDE'S INN.** *County M (54512). 715/385-2233.* Hrs: 4-10 pm. Closed Easter, Dec 25. Continental menu. Bar. Dinner $6.50-$19.95. Child's menu. Specialties: beef Wellington, Black Forest schnitzel. Own ice cream, desserts. Cr cds: MC, V.

[D] [≈]

Burlington

(G-6) *See also Delavan, Elkhorn, Fontana, Lake Geneva*

Settled 1835 **Pop** 8,855 **Elev** 766 ft
Area code 262 **Zip** 53105
Information Chamber of Commerce, 112 E Chesnut St, PO Box 156; 262/763-6044
Web www.burlingtonareachamber. com

Originally called Foxville, Burlington was renamed for the city in Vermont by a group of settlers arriving in 1835. It is the home of the Liar's Club, an organization dedicated to the preservation of the art of telling tall tales. A prize is awarded each year to the contributor who submits the most incredible "stretcher."

What to See and Do

Green Meadows Farm. Operating farm offers daily guided tours; pony rides, tractor-drawn hayrides; more than 20 "hands-on" animal areas; picnic areas. (May-June, Tues-Sat; July-Labor Day, Oct, daily; closed Sept) Pumpkin picking in Oct. 33603 High Dr, 5 mi N via WI 36, 3 mi W of Waterford on WI 20. Phone 262/534-2891. ¢¢

Spinning Top Exploratory Museum. Exhibits and displays dealing with tops, yo-yos, gyroscopes; top games, demonstrations; 35 tops for hands-on experiments. Video presentations. 533 Milwaukee Ave. Phone 262/763-3946. ¢¢

Walking tours.

Historic Burlington. Visit 22 historic spots in the city, incl the Lincoln Monument and the Meinhardt Homestead.

Tall Tales Trail. Seventeen-stop walking tour featuring tall tales preserved on plaques and mounted on public buildings and store-fronts.

Special Events

Chocolate City Festival. Two-day, city-wide celebration incl arts and crafts fair (fee), parade, entertain-ment. Wkend after Mother's Day. Phone 262/763-3300.

Aquaducks Water Ski Show. Fischer Park on Browns Lake. Performance each Sat evening; rain date Sun. June-Labor Day. Phone 262/763-6044.

Motel/Motor Lodge

★ ★ **AMERICINN MOTEL.** *205 S Browns Lake Dr (53105). 262/534-2125; toll-free 800/634-3444. www.americinn.com.* 50 rms, 2 story. May-Oct: S, D $62-$87; each addl $6; suites $74-$99; under 12 free; lower rates rest of yr. Crib free. TV; cable (premium). Sauna. Indoor pool; whirlpool. Complimentary continen-tal bkfst. Restaurant opp 11:30 am-10:30 pm. Ck-out 11 am. Meeting rm. Cr cds: A, D, DS, MC, V.

D ⟅ ⟆ ⟇ SC

Cable

See also Hayward

Pop 817 **Elev** 1,370 ft **Area code** 715 **Zip** 54821

Information Cable Area Chamber of Commerce, PO Box 217; 715/798-3833 or 800/533-7454

Web www.cable4fun.com

What to See and Do

Skiing. Mount Telemark Ski Area. Area has two chairlifts, two T-bars, rope tow; alpine and nordic ski schools, rentals, patrol, snowmaking; nursery, restaurants, cafeteria, bar, lodge. Longest run ½ mi; vertical drop 370 ft. (Thanksgiving-Mar, daily) X-country trails (Dec-Mar, daily; rentals), more than 40 mi of trails. Hiking, bridle, and bicycle trails rest of yr; also 18-hole golf,

eight tennis courts (four indoor). 3 mi E on County M. Phone 715/798-3999.

Special Event

American Birkebeiner. X-country ski race. More than 6,000 participants from 40 states and 15 countries. 55 km. Late Feb. Phone 715/634-5025.

Cedarburg

(F-6) *See also Milwaukee, Port Washing-ton*

Pop 9,895 **Elev** 780 ft **Area code** 262 **Zip** 53012

Information Chamber of Commerce, PO Box 104; 262/377-9620 or 800/CDR-BURG

Web www.cedarburg.org

Cedarburg, surrounded by rich farm-lands and protected forests and wet-lands, has many beautiful old homes built in the 1800s. Many buildings in the historic downtown area have been restored.

What to See and Do

Cedar Creek Settlement and Winery. Stone woolen mill (1864) converted into a winery; houses shops, art stu-dios, and restaurants. Winery makes strawberry, cranberry, and grape wines; museum of antique wine-making tools. (Daily; closed hols) W6340 Bridge Rd, at N Washington. Phone 262/377-8020. ¢

Special Events

Winter Festival. Ice carving and snow sculpture contests, bed and barrel races across ice, winter softball and volleyball, Alaskan malamute weight pull, snow goose egg hunt; torchlight parade, horse-drawn sleigh rides. First full wkend Feb. Phone 262/377-9620.

Stone and Century House Tour. Tour of historic homes in the area. First full wkend June. Phone 262/375-3676.

Strawberry Festival. Strawberry foods, contests, craft fair, entertainment. Fourth full wkend June. Phone 262/377-9620.

Ozaukee County Fair. W65 N796 Washington Ave (Firemen's Park and County Grounds). Educational and commercial exhibits, carnival, entertainment. Late July-early Aug. Phone 262/377-9620.

Wine and Harvest Festival. Cedar Creek Winery. Grape-stomping contests, farmers market, arts and crafts fair, scarecrow contest; entertainment, food. Third wkend Sept. Phone 262/377-9620.

Motels/Motor Lodges

★★ **BEST WESTERN QUIET HOUSE SUITES.** *10330 N Port Washington Rd, Mequon (53092). 262/241-3677; fax 262/241-3707; res 800/780-7234. www.bestwestern.com.* 54 rms, 2 story. S $101-$190; D $111-$200; each addl $10; suites $160-$184. Pet accepted; $15. TV; cable (premium). Indoor/outdoor pool; whirlpool. Complimentary continental bkfst. Restaurant adj 11 am-11 pm. Ck-out 11 am. Business servs avail. In-rm modem link. Exercise equipt. Cr cds: A, C, D, DS, MC, V.
🄳 🔧 🌊 🏋 🔌 🔥

★ **CHALET MOTEL.** *10401 N Port Washington Rd, Mequon (53092). 262/241-4510; fax 262/241-5542; toll-free 800/343-4510.* 41 rms, 2 story. May-Oct: S $61-$88; D $68-$98; each addl $7; suites $85-$150; under 12 free; wkly rates; higher rates special events, hols; lower rates rest of yr. Crib free. Pet accepted, some restrictions. TV; cable (premium). Restaurant 6 am-9 pm; Fri to 9:30 pm; Sat, Sun from 7 am. Bar. Ck-out 11 am. Meeting rm. Business servs avail. Many refrigerators. Cr cds: A, C, D, DS, MC, V.
🄳 🔧 🔌 🔥

B&Bs/Small Inns

★ **STAGECOACH INN BED AND BREAKFAST.** *W61 N 520 Washington Ave (53012). 262/375-0208; fax 262/375-6170; toll-free 888/375-0208. www.stagecoach-inn-wi.com.* 12 rms, 3 story, 6 suites. Phone avail. S, D $80-$110; each addl $10; suites $110-$145. TV; cable. Complimentary continental bkfst. Coffee in rms. Restaurant nearby. Bar. Ck-out

11 am, ck-in 4 pm. Business servs avail. X-country ski 3 mi. Restored stagecoach inn (1853); antiques. Some in-rm whirlpools, fireplaces. Totally nonsmoking. Cr cds: A, D, DS, MC, V.
🔧 🔌 🔥 🐾

★★★ **WASHINGTON HOUSE INN.** *W62 N573 Washington Ave (53012). 262/375-3550; fax 262/375-9422; toll-free 800/554-4717. www.washingtonhouseinn.com.* 34 rms, 3 story. S, D $89-$219; each addl $10. TV; cable (premium), VCR avail. Complimentary continental bkfst buffet. Restaurant opp. Ck-out noon, ck-in 3 pm. Meeting rm. Business center. X-country ski 5 mi. Sauna. Many in-rm whirlpools; some fireplaces. In a Victorian Cream City brick building (1886); antiques, historic memorabilia. Rms named after city's pioneers. Cr cds: A, D, DS, MC, V.
🄳 🔌 🐾 🔧

Restaurants

★★★ **BODER'S ON THE RIVER.** *11919 N River Rd, Mequon (53092). 262/242-0335.* Hrs: 11:30 am-2 pm, 5:30-8 pm; Fri 5-9 pm; Sat 5:30-9 pm; Sun 11:30 am-2 pm, 4-7 pm; Sun brunch. Closed Mon; hols. Res accepted. Bar. Wine list. Complete meals: lunch $6.50-$10.95, dinner $12.95-$23.95. Sun brunch $14.95. Child's menu. Specializes in roast duck, sauteed fresh chicken livers. Own baking. Country inn (1840); fireplaces. Family-owned. Cr cds: A, D, DS, MC, V.
🄳

★ **KOWLOON.** *W63 N145 Washington Ave (53012). 262/375-3030.* Hrs: 11:30 am-9 pm; Fri to 10 pm; Sat 4:30-10 pm; Sun 4-9 pm. Closed Mon. Chinese menu. Bar. Lunch $2.50-$4.35, dinner $4.75-$7.75. Buffet: lunch $4.35, dinner $6.50. Specializes in Szechuan dishes. Chinese lanterns and fans. Cr cds: A, D, DS, MC, V.
🄳 🔧

★★ **RIVERSITE.** *11120 N Cedarburg Rd, Mequon (53092). 262/242-6050.* Hrs: 5-10 pm. Closed Sun; hols. Res accepted. Bar. Dinner $14.95-$26.95. Specializes in seafood, steak. Overlooking Milwaukee River. Cr cds: A, MC, V.

D 🔌

Chippewa Falls

(C-2) *See also Eau Claire, Menomonie*

Settled 1836 **Pop** 12,727 **Elev** 902 ft
Area code 715 **Zip** 54729
Information Chamber of Commerce, 10 S Bridge St; 715/723-0331
Web www.chippewachamber.org

Water has replaced lumber as the prime natural resource of this city on the Chippewa River. Jean Brunet, a pioneer settler, built a sawmill and then a dam here. Soon the area was populated by lumberjacks. Today, hydroelectric power is channeled to the industries of Chippewa Falls, which has water noted for its purity.

What to See and Do

Brunet Island State Park. A 1,032-acre river island park. Swimming, fishing (pier), boating, canoeing; nature and hiking trails, cross-country skiing, picnicking, playground, camping (electric hookups, dump station). Standard fees. (Daily) N via US 53, then E on WI 64 in Cornell. Phone 715/239-6888. ¢¢

Chippewa Falls Zoo. Concentrates on native animals. Also picnic tables, playground, tennis courts, pool. Fee for some activities. (May-Oct, daily) Irvine Park, N on WI 124. Phone 715/723-3890. **FREE**

Cook-Rutledge Mansion. (1870s) Restored Victorian mansion. Guided tours (June-Aug, Thurs-Sun; rest of yr, by appt). 505 W Grand Ave. Phone 715/723-7181. ¢¢

Lake Wissota State Park. A 1,062-acre park with swimming, waterskiing, fishing, boating, canoeing; hiking, x-country skiing, picnicking, playground, concession, camping (dump station, electro-hookups; res accepted). Observation points. Standard fees. (Daily) 8 mi E on WI 29. Phone 715/382-4574. ¢¢

Special Events

Northern Wisconsin State Fair. Fairgrounds. Phone 715/723-2861. Early or mid-July.

Pure Water Days. Downtown. Canoe paddling, sport competitions, contests, parade, dances, beer garden, food. Second wkend Aug. Phone 715/723-0331.

Motels/Motor Lodges

★ ★ **AMERICINN MOTEL AND SUITES.** *11 W South Ave (54729). 715/723-5711; fax 715/723-5254; toll-free 800/634-3444. www.americinn. com.* 62 rms, 2 story. S $57-$88; D $65-$91; suites $58.90-$104.90; under 18 free. Pet accepted; $25. TV; cable (premium). Complimentary coffee in lobby. Complimentary continental bkfst. Ck-out 11 am. Business servs avail. In-rm modem link. Health club privileges. Indoor pool; whirlpool. Some refrigerators. Cr cds: A, D, DS, MC, V.

D 🐾 🌊 🛶 🔥

★ **COUNTRY INN.** *1021 W Park Ave (54729). 715/720-1414; fax 715/720-1414.* 62 rms, 2 story. May-Sept: S $54.90-$98.90; D $62.90-$106.90; each addl $8; under 18 free; lower rates rest of yr. Crib avail. TV; cable (premium). Complimentary continental bkfst. Coffee in rms. Restaurant nearby. Ck-out 11 am. Business servs avail. In-rm modem link. Indoor pool; whirlpool. Some refrigerators. Cr cds: A, D, DS, MC, V.

D 🌊 🛶 🔥

★ **GLEN LOCH MOTEL.** *1225 Jefferson Ave (54729). 715/723-9121; fax 715/723-7020; toll-free 800/470-2755.* 19 rms. S $30; D $36-$44; each addl $4. TV; cable (premium). Complimentary coffee in lobby. Ck-out 11 am. Picnic tables. Cr cds: MC, V.

🛶 🔥 SC

★ **IMA INDIANHEAD.** *501 Summit Ave (54729). 715/723-9171; fax 715/723-6142.* 27 rms. S, D $40-$46; each addl $5. Crib avail. Pet accepted. TV; cable (premium), VCR avail. Complimentary coffee in lobby. Restaurant adj. Ck-out 11 am. Valet serv. Some refrigerators. On bluff overlooking city. Cr cds: A, DS, MC, V.

D 🐾 🏊 ➗ 🔥

★★ **PARK INN.** *1009 W Park Ave (54729). 715/723-2281; fax 715/723-2283; toll-free 800/446-9320. www. parkinn.com.* 67 rms. S $60-$79; D $67-$89; each addl $7. Crib avail. Pet accepted, some restrictions. TV; cable. Indoor pool; whirlpool. Restaurants 6:30 am-1:30 pm, 5-9:30 pm. Bar. Ck-out noon. Meeting rms. Business servs avail. Valet serv. Sundries. Some wet bars. Cr cds: A, C, D, DS, MC, V.

D 🐾 ➖ ➗ SC 🔥

Restaurants

★★ **EDELWEISS STEAK HOUSE AND MOTEL.** *8988 WI 124 (54729). 715/723-7881.* Hrs: 4:30-9:30 pm; Sun 10:30 am-2 pm, 4:30-9:30 pm. Closed Mon (winter); Dec 24, 25. German, American menu. Res accepted. Bar to 1 am. Dinner $6.75-$16.95. Bavarian decor; beamed ceiling; loft dining area. Cr cds: DS, MC, V.

D ➖

★ **LINDSAY'S ON GRAND.** *24 W Grand Ave (54729). 715/723-4025.* Hrs: 6 am-9 pm. Closed Jan 1, Thanksgiving, Dec 25. Bkfst $2.75-$4.85, lunch, dinner $4.55-$7.95. Child's menu. Specialties: cod fillet, glazed ham steak. Own pasta. Casual family restaurant.

D

Crandon

See also Rhinelander, Three Lakes

Pop 1,958 **Elev** 1,629 ft
Area code 715 **Zip** 54520
Information Chamber of Commerce, 201 S Lake Ave, PO Box 88; 715/478-3450 or 800/334-3387
Web www.crandonwi.com

What to See and Do

Camp Five Museum and "Lumberjack Special" Steam Train Tour. Old steam train ride to Camp Five Museum complex; harness and an active blacksmith shop, 1900 country store, logging museum with audiovisual presentation, nature center with diorama featuring area wildlife, 30-min guided forest tour, hayrack/pontoon boat trip (fee); children's playground, concession. (Mid-June-late Aug, four departures daily; closed Sun) 11 mi E on US 8 and WI 32 in Laona. Phone 715/674-3414. ¢¢¢

Motel/Motor Lodge

★ **FOUR SEASONS MOTEL.** *304 W Glen St (54520). 715/478-3377; fax 715/478-3785; res 888/816-6835. www.fourseasons-motel.com.* 20 rms. S $38; D $50; under 6 free. Crib free. TV; cable (premium). Coffee in rms. Ck-out 11 am. Business servs avail. Refrigerators. Cr cds: DS, MC, V.

D 🐾 ➗ 🔥

Delavan

(G-5) *See also Beloit, Burlington, Elkhorn, Fontana, Lake Geneva*

Settled 1836 **Pop** 6,073 **Elev** 940 ft
Area code 262 **Zip** 53115
Information Delavan Chamber of Commerce, 52 E Walworth Ave; 262/728-5095 or 800/624-0052
Web www.delavanwi.org

Between 1847 and 1894, Delavan was the headquarters of 28 different circuses. The original P. T. Barnum circus was organized here during the winter of 1870-1871 by William C. Coup. Spring Grove and St. Andrew's cemeteries are "last lot" resting places for more than 100 members of the 19th-century circus colony. Today many flowering crabapple trees grace the town, blooming usually in mid-May.

Restaurant

★★ **MILLIE'S.** *N 2484 County O (53115). 262/728-2434.* Hrs: 8 am-4 pm. Closed Mon (exc July-Aug); Thanksgiving, Dec 25; also Tues-Fri Jan-Feb. Bar. Bkfst $3.50-$7.95, lunch, dinner $4.95-$11.95. Specializes in Pennsylvania Dutch-style cooking. Own pancakes. Antique fur-

Devil's Lake

niture. On 80-acre farm; English gardens, gazebo.

D ⊣

Devil's Lake State Park

See also Baraboo, Portage, Prairie du Sac, Wisconsin Dells

(3 mi S of Baraboo on WI 123)

These 11,050 acres, with spring-fed Devil's Lake as the greatest single attraction, form Wisconsin's most beautiful state park. Remnants of an ancient mountain range surround the lake, providing unique scenery. The lake, 1¼ miles long, is in the midst of sheer cliffs of quartzite that rise as high as 500 feet above the water. Unusual rock formations may be found at the top of the bluffs. The park has a naturalist in residence who may be contacted for information concerning year-round nature hikes and programs. Sandy swimming beaches with bathhouses, concessions, and boat landings are at either end. No motorboats permitted. The park provides hiking and x-country skiing trails, picnic grounds, improved tent and trailer facilities (electric hookups, dump station), and a nature center. The lake is restocked yearly. Native American

mounds include the Eagle, Bear, and Lynx mounds. General tourist supplies are available at the north and south shores. Standard fees. (Daily) Contact Park Superintendent, S5975 Park Rd, Baraboo 53913. Phone 608/356-8301. Per vehicle ¢¢¢

Ice Age National Scientific Reserve. Naturalists explain evidence of Wisconsin glaciation; exhibits of local Ice Age features; trails; under development. Also included in the Reserve are Northern Unit Kettle Moraine State Forest (see FOND DU LAC) and two state parks, Mill Bluff (see TOMAH) and Interstate (see ST. CROIX FALLS). Per vehicle ¢¢

Dodgeville

See also Mineral Point, Mount Horeb, New Glarus, Platteville

Settled 1827 **Pop** 3,882 **Elev** 1,222 ft
Area code 608 **Zip** 53533
Information Dodgeville Chamber of Commerce, 178 1/2 N Iowa St, Suite 201; 608/935-5993
Web www.dodgeville.com

What to See and Do

Governor Dodge State Park. A 5,029-acre park with 95-acre and 150-acre lakes. Rock formations, white pine. Swimming, bathhouse, fishing, boating (electric motors only; ramps), canoeing (rentals); bicycle, hiking, and bridle trails; x-country skiing, snowmobiling, picnicking, playgrounds, concession, camping (electric hookups, dump station), backpack campsites, horse campground. Nature programs (June-Aug). Standard fees. (Daily) 3 mi N via US 151, WI 23. Phone 608/935-2315.

Motels/Motor Lodges

★★ **DON Q INN.** *3656 WI 23 (53533). 608/935-2321; fax 608/935-2416; toll-free 800/666-7848. www. fantasuite.com.* 60 rms, 3 story. Mid-May-Oct: S, D $69-$89; each addl $10; specialty rms $109-$224; under 18 free; lower rates rest of yr. Crib $8. TV. Indoor/outdoor pool; whirlpool. Complimentary continental bkfst (Mon-Sat). Restaurant 5-8:30 pm. Ck-out noon. Meeting rms. X-country ski 1½ mi. Some in-rm whirlpools. Game rm. Imaginatively furnished; rustic decor. Cr cds: A, D, DS, MC, V.

⬛⬛⬛⬛⬛⬛

★★ **NEW CONCORD INN.** *3637 State Rd 23 (53533). 608/935-3770; fax 608/935-9605; toll-free 800/348-9310. www.concordinn.com.* 63 rms, 3 story. May-Oct: S, D $74-$129; each addl $6; suites $82; under 12 free; lower rates rest of yr. Crib $6. TV; cable (premium). Indoor pool; whirlpool. Complimentary continental bkfst. Restaurant nearby. Ck-out 11 am. X-country ski 2 mi. Game rm. Some refrigerators. Cr cds: A, DS, MC, V.

⬛⬛⬛⬛⬛⬛⬛

Door County

Famous for its fish boils, foliage, and 250 miles of shoreline, Door County is a peninsula with Green Bay on the west and Lake Michigan on the east. Its picturesque villages, rolling woodlands, limestone bluffs, and beautiful vistas are the reason the area is often referred to as the Cape Cod of the Midwest.

Door County offers year-round recreational opportunities. Spring and summer bring fishing, sailing, beachcombing, camping, hiking, biking, and horseback riding. Thousands of acres of apple and cherry blossoms color the landscape in late May. There is excellent scuba diving in the *Portes des Mortes* (Death's Door) Straits at the tip of the peninsula, where hundreds of shipwrecks lie in the shifting freshwater sands. Fall colors can be viewed from the endless miles of trails and country roads, which become cross-country ski routes in winter.

Many artists reside here, as is evidenced by the towns' shops, galleries, and boutiques. Summertime theater and concerts also attract tourists.

The taste of the peninsula is unquestionably the legendary fish boil. Trout or whitefish and potatoes and onions are cooked in a cauldron over an open fire. When the fish has almost finished cooking, kerosene is thrown onto the fire, creating a huge flame and causing the unwanted oils to boil out and over the pot. (See restaurant listings in individual towns.)

Door County Chamber of Commerce, 1015 Green Bay Rd, PO Box 406, Sturgeon Bay, 54235, 920/743-4456 or 800/527-3529, has winter and summer schedules of events, maps and details on recreational facilities. For a free vacation guide, phone 800/52-RELAX.

The following towns in Door County are included in the *Mobil Travel Guide* (For full information on any one of them, see the individual alphabetical listing): Bailey's Harbor, Egg Harbor, Ellison Bay, Ephraim, Fish Creek, Sister Bay, Sturgeon Bay, and Washington Island.

Special Event

Festival of Blossoms. Phone 920/743-4456. Month of May.

Eagle River

See also Land O' Lakes, Rhinelander, St. Germain, Three Lakes

Pop 1,374 **Elev** 1,647 ft
Area code 715 **Zip** 54521
Information Eagle River Area Chamber of Commerce, PO Box 1917; 715/479-6400 or 800/359-6315
Web www.eagle-river.com

The bald eagles that gave this town its name are still occasionally seen, and the Eagle chain of 28 lakes, the largest inland chain of freshwater lakes in the world, is an outstanding tourist attraction. Eagle River has developed as a center of winter sports. The result is lake vacationers in summer and ski fans, both cross-country and downhill, and snowmobilers in winter. There are more than 11 miles of cross-country ski trails on Anvil Lake trail, and 600 miles of snowmobile trails and several hiking areas are in the Nicolet National Forest. A Ranger District office of the Nicolet National Forest (see THREE LAKES) is located here.

What to See and Do

Trees For Tomorrow Natural Resources Education Center. Demonstration forests, nature trail; "talking tree." (Daily) Outdoor skills and natural resource programs with emphasis on forest ecology and conservation. X-country skiing. Orienteering. Natural resources workshops (fee). Guided tours (Tues and Thurs, summer). 519 Sheridan St. Phone 715/479-6456. **FREE**

Special Events

World Championship Snowmobile Derby. 1½ mi N on US 45. Third wkend Jan. Phone 715/479-4424.

Klondike Days. Oval sled dog races, winter events. Mid- Feb. Phone 715/479-4456.

National Championship Musky Open. Third wkend Aug. Phone 715/479-6400.

Cranberry Fest. Cranberry bog tours, events. First wkend Oct. Phone 800/359-6315.

Motels/Motor Lodges

★ ★ **DAYS INN.** 844 Railroad St N (54521). 715/479-5151; fax 715/479-8259; toll-free 800/329-7466. www.daysinn.com. 93 rms, 2 story. June-Oct: S $54-$99; D $59-$99; each addl $5; under 18 free; wkends (2-day min); higher rates for special events; lower rates rest of yr. Crib free. Pet accepted. TV; cable. Indoor pool; whirlpool, sauna. Complimentary continental bkfst. Coffee in rms. Restaurant adj 5 am-9 pm. Ck-out 11 am. Coin lndry. Meeting rm. Business servs avail. In-rm modem link. X-country ski ½ mi. Game rm. Some in-rm whirlpools; refrigerators. Cr cds: A, MC, V.

★ ★ **EAGLE RIVER INN AND RESORT.** 5260 WI 70 W (54521). 715/479-2000; fax 715/479-9198; toll-free 866/479-2060. www.eriver-inn.com. 36 rms, 2 story, 7 suites, 8 kits. Late June-Aug, Christmas wk, wkends Jan-Feb: S $59-79; D $79-$109; each addl $10; suites $149-$179; kit. units $79-$119; under 12 free; lower rates rest of yr. wkly rates; ski, plans; Crib $10. TV; cable. Indoor pool; whirlpool. Restaurant 4-9 pm in season. Bar. Ck-out 11 am. Meeting rms. Business servs avail. Gift shop. X-country ski 2 mi. Exercise equipt; sauna. Game rm. Miniature golf. Boats. In-rm whirlpool in some suites. Balconies. Picnic tables. On lake; dock. Cr cds: A, DS, MC, V.

★ **WHITE EAGLE.** 4948 WI 70 W (54521). 715/479-4426; fax 715/479-3570; toll-free 800/782-6488. www.whiteeaglemotel.com. 22 rms. No A/C. Mid-June-mid-Oct: S, D $52-$75; each addl $5; lower rates rest of yr. Crib free. Pet accepted; $10. TV; cable (premium). Heated pool; whirlpool. Sauna. Complimentary coffee. Restaurant nearby. Ck-out 10:30 am. X-country ski 3 mi. Snowmobile trails. Paddleboat, pontoon boat. Refrigerators avail. Picnic tables. On Eagle River; private piers. Driving range, miniature golf opp. Cr cds: DS, MC, V.

Resorts

★ ★ **CHANTICLEER INN.** 1458 E Dollar Lake Rd (54521). 715/479-4486; fax 715/479-0004; toll-free 800/752-9193. www.chanticleerinn.com. 13 motel rms, 2 story, 8 kit. villas, 50 units (1-3 bedrm) in 20 town houses, 20 with kit., most A/C. S, D $69-$125; each addl $10; under 16 free; golf, package plans; higher rates: winter hols, snowmobile derby. Crib $10. TV. Playground. Complimentary coffee in motel rms. Dining rm 8-10 am, 5:30-9:30 pm. Box lunches, snacks. Bar. Ck-out 10:30 am, ck-in 3 pm. Grocery, package store 2½ mi. Coin lndry. Meeting rms. Business servs avail. Gift shop. Free airport transportation. 2 tennis courts, 1 lighted. 9-hole golf adj, daily greens fee. 2 sand beaches; boats, motors, canoes, pontoon boats. X-country ski on site. Rec rm. Fishing guides, clean and store area. Fireplace in villas/condos. Private patios or balconies in townhouses and suites. Cr cds: A, DS, MC, V.

⬛⬛⬛⬛⬛⬛⬛

★ **GYPSY VILLA RESORT.** *950 Circle Dr (54521). 715/479-8644; fax 715/479-8780; toll-free 800/232-9714. www.gypsyvilla.com.* 21 kit. cottages (1-4-bedrm), 6 A/C. Kit. cottages $445-$1,918/wk (2-6 persons); daily rates; MAP avail. Crib free. Garage parking (fee). Pet accepted, some restrictions; fee. TV; VCR avail. Wading pool; whirlpool. Playground. Free supervised children's activities (June-Aug). Ck-out noon, ck-in 3 pm. Coin lndry. Meeting rms. Phone avail. Business servs avail. Grocery, package store 2 mi. Tennis. Private swimming beach. Boats, waterskiing. Bicycles. Lawn games. Soc dir. Game rm. Exercise equipt; sauna. Fish/hunt guides. Fireplaces; some in-rm whirlpools. Private patios. Picnic tables, grills. Most cottages on Cranberry Island. Cr cds: A, MC, V.

⬛⬛⬛⬛⬛⬛⬛ SC

Restaurant

★ **BAERTSCHY'S PINE GABLES SUPPER CLUB.** *5009 WI 70 W (54521). 715/479-7689.* Hrs: 4:30-closing. Closed Tues. German, American menu. Bar. Dinner $6.95-$15.95. Own soups, dressings. Rustic decor. Cr cds: A, D, DS, MC, V.

D ⬛

Eau Claire

(D-2) *See also Chippewa Falls, Menomonie*

Settled 1844 **Pop** 56,856 **Elev** 796 ft
Area code 715
Information Eau Claire Convention Bureau, 3625 Gateway Dr, Suite F, 54701; 715/831-2345 or 800/344-3866
Web www.eauclaire-info.com

Once a wild and robust lumber camp and sawmill on the shores of the Eau Claire and Chippewa rivers, the city

has turned to diversified industry. The name is French for "clear water."

What to See and Do

Chippewa Valley Museum. "Paths of the People" Ojibwe exhibit, "Settlement and Survival" 1850-1925 history of Chippewa Valley. Street scene, 21-rm doll house, agricultural wing, old-fashioned ice cream parlor, research library. Log house (1860); Sunnyview School (1880). Gift shop. (Tues-Sun) Carson Park. Phone 715/834-7871. ¢¢

Dells Mills Museum. (1864) Historic five-story water-powered flour and grist mill built of hand-hewn timbers; wooden pegged. One-rm schoolhouse museum. Gun shop, antique shop. (May-Oct, daily) 20 mi SE via WI 12, 3 mi N of Augusta via WI 27 on County V. Phone 715/286-2714. ¢¢¢

⭐ **Paul Bunyan Logging Camp.** Restored 1890s logging camp with bunkhouse, cook shack, blacksmith shop, dingle, filers shack, barn; heavy equipment display. Artifacts, film at interpretive center. (First Mon in Apr-first Mon in Oct) Carson Park, Clairemont Ave to Menomonie St, E to Carson Park Dr. Phone 715/835-6200. ¢¢

University of Wisconsin-Eau Claire. (1916) 10,500 students. Planetarium, bird museum, greenhouses; dramatic productions, musical events, art gallery (free). Putnam Park arboretum, a 230-acre tract of forest land kept in its natural state, has self-guided nature trails. Park and Garfield aves. Phone 715/836-2637.

Motels/Motor Lodges

★ **ANTLERS MOTEL.** *2245 S Hastings Way (54701). 715/834-5313; fax 715/839-7582; toll-free 800/423-4526.* 33 rms, 1-2 story. S $48-$55; D $56-$62; each addl $5. Crib free. TV; cable (premium). Playground. Restaurant adj open 24 hrs. Ck-out 11 am. Cr cds: A, MC, V.

⬛

★★ **BEST WESTERN ATRIUM INN.** *2851 Hendrickson Dr (54701). 715/835-2242; fax 715/835-1027; toll-free 800/528-1234. www.bestwestern. com.* 109 rms, 2 story. S $64-$78; D $75-$90; each addl $12; under 18 free. Crib free. TV; cable (premium), VCR avail. Indoor pool; whirlpool. Complimentary full bkfst Sat-Sun. Complimentary continental bkfst Mon-Fri. Coffee in rms. Restaurant 6:30 am-2 pm, 5-9 pm; Sat, Sun 7 am-2 pm, 5-9 pm. Bar 4 pm-1 am, Sun noon-9 pm; entertainment. Ck-out 11 am. Meeting rms. Business servs avail. In-rm modem link. Valet serv. Sundries. Free airport, bus depot transportation. Exercise equipt. Sauna. Domed recreation area. Game rm. Cr cds: A, C, D, DS, MC, V.

⊡ ⇌ 🏋 ✈ 🔥

★ ★ **BEST WESTERN WHITE HOUSE INN.** *1828 S Hastings Way (54701). 715/832-8356; fax 715/836-9686; toll-free 877/213-1600. www. bestwestern.com.* 66 rms, 1-2 story. S, D $64-67; each addl $5. Crib $5. Pet accepted; $10/day. TV; cable (premium). Indoor pool; whirlpool. Complimentary continental bkfst. Restaurant 4:30-11 pm. Ck-out 11 am. Business servs avail. In-rm modem link. Valet serv. Sauna. Health club privileges. Game rm. Refrigerators; some in-rm whirlpools. Sun deck. Cr cds: A, C, D, DS, MC, V.

⊡ ⇤ ⇌ ⊠ 🔥 SC

★ ★ **COMFORT INN.** *3117 Craig Rd (54701). 715/833-9798; res 800/228-5150. www.comfortinn.com.* 56 rms, 2 story. June-Aug: S $62.95-$70.95; D $67.95-$75.95; each addl $5; under 18 free; lower rates rest of yr. Crib avail. Pet accepted. TV; cable (premium). Indoor pool. Complimentary continental bkfst. Restaurant nearby. Ck-out 11 am. Business servs avail. In-rm modem link. Game rm. X-country ski 2 mi. Cr cds: A, C, D, DS, MC, V.

⊡ ⇤ ⇢ ⇌ ⊠ 🔥

★ **EXEL INN.** *2305 Craig Rd (54701). 715/834-3193; fax 715/839-9905; toll-free 800/367-3935.* 100 rms, 2 story. S $33.99-$45; D $44.99-$60; each addl $5. Crib free. Pet accepted. TV; cable (premium). Complimentary continental bkfst. Coffee in rms. Restaurant adj open 24 hrs. Ck-out noon. Business servs avail. Exercise equipt. Cr cds: A, C, D, DS, MC, V.

⊡ ⇤ 🏋 ⊠ 🔥 SC

★ ★ **HAMPTON INN.** *2622 Craig Rd (54701). 715/833-0003; fax 715/833-*0915; toll-free 800/426-7866. www. hamptoninn.com.* 106 rms, 3 story. S $59-$74; D $64-$79; under 18 free; higher rates wkends. Crib avail. TV; cable (premium). Indoor pool; whirlpool. Complimentary continental bkfst. Restaurant opp 6 am-11 pm. Ck-out noon. Meeting rms. Business servs avail. In-rm modem link. X-country ski 2 mi. Exercise equipt. Cr cds: A, C, D, DS, MC, V.

⊡ ⇤ ⇌ 🏋 ⊠ 🔥 SC

★ **HEARTLAND INN.** *4075 Commonwealth Ave (54701). 715/839-7100; fax 715/839-7050; toll-free 800/334-3277. www.heartlandinn.com.* 88 rms, 2 story. S $65-$75; D $70-$80; each addl $5; under 17 free. Crib avail. Pet accepted. TV; cable (premium), VCR avail. Indoor pool; whirlpool. Complimentary continental bkfst. Coffee in rms. Restaurant nearby. Ck-out noon. Meeting rms. Business servs avail. In-rm modem link. Coin lndry. Game rm. Sundries. X-country ski 5 mi. Sauna. Cr cds: A, D, DS, MC, V.

⊡ ⇌ ⊠ 🔥 SC ⇤ ⇢

★ **MAPLE MANOR MOTEL.** *2507 S Hastings Way (54701). 715/834-2618; fax 715/834-1148; toll-free 800/624-3763. www.themaplemanor.com.* 36 rms. S $29-$35; D $35-$45; each addl $5; wkly rates. Crib $3. Pet accepted. TV; cable (premium). Complimentary full bkfst. Restaurant 6:30 am-1:30 pm. Bar to 11 pm. Ck-out 11:30 am. Sundries. Many refrigerators. Picnic tables. Cr cds: A, D, DS, MC, V.

⇤ ⊠ 🔥 SC

★ ★ **QUALITY INN.** *809 W Clairemont Ave (54701). 715/834-6611; toll-free 800/638-7949. www.quality inn-eauclaire.com.* 120 rms, 2 story. S $52-$75; D $60-$80; each addl $10; suites $119-$139; under 18 free; Sun rates. Crib free. Pet accepted. TV; cable (premium), VCR avail. 2 pools, 1 indoor; whirlpool. Complimentary full bkfst. Restaurant 6 am-10 pm; Fri, Sat to 10:30 pm. Bar 11-2 am; entertainment Tues-Sat. Ck-out noon. Meeting rms. Business servs avail. In-rm modem link. Valet serv. Sundries. Sauna. Rec rm. Private patios, balconies. Cr cds: A, C, D, DS, ER, JCB, MC, V.

⊡ ⇤ ⇌ ⊠ 🔥 SC

★★ **RAMADA INN CONFERENCE CENTER.** *1202 W Clairemont Ave (54701). 715/834-3181; fax 715/834-1630; www.ramada.com.* 233 rms, 2-5 story. S $59-99; D $69-$109; each addl $10. Crib free. Pet accepted. TV; cable (premium). 2 indoor pools. Restaurant. Bar; Sun from noon. Complimentary continental bkfst Mon-Fri. Ck-out 11 am. Meeting rms. Business servs avail. In-rm modem link. Exercise equipt. Coin lndry. Valet serv. Free airport transportation. Cr cds: A, D, DS, MC, V.

[icons]

★ **ROADSTAR INN.** *1151 W MacArthur Ave (54701). 715/832-9731; fax 715/832-0690; toll-free 800/445-4667.* 62 rms, 2 story. S $38-$48; D $47-$54; each addl $3; under 16 free. Crib avail. TV; cable (premium). Complimentary continental bkfst. Restaurant nearby. Ck-out 11 am. Some refrigerators. Cr cds: A, C, D, DS, MC, V.

[icons]

B&B/Small Inn

★★★ **FANNY HILL VICTORIAN INN.** *3919 Crescent Ave (54703). 715/836-8184; fax 715/836-8180; toll-free 800/292-8026. www.fannyhill.com.* 11 rms. S, D $79-$175; package plans. TV; cable (premium). Complimentary full bkfst. Restaurant (see also FANNY HILL INN AND DINNER THEATRE). Ck-out 11 am, ck-in 2:30 pm. Business servs avail. X-country ski adj. Dinner theater on premises. Victorian garden overlooking Chippewa River. Totally nonsmoking. Cr cds: A, C, D, DS, MC, V.

[icons]

Restaurant

★★ **FANNY HILL INN AND DINNER THEATRE.** *3919 Crescent Ave (54703). 715/836-8184. www.fanny hill.com.* Hrs: 5-9 pm; Sun brunch 10 am-2 pm. Closed Mon, Tues (summer only); Dec 24-25. Res accepted; required for dinner theatre. Continental menu. Bar. A la carte entrees: dinner $12.95-$25.95. Sun brunch $9.95. Specializes in steak, seafood. Dinner theater Thurs-Sun. Family-owned. Cr cds: A, D, DS, MC, V.

[icon]

Egg Harbor (Door County)

See also Door County

Pop 183 **Elev** 600 ft **Area code** 920 **Zip** 54209

Information Door County Chamber of Commerce, 1015 Green Bay Rd, PO Box 406, Sturgeon Bay 54235; 920/743-4456 or 800/527-3529

Web www.doorcountyvacations.com

This town in Door County (see) is on the shores of Green Bay.

Special Event

Birch Creek Music Center. 3 mi E via County E. Concert series in unique barn concert hall. Early-mid-July: percussion series; mid-July-mid-Aug: big band series. Phone 920/868-3763. Other concerts and events through Labor Day.

Motels/Motor Lodges

★★ **ALPINE INN.** *7715 Alpine Rd, Egg Harbor (54209). 920/868-3000.* 52 motel rms, 3 story, 5 suites; 30 kit. cottages. No elvtr. No rm phones. Mid-June-Labor Day: S $60.50-$82; D $71-$96; each addl $10; suites $96; kit. cottages $104-$271 or $640-$1,146/wk; MAP avail; family, wkly rates; golf plan; lower rates Memorial Day-mid-June, Labor Day-mid-Oct. Closed rest of yr. Crib $5. Pet accepted, some restrictions. TV. Heated pool. Playground. Supervised children's activities (July-Aug); ages 3-8. Restaurant 7:30-11 am, 5:45-8:30 pm. Bar to midnight. Ck-out 10 am. Meeting rms. Business servs avail. Bellhops. Gift shop. Tennis. 27-hole golf, greens fee, putting green. Game rm. Rec rm. Some refrigerators; microwaves avail; wet bar in cottages. Picnic tables, grills. Swimming beach. Cr cds: A, DS, MC, V.

[icons]

★★★ **ASHBROOKE SUITES.** *7942 Egg Harbor Rd, Egg Harbor (54209). 920/868-3113; fax 920/868-2837; toll-free 877/868-3113. www.ashbrooke. net.* 36 rms, 2 story. Late June-mid-Oct (2-day min): S, D $111-$185; lower rates Dec-late June. Closed Dec; also wkdays Nov-Apr. Children over 13 yrs only. TV; cable (premium). Indoor pool; whirlpool. Complimentary continental bkfst. Complimentary coffee in rms. Restaurant adj 7 am-9 pm. Ck-out 11 am. Meeting rm. Business servs avail. X-country ski 5 mi. Exercise equipt; sauna. Refrigerators, microwaves, wet bars; some in-rm whirlpools, fireplaces. Totally nonsmoking. Cr cds: A, MC, V.

⬛ 🔧 🔧 🏊 🏊 🏃 🔧 🔧

★★★ **BAY POINT INN.** *7933 WI 42, Egg Harbor (54209). 920/868-3297; fax 920/868-2876; toll-free 800/707-6660. www.baypointinn.com.* 10 kit. suites, 2 story. June-Sept: kit. suites $165-$235; each addl $12; wkly rates; lower rates rest of yr. Crib avail. TV; VCR (free movies). Heated pool; whirlpool. Complimentary continental bkfst. Restaurant nearby. Ck-out 11 am. Business center. X-country ski 6 mi. Microwaves; some fireplaces; whirlpool in suites. Balconies. Picnic tables, grills. Cr cds: A, D, DS, MC, V.

⬛ 🔧 🏊 🔧 SC 🏃

★★★ **EGG HARBOR LODGE.** *7965 WI 42, Egg Harbor (54209). 920/868-3115. www.eggharborlodge.com.* 25 rms, 3 story. July-Aug: S $86-$130, D $111-$250; addl $25; wkend rates vary; studio rms $135-$250; lower rates May-June, Sept-Oct. Closed rest of yr. Children over 17 yrs only. TV; cable (premium). Heated pool; whirlpool. Complimentary coffee in rms. Restaurant nearby. Ck-out 11 am. Tennis. Putting green. Refrigerators; some wet bars, in-rm whirlpools; microwaves avail. Private patios, balconies. Cr cds: A, MC, V.

🔧 🔧 🔧 🏊 🔧 🔧

★★ **LANDING RESORT.** *7741 Egg Harbor Rd , Egg Harbor (54209). 920/868-3282; fax 920/868-2689; toll-free 800/851-8917. www.thelandingresort.com.* 60 kit. units, 2 story. June-Aug: S $111-$125; D $134-$205; each addl $10; under 7 free; wkly rates; lower rates rest of yr. Crib $5. TV; cable (premium), VCR (movies $3). 2 pools, 1 indoor; whirlpool. Playground. Restaurant nearby. Ck-out 11 am. Business servs avail. Tennis. Game rm. Microwaves. Private

patios. Picnic tables, grills. On 5 wooded acres. Cr cds: DS, MC, V.

⬛ 🔧 🏊 🔧 🔧

★ **LULL-ABI MOTEL.** *7928 Egg Harbor Rd, Egg Harbor (54209). 920/868-3135; fax 920/868-1695. www.lullabimotel.com.* 23 rms, 2 story, 5 suites. July-Oct: D $56-$88; each addl $15; suites $84-$99; lower rates rest of yr. TV; cable (premium). Complimentary coffee in lobby. Restaurant nearby. Ck-out 11 am. Whirlpool. Refrigerator, microwave, minibar in suites. Cr cds: A, DS, MC, V.

⬛ 🔧

Restaurants

★ **GRANT'S OLDE STAGE STATION TAVERN.** *7778 Egg Harbor Rd, Egg Harbor (54209). 920/868-3247.* Hrs: 8-2 am. Closed Dec 25. Italian, Amer menu. Bar. Bkfst $1.50-$7.50, lunch $3.95-$9.95, dinner $4.50-$15.50. Buffet: bkfst $6.95. Child's menu. Specializes in broasted chicken, chicken pot pie. Own desserts, bakery. Former stagecoach stop (1889). Outdoor dining. Cr cds: MC, V.

⬛ 🔧

★ **VILLAGE CAFE.** *7918 Egg Harbor Rd, Egg Harbor (54209). 920/868-3342.* Hrs: 7 am-2 pm. Closed Nov-May. Wine, beer. Bkfst $2.55-$6.15, lunch $4.95-$6.45. Specializes in bkfst entrees. Outdoor dining on screened-in deck. Cr cds: DS, MC, V.

⬛

Elkhart Lake

See also Fond du Lac, Sheboygan

Pop 1,019 **Elev** 945 ft **Area code** 920 **Zip** 53020

Information Chamber of Commerce, 41 E Rhine St, PO Box 425; 920/876-2922

Web www.elkhartlake.com

This lake resort, famous for its good beaches, is one of the state's oldest vacation spots.

What to See and Do

Broughton-Sheboygan County Marsh. A 14,000-acre wildlife area. Fishing, boating, canoeing; duck hunting, camping (53 sites; hookups), lodge, restaurant. Standard fees. 1 mi NE on County J. Phone 920/876-2535. **FREE**

Little Elkhart Lake. A 131-acre lake with heavy concentrations of pike, walleye, bass, and panfish.

Old Wade House Historic Site. Restored Old Wade House (1850), early stagecoach inn. Nearby are smokehouse, blacksmith shop, mill dam site; and Jung Carriage Museum housing more than 100 restored horse and hand-drawn vehicles. Picnicking, concession. Horse-drawn carriage rides. (May-Oct, call for schedule) 2 mi U on County P, then SW via County P and A in Greenbush. Phone 920/526-3271. ¢¢¢

Timm House. (1892) Ten-rm, Victorian-style house contains period furniture; guided tours. (June-Sept, Sun; rest of yr, by appt) Approx 15 mi N via WI 32, NW via WI 57 in New Holstein at 1600 Wisconsin Ave. Phone 920/898-9006. ¢ Admission incl

Pioneer Corner Museum. Exhibits of early German immigrant furniture; extensive button collection; general store and post office; Panama Canal memorabilia. (June-Sept, Sun; rest of yr, by appt) Main St. Phone 920/898-9006.

Special Event

Road America. 1½ mi S on WI 67. Located on 525 rolling, wooded acres; a closed-circuit 4-mi sports car racecourse with 14 turns. One of the most popular events of the season is the CART Indy race, which draws top-name race teams. Mon-Fri, June-Sept. Phone 800/365-7223.

Resorts

★ ★ ★ **OSTHOFF RESORT.** *101 Osthoff Ave (53020). 920/876-3366; fax 920/876-3228; res 800/876-3399. www.osthoff.com.* 145 kit. suites, 4 story. May-mid-Oct: suites $185-$440; under 18 free; family rates; package plans; wkends, hols 2-3 day min (in season); higher rates special events; lower rates rest of yr. Crib $5.

TV; cable (premium), VCR avail (movies). Complimentary coffee in rms. Restaurant 7 am-10 pm. Box lunches. Snack bar. Picnics. Bar 8 am-11 pm. Ck-out noon, ck-in 3 pm. Grocery. Coin lndry. Package store. Business servs avail. Bellhops. Valet serv. Beauty shop. Sports dir. Lighted tennis. 36-hole golf privileges, pro. Boats. Waterskiing. X-country ski onsite. Snowmobiles. Hiking. Bicycle rentals. Lawn games. Social dir. Rec rm. Game rm. Exercise equipt; sauna. Massage. Spa. Fishing/hunting guides; clean and store. 3 pools, 1 indoor; whirlpool, poolside serv. Playground. Supervised children's activities; ages 4-12. Wet bars, fireplaces; many in-rm whirlpools. Balconies. Picnic tables, grills. On lake. Totally nonsmoking. Cr cds: A, D, DS, MC, V.

⊡ 🛆 🏊 🏌 🛶 🕴 🎿 🔥 🏌

★ **VICTORIAN VILLAGE ON ELKHART LAKE.** *279 S Lake St (53020). 920/876-3323; fax 920/876-3484; toll-free 877/860-9988. www.vicvill.com.* 120 units, 17 in main building. MAP, June-Sept: S, D $100-$195; children $17.95-$19.95; wkly rates; EP avail; wkend packages; lower rates rest of yr. Crib free. TV; VCR avail. 2 pools, 1 indoor. Free supervised children's activities (June-Sept); ages 3-12. Dining rm 8-10 am, 6:30-8 pm. Box lunches, snack bar, picnics. Bar 8-1 am. Ck-out 11:30 am, ck-in 4 pm. Convention facilities. Business servs avail. In-rm modem link. Sports dir. Miniature golf. Private beach; swimming, waterskiing; boats, motors, rowboats, canoes, sailboats, paddleboats, pontoons, jet skis. Hiking trails. Lawn games. Soc dir; entertainment. Game rm. Rec rm. Balconies. Picnic tables. Dock. Cr cds: A, DS, MC, V.

⊡ 🏊 🛆 🎿 🔥

B&Bs/Small Inns

★ ★ ★ **52 STAFFORD.** *52 S Stafford St, Plymouth (53073). 920/893-0552; fax 920/893-1800. www.classicinns. com.* 19 rms, 3 story, 4 suites. No elvtr. S, D $79.50-$129.50; suites $129.50. Crib free. TV; cable. Complimentary continental bkfst. Dining rm 5-9 pm; Fri, Sat to 10 pm. Ck-out 10:30 am, ck-in 3 pm. Business servs avail. X-country ski 12 mi. Many in-

rm whirlpools. Four-poster beds. Built 1892; restored and furnished as an Irish guest house. Cr cds: A, D, DS, MC, V.
⊠ ⊠ ⊠

★★ **YANKEE HILL INN BED AND BREAKFAST.** *405 Collins St, Plymouth (53073). 920/892-2222; fax 920/892-6228. www.yankeehillinn.com.* 12 rms, 5 with A/C, 3 with shower only, 2 story. S, D $78-$106; each addl $15. TV in common rm; cable, VCR avail. Complimentary full bkfst. Restaurant nearby. Ck-out 11 am, ck-in 3 pm. Business servs avail. Luggage handling. Gift shop. Downhill/x-country ski 1 mi. Many in-rm whirlpools; microwaves avail. Picnic tables, grills. 2 separate houses: Henry H. Huson house built in 1870; Gothic Italianate home. Gilbert L. Huson house built in 1891; Queen Anne home. Totally nonsmoking. Cr cds: A, DS, MC, V.
⊠ ⊠ ⊠

Elkhorn

(G-5) *See also Burlington, Fort Atkinson, Janesville, Waukesha*

Settled 1837 **Pop** 5,337 **Elev** 1,033 ft **Area code** 262 **Zip** 53121
Information Chamber of Commerce, 114 W Court St; 262/723-5788
Web www.elkhorn-wi.org

What to See and Do

Skiing. Alpine Valley Ski Resort. Resort has quad, five triple, three double chairlifts; four rope tows; patrol, school, rentals; snowmaking; restaurant, cafeteria, bar. Longest run 3,000 ft; vertical drop 388 ft. (Dec-mid-Mar, daily; closed Dec 24 afternoon) Night skiing. Also motel; indoor/outdoor pools, whirlpool; golf, tennis. 1½ mi S off I-43 on County D and Townline Rd near East Troy. Phone 262/642-7374. ¢¢¢¢

Watson's Wild West Museum. Re-creation of general store; storytelling, western-style barbecues. (May-Oct, Tues-Sun) W 4865 Potter Rd. Phone 262/723-7505. ¢¢

Webster House. Restored 19th-century home of Joseph Philbrick Webster, composer of "Sweet Bye and Bye" and "Lorena." Mounted game bird collection. (Memorial Day-mid-Oct, Wed-Sat afternoons; Apr, by appt) 9 E Rockwell St. Phone 262/723-4248. ¢¢

Special Events

Festival of Summer. Town Sq. Arts and crafts fair; custom car show. First wkend Aug. Phone 262/723-5788.

Walworth County Fair. NE via WI 11 E to city limits. Agricultural fair, grandstand entertainment, and harness racing. Phone 262/723-3228. Six days ending Labor Day.

Ellison Bay (Door County)

See also Door County

Pop 250 **Elev** 610 ft **Area code** 920 **Zip** 54210
Information Door County Chamber of Commerce, 1015 Green Bay Rd, PO Box 406, Sturgeon Bay 54235; 920/743-4456 or 800/527-3529
Web www.doorcountyvacations.com

This resort area is near the northern end of Door County (see). Fishing and boating are popular here; public launching ramps and charter boats are available. This is also considered a good area for scuba diving.

What to See and Do

Death's Door Bluff. Near top of peninsula between the mainland and Washington Island (see). According to legend, 300 Native Americans, attempting a surprise attack, were betrayed and dashed to death against the rocks. Also named because of the large number of ships lost here.

Door County Maritime Museum. Artifacts of fishing and shipbuilding industries; fishing tug open to public; Great Lakes sailing and US Coast Guard; nautical painting; also film on history of commercial fishing. (July-mid-Oct, days vary; Memorial Day-June, Fri-Sun; closed rest of yr) 5 mi E and N on WI 42 in Gills Rock. Phone 920/854-2860. ¢

Ferry to Washington Island. (see) Enclosed cabin plus open deck seating. 30-min trip. (Yr-round) Also accommodates cars and bicycles (fees vary). (Daily) 8 mi E and N on WI 42 to Northport Pier, in Gills Rock. Contact Washington Island Ferry Line. Phone 920/847-2546. ¢¢¢

Newport State Park. A 2,370-acre wilderness park with 11 mi of Lake Michigan shoreline. Beach. Hiking, x-country ski trails; picnicking, backpack and winter camping. Standard fees. NE of town on County Rd NP. Phone 920/854-2500. ¢¢

Special Event

Old Ellison Bay Days. Parade, fishing contests, fish boil, bazaars, fireworks. Late June. Phone 920/743-4456.

Motels/Motor Lodges

★ ★ **GRAND VIEW MOTEL.** *11885 WI 42, Ellison Bay (54210). 920/854-5450; fax 920/854-7538; toll-free 800/258-8208. www.doorcounty vacations.com.* 28 units, 2 story. Late June-mid-Oct: S, D $82-$138; each addl $7; under 14, $3; suites $138; lower rates early Apr-late June, midlate Oct. Closed rest of yr. Crib avail. TV; VCR avail. Complimentary continental bkfst. Ck-out 11 am. Bellhops. Sundries. Bicycles. Rec rm. Refrigerators; some in-rm whirlpools, fireplaces. Private patios, balconies. Totally nonsmoking. Cr cds: A, MC, V.
D ⊠

★ **SHORELINE RESORT.** *12747 WI 42, Ellison Bay (54210). 920/854-2606; fax 920/854-5971. www.the shorelineresort.com.* 16 rms, 2 story. July-Aug: S, D $89-$94; kit. unit $99; lower rates May-June, Sept-Oct. Closed rest of yr. Crib free. TV. Restaurant adj 7 am-9 pm. Wine, beer. Ck-out 11 am. Business servs avail. Gift shop. Refrigerators, microwaves. Balconies. Picnic tables, grills. Overlooks Green Bay. Totally nonsmoking. Cr cds: DS, MC, V.
D ⊠ 🖗

Resort

★ ★ **WAGON TRAIL.** *1041 County Rd ZZ, Ellison Bay (54210). 920/854-2385; fax 920/854-5278. toll-free 888/559-2466. www.wagontrail.com.* 72 rms in 2-story lodge, 8 suites, 16 kits; 30 houses, 8 kit. cottages. July-Aug: S, D $109-$169; each addl $10; suites $159-$239; kit. cottages $175-$250; houses $175-$260; under 18 free in lodge; lower rates rest of yr. Crib free. TV; cable. Indoor pool; whirlpool. Playground. Restaurant. Box lunches. Ck-out 10 am, ck-in 3 pm. Coin lndry. Meeting rms. Business servs avail. Package store 1 mi. Gift shop. Bakery shop. Tennis. Private beach, marina. Boats; motors. X-country ski on site; rentals. Exercise rm; sauna. Bicycle rentals. Lawn games. Game rm. Some refrigerators, in-rm whirlpools; microwaves avail. Some patios, fireplaces in cottages. Picnic tables, grills. On shores of Rowley's Bay; extensive wooded grounds. Cr cds: DS, MC, V.
D ⊠ 🖗 ⚓ 🏃 ⊠ 🖗

B&B/Small Inn

★ ★ **HARBOR HOUSE INN.** *12666 WI 42, Ellison Bay (54210). 920/854-5196; fax 920/854-9917. www.doorcounty-inn.com.* 15 units, 9 with shower only, 14 with A/C, 2 story. No rm phones. July-Aug: S, D $65-$125; each addl $15; cabins $105-$135; wkly rates; wkends (3-day min); lower rates May-June, Sept-Oct. Closed rest of yr. Pet accepted, some restrictions. TV. Playground. Complimentary continental bkfst. Restaurant nearby. Ck-out 10 am, ck-in 2 pm. Sauna. Whirlpool. Refrigerators; microwaves avail. Balconies. Picnic tables, grills. Lake view, beach access. Victorian-style house built 1904; many antiques. Totally nonsmoking. Cr cds: A, MC, V.
🐾 🐈 ⊠ 🖗

Restaurants

★ **SHORELINE.** *12747 WI 42, Ellison Bay (54210). 920/854-2950.* Hrs: 7 am-9 pm. Closed Nov-Apr. Wine, beer. Bkfst $1.95-$5.95, lunch $1.75-$7.25, dinner $4.95-$13.95. Child's menu. Specializes in whitefish, perch. View of the bay. Cr cds: DS, MC, V.
D ⊠

★ **VIKING.** *12029 WI 42, Ellison Bay (54210). 920/854-2998. www.door countyfishboil.com.* Hrs: 6 am-9 pm; to 7 pm in winter. Closed Easter, Thanksgiving, Dec 25. Wine, beer. Bkfst $1.99-$8.95, lunch $2.60-$7.95, dinner $7.25-$14.95. Fish boil $11.25. Child's menu. Specializes in fresh fish, whitefish chowder. Outdoor dining. Cr cds: A, DS, MC, V.
⬛ ▱

Ephraim (Door County)

See also Door County

Founded 1853 **Pop** 261 **Elev** 600 ft
Area code 920 **Zip** 54211
Information Door County Chamber of Commerce, 1015 Green Bay Rd, PO Box 406, Sturgeon Bay 54235; 920/743-4456 or 800/527-3529
Web www.doorcountyvacations.com

Moravian colonists founded the second Ephraim here after leaving the first town of that name, now a part of Green Bay; a monument at the harbor commemorates the landing of Moravians in 1853. The village is now a quaint resort community and a center for exploration of the north and west shores of Door County (see).

Special Event

Fyr-Bal Fest. Scandinavian welcome to summer. Fish boil, Blessing of the Fleet, art fair, lighting of the bonfires on the beach at dusk, coronation of Viking Chieftain. Three days mid-June. Phone 920/854-4989.

Motels/Motor Lodges

★★ **EDGEWATER RESORT MOTEL.** *10040 Hwy 42, Ephraim (54211). 920/854-2734; fax 920/854-4127. www.edge-waterresort.com.* 38 units, 2 story. July-Aug, Sept-Oct (wkends): S, D $90-$146; lower rates May-June. Closed Nov-Apr. Crib free. TV; cable (premium). Heated pool. Restaurant (see also OLD POST OFFICE RESTAURANT). Ck-out 11

am. Refrigerators. On Green Bay. Cr cds: DS, MC, V.
🐾 ▱ 🔥

★★ **EPHRAIM GUEST HOUSE.** *3042 Cedar St, Ephraim (54211). 920/854-2319; toll-free 800/589-8423. www.ephraimguesthouse.com.* 14 kit. suites, 2 story. July-late Aug: S, D $110-$185; each addl $12; under 8 free; lower rates rest of yr. Crib free. TV; cable (premium), VCR. Whirlpool. Restaurant nearby. Ck-out 11 am. Coin lndry. X-country ski 3 mi. Some in-rm whirlpools, fireplaces. Private patios, balconies. Picnic tables, grills. Bay 1 blk. Cr cds: A, DS, MC, V.
⬛ 🐾 ▱ 🔥 SC

★ **EPHRAIM MOTEL.** *10407 Water St, Ephraim (54211). 920/854-5959; toll-free 800/451-5995. www.ephraim motel.com.* 28 rms, 2 story. July-mid-Aug, Oct: S, D $85-$90 each addl $10; under 6 free; lower rates May-June, Sept. Closed rest of yr. Crib free. TV; cable. Heated pool. Complimentary continental bkfst. Restaurants nearby. Ck-out 11 am. Meeting rm. Refrigerators, microwaves. Balconies. Totally non-smoking. Cr cds: MC, V.
⬛ ▱ 🔥 ▱

★★ **EPHRAIM SHORES MOTEL.** *10018 Water St, Ephraim (54211). 920/854-2371; fax 920/854-4926. www.ephraimshores.com.* 46 rms, 2 story. D $90-$130; each addl $10; suites $155-$210; under 12, $4; 12-18, $8; under 4 free. Crib $3. TV; cable. Indoor pool; whirlpool. Playground. Coffee in rms. Restaurant 8 am-8 pm. Ck-out 10:30 am. Business servs avail. Sundries. Game rm. Exercise equipt. Rec rm. Bicycles. Refrigerators; some in-rm whirlpools. Sun deck. On Green Bay, overlooking Eagle Harbor. Totally nonsmoking. Cr cds: MC, V.
⬛ ▱ 🏋 ▱ 🔥

★★ **EVERGREEN BEACH.** *9944 Water St, Ephraim (54211). 920/854-2831; fax 920/854-9222; toll-free 800/420-8130. www.evergreenbeach. com.* 30 rms, 1-2 story. Memorial Day wknd-Labor Day: D $99-$128; each addl $10-$15; family rates; lower rates June, after Labor Day-late Oct. Closed rest of yr. Crib $5. TV; cable (premium). Heated pool. Playground. Complimentary continental bkfst. Coffee in rms. Restaurant nearby. Ck-out 10:30 am. Business servs avail. Lawn games. Refrigerators; many microwaves. Many balconies. On Eagle Harbor; private beach. Totally nonsmoking. Cr cds: A, DS, MC, V.

⊡ ⊠ ⊠ ⊠

★★ **PINE GROVE MOTEL.** *10080 Water St, Ephraim (54211). 920/854-2321; fax 920/854-2511; toll-free 800/292-9494.* 44 rms, 2 story. May-Oct: S $55-$75; D $88-$103; each addl $12; suites $170; wkly rates. Closed rest of yr. Crib free. TV; cable (premium). Indoor pool; whirlpool. Complimentary coffee. Ck-out 11 am. Coin lndry. Business servs avail. Sundries. Game rm. Exercise equipt. Refrigerators; some in-rm whirlpools. Balconies. On bay; gazebo, private sand beach. Cr cds: DS, MC, V.

⊠ ⊼ ⊠ ⊠

★★ **SOMERSET INN AND SUITES.** *10401 N Water St, Ephraim (54211). 920/854-1819; fax 920/854-9087; toll-free 800/809-1819. www.somerset inndc.com.* 20 rms, 2 story, 18 suites. Late June-Aug, wkends in fall: S, D $79-$99; each addl $10; suites $119-$139; lower rates rest of yr. Crib free. TV; cable (premium). 2 pools, 1 indoor; whirlpool. Playground. Complimentary coffee in rms. Restaurant nearby. Ck-out 11 am. X-country ski 1 mi. Refrigerators, microwaves; some in-rm whirlpools. Balconies. Picnic tables, grills. Totally nonsmoking. Cr cds: DS, MC, V.

⊡ ⊠ ⊠ ⊠ ⊠

★ **TROLLHAUGEN LODGE.** *10176 WI 42 , Ephraim (54211). 920/854-2713; res 800/854-4118. www. trollhaugenlodge.com.* 13 rms, showers only. July-Aug, 3 wkends in Oct: S, D $71-$99; kit. cottage $125; each addl $5-$10; wkly rates; wkends (2-day min); higher rates special events; lower rates Sept-Oct, mid-Apr-June. Closed rest of yr. TV; cable, VCR avail. Complimentary continental bkfst. Restaurant nearby. Ck-out 10 am. Refrigerators; many microwaves; some fireplaces. Some balconies. Picnic tables, grills. Cr cds: DS, MC, V.

⊠ ⊠

B&Bs/Small Inns

★★★ **EAGLE HARBOR INN.** *9914 Water St, Ephraim (54211). 920/854-2121; fax 920/854-2121; toll-free 800/324-5427. www.eagleharbor.com.* 9 inn rms, 1-2 story, 32 suites. S, D $64-149; suites, July-Aug: $165-$229; lower rates rest of yr. TV; cable (premium), VCR. Indoor pool. Playground. Complimentary bkfst. Restaurant nearby. Ck-out 10 am, ck-in 3 pm. Meeting rm. Business servs avail. In-rm modem link. X-country ski 1 mi. Exercise equipt; sauna. Massage. Microwaves avail. In-rm whirlpool, fireplace in suites. Picnic tables, grills. Opp beach. Decorated with turn-of-the-century antiques. Cr cds: DS, MC, V.

⊡ ⊠ ⊠ ⊠ ⊠

★★ **EPHRAIM INN.** *9994 Pioneer Ln, Ephraim (54211). 920/854-4515; fax 920/854-1859; res 800/622-2193. www.theephraiminn.com.* 16 rms, 2 story. S, D $105-$165. Closed Nov-Apr (Mon-Thurs). Children over 12 yrs only. TV. Complimentary full bkfst. Ck-out 11 am, ck-in 3 pm. Opp beach. Overlooks Green Bay. Each rm has different theme. Cr cds: A, DS, MC, V.

⊡ ⊠ ⊠

★ **FRENCH COUNTRY INN BED AND BREAKFAST.** *3052 Spruce Ln, Ephraim (54211). 920/854-4001; fax 920/854-4001.* 7 rms in main bldg, 5 share bath, 2 story, 1 kit. cottage. No A/C. May-Oct: S, D $62-$89; kit. cottage $89-$99; wkly rates; lower rates rest of yr. Children over 12 yrs only in main bldg. Crib free. TV in cottage. Complimentary continental bkfst. Restaurant nearby. Ck-out 11 am, ck-in 3 pm. X-country ski 1 mi. 2 sitting rms; antiques. Built 1912. Near bay. Totally nonsmoking. Cr cds: A, MC, V.

⊠ ⊠ ⊠

Restaurants

★ **OLD POST OFFICE RESTAURANT.** *10040 Water St, Ephraim (54211). 920/854-4034.* Hrs: 7:30-11 am, 5:30-8 pm. Closed Nov-Apr. Res accepted. Bkfst $2.50-$7.50. Fish boil $13.25. Child's menu. Overlooks bay. Cr cds: C, DS, MC, V.

⊡ ⊠

★ ★ **PAULSON'S OLD ORCHARD INN.** *10341 WI 42, Ephraim (54211).* *920/854-5717.* Hrs: 8 am-8 pm; winter hrs vary. Bkfst, lunch $5-$8, dinner $9-$15. Specialties: Swedish meatballs, eggs Benedict. Own desserts. Fireplace, cathedral ceiling. Victorian gift shop. English country gardens in summer. Cr cds: C, DS, MC, V.

D

★ **SUMMER KITCHEN.** *10425 Water St, Ephraim (54211). 920/854-2131.* Hrs: 8 am-9 pm. Closed Nov-Apr. Bkfst $3.75-$6.95, lunch $2.15-$14.95, dinner $3.75-$18.95. Specializes in barbecued dishes. Own soups, desserts. Patio dining. Gazebo. Cr cds: MC, V.

D

Fish Creek (Door County)

See also Door County

Pop 200 **Elev** 583 ft **Area code** 920 **Zip** 54212

Information Door County Chamber of Commerce, 1015 Green Bay Rd, PO Box 406, Sturgeon Bay 54235; 920/743-4456 or 800/52-RELAX

Web www.doorcountyvacations.com

This picturesque Green Bay resort village, with its many interesting shops, is in Door County (see).

What to See and Do

Peninsula State Park. A 3,763-acre park with nine mi of waterfront incl sandy and cobblestone beaches; caves, cliffs; observation tower. Swimming, fishing, boating, water-skiing; hiking, bicycle trails; x-country skiing, snowmobiling, picnic grounds, playground, concession, camping (471 sites, hookups, dump station). Naturalist programs. Eighteen-hole golf course (mid-May-mid-Oct). Standard fees. N off WI 42. Phone 920/868-3258. ¢¢¢

Special Event

American Folklore Theatre. Peninsula State Park Amphitheater (see). Original folk musical productions based on American lore and literature. Limited fall season. Phone 920/868-1100. Mon-Sat, July-Aug.

Motels/Motor Lodges

★ **BEOWULF LODGE.** *3775 WI 42, Fish Creek (54212). 920/868-2046; fax 920/868-2381; toll-free 800/433-7592. www.beowulflodge.com.* 60 rms, 2 story, 9 suites, 26 kits. May-Oct: S, D $85-$95; suites $120-$145; kit. units $95; lower rates rest of yr. Crib $10. TV; cable, VCR avail. Indoor pool; whirlpool. Complimentary coffee in lobby. Restaurant nearby. Ck-out 10 am. Coin lndry. Business servs avail. Tennis. Downhill ski 20 mi; x-country ski on site. Game rm. Some refrigerators; microwaves avail. Picnic tables, grills. Cr cds: DS, MC, V.

D ⊠ ⊱ ⋈ ⋈ ⋈

★ **BY THE BAY MOTEL.** *Hwy 42, Fish Creek (54212). 920/868-3456. www.bythebaymotel.com.* 15 rms, 2 story. Mid-June-Labor Day and Oct: S, D $84-$120; each addl $8; some lower rates off-season. Closed Nov-Apr. Crib $5. TV; cable (premium). Restaurant adj 7 am-9 pm. Ck-out 10:30 am. Business servs avail. Public beach opp. Totally nonsmoking. Cr cds: A, DS, MC, V.

D ⋈ ⋈

★ **CEDAR COURT.** *9429 Cedar St, Fish Creek (54212). 920/868-3361; fax 920/868-2541. www.cedarcourt.com.* 11 rms, 2 story, 9 kit. cottages. Late June-Aug: S $62-$85; D $78-$120; suites $115; cottages $115-$235; each addl $10; under 12 free; wkly, 3-day wkend rates; ski plan; honeymoon package; lower rates rest of yr. Crib free. TV; cable, VCR avail. Heated pool. Complimentary coffee in rms. Restaurant nearby. Ck-out 11 am. Business servs avail. Downhill ski 20 mi; x-country ski 1 mi. Refrigerators; some in-rm whirlpools; microwaves avail. Balconies. Picnic tables, grills. Totally nonsmoking. Cr cds: DS, MC, V.

D ⋈ ⋈ ⋈ ⋈

Door County Marina

★★ **HOMESTEAD.** *4006 WI 42, Fish Creek (54212). 920/868-3748; fax 920/868-2874; toll-free 800/686-6621. www.homesteadsuites.com.* 33 units in 2 bldgs, 2 story, 23 suites. July-Aug: S, D $79-$129; each addl $10; suites $139-$179; under 17 free; each addl $10; package plans; lower rates rest of yr. TV; cable (premium), VCR avail (movies $4). Indoor pool; whirlpool. Complimentary continental bkfst. Restaurant nearby. Ck-out 11 am. Business servs avail. In-rm modem link. Sundries. X-country ski adj. Bike trail adj. Exercise equipt; sauna. Game rm. Refrigerators; many wet bars; microwave in suites. Balconies. Picnic tables. Adj to Peninsula State Park. Totally non-smoking. Cr cds: DS, MC, V.

⬜🔲🔳🏃🎿🔥

★ **JULIE'S PARK CAFE AND MOTEL.** *4020 WI 42, Fish Creek (54212). 920/868-2999; fax 920/868-9837. www.juliesmotel.com.* 12 units. Late-June-late Aug: S, D $77-$92; each addl $10; lower rates rest of yr. Crib free. Pet accepted, some restrictions; $15/day. TV; cable (premium). Restaurant 7 am-10 pm. Ck-out 10 am. X-country ski adj. Gazebo. Totally nonsmoking. Cr cds: A, MC, V.

🔥🐾🔲🎿

B&Bs/Small Inns

★★ **BEACH HOUSE.** *4117 Main St, Fish Creek (54212). 920/868-2444; fax 920/868-9833.* 4 inn rms, 3 kit. suites, 6 kit. cottages. No A/C in cottages. July-Aug: S, D $85-$165; suites $155-$175; kit. cottages $85-$145; wkend, wkly rates; lower rates rest of yr. Adults only (inn). Crib free. TV; cable (premium), VCR. Complimentary continental bkfst (inn guests). Restaurants nearby. Ck-out 11 am, ck-in 3 pm. Downhill ski 20 mi; x-country ski 5 blks. Some in-rm whirlpools, fireplaces; microwaves avail. Picnic tables, grills. Built 1902; many antiques, library. Set atop hill; overlooks harbor. Bikes. Totally non-smoking (inn). Cr cds: A, MC, V.

🔲🎿🔥

★★ **HARBOR GUEST HOUSE.** *9484 Spruce St, Fish Creek (54212). 920/868-2284; fax 920/868-1535. www.harborguesthouse.com.* 7 kit. suites (1-2-bedrm), 2 story. July-mid-Oct: kit. suites $168-$285; family rates; lower rates rest of yr. Crib $5. TV; cable (premium). Complimentary coffee in rms. Restaurant nearby. Ck-out 10 am, ck-in 3 pm. X-country ski on site. Boat slips avail. Microwaves, fireplaces. Some balconies. Grills. View of Green Bay. Cr cds: MC, V.

⬛ ⬛ ⬛ ⬛

★ ★ **SETTLEMENT COURTYARD INN.** *9126 WI 42, Fish Creek (54212). 920/868-3524; fax 920/868-3048. www.dcty.com/settlement.* 32 kit units, 2 story. July-Oct: S $74-$119; D $79-$129; each addl $12; suites $129-$174; under 4 free; wkly rates; lower rates rest of yr. Crib free. TV; VCR avail. Continental bkfst in season. Restaurant nearby. Ck-out 10:30 am, ck-in 3 pm. Business servs avail. X-country ski on site. Fireplaces; microwaves avail. Hiking trails. Cr cds: A, DS, MC, V.

⬛ ⬛ ⬛

★ ★ ★ **THE WHISTLING SWAN INN.** *4192 Main St, Fish Creek (54212). 920/868-3442; fax 920/868-1703; res 888/277-4289. www.whistlingswan.com.* 7 units, 2 story, 2 suites. D, suites $114-$157. Crib free. TV avail; cable (premium). Complimentary full bkfst. Restaurant adj 7:30 am-8 pm. Ck-out 11 am, ck-in 3 pm. Business servs avail. Renovated country inn (1887); antique furnishings. Near lake, swimming beach. Totally nonsmoking. Cr cds: A, DS, MC, V.

⬛ ⬛ ⬛ ⬛

★ ★ **WHITE GULL INN.** *4225 Main St, Fish Creek (54212). 920/868-3517; fax 920/868-2367; toll-free 888/364-9542. www.whitegullinn.com.* 9 rms, 1-2 story, 5 cottages. S $115; D $160; cottages $194-$305; winter mid-wk packages. Crib free. TV in cottages; cable (premium), VCR (free movies). Restaurant (see also WHITE GULL INN). Ck-out 11 am, ck-in 3 pm. Business servs avail. Free airport transportation. X-country ski 1 mi. Fireplaces. Balconies. Built 1896; library, antiques. Cr cds: A, C, D, DS, MC, V.

⬛ ⬛ ⬛

Restaurants

★ ★ **C AND C SUPPER CLUB.** *WI 42, Fish Creek (54212). 920/868-3412.* Hrs: 4:45-10 pm; Nov-Apr hrs vary. Res accepted. Bar 11-2 am. Dinner $9.75-$21.99. Child's menu. Specializes in steak, seafood, pasta. Salad

bar. Entertainment Fri, Sat. Parking. Cr cds: D, DS, MC, V.

⬛ ⬛

★ **COOKERY.** *WI 42, Fish Creek (54212). 920/868-3634.* Hrs: 7 am-9 pm; Nov-Apr, wkends only. Wine, beer. Bkfst $2.95-$7.25, lunch $2.59-$8.99, dinner $5.99-$12.99. Child's menu. Bakery and deli. Parking. Gift shop. Totally nonsmoking. Cr cds: MC, V.

⬛ ⬛

★ ★ ★ **KORTES' ENGLISH INN.** *3713 Hwy 42, Fish Creek (54212). 920/868-3076. www.theenglishinn.com.* Hrs: 5:30-9 pm. Closed Nov-Apr. Continental menu. Bar 4 pm-2 am. Extensive wine list. Complete menu: dinner $9.50-$26. Child's menu. Specializes in lamb, veal, seafood. Seafood buffet Fri. Own baking. Entertainment. Extensive dessert list. Parking. Old World decor; stained glass, wooden beams, local artwork. Cr cds: D, MC, V.

⬛

★ **PELLETIER'S.** *4199 Main St, Fish Creek (54212). 920/868-3313.* Hrs: 7:30 am-8 pm. Closed Nov-mid-May. Res accepted; required fish boil. Wine, beer. Bkfst $2.25-$6.25, lunch $3.25-$9.95. Fish boil dinner: $11.25. Specializes in crêpes, fish boil. Own soups. Parking. Patio dining. Nautical decor. Family-owned.

⬛

★ ★ **SUMMERTIME.** *1 N Spruce St, Fish Creek (54212). 920/868-3738. www.thesummertime.com.* Hrs: 7:30 am-10 pm; Fri, Sat to 11 pm. Res accepted. Wine, beer. Bkfst $1.95-$7.95, lunch $2.75-$9.95, dinner $6.95-$30. Specializes in South African-style barbecue ribs, Italian and Greek cuisine. Own baking. Outdoor dining. Cr cds: A, MC, V.

⬛ ⬛

★ ★ **WHITE GULL INN.** *4225 Main St, Fish Creek (54212). 920/868-3517. www.whitegullinn.com.* Hrs: 7:30 am-2:30 pm, 5-8 pm. Closed Thanksgiving, Dec 25. Res accepted. Wine, beer. Bkfst, lunch, $4-$8; dinner $14.95-$24.95. Fish boil Wed, Fri-Sun eves: $14.95. Child's menu. Parking.

Turn-of-the-century decor. Family-owned. Cr cds: A, D, DS, MC, V.

D

Fond du Lac

(E-6) *See also Green Lake, Oshkosh, Waupun*

Settled 1835 **Pop** 42,000 **Elev** 760 ft
Area code 920
Information Convention & Visitors Bureau, 171 S Pioneer Rd St; 920/923-3010 or 800/937-9123, ext 71
Web www.fdl.com

Located at the foot of Lake Winnebago and named by French explorers in the 1600s, Fond du Lac, "foot of the lake," was an early outpost for fur trading, later achieving prominence as a lumbering center and railroad city.

What to See and Do

Galloway House and Village. Restored 30-rm Victorian mansion with four fireplaces, carved woodwork, and stenciled ceilings; village of late 1800s; 24 buildings incl one-rm schoolhouse, print shop, general store, operating gristmill, museum with collection of Native American artifacts; war displays; other area artifacts. (Memorial Day-Labor Day, daily; rest of Sept, Sat and Sun) 336 Old Pioneer Rd. Phone 920/922-6390. ¢¢¢

Kettle Moraine State Forest, Northern Unit. The forest's 30,000 acres incl Long and Mauthe Lake Recreation Areas, scenic Kettle Moraine Dr. Swimming, waterskiing, fishing, boating, canoeing. There are 58 mi of hiking and bridle trails. Snowmobiling, x-country skiing, picnicking, camping avail (338 sites, hookups, dump station), incl primitive and winter camping. Observation tower. Forest Supervisor is in Campbellsport. Standard fees. (Daily) 17 mi SE on US 45 to Waucousta, then E on County F. ¢¢¢¢ Also here is

Ice Age Visitors Center. Films, slides, and panoramas show visitors how glaciers molded Wisconsin's terrain; naturalists answer

questions. (Daily; closed Jan 1, Dec 25) Phone 920/533-8322. **FREE**

Lakeside Park. A 400-acre park on Lake Winnebago. Boating (ramps, canoe rentals); petting zoo, playground, rides, picnic area; lighthouse. (June-Aug, daily) (See SPECIAL EVENT) N end of Main St. Phone 920/989-6846. **FREE**

Lake Winnebago. Boating, sailing, windsurfing, waterskiing, fishing, ice-fishing, sturgeon spearing (last two wks Feb), ice-boating, snowmobiling. Phone 800/937-9123.

🌟 **Octagon House.** A 12-rm octagonal house built in 1856 by Isaac Brown and designed by Orson Fowler has hidden rm, secret passageways, and an underground tunnel. Period antiques, dolls, clothing; native American display, ship collection, spinning wheel demonstrations. Carriage house has pony carriages. 90-min guided tours Mon, Wed, Fri, afternoons. 276 Linden St. Phone 920/922-1608. ¢¢

St. Paul's Cathedral. Episcopal. English Gothic limestone structure with wood carvings from Oberammergau, Germany, rare ecclesiastical artifacts, and a variety of stained-glass windows; cloister garden. Self-guided tours (by appt). 51 W Division. Phone 920/921-3363.

Silver Wheel Manor. A 30-rm mansion that was once part of 400-acre farm established 1860; antique furnishings; collection of more than 1,200 dolls and accessories; model trains; circus rm, photography rm. (Mon, Wed, Fri, Sat, mornings) N 6221 County K; E on WI 23, S on County K. Phone 920/922-1608. ¢¢¢

Special Event

Walleye Weekend Festival and Mercury Marine National Walleye Tournament. Lakeside Park. Fish fry, food, entertainment, sports competions. Second wkend June. Phone 920/923-6555.

Motels/Motor Lodges

★ **DAYS INN.** *107 N Pioneer Rd (54935). 920/923-6790; toll-free 800/329-7466. www.daysinn.com.* 59 rms, 2 story. S $49.95-$55.95; D $65.95-$70.95; each addl $6; under 17 free. Crib free. Pet accepted; $3. TV; cable (premium). Complimentary continental bkfst. Ck-out 11 am. Business servs avail. In-rm modem link. Cr cds: A, C, D, DS, JCB, MC, V.

D 🐾 🏊 📶 **SC**

★ **ECONO LODGE.** *649 W Johnson St (54935). 920/923-2020; fax 920/929-9352; toll-free 800/553-2666. www.econolodge.com.* 48 rms, 2 story. S $54-$69; D $54-$74; each addl $5; higher rates special events. Crib $3. TV; cable (premium). Indoor pool; whirlpool. Complimentary continental bkfst. Restaurant nearby. Ck-out 11 am. Business servs avail. Refrigerators. Cr cds: A, C, D, DS, MC, V.

D 🏊 📶 **SC**

★★ **HOLIDAY INN.** *625 W Rolling Meadows Dr (54937). 920/923-1440; fax 920/923-1366. www.holiday-inn.com.* 139 rms, 2 story. S $72-$115; D $82-$125; under 19 free. Crib free. Pet accepted. TV; cable (premium), VCR avail. Indoor pool; whirlpool. Complimentary continental bkfst Mon-Fri. Coffee in rms. Restaurant 7 am-10 pm. Bar 11-1 am. Ck-out 11 am. Coin lndry. Meeting rms. In-rm modem link. Bellhops. Valet serv. Sundries. Free airport transportation. Exercise equipt; sauna. Rec rm. Golf course opp. Microwaves avail. Cr cds: A, MC, V.

D 🐾 🏋 🏊 ✈ 📶 **SC**

★ **NORTHWAY MOTEL.** *301 S Pioneer Rd (54935). 920/921-7975; fax 920/921-7983; toll-free 800/850-7339. www.visitwisconsin.com/fondulac.* 19 rms. June-Oct: S $30-$35; D $49-$55; each addl $5; under 12 free; wkly rates; higher rates special events; lower rates rest of yr. Crib $4. Pet accepted; $7. TV; cable. Complimentary continental bkfst. Coffee in rms. Ck-out 11 am. X-country ski 10 mi. Refrigerators, microwaves avail. Picnic tables, grills. Cr cds: A, DS, MC, V.

D 🐾 🏊 📶 **SC**

★★ **RAMADA PLAZA.** *1 N Main St (54935). 920/923-3000; fax 920/923-2561; res 800/274-1712. www.ramada.com.* 132 rms, 8 story. Mid-June-late Aug: S $69-$109; D $76-$119; each addl $10; suites $95-$200; under 18 free; higher rates special events; lower rates rest of yr. Crib free. TV; cable (premium). Complimentary coffee in rms. Restaurant 6:30 am-

2:30 pm, 5-9 pm. Bar; entertainment wkends. Ck-out 11 am. Meeting rms. Business servs avail. In-rm modem link. X-country ski 2 mi. Exercise equipt; sauna. Massage. Indoor pool; whirlpool. Refrigerator, wet bar in suites; microwaves avail. Luxury level. Cr cds: A, C, D, DS, JCB, MC, V.

D 🏊 🏊 🏋 📶 🔥 **SC**

Restaurants

★ **SALTY'S SEAFOOD AND SPIRITS.** *503 N Park Ave (54935). 920/922-9940.* Hrs: 11 am-10 pm; wkends to 11 pm. Closed hols. Bar. Lunch, dinner $3.95-$12.95. Specializes in seafood, prime rib, steak. Salad bar. Nautical decor. Cr cds: A, DS, MC, V.

D

★★ **SCHREINER'S.** *168 N Pioneer Rd (54935). 920/922-0590. www.fdlchowder.com.* Hrs: 6:30 am-9 pm; mid-July-mid-Aug to 10 pm. Closed Thanksgiving; Dec 24 eve, 25. Serv bar. Bkfst $4.50-$6, lunch, dinner $5.50-$10. Child's menu. Specializes in New England clam chowder, fresh baked goods. Colonial decor. Family-owned. Cr cds: A, MC, V.

D

Fontana

See also Beloit, Burlington, Delavan, Elkhorn, Lake Geneva

Pop 1,635 **Elev** 900 ft **Area code** 262 **Zip** 53125

Located on the western shore of Geneva Lake in territory once occupied by the Potawatomi, this town was named for its many springs.

Resort

★★★ **ABBEY RESORT & FONTANA SPA.** *269 Fontana Blvd (53125). 262/275-6811; fax 262/275-3264; toll-free 800/558-2405. www.theabbeyresort.com.* 334 rms, 2 story, 20 condos. S, D $99-$250; each addl $12; under 17 free; suites $250-$400; kit. units $400-$475; package plans. Crib free. TV; cable, VCR. 5 pools, 2 indoor; whirlpool, poolside serv. Supervised children's activities; ages 5-12. Dining rms 7 am-10 pm. Snack bar. Bars 11-2 am. Ck-out noon, ck-in 4 pm. Convention facilities. Business center. In-rm modem link. Valet serv. Concierge. Gift shop. Barber, beauty shop. Airport transportation. Tennis. Waterskiing, marina, boats. Downhill ski 10 mi; x-country ski 2 mi. Bicycles. Lawn games. Rec dir. Rec rm. Game rm. Exercise equipt; sauna. Massage. Full service spa. Private patios and balconies (condos). On Geneva Lake. Cr cds: A, C, D, DS, MC, V.

Fort Atkinson

(F-5) *See also Elkhorn, Janesville, Madison, Watertown*

Settled 1836 **Pop** 10,227 **Elev** 790 ft
Area code 920 **Zip** 53538
Information Chamber of Commerce, 244 N Main St; 920/563-3210 or 888/733-3678
Web www.fortchamber.com

In 1872, William Dempster Hoard, later governor of Wisconsin, organized the Wisconsin State Dairyman's Association here. He toured the area, drumming up support by preaching the virtues of the cow, "the foster mother of the human race." More than any other man, Hoard was responsible for Wisconsin's development as a leading dairy state. Nearby are Lake Koshkonong, a popular recreation area, and Lake Ripley, where Ole Evinrude invented the outboard motor in 1908.

What to See and Do

Hoard Historical Museum. Housed in historic home (1864), museum features pioneer history and archaeology of the area; period rms, antique quilt, bird rm, old costumes and clothing, antique firearms; reference library; permanent and changing displays. (June-Aug, Tues-Sun; rest of yr, Tues-Sat; closed Thanksgiving, Dec 25) 407 Merchants Ave. Phone 920/563-7769. **FREE** Also here is

Dwight Foster House. (1841) Historic home of city's founder; five-rm, two-story Greek Revival frame house is furnished in the period, with many original pieces. (June-Aug, Tues-Sun; rest of yr, Tues-Sat; closed Thanksgiving, Dec 25) Phone 920/563-7769. **FREE**

National Dairy Shrine Museum. Traces development of the dairy industry for past 100 yrs. Collection of memorabilia; exhibits incl old creamery, replica of early dairy farm kitchen, old barn, and milk-hauling equipt. Multimedia presentation. (June-Aug, Tues-Sun; rest of yr, Tues-Sat; closed Thanksgiving, Dec 25) Phone 920/563-7769. **FREE**

Panther Intaglio. Panther-shaped prehistoric earthwork; dates to A.D. 1000. Discovered by Increase Lapham in 1850. 1236 Riverside Dr.

Motel/Motor Lodge

★ **SUPER 8 FORT ATKINSON.** *225 S Water St E (53538). 920/563-8444; toll-free 800/800-8000. www.super8. com.* 40 rms, 3 story. S $48-$60; D $50-$71; each addl $10; suites $110; under 12 free; higher rates wkends, hols, special events. Crib $5. Pet accepted, some restrictions. TV; cable. Complimentary continental bkfst. Restaurant nearby. Bar 4 pm-midnight; Fri, Sat to 1 am; entertainment. Ck-out 11 am. Meeting rms. Sundries. Downhill/x-country ski 5 mi. Overlooks Rock River. Patio and deck chairs on riverbank. Cr cds: A, C, D, DS, MC, V.

Galesville

See also La Crosse

Pop 1,278 **Elev** 712 ft **Area code** 608
Zip 54630

What to See and Do

State parks. Fishing, boating, canoeing; hiking, picnicking, playgrounds, camping (electric hookups, dump stations). Standard fees.

Merrick State Park. A 324-acre park along Mississippi River.

Canoeing; camping. (Daily) 22 mi NW on WI 35. Phone 608/687-4936.

Perrot State Park. Trempealeau Mtn, a beacon for voyageurs for more than 300 yrs, is in this 1,425-acre park. Nicolas Perrot set up winter quarters here in 1686; a French fort was built on the site in 1731. X-country skiing. Vistas, bluffs. Standard fees. (Daily) 2 mi W on Trempealeau. Phone 608/534-6409. ¢¢¢

Motel/Motor Lodge

★ **SONIC MOTEL.** *21278 W State St (54630). 608/582-2281.* 24 rms, 2 kits. S $36.95; D $40.95-$48.95. Crib free. TV; cable (premium). Complimentary coffee in rms. Ck-out 11 am. Gift shop. X-country ski 5 mi. Cr cds: MC, V.

Green Bay

(D-6) *See also Appleton*

Pop 96,466 **Elev** 594 ft **Area code** 920

Information Visitor & Convention Bureau, 1901 S Oneida St, 54307-0596; 920/494-9507 or 888/867-3342

Web www.greenbay.org

The strategic location that made Green Bay a trading center as far back as 1669 today enables this port city to handle nearly 1.8 million tons of cargo a year. The region was claimed for the King of France in 1634, and was named La Baye in 1669 when it became the site of the mission of St. Francis. It then saw the rise of fur trading, a series of Native American wars, and French, British, and US conflicts. Although it became part of the United States in 1783, Green Bay did not yield to American influence until after the War of 1812, when agents of John Jacob Astor gained control of the fur trade. The oldest settlement in the state, Green Bay is a paper and cheese producing center as well as a hub for health care and insurance. It

is also famous for its professional football team, the Green Bay Packers.

What to See and Do

Children's Museum of Green Bay. Hands-on exhibits and interactive programs. Areas incl the Hospital, Submarine, Fire Truck, Police Station, Bank, and Grocery Store. (Daily; closed hols) Upper Level Washington Commons Mall. Phone 920/432-4397. ¢¢

Green Bay Botanical Gardens. Educational and recreational facility. Formal rose garden; children's garden; four season garden; gift shop. (Tues-Sun, daily) 2600 Larsen Rd. Phone 920/490-9457. ¢

Green Bay Packer Hall of Fame. History of team from 1919 to present; a unique collection of multimedia presentations, memorabilia, hands-on activites, NFL films. (Daily; closed hols) Brown County Expo Centre, 855 Lombardi Ave; across from Lambeau Field. Phone 920/499-4281. ¢¢¢

Hazelwood Historic Home Museum. (1837-1838) Greek Revival house where state constitution was drafted. (Memorial Day-Labor Day, Mon-Fri; rest of yr, by appt) 1008 S Monroe Ave. Phone 920/437-1840. ¢¢

Heritage Hill State Park. Forty-acre living history museum; complex of 26 historical buildings illustrate the development of northeast Wisconsin. (Memorial Day-Labor Day, Tues-Sun; Dec, Sat-Sun) Christmas festival (Fri-Sun in Dec). 2640 S Webster. Phone 920/448-5150. ¢¢¢

🌟 **National Railroad Museum.** Seventy-five steam locomotives, diesels, and cars; train rides; exhibit building; theater; gift shop. (May-mid-Oct, daily; wkdays rest of yr) 2285 S Broadway. Phone 920/437-7623.

Neville Public Museum. Science, history, and art collections and exhibits. (Daily; closed Mon, hols) 210 Museum Pl. Phone 920/448-4460. **DONATION**

Northeastern Wisconsin Zoo. Over 43 acres of animals in natural settings. Children's zoo. Exhibits incl Wisconsin Trail, International and Northern trail. (Daily) 4378 Reforestation Rd. Phone 920/434-7841. ¢

Oneida Nation Museum. Permanent and "hands-on" exhibits tell story of

Oneida Nation. (Tues-Fri; closed hols) W892 EE Rd, 7 mi SW on US 41 to County Rd EE. Phone 920/869-2768. ¢

Professional sports team. Green Bay Packers (NFL). Lambeau Field, 1265 Lombardi Ave. Phone 920/496-5700.

University of Wisconsin-Green Bay. (1965) 5,000 students. Campus built on 700 acres. Weidner Center for the Performing Arts. Also here is Cofrin Memorial Arboretum; nine-hole golf course (fee); Bayshore picnic area. Tours of campus (by appt). N Nicolet Dr, 4 mi NE on WI 54, 57. Phone 920/465-2000.

Special Event

Waterboard Warriors. Brown County Fairgrounds. Waterski shows performed by skiers from the area. Tues and Thurs (evenings). June-Aug. Phone 920/468-1967.

Motels/Motor Lodges

★★ **BAYMONT INN.** 2840 S Oneida St (54304). 920/494-7887; fax 920/494-3370; toll-free 877/229-6668. www.baymontinn.com. 78 rms, 2 story. S $64; D $72; under 18 free; higher rates: wkends, special events, football games. Crib free. Pet accepted, some restrictions. TV; cable (premium), VCR avail (movies). Complimentary continental bkfst. Complimentary coffee in rms. Restaurant adj. Ck-out noon. Meeting rms. Business center. X-country ski 10 mi. Health club privileges. Microwaves avail. Cr cds: A, C, D, DS, MC, V.

★★ **BEST WESTERN MIDWAY HOTEL.** 780 Packer Dr (54304). 920/499-3161; fax 920/499-9401; toll-free 800/528-1234. www.bestwestern.com. 145 rms, 2 story. S $70-$76; D $81-$100; each addl $7; under 18 free. Crib free. TV. Indoor pool; whirlpool. Complimentary continental bkfst. Coffee in rms. Restaurant 7 am-10 pm. Bar 11-1 am. Ck-out 11 am. Meeting rms. Business servs avail. In-rm modem link. Bellhops. Valet serv. Sundries. Free airport transportation. Downhill ski 10 mi; x-country ski 5 mi. Exercise equipt; sauna. Health club privileges. Game

rm. Lambeau Field adj. Cr cds: A, C, D, DS, MC, V.

★★ **COMFORT INN.** 2841 Ramada Way (54304). 920/498-2060; toll-free 800/288-5150. www.comfortinn.com. 60 rms, 2 story. S $54-$79; D $64-$89; each addl $5; under 17 free; higher rates: Packers football games, EAA Fly-in, Dec 31; lower rates wkdays. Crib free. Pet accepted, some restrictions. TV; cable (premium). Indoor pool; whirlpool. Complimentary continental bkfst. Coffee in rms. Restaurant nearby. Ck-out 11 am. Business servs avail. In-rm modem link. Valet serv. X-country ski 5 mi. Health club privileges. Cr cds: A, C, D, DS, ER, JCB, MC, V.

★ **DAYS INN.** 406 N Washington St (54301). 920/435-4484; fax 920/435-3120; res 800/329-7466. www.daysinn. com. 98 rms, 5 story. S $55-$85; D $65-$95; suites $70-$100; each addl $5; under 18 free. Crib free. Pet accepted; fee. TV. Indoor pool. Complimentary continental bkfst. Restaurant 6:30 am-2 pm, 5-9 pm. Bar 3 pm-midnight. Ck-out noon. Meeting rms. Business servs avail. In-rm modem link. Valet serv. Sundries. Health club privileges. Microwaves avail. Overlooks Fox River. Cr cds: A, C, D, DS, JCB, MC, V.

★ **EXEL INN.** 2870 Ramada Way (54304). 920/499-3599; fax 920/498-4055. www.exelinns.com. 104 rms, 2 story. S $44.99-$54.99; D $51.99-$56.99; each addl $5; under 18 free. Crib free. Pet accepted, some restrictions. TV; cable. Complimentary continental bkfst. Restaurant adj open 24 hrs. Ck-out noon. Business servs avail. In-rm modem link. Health club privileges. Cr cds: A, D, DS, MC, V.

★★ **FAIRFIELD INN.** 2850 S Oneida St (54304). 920/497-1010; fax 920/497-3098; toll-free 800/228-2800. www.fairfieldinn.com. 63 rms, 3 story. May-Sept: S $63; D $69; each addl $6; under 18 free; higher rates special events; lower rates rest of yr. TV; cable (premium). Complimentary continental bkfst. Restaurant adj open 24 hrs. Ck-out noon. Business servs avail. X-country ski 3 mi. Health club privileges. Indoor pool; whirlpool. Cr cds: A, C, D, DS, MC, V.

⬛ ⬛ ⬛ ⬛

★ ★ **HOLIDAY INN.** *200 Main St (54301). 920/437-5900; fax 920/437-1192; toll-free 800/457-2929. www. holiday-inn.com.* 146 rms, 7 story. S, D $89-$109; family rates. Crib free. Pet accepted, some restrictions. TV; cable (premium). Indoor pool; whirlpool. Coffee in rms. Restaurant 6 am-10 pm. Bar 10-1 am; entertainment. Ck-out noon. Coin lndry. Meeting rms. Business servs avail. Bellhops. Valet serv. Sundries. Sauna. Health club privileges. On Fox River; marina. Luxury level. Cr cds: A, C, D, DS, ER, JCB, MC, V.

⬛ ⬛ ⬛ ⬛ ⬛

★ ★ **HOLIDAY INN AIRPORT.** *2580 S Ashland Ave (54304). 920/499-5121; fax 920/499-6777; toll-free 800/465-4329. www.holiday-inn.com.* 147 rms, 2 story. June-Aug: S $80-$95; D $90-$105; each addl $10; suites $125; under 18 free; lower rates rest of yr. Crib free. TV; cable (premium). Indoor pool; whirlpool. Complimentary coffee in rms. Restaurant 6:30 am-1:30 pm, 5:30-10 pm. Ck-out noon. Meeting rms. Business center. Bellhops. Free airport transportation. Health club privileges. Game rm. Some refrigerators. Cr cds: A, MC, V.

⬛ ⬛ ⬛ ⬛ ⬛ SC ⬛

★ **MARINER MOTEL.** *2222 Riverside Dr (54301). 920/437-7107; fax 920/437-2877.* 23 rms, 2 story. S $39.95-$50; D $44.95-$58.95; each addl $5; under 18 free; higher rates special events. Crib $5. TV; cable. Complimentary continental bkfst. Restaurant 11:30 am-2 pm, 5-9 pm; Fri, Sat to 10 pm. Ck-out 11 am. Meeting rms. Beauty shop. X-country ski 10 mi. Health club privileges. Lawn games. Refrigerators; microwaves avail. Patios. Gazebo. On Fox River; dock. Cr cds: A, C, D, DS, MC, V.

⬛ ⬛ ⬛ ⬛ SC

★ **ROAD STAR INN.** *1941 True Ln (54304). 920/497-2666; fax 920/497-4754; toll-free 800/445-4667.* 63 rms, 2 story. July-Oct: S $45; D $50; each addl $3; under 15 free; higher rates: special events, wkends; lower rates

rest of yr. Pet accepted. TV; cable. Complimentary continental bkfst. Restaurant nearby. Ck-out 11 am. Some refrigerators, wet bars. Cr cds: A, C, D, DS, MC, V.

⬛ ⬛ ⬛ ⬛

★ **SKY LITE.** *2120 S Ashland Ave (54304). 920/494-5641; fax 920/494-4032.* 23 rms, some kits. S $29.50-$35; D $39.50-$56; under 12 free. Crib $5. Pet accepted, some restrictions. TV; cable (premium). Restaurant nearby. Ck-out 11 am. Coin lndry. Sundries. Microwaves avail. Picnic tables. Cr cds: A, DS, MC, V.

⬛ ⬛ ⬛ ⬛

★ **SUPER 8.** *2868 S Oneida St (54304). 920/494-2042; fax 920/494-6959. www.super8.com.* 84 rms, 2 story. Mid-June-Oct: S $55-$60; D $65-$70; lower rates rest of yr. Crib free. Pet accepted. TV; cable, VCR avail. Complimentary continental bkfst. Restaurant nearby. Ck-out 11 am. Coin lndry. Meeting rm. Business servs avail. In-rm modem link. Sauna. Health club privileges. Whirlpool. Microwaves avail. Cr cds: A, C, D, DS, MC, V.

⬛ ⬛ ⬛ ⬛

Hotel

★ ★ ★ **RADISSON INN.** *2040 Airport Dr (54313). 920/494-7300; fax 920/494-9599. www.radisson.com.* 299 rms, 3-6 story. S $99; D $119; each addl $10; suites $159-$279; under 18 free; wkend rates. TV; cable. Indoor pool; whirlpool. Coffee in rms. Restaurant 6 am-10 pm; wkends 7 am-11 pm. Bar 11-1:30 am; entertainment. Meeting rms. Business servs avail. In-rm modem link. Bellhops. Valet serv. Guest lndry. Free airport transportation. Exercise equipt; sauna. Health club privileges. Some bathrm phones, in-rm whirlpools, refrigerators, fireplaces. Cr cds: A, DS, MC, V.

⬛ ⬛ ⬛ ⬛ ⬛ ⬛

B&Bs/Small Inns

★ ★ ★ **ASTOR HOUSE.** *637 S Monroe Ave (54301). 920/432-3585; fax 920/436-3145; toll-free 888/303-6370. www.astorhouse.com.* 5 rms, 4 with shower only, 3 story. S $85-$99; D

$115-$152. TV; cable, VCR (movies). Complimentary continental bkfst. Restaurant nearby. Ck-out 11 am, ck-in 4-6 pm. In-rm modem link. Luggage handling. X-country ski 10 mi. Refrigerators; some in-rm whirlpools, fireplaces. Built in 1888; antiques. Totally nonsmoking. Cr cds: A, DS, MC, V.

★ ★ ★ **JAMES STREET INN.** *201 James St, De Pere (54115). 920/337-0111; fax 920/337-6135. www.james streetinn.com.* 30 rms, 4 story. S $79-$129; D $89-$139; each addl $5; suites $89-$199; under 12 free. Crib free. TV; cable (premium), VCR avail (movies). Complimentary continental bkfst; afternoon refreshments. Restaurant nearby. Ck-out noon, ck-in 3 pm. Business servs avail. X-country ski 2 mi. Minibars; some in-rm whirlpools, microwaves. Old flour mill built 1858. Cr cds: A, D, DS, MC, V.

Restaurants

★ ★ **EVE'S SUPPER CLUB.** *2020 Riverside Dr (54301). 920/435-1571.* Hrs: 11 am-2 pm, 5-10 pm; Sat from 5 pm. Closed Sun; Thanksgiving, Dec 24, 25. Res accepted Mon-Thurs. Bar. Lunch $2.50-$10.95, dinner $5.95-$35. Specializes in steak, seafood. View of Fox River. Cr cds: A, D, DS, MC, V.

★ ★ **RIVER'S BEND.** *792 Riverview Dr, Howard (54303). 920/434-1383.* Hrs: 11:30 am-2 pm, 5-10 pm; Fri to 10:30 pm; Sat 5-10:30 pm; Sun 4:30-9 pm. Closed hols. Res accepted. Bar to 1 am. Lunch $3.95-$8, dinner $7-$29. Child's menu. Specializes in prime rib, steak, seafood. Salad bar. Local artwork on display. Overlooks Duck Creek. Cr cds: A, D, DS, MC, V.

★ ★ **WELLINGTON.** *1060 Hansen Rd (54304). 920/499-2000.* Hrs: 11:30 am-2 pm, 5-10 pm; Sat from 5 pm. Closed Sun; hols. Res accepted Mon-Fri. Lunch $6-$9.50, dinner $15.50-$19.50. Child's menu. Specialty: beef Wellington. Outdoor dining. Cr cds: A, D, MC, V.

Green Lake

See also Fond du Lac, Waupun

Pop 1,064 **Elev** 828 ft **Area code** 920 **Zip** 54941

Information Chamber of Commerce, 550 Mill St, PO Box 386; 920/294-3231 or 800/253-7354

This county seat, known as the oldest resort community west of Niagara Falls, is a popular four-season recreational area. Green Lake, 7,325 acres, is the deepest natural lake in the state and affords good fishing, including lake trout, swimming, sailing, powerboating, and iceboating.

What to See and Do

Green Lake Conference Center/American Baptist Assembly. A 1,000-acre all-yr vacation-conference center. Activities incl indoor swimming, fishing; x-country skiing (rentals), toboganning, ice-skating, camping (fee), hiking, biking, tennis, 36-hole golf. (Daily) Phone 920/294-3323. ¢

Lake Cruises. A 1¼-hr narrated cruise. (June-Aug, daily; May, Sept-Oct, Sat-Sun) Also dinner, brunch cruises; private charters. At Heidel House, Illinois Ave. Phone 920/294-3344. ¢¢

Motels/Motor Lodges

★ ★ **AMERICINN MOTEL AND SUITES.** *1219 W Fond du Lac St, Ripon (54971). 920/748-7578; fax 920/748-7897; res 800/634-3444. www.americinn.com.* 42 rms, 2 story. July-Aug: S $63-$73; D $70-$80; each addl $6; suites $99-$119; under 12 free; higher rates special events; lower rates rest of yr. Crib free. TV; cable (premium). Complimentary continental bkfst. Complimentary coffee in rms. Restaurant nearby. Meeting rms. Business servs avail. Ck-out 11 am. X-country ski 6 mi. Sauna. Indoor pool; whirlpool. Some refrigerators. Cr cds: A, DS, MC, V.

★ **BAYVIEW MOTEL & RESORT.** *439 Lake St (54941). 920/294-6504; fax 920/294-0888. www.vbe. com/~bayview.* 17 rms, 2 story, 7 kits. May-Oct: S $84; D $94; each addl $6;

suites $190; golf plans; lower rates rest of yr. Crib $10. TV; cable. Coffee in rms. Restaurant nearby. Ck-out 10 am. X-country ski 5 mi. Pontoon, fishing boats; motors, launching ramp, dockage, boat trailer parking. Fish clean/store. Picnic tables, grills. On lake. Cr cds: MC, V.

Resort

★ ★ ★ **HEIDEL HOUSE.** *643 Illinois Ave (54941). 920/294-3344; fax 920/294-6128; res 800/444-2812. www.heidelhouse.com.* 205 rms, 4 story. S, D $155-$315; each addl $15; under 17 free. Crib avail. 2 heated pools; whirlpool. TV; cable (premium), VCR avail. Complimentary coffee, newspaper in rms. Restaurant 6 am-10 pm. Ck-out noon. Meeting rms. Business center. Gift shop. Game rm. Exercise rm. Tennis. Some refrigerators, minibars. Cr cds: A, C, D, DS, MC, V.

B&Bs/Small Inns

★ ★ **CARVER'S ON THE LAKE.** *N5529 Co Rd A (54941). 920/294-6931. www.carversonthelake.com.* 9 rms, 2 with shower only, 2 story. Some rm phones. Memorial Day-Sept: S, D $75-$175; kit. units $95-$165; wkly rates; wkends (2-day min); lower rates rest of yr. TV; cable. Complimentary continental bkfst. Restaurant (see also CARVER'S ON THE LAKE). Ck-out 11 am, ck-in 3 pm. 18-hole golf privileges. X-country ski adj. Some in-rm whirlpools, fireplaces. Picnic tables. On lake. Built 1925; antiques. Totally nonsmoking. Cr cds: MC, V.

★ **OAKWOOD LODGE.** *365 Lake St (54941). 920/294-6580.* 12 rms, 2 story. No A/C. No rm phones. May-Sept: S, D $85-$120; each addl $20; golf plans; lower rates rest of yr. Crib free. TV in sitting rm; cable (premium), VCR avail. Complimentary full bkfst. Ck-out 11 am, ck-in 3 pm. X-country ski 5 mi. In-rm whirlpool. Some balconies. Grills. Built 1866; antique furnishings. On Green Lake; swimming. Totally nonsmoking. Cr cds: MC, V.

Restaurants

★ ★ **ALFRED'S SUPPER CLUB.** *506 Hill St (54941). 920/294-3631. www. foodspot.com/alfreds.* Hrs: 5-11 pm. Closed Mon in winter. Res accepted. Italian, American menu. Bar. Dinner $18-$28. Child's menu. Specializes in steak, pasta. Salad bar. Cr cds: A, DS, MC, V.

★ ★ ★ **CARVER'S ON THE LAKE.** *N5529 County Rd A (54941). 920/294-6931. www.carversonthelake.com.* Hrs: 5 pm to closing. Closed Mon. Res accepted. Bar. Wine list. Dinner $18-$28. Child's menu. Specializes in fresh seafood, regional dishes, pasta. Own baking. Dining in old English country house; antiques. Cr cds: MC, V.

★ ★ **NORTON'S MARINE DINING ROOM.** *380 S Lawson Dr (54941). 920/294-6577.* Hrs: 11 am-3 pm, 5-10 pm. Closed Dec 24, 25. Bar to 2 am. Lunch $3.25-$11.95, dinner $8.50-$39.95. Specializes in steak, seafood. Outdoor dining. Overlooks Green Lake. Cr cds: A, MC, V.

Hayward

See also Cable, Spooner

Settled 1881 **Pop** 1,897 **Elev** 1,198 ft
Area code 715 **Zip** 54843

Information Hayward Area Chamber of Commerce, 101 W 1st St; 715/634-8662

Web www.haywardlakes.com

A Ranger District office of the Chequamegon National Forest (see PARK FALLS) is located here.

What to See and Do

National Freshwater Fishing Hall of Fame. A 143-ft long and 4½-story high walk-thru "muskie"; the mouth serves as an observation deck. Museum and educational complex contains more than 400 mounts representing many world species; world records and record photo gallery and library; thousands of angling artifacts; 350 outboard motor relics. Project covers six acres and incl five other museum display buildings. (Mid-Apr-Nov, daily) Snack shop, gift shop, playground with fish theme. 10360 Hall of Fame Dr, Jct Hwy B & WI 27. Phone 715/634-4440. ¢¢

Special Event

Lumberjack World Championship. On County B. Logrolling, tree chopping, climbing, and sawing. Late July. Phone 715/634-2484.

Motels/Motor Lodges

★★ **AMERICINN OF HAYWARD.** *15601 US 63 N (54843). 715/634-2700; fax 715/634-3958; res 800/634-3444. www.americinn.com.* 42 rms, 2 story. S $55-$91; D $55-$101; each addl $71.90-$81.90; each addl $6; suites $81.90-$99.90; under 18 free; higher rates special events. Crib free. Pet accepted, some restrictions; $6. TV; cable (premium), VCR avail. Complimentary continental bkfst. Restaurant nearby. Ck-out 11 am. Meeting rms. Business servs avail. Downhill ski 20 mi; x-country ski adj. Sauna. Indoor pool; whirlpool. Game rm. Rec rm. Some in-rm whirlpools, refrigerators, microwaves. Picnic tables. Cr cds: A, DS, MC, V.
🄳 🍴 🏊 ≈ ⚒

★★ **BEST WESTERN NORTHERN PINE INN.** *9966 N WI 27 (54843). 715/634-4959; fax 715/634-8999; toll-free 800/777-7996. www.bestwestern.com.* 39 rms. June-mid-Sept, mid-Dec-Feb: S $59-$79; D $64-$89; each addl $5; suites $89-$99; under 12 free; lower rates rest of yr. Crib avail. Pet accepted. TV; cable. Indoor pool; whirlpool. Playground. Complimentary continental bkfst. Ck-out 11 am. Meeting rms. Business servs avail. Downhill ski 20 mi; x-country ski 1 mi. Sauna. Game rm. Some refrigerators, in-rm whirlpools; microwaves avail. Some patios. Picnic tables. Cr cds: A, C, D, DS, MC, V.
🄳 🍴 🏊 ≈ ⚒

★ **CEDAR INN.** *15659 WI 27 (54843). 715/634-5332; fax 715/634-1343; toll-free 800/776-2478. www.*

haywardlakes.com/cedarinn.htm. 23 rms. Memorial Day-early Oct: S $46-$56; D $51-$71; each addl $5; suites $100-$140; under 5 free; higher rates Birkebeiner Ski Race; lower rates rest of yr. Crib $5. TV; cable (premium). Complimentary continental bkfst. Restaurant nearby. Ck-out 10:30 am. Business servs avail. In-rm modem link. X-country ski 3 mi. Sauna. Whirlpool. Refrigerators; microwaves avail. Cr cds: A, DS, MC, V.
🄳 🏊 ≈ ⚒

★★ **COUNTRY INN AND SUITES.** *WI 27 S (54843). 715/634-4100; fax 715/634-2403; toll-free 800/456-4000. www.countryinns.com.* 66 rms, 2 story, 8 suites. June-Sept: S, D $78-$108; each addl $6; suites $88-$120; under 18 free; wknd rates; higher rates special events; lower rates rest of yr. Crib free. Pet accepted, some restrictions. TV; cable (premium). Complimentary continental bkfst. Coffee in rms. Restaurant 11 am-10:30 pm; closed Dec. Bar 11 am-midnight. Ck-out noon. Meeting rms. Business servs avail. In-rm modem link. X-country ski 4 mi. Indoor pool; whirlpool. Game rm. Bathrm phones, refrigerators, microwaves, wet bars; some in-rm whirlpools. Cr cds: A, D, DS, MC, V.
🄳 🍴 🏊 ≈ ⚒

★ **NORTHWOODS MOTEL.** *9854 WI 27 N (54843). 715/634-8088; fax 715/634-0714; toll-free 800/232-9202. www.haywardlakes.com.* 9 rms. S $35-$55; D $45-$60; each addl $5; kit. suite $65; family rates; higher rates special events (3-day min). Crib free. Pet accepted. TV; cable. Complimentary coffee in lobby. Ck-out 10 am. Downhill ski 19 mi; x-country ski 3 mi. Cr cds: DS, MC, V.
🄳 🍴 🏊 ⚒ SC

★ **SUPER 8.** *10444 N WI 27 S (54843). 715/634-2646; fax 715/634-6482. www.super8.com.* 46 rms, 1-2 story. Apr-Sept: S $50-$60; D $60-$82; each addl $5; under 12 free; higher rates special events; lower rates rest of yr. Crib $5. Pet accepted. TV; cable (premium). Indoor pool; whirlpool. Complimentary coffee in lobby. Restaurant adj 5:30 am-9 pm. Ck-out 11 am. X-country ski 2 mi. Game rm. Cr cds: A, D, MC, V.
🄳 🍴 🏊 ≈ ⚒

Restaurant

★ **KARIBALIS.** *10590 Main St (54843).* 715/634-2462. Hrs: Memorial Day-Labor Day: 11 am-10 pm; Sun to 9 pm. Closed Easter, Thanksgiving, Dec 25. Res accepted. Bar to midnight. Lunch $5.50-$7.95, dinner $5.95-$13.50. Child's menu. Specializes in steak, seafood, pasta. Salad bar. Outdoor dining. Family-owned. Cr cds: A, DS, MC, V.

🅳 ⊸

Hudson (C-1)

Pop 6,378 **Elev** 780 ft **Area code** 715 **Zip** 54016

Information Hudson Area Chamber of Commerce, 502 2nd St; 715/386-8411 or 800/657-6775

Web www.hudsonwi.org

What to See and Do

Octagon House. (1855) Octagonal home furnished in the style of gracious living of the 1800s; garden house museum with country store and lumbering and farming implements; carriage house museum with special display areas. (May-Oct, Tues-Sun; first three wks Dec; closed hols) 1004 3rd St. Phone 715/386-2654. ¢¢

Willow River State Park. A 2,800-acre park with swimming, fishing, boating, canoeing; x-country skiing, picnicking, camping (hookups, dump station). Naturalist programs (summer only). River scenery with two dams. Standard fees. (Daily) 5 mi N on County A. Phone 715/386-5931. ¢¢

Motels/Motor Lodges

★★ **BEST WESTERN HUDSON HOUSE INN.** *1616 Crest View Dr (54016).* 715/386-2394; fax 715/386-3167; toll-free 800/528-1234. www.bestwestern.com. 100 rms, 1-2 story. S $60-$82; D $69-$90; each addl $6; studio rm $81-$160; under 13 free. Crib free. TV; cable (premium). Indoor pool. Restaurant 5-9 pm. Rm serv from 9 am. Bar 11:30-1 am; entertainment Fri, Sat. Ck-out 11 am. Meeting rms. Business servs avail. In-rm modem link. Sundries. Beauty shop. Downhill ski 8 mi. Cr cds: A, C, D, DS, MC, V.

🏊 ⊷ 🖼 🐾 SC

★★ **COMFORT INN.** *811 Dominion Dr (54016).* 715/386-6355; fax 715/386-9778; toll-free 800/725-8987. www.comfortinn.com. 60 rms, 2 story. S $44.95-$62.95; D $47.95-$72.95; each addl $5; under 18 free. Crib free. Pet accepted, some restrictions; $50. TV; cable (premium), VCR avail. Indoor pool; whirlpool. Complimentary continental bkfst. Restaurant nearby. Ck-out 11 am. Guest lndry. Business servs avail. Cr cds: A, D, DS, MC, V.

🅳 🐾 ⊷ 🖼 🐾

B&B/Small Inn

★★★ **PHIPPS INN.** *1005 3rd St (54016).* 715/386-0800; fax 715/386-9002; toll-free 888/865-9388. www.phippsinn.com. 6 rms, 3 story, 3 suites. No rm phones. S, D $120-$209. Complimentary full bkfst; afternoon refreshments. Ck-out 11 am, ck-in 4-6 pm. Downhill ski 10 mi; x-country ski 7 mi. In-rm whirlpools. Restored Queen Anne-style Victorian mansion (1884); formal music rm with baby grand piano, two parlors, 3 porches. Totally nonsmoking. Cr cds: MC, V.

🏊 🖼 🐾

Hurley

See also Manitowish Waters

Founded 1885 **Pop** 1,782 **Elev** 1,493 ft **Area code** 715 **Zip** 54534

Information Chamber of Commerce, 316 Silver St; 715/561-4334

Web www.hurleywi.com

Originally a lumber and mining town, Hurley is now a winter sports center.

What to See and Do

Iron County Historical Museum. Exhibits of county's iron mining past; local artifacts, photo gallery.

(Daily; closed Dec 25) Iron St at 3rd Ave S. Phone 715/561-2244. **FREE**

Skiing. Whitecap Mountain Ski Area. Area has six chairlifts, rope tow; patrol, school, rentals; nursery; restaurant, cafeteria, concession area. Longest run 1½ mi; vertical drop 450 ft. (Nov-Mar, daily) Half-day rates. 8 mi W on WI 77 to Iron Belt, then 3 mi W on County E. Phone 561/277-6800. ¢¢¢¢

Special Events

Iron County Heritage Festival. 316 Silver St. Various heritage themes and costumed cast of characters. Last Sat July. Phone 715/561-4334.

Paavo Nurmi Marathon. Begins in Upson, SW via WI 77. Oldest marathon in state. Related activities Fri-Sat. Second wkend Aug. Phone 715/561-3290.

Red Light Snowmobile Rally. Second wkend Dec. Phone 715/561-4334.

Motel/Motor Lodge

★ ★ **RAMADA INN.** *1000 10th Ave N (54534). 715/561-3030; fax 715/561-4280. www.ramada.com.* 100 rms, 2 story. S $48-$65; D $62-$77; each addl $6; under 19 free; higher rates some winter hol wks and winter wkends. Crib free. Pet accepted. TV; cable. Indoor pool; whirlpool. Restaurant 7 am-2 pm, 5:30-10 pm. Bar 11-1 am. Ck-out noon. Coin lndry. Meeting rms. Business servs avail. Valet serv. Downhill/x-country ski 15 mi. Snowmobile trails. Game rm. Cr cds: A, D, DS, MC, V.

Janesville

(G-5) *See also Beloit, Fort Atkinson, Madison*

Founded 1836 **Pop** 52,133 **Elev** 858 ft **Area code** 608

Information Janesville Area Convention & Visitors Bureau, 51 S Jackson St, 53545; 608/757-3171 or 800/487-2757

Web www.janesville.com

In 1836, pioneer Henry F. Janes carved his initials into a tree on the bank of the Rock River. The site is now the intersection of the two main streets of industrial Janesville. Janes went on to found other Janesvilles in Iowa and Minnesota. Wisconsin's Janesville has a truck and bus assembly plant that offers tours. Because of its 1,900 acres of parkland, Janesville has been called "Wisconsin's Park Place."

What to See and Do

General Motors Corporation. Guided tours (Mon-Thurs; closed hols). No cameras. Res required. 1000 Industrial Ave. Phone 608/756-7681. **FREE**

Lincoln-Tallman Restorations. Tallman House (1855-1857), 26-rm antebellum mansion of Italianate design considered among the top 10 mid-19th-century structures for the study of American culture at the time of the Civil War. Restored Greek Revival Stone House (1842). Horse Barn (1855-1857) serves as visitor center and museum shop. Tours (daily). 440 N Jackson St, 4 blks N on US 14 Business. Phone 608/752-4519. ¢¢

Milton House Museum. (1844) Hexagonal building constructed of grout; underground railroad tunnel connects it with original log cabin; country store; guided tours. (Memorial Day-Labor Day, daily; May, Sept-mid-Oct, wkends, also Mon-Fri by appt) 18 S Janesville St in Milton, 8 mi NE at jct WI 26, 59. Phone 608/868-7772. ¢

Municipal parks. Riverside. Wading pool, fishing, boat launch; picnicking, hiking, x-country skiing, tennis courts, 18-hole golf, concession. N Washington St, N on US 14 Business. **Palmer.** Wading pool, swimming beach; picnicking, tennis courts, exercise course, nine-hole golf, concession. E Racine St, E on US 14 Business, exit WI 11. **Traxler.** Boat launching ramps for Rock River, fishing, children's fishing pond; picnicking, ice-skating; water ski shows, rose gardens. (Daily, May-Sept) N Parker Dr, ½ mi N on US 51. **Rockport.** Swimming pool, bathhouse; x-country skiing, hiking. 2800 Rockport Rd. Phone 608/755-3025. **FREE**

Rotary Gardens. Fifteen-acre botanical garden (Daily). Gift shop. 1455 Palmer Dr. Phone 608/752-3885.

Special Event

Rock County 4-H Fair. Rock County 4-H Fairgrounds. One of the largest 4-H fairs in country. Exhibits, competitions, carnival, grandstand shows, concerts. Phone 608/754-1470. Last wk July.

Motels/Motor Lodges

★ ★ **BEST WESTERN.** *3900 Milton Ave (53546). 608/756-4511; fax 608/756-0025; toll-free 800/334-4271. www.bestwestern.com.* 105 rms, 3 story. May-Sept: S, D $65-$90; each addl $5; suites $95-$140; under 18 free; lower rates rest of yr. Crib free. Pet accepted, some restrictions; fee. TV; cable. Indoor pool; whirlpool. Complimentary coffee in rms. Restaurant 6-9 pm; wkends 7 am-10 pm. Bar 4 pm-1 am. Ck-out 11 am. Meeting rms. Business servs avail. Airport transportation. Exercise equipt. Game rm. Cr cds: A, C, D, DS, MC, V.
🄳 🐾 ⚓ 🏋 ✈ 🦊 SC

★ ★ **RAMADA INN.** *3431 Milton Ave (53545). 608/756-2341; fax 608/756-4183; toll-free 800/433-7787. www. ramada.com.* 189 rms, 2 story. S $66-$72; D $72-$80; suites $125-$150; each addl $10; under 18 free. Crib free. TV; cable (premium). Complimentary continental bkfst (Mon-Fri). Coffee in rms. Indoor pool; whirlpool. Restaurant 6 am-1:30 pm, 5-10 pm. Bar 11-1 am. Ck-out noon. Meeting rms. Business servs avail. Sundries. Gift shop. Putting green. Exercise equipt; sauna. Game rm. Cr cds: A, C, D, DS, ER, JCB, MC, V.
🄳 ⚓ 🏋 🌙 🔥

Kenosha

(G-6) *See also Lake Geneva, Milwaukee, Racine, see also Waukegan, IL*

Settled 1835 **Pop** 80,352 **Elev** 610 ft
Area code 262
Information Kenosha Area Convention & Visitors Bureau, 812 56th St, 53140; 262/654-7307 or 800/654-7309
Web www.kenoshacvb.com

A major industrial city, port, and transportation center, Kenosha was settled by New Englanders. The city owns 84 percent of its Lake Michigan frontage, most of it developed as parks.

What to See and Do

Bong State Recreation Area. A 4,515-acre area. Swimming, fishing, boating; hiking, bridle, and off-road motorcycle trails; x-country skiing, snowmobiling, picnicking, guided nature hikes, nature center, special events area; family, group camping (fee). 17 mi W via WI 142; 9 mi W of I-94. Phone 262/878-5600. ¢¢

Carthage College. (1847) 2,100 students. Civil War Museum in Johnson Art Center (Mon-Fri; closed hols). 2001 Alford Park Dr, WI 32, northern edge of city on lakeside. Phone 262/551-8500. **FREE**

Factory outlet stores. More than 170 outlet stores can be found at **Original Outlet Mall**, 7700 120th Ave; and **Prime Outlets at Pleasant Prairie**, 11211 120th Ave; 262/857-2101. (Daily)

Kemper Center. Approx 11 acres. Several buildings incl Italianate Victorian mansion (1860); complex has more than 100 different trees, rose collection; mosiac mural; outdoor tennis courts, picnic area; also Anderson Art Gallery (Thurs-Sun afternoons). Guided tours by appt. (Office, Mon-Fri; grounds, daily) 6501 3rd Ave. Phone 262/657-6005. **FREE**

Kenosha County Historical Society and Museum. Items and settings of local and Wisconsin history, Native American material, folk and decorative art. Research library. (Tues-Sun afternoons; closed hols) 220 51st Pl. Phone 262/654-5770. **FREE**

Rambler Legacy Gallery. Lorado Taft dioramas of famous art studios; Native American, Oceanic, and African arts; Asian ivory and porcelain, Wisconsin folk pottery; mammals exhibit, dinosaur exhibit. Changing art, natural history exhibits. (Daily; closed hols) Civic Center. 5500 1st Ave. Phone 262/653-4140. **Donation**

Dog racing

Southport Marina. Two-mi walkway on Lake Michigan; playground. (Daily) From 97th to 57th Sts. Phone 262/657-5565. **FREE**

University of Wisconsin-Parkside. (1968) 5,100 students. A 700-acre campus. Buildings are connected by glass-walled interior corridors that radiate from $8-million tri-level Wyllie Library Learning Center. Nature, x-country ski trails. Tours. Wood Rd. Phone 262/595-2355.

Special Event

Bristol Renaissance Fair. 6 mi SW via I-94, Russell Rd exit, just N of the IL/WI state line. Re-creation of a 16th-century European marketplace featuring royal knights and swordsmen, master jousters, musicians, mimes, dancers, and hundreds of crafters and food peddlers. Richly gowned ladies, tattered beggars, barbarians, and soldiers stroll the grounds. Procession is heralded by trumpets and the royal drum corps. Phone 847/395-7773 or 800/52-FAIRE. Nine wkends beginning last wkend June.

Motels/Motor Lodges

★★ **BAYMONT INN.** *7540 118th Ave, Pleasant Prairie (53158). 262/857-*7911; fax 414/857-2370. www.baymontinn.com.* 95 rms, 2 story. S $69-$79; each addl $7; higher rates wkends; under 18 free. Crib free. Pet accepted. TV; cable (premium). Complimentary continental bkfst. Complimentary coffee in rms. Restaurant adj open 24 hrs. Ck-out noon. Business servs avail. In-rm modem link. Valet serv. Downhill ski 15 mi. Cr cds: A, D, DS, MC, V.

[D] [symbols] [SC]

★★ **HOLIDAY INN EXPRESS HARBORSIDE.** *5125 6th Ave (53140). 262/658-3281; fax 262/658-3420. www.holiday-inn.com.* 111 rms, 5 story. S $74-$125; D $89-$139; under 19 free. Crib free. Pet accepted. TV; cable (premium). Sauna. Indoor pool; whirlpool. Ck-out 11 am. Meeting rms. Business servs avail. On Lake Michigan. Cr cds: A, D, DS, JCB, MC, V.

[D] [symbols]

★ **KNIGHTS INN.** *7221 122nd Ave (53142). 414/857-2622; fax 414/857-2375. www.knightsinn.com.* 113 rms, 14 kits. June-Oct: S, D $47.95-$69.95; each addl $5; kit. units $62.95-$68.95; under 18 free; higher rates wkends; lower rates rest of yr. Crib free. Pet accepted. TV. Complimentary coffee in lobby. Restaurant nearby. Ck-out noon. Business servs avail. Cr cds: A, C, D, DS, MC, V.

D 🐾 🖼 🖌 SC

Restaurants

★ ★ **HOUSE OF GERHARD.** *3927 75th St (53142). 262/694-5212.* Hrs: 11:30 am-10 pm. Closed Sun; Dec 24-25; also 1 wk early July. Res accepted. German, American menu. Bar. Lunch $4.50-$11.95, dinner $8.95-$16. Child's menu. Specialties: schnitzel, rouladen, Cajun dishes. German decor. Family-owned. Cr cds: A, DS, MC, V.

🖼

★ ★ **MANGIA TRATTORIA.** *5717 Sheridan Rd (53140). 262/652-4285.* Hrs: 11:30 am-2 pm, 5-9 pm; Fri to 10 pm; Sat 5-10 pm; Sun 3-8 pm. Closed hols. Res accepted. Italian menu. Bar. Lunch, dinner $9-$20. Specializes in pasta, fresh seafood, wood-burning oven pizza. Outdoor dining. Cr cds: A, D, DS, MC, V.

D 🖼

★ ★ ★ **RAY RADIGAN'S.** *11712 S Sheridan Rd, Pleasant Prairie (53158). 262/694-0455.* Hrs: 11 am-10 pm; Sun from noon. Closed Mon; Dec 24-25. Res accepted. Bar. Lunch $5-$10, dinner $11.95-$30. Specializes in fresh seafood, steak. Own baking. Family-owned. Cr cds: A, D, DS, MC, V.

🖼

Kohler

See also Sheboygan

Pop 1,965 **Area code** 920 **Zip** 53044
Information Sheboygan County Chamber of Commerce, 712 Riverfront Dr, Suite 101, Sheboygan 53081; 920/457-9495 or 800/457-9497

Web www.sheboygan.org

Kohler, a small village located one hour north of Milwaukee, has gained a reputation as a destination unlike anything else in the United States. It was born as one of the earliest planned communities. Designed by the Olmstead Brothers of Boston, Kohler began as a "garden at the factory gate" and headquarters for the country's largest plumbing manufacturer. Running through Kohler is seven miles of the Sheboygan River and a 500-acre wildlife sanctuary, with some of the best salmon and trout fishing in the Unites States.

What to See and Do

Waelderhaus. Reproduction of Kohler family home in Austrian Alps. Guided tours (afternoons, three departures daily; closed hols). 1 mi S off County PP, on W Riverside Dr in Kohler. Phone 920/452-4079. **FREE**

Hotel

★ ★ ★ **INN ON WOODLAKE.** *705 Woodlake Rd (53044). 920/452-7800; fax 920/452-6288; toll-free 800/919-3600. www.innonwoodlake.com.* 121 rms, 3 story. May-Oct: S $149-$295; D $169-$315; each addl $10; under 16 free; lower rates rest of yr. Crib free. TV; cable (premium), VCR avail (movies). Indoor pool; whirlpool, sauna. Complimentary continental bkfst. Restaurant adj 11 am-10 pm. Ck-out noon. Tennis privileges. Golf privileges. Exercise equipt. Health club privileges. X-country ski. Some refrigerators. Cr cds: A, D, DS, MC, V.

D 🏊 🎿 ⛳ 🛏 🧍 🖼 🖌

Resort

★ ★ ★ ★ **THE AMERICAN CLUB.** *444 Highland Dr (53044). 920/457-8000; fax 920/457-0299; toll-free 800/344-2838. www.americanclub.com.* Built in 1918 and opened as a resort in 1981, this National Register historic landmark used to house workers from Kohler Company, the well-known kitchen and bath manufacturer. All 237 guest rooms have luxurious whirlpool baths. The Sports Core Salon and Day Spa, restaurants, and golf courses are just a few of the attractions in this immaculate town. 236 rms, 3 story. May-Oct: S $235-$960; D $265-$990; each addl $15; under 17 free; lower rates rest of year. Crib free. TV; cable (premium); VCR avail (movies). Complimentary afternoon tea. Restaurant (see THE IMMIGRANT).

Rm serv 24 hrs. Bar 11:30- 1 am; entertainment, dancing. Ck-out noon. Meeting rms. In-rm modem link. Concierge. Gift shop. Indoor/outdoor tennis. Exercise rm. 72-hole golf; driving range, putting green. X-country ski on site. Spa. Hunting, trap shooting, and fishing. In-rm whirlpools, wet bars, honor bar; some bathrm phones, refrigerators. Carriage rides; bicycles. Cr cds: A, C, D, DS, JCB, MC, V.

🅓 ⚓ 🏄 🏋 🎿 🏃 � 🔥 SC

Restaurant

★ ★ ★ **THE IMMIGRANT.** 444 *Highland Dr (53044). 920/457-8000. www. americanclub.com.* Hrs: 6-10 pm; Closed Sun, Mon. Res required. Bar. Wine cellar. Regional American menu. A la carte entrees: dinner $32-$40. Specializes in fresh fish, game, beef. Own baking. Entertainment Fri, Sat. Six elegant dining areas with distinct ethnic decor. Jacket. Cr cds: A, D, DS, MC, V.

🅓

Lac du Flambeau

See also Manitowish Waters, Minocqua, Woodruff

Pop 1,423 **Elev** 1,635 ft
Area code 715 **Zip** 54538
Information Chamber of Commerce, PO Box 158; 715/588-3346 or 877/588-3346
Web www.lacduflambeauchamber. com

The French gave this village the name "Lake of the Torch" because of the Chippewa practice of fishing and canoeing at night by the light of birch bark torches. Located in the center of the Lac du Flambeau Reservation, the village is tribal headquarters for more than 1,200 Chippewa still living in the area. It is also the center for a popular, lake-filled north woods recreation area. The reservation boasts 126 spring-fed lakes and its own fish hatchery.

What to See and Do

Chequamegon National Forest. (See PARK FALLS) S on County D, then W on WI 70. Phone 715/362-1300.

Lac du Flambeau Chippewa Museum and Cultural Center. Displays of Native American artifacts, fur trading, and historical items. Chippewa craft workshops (May-Oct). (Mon-Sat; also by appt) Downtown. Phone 715/588-3333. ¢¢

Waswagoning Ojibwe Village. Twenty acres of Ojibwe culture with guided tours. (Memorial Day-Labor Day) 1 mi N on County H. Phone 715/588-3560. ¢¢¢

Special Events

Powwows. At Indian Bowl, fronting on Lake Interlaken. Dancing by Waswa-gon Dancers. Tues eves. July-mid-Aug. Phone 715/588-3333.

Colorama. Last Sat Sept. Phone 715/588-3346.

Resort

★ ★ **DILLMAN'S BAY PROPERTIES.** *3285 Sandlake Lodge Ln (54538). 715/588-3143; fax 715/588-3110. www.dillmans.com.* 16 units, 18 cottages. No A/C. EP, mid-May-mid-Oct: daily, from $51/person; wkly, from $343/person; family rates. Closed rest of yr. Crib free. Pet accepted. TV in lobby, some rms. Playground. Dining by res. Ck-out 10 am, ck-in noon. Package store. Meeting rms. Sports dir in summer. Tennis. Practice fairway. Sand beaches; waterskiing; windsurfing; scuba diving; boats, motors, kayaks, sailboats, canoes, pontoon boats; private launch, covered boathouse. Bicycles. Lawn games. Hiking trails. Soc dir; wine and cheese party Sun. Nature study, photography, painting workshops. Rec rm. Fishing clean and store area. Some fireplaces; refrigerator, microwave in suites and cottages. On 250 acres. Cr cds: MC, V.

🅓 🐎 ⚓ 🏃 🛏 🔥 SC

La Crosse

(E-3) *See also Galesville, Sparta*

Settled 1842 **Pop** 51,003 **Elev** 669 ft
Area code 608
Information La Crosse Area Convention and Visitor Bureau, 410 E Veterans Memorial Dr, 54601; 608/782-2366 or 800/658-9424
Web www.explorelacrosse.com

An agricultural, commercial, and industrial city, La Crosse is washed by the waters of the Mississippi, the Black, and La Crosse rivers. Once a trading post, it was named by the French for the native game the French called lacrosse. More than 200 businesses and industries operate here today.

What to See and Do

Goose Island County Park. Beach, fishing, boat ramps; hiking trails, picnicking, camping (electric hookups). (Mid-Apr-mid-Oct, daily) 3 mi S on WI 35, then 2 mi W on County GI. Phone 608/788-7018. ¢¢¢

Granddad Bluff. Tallest (1,172 ft) of the crags that overlook the city; it provides a panoramic view of the winding Mississippi, the tree-shaded city, and the Minnesota and Iowa bluffs. Picnic area. (May-late Oct, daily) Surfaced path to shelter house and top of bluff for the disabled. Bliss Rd, 2 mi E. Phone 608/789-7533. **FREE**

Hixon House. (ca 1860) Fifteen-rm home; Victorian and Asian furnishings. Visitor information center and gift shop in building that once served as wash house. (Memorial Day-Labor Day, daily) 429 N 7th St. Phone 608/782-1980. ¢¢

Industrial tour. City Brewery. One-hr guided tours. Gift shop. (Mon-Sat; closed hols) 1111 S 3rd St. Phone 608/420-0800. **FREE**

La Crosse Queen **Cruises.** Sightseeing cruise on the Mississippi River aboard 150-passenger, double-deck paddlewheeler (early May-mid-Oct, daily). Also dinner cruise (Fri night, Sat and Sun). Charters (approx Apr-Oct). Boat Dock, Riverside Park, W end of State St. Phone 608/784-2893.

Pump House Regional Arts Center. (Western Wisconsin Regional Arts) Regional art exhibits; performing arts (wkends). (Tues-Sat; closed hols) 119 King St. Phone 608/785-1434. **DONATION**

Skiing. Mount La Crosse Ski Area. Area has three chairlifts, rope tow; patrol, rentals, school; snowmaking; night skiing; cafeteria, bar. Longest run 1 mi; vertical drop 516 ft. (Thanksgiving-mid-Mar, daily; closed Dec 25) Half-day rates on weekends, holidays. X-country trails (Dec-mid-Mar, daily). 2 mi S on WI 35. Phone 608/788-0044.

Swarthout Museum. Changing historical exhibits ranging from prehistoric times to the 20th century. (Memorial Day-Labor Day, Tues-Sat; rest of yr, Tues-Sun; closed hols) 112 S 9th St. Phone 608/782-1980. **FREE**

Special Events

La Crosse Interstate Fair. 11 mi E on I-90 in West Salem. Stock car racing, farm exhibits; carnival, entertainment. Mid-July. Phone 800/658-9424.

Riverfest. Riverside Park. Five-day festival with river events, music, food, entertainment, fireworks, children's events. Early July. Phone 608/782-6000.

Oktoberfest. Oktoberfest Strasse, S side of town. Six days beginning last wkend Sept or first wkend Oct. Phone 800/658-9424.

Motels/Motor Lodges

★ ★ **BEST WESTERN.** *1835 Rose St (54603). 608/781-7000; fax 608/781-3195. www.bestwestern.com.* 121 rms, 2 story. S $54-$76; D $68-$95; each addl $10; under 18 free. Crib free. TV; cable (premium), VCR. Indoor pool; whirlpool. Complimentary coffee in rms. Restaurant 6:30 am-10 pm. Rm serv to 9 pm. Bar 11:30-1 am; entertainment Tues-Sat. Ck-out noon. Meeting rms. Business servs avail. In-rm modem link. Valet serv. Sundries. Downhill/x-country ski 10 mi. Minature golf. Exercise equipt; sauna. Rec rm. On river; dockage.

Private beach. Cr cds: A, C, D, DS, MC, V.

⬛ 🏊 🛏 🧍 📶 🔥

★ **DAYS INN HOTEL AND CONFERENCE CENTER.** *101 Sky Harbour Dr (54603). 608/783-1000; fax 608/783-2948. www.daysinn.com.* 148 rms, 2 story. S, D $64.99-$99.99; each addl $5; under 18 free. Crib free. Pet accepted; fee. TV; cable. Sauna. Indoor pool; whirlpool. Complimentary coffee in rms. Restaurant 6:30 am-2 pm, 5-9 pm. Bar 4:30 pm-1 am. Ck-out 11 am. Meeting rms. Business servs avail. Valet serv. Sundries. Exercise equipt. Downhill/x-country ski 10 mi. Game rm. Cr cds: A, C, D, DS, ER, JCB, MC, V.

⬛ 🏊 🛏 🧍 📶 🔥

★ **EXEL INN.** *2150 Rose St (54603). 608/781-0400; fax 608/781-1216; toll-free 800/367-3935. www.exelinns.com.* 102 rms, 2 story. S $31.99-$47.99; D $38.99-$54.99; each addl $4; suite $80-$100; under 19 free. Crib free. Pet accepted. TV. Complimentary continental bkfst. Coffee in rms. Restaurant nearby. Ck-out noon. Coin lndry. Downhill/x-country ski 10 mi. Game rm. Cr cds: A, C, D, DS, ER, MC, V.

⬛ 🏊 📶 🔥 🐾

★★ **HAMPTON INN.** *2110 Rose St (54603). 608/781-5100; fax 608/781-3574; toll-free 800/426-7866. www. hamptoninn.com.* 101 rms, 2 story. S, D $69-$109; under 19 free. Crib free. TV; cable. Indoor pool. Complimentary continental bkfst. Restaurant adj open 24 hrs. Ck-out noon. Exercise Equipt. Meeting rms. Whirlpool. Cr cds: A, C, D, DS, JCB, MC, V.

⬛ 🛏 🧍 📶 🔥 SC

★ **NIGHT SAVER INN.** *1906 Rose St (54603). 608/781-0200; toll-free 800/658-9497. www.visitor-guide.com/ nightsaver.* 73 rms, 2 story. Mid-May-Oct: S $44; D $54; under 12 free; lower rates rest of yr. Crib avail. TV; cable (premium), VCR avail. Complimentary continental bkfst. Restaurant opp 6 am-11 pm. Ck-out 11 am. Business servs avail. In-rm modem link. Downhill ski 8 mi; x-country ski 1 mi. Exercise equipt. Whirlpool. Cr cds: A, C, D, DS, MC, V.

🏊 🧍 📶 🔥

★ **ROADSTAR INN.** *2622 Rose St (54603). 608/781-3070; fax 608/781-5114; toll-free 800/445-4667.* 110 rms, 2 story. S $42-$62; D $47-$67; each addl $5; under 15 free; higher rates special events. TV; cable (premium). Complimentary continental bkfst. Restaurant adj open 24 hrs. Ck-out noon. Downhill/x-country ski 8 mi. Some refrigerators, wet bars. Cr cds: A, D, DS, MC, V.

⬛ 🏊 📶 🔥 SC

★ **SUPER 8.** *1625 Rose St (54603). 608/781-8880; fax 608/781-4366; toll-free 800/800-8000. www.super8.com.* 82 rms, 2 story. S $69-$92; D $82-$102; each addl $5; under 18 free. Crib free. TV. Indoor pool; whirlpool. Complimentary continental bkfst. Restaurant nearby. Ck-out 11 am. Coin lndry. Exercise equipt. Meeting rms. Sundries. Downhill/x-country ski 10 mi. Some in-rm whirlpools. Cr cds: A, D, DS, MC, V.

⬛ 🏊 🛏 🧍 📶 🔥 SC

Hotel

★★★ **RADISSON HOTEL LA CROSSE.** *200 Harborview Plz (54601). 608/784-6680; fax 608/782-6430. www.radisson.com.* 169 units, 8 story. S $89-$109; D $99-$139; each addl $10; suites $185-$420; under 18 free. Pet accepted. TV; cable. Indoor pool; whirlpool. Restaurant 6:30 am-11 pm. Bar 11-1 am; entertainment Fri-Sat. Ck-out noon. Meeting rms. Business servs avail. Free airport, bus depot transportation. Downhill/x-country ski 8 mi. Exercise equipt. Overlooks Mississippi River. Cr cds: A, MC, V.

⬛ 🐾 🏊 🛏 🧍 ✈ 📶 🔥 SC

Restaurants

★★ **FREIGHTHOUSE.** *107 Vine St (54601). 608/784-6211.* Hrs: 4:30-10 pm; Fri, Sat 5-10:30 pm. Closed Easter, Thanksgiving, Dec 24-25. Bar to 1 am. Dinner $11.95-$35.95. Specialties: Alaskan king crab, prime rib. Outdoor dining overlooking river. Former freight house of the Chicago, Milwaukee, and St. Paul Railroad (1880). Cr cds: A, D, DS, MC, V.

⬛

★★ **PIGGY'S.** *328 S Front St (54601). 608/784-4877. www.piggys.com.* Hrs:

5-10 pm; Sat, Sun from 4 pm. Closed Memorial Day, Labor Day, Dec 24-25. Res accepted. Bar. Dinner $16.95-$28.95. Child's menu. Specializes in ribs, pork chops, prime steaks. View of Mississippi River. Cr cds: A, D, DS, MC, V.

D

Ladysmith

Pop 3,938 **Elev** 1,144 ft
Area code 715 **Zip** 54848
Information Rusk County Visitor Center, 205 W 9th St; 715/532-2642 or 800/535-7875
Web www.ruskcounty.org

Ladysmith, county seat of Rusk County, is located along the Flambeau River. The economy is based on processing lumber and marketing dairy and farm produce. There are fishing and canoeing facilities in the area.

What to See and Do

Flambeau River State Forest. A 91,000-acre forest. Canoeing river, swimming, fishing, boating; backpacking, nature and hiking trails, mountain biking, x-country skiing, snowmobiling, picnicking, camping (dump station). Standard fees. (Daily) E on US 8 to Hawkins, then N on County M to County W, near Winter. Phone 715/332-5271. ¢¢

Special Events

Northland Mardi Gras. Memorial Park. Third wkend July. Phone 715/532-2642.

Rusk County Fair. Four days mid-Aug. Phone 715/532-2639.

Leaf it to Rusk Fall Festival. Last wkend Sept. Phone 715/532-2642.

Motels/Motor Lodges

★★ **BEST WESTERN EL RANCHO.** 8500 W Flambeau Ave (54848). 715/532-6666; fax 715/532-7551; res 800/780-7234. www.bestwestern.com. 27 rms. S $46-$50; D $54-$62; each addl $4; under 12 free. Crib $9. Pet accepted. TV; cable (premium).

Restaurant 11 am-2 pm, 4:30-9:30 pm. Bar to 1 am. Ck-out 11 am. Business servs avail. Downhill ski 15 mi; x-country ski on site. Cr cds: A, C, D, DS, MC, V.

D 🐾 🏊 ⛷ 🔥

★ **EVERGREEN MOTEL.** 1201 Lake Ave W (54848). 715/532-3168; fax 715/532-3168; toll-free 800/828-3168. 20 rms. S $30; D $40; each addl $4. Crib $4. Pet accepted, some restrictions. TV; cable (premium). Complimentary coffee in rms. Restaurant nearby. Ck-out 11 am. Downhill/x-country ski 7 mi. Picnic tables. Cr cds: A, DS, MC, V.

D 🐾 🏊 ⛷ 🔥

Lake Geneva

(G-6) *See also Burlington, Elkhorn, Fontana, Kenosha*

Settled 1840 **Pop** 5,979 **Elev** 880 ft
Area code 262 **Zip** 53147
Information Geneva Lake Area Chamber of Commerce, 201 Wrigley Dr; 262/248-4416 or 800/345-1020
Web www.lakegenevawi.com

This is a popular and attractive four-season resort area. Recreational activities include boating, fishing, swimming, horseback riding, camping, hiking, biking, golf, tennis, skiing, cross-country skiing, ice fishing, snowmobiling, and ice boating.

What to See and Do

Big Foot Beach State Park. A 272-acre beach park on Geneva Lake. Swimming (lifeguard on duty mid-June-Labor Day, wknds only), fishing; picnicking, playground, winter sports, camping. Standard fees. (Daily) 1 mi S on WI 120. Phone 262/248-2528. ¢¢¢

Excursion boats. Two-hr round-trip and one-hr rides; also lunch, Sun brunch, dinner cruises. (May-Oct, daily) Res required. Mail boat (mid-June-mid-Sept, once daily). Riviera Docks. Phone 262/248-6206. ¢¢¢¢

Geneva Lake. This 5,230-acre lake provides a variety of game fish in clear waters. The surrounding hills are heavily wooded with elm, maple, and oak trees.

Skiing.

Grand Geneva Resort. Area has three chairlifts, two rope tows; patrol, school, rentals; snowmaking; lodging (see RESORT); restaurant, cafeteria, concession, bar. Longest run ¼ mi; vertical drop 211 ft (Dec-Mar, daily) X-country trails, night skiing. 2 mi E at jct US 12 and WI 50. Phone 800/558-3417. ¢¢¢¢

Wilmot Mountain. Quad, three triple, four double chairlifts, six rope tows; patrol, school, rentals, snowmaking; restaurant, cafeteria, bar. Longest run 2,500 ft; vertical drop 230 ft. Night skiing. (Mid Nov-Mar, daily; closed Dec 24 eve) 3 mi N of Antioch, IL on IL 83, then W on WI County C; 1 mi S of Wilmot, WI on IL state line. Phone 262/862-2301.

Special Events

Winterfest. Riviera Park at the lakefront. Host of US Snow Sculpting Championships. Early Feb. Phone 262/248-4416.

Venetian Festival. Flatiron Park. Rides, games, food; lighted boat parade and fireworks. Third wkend Aug. Phone 262/248-4416.

Motels/Motor Lodges

★★ **AMBASSADOR.** *415 S Wells St (53147). 262/248-3452; fax 262/248-0605.* 18 rms. Late May-mid-Sept: S $65-$135; lower rates rest of yr. TV. Indoor pool; whirlpool, sauna. Complimentary continental bkfst. Restaurant nearby. Ck-out 11 am. Meeting rms. Business servs avail. Tennis. Downhill/x-country ski 2 mi. Miniature golf adj. Some refrigerators, whirlpools. Totally nonsmoking. Cr cds: A, DS, MC, V.

D ➤ ⛷ ≈ 🖾 🐾

★ **BUDGET HOST DIPLOMAT.** *1060 S Wells St (53147). 262/248-1809; fax 262/248-1809; toll-free 800/264-5678. www.budgethost.com.* 23 rms, 2 story. Apr-Oct: S $41-$71; D $51-$110; under 12 free; ski plan; higher rates some hols; lower rates rest of yr. Crib free. TV; cable (premium), VCR avail. Pool. Complimentary coffee in lobby. Ck-out 11 am.

Business servs avail. Downhill/x-country ski 2 mi. Balconies. Picnic tables. Cr cds: A, DS, MC, V.

D ➤ ≈ 🖾 🐾

★★★ **INTERLAKEN RESORT AND COUNTRY SPA.** *W 4240 WI 50 (53147). 262/248-9121; fax 262/245-5016; toll-free 800/225-5558. www.interlakenresort.com.* 144 rms in 3-story lodge, 100 kit. villas. Lodge: S, D $49-$189; each addl $10; villas for 1-6, $99-$229; under 12 free; package plans avail. Crib free. TV; VCR (movies). 3 pools, 1 indoor; wading pool, whirlpool, poolside serv. Free supervised children's activites (June-Labor Day; also hols). Restaurant 7 am-10 pm. Bar 11-1 am; wkend entertainment. Ck-out noon. Meeting rms. Business servs avail. Valet serv. Concierge (seasonal). Sundries. Gift shop. Barber, beauty shop. Tennis. Downhill ski 5 mi; x-country ski on site. Snowmobiles; ice skates. Exercise equipt; sauna, steam rm. Game rm. Boats, waterskiing, windsurfing. Cr cds: A, C, D, DS, MC, V.

D 🚲 ➤ 🏃 ≈ 🚶 🖾 🐾

Resort

★★★ **GRAND GENEVA RESORT AND SPA.** *7036 Grand Geneva Way (53147). 262/248-8811; fax 262/249-4763; toll-free 800/558-3417. www.grandgeneva.com.* 355 rms, 3 story. S, D $179-$279; each addl $10; under 18 free. Crib free. TV; cable (premium), VCR (movies). 3 pools, 2 indoor; whirlpool. Playground. Supervised children's activities; ages 4-12. Complimentary coffee in rms. Restaurants 6:30 am-10 pm; Fri (see also RISTORANTE BRISSAGO). Bar 11:30-2 am; entertainment. Ck-out noon, ck-in 4 pm. Convention facilities. Business center. In-rm modem link. Valet serv. Gift shop. Airport transportation. Indoor, outdoor tennis, pro. 36-hole golf, pro, driving range, putting green. Paddleboats, hydrobikes. Downhill/x-country ski on site. Bicycle rentals. Exercise rm; sauna, steam rm. Spa center. Private patios, balconies. 1,300 acres of wooded, meadowland with private lake. Cr cds: A, C, D, DS, JCB, MC, V.

D ➤ 🏌 🏃 ≈ 🚶 ✈ 🖾 🐾 🏃

B&B/Small Inn

★★ **FRENCH COUNTRY INN.** *W 4190 West End Rd (53147). 262/245-5220; fax 262/245-9060. www.french countryinn.com.* 34 rms, 2 story. May-Oct: S, D $135-$185; suites $145-$275; lower rates rest of yr. Crib free. TV; cable (premium). Pool. Dining rm 5-10 pm; Fri, Sat to 10:30 pm. Complimentary full bkfst; afternoon refreshments. Ck-out noon, ck-in 3 pm. Business servs avail. Golf privileges. Downhill ski 12 mi; x-country ski 1 mi. On lake; beach. Portions of guest house built in Denmark and shipped to US for Danish exhibit at the 1893 Columbian Exposition in Chicago. Cr cds: MC, V.

D ⊠ ⩯ ⊠ 🕭

Restaurants

★ **POPEYE'S GALLEY AND GROG.** *811 Wrigley Dr (53147). 262/248-4381.* Hrs: 11 am-10 pm; Fri, Sat to 11 pm; winter 11:30 am-9 pm; Fri, Sat to 10 pm. Closed Dec 25. Bar. Lunch, dinner $5.95-$15.95. Child's menu. Parking. Nautical decor. Glass-enclosed deck with view of Geneva Lake. Cr cds: A, DS, MC, V.

D ⊐

★★★ **RISTORANTE BRISSAGO.** *7036 Grand Geneva Way (53147). 262/248-8811. www.grandgeneva.com.* Hrs: 5:30-10 pm; Fri, Sat to 11 pm. Closed Mon. Res accepted. Italian menu. Bar. Wine list. A la carte entrees: dinner $9.75-$27. Specialties: osso buco Milanese, gamberi Mediterraneo, antipasto. Valet parking. Views of lake and wooded hills. Cr cds: A, D, DS, MC, V.

D

★★★ **ST. MORITZ.** *327 Wrigley Dr (53147). 262/248-6680.* Hrs: 5:30-10 pm. Closed Mon. Res accepted. Continental menu. Bar. Wine cellar. Dinner $14.95-$24.95. Child's menu. Specializes in veal, fresh fish. Own baking. Parking. Historic Queen Anne house (1885); ornately decorated; 12 fireplaces. Cr cds: A, D, DS, MC, V.

D ⊐

Land O' Lakes

See also Boulder Junction, Eagle River

Pop 700 **Elev** 1,700 ft **Area code** 715 **Zip** 54540

Information Chamber of Commerce, US 45, PO Box 599; 715/547-3432 or 800/236-3432

Web www.ci.land-o-lakes.wi.us

This lovely village, on the Michigan border amid more than 100 lakes, serves as a center for tourist traffic. Fishing and boating in the area are exceptional. East of town is Lac Vieux Desert, source of the Wisconsin River.

Motel/Motor Lodge

★ **PINEAIRE RESORT MOTEL.** *2091 WI 45 (54540). 906/544-2313.* 9 cottages, 7 with shower only. No A/C, rm phones. Cottages $35-$45; each addl $5; under 8 free. Crib free. Pet accepted. TV. Restaurant nearby. Ck-out 10 am. X-country ski on site. Snowmobiling. Picnic tables, grills. Cr cds: A, MC, V.

🐾 🐾 ⊠ 🕭

Resort

★★ **SUNRISE LODGE.** *5894 W Shore Rd (54540). 715/547-3684; fax 715/547-6110; toll-free 800/221-9689. www.sunriselodge.com.* 22 units in 21 cottages, 18 kits. No A/C in cottages. May-Oct, AP: S $80; D $150; EP: S $49; D $59; wkly, family rates; fall plan; Nov-Apr, EP only: D $55-$125. Crib avail. Pet accepted. Playground. Dining rm 7:30-10 am, 11:30 am-2 pm, 5-7:30 pm; Sun 7:30-11 am, noon-3 pm; wkends only in winter. Box lunches. Meeting rm. Business servs avail. Airport, bus depot transportation. Tennis. Miniature golf. Private beach; boats, motors, canoes. X-country ski on site. Lawn games. Exercise trail. Nature trail. Bicycles. Rec rm. Fish/hunt guides; clean and store area. Refrigerators. Picnic tables, grills. Spacious grounds. On Lac Vieux Desert. Cr cds: DS, MC, V.

D 🐾 🐾 ⊠ 🎿 ✈ 🕭

Madison

(F-5) *See also Mount Horeb, New Glarus, Prairie du Sac*

Settled 1837 **Pop** 191,262 **Elev** 863 ft
Area code 608
Information Greater Madison Convention & Visitors Bureau, 615 E Washington Ave, 53703; 608/255-2537 or 800/373-6376
Web www.visitmadison.com

Madison was a virgin wilderness in 1836 when the territorial legislature selected the spot for the capital and the state university. Today this "City of Four Lakes," located on an isthmus between Lake Mendota and Lake Monona, is a recreational, cultural, and manufacturing center. Both the university and state government play important roles in the community.

Madison has a rich architectural heritage left by Frank Lloyd Wright and the Prairie School movement. There are a number of Wright buildings here; many are private homes and not open to the public but may be viewed from the outside.

What to See and Do

Dane County Farmers' Market. Festive open-air market selling Wisconsin produce and agricultural products. (Two locations) Capitol Sq (May-Oct, Sat) and 200 Martin Luther King, Jr. Blvd. (May-Oct, Sat) Phone 608/424-6714.

Edgewood College. (1927) 1,725 students. A 55-acre campus on Lake Wingra; Native American burial mounds. 855 Woodrow St. Phone 608/257-4861.

Frank Lloyd Wright architecture.

First Unitarian Society. A classic example of Wright's Prairie School work. (May-Sept, Mon-Fri afternoons, also Sat mornings; closed hols and two wks Aug) 900 University Bay Dr. Phone 608/233-9774. ¢¢

Self-driving tour. These are private homes and not open to the public. However, they may be viewed from the outside. **Airplane House** (1908), 120 Ely Place; **Dr. Arnold Jackson House** (1957), 3515 W Beltline Hwy; **Lamp House** (1899), 22 N Butler St; **J. C. Pew House** (1939), 3650 Lake Mendota Dr; **Louis Sullivan's Bradley House,** 106 N Prospect; **"Jacobs I" House** (1937), 441 Toepfer Ave.

Henry Vilas Park Zoo. World-famous for successful orangutan, Siberian tiger, spectacle bear, penguin, and camel breeding programs. Zoo exhibits incl 600 specimens consisting of 140 species. Petting zoo, picnic area on an island in Lake Wingra's lagoon, bathing beach, tennis courts. (Daily) 702 S Randall Ave on Lake Wingra. Phone 608/258-9490. **FREE**

Lake Kegonsa State Park. A 343-acre park. Swimming, waterskiing, fishing, boating; hiking and nature trails, picnicking, playground, camping (May-mid-Oct, dump station). Standard fees. (Daily) 13 mi SE via I-90, then S on County N. Phone 608/873-9695. ¢¢

Madison Art Center. Features modern and contemporary art by international, national, regional, and local artists; permanent collection. Tours (by appt, fee). (Tues-Sun; closed hols) 211 State St in Civic Center. Phone 608/257-0158. **FREE**

Madison Children's Museum. Hands-on museum. Special craft and activity programs every wkend. (Tues-Sun, daily; closed hols) 100 State St. Phone 608/256-6445. ¢¢

Olbrich Botanical Gardens. Contains 14 acres of horticultural displays incl annuals, perennials, shrubs, hybrid roses, lilies, dahlias, spring bulbs, rock and herb gardens. All-American Rose Selection Demonstration Garden. Garden building has a tropical conservatory housed inside a 50-ft high glass pyramid; tropical ferns, palms, flowering plants; waterfall, stream. (Daily; closed Dec 25) 3330 Atwood Ave. Phone 608/246-4551. ¢

State Capitol. Dominates the center of the city. The white granite building has a classic dome topped by Daniel Chester French's gilded bronze statue *Wisconsin.* Tours (daily; closed most hols). Capitol Sq. Phone 608/266-0382. **FREE**

State Historical Museum. Permanent exhibits explore the history of Native

American life in Wisconsin; gallery with changing Wisconsin, US history exhibits. Theater. (Tues-Sat) 30 N Carroll St, located on Capitol Sq, jct State, Mifflin, and Carroll sts. Phone 608/264-6555. **FREE**

University of Wisconsin-Madison. (1849) 41,948 students. The 929-acre campus extends for more than 2 mi along S shore of Lake Mendota. 7 blks W of Capitol. Maps and general information at Visitor and Information Place, N Park and Langdon Sts; or at Campus Assistance Center, 420 N Lake St. Phone 608/263-2400. On campus are

Carillon Tower. 56 bells; afternoon concerts (Sun). Phone 608/263-1900.

Elvehjem Museum of Art. Paintings, sculpture, decorative arts, prints, Japanese woodcuts, other artworks from 2300 B.C. to present day; changing exhibits; 80,000-volume Kohler Art Library. (Tues-Sun; closed Jan 1, Thanksgiving, Dec 25) 800 University Ave. Phone 608/263-2246. **FREE**

Geology Museum. Six-ft rotating globe, rocks, minerals, a black light display, a walk-through cave, meteorites, and fossils incl the skeletons of a giant mastodon and dinosaurs. (Mon-Fri, daily, also Sat mornings; closed hols) 1215 W Dayton St, corner of W Dayton and Charter sts. Phone 608/262-2399. **FREE**

Memorial Library. More than five million volumes; collection of rare books. Langdon and Lake sts. Phone 608/262-3193.

Observatory and Willow drives. Scenic drives along shore of Lake Mendota.

Washburn Observatory. Public viewing first and third Wed eves of each month (weather permitting). 1401 Observatory Dr. Phone 608/262-9274. **FREE**

USDA Forest Products Laboratory. Devoted to scientific and technical research on properties, processing, and uses of wood and wood products. Guided tour (one departure, Mon-Thurs afternoons; closed hols). 1 Gifford Pinchot Dr off N Walnut St. Phone 608/231-9200. **FREE**

Wisconsin Veterans Museum. Dioramas, exhibits of events from Civil War to Persian Gulf War. (June-Sept, daily; rest of yr, Mon-Sat; closed hols) 30 W Mifflin St. Phone 608/267-1799. **FREE**

Special Events

Concerts on the Square. Six-week series; Wed evenings. Late June-early Aug. Phone 608/257-0638.

Paddle & Portage Canoe Race. Downtown isthmus. July. Phone 608/255-1008.

Art Fair on the Square. Capitol Concourse. Exhibits by 500 artists and craftspersons; food, entertainment. Contact Madison Art Center. Mid-July. Phone 608/257-0158.

Dane County Fair. Alliant Energy Center. Mid-July. Phone 608/224-0500.

Motels/Motor Lodges

★★ **BEST WESTERN.** *650 Grand Canyon Dr (53719). 608/833-4200; fax 608/833-5614; res 800/847-7919. www.bestwestern.com.* 101 suites, 2 story. S $60-$99; D $60-$109; Suites $63-$110; each addl $5; under 17 free. Crib free. Pet accepted. TV; cable. Complimentary full bkfst. Ck-out noon. Coin lndry. Meeting rms. Business servs avail. In-rm modem link. Exercise equipt. Health club privileges. Refrigerators, wet bars; microwaves avail. Cr cds: A, C, D, DS, MC, V.

[D] [🐾] [🏋] [🔁] [🔥] [SC]

★★ **BEST WESTERN INN ON THE PARK.** *22 S Carroll St (53703). 608/257-8811; fax 608/257-5995; res 800/279-8811.* www.bestwestern.com. 213 rms, 9 story. S $84-$109; D $89-$149; each addl $10; suites $99-$179; under 12 free; higher rates special events. Crib free. TV; cable (premium). Heated pool; whirlpool. Restaurants 6 am-11 pm. Bar 2 pm-closing. Ck-out noon. Meeting rms. Business servs avail. In-rm modem link. Gift shop. Free covered parking; valet. Free airport transportation. Exercise equipt. Some in-rm whirlpools. Cr cds: A, C, D, DS, MC, V.

[D] [🔁] [🏋] [✈] [🔁] [🐾]

★ **ECONO LODGE.** *4726 E Washington Ave (53704). 608/241-4171; fax 608/241-1715; res 800/553-2666.*

www.econolodge.com. 97 rms, 2 story. S $49-$60; D $55-$80; each addl $4; theme rms $60-$85; under 18 free. Crib $3. TV; cable. Complimentary continental bkfst. Restaurant nearby. Ck-out 11 am. Lndry facilities. Meeting rm. Business servs avail. Sundries. Some microwaves. Cr cds: A, MC, V.

⬛ 🔲 🔲 🔲 SC

★★★ **THE EDGEWATER.** *666 Wisconsin Ave (53703). 608/256-9071; fax 608/256-0910; toll-free 800/922-5512. www.theedgewater.com.* 116 rms, 8 story. S, D $79-$160; suites $189-$389. Crib free. Pet accepted, some restrictions. TV; cable (premium). Restaurant (see also ADMIRALTY). Rm serv 6:30 am-10:30 pm. Bar 11-12:30 am. Ck-out noon. Meeting rms. Business servs avail. Bellhops. Valet serv. Free garage. Free airport transportation. Massage. Health club privileges. Some microwaves. On Lake Mendota; swimming beach. Cr cds: A, MC, V.

⬛ 🔲 🔲 🔲 🔲 🔲

★ **EXEL INN.** *4202 E Towne Blvd (53704). 608/241-3861; fax 608/241-9752; toll-free 800/356-8013. www.exelinns.com.* 101 rms, 2 story. May-Sept: S $39.99-$54; D $48.99-$63; each addl $4; under 18 free; wkly rates; higher rates special events; lower rates rest of yr. Crib free. Pet accepted, some restrictions. TV; cable (premium). Complimentary continental bkfst. Coffee in rms. Restaurant nearby. Ck-out noon. Business servs avail. In-rm modem link. Sundries. Coin lndry. X-country ski 3 mi. Exercise equipt. Health club privileges. Game rm. Some refrigerators; microwaves avail. Cr cds: A, C, D, DS, MC, V.

⬛ 🔲 🔲 🔲 🔲 🔲 SC

★★ **FAIRFIELD INN.** *4765 Hayes Rd (53704). 608/249-5300; fax 608/240-9335; res 800/228-2800. www.fairfieldinn.com.* 135 rms, 3 story. S, D $54-$89; under 18 free. Crib free. TV; cable (premium). Heated pool. Complimentary continental bkfst. Restaurants nearby. Ck-out noon. Business servs avail. Cr cds: A, C, D, DS, MC, V.

⬛ 🔲 🔲 🔲 SC

★★ **HAMPTON INN.** *4820 Hayes Rd (53704). 608/244-9400; fax 608/244-7177; toll-free 800/426-7866. www.*

hampton-inn.com. 116 rms, 4 story. S $69-$89; D $79-$99; under 19 free; higher rates special events. Crib free. TV; cable. Indoor pool; whirlpool. Complimentary continental bkfst. Coffee in rms. Restaurant nearby. Ck-out noon. Meeting rms. Business servs avail. X-country ski 10 mi. Exercise equipt. Microwaves avail. Cr cds: A, C, D, DS, MC, V.

⬛ 🔲 🔲 🔲 🔲 🔲

★ **HOWARD JOHNSON PLAZA HOTEL.** *525 W Johnson St (53703). 608/251-5511; fax 608/251-4824; toll-free 800/446-4656. www.hojo.com.* 163 rms, 7 story. S $82-$135; D $92-$145; each addl $10; studio rms $92-$145; suite $125-$150; under 18 free. Crib free. TV; cable. Indoor pool; whirlpool. Coffee in rms. Restaurant 6 am-10 pm. Bar 4:30 pm-12:45 am. Ck-out noon. Meeting rms. Business servs avail. Valet serv. Sundries. Free airport transportation. X-country ski 1 mi. Exercise equipt. Health club privileges. Refrigerators, microwaves avail. Cr cds: A, C, D, DS, ER, JCB, MC, V.

⬛ 🔲 🔲 🔲 🔲 🔲 🔲 SC

★★ **IVY INN HOTEL.** *2355 University Ave (53705). 608/233-9717; fax 608/233-2660; toll-free 877/IVY-INN1. www.ivyinnhotel.com.* 57 rms, 2 story. S $91-$111; D $101-$111; each addl $10; under 13 free. Crib free. Pet accepted. TV; cable. Restaurant 7 am-2 pm, 5-8 pm. Bar 4 pm-midnight. Ck-out noon. Business servs avail. Valet serv. Sundries. Cr cds: A, D, DS, MC, V.

⬛ 🔲 🔲 🔲 🔲

★ **SELECT INN.** *4845 Hayes Rd (53704). 608/249-1815; toll-free 800/641-1000. www.selectinn.com.* 97 rms, 3 story. June-mid-Sept: S $43.90-$63.90; D $51.90-$70; each addl $4; under 18 free. Pet accepted; $25 deposit. TV; cable. Complimentary continental bkfst. Restaurant nearby. Ck-out 11 am. Meeting rm. Business servs avail. Sundries. Whirlpool. Some refrigerators, microwaves, minibars. Cr cds: A, C, D, DS, MC, V.

⬛ 🔲 🔲 🔲 SC

Hotels

★★★ **MADISON CONCOURSE HOTEL AND GOVERNOR'S CLUB.** *1 W Dayton St (53703). 608/257-*

6000; fax 608/257-5280; toll-free 800/356-8293. www.concoursehotel. com. 356 rms, 13 story. S $109-$159; D $119-$169; each addl $10; suites $200-$350; under 18 free. Crib free. TV; cable. Pool; whirlpool. Coffee in rms. Restaurant 6:30 am-10 pm. Bar 11-1 am; entertainment. Ck-out noon. Convention facilities. Business center. Barber. Gift shop. Free garage. Airport transportation. X-country ski 3 mi. Exercise equipt; sauna, steam rm. Health club privileges. Some in-rm whirlpools. Luxury level. Cr cds: A, C, D, DS, MC, V.

★★★ **MARRIOTT MADISON WEST.** *1313 John Q. Hammons Dr (53562). 608/831-2000; fax 608/831-2040; toll-free 888/236-2427. www. marriott.com.* 295 rms, 10 story. S, D $115-$199; each addl $15; under 17 free. Crib avail. Pet accepted. Indoor pool. TV; cable (premium), VCR avail. Complimentary coffee, newspaper in rms. Restaurant 6 am-10 pm. Ck-out noon. Meeting rms. Business center. Gift shop. Some refrigerators, minibars. Cr cds: A, C, D, DS, MC, V.

★★★ **SHERATON.** *706 John Nolen Dr (53713). 608/251-2300; fax 608/251-1189; toll-free 800/325-3535. www.sheraton.com.* 237 rms, 7 story. S $99; D $119; each addl $10; under 18 free; wkend rates. Crib free. TV; cable. Indoor pool; whirlpool. Restaurant 11:30 am-2 pm, 5-10 pm. Bar 5 pm-1 am. Rm serv 6:30-11 am. Ck-out noon. Meeting rms. Gift shop. Exercise equipt; sauna. Game rm. Luxury level. Cr cds: A, C, D, DS, ER, JCB, MC, V.

B&Bs/Small Inns

★★★ **ANNIE'S BED AND BREAKFAST.** *2117 Sheridan Dr (53704). 608/244-2224. www.bbinternet.com/ annies.* 2, 2-bedrm suites, 2 story. Suites $97-$189; each addl $40; 2-day min. Children over 12 only. TV; VCR avail (free movies). Complimentary full bkfst. Complimentary coffee in library. Ck-out noon, ck-in 4-6 pm. Business servs avail. In-rm modem link. X-country ski adj.

Health club privileges. Whirlpool. Refrigerators. Picnic tables. Rustic cedar shake and stucco house; extensive gardens, gazebo, lily pond. Overlooks park. Near Lake Mendota. Cr cds: A, MC, V.

★★ **COLLINS HOUSE B&B.** *704 E Gorham St (53703). 608/255-4230; fax 608/255-0830. www.collinshouse.com.* 5 rms, 3 story. S $95-$170; D $105-$180. Crib free. TV in sitting rm; VCR avail (free movies). Complimentary bkfst. Restaurant nearby. Ck-out noon, ck-in 4 pm. X-country ski 3 mi. Some in-rm whirlpools, fireplaces; microwaves avail. Balconies. Former residence of lumber industry executive (1911); example of Prairie School style of architecture. View of Lake Mendota. Totallly nonsmoking. Cr cds: A, MC, V.

Extended Stay

★★ **RESIDENCE INN BY MARRIOTT.** *501 D'Onofrio Dr (53719). 608/833-8333; fax 608/833-2693; toll-free 800/331-3131. www.residenceinn. com.* 80 kit. suites, 2 story. Kit. suites $120-$175; higher rates special events. Crib free. Pet accepted, some restrictions. TV; cable. Heated pool; whirlpool. Complimentary continental bkfst. Coffee in rms. Restaurant nearby. Ck-out noon. Coin lndry. Meeting rms. Valet serv. Exercise equipt. Health club privileges. Microwaves; refrigerators. Private patios, balconies; fireplaces. Picnic tables, grills. Cr cds: A, D, DS, MC, V.

Restaurants

★★★ **ADMIRALTY.** *666 Wisconsin (53703). 608/256-9071. www.the edgewater.com.* Hrs: 6:30-10 am, 11 am-2 pm, 5-10 pm; Sun brunch 11 am-2 pm. Res accepted. Continental menu. Bar. Wine cellar. Bkfst $4.75-$12.95, lunch $7.95-$18.95, dinner $16-$30. Sun buffet $21.95. Specializes in fresh fish. Tableside cooking. Entertainment Fri, Sat (summer, fall). Parking. Outdoor dining. Overlooks

Lake Mendota. Family-owned. Cr cds: A, D, MC, V.

[D]

★★ **CHINA HOUSE.** *1256 S Park St (53715). 608/257-1079.* Hrs: 11:30 am-10 pm; Fri, Sat to 11 pm. Res accepted. Chinese menu. Bar. A la carte entrees: lunch $3.75-$4.75, dinner $5.95-$9.25. Specializes in Szechwan and Hunan cuisine. Parking. Chinese decor. Cr cds: A, C, MC, V.

[D]

★★ **COACHMAN'S GOLF RESORT.** *984 County Trunk A, Edgerton (53534). 608/884-8484. www.coachman.com.* Hrs: 11 am-9 pm; Fri, Sat to 10 pm; Sun brunch 9 am-2 pm. Closed Dec 24 evening, Dec 25. Res accepted. Bar. Lunch $4-$7, dinner $7.75-$16.95. Sun brunch $10.50. Specializes in roast duck, charcoal-grilled steak. Salad bar. Parking. English country inn atmosphere. Guest rms avail. Cr cds: A, DS, MC, V.

[D]

★ **ESSEN HAUS.** *514 E Wilson St (53703). 608/255-4674.* Hrs: 5-10 pm; Fri to 11 pm; Sat 4-11 pm; Sun 3-9 pm. Closed Mon; Jan 1, Dec 24-25. Res accepted. German, American menu. Bar from 3 pm. Dinner $12.95-$18.95. Specializes in authentic German cuisine, prime rib, fresh fish. Child's menu. Entertainment. Parking. Old World atmosphere; extensive stein collection. Cr cds: MC, V.

[D]

★★★ **L'ETOILE.** *25 N Pinckney (53703). 608/251-0500.* Hrs: from 5:30 pm; Fri, Sat from 5 pm. Closed Sun; hols. Res accepted. French, American menu. Bar. Dinner $20-$30. Specializes in seasonal and regional dishes. Menu changes daily. Contemporary decor; original artwork. View of capitol. Cr cds: D, DS, MC, V.

★★ **MARINER'S INN.** *5339 Lighthouse Bay Dr (53704). 608/246-3120. www.marinersinn.com.* Hrs: from 5 pm; Fri-Sun from 4:30 pm. Closed some hols. Bar. Dinner $14.99-$19.99. Specializes in steak, seafood, legendary hash browns. Own cheesecake. Parking. Nautical decor. View

of lake; dockage. Family-owned. Cr cds: MC, V.

[D] [⊡]

★ **NAU-TI-GAL.** *5360 Westport Rd (53704). 608/246-3130. www.nautigal. com.* Hrs: 11:30 am-10 pm; Fri, Sat to 10:30 pm (summer); Sun 10 am-9 pm; Sun brunch to 2 pm. Closed Jan 1, Thanksgiving, Dec 25; also Super Bowl Sun, Mon Nov-Feb. Bar. Lunch $3.50-$8, dinner $7.99-$18. Sun brunch $12.99. Specializes in seafood. Outdoor dining. Nautical decor. Cr cds: MC, V.

[D] [⊡]

★★ **QUIVEY'S GROVE.** *6261 Nesbitt Rd (53719). 608/273-4900. www. quiveysgrove.com.* Hrs: 11 am-10 pm. Closed Sun; hols. Res accepted. Bar. Lunch $5.75-$7.50, dinner $7.75-$22.50. Child's menu. Specializes in regional Wisconsin dishes, turtle pie. Parking. Converted historic mansion and stables (1855); many antiques. Cr cds: A, DS, MC, V.

[D]

★ **SA-BAI THONG.** *2840 University Ave (53705). 608/238-3100. www. sabaithong.com.* Hrs: 11 am-9 pm; Fri, Sat to 10 pm; Sun from 5 pm. Closed Jan 1, Thanksgiving, Dec 25. Res accepted. Thai menu. Wine, beer. A la carte entrees: lunch $4.95-$6.25, dinner $6.95-$14.95. Specializes in seafood, curry dishes. Contemporary Thai decor. Totally nonsmoking. Cr cds: A, DS, MC, V.

[D]

Unrated Dining Spot

ELLA'S DELI. *2902 E Washington Ave (53704). 608/241-5291.* Hrs: 10 am-11 pm; Fri, Sat to midnight. Closed Thanksgiving, Dec 24-25. Kosher-style deli menu. Bkfst $2.50-$5, lunch $3.50-$5.50, dinner $3.50-$6.50. Specializes in deli sandwiches, ice cream sundaes. Parking. Numerous cartoon character and clown decorations throughout dining area. Outdoor carousel. Cr cds: MC, V.

[D]

Manitowish Waters

See also Boulder Junction, Lac du Flambeau, Minocqua, Woodruff

Pop 686 **Elev** 1,611 ft **Area code** 715 **Zip** 54545

Information Chamber of Commerce, PO Box 251, 54545; 715/543-8488 or 888/626-9877

Web www.manitowishwaters.org

Manitowish Waters is in Northern Highland-American Legion State Forest (see BOULDER JUNCTION), which abounds in small and medium-size lakes linked by streams. Ten of the fourteen lakes are navigable without portaging, making them ideal for canoeing. There are 16 campgrounds on lakes in the forest (standard fees) and 135 overnight campsites on water trails. Canoe trips, fishing, swimming, boating, waterskiing, and snowmobiling are popular here.

What to See and Do

Cranberry bog tours. Tours begin with a video and samples, then follow guides in own vehicle. (Late July-early Oct, Fri) Community Center. Phone 715/543-8488.

Motel/Motor Lodge

★ **GREAT NORTHERN.** *US 51 S, Mercer (54547). 715/476-2440; fax 715/476-2205.* 80 rms, 2 story. No A/C. S, D $64-$84; each addl $10; under 10 free. Crib $5/day. Pet accepted; $10/day. TV; cable (premium). Sauna. Indoor pool; whirlpools. Complimentary continental bkfst. Restaurant. Bar 5 pm-2 am. Ck-out 11 am. Meeting rms. Business servs avail. Gift shop. X-country ski 1 mi. Game rm. On lake; swimming beach, boats. Cr cds: DS, MC, V.

🄳 🐕 🛶 ⤵ ➤ 🔖 🐾 SC

Restaurants

★★ **LITTLE BOHEMIA.** *County W (54545). 715/543-8433. www.littlebohemia.net.* Hrs: 4-11 pm; June-Aug expanded hrs. Closed Wed; Feb and Mar. Res accepted. No A/C. Bar. Dinner $10.95-$22.95. Child's menu. Specializes in ribs, steak, roast duck. Rustic decor. Site of a 1930s shootout between John Dillinger and the FBI; musuem. Cr cds: DS, MC, V. 🖳

★★ **SWANBERG'S BAVARIAN INN.** *County W (54545). 715/543-2122.* Hrs: 11:30 am-9 pm. Closed Sun. Res accepted. Continental menu. Bar. Lunch $3.50-$7.50, dinner $6.95-$25. Child's menu. Specialties: beef rouladen, Wiener schnitzel. Cr cds: DS, MC, V. 🄳

Manitowoc

(E-6) *See also Green Bay, Sheboygan, Two Rivers*

Settled 1836 **Pop** 32,520 **Elev** 606 ft **Area code** 920 **Zip** 54220

Information Manitowoc-Two Rivers Area Chamber of Commerce, 1515 Memorial Dr, PO Box 903, 54221-0903; 920/684-5575 or 800/262-7892

Web www.mtvcchamber.com

A shipping, shopping, and industrial center, Manitowoc has an excellent harbor and a geographical position improved by the completion of the St. Lawrence Seaway. Shipbuilding has been an important industry since the earliest days. During World War II Manitowoc shipyards produced nearly 100 vessels for the United States Navy including landing craft, wooden minesweepers, sub chasers, and 28 submarines. Manitowoc is the home of one of the largest manufacturers of aluminum ware and is a leader in the state's canning industry. Nearby lakes and streams provide excellent fishing.

What to See and Do

Lake Michigan car ferry. Departs from dock at S Lakeview Dr. (Early May-Oct, daily; advance res strongly recommended) Trips to Ludington, MI. Phone 920/684-0888.

Lincoln Park Zoo. Array of animals in attractive settings; picnic, recreational facilities. (Daily) 1215 N 8th St. Phone 920/683-4537. **FREE**

Pine Crest Historical Village. Site of 22 historic buildings depicting a typical turn-of-the-century Manitowoc county village. (May-Labor Day, daily; Sept-mid-Oct, Fri-Sun; also two wkends late Nov-early Dec) I-43 exit 152, then 3 mi W on County JJ, then left on Pine Crest Lane. Phone 920/684-5110. ¢¢¢

Rahr-West Art Museum. Victorian house with period rms; American art; collection of Chinese ivory carvings. Modern art wing featuring changing exhibits. (Daily; closed hols) 610 N 8th St at Park St. Phone 920/683-4501. **DONATION**

Skiing. Hidden Valley Ski Area. Area has double chairlift, two surface lifts; patrol, school, rentals; snowmaking; snack bar, bar. Longest run 2,600 ft; vertical drop 200 ft. (Dec-Mar, Fri-Sun; night skiing Tues-Fri). 13 mi N via I-43, exit 164, ½ mi S on County R to E Hidden Valley Rd. Phone 920/682-5475. ¢¢¢¢¢

Wisconsin Maritime Museum. Exhibits depict 150 yrs of maritime history including model ship gallery; narrated tours through the USS *COBIA,* a 312-ft WWII submarine. (Daily; closed hols) 75 Maritime Dr. Phone 920/684-0218. ¢¢¢

Marinette

(C-6) *See also Oconto, Peshtigo, also see Menominee, MI*

Settled 1795 **Pop** 11,843 **Elev** 598 ft
Area code 715 **Zip** 54143
Information Chamber of Commerce, 601 Marinette Ave, PO Box 512; 715/735-6681 or 800/236-6681
Web www.cybrzn.com/chamber

Located along the south bank of the Menominee River, Marinette is named for Queen Marinette, daughter of a Menominee chief. An industrial and port city, it is also the retail trade center for the surrounding recreational area.

What to See and Do

City Park. Picnicking, camping (electric hookups, dump station; May-Sept). Carney Ave. Phone 715/732-0558. ¢¢

Fishing, whitewater rafting, canoeing. Trout streams, lakes, and the Peshtigo River nearby. Inquire at Chamber of Commerce.

Marinette County Historical Museum. Features logging history of area; miniature wood carvings of logging camp; Native American artifacts. Tours by appt. (Memorial Day-Sept, daily) On Stephenson Island, US 41 at state border. Phone 715/732-0831. **DONATION**

Special Event

Theatre on the Bay. 750 W Bay Shore St, University of Wisconsin Center/Marinette County. Comedies, dramas, musicals. Phone 715/735-4300. June-Aug.

Motels/Motor Lodges

★★ **BEST WESTERN.** *1821 Riverside Ave (54143).* 715/732-1000; fax 715/732-0800; toll-free 800/338-3305. *www.bestwestern.com.* 120 rms, 6 story. S $75-$79; D $79-$85; each addl $6; under 18 free. Crib free. TV; cable; VCR avail (movies). Indoor pool. Complimentary bkfst buffet Mon-Fri. Coffee in rms. Restaurant 6 am-10 pm. Bar 11-1 am. Ck-out noon. Meeting rm. Business servs avail. Valet serv. Sundries. X-country ski 1 mi. Game rm. Cr cds: A, C, D, DS, ER, JCB, MC, V.
D 🎣 ⛺ 🛏 🐾 **SC**

★ **SUPER 8 MOTEL.** *1508 Marinette Ave (54143).* 715/735-7887; fax 715/735-7455; res 800/800-8000. *www.super8.com.* 68 rms, 2 story. Mid-May-Sept: S $46; D $52; under 12 free; lower rates rest of yr. Crib free. Pet accepted, some restrictions. TV; cable (premium). Complimentary continental bkfst. Ck-out 11 am. Meeting rms. Business servs avail. X-country ski 5 mi. Sauna. Whirlpool. Cr cds: A, D, DS, MC, V.
D 🐾 🎣 🛏 🐾 **SC**

B&B/Small Inn

★★ **LAUERMAN GUEST HOUSE INN.** *1975 Riverside Ave (54143).*

715/732-7800. 7 rms, 3 story. S $53; D $75; each addl $10. Complimentary full bkfst. Ck-out 11 am, ck-in 2 pm. Free airport, bus depot transportation. X-country ski 1 mi. Some in-rm whirlpools. Balcony. House (1910) across from Menominee River; antiques. Lake, swimming nearby. Cr cds: A, DS, MC, V.

☒ ✈ 🐾 **SC**

Marshfield

(D-4) *See also Stevens Point, Wisconsin Rapids*

Settled 1872 **Pop** 19,291 **Elev** 1,262 ft
Area code 715 **Zip** 54449
Information Visitors & Promotion Bureau, 700 S Central St, PO Box 868; 715/384-3454 or 800/422-4541
Web www.mtecnserv.com/macci

Marshfield, a city that once boasted one sawmill and 19 taverns, was almost destroyed by fire in 1887. It was rebuilt on a more substantial structural and industrial basis. This is a busy northern dairy center, noted for its large medical clinic, manufactured housing wood products, and steel fabrication industries.

What to See and Do

Upham Mansion. (1880) Italianate, mid-Victorian house built entirely of wood. Some original furniture, custom-made in the factory of the owner. (Wed and Sun afternoons) 212 W Third St. Phone 715/387-3322. **FREE**

Wildwood Park and Zoo. Zoo houses a variety of animals and birds, mostly native to Wisconsin. (Mid-May-late Sept, daily; rest of yr, Mon-Fri) off WI 13 (Roddis Ave), S of business district or off 17th St from Central Ave S. Phone 715/384-4642. **FREE**

Special Events

Dairyfest. Salute to the dairy industry. First wkend June. Phone 800/422-4541.

Central Wisconsin State Fair. Fair Park. Vine Ave and 14th St. Phone

715/387-1261. Six days ending Labor Day.
Fall Festival. Phone 800/422-4541. Mid-Sept.

Mauston

See also Wisconsin Dells

Settled 1840 **Pop** 3,439 **Elev** 883 ft
Area code 608 **Zip** 53948
Information Greater Mauston Area Chamber of Commerce, 503 WI 82, PO Box 171; 608/847-4142

What to See and Do

Buckhorn State Park. A 2,504-acre park with facilities for swimming, waterskiing, fishing, boating, canoeing; hunting, hiking, nature trails, picnicking, playground, backpack and canoe camping. (Daily) Standard fees. 11 mi N via County Rds 58 and G, near Necedah. Phone 608/565-2789. ¢¢

Motels/Motor Lodges

★ **K AND K MOTEL.** *219 US 12/16, Camp Douglas (54618).* 608/427-3100; fax 608/427-3824. 14 rms. S $30-$35; D $37.95-$50; each addl $5; higher rates special events. Crib free. Pet accepted; fee. TV; cable, VCR avail (movies $5). Coffee in lobby. Restaurant opp 11 am-10 pm. Ck-out 10 am. Coin lndry. Business servs avail. Refrigerators, microwaves. Cr cds: A, MC, V.

D 🐾 🐾 🖾 🐾 **SC**

★ **TRAVELODGE OF NEW LISBON.** *1700 E Bridge St, New Lisbon (53950).* 608/562-5141; fax 608/562-6205; toll-free 888/895-6200. www.travelodge.com. 61 rms. S $50-$69; D $52-$100; each addl $5; studio rms $49-$59. Crib free. TV; cable. Playground. Complimentary continental bkfst. Coffee in rms. Restaurant 6:30 am-9 pm. Bar 11:30-1 am. Ck-out 11 am. Meeting rm. Rec rm. Cr cds: A, D, DS, JCB, MC, V.

D 🖾 🐾 **SC**

Guest Ranch

★ ★ **WOODSIDE RANCH TRAD-ING POST.** *W 4015 WI 82 (53948). 608/847-4275; toll-free 800/646-4275. www.woodsideranch.com.* 14 rms in 2-story lodge, 23 cottages (1-, 2- and 3-bedrm). No rm phones. AP, late June-late Sept, late Dec-late Feb: S $210/wk; D $370/wk; each addl $175-$420/wk; lower rates rest of yr. Crib free. Pet accepted. TV in lobby. Sauna. Pool; wading pool, poolside serv. Playground. Free supervised children's activities. Complimentary coffee in lobby. Dining rm; sittings at 8 am, 12:30 and 5:30 pm. Snack bar, picnics. Bar 8-2 am; entertainment Tues, Sat. Ck-out 10 am, ck-in 1:30 pm. Coin lndry. Grocery, package store 5 mi. Gift shop. Sports dir. Tennis. Swimming. Boats. Downhill/x-country ski on site. Sleighing, sledding. Hiking. Soc dir. Rec rm. Game rm. Fireplace in cottages. On 1,400 acres. Cr cds: DS, MC, V.
🄳 🐾 🛖 ⛷ 🏊 🌲 🔥

Menasha

(see Neenah-Menasha)

Menomonee Falls

(F-6) *See also Milwaukee, Wauwatosa*

Settled 1843 **Pop** 26,840 **Elev** 840 ft **Area code** 262 **Zip** 53051

Information Menomonee Falls Chamber of Commerce, N 88 W 16621 Appleton Ave, PO Box 73, 53052; 262/251-6565 or 800/801-6565

What to See and Do

Bugline Recreation Trail. A 12.2-mi trail located on the former Chicago, Milwaukee, St. Paul, and Pacific Railroad right-of-way. Bicycling, hiking, jogging, horseback riding (some areas), x-country skiing, snowmobiling. Dogs allowed (on leash). Appleton Ave.

Old Falls Village. Miller-Davidson farmhouse (1858) of Greek Revival style, decorative arts museum, 1851 schoolhouse, carriage house, barn museum, 1890 railroad depot, two restored log cabins,1873 Victorian cottage; extensive grounds, picnic area. (May-Sept, Sun; also by appt) ½ mi N on County Line Rd. Phone 262/255-8346. ¢

Sub-Continental Divide. Water falling west of this crest of land goes into the Fox River Watershed and eventually into the Gulf of Mexico via the Mississippi River. Water falling on the east side goes into the Menomonee River watershed and enters the St. Lawrence Seaway by flowing through the Great Lakes. Main St, 1 blk W of Town Line Rd. Phone 262/251-6565.

Motel/Motor Lodge

★ **SUPER 8 MOTEL.** *N96 W17490 County Line Rd, Germantown (53022). 262/255-0880; fax 262/255-7741; toll-free 800/800-8000. www.super8.com.* 81 rms, 2 story. June-Sept: S $65-$79; D $79-$90; each addl $5; suites $80-$100; under 12 free; lower rates rest of yr. Crib free. Pet accepted; $50 refundable. TV; cable (premium). Indoor pool; whirlpool. Complimentary continental bkfst. Restaurant adj open 24 hrs. Ck-out 11 am. Coin lndry. Business servs avail. Cr cds: A, C, D, DS, MC, V.
🄳 🐾 🏊 🍽 🔥 🆂🅲

Restaurants

★ ★ ★ **FOX AND HOUNDS.** *1298 Freiss Lake Rd, Hubertus (53033). 262/628-1111. www.ratzsch.com.* Hrs: 5-10 pm. Closed Mon; Jan 1, Dec 24. Res accepted. Bar. A la carte entrees: dinner $14-$25. Child's menu. Specialties: braised lamb shanks, stuffed pork chops, duck. Own baking. Extensive wine and beer selection. Early American atmosphere in rambling stone and timber building (1843). Fireplaces. Family-owned. Cr cds: A, D, DS, MC, V.
🄳 🍽

★ ★ **JERRY'S OLD TOWN INN.** *N 116 W 15841 Main St, Germantown (53022). 262/251-4455.* Hrs: 4-10 pm; Fri, Sat to 10:30 pm; Sun to 9 pm. Res accepted. Bar. Dinner $17.95-

$29.95. Child's menu. Specialty: barbecue baby-back pork ribs. Own baking. Casual dining; pig theme throughout. Cr cds: A, MC, V.

D

★ ★ **LOHMANN'S STEAK HOUSE.** *W183 N9609 Appleton Ave, Germantown (53051). 262/251-8430. www. foodspot.com/lohmanns.* Hrs: 11:30 am-2 pm, 5-10 pm. Closed Sun; hols. Res accepted. Bar. Lunch $4.50-$10.25, dinner $10.50-$42. Child's menu. Specializes in prime rib, steak, seafood. Fireplace. Family-owned. Cr cds: A, D, DS, MC, V.

D 🔧

Menomonie

(D-2) *See also Chippewa Falls, Eau Claire*

Settled 1859 **Pop** 13,547 **Elev** 877 ft
Area code 715 **Zip** 54751
Information Chamber of Commerce, 700 Wolske Bay Rd, Suite 200; 715/235-9087 or 800/283-1862

Located on the banks of the Red Cedar River, Menomonie is home of the University of Wisconsin-Stout and was once headquarters for one of the largest lumber corporations in the country. The decline of the lumber industry diverted the economy to dairy products. Recently several new industries have located here, giving the city a more diversified economic base.

What to See and Do

Caddie Woodlawn Park. Two century-old houses and log smokehouse in five-acre park; memorial to pioneer girl Caddie Woodlawn. Picnicking. (Daily) 10 mi S on WI 25. Phone 715/235-2070. **FREE**

Empire in Pine Lumber Museum. Lumbering artifacts, slides of life in lumber camps; primitive furniture, displays incl original pay office. (Early May-Oct, daily; mid-Apr-early May, by appt) 7 mi S on WI 25 in Downsville. Phone 715/664-8690. **FREE**

Mabel Tainter Memorial Building. Hand-stenciled and ornately carved cultural center constructed in 1889 by lumber baron Andrew Tainter in memory of his daughter Mabel. Theater with performing arts season; reading room, pipe organ. Gift shop. Guided tours (daily). 205 Main St. Phone 715/235-9726. ¢¢

Wilson Place Museum. Victorian mansion (1846); former residence of Senator James H. Stout, founder of University of Wisconsin. Almost all original furnishings. Guided tours (Memorial Day-Labor Day, daily; closed Jan 1, Thanksgiving, Dec 25) Wilson Cir. Phone 715/235-2283. ¢¢

Special Events

Winter Carnival. Wakanda Park. Second wkend Feb. Phone 715/235-9087.

Victorian Christmas. Wilson Place Museum. Daily, mid-Nov-Dec. Phone 715/235-2283.

Motels/Motor Lodges

★ ★ **BEST WESTERN HOLIDAY MANOR.** *1815 N Broadway (54751). 715/235-9651; fax 715/235-6568; res 800/528-1234. www.bestwestern.com.* 135 rms. S $53-$68; D $69-$105; each addl $4; under 12 free; higher rates special events. Crib $4. Pet accepted, some restrictions; $10. TV; cable (premium). Indoor pool. Restaurant opp open 24 hrs. Bar 4 pm-2 am. Ck-out 11 am. Meeting rms. Business servs avail. Valet serv. Sundries. X-country ski 2 mi. Cr cds: A, C, D, DS, MC, V.

D 🔧 🐾 🏊 ❄️ 🐕 **SC**

★ **BOLO COUNTRY INN.** *207 Pine Ave (54751). 715/235-5596; fax 715/235-5596. www.thebolocountryinn. com.* 25 rms. S, D $49-$79. Pet accepted. TV; cable (premium). Complimentary continental bkfst. Restaurant 11 am-10 pm. Bar 11-1 am. Ck-out noon. Meeting rms. Picnic tables. Cr cds: A, MC, V.

D 🐾 ❄️ 🔥

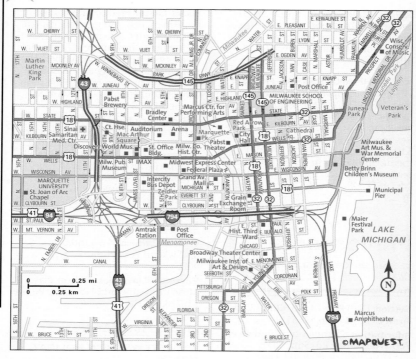

Milwaukee (F-6)

Settled 1822 **Pop** 628,088 **Elev** 634 ft
Area code 414

Information Greater Milwaukee Convention & Visitors Bureau, 101 W Wisconsin Ave, 53203; 414/273-3950 or 800/231-0903

Web www.officialmilwaukee.com

Suburbs Menomonee Falls, Port Washington, Waukesha, Wauwatosa.

Thriving and progressive, Milwaukee has retained its *Gemütlichkeit*—though today's lively conviviality is as likely to be expressed at a soccer game or at a symphony concert as at the beer garden. This is not to say that raising beer steins has noticeably declined as a popular local form of exercise. While Milwaukee is still the beer capital of the nation, its leading single industry is not brewing but the manufacture of X-ray apparatus and tubes.

Long a French trading post and an early campsite between Chicago and

Green Bay, the city was founded by Solomon Juneau, who settled on the east side of the Milwaukee River. English settlement began in significant numbers in 1833, and was followed by an influx of Germans, Scandinavians, Dutch, Bohemians, Irish, Austrians, and large numbers of Poles. By 1846, Milwaukee was big and prosperous enough to be incorporated as a city. In its recent history, perhaps the most colorful period was from 1916-40 when Daniel Webster Hoan, its Socialist mayor, held the reins of government.

The city's Teutonic personality has dimmed, becoming only a part of the local color of a city long famous for good government, a low crime rate, and high standards of civic performance.

With a history going back to the days when the Native Americans called this area Millioki, "gathering place by the waters," Milwaukee has undergone tremendous development since World War II. The skyline changed with new building, an expressway system was constructed, the St. Lawrence Seaway opened new markets, new cultural activities were introduced, and 44 square miles were tacked onto the city's girth.

Today a city of 96.5 square miles on the west shore of Lake Michigan, where the Milwaukee, Menomonee, and Kinnickinnic rivers meet, Milwaukee is the metropolitan center of five counties. "The machine shop of America" ranks among the nation's top industrial cities and is a leader in the output of diesel and gasoline engines, outboard motors, motorcycles, tractors, wheelbarrows, padlocks, and, of course, beer.

As a result of the St. Lawrence Seaway, Milwaukee has become a major seaport on America's new fourth seacoast. Docks and piers handle traffic of ten lines of oceangoing ships.

The city provides abundant tourist attractions including professional and college basketball, hockey, and football, major league baseball, top-rated polo, soccer, and auto racing. There is also golf, tennis, swimming, sailing, fishing, hiking, skiing, tobogganing, and skating. For the less athletic, Milwaukee has art exhibits, museums, music programs, ballet, and theater including the Marcus Center for Performing Arts. Its many beautiful churches include St. Josaphat's Basilica, St. John Cathedral, and the Gesu Church.

Additional Visitor Information

The Greater Milwaukee Convention & Visitors Bureau, 101 W Wisconsin Ave, 53203; 414/273-3950 or 800/231-0903 and a visitor center at 400 Wisconsin Ave (daily)

Transportation

Car Rental Agencies. See IMPORTANT TOLL-FREE NUMBERS.

Public Transportation. Milwaukee County Transit System; 414/344-6711.

Rail Passenger Service. Amtrak 800/872-7245.

Airport Information

General Mitchell International Airport. Information 414/747-5300; 414/747-5245 (lost and found); 414/936-1212 (weather).

What to See and Do

Annunciation Greek Orthodox Church. Domed structure designed by Frank Lloyd Wright. 9400 W Congress St. Phone 414/461-9400.

Betty Brinn Children's Museum. Hands-on exhibits; workshops; performances. (June-Labor Day, daily) 929 E Wisconsin Ave, near the lakefront. Phone 414/291-0888. ¢¢

Bradford Beach. The city's finest bathing beach, with bathhouse, concessions. **FREE**

Captain Frederick Pabst Mansion. (1893) Magnificent house of the beer baron; exquisite woodwork, wrought iron, and stained glass; restored interior. Guided tours. (Daily; closed hols) 2000 W Wisconsin Ave, downtown. Phone 414/931-0808. ¢¢¢

Charles Allis Art Museum. Art treasures from the United States, Near East, Far East, and Europe dating from 600 B.C. to the 1900s; personal collection of Charles Allis in his preserved Tudor-style mansion. (Wed-Sun afternoons) 1801 N Prospect Ave, near the lakefront. Phone 414/278-8295. ¢¢

City Hall. (1895) Milwaukee landmark of Flemish Renaissance design. Common Council Chamber and Anteroom retain their turn-of-the-century character; ornately carved woodwork, leaded glass, stenciled ceilings, and two large stained glass windows; ironwork balconies surround eight-story atrium. (Mon-Fri; closed hols) 200 E Wells St, downtown. Phone 414/286-3285. **FREE**

Court of Honor. Three-blk area serving as a monument to the city's Civil War dead. Bounded by Marquette University on the west and the downtown business district on the east, it contains an 18-story YMCA building, the Public Library, many towering churches, and statues of historic figures.

Iroquois Boat Line Tours. View lakefront, harbor, lighthouse, breakwater, and foreign ships in port. (Late June-Aug, daily) Board at Clybourn St Bridge on W bank of Milwaukee River. Phone 414/294-9450. ¢¢¢

Kilbourntown House. (1844) Excellent example of Greek Revival architecture; restored and furnished in the 1844-1864 period. (Late June-Labor

Day, Tues, Thurs, Sat-Sun) 4400 W Estabrook Dr, in Estabrook Park, 5 mi N on I-43, Capitol Dr E exit. Phone 414/273-8288. **FREE**

Marcus Center for the Performing Arts. Strikingly beautiful structure, overlooking the Milwaukee River, with four theaters, reception areas, and parking facility connected by a skywalk. Outdoor riverfront Peck Pavilion. 929 N Water St, downtown. Phone 414/273-7206. Also here is

Milwaukee Ballet. Classical and contemporary ballet presentations. (Sept-May) Phone 414/643-7677.

Marquette University. (1881) 11,000 students. Wisconsin Ave and 11th-17th Sts, downtown. Phone 414/288-3178. On campus are

Haggerty Museum of Art. Paintings, prints, drawings, sculpture, and decorative arts; changing exhibits. (Daily) 13th and Clybourn Sts. Phone 414/288-1669. **FREE**

Marquette Hall's 48-bell carillon. One of the largest in the country. Occasional concerts. 1217 W Wisconsin Ave. Phone 414/288-7250. **FREE**

St. Joan of Arc Chapel. 15th century French chapel reconstructed on Marquette's campus in 1964. Tours (daily). 14th St and W Wisconsin Ave. Phone 414/288-6873.

Miller Brewing Company. One-hour guided tour, incl outdoor walking. (May-Sept, Mon-Sat; rest of yr, Tues-Sat; closed hols) 4251 W State St.

Milwaukee County Historical Center. Milwaukee history and children's exhibits; archive library housed in bank building (1913). (Daily; closed hols) 910 N Old World, 3rd St at Pere Marquette Park, downtown. Phone 414/273-8288. **FREE**

Milwaukee County Zoo. On 194 wooded acres. Mammals, birds, reptiles, and fish exhibited in continental groupings with native backdrops. World-

renowned predator/prey outdoor exhibits. Miniature train travels on a 1¼-mi track (fee); guided tours on Zoomobile (fee). Park (daily). 10001 W Blue Mound Rd, 6 mi W. Phone 414/771-3040. ¢¢

Milwaukee Public Museum. Natural and human history museum; unique "walk-through" dioramas and exhibits; life-size replicas of dinosaurs. Rain forest, Native American, and special exhibits. IMAX Dome Theater. Shops; restaurant. (Daily) 800 W Wells St, downtown. Phone 414/278-2700. ¢¢

Discovery World Museum of Science, Economics and Technology. Museum with more than 140 participatory exhibits. Entrepreneurial village, stock wall, and Into Einstein's Brain show. (Daily; closed hols) 815 N James Lovell St, downtown. Phone 414/765-9960.

Humphrey IMAX Dome Theater. A 275-seat theater; giant wrap-around domed screen. Phone 414/319-4629. ¢¢

Mitchell Park Horticultural Conservatory. Superb modern design, three self-supporting domes (tropical, arid, and show dome) feature outstanding seasonal shows and beautiful exhibits all yr. Each dome is almost half the length of a football field in diameter and nearly as tall as a seven-story building. Also gift shop, picnic area; parking (free). (Daily) 524 S Layton Blvd at W Pierce St. Phone 414/649-9800. ¢¢

Old World Third Street. Downtown walking tour for gourmets, historians, and lovers of antiques and

Clowns on parade at Circus World Museum, Baraboo

atmosphere. Incl the *Milwaukee Journal* Company's history of the newspaper. Most shops (Mon-Sat). Between W Wells St and W Highland Blvd.

Pabst Theater. (1895) Center of Milwaukee's earlier cultural life; restored to its original elegance. Lavish decor and excellent acoustics enhance the charm of the theater. Musical and dramatic events. Tours (Sat; free). 144 E Wells St, downtown. Phone 414/286-3663.

Park system. One of the largest in the nation, with 14,681 acres; 137 parks and parkways, community centers, five beaches, 19 pools, 16 golf courses, 134 tennis courts, and winter activities incl x-country skiing, skating, sledding. Fees vary. Phone 414/257-6100. Of special interest is

> **Whitnall Park.** A 640-acre park with Boerner Botanical Gardens (parking fee) featuring the Rose Garden, one of the All-American Selection Gardens; also nature trails, woodlands, formal gardens, wildflowers, shrubs, test gardens, fruit trees, rock, and herb gardens; Wehr Nature Center. Eighteen-hole golf (fee). (Early Apr-mid-Oct, daily) S 92nd St and Whitnall Park Dr. Phone 414/425-1130. **FREE**

Port of Milwaukee. Incl Inner Harbor, formed by Milwaukee, Menomonee, and Kinnickinnic rivers, and the commercial municipal port development in the Outer Harbor on the lakefront. Ships flying foreign flags may be seen at Jones Island on Milwaukee's south side. Phone 414/286-3511.

Professional sports.

> **Milwaukee Brewers (MLB).** Miller Park, 1 Brewers Way.

> **Milwaukee Bucks (NBA).** Bradley Center, 1001 N 4th St. Phone 414/227-0500.

Schlitz Audubon Center. Center has 225 acres of shoreline, grassland, bluff, ravine, and woodland habitats with a variety of plants and wildlife incl fox, deer, skunk, and opossum; self-guided trails; some guided programs. (Tues-Sun). 1111 E Brown Deer Rd. Phone 414/352-2880. ¢¢

University of Wisconsin-Milwaukee. (1956) 25,400 students. The Manfred Olson Planetarium (fee) offers programs Fri and Sat evenings during academic yr. Phone 414/229-4961.

Villa Terrace Decorative Arts Museum. (1923) this Italian Renaissance-style house serves as a museum for decorative arts. Guided tours (res required). (Wed-Sun afternoons; closed Jan 1, Dec 25) 2220 N Terrace Ave, near the lakefront. Phone 414/271-3656. ¢¢

⭐ **War Memorial Center.** An imposing modern monument to honor the dead by serving the living; designed by Eero Saarinen. Phone 414/273-5533. Provides facilities for civic groups and houses the

> **Milwaukee Art Museum.** Permanent collection of American and European masters; folk, decorative and contemporary art. Special exhibits; films and tours. (Tues-Sun; closed Jan 1, Thanksgiving, Dec 25) 700 N Lincoln Memorial Dr, near the lakefront. Phone 414/224-3200. ¢¢

Special Events

Summerfest. Lakefront, E of downtown. Eleven different music stages; food. Late June-early July. Phone 800/273-3378.

Great Circus Parade. Downtown. This re-creation of an old-time circus parade incl bands, costumed units, animals, and unusual collection of horsedrawn wagons from the Circus World Museum. Mid-July. Phone 608/356-8341.

Wisconsin State Fair. State Fair Park in West Allis, bounded by I-94, Greenfield Ave, 76th and 84th sts. Entertainment, 12 stages, auto races, exhibits, contests, demonstrations, fireworks. Phone 414/266-7000 or 800/884-FAIR. Aug 3-13.

Holiday Folk Fair. The Wisconsin Center. Continuous ethnic entertainment, 300 types of food from around the world, cultural exhibits, workshops. Phone 414/225-6225. Wkend before Thanksgiving.

Ethnic Festivals. Incl African, Arabian, German, Italian, Irish, Asian, Mexican, and Polish, take place throughout the summer. Convention and Visitors Bureau has information. May-Sept. Phone 414/273-3950.

Motels/Motor Lodges

★★ **BAYMONT INN & SUITES.**
5442 N Lovers Ln (53225). 414/535-1300; fax 414/535-1724; toll-free 800/428-3438. www.baymontinn.com. 140 rms, 3 story. S $84-$94; D $94-$104; each addl $7; suites $80-$105; under 18 free. Pet accepted, some restrictions. TV; cable (premium), VCR avail. Complimentary continental bkfst. Complimentary coffee in rms. Restaurant nearby. Ck-out noon. Meeting rm. Business servs avail. In-rm modem link. Exercise equipt. Valet serv. Microwaves avail. Cr cds: A, C, D, DS, MC, V.
⬚ ⬚ ⬚ ⬚ ⬚

★★ **BEST WESTERN MIDWAY HOTEL.** *251 N Mayfair Rd (53226). 414/774-3600; fax 414/774-5015; toll-free 800/528-1234. www.bestwestern. com.* 116 rms, 3 story. S $94-$129; D $104-$139; each addl $10; under 18 free. Crib free. TV; cable (premium). Indoor pool; whirlpool. Complimentary coffee in rms. Restaurant 6 am-10 pm. Bar 11-1:30 am. Ck-out noon. Coin lndry. Meeting rms. Business servs avail. In-rm modem link. Bellhops. Sundries. Valet serv. Free airport, RR station, bus depot transportation. Health club privileges. Exercise equipt; sauna. Some refrigerators. Cr cds: A, C, D, DS, MC, V.
⬚ ⬚ ⬚ ⬚ ⬚ ⬚

★★ **CLARION HOTEL.** *5311 S Howell Ave (53207). 414/481-2400; fax 414/481-4471. www.clarionhotel.com.* 180 rms, 3 story. S, D $80-$99; suites $99-$160; each addl $5; under 18 free. Crib $7. TV; cable (premium). Indoor pool. Complimentary continental bkfst. Restaurant 7 am-10 pm; Sun 9 am-9 pm. Bar 11 am-11 pm. Ck-out 11 am. Coin lndry. Meeting rms. Business servs avail. Bellhops. Free airport transportation. Downhill ski 8 mi. Exercise equipt. Cr cds: A, C, D, DS, JCB, MC, V.
⬚ ⬚ ⬚ ⬚ ⬚ ⬚ ⬚

★ **EXEL INN.** *1201 W College Ave (53154). 414/764-1776; fax 414/762-8009; res 800/367-3935. www.exelinn. com.* 110 rms, 2 story. S $39.99-$79.99; D $49.99-$89.99; each addl $4; under 18 free. Crib free. Pet accepted. TV; cable (premium). Complimentary continental bkfst. Restau-

rant opp 6 am-noon. Ck-out noon. Coin lndry. Business servs avail. In-rm modem link. Free airport transportation. Microwaves avail. Cr cds: A, C, D, DS, MC, V.
⬚ ⬚ ⬚ ⬚ ⬚

★ **EXEL INN.** *5485 N Port Washington Rd, Glendale (53217). 414/961-7272; fax 414/961-1721; toll-free 800/367-3935. www.exelinn.com.* 125 rms, 3 story. S $49.99-$63.99; D $59.99-$76.99; each addl $7; under 17 free; wkend rates; higher rates special events. Crib free. Pet accepted, some restrictions. TV; cable (premium). Complimentary continental bkfst. Restaurant adj open 24 hrs. Ck-out noon. Coin lndry. Business servs avail. In-rm modem link. Sundries. Game rm. Some in-rm whirlpools; microwaves avail. Cr cds: A, C, D, DS, MC, V.
⬚ ⬚ ⬚ ⬚ SC

★★★ **FOUR POINTS BY SHERATON AIRPORT.** *4747 S Howell Ave (53207). 414/481-8000; fax 414/481-8065; toll-free 800/558-3862. www. fourpoints.com.* 508 rms, 6 story. S, D $89-$132; each addl $10; suites $250-$295; under 17 free; package plans. Crib free. TV; cable (premium). 2 heated pools, 1 indoor; whirlpool. Restaurants 6 am-10 pm. Bar 11-2 am. Ck-out noon. Meeting rms. Business center. In-rm modem link. Gift shop. Barber, beauty shop. Free airport transportation. Indoor tennis. Exercise equipt; sauna. Game rm. Some refrigerators. Cr cds: A, C, D, DS, MC, V.
⬚ ⬚ ⬚ ⬚ ⬚ ⬚ SC ⬚

★★ **HAMPTON INN.** *5601 N Lovers Ln Rd (53225). 414/466-8881; fax 414/466-3840; toll-free 800/426-7866. www.hamptoninn.com.* 107 rms, 4 story. S, D $82-$109; under 18 free; higher rates: special events, summer wkends. Crib free. TV; cable. Indoor pool; whirlpool. Complimentary continental bkfst. Restaurant adj. Ck-out noon. Meeting rm. Business servs avail. In-rm modem link. Valet serv. Exercise equipt. Microwaves avail. Cr cds: A, C, D, DS, MC, V.
⬚ ⬚ ⬚ ⬚ ⬚ SC

★★ **HOLIDAY INN.** *611 W Wisconsin Ave (53203). 414/273-2950; fax 414/273-7662; toll-free 800/465-4329. www.holiday-inn.com.* 247 rms, 10 story. S $99-$129; D $109-$139; each addl $10; suites $119-$199; under 18 free; higher rates special events. TV; cable (premium). Pool. Coffee in rms. Restaurant 6 am-10 pm. Bar from 4 pm. Ck-out noon. Meeting rms. Business center. In-rm modem link. Valet serv. Free valet parking. Exercise equipt. Cr cds: A, C, D, DS, ER, JCB, MC, V.

`D ≈ 🏃 ➦ 🔥 SC 🏃`

★ ★ **HOSPITALITY INN.** *4400 S 27th St (53220). 414/282-8800; fax 414/282-7713; toll-free 800/825-8466. www.hospitalityinn.com.* 167 rms in 2 bldgs, suites. S, D $60-$200. TV; cable (premium). 2 indoor pools; whirlpool. Complimentary continental bkfst. Ck-out noon. Meeting rms. Free airport transportation. Exercise equipt. Refrigerators, microwaves; in-rm whirlpools. Cr cds: A, MC, V.

`D ≈ 🏃 ✈ ➦ 🔥 SC`

★ ★ **MANCHESTER SUITES-AIR-PORT.** *200 W Grange Ave (53207). 414/744-3600; fax 414/744-4188; toll-free 800/723-8280. www.manchester suites.com.* 123 suites, 4 story. S, D $85-$109; each addl $8; under 14 free. Crib free. TV; cable (premium). Complimentary full bkfst. Coffee in rms. Ck-out noon. Meeting rm. Business servs avail. In-rm modem link. Valet serv. Sundries. Free airport transportation. Health club privileges. Refrigerators, microwaves, wet bars. Cr cds: A, MC, V.

`✈ 🔥`

★ ★ **MANCHESTER SUITES NORTHWEST.** *11777 W Silver Spring Dr (53225). 414/462-3500; fax 414/462-8166; toll-free 800/723-8280. www.manchestersuites.com.* 123 suites, 4 story. Suites $79-$129; under 14 free. Crib free. TV; cable. Complimentary full bkfst. Coffee in rms. Restaurant nearby. Ck-out noon. Meeting rm. Business servs avail. In-rm modem link. Valet serv. Exercise equipt. Sundries. Refrigerators, microwaves, wet bars. Cr cds: A, MC, V.

`D 🏃 ➦ 🔥 SC`

★ ★ **RAMADA INN.** *633 W Michigan St (53203). 414/272-8410; fax 414/272-4651; toll-free 800/228-2828. www.ramada.com.* 154 rms, 7 story. S $80-$100; D $90-$117; each addl $10; suites $105-$170; under 18 free; wkend rates. Crib free. TV; cable (premium), VCR avail (movies). Heated pool. Coffee in rms. Restaurant 6 am-10 pm. Bar 11-2 am. Ck-out noon. Meeting rms. Business servs avail. In-rm modem link. Valet serv. Downhill ski 15 mi; x-country ski 7 mi. Exercise equipt. Cr cds: A, C, D, DS, JCB, MC, V.

`D ≈ ≈ 🏃 ➦ 🔥 SC`

★ **RED ROOF INN.** *6360 S 13th St, Oak Creek (53154). 414/764-3500; fax 414/764-5138; toll-free 800/843-7663. www.redroof.com.* 108 rms, 2 story. S $41.99-$58.99; D $45.99-$69.99; under 18 free. Crib free. Pet accepted. TV; cable (premium). Complimentary coffee in lobby. Ck-out noon. Business servs avail. Cr cds: A, C, D, DS, MC, V.

`D 🐾 ➦ 🔥`

★ ★ **WESTWOOD INN HOTEL & SUITES.** *201 N Mayfair Rd (53226). 414/771-4400; fax 414/771-4517; toll-free 800/531-3966. www. westwoodhotel.com.* 230 rms, 3 story. May-Sept: S $84; D $99; under 18 free; lower rates rest of yr. Crib free. Pet accepted, some restrictions. TV; cable (premium). Indoor pool; whirlpool. Playground. Restaurant 6 am-1 pm, 5-9 pm. Bar 3 pm-1 am; Fri, Sat to 2 am. Ck-out noon. Coin lndry. Meeting rms. Business servs avail. Valet serv. Exercise equipt; sauna. Picnic tables. Cr cds: A, D, DS, MC, V.

`D 🐾 ≈ 🏃 ➦ 🔥`

Hotels

★ ★ ★ **HILTON.** *509 W Wisconsin Ave (53203). 414/271-7250; fax 414/271-1039. www.hilton.com.* 500 rms, 25 story. S, D $99-$199; each addl $20; suites $225-$1,000; under 18 free; wkend plan. Crib free. TV; cable (premium). Indoor pool. Restaurant 6:30 am-10 pm. Bar 11-1 am. Ck-out noon. Convention facilities. Business servs avail. In-rm modem link. Concierge. Gift shop. Barber, beauty shop. Exercise equipt; sauna. Cr cds: A, C, D, DS, MC, V.

`D ≈ 🏃 ➦ 🔥`

★ ★ ★ **HILTON INN.** *4700 N Port Washington Rd (53212). 414/962-6040; fax 414/962-6166; toll-free*

800/445-8667. www.hilton.com. 163 rms, 5 story. S $109-$137; D $124-$152; each addl $15; suites $180-$370; studio rms $120-$135; family rates. TV; cable (premium). Indoor pool. Coffee in rms. Restaurant 6:30 am-10 pm. Bar 11 am-midnight. Ck-out noon. Meeting rms. Business servs avail. In-rm modem link. Exercise equipt. Some refrigerators. Overlooks river. Cr cds: A, C, D, DS, ER, JCB, MC, V.

⊡ ⇌ 🛉 ⊠ 🐾 SC

★★ **HOTEL WISCONSIN.** 720 N Old World 3rd St (53203). 414/271-4900; fax 414/271-9998. 234 rms, 11 story. Mid-June-Sept: S, D $69-$76; each addl $8; suites $85; kit. units $69-$82; under 17 free; lower rates rest of yr. Crib free. Pet accepted. TV; cable (premium), VCR avail. Restaurant 6 am-10 pm. Ck-out 11 am. Meeting rm. Business servs avail. Concierge. Sundries. Valet serv. Coin lndry. Game rm. Health club privileges. Some refrigerators; microwaves avail. Cr cds: A, D, DS, MC, V.

🐾 🛉 ⊠ 🐾

★★★ **HYATT REGENCY.** 333 W Kilbourn Ave (53203). 414/276-1234; fax 414/276-6338; toll-free 800/233-1234. www.hyatt.com. 484 rms, 22 story. S $109-$179; D $134-$204; each addl $25; parlor rms $100-$150; suites $295-$750; under 18 free; wkend rates; package plans. TV; cable (premium), VCR avail (movies). Restaurants 6:30 am-midnight (see also POLARIS). Bar from 11 am, Fri, Sat to 2 am. Ck-out noon. Convention facilities. Business center. Concierge. Gift shop. Exercise equipt. Cr cds: A, C, D, DS, MC, V.

⊡ 🛉 ⊠ 🐾 🛉

★★ **PARK EAST.** 916 E State St (53202). 414/276-8800; fax 414/765-1919; toll-free 800/328-7275. www.parkeasthotel.com. 159 rms, 5 story. S $98-$120; D $108-$129; each addl $10; suites $120-$200; under 18 free. Crib $5. TV; cable (premium), VCR (movies). Complimentary continental bkfst. Restaurant 11 am-11 pm. Ck-out noon. Meeting rms. Business servs avail. Exercise equipt. Health club privileges. Some in-rm whirlpools, refrigerators, wet bars; microwaves avail. Cr cds: A, MC, V.

⊡ 🛉 🐾

★★★ **THE PFISTER.** 424 E Wisconsin Ave (53202). 414/273-8222; fax 414/273-8082; toll-free 800/558-8222. www.thepfister.com. 307 rms, 23 story. S, D $265-$285; each addl $20; suites $300-$1,050; under 18 free; wkend rates. Crib free. Parking $10; valet avail. TV; cable, VCR avail (movies). Indoor pool. Restaurant 6:30 am-11 pm (see also ENGLISH ROOM). Rm serv 24 hrs. Bars 11-2 am. Entertainment. Ck-out noon. Ck-in 3 pm. Convention facilities. Business servs avail. In-rm modem link. Concierge. Gift shop. Barber, beauty shop. Airport transportation avail. Exercise equipt. Bathrm phones. Minibars. Cr cds: A, C, D, DS, JCB, MC, V.

🐾 ⊡ ⇌ 🛉 ⊠ 🐾 SC

★★★ **RADISSON HOTEL MILWAUKEE AIRPORT.** 6331 S 13th St (53221). 414/764-1500; fax 414/764-6531; toll-free 800/303-8002. www.radisson.com. 159 rms, 3 story. S $69-$100; D $79-$120; each addl $10; under 18 free. Crib free. Pet accepted. TV. Indoor pool. Playground. Restaurant 6 am-1 pm, 5-10 pm; Sat, Sun from 7 am. Bar. Ck-out 11 am. Coin lndry. Meeting rms. Business servs avail. Bellhops. Sundries. Free airport transportation. Exercise equipt; saunas. Game rm. Balconies. Cr cds: A, MC, V.

🐾 ⇌ 🛉 ✈

★★★ **RADISSON HOTEL MILWAUKEE WEST.** 2303 N Mayfair Rd (53226). 414/257-3400; fax 414/257-0900. www.radisson.com. 150 rms, 8 story. S $99-$169; D $109-$179; each addl $10; under 18 free; lower rates wkends. Crib free. TV; cable (premium). Sauna. Indoor pool. Coffee in rms. Restaurant 6 am-2 pm, 5-10 pm. Bar 11-2 am. Ck-out noon. Meeting rms. Business servs avail. In-rm modem link. Ecercise equipt. Bellhops. Sundries. Free airport transportation. X-country ski 2 mi. Cr cds: A, C, D, DS, JCB, MC, V.

⊡ ⇌ ⇌ 🛉 ✈ ⊠ 🐾 SC

★★★ **SHERATON BROOKFIELD.** 375 S Moorland Rd (53005). 262/786-1100. www.sheraton.com. 389 rms, 12 story. S, D $169-$235; each addl $20; under 17 free. Crib avail. Pet accepted. 2 heated pools. TV; cable (premium), VCR avail. Complimentary coffee, newspaper in rms. Restaurant 6 am-10 pm. Ck-out noon. Meeting rms. Business center. Gift shop. Exercise rm. Some refrigerators, minibars. Cr cds: A, C, D, DS, MC, V.

★★ **SHERATON INN.** *8900 N Kildeer Ct, Brown Deer (53209). 414/355-8585; fax 414/355-3566. www.sheraton.com.* 149 rms, 6 story. S $124-$137; D $150-$180; each addl $10; suites $180-$285; under 18 free; wkend rates. Crib free. TV; cable (premium), VCR avail. Indoor/outdoor pool; whirlpool, poolside serv. Coffee in rms. Restaurant 6:30 am-10:30 pm. Bar 10-2 am. Ck-out noon. Meeting rms. Business servs avail. In-rm modem link. Bellhops. Valet serv. Barber. Airport transportation. X-country ski 3 mi. Sauna. Health club privileges. Some refrigerators; microwaves avail. Cr cds: A, C, D, DS, JCB, MC, V.

★★ **WYNDHAM HOTEL.** *139 E Kilbourn Ave (53202). 414/276-8686; fax 414/276-8007; toll-free 800/822-4200. www.wyndham.com.* 221 rms, 10 story, 77 suites. S, D $150-$192; each addl $10; under 18 free; wkend rates. Crib free. Garage $10. TV; cable, VCR avail. Complimentary coffee in rms. Restaurant 6:30 am-2 pm, 5-10 pm. Bar 11-2 am; entertainment Fri-Sat. Ck-out noon. Meeting rms. Business servs avail. Gift shop. Exercise equipt; sauna, steam rm. Whirlpool. Cr cds: A, C, D, DS, MC, V.

All Suite

★★★ **EMBASSY SUITES-MILWAUKEE WEST.** *1200 S Moorland Rd, Brookfield (53005). 262/782-2900; fax 414/796-9159; toll-free 800/444-6404. www.embassysuites.com.* 203 suites, 5 story. S, D, suites $109-$500; each addl $20; under 12 free; wkend rates; package plans. Crib free. Pet accepted, some restrictions. TV; cable (premium). Indoor pool; whirlpool. Complimentary full bkfst. Complimentary coffee in rms. Restaurant 11 am-11 pm. Bar to 1 am. Ck-out noon. Meeting rms. Business center. In-rm modem link. Concierge. Free airport transportation. Tennis privileges. Golf privileges. Exercise equipt; sauna, steam rm. Game rm. Refrigerators, microwaves, wet bars. Cr cds: A, MC, V.

Restaurants

★ **AU BON APPETIT.** *1016 E Brady St (53202). 414/278-1233. www.aubonappetit.com.* Hrs: 5-9 pm; Fri, Sat to 10 pm. Closed Sun, Mon; hols. Res accepted. Mediterranean menu. Wine. Dinner $6.95-$11.95. Specializes in Lebanese dishes, hummos, tabouleh. Own baking. Street parking. Casual, intimate restaurant; Mediterranean decor. Cr cds: MC, V.

★ **BALISTRERI'S BLUE MOUND INN.** *6501 W Blue Mound Rd (53213). 414/258-9881. www.balistreris.com.* Hrs: 11-1 am; Fri to 2 am; Sat 4 pm-2 am; Sun 4 pm-1 am. Closed Thanksgiving, Dec 24, 25. Res accepted. Italian, American menu. Bar. Lunch, dinner $6-$20. Specialties: veal Balistreri, pollo carcioffi, whitefish Frangelico. Own pasta. Casual, contemporary decor. Cr cds: A, D, DS, MC, V.

★★★ **BARTOLOTTA'S LAKE PARK BISTRO.** *3133 E Newberry Blvd (53211). 414/962-6300. www.foodspot.com.* Hrs: 11:30 am-2 pm, 5:30-9 pm; Fri to 10 pm; Sat 5-10 pm; Sun 10:30 am-2 pm (brunch), 5-8 pm. Closed hols. Res accepted. French menu. Bar. Lunch $7-$15, dinner $12-$22. Sun brunch $17.95-$21.95. Child's menu. Specializes in New York strip, Atlantic salmon. Own baking. Former park pavilion; overlooks Lake Michigan. Cr cds: A, D, DS, MC, V.

★★ **BAVARIAN INN.** *700 W Lexington Blvd (53217). 414/964-0300.* Hrs: 11:30 am-2:30 pm, 5-9 pm; Fri to 10 pm; Sat 5-9 pm; Sun brunch 10:30 am-2 pm. Closed Mon; Jan 1, July 4, Dec 24, 25. Res accepted. German, American menu. Bar. Lunch $4.95-$9.95, dinner $7.95-$14.95. Sun brunch $12.95. Child's menu. Specializes in schnitzel. Accordionist Fri-Sun. Parking. Chalet-style building; large fireplace, timbered ceilings, stein and Alpine bell collections. Cr cds: A, DS, MC, V.

D

★★★ **BOULEVARD INN.** *925 E Wells St (53202). 414/765-1166. www.boulevardinn.com.* Hrs: 11:30 am-9 pm; Fri, Sat to 10 pm; Sun from 10:30 am; Sun brunch to 2 pm. Closed hols. Res accepted. Bar. Wine list. Lunch $7.50-$11.50, dinner $19.95-$35.95. Sun brunch $13.95. Child's menu. Specializes in fresh fish, veal, German dishes. Own baking. Pianist. Valet parking. Some tableside preparation. Overlooks Lake Michigan. Family-owned. Cr cds: A, C, D, MC, V.

D

★★ **BUCA DI BEPPO.** *1233 N Van Buren Ave (53202). 414/224-8672. www.bucadibeppo.com.* Italian menu. Specializes in pasta, chicken cacciatore, tiramisu. Hrs: 5-10 pm; Fri to 11 pm; Sat, Sun from 4 pm. Closed Thanksgiving, Dec 24, 25. Res accepted. Bar. Dinner a la carte entrees: $9.95-$22.95. Eclectic decor. Cr cds: A, D, DS, MC, V.

★ **COUNTY CLARE.** *1234 N Astor St (53202). 888/942-5273. www.countyclare-inn.com.* Hrs: 11:30 am-10 pm; Sun to 9 pm. Closed hols. Irish menu. Bar to 1 am. Lunch $3.50-$9.50, dinner $3.50-$10.95. Specialties: Irish smoked salmon, corned beef and cabbage, Irish root soup. Traditional Irish music Sun. Irish pub decor with cut glass and dark woods. Cr cds: A, D, DS, MC, V.

D

★ **DOS BANDIDOS.** *5932 N Green Bay Ave (53209). 414/228-1911.* Hrs: 11 am-10:30 pm; Fri to 11:30 pm; Sat noon-11:30 pm; Sun 4-9 pm. Closed hols. Mexican, American menu. Bar. Lunch $3.95-$6.50, dinner $7.25-$11.95. Specializes in steak and chicken fajitas, spinach enchiladas, vegetarian dishes. Parking. Patio dining. Mexican cantina decor. Cr cds: A, DS, MC, V.

D

★★ **EAGAN'S.** *1030 N Water St (53202). 414/271-6900.* Hrs: 11 am-11 pm; Fri, Sat to 1 am; Sun brunch 11 am-2 pm. Closed hols. Bar. Lunch, dinner $6.95-$15.95. Sun brunch $6.95-$14.95. Specializes in seafood. Outdoor dining. Contemporary decor. Totally nonsmoking. Cr cds: A, D, DS, MC, V.

D

★★ **ELM GROVE INN.** *13275 Watertown Plank Rd, Elm Grove (53122). 262/782-7090. www.elmgroveinn.com.* Hrs: 11:30 am-2 pm, 5-9:30 pm; Sat from 5 pm. Closed Sun; hols. Res accepted. Continental menu. Bar to midnight. Lunch $7.50-$13, dinner $17-$32. Specializes in fresh fish, veal, beef. Own baking. 1850s bldg has high-backed chairs, stained glass and large fireplace. Cr cds: A, DS, MC, V.

D

★★★ **ELSA'S ON THE PARK.** *833 N Jefferson St (53202). 414/765-0615. www.elsas.com.* Specializes in half pound sirloin burger, chicken wings. Hrs: 11 am-2 pm; Fri to 2:30 pm; Sat 5 pm-2:30 am; Sun 5 pm-2 am. Wine, beer. Lunch, dinner $4.75-$10. Entertainment. Cr cds: A, MC, V.

D ⊒

★★★ **ENGLISH ROOM.** *424 E Wisconsin Ave (53202). 414/390-3832.* Hrs: 5:30-10 pm; Sat to 11 pm; Sun from 5 pm. Res accepted. Bar. Extensive wine list. Dinner $15-$25. Valet parking. Established 1893; past patrons incl Teddy Roosevelt and Enrico Caruso. Cr cds: MC, V.

D SC ⊒

★★★ **GRENADIER'S.** *747 N Broadway Ave (53202). 414/276-0747. www.grenadiers.com.* For more than 20 years, this French continental restaurant has attracted locals and visitors alike to its elegant, romantic dining room. Specializes in Dover sole, lamb curry Calcutta, fresh seared tuna on ocean salad. Own pastries. Hrs: 11:30 am-10 pm; Sat from 5:30 pm. Closed Sun; hols. Res accepted. Bar. Wine cellar. Lunch a la carte entrees: $9.95-$15.95, dinner a la carte entrees: $19-$39. Degustation menu: dinner $34.95. Entertainment: pianist. Valet parking (dinner). Jacket recommended. Cr cds: A, D, DS, MC, V.

D ⊒

★ **IZUMI'S.** *2178 N Prospect Ave (53209). 414/271-5278.* Hrs: 11:30 am-2 pm, 5-10 pm; Fri, Sat 5-10:30 pm; Sun 4-9 pm. Closed hols. Res accepted. Japanese menu. Wine, beer.

Lunch $4.95-$12.95, dinner $9-$23. Specializes in sushi, sukiyaki, teriyaki dishes. Parking. Contemporary Japanese decor. Cr cds: A, MC, V.
`D`

★★ **JACK PANDL'S WHITEFISH BAY INN.** *1319 E Henry Clay St, Whitefish Bay (53217). 414/964-3800. www.jackpandls.com.* Hrs: 11:30 am-2:30 pm, 5-9 pm; Fri, Sat to 10:30 pm; Sun 10:30 am-2:30 pm, 4-8 pm. Res accepted. Bar. Lunch $5.95-$9.95, dinner $7.95-$21.95. Child's menu. Specialties: whitefish, German pancakes, Schaum torte. Parking. Established in 1915; antique beer stein collection. Family-owned. Cr cds: A, DS, MC, V.

★★ **KARL RATZSCH'S.** *320 E Mason St (53202). 414/276-2720.* Hrs: 4-9:30 pm; Sat to 10:30 pm; Sun to 9 pm. Closed hols. Res accepted. German, American menu. Bar. Dinner $16.95-$24. Child's menu. Specializes in planked whitefish, roast goose shank, aged prime steak. Pianist evenings. Valet parking. Collection of rare steins, glassware. Old World Austrian atmosphere. Family-owned. Cr cds: A, DS, MC, V.

★★ **KING AND I.** *823 N 2nd St (53203). 414/276-4181.* Hrs: 11:30 am-10 pm; Sat 5-11 pm; Sun 4-9 pm. Closed hols. Res accepted. Thai menu. Bar. Lunch $5-$10, dinner $9-$18. Specialties: volcano chicken, fresh red snapper, crispy duck. Southeast Asian decor; enameled wood chairs, hand-carved teakwood, native artwork. Cr cds: A, D, DS, MC, V.
`D`

★ **THE KNICK.** *1030 E Juneau Ave (53202). 414/272-0011.* Hrs: 6:30 am-10 pm; Fri, Sat to 11 pm; Sun 9 am-10 pm. Sun brunch 9 am-3 pm. Closed Thanksgiving, Dec 25. Res accepted. Bar. Bkfst, lunch $3.95-$7.95, dinner $10.95-$19.95. Sun brunch $3.95-$7.95. Specializes in seafood, pasta. Outdoor dining. Casual decor. Totally nonsmoking. Cr cds: A, MC, V.
`D`

★★ **MADER'S.** *1037 N Old World 3rd St (53203). 414/271-3377. www.maders.com.* Hrs: 11:30 am-9 pm; Fri, Sat to 10 pm; Sun 10:30 am-9 pm; Sun brunch to 2 pm. Res accepted.

German, Continental menu. Bar. Lunch $4.95-$12, dinner $13.95-$28. Sun Viennese brunch $14.95. Child's menu. Specialties: Rheinischer sauerbraten, Wiener schnitzel, roast pork shank. Valet parking. Old World German decor; antiques. Gift shop. Family-owned. Cr cds: A, D, DS, MC, V.
`D`

★★★ **MANIACI'S CAFE SICILIANO.** *6904 N Santa Monica Blvd, Fox Point (53217). 414/352-5757.* Hrs: 4-10 pm. Closed Sun; hols; also wk of July 4. Res accepted. Continental menu. Serv bar. Wine cellar. Dinner $17.50-$32.95. Child's menu. Specializes in veal, fish, pasta. Own pasta. Sicilian decor with brick columns, tile floors. Family-owned. Cr cds: A, MC, V.

★★★ **MIMMA'S CAFE.** *1307 E Brady St (53202). 414/271-7337. www.mimmas.com.* Hrs: 5-10 pm; Fri, Sat to midnight; Sun from 5 pm. Closed Sun; hols. Res accepted. Italian menu. Bar. A la carte entrees: dinner $8-$30. Specializes in pasta, seafood, veal. Contemporary decor. Cr cds: A, D, DS, MC, V.
`D`

★★ **NORTH SHORE BISTRO.** *8649 N Port Washington Rd, Fox Point (53217). 414/351-6100.* Hrs: 11 am-10 pm; Sat to 11 pm; Sun from 4 pm. Closed hols. Res accepted. Bar. Lunch $6-$9.25, dinner $6-$24.95. Specializes in seafood, steak, pasta. Outdoor dining. Casual bistro atmosphere. Cr cds: A, MC, V.
`D`

★ **OLD TOWN SERBIAN GOURMET HOUSE.** *522 W Lincoln Ave (53207). 414/672-0206. www.wwbci.com/oldtown.* Hrs: 11:30 am-2:30 pm, 5-11 pm; Sat, Sun from 5 pm. Closed Mon; hols. Res accepted. Serbian, American menu. Bar. Lunch $5-$9, dinner $12-$20. Child's menu. Entertainment (wkends). Parking. Family-owned. Cr cds: A, DS, MC, V.

★★★ **OSTERIA DEL MONDO.** *1028 E Juneau Ave (53202). 414/291-3770. www.osteria.com.* Hrs: 5-10:30 pm; Fri, Sat to 11 pm, Sun to 9 pm;

Sun brunch 10 am-3 pm; hrs vary seasonally. Closed hols. Res accepted. Italian menu. Bar. Dinner $12.95-$22.95. Sun brunch $9.95-$19.95. Specializes in seafood, pasta. Street parking. Outdoor dining. Italian decor. Totally nonsmoking. Cr cds: A, D, MC, V.
D

★★★ **PANDL'S BAYSIDE.** *8825 N Lake Dr (53217). 414/352-7300. www.pandls.com.* Hrs: 11:30 am-9:30 pm; Fri-Sat to 10:30 pm; Sun 10 am-8:30 pm; Sun brunch to 2 pm. Closed Labor Day, Dec 25. Res accepted. Bar. Lunch, dinner $7.50-$26.95. Sun brunch $18.95. Child's menu. Specializes in fresh fish, prime meats. Salad bar (dinner). Own pastries. Parking. Family-owned. Cr cds: A, C, D, DS, MC, V.
D

★ **PLEASANT VALLEY INN.** *9801 W Dakota St (53227). 414/321-4321. www.foodspot.com/pleasantvalleyinn.* Hrs: 5-9 pm; Fri, Sat to 10 pm; Sun 4-8 pm. Closed Mon; hols. Res accepted. Bar. Dinner $14-$24. Child's menu. Specializes in steak, seafood. Casual decor. Cr cds: A, D, DS, MC, V.

★★ **POLARIS.** *333 W Kilbourn Ave (53203). 414/270-6130.* Hrs: 5-11 pm. Closed Jan 1, Thanksgiving, Dec 25. Res accepted. Bar. A la carte entrees: dinner $16.50-$25. Specializes in prime rib au jus, grilled veal chops, chicken tortellini. Parking. Revolving restaurant on 22nd floor. Cr cds: A, D, DS, MC, V.
D

★★ **PORTERHOUSE.** *800 W Layton Ave (53221). 414/744-1750. www.foodspot.com/porterhouse.* Hrs: 11 am-2:30 pm, 5-10 pm; Fri, Sat to 11 pm; Sun 4-9 pm. Closed Mon. Res accepted. Bar. Lunch $4.50-$10.95, dinner $9.95-$31.95. Child's menu. Specializes in char-broiled steak, ribs, seafood. Parking. Cr cds: A, D, DS, MC, V.
D

★ **RED ROCK CAFE.** *4022 N Oakland Ave (53211). 414/962-4545.* Hrs: 11 am-2 pm, 5-9 pm; Fri, Sat to 10 pm; Sun from 5 pm. Closed Mon; hols. Bar. Lunch $6.95-$11.95, dinner $8.25-$22.50. Child's menu. Specializes in seafood. Nautical decor. Totally nonsmoking. Cr cds: MC, V.
D SC

★★ **RIVER LANE INN.** *4313 W River Ln, Brown Deer (53223). 414/354-1995.* Hrs: 11:30 am-2:30 pm, 5-10 pm. Closed Sun; hols. Bar. Lunch $6.75-$10.95, dinner $15.95-$20.95. Specializes in seafood. Casual decor. Cr cds: A, DS, MC, V.
D

Schlitz Brewing Company

★ **ROYAL INDIA.** *3400 S 27th St (53215). 414/647-9600.* Hrs: 11 am-3 pm, 5-10 pm; Fri, Sat to 10:30 pm. Res accepted. Indian menu. Wine, beer. Buffet: lunch $6.95. Dinner $5.95-$11.95. Specializes in tandoori dishes, seafood, lamb. Own baking. Casual Indian decor. Totally non-smoking. Cr cds: A, MC, V.

D

★ ★ ★ **SANFORD.** *1547 N Jackson St (53202). 414/276-9608. www. sandfordrestaurant.com.* The site, once a grocery store owned by chef Sanford D'Amato's family, houses a modern, sophisticated dining room offering internationally flavored, New American cuisine from an a la carte menu. An additional, five-course ethnic tasting menu is also offered on weeknights. Specializes in sea scallops, grilled breast of duck, cumin wafers with grilled marinated tuna. Hrs: 5:30-8:45 pm; Fri to 9 pm; Sat 5-9 pm. Closed Sun; hols. Res accepted. Serv bar. Wine cellar. Dinner $23.95-$29.95. Tasting menus: 3-, 4-, and 5-course, $45-$65, 7-course, $75. Free valet parking. Cr cds: A, D, DS, MC, V.

D

★ **SAZ'S STATE HOUSE.** *5539 W State St (53208). 414/453-2410. www.sazbbq.com.* Hrs: 11 am-9:30 pm; Fri, Sat to 11 pm; Sun to 9 pm; Sun brunch 10:30 am-2:30 pm. Closed Dec 24, 25. Bar. Lunch $5-$10, dinner $7.50-$19.95. Specializes in barbecued ribs, fresh fish, chicken. Parking. Outdoor dining. 1905 roadhouse. Cr cds: A, DS, MC, V.

D ⬛

★ ★ **SELENSKY'S GRAND CHAMPION GRILL.** *4395 S 76th St, Greenfield (53220). 414/327-9100.* Hrs: 3:30-11 pm; Sun 2:30-9 pm. Closed Mon; Jan 1, July 4, Dec 25. Bar. Dinner $8.95-$18.95. Child's menu. Specializes in prime rib, steak, fresh seafood. Casual decor. Cr cds: MC, V.

D ⬛

★ ★ **SINGHA THAI.** *2237 S 108th St, West Allis (53227). 414/541-1234.* Hrs: 11 am-9 pm; Fri, Sat to 10 pm. Closed hols. Res accepted. Thai menu. Lunch $5-$10, dinner $6-$15. Specializes in noodle dishes, curry dishes. Casual atmosphere. Cr cds: MC, V.

D

★ ★ ★ **STEVEN WADE'S CAFE.** *17001 Greenfield Ave, New Berlin (53151). 262/784-0774. www.foodspot. comstevenwades.* Hrs: 11:30 am-2 pm, 5:30-10 pm; Mon, Sat from 5:30 pm. Closed Sun; hols. Res accepted. Contemporary American menu. Lunch $8-$14, dinner $16-$25. Specializes in wild game, pasta, seafood. Intimate atmosphere. Totally nonsmoking. Cr cds: A, DS, MC, V.

D SC

★ **THREE BROTHERS.** *2414 S St. Clair St (53207). 414/481-7530.* Hrs: 5-10 pm; Fri, Sat 4-11 pm; Sun 4-10 pm. Closed Mon; hols. Res accepted. Serbian menu. Serv bar. Dinner $10.95-$14.95. Specialties: burek, roast lamb, gulash. Serbian artwork on display.

D ⬛

★ **TRES HERMANOS.** *1332 W Lincoln Ave (53215). 414/384-9050.* Hrs: 11 am-midnight. Closed Thanksgiving, Dec 25. Res accepted. Mexican menu. Bar. Lunch $1.75-$5.99, dinner $1.75-$15. Child's menu. Specializes in seafood, burritos, tacos. Salad bar. Entertainment Fri, Sat. Mexican decor. Totally nonsmoking. Cr cds: A, D, DS, MC, V.

D

★ ★ **WEISSGERBER'S 3RD STREET PIER.** *1110 N Old World 3rd St (53203). 414/272-0330. www. weissgerbers.com.* Hrs: 5-10 pm; Sat from 5 pm; Sun 4-9 pm. Res accepted. Bar. Dinner $15.95-$34.95. Child's menu. Specializes in seafood, steak. Own desserts. Jazz Fri, Sat. Valet parking. Outdoor dining. Lunch, dinner cruises on Lake Michigan avail. In restored landmark building on Milwaukee River. Cr cds: A, D, DS, MC, V.

D ⬛

★ ★ **WEST BANK CAFE.** *732 E Burleigh St (53212). 414/562-5555.* Hrs: 5:30-9:30 pm; Fri, Sat to 10 pm. Closed hols. Chinese, Vietnamese menu. Serv bar. Dinner $7-$16. Specializes in Vietnamese dishes. Own baking. Street parking. Contemporary Oriental decor. Totally non-smoking. Cr cds: A, MC, V.

D

★ **YEN CHING.** *7630 W Good Hope Rd (53223).* 414/353-6677. Hrs: 11:30 am-2 pm, 4:30-9:30 pm; Fri, Sat 4:30-10 pm; Sun 11:30 am-2:30 pm, 4:30-9 pm. Mandarin menu. Serv bar. Lunch $4.25-$5.50, dinner $6.50-$12. Specializes in beef, chicken, seafood. Parking. Oriental decor. Cr cds: A, D, DS, MC, V.

D ⊸

Unrated Dining Spots

THE CHOCOLATE SWAN. *13320 Watertown Plank Rd, Elm Grove (53122).* 262/784-7926. Hrs: 11 am-6 pm; Fri to 8:30 pm; Sat from 10 am. Closed Sun; hols. Dessert menu only. Desserts $1.75-$5.75. Specialties: Mary's chocolate interlude, yellow strawberry log. Tea room ambiance. Totally nonsmoking. Cr cds: C, MC, V.

SAFE HOUSE. *779 N Front St (53202).* 414/271-2007. www.safe-house.com. Hrs: 11:30-2 am; Fri, Sat to 2:30 am; Sun 4 pm-midnight. Res accepted. Bar. Lunch, dinner $4.25-$12.95. Specializes in sandwiches, specialty drinks. DJ Fri, Sat, magician Sun-Thurs. Spy theme decor. Cr cds: A, MC, V.

Mineral Point

See also Dodgeville, New Glarus, Platteville

Settled 1827 **Pop** 2,428 **Elev** 1,135 ft
Area code 608 **Zip** 53565
Information Chamber/Main St, 225 High St; 608/987-3201 or 888/764-6894
Web www.mineralpoint.com

The first settlers were New Englanders and Southerners attracted by the lead (galena) deposits. In the 1830s miners from Cornwall, England settled here. These "Cousin Jacks," as they were called, introduced superior mining methods and also built the first permanent homes, duplicating the rock houses they had left in Cornwall. Since the mines were in

sight of their homes their wives called them to meals by stepping to the door and shaking a rag—so the town was first called "Shake Rag."

Visitors to Mineral Point can experience the way small towns used to be. The city offers a wide variety of shopping opportunities, including artisan galleries and working studios, antique shops, and specialty shops.

What to See and Do

Mineral Point Toy Museum. Antique and collectible doll houses, toys, and trains. (May-Oct, Fri-Sun, daily) 215 Commerce. Phone 608/987-3160. ¢¢

Pendarvis, Cornish Restoration. Guided tour of six restored log and limestone homes of Cornish miners (ca 1845). Also 40-acre nature walk in old mining area (free), which has mine shafts, wildflowers, and abandoned "badger holes." (May-Oct, daily) 114 Shake Rag St. Phone 608/987-2122. ¢¢¢

Motel/Motor Lodge

★ **REDWOOD MOTEL.** *625 Dodge St (53565).* 608/987-2317; fax 608/987-2317; toll-free 800/321-1958. 28 rms, 2 story. May-Oct: S $35-$55; D $43-$55; each addl $5; lower rates rest of yr. TV; cable. Restaurant adj 6 am-8 pm. Ck-out 11 am. Business servs avail. Miniature golf. Cr cds: DS, MC, V.

D ⊸ ⊛ SC

Minocqua

See also Boulder Junction, Eagle River, Lac du Flambeau, Rhinelander, St. Germain, Woodruff

Pop 3,522 **Elev** 1,603 ft
Area code 715 **Zip** 54548
Information Minocqua-Arbor Vitae-Woodruff Area Chamber of Commerce, 8216 US 51, PO Box 1006; 715/356-5266 or 800/446-6784
Web www.minocqua.org

Minocqua is a four-season resort area known for its thousands of acres of lakes. The area contains one of the largest concentrations of fresh water bodies in America. Minocqua, the

"Island City," was once completely surrounded by Lake Minocqua. Now youth camps and resorts are along the lakeshore.

What to See and Do

Area has 3,200 lakes, streams, and ponds. Contain every major type of freshwater fish found in Wisconsin. Also clear water for diving. The Min-Aqua-Bat waterski shows are held mid-June-mid-Aug on Wed, Fri, and Sun eves. For winter sports enthusiasts there are thousands of miles of groomed snowmobile and hundreds of miles of x-country ski trails. Inquire at Chamber of Commerce.

Circle M Corral Family Fun Park. Horseback riding, bumper boats, go-carts; train ride with robbery aboard replica C. P. Huntington; water slide; miniature golf; children's rides. Picnic area, snack bar. (Mid-May-mid-Oct, daily) 2½ mi W of US 51 on WI 70 W. Phone 715/356-4441. ¢¢

Jim Peck's Wildwood. A wildlife park featuring hundreds of tame animals and birds native to the area; many can be pet at baby animal nursery; walk among tame deer; trout and musky ponds. Picnic area; nature walk; adventure boat rides; gift shop, snack wagon. (May-mid-Oct, daily) US 51 to WI 70, then 2 mi W. Phone 715/356-5588. ¢¢

Minocqua Museum. Ongoing display of Island City's unique history. Main gallery exhibits change annually; some permanent exhibits. (June-Sept, daily; or by appt) US 51 to 416 Chicago Ave, downtown. Phone 715/356-7666. **DONATION**

Minocqua Winter Park Nordic Center. Center has over 35 mi of groomed and tracked x-country trails; two groomed telemarking slopes; more than one mi of lighted trails for night skiing (Thurs-Fri only). School, shop, rentals. Heated chalet, concessions. (Dec-Mar, Thurs-Tues) 6 mi W on WI 70 to Squirrel Lake Rd, then approx 6 mi S, follow the signs. Phone 715/356-3309. ¢¢¢¢

Northwoods Wildlife Center. Wildlife hospital, wildlife educational center with tours and scheduled programs. (Mon-Sat, daily) US 51 to WI 70, then 1 mi W. Phone 715/356-7400. **DONATION**

Wilderness Cruise. Two-hr cruise on the Willow Flowage aboard the *Wilderness Queen*. Also brunch, dinner, and sightseeing cruises. (Mid-May-Oct, call for hours; res required) 7 mi S on US 51, then 7 mi on County Y to Willow Dam Rd in Hazelhurst. Phone 715/453-3310. ¢¢¢¢

Special Event

Northern Lights Playhouse. 10 mi S of Minocqua on US 51 in Hazelhurst. Professional repertory theater presents Broadway plays, musicals, and comedies; also Children's Theatre. Phone 715/356-7173. Memorial Day-early Oct. ¢¢¢

Motels/Motor Lodges

★ **AQUA AIRE MOTEL.** *806 WI 51N (54548). 715/356-3433; fax 715/358-9701. www.north-wis.com/aquaaire.* 10 rms, shower only. June-Aug: S $80; D $90; each addl $5; under 3 free; wkly rates; higher rates special events; lower rates rest of yr. Crib free. Pet accepted, some restrictions. TV; cable (premium). Restaurant opp 7 am-2:30 pm. Ck-out 11 am. Business servs avail. X-country ski 7 mi. Refrigerators; microwaves avail. Picnic tables. Cr cds: A, DS, MC, V.

★★ **NEW CONCORD INN.** *320 Front St (54548). 715/356-1800; fax 715/356-6955; res 800/356-8888. www.newconcordinn.com.* 53 rms, 3 story. July-Sept, Dec-Feb: S, D $88-$115; each addl $7; suites $130; under 12 free; lower rates rest of yr. Crib $5. TV; cable (premium), VCR avail. Indoor pool; whirlpool. Complimentary continental bkfst. Restaurant nearby. Ck-out 11 am. Meeting rms. Business servs avail. Sundries. Game rm. Some in-rm whirlpools, refrigerators. Opp beach. Cr cds: A, MC, V.

Restaurants

★★ **NORWOOD PINES.** *10171 US 70W (54548). 715/356-3666. www.norwoodpines.com.* Hrs: 5-10 pm. Closed Sun; Dec 24-25. Dinner $8.95-$33. Friday fish fry $8.95. Child's menu. Specializes in veal,

A STROLL THROUGH A SWISS MOUNTAIN VILLAGE (IN WISCONSIN!)

Snuggled in the Little Sugar River valley, tiny New Glarus resembles a Swiss mountain village. And with good reason. The town was founded in 1845 by 108 immigrants from the Swiss canton of Glarus who traveled to America to escape poverty and unemployment. Today, it is not unusual to see dairy herds grazing among the pretty hills, nor is it startling to hear a yodel echo across the valley. In fact, every year on the first Sunday in August, yodelers, alphornists, and folk dancers gather here to celebrate Swiss Independence Day.

Gather brochures at the New Glarus Information Center at Railroad Street and Sixth Avenue, then walk one block east to First Street, the town's main business thoroughfare. On the corner is the New Glarus Hotel, built in 1853 by Swiss settlers. Its main dining room occupies an old opera house (where talking movies were introduced in 1930). On an enclosed upper balcony, picture windows look out onto picturesque shops and over rooftops to surrounding green hills. Veal dishes include geschetzlets (thin slices lightly browned and served with a white wine sauce). Don't miss the baked-on-the-premises rhubarb-custard torte. The hotel has lodging in six guest rooms. Across the street are three good "foodie" stops. Chalet-style Schoco-Laden is a retail outlet for imported chocolates, homemade fudge, ice cream, and locally made cheeses. Ruef's Meat Market offers a variety of wurst, including fresh and smoked brats and landjaeger sausages favored by Swiss hunters (dried sausage that makes a great munchie). New Glarus Bakery and Tea Room is the spot for an afternoon respite or to buy tempting baked goods that include rich, dense stollen (German sweet bread).

Wandering downtown's few short blocks, visitors quickly realize just how much the village resembles a Swiss mountain town. Chalet-style buildings feature carved balconies decorated by colorful coats of arms, Swiss flags and banners, and window boxes spilling with bright red geraniums. Many businesses bear Swiss-German inscriptions proclaiming the nature of the commerce conducted within. The clank of cowbells welcomes you to shops selling lace, embroidery, and raclette grills. Just east of First Street on Seventh Avenue, the Chalet of the Golden Fleece Museum replicates a Swiss Bernese mountain chalet. Rocks and logs on the roof reflect a Swiss practice designed to protect slate shingles from strong mountain winds. The museum houses a collection of more than 3,000 Swiss items, from dolls to kitchenware, as well as artifacts collected from around the world (such as a jeweled watch once owned by King Louis XVI, 2,000-year-old Etruscan earrings, and Gregorian chants on parchment dating from 1485). Continue east on Seventh Avenue to the Swiss Historical Village Museum, a replica pioneer village with log cabins, log church, and a one-room schoolhouse. Operated by the local historical society, the museum preserves the history and records of New Glarus and tells the story of Swiss immigration and colonization. Its 14 buildings include a traditional Swiss bee house, a replica cheese factory, blacksmith's shop, general store, and a print shop that displays equipment used to print the *New Glarus Post* from 1897 to 1967.

steak, seafood. Pianist, sing-along Fri, Sat. Parking. Cr cds: D, DS, MC, V.
[D]

★ **PAUL BUNYAN'S.** *8653 WI 51N (54548). 715/356-6270. www.paul bunyans.com.* Hrs: 7 am-9 pm. Closed Oct-Apr. Bar. Complete meals: bkfst $6.95, lunch $5.95-$7.50, dinner $9.95-$10.95. Fri fish fry $8.50. Child's menu. Specializes in lumberjack-style meals. 2 entrees daily; family-style serv. Replica of typical 1890

logging camp. Family-owned. Cr cds: DS, MC, V.
[D]

★ **RED STEER.** *8230 WI 51 S (54548). 715/356-6332.* Hrs: 5 pm-closing. Closed Thanksgiving, Dec 24-25. Res accepted. Bar. Dinner $10.95-$19.95. Child's menu. Specializes in charcoal-broiled steak, seafood, ribs. Rustic decor. Cr cds: A, D, DS, MC, V.

★ **SPANG'S.** *318 Milwaukee St (54548). 715/356-4401.* Hrs: 5-10 pm. Closed Easter, Thanksgiving, Dec 24-25. Italian menu. Bar. Dinner $6.25-$13.95. Child's menu. Specializes in pasta, pizza. Cr cds: A, DS, MC, V.
[D] [⊒]

Monroe

(G-4) *See also Janesville, New Glarus*

Pop 10,241 **Elev** 1,099 ft
Area code 608 **Zip** 53566
Information Chamber of Commerce, 1505 9th St; 608/325-7648
Web www.monroechamber.org

A well-known community of Swiss heritage in an area of abundant dairy production, Monroe is the site of a unique courthouse with a 120-foot tall clock tower.

What to See and Do

Alp and Dell Cheesery, Deli, and Country Cafe. Watch cheesemaking process (Mon-Fri). Self-guided tours. Retail store (daily). 657 2nd St. Phone 608/328-3355.

Yellowstone Lake State Park. A 968-acre park on Yellowstone Lake. Swimming, waterskiing, fishing, boating (rentals); hiking, x-country skiing, snowmobiling, picnicking, playground, concession, camping (electric, dump station; res accepted through reserve America), winter camping. Standard fees. (Daily) 16 mi NW on WI 81 to Argyle, then N on County N, then W on Lake Rd. Phone 608/523-4427. ¢¢

Special Event

Balloon Rally. Phone 608/325-7648. Mid-June.

Motel/Motor Lodge

★ **KNIGHTS INN.** *250 N 18th Ave (53566). 608/325-4138; fax 608/325-1282; toll-free 800/325-1178. www. knightsinn.com.* 65 rms, 2 story. S $30-$40; D $59-$69; each addl $4; under 13 free. Crib free. TV; cable (premium). Complimentary coffee in lobby. Restaurant nearby. Ck-out 11

am. Business servs avail. In-rm modem link. Cr cds: A, DS, MC, V.
[D] [⊒] [🐾]

Mount Horeb

See also Dodgeville, Madison, New Glarus

Pop 4,182 **Elev** 1,230 ft
Area code 608 **Zip** 53572
Information Chamber of Commerce, PO Box 84; 608/437-5914 or 888/765-5929

What to See and Do

Blue Mound State Park. A 1,150-acre park with scenic views and lookout towers. Swimming pool; nature, mountain bike trails, hiking, and x-country ski trails; picnicking, playgrounds, camping (dump station). Standard fees. (Daily) W on US 18, 1 mi NW of Blue Mounds. Phone 608/437-5711. ¢¢

Cave of the Mounds. Colorful onyx formations in limestone cavern, rooms on two levels. Registered National Natural Landmark. One-hr guided tours. (Yr-round, call for hours) Also picnic grounds, gardens, snack bar, and gift shops. 4 mi W on US 18/151, then follow signs to Cave of the Mounds. Phone 608/437-3038. ¢¢

🌟 **Little Norway.** Norwegian pioneer farmstead built in 1856; museum of Norse antiques. Guided tours (45 min). (May-late Oct, daily) W via US 18/151 to Cave of the Mounds Rd, then follow signs to County JG. Phone 608/437-8211. ¢¢

Mount Horeb Mustard Museum. Large collection of mustards, mustard memorabilia, and samplings. (Daily) 100 W Main St. Phone 608/437-3986.

Motel/Motor Lodge

★★ **KARAKAHL COUNTRY INN.** *1405 US 18 Business and 151 E (53572). 608/437-5545; fax 608/437-5908; toll-free 888/621-1884. www.karakahl.com.* 76 rms, 1-2 story. Mid-May-mid-Oct: S $59-$64; D $69-$174; each addl $5; under 18 free;

lower rates rest of yr; crib $4. Pet accepted, some restrictions; $5. TV; cable. Saunas. Indoor pool. Complimentary continental bkfst. Restaurant 7 am-2 pm, 5-8 pm; Fri, Sat to 10 pm; closed Sun eve. Bar 5 pm-1 am. Ck-out noon. Business servs avail. X-country ski 2 blks. Cr cds: A, DS, MC, V.

🅳 🐾 🏊 ⛓ 🎿 🔥

Neenah-Menasha

(E-6) *See also Appleton, Green Bay, Oshkosh*

Settled 1843 **Pop** 23,219 **Elev** 750 ft
Area code 920 **Zip** Neenah, 54956; Menasha, 54952
Information Fox Cities Convention & Visitor Bureau, 3433 W College Ave, Appleton, 54914; 920/734-3358 or 800/236-6673
Web www.foxcities.org

Wisconsin's great paper industry started in Neenah and its twin city, Menasha. The two cities, located on Lake Winnebago, are still among the nation's leaders in dollar volume of paper products. Many paper product factories are located here in addition to large wood product plants, printing and publishing houses, foundries, and machine shops.

What to See and Do

Barlow Planetarium. 3-D projections explain the stars. (Thurs, Fri eves; Sat, Sun afternoons-eves) 1478 Midway Rd, Menasha. Phone 920/832-2848. ¢¢

Bergstrom-Mahler Museum. More than 1,800 glass paperweights; antique German glass; American regional paintings; changing exhibits. (Tues-Sun; closed hols) Museum shop, specializing in glass. 165 N Park Ave, Neenah. Phone 920/751-4658. **DONATION**

Doty Cabin. Home of Wisconsin's second territorial governor, James Duane Doty. Boating (ramp); tennis courts, picnic facilities, playgrounds; park (daily), cabin (June-mid-Aug, daily, afternoons). Doty Park, Web-

ster and Lincoln sts, Neenah. Phone 920/751-4614. **DONATION**

High Cliff State Park. A 1,139-acre park with beautiful wooded bluffs. Swimming, bathhouse, waterskiing, fishing, boating (marina); nature, hiking, snowmobile, and x-country ski trails; picnicking, playgrounds, concession, camping (dump station). Naturalist program. Standard fees. (Daily) 9 mi E, off WI 114, on opposite shore of Lake Winnebago. Phone 920/989-1106. ¢¢ In the park is

> **High Cliff General Store Museum.** Museum depicts life in the area from 1850 to the early 1900s. Store was once the center of activity of the lime kiln community and housed the post and telegraph offices. Relic of old lime kiln oven nearby. (Mid-May-Sept, Sat-Sun and hols) Phone 920/989-1106. **FREE**

Smith Park. Monument to Jean Nicolet, who came in 1634 to arrange peace between Native American tribes. Tennis courts, x-country skiing, picnic areas, pavilion, playground. Native American effigy mounds; formal gardens; historic railroad caboose representing birthplace of Central Wisconsin Railroad. (Daily) Keyes St, Menasha. Phone 920/967-5106. **FREE**

New Glarus

See also Madison, Monroe, Mount Horeb

Settled 1845 **Pop** 1,899 **Elev** 900 ft
Area code 608 **Zip** 53574
Information New Glarus Tourism, PO Box 713; 608/527-2095 or 800/527-6838

When bad times struck the Swiss canton of Glarus in 1844, a group of 193 set out for the New World and settled New Glarus. Their knowledge of dairying brought prosperity. The town is still predominantly Swiss in character and ancestry.

What to See and Do

Chalet of the Golden Fleece. Replica of Swiss chalet, with more than 3,000 Swiss items. Guided tours. (May-Oct, daily) 618 2nd St at 7th Ave. Phone 608/527-2614. ¢¢

New Glarus Woods State Park. Park has 38 campsites in 425 acres of wooded valleys. Picnicking, playgrounds. Standard fees. (Daily) 1 mi S on WI 69. Phone 608/527-2335. ¢¢

Sugar River State Trail. A 24-mi trail follows abandoned railroad bed between New Glarus and Brodhead to the southeast. Hiking, biking, snowmobiling, and x-country skiing. (Daily) Phone 608/527-2334. ¢¢

⭐ **Swiss Historical Village.** Replicas of first buildings erected by settlers, incl blacksmith shops, cheese factory, schoolhouse, and print shop; original furnishings and tools; guided tours. (May-Oct, daily) 612 7th Ave. Phone 608/527-2317. ¢¢¢

Special Events

Heidi Festival. Mid-June. Phone 608/527-2095.

Swiss Volksfest. Wilhelm Tell Shooting Park, ½ mi N on County O. Singing, yodeling, dancing. Honors birth of Swiss confederation in 1291. First Sun Aug. Phone 608/527-2095.

Wilhelm Tell Festival. Alpine Festival, Swiss entertainment, Sat. Schiller's drama, *Wilhelm Tell,* in German, Sun; in English, Sat, Mon. Tell Amphitheater, 1¼ mi E on County W. Also fine arts show, Village Park, Sun. Labor Day wkend. Phone 608/527-2095.

Motels/Motor Lodges

★ ★ **CHALET LANDHAUS INN.** *801 WI 69 (53574). 608/527-5234; fax 608/527-2365; res 800/944-1716. www.chaletlandhaus.com.* 67 rms, 3-4 story. May-Oct: S $74-$85; D $89-$109; each addl $18; suites $99-$160; family rms $109-$145; under 8 free; lower rates rest of yr. Crib $12. TV; cable. Restaurant 7-11 am, 5:30-9 pm; Sun, Mon to 11 am. Ck-out 11 am. Indoor pool. Whirlpool. Exercise equipt. Meeting rms. Business servs avail. X-country ski 2 mi. Whirlpool in suites. Some balconies. Cr cds: A, DS, MC, V.

D ⛽ 🏊 🛎 🔒 🔥 SC

★ **SWISS-AIRE MOTEL.** *1200 WI 69 (53574). 608/527-2138; fax 608/527-5818; toll-free 800/798-4391. www.swissaire.com.* 26 rms. May-Oct: S $45-$79; D $59-$115; each addl $6; under 5 free; lower rates rest of yr. Crib free. Pet accepted. TV; cable. Heated pool. Complimentary continental bkfst. Ck-out 11 am. Meeting rms. Picnic tables. Cr cds: AMEX, DS, MC, V.

🐾 🏊 🔒 🔥

B&B/Small Inn

★ ★ **COUNTRY HOUSE.** *180 WI 69 (53574). 608/527-5399.* 4 rms, 2 story. S, D $65-$110. Complimentary full bkfst. Ck-out 11 am, ck-in 4-7 pm. Built in 1892; antiques. Totally nonsmoking. Cr cds: MC, V.

🔒 🐾

Restaurant

★ ★ **NEW GLARUS HOTEL.** *100 6th Ave (53574). 608/527-5244. www.newglarushotel.com.* Hrs: 11 am-9 pm; Fri, Sat to 10 pm; Sun brunch 10:30 am-3 pm. Closed Thanksgiving, Dec 24-25; also Tues in Nov-Apr. Res accepted. Swiss, American menu. Bar. Lunch $3.50-$9, dinner $5-$15. Sun brunch $12.50. Child's menu. Specialties: beef and cheese fondues, piccata schnitzel, three filet (pork, veal, beef). Own baking. Polka Fri, Sat; yodeling (summer). Cr cds: A, DS, MC, V.

D 🔒

Oconomowoc

See also Milwaukee, Watertown

Pop 10,993 **Elev** 873 ft **Area code** 262 **Zip** 53066

Information Greater Oconomowoc Area Chamber of Commerce, 152 E Wisconsin Ave; 262/567-2666

Web www.oconomowoc.com

Native Americans called this place "the gathering of waters," because of its location between Fowler Lake and Lac La Belle.

What to See and Do

Honey of a Museum. Bee Tree provides a close-up view of bee activities; pollination and beeswax exhibits; multimedia show about beekeeping yesterday, today, and around the world; nature walk, honey tasting. (Mid-May-Oct, daily; rest of yr, Mon-Fri; closed hols) Honey Acres, 10 mi N, on WI 67 just N of Ashippun. Phone 920/474-4411. **FREE**

Skiing. Highlands Ski Hill. Area has two chairlifts, rope tow; patrol, school, rentals; snowmaking; bar. Longest run 2,200 ft; vertical drop 196 ft. (Nov-Mar, daily). WI 67 and I-94. Phone 262/567-2577. ¢¢¢¢

Motel/Motor Lodge

★★ **COUNTRY PRIDE INN.** *2412 Milwaukee St, Delafield (53018). 262/646-3300; fax 262/646-3491.* 56 rms, 2 story. May-Sept: S $52; D $62; suites $85-$125; each addl $5; lower rates rest of yr. Crib $5. TV; cable (premium). Indoor pool; whirlpool. Complimentary coffee in lobby. Restaurant adj 6 am-11 pm. Ck-out 11 am. Meeting rm. Business servs avail. Sundries. Downhill ski 6 mi; x-country ski ¼ mi. Sauna. Some in-rm whirlpools. Cr cds: A, DS, MC, V.
D 🏂 ≼ ≈ ⊠ 🔥

Resort

★★★ **OLYMPIA RESORT AND SPA.** *1350 Royale Mile Rd (53066). 414/567-0311; fax 414/567-5934; toll-free 800/558-9573. www.olympiaresort. com.* 256 units, 3-4 story. S, D $99-$129; each addl $20; suites $189-$249; family, ski and golf plans. TV. 2 pools, 1 indoor; whirlpool, pool-side serv. Coffee in rms. Dining rm 6:30 am-10 pm. Bars 11-2 am. Ck-out noon, ck-in 4 pm. Meeting rms. Business servs avail. Grocery 1 blk. Deli. Valet serv. Beauty shop. Indoor, outdoor tennis. 18-hole golf, greens fee, pro, driving range. Downhill ski. Entertainment Fri, Sat; movies. Game rm. Exercise rm; sauna, steam rm. Some refrigerators. Fireplace in suites. Cr cds: A, C, D, DS, MC, V.
D 🏂 ≼ 🏌 ⛸ ≈ 🎿 ⊠ 🔥 SC

B&B/Small Inn

★★ **INN AT PINE TERRACE.** *351 E Lisbon Rd (53066). 262/567-7463; toll-free 888/526-0588. www.innatpine terrace.com.* 12 rms, 3 story. S, D $75-$175; each addl $15. TV; cable (premium). Heated pool. Complimentary continental bkfst; afternoon refreshments. Restaurant nearby. Exercise equipt. Ck-out 10:30 am, ck-in 3 pm. Restored mansion (1879); antique furnishings. Cr cds: A, D, DS, MC, V.
D ≈ 🏌 ⊠ 🔥

Restaurants

★★★ **GOLDEN MAST INN.** *1270 Lacy Ln, Okauchee (53066). 262/567-7047. www.weissgerbers.com.* Hrs: 5-11 pm; Sun 11 am-9; Sun brunch 11 am-2 pm. Closed Mon in Oct-Apr. Res accepted. German, American menu. Bar. Wine cellar. Dinner $15.95-$34.95. Child's menu. Specializes in Wiener schnitzel, Kasseler rippchen, seafood. Outdoor dining in beer garden. German decor; antiques, fireplace. View of lake and landscaped grounds. Family-owned. Cr cds: A, DS, MC, V.
D ⊸

★ **RED CIRCLE INN.** *33013 Watertown Plank Rd, Nashotah (53058). 262/367-4883.* Hrs: 5-9:30 pm. Closed Sun and Mon; hols. Res accepted. Bar from 4 pm. Dinner $17.95-$25. Specializes in veal, fresh fish, steak. Former stagecoach stop; one of oldest restaurants in state (est 1848). Cr cds: A, DS, MC, V.
D ⊸

Oconto

See also Green Bay, Marinette, Menomonie, Peshtigo

Pop 4,474 **Elev** 591 ft **Area code** 920 **Zip** 54153

On Green Bay at the mouth of the Oconto River, Oconto was the home of Copper Culture people 4,500 years ago.

What to See and Do

Beyer Home. (ca 1868) Victorian house with furnishings of 1880-1890s. Adj museum annex has exhibits of Copper Culture people and antique vehicles. (June-Labor Day, Mon-Sat, also Sun afternoons) 917 Park Ave. Phone 920/834-6206. ¢¢

Wisconsin countryside

North Bay Shore County Park.
Swimming, fishing, boating; tent and
trailer sites, camping (late May-late
Sept; fee). Fall Salmon Run. (Daily) 9
mi N on County Y. Phone 920/834-
6825. **FREE**

Oshkosh (E-6)

Settled 1836 **Pop** 55,006 **Elev** 767 ft
Area code 920

Information Oshkosh Convention &
Visitors Bureau, 2 N Main St, 54901;
920/236-5250 or 800/876-5250

Web www.oshkoshcvb.org

Named for the Chief of the Menominee, Oshkosh is located on the west
shore of Lake Winnebago, the largest
freshwater lake within the state. The
city is known for the many recreational activities offered by its lakes
and rivers. This is the original home
of the company that produces the
famous overalls that help make
Oshkosh a household word. The
economy of the town, once called
"Sawdust City," is centered on transportation equipment manufacturing,
tourism, and candle making.

What to See and Do

⭐ **EAA Air Adventure Museum.** More
than 90 aircraft on display incl
home-built aircraft, antiques, classics,
ultralights, aerobatic and rotary-
winged planes. Special World War II
collection. Extensive collections of
aviation art and photography; special
displays of engines, propellers, and
scale models. Five theaters. Antique
airplanes fly on wkends (May-Oct).
(Daily; closed hols) 3000 Poberezny
Rd. Phone 920/426-4818. **¢¢**

Grand Opera House. A restored 1883
Victorian Theater, offers a variety of
performing arts. 100 High Ave, PO
Box 1004. Phone 920/424-2350.

Menominee Park. Swimming beach
(lifeguard), fishing, sailing, paddleboats; tennis courts, picnic shelters,
concession. Train rides, children's
zoo (late May-early Sept, daily). Fee
for some activities. (Daily) On Lake
Winnebago, enter off Hazel or Mer-
ritt sts. Phone 920/236-5080.

Oshkosh Public Museum. Housed in
turn-of-the-century, Tudor-style mansion with Tiffany stained-glass win-

dows and interior; also occupies adj addition. Apostles Clock, china and glassware collection; life-sized dioramas depicting French exploration, British occupation, pioneer settlement, and native wildlife; antique fire and train equipt; meteorites; Native American exhibits; fine and decorative art; 1913 Harley-Davidson; miniature lumber company. (Tues-Sun; closed hols) 1331 Algoma Blvd. Phone 920/424-4731. **FREE**

Paine Art Center and Arboretum. Tudor-revival house; period rms, European and American paintings and sculpture, Asian rugs, furniture and decorative arts; changing art exhibitions. Arboretum and display gardens. (Tues-Sun afternoons; closed hols) 1410 Algoma Blvd, at jct WI 21, 110. Phone 920/235-6903. ¢¢

Rebel Alliance Theater. Non-profit organization dedicated to bringing the live theater experience to Fox Valley. 445 N Main St. Phone 920/426-8580.

University of Wisconsin-Oshkosh. (1871) 11,000 students. Priebe Art Gallery, Reeve Memorial Union, Kolf Sports and Recreation Center. Campus tours (Mon-Fri; Sat by appt). 800 Algoma Blvd. Phone 920/424-0202.

Special Events

Sawdust Days. Commemorates lumbering era. Early July. Phone 920/235-5584.

Oshkosh Public Museum Art Fair. On Oshkosh Public Museum grounds. Featuring original fine art by over 200 quality artists from around the country. Music, entertainment, concessions. Phone 920/424-4731. Early July.

EAA Air Venture. (Experimental Aircraft Association). Held at Wittman Regional Airport. One of the nation's largest aviation events. More than 500 educational forums, workshops, and seminars; daily air shows; exhibits; more than 12,000 aircraft. Late July-early Aug. Phone 920/426-4800.

Motels/Motor Lodges

★★ **BAYMONT INN.** *1950 Omro Rd (54901). 920/233-4190; fax 920/233-8197; res 800/428-3438. www.baymontinn.com.* 100 rms, 2 story. June-Aug: S, D $67.95-$85.95; each

addl $7; under 18 free; wkly rates; higher rates special events; lower rates rest of yr. Crib avail. Pet accepted, some restrictions. TV; cable. Complimentary continental bkfst. Complimentary coffee in rms. Restaurant adj 7 am-10 pm. Ck-out noon. Meeting rms. Business servs avail. In-rm modem link. Valet serv. X-country ski 2 mi. Cr cds: A, D, DS, MC, V.

D 🔌 🎿 ⚓ 🖥 🐾

★★ **FAIRFIELD INN.** *1800 S Koeller St (54901). 920/233-8504; fax 920/233-8504. www.fairfieldinn.com.* 57 rms, 3 story, 11 suites. June-Sept: S $59.95-$61.95; D $62.95-$77.95; each addl $6; suites $67.95-$79.95; under 18 free; lower rates rest of yr. Crib $5. TV; cable (premium). Indoor pool; whirlpool. Complimentary continental bkfst. Restaurant nearby. Ck-out noon. Meeting rms. Business servs avail. In-rm modem link. Game rm. Some refrigerators, microwaves. Cr cds: A, D, DS, MC, V.

D 🏊 🖥 🐾

★★ **HOLIDAY INN EXPRESS HOTEL AND SUITES.** *2251 Westowne Ave (54904). 920/303-1300; fax 920/303-9330; res 800/465-4329. www.holiday-inn.com.* 68 rms, 3 story, 38 suites. June-Aug: S $75-$99; D $85-$99; suites $99-$175; under 19 free; higher rates special events; lower rates rest of yr. Crib avail. Pet accepted. TV; cable. Complimentary continental bkfst. Complimentary coffee in rms. Restaurant nearby. Ck-out 11 am. Meeting rms. Business servs avail. In-rm modem link. Coin lndry. Free airport transportation. Downhill ski; x-country ski 2 mi. Exercise equipt. Indoor pool; whirlpool. Many refrigerators, microwaves, minibars; some in-rm whirlpools. Cr cds: A, C, D, DS, ER, JCB, MC, V.

D 🔌 🎿 🏊 👤 ✈ 🖥 🐾 SC

★ **HOWARD JOHNSON INN.** *1919 Omro Rd (54902). 414/233-1200; fax 414/233-1135. www.hojo.com.* 100 rms, 2 story. May-Aug: S $55-$75; D $60-$80; each addl $5; under 18 free; lower rates rest of yr. Crib free. Pet accepted, some restrictions. TV; cable. Indoor pool; whirlpool. Coffee in rms. Restaurant adj 6 am-10 pm. Bar 4 pm-1 am. Ck-out noon. Meeting rm. Business servs avail. Private patios, balconies. Cr cds: A, C, D, DS, MC, V.

⭐⭐ **RAMADA INN.** *500 S Koeller St (54902). 920/235-3700; fax 920/235-6268; res 888/298-2054. www.ramada. com.* 125 rms, 2 story. S, D $59.95-89.95; each addl $10; under 18 free; wkend rates. Pet accepted. TV; cable (premium). Indoor pool; whirlpool, poolside serv. Restaurant 7 am-10 pm. Ck-out noon. Coin lndry. Meeting rms. Business center. Bellhops. Valet serv. Sundries. Free airport transportation. Exercise equipt; sauna. Microwaves avail. Cr cds: A, C, D, DS, MC, V.

Hotel

⭐⭐⭐ **PARK PLAZA INTERNATIONAL.** *1 N Main St (54901). 920/231-5000; fax 920/231-8383; toll-free 800/365-4458. www.parkplaza oshkosh.com.* 179 rms, 8 story. S, D $95-$122; suites $145; under 18 free. Pet accepted, some restrictions. TV; cable (premium), VCR avail. Indoor pool; whirlpool, poolside serv. Restaurant 6:30 am-10 pm. Bar 11-1 am. Ck-out noon. Meeting rms. Business servs avail. In-rm modem link. Concierge. Free covered parking. Free airport transportation. Exercise equipt. Health club privileges. Some refrigerators; microwaves avail. View of river. Luxury level. Cr cds: A, D, DS, MC, V.

Resort

⭐⭐⭐ **PIONEER RESORT AND MARINA.** *1000 Pioneer Dr (54902). 920/233-1980; fax 920/426-2115; toll-free 800/683-1980. www.pioneerresort. com.* 192 rms, 2-3 story. Memorial Day-Labor Day: S, D $89-$139; each addl $10; suites $299; under 18 free; package plans. Crib free. TV; cable (premium), VCR avail. 2 pools, 1 indoor; wading pool, whirlpool. Supervised children's activities; ages 5-12. Restaurants 7 am-10 pm. Bar 10:30-1 am. Ck-out noon. Business servs avail. In-rm modem link. Free airport transportation. Tennis. Exercise equipt. Massage. Social dir. Lawn games. Guest bicycles. Some in-rm

whirlpools, microwaves. On lake; boat rentals, marina, sailing. Cr cds: A, D, DS, MC, V.

Restaurants

⭐ **FIN 'N FEATHER SHOWBOATS.** *22 W Main St, Winneconne (54986). 920/582-4305. www.fin-n-feathershowboats.com.* Hrs: 8 am-11 pm; winter months to 10 pm; Sun brunch 9 am-3 pm. Closed Dec 25. Res accepted. Bar to 2:30 am. Bkfst $1.95-$6.95, lunch, dinner $2.65-$24.95. Sun brunch buffet $9.95. Specializes in fish, Angus steak, pasta. Salad bar. Replica of riverboat; excursions avail on Showboat II. Family-owned. Cr cds: A, MC, V.

⭐⭐ **ROBBINS.** *1810 Omro Rd (54901). 920/235-2840.* Hrs: 11 am-10 pm; Fri, Sat to 11 pm; Sun to 9 pm. Closed Dec 25. Res accepted. Continental menu. Bar to 2 am. Lunch $4.45-$7.25, dinner $6.45-$18.95. Child's menu. Specializes in steak, seafood, pasta. Semi-formal atmosphere; elaborate cut-glass panel at entrance. Cr cds: DS, MC, V.

⭐ **WISCONSIN FARMS.** *2450 Washburn (54904). 920/233-7555. www. foodspot.com/wifarmsrest/index.html.* Hrs: 5 am-7 pm; Fri, Sat to 9 pm. Closed Thanksgiving, Dec 25. Res accepted. Bkfst $1.35-$7.95, lunch $3.50-$15.99, dinner $5-$20. Child's menu. Specializes in beef, cheesecake. Country atmosphere. Cr cds: DS, MC, V.

Park Falls

See also Lac du Flambeau, Manitowish Waters

Pop 3,104 **Elev** 1,490 ft
Area code 715 **Zip** 54552

Information Park Falls Area Chamber of Commerce, 400 S 4th Ave S, Suite 8; 715/762-2703 or 800/762-2709

Web www.parkfalls.com

Park Falls has been proclaimed "ruffed grouse capital of the world," since more than 5,000 acres within this area have been used to create a natural habitat for the bird.

What to See and Do

Chequamegon National Forest. Aspen, maple, pine, spruce, balsam, and birch on 855,000 acres. Rainbow Lake and Porcupine Lake Wildernes areas; Great Divide National Scenic Byway. Canoeing on south fork of Flambeau River, the north and south forks of the Chippewa River and Namekagon River; muskellunge, northern pike, walleye, and bass fishing; hunting for deer, bear, and small game; archery. Blueberry and raspberry picking. Swimming, boat launching; Ice Age and North Country national scenic trails; hiking, motorcycle, x-country ski, and snowmobile trails; camping (May-Sept; some sites to Dec) on a first-come basis (fee). Pets must be leashed. Resorts and cabins are located in and near the forest. (Daily) E on WI 29, 70, or US 8 and 2; also NW on WI 13 and 63. A District Ranger office is located here. Phone 715/762-2461. **FREE**

Concrete Park. Fred Smith's concrete and glass statues incl northwoods people, folklore, fantasies, historic personages, Native Americans, angels, and animals. (Daily) 22 mi S via WI 13 in Phillips. Phone 800/762-2709. **FREE**

Old Town Hall Museum. Artifacts of logging era (1876-1930); replica of turn-of-the-century living rm and kitchen; county historic display; old opera house. (June-Labor Day, Fri and Sun afternoons) W 7213 Pine St. Phone 715/762-4571. **FREE**

Post Office Lumberjack Mural. In 1938 the US Government provided artists the opportunity to submit artwork to be displayed in local post offices throughout the country. The Park Falls Post Office features one of the 2,200 that were finally selected. The restored mural, covering one entire wall, depicts the history of logging. (Mon-Sat) 109 N 1st St. Phone 715/762-4575.

Special Event

Flambeau Rama. Downtown. Four-day event incl parades, arts and crafts show, Evergreen Road Run, games. Early Aug. Phone 715/762-2703.

Peshtigo

See also Marinette, Oconto

Pop 3,154 **Elev** 600 ft **Area code** 715 **Zip** 54157
Information City Clerk, City Hall, 331 French St, PO Box 100; 715/582-3041

On October 8, 1871, the same day that the Chicago fire claimed 250 lives, 800 people died in Peshtigo, virtually unpublicized, when the entire town burned to the ground in a disastrous forest fire. A monument to those who died in the fire is located in the Peshtigo Fire Cemetery on Oconto Ave. The city is now a manufacturing center.

What to See and Do

Badger Park. Swimming, fishing (northern, bass, coho salmon); tent and trailer sites (electric hookups), playground. (May-Oct, daily) N Emery Ave on Peshtigo River. Phone 715/582-4321. ¢¢¢

Peshtigo Fire Museum. Local historical items. (Memorial Day-early Oct, daily) 400 Oconto Ave. Phone 715/582-3244. **FREE**

Platteville

(G-3) *See also Mineral Point*

Pop 9,708 **Elev** 994 ft **Area code** 608 **Zip** 53818
Information Chamber of Commerce, 275 US 151 W, PO Box 16; 608/348-8888
Web www.platteville.com

Sport fishing is very popular in the many streams in the area as are ice fishing on the Mississippi River and hunting for upland game, waterfowl, and deer. The world's largest letter

"M" was built on Platteville Mound in 1936 by mining engineering students; it is lit twice each year for the University of Wisconsin-Platteville's homecoming and Miner's Ball.

What to See and Do

Mining Museum. Traces the development of lead and zinc mining in the area. Guided tour incl a walk down into Bevans Lead Mine and a mine train ride (May-Oct, daily). Changing exhibits (Nov-Apr, Mon-Fri). 385 E Main St. Phone 608/348-3301. ¢¢¢ Admission incl

> **Rollo Jamison Museum.** Museum contains a large collection of everyday items collected by Jamison during his lifetime, incl horse-drawn vehicles, tools, and musical instruments. 405 Main St. Phone 608/348-3301.

Stone Cottage. (1837) Much of the interior is the original furnishing of the home; two-ft thick walls of dolomite Galena limestone. Was private residence until 1960s. Corner of West, Madison, and US 81. Phone 608/348-8888. ¢

Special Events

Wisconsin Shakespeare Festival. In Center for the Arts on campus of University of Wisconsin-Platteville. Nightly Tues-Sun; matinees Wed, Sat, and Sun. Phone 608/342-1298. Early July-early Aug. Phone 608/342-1398.

Dairy Days Celebration. Carnival, parade, food, live music, tractor and truck pulls, car show, 4-H exhibits. First wkend after Labor Day. Phone 608/348-8888.

Motels/Motor Lodges

★ ★ **BEST WESTERN.** *420 W Maple St, Lancaster (53813). 608/723-4162; fax 608/723-4843. www.bestwestern. com.* 22 rms, 2 story. S $45; D $62; under 12 free. Crib free. TV; cable (premium). Complimentary continental bkfst. Restaurant nearby. Ck-out 11 am. Coin lndry. Cr cds: A, C, D, DS, MC, V.
🔲 🐾 ▧ 🔥

★ **SUPER 8 - PLATTEVILLE.** *100 WI 80/81 S (53818). 608/348-8800; fax 608/348-7233. www.super8.com.* 46 rms, 2 story. S $41-$47; D $48-$64; each addl $5; suites $125. Crib $4. Pet accepted; $10. TV; cable (premium). Complimentary continental bkfst. Restaurant adj open 24 hrs. Ck-out 11 am. Coin lndry. Meeting rms. Some bathrm phones, refrigerators. Overlooks stream. Gazebo. Cr cds: A, MC, V.
🐾 🔥

B&B/Small Inn

★ **WISCONSIN HOUSE.** *2105 Main St, Hazel Green (53811). 608/854-2233. www.wisconsinhouse.com.* 8 rms, 2 share bath, 3 story, 2 suites. No rm phones. S, D $75-$110; each addl $15; suites $125; wkday rates. TV in sitting rm; cable, VCR avail. Complimentary full bkfst. Dinner avail Sat. Ck-out 10 am, ck-in 3 pm. X-country ski 5 mi. Balconies. Built 1846; former stagecoach stop. Totally nonsmoking. Cr cds: A, DS, MC, V.
▧ ▧ 🔥

Restaurant

★ ★ **TIMBERS.** *670 Ellen St (53818). 608/348-2406.* Hrs: 11 am-1:30 pm, 5-10 pm; Sun 3-9 pm; Sun brunch 10:30 am-2 pm. Res accepted. Continental menu. Bar from 11 am. Lunch $3.75-$7.50, dinner $9.50-$19.95. Sun brunch $11.95. Child's menu. Specializes in steak, seafood. Pianist wkends, organist nightly. Large custom-built electronic theater pipe organ. Cr cds: A, D, DS, MC, V.
🔲 ▧

Portage

(E-4) *See also Baraboo, Prairie du Sac, Wisconsin Dells*

Settled 1835 **Pop** 8,640 **Elev** 800 ft
Area code 608 **Zip** 53901

Information Chamber of Commerce, 301 W Wisconsin St; 608/742-6242 or 800/474-2525

Portage is built on a narrow strip of land separating the Fox and Wisconsin rivers. In the early flow of traffic, goods were hauled from one river to another, providing the name for the city. Before permanent settlement, Fort Winnebago occupied this site; several historic buildings remain. Modern Portage is the business center of Columbia County.

What to See and Do

Fort Winnebago Surgeons' Quarters. Original log house (1828), surviving from Old Fort Winnebago, used by medical officers stationed at the fort. Restored; many original furnishings. Garrison school (1850-1960). (Mid-May-mid-Oct, daily) 1 mi E on WI 33. Phone 608/742-2949. ¢¢

Home of Zona Gale. Greek Revival house built in 1906 for the Pulitzer Prize-winning novelist; some original furnishings. (Mon-Fri, by appt) 506 W Edgewater St. Phone 608/742-7744. ¢

Old Indian Agency House. (1832) Restored house of John Kinzie, US Indian Agent to the Winnebago and an important pioneer; his wife Juliette wrote *Wau-bun,* an early history of their voyages to Fort Winnebago. Period furnishings. (May-Oct, daily; rest of yr, by appt) 1 mi E on WI 33 to Agency House Rd. Phone 608/742-6362. ¢¢

Silver Lake. Swimming, beach, lifeguards, waterskiing, fishing (rainbow trout, largemouth bass, northern pike, panfish, muskie, walleye), boating (public landing); picnic area (shelter), playground. Parking. (Early June-Labor Day, daily) N side of town. Phone 608/742-2176. **FREE**

Skiing. Cascade Mountain Ski Area. Two double, three quad, three triple chairlifts, rope tow; patrol, school, snowmaking; snack bar, cafeteria, dining rm, bar. Twenty-seven runs; longest run one mi; vertical drop 460 ft. Night skiing. (Mid-Nov-Mar, daily) NW on I-90/94, then ¼ mi W on WI 33 to Cascade Mtn Rd. Phone 608/742-5588.

Motel/Motor Lodge

★ ★ **RIDGE MOTOR INN.** *2900 New Pinery Rd (53901). 608/742-5306; fax 608/742-5306; toll-free 877/742-5306.* 113 rms, 3 story, 9 kit. suites. June-Aug: S $49-$69; D $59-$79; each addl $5; kit. suites $100-$135; under 12 free; wkend rates; lower rates rest of yr. Crib $4. TV; cable (premium), VCR avail (movies). Indoor pool;

whirlpool. Complimentary coffee in rms. Restaurant 6 am-10 pm. Bar. Ck-out 11 am. Coin lndry. Meeting rms. Business servs avail. Downhill ski 4 mi; x-country ski 16 mi. Exercise rm; sauna, steam rm. Massage. Game rm. Cr cds: A, C, D, DS, MC, V.

D ⊠ ⇌ 🛪 🛍 🔥

Port Washington

(F-6) *See also Cedarburg, Milwaukee, Sheboygan*

Settled 1830 **Pop** 9,338 **Elev** 612 ft **Area code** 262 **Zip** 53074
Information Tourist Center located in the Pebble House, 126 E Grand Ave, PO Box 153; 262/284-0900 or 800/719-4881
Web www.discoverusa.com/wi/ptwash

Located along the shore of Lake Michigan, Port Washington has many pre-Civil War homes. The Port Washington Marina, one of the finest on Lake Michigan, provides exceptional facilities for boating and fishing.

What to See and Do

Eghart House. Built in 1872; Victorian furnishings from 1850-1900 in hall, parlor, dining-living rm, bedrm, kitchen, and pantry. Tours. (Late May-Labor Day, Sun afternoons; wkdays by appt) 316 Grand Ave. Phone 262/284-2875. ¢

Motels/Motor Lodges

★ ★ **BEST WESTERN HARBOR-SIDE.** *135 E Grand Ave (53074). 262/284-9461; fax 262/284-3169; res 800/528-1234. www.bestwestern.com.* 96 rms, 5 story. S $59-$199; D $89-$199; each addl $10; under 12 free. Crib free. Pet accepted; some restrictions. Sauna. Indoor pool; whirlpool. Complimentary continental bkfst. Restaurant 6:30-10 am. Bar 4 pm-1 am. Ck-out 11 am. Exercise equipt. Meeting rms. Business servs avail. Valet serv. Game rm. On Lake Michigan; dock. Some whirlpools. Cr cds: A, D, DS, MC, V.

⊡ 🐾 ⊠ 🏄 ⊠ 🔥

★ ★ **WEST BEND FANTASUITES.** *2520 W Washington St, West Bend (53095). 262/338-0636; fax 262/338-4290; toll-free 800/727-9727. www. fantasuite.com.* 86 rms, 2 story, 25 theme suites. S $59-$67; D $69-$77; each addl $8; suites $99-$179; under 18 free. Crib free. TV; cable (premium), VCR avail (movies). Sauna. Indoor/outdoor pool; whirlpool. Complimentary continental bkfst. Bar. Ck-out noon. Meeting rms. Business servs avail. Valet serv. Game rm. Uniquely decorated suites with varying themes. Cr cds: A, C, D, DS, MC, V.

⊡ ⊠ ⊠ 🔥

Restaurants

★ ★ **BUCHEL'S COLONIAL HOUSE.** *1000 S Spring St (53074). 262/284-2212.* Hrs: 5-10 pm. Closed Sun-Mon; hols. Res accepted. Continental menu. Bar. Dinner $11.50-$20. Child's menu. Specializes in homemade soup, veal. Colonial, nautical decor. Cr cds: MC, V.

⊡

★ ★ **SMITH BROTHERS' FISH SHANTY.** *100 N Franklin St (53074). 262/284-5592. www.foodspot.com.* Hrs: 11 am-10 pm; Fri, Sat to 11 pm. Closed Thanksgiving, Dec 25. Res accepted. Bar. Lunch $4.95-$10.95, dinner $7.50-$15.50. Child's menu. Specialties: seafood, lemon meringue pie. Outdoor deck dining. Nautical decor. View of Port Washington harbor and marina. Cr cds: DS, MC, V.

⊡ ⊟

Prairie du Chien (F-3)

Settled 1736 **Pop** 5,659 **Elev** 642 ft **Area code** 608 **Zip** 53821

Information Chamber of Commerce, 211 S Main St, PO Box 326; 608/326-2032 or 800/732-1673

Web www.prairieduchien.org

This is the second oldest European settlement in Wisconsin, and dates to June 1673. Marquette and Jolliet discovered the Mississippi River just south of the prairie that the French adventurers then named Prairie du Chien ("prairie of the dog") for Chief Alim, whose name meant "dog." The site became a popular gathering place and trading post. The War of 1812 led to the construction of Fort Shelby and Fort Crawford on an ancient Native American burial ground in the village. Stationed here were Jefferson Davis, later president of the Confederacy, and Zachary Taylor, later president of the United States. In 1826, Hercules Dousman, an agent for John Jacob Astor's American Fur Company, came and built a personal fortune, becoming Wisconsin's first millionaire. When Fort Crawford was moved, Dousman bought the site and erected Villa Louis, the "House of the Mound," a palatial mansion.

What to See and Do

Fort Crawford Museum. Relics of 19th-century medicine, Native American herbal remedies, drugstore, dentist and physicians' offices. Educational health exhibits; Dessloch Theater displays "transparent twins." Dedicated to Dr. William Beaumont, who did some of his famous digestive system studies at Fort Crawford. (May-Oct, daily) 717 S Beaumont Rd. Phone 608/326-6960. ¢¢

★ **Kickapoo Indian Caverns and Native American Museum.** Largest caverns in Wisconsin, used by Native Americans for centuries as a shelter. Sights incl subterranean lake, Cathedral Room, Turquoise Room, Stalactite Chamber, and Chamber of the Lost Waters. Guided tours. (Mid-May-Oct, daily) W 200 Rhein Hollow, 6 mi S on US 18, then 9 mi E on WI 60 in Wauzeka. Phone 608/875-7723. ¢¢¢

Nelson Dewey State Park. This 756-acre park offers nature, hiking trails; camping (hookups). Standard fees. (Daily) 35 mi S via US 18, WI 35 ,and 133 near Cassville. Phone 608/725-5374. Also here is

Stonefield. Named for a rock-studded, 2,000-acre farm that Dewey (first elected governor of WI) established on the bluffs of the Mississippi River. State Agricultural Museum contains display of farm machinery. Site also features recreation of an 1890 Stonefield Village incl blacksmithy, general store, print shop, school, church, and 26 other buildings. Horse-drawn wagon rides (limited hrs; fee). (Memorial Day-early Oct, Wed-Sun) Phone 608/725-5210. ¢¢¢

★ **Villa Louis.** (1870) Built on site of Fort Crawford. Restored to its 19th-century splendor. Contains original furnishings, collection of Victorian decorative arts. Surrounded by extensive grounds, bounded by the Mississippi River. Tours incl Fur Trade Museum. (May-Oct, Tues-Sun) 521 Villa Louis Rd, off US 18. Phone 608/326-2721. ¢¢¢

Wyalusing State Park. A 2,654-acre park at the confluence of the Mississippi and Wisconsin rivers. Sentinel Ridge (500 ft) provides a commanding view of the area; valleys, caves, waterfalls, springs; Native American effigy mounds. Swimming beach nearby, fishing, boating (landing), canoeing; 18 mi of nature, hiking, and x-country ski trails; picnicking, playground, concession, camping (electric hookups, dump station). Nature center; naturalist programs (summer). Standard fees. (Daily) 7 mi SE on US 18, then W on County C, X. Phone 608/996-2261. ¢¢

Motels/Motor Lodges

★★ **BEST WESTERN QUIET HOUSE & SUITES.** *Hwys 18 & 35 S (53821). 608/326-4777; fax 608/326-4787. www.bestwestern.com.* 42 suites, 2 story. S $91; D $111; each addl $10. Pet accepted. TV; cable (premium). Indoor pool; whirlpool. Restaurant opp 5 am-10 pm. Ck-out 11 am. Business servs avail. In-rm modem link. Sundries. Exercise equipt. Some in-rm whirlpools. Cr cds: A, C, D, DS, MC, V.
D 🏌 ☒ 🏊 ☒ 🐾

★ **BRISBOIS MOTOR INN.** *533 N Marquette Rd (53821). 608/326-8404; fax 608/326-0001; toll-free 800/356-5850. www.brisboismotorinn.com.* 46 rms. S $49-$59; D $67-$84; each addl $5; under 17 free. Crib free. TV; cable (premium). Heated pool. Playground.

Complimentary continental bkfst. Restaurant adj 6 am-11 pm. Ck-out 11 am. Meeting rm. Free airport transportation. X-country ski 2 mi. Cr cds: A, D, DS, MC, V.
D ☒ ✈ ☒ 🐾

★ **HOLIDAY MOTEL.** *1010 S Marquette Rd (53821). 608/326-2448; fax 608/326-2413; toll-free 800/962-3883. www.holidaymotelpdc.com.* 18 rms, 1-2 story. May-Oct: S $45-$55; D $60-$75; suite $98; each addl $5; under 16 free; lower rates rest of yr. Crib free. TV; cable (premium). Complimentary coffee. Restaurant nearby. Ck-out 11 am. Business servs avail. Cr cds: A, DS, MC, V.
D ☒ 🐾

★ **PRAIRIE MOTEL.** *1616 S Marquette Rd (53821). 608/326-6461; toll-free 800/526-3776.* 32 rms. May-Oct: S $49-$55; D $55-$65; family rates; lower rates rest of yr. Pet accepted. TV; cable (premium). Heated pool. Playground. Complimentary coffee in rms. Ck-out 11 am. X-country ski 2 mi. Miniature golf. Lawn games. Some refrigerators. Picnic tables, grills. Cr cds: DS, MC, V.
🐾 ☒ ☒ ☒ 🐾

Prairie du Sac

See also Baraboo, Madison, Spring Green

Pop 2,380 **Elev** 780 ft **Area code** 608 **Zip** 53578

Information Sauk Prairie Area Chamber of Commerce, 207 Water St, Sauk City 53583; 608/643-4168

A favorite launching area for canoeists on the Wisconsin River. It is possible to see bald eagles south of the village at Ferry Bluff, where many of them winter. Watching them feed on fish in the open water is a favorite winter pastime.

What to See and Do

Wollersheim Winery. (1857) Guided tours, wine tasting, cheese, gift shop. (Daily; closed hols) 7876 WI 188. Phone 608/643-6515. ¢¢

Special Event

Harvest Festival. Wollersheim Winery. Grape stompers competition; music; cork toss; grape spitting contest; foods. First full wkend Oct. Phone 608/643-6515.

Racine

(G-6) *See also Burlington, Kenosha, Milwaukee*

Founded 1834 **Pop** 84,298 **Elev** 626 ft
Area code 262
Information Racine County Convention and Visitors Bureau, 345 Main St, 53403; 262/634-3293 or 800/C-RACINE
Web www.racine.org

Racine is situated on a thumb of land jutting into Lake Michigan. The largest concentration of people of Danish descent in the United States can be found here; in fact, West Racine is known as "Kringleville" because of its Danish pastry. There are more than 300 manufacturing firms located here.

What to See and Do

Architectural tour. A 45-min tour of SC Johnson Wax world headquarters designed by Frank Lloyd Wright (Fri; closed hols). 1525 Howe St. Res required. Phone 262/260-2154. **FREE**

Charles A. Wustum Museum of Fine Arts. Painting, photography, graphics, crafts, and sculpture displays; works of local, regional, and nationally known artists are featured. Permanent and changing exhibits. Also park and formal gardens. (Daily; closed hols) 2519 Northwestern Ave. Phone 262/636-9177. **FREE**

Racine Heritage Museum. Cultural history of Racine incl permanent and temporary exhibits, archive, and photographic collection. (Tues-Sat; closed hols) 701 S Main St. Phone 262/636-3926. **FREE**

Racine Zoological Gardens. Extensive animal collection, picnic area, swimming (beach). (Daily; closed Dec 25) 2131 N Main St. Phone 262/636-9189. **FREE**

Special Event

Salmon-A-Rama. Lakefront. Fishing contest. Two wkends. Mid-July. Phone 262/636-9229.

Motels/Motor Lodges

★ **KNIGHTS INN.** *1149 Oakes Rd (53406). 262/886-6667; fax 262/886-6667; toll-free 800/418-8977. www. knightsinn.com. 107 rms, 1 story.*

Cattle grazing

June-Labor Day: S $40-$49; D $49-$59; each addl $7; suites $47.95-$58.95; kit. units $58.95-$62.95; under 18 free; lower rates rest of yr. Crib free. Pet accepted. TV; cable (premium), VCR avail (movies). Complimentary continental bkfst. Restaurant nearby. Ck-out noon. Cr cds: A, D, DS, MC, V.

D ⊕ ⊠ ⊠ SC

★ **RIVERSIDE DAYS INN.** *3700 Northwestern Ave (53405). 262/637-*

9311; fax 262/637-4575; toll-free
888/242-6494. www.daysinn.com. 112
rms, 2 story. S $49-$89; D $59-$99;
each addl $6; under 18 free. Crib
free. Pet accepted. TV; cable (premium). Heated pool. Complimentary
coffee in rms. Restaurant 6 am-2 pm,
5:30-9 pm. Bar 4 pm-2 am. Ck-out 11
am. Coin lndry. Meeting rms. Business servs avail. In-rm modem link.
Bellhops. Valet serv. Sundries. Exercise equipt. X-country ski 3 mi.
Game rm. Lawn games. Picnic tables.
On Root River. Cr cds: A, C, D, DS,
MC, V.

D 🔦 🛄 🏊 🎿 🕴 🛄 🐾 SC

Hotel

★★★ **MARRIOTT RACINE.** 7111
Washington Ave (53406). 262/886-
6100; fax 262/886-1048. www.
marriott.com. 222 rms, 5 story. S, D
$145-$175; each addl $20; under 17
free. Crib avail. Indoor pool. TV;
cable (premium), VCR avail. Complimentary coffee, newspaper in rms.
Restaurant 6 am-10 pm. Ck-out
noon. Meeting rms. Business center.
Gift shop. Exercise rm. Some refrigerators, minibars. Cr cds: A, C, D, DS,
MC, V.

🐾 🛄 🕴 🕴

Restaurants

★ **GREAT WALL.** 6025 Washington
Ave (53406). 262/886-9700. Hrs: 11
am-8:30 pm; Fri to 9:30 pm; Sat 4-
9:30 pm; Sun 11 am-2 pm. Closed
Mon; hols. Res accepted. Pan-Asian
menu. Bar. Lunch $4.50-$5.25, dinner $6.75-$15.50. Buffet 11 am-2 pm:
lunch $5.25, Sun $6.50. Specializes
in Szechwan and Mandarin dishes.
Chinese decor. Cr cds: A, DS, MC, V.

D ➡

★★ **HOB NOB.** 277 S Sheridan Rd
(53403). 262/552-8008. Hrs: 5-10 pm;
Sun from 4 pm. Closed Dec 24, 25;
also Super Bowl Sun. Res accepted.
Bar. Dinner $9.95-$19.95. Specializes
in seafood, steak, duck. View of Lake
Michigan. Cr cds: A, D, DS, MC, V.

D ➡

Reedsburg

(F-4) See also Baraboo, Portage, Prairie
du Sac, Wisconsin Dells

Pop 5,834 **Elev** 926 ft **Area code** 608
Zip 53959
Information Chamber of Commerce,
240 Railroad St, PO Box 142;
608/524-2850 or 800/844-3507

Self-proclaimed "butter capital of
America," Reedsburg is the home of
one of the largest butter producing
plants in the world. The Wisconsin
Dairies plant produces more than
50,000,000 pounds of butter here
each year.

What to See and Do

Carr Valley Cheese Factory. Observation area for viewing production of
cheddar cheese. (Mon-Sat; closed Jan
1, Dec 25) 9 mi W on County K, G
in La Valle. Phone 608/986-2781.
FREE

Foremost Farms. Viewing window
for butter making process. (Mon-Fri)
501 S Pine. Phone 608/524-2351.
FREE

**Historical Society Log Village and
Museum.** Log cabin with loft, Oetz-
man log house (1876), log church
and library, one-rm schoolhouse,
blacksmith shop; completely furnished kitchen, living rm, and
bedrm; apothecary shop; Native
American and army memorabilia.
Located on 52 acres of pine forest
and farm fields. (June-Sept, Sat-Sun)
3 mi E via WI 33. Phone 608/524-
2807. **DONATION**

Museum of Norman Rockwell Art.
One of the largest collections of Norman Rockwell memorabilia spans the
artist's 65-yr career. Video. Gift shop.
(Mid-May-Oct, daily; rest of yr, Tues-
Sun; closed hols) 227 S Park. Phone
608/524-2123. ¢¢¢

Park Lane Model Railroad Museum.
Features working model railroad lay-
outs; hundreds of individual cars on
display. (Mid-May-mid-Sept, daily) 8
mi E on WI 23 at Herwig Rd. Phone
608/254-8050. ¢¢

Special Event

Butter Festival. Nishan Park. Four-
day festival with parade, tractor and

horse pulls, carnival rides, events, arts and crafts, food. Six days mid-June. Phone 608/524-2850.

Rhinelander

(B-5) *See also Crandon, Eagle River, Minocqua, Three Lakes*

Settled 1880 **Pop** 7,427 **Elev** 1,560 ft **Area code** 715 **Zip** 54501
Information Rhinelander Area Chamber of Commerce, 450 W Kemp St, PO Box 795; 715/365-7464 or 800/236-4386
Web www.ci.rhinelander.wi.us

Rhinelander is the gateway to the "world's most concentrated lake region." It lies at the junction of the Wisconsin and Pelican rivers. 232 lakes, 11 trout streams, and two rivers within a 12-mile radius make the city a thriving resort center. Fishing is good in lakes and streams, and there is hunting for upland game and deer. The logging industry, which built this area, still thrives and the many miles of old logging roads are excellent for hiking and mountain biking. Paved bicycle trails, cross-country skiing, and snowmobiling are also popular in this north-woods area.

Rhinelander is headquarters for the Nicolet National Forest (see THREE LAKES); phone 715/362-3415.

What to See and Do

⭐ **Rhinelander Logging Museum.** Most complete displays of old-time lumbering in Midwest. On grounds are "Five Spot," last narrow-gauge railroad locomotive to work Wisconsin's northwoods, and a restored depot dating from late 1800s. Also on premises is one-rm schoolhouse. Museum houses the "hodag," called "the strangest animal known to man." Created as a hoax, it has become the symbol of the city. (Memorial Day-Labor Day, daily) In Pioneer Park, on US 8, WI 47. Phone 715/369-5004. **DONATION** Also on the grounds is

Civilian Conservation Corps Museum. Houses photographs,

memorabilia, artifacts, tools, and papers that record much of the history of the CCC. The manner of clothing worn, how the enrolee was housed and fed, and the tools used in project work are on the display. (Last wk May-first wk Sept, daily) Phone 800/236-4386. **FREE**

Special Events

Art Fair. Courthouse lawn. Second Sat June. Phone 715/365-7464.
Hodag Country Festival. Three-day country music festival featuring top-name entertainment. Phone 800/762-3803. Mid-July. Phone 715/369-1300.
Oktoberfest. Downtown. German music, food. Phone 800/236-4386. Mid-Oct. Phone 715/365-7464.

Motels/Motor Lodges

★ ★ **AMERICINN.** *648 W Kemp St (54501). 715/369-9600; fax 715/369-9613; toll-free 800/634-3444. www. americinn.com.* 52 rms, 3 with shower only, 2 story. Mid-June-Labor Day: S $59-$69; D $67-$77; each addl $6; suites $105.90-$110.90; under 12 free; lower rates rest of yr. Pet accepted, some restrictions. TV; cable (premium), VCR avail. Sauna. Indoor pool; whirlpool. Complimentary continental bkfst. Restaurant opp 6 am-11 pm. Ck-out 11 am. Meeting rm. Business servs avail. Sundries. Valet serv. Coin lndry. X-country ski 1 mi. Putting green. Some refrigerators, in-rm whirlpools. Cr cds: A, D, DS, MC, V.
🄳 🐾 🐃 🏊 ⛷ ⛄ 🐾 🅂🄲

★ ★ **BEST WESTERN CLARIDGE MOTOR INN.** *70 N Stevens St (54501). 715/362-7100; fax 715/362-3883; res 800/427-1377. www. bestwestern.com.* 80 rms, 2-4 story. July-Oct: S $60-$70; D $70-$80; each addl $8; suites $84-$115; under 18 free. Pet accepted. TV; cable. Indoor pool; whirlpool. Coffee in rms. Restaurant 6:30 am-2 pm, 5-10 pm; Sun, hols to 9 pm. Rm serv 5-9 pm. Bar 11 am-2 pm, 4 pm-midnight. Ck-out 11 am. Lndry facilities. Meeting rms. Business servs avail. Valet serv. Sundries. Free airport transportation.

X-country ski 5 mi. Exercise equipt. Cr cds: A, C, D, DS, MC, V.

★★ **HOLIDAY INN.** *668 W Kemp St (54501).* 715/369-3600; fax 715/369-3601; toll-free 800/465-4329. *www.holiday-inn.com.* 101 rms, 2 story. S $55-$64; D $64-$79; each addl $8. Crib free. Pet accepted. TV; cable, VCR avail (movies). Indoor pool; whirlpool. Restaurant 6:30 am-2 pm, 5-10 pm; Sun from 7 am. Bar 11:30 am-midnight; entertainment. Ck-out 11 am. Coin lndry. Meeting rms. Business servs avail. Sundries. Free airport transportation. Downhill ski 20 mi; x-country ski 5 mi. Golf, 1 mi. Exercise equipt; sauna. Game rm. Cr cds: A, C, D, DS, JCB, MC, V.

Resorts

★ **HOLIDAY ACRES RESORT.** *4060 S Shore Dr (54501).* 715/369-1500; fax 715/369-3665; toll-free 800/261-1500. *www.holidayacres.com.* 30 rms in 2-story lodge, 30 kit. cottages (1-4 bedrm; boat incl; maid serv avail). Lodge, mid-June-late Aug, also Fri, Sat Dec 24-mid-Mar: S, D $94-$134; each addl $11.50; cottages for 2-8, $89-$264; winter wkend packages; lower rates rest of yr. Pet accepted; $6. TV; cable, VCR avail (movies). Indoor pool, whirlpools, sauna. Playground. Coffee in rms. Dining rm 5 am-10 pm. Box lunches, coffee shop. Bar 4 pm-1 am. Ck-out 11 am (cottages in summer, 10 am). Meeting rms. Business servs avail. Grocery, package store 3 mi. Gift shop in season. Airport transportation. Tennis. Sand beach; boats, motors, rafts, canoes, sailboat, windsurfing. Downhill ski 20 mi; x-country ski on site. Snowmobile trails. Bicycles. Lawn games. Fireplace in 24 cottages, 2 lodge rms; some screened porches. 1000 acres on Lake Thompson. Cr cds: A, C, D, DS, MC, V.

★ **KAFKA'S RESORT.** *4281 W Lake George Rd (54501).* 715/369-2929; toll-free 800/426-6674. *www.kafkas-resort.com.* 10 kit. cottages (2-3 bedrm; boat incl). No A/C. Mid-June-Aug: cottages for 2-6, $500-$750/wk; lower rates rest of yr. TV; cable. Play-

ground. Bar 1 pm-midnight. Ck-out 9 am, ck-in 2 pm. Grocery, package store 2 mi. No maid serv. Free airport transportation. Private beach, swimming; boats, motors, canoes. Downhill ski 20 mi; x-country ski 5 mi. Tennis, 2 mi. Snowmobiling. Lawn games. Rec rm. Fishing guides, clean and store area. Picnic tables, grills. Cr cds: A, MC, V.

Restaurants

★★ **RHINELANDER CAFE AND PUB.** *33 N Brown St (54501).* 715/362-2918. Hrs: 8 am-11 pm. Closed Thanksgiving, Dec 25. Bar 10:30-1 am. Bkfst $1.50-$5.75, lunch $5-$10, dinner $8-$25. Child's menu. Specializes in prime rib, roast duck. Nautical decor. Family-owned. Cr cds: A, D, DS, MC, V.

★ **TULA'S.** *232 S Courtney (54501).* 715/369-5248. *www.newnorth.net/taselberg/tulas.* Hrs: 6 am-9 pm. Closed Dec 25. Res accepted. Bar 11 am-midnight. Bkfst $2.29-$6.95, lunch $2.79-$6.99, dinner $2.79-$14.95. Child's menu. Specializes in fish. Own soups. Outdoor dining. Cr cds: DS, MC, V.

Rice Lake

(C-2) *See also Spooner*

Pop 7,998 **Elev** 1,140 ft
Area code 715 **Zip** 54868
Information Rice Lake Area Chamber of Commerce, 37 S Main St; 715/234-2126 or 800/523-6318
Web www.chamber.rice-lake.wi.us

Formerly headquarters for the world's largest hardwood mills, Rice Lake has an economy based on industry and retail trade. The city and lake were named for nearby wild rice sloughs, which were an important Sioux and Chippewa food source. Surrounded by 84 lakes, the city is in a major recreation area.

Special Events

Aquafest. June. Phone 800/523-6318.
County Fair. July. Phone 800/523-6318.

Motels/Motor Lodges

★★ **AMERICINN MOTEL AND SUITES.** *2906 Pioneer Ave (54868). 715/234-9060; fax 715/736-9060; res 800/634-3444. www.americinn.com.* 43 rms, 2 story. June-Sept: S $52-$61; D $58-$79; each addl $6; under 13 free; lower rates rest of yr. Crib free. TV; cable (premium). Complimentary continental bkfst. Restaurant nearby. Ck-out 11 am. Business servs avail. In-rm modem link. Downhill ski 10 mi; x-country ski 1 mi. Indoor pool; whirlpool. Playground. Some refrigerators. Cr cds: A, C, D, DS, MC, V.
⬛ 🏊 〰️ 🎿 🔥 **SC**

★★ **CURRIER'S LAKEVIEW MOTEL.** *2010 E Sawyer St (54868). 715/234-7474; fax 715/736-1501; toll-free 800/433-5253. www.curriers lakeview.com.* 19 rms, 2 story, 8 kits. Mid-May-mid-Sept: S $37-$65; D $52-$85; kit. units for 2-8, $4 addl; lower rates rest of yr. Crib $2. Pet accepted. TV; cable (premium). Continental bkfst. Ck-out 11 am. Meeting rm. Free airport transportation. Downhill/x-country ski 18 mi. Snowmobile trails. Refrigerators. Private beach; boats, motors, dockage; paddle boats, canoes, pontoons. Picnic tables, grill. Wooded grounds; on lake; park adj. Cr cds: A, DS, MC, V.
🚣 🐾 🎿 ✈️ 🎿 🔥

★ **SUPER 8.** *115 2nd St, Chetek (54728). 715/924-4888; fax 715/924-2538. www.super8.com.* 40 rms, 2 story. June-Sept: S $60-$68; D $70-$85; each addl $6; under 12 free; lower rates rest of yr. Crib free. TV; cable (premium). Complimentary continental bkfst. Restaurant nearby. Ck-out 11 am. Business servs avail. In-rm modem link. Indoor pool; whirlpool. Cr cds: A, D, DS, MC, V.
⬛ 🐾 〰️ 🎿 🔥

B&B/Small Inn

★★★★ **CANOE BAY.** *115 2nd St, Chetek (54728). 715/924-4594; fax 715/924-4594. www.canoebay.com.* This secluded, 280-acre wilderness spot might seem an unlikely location for luxury at its finest, but this resort delivers. Choose from the five-room inn, the four-room lodge, or several cottages, all with Adirondack or Frank Lloyd Wright-inspired design and completely wooded or lake-view locations. The exceptional restaurant provides breakfast in bed, gourmet lunch baskets, and a four-course, daily-changing dinner menu. 19 units, 5 rms in inn, 4 rms in lodge, 10 cottages. S, D $270-$725. Adults only. TV; cable (premium), VCR (movies). Complimentary bkfst, coffee in rms. Restaurant sitting 6-8 pm. Rm serv noon-8 pm. Ck-out 11 am, ck-in 3 pm. Concierge serv. Business servs avail. 9-hole golf privileges. X-country ski on site. Ice skating. Spa. Exercise equipt. Refrigerators; microwaves avail. Picnic tables. On 2 lakes. Totally nonsmoking. Cr cds: A, DS, MC, V.
⬛ 🐾 🎿 🎿 🎿 〰️ 🔥

Restaurants

★ **MARK'S.** *2900 S Main (54868). 715/234-3660.* Hrs: 8 am-9 pm; Sat to 5:30 pm; Sun to 5 pm. Closed Thanksgiving, Dec 25. Res accepted. Bkfst $1.79-$5.29, lunch $3.95-$5.95, dinner $5.95-$7.95. Specializes in chicken, seafood. Informal family atmosphere. Cr cds: A, D, DS, MC, V.
⬛ 🍽️

★ **NORSKE NOOK.** *2900 Pioneer Ave (54868). 715/234-1733. www.norske nook.com.* Hrs: 5:30 am-10 pm; Sun 8 am-8 pm. Closed Thanksgiving, Dec 25. Res accepted. Bkfst, lunch, dinner $3.25-$12. Child's menu. Specialzies in hot sandwiches, pies. Old-style family restaurant. Cr cds: DS, MC, V.
⬛

Richland Center

(F-3) *See also Reedsburg, Spring Green*

Settled 1849 **Pop** 5,018 **Elev** 731 ft
Area code 608 **Zip** 53581

Information Richland Chamber of Commerce, 174 S Central, PO Box 128; 608/647-6205 or 800/422-1318
Web www.richlandcounty.com

This is the birthplace of famed architect Frank Lloyd Wright (1867).

What to See and Do

Eagle Cave. Large onyx cavern contains stalactites, stalagmites, fossils. Camping (hookups; fee); marked trails, picnicking, deer farm; fishing, swimming, horseback riding; hay rides; game rm. 220 acres. Guided cave tours (Memorial Day-Labor Day, daily) 12 mi SW via WI 80 and 60. Phone 608/537-2988. ¢¢

Special Events

Wisconsin High School State Rodeo Finals. Late June. Phone 608/647-6859.
Richland County Fair. Early-Sept. Phone 608/647-6859.

St. Croix Falls

Settled 1837 **Pop** 1,640 **Elev** 900 ft
Area code 715 **Zip** 54024

Headquarters for the Interstate State Park, St. Croix Falls has become a summer and winter resort area. The oldest community in Polk County, it depends on farming, industry, dairying, and the tourist trade. Lions Park north of town has picnicking and boat launching, and there are many miles of groomed snowmobile trails in Polk County. Fishing for catfish, walleye, sturgeon, and panfish is excellent in the St. Croix River and the many area lakes.

What to See and Do

Crex Meadows Wildlife Area. This 30,000-acre state-owned wildlife area is a prairie-wetlands habitat; breeding wildlife species incl giant Canada geese, 11 species of ducks, sharp-tailed grouse, sandhill cranes, bald eagles, ospreys, trumpeter swans, and loons. Wildlife observation and photography; guided (by appt) and self-guided tours. Canoeing; hunting, trapping (fall); hiking, picnicking,

camping (Sept-Dec). (Daily) N via WI 87, 1 mi N of Grantsburg. Phone 715/463-2896. **FREE**

Governor Knowles State Forest. A 33,000-acre forest extending north and south along the St. Croix River. Fishing, boating, canoeing; hiking, bridle, snowmobile (fee), and x-country ski trails; picnicking, group camping. (Daily) Headquarters 27 mi N via WI 87, just N of Grantsburg on WI 70. Phone 715/463-2898.

⭐ **Interstate State Park.** A 1,325-acre park; Wisconsin's oldest state park. Swimming, fishing, boating, canoeing; nature, hiking, and x-country ski trails; picnicking, camping (dump station). Permanent naturalist; naturalist programs. Part of the Ice Age National Scientific Reserve. The Reserve operates a visitor center here. (Daily) Standard fees. 2 blks S of US 8 on WI 35. Phone 715/483-3747. ¢¢¢
In the park is

    The Gorge of the St. Croix River. Forms the Dalles of the St. Croix, with volcanic rock formation, sheer rock walls, some over 200 ft tall; series of potholes, wooded hills and valley; state trout hatchery is located just N of Interstate Park (daily).

St. Croix National Scenic Riverway. Northern unit, 200 mi of scenic riverway in mixed pine and hardwood forest. Southern unit, 52 mi of scenic riverway in mixed pine and hardwood forests, high rocky bluffs. National Park Visitor centers (daily). Phone 715/483-3284.

Skiing. Trollhaugen Ski Resort. Resort has three chairlifts, seven rope tows; patrol, school, rentals; snowmaking; bars, cafeterias, restaurant. 22 runs. (Early Nov-Mar, daily) 3 mi S on WI 35 to Dresser, then ¾ mi E on County F. Phone 715/755-2955. ¢¢¢¢

Motel/Motor Lodge

★ ★ **DALLES HOUSE MOTEL.** WI 35 S (54024). 715/483-3206; fax 715/483-3207. 50 rms, 2 story. S, D $43-$85; each addl $6. Crib $7. Pet accepted. Sauna. Indoor pool; whirlpools. Restaurant 8 am-11 pm. Ck-out 11 am. Coin lndry. Meeting rm. Business servs avail. In-rm modem link. Downhill ski 3 mi; x-country ski ¼

mi. Interstate State Park adj. Cr cds:
A, MC, V.

St. Germain

See also Eagle River, Minocqua, Three Lakes, Woodruff

Pop 1,100 **Elev** 1,627 ft
Area code 715 **Zip** 54558

Cottage Colony

★ ★ **ESCH'S SERENITY BAY.** *1276 Halberstadt Rd (54558). 715/479-8866. www.eschsresort.com.* 9 kit. cottages (2-3 bedrm). No A/C. Mid-June-mid-Aug: wkly (with boat), 4-6 persons, $975-$1,325; each addl $100; daily rates; lower rates May-mid-June, mid-Aug-Oct. Closed rest of yr. No maid serv. Linens rented. Crib $10. TV; cable (premium), VCR avail. Playground. Restaurant nearby. Ck-out 9 am, ck-in 3 pm. Grocery, coin lndry, package store 2½ mi. Business servs avail. Tennis. 500-ft sand beach; waterskiing, equipt; boats, motors, paddleboat, pontoon boat. Lawn games. Fireplaces. Private porches, decks. Picnic tables, barbecue pits. Set in pines on shore of Little St. Germain Lake. Cr cds: A, MC, V.

Restaurants

★ **ELIASON'S SOME PLACE ELSE.** *438 WI 70 (54558). 715/542-3779.* Hrs: 5-9 pm. Closed Mon; Dec 24-25; also Nov. Bar. Dinner $4.95-$19.95. Fri fish fry $7.50. Specializes in prime rib, lobster. Entertainment Fri, Sat. Country decor. Gift shop. Family-owned. Cr cds: MC, V.

★ **SPANG'S.** *WI 70 (54558). 715/479-9400.* Hrs: 5-10 pm. Closed Easter, Thanksgiving, Dec 24-25. Italian, American menu. Bar. Dinner $7.25-$15.25. Child's menu. Specializes in pasta, pizza. Garden lounge. Old World atmosphere. Family-owned. Cr cds: A, DS, MC, V.

Sayner

See also Boulder Junction, Eagle River, Minocqua, Woodruff

Pop 450 **Elev** 1,675 ft **Area code** 715
Zip 54560

Centrally located in the Northern Highland-American Legion State Forest and boasting 42 sparkling lakes, the Sayner-Star Lake area offers camping, waterskiing, and excellent all-year fishing. Considered the birthplace of the snowmobile, Sayner is near miles of scenic well-groomed trails.

Resort

★ ★ **FROELICH'S SAYNER LODGE.** *3221 Plum Lake Dr (54560). 715/542-3261. www.saynerlodge.com.* 11 lodge rms, 2 story, 25 cottages (1-3 bedrm). No A/C exc public rms. Late May-Oct: S, D $50-$60; cabana: $70; cottage $80-$210. Closed rest of yr. Pet accepted, some restrictions. TV; VCR avail. Heated pool. Playground. Complimentary continental bkfst. Bar 4 pm-12:30 am; closed Mon, Tues. Ck-out 10 am, ck-in 2 pm. Grocery, coin lndry, package store ¾ mi. Airport transportation. Tennis. Boats, motors, canoe, pontoon boat; waterskiing. Lawn games. Hiking trails. Rec rm. Fishing guides. Library. Screened porch in most cottages; some fireplaces. On Plum Lake. Cr cds: MC, V.

Shawano (D-5)

Settled 1843 **Pop** 7,598 **Elev** 821 ft
Area code 715 **Zip** 54166
Information Chamber of Commerce, 1404 E Green Bay St, PO Box 38; 715/524-2139 or 800/235-8528
Web www.shawano.com

A city born of the lumber boom, Shawano is now a retail trade center for the small surrounding farms and produces dairy and wood products.

What to See and Do

Shawano Lake. Lake is four mi wide and seven mi long. Fishing, boating (ramps); ice fishing, hunting. 300 mi of snowmobile trails, 8 mi of x-country ski trails. Camping (fee). 2 mi E on WI 22. Phone 800/235-8528.

Special Event

Flea Market. Shawano County Fairgrounds. Phone 715/526-9769. Sun, Apr-Oct.

Motels/Motor Lodges

★ ★ **AMERICINN.** *1330 E Green Bay St (54166). 715/524-5111; fax 715/526-3626; res 800/634-3444. www.americinn.com.* 47 rms, 2 story. S, D $54.90-$64.90; each addl $6-$10; suites $69.90-$103.90; under 12 free. Crib free. TV; cable (premium), VCR avail. Sauna. Indoor pool; whirlpool. Complimentary continental bkfst. Restaurant nearby. Ck-out 11 am. Meeting rms. Business servs avail. In-rm modem link. Refrigerator in suites. Cr cds: A, D, DS, MC, V.
D ⊠ ⊠ 🐾

★ ★ **BEST WESTERN VILLAGE HAUS.** *201 N Airport Dr (54166). 715/526-9595; fax 715/526-9826; toll-free 800/553-4479. www.bestwestern. com.* 89 rms, 2 story. June-Aug: S, D $65-$106; each addl $6; under 13 free; lower rates rest of yr. Crib free. TV; cable. Indoor pool; whirlpool. Complimentary continental bkfst. Restaurant 6 am-9 pm; Sat 7 am-10 pm. Bar 3 pm-2 am. Ck-out 11 am. Meeting rms. Business servs avail. Sundries. X-country ski 5 mi. Game rm. Near lake, river; beach swimming. Cr cds: A, C, D, DS, MC, V.
D ⊠ ⊠ ⊠ SC

Restaurant

★ **ANELLO'S TORCHLIGHT.** *1276 E Green Bay St (54166). 715/526-5680.* Hrs: 11 am-2 pm, 4-10 pm; Mon from 4 pm; Fri to 11 pm, Sat 4-11 pm; Sun 4-9 pm. Closed Thanksgiving. Res accepted. Italian, American menu. Bar. Lunch $4-$7.95. Complete meals: dinner $5.95-$26.95.

Salad bar. Castle motif; full suit of armor. Cr cds: A, DS, MC, V.

Sheboygan

(E-6) *See also Manitowoc, Port Washington*

Settled 1818 **Pop** 49,676 **Elev** 633 ft **Area code** 262 and 920
Information Sheboygan County Convention & Visitors Bureau, 712 Riverfront Dr, 53081; 920/457-9495, ext 900 or 800/457-9497, ext 900
Web www.sheboygan.org

A harbor city on the west shore of Lake Michigan, Sheboygan is a major industrial city and a popular fishing port.

What to See and Do

John Michael Kohler Arts Center. Changing contemporary art exhibitions, galleries, shop, historic house; theater, dance, and concert series. (Daily; closed hols) 608 New York Ave. Phone 262/458-6144. **FREE**

Kohler-Andrae State Park. Incl 1,000 acres of woods and sand dunes. Swimming, bathhouse; nature and x-country ski trails, picnicking, playgrounds, concession, camping (105 sites, electric hookups, dump station), winter camping. Nature center (closed winter). Standard fees. (Daily) S on I-43 exit 120, on Lake Michigan. Phone 920/451-4080. ¢¢

Lakeland College. (1862) 2,500 students. On campus are Lakeland College Museum (Wed-Thurs, also by appt; free) and Bradley Fine Arts Gallery (Mon-Fri afternoon during school yr; free). 10 mi NW on County M off County A (access to County A from WI 42 and 57). Phone 262/565-2111.

Scenic drives. Along lakeshore on Broughton Dr, Riverfront Dr, Lakeshore Dr.

Sheboygan County Historical Museum. Exhibit center plus Judge David Taylor home (1850); two-story loghouse (1864) furnished with pioneer items; restored barn; 1867 cheese factory. (Apr-Oct, Tues-Sat; closed Good Friday, Easter, July

4) 3110 Erie Ave. Phone 920/458-1103. ¢¢

Special Events

Polar Bear Swim. Deland Park. More than 350 swimmers brave Lake Michigan's icy winter waters. Jan 1. Phone 920/457-9491.

Great Cardboard Boat Regatta. Rotary Riverview Park. Human-powered cardboard craft compete in various classes for fun and prizes. Part of city-wide Independence Day festivities. July 4. Phone 920/458-6144.

Outdoor Arts Festival. On the grounds of John Michael Kohler Arts Center. Multi-arts event features works by 125 juried artists; demonstrations, entertainment, refreshments. Third full wkend July. Phone 920/458-6144.

Holland Fest. 1 mi W off I-43 via exit 113 in Cedar Grove. Dutch traditions: wooden-shoe dancing, street scrubbing, folk fair, food, music, art fair, parade. Phone 920/668-6118. Last Fri and Sat July. Phone 920/457-9491.

Bratwurst Day. Kiwanis Park. Early Aug. Phone 920/457-9491.

Motels/Motor Lodges

★ ★ **BAYMONT INN.** *2932 Kohler Memorial Dr (53081).* 920/457-2321; fax 920/457-0827; toll-free 800/301-0200. www.baymontinn.com. 98 rms, 2 story. S $46-$52; D $52-$60; under 18 free. Crib free. Pet accepted, some restrictions. TV; cable (premium). Complimentary continental bkfst. Complimentary coffee in rms. Restaurants adj 6 am-11 pm. Ck-out noon. Business servs avail. Cr cds: A, MC, V.
🅳 🐾 ⛱ 🔥 **SC**

★ **BEST VALUE INN PARKWAY.** *3900 Motel Rd (53081).* 920/458-8338; fax 920/459-7470; toll-free 888/315-2378. www.bestvalueinn.com. 32 rms. June-Sept: S, D $69.90-$85.90; each addl $3; higher rates special events; lower rates rest of yr. Crib $6. Pet accepted. TV; cable (premium). Complimentary coffee in rms. Restaurant nearby. Ck-out 11 am. Business servs avail. Sundries. X-country ski 2 mi. Refrigerators;

microwaves avail. Picnic tables, grills. Cr cds: A, MC, V.
🐾 ⛱ 🔥

Restaurants

★ ★ **CITY STREETS RIVERSIDE.** *712 Riverfront Dr (53081).* 920/457-9050. Hrs: 11 am-2 pm, 5-9 pm; Fri to 10 pm; Sat 5-10 pm. Closed Sun; hols. Res accepted. Bar to 2 am. Lunch $4.50-$8.50, dinner $5.95-$24.95. Specializes in prime rib, seafood. Beamed ceiling. Cr cds: DS, MC, V.
🅳 🖃

★ ★ **RICHARD'S.** *501 Monroe St, Sheboygan Falls (53085).* 920/467-6401. Hrs: 11 am-2 pm, 5-10 pm; Sat-Mon from 5 pm. Res accepted. Bar 5 pm-2 am. Lunch $4-$10, dinner $10-$35. Specialties: oysters Rockefeller, veal chops, prime rib. Former stagecoach inn (ca 1840s). Cr cds: D, DS, MC, V.
🅳 🖃

Sister Bay (Door County)

See also Door County

Pop 675 **Elev** 587 ft **Area code** 920 **Zip** 54234

Information Door County Chamber of Commerce, 1015 Green Bay Rd, PO Box 406, Sturgeon Bay 54235; 920/743-4456 or 800/527-3529

Web www.doorcountyvacations.com

This town is near the northern tip of Door County (see). Sister Bay was settled in 1857 by Norwegian immigrants. Today it's known for its shopping, dining, and boating opportunities, but still retains a distinct Scandinavian flavor.

Special Event

Sister Bay Fall Festival. Fish boil, fireworks, parade, street auction. Mid-Oct. Phone 920/743-4456.

Motels/Motor Lodges

★ **BLUFFSIDE MOTEL.** *403 Bluffside Ln, Sister Bay (54234).* 920/854-2530.

toll-free 877/854-2530. www.bluffside.com. 16 units, 1-2 story, 1 suite. July-Labor Day, late Sept-Oct: S, D $65-$89; each addl $6; suite $125-$150; lower rates May-June, wkdays after Labor Day-late Sept. Closed rest of yr. Crib free. TV; cable. Complimentary coffee in rms. Restaurant nearby. Ck-out 10 am. Free airport transportation. Refrigerators; microwaves avail. Picnic tables, grills. Cr cds: MC, V.

[symbols]

★★★ **THE CHURCH HILL INN.** 425 Gateway Dr, Sister Bay (54234). 920/854-4885; fax 920/854-4634; toll-free 800/422-4906. www.churchhillinn.com. 34 rms, 2 story. S $75-$105; D $65-$154; each addl $19; higher rates wkends. Children over 10 yrs only. TV; cable. VCR avail (movies). Heated pool; whirlpool. Complimentary full bkfst; afternoon refreshments. Ck-out 10:30 am. Meeting rms. Business servs avail. X-country ski 4 mi. Exercise equipt; sauna. Some refrigerators, in-rm whirlpools. Balconies. Common rms with fireplaces. Totally nonsmoking. Cr cds: MC, V.

[symbols]

★ **COACHLITE INN.** 830 S Bay Shore Dr, Sister Bay (54234). 920/854-5503; fax 920/854-9011; toll-free 800/745-5031. www.coachliteinn.com. 21 rms, 2 story, 2 suites. Late July-late Aug: S, D $84-$99; each addl $7; suites $115-$150; lower rates rest of yr. Crib $3. TV; cable. Complimentary coffee in lobby. Restaurant nearby (open in season). Ck-out 10 am. X-country ski 3 mi. Some in-rm whirlpools, microwaves. Balconies. Picnic tables. Gazebo. Cr cds: MC, V.

[symbols]

★★★ **COUNTRY HOUSE RESORT.** 715 Highland Rd, Sister Bay (54234). 920/854-4551; fax 920/854-9809; toll-free 800/424-0041. www.country-house.com. 46 rms, 2 story. May-Oct: S, D $84-$142; each addl $22; suites $223-$279; lower rates rest of yr. Children over 13 yrs only. TV; cable (premium). Pool; whirlpool. Complimentary continental bkfst. Coffee in rms. Ck-out 11 am. Meeting rm. Business servs avail. Tennis. Rowboats, dock facilities. Bicycles. Lawn games. Refrigerators; some in-rm whirlpools, microwaves. Private balconies overlook water. Picnic tables, grills. Along

Green Bay shoreline, on 16 wooded acres. Cr cds: A, DS, MC, V.

[symbols]

★ **EDGE OF TOWN MOTEL.** 11092 WI 42, Sister Bay (54234). 920/854-2012. 10 rms. No rm phones. Mid-June-Oct: S $39-$62; $59-$72; each addl $7; family rates; lower rates rest of yr. Crib free. Pet accepted, some restrictions; $7. TV; cable (premium). Complimentary coffee in lobby. Restaurant nearby. Ck-out 11 am. Refrigerators, microwaves. Cr cds: DS, MC, V.

[symbols]

★★ **HELMS FOUR SEASONS RESORT.** 414 Mill Rd, Sister Bay (54234). 920/854-2356; fax 920/854-1836. www.helmsfourseasons.com. 41 rms, 2 story, 9 kit. apts. Mid-June-late Oct: S, D $104-$113; each addl $8-$10; kit. apts $134-$215; lower rates rest of yr. Crib free. TV; cable. Indoor pool; whirlpool. Complimentary continental bkfst (Labor Day-Memorial Day). Restaurant nearby. Ck-out 10 am. Coin lndry. Meeting rm. Gift shop. Sundries. Free airport transportation. X-country ski 5 mi. Snowmobiling. Sun deck. Refrigerators; some fireplaces. Many private patios, balconies. On Sister Bay, dock. Cr cds: MC, V.

[symbols]

★★ **HOTEL DU NORD.** 11000 Bayshore Dr, Sister Bay (54234). 920/854-4221; fax 920/854-2710; toll-free 800/582-6667. www.hoteldunord.com. 56 rms, 2 story. S, D $85-$165. Crib free. TV; VCR avail (movies). Heated pool; whirlpool. Continental bkfst. Restaurant (see also HOTEL DU NORD). Ck-out 11 am. Coin lndry. Business servs avail. Sundries. Some in-rm whirlpools. On Green Bay. Cr cds: A, MC, V.

[symbols]

★★ **THE INN AT LITTLE SISTER HILL.** 2715 Little Sister Hill Rd, Sister Bay (54234). 920/854-2328; fax 920/854-2696; toll-free 800/768-6317. www.doorcountyinn.com. 26 kit. suites, 2 story. D $69-$119. June-Oct: kit. suites $109-$169; each addl $10; lower rates rest of yr. Crib $10. TV; cable, VCR (movies). Heated pool. Playground. Complimentary coffee in lobby. Ck-out 11 am. Coin lndry. Meeting rm. Refrigerators, microwaves. Some balconies. Picnic tables, grills. Cr cds: DS, MC, V.

⬜ 〰 🏊 🔥 SC

★★ **NORDIC LODGE.** *2721 Nordic Dr, Sister Bay (54234). 920/854-5432; fax 920/854-5974. toll-free 866/854-5432. www.thenordiclodge.com.* 33 rms, 2 story. July-Oct: D $92-$96; each addl $5-$10; under 2 free; higher rates: Fall Festival, some hols; lower rates rest of yr. Crib free. TV; cable (premium). Indoor pool; whirlpool. Complimentary continental bkfst. Ck-out 11 am. Refrigerators; microwaves avail. Balconies. Picnic tables, grills. Golf course opp. Near Pebble Beach. Totally nonsmoking. Cr cds: MC, V.

⬜ 🐾 🎿 〰 〰 🔥

★★ **OPEN HEARTH LODGE.** *1109 S Bayshore Dr, Sister Bay (54234). 920/854-4890; fax 920/854-7486. www.openhearthlodge.com.* 32 rms, 2 story. July-Oct: D $89-$99; each addl $3-$10; lower rates rest of yr. Crib free. TV; cable. Indoor pool; whirlpool. Playground. Complimentary continental bkfst. Complimentary coffee. Restaurant nearby. Ck-out 11 am. Refrigerators; microwaves avail. Cr cds: A, DS, MC, V.

⬜ 〰 〰 🔥

★ **SCANDIA COTTAGES.** *11062 Beach Rd, Sister Bay (54234). 920/854-2447. www.scandiacottages.com.* 6 kit. cottages, 1 motel rm. No rm phones. June-Oct, Dec-Feb: kit. cottages $65-$150; each addl $5-$10; family, wkly rates; ski plan; lower rates rest of yr. Crib free. Pet accepted. TV; cable. Restaurant nearby. Ck-out 10 am. X-country ski 4 mi. Picnic tables, grills. Bay nearby. Totally nonsmoking. Cr cds: A, MC, V.

⬜ 🐾 🎿 〰 〰 🔥

★ **VOYAGER INN AT DOOR COUNTY.** *232 WI 57, Sister Bay (54234). 920/854-4242; fax 920/854-2670. www.voyagerinndc.com.* 29 rms. July-Aug, wknds Sept-mid-Oct: S, D $63-$84; each addl $7; lower rates May-June. Closed rest of yr. Crib $5. Heated pool; whirlpool. Restaurant nearby. Ck-out 11 am. Business servs avail. Sauna. Refrigerators; microwaves avail. Some balconies, patios. Cr cds: DS, MC, V.

〰 〰 🔥

Resort

★ **LITTLE SISTER RESORT AT PEBBLE.** *360 Little Sister Rd, Sister Bay (54234). 920/854-4013; fax 920/854-5076. www.littlesisterresort.com.* 6 chalets, 13 cottages (1-2-bedrm). MAP only, July-Aug: wkly, chalets, cottages $425-$550/person; family rates; lower rates rest of yr. Closed Nov-Apr. Crib $7. TV; cable (premium). Playground. Ck-out 10 am. Grocery store 2 mi. Coin lndry. Tennis. Hiking. Bicycles. Lawn games. Boat rentals. Balconies. Picnic tables. On swimming beach. Cr cds: MC, V.

⬜ ⚓ 〰 🎿 🔥

Restaurants

★ **AL JOHNSON'S SWEDISH RESTAURANT.** *702 Bay Shore Dr, Sister Bay (54234). 920/854-2626.* Hrs: 6 am-9 pm; Nov-Apr to 8 pm. Closed Thanksgiving, Dec 25. Swedish, American menu. Bkfst (all day) $2.95-$8.75; lunch $3.50-$11.95. Complete meals: dinner $13.25-$17.95. Child's menu. Specializes in Swedish pancakes, meatballs. Swedish-style structure, decor. Gift shop. Goats graze on grass-covered roof. Family-owned. Cr cds: A, DS, MC, V.

★★ **HOTEL DU NORD.** *11000 Bay Shore Dr, Sister Bay (54234). 920/854-7972. www.hoteldunord.com.* Hrs: 7:30 am-2 pm, 5:30-10 pm; Sun brunch 9:30 am-12:30 pm. Res accepted. Bar 4:30 pm-midnight. Bkfst $4-$8, lunch $6-$10, dinner $16.25-$22. Sun brunch $11.95. Child's menu. Overlooks Green Bay. Cr cds: A, D, MC, V.

⬜

★ **NORTHERN GRILL AND PIZZA.** *321 Country Walk Dr, Sister Bay (54234). 920/854-9590.* Hrs: 11 am-11 pm. Bar. Lunch $2.50-$5.25, dinner $9.95-$14.95. Child's menu. Specializes in homemade pizza, smoked barbeque ribs, local fish. Outdoor dining. Cr cds: DS, MC, V.

⬜

Sparta

(E-3) *See also Black River Falls, La Crosse, Tomah*

Settled 1849 **Pop** 7,788 **Elev** 793 ft
Area code 608 **Zip** 54656
Information Chamber of Commerce, 111 Milwaukee St; 608/269-4123 or 608/269-2453

Sparta is the home of several small industries manufacturing, among other items, dairy products, brushes, and automobile parts. The area is also well-known for its biking trails. Fort McCoy, a US Army base, is five miles northeast on WI 21.

What to See and Do

Elroy-Sparta State Trail. Built on an old railroad bed, this 32-mi hard-surfaced (limestone screenings) trail passes through three tunnels and over 23 trestles. Biking (fee). (Apr-Oct, daily) Phone 608/337-4775. ¢¢

Motels/Motor Lodges

★ **BEST NIGHTS INN.** *303 W Wisconsin St (54656). 608/269-3066; fax 608/269-3175; toll-free 800/201-0234. www.bestnightsinn.com.* 31 rms. Mid-May-Oct: S $38-$72; D $48-$89; each addl $7; under 16 free; lower rates rest of yr. Crib avail. Pet accepted. TV; cable. Heated pool. Restaurant opp open 24 hrs. Ck-out 11 am. Refrigerators. Cr cds: A, DS, MC, V.
🄳 🐾 ⌘ 🛏 🆗

★ **BUDGET HOST HERITAGE MOTEL.** *704 W Wisconsin St (54656). 608/269-6991; toll-free 800/658-9484.* 22 rms, 2 story. S $35; D $52; each addl $3. Crib $5. Pet accepted. TV; cable (premium). Pool; whirlpool. Restaurant adj open 24 hrs. Ck-out 11 am. Cr cds: A, C, DS, MC, V.
🐾 ⌘ 🛏 🆗

★★ **COUNTRY INN BY CARLSON.** *737 Avon Rd (54656). 608/269-3110; fax 608/269-6726. www.countryinns.com.* 61 rms, 2 story. S $60-$68; D $62-$70; suites $64-$121; under 18 free. Crib avail. Pet accepted. TV; cable (premium), VCR avail (movies). Indoor pool; whirlpool. Complimentary continental bkfst. Restaurant adj 24 hrs. Bar from 4 pm. Ck-out noon.

Coin lndry. Meeting rms. Business servs avail. Downhill ski 7 mi; x-country ski 1 mi. Some refrigerators. Cr cds: A, D, DS, MC, V.
🄳 🐾 ⌘ 🛏 🆗

★ **DOWNTOWN MOTEL.** *509 S Water St (54656). 608/269-3138.* 17 rms. S $32-$39.95; D $36-$45; each addl $3; under 12 free. Crib free. TV; cable (premium). Restaurant 6 am-1 pm. Ck-out 11 am. Cr cds: DS, MC, V.
🛏 🆗

B&B/Small Inn

★★ **JUSTIN TRAILS COUNTRY INN.** *7452 Kathryn Ave (54656). 608/269-4522; fax 608/269-3280; toll-free 800/488-4521. www.justintrails.com.* 4 rms, 1-2 story, 3 cottages. S $80; D $80-$145; cottages $175-$325; family rates. Crib free. Pet accepted. Complimentary full bkfst. Ck-out noon, ck-in 3 pm. X-country ski on site. Library/sitting rm. Restored 1920s farmhouse; log cabins. Cr cds: A, D, DS, MC, V.
🐾 ⌘ 🛏 🆗

Spooner

See also Hayward, Rice Lake

Settled 1883 **Pop** 2,464 **Elev** 1,065 ft
Area code 715 **Zip** 54801
Information Spooner Area Chamber of Commerce, 122 N River St; 715/635-2168 or 800/367-3306
Web www.spoonerwisconsin.com

Once a busy railroad town, Spooner is now a popular destination for fishermen and nature lovers.

What to See and Do

Railroad Memories Museum. Memorabilia, model railroad in old Chicago & Northwestern depot. (Mid May-mid-Oct, daily) 424 Front St. Phone 715/635-3325. ¢¢

St. Croix National Scenic Riverway. One of two in the US; excellent canoeing (Class #1 rapids) and tubing. (See ST. CROIX FALLS) Contact Chamber of Commerce or National

Park Service Information Station in Trego. Phone 715/635-8346.

Trego Lake Park. Heavily wooded area on the Namekagon River (Wild River). Fishing, boating, canoeing, inner tubing; hiking, picnicking, camping (electric hookups). (May-Sept) ¼ mi N, jct US 53, 63 in Trego. Phone 715/635-9931. ¢¢

Special Events

Spooner Car Show. Early June. Phone 715/635-3740.

Spooner Rodeo. PRCA approved. Country music. Mid-July. Phone 800/367-3306.

Motels/Motor Lodges

★ **COUNTRY HOUSE.** *717 S River St (54801). 715/635-8721.* 22 rms. June-Oct: S $39-$75; D $54-$85; each addl $5; under 12 free; lower rates rest of yr. Crib $4. Pet accepted, some restrictions; fee. TV; cable, VCR avail. Complimentary coffee in rms. Restaurant adj 6:30 am-9 pm. Ck-out 11 am. Business servs avail. Cr cds: A, C, D, DS, MC, V.

🄳 ⬛ ⬛ ⬛

★ **GREEN ACRES MOTEL.** *N 4809 US 63 S (54801). 715/635-2177; res 800/373-5293.* 21 rms. Late May-Aug: S, D $59-$76; each addl $5; higher rates rodeo; lower rates rest of yr. Crib $5. Pet accepted, some restrictions; $5. TV; cable (premium). Complimentary coffee in lobby. Ck-out 10 am. Business servs avail. X-country ski 2 mi. Playground. Lawn games. Microwaves avail. Picnic tables, grills. Cr cds: A, DS, MC, V.

🄳 ⬛ ⬛ ⬛ ⬛

Restaurant

★ **JIMBO'S CLUB 70.** *WI 70 (54801). 715/635-9300.* Hrs: 4-9 pm; Fri, Sat to 10 pm. Closed Sun-Tues; Jan 1, Dec 24, 25. Res accepted. Italian, American menu. Bar. Dinner $6.95-$14.95. Child's menu. Specializes in steak, seafood, pasta. Own pasta. Contemporary decor; ceiling fans, large windows. Cr cds: MC, V.

🄳 ⬛

Spring Green

See also Dodgeville, Mineral Point, Prairie du Sac

Pop 1,283 **Elev** 729 ft **Area code** 608 **Zip** 53588

Information Chamber of Commerce, PO Box 3; 608/588-2042 or 800/588-2042

Web www.springgreen.com

This is where Frank Lloyd Wright grew up, built his home (Taliesin East), and established the Taliesin Fellowship for the training of apprentice architects.

What to See and Do

✪ **House on the Rock.** Designed and built by Alexander J. Jordan atop a chimney-like rock, 450 ft above a valley. Waterfalls, trees throughout house; collections of antiques, Asian objets d'art, and automated music machines (many of the musical exhibits require addl money to activate the automation mechanism). Restaurant. (Mid-March-late Oct, daily) 9 mi S on WI 23. Phone 608/935-3639. ¢¢¢¢

✪ **Taliesin.** Features Frank Lloyd Wright's home, studio, farm, and school. (May-Oct, daily) 3 mi S on WI 23. Phone 608/588-7948. ¢¢¢¢

Tower Hill State Park. Park has 77 acres of wooded hills and bluffs overlooking the Wisconsin River. Site of Pre-Civil War shot tower and early lead-mining village of Helena. Fishing, canoeing; picnicking (shelter), playgrounds, camping. Standard fees. (Daily) 3 mi E on US 14, then S on County Hwy C. Phone 608/588-2116. ¢

Special Event

American Players Theatre. Rte 3, Golf Course Rd. Theater arts center for the classics. Summer performances in outdoor amphitheater (Tues-Sun; also matinees Tues-Fri in Sept and Oct) Phone 608/588-2361. Mid-June-early Oct.

Motels/Motor Lodges

★ **PRAIRIE HOUSE MOTEL.** *E4884 US 14 (53588). 608/588-2088; fax 608/588-7965; toll-free 800/588-2088. www.execpc.com/~phouse.* 51 rms, 1 story. July-Aug: S $47-$80; D $57-$80; each addl $5; under 18 free; lower rates rest of yr. Crib $5. TV. Complimentary coffee in lobby. Restaurant nearby. Ck-out 11 am. Meeting rm. X-country ski 5 mi. Exercise equipt; sauna. Whirlpool. Some refrigerators. Cr cds: A, DS, MC, V.

D ⚡ 🏋 ⛷ 🔥

★ ★ **ROUND BARN LODGE.** *US 14 (53588). 608/588-2568; fax 608/588-2100. www.roundbarn.com.* 44 rms, 2 story. June-Aug: S, D $79.50-$99.50; each addl $5; suites $109.50-$119.50; under 6 free; lower rates rest of yr. Crib free. TV; cable (premium). Indoor/outdoor pool; whirlpool. Complimentary coffee in lobby. Restaurant 7 am-9 pm. Ck-out 11 am. Meeting rm. X-country ski 5 mi. Cr cds: A, D, DS, MC, V.

D ⚡ 🏊 ⛷ 🔥

Restaurant

★ ★ **POST HOUSE.** *127 E Jefferson (53588). 608/588-2595. www.post housespringgreen.com.* Hrs: 11 am-2 pm, 5-9 pm; Fri, Sat to 10 pm; Sun 11 am-8 pm. Closed Mon, Tues (Nov-Apr); hols. Res accepted. Bar. Lunch $5.75-$7, dinner $8.50-$14.50. Child's menu. Specializes in prime rib, roast duck. Outdoor dining. Contemporary American decor. Cr cds: MC, V.

D

Stevens Point

(D-4) *See also Marshfield, Wisconsin Rapids*

Settled 1838 **Pop** 23,006 **Elev** 1,093 ft
Area code 715 **Zip** 54481
Information Stevens Point Area Convention and Visitors Bureau, 23 Park Ridge Dr; 715/344-2556 or 800/236-4636
Web www.spacvb.com

A diversified community on the Wisconsin River near the middle of the state, Stevens Point was established as a trading post by George Stevens, who bartered with the Potawatomi. Incorporated as a city in 1858, today it has a number of industries and markets the dairy produce and vegetable crops of Portage County.

What to See and Do

George W. Mead Wildlife Area. Preserved and managed for waterfowl, fur bearers, deer, prairie chickens, ruffed grouse, and other game and nongame species. Limited fishing; hunting, bird-watching, hiking. (Mon-Fri) 15 mi NW on US 10 to Milladore, then 5 mi N on County S. Phone 715/457-6771. **FREE**

Stevens Point Brewery. (1857) The brewery tour has been described as one of the most interesting in the country. (Mon-Sat, res suggested). 2617 Water St, corner of Beer and Water sts. Phone 715/344-9310. ¢

University of Wisconsin-Stevens Point. (1894) 8,500 students. Across the entire front of the four-story Natural Resources Building is the world's largest computer-assisted mosaic mural. Museum of Natural History has one of the most complete collections of preserved birds and bird eggs in the country (academic yr, daily). Planetarium show in Science Hall (academic yr, Sun). Fine Arts Center houses 1,300 American Pattern glass goblets. 2100 Main St. Phone 715/346-4242.

Motels/Motor Lodges

★ ★ **BAYMONT INN & SUITES.** *4917 Main St (54481). 715/344-1900; fax 715/344-1254; res 800/428-3438. www.baymontinn.com.* 80 rms, 3 story. S $39.95-$44.95; D $47.95-$51.95; under 19 free. Crib free. Pet accepted. TV; cable (premium). Complimentary continental bkfst. Complimentary coffee in rms. Restaurant adj open 24 hrs. Ck-out noon. Coin lndry. Meeting rms. Business servs avail. In-rm modem link. X-country ski 1 mi. Cr cds: A, MC, V.

D 🐾 ⚡ ⛷ 🔥 SC

★ ★ ★ **COMFORT SUITES.** *300 N Division St (54481). 715/341-6000; fax 715/341-8908; res 800/221-2222. www.comfortsuites.com.* 105 suites, 3 story. S, D $84-$139; each addl $10; under 18 free. Crib free. TV; VCR (movies). Indoor pool; whirlpool. Complimentary continental bkfst. Complimentary coffee in rms. Restaurant adj open 24 hrs. Ck-out noon. Coin lndry. Meeting rms. Business servs avail. In-rm modem link. Valet serv. Sundries. Golf, tennis, 3 mi. X-country ski 2 mi. Exercise equipt. Refrigerators; some in-rm whirlpools, wet bars. Cr cds: A, D, DS, MC, V.

★★ **HOLIDAY INN.** *1501 Northpoint Dr (54481). 715/341-1340; fax 715/341-9446; toll-free 800/922-7880. www.holiday-inn.com.* 295 rms, 2-6 story. S $79-$99; D $89-$109; each addl $10; suites $99-$168; under 18 free. Crib free. Pet accepted. TV; cable, VCR (movies). Indoor pool; whirlpool, poolside serv. Restaurant 6:30 am-10 pm; Fri, Sat to 11 pm. Bar 11-1 am; entertainment. Ck-out 11 am. Coin lndry. Convention facilities. Business servs avail. In-rm modem link. Valet serv. Sundries. Gift shop. Free airport transportation. Golf, tennis, 1 mi. Downhill ski 20 mi; x-country ski 1 mi. Exercise equipt; sauna. Cr cds: A, D, DS, MC, V.

★ **POINT MOTEL.** *209 Division St (54481). 715/344-8312; fax 715/344-8312.* 44 rms, 2 story. S $33; D $37-$42; each addl $4. Crib $4. Pet accepted. TV; cable, VCR avail. Complimentary continental bkfst. Ck-out 11 am. Meeting rm. Cr cds: A, D, DS, MC, V.

Restaurant

★★★ **THE RESTAURANT AND PAGLIACCI'S.** *1800 N Point Dr (54481). 715/346-6010.* Hrs: 5-9 pm; Fri, Sat to 10 pm. Closed Sun; hols. Res accepted. Bar. Wine list. A la carte entrees: dinner $5-$17. Specializes in pasta, veal, seafood. Own baking. Outdoor dining. Cr cds: A, MC, V.

Sturgeon Bay (Door County)

(D-7) *See also Algoma, Door County, Green Bay*

Settled 1870 **Pop** 9,176 **Elev** 588 ft
Area code 920 **Zip** 54235
Information Door County Chamber of Commerce, 1015 Green Bay Rd, PO Box 406; 920/743-4456 or 800/527-3529
Web www.doorcountyvacations.com

Sturgeon Bay, in Door County (see), sits at the farthest inland point of a bay where swarms of sturgeon were once caught and piled like cordwood along the shore. The historic portage from the bay to Lake Michigan, used for centuries by Native Americans and early explorers, began here. The Sturgeon Bay ship canal now makes the route a waterway used by lake freighters and pleasure craft. The city is the county seat and trading center. Two shipyards and a number of other industries are located here. Ten million pounds of cherries are processed every year in Door County.

What to See and Do

Cave Point County Park. Wave-worn grottoes and caves in limestone bluffs. Sand dunes, beautiful landscapes nearby. 10 mi NE via WI 57, County Hwy D. Phone 920/823-2400.

Door County Maritime Museum. Shipbuilding history and artifacts; boats on display; actual pilothouse of a Great Lakes ore carrier. (Daily) 120 N Madison. Phone 920/743-5958. ¢¢

🌟 **Door County Museum.** Old-time stores; fire dept with antique trucks; county memorabilia and photographs. Video presentation. Gift shop. (May-Oct, daily) 4th Ave and Michigan St. Phone 920/743-5809. **DONATION**

The Farm. Farm animals and fowl in natural surroundings; pioneer farmstead; wildlife display. (Memorial Day-Mid Oct, daily) 4 mi N on WI 57. Phone 920/743-6666. ¢¢

Potawatomi State Park. 1,200-acre woodland along the shores of Sturgeon Bay. Limestone bluffs. Waterskiing, fishing, boating, canoeing; nature, hiking, snowmobile, x-country ski, and bicycle trails; downhill skiing. Picnicking, playgrounds, camping (125 sites, 23 hookups), winter camping. Standard fees. 2 mi NW. Phone 920/746-2890.

Robert La Salle County Park. Site where La Salle and his band of explorers were rescued from starvation by friendly Native Americans. Monument marks location of La Salle's fortified camp. Picnicking. SE on Lake Michigan. Phone 800/527-3529.

US Coast Guard Canal Station. At entrance to ship canal on Lake Michigan. Coast Guard provides maritime law enforcement patrols, search and rescue duties, weather reports; lighthouse. Tours (by appt). 2501 Canal Rd. Phone 920/743-3367. **FREE**

Special Events

Shipyards Tour. Early May. Phone 920/746-2286.

Annual Sturgeon Bay Harvest Fest. Art show, huge craft show, farmers market, food booths, music and entertainment. Late Sept. Along Third Ave. Phone 800/301-6695.

Motels/Motor Lodges

★ ★ **BAY SHORE INN.** *4205 N Bay Shore Dr (54235). 920/743-4551; fax 920/743-3299; toll-free 800/556-4551. www.bayshoreinn.net.* 30 kit. suites, 3 story. July-Aug: S, D $79-$179; hol wkends (2-3-day min); lower rates rest of yr. Crib $5. TV; cable (premium), VCR. 2 pools, 1 indoor; whirlpool. Playground. Complimentary coffee in rms. Ck-out 11 am. Coin lndry. Meeting rms. Business servs avail. Tennis. X-country ski 6 mi. Bicycles, paddle boats. Game rm. In-rm whirlpools, microwaves. Balconies. Picnic tables, grills. On swimming beach. Cr cds: A, DS, MC, V.

★ ★ **BEST WESTERN MARITIME INN.** *1001 N 14th Ave (54235). 920/743-7231; fax 920/743-9341. www.bestwestern.com.* 90 rms, 2 story. July-Oct: S $81-$90; D $88-$99; each addl $7; suites $145-$160; under 12 free; package plans; lower

rates rest of yr. TV; cable (premium). Indoor pool; whirlpool. Complimentary continental bkfst. Restaurant nearby. Ck-out 11 am. Business servs avail. Downhill/x-country ski 5 mi. Game rm. Refrigerators; microwaves avail. Some in-rm whirlpools. Cr cds: A, C, D, DS, MC, V.

★ **CHAL-A MOTEL .** *3910 WI 42 and 57 (54235). 920/743-6788.* 20 rms. S $29-$49; D $34-$54; each addl $4. Crib $5. TV. Complimentary coffee in lobby. Ck-out 10:30 am. Downhill ski 7 mi. Museum on premises; features collections of cars, toys, and dolls. Cr cds: MC, V.

★ ★ **CHERRY HILLS LODGE.** *5905 Dunn Rd (54235). 920/743-4222; fax 920/743-4222; toll-free 800/545-2307. www.golfdoorcounty.com.* 31 rms, 2 story. July-Aug, wkends in Sept: S, D $115-$155; each addl $15; golf plan; lower rates rest of yr. TV. Heated pool; whirlpool. Dining rm 7-10:30 am, 11 am-2 pm, 6-9 pm. Bar; entertainment. Ck-out 11 am. Meeting rms. Business servs avail. Gift shop. 18-hole golf, greens fee $19-$28. Downhill/x-country ski 7 mi. Refrigerators, minibars. Patios, balconies. Picnic tables. Totally nonsmoking. Cr cds: A, C, D, DS, MC, V.

★ ★ **CLIFF DWELLERS RESORT.** *3540 N Duluth Ave (54235). 920/743-4260.* 16 lodge rms, 1-2 story; 12 kit. cottages (1-2 bedrm). Mid-June-Oct: S, D $95-$105; each addl $10-$15; cottages $105-$175; package plans; lower rates May-mid-June. Closed rest of yr. Crib avail. TV; cable. Heated pool; whirlpool. Bkfst tray in rms. Ck-out 11 am. Tennis. Sauna. Rowboats. Bicycles. Sun deck. Lawn games. Balconies. Refrigerators, microwaves avail. Grills. Overlooks Sturgeon Bay. Cr cds: A, DS, MC, V.

★ **HOLIDAY MOTEL.** *29 N 2nd Ave (54235). 920/743-5571; fax 920/743-5395.* 18 rms, 2 story. July-Aug: S $26-$50; D $39-$69; each addl $5; under 18 free; wkly rates; higher rates: wkends Sept, Oct; wkends (2-day min); lower rates rest of yr. Crib free. Pet accepted, some restrictions;

$5. TV; cable, VCR avail (free movies). Complimentary continental bkfst. Restaurant nearby. Ck-out 11 am. Business servs avail. X-country ski 4 mi. Refrigerators; microwaves avail. Cr cds: A, D, DS, MC, V.

⬛🔾➤◀🔥

★★ **LEATHEM SMITH LODGE AND MARINA.** *1640 Memorial Dr (54235). 920/743-5555; fax 920/743-5355; toll-free 800/336-7947. www.leathemsmithlodge.com.* 63 rms, 2 story, 16 suites. Late June-Aug and late Dec: S, D $99-$108; each addl $15; suites $135-$210; under 12 free; 2-day min hols (some higher rates); lower rates rest of yr. Crib $10. TV; cable, VCR avail (movies $3.75). Heated pool; poolside serv. Playground. Ck-out 11 am. Meeting rms. Business servs avail. Gift shop. Tennis. 9-hole par 3 golf; greens fee $6, putting green. Downhill/x-country ski 6 mi. Lawn games. Some refrigerators, microwaves. 48-slip marina with boat ramp. Cr cds: A, MC, V.

⬛🔾🎿⛷➤⛵◀🔥

★★ **WHITE BIRCH INN.** *1009 S Oxford (54235). 920/743-3295; fax 920/743-6587.* 14 units, 2 story, 3 suites. May-mid-Oct: S, D $75-$150; each addl $10; lower rates rest of yr. Crib free. TV. Complimentary continental bkfst. Restaurant 11:30 am-1:30 pm, 5:30-9:30 pm; Sat from 5 pm. Ck-out 11:30 am. Gift shop. Free airport transportation. X-country ski 6 mi. Picnic tables. Southwestern decor; Native American artifacts. Cr cds: MC, V.

🔥⬛➤✈◀

Resort

★★★ **STONE HARBOR RESORT.** *107 N 1st Ave (54235). 920/746-0700. www.stoneharbor-resort.com.* 126 rms, 5 story. S, D $175-$275; each addl $25; under 17 free. Crib avail. Indoor pool. TV; cable (premium), VCR avail. Complimentary coffee, newspaper in rms. Restaurant 6 am-10 pm. Ck-out noon. Meeting rms. Business center. Gift shop. Whirlpool, sauna. Exercise rm. Some refrigerators, minibars. Cr cds: A, C, D, DS, MC, V.

⛵✈🔥🏃

B&Bs/Small Inns

★★★ **BARBICAN INN.** *132 N 2nd Ave (54235). 920/743-4854; toll-free 877/427-8491. www. barbicanbandb.com.* 18 suites in 3 houses, 2 story. No rm phones. D $120-$185; package rates. TV; cable (premium), VCR. Complimentary continental bkfst. Restaurant nearby. Ck-out 11 am, ck-in 2 pm. Downhill/x-country ski 10 mi. In-rm whirlpools, refrigerators, fireplaces. Restored Victorian houses (1873); antiques. Former residence of local lumber baron. Cr cds: MC, V.

⬛➤🔥

★★ **CHADWICK INN.** *25 N 8th Ave (54235). 920/743-2771; fax 920/743-4386. www.thechadwickinn.com.* 3 suites, 3 story. June-Oct: suites $110-$125; lower rates rest of yr. TV; cable (premium), VCR avail. Complimentary continental bkfst in rms. Restaurant nearby. Ck-out noon, ck-in 2 pm. Some street parking. Free airport transportation. Downhill/x-country ski 5 mi. In-rm whirlpools, fireplaces. Balconies. Built 1895; original woodwork, antique glassware, Chickering piano (1823). Cr cds: A, MC, V.

➤✈◀🔥

★★★ **CHANTICLEER GUEST HOUSE.** *4072 Cherry Rd (County HH) (54235). 920/746-0334; fax 920/746-1368. www.chanticleer guesthouse.com.* 8 rms, 3 story. S, D $130-$220; wkly rates; 2-day min wkends, 3-day min hol wkends. Adults only. TV; VCR. Heated pool. Complimentary continental bkfst; afternoon refreshments. Complimentary coffee in lobby. Ck-out 11 am, ck-in 2 pm. Luggage handling. X-country ski on site. Sauna. Refrigerators, microwaves, in-rm whirlpools, fireplaces. Balconies. Picnic tables. Country house built 1916 on 30 acres; gazebo and sheep. Hiking trail. Cr cds: DS, MC, V.

⬛➤⛵◀🔥

★ **GRAY GOOSE BED AND BREAKFAST.** *4258 Bay Shore Dr (54235). 920/743-9100; fax 920/743-9165. www.ggoosebb.com.* 4 air-cooled rms, 2 with shower only, 2 story, 1 suite. No rm phones. May-Oct: S, D $100-$135; each addl $15; suites $125; under 12 free; hols 2-day min; lower rates rest of yr. Children over 12 yrs only. Premium cable TV in common rm, VCR avail (movies). Complimentary full bkfst. Ck-out 11 am, ck-in 3 pm. Downhill ski 10 mi; x-country ski 5 mi. Some fireplaces; microwaves avail. Built 1862. Totally nonsmoking. Cr cds: A, MC, V.

★★★ **INN AT CEDAR CROSSING.** *336 Louisiana St (54235). 920/743-4200; fax 920/743-4422. www.innatcedarcrossing.com.* 9 rms, 2 story. D $119-$159; each addl $20; suites $135-$179; package plans. TV in lobby; cable (premium), VCR (free movies). Complimentary bkfst. Restaurant (see also INN AT CEDAR CROSSING). Ck-out 11 am, ck-in 2 pm. Business servs avail. Free airport transportation. Downhill/x-country ski 5 mi. Some in-rm whirlpools, fireplaces. Balconies. Built 1884. Antique furnishings. Totally nonsmoking. Cr cds: A, DS, MC, V.

★★★ **SCOFIELD HOUSE BED AND BREAKFAST.** *908 Michigan St (54235). 920/743-7727; fax 920/743-7727; toll-free 888/463-0204. www.scofieldhouse.com.* 6 rms, 3 story. No rm phones. S, D $93-$196; each addl $20; no childern under 14. TV; cable (premium), VCR (free movies). Complimentary full bkfst; afternoon refreshments. Restaurant nearby. Ck-out 11 am, ck-in 3 pm. Downhill/x-country ski 6 mi. Many in-rm whirlpools. Many balconies. Former mayor's residence (1902); antiques, stained glass. Totally nonsmoking. Cr cds: A, MC, V.

★★★ **WHITE LACE INN.** *16 N 5th Ave (54235). 920/743-1105; fax 920/743-8180; toll-free 877/948-5223. www.whitelaceinn.com.* 18 rms, 2 story. D $129-$219; ski rates; lower rates Sun-Thurs Nov-Apr. Adults only. TV in most rms; VCR avail. Complimentary bkfst. Ck-out 11 am, ck-in 3 pm. Downhill/x-country ski 5 mi. Some in-rm whirlpools; microwaves avail. Balconies. Four buildings built 1880, 1900. White-columned front porch. Antiques; some fireplaces. Totally nonsmoking. Cr cds: A, DS, MC, V.

Restaurants

★★ **INN AT CEDAR CROSSING.** *112 N 3rd Ave (54235). 920/743-4249. www.innatcedarcrossing.com.* Hrs: 7 am-9 pm; Fri, Sat to 9:30 pm. Closed Dec 25. Res accepted. Bar. Bkfst $1.95-$6.95, lunch $4.95-$8.95, dinner $8.95-$32. Specializes in poultry, fresh fish. Own desserts. Victorian storefront (1884); antique furnishings, fireplaces. Totally nonsmoking. Cr cds: A, DS, MC, V.

★★ **MILL SUPPER CLUB.** *4128 WI 42/57 (54235). 920/743-5044.* Hrs: 4:30 pm-1 am. Closed Mon; Easter, Thanksgiving, Dec 24, 25. Bar. Dinner $7.95-$36.95. Child's menu. Specializes in family-style chicken, prime rib, seafood. Family-owned. Cr cds: MC, V.

Superior (A-2)

Founded 1852 **Pop** 27,134 **Elev** 642 ft
Area code 715 **Zip** 54880
Information Tourist Information Center, 305 Harborview Parkway; 800/942-5313
Web www.visitsuperior.com

At the head of Lake Superior, with the finest natural harbor on the Great Lakes, Superior-Duluth has been one of the leading ports in the country in volume of tonnage for many years. The Burlington Northern Docks and taconite pellet handling complex are the largest in the United States. More than 200 million bushels of grain are shipped in and out of the area's elevators each year. Here is the largest coal-loading terminal in the United States with 12 coal docks in the Superior-Duluth area, also a briquet plant, a shipyard, a refinery, and a flour mill. Production of dairy products is also a major industry. Long before its founding date, the city was the site of a series of trading posts. The University of Wisconsin-Superior is located here.

What to See and Do

Amnicon Falls State Park. An 825-acre park with many small waterfalls and interesting rock formations. Hiking, picnicking, camping. Standard fees. (Daily) 10 mi E on US 2. Phone 715/398-3000. ¢¢

Barker's Island. Boating (launching ramps, marina); picnic facilities, lodging, dining. From E 2nd St and 6th Ave E, off US 2, 53, WI 13. Phone 800/942-5313. Also here are

Duluth-Superior Excursions. A 1¾-hr narrated tour of Superior-Duluth Harbor and Lake Superior on excursion boats(Mid-May-mid-Oct, daily) Also lunch and dinner cruises. ¢¢¢¢

The S.S. Meteor. (1896) Last remaining whaleback freighter, the *Meteor* is moored here and is open to visitors as a maritime museum. (May-Sept, daily) Phone 715/392-5712. ¢¢

Brule River State Forest. On 40,218 acres. Fishing, boating, canoeing; nature, hiking, snowmobile, and x-country ski trails; picnicking, camping. Standard fees. (Daily) 30 mi SE via US 2. Phone 715/372-4866. ¢¢¢

Fairlawn Mansion and Museum. Restored 42-rm Victorian mansion overlooking Lake Superior. First floor and exterior fully restored and furnished. (Daily; closed most hols) 906 E 2nd St. Phone 715/394-5712. ¢¢¢

Old Fire House and Police Museum. Firehouse (1898) serving as a museum devoted to the history of police and fire fighting. Historical vehicles, artifacts. (June-Aug; daily) 23rd Ave E and 4th St. Phone 715/398-7558. ¢¢

Pattison State Park. Has 1,476 acres of sand beach and woodlands. Swimming, fishing, canoeing; nature, hiking, and x-country ski trails; picnic grove, playgrounds, primitive and improved camping (electric hookups, dump station). Nature center. Outstanding park attraction is Big Manitou Falls (165-ft drop), the highest waterfall in the state. Little Manitou Falls (31-ft drop) is located upstream of the main falls. Standard fees. (Daily) 15 mi S on WI 35. Phone 715/399-3111. ¢¢

Superior Municipal Forest. Has 4,500 acres of scenic woods bordering the shores of the St. Louis River. Fishing, boating; hiking, jogging, x-country skiing, archery. N 28th St and Billings Dr. **FREE**

Wisconsin Point. Popular for picnicking by light of driftwood fires. Swimming, fishing; bird-watching. On shores of Lake Superior. Phone 800/942-5313. **FREE**

Special Events

Head-of-the-Lakes Fair. Fairgrounds, 48th and Tower Ave. Phone 715/394-7848. July.

Miller Lite Northern Nationals Stock Car Races. Superior Speedway. Phone 715/394-7848. Sept.

Motels/Motor Lodges

★ ★ **BARKER'S ISLAND INN.** *300 Marina Dr (54880). 715/392-7152; fax 715/392-1180; toll-free 800/344-7515. www.barkersislandinn.com.* 112 rms, 2 story. Mid-June-mid-Oct: S, D $65-$109; suites $135; wkday rates; higher rates: Grandma's Marathon, Dec 31; lower rates rest of yr. Crib free. TV; cable. Sauna. Indoor pool; whirlpool. Restaurant 7 am-9 pm. Bar noon-1 am (summer), 4 pm-1 am (winter). Ck-out 11 am. Coin lndry. Meeting rms. Business servs avail. Sundries. Lighted tennis. Downhill ski 10 mi; x-country ski 5 mi. Game rm. Cr cds: A, C, D, DS, MC, V.

⊡ ⊠ ⊭ ⊠ ⊠ ⊠

★ ★ **BEST WESTERN BAY WALK INN.** *1405 Susquehanna Ave (54880). 715/392-7600; fax 715/392-7680. www.bestwestern.com.* 50 rms, 2 story. June-Sept: S $50-$75; D $55-$81; each addl $6; suites $80-$125; under 16 free; higher rates special events; lower rates rest of yr. Crib free. Pet accepted, some restrictions. TV; cable (premium), VCR avail (movies). Sauna. Indoor pool; whirlpool. Complimentary continental bkfst. Restaurant adj 11 am-9 pm. Ck-out 11 am. Coin lndry. Business servs avail. Downhill ski 7 mi; x-country ski 1 mi. Game rm. Exercise equipt. Some refrigerators. Cr cds: A, C, D, DS, ER, JCB, MC, V.

⊡ ⊠ ⊠ ⊠ ⊼ ⊠ ⊠

★ ★ **BEST WESTERN BRIDGEVIEW.** *415 Hammond Ave (54880). 715/392-8174; fax 715/392-8487; toll-free 800/777-5572. www.bestwestern.com.* 96 rms, 2 story. Mid-June-Sept: S

Breathtaking Wisconsin scenery

$60-$100; D $70-$100; each addl $5; under 18 free; lower rates rest of yr. Pet accepted. TV; cable (premium). Sauna. Indoor pool; whirlpool. Complimentary continental bkfst. Restaurant nearby. Bar 5-10:30 pm, to midnight wkends. Ck-out noon. Coin lndry. Meeting rm. Business servs avail. Sundries. Downhill/x-country ski 8 mi. Some refrigerators, microwaves. Cr cds: A, C, D, DS, ER, JCB, MC, V.

★ **SUPER 8.** *4901 E 2nd St (54880). 715/398-7686; fax 715/398-7339. www.super8.com.* 40 rms, 2 story. May-Sept: S, D $64-$74; under 12 free; lower rates rest of yr. Crib free. TV; cable (premium). Complimentary continental bkfst. Restaurant adj 7 am-11 pm. Ck-out 11 am. Business servs avail. Downhill ski 20 mi; x-country ski adj. Cr cds: A, C, D, DS, MC, V.

Restaurant

★★ **SHACK SMOKEHOUSE AND GRILLE.** *3301 Belknap St (54880).*
715/392-9836. www.shackonline.com. Hrs: 11 am-9 pm; Fri, Sat to 10 pm; Sun 11 am-8 pm. Closed Dec 24, 25. Res accepted. Bar 10 am-midnight. Lunch $4.99-$6.99, dinner $9.99-$17.99. Specializes in authentic hickory-smoked barbeque, local seafood, prime rib. Own soups. Family-owned. Cr cds: DS, MC, V.

Three Lakes

See also Crandon, Eagle River, Rhinelander, St. Germain

Pop 1,900 **Elev** 1,637 ft
Area code 715 **Zip** 54562
Information Three Lakes Information Bureau, 1704 Superior St, PO Box 268; 715/546-3344 or 800/972-6103
Web www.threelakes.com

Between Thunder Lake and the interlocking series of 28 lakes on the west boundary of Nicolet National Forest, Three Lakes is a provisioning point for parties exploring the forest and lake country.

What to See and Do

Schequamegon-Nicolet National Forest. Forest has 661,000 acres, and is 62 mi long and 36 mi wide; elevation ranges from 860 ft to 1,880 ft. Noted for scenic drives through pine, spruce, fir, sugar maple, oak, and birch trees. More than 1,200 lakes and 1,100 mi of trout streams. Fishing for trout, pike, bass, muskellunge and walleye, and hunting for deer, bear, grouse, and waterfowl. Swimming, canoeing, boating, rafting; interpretive nature trails, hiking. More than 122 mi of x-country ski trails, 520 mi of snowmobile trails, snowshoeing. Three wilderness areas and several non-motorized walk-in areas provide more than 33,000 acres for backpacking and primitive camping. Picnicking, camping, and other outdoor recreational activities in general forest zone are unrestricted and no permits are required. Within developed areas, camping and picnicking are restricted to designated sites and most are on a first-come basis; res are available for selected campgrounds. Fees are charged at most developed campgrounds. (Daily) N on WI 32. Phone 715/479-2827. **FREE**

Three Lakes Winery. Produces fruit wines. Winery tours (late May-mid-Oct, daily); wine tasting rm (all yr; must be 21 or over to taste wine). Corner of WI 45 and County A. Phone 715/546-3080. **FREE**

Tomah

(E-3) *See also Sparta*

Pop 7,570 **Elev** 960 ft **Area code** 608
Zip 54660
Information Greater Tomah Area Chamber of Commerce, 306 Arthur St, PO Box 625; 608/372-2166 or 800/94-TOMAH
Web www.tomahwisconsin.com

Tomah is Wisconsin's "Gateway to Cranberry Country." This was also the home of Frank King, the creator of the comic strip "Gasoline Alley";

the main street was named after him. Lake Tomah, on the west edge of town, has boating, waterskiing, fishing, ice-fishing, and snowmobiling.

What to See and Do

Little Red Schoolhouse Museum. Built in 1864, in use until 1965; many original furnishings, books. (Memorial Day-Labor Day, afternoons) Superior Ave in Gillett Park. Phone 608/372-2166. **FREE**

Mill Bluff State Park. Has 1,258 acres with rock bluffs. Swimming; picnicking, camping. Being developed as part of Ice Age National Scientific Reserve. Standard fees. (Daily) 7 mi E, off US 12, 16. Phone 608/427-6692. ¢¢

Necedah National Wildlife Refuge. Water birds may be seen during seasonal migrations; lesser numbers present during the summer. Resident wildlife incl deer, wild turkey, ruffed grouse, wolf, and bear. Viewing via 11-mi self-guided auto tour or one-mi self-guided foot trail. (All yr, daily; office, Mon-Fri; foot trail, mid-Mar-mid-Nov only; auto tour is along township roads, which may close due to inclement weather) 6 mi E via WI 21 near Necedah. Phone 608/565-2551. **FREE**

Wildcat Mountain State Park. Has 3,470 acres of hills and valleys. Trout fishing in Kickapoo River, Billings and Cheyenne creeks. Canoeing; nature, hiking, bridle, and x-country ski trails; picnicking, playgrounds, camping. Observation points provide panoramic view of countryside. Standard fees. (Daily) 25 mi S via WI 131, 33, near Ontario. Phone 608/337-4775. ¢¢

Special Event

Cranberry Festival. Main St in Warrens. Late Sept. Phone 608/378-4200.

Motels/Motor Lodges

★★ **COMFORT INN.** *305 Wittig Rd (54660). 608/372-6600; fax 608/372-6600; toll-free 800/288-5150. www. comfortinn.com.* 52 rms, 2 story. May-Aug: S, D $69.95-$79.95; each addl $5; under 18 free; lower rates rest of yr. Crib avail. Pet accepted. TV; cable (premium). Indoor pool; whirlpool.

Complimentary continental bkfst. Restaurant adj. Ck-out 11 am. Business servs avail. Downhill ski 15 mi; x-country ½ mi. Some refrigerators. Cr cds: A, C, D, DS, MC, V.

★★ **HOLIDAY INN.** *WI 21 (54660). 608/372-3211; fax 608/372-3243. www.holiday-inn.com.* 100 rms, 2 story. Mid-May-Labor Day: S $72; D $85; each addl $6; family rates; lower rates rest of yr. Crib free. Pet accepted, some restrictions. TV. Sauna. Heated pool; whirlpool, poolside serv. Restaurant 6 am-2 pm, 5-10 pm. Bar. Ck-out noon. Coin lndry. Meeting rms. Business servs avail. In-rm modem link. Valet serv. Sundries. X-country ski ½ mi. Exercise equipt. Game rm. Rec rm. Some refrigerators. Cr cds: A, C, D, DS, MC, V.

★ **LARK INN.** *229 N Superior Ave (54660). 608/372-5981; fax 608/372-3009; toll-free 800/447-5275. www.larkinn.com.* 25 rms, 1-2 story, 3 kits. S $49-$58; D $59-$68; each addl $5; kits. $60-$70; under 16 free. Crib $3. Pet accepted. TV; cable (premium), VCR avail (movies $2.50). Restaurant 6 am-11 pm. Ck-out 11 am. Coin lndry. Sundries. Downhill ski 10 mi; x-country ski 1 mi. Some refrigerators. Picnic tables. Cr cds: A, C, D, DS, MC, V.

★ **REST WELL MOTEL.** *25491 US 12 (54660). 608/372-2471.* 12 rms, 10 with shower only. No rm phones. S $35-$40; D $25-$55. Pet accepted. TV. Ck-out 10 am. Downhill ski 10 mi; x-country 1 mi. Cr cds: MC, V.

★ **SUPER 8.** *1008 E McCoy Blvd (54660). 608/372-3901; fax 608/372-5792. www.super8.com.* 65 rms, 2 story. Mid-June-late Sept: S, D $49-$79; each addl $5; under 19 free; lower rates rest of yr. Crib free. Pet accepted. TV; cable. Complimentary continental bkfst. Restaurant adj open 24 hrs. Ck-out 11 am. Coin lndry. Business servs avail. Downhill ski 12 mi; x-country ski 1 mi. Some refrigerators. Cr cds: A, C, D, DS, MC, V.

Restaurant

★★ **BURNSTAD'S.** *701 E Clifton St (54660). 608/372-3277. www.burnstads.com.* Hrs: 8 am-8 pm; Closed Jan 1, Dec 25. Res accepted. Continental menu. Bkfst $1.95-$6.25, lunch $4.75-$7.95, dinner $7.95-$14.95. Specialties: European pirozhki, shrimp de Jonghe. Family-owned. Totally non-smoking. Cr cds: A, D, DS, MC, V.

Two Rivers

(E-7) *See also Green Bay, Manitowoc, Sheboygan*

Pop 13,030 **Elev** 595 ft **Area code** 920 **Zip** 54241

Information Manitowoc-Two Rivers Area Chamber of Commerce, 1515 Memorial Dr, PO Box 903, Manitowoc 54221-0903; 920/684-5575 or 800/262-7892

Web www.manitowoc.com

A fishing fleet in Lake Michigan and light industry support Two Rivers.

What to See and Do

Point Beach State Forest. A 2,900-acre park with heavily wooded areas, sand dunes, and beach along Lake Michigan. Nature, hiking, snowmobile, and x-country ski trails; ice skating. Picnicking, playgrounds, concession, improved camping, winter camping. Nature center. Standard fees. (Daily) 5 mi N on County Trunk Hwy O. Phone 920/794-7480. ¢¢

Rogers Street Fishing Village Museum. Artifacts of commercial fishing industry; 60-yr-old diesel engine; artifacts from sunken vessels; 1886 lighthouse; life-size woodcarvings. Art and craft galleries feature local area artists. (June-Aug, daily) 2102 Jackson St. Phone 920/793-5905. ¢

Washington Island (Door County)

See also Door County

Settled 1869 **Pop** 623 **Elev** 600 ft
Area code 920 **Zip** 54246
Information Door County Chamber of Commerce, 1015 Green Bay Rd, PO Box 406, Sturgeon Bay 54235; 920/743-4456 or 800/527-3529
Web www.doorcountyvacations.com

Washington Island, six miles off the coast of Door County is one of the oldest Icelandic settlements in the United States. Many Scandinavian festivals are still celebrated. Surrounding waters offer excellent fishing. The island may be reached by ferry (see ELLISON BAY).

What to See and Do

Rock Island State Park. Reached by privately-operated ferry (June-Oct, daily; fee) from Jackson Harbor located at the NE corner of island. This 912-acre park was the summer home of electric tycoon, C. H. Thordarson. Buildings in Icelandic architectural style. Potawatomi Lighthouse (1836) on northern point. Swimming, fishing, boating; nature trail, more than 9 mi of hiking and snowmobile trails, picnicking, primitive camping (no supplies available). No vehicles permitted. Standard fees. (Daily) Little Lake Rd, NW corner of island. Phone 920/847-2235.

Washington Island Museum. Native American artifacts; antiques; rocks and fossils. (May-mid-Oct, daily) Little Lake Rd, NW corner of island. Phone 920/847-2522.

Special Event

Scandinavian Dance Festival. Dance festival and Viking Games. Early Aug. Phone 920/847-2179.

Motels/Motor Lodges

★★ **FINDLAY'S HOLIDAY INN AND VIKING VILLAGE.** *Main Rd* (54246). 920/847-2526; fax 920/847-2752; toll-free 800/522-5469. *www.holidayinn.net.* 16 rms, some A/C. S $76-$85; D $85-$115; under 6 free; wkly rates. Crib free. TV. Restaurant (see also FINDLAY'S HOLIDAY INN). Ck-out 10 am. Business servs avail. Gift shop. Health club privileges. Lawn games. On Lake Michigan; beach. Cr cds: MC, V.
[D] [🐾] [🔥]

★ **VIKING VILLAGE MOTEL.** *Main Rd* (54246). 920/847-2551; res 888/847-2144. 12 kit units. No A/C. S $75-$85; D $85-$110; each addl $5; suites $95-$120; under 6 free; wkly rates. Crib free. Pet accepted. TV. Coffee in rms. Restaurant 7 am-1:30 pm, 5:30-7:30 pm. Ck-out 10 am. Health club privileges. Refrigerators; some microwaves, fireplaces. Cr cds: MC, V.
[D] [🐾] [🐾] [🔥]

Restaurant

★★ **FINDLAY'S HOLIDAY INN.** *Main Rd* (54246). 920/847-2526. *www.holidayinn.net.* Hrs: 7-10:30 am, 11:30 am-2 pm, 5:30-7:30 pm. (Dinner Tues, Fri only) Closed Nov-Apr. Res accepted. Wine, beer. Bkfst $2-$7, lunch $3.50-$10, dinner $5-$12. Specializes in seafood. Salad bar. Entertainment. Norwegian decor. Totally nonsmoking. Cr cds: MC, V.
[D]

Watertown

(F-5) *See also Beaver Dam, Fort Atkinson, Oconomowoc*

Settled 1836 **Pop** 19,142 **Elev** 823 ft
Area code 262 **Zip** 53094
Information Chamber of Commerce, 519 E Main St; 262/261-6320

Waterpower, created where the Rock River falls 20 feet in two miles, attracted the first New England settlers. A vast number of German immigrants followed, including Carl Schurz, who became Lincoln's minister to Spain and Secretary of the Interior under President Hayes. His wife, Margarethe Meyer Schurz, established the first kindergarten in the United States. Watertown, with diversified industries, is in the center of an important farming and dairy community.

What to See and Do

⭐ **Octagon House and First Kindergarten in USA.** Completed in 1854 by John Richards, the 57-rm mansion has 40-ft spiral cantilever hanging staircase; Victorian-style furnishings throughout, many original pieces. On grounds are restored kindergarten founded by Margarethe Meyer Schurz in 1856 and 100-yr-old barn with early farm implements. (May-Oct, daily) 919 Charles St. Phone 262/261-2796. ¢¢

Special Event

Riverfest. Four-day event; craft show, carnival, raft race, entertainment. Early Aug. Phone 920/261-6320.

Waukesha

(F-6) *See also Milwaukee*

Settled 1834 **Pop** 56,958 **Elev** 821 ft
Area code 262
Information Waukesha Area Convention & Visitors Bureau, 223 Wisconsin Ave, 53186; 262/542-0330 or 800/366-8474
Web www.wauknet.com/visit

Mineral springs found here by pioneer settlers made Waukesha famous as a health resort; in the latter half of the 19th century, it was one of the nation's most fashionable. Before that it was an important point on the Underground Railroad. The *American Freeman* (1844-1848) was published here. Today the city is enjoying important industrial growth. Carroll College lends the city a gracious academic atmosphere. The name Waukesha (*by the little fox*) comes from the river that runs through it. The river, along with the city's many parks and wooded areas, adds to a beautiful atomosphere for leisure activities.

What to See and Do

Kettle Moraine State Forest, Southern Unit. Contains 20,000 acres of rough, wooded country as well as Ottawa and Whitewater lakes. Swimming, waterskiing, fishing, boating, canoeing. Trails: hiking, 74 mi; bridle, 50 mi; snowmobile, 52 mi; x-country ski, 40 mi; nature, 3 mi. Picnicking, playground, primitive and improved camping (electric hookups, dump station), winter camping. Standard fees. (Daily) 17 mi SW on WI 59. Phone 262/594-2135. ¢¢

⭐ **Old World Wisconsin.** A 576-acre outdoor museum with more than 65 historic structures (1840-1915) reflecting various ethnic backgrounds of Wisconsin history. Restored buildings incl church, town hall, schoolhouse, stagecoach inn, blacksmith shop, and ten complete 19th-century farmsteads. All buildings furnished in period artifacts; staffed by costumed interpreters. Tram system; restaurant. (May-Oct, daily) 14 mi SW on WI 67; 1 ½ mi S of Eagle. Phone 262/594-6300. ¢¢¢

Waukesha County Museum. Historical exhibits (Tues-Sat, also Sun afternoons; closed hols). Research library (Tues-Sat; closed hols; fee). 101 W Main St at East Ave. Phone 262/548-7186. **FREE**

Special Events

Waukesha JanBoree. Three days of winter activities. Late Jan. Phone 262/524-3737.

Fiesta Waukesha. On Fox River banks. Music, folklore, dance, diverse food, and cultural activities. Mid-June. Phone 262/547-0887.

Waukesha County Fair. Incl performances by top-name Country and Western and rock artists. Phone 262/544-5922. Mid-July.

Holiday Fair, Christmas Walk, and Annual Parade. Downtown. Merchants offer special bargains, festive treats. Mid-Nov. Phone 262/549-6154.

Motels/Motor Lodges

★ ★ **FAIRFIELD INN.** *20150 W Blue Mound Rd, Brookfield (53045). 262/785-0500; fax 262/785-1966; res 800/228-2800. www.fairfieldinn.com.*

135 rms, 3 story. S $54.95-$95.95; D $64.95-$95.95; each addl $10; under 18 free. Crib free. TV; cable (premium). Pool. Complimentary continental bkfst. Restaurant adj 6-1 am. Ck-out noon. Business servs avail. In-rm modem link. Cr cds: A, D, DS, MC, V.

D 🏊 ⛷ 🔥 🐾

★★ **HAMPTON INN.** *575 N Barker Rd, Brookfield (53045). 262/796-1500; fax 262/796-0977; toll-free 800/426-7866. www.hamptoninn.com.* 120 rms, 4 story. S, D $89-$104; under 18 free; higher rates special events. Crib free. TV; cable (premium). Indoor pool; whirlpool. Complimentary continental bkfst. Restaurant adj 6 am-3 am. Ck-out noon. Meeting rm. Business servs avail. Sundries. Cr cds: A, C, D, DS, MC, V.

D 🏊 ⛷ 🔥 **SC**

★ **RAMADA LIMITED WAUKESHA-MILWAUKEE WEST.** *2111 E Moreland Blvd (53186). 262/547-7770; fax 262/547-0688; toll-free 888/298-2054. www.ramada.com.* 92 rms, 2 story. July-Aug: S, D $75-$99; each addl $6; under 19 free; higher rates special events; lower rates rest of yr. Crib avail. TV; cable (premium); VCR avail. Sauna. Whirlpool. Exercise equipt. Complimentary continental bkfst. Restaurant adj. Ck-out 11 am. Business servs avail. Some refrigerators. Cr cds: A, D, DS, MC, V.

D 🏋 ⛷ 🐾

★ **SELECT INN.** *2510 Plaza Ct (53186). 262/786-6015; fax 262/786-5784; toll-free 800/641-1000. www.selectinn.com.* 101 rms, 2-3 story. No elvtr. S, D $59-$74; under 12 free. Pet accepted; $25 refundable. TV; cable. Complimentary continental bkfst. Ck-out 11 am. Meeting rm. Business servs avail. X-country ski 5 mi. Some refrigerators. Cr cds: A, C, D, DS, MC, V.

D 🐾 ⛷ 🔥 **SC**

★★ **WYNDHAM GARDEN HOTEL.** *18155 Bluemound Rd, Brookfield (53045). 262/792-1212; fax 262/792-1201; toll-free 800/822-4200. www.wyndham.com.* 178 rms, 3 story. S, D $69-$179; wkend rates; higher rates special events. Crib avail. TV; cable, VCR avail. Indoor pool; whirlpool. Complimentary coffee in rms.

Restaurant 7 am-9 pm. Bar 4 pm-midnight. Ck-out noon. Meeting rms. Business servs avail. In-rm modem link. Sundries. Valet serv. Free Milwaukee airport transportation. Exercise equipt. Game rm. Balconies. Picnic tables. Cr cds: A, DS, JCB, MC, V.

D 🏊 🏋 ✈ ⛷ 🔥 **SC**

Hotel

★★★ **MARRIOTT WAUKESHA.** *W 231 N 1600 (53186). 262/574-0888. www.marriott.com.* 283 rms, 6 story. S, D $150-$199; each addl $20; under 17 free. Crib avail. Indoor pool. TV; cable (premium), VCR avail. Complimentary coffee, newspaper in rms. Restaurant 6 am-10 pm. Ck-out 11 am. Meeting rms. Business center. Gift shop. Whirlpool. Exercise rm. Some refrigerators, minibars. Cr cds: A, C, D, DS, MC, V.

🏊 🏋 🚶 🔥 🐾

Restaurants

★★ **SEVEN SEAS.** *1807 Nagawicka Rd, Hartland (53029). 262/367-3903. www.weissgerbers.com.* Hrs: 5-10 pm; Sun brunch from 11 am; Sun 4-9 pm. Closed Tues (Oct-Apr). Res accepted. German, American menu. Bar. Dinner $14.95-$42. Sun brunch $14.95. Child's menu. Specializes in Wiener schnitzel, roast duck, seafood. Outdoor dining. Overlooks Lake Nagawicka; nautical decor. Cr cds: A, D, DS, MC, V.

D

★★★ **WEISSGERBER'S GASTHAUS INN.** *2720 N Grandview Blvd (53188). 262/544-4460. www.weissgerbers.com.* Hrs: 11:30 am-2:30 pm, 5-10 pm; Sat from 5 pm; Sun 4-9 pm. Res accepted. German, American menu. Bar. Lunch $6-$10, dinner $16-$22. Specialties: stuffed pork chops, pork shanks, Wiener schnitzel. Own desserts. Outdoor beer garden. Cathedral ceiling; fireplace. Cr cds: A, DS, MC, V.

D

Waupaca

See also Stevens Point, Wautoma

Pop 4,957 **Elev** 870 ft **Area code** 715
Zip 54981
Information Waupaca Area Chamber of Commerce, 221 S Main; 715/258-7343 or 888/417-4040
Web www.waupacaareachamber.com

This community, near a chain of 22 lakes to the southwest, is a boating, fishing, and tourist recreation area.

What to See and Do

Canoeing and tubing. Two- to three-hr trips. (May-Labor Day) Contact Chamber of Commerce. On the Crystal and Little Wolf rivers.

Covered Bridge. A 40-ft lattice design with 400 handmade oak pegs used in its construction. 3 mi S on Hwy K near the Red Mill Colonial Shop. Phone 715/258-7343.

Hartman Creek State Park. A 1,400-acre park with 300-ft sand beach on Hartman Lake. Swimming, fishing, boating (no gasoline motors), canoeing; nature, hiking, snowmobile, and x-country ski trails; picnicking, camping (dump station), winter camping. Standard fees. (Daily) 6 mi W via WI 54, then 1½ mi S on Hartman Creek Rd. Phone 715/258-2372. ¢¢

Scenic cruises. Sternwheeler *Chief Waupaca* offers 1½-hr cruises on eight lakes of the Chain O' Lakes. Also cruises aboard motor yacht *Lady of the Lakes*. (Memorial Day-Sept, daily) Private evening charters arranged. 4 mi SW via WI 54 and County QQ at Clear Water Harbor. Phone 715/258-2866. ¢¢

South Park. Offers swimming beach, bathhouse, fishing dock, boat landing; picnicking. Mirror and Shadow lakes, S end of Main St. Phone 715/258-7343. Also in park is

Hutchinson House Museum. Restored 12-rm Victorian pioneer home (1854); furnishings, artifacts; herb garden; Heritage House. Contact the Chamber of Commerce. End of Main St in South Park. Phone 715/258-7343. ¢

Special Events

Strawberry Fest. Arts and crafts, entertainment, fresh strawberries. Third Sat June. Phone 715/258-7343.

Fall-O-Rama. Arts and crafts fair, entertainment, food. Third Sat Sept. Phone 715/258-7343.

Motel/Motor Lodge

★★ **BAYMONT INN & SUITES.** *110 Grand Seasons Dr (54981). 715/258-9212; fax 715/258-4294; toll-free 877/880-1054. www.baymontinn.com.* 88 rms, 3 story. Late May-early Sept: S $69-$79; D $79-$109; each addl $10; suites $89-$140; under 18 free; family rates; package plans; higher rates special events; lower rates rest of yr. Crib free. Pet accepted. TV; cable (premium). Complimentary continental bkfst (Mon-Sat). Restaurant 10 am-10 pm. Bar to 2 am. Ck-out 11 am. Meeting rms. Business servs avail. Sundries. Coin lndry. Downhill ski 10 mi; x-country ski 2 mi. Exercise equipt; sauna. Massage. Indoor pool; whirlpool. Game rm. In-rm whirlpool, refrigerator, microwave in suites. Picnic tables. Cr cds: A, MC, V.

[symbols]

Waupun

(E-5) *See also Beaver Dam, Fond du Lac, Green Lake*

Founded 1839 **Pop** 8,207 **Elev** 904 ft
Area code 920 **Zip** 53963
Information Chamber of Commerce, 434 E Main; 920/324-3491

The city's Native American name means "Early Dawn of Day." Diversified crops, light industry, and three state institutions contribute to this small city's economy.

What to See and Do

City of Sculpture. First bronze casting of famous sculpture by James Earl Frazer, designer of Indian head nickel. Also six other historical bronze statues. Madison St at Shaler Park.

Fond du Lac County Park. Park has 100 acres of virgin timber on Rock

River. Swimming pool (mid-June-Aug, daily; fee); picnic area (tables, fireplaces), playgrounds, camping (mid-May-Nov, daily). Park (all yr). W on WI 49 to County Trunk MMM. Phone 920/324-2769. ¢¢¢

Horicon National Wildlife Refuge. Large flocks of Canadian geese and various species of ducks can be seen Oct, Nov, Mar, Apr. Many visitors stop during migratory seasons to watch the birds resting and feeding on the Horicon Marsh (daylight hrs). Limited hunting and fishing (inquire for dates); canoeing. Hiking trails. (Daily) Visitor Center, 6½ mi E on WI 49, then 4 mi S on Dodge County Z. Phone 920/387-2658. **FREE**

Motel/Motor Lodge

★ **INN TOWN.** *27 S State St (53963). 920/324-4211; fax 920/324-6921; toll-free 800/433-6231.* 16 rms. S $33-$40; D $46-$53; each addl $3. Crib $3. Pet accepted. TV; cable (premium). Coffee in rms. Restaurant nearby. Ck-out 10 am. Refrigerators; microwaves avail. Cr cds: A, DS, MC, V.

Wausau

(C-4) *See also Antigo, Stevens Point*

Settled 1839 **Pop** 37,060 **Elev** 1,195 ft **Area code** 715 **Zip** 54401
Information Wausau Area Convention and Visitors Bureau, 300 3rd St, Suite 200, PO Box 6190, 54402-6190; 715/845-6231, ext 324 or 800/236-9728
Web www.wausauchamber.com

Known as Big Bull Falls when it was settled as a lumber camp, the town was renamed Wausau, Native American for "Faraway Place." When the big timber was gone, the lumber barons started paper mills; paper products are still one of the city's many industries.

What to See and Do

Leigh Yawkey Woodson Art Museum. Collection of wildlife art, porcelain,

and glass; changing exhibits. (Tues-Sun; closed hols) 700 N 12th St. Phone 715/845-7010. **FREE**

Marathon County Historical Museum. Former home of early lumberman Cyrus C. Yawkey. Victorian period rms; model railroad display; changing theme exhibits. (Tues-Thurs, Sat and Sun; closed hols) 403 McIndoe St. Phone 715/848-6143. **FREE**

Rib Mountain State Park. An 860-acre park; summit of Rib Mtn is one of the highest points (1,940 ft) in the state; 60-ft observation tower. Hiking trails that wind past rocky ridges and natural oddities in quartzite rocks. View of miles of Wisconsin River Valley, the city and countryside. Picnicking, playgrounds, concession, camping. Standard fees. (Daily) 4 mi SW on County N. Phone 715/842-2522. ¢¢ In park is

Granite Peak Ski Area. Area has three chairlifts, rope tow; patrol, school, rentals; snowmaking; cafeteria, bar. Longest run 3,800 ft; vertical drop 624 ft. (Late Nov-mid-Apr, daily) 2 mi SW via WI 51 and 29, NN exit. Phone 715/845-2846. ¢¢¢¢

Special Events

Wisconsin Valley Fair. Marathon Park. Early Aug. Phone 715/355-8788.

Big Bull Falls Blues Festival. Mid-Aug. Phone 715/355-8788.

Motels/Motor Lodges

★★ **BAYMONT INN.** *1910 Stewart Ave (54401). 715/842-0421; fax 715/845-5096; res 800/428-3438. www.baymontinn.com.* 96 rms, 2 story. S $59-$64; D $64-$69; under 18 free. Crib free. Pet accepted. TV; cable. Indoor pool. Continental bkfst. Coffee in rms. Restaurant nearby. Ck-out noon. Business servs avail. In-rm modem link. Downhill/x-country ski 2 mi. Cr cds: A, C, D, DS, MC, V.

★★ **BEST WESTERN MIDWAY HOTEL.** *2901 Martin Ave (54401). 715/842-1616; fax 715/845-3726; toll-free 800/528-1234. www.bestwestern. com.* 98 rms, 2 story. S, D $70; each addl $12; under 18 free. Crib free.

TV; cable. Indoor pool; whirlpool. Playground. Coffee in rms. Complimentary Continental bkfst. Restaurant 6 am-10 pm. Bar; entertainment. Ck-out noon. Meeting rms. Business servs avail. In-rm modem link. Valet serv. Free airport transportation. Downhill ski 1 mi; x-country ski 3 mi. Rec rm. Exercise equipt; sauna. Lawn games. Some refrigerators, microwaves. Picnic tables. Cr cds: A, C, D, DS, MC, V.

⚃ 🏊 🏖 🔌 🐾

★ **EXEL INN.** *116 S 17th Ave (54401). 715/842-0641; fax 715/848-1356; res 800/367-3935. www. exelinns.com.* 122 rms, 2 story. S $36.99-$46.99; D $43.99-$52.99; each addl $4; under 18 free. Crib free. Pet accepted. TV; cable (premium). Complimentary continental bkfst. Complimentary coffee in rms. Restaurant nearby. Ck-out noon. Business servs avail. Lndry facilities. Downhill ski 3 mi; x-country ski 3 mi. Game rm. View of Rib Mtn. Cr cds: A, MC, V.

⚃ 🏊 🏖 🔌 🐾 SC

★★ **RAMADA INN.** *201 N 17th Ave (54401). 715/845-4341; fax 715/845-4990; res 888/298-2054. www.ramada. com.* 233 rms, 6 story. S $59; D $69-$99; each addl $10. suites $119-$179; under 18 free; higher rates special events. Crib free. TV; cable (premium), VCR avail. Complimentary continental bkfst. Complimentary coffee in rms. Restaurant 6:30 am-10 pm. Bar from 3 pm. Ck-out noon. Meeting rms. Business servs avail. In-rm modem link. Valet serv. Coin lndry. Free airport transportation. Downhill/x-country ski 2 mi. Exercise equipt; sauna. Indoor pools; wading pool, whirlpool. Game rms. Refrigerators, microwaves; some in-rm whirlpools. Many balconies. Cr cds: A, D, MC, V.

✈ 🏖 🏊 🔌 🐾

★ **RIB MOUNTAIN INN.** *2900 Rib Mtn Way (54401). 715/848-2802; fax 715/848-1908; toll-free 877/960-8900. www.ribmtninn.com.* 16 rms, 2 story, 4 villas, 4 townhouses. S, D $69-$150; villas $109-$160; townhouses $160-$195; wkly, monthly rates; ski plan; higher rates: ski season, wkends. Pet accepted. TV; cable (premium), VCR (movies). Continental bkfst. Ck-out 11 am. Business servs avail. Driving range. Downhill ski ¼ mi; x-country ski 7 mi. Sauna. Lawn games. Refrigerators, fireplaces. Patios, balconies. Picnic tables, grills. On Rib Mtn. Adj to state park. Cr cds: A, C, D, DS, MC, V.

⚃ 🐾 🏖 🔌 🐾

★ **SUPER 8.** *2006 Stewart Ave (54401). 715/848-2888; fax 715/842-9578. www.super8.com.* 88 rms, 2 story. S $47-$54; D $54-$69; each addl $10; under 18 free. Crib free. Pet accepted. TV; cable. Indoor pool; whirlpool. Complimentary continental bkfst. Ck-out noon. Business servs avail. Valet serv. Sundries. Cr cds: A, D, DS, MC, V.

⚃ 🐾 🏖 🔌 🐾

B&B/Small Inn

★★ **ROSENBERRY INN.** *511 Franklin St (54403). 715/842-5733; fax 715/843-5659; toll-free 800/336-3799. www.rosenberryinn.com.* 8 rms, 3 story. A/C in 4 rms. No rm phones. S $70; D $100; each addl $15. TV in sitting rm; cable. Complimentary full bkfst. Restaurant nearby. Ck-out 11 am, ck-in 2 pm. Downhill/x-country ski 5 mi. Some in-rm whirlpools. Two historic homes built 1908; Prairie School-style architecture, antiques. Cr cds: MC, V.

🏖 🔌 🐾

Restaurants

★ **CARMELO'S.** *3607 N Mountain Rd (54401). 715/845-5570.* Hrs: 5-10 pm; Sun, Mon to 9 pm. Closed hols. Res accepted. Italian menu. Bar. Dinner $7.25-$15.75. Specializes in pasta. Parking. Family-owned. Cr cds: A, DS, MC, V.

⚃

★★ **GULLIVER'S LANDING.** *1701 Mallard Ln (54401). 715/849-8409.* Hrs: 11 am-10 pm; wkends to 11 pm. Closed hols. Res accepted. Bar. Dinner $7.95-$29.95. Child's menu. Specializes in steaks, seafood. Own breads. Parking. Outdoor dining. Nautical decor; aquariums. Dockage. Cr cds: A, DS, MC, V.

⚃ 🔌

★★ **MICHAEL'S.** *2901 Rib Mtn Dr (54401). 715/842-9856.* Hrs: 5-10 pm. Closed Sun; hols. Res accepted. Continental menu. Bar from 4 pm. Dinner $6.95-$19.95. Child's menu. Specializes in seafood, veal, beef. Parking. Wildlife pictures on walls. Cr cds: A, DS, MC, V.

D

★ ★ **WAGON WHEEL SUPPER CLUB.** *3901 N 6th St (54403). 715/675-2263. www.islpage.com/i/ wagonwheel.* Hrs: 5-10 pm. Closed Sun. Res accepted Mon-Thurs. Bar. A la carte entrees: dinner $11.75-$49.50. Specializes in charcoal-broiled steak, barbecued ribs, seafood. Parking. Rustic atmosphere. Family-owned. Cr cds: A, DS, MC, V.

D ⊒

★ **WAUSAU MINE CO.** *3904 W Stewart Ave (54401). 715/845-7304.* Hrs: 11 am-midnight. Closed Easter, Thanksgiving, Dec 24-25. Res accepted Sun-Thurs. Bar. Lunch, dinner $3.95-$16.75. Child's menu. Parking. Cr cds: A, DS, MC, V.

D SC ⊒

Wautoma

See also Green Lake, Waupaca

Pop 1,784 **Elev** 867 ft **Area code** 920 **Zip** 54982

What to See and Do

Skiing. Nordic Mountain Ski Area. Triple, double chairlifts, T-bar, poma-lift, two rope tows; patrol, school, rentals; snowmaking; restaurant, cafeteria, concession, bar. Longest run 1 mi; vertical drop 265 ft. Night skiing. (Dec-mid-Mar, Thurs-Tues; closed Dec 25); 13 mi of x-country trails (wkends only; free). 8 mi N via WI 152. Phone 920/787-3324. ¢¢¢¢

Wild Rose Pioneer Museum. Historical complex of buildings incl Elisha Stewart House, containing furniture of the late 19th century; pioneer hall; outbuildings; carriage house; blacksmith shop, cobbler shop, replica of general store, one-rm schoolhouse, apothecary; weaving rm; gift shop. Tours. (Mid-June-Labor Day, Wed and Sat afternoons; also by appt during summer) 8 mi N on WI

22, Main St, in Wild Rose. Phone 920/622-3364. ¢

Wauwatosa

See also Menomonee Falls, Milwaukee

Settled 1835 **Pop** 49,366 **Elev** 634 ft **Area code** 414
Information Chamber of Commerce, 7707 W State St, 53213; 414/453-2330

What to See and Do

Lowell Damon House. (1844) Community's oldest home is a classic example of colonial architecture; period furnishings. Tours (Sun, Wed; closed hols). 2107 Wauwatosa Ave. Phone 414/273-8288. **FREE**

Motels/Motor Lodges

★ **EXEL INN.** *115 N Mayfair Rd (53226). 414/257-0140; fax 414/475-7875; res 800/367-3935. www. exelinns.com.* 122 rms, 2 story. S $44.99-$66.99; D $65.99-$79.99; suites $105-$132; each addl (up to 4) $4; under 17 free. Crib free. Pet accepted, some restrictions. TV; cable (premium). Complimentary continental bkfst. Ck-out noon. Business servs avail. Cr cds: A, C, D, DS, MC, V.

D ◄ ⊒ ⋈ SC

★ **FORTY WINKS INN.** *11017 W Bluemound Rd (53226). 414/774-2800; fax 414/774-9134; toll-free 800/946-5746.* 31 rms (12 with shower only), 2 story. June-Aug: S, D $60-$75; each addl $6; kit. units $65-$85; lower rates rest of yr. Crib $5. TV; cable (premium). Complimentary coffee in lobby. Restaurant nearby. Ck-out 11 am. Sundries. X-country ski 1 mi. Some refrigerators. Cr cds: A, DS, MC, V.

D ⊱ ⊒ ⋈

★ ★ **HOLIDAY INN EXPRESS.** *11111 W North Ave (53226). 414/778-0333; fax 414/778-0331. www.holiday-inn.com.* 122 rms, 3 story, 8 suites. S, D $94-$109; suites $109-$119; under

18 free. Crib free. TV; cable (premium), VCR avail. Complimentary continental bkfst. Restaurant adj open 24 hrs. Ck-out noon. Meeting rms. Business servs avail. Valet serv. Health club privileges. Some refrigerators. Some balconies. Cr cds: A, C, D, DS, JCB, MC, V.

D ⊠ 🖾 SC

Restaurants

★ ★ ★ **BARTOLOTTA'S.** *7616 W State St (53213). 414/771-7910. www.bartolottas.com.* Hrs: 5:30-10 pm; Fri, Sat to 10:30 pm. Closed Sun; hols. Res accepted. Italian menu. Bar. Dinner $17-$28.95. Child's menu. Specialties: sauteed veal chop with marsala cream sauce, grilled seafood. Entertainment. Outdoor dining. Italian decor. Totally nonsmoking. Cr cds: A, D, DS, MC, V.

D

★ ★ **JAKE'S.** *6030 W North Ave (53213). 414/771-0550.* Hrs: 5-10 pm; Sun to 9 pm. Closed hols; also Super Bowl Sun. Bar. Dinner $10.95-$23.95. Child's menu. Specializes in steak, fresh seafood, roast duck. Family-owned. Totally nonsmoking. Cr cds: A, MC, V.

D

Wisconsin Dells

See also Baraboo, Mauston, Portage, Prairie du Sac

Settled 1856 **Pop** 2,393 **Elev** 912 ft
Area code 608 **Zip** 53965
Information Wisconsin Dells Visitor & Convention Bureau, 701 Superior St, PO Box 390; 608/254-4636 or 800/22-DELLS
Web www.wisdells.com

Until 1931 this city was called Kilbourn, but it changed its name in the hope of attracting tourists to the nearby Dells. It seems to have worked—Wisconsin Dells has become the state's prime tourist attraction.

What to See and Do

Beaver Springs Fishing Park and Riding Stables. Guided one-hr rides. Spring-fed ponds stocked with trout, catfish, bass, and other fish. Pay for fish caught. Pole rental. (Apr-Oct, daily) 600 Trout Rd, ½ mi S on WI 13. Phone 608/254-2735. ¢¢

Dells Boat Tours. Guided sightseeing tours through the Dells Scenic Riverway. View of towering sandstone cliffs, narrow fern-filled canyons, and unique rock formations. Upper Dells tour is two hrs with scenic shore landings at Stand Rock and Witches Gulch; Lower Dells tour is one hr and features the Rocky Island region, caverns and cliffs; complete tour is Upper and Lower Dells combined. (Mid-Apr-Oct, daily, departures every 30 min in July and Aug) Phone 608/254-8555. ¢¢¢¢

Duck tours.

⭐ **Dells Ducks.** One-hr land/water tour of scenic rock formations along Wisconsin River. (Late May-late Oct, daily) 1½ mi S on US 12. Phone 608/254-6080. ¢¢¢¢

Original Wisconsin Ducks. One-hr, 8½-mi land and water tours on the Original Wisconsin Ducks. (Apr-Oct, daily) 1 mi S on US 12. Phone 608/254-8751. ¢¢¢¢

H. H. Bennett Studio and History Center. (1865) Oldest photographic studio in the United States. The landscape and nature photography of H. H. Bennett helped make the Dells area famous. The studio is still in operation and it is possible to purchase enlargements made from Bennett's original glass negatives. (Memorial Day-Labor Day, daily; rest of yr, by appt) 215 Broadway. Phone 608/253-3523.

Riverview Park & Waterworld. Wave pool, speed slides, tube rides, and kids pools. Grand Prix, go-carts, dune cat track. Park (late May-early Sept); admission free; fee for activities. Waterworld (late May-early Sept, daily). ¼ mi S on US 12. Phone 608/254-2608. ¢¢¢¢

Skiing.

Christmas Mountain Village. Area has two double chairlifts, rope tow; patrol, school, rentals; snowmaking; restaurant, bar, snack bar. Lodge. Seven power-tilled runs; longest run ½ mi; vertical drop

250 ft. (Mid-Dec-mid-Mar, daily; closed Dec 24 eve) X-country trails; night skiing. 4 mi W on County H. Phone 608/254-3971. ¢¢¢¢

Tommy Bartlett's Thrill Show. Water ski theme, "Hooray for Hollywood," features juggling jokester, the Nerveless Knocks, "Mr. Sound Effects" Wes Harrison, and colorful entrancing waters; also laser light show (evening performances only). (Late May-early Sept, daily) 3 mi S on US 12, in Lake Delton. Phone 608/254-2525. ¢¢¢¢ Also here is

> **Tommy Bartlett's Robot World & Exploratory.** More than 150 hands-on exhibits, incl the world's only Russian Mir Space Station core module. Principles of light, sound, and motion are explored. Features robot-guided tour. (Daily) 3 mi S on US 12. Phone 608/254-2525. ¢¢¢

Wisconsin Deer Park. A 28-acre wildlife exhibit. (May-mid-Oct, daily) ½ mi S on US 12. Phone 608/253-2041. ¢¢¢

Motels/Motor Lodges

★ ★ **AMERICAN WORLD RESORT AND SUITES.** *400 Wiconsin Dells Pkwy (53965). 608/253-4451; fax 608/254-4770; toll-free 800/433-3557. www.americanworld.com.* 94 rms, 6 bldgs, 1-3 story. Memorial Day-Labor Day: S, D $69-$119; each addl $7; suites $129-$189; wkly rates; higher rates hol wkends; lower rates rest of yr. TV; cable. 6 pools; 3 indoor, whirlpools. Restaurant nearby. Ck-out 10 am. Coin lndry. Business servs avail. Tennis. Downhill ski 7 mi; x-country ski 3 mi. Lawn games. Some refrigerators, in-rm whirlpools; microwaves. Balconies. Picnic tables. RV park. Cr cds: A, D, DS, MC, V.
D ⚓ 🎿 ≋ ▨ 🐾 SC

★ ★ **BAKERS SUNSET BAY RESORT.** *921 Canyon Rd (53965). 608/254-8406; fax 608/253-2062; toll-free 800/435-6515. www.sunsetbayresort.com.* 74 units, 21 suites, 16 mini-suites, 4 cottages, 1-2 story. July-Aug: S, D $105-$195; kit. cottages $700-$985/wk; lower rates rest of yr. Crib $7. TV; cable (premium). 4 pools, 2 indoor; wading pool. Playground. Complimentary continental bkfst (off-season). Ck-out 10 am. Meeting rm. Business servs avail. Lawn games. Exercise equipt. Sauna. Game rm. Some fireplaces, microwaves. Balconies. Picnic tables. On lake; swimming beach, pontoon boats. Cr cds: A, MC, V.
D ☎ ≋ ✗ ▨ 🐾 SC

★ ★ **BEST WESTERN AMBASSADOR INN.** *610 Frontage Rd S (53965). 608/254-4477; fax 608/253-6662; toll-free 800/828-6888. www.*

Tour of the Wisconsin River aboard an amphibious Dell Duck

bestwestern.com. 181 units, 3 story, 27 suites. Late June-mid-Oct: S, D $78-$98; each addl $6; suites $98-$198; under 17 free; lower rates rest of yr. Crib $5. TV; cable (premium), VCR avail (movies). 2 pools, 1 indoor; wading pool, whirlpool. Complimentary coffee. Restaurant nearby. Ck-out 11 am. Coin lndry. Meeting rms. Business servs avail. Sundries. Gift shop. Downhill/x-country ski 4 mi. Sauna. Game rm. Refrigerator, minibar in suites; microwaves avail. Picnic tables. Cr cds: A, C, D, DS, MC, V.

⊡ ⤢ ⊠ ⊠ ⚒ SC

★★ **BLACKHAWK MOTEL.** *720 Race St (53965). 608/254-7770; fax 608/253-7333. www.blackhawkmotel. com.* 75 motel rms, 1-2 story, 9 kit. cottages. Mid-June-Labor Day: S, D $65-$110; each addl $5; suites $100-$160; cottages for 2-7, $65-$170; lower rates Apr-mid-June, after Labor Day-Oct. Closed rest of yr. Crib $5. TV; cable (premium), VCR avail (movies). Indoor/outdoor pool; wading pool, whirlpools. Playground. Complimentary coffee in lobby. Restaurant nearby. Ck-out 11 am; off-season, noon. Coin lndry. Saunas. Game rm. Some in-rm whirlpools; refrigerators, microwaves avail. Water slides. Cr cds: A, C, D, DS, MC, V.

⊡ ⤢ ⊠ ⚒

★★ **CAROUSEL INN AND SUITES.** *1031 Wisconsin Dells Pkwy (53965). 608/254-6554; fax 608/254-6554; toll-free 800/648-4765. www.carousel-inn.com.* 102 rms, 16 with shower only, 2 story. July-Aug: S, D $140; suites $240; under 18 free; higher rates wkends, hols; lower rates May-June, Sept. Closed rest of yr. Crib $10. TV; cable (premium), VCR avail (movies $5). Indoor pool; whirlpool. Playground. Ck-out 11 am. Business servs avail. Gift shop. Game rm. Refrigerators. Some in-rm whirlpools. Balconies. Indoor water slide, outdoor waterpark. Cr cds: A, DS, MC, V.

⊡ ⤢ ⊠ ⚒

★ **CHIPPEWA MOTEL.** *1114 Broadway (53965). 608/253-3982; fax 608/254-2577. www.chippewamotel. com.* 50 rms, 2 story. Mid-June-Labor Day: S, D $78-$105; suites $125-$170; family rates; lower rates rest of yr. Crib $4. TV; cable (premium). Indoor pool; whirlpool. Playground.

Restaurant opp 7 am-10 pm. Ck-out 10 am. Coin lndry. Business servs avail. Sauna. Game rm. Some in-rm whirlpools; microwaves avail. Picnic tables. Cr cds: A, DS, MC, V.

⊡ ⤢ ⚒

★★ **COMFORT INN.** *703 Frontage Rd N (53965). 608/253-3711; fax 608/254-2164; res 800/228-5150. www.comfortinn.com.* 75 rms, 3 story. Memorial Day-Labor Day: S, D $99-$150; each addl $6; higher rates spring and fall wkends; lower rates rest of yr. Crib free. TV; cable (premium). Indoor pool; whirlpool. Complimentary continental bkfst. Restaurant adj 6:30 am-1 pm, 5-9 pm. Ck-out 11 am. Business servs avail. Game rm. Refrigerators, microwaves. Cr cds: A, DS, MC, V.

⊡ ⤢ ⊠ ⚒

★ **DAYS INN.** *944 WI 12/16 (53965). 608/254-6444; fax 608/254-6444. www.daysinn.com.* 100 rms, 2 story. Late June-Aug: S $85-$99; D $105-$135; each addl $5; suites $119-$152; under 12 free; lower rates rest of yr. Crib free. TV; cable (premium). Indoor/outdoor pool; whirlpool. Restaurant adj open 24 hrs. Ck-out 11 am. Business servs avail. Downhill/x-country ski 7 mi. Sauna. Microwaves avail. Cr cds: A, D, DS, MC, V.

⊡ ⤢ ⊠ ⚒

★★ **INDIAN TRAIL MOTEL.** *1013 Broadway (53965). 608/253-2641. www.indiantrailmotel.com.* 45 rms. July-Labor Day: S $50-$60; D $60-$100; lower rates Apr-June, after Labor Day-Oct. Closed rest of yr. Crib $5. TV; cable (premium). 2 pools, 1 indoor; whirlpool. Playground. Restaurant adj 7 am-10 pm. Ck-out 10 am. Lawn games. Refrigerators, microwaves, in-rm whirlpools. On 11 acres. Cr cds: A, DS, MC, V.

⤢ ⊠ ⚒

★ **INTERNATIONAL MOTEL.** *1311 E Broadway (53965). 608/254-2431.* 45 rms. July-Labor Day: S $35-$65; D $45-$90; lower rates May-June, after Labor Day-mid-Oct. Closed rest of yr. Crib $5. Pet accepted, some restrictions. TV; cable (premium). Heated pool; wading pool. Playground. Complimentary coffee in lobby. Restaurant adj 7 am-midnight. Ck-out 11 am. Game rm. Refrigerators avail. Balconies. Picnic tables on patio. Cr cds: A, C, D, DS, MC, V.

⊡ 🐾 ☲ 🕸 🔥

★ **LUNA INN AND SUITES.** *1111 Wisconsin Dells Pkwy, Wisconsin Dells (53965). 608/253-2661; res 800/999-5862. www.lunainn.com.* 70 rms, 1-2 story. Mid-June-mid-Sept: S $65-$80; D $78-$99; each addl $8; suites $80-$178; lower rates mid-Sept-mid-Nov, mid-Apr-mid-June. Closed rest of yr. Crib $5. TV; cable (premium), VCR. 2 pools, 1 indoor; whirlpool. Game room. Coffee in lobby. Restaurant adj 7 am-10 pm. Ck-out 10:30 am. Some refrigerators, microwaves. Cr cds: DS, MC, V.

⊡ ☲ 🕸 🔥

★★ **MAYFLOWER.** *910 Wisconsin Dells Pkwy (53965). 608/253-6471; fax 608/253-7617; toll-free 800/345-7407; www.dells.com/mayflower.* 72 rms, 1-2 story. Mid-June-early Sept: S, D $98-$128; each addl $6; lower rates rest of yr. Crib $6. TV; cable (premium). 2 pools, 1 indoor; wading pool, whirlpool. Playground. Restaurant adj. Ck-out 11 am. Coin lndry. Business servs avail. Downhill ski 7 mi; x-country ski 3 mi. Sauna. Game rm. Refrigerators, microwaves; some in-rm whirlpools. Balconies. Picnic tables. Cr cds: A, D, MC, V.

☲ ☲ ✈ 🔥

★ **PARADISE MOTEL.** *1700 Wisconsin Dells Pkwy (53965). 608/254-7333; fax 608/253-2350; res 800/254-7556.* 45 rms. Mid-June-Labor Day: S, D $60-$95; suites $85-$155; family of 6-8, $85-$175; lower rates rest of yr. Crib $5. TV; cable (premium). Heated pool; wading pool, whirlpool. Playground. Restaurant nearby. Ck-out 11 am. Refrigerators; some in-rm whirlpools. Cr cds: A, DS, MC, V.

⊡ ☲ 🕸 🔥 SC

★★ **RIVER INN.** *1015 River Rd (53965). 608/253-1231; fax 608/253-6145; toll-free 800/659-5395.* 54 rms, 5 story. June-Sept: S, D $84-$159; suites $114-$159; lower rates rest of yr. TV; cable (premium). 2 pools, 1 indoor; whirlpool. Playground. Coffee in rms. Restaurant 8 am-10 pm (in season). Bar 4 pm-1 am. Ck-out 11 am. Business servs avail. Downhill/x-country ski 7 mi. Exercise equipt; sauna. Refrigerators; some

microwaves. Some balconies, patios. Cr cds: A, D, DS, MC, V.

⊡ ☲ ✈ 🎿 🕸 🔥

★★ **RIVIERA MOTEL AND SUITES.** *811 Wisconsin Dells Pkwy (53965). 608/253-1051; fax 608/253-9038; toll-free 800/800-7109. www.rivierasuites. com.* 58 rms. July-Aug: D $99-$225; lower rates rest of yr. Crib $7. TV; cable (premium). 2 pools, 1 indoor; whirlpool, water slide. Restaurant nearby. Ck-out 10:30 am. Business servs avail. Sauna. Some in-rm whirlpools, microwaves, fireplaces. Picnic table, grill. Cr cds: DS, MC, V.

⊡ ☲ 🕸 🔥

★ **SUPER 8 MOTEL.** *800 Cty Hwy H (53965). 608/254-6464; fax 608/254-2692. www.super8.com.* 123 rms, 3 story. June-Sept: S $69.99; D $87.99; each addl $6; suites $150; golf plans; lower rates rest of yr. Crib $4. Pet accepted, some restrictions. TV; cable. Complimentary continental bkfst. Complimentary coffee in rms. Restaurant adj 6-1 am. Ck-out 11 am. Business servs avail. Downhill ski 5 mi; x-country ski 3 mi. Sauna. Indoor pool; whirlpool. Picnic tables. Cr cds: A, C, D, DS, MC, V.

⊡ 🐾 ✈ ☲ 🕸 🔥

★★ **WINTERGREEN RESORT AND CONFERENCE CENTER.** *60 Gassek Rd (53940). 608/254-2285; fax 608/253-6235; toll-free 800/648-4765. www.wintergreen-resort.com.* 111 rms, 3 story. July-Aug: S, D $119-$179; each addl $8; suites $159-$339; under 18 free; wkly rates; package plans; higher rates wkends (2-day min); lower rates rest of yr. Crib $10. TV; cable (premium). 2 pools, 1 indoor; wading pool, whirlpool. Playground. Restaurant 7 am-9 pm. Ck-out 11 am. Coin lndry. Meeting rms. Business servs avail. Sundries. Gift shop. Downhill ski 12 mi; x-country ski 2 mi. Exercise equipt; sauna. Game rm. Refrigerators, microwaves, minibars; some in-rm whirlpools. Balconies. Picnic tables. Indoor/outdoor water park. Cr cds: A, DS, MC, V.

⊡ ✈ ☲ 🎿 🕸 🔥

Resorts

★★★ **CHULA VISTA RESORT AND CONFERENCE CENTER.** *4031 N*

River Rd (53965). 608/254-8366; fax 608/254-7653; toll-free 800/388-4782. www.chulavistaresort.com. 260 rms. Memorial Day-Labor Day: S $89-$159; D $99-$169; each addl $5; suites $165-$299; lower rates rest of yr. Crib $10. TV; cable (premium). 5 pools, 1 indoor; wading pool, whirl-pool, poolside serv. Dining rm 7:30 am-11 pm. Bar. Ck-out 10:30 am, ck-in 3 pm. Convention facilities. Business servs avail. Gift shop. Package store. Airport, RR station, bus depot transportation. Tennis. Golf. Downhill ski 5 mi. Snowmobiling. Hiking trails. Exercise equipt; sauna, steam rm. Miniature golf. Microwaves; some in-rm whirlpools. Balconies. Cr cds: A, D, DS, MC, V.
D ⚡ 🏋 ⚓ 🧑 ✈ ⛵ 🐾 🎿

★ ★ ★ **KALAHARI RESORT.** 1305 Kalahari Dr (53965). 608/254-5466. www.kalahariresort.com. 272 rms, 4 story. S, D $199-$299; each addl $15; under 17 free. Crib avail. Heated pool. TV; cable (premium); VCR avail. Complimentary coffee, newspaper in rms. Restaurant 6 am-10 pm. Ck-out 11 am. Meeting rms. Business center. Gift shop. Exercise rm. Some refrigerators, minibars. Extensive water park. Cr cds: A, C, D, DS, MC, V.
⚓ 🧑 🐾 🎿

Cottage Colony

★ ★ **MEADOW BROOKE RESORT.** 1533 River Rd (53965). 608/253-3201; fax 608/254-7751. 18 units, 2 story, 14 with kit., 14 cabins. No rm phones. July-Labor Day: S, D $79-$119; cabins for 4, $89-$199; kit. cabins $99-$139; family rates; lower rates May-June, after Labor Day-Oct. Closed rest of yr. TV; cable (premium). Heated pool. Playground. Restaurant nearby. Ck-out 10 am, ck-in 3 pm. Grocery 1 mi. Package store 1 mi. Hiking. Lawn games. Refrigerators, microwaves. Some balconies. Picnic tables, grills. Extensive wooded grounds. Cr cds: A, DS, MC, V.
D ⚓ 🐾

Restaurants

★ ★ **DEL-BAR.** 800 Wisconsin Dells Pkwy, Lake Delton (53940). 608/253-1861. www.del-bar.com. Hrs: 4:30-10

pm; June-Aug to 10:30 pm. Closed Thanksgiving, Dec 25. Bar. Dinner $12-$25. Friday fish fry $9.95. Specializes in custom-cut steak, pasta, fresh seafood. Parking. Family-owned. Cr cds: A, D, DS, MC, V.
D SC 🍴

★ ★ **FISCHER'S.** 441 Wisconsin Dells Pkwy S, Lake Delton (53965). 608/253-7531. Hrs: 4-11 pm. Closed Thanksgiving, Dec 24-25. Res accepted. Bar. Dinner $7-$19. Specializes in steak, barbecue ribs, fresh seafood. Child's menu. Parking. Family-owned. Cr cds: DS, MC, V.
D

★ ★ **WALLY'S HOUSE OF EMBERS.** 935 Wisconsin Dells Pkwy, Lake Delton (53940). 608/253-6411. www.dells.com/embers. Hrs: 4:30 pm-midnight. Res accepted. Bar. Dinner $9.90-$22.90. Child's menu. Specializes in hickory-smoked ribs, steak, fresh seafood. Entertainment wkends. Outdoor gazebo; garden. Family-owned. Cr cds: A, MC, V.
D 🍴

★ **WINTERGREEN GRILLE.** 60 Gasser Rd #A, Lake Delton (53940). 608/254-7686. www.dells.com/wintergrn.html. Hrs: 7 am-9 pm. Sun bkfst buffet 8-11:30 am Memorial Day-Labor Day. American, Italian menu. Wine, beer. Bkfst $3.50-$7.95, lunch $4.75-$7.95, dinner $9.95-$17.95. Sun buffet $5.95. Child's menu. Specializes in ribs, pizza. Parking. Cr cds: A, D, DS, MC, V.
D

Wisconsin Rapids

(D-4) See also Marshfield, Stevens Point

Pop 18,245 **Elev** 1,028 ft
Area code 715 **Zip** 54494
Information Wisconsin Rapids Area Convention & Visitors Bureau, 1120 Lincoln St; 715/422-4856 or 800/554-4484
Web www.wctc.net/chamber

A paper manufacturing and cranberry center, Wisconsin Rapids was formed in 1900 by consolidating the two towns of Grand Rapids and Centralia after the Wisconsin River had devastated large sections of both communities. At first the combined town was called Grand Rapids, but the name was changed when confusion with the Michigan city developed. Cranberry marshes here produce the largest inland cranberry crop in the world.

What to See and Do

Forest tour. Self-guided walking or x-country skiing tour of site of Consolidated Papers' first tree nursery, now planted with various types of hard and soft woods; 27 marked points of special interest on 60 acres. (Daily) 5 mi NE on County U, on banks of Wisconsin River. Phone 715/422-3789. **FREE**

Grotto Gardens. A six-acre garden park with series of religious tableaux, statues, and grottoes (daily). Picnic grounds. Gift shop/information center (Memorial Day-Labor Day, daily). 7 mi N via WI 34, County C in Rudolph. Phone 715/435-3120. ¢

South Wood County Historical Corporation Museum. Historical museum in town mansion. (June-Aug, Sun-Thrus, afternoons) 540 3rd St S. Phone 715/423-1580. **FREE**

Special Event

River Cities Fun Fest. Tours, car show, arts and crafts fair, water ski shows. First wkend Aug. Phone 715/423-1830.

Motels/Motor Lodges

★★ **BEST WESTERN RAPIDS MOTOR INN.** *911 Huntington Ave (54494). 715/423-3211; fax 715/423-2875; res 800/528-1234. www.best western.com.* 43 rms, 2 story. S $46-$54; D $49-$60; each addl $6; under 12 free; package plans. Crib $6. Pet accepted. TV; cable (premium). Complimentary continental bkfst. Restaurant opp open 24 hrs. Ck-out 11 am. Meeting rms. In-rm modem link. Whirlpool. X-country ski 2 mi. Refrigerators avail. Cr cds: A, C, D, DS, MC, V.
🅳 🐾 ⛷ 🗑 🐾 SC

★ **CAMELOT.** *9210 WI 13 S (54494). 715/325-5111.* 14 rms, 6 with shower only. S $35-$40; D $45-$50; each addl $2; higher rates special events. Crib $5. Pet accepted. TV; cable (premium), VCR (movies). Complimentary coffee in rms. Restaurant opp 5:30 am-8 pm. Ck-out 11 am. Downhill ski 20 mi; x-country ski 2 mi. Pool. Refrigerators; microwaves avail. Picnic tables. Cr cds: A, MC, V.
🐾 ⛷ 🗑 🐾

★ **ECONO LODGE.** *3300 8th St S (54494). 715/423-7000; fax 715/423-7150; res 800/755-1488. www.econo lodge.com.* 55 rms, 2 story. S $39.95-$44; D $49.95-$54; each addl $5; under 18 free; wkends 2-day min. Crib free. $10. TV; cable. Complimentary coffee in rms. Restaurant 6:30 am-10 pm. Bar 3 pm-2 am. Ck-out 11 am. Meeting rms. Business servs avail. In-rm modem link. Many refrigerators, microwaves. Cr cds: A, D, DS, MC, V.
🅳 🗑 🐾

★★★ **HOTEL MEAD.** *451 E Grand Ave (54494). 715/423-1500; fax 715/422-7064; res 800/843-6323. www.hotelmead.com.* 157 rms, 5 story, 51 suites. S $99; D $109; each addl $10; suites $109-$115; under 18 free; package plans. Crib avail. $15. TV; cable (premium). Complimentary coffee in rms. Restaurant 6:30 am-10 pm. Bar 11-1 am. Ck-out noon. Meeting rms. Business servs avail. In-rm modem link. Valet serv. Sundries. 18-hole golf privileges. X-country ski 2 mi. Exercise equipt. Indoor pool; whirlpool, poolside serv. Refrigerators; some bathrm phones, microwaves, wet bars. Cr cds: A, C, D, DS, MC, V.
🅳 ⛷ 🏋 ⟷ 🏌 🗑 🐾

★ **MAPLES MOTELS.** *4750 8th St S (54494). 715/423-2590; fax 715/423-2592.* 27 rms, 2 with shower only, 16 kit. units. S $35-$40; D $45-$55; each addl $5; kit. units $50-$70. Crib $5. Pet accepted. TV; cable, VCR. Complimentary coffee in suites. Restaurant opp 5-2 am. Ck-out 11 am. Business servs avail. In-rm modem link. X-country ski 2 mi. Pool. Game rm. Refrigerators; microwave in suites. Picnic tables, grills. Cr cds: A, MC, V.
🐾 ⛷ ⟷ 🐾

★★ **QUALITY INN.** *3120 8th St
(54494). 715/423-5506; fax 715/423-
7150; res 800/755-1336. www.quality
inn.com.* 36 rms, 2 story. No rm
phones. S $60-$66; D $66-$72; each
addl $6; under 18 free. TV; cable
(premium). Indoor pool. Complimentary continental bkfst. Complimentary coffee in rms. Restaurant
nearby. Ck-out 11 am. Meeting rm.
Health club privileges. Cr cds: A, C,
D, DS, MC, V.

[D] [≈] [≋] [🐾] [SC]

Woodruff

*See also Boulder Junction, Eagle River,
Lac du Flambeau, Minocqua,
Rhinelander, St. Germain*

Pop 2,000 **Elev** 1,610 ft
Area code 715 **Zip** 54568
Information Minocqua-Arbor Vitae-
Woodruff Area Chamber of Com-
merce, 8216 US 51 S, Minocqua,
54548; 715/356-5266 or 800/446-
6784
Web www.minocqua.org

Woodruff is a four-seasons playground for families and outdoor
recreationalists alike. The area has
one of the largest concentrations of
fresh water bodies in America, providing unlimited fishing and water
activities.

What to See and Do

Kastle Rock. 18-hole miniature golf
with 500-ft train track. (May-Aug,
daily) US 51 to County Trunk J, 2
blks E. Phone 715/356-6865. ¢¢¢
Woodruff State Fish Hatchery.
Hatchery (mid-Apr-mid-June). Tours
(Memorial Day-Labor Day, Mon-Fri)
2½ mi SE on County Trunk J. Phone
715/356-5211. **FREE**

Special Event

Scheer's Lumberjack Show. US 51, 2
mi N of Minocqua to WI 47. World
champion lumberjacks provide entertainment, live music. Phone
715/356-4050. June-Aug. Phone
715/634-6923.

ATTRACTION LIST

Attraction names are listed in alphabetical order followed by a symbol identifying their classification and then city. The symbols for classification are: [S] for Special Events and [W] for What to See and Do

Abraham Lincoln National Railsplitter Contest & Crafts Festival [S] *Lincoln, IL*

Actors Theater [S] *Columbus, OH*

Adlai E. Stevenson Memorial Room [W] *Bloomington, IL*

Adler Planetarium & Astronomy Museum [W] *Chicago, IL*

Administrative Building [W] *South Bend, IN*

Adventure Copper Mine [W] *Ontonagon, MI*

Adventure Island [W] *Cadillac, MI*

Advil Western Open Golf Tournament [S] *Lockport, IL*

A. E. Seaman Mineralogical Museum [W] *Houghton, MI*

African Safari Wildlife Park [W] *Port Clinton, OH*

Ahnapee State Trail [W] *Algoma, WI*

Air & Water Show [S] *Chicago, IL*

Airport Playfield [W] *Cincinnati, OH*

Air Show Parade [S] *Vandalia, OH*

Akron Art Museum [W] *Akron, OH*

Akron Civic Theatre [W] *Akron, OH*

Akron Symphony Orchestra [S] *Akron, OH*

Akron Zoological Park [W] *Akron, OH*

Albert E. Sleeper State Park [W] *Port Austin, MI*

All-American Soap Box Derby [S] *Akron, OH*

Allen County Fair [S] *Lima, OH*

Allen County-Fort Wayne Historical Society Museum [W] *Fort Wayne, IN*

Allen County Museum [W] *Lima, OH*

Allen Memorial Art Museum [W] *Oberlin, OH*

Allstate Arena [W] *Chicago, IL*

Allstate Arena [W] *Chicago O'Hare Airport Area, IL*

Alma College [W] *Alma, MI*

Aloha [W] *Cheboygan, MI*

Alp and Dell Cheesery, Deli, and Country Cafe [W] *Monroe, WI*

Alpena County Fair [S] *Alpena, MI*

Alpenfest [S] *Gaylord, MI*

Alpine Valley Ski Area [W] *Cleveland, OH*

Alton Belle Riverboat Casino [W] *Alton, IL*

Alton Museum of History and Art [W] *Alton, IL*

Alum Creek State Park [W] *Delaware, OH*

Americana Amusement Park [W] *Middletown (Butler County), OH*

American Birkebeiner [S] *Cable, WI*

American Folklore Theatre [S] *Fish Creek (Door County), WI*

American Museum of Magic [W] *Marshall, MI*

American Passion Play, The [S] *Bloomington, IL*

American Players Theatre [S] *Spring Green, WI*

American Sightseeing Tours [W] *Chicago, IL*

Amish Acres [W] *Nappanee, IN*

Amish Acres Arts & Crafts Festival [S] *Nappanee, IN*

Amish Country Tours [W] *Arcola, IL*

Amishville [W] *Geneva (Adams County), IN*

Amnicon Falls State Park [W] *Superior, WI*

Andersen Water Park & Wave Pool [W] *Saginaw, MI*

Anderson Japanese Gardens [W] *Rockford, IL*

Anderson University [W] *Anderson, IN*

Andrew J. Blackbird Museum [W] *Harbor Springs, MI*

Angel Mounds State Historic Site [W] *Evansville, IN*

Angel Museum [W] *Beloit, WI*

Ann Arbor Summer Festival [S] *Ann Arbor, MI*

Annual Ski Jumping Championships [S] *Ishpeming, MI*

Annual Sturgeon Bay Harvest Fest [S] *Sturgeon Bay (Door County), WI*

Annunciation Greek Orthodox Church [W] *Milwaukee, WI*

Antioch College [W] *Springfield, OH*

Antique Alley [W] *Richmond, IN*

Antique Auto & Race Car Museum [W] *Bedford, IN*

Antique Car Parade [S] *Hamilton, OH*

Antique shopping [W] *Kankakee, IL*

Antique Town Rods Car Show [S] *Galena, IL*

Apollo [W] *Chicago, IL*

Apostle Islands Cruise Service [W] *Bayfield, WI*

Apostle Islands National Lakeshore [W] *Bayfield, WI*

Appeal to the Great Spirit [W] *Muncie, IN*

Apple Butter Stirrin' [S] *Coshocton, OH*

Applefest [S] *Lebanon, OH*

Apple Fest [S] *Mount Pleasant, MI*

Apple Festival [S] *Bayfield, WI*

Apple Festival [S] *Charlevoix, MI*

Apple Festival [S] *Elyria, OH*

Aquaducks Water Ski Show [S] *Burlington, WI*

Aquafest [S] *Rice Lake, WI*

Aquarium [W] *Detroit, MI*

Architectural Tour [W] *Midland, MI*

Architectural tour [W] *Racine, WI*

Architectural tours [W] *Chicago, IL*

Area has 3,200 lakes, streams, and ponds [W] *Minocqua, WI*

Argyle Lake State Park [W] *Macomb, IL*

Arie Crown [W] *Chicago, IL*

Arms Family Museum of Local History, The [W] *Youngstown, OH*

Arnold Transit Company [W] *Mackinac Island, MI*

Arnold Transit Company [W] *St. Ignace, MI*

Art Center [W] *Mount Clemens, MI*

Art Chicago [S] *Chicago, IL*

Art Fair [S] *Rhinelander, WI*

Art Fair on the Square [S] *Madison, WI*

Art Institute of Chicago, The [W] *Chicago, IL*

Art in the Park [S] *Copper Harbor, MI*

Art in the Park [S] *Petoskey, MI*

"Art on the Bay"—Thunder Bay Art Show [S] *Alpena, MI*

Art on the Rocks [S] *Marquette, MI*

Arts and Crafts Dockside and St. Ignace Powwow [S] *St. Ignace, MI*

Ashtabula County Fair [S] *Ashtabula, OH*

Ashtabula County History Museum, Jennie Munger Gregory Memorial [W] *Geneva-on-the-Lake, OH*

Astor House Antique Doll & Indian Artifact Museum [W] *Copper Harbor, MI*

Atheneum Visitors' Center, The [W] *New Harmony, IN*

Atwood Lake Park [W] *New Philadelphia, OH*

Auburn-Cord-Duesenberg Museum [W] *Auburn, IN*

Auburn-Cord-Duesenberg Festival [S] *Auburn, IN*

Auditorium [W] *Chicago, IL*

Auditorium Building [W] *Chicago, IL*

Au Glaize Village [W] *Defiance, OH*

Aullwood Audubon Center and Farm [W] *Dayton, OH*

Aurora Farmers Fair [S] *Aurora, IN*

Aurora Historical Museum [W] *Aurora, IL*

Au Sable River Festival [S] *Grayling, MI*

Au Sable River International Canoe Marathon [S] *Oscoda, MI*

Auto ferry service [W] *Ludington, MI*

Auto racing [S] *Mansfield, OH*

Autumn Fest [S] *Marshall, IL*

Autumn Fest [S] *Wheaton, IL*

Autumn Leaves Craft Festival [S] *Marietta, OH*

Autumn on Parade [S] *Oregon, IL*

Back to the Days of Kosciuszko [S] *Warsaw, IN*

Badger Park [W] *Peshtigo, WI*

Bagelfest [S] *Mattoon, IL*

Baha'i House of Worship [W] *Wilmette, IL*

Baileys Harbor Brown Trout Tournament [S] *Baileys Harbor (Door County), WI*

Bald Knob [W] *Carbondale, IL*

Ball Corporation Museum [W] *Muncie, IN*

BalletMet [S] *Columbus, OH*

Balloon Fest [S] *Centralia, IL*

Balloon Rally [S] *Monroe, WI*

Ball State University [W] *Muncie, IN*

Balmoral Park Race Track [W] *Chicago, IL*

Balzekas Museum of Lithuanian Culture [W] *Chicago, IL*

Banana Split Festival [S] *Wilmington, OH*

Barker Mansion [W] *Michigan City, IN*

Barker's Island [W] *Superior, WI*

Barlow Planetarium [W] *Neenah-Menasha, WI*

Basilica of the Sacred Heart, The [W] *South Bend, IN*

Bass Festival [S] *Iron River, MI*

Batcolumn [W] *Chicago, IL*

Battery Park [W] *Sandusky, OH*

Battle of Corydon Memorial Park [W] *Corydon, IN*

Bavarian Festival [S] *Frankenmuth, MI*

Baxter's Vineyards [W] *Nauvoo, IL*

Bay City State Recreation Area [W] *Bay City, MI*

Bay County Historical Museum [W] *Bay City, MI*

Bay Days Festival [S] *Ashland, WI*

Bayfield Festival of Arts [S] *Bayfield, WI*

BB Riverboats [W] *Cincinnati, OH*

Beach Waterpark, The [W] *Mason, OH*

Bearcreek Farms [W] *Geneva (Adams County), IN*

Beaumont Memorial [W] *Mackinac Island, MI*

Beaver Creek State Park [W] *East Liverpool, OH*

Beaver Dam Lake [W] *Beaver Dam, WI*

Beaver Island Boat Company [W] *Charlevoix, MI*

Beaver Springs Fishing Park and Riding Stables [W] *Wisconsin Dells, WI*

Beck Center for the Arts [W] *Cleveland, OH*

Belle Isle [W] *Detroit, MI*

Belle Isle Zoo [W] *Detroit, MI*

Beloit College [W] *Beloit, WI*

Belvedere Mansion [W] *Galena, IL*

Bendix Woods [W] *South Bend, IN*

Ben Hur Museum [W] *Crawfordsville, IN*

Benjamin Blacksmith Shop [W] *Mackinac Island, MI*

Benjamin Wegerzyn Horticultural Center [W] *Dayton, OH*

Benzie Area Historical Museum [W] *Beulah, MI*

Bergstrom-Mahler Museum [W] *Neenah-Menasha, WI*

Berlin Raceway [W] *Grand Rapids, MI*

Betty Brinn Children's Museum [W] *Milwaukee, WI*

Beyer Home [W] *Oconto, WI*

Bicentennial Commons at Sawyer Point [W] *Cincinnati, OH*

Bicentennial Park Theater/Band Shell Complex [W] *Joliet, IL*

Big Bull Falls Blues Festival [S] *Wausau, WI*

Big Foot Beach State Park [W] *Lake Geneva, WI*

Big Powderhorn Mountain [W] *Ironwood, MI*

Bill Monroe Bluegrass Hall of Fame [W] *Nashville, IN*

Billy Graham Center Museum [W] *Wheaton, IL*

Binder Park Zoo [W] *Battle Creek, MI*

Biological Sciences Greenhouse [W] *Macomb, IL*

Birch Creek Music Center [S] *Egg Harbor (Door County), WI*

Bird Haven-Robert Ridgway Memorial [W] *Olney, IL*

Birks Museum [W] *Decatur, IL*

Bishop Hill Jordbruksdagarna [S] *Bishop Hill, IL*

Bishop Hill Museum [W] *Bishop Hill, IL*

Bishop Hill State Historic Site [W] *Bishop Hill, IL*

Bittersweet Ski Area [W] *Kalamazoo, MI*

Bjorklunden [W] *Baileys Harbor (Door County), WI*

Blackberry Historical Farm Village [W] *Aurora, IL*

Blackhand Gorge [W] *Newark, OH*

Blackhawk [W] *Elgin, IL*

Black Hawk State Historic Site [W] *Rock Island, IL*

Blackjack [W] *Ironwood, MI*

Black River Falls State Forest [W] *Black River Falls, WI*

Black River Harbor [W] *Ironwood, MI*

Blandford Nature Center [W] *Grand Rapids, MI*

Blessing of the Fleet [S] *Ashtabula, OH*

Bloomington Antique Mall [W] *Bloomington, IN*

Blossom Music Center [S] *Akron, OH*

Blossomtime Festival [S] *St. Joseph, MI*

Blueberry Festival [S] *Muskegon, MI*

Blueberry Festival [S] *South Haven, MI*

Bluegrass and Chowder Festival [S] *Salem, IL*

Blue Mound State Park [W] *Mount Horeb, WI*

Blue River Canoe Trips [W] *New Albany, IN*

Blue Rock State Park [W] *Zanesville, OH*

Bluespring Caverns [W] *Bedford, IN*
BoarsHead Theater [W] *Lansing, MI*
Boat Regatta [S] *Put-in-Bay, OH*
Boat trips [W] *Coshocton, OH*
Boat trips [W] *Sandusky, OH*
Boat trips to Manitou Islands [W] *Leland, MI*
Bob Evans Farm [W] *Gallipolis, OH*
Bob Evans Farm Festival [S] *Gallipolis, OH*
Bong State Recreation Area [W] *Kenosha, WI*
Bonneyville Mill [W] *Goshen, IN*
Boonshoft Museum of Discovery [W] *Dayton, OH*
Boston Mills [W] *Akron, OH*
Bowling Green State University [W] *Bowling Green, OH*
Boyd's Crystal Art Glass [W] *Cambridge, OH*
Boyne Highlands [W] *Harbor Springs, MI*
Bradford Beach [W] *Milwaukee, WI*
Branch County 4-H Fair [S] *Coldwater, MI*
Brandywine [W] *Akron, OH*
Bratwurst Day [S] *Sheboygan, WI*
Brenke River Sculpture and Fish Ladder [W] *Lansing, MI*
Brewery Arcade [W] *Portsmouth, OH*
Briar Street [W] *Chicago, IL*
Bridgefest [S] *Houghton, MI*
Brigham Young Home [W] *Nauvoo, IL*
Bristol Renaissance Fair [S] *Kenosha, WI*
Brockway Mountain Challenge [S] *Copper Harbor, MI*
Brockway Mountain Drive [W] *Copper Harbor, MI*
Bronner's Christmas Wonderland [W] *Frankenmuth, MI*
Bronson Park [W] *Kalamazoo, MI*
Bronson Polish Festival Days [S] *Coldwater, MI*
Brookfield Zoo [W] *Brookfield, IL*
Brookfield Zoo [W] *Chicago, IL*
Brookside Park [W] *Cleveland, OH*
Brookville Lake State Reservoir [W] *Connersville, IN*
Broughton-Sheboygan County Marsh [W] *Elkhart Lake, WI*
Brower [W] *Big Rapids, MI*
Brown County Art Gallery [W] *Nashville, IN*
Brown County Art Guild [W] *Nashville, IN*
Brown County Playhouse [S] *Nashville, IN*

Brown County State Park [W] *Bloomington, IN*
Brown County State Park [W] *Nashville, IN*
Brown Trout Festival [S] *Alpena, MI*
Brule River State Forest [W] *Superior, WI*
Brunet Island State Park [W] *Chippewa Falls, WI*
Brussels Ferry [W] *Alton, IL*
Buchanan Center for the Arts [W] *Monmouth, IL*
Buck Creek State Park [W] *Springfield, OH*
Buckeye Central Scenic Railroad [W] *Newark, OH*
Buckeye Lake State Park [W] *Newark, OH*
Buckhorn State Park [W] *Mauston, WI*
Buckingham Fountain [W] *Chicago, IL*
Buffalo Chip Throwing Contest [S] *Terre Haute, IN*
Buffalo Rock State Park [W] *Ottawa, IL*
Buffalo Trace Park [W] *Corydon, IN*
Bugline Recreation Trail [W] *Menomonee Falls, WI*
Burdette Park [W] *Evansville, IN*
Burnidge [W] *Elgin, IL*
Burpee Museum of Natural History [W] *Rockford, IL*
Burr Oak [W] *Athens, OH*
Burt Lake State Park [W] *Indian River, MI*
Butler County Fair [S] *Hamilton, OH*
Butler County Historical Museum (Benninghofen House) [W] *Hamilton, OH*
Butler Institute of American Art, The [W] *Youngstown, OH*
Butler University [W] *Indianapolis, IN*
Butler Winery [W] *Bloomington, IN*
Butter Festival [S] *Reedsburg, WI*
Caddie Woodlawn Park [W] *Menomonie, WI*
Caesar Creek State Park [W] *Wilmington, OH*
Cahokia Courthouse State Historic Site [W] *Cahokia, IL*
Cahokia Mounds State Historic Site [W] *Cahokia, IL*
Calumet Theatre [W] *Calumet, MI*
Cambridge Glass Museum, The [W] *Cambridge, OH*
Camp Chase Confederate Cemetery [W] *Columbus, OH*

Camp Five Museum and "Lumberjack Special" Steam Train Tour [W] *Crandon, WI*

Camp Perry Military Reservation [W] *Port Clinton, OH*

Campus Martius, Museum of the Northwest Territory [W] *Marietta, OH*

Canada [W] *Detroit, MI*

Canal Fulton and Museum [W] *Massillon, OH*

Candlelight Christmas [S] *Peoria, IL*

Candlelight Tour of New Salem [S] *Petersburg, IL*

Cannonsburg [W] *Grand Rapids, MI*

Canoeing [W] *Indian River, MI*

Canoeing and tubing [W] *Waupaca, WI*

Canoe trips [W] *Grayling, MI*

Cantigny [W] *Wheaton, IL*

Canton Classic Car Museum [W] *Canton, OH*

Canton Cultural Center for the Arts, The [W] *Canton, OH*

Canton Garden Center [W] *Canton, OH*

Capitol Complex Visitors Center [W] *Springfield, IL*

Cappon House [W] *Holland, MI*

Captain Frederick Pabst Mansion [W] *Milwaukee, WI*

Cardinal Greenway Rail Trail [W] *Richmond, IN*

Carew Tower [W] *Cincinnati, OH*

Carillon Park [W] *Dayton, OH*

Carillon Tower [W] *Madison, WI*

Carl Sandburg State Historic Site [W] *Galesburg, IL*

Carnation Festival [S] *Alliance, OH*

Carnegie Center for Art and History [W] *New Albany, IN*

Carousel Concepts [W] *Marion, OH*

Carrousel Magic! [W] *Mansfield, OH*

Carr Valley Cheese Factory [W] *Reedsburg, WI*

Carry Nation Festival [S] *Holly, MI*

Car Show Swap Meet [S] *Coldwater, MI*

Carson Pirie Scott [W] *Chicago, IL*

Carthage College [W] *Kenosha, WI*

Cascade & Elywood parks [W] *Elyria, OH*

Cascade Mountain Ski Area [W] *Portage, WI*

Cascades Falls Park [W] *Jackson, MI*

Cascades-Sparks Museum [W] *Jackson, MI*

Cass County Historical Museum (Jerolaman-Long House) [W] *Logansport, IN*

Castle Museum of Saginaw County History [W] *Saginaw, MI*

Castle Rock [W] *St. Ignace, MI*

Castle Rock State Park [W] *Oregon, IL*

Catawba Island State Park [W] *Port Clinton, OH*

Cathedral of the Immaculate Conception and Museum [W] *Fort Wayne, IN*

Cave of the Mounds [W] *Mount Horeb, WI*

Cave Point County Park [W] *Sturgeon Bay (Door County), WI*

Cedar Creek Settlement and Winery [W] *Cedarburg, WI*

Cedarhurst [W] *Mount Vernon, IL*

Cedarhurst Craft Fair [S] *Mount Vernon, IL*

Cedar Point [W] *Sandusky, OH*

Celebration: A Festival of the Arts [S] *Charleston, IL*

Celina Lake Festival [S] *Celina, OH*

Center for Belgian Culture [W] *Moline, IL*

Center for Cultural & Natural History [W] *Mount Pleasant, MI*

Centralia Carillon [W] *Centralia, IL*

Central Michigan University [W] *Mount Pleasant, MI*

Central Wisconsin State Fair [S] *Marshfield, WI*

Century Center [W] *South Bend, IN*

Cereal City Festival [S] *Battle Creek, MI*

Cernan Earth and Space Center [W] *Chicago O'Hare Airport Area, IL*

Chadwick Arboretum [W] *Columbus, OH*

Chain O'Lakes Area [W] *Antioch, IL*

Chain O'Lakes State Park [W] *Antioch, IL*

Chalet Cross-Country [W] *Clare, MI*

Chalet of the Golden Fleece [W] *New Glarus, WI*

Champaign County Historical Museum [W] *Champaign/Urbana, IL*

Charles A. Grignon Mansion [W] *Appleton, WI*

Charles Allis Art Museum [W] *Milwaukee, WI*

Charles A. Wustum Museum of Fine Arts [W] *Racine, WI*

Charles Gates Dawes House [W] *Evanston, IL*

Cheboygan [W] *Cheboygan, MI*

Cheboygan County Fair [S] *Cheboygan, MI*

Cheboygan Opera House [W] *Cheboygan, MI*

Chequamegon National Forest [W] *Lac du Flambeau, WI*

Chequamegon National Forest [W] *Park Falls, WI*

Chester Gould-Dick Tracy Museum [W] *Woodstock, IL*

Chicago [W] *Chicago, IL*

Chicago Academy of Sciences' Peggy Notebaert Nature Museum [W] *Chicago, IL*

Chicago Athenaeum—The Museum of Architecture and Design [W] *Schaumburg, IL*

Chicago Auto Show [S] *Chicago, IL*

Chicago Blackhawks (NHL) [W] *Chicago, IL*

Chicago Blues Festival [S] *Chicago, IL*

Chicago Botanic Garden [W] *Chicago, IL*

Chicago Botanic Garden [W] *Northbrook, IL*

Chicago Bulls (NBA) [W] *Chicago, IL*

Chicago Children's Museum [W] *Chicago, IL*

Chicago Cubs (MLB) [W] *Chicago, IL*

Chicago Cultural Center [W] *Chicago, IL*

Chicago Fire Academy [W] *Chicago, IL*

Chicago Highlights Bus Tour [W] *Chicago, IL*

Chicago Historical Society [W] *Chicago, IL*

Chicago International Film Festival [S] *Chicago, IL*

Chicago Loop Synagogue [W] *Chicago, IL*

Chicago Motor Coach Company [W] *Chicago, IL*

Chicago Neighborhood Tours [W] *Chicago, IL*

Chicago Place [W] *Chicago, IL*

Chicago River Boat Tour [W] *Chicago, IL*

Chicago Symphony Orchestra [W] *Chicago, IL*

Chicago Temple [W] *Chicago, IL*

Chicago to Mackinac Races [S] *Chicago, IL*

Chicago Tribune Tower [W] *Chicago, IL*

Chicago Trolley Company [W] *Chicago, IL*

Chicago White Sox (MLB) [W] *Chicago, IL*

Chicago Wolves (IHL) [W] *Chicago, IL*

Chief Menominee Monument [W] *Plymouth, IN*

Children's Museum [W] *Decatur, IL*

Children's Museum [W] *Detroit, MI*

Children's Museum [W] *Indianapolis, IN*

Children's Museum of Green Bay [W] *Green Bay, WI*

Children's Science & Technology Museum [W] *Terre Haute, IN*

Children's Zoo [W] *Saginaw, MI*

Chippewa Falls Zoo [W] *Chippewa Falls, WI*

Chippewa Nature Center [W] *Midland, MI*

Chippewa Valley Museum [W] *Eau Claire, WI*

Chocolate City Festival [S] *Burlington, WI*

Christmas Candle Lightings [S] *Coshocton, OH*

Christmas Candlelight Tour [S] *Lancaster, OH*

Christmas in the Park [S] *Brazil, IN*

Christmas in the Village [S] *Naperville, IL*

Christmas in Zoar [S] *New Philadelphia, OH*

Christmas Mountain Village [W] *Wisconsin Dells, WI*

Christmas on the Square [S] *Corydon, IN*

Christmas Walk [S] *Geneva, IL*

Christy Woods [W] *Muncie, IN*

Cincinnati Art Museum [W] *Cincinnati, OH*

Cincinnati Ballet [S] *Cincinnati, OH*

Cincinnati Bengals (NFL) [W] *Cincinnati, OH*

Cincinnati Fire Museum [W] *Cincinnati, OH*

Cincinnati History Museum [W] *Cincinnati, OH*

Cincinnati Opera [S] *Cincinnati, OH*

Cincinnati Playhouse in the Park [W] *Cincinnati, OH*

Cincinnati Reds (MLB) [W] *Cincinnati, OH*

Cincinnati Symphony Orchestra [S] *Cincinnati, OH*

Cincinnati Zoo and Botanical Garden [W] *Cincinnati, OH*

Cinergy Children's Museum [W] *Cincinnati, OH*

Circle M Corral Family Fun Park [W] *Minocqua, WI*

Circus City Festival [S] *Peru, IN*

Circus Museum [W] *Peru, IN*

Circus World Museum [W] *Baraboo, WI*

City Folk Festival [S] *Dayton, OH*

City Greenhouses and Conservatory [W] *South Bend, IN*

City Hall [W] *Cincinnati, OH*

City Hall [W] *Cleveland, OH*

City Hall [W] *Columbus, OH*

City Hall [W] *Milwaukee, WI*

City Hall and Bell Tower [W] *Bay City, MI*

City Market [W] *Indianapolis, IN*

City of Douglas [W] *Saugatuck, MI*

City of Joseph Pageant [S] *Nauvoo, IL*

City of Sculpture [W] *Waupun, WI*

City Park [W] *Marinette, WI*

Civic Center [W] *Detroit, MI*

Civic Garden Center of Greater Cincinnati [W] *Cincinnati, OH*

Civic Opera Building [W] *Chicago, IL*

Civic Opera House [W] *Chicago, IL*

Civilian Conservation Corps Museum [W] *Rhinelander, WI*

Civil War Days [S] *Rockville, IN*

Civil War Encampment & President Hayes Birthday Reunion [S] *Fremont, OH*

Civil War Living History Days [S] *Glenview, IL*

Civil War Muster & Battle Reenactment [S] *Jackson, MI*

Clare County Fair [S] *Harrison, MI*

Clark County Fair [S] *Springfield, OH*

Clarke Historical Library [W] *Mount Pleasant, MI*

Clay County Historical Museum [W] *Brazil, IN*

Clear Fork Reservoir [W] *Mansfield, OH*

Clear Fork Ski Area [W] *Mansfield, OH*

Clegg Botanical Garden [W] *Lafayette, IN*

Clements Canoes [W] *Crawfordsville, IN*

Clendening Lake Marina [W] *Gnadenhutten, OH*

Cleveland Arcade, The [W] *Cleveland, OH*

Cleveland Botanical Garden [W] *Cleveland, OH*

Cleveland Browns (NFL) [W] *Cleveland, OH*

Cleveland Cavaliers (NBA) [W] *Cleveland, OH*

Cleveland Hopkins International Airport [W] *Cleveland, OH*

Cleveland Indians (MLB) [W] *Cleveland, OH*

Cleveland Institute of Art [W] *Cleveland, OH*

Cleveland Institute of Music [W] *Cleveland, OH*

Cleveland Metroparks [W] *Cleveland, OH*

Cleveland Metroparks Zoo [W] *Cleveland, OH*

Cleveland Museum of Art, The [W] *Cleveland, OH*

Cleveland Museum of Natural History [W] *Cleveland, OH*

Cleveland National Air Show [S] *Cleveland, OH*

Cleveland Orchestra, The [W] *Cleveland, OH*

Cleveland Play House [W] *Cleveland, OH*

Cleveland Rockers (WNBA) [W] *Cleveland, OH*

Cleveland State University [W] *Cleveland, OH*

Clifty Falls State Park [W] *Madison, IN*

Clinch Park [W] *Traverse City, MI*

Clowes Memorial Hall [W] *Indianapolis, IN*

Clowes Pavilion [W] *Indianapolis, IN*

Coast Guard Festival [S] *Grand Haven, MI*

Cobo Hall-Cobo Arena [W] *Detroit, MI*

Coleman A. Young Municipal Center [W] *Detroit, MI*

Coles County Courthouse [W] *Charleston, IL*

Coles County Fair [S] *Charleston, IL*

Colgate Clock [W] *Jeffersonville, IN*

College Football Hall of Fame [W] *South Bend, IN*

College of Wooster [W] *Wooster, OH*

Colonel Eli Lilly Civil War Museum [W] *Indianapolis, IN*

Colonial Michilimackinac [W] *Mackinaw City, MI*

Colonial Michilimackinac Pageant [S] *Mackinaw City, MI*

Colony Blacksmith Shop [W] *Bishop Hill, IL*

Colony Church [W] *Bishop Hill, IL*

Colony Store [W] *Bishop Hill, IL*

Colorama [S] *Lac du Flambeau, WI*

Columbian Park [W] *Lafayette, IN*

Columbus Area Visitors Center [W] *Columbus, IN*

Columbus Bluegrass & Craft Show [S] *Columbus, IN*

Columbus Blue Jackets (NHL) [W] *Columbus, OH*

Columbus Crew (MLS) [W] *Columbus, OH*

Columbus Museum of Art [W] *Columbus, OH*

Columbus Symphony Orchestra [W] *Columbus, OH*

Columbus Zoo [W] *Columbus, OH*

Commons, The [W] *Columbus, IN*

Community Circle Theater [S] *Grand Rapids, MI*

Community House Number 2 [W] *New Harmony, IN*

Concerts on the Square [S] *Madison, WI*

Concrete Park [W] *Park Falls, WI*

Confederate Soldiers' Cemetery [W] *Alton, IL*

Conneaut Historical Railroad Museum [W] *Ashtabula, OH*

Conner Prairie [W] *Indianapolis, IN*

Conservatory of Music [W] *Oberlin, OH*

Constitution Elm Monument [W] *Corydon, IN*

Contemporary Arts Center [W] *Cincinnati, OH*

Cook-Rutledge Mansion [W] *Chippewa Falls, WI*

Copper Falls State Park [W] *Ashland, WI*

Copper Harbor Lighthouse Tour [W] *Copper Harbor, MI*

Copper Peak Ski Flying [W] *Ironwood, MI*

Copshaholm [W] *South Bend, IN*

Corn Fest [S] *De Kalb, IL*

Cornish Pumping Engine & Mining Museum [W] *Iron Mountain, MI*

Corn Stock Theater [W] *Peoria, IL*

Corydon Capitol State Historic Site [W] *Corydon, IN*

Coshocton Canal Festival [S] *Coshocton, OH*

COSI Columbus, Ohio's Center of Science & Industry [W] *Columbus, OH*

COSI Toledo [W] *Toledo, OH*

Cosley Animal Farm & Museum [W] *Wheaton, IL*

Country Concert at Hickory Hill Lakes [S] *Sidney, OH*

County Court House and Administration Building [W] *Cleveland, OH*

County Fair [S] *Rice Lake, WI*

County Museum [W] *Nashville, IN*

County recreation areas [W] *Flint, MI*

Court of Honor [W] *Milwaukee, WI*

Covered Bridge [W] *Waupaca, WI*

Covered Bridge Festival [S] *Ashtabula, OH*

Cowan Lake State Park [W] *Wilmington, OH*

Crab Orchard National Wildlife Refuge [W] *Marion, IL*

Cranberry bog tours [W] *Manitowish Waters, WI*

Cranberry Fest [S] *Eagle River, WI*

Cranberry Festival [S] *Tomah, WI*

Cranbrook Academy of Art and Museum [W] *Bloomfield Hills, MI*

Cranbrook Educational Community [W] *Bloomfield Hills, MI*

Cranbrook Gardens [W] *Bloomfield Hills, MI*

Cranbrook House [W] *Bloomfield Hills, MI*

Cranbrook Institute of Science [W] *Bloomfield Hills, MI*

Crane Creek State Park [W] *Toledo, OH*

Crane Park [W] *Kalamazoo, MI*

Cream of Wheaton [S] *Wheaton, IL*

Creegan Company [W] *Steubenville, OH*

Crex Meadows Wildlife Area [W] *St. Croix Falls, WI*

Crispus Attucks Museum [W] *Indianapolis, IN*

Crocker House [W] *Mount Clemens, MI*

Crosby Festival of the Arts [S] *Toledo, OH*

Cross-Country Ski Weekend [S] *Peru, IL*

Cross in the Woods [W] *Indian River, MI*

Crossroads Village/Huckleberry Railroad [W] *Flint, MI*

Crown Hill Cemetery [W] *Indianapolis, IN*

Crown Space Center [W] *Chicago, IL*

Crystal Cave [W] *Put-in-Bay, OH*

Crystal Traditions [W] *Tiffin, OH*

Culbertson Mansion State Historic Site [W] *New Albany, IN*

Cultural Gardens [W] *Cleveland, OH*

Cuneo Museum & Gardens [W] *Libertyville, IL*

Curious Kids Museum [W] *St. Joseph, MI*

Curwood Castle [W] *Owosso, MI*

Curwood Festival [S] *Owosso, MI*

Custer's Last Stand Festival of Arts [S] *Evanston, IL*

Custom House Museum [W] *Cairo, IL*

Cuyahoga County Fair [S] *Cleveland, OH*

Cuyahoga River Gorge Reservation [W] *Akron, OH*

Cuyahoga Valley Line Steam Railroad [W] *Cleveland, OH*

Cuyahoga Valley National Park [W] *Akron, OH*

Cuyahoga Valley Scenic Railroad [W] *Akron, OH*

Dahlem Environmental Education Center [W] *Jackson, MI*

Dairy Days Celebration [S] *Platteville, WI*

Dairyfest [S] *Marshfield, WI*

Dam Fest [S] *Hamilton, OH*

Dana-Thomas House State Historic Site [W] *Springfield, IL*

Dane County Fair [S] *Madison, WI*

Dane County Farmers' Market [W] *Madison, WI*

Dan Quayle Center, Home of the United States Vice-Presidential Museum, The [W] *Huntington, IN*

Daughters of Union Veterans of the Civil War Museum [W] *Springfield, IL*

David Adler Cultural Center [W] *Libertyville, IL*

David Crabill House [W] *Springfield, OH*

David Lenz House [W] *New Harmony, IN*

Davisburg Candle Factory [W] *Holly, MI*

Dawes Arboretum [W] *Newark, OH*

Days Fest [S] *Salem, IL*

Dayton Air Show [S] *Dayton, OH*

Dayton Art Institute, The [W] *Dayton, OH*

Dayton Art Institute Concert Series, The [S] *Dayton, OH*

Dayton Lane Historic Area Walking Tour [W] *Hamilton, OH*

Death's Door Bluff [W] *Ellison Bay (Door County), WI*

Deer Acres [W] *Bay City, MI*

Deere & Company [W] *Moline, IL*

Deer Forest [W] *St. Joseph, MI*

Degenhart Paperweight and Glass Museum [W] *Cambridge, OH*

Delaware County Fair [S] *Delaware, OH*

Delaware County Fair [S] *Muncie, IN*

Delaware County Historical Society Museum [W] *Delaware, OH*

Delaware Mine Tour [W] *Copper Harbor, MI*

Delaware State Park [W] *Delaware, OH*

Delhi [W] *Ann Arbor, MI*

Dells Boat Tours [W] *Wisconsin Dells, WI*

Dells Ducks [W] *Wisconsin Dells, WI*

Dells Mills Museum [W] *Eau Claire, WI*

Delta County Historical Museum and Sand Point Lighthouse [W] *Escanaba, MI*

*Delta Queen*and*Mississippi Queen* [W] *Cincinnati, OH*

Deming Park [W] *Terre Haute, IN*

Dennos Art Center [W] *Traverse City, MI*

DePaul University [W] *Chicago, IL*

DePauw University [W] *Greencastle, IN*

Detroit Grand Prix [S] *Detroit, MI*

Detroit Historical Museum [W] *Detroit, MI*

Detroit Institute of Arts [W] *Detroit, MI*

Detroit Lions (NFL) [W] *Detroit, MI*

Detroit Pistons (NBA) [W] *Detroit, MI*

Detroit Pistons (NBA) [W] *Pontiac, MI*

Detroit Public Library [W] *Detroit, MI*

Detroit Red Wings (NHL) [W] *Detroit, MI*

Detroit Shock (WNBA) [W] *Detroit, MI*

Detroit Symphony Orchestra Hall [W] *Detroit, MI*

Detroit Tigers (MLB) [W] *Detroit, MI*

Detroit Zoo [W] *Detroit, MI*

Detwiler/Bay View Park [W] *Toledo, OH*

Devil's Head Resort [W] *Baraboo, WI*

Devil's Lake State Park [W] *Baraboo, WI*

Dexter-Huron [W] *Ann Arbor, MI*

Dickens Festival [S] *Holly, MI*

Dickson Mounds State Museum [W] *Havana, IL*

Diesel Locomotive Excursion [W] *French Lick, IN*

Dillon State Park [W] *Zanesville, OH*

Dinosaur Gardens Prehistoric Zoo [W] *Alpena, MI*

Discovery Center Museum [W] *Rockford, IL*

Discovery World Museum of Science, Economics and Technology [W] *Milwaukee, WI*

Dittrick Museum of Medical History [W] *Cleveland, OH*

Dobbs Park & Nature Center [W] *Terre Haute, IN*

Dodge County Fair [S] *Beaver Dam, WI*

Dodge County Historical Museum [W] *Beaver Dam, WI*

Donald E. Stevens Convention Center [W] *Chicago, IL*

Donley's Wild West Town [W] *Union, IL*

Door County Maritime Museum [W] *Ellison Bay (Door County), WI*

Door County Maritime Museum [W] *Sturgeon Bay (Door County), WI*

Door County Museum [W] *Sturgeon Bay (Door County), WI*

Door Prairie Museum [W] *La Porte, IN*

Dossin Great Lakes Museum [W] *Detroit, MI*

Doty Cabin [W] *Neenah-Menasha, WI*

Dover Lake Waterpark [W] *Akron, OH*

Dow Gardens [W] *Midland, MI*

Dowling House [W] *Galena, IL*

Down Memory Lane Parade and Straits Area Antique Auto Show [S] *St. Ignace, MI*

Downtown Traverse City Art Fair [S] *Traverse City, MI*

Dr. William Hutchings Hospital Museum [W] *Madison, IN*

Duck tours [W] *Wisconsin Dells, WI*

Dulcimer Days [S] *Coshocton, OH*

Duluth-Superior Excursions [W] *Superior, WI*

Dunham Tavern Museum [W] *Cleveland, OH*

Du Page County Fair [S] *Wheaton, IL*

Du Page County Historical Museum [W] *Wheaton, IL*

Du Quoin State Fair [S] *Du Quoin, IL*

DuSable Museum of African-American History [W] *Chicago, IL*

Dutch Village [W] *Holland, MI*

Dwight Foster House [W] *Fort Atkinson, WI*

EAA Air Adventure Museum [W] *Oshkosh, WI*

EAA Air Venture [S] *Oshkosh, WI*

Eagle Cave [W] *Richland Center, WI*

Eagle Creek Park [W] *Indianapolis, IN*

Earlham College [W] *Richmond, IN*

Early West Street Log Structures [W] *New Harmony, IN*

Easley's Winery [W] *Indianapolis, IN*

Eastern Illinois University [W] *Charleston, IL*

Eastern Market [W] *Detroit, MI*

Eastern Michigan University [W] *Ypsilanti, MI*

East Fork State Park [W] *Cincinnati, OH*

East Harbor State Park [W] *Port Clinton, OH*

East Lansing Art Festival [S] *Lansing, MI*

East Race Waterway [W] *South Bend, IN*

Eastwood Lake [W] *Dayton, OH*

Echo Valley [W] *Kalamazoo, MI*

Eck Visitors Center [W] *South Bend, IN*

Eden Park [W] *Cincinnati, OH*

Edgar Lee Masters Memorial Home [W] *Petersburg, IL*

Edgewater Park [W] *Cleveland, OH*

Edgewood College [W] *Madison, WI*

Educational Memorabilia Center, The [W] *Bowling Green, OH*

Edwards Place [W] *Springfield, IL*

Effigy Tumuli Sculpture [W] *Ottawa, IL*

Eghart House [W] *Port Washington, WI*

1850 Doctor's Office [W] *New Harmony, IN*

1800s Craft Fair [S] *Lincoln, IL*

1810 House, The [W] *Portsmouth, OH*

1830 Owen House [W] *New Harmony, IN*

Eiteljorg Museum of American Indian and Western Art [W] *Indianapolis, IN*

Elgin Area Historical Society Museum [W] *Elgin, IL*

Elgin Public Museum [W] *Elgin, IL*

Elgin Symphony Orchestra [S] *Elgin, IL*

Elkhart County Historical Museum [W] *Elkhart, IN*

Ella Sharp Museum [W] *Jackson, MI*

Ella Sharp Park [W] *Jackson, MI*

Ellwood House Museum [W] *De Kalb, IL*

Elmhurst Historical Museum [W] *Elmhurst, IL*

Elroy-Sparta State Trail [W] *Sparta, WI*

Elvehjem Museum of Art [W] *Madison, WI*

Elwood Haynes Museum [W] *Kokomo, IN*

Embassy Theatre [W] *Fort Wayne, IN*

Empire in Pine Lumber Museum [W] *Menomonie, WI*

Empress Casino Joliet [W] *Joliet, IL*

Enshrinement Festival [S] *South Bend, IN*

Entertainment [S] *Indianapolis, IN*

Erie County Fair [S] *Sandusky, OH*

Erieview Park [W] *Geneva-on-the-Lake, OH*

Erlander Home Museum [W] *Rockford, IL*

Ernest Hemingway Museum [W] *Oak Park, IL*

Ethnic Festival [S] *Springfield, IL*

Ethnic Festivals [S] *Milwaukee, WI*

Euclid Beach Park [W] *Cleveland, OH*

Eugene V. Debs Home [W] *Terre Haute, IN*

Eureka College [W] *Peoria, IL*

Evanston Ecology Center [W] *Evanston, IL*

Evansville Freedom Festival [S] *Evansville, IN*

Evansville Museum of Arts, History and Science [W] *Evansville, IN*

Evansville Philharmonic Orchestra [S] *Evansville, IN*

Excursion boats [W] *Lake Geneva, WI*

Executive Mansion [W] *Springfield, IL*

Exhibit Museum of Natural History [W] *Ann Arbor, MI*

Factory Outlet Stores [W] *Frankenmuth, MI*

Factory outlet stores [W] *Kenosha, WI*

F. A. Deleglise Cabin [W] *Antigo, WI*

Fair at New Boston [S] *Springfield, OH*

Fairfield County Fair [S] *Lancaster, OH*

Fairlawn Mansion and Museum [W] *Superior, WI*

Fairmount, Hometown of James Dean [W] *Marion, IN*

Fairmount Museum Days/Remembering James Dean [S] *Marion, IN*

Fairmount Park [W] *Collinsville, IL*

Fairport Harbor Lighthouse and Marine Museum [W] *Painesville, OH*

Fairview Park [W] *Centralia, IL*

Fairview Park [W] *Decatur, IL*

Fall Festival [S] *Marshfield, WI*

Fall Festival [S] *Midland, MI*

Fall Festival [S] *Plymouth, MI*

Fall Festival, Car Show, and 5-K Pumpkin Run/Walk [S] *Connersville, IN*

Fall Festival of Arts & Crafts [S] *Olney, IL*

Fall Festival of Leaves [S] *Chillicothe, OH*

Fall foliage hikes and tours [S] *Portsmouth, OH*

Fall Harvest Days [S] *Dearborn, MI*

Fall-O-Rama [S] *Waupaca, WI*

Fall Tour of Homes [S] *Galena, IL*

Farm, The [W] *Sturgeon Bay (Door County), WI*

Farm City Festival [S] *Mount Clemens, MI*

Farmington Founders Festival [S] *Farmington, MI*

Farrington's Grove Historical District [W] *Terre Haute, IN*

Father Marquette National Memorial [W] *St. Ignace, MI*

Fayette [W] *Manistique, MI*

Fayette County Free Fair [S] *Connersville, IN*

Feast of the Flowering Moon [S] *Chillicothe, OH*

Feast of the Hunters' Moon [S] *Lafayette, IN*

Feast of the Ste. Claire [S] *Port Huron, MI*

Federal Building [W] *Columbus, OH*

Federal Building [W] *Sault Ste. Marie, MI*

Federal Buildings [W] *Cleveland, OH*

Fenner Nature Center [W] *Lansing, MI*

Fenn Valley Vineyards and Wine Cellar [W] *Saugatuck, MI*

Fenton Art Glass Company [W] *Marietta, OH*

Fermi National Accelerator Laboratory [W] *Aurora, IL*

Ferne Clyffe State Park [W] *Carbondale, IL*

Fernwood Botanic Gardens [W] *Niles, MI*

Ferrous Frolics [S] *Iron River, MI*

Ferry services [W] *Mackinac Island, MI*

Ferry service to Isle Royale National Park [W] *Copper Harbor, MI*

Ferry service to Isle Royale National Park [W] *Houghton, MI*

Ferry to Washington Island [W] *Ellison Bay (Door County), WI*

Festival [S] *Grand Rapids, MI*

Festival of Blossoms [S] *Door County, WI*

Festival of Summer [S] *Elkhorn, WI*

Festival of the Arts [S] *Iron Mountain, MI*

Festival of the Fish [S] *Vermilion, OH*

Festival of the Gnomes [S] *Joliet, IL*

Festival of the Hills [S] *Ironton, OH*

Festival of the Vine [S] *Geneva, IL*

Fiddlers' Gathering [S] *Lafayette, IN*

Field Museum [W] *Chicago, IL*

Fiesta Waukesha [S] *Waukesha, WI*

Finnish-American Heritage Center [W] *Hancock, MI*

Firefly Festival of the Performing Arts [S] *South Bend, IN*

First Division Museum [W] *Wheaton, IL*

First Street Historic District [W] *Menominee, MI*

First Unitarian Society [W] *Madison, WI*

Fisher Building [W] *Detroit, MI*

Fishing [W] *Ashland, WI*

Fishing [W] *Cheboygan, MI*

Fishing, whitewater rafting, canoeing [W] *Marinette, WI*

Fish Ladder [W] *Grand Rapids, MI*

500 Festival [S] *Indianapolis, IN*

500-Miler Snowmobile Run [S] *Grand Marais, MI*

Flambeau Rama [S] *Park Falls, WI*

Flambeau River State Forest [W] *Ladysmith, WI*

Flamingo [W] *Chicago, IL*

Flanagan House [W] *Peoria, IL*

Flea Market [S] *Shawano, WI*

Flint College and Cultural Corporation [W] *Flint, MI*

Flint Institute of Arts [W] *Flint, MI*

Flint Ridge State Memorial [W] *Newark, OH*

Floodwall Murals Project [W] *Portsmouth, OH*

Foellinger-Freimann Botanical Conservatory [W] *Fort Wayne, IN*

Foellinger Theatre [S] *Fort Wayne, IN*

Folkfest [S] *Manistique, MI*

Fond du Lac County Park [W] *Waupun, WI*

Ford International Detroit Jazz Festival [S] *Detroit, MI*

Ford Lake Park [W] *Ypsilanti, MI*

Foremost Farms [W] *Reedsburg, WI*

Forest City Queen [W] *Rockford, IL*

Forest Glen Preserve [W] *Danville, IL*

Forest Park [W] *Brazil, IN*

Forest Park Nature Center [W] *Peoria, IL*

Forest preserves [W] *Elgin, IL*

Forest tour [W] *Wisconsin Rapids, WI*

Forks of the Wabash [W] *Huntington, IN*

Forks of the Wabash Pioneer Festival [S] *Huntington, IN*

For-Mar Nature Preserve and Arboretum [W] *Flint, MI*

Fort Ancient State Memorial [W] *Columbus, OH*

Fort Ancient State Memorial [W] *Lebanon, OH*

Fort Ancient State Memorial [W] *Wilmington, OH*

Fort Crawford Museum [W] *Prairie du Chien, WI*

Fort Custer State Recreation Area [W] *Battle Creek, MI*

Fort Defiance Days [S] *Defiance, OH*

Fort Defiance State Park [W] *Cairo, IL*

Fort Hill State Memorial [W] *Columbus, OH*

Fort Knox II [W] *Vincennes, IN*

Fort Laurens State Memorial [W] *New Philadelphia, OH*

Fort Mackinac [W] *Mackinac Island, MI*

Fort Meigs State Memorial [W] *Toledo, OH*

Fort Ouiatenon [W] *Lafayette, IN*

Fort St. Joseph Museum [W] *Niles, MI*

Fort Wayne Children's Zoo [W] *Fort Wayne, IN*

Fort Wayne Museum of Art [W] *Fort Wayne, IN*

Fort Wilkins State Park [W] *Copper Harbor, MI*

Fort Winnebago Surgeons' Quarters [W] *Portage, WI*

Fountain Square Plaza [W] *Cincinnati, OH*

Four Flags Area Apple Festival [S] *Niles, MI*

The Four Seasons [W] *Chicago, IL*

Fourth Presbyterian Church [W] *Chicago, IL*

Fourth St Art Fair [S] *Bloomington, IN*

Fowler Park Pioneer Village [W] *Terre Haute, IN*

Fox Cities Children's Museum [W] *Appleton, WI*

Fox Ridge State Park [W] *Charleston, IL*

Fox River Trolley Museum [W] *Elgin, IL*

France Park [W] *Logansport, IN*

Frances E. Willard Home/National Woman's Christian Temperance Union [W] *Evanston, IL*

Francis Stupey Log Cabin [W] *Highland Park, IL*

Frankenmuth Historical Museum [W] *Frankenmuth, MI*

Frankenmuth Oktoberfest [S] *Frankenmuth, MI*

Frankenmuth Riverboat Tours [W] *Frankenmuth, MI*

Franklin House [W] *Chillicothe, OH*

Frank Lloyd Wright architecture [W] *Madison, WI*

Frank Lloyd Wright Home and Studio [W] *Oak Park, IL*

Frederick C. Crawford Auto-Aviation Collection [W] *Cleveland, OH*

Frederik Meijer Gardens and Sculpture Park [W] *Grand Rapids, MI*

Freeport Arts Center [W] *Freeport, IL*

French Art Colony [W] *Gallipolis, OH*

Friends Creek Regional Park [W] *Decatur, IL*

Frontier Day [S] *Terre Haute, IN*

Frostbite Open [S] *Harrison, MI*

Fullersburg Woods Environmental Center [W] *Oak Brook, IL*

Funk Prairie Home [W] *Bloomington, IL*

Fyr-Bal Fest [S] *Ephraim (Door County), WI*

Galena Arts Festival [S] *Galena, IL*

Galena Country Fair [S] *Galena, IL*

Galena-Jo Daviess County History Museum [W] *Galena, IL*

Galena Post Office & Customs House [W] *Galena, IL*

Gallery Shop [W] *Newark, OH*

Galloway House and Village [W] *Fond du Lac, WI*

Galpin Wildlife and Bird Sanctuary [W] *Milan, OH*

Gardenview Horticultural Park [W] *Strongsville, OH*

Garfield Farm Museum [W] *Geneva, IL*

Garfield Park and Conservatory [W] *Chicago, IL*

Garfield Park and Conservatory [W] *Indianapolis, IN*

Gaylord Building [W] *Lockport, IL*

Geauga County Historical Society-Century Village [W] *Chardon, OH*

Geauga County Maple Festival [S] *Chardon, OH*

Gebhard Woods State Park [W] *Morris, IL*

General Motors Corporation [W] *Janesville, WI*

Genesee-C. S. Mott Lake [W] *Flint, MI*

Genesius Guild [S] *Rock Island, IL*

Gene Stratton Porter Historic Site [W] *Auburn, IN*

Geneva Grape Jamboree [S] *Geneva-on-the-Lake, OH*

Geneva Historical Society Museum [W] *Geneva, IL*

Geneva Lake [W] *Lake Geneva, WI*

Geneva State Park [W] *Geneva-on-the-Lake, OH*

Geology Museum [W] *Madison, WI*

George Keppler House [W] *New Harmony, IN*

George L. Luthy Memorial Botanical Garden [W] *Peoria, IL*

George Rogers Clark National Historical Park [W] *Vincennes, IN*

George W. Mead Wildlife Area [W] *Stevens Point, WI*

Georgian, The [W] *Lancaster, OH*

Gerald R. Ford Museum [W] *Grand Rapids, MI*

Gerald R. Ford Presidential Library [W] *Ann Arbor, MI*

Germanfest [S] *Fort Wayne, IN*

German Friendship Garden, The [W] *Richmond, IN*

Germania Maennerchor Volkfest [S] *Evansville, IN*

German Village [W] *Columbus, OH*

German Village Walking Tour [W] *Hamilton, OH*

Giant City State Park [W] *Carbondale, IL*

Gillette Visitor Center [W] *Muskegon, MI*

Gillson Park [W] *Wilmette, IL*

Gilmore-CCCA Museum [W] *Kalamazoo, MI*

Glacial Grooves State Memorial [W] *Kelleys Island, OH*

Gladiolus Festival [S] *Kankakee, IL*

Gladiolus fields [W] *Kankakee, IL*

Glamorgan Castle [W] *Alliance, OH*

Glass Heritage Festival [S] *Tiffin, OH*

Glass Heritage Gallery [W] *Tiffin, OH*

Glendower State Memorial Museum [W] *Lebanon, OH*

Glen Miller Park [W] *Richmond, IN*

Glen Oak Park & Zoo [W] *Peoria, IL*

Glockenspiel [W] *Frankenmuth, MI*

Gnadenhutten Historical Park and Museum [W] *Gnadenhutten, OH*

Gogebic County Fair [S] *Ironwood, MI*

Golf Center at Kings Island [W] *Mason, OH*

Goodman [W] *Chicago, IL*

Goodtime III boat cruise [W] *Cleveland, OH*

Goodyear World of Rubber [W] *Akron, OH*

Goose Island County Park [W] *La Crosse, WI*

Gordon Park [W] *Cleveland, OH*

Gorge of the St. Croix River, The [W] *St. Croix Falls, WI*

Governor Dodge State Park [W] *Dodgeville, WI*

Governor Hendricks' Headquarters [W] *Corydon, IN*

Governor Knowles State Forest [W] *St. Croix Falls, WI*

Grace Episcopal Church [W] *Galena, IL*

Graceland Cemetery Tour [W] *Chicago, IL*

Grand American World Trapshooting Championship of the Amateur Trapshooting Association of America [S] *Vandalia, OH*

Granddad Bluff [W] *La Crosse, WI*

Grande Levée [S] *Vandalia, IL*

Grand Geneva Resort [W] *Lake Geneva, WI*

Grand Haven State Park [W] *Grand Haven, MI*

Grand Lake-St. Marys State Park [W] *Celina, OH*

Grand Opera House [W] *Oshkosh, WI*

Grand Rapids Art Museum [W] *Grand Rapids, MI*

Grand Victoria Riverboat Casino [W] *Elgin, IL*

Granite Peak Ski Area [W] *Wausau, WI*

Grant Park [W] *Chicago, IL*

Grant Park July 3 Concert [S] *Chicago, IL*

Grant Park Music Festival [S] *Chicago, IL*

Grape Festival [S] *Nauvoo, IL*

Graue Mill and Museum [W] *Oak Brook, IL*

Grave of Joseph Smith [W] *Nauvoo, IL*

Gray Line bus tours [W] *Detroit, MI*

Gray Line Tours [W] *Chicago, IL*

Great Cardboard Boat Regatta [S] *Sheboygan, WI*

Great Circus Parade [S] *Milwaukee, WI*

Greater Columbus Arts Festival [S] *Columbus, OH*

Greater Lafayette Museum of Art [W] *Lafayette, IN*

Great Lakes Kite Festival [S] *Grand Haven, MI*

Great Lakes Marine and US Coast Guard Memorial Museum [W] *Ashtabula, OH*

Great Lakes Rendezvous [S] *Saginaw, MI*

Great Lakes Science Center [W] *Cleveland, OH*

Great Schooner Race [S] *Bayfield, WI*

Green Bay Botanical Gardens [W] *Green Bay, WI*

Green Bay Packer Hall of Fame [W] *Green Bay, WI*

Greenfield Village [W] *Dearborn, MI*

Green Lake Conference Center/American Baptist Assembly [W] *Green Lake, WI*

Green Meadows Farm [W] *Burlington, WI*

Greentown Glass Festival [S] *Kokomo, IN*

Greenwich Village Art Fair [S] *Rockford, IL*

Gross Point Lighthouse [W] *Evanston, IL*

Grotto Gardens [W] *Wisconsin Rapids, WI*

Grotto of Our Lady of Lourdes [W] *South Bend, IN*

Grovefest [S] *Glenview, IL*

Grove National Historic Landmark, The [W] *Glenview, IL*

Gruenewald Historic House [W] *Anderson, IN*

Grundy County Corn Festival [S] *Morris, IL*

Guided tours [W] *South Bend, IN*

Gurnee Mills Mall [W] *Gurnee, IL*

Gwen Frostic Prints [W] *Beulah, MI*

Hackley and Hume Historic Site [W] *Muskegon, MI*

Haeger Factory Outlet [W] *Dundee, IL*

Haggerty Museum of Art [W] *Milwaukee, WI*

Hale Farm and Village [W] *Akron, OH*

Halfway Tavern [W] *Salem, IL*

Hall Auditorium [W] *Oberlin, OH*

Halloween Harvest Festival [S] *Saugatuck, MI*

Hamilton County Courthouse [W] *Cincinnati, OH*

Hammond Fest [S] *Hammond, IN*

Hanchett-Bartlett Homestead [W] *Beloit, WI*

Hancock Historical Museum [W] *Findlay, OH*

Hanna Fountain Mall [W] *Cleveland, OH*

Hannah Lindahl Children's Museum [W] *Mishawaka, IN*

Harbor Days [S] *Saugatuck, MI*

Harborfest [S] *South Haven, MI*

Harbor Steamer [W] *Grand Haven, MI*

Harbor Trolleys [W] *Grand Haven, MI*

Harding Memorial [W] *Marion, OH*

Harmonie State Park [W] *New Harmony, IN*

Harmonist Cemetery [W] *New Harmony, IN*

Harness racing [S] *Jackson, MI*

Harness racing. Scioto Downs [S] *Columbus, OH*

Harrah's Joliet Casino [W] *Joliet, IL*

Harriet Beecher Stowe Memorial [W] *Cincinnati, OH*

Harrison County Fair [S] *Corydon, IN*

Harry London Chocolate Factory [W] *Canton, OH*

Hartman Creek State Park [W] *Waupaca, WI*

Hart Plaza and Dodge Fountain [W] *Detroit, MI*

Hartung's Automotive Museum [W] *Glenview, IL*

Hartwick Pines State Park [W] *Grayling, MI*

Harvest Festival [S] *Akron, OH*

Harvest Festival [S] *Prairie du Sac, WI*

Harvest Frolic and Trades Fair [S] *Charleston, IL*

Harvest Homecoming [S] *New Albany, IN*

Haunted Depot, The [W] *Sault Ste. Marie, MI*

Haunted Hydro [S] *Fremont, OH*

Hawthorne Race Course [W] *Chicago, IL*

Hawthorne Race Course [W] *Cicero, IL*

Hayes Presidential Center, Spiegel Grove [W] *Fremont, OH*

Hayes Regional Arboretum [W] *Richmond, IN*

Haymarket Riot Monument [W] *Chicago, IL*

Haynes Apperson Festival [S] *Kokomo, IN*

Haynes Memorial [W] *Kokomo, IN*

Hazel Park [W] *, MI*

Hazelwood Historic Home Museum [W] *Green Bay, WI*

Headlands Beach State Park [W] *Mentor, OH*

Head-of-the-Lakes Fair [S] *Superior, WI*

Health Museum of Cleveland [W] *Cleveland, OH*

Heber C. Kimball Home [W] *Nauvoo, IL*

Hebrew Union College—Jewish Institute of Religion [W] *Cincinnati, OH*

Heidi Festival [S] *New Glarus, WI*

Henes Park [W] *Menominee, MI*

Henry County Historical Society Museum [W] *New Castle, IN*

Henry County Memorial Park [W] *New Castle, IN*

Henry Ford Estate-Fair Lane [W] *Dearborn, MI*

Henry Ford Museum [W] *Dearborn, MI*

Henry Ford Museum and Greenfield Village [W] *Dearborn, MI*

Henry Vilas Park Zoo [W] *Madison, WI*

Henson Robinson Zoo [W] *Springfield, IL*

Herbert H. Dow Historical Museum [W] *Midland, MI*

Heritage Days [S] *Peru, IN*

Heritage Festival [S] *Piqua, OH*

Heritage Hill State Park [W] *Green Bay, WI*

Heritage Village Museum [W] *Cincinnati, OH*

Hesburgh Library [W] *South Bend, IN*

H. H. Bennett Studio and History Center [W] *Wisconsin Dells, WI*

Hiawatha Music Festival [S] *Marquette, MI*

Hiawatha National Forest [W] *Escanaba, MI*

Hiawatha—World's Tallest Indian [W] *Ironwood, MI*

Hickories Museum, The [W] *Elyria, OH*

Hickory Hills [W] *Traverse City, MI*

Hieronymus Mueller Museum [W] *Decatur, IL*

Higgins Lake [W] *Houghton Lake, MI*

High Cliff General Store Museum [W] *Neenah-Menasha, WI*

High Cliff State Park [W] *Neenah-Menasha, WI*

Highland [W] *Pontiac, MI*

Highland Festival & Games [S] *Alma, MI*

Highland Park [W] *Kokomo, IN*

Highland Park Historical Society [W] *Highland Park, IL*

High-level bridges [W] *Cleveland, OH*

Hillforest [W] *Aurora, IN*

Hinkle Fieldhouse and Butler Bowl [W] *Indianapolis, IN*

Hiram Butrick Sawmill [W] *Antioch, IL*

Historical Military Armor Museum [W] *Anderson, IN*

Historical Museum [W] *Arlington Heights, IL*

Historical Museum [W] *Downers Grove, IL*

Historical Society Log Village and Museum [W] *Reedsburg, WI*

Historic Battle Alley [W] *Holly, MI*

Historic Billie Creek Village [W] *Rockville, IN*

Historic Burlington [W] *Burlington, WI*

Historic Cemetery Walk [S] *Elgin, IL*

Historic District [W] *La Grange, IL*

Historic Francis Park [W] *Kewanee, IL*

Historic Holy Family Mission Log Church [W] *Cahokia, IL*

Historic Home Tour [S] *Marshall, MI*

Historic Indian Museum [W] *Piqua, OH*

Historic Lockerbie Square [W] *Indianapolis, IN*

Historic Loveland Castle [W] *Cincinnati, OH*

Historic Lyme Village [W] *Bellevue, OH*

Historic Trinity Lutheran Church [W] *Detroit, MI*

Historic West 8th Street [W] *Anderson, IN*

Hixon House [W] *La Crosse, WI*

Hoard Historical Museum [W] *Fort Atkinson, WI*

Ho-Chunk Casino & Bingo [W] *Baraboo, WI*

Hodag Country Festival [S] *Rhinelander, WI*

Hog Capital of the World Festival [S] *Kewanee, IL*

Holcomb Observatory & Planetarium [W] *Indianapolis, IN*

Holiday Fair, Christmas Walk, and Annual Parade [S] *Waukesha, WI*

Holiday Folk Fair [S] *Milwaukee, WI*

Holiday World & Splashin' Safari [W] *Santa Claus, IN*

Holland Fest [S] *Sheboygan, WI*

Holland Museum [W] *Holland, MI*

Holland State Park [W] *Holland, MI*

Holloway Reservoir [W] *Flint, MI*

Holy Name Cathedral [W] *Chicago, IL*

Home of Zona Gale [W] *Portage, WI*

Honey of a Museum [W] *Oconomowoc, WI*

Honeywell Center [W] *Wabash, IN*

Honolulu House Museum [W] *Marshall, MI*

Hook's American Drug Store Museum [W] *Indianapolis, IN*

Hoopeston Sweet Corn Festival [S] *Danville, IL*

Hoosier National Forest [W] *Bedford, IN*

Hoosier National Forest [W] *Nashville, IN*

Hoover Historical Center [W] *Canton, OH*

Hoover Reservoir Area [W] *Columbus, OH*

Hope College [W] *Holland, MI*

Hopewell Culture National Historical Park [W] *Chillicothe, OH*

Hopewell Culture National Historical Park [W] *Columbus, OH*

Horicon National Wildlife Refuge [W] *Waupun, WI*

Horse racing [W] *Chicago, IL*

Horse racing [W] *Cicero, IL*

Horse racing [S] *Detroit, MI*

Horse racing. Toledo Raceway Park [S] *Toledo, OH*

Horseshoe Lake State Conservation Area [W] *Cairo, IL*

Hot-Air Balloon Festival [S] *Coshocton, OH*

Hot-Air Balloon Jubilee [S] *Jackson, MI*

Houghton County Fair [S] *Hancock, MI*

Houghton Lake [W] *Houghton Lake, MI*

House on the Rock [W] *Spring Green, WI*

Howard County Fair [S] *Kokomo, IN*

Howard Steamboat Museum [W] *Jeffersonville, IN*

Hower House [W] *Akron, OH*

Huddleston Farmhouse Inn Museum [W] *Richmond, IN*

Hudson Mills [W] *Ann Arbor, MI*

Hueston Woods State Park [W] *Oxford, OH*

Humphrey IMAX Dome Theater [W] *Milwaukee, WI*

Huntington County Heritage Days [S] *Huntington, IN*

Huntington Reservoir [W] *Huntington, IN*

Huron City Museum [W] *Port Austin, MI*

Huron-Clinton Metroparks [W] *Ann Arbor, MI*

Huron-Clinton Metroparks [W] *Detroit, MI*

Huron Lightship Museum [W] *Port Huron, MI*

Huron-Manistee National Forest [W] *Manistee, MI*

Huron-Manistee National Forest [W] *Oscoda, MI*

Hutchinson House Museum [W] *Waupaca, WI*

Ice Age Visitors Center [W] *Fond du Lac, WI*

Ice Sculpture Spectacular [S] *Plymouth, MI*

Illinois and Michigan Canal Museum [W] *Lockport, IL*

Illinois and Michigan Canal State Trail [W] *Morris, IL*

Illinois Beach State Park [W] *Waukegan, IL*

Illinois Institute of Technology [W] *Chicago, IL*

Illinois Railway Museum [W] *Union, IL*

Illinois River National Wildlife and Fish Refuges [W] *Havana, IL*

Illinois Shakespeare Festival [S] *Bloomington, IL*

Illinois Snow Sculpting Competition [S] *Rockford, IL*

Illinois State Fair [S] *Springfield, IL*

Illinois State Museum [W] *Springfield, IL*

Illinois State University [W] *Bloomington, IL*

Illinois Waterway Visitor Center [W] *Peru, IL*

Illinois Wesleyan University [W] *Bloomington, IL*

Impression 5 Science Center [W] *Lansing, MI*

Independence Dam State Park [W] *Defiance, OH*

Indiana Basketball Hall of Fame, The [W] *New Castle, IN*

Indiana Beach [W] *Logansport, IN*

Indiana Black Expo [S] *Indianapolis, IN*

Indiana Convention Center & RCA Dome [W] *Indianapolis, IN*

Indiana Dunes National Lakeshore [W] *Michigan City, IN*

Indiana Fever (WNBA) [W] *Indianapolis, IN*

Indiana Flower & Patio Show [S] *Indianapolis, IN*

Indiana Football Hall of Fame [W] *Richmond, IN*

Indiana Heritage Quilt Show [S] *Bloomington, IN*

Indiana Military Museum [W] *Vincennes, IN*

Indiana Pacers (NBA) [W] *Indianapolis, IN*

Indianapolis 500 [S] *Indianapolis, IN*

Indianapolis Colts (NFL) [W] *Indianapolis, IN*

Indianapolis Motor Speedway and Hall of Fame Museum [W] *Indianapolis, IN*

Indianapolis Museum of Art-Columbus [W] *Columbus, IN*

Indianapolis Museum of Art [W] *Indianapolis, IN*

Indianapolis Sightseeing [W] *Indianapolis, IN*

Indianapolis Zoo [W] *Indianapolis, IN*

Indiana State Chili Cook-off [S] *Vincennes, IN*

Indiana State Fair [S] *Indianapolis, IN*

Indiana State Museum [W] *Indianapolis, IN*

Indiana State University [W] *Terre Haute, IN*

Indiana Territory Site [W] *Vincennes, IN*

Indiana University [W] *Bloomington, IN*

Indiana University—Purdue University Indianapolis [W] *Indianapolis, IN*

Indiana World War Memorial Plaza [W] *Indianapolis, IN*

Indian Dormitory [W] *Mackinac Island, MI*

Indian Lake [W] *Manistique, MI*

Indian Lake State Park [W] *Bellefontaine, OH*

Industrial tour. City Brewery [W] *La Crosse, WI*

Industrial tours [W] *Cambridge, OH*

Industrial tours [W] *Marietta, OH*

Industrial tours [W] *Tiffin, OH*

Industrial tour. Zimmerman Art Glass [W] *Corydon, IN*

Ingram's Log Cabin Village [W] *Salem, IL*

Inland Seas Maritime Museum [W] *Vermilion, OH*

Inscription Rock State Memorial [W] *Kelleys Island, OH*

Interlochen Arts Camp [S] *Traverse City, MI*

Interlochen Center for the Arts [W] *Traverse City, MI*

Interlochen State Park [W] *Traverse City, MI*

International Auto Show [S] *Detroit, MI*

International Carillon Festival [S] *Springfield, IL*

International Crane Foundation [W] *Baraboo, WI*

International Festival Week [S] *Lorain, OH*

International Food Festival [S] *Marquette, MI*

International Institute of Metropolitan Detroit [W] *Detroit, MI*

International Museum of Surgical Science [W] *Chicago, IL*

Interstate State Park [W] *St. Croix Falls, WI*

Irish Festival [S] *Clare, MI*

Iron County Fair [S] *Iron River, MI*

Iron County Heritage Festival [S] *Hurley, WI*

Iron County Historical Museum [W] *Hurley, WI*

Iron County Museum [W] *Iron River, MI*

Iron Mountain Iron Mine [W] *Iron Mountain, MI*

Iroquois Boat Line Tours [W] *Milwaukee, WI*

Island Park and Alpena Wildfowl Sanctuary [W] *Alpena, MI*

Isle Royale Queen III Evening Cruises [W] *Copper Harbor, MI*

St. Charles Belle II and *Fox River Queen* [W] *St. Charles, IL*

Italian Fest [S] *Collinsville, IL*

Jackson County Fair [S] *Jackson, MI*

Jamboree in the Hills [S] *St. Clairsville, OH*

James Dean/Fairmount Historical Museum [W] *Marion, IN*

James Dean Memorial Gallery, The [W] *Marion, IN*

James M. Thomas Telecommunication Museum [W] *Chillicothe, OH*

James Whitcomb Riley Festival [S] *Greenfield, IN*

James Whitcomb Riley Home [W] *Greenfield, IN*

James Whitcomb Riley Home [W] *Indianapolis, IN*

Jane Addams' Hull House [W] *Chicago, IL*

Japanese Cultural Center & Tea House [W] *Saginaw, MI*

Jazz Festival [S] *Chicago, IL*

Jefferson County Courthouse [W] *Steubenville, OH*

Jefferson County Historical Association Museum and Genealogical Library [W] *Steubenville, OH*

Jennison Nature Center [W] *Bay City, MI*

Jeremiah Sullivan House [W] *Madison, IN*

Jesse Besser Museum [W] *Alpena, MI*

Jim Peck's Wildwood [W] *Minocqua, WI*

John Ball Zoo [W] *Grand Rapids, MI*

John Brown Home [W] *Akron, OH*

John Bryan State Park [W] *Springfield, OH*

John Carroll University [W] *Cleveland, OH*

John Deere Commons [W] *Moline, IL*

John Deere Historic Site [W] *Dixon, IL*

John G. Blank Center for the Arts [W] *Michigan City, IN*

John G. Shedd Aquarium [W] *Chicago, IL*

John Hancock Center [W] *Chicago, IL*

John Hauck House Museum [W] *Cincinnati, OH*

John Johnston Home [W] *Piqua, OH*

John Michael Kohler Arts Center [W] *Sheboygan, WI*

Johnny Appleseed Festival [S] *Fort Wayne, IN*

Johnny's Game and Fish Park [W] *Cadillac, MI*

Johnson-Humrickhouse Museum [W] *Coshocton, OH*

Johnson Sauk Trail State Park [W] *Kewanee, IL*

John Stark Edwards House [W] *Warren, OH*

John Wood Mansion [W] *Quincy, IL*

Jordan Hall and Greenhouse [W] *Bloomington, IN*

Joseph Moore Museum of Natural Science [W] *Richmond, IN*

Joseph Smith Historic Center [W] *Nauvoo, IL*

Joseph Smith Homestead [W] *Nauvoo, IL*

Joyce Center [W] *South Bend, IN*

Jubilee College State Historic Site [W] *Peoria, IL*

Jubilee College State Park [W] *Peoria, IL*

Julmarknad [S] *Bishop Hill, IL*

June Tour of Historic Homes [S] *Galena, IL*

J. W. Wells State Park [W] *Menominee, MI*

Kalamazoo Air Zoo [W] *Kalamazoo, MI*

Kalamazoo College [W] *Kalamazoo, MI*

Kalamazoo County Fair [S] *Kalamazoo, MI*

Kalamazoo County Flowerfest [S] *Kalamazoo, MI*

Kalamazoo Institute of Arts [W] *Kalamazoo, MI*

Kalamazoo Nature Center [W] *Kalamazoo, MI*

Kalamazoo Valley Museum [W] *Kalamazoo, MI*

Kane County Flea Market [W] *St. Charles, IL*

Kangaroo Lake [W] *Baileys Harbor (Door County), WI*

Kankakee County Fair [S] *Kankakee, IL*

Kankakee County Historical Society Museum [W] *Kankakee, IL*

Kankakee River Fishing Derby [S] *Kankakee, IL*

Kankakee River State Park [W] *Kankakee, IL*

Kankakee River Valley Bicycle Classic [S] *Kankakee, IL*

Kankakee River Valley Regatta [S] *Kankakee, IL*

Karamu House and Theater [W] *Cleveland, OH*

Kastle Rock [W] *Woodruff, WI*

Keewatin Marine Museum [W] *Saugatuck, MI*

Kelleys Island State Park [W] *Kelleys Island, OH*

Kellogg's Cereal City USA [W] *Battle Creek, MI*

Kelsey Museum of Ancient and Medieval Archaeology [W] *Ann Arbor, MI*

Kelso Hollow Outdoor Theatre [W] *Lincoln's New Salem State Historic Site, IL*

Kemper Center [W] *Kenosha, WI*

Kempf House Center for Local History [W] *Ann Arbor, MI*

Kennedy Museum of Art [W] *Athens, OH*

Kenosha County Historical Society and Museum [W] *Kenosha, WI*

Kensington Metropark [W] *Farmington, MI*

Kent State University [W] *Kent, OH*

Kettle Moraine State Forest, Northern Unit [W] *Fond du Lac, WI*

Kettle Moraine State Forest, Southern Unit [W] *Waukesha, WI*

Kewaunee County Historical Museum [W] *Algoma, WI*

Keweenaw National Historical Park [W] *Calumet, MI*

Kickapoo Indian Caverns and Native American Museum [W] *Prairie du Chien, WI*

Kickapoo State Park [W] *Danville, IL*

Kilbourntown House [W] *Milwaukee, WI*

Kimball House Museum [W] *Battle Creek, MI*

Kimmell Park [W] *Vincennes, IN*

Kingman Museum of Natural History [W] *Battle Creek, MI*

Kingsbury Fish and Wildlife Area [W] *La Porte, IN*

King's Glass Engraving [W] *Tiffin, OH*

Kingwood Center and Gardens [W] *Mansfield, OH*

Klondike Days [S] *Eagle River, WI*

Knoles Log Home [W] *Chillicothe, OH*

Knox College [W] *Galesburg, IL*

Kohl Children's Museum [W] *Wilmette, IL*

Kohler-Andrae State Park [W] *Sheboygan, WI*

Kokomo's Family Fun Center [W] *Saginaw, MI*

Krannert Art Museum [W] *Champaign/Urbana, IL*

Krannert Pavilion [W] *Indianapolis, IN*

Krape Park [W] *Freeport, IL*

Krasl Art Center [W] *St. Joseph, MI*

Krasl Art Fair [S] *St. Joseph, MI*

Krohn Conservatory [W] *Cincinnati, OH*

Labor Day Arts Fair [S] *Big Rapids, MI*

Labyrinth, The [W] *New Harmony, IN*

Lac du Flambeau Chippewa Museum and Cultural Center [W] *Lac du Flambeau, WI*

La Crosse Interstate Fair [S] *La Crosse, WI*

La Crosse Queen Cruises [W] *La Crosse, WI*

Ladd Arboretum [W] *Evanston, IL*

Ladies' Getaway [S] *Galena, IL*

La Grande Vitesse [W] *Grand Rapids, MI*

Lake Antoine Park [W] *Iron Mountain, MI*

Lake Centralia [W] *Centralia, IL*

Lake County Fair [S] *Grayslake, IL*

Lake County Fair [S] *Painesville, OH*

Lake Cruises [W] *Green Lake, WI*

Lake Decatur [W] *Decatur, IL*

Lake de Pue [W] *Peru, IL*

Lake Erie Island State Park [W] *Put-in-Bay, OH*

Lake Erie Nature and Science Center [W] *Cleveland, OH*

Lakefront Music Fest [S] *Michigan City, IN*

Lake Hope [W] *Athens, OH*

Lake Jacksonville [W] *Jacksonville, IL*

Lake Kegonsa State Park [W] *Madison, WI*

Lakeland College [W] *Sheboygan, WI*

Lake Mattoon [W] *Mattoon, IL*

Lake Michigan car ferry [W] *Manitowoc, WI*

Lake Monroe [W] *Bloomington, IN*

Lake of Egypt [W] *Marion, IL*

Lake of the Woods County Preserve [W] *Champaign/Urbana, IL*

Lakeport State Park [W] *Port Huron, MI*

Lakeside Park [W] *Fond du Lac, WI*

Lakeside Rose Garden [W] *Fort Wayne, IN*

Lake Storey Recreational Area [W] *Galesburg, IL*

Lake Superior Big Top Chautauqua [W] *Bayfield, WI*

Lake Superior State University [W] *Sault Ste. Marie, MI*

Lake Vesuvius [W] *Ironton, OH*

Lake View Cemetery [W] *Cleveland, OH*

Lakeview Museum of Arts and Sciences [W] *Peoria, IL*

Lakeview Park [W] *Lorain, OH*

Lake Waveland [W] *Crawfordsville, IN*

Lake Winnebago [W] *Fond du Lac, WI*

Lake Wissota State Park [W] *Chippewa Falls, WI*

Lambs Farm [W] *Libertyville, IL*

Lancaster Festival [S] *Lancaster, OH*

Lane-Hooven House [W] *Hamilton, OH*

Lane Place [W] *Crawfordsville, IN*

Lanier State Historic Site [W] *Madison, IN*

La Porte County Fair [S] *La Porte, IN*

La Porte County Historical Society Museum [W] *La Porte, IN*

La Salle County Historical Museum [W] *Peru, IL*

Lawnfield (James A. Garfield National Historic Site) [W] *Mentor, OH*

Law Quadrangle [W] *Ann Arbor, MI*

Lawrence County Fair [S] *Ironton, OH*

Lawrence County Historical Museum [W] *Bedford, IN*

Lawrence County Museum [W] *Ironton, OH*

Lawrence University [W] *Appleton, WI*

Leaf it to Rusk Fall Festival [S] *Ladysmith, WI*

Lebanon Raceway [S] *Lebanon, OH*

Ledges, The [W] *Lansing, MI*

Leeper Park Art Fair [S] *South Bend, IN*

Leeper Park Tennis [W] *South Bend, IN*

Leesville Lake [W] *New Philadelphia, OH*

Leigh Yawkey Woodson Art Museum [W] *Wausau, WI*

Leila Arboretum [W] *Battle Creek, MI*

Lemon Lake County Park [W] *Merrillville, IN*

Levi Coffin House State Historic Site [W] *Richmond, IN*

Liberty Hyde Bailey Birthsite Museum [W] *South Haven, MI*

Library Park [W] *Fremont, OH*

Lichtenberger Building/Maximilian-Bodmer Exhibit [W] *New Harmony, IN*

Licking County Historical Society Museum [W] *Newark, OH*

Lieber State Recreation Area [W] *Greencastle, IN*

Lighthouse Place Outlet Center [W] *Michigan City, IN*

Lilac Festival [S] *Mackinac Island, MI*

Lilly Pavilion of Decorative Arts [W] *Indianapolis, IN*

Limberlost State Historic Site [W] *Geneva (Adams County), IN*

Lincoln Depot [W] *Springfield, IL*

Lincoln-Herndon Law Office Building [W] *Springfield, IL*

Lincoln Home National Historic Site [W] *Springfield, IL*

Lincoln Log Cabin State Historic Site [W] *Charleston, IL*

Lincoln Memorial Garden & Nature Center [W] *Springfield, IL*

Lincoln Park [W] *Chicago, IL*

Lincoln Park Conservatory [W] *Chicago, IL*

Lincoln Park Railway Exhibit [W] *Lima, OH*

Lincoln Park Zoo [W] *Manitowoc, WI*

Lincoln Park Zoological Gardens [W] *Chicago, IL*

Lincoln shrines [W] *Springfield, IL*

Lincoln's New Salem State Historic Site [W] *Petersburg, IL*

Lincoln Statue Park [W] *Dixon, IL*
Lincoln-Tallman Restorations [W] *Janesville, WI*
Lincoln Tomb State Historic Site [W] *Springfield, IL*
Lincoln Trail State Park [W] *Marshall, IL*
"Little 500" [S] *Anderson, IN*
Little 500 Bicycle Race [S] *Bloomington, IN*
Little Brick House Museum [W] *Vandalia, IL*
Little Elkhart Lake [W] *Elkhart Lake, WI*
Little Girl's Point Park [W] *Ironwood, MI*
Little Miami Scenic State Park [W] *Wilmington, OH*
Little Netherlands [W] *Holland, MI*
Little Norway [W] *Mount Horeb, WI*
Little Red Schoolhouse [W] *Hammond, IN*
Little Red Schoolhouse Museum [W] *Tomah, WI*
Little Traverse Historical Museum [W] *Petoskey, MI*
Little Wyandotte Cave [W] *Wyandotte, IN*
Living Word Outdoor Drama, The [S] *Cambridge, OH*
Lizzadro Museum of Lapidary Art [W] *Elmhurst, IL*
L. Mawby Vineyards/Winery [W] *Traverse City, MI*
Logan County Fair [S] *Bellefontaine, OH*
Logan County Fair [S] *Lincoln, IL*
Log Cabin Tour [S] *Nashville, IN*
Log Cabin Visitors Center [W] *Vincennes, IN*
Long Grove Village [W] *Arlington Heights, IL*
Loop Walking Tours [W] *Chicago, IL*
Lorain Harbor [W] *Lorain, OH*
Lords Park [W] *Elgin, IL*
Lotus World Music and Arts Festival [S] *Bloomington, IN*
Lowden Memorial State Park [W] *Oregon, IL*
Lowell Damon House [W] *Wauwatosa, WI*
Loyola University [W] *Chicago, IL*
LPGA State Farm Classic [S] *Springfield, IL*
Luce County Historical Museum [W] *Newberry, MI*
Lucia Nights [S] *Bishop Hill, IL*
Ludington Park [W] *Escanaba, MI*
Ludington Pumped Storage Hydro-electric Plant [W] *Ludington, MI*
Ludington State Park [W] *Ludington, MI*
Luge Run [S] *Muskegon, MI*
Lumberjack Days [S] *Newberry, MI*
Lumberjack World Championship [S] *Hayward, WI*
Lyric Opera of Chicago [W] *Chicago, IL*
Maasto Hiihto Ski Trail [W] *Hancock, MI*
Mabel Hartzell Museum [W] *Alliance, OH*
Mabel Tainter Memorial Building [W] *Menomonie, WI*
MacDonell House [W] *Lima, OH*
Mackinac Bridge [W] *Mackinaw City, MI*
Mackinac Bridge Museum [W] *Mackinaw City, MI*
Mackinac Bridge Walk [S] *Mackinaw City, MI*
Mackinac Bridge Walk [S] *St. Ignace, MI*
Mackinac Island Carriage Tours, Inc [W] *Mackinac Island, MI*
Mackinac Island ferries [W] *Mackinaw City, MI*
Mackinac Island ferries [W] *St. Ignace, MI*
Mackinac Island State Park [W] *Mackinac Island, MI*
Mackinac Race [S] *Port Huron, MI*
Mackinaw Mush Sled Dog Race [S] *Mackinaw City, MI*
Macon County Historical Society Museum [W] *Decatur, IL*
Madame Walker Theatre Center [W] *Indianapolis, IN*
Madeline Island [W] *Bayfield, WI*
Madeline Island Ferry Line [W] *Bayfield, WI*
Madeline Island Historical Museum [W] *Bayfield, WI*
Madison Art Center [W] *Madison, WI*
Madison Children's Museum [W] *Madison, WI*
Madison County Historical Museum [W] *Edwardsville, IL*
Madison In Bloom [S] *Madison, IN*
Madison Train Station Museum [W] *Madison, IN*
Madonna of the Trails [W] *Richmond, IN*
Madrigal Feasts [S] *Bloomington, IN*
Mad River and NKP Railroad Society Museum [W] *Bellevue, OH*

Magic Waters [W] *Rockford, IL*

Magnolia Manor [W] *Cairo, IL*

Malabar Farm State Park [W] *Mansfield, OH*

Manistee County Historical Museum [W] *Manistee, MI*

Maple City Summerfest [S] *Monmouth, IL*

Maple Lake [W] *Paw Paw, MI*

Maple Sugar Festival [S] *Northbrook, IL*

Maple Sugarin' Days [S] *Terre Haute, IN*

Maple Syrup Festival [S] *Midland, MI*

Maple Syrup Festival [S] *Mount Pleasant, MI*

Maple Syrup Time [S] *Springfield, IL*

Marathon County Historical Museum [W] *Wausau, WI*

Marcus Center for the Performing Arts [W] *Milwaukee, WI*

Marengo Cave Park [W] *Corydon, IN*

Marina City [W] *Chicago, IL*

Mariners' Church [W] *Detroit, MI*

Marinette County Historical Museum [W] *Marinette, WI*

Marion County Fair [S] *Marion, OH*

Marion County Fair [S] *Salem, IL*

Marion Easter Pageant [S] *Marion, IN*

Marion E. Wade Center [W] *Wheaton, IL*

Marquette County Historical Museum [W] *Marquette, MI*

Marquette Hall's 48-bell carillon [W] *Milwaukee, WI*

Marquette Mission Park and Museum of Ojibwa Culture [W] *St. Ignace, MI*

Marquette Park [W] *Mackinac Island, MI*

Marquette University [W] *Milwaukee, WI*

Marriott Lincolnshire Resort Theater [W] *Chicago, IL*

Marshall County Blueberry Festival [S] *Plymouth, IN*

Marshall County Historical Museum [W] *Plymouth, IN*

Marshall Field's [W] *Chicago, IL*

Marshall M. Fredericks Sculpture Gallery [W] *Saginaw, MI*

Martha Kinney Cooper Ohioana Library [W] *Columbus, OH*

Mary Fendrich Hulman Pavilion [W] *Indianapolis, IN*

Mary Gray Bird Sanctuary of the Indiana Audubon Society [W] *Connersville, IN*

Mary Jane Thurston State Park [W] *Bowling Green, OH*

Mason County Campground and Picnic Area [W] *Ludington, MI*

Masonic Temple [W] *Dayton, OH*

Massillon Museum [W] *Massillon, OH*

Materials Park Geodesic Dome [W] *Chardon, OH*

Matrix: Midland Festival [S] *Midland, MI*

Matthaei Botanical Gardens [W] *Ann Arbor, MI*

Matthews Covered Bridge [W] *Marion, IN*

Matthiessen State Park [W] *Peru, IL*

Maumee Bay State Park [W] *Toledo, OH*

May Festival [S] *Cincinnati, OH*

Maywood Park Race Track [W] *Chicago, IL*

Mazza Museum, International Art from Picture Books. [W] *Findlay, OH*

McCormick Place Convention Complex [W] *Chicago, IL*

McCormick's Creek State Park [W] *Bloomington, IN*

McGuffey Museum [W] *Oxford, OH*

McHenry County Historical Museum [W] *Union, IL*

McKinley Memorial [W] *Columbus, OH*

McKinley Museum of History, Science and Industry [W] *Canton, OH*

McKinley National Memorial [W] *Canton, OH*

Meadow Brook Art Gallery [W] *Pontiac, MI*

Meadow Brook Hall [W] *Pontiac, MI*

Meadow Brook Music Festival [S] *Detroit, MI*

Meadow Brook Music Festival [S] *Pontiac, MI*

Meadow Brook Theatre [S] *Detroit, MI*

Meadow Brook Theatre [W] *Pontiac, MI*

Mecosta County Parks [W] *Big Rapids, MI*

Meier's Wine Cellars [W] *Cincinnati, OH*

Memorial Library [W] *Madison, WI*

Mennonite Historical Library [W] *Goshen, IN*

Menominee Marina [W] *Menominee, MI*

Menominee Park [W] *Oshkosh, WI*

Menominee Range Historical Museum [W] *Iron Mountain, MI*

Mercer County Courthouse [W] *Celina, OH*

Mercer County Historical Museum, the Riley Home [W] *Celina, OH*

Merchandise Mart [W] *Chicago, IL*

Mercury, the Skyline Cruiseline [W] *Chicago, IL*

Merrick Rose Garden [W] *Evanston, IL*

Merrick State Park [W] *Galesville, WI*

Merrifield Park [W] *Mishawaka, IN*

Merrill Lake [W] *Big Rapids, MI*

Merry-Go-Round Museum [W] *Sandusky, OH*

Mesick Mushroom Festival [S] *Traverse City, MI*

Mesker Park Zoo [W] *Evansville, IN*

Metamora Courthouse State Historic Site [W] *Peoria, IL*

Metro Beach Metropark [W] *Mount Clemens, MI*

Mexican Fine Arts Center Museum [W] *Chicago, IL*

Meyer May House [W] *Grand Rapids, MI*

Miami and Erie Canal [W] *Piqua, OH*

Miami County Museum [W] *Peru, IN*

Miami Indian Historical Site [W] *Marion, IN*

Miami University [W] *Oxford, OH*

Michael Jordan Golf Center [W] *Aurora, IL*

Michel Brouillet Old French House [W] *Vincennes, IN*

Michigan Antique Festivals [S] *Midland, MI*

Michigan Avenue [W] *Chicago, IL*

Michigan City Summer Festival [S] *Michigan City, IN*

Michigan Consolidated Gas Company Building [W] *Detroit, MI*

Michigan Fiddlers' Jamboree [S] *Newberry, MI*

Michigan Historical Museum [W] *Lansing, MI*

Michigan Maritime Museum [W] *South Haven, MI*

Michigan Renaissance Festival [S] *Holly, MI*

Michigan's Adventure Amusement Park [W] *Muskegon, MI*

Michigan's Own Military & Space Museum [W] *Frankenmuth, MI*

Michigan Space Center [W] *Jackson, MI*

Michigan Speedway [S] *Jackson, MI*

Michigan State Fair [S] *Detroit, MI*

Michigan State University [W] *Lansing, MI*

Michigan Technological University [W] *Houghton, MI*

Mid-Continent Railway Museum [W] *Baraboo, WI*

MiddFest [S] *Middletown (Butler County), OH*

Middlefork Reservoir [W] *Richmond, IN*

Midland Center for the Arts [W] *Midland, MI*

Midsommar [S] *Bishop Hill, IL*

Midway Village & Museum Center [W] *Rockford, IL*

Midwest Carvers Museum [W] *Homewood, IL*

Midwest Museum of American Art [W] *Elkhart, IN*

Milan Historical Museum [W] *Milan, OH*

Mill Bluff State Park [W] *Tomah, WI*

Mill Creek [W] *Mackinaw City, MI*

Mill Creek Park [W] *Marshall, IL*

Mill Creek Park [W] *Youngstown, OH*

Miller Brewing Company [W] *Milwaukee, WI*

Miller Lite Northern Nationals Stock Car Races [S] *Superior, WI*

Miller Park Zoo [W] *Bloomington, IL*

Millikin Place [W] *Decatur, IL*

Milton House Museum [W] *Janesville, WI*

Milwaukee Art Museum [W] *Milwaukee, WI*

Milwaukee Ballet [W] *Milwaukee, WI*

Milwaukee Brewers (MLB) [W] *Milwaukee, WI*

Milwaukee Bucks (NBA) [W] *Milwaukee, WI*

Milwaukee County Historical Center [W] *Milwaukee, WI*

Milwaukee County Zoo [W] *Milwaukee, WI*

Milwaukee Public Museum [W] *Milwaukee, WI*

Mineral Point Toy Museum [W] *Mineral Point, WI*

Mining Museum [W] *Platteville, WI*

Minnetrista Cultural Center [W] *Muncie, IN*

Minocqua Museum [W] *Minocqua, WI*

Minocqua Winter Park Nordic Center [W] *Minocqua, WI*

Minor League Baseball [S] *South Bend, IN*

Mint Festival [S] *Lansing, MI*

Miro's *Chicago* [W] *Chicago, IL*

Mirror Lake State Park [W] *Baraboo, WI*

Mississinewa 1812 [S] *Marion, IN*

Mississinewa Lake [W] *Marion, IN*

Mitchell Museum of the American Indian [W] *Evanston, IL*

Mitchell Park Horticultural Conservatory [W] *Milwaukee, WI*

Monadnock Building [W] *Chicago, IL*

Monastery of the Immaculate Conception [W] *Jasper, IN*

Monroe County Fair [S] *Bloomington, IN*

Monroe County Fair [S] *Monroe, MI*

Monroe County Historical Society Museum [W] *Bloomington, IN*

Monroe County Historical Museum [W] *Monroe, MI*

Montague City Museum [W] *Whitehall, MI*

Montgomery County Fair [S] *Dayton, OH*

Montreal Canoe Weekends [S] *Peru, IL*

Mont Ripley Ski Area [W] *Houghton, MI*

Monument to the Native American [W] *Oregon, IL*

Moore Home State Historic Site [W] *Charleston, IL*

Moraine Hills State Park [W] *McHenry, IL*

Morris-Butler House [W] *Indianapolis, IN*

Morton Arboretum [W] *Downers Grove, IL*

Mosquito Lake State Park [W] *Warren, OH*

Mosser Glass [W] *Cambridge, OH*

Motown Museum [W] *Detroit, MI*

Moundbuilders State Memorial [W] *Newark, OH*

Mound Cemetery [W] *Marietta, OH*

Mounds State Park [W] *Anderson, IN*

Mount Adams [W] *Cincinnati, OH*

Mount Airy Forest and Arboretum [W] *Cincinnati, OH*

Mount Ashwabay Ski Area [W] *Bayfield, WI*

Mount Gilead State Park [W] *Mount Gilead, OH*

Mount Horeb Mustard Museum [W] *Mount Horeb, WI*

Mount La Crosse Ski Area [W] *La Crosse, WI*

Mount Marquette Scenic Outlook Area [W] *Marquette, MI*

Mount Pleasant [W] *Lancaster, OH*

Mount Pulaski Courthouse State Historic Site [W] *Lincoln, IL*

Mount Telemark Ski Area [W] *Cable, WI*

Mount Union College [W] *Alliance, OH*

Mount Zion [W] *Ironwood, MI*

Mozart Festival [S] *Woodstock, IL*

Mumaugh Memorial [W] *Lancaster, OH*

Muncie Children's Museum [W] *Muncie, IN*

Muncie Dragway [S] *Muncie, IN*

Munger Potato Festival [S] *Bay City, MI*

Municipal Band Concerts [S] *Springfield, IL*

Municipal Marina [W] *Grand Haven, MI*

Municipal parks. Riverside [W] *Janesville, WI*

Municipal Pier [W] *Lorain, OH*

Murphy Auditorium [W] *New Harmony, IN*

Museum of African-American History [W] *Detroit, MI*

Museum of Art [W] *Ann Arbor, MI*

Museum of Art [W] *Muncie, IN*

Museum of Arts and History [W] *Port Huron, MI*

Museum of Broadcast Communications [W] *Chicago, IL*

Museum of Ceramics [W] *East Liverpool, OH*

Museum of Contemporary Art [W] *Chicago, IL*

Museum of Contemporary Photography [W] *Chicago, IL*

Museum of Holography/Chicago [W] *Chicago, IL*

Museum of Natural History [W] *Champaign/Urbana, IL*

Museum of Natural History & Science [W] *Cincinnati, OH*

Museum of Norman Rockwell Art [W] *Reedsburg, WI*

Museum of Science and Industry [W] *Chicago, IL*

Museum Ship Valley Camp and Great Lakes Maritime Museum [W] *Sault Ste. Marie, MI*

Musical Fountain [W] *Grand Haven, MI*

Music and Arts Festival [S] *Grand Marais, MI*

Music-Drama Center [W] *Appleton, WI*

Muskegon Air Fair [S] *Muskegon, MI*

Muskegon Museum of Art [W] *Muskegon, MI*

Muskegon Shoreline Spectacular [S] *Muskegon, MI*

Muskegon State Park [W] *Muskegon, MI*

Muskegon Summer Celebration [S] *Muskegon, MI*

Muskegon Trolley Company [W] *Muskegon, MI*

Muskingum County Fair [S] *Zanesville, OH*

Muskingum Park [W] *Marietta, OH*

Muskingum Watershed Conservancy District. Seneca Lake Park [W] *Cambridge, OH*

Muskingum Watershed Conservancy District. Charles Mill Lake Park [W] *Mansfield, OH*

Muskingum Watershed Conservancy District [W] *New Philadelphia, OH*

Musky Jamboree/Arts and Crafts Fair [S] *Boulder Junction, WI*

MV *City of Sandusky.* [W] *Sandusky, OH*

MV *Pelee Islander.* [W] *Sandusky, OH*

Naper Settlement [W] *Naperville, IL*

NASA Lewis Visitor Center [W] *Cleveland, OH*

National Automotive and Truck Museum [W] *Auburn, IN*

National Championship Musky Open [S] *Eagle River, WI*

National Championship Boat Races [S] *Peru, IL*

National Cherry Festival [S] *Traverse City, MI*

National Dairy Shrine Museum [W] *Fort Atkinson, WI*

National Forest Festival [S] *Manistee, MI*

National Freshwater Fishing Hall of Fame [W] *Hayward, WI*

National Heisey Glass Museum [W] *Newark, OH*

National Inventors Hall of Fame [W] *Akron, OH*

National Matches [S] *Port Clinton, OH*

National New York Central Railroad Museum [W] *Elkhart, IN*

National Railroad Museum [W] *Green Bay, WI*

National Road-Zane Grey Museum [W] *Zanesville, OH*

National Shrine of Our Lady of the Snows [W] *Belleville, IL*

National Ski Hall of Fame and Ski Museum [W] *Ishpeming, MI*

National Sweet Corn Festival [S] *Peru, IL*

National Tractor Pulling Championship [S] *Bowling Green, OH*

National Vietnam Veterans Art Museum [W] *Chicago, IL*

Native American Museum [W] *Terre Haute, IN*

Naturealm Visitors Center [W] *Akron, OH*

Nature Center at Shaker Lakes [W] *Beachwood, OH*

Nautica Queen boat cruise [W] *Cleveland, OH*

Nauvoo Restoration, Inc, Visitor Center [W] *Nauvoo, IL*

Nauvoo State Park [W] *Nauvoo, IL*

Navy Pier [W] *Chicago, IL*

Navy Pier Art Fair [S] *Chicago, IL*

NCAA Hall of Champions [W] *Indianapolis, IN*

Necedah National Wildlife Refuge [W] *Tomah, WI*

Neil Armstrong Museum [W] *Wapakoneta, OH*

Nelson Dewey State Park [W] *Prairie du Chien, WI*

Neville Public Museum [W] *Green Bay, WI*

New American Theater [S] *Rockford, IL*

Newark Earthworks [W] *Newark, OH*

Newberry Library, The [W] *Chicago, IL*

Newcom Tavern [W] *Dayton, OH*

New Glarus Woods State Park [W] *New Glarus, WI*

New Lincoln Museum, The [W] *Fort Wayne, IN*

Newport State Park [W] *Ellison Bay (Door County), WI*

Newton Memorial Arts Building [W] *Milan, OH*

Niabi Zoo [W] *Moline, IL*

Nichols Arboretum [W] *Ann Arbor, MI*

Nike Town [W] *Chicago, IL*

900 North Michigan Shops [W] *Chicago, IL*

North Bay Shore County Park [W] *Oconto, WI*

North Campus [W] *Ann Arbor, MI*

Northeastern Wisconsin Zoo [W] *Green Bay, WI*

Northern Highland-American Legion State Forest [W] *Boulder Junction, WI*

Northern Illinois University [W] *De Kalb, IL*

Northern Indiana Center for History [W] *South Bend, IN*

Northern Lights Playhouse [S] *Minocqua, WI*

Northern Michigan University [W] *Marquette, MI*
Northern Wisconsin State Fair [S] *Chippewa Falls, WI*
Northland College [W] *Ashland, WI*
Northland Mardi Gras [S] *Ladysmith, WI*
North Pier Chicago [W] *Chicago, IL*
North Shore Center for the Performing Arts [W] *Chicago, IL*
North Shore Center for the Performing Arts [W] *Skokie, IL*
Northville Downs [W] , *MI*
Northwestern University Chicago Campus [W] *Chicago, IL*
Northwestern University [W] *Evanston, IL*
Northwest Ohio Rib-Off [S] *Toledo, OH*
Northwoods Wildlife Center [W] *Minocqua, WI*
Notre Dame Stadium [W] *South Bend, IN*
Nub's Nob [W] *Harbor Springs, MI*
Oak Hill Cottage [W] *Mansfield, OH*
Oakhurst Gardens [W] *Muncie, IN*
Oakland Cemetery [W] *Petersburg, IL*
Oakland University [W] *Pontiac, MI*
Oak Park Visitors Center [W] *Oak Park, IL*
Oak Street [W] *Chicago, IL*
Oberlin College [W] *Oberlin, OH*
Observatory and Willow drives [W] *Madison, WI*
Octagon Earthworks [W] *Newark, OH*
Octagon House [W] *Fond du Lac, WI*
Octagon House [W] *Hudson, WI*
Octagon House and First Kindergarten in USA [W] *Watertown, WI*
Ogle County Historical Society Museum [W] *Oregon, IL*
Ohio Agricultural Research and Development Center [W] *Wooster, OH*
Ohio Ballet [S] *Akron, OH*
Ohio Caverns [W] *Bellefontaine, OH*
Ohio Ceramic Center [W] *Zanesville, OH*
Ohio Heritage Days [S] *Mansfield, OH*
Ohio Historical Center [W] *Columbus, OH*
Ohio River Museum State Memorial [W] *Marietta, OH*
Ohio River Sternwheel Festival [S] *Marietta, OH*
Ohio's Prehistoric Native American Mounds [W] *Columbus, OH*

Ohio State Capitol [W] *Columbus, OH*
Ohio State Fair [S] *Columbus, OH*
Ohio State Reformatory [W] *Mansfield, OH*
Ohio State University [W] *Columbus, OH*
Ohio University [W] *Athens, OH*
Ohio Valley Summer Theater [S] *Athens, OH*
Ohio Village [W] *Columbus, OH*
Ohio Wesleyan University [W] *Delaware, OH*
Ohio Winter Ski Carnival [S] *Mansfield, OH*
Oktoberfest [S] *La Crosse, WI*
Oktoberfest [S] *Rhinelander, WI*
Oktoberfest-Zinzinnati [S] *Cincinnati, OH*
Olbrich Botanical Gardens [W] *Madison, WI*
Old Bag Factory, The [W] *Goshen, IN*
"Old Ben" [W] *Kokomo, IN*
Old Canal Days [S] *Lockport, IL*
Old Capitol Day [S] *Corydon, IN*
Old Car Festival [S] *Dearborn, MI*
Old Carthage Jail [W] *Nauvoo, IL*
Old Cathedral Library and Museum [W] *Vincennes, IN*
Old Cathedral Minor Basilica, The [W] *Vincennes, IN*
Old Courthouse Museum [W] *Bloomington, IL*
Old Ellison Bay Days [S] *Ellison Bay (Door County), WI*
Oldest Stone House Museum [W] *Cleveland, OH*
Olde Time Music Fest [S] *Coshocton, OH*
Old Falls Village [W] *Menomonee Falls, WI*
Old Fashioned Arts and Crafts Christmas [S] *Rockville, IN*
Old Fire House and Police Museum [W] *Superior, WI*
Old French Cemetery, The [W] *Vincennes, IN*
Old Indian Agency House [W] *Portage, WI*
Old Jail Museum [W] *Crawfordsville, IN*
Old Jail Museum Breakout [S] *Crawfordsville, IN*
Old Lighthouse Museum [W] *Michigan City, IN*
Old Log Jail and Chapel-in-the-Park Museums [W] *Greenfield, IN*
Old Market House State Historic 1846 Site [W] *Galena, IL*

Old Presque Isle Lighthouse and Museum [W] *Alpena, MI*

Old Settlers' Memorial Log Cabin [W] *Dixon, IL*

Old State Bank, Indiana State Memorial [W] *Vincennes, IN*

Old State Capitol State Historic Site [W] *Springfield, IL*

Old Stone Annex Building [W] *Lockport, IL*

Old Town Hall Museum [W] *Park Falls, WI*

Old Wade House Historic Site [W] *Elkhart Lake, WI*

Old Waterworks Building [W] *Manistee, MI*

Old Woman Creek National Estuarine Research Reserve [W] *Sandusky, OH*

Old World Third Street [W] *Milwaukee, WI*

Old World Wisconsin [W] *Waukesha, WI*

Olentangy Indian Caverns and Ohio Frontierland [W] *Delaware, OH*

Oliver P. Parks Telephone Museum [W] *Springfield, IL*

Oliver Winery [W] *Bloomington, IN*

Olivet Nazarene University [W] *Kankakee, IL*

Omnimax Theater [W] *Cincinnati, OH*

Oneida Nation Museum [W] *Green Bay, WI*

100 Center Complex [W] *Mishawaka, IN*

114th Infantry Flag Retreat Ceremony [S] *Springfield, IL*

One-Room Schoolhouse [W] *Salem, IL*

On the Waterfront Big Band Concert Series [S] *Grand Haven, MI*

Opera/Columbus [S] *Columbus, OH*

Orange County Pumpkin Festival [S] *French Lick, IN*

Orchard Beach State Park [W] *Manistee, MI*

Oregon Public Library Art Gallery [W] *Oregon, IL*

Oriental Garden [W] *Decatur, IL*

Oriental Institute Museum [W] *Chicago, IL*

Original Wisconsin Ducks [W] *Wisconsin Dells, WI*

Orpheum Children's Science Museum [W] *Champaign/Urbana, IL*

Osborne Spring Park [W] *Bedford, IN*

O'Shaughnessy Reservoir [W] *Columbus, OH*

Oshkosh Public Museum [W] *Oshkosh, WI*

Oshkosh Public Museum Art Fair [S] *Oshkosh, WI*

Other places [W] *Mackinac Island, MI*

Otsego County Fair [S] *Gaylord, MI*

Otsego Lake State Park [W] *Gaylord, MI*

Ottawa County Historical Museum [W] *Port Clinton, OH*

Ottawa National Forest [W] *Ironwood, MI*

Ottawa Park [W] *Toledo, OH*

Ottawa's Riverfest Celebration [S] *Ottawa, IL*

Otter Creek Golf Course [W] *Columbus, IN*

Ouabache Trails Park [W] *Vincennes, IN*

Our House State Memorial [W] *Gallipolis, OH*

Our Lady of Sorrows Basilica [W] *Chicago, IL*

Outagamie Museum [W] *Appleton, WI*

Outdoor Art [W] *Chicago, IL*

Outdoor Arts Festival [S] *Sheboygan, WI*

Outdoor Summer Music Festival [S] *Oxford, OH*

Ox Bow [W] *Goshen, IN*

Ozaukee County Fair [S] *Cedarburg, WI*

Paavo Nurmi Marathon [S] *Hurley, WI*

Pabst Theater [W] *Milwaukee, WI*

Paddle & Portage Canoe Race [S] *Madison, WI*

Paddle-wheeler boat trips [W] *Oscoda, MI*

Paine Art Center and Arboretum [W] *Oshkosh, WI*

Paint Creek State Park [W] *Chillicothe, OH*

Palms Book [W] *Manistique, MI*

Pando [W] *Grand Rapids, MI*

Panther Intaglio [W] *Fort Atkinson, WI*

Paramount Arts Centre [W] *Aurora, IL*

Paramount's Kings Island [W] *Cincinnati, OH*

Paramount's Kings Island [W] *Mason, OH*

Paramount Theatre and Centre Ballroom [W] *Anderson, IN*

Paris [W] *Big Rapids, MI*

Parke County Covered Bridge Festival [S] *Rockville, IN*

Parke County Maple Fair [S] *Rockville, IN*

Park facilities [W] *Anderson, IN*

Park Lane Model Railroad Museum [W] *Reedsburg, WI*

Park of Roses [W] *Columbus, OH*

Parks [W] *Goshen, IN*

Parks [W] *South Bend, IN*

Parks [W] *Toledo, OH*

Park system [W] *Milwaukee, WI*

Pattison State Park [W] *Superior, WI*

Paul Bunyan Days [S] *Oscoda, MI*

Paul Bunyan Logging Camp [W] *Eau Claire, WI*

Paul Dresser Birthplace State Shrine and Memorial [W] *Terre Haute, IN*

Paul Laurence Dunbar House State Memorial [W] *Dayton, OH*

Peace Museum [W] *Chicago, IL*

Pendarvis, Cornish Restoration [W] *Mineral Point, WI*

Peninsula State Park [W] *Fish Creek (Door County), WI*

Pennsylvania House [W] *Springfield, OH*

Penrod Arts Fair [S] *Indianapolis, IN*

Peony Festival & Parade [S] *Van Wert, OH*

Peoria Historical Society Buildings [W] *Peoria, IL*

Peoria Players [W] *Peoria, IL*

Perchville USA [S] *Tawas City, MI*

Pere Marquette Memorial Cross [W] *Ludington, MI*

Pere Marquette State Park [W] *Alton, IL*

Performing arts—City [W] *Chicago, IL*

Performing arts—Outlying Areas [W] *Chicago, IL*

Perkins Mansion [W] *Akron, OH*

Perkins Observatory [W] *Delaware, OH*

Perrot State Park [W] *Galesville, WI*

Perry's Cave [W] *Put-in-Bay, OH*

Perry's Victory and International Peace Memorial [W] *Port Clinton, OH*

Perry's Victory and International Peace Memorial [W] *Put-in-Bay, OH*

Peshtigo Fire Museum [W] *Peshtigo, WI*

Petoskey State Park [W] *Petoskey, MI*

Pet Parade [S] *La Grange, IL*

Petrillo Music Shell [W] *Chicago, IL*

Pettengill-Morron House [W] *Peoria, IL*

Petunia Festival [S] *Dixon, IL*

Pheasant Run Dinner Theatre [W] *Chicago, IL*

Piano Factory, The [W] *St. Charles, IL*

Piasa Bird Painting Reproduction [W] *Alton, IL*

Piatt Castles [W] *Bellefontaine, OH*

Pictured Rocks Boat Cruise [W] *Munising, MI*

Pictured Rocks National Lakeshore [W] *Grand Marais, MI*

Pictured Rocks National Lakeshore [W] *Munising, MI*

Pictured Rocks Road Race [S] *Munising, MI*

Pilcher Park [W] *Joliet, IL*

Pilgrimage [S] *Lancaster, OH*

Pine Crest Historical Village [W] *Manitowoc, WI*

Pine Mountain Ski Jumping Tournament [S] *Iron Mountain, MI*

Pinhook [W] *South Bend, IN*

Pioneer Cemetery [W] *Monmouth, IL*

Pioneer Corner Museum [W] *Elkhart Lake, WI*

Pioneer Day Festival [S] *Richmond, IN*

Pioneer Days [S] *Terre Haute, IN*

Pioneer Farm & House Museum [W] *Oxford, OH*

Pioneer Mothers Memorial Forest [W] *Bedford, IN*

Pioneer Settlement [W] *Lockport, IL*

Pioneer Trail Park and Campground [W] *Escanaba, MI*

Piqua Historical Area [W] *Piqua, OH*

P. J. Hoffmaster State Park [W] *Muskegon, MI*

Planetarium [W] *Peoria, IL*

Platte River State Anadromous Fish Hatchery [W] *Beulah, MI*

Playhouse Square Center [W] *Cleveland, OH*

Pleasant Home Mansion [W] *Oak Park, IL*

Point Beach State Forest [W] *Two Rivers, WI*

Pokagon State Park [W] *Angola, IN*

Polar Bear Swim [S] *Sheboygan, WI*

Polar Ice Cap Golf Tournament [S] *Grand Haven, MI*

Polish Museum of America [W] *Chicago, IL*

Pontiac Lake [W] *Pontiac, MI*

Popcorn Festival [S] *Marion, OH*

Popcorn Festival [S] *Valparaiso, IN*

Porcupine Mountains Wilderness State Park [W] *Ontonagon, MI*

Portage Lakes State Park [W] *Akron, OH*

Portage Princess Cruise [W] *Akron, OH*

Porter County Fair [S] *Valparaiso, IN*

Port of Milwaukee [W] *Milwaukee, WI*

Port of Toledo [W] *Toledo, OH*

Post Office Lumberjack Mural [W] *Park Falls, WI*

Postville Court House State Historic Site [W] *Lincoln, IL*

Potato Creek State Park [W] *South Bend, IN*

Potawatomi State Park [W] *Sturgeon Bay (Door County), WI*

Potawatomi Zoo [W] *South Bend, IN*

Potter Park Zoo [W] *Lansing, MI*

Pottery Lovers Celebration [S] *Zanesville, OH*

Pottery tours. Hall China Company. [W] *East Liverpool, OH*

Pottwatomie Park [W] *St. Charles, IL*

Power Center for the Performing Arts [W] *Ann Arbor, MI*

Powwows [S] *Lac du Flambeau, WI*

Prairie Avenue Historic District [W] *Chicago, IL*

Prairie Creek Reservoir [W] *Muncie, IN*

"Prairie Tales" at New Salem [S] *Petersburg, IL*

President Benjamin Harrison Home [W] *Indianapolis, IN*

President Harding's Home and Museum [W] *Marion, OH*

Presque Isle Park [W] *Marquette, MI*

Pride of Oregon [W] *Oregon, IL*

Pride of the Fox RiverFest [S] *St. Charles, IL*

Print Shop [W] *Nauvoo, IL*

Professional sports [W] *Chicago, IL*

Professional sports [W] *Cincinnati, OH*

Professional sports [W] *Cleveland, OH*

Professional sports [W] *Columbus, OH*

Professional sports [W] *Detroit, MI*

Professional sports [W] *Indianapolis, IN*

Professional sports [W] *Milwaukee, WI*

Professional sports [W] *Pontiac, MI*

Professional sports team. Green Bay Packers (NFL) [W] *Green Bay, WI*

Pro Football Hall of Fame [W] *Canton, OH*

Pro Football Hall of Fame Festival [S] *Canton, OH*

Public Auditorium and Convention Center [W] *Cleveland, OH*

Public Landing [W] *Cincinnati, OH*

Public Library [W] *Cleveland, OH*

Public Museum of Grand Rapids, The [W] *Grand Rapids, MI*

Pump House Regional Arts Center [W] *La Crosse, WI*

Punderson State Park [W] *Chardon, OH*

Purdue University [W] *Lafayette, IN*

Pure Water Days [S] *Chippewa Falls, WI*

Put-in-Bay Tour Train [W] *Put-in-Bay, OH*

Quad City Botanical Center [W] *Rock Island, IL*

Quaker Square [W] *Akron, OH*

Quincy Chain of Lakes Tip-Up Festival [S] *Coldwater, MI*

Quincy Museum [W] *Quincy, IL*

Quincy Steam Hoist, Shaft House, Tram Rides, and Underground Mine Tours [W] *Hancock, MI*

Raccoon Lake [W] *Centralia, IL*

Raccoon Lake State Recreation Area [W] *Rockville, IN*

Racine Heritage Museum [W] *Racine, WI*

Racine Zoological Gardens [W] *Racine, WI*

Racing Rapids Action Park [W] *Dundee, IL*

Raggedy Ann Festival [S] *Arcola, IL*

Raging Rivers Waterpark [W] *Alton, IL*

Rahr-West Art Museum [W] *Manitowoc, WI*

Railroad Days [S] *Galesburg, IL*

Railroad Memories Museum [W] *Spooner, WI*

Ralph Mueller Planetarium [W] *Cleveland, OH*

Rambler Legacy Gallery [W] *Kenosha, WI*

Ramsdell Theatre and Hall [W] *Manistee, MI*

Ramsey Lake State Park [W] *Vandalia, IL*

Ravinia Festival [W] *Chicago, IL*

Ravinia Festival [S] *Chicago, IL*

Ravinia Festival [S] *Highland Park, IL*

RCA Championships (tennis) [S] *Indianapolis, IN*

Rebel Alliance Theater [W] *Oshkosh, WI*

Red Arrow Highway [W] *New Buffalo, MI*

Red Brick Rally Car Show [S] *Oxford, OH*

Red Light Snowmobile Rally [S] *Hurley, WI*

Regatta and Governor's Cup Race [S] *Madison, IN*

Reitz Home Museum [W] *Evansville, IN*

Renaissance Center [W] *Detroit, MI*

Rend Lake [W] *Benton, IL*

Rend Lake Water Festival [S] *Benton, IL*

R. E. Olds Transportation Museum [W] *Lansing, MI*

Republican Party founding site [W] *Jackson, MI*

Rhinelander Logging Museum [W] *Rhinelander, WI*

Rialto Square Theatre [W] *Joliet, IL*

Rib Mountain State Park [W] *Wausau, WI*

Richard J. Daley Center and Plaza [W] *Chicago, IL*

Richard W. Bock Museum [W] *Greenville, IL*

Richland Carrousel Park [W] *Mansfield, OH*

Richland County Fair [S] *Mansfield, OH*

Richland County Fair [S] *Olney, IL*

Richland County Fair [S] *Richland Center, WI*

Richland County Museum [W] *Mansfield, OH*

River Cities Fun Fest [S] *Wisconsin Rapids, WI*

River cruises [W] *Cincinnati, OH*

River Days Festival [S] *Portsmouth, OH*

River Downs Race Track [S] *Cincinnati, OH*

River excursions [W] *Kankakee, IL*

Riverfest [S] *Beloit, WI*

Riverfest [S] *Cincinnati, OH*

Riverfest [S] *La Crosse, WI*

Riverfest [S] *Niles, MI*

Riverfest [S] *Watertown, WI*

Riverfront Festivals [S] *Detroit, MI*

River Raisin Battlefield Visitor Center [W] *Monroe, MI*

River Trail Nature Center [W] *Northbrook, IL*

Riverview Park & Waterworld [W] *Wisconsin Dells, WI*

Road America [S] *Elkhart Lake, WI*

Robbins-Hunter Museum in the Avery Downer House [W] *Newark, OH*

Robert Crown Center for Health Education [W] *Hinsdale, IL*

Robert Henry Fauntleroy House [W] *New Harmony, IN*

Robert La Salle County Park [W] *Sturgeon Bay (Door County), WI*

Robert R. McCormick Museum [W] *Wheaton, IL*

Roberts Municipal Stadium [W] *Evansville, IN*

Robert T. Longway Planetarium [W] *Flint, MI*

Robie House [W] *Chicago, IL*

Robinson-Ransbottom Pottery Company [W] *Zanesville, OH*

Rock and Roll Hall of Fame and Museum [W] *Cleveland, OH*

Rock County 4-H Fair [S] *Janesville, WI*

Rock Cut State Park [W] *Rockford, IL*

Rockefeller Greenhouse [W] *Cleveland, OH*

Rockefeller Memorial Chapel [W] *Chicago, IL*

Rockefeller Park [W] *Cleveland, OH*

Rockford Art Museum [W] *Rockford, IL*

Rockford Speedway [S] *Rockford, IL*

Rockford Trolley [W] *Rockford, IL*

Rock Island Arsenal and US Army Armament, Munitions and Chemical Command [W] *Rock Island, IL*

Rock Island State Park [W] *Washington Island (Door County), WI*

Rockome Gardens [W] *Arcola, IL*

Rock Springs Center for Environmental Discovery [W] *Decatur, IL*

Rogers Street Fishing Village Museum [W] *Two Rivers, WI*

Rollo Jamison Museum [W] *Platteville, WI*

Rombach Place—Museum of Clinton County Historical Society [W] *Wilmington, OH*

Ronald Reagan's Boyhood Home [W] *Dixon, IL*

Roofless Church [W] *New Harmony, IN*

Rookery, The [W] *Chicago, IL*

Roosevelt University [W] *Chicago, IL*

Roscoe Village [W] *Coshocton, OH*

Rose Festival [S] *Jackson, MI*

Ross County Historical Society Museum [W] *Chillicothe, OH*

Ross County Historical Society Museum [W] *Columbus, OH*

Rossi Pasta [W] *Marietta, OH*

Rossville Walking Tour [W] *Hamilton, OH*

Rotary Gardens [W] *Janesville, WI*

Route 66 Raceway [S] *Joliet, IL*

Royal George [W] *Chicago, IL*

Roy Rogers Festival [S] *Portsmouth, OH*

Rum Village [W] *South Bend, IN*

Run on Water [S] *Bayfield, WI*

Rusk County Fair [S] *Ladysmith, WI*

Ruthmere [W] *Elkhart, IN*

Sacra Via Street [W] *Marietta, OH*

Saginaw Art Museum [W] *Saginaw, MI*

Saginaw County Fair [S] *Saginaw, MI*

Saginaw Harness Raceway [S] *Saginaw, MI*

Sailboat Race Week [S] *Bayfield, WI*

Sailing Festival [S] *St. Joseph, MI*

Sailing races [S] *Mackinac Island, MI*

St. Charles History Museum [W] *St. Charles, IL*

St. Croix National Scenic Riverway [W] *Spooner, WI*

St. Croix National Scenic Riverway [W] *St. Croix Falls, WI*

St. Francis Solanus Indian Mission [W] *Petoskey, MI*

St. Helen Lake [W] *Houghton Lake, MI*

St. Joan of Arc Chapel [W] *Milwaukee, WI*

St. Julian Wine Company [W] *Paw Paw, MI*

St. Mary-of-the-Woods College [W] *Terre Haute, IN*

St. Mary's College [W] *South Bend, IN*

St. Patrick's Day Parade [S] *Chicago, IL*

St. Patrick's Park [W] *South Bend, IN*

St. Paul's Cathedral [W] *Fond du Lac, WI*

St. Stanislaus Polish Festival [S] *Bay City, MI*

Salamonie Reservoir, Dam, and Forest [W] *Wabash, IN*

Salmon-A-Rama [S] *Racine, WI*

Salomon Wolf House [W] *New Harmony, IN*

Salt Fork Arts and Crafts Festival [S] *Cambridge, OH*

Salt Fork State Park [W] *Cambridge, OH*

Sandburg Days Festival [S] *Galesburg, IL*

Santa Maria Replica [W] *Columbus, OH*

Santa's Village Theme Park [W] *Dundee, IL*

Sauder Farm & Craft Village [W] *Wauseon, OH*

Saugatuck Dune Rides [W] *Saugatuck, MI*

Sauk County Historical Museum [W] *Baraboo, WI*

Sauk Trail Heritage Days [S] *Kewanee, IL*

Sawdust Days [S] *Oshkosh, WI*

Sayles House [W] *Milan, OH*

Scandinavian Dance Festival [S] *Washington Island (Door County), WI*

Scarecrow Festival [S] *St. Charles, IL*

Scenic cruises [W] *Waupaca, WI*

Scenic drive [W] *Oregon, IL*

Scenic drive [W] *Traverse City, MI*

Scenic drives [W] *Cincinnati, OH*

Scenic drives [W] *Sheboygan, WI*

Scheer's Lumberjack Show [S] *Woodruff, WI*

Schequamegon-Nicolet National Forest [W] *Three Lakes, WI*

Schingoethe Center for Native American Cultures [W] *Aurora, IL*

Schlitz Audubon Center [W] *Milwaukee, WI*

Schoenbrunn Village State Memorial [W] *New Philadelphia, OH*

Schofield House [W] *Madison, IN*

Scholle House [W] *New Harmony, IN*

Schoolcraft County Snowmobile Poker Run [S] *Manistique, MI*

School Section Lake [W] *Big Rapids, MI*

Schooner *Madeline* [W] *Traverse City, MI*

Scioto County Fair [S] *Portsmouth, OH*

SciTech—Science and Technology Interactive Center [W] *Aurora, IL*

Scottish Rite Cathedral [W] *Bay City, MI*

Scottish Rite Cathedral [W] *Indianapolis, IN*

Scovill Family Park Complex [W] *Decatur, IL*

Scovill Park and Zoo [W] *Decatur, IL*

Seafood Festival [S] *Marquette, MI*

Sears Tower [W] *Chicago, IL*

Second City [W] *Chicago, IL*

Seeley G. Mudd Center [W] *Oberlin, OH*

Seiberling Mansion [W] *Kokomo, IN*

Seip Mound State Memorial [W] *Chillicothe, OH*

Seip Mound State Memorial [W] *Columbus, OH*

Self-driving tour [W] *Madison, WI*

Seneca Caverns [W] *Bellevue, OH*

Seneca County Museum [W] *Tiffin, OH*

Seney National Wildlife Refuge [W] *Newberry, MI*

Serpent Mound State Memorial [W] *Columbus, OH*

Seven Caves [W] *Chillicothe, OH*

Shades State Park [W] *Crawfordsville, IN*

Shades State Park [W] *Rockville, IN*

Shawano Lake [W] *Shawano, WI*

Shawnee National Forest [W] *Marion, IL*

Shawnee State Forest [W] *Portsmouth, OH*

Shawnee State Park [W] *Portsmouth, OH*

Sheboygan County Historical Museum [W] *Sheboygan, WI*

Sheean Library [W] *Bloomington, IL*

Sheldon Swope Art Museum [W] *Terre Haute, IN*

Shepler's [W] *St. Ignace, MI*

Shepler's Mackinac Island Ferry [W] *Mackinac Island, MI*

Shepler's Mackinac Island Ferry [W] *Mackinaw City, MI*

Sherman House Museum [W] *Lancaster, OH*

Shiawassee County Fair [S] *Owosso, MI*

Shipyards Tour [S] *Sturgeon Bay (Door County), WI*

Shoot Time in Manistee [S] *Manistee, MI*

Shore Drive [W] *Harbor Springs, MI*

Shoreline Marine Company [W] *Chicago, IL*

Showboat *Becky Thatcher.* [S] *Marietta, OH*

Shubert [W] *Chicago, IL*

Sightseeing [W] *Galena, IL*

Sightseeing [W] *Rockford, IL*

Sightseeing boat tours [W] *Chicago, IL*

Sightseeing bus tours [W] *Chicago, IL*

Sightseeing cruises [W] *Saugatuck, MI*

Sightseeing tours [W] *Cleveland, OH*

Silvercreek and Stephenson Railroad [W] *Freeport, IL*

Silver Lake [W] *Portage, WI*

Silver Wheel Manor [W] *Fond du Lac, WI*

Sinnissippi Gardens [W] *Rockford, IL*

Sister Bay Fall Festival [S] *Sister Bay (Door County), WI*

Six Flags Great America [W] *Chicago, IL*

Six Flags Great America [W] *Gurnee, IL*

Six Flags Worlds of Adventure [W] *Aurora, OH*

Ski area [W] *Ontonagon, MI*

Ski areas [W] *Traverse City, MI*

Ski Brule [W] *Iron River, MI*

Skiing [W] *Akron, OH*

Skiing [W] *Grand Rapids, MI*

Skiing [W] *Harbor Springs, MI*

Skiing [W] *Ironwood, MI*

Skiing [W] *Kalamazoo, MI*

Skiing [W] *Lake Geneva, WI*

Skiing [W] *Mansfield, OH*

Skiing [W] *Wisconsin Dells, WI*

Skiing. Alpine Valley Ski Resort [W] *Elkhorn, WI*

Skiing. Alpine Valley Ski Resort [W] *Pontiac, MI*

Skiing. Boyne Mountain [W] *Boyne City, MI*

Skiing. Caberfae Peaks Ski Resort [W] *Cadillac, MI*

Skiing. Chestnut Mountain Resort [W] *Galena, IL*

Skiing. Crystal Mountain Resort [W] *Beulah, MI*

Skiing. Hidden Valley Ski Area [W] *Manitowoc, WI*

Skiing. Highlands Ski Hill [W] *Oconomowoc, WI*

Skiing. Indianhead Mountain-Bear Creek Ski Resort [W] *Wakefield, MI*

Skiing. Mad River Mountain Ski Resort [W] *Bellefontaine, OH*

Skiing. Marquette Mountain Ski Area [W] *Marquette, MI*

Skiing. Mount Holly Ski Area [W] *Holly, MI*

Skiing. Nordic Mountain Ski Area [W] *Wautoma, WI*

Skiing. Paoli Peaks Ski Area [W] *French Lick, IN*

Skiing. Pine Mountain Lodge [W] *Iron Mountain, MI*

Skiing. Shanty Creek Resort [W] *Bellaire, MI*

Skiing. Snowsnake Mountain [W] *Harrison, MI*

Skiing. Treetops Sylvan Resort [W] *Gaylord, MI*

Skiing. Trollhaugen Ski Resort [W] *St. Croix Falls, WI*

Ski World [W] *Nashville, IN*

Skydive Chicago, Inc [W] *Ottawa, IL*

Skyline Ski Area [W] *Grayling, MI*

Slavic Village Harvest Festival [S] *Cleveland, OH*

Sloan Museum [W] *Flint, MI*

Smith Park [W] *Neenah-Menasha, WI*

Smith's Mansion [W] *Nauvoo, IL*

Smith's Red Brick Store [W] *Nauvoo, IL*

Snite Museum of Art [W] *South Bend, IN*

Snowmobiling [W] *Copper Harbor, MI*

Snow Trails [W] *Mansfield, OH*

Soaring Eagle Casino [W] *Mount Pleasant, MI*

Sojourner Truth Grave [W] *Battle Creek, MI*

Soldiers Memorial [W] *Oregon, IL*

Soldiers, Sailors and Pioneers Monument [W] *Hamilton, OH*

"Soo" Locks [W] *Sault Ste. Marie, MI*

Soo Locks Boat Tours [W] *Sault Ste. Marie, MI*

Sorghum & Cider Fair [S] *Rockville, IN*

Sorg Opera Company [W] *Middletown (Butler County), OH*

South Bend Regional Museum of Art [W] *South Bend, IN*

South Bend Summer in the City Festival [S] *South Bend, IN*

Southern Illinois Arts & Crafts Marketplace [W] *Benton, IL*

Southern Illinois University [W] *Carbondale, IL*

Southern Illinois University at Edwardsville [W] *Edwardsville, IL*

Southern Ohio Museum and Cultural Center [W] *Portsmouth, OH*

South Park [W] *Waupaca, WI*

Southport Marina [W] *Kenosha, WI*

Southwind Park [W] *Bellefontaine, OH*

South Wood County Historical Corporation Museum [W] *Wisconsin Rapids, WI*

Sparks Illuminated Cascades Waterfalls [W] *Jackson, MI*

Spertus Museum [W] *Chicago, IL*

Spinning Top Exploratory Museum [W] *Burlington, WI*

Spirit of Chicago [W] *Chicago, IL*

Spirit of Peoria [W] *Peoria, IL*

Spirit of Vincennes Rendezvous [S] *Vincennes, IN*

Splashin' Safari Water Park [W] *Santa Claus, IN*

Spooner Car Show [S] *Spooner, WI*

Spooner Rodeo [S] *Spooner, WI*

Spoon River Scenic Drive Fall Festival [S] *Havana, IL*

Spoon River Valley Scenic Drive [S] *Peoria, IL*

Sportsman's Park [W] *Cicero, IL*

Sportsman's Park Race Track [W] *Chicago, IL*

Spring/Fall Bike Tours [S] *Mackinaw City, MI*

Springfield Air Rendezvous [S] *Springfield, IL*

Springfield Art Association [W] *Springfield, IL*

Springfield Arts Festival [S] *Springfield, OH*

Springfield Children's Museum [W] *Springfield, IL*

Springfield Muni Opera [S] *Springfield, IL*

Springfield Museum of Art [W] *Springfield, OH*

Spring Flower Show [S] *Chicago, IL*

Spring Hill [W] *Massillon, OH*

Spring Lake Park [W] *Macomb, IL*

Spring Mill State Park [W] *Bedford, IN*

Spring Old Car Club Spring Festival [S] *Lancaster, OH*

Square 13 [W] *Lancaster, OH*

Squire Boone Caverns and Village [W] *Corydon, IN*

S. Ray Miller Antique Auto Museum [W] *Elkhart, IN*

S.S. *Meteor*, The [W] *Superior, WI*

SS *Willis B. Boyer* Museum Ship [W] *Toledo, OH*

Stacy's Tavern Museum [W] *Glen Ellyn, IL*

Stage Coach Theater [S] *De Kalb, IL*

Stagecoach Trail Festival [S] *Galena, IL*

Stambaugh Auditorium [W] *Youngstown, OH*

Stanbery-Rising [W] *Lancaster, OH*

Stan Hywet Hall and Gardens [W] *Akron, OH*

Starlight Theatre [W] *Indianapolis, IN*

Star Line Ferry [W] *Mackinac Island, MI*

Star Line Ferry [W] *Mackinaw City, MI*

Star Line Ferry [W] *St. Ignace, MI*

Star of Saugatuck [W] *Saugatuck, MI*

Star Plaza Theatre [W] *Merrillville, IN*

Starved Rock State Park [W] *Ottawa, IL*

Starved Rock State Park [W] *Peru, IL*

State Capitol [W] *Indianapolis, IN*

State Capitol [W] *Madison, WI*

State Capitol [W] *Springfield, IL*

State Capitol Building [W] *Lansing, MI*

State Historical Museum [W] *Madison, WI*

State parks [W] *Athens, OH*

State parks [W] *Cheboygan, MI*

State parks [W] *Galesville, WI*

State parks [W] *Manistique, MI*

State recreation areas [W] *Pontiac, MI*

State Street [W] *Chicago, IL*

Statue of Father Marquette [W] *Marquette, MI*

Steamboat Days Festival [S] *Jeffersonville, IN*

Steamboat Festival [S] *Peoria, IL*

Steamship *William G. Mather* Museum [W] *Cleveland, OH*

Stearman Fly-In Days [S] *Galesburg, IL*

Stearns Park [W] *Ludington, MI*

Steeple Building [W] *Bishop Hill, IL*

Stengel True Museum [W] *Marion, OH*

Stephen A. Forbes State Park [W] *Salem, IL*

Stephenson County Fair [S] *Freeport, IL*

Stephenson County Historical Museum [W] *Freeport, IL*

Stephenson Island [W] *Menominee, MI*

Steppenwolf [W] *Chicago, IL*

Sterling State Park [W] *Monroe, MI*

Sternwheeler *The Lorena* [W] *Zanesville, OH*

Stevens Point Brewery [W] *Stevens Point, WI*

Stone and Century House Tour [S] *Cedarburg, WI*

Stone Cottage [W] *Platteville, WI*

Stonefield [W] *Prairie du Chien, WI*

Stony Creek Metropark [W] *Troy, MI*

Strawberry Fest [S] *Waupaca, WI*

Strawberry Festival [S] *Cedarburg, WI*

Strawberry Festival [S] *Crawfordsville, IN*

Street Art Fair [S] *Ann Arbor, MI*

Stronghold Castle [W] *Oregon, IL*

Strouds Run [W] *Athens, OH*

Studebaker National Museum, The [W] *South Bend, IN*

Sturgeon & Pigeon River Outfitters [W] *Indian River, MI*

Sub-Continental Divide [W] *Menomonee Falls, WI*

Sugar Creek Canoe Race [S] *Crawfordsville, IN*

Sugar Loaf Mountain [W] *Marquette, MI*

Sugar Loaf Resort [W] *Traverse City, MI*

Sugar River State Trail [W] *New Glarus, WI*

Suicide Bowl [W] *Ishpeming, MI*

Summer concerts [S] *Whitehall, MI*

Summerfest [S] *Milwaukee, WI*

Summerfest [S] *Mishawaka, IN*

Summer Festival [S] *Glenview, IL*

Summer Festival [S] *Springfield, IL*

Summer Festival at New Salem [S] *Petersburg, IL*

Summit County Historical Society [W] *Akron, OH*

Summit Lake State Park [W] *New Castle, IN*

Sunday Polo [S] *Oak Brook, IL*

SunWatch Prehistoric Indian Village and Archaeological Park [W] *Dayton, OH*

Superior Municipal Forest [W] *Superior, WI*

Suwanee Park [W] *Dearborn, MI*

Swan City Car Show [S] *Beaver Dam, WI*

Swarthout Museum [W] *La Crosse, WI*

Swedish-American Museum Center [W] *Chicago, IL*

Swedish Days [S] *Geneva, IL*

Sweetcorn-Watermelon Festival [S] *Mount Vernon, IL*

Swimming, picnicking [W] *Charlevoix, MI*

Swiss Festival [S] *New Philadelphia, OH*

Swiss Historical Village [W] *New Glarus, WI*

Swiss Valley Ski Area [W] *Three Rivers, MI*

Swiss Volksfest [S] *New Glarus, WI*

Sycamore stump [W] *Kokomo, IN*

Symphony Center [W] *Chicago, IL*

Tahquamenon Falls State Park [W] *Hulbert, MI*

Tahquamenon Falls State Park [W] *Newberry, MI*

Talbot-Hyatt Pioneer Garden [W] *Madison, IN*

Taliesin [W] *Spring Green, WI*

Talisman Riverboat [W] *Lincoln's New Salem State Historic Site, IL*

Tall Ship *Malabar* [W] *Traverse City, MI*

Tall Tales Trail [W] *Burlington, WI*

Tappan Lake Park [W] *Gnadenhutten, OH*

Taste of Chicago [S] *Chicago, IL*
Taste of Glen Ellyn [S] *Glen Ellyn, IL*
Taste of Saugatuck [S] *Saugatuck, MI*
Tawas Bay Waterfront Art Show [S] *Tawas City, MI*
T. C. Steele State Historic Site [W] *Nashville, IN*
Tecumseh! [S] *Chillicothe, OH*
Temple Museum of Religious Art [W] *Cleveland, OH*
Terra Museum of American Art [W] *Chicago, IL*
Theater [W] *Peoria, IL*
Theaters [W] *Chicago, IL*
Theatre Building [W] *Chicago, IL*
Theatre Company-University of Detroit Mercy, The [S] *Detroit, MI*
Theatre on the Bay [S] *Marinette, WI*
Thistledown Racing Club [W] *Beach-wood, OH*
Thomas A. Edison Birthplace Museum [W] *Milan, OH*
Thomas Rees Memorial Carillon [W] *Springfield, IL*
Thompson State Fish Hatchery [W] *Manistique, MI*
Thoroughbred racing. Beulah Park Jockey Club [S] *Columbus, OH*
Thrall's Opera House [W] *New Harmony, IN*
Three Lakes Winery [W] *Three Lakes, WI*
Three Rivers Festival [S] *Fort Wayne, IN*
Thunderbird Museum [W] *Black River Falls, WI*
Tibbits Opera House [W] *Coldwater, MI*
Tibbits Professional Summer Theatre Series [S] *Coldwater, MI*
Tiffin-Seneca Heritage Festival [S] *Tiffin, OH*
Tillich Park [W] *New Harmony, IN*
Timber Ridge Ski Area [W] *Kalama-zoo, MI*
Timm House [W] *Elkhart Lake, WI*
Tinker Swiss Cottage Museum [W] *Rockford, IL*
Tippecanoe Battlefield Museum and Park [W] *Lafayette, IN*
Tippecanoe County Historical Museum [W] *Lafayette, IN*
Tippecanoe Lake [W] *Warsaw, IN*
Tip-Up-Town USA Ice Festival [S] *Houghton Lake, MI*
Tobico Marsh [W] *Bay City, MI*
Toledo Botanical Garden [W] *Toledo, OH*

Toledo Museum of Art, The [W] *Toledo, OH*
Toledo Symphony, The [W] *Toledo, OH*
Toledo Zoo, The [W] *Toledo, OH*
Tomahawk Trails Canoe Livery [W] *Indian River, MI*
Tommy Bartlett's Robot World & Exploratory [W] *Wisconsin Dells, WI*
Tommy Bartlett's Thrill Show [W] *Wisconsin Dells, WI*
Toonerville Trolley and Riverboat Trip to Tahquamenon Falls [W] *Soo Junction, MI*
Touching on Traditions [S] *Elgin, IL*
Tourist Park [W] *Marquette, MI*
Tour of homes [S] *Sandusky, OH*
Tours [W] *Oberlin, OH*
Tower City Center [W] *Cleveland, OH*
Tower Hill State Park [W] *Spring Green, WI*
Tower of History [W] *Sault Ste. Marie, MI*
Traditional Music Festival [S] *Peters-burg, IL*
Trailside Equestrian Center at Lock-wood Park [W] *Rockford, IL*
Trailside Nature Center [W] *Cincin-nati, OH*
Trapshooting Hall of Fame and Museum [W] *Vandalia, OH*
Trees For Tomorrow Natural Resources Education Center [W] *Eagle River, WI*
Trego Lake Park [W] *Spooner, WI*
Tri-City JazzFest [S] *Cleveland, OH*
Tri-State Pottery Festival [S] *East Liv-erpool, OH*
Trolley Fest [S] *Elgin, IL*
Trolley tours [W] *Marietta, OH*
Trolley Tours of Cleveland [W] *Cleveland, OH*
Trout Derby [S] *Portsmouth, OH*
Troy Museum and Historical Village [W] *Troy, MI*
Trumpet in the Land [S] *New Philadel-phia, OH*
Tulip Time Festival [S] *Holland, MI*
Turfway Park Race Course [S] *Cincin-nati, OH*
Turkey Run State Park [W] *Craw-fordsville, IN*
Turkey Run State Park [W] *Rockville, IN*
Turtlecreek Valley Railway [W] *Lebanon, OH*
Tuscora Park [W] *New Philadelphia, OH*

Twin Soo Tour [W] *Sault Ste. Marie, MI*

Tyler Creek [W] *Elgin, IL*

Ulysses S. Grant Home State Historic Site [W] *Galena, IL*

Union Cemetery [W] *Steubenville, OH*

Union Terminal [W] *Cincinnati, OH*

United Center [W] *Chicago, IL*

United States Air Force Museum [W] *Dayton, OH*

United States Post Office [W] *Chicago, IL*

Unity Temple [W] *Oak Park, IL*

University Museum [W] *Carbondale, IL*

University of Akron, The [W] *Akron, OH*

University of Chicago [W] *Chicago, IL*

University of Cincinnati [W] *Cincinnati, OH*

University of Dayton [W] *Dayton, OH*

University of Illinois [W] *Champaign/Urbana, IL*

University of Illinois at Chicago [W] *Chicago, IL*

University of Michigan [W] *Ann Arbor, MI*

University of Notre Dame [W] *South Bend, IN*

University of Southern Indiana [W] *Evansville, IN*

University of Toledo [W] *Toledo, OH*

University of Wisconsin-Eau Claire [W] *Eau Claire, WI*

University of Wisconsin-Green Bay [W] *Green Bay, WI*

University of Wisconsin-Parkside [W] *Kenosha, WI*

University of Wisconsin-Madison [W] *Madison, WI*

University of Wisconsin-Milwaukee [W] *Milwaukee, WI*

University of Wisconsin-Oshkosh [W] *Oshkosh, WI*

University of Wisconsin-Stevens Point [W] *Stevens Point, WI*

Untitled [W] *Chicago, IL*

Untitled Sounding Sculpture [W] *Chicago, IL*

Untouchable Tours [W] *Chicago, IL*

UP 200 Dog Sled Race [S] *Marquette, MI*

Upham Mansion [W] *Marshfield, WI*

Upper Harbor ore dock [W] *Marquette, MI*

Upper Peninsula Championship Rodeo [S] *Iron River, MI*

Upper Peninsula Children's Museum [W] *Marquette, MI*

Upper Peninsula Firefighters Memorial Museum [W] *Calumet, MI*

Upper Peninsula State Fair [S] *Escanaba, MI*

US Air & Trade Show [S] *Vandalia, OH*

US Coast Guard Canal Station [W] *Sturgeon Bay (Door County), WI*

US Coast Guard Cutter *Mackinaw*, The [W] *Cheboygan, MI*

USDA Forest Products Laboratory [W] *Madison, WI*

US Open Drum and Bugle Corps Competition [S] *Marion, OH*

USS *COD* [W] *Cleveland, OH*

USS *Silversides* and Maritime Museum [W] *Muskegon, MI*

Valley Gem Sternwheeler [W] *Marietta, OH*

Valley Vineyards Winery [W] *Lebanon, OH*

Van Buren State Park [W] *South Haven, MI*

Vandalia Statehouse State Historic Site [W] *Vandalia, IL*

Van Riper State Park [W] *Ishpeming, MI*

Van Wert County Fair [S] *Van Wert, OH*

Van Wert County Historical Society Museum [W] *Van Wert, OH*

Veldheer's Tulip Gardens and Deklomp Wooden Shoe & Delftware Factory [W] *Holland, MI*

Venetian Festival [S] *Charlevoix, MI*

Venetian Festival [S] *Lake Geneva, WI*

Venetian Festival [S] *St. Joseph, MI*

Venetian Night [S] *Chicago, IL*

Vermilion County Museum [W] *Danville, IL*

Vesper Cruises [S] *Mackinaw City, MI*

Veterans Armed Forces Celebration [S] *Connersville, IN*

Veterans' Memorial Building [W] *Detroit, MI*

Victorian Chautauqua [S] *Jeffersonville, IN*

Victorian Christmas [S] *Aurora, IN*

Victorian Christmas [S] *Menomonie, WI*

Victorian Port City Festival [S] *Manistee, MI*

Victory Gardens [W] *Chicago, IL*

Vigo County Historical Museum [W] *Terre Haute, IN*

Village Exhibit Tour [W] *Coshocton, OH*

Village of Elsah [W] *Alton, IL*
Village tours [W] *Bishop Hill, IL*
Villa Louis [W] *Prairie du Chien, WI*
Villa Terrace Decorative Arts
      Museum [W] *Milwaukee, WI*
Vincennes University [W] *Vincennes,
      IN*
Vinegar Hill Lead Mine & Museum
      [W] *Galena, IL*
Visitor activities [W] *Munising, MI*
Volo Auto Museum and Village [W]
      McHenry, IL
Von Stiehl Winery [W] *Algoma, WI*
Voyageurs Landing [W] *Elgin, IL*
Wabash Avenue [W] *Chicago, IL*
Wabash County Historical Museum
      [W] *Wabash, IN*
Wabash Valley Festival [S] *Terre
      Haute, IN*
Wade Park [W] *Cleveland, OH*
Waelderhaus [W] *Kohler, WI*
Walking tours [W] *Burlington, WI*
Walking tours of Pullman Historic
      District [W] *Chicago, IL*
Walleye Weekend Festival and Mer-
      cury Marine National Walleye
      Tournament [S] *Fond du Lac,
      WI*
Walworth County Fair [S] *Elkhorn,
      WI*
War Memorial Center [W] *Milwau-
      kee, WI*
Warner Vineyards [W] *Paw Paw, MI*
Warren County Fair [S] *Lebanon, OH*
Warren County Historical Society
      Museum [W] *Lebanon, OH*
Warren County Prime Beef Festival
      [S] *Monmouth, IL*
Warren Dunes State Park [W] *St.
      Joseph, MI*
Warther Museum [W] *New Philadel-
      phia, OH*
Washburn Observatory [W] *Madison,
      WI*
Washington Boulevard Trolley Car
      [W] *Detroit, MI*
Washington Island Museum [W]
      *Washington Island (Door
      County), WI*
Washington Park [W] *Michigan City,
      IN*
Waswagoning Ojibwe Village [W]
      Lac du Flambeau, WI
Waterboard Warriors [S] *Green Bay,
      WI*
Waterfront Art Fair [S] *Charlevoix, MI*
Waterfront Festival [S] *Menominee,
      MI*
Waterloo Farm Museum [W] *Jackson,
      MI*

Waterloo State Recreation Area [W]
      Jackson, MI
Water Tower [W] *Chicago, IL*
Water Tower Place [W] *Chicago, IL*
Waterway Daze [S] *Joliet, IL*
Waterworks Park [W] *Canton, OH*
Watson's Wild West Museum [W]
      Elkhorn, WI
Waukesha County Fair [S] *Wauke-
      sha, WI*
Waukesha County Museum [W]
      Waukesha, WI
Waukesha JanBoree [S] *Waukesha,
      WI*
Wayne County Fair [S] *Wooster, OH*
Wayne County Historical Museum
      [W] *Richmond, IN*
Wayne County Historical Society
      Museum [W] *Wooster, OH*
Wayne Fitzgerrell State Recreation
      Area [W] *Benton, IL*
Wayne National Forest [W] *Athens,
      OH*
Wayne National Forest [W] *Ironton,
      OH*
Wayne State University [W] *Detroit,
      MI*
Webb House Museum [W] *Newark,
      OH*
Webster House [W] *Elkhorn, WI*
Welcome to My Garden Tour [S]
      Marshall, MI
Wendella [W] *Chicago, IL*
Wesselman Park [W] *Evansville, IN*
West Branch State Park [W] *Kent,
      OH*
Western Illinois University [W]
      Macomb, IL
Western Michigan University [W]
      Kalamazoo, MI
Western Reserve Historical Society
      Museum and Library [W]
      Cleveland, OH
Wexner Center for the Arts [W]
      Columbus, OH
Wheaton College [W] *Wheaton, IL*
Wheeler Park [W] *Geneva, IL*
Wheels O' Time Museum [W] *Peoria,
      IL*
Whitcomb Conservatory [W]
      Detroit, MI
Whitecap Mountain Ski Area [W]
      Hurley, WI
White Lake Arts & Crafts Festival [S]
      Whitehall, MI
White Pines Forest State Park [W]
      Oregon, IL
White Pine Village [W] *Ludington,
      MI*

White River Light Station Museum [W] *Whitehall, MI*

Whitewater Canal State Historic Site [W] *Batesville, IN*

Whitewater Memorial State Park [W] *Connersville, IN*

Whitewater Valley Railroad [W] *Connersville, IN*

Whitnall Park [W] *Milwaukee, WI*

Wicker Memorial Park [W] *Hammond, IN*

Wildcat Mountain State Park [W] *Tomah, WI*

Wilderness Center, The [W] *Massillon, OH*

Wilderness Cruise [W] *Minocqua, WI*

Wilderness State Park [W] *Mackinaw City, MI*

Wildflower Pilgrimage [S] *Peru, IL*

Wildlife Prairie Park [W] *Peoria, IL*

Wild Rose Pioneer Museum [W] *Wautoma, WI*

Wilds, The [W] *Zanesville, OH*

Wildwood Cultural Center [W] *Mentor, OH*

Wildwood Park [W] *Cleveland, OH*

Wildwood Park and Zoo [W] *Marshfield, WI*

Wilford Woodruff Home [W] *Nauvoo, IL*

Wilhelm Tell Festival [S] *New Glarus, WI*

Willard Beach [W] *Battle Creek, MI*

William Henry Harrison Mansion (Grouseland) [W] *Vincennes, IN*

William Howard Taft National Historic Site [W] *Cincinnati, OH*

William Jennings Bryan Birthplace/Museum [W] *Salem, IL*

William Mitchell State Park [W] *Cadillac, MI*

William M. Staerkel Planetarium [W] *Champaign/Urbana, IL*

William Reddick Mansion (1855) [W] *Ottawa, IL*

Williamson County Fair [S] *Marion, IL*

Willow River State Park [W] *Hudson, WI*

Wilmette Historical Museum [W] *Wilmette, IL*

Wilmington College [W] *Wilmington, OH*

Wilmot Mountain [W] *Lake Geneva, WI*

Wilmot Mountain Ski Area [W] *Antioch, IL*

Wilson Place Museum [W] *Menomonie, WI*

Wilson State Park [W] *Harrison, MI*

Windmill Island [W] *Holland, MI*

Wine and Harvest Festival [S] *Cedarburg, WI*

Wine and Harvest Festival [S] *Kalamazoo, MI*

Winery at Wolf Creek, The [W] *Akron, OH*

Winery tours [W] *Paw Paw, MI*

Wing House Museum [W] *Coldwater, MI*

Winnebago County Fair [S] *Rockford, IL*

Winnebago Pow-Wow [S] *Black River Falls, WI*

Winter Carnival [S] *Houghton, MI*

Winter Carnival [S] *Menomonie, WI*

Winter Delights [S] *Chicago, IL*

Winterfest [S] *Gaylord, MI*

Winterfest [S] *Grand Haven, MI*

Winterfest [S] *Lake Geneva, WI*

Winterfest [S] *Mackinaw City, MI*

Winter Festival [S] *Cedarburg, WI*

Winter Wilderness Weekend [S] *Peru, IL*

Winter Wolf Festival [S] *Grayling, MI*

Wisconsin Deer Park [W] *Wisconsin Dells, WI*

Wisconsin High School State Rodeo Finals [S] *Richland Center, WI*

Wisconsin Maritime Museum [W] *Manitowoc, WI*

Wisconsin Point [W] *Superior, WI*

Wisconsin Shakespeare Festival [S] *Platteville, WI*

Wisconsin State Fair [S] *Milwaukee, WI*

Wisconsin Valley Fair [S] *Wausau, WI*

Wisconsin Veterans Museum [W] *Madison, WI*

Wittenberg University [W] *Springfield, OH*

WIU Museum [W] *Macomb, IL*

W. K. Kellogg Bird Sanctuary of Michigan State University [W] *Battle Creek, MI*

Wolcott Museum Complex [W] *Toledo, OH*

Woldumar Nature Center [W] *Lansing, MI*

Wolf Park [W] *Lafayette, IN*

Wollersheim Winery [W] *Prairie du Sac, WI*

Wonderful World of Ohio Mart [S] *Akron, OH*

Wood-Bee Carvers Show [S] *Iron Mountain, MI*

Wood County Fair [S] *Bowling Green, OH*

Wooden Shoe Factory [W] *Holland, MI*

Woodland Cemetery and Arboretum [W] *Dayton, OH*

Woodlawn Nature Center [W] *Elkhart, IN*

Woodruff State Fish Hatchery [W] *Woodruff, WI*

Woodstock Opera House [W] *Woodstock, IL*

Woolly Bear Festival [S] *Vermilion, OH*

Workingmen's Institute [W] *New Harmony, IN*

World Championship Snowmobile Derby [S] *Eagle River, WI*

World Heritage Museum [W] *Champaign/Urbana, IL*

World's Largest Weather Vane [W] *Whitehall, MI*

Wright Brothers Memorial [W] *Dayton, OH*

Wright Cycle Shop [W] *Dayton, OH*

Wright Earthworks [W] *Newark, OH*

Wright-Patterson Air Force Base [W] *Dayton, OH*

Wright State University [W] *Dayton, OH*

Wrigley Building [W] *Chicago, IL*

Wriston Art Center [W] *Appleton, WI*

Wyalusing State Park [W] *Prairie du Chien, WI*

Wyandot Lake Amusement & Water Park [W] *Columbus, OH*

Wyandotte Caves [W] *Wyandotte, IN*

Wyatt Earp Birthplace [W] *Monmouth, IL*

Xavier University [W] *Cincinnati, OH*

Yankee Peddler Festival [S] *Akron, OH*

Yellowstone Lake State Park [W] *Monroe, WI*

Yellowwood State Forest [W] *Nashville, IN*

Ye Olde Mill [W] *Newark, OH*

Yoctangee Park [W] *Chillicothe, OH*

Youngstown Historical Center of Industry & Labor [W] *Youngstown, OH*

Youngstown Playhouse [W] *Youngstown, OH*

Youngstown State University [W] *Youngstown, OH*

Youngstown Symphony Center [W] *Youngstown, OH*

Ypsilanti Heritage Festival [S] *Ypsilanti, MI*

Ypsilanti Historical Museum [W] *Ypsilanti, MI*

Ypsilanti Monument and Water Tower [W] *Ypsilanti, MI*

Zane Caverns [W] *Bellefontaine, OH*

Zane Grey Birthplace [W] *Zanesville, OH*

Zane Square Arts & Crafts Festival [S] *Lancaster, OH*

Zane's Trace Commemoration [S] *Zanesville, OH*

Zanesville Art Center [W] *Zanesville, OH*

Zoar Harvest Festival [S] *New Philadelphia, OH*

Zoar State Memorial [W] *New Philadelphia, OH*

LODGING LIST

Establishment names are listed in alphabetical order followed by a symbol identifying their classification and then city and state. The symbols for classification are: [AS] for All Suites, [BB] for B&Bs/Small Inns, [CAS] for Casinos, [CC] for Cottage Colonies, [CON] for Villas/Condos, [CONF] for Conference Centers, [EX] for Extended Stays, [HOT] for Hotels, [MOT] for Motels/Motor Lodges, [RAN] for Guest Ranches, and [RST] for Resorts

ABBEY RESORT & FONTANA SPA [RST] *Fontana, WI*
ADAM'S MARK [HOT] *Columbus, OH*
ADAM'S MARK [HOT] *Northbrook, IL*
AIRPORT PLAZA INN [MOT] *Detroit Wayne County Airport Area, MI*
AL & SALLY'S [MOT] *Michigan City, IN*
ALDRICH GUEST HOUSE [BB] *Galena, IL*
ALGER FALLS MOTEL [MOT] *Munising, MI*
ALLEN'S VICTORIAN PINES LODGING [MOT] *Galena, IL*
ALLERTON CROWNE PLAZA HOTEL [HOT] *Chicago, IL*
ALLISON HOUSE INN [BB] *Nashville, IN*
ALPINE INN [MOT] *Egg Harbor (Door County), WI*
AMBASSADOR [MOT] *Lake Geneva, WI*
AMERICAN CLUB, THE [RST] *Kohler, WI*
AMERICAN WORLD RESORT AND SUITES [MOT] *Wisconsin Dells, WI*
AMERICINN [MOT] *Rhinelander, WI*
AMERICINN [MOT] *Shawano, WI*
AMERICINN MOTEL [MOT] *Burlington, WI*
AMERICINN MOTEL AND SUITES [MOT] *Chippewa Falls, WI*
AMERICINN MOTEL AND SUITES [MOT] *Green Lake, WI*
AMERICINN MOTEL AND SUITES [MOT] *Rice Lake, WI*
AMERICINN OF HAYWARD [MOT] *Hayward, WI*
AMERIHOST INN [MOT] *Athens, OH*
AMERIHOST INN [MOT] *Grand Rapids, MI*
AMERIHOST INN [MOT] *Lancaster, OH*
AMERIHOST INN [MOT] *Zanesville, OH*
AMERIHOST INN WILMINGTON [MOT] *Wilmington, OH*

AMERISUITES [MOT] *Arlington Heights, IL*
AMERISUITES [MOT] *Cincinnati, OH*
AMERISUITES [MOT] *Columbus, OH*
AMERISUITES [MOT] *Indianapolis, IN*
AMWAY GRAND PLAZA HOTEL [HOT] *Grand Rapids, MI*
ANNIE'S BED AND BREAKFAST [BB] *Madison, WI*
ANNIE WIGGINS GUEST HOUSE [BB] *Galena, IL*
ANTLERS MOTEL [MOT] *Eau Claire, WI*
AQUA AIRE MOTEL [MOT] *Minocqua, WI*
ARBOR HILL [BB] *La Porte, IN*
ARCHWAY MOTEL [MOT] *Charlevoix, MI*
ASHBROOKE SUITES [MOT] *Egg Harbor (Door County), WI*
ASTOR HOUSE [BB] *Green Bay, WI*
ASTOR HOUSE-MINNETONKA RESORT [MOT] *Copper Harbor, MI*
ATHENEUM SUITE HOTEL, THE [AS] *Detroit, MI*
ATWOOD [RST] *New Philadelphia, OH*
AUBURN INN [MOT] *Auburn, IN*
AURORA BOREALIS MOTOR INN [MOT] *St. Ignace, MI*
AVALON INN & RESORT [MOT] *Warren, OH*
BAKERS SUNSET BAY RESORT [MOT] *Wisconsin Dells, WI*
BARBICAN INN [BB] *Sturgeon Bay (Door County), WI*
BARICELLI INN [BB] *Cleveland, OH*
BARKER'S ISLAND INN [MOT] *Superior, WI*
BATTLE CREEK INN [MOT] *Battle Creek, MI*
BAYFIELD INN [MOT] *Bayfield, WI*
BAYMONT INN [MOT] *Decatur, IL*
BAYMONT INN [MOT] *Glenview, IL*
BAYMONT INN [MOT] *Green Bay, WI*
BAYMONT INN [MOT] *Gurnee, IL*
BAYMONT INN [MOT] *Jackson, MI*
BAYMONT INN [MOT] *Kenosha, WI*

BAYMONT INN [MOT] *Oak Lawn, IL*
BAYMONT INN [MOT] *Oshkosh, WI*
BAYMONT INN [MOT] *Sheboygan, WI*
BAYMONT INN [MOT] *Wausau, WI*
BAYMONT INN & SUITES [MOT]
    Hinsdale, IL
BAYMONT INN & SUITES [MOT]
    Milwaukee, WI
BAYMONT INN & SUITES [MOT]
    Stevens Point, WI
BAYMONT INN & SUITES [MOT]
    Waupaca, WI
BAY POINT INN [MOT] *Egg Harbor
    (Door County), WI*
BAY SHORE INN [MOT] *Sturgeon Bay
    (Door County), WI*
BAYSHORE RESORT [MOT] *Traverse
    City, MI*
BAY VALLEY HOTEL & RESORT [RST]
    Bay City, MI
BAY VALLEY INN [MOT] *Frankfort, MI*
BAYVIEW [MOT] *Escanaba, MI*
BAY VIEW AT MACKINAC [BB]
    Mackinac Island, MI
BAY VIEW BEACHFRONT MOTEL
    [MOT] *St. Ignace, MI*
BAYVIEW MOTEL & RESORT [MOT]
    Green Lake, WI
BAYWINDS INN [MOT] *Petoskey, MI*
BEACHCOMBER MOTEL ON THE
    WATER [MOT] *Mackinaw City,
    MI*
BEACH CONDOMINIUMS [MOT]
    Traverse City, MI
BEACH HOUSE [BB] *Fish Creek (Door
    County), WI*
BEL-AIRE MOTEL [MOT] *Muskegon,
    MI*
BELDEN-STRATFORD [HOT] *Chicago,
    IL*
BELLA VISTA MOTEL [MOT] *Copper
    Harbor, MI*
BELLEVILLE INN [MOT] *Belleville, IL*
BELL TOWER HOTEL [HOT] *Ann
    Arbor, MI*
BENTON HOTEL SUITES [MOT] *St.
    Joseph, MI*
BEOWULF LODGE [MOT] *Fish Creek
    (Door County), WI*
BEST INN [MOT] *Marion, IL*
BEST INNS [MOT] *Bloomington, IL*
BEST INNS [MOT] *Carbondale, IL*
BEST INNS [MOT] *Mount Vernon, IL*
BEST INNS [MOT] *Waukegan, IL*
BEST INNS OF AMERICA [MOT]
    Anderson, IN
BEST INNS OF AMERICA [MOT]
    Effingham, IL
BEST INNS OF AMERICA [MOT]
    South Bend, IN

BEST INNS OF AMERICA [MOT]
    Springfield, IL
BEST NIGHTS INN [MOT] *Sparta, WI*
BEST VALUE INN [MOT] *Mansfield,
    OH*
BEST VALUE INN PARKWAY [MOT]
    Sheboygan, WI
BEST WESTERN [MOT] *Black River
    Falls, WI*
BEST WESTERN [MOT] *Cadillac, MI*
BEST WESTERN [MOT] *Cambridge,
    OH*
BEST WESTERN [MOT] *Detroit, MI*
BEST WESTERN [MOT] *Grand Haven,
    MI*
BEST WESTERN [MOT] *Homewood, IL*
BEST WESTERN [MOT] *Janesville, WI*
BEST WESTERN [MOT] *La Crosse, WI*
BEST WESTERN [MOT] *Madison, WI*
BEST WESTERN [MOT] *Marietta, OH*
BEST WESTERN [MOT] *Marinette, WI*
BEST WESTERN [MOT] *Munising, MI*
BEST WESTERN [MOT] *Platteville, WI*
BEST WESTERN [MOT] *Portsmouth,
    OH*
BEST WESTERN [MOT] *Richmond, IN*
BEST WESTERN [MOT] *St. Joseph, MI*
BEST WESTERN [MOT] *Wapakoneta,
    OH*
BEST WESTERN [MOT] *Warren, OH*
BEST WESTERN AIRPORT INN [MOT]
    Marion, IL
BEST WESTERN AIRPORT INN [MOT]
    Moline, IL
BEST WESTERN AIRPORT PLAZA
    [MOT] *Fort Wayne, IN*
BEST WESTERN AMBASSADOR INN
    [MOT] *Wisconsin Dells, WI*
BEST WESTERN BAY WALK INN
    [MOT] *Superior, WI*
BEST WESTERN BELLEVUE RESORT
    INN [MOT] *Bellevue, OH*
BEST WESTERN BREAKERS [MOT]
    Manistique, MI
BEST WESTERN BRIDGEVIEW [MOT]
    Superior, WI
BEST WESTERN CAMPUS INN [MOT]
    Beaver Dam, WI
BEST WESTERN CEDAR POINT
    [MOT] *Sandusky, OH*
BEST WESTERN CLARIDGE MOTOR
    INN [MOT] *Rhinelander, WI*
BEST WESTERN CLOCKTOWER
    RESORT [HOT] *Rockford, IL*
BEST WESTERN COLONIAL INN
    [MOT] *Rockford, IL*
BEST WESTERN COPPER CROWN
    [MOT] *Hancock, MI*
BEST WESTERN COUNTRY INN
    [MOT] *Ishpeming, MI*

BEST WESTERN COUNTRY VIEW INN [MOT] *Greenville, IL*

BEST WESTERN CREEKSIDE INN [MOT] *Bay City, MI*

BEST WESTERN DEL MAR [MOT] *Wauseon, OH*

BEST WESTERN DUTCHMAN INN [MOT] *Jasper, IN*

BEST WESTERN EL RANCHO [MOT] *Ladysmith, WI*

BEST WESTERN EXECUTIVE INN [MOT] *Iron Mountain, MI*

BEST WESTERN FOUR SEASONS MOTEL [MOT] *Traverse City, MI*

BEST WESTERN FOX VALLEY INN [MOT] *Aurora, IL*

BEST WESTERN GEORGIAN HOUSE LAKEFRONT [MOT] *St. Ignace, MI*

BEST WESTERN GOVERNOR DODGE MOTOR INN [MOT] *Platteville, WI*

BEST WESTERN GRANDVILLAGE INN [MOT] *Grand Rapids, MI*

BEST WESTERN GREENFIELD INN [MOT] *Dearborn, MI*

BEST WESTERN GREEN TREE INN [MOT] *Jeffersonville, IN*

BEST WESTERN HARBORSIDE [MOT] *Port Washington, WI*

BEST WESTERN HERITAGE INN [MOT] *Collinsville, IL*

BEST WESTERN HITCH INN POST [MOT] *Libertyville, IL*

BEST WESTERN HOLIDAY HOUSE [MOT] *Ashland, WI*

BEST WESTERN HOLIDAY MANOR [MOT] *Menomonie, WI*

BEST WESTERN HOSPITALITY INN [MOT] *Kalamazoo, MI*

BEST WESTERN HUDSON HOUSE INN [MOT] *Hudson, WI*

BEST WESTERN INN [MOT] *Akron, OH*

BEST WESTERN INN [MOT] *Goshen, IN*

BEST WESTERN INN [MOT] *Lancaster, OH*

BEST WESTERN INN [MOT] *Mackinaw City, MI*

BEST WESTERN INN [MOT] *Manistee, MI*

BEST WESTERN INN [MOT] *St. Charles, IL*

BEST WESTERN INN [MOT] *Wooster, OH*

BEST WESTERN INN [MOT] *Youngstown, OH*

BEST WESTERN INN FRANKLIN SQUARE [MOT] *Houghton, MI*

BEST WESTERN INN OF CHICAGO [MOT] *Chicago, IL*

BEST WESTERN INN ON THE PARK [MOT] *Madison, WI*

BEST WESTERN INN SPRINGDALE [MOT] *Cincinnati, OH*

BEST WESTERN KING'S INN [MOT] *Houghton, MI*

BEST WESTERN LAKEVIEW MOTOR [MOT] *Minocqua, WI*

BEST WESTERN MARIEMONT INN [MOT] *Cincinnati, OH*

BEST WESTERN MARITIME INN [MOT] *Sturgeon Bay (Door County), WI*

BEST WESTERN MIDWAY HOTEL [MOT] *Appleton, WI*

BEST WESTERN MIDWAY HOTEL ELK GROVE [MOT] *Chicago O'Hare Airport Area, IL*

BEST WESTERN MIDWAY HOTEL [MOT] *Eau Claire, WI*

BEST WESTERN MIDWAY HOTEL [MOT] *Grand Rapids, MI*

BEST WESTERN MIDWAY HOTEL [MOT] *Green Bay, WI*

BEST WESTERN MIDWAY HOTEL [MOT] *Lansing, MI*

BEST WESTERN MIDWAY HOTEL [MOT] *Milwaukee, WI*

BEST WESTERN MIDWAY HOTEL [MOT] *Wausau, WI*

BEST WESTERN NORTH [MOT] *Columbus, OH*

BEST WESTERN NORTHERN PINE INN [MOT] *Hayward, WI*

BEST WESTERN OF ALPENA [MOT] *Alpena, MI*

BEST WESTERN OLD CAPITOL INN [MOT] *Corydon, IN*

BEST WESTERN PARADISE INN [MOT] *Champaign/Urbana, IL*

BEST WESTERN PARK PLAZA [MOT] *Muskegon, MI*

BEST WESTERN PIONEER INN [MOT] *Escanaba, MI*

BEST WESTERN PORCUPINE MOUNTAIN LODGE [MOT] *Ontonagon, MI*

BEST WESTERN QUIET HOUSE SUITES [MOT] *Cedarburg, WI*

BEST WESTERN QUIET HOUSE & SUITES [MOT] *Galena, IL*

BEST WESTERN QUIET HOUSE & SUITES [MOT] *Prairie du Chien, WI*

BEST WESTERN RAINTREE INN [MOT] *Effingham, IL*

BEST WESTERN RAPIDS MOTOR INN [MOT] *Wisconsin Rapids, WI*

BEST WESTERN REAGAN HOTEL [MOT] *Dixon, IL*

BEST WESTERN REGENCY INN [MOT] *Antioch, IL*

BEST WESTERN RIVER NORTH
    HOTEL [MOT] *Chicago, IL*
BEST WESTERN RIVER TERRACE
    [MOT] *Cheboygan, MI*
BEST WESTERN ROYAL CREST [MOT]
    Gaylord, MI
BEST WESTERN SAULT STE. MARIE
    [MOT] *Sault Ste. Marie, MI*
BEST WESTERN STERLING INN
    BANQUET & CONFERENCE
    CENTER [MOT] *Warren, MI*
BEST WESTERN SUITES [MOT]
    Columbus, OH
BEST WESTERN SYCAMORE INN
    [MOT] *Oxford, OH*
BEST WESTERN UNIVERSITY INN
    [MOT] *Bloomington, IL*
BEST WESTERN VALLEY PLAZA
    RESORT [MOT] *Midland, MI*
BEST WESTERN VILLAGE HAUS
    [MOT] *Shawano, WI*
BEST WESTERN WHITE HOUSE INN
    [MOT] *Eau Claire, WI*
BEST WESTERN WORTHINGTON
    INN [MOT] *Charleston, IL*
BIRCHWOOD INN [MOT] *Harbor
    Springs, MI*
BLACKHAWK MOTEL [MOT]
    Michigan City, IN
BLACKHAWK MOTEL [MOT]
    Wisconsin Dells, WI
BLACK RIVER LODGE [MOT]
    Ironwood, MI
BLUE CHIP HOTEL AND CASINO
    [HOT] *Michigan City, IN*
BLUE WATER INN [MOT] *St. Clair, MI*
BLUFFSIDE MOTEL [MOT] *Sister Bay
    (Door County), WI*
BOLO COUNTRY INN [MOT]
    Menomonie, WI
BONNYMILL [BB] *Flint, MI*
BOOK INN BED & BREAKFAST [BB]
    South Bend, IN
BOTSFORD INN [BB] *Detroit, MI*
BOULEVARD INN [HOT] *St. Joseph,
    MI*
BOYNE HIGHLANDS RESORT [RST]
    Harbor Springs, MI
BOYNE MOUNTAIN [RST] *Boyne City,
    MI*
BRAXTAN HOUSE INN BED &
    BREAKFAST [BB] *French Lick, IN*
BREEZE INN TO THE CHALET [MOT]
    Cedarburg, WI
BRIGHTWOOD INN [BB] *Peru, IL*
BRISBOIS MOTOR INN [MOT] *Prairie
    du Chien, WI*
BROWN COUNTRY INN [MOT]
    Nashville, IN
BUDGET HOST CRESTVIEW INN
    [MOT] *Sault Ste. Marie, MI*

BUDGET HOST DIPLOMAT [MOT]
    Lake Geneva, WI
BUDGET HOST HERITAGE MOTEL
    [MOT] *Sparta, WI*
BUDGET HOST INN [MOT] *St. Ignace,
    MI*
BUDGET HOST INN [MOT]
    Wapakoneta, OH
BUDGET HOST/MANISTIQUE
    MOTOR INN [MOT]
    Manistique, MI
BUDGET INN [MOT] *Lincoln, IL*
BURR OAK RESORT [RST] *Athens, OH*
BUXTON INN [BB] *Newark, OH*
BY THE BAY MOTEL [MOT] *Fish
    Creek (Door County), WI*
CADILLAC SANDS RESORT [MOT]
    Cadillac, MI
CAMELOT [MOT] *Wisconsin Rapids,
    WI*
CANOE BAY [BB] *Rice Lake, WI*
CANTERBURY HOTEL [HOT]
    Indianapolis, IN
CAROUSEL INN AND SUITES [MOT]
    Wisconsin Dells, WI
CARVER'S ON THE LAKE [BB] *Green
    Lake, WI*
CASTLETON BY MARRIOTT
    COURTYARD [MOT]
    Indianapolis, IN
CEDAR COURT [MOT] *Fish Creek
    (Door County), WI*
CEDAR INN [MOT] *Hayward, WI*
CEDAR MOTOR INN [MOT]
    Marquette, MI
CEDARS MOTEL [MOT] *Ashtabula,
    OH*
CELIBETH HOUSE [BB] *Manistique,
    MI*
CHADWICK INN [BB] *Sturgeon Bay
    (Door County), WI*
CHAL-A MOTEL [MOT] *Sturgeon Bay
    (Door County), WI*
CHALET LANDHAUS INN [MOT]
    New Glarus, WI
CHANCELLOR INN [HOT]
    Champaign/Urbana, IL
CHANTICLEER GUEST HOUSE [BB]
    Sturgeon Bay (Door County), WI
CHANTICLEER INN [RST] *Eagle River,
    WI*
CHARACTER INN [HOT] *Flint, MI*
CHECKERBERRY INN, THE [BB]
    Goshen, IN
CHEQUAMEGON [HOT] *Ashland, WI*
CHERRY HILLS LODGE [MOT]
    Sturgeon Bay (Door County), WI
CHERRY VALLEY LODGE [MOT]
    Newark, OH
CHICAGO PIKE [BB] *Coldwater, MI*

CHIMNEY CORNERS RESORT [RST] *Frankfort, MI*

CHIPPEWA MOTEL [MOT] *Houghton, MI*

CHIPPEWA MOTEL [MOT] *Wisconsin Dells, WI*

CHIPPEWA MOTOR LODGE [MOT] *Mackinaw City, MI*

CHULA VISTA RESORT AND CONFERENCE CENTER [RST] *Wisconsin Dells, WI*

CHURCH HILL INN, THE [MOT] *Sister Bay (Door County), WI*

CINCINNATIAN HOTEL, THE [HOT] *Cincinnati, OH*

CITY SUITES [HOT] *Chicago, IL*

CLARIDGE [HOT] *Chicago, IL*

CLARION FOURWINDS RESORT [RST] *Bloomington, IN*

CLARION HOTEL [MOT] *Milwaukee, WI*

CLARION HOTEL [MOT] *Toledo, OH*

CLARION HOTEL CLEVELAND WEST [MOT] *Cleveland, OH*

CLARION HOTEL EXECUTIVE PLAZA [HOT] *Chicago, IL*

CLARION INN RIVERS EDGE [MOT] *Sandusky, OH*

CLARION INN SANDUSKY [MOT] *Sandusky, OH*

CLEVELAND BEACHWOOD SUPER 8 [MOT] *Beachwood, OH*

CLIFF DWELLERS RESORT [MOT] *Sturgeon Bay (Door County), WI*

CLUBHOUSE INN [MOT] *Oak Brook, IL*

COACHLITE INN [MOT] *Sister Bay (Door County), WI*

COLLINS HOUSE B&B [BB] *Madison, WI*

COLONIAL INN [MOT] *Harbor Springs, MI*

COLONY [MOT] *Brookfield, IL*

COMFORT INN [MOT] *Alliance, OH*

COMFORT INN [MOT] *Alma, MI*

COMFORT INN [MOT] *Anderson, IN*

COMFORT INN [MOT] *Arcola, IL*

COMFORT INN [MOT] *Ashtabula, OH*

COMFORT INN [MOT] *Aurora, IL*

COMFORT INN [MOT] *Bellefontaine, OH*

COMFORT INN [MOT] *Beloit, WI*

COMFORT INN [MOT] *Brecksville, OH*

COMFORT INN [MOT] *Canton, OH*

COMFORT INN [MOT] *Celina, OH*

COMFORT INN [MOT] *Champaign/Urbana, IL*

COMFORT INN [MOT] *Chicago, IL*

COMFORT INN [MOT] *Chillicothe, OH*

COMFORT INN [MOT] *Danville, IL*

COMFORT INN [MOT] *Dayton, OH*

COMFORT INN [MOT] *Defiance, OH*

COMFORT INN [MOT] *Downers Grove, IL*

COMFORT INN [MOT] *Eau Claire, WI*

COMFORT INN [MOT] *Elyria, OH*

COMFORT INN [MOT] *Evansville, IN*

COMFORT INN [MOT] *Farmington, MI*

COMFORT INN [MOT] *Galesburg, IL*

COMFORT INN [MOT] *Grand Rapids, MI*

COMFORT INN [MOT] *Green Bay, WI*

COMFORT INN [MOT] *Gurnee, IL*

COMFORT INN [MOT] *Hudson, WI*

COMFORT INN [MOT] *Iron Mountain, MI*

COMFORT INN [MOT] *Ironwood, MI*

COMFORT INN [MOT] *Lincoln, IL*

COMFORT INN [MOT] *Mackinaw City, MI*

COMFORT INN [MOT] *Mansfield, OH*

COMFORT INN [MOT] *Marietta, OH*

COMFORT INN [MOT] *Marion, IL*

COMFORT INN [MOT] *Marion, OH*

COMFORT INN [MOT] *Mount Pleasant, MI*

COMFORT INN [MOT] *Munising, MI*

COMFORT INN [MOT] *Newberry, MI*

COMFORT INN [MOT] *Peru, IL*

COMFORT INN [MOT] *Piqua, OH*

COMFORT INN [MOT] *Port Huron, MI*

COMFORT INN [MOT] *Richmond, IN*

COMFORT INN [MOT] *Rockford, IL*

COMFORT INN [MOT] *Sault Ste. Marie, MI*

COMFORT INN [MOT] *Sidney, OH*

COMFORT INN [MOT] *Springfield, IL*

COMFORT INN [MOT] *St. Ignace, MI*

COMFORT INN [MOT] *St. Joseph, MI*

COMFORT INN [MOT] *Toledo, OH*

COMFORT INN [MOT] *Tomah, WI*

COMFORT INN [MOT] *Wisconsin Dells, WI*

COMFORT INN [MOT] *Youngstown, OH*

COMFORT INN [MOT] *Zanesville, OH*

COMFORT INN & CONFERENCE CENTER [MOT] *Edwardsville, IL*

COMFORT INN & EXECUTIVE SUITES [MOT] *Lansing, MI*

COMFORT INN CLEVELAND AIRPORT [MOT] *Cleveland, OH*

COMFORT INN MILAN [MOT] *Milan, OH*

COMFORT INN NAVAL TRAINING CENTER [MOT] *Waukegan, IL*

COMFORT INN NORTH [MOT] *Joliet, IL*

COMFORT INN NORTH EAST [MOT] *Cincinnati, OH*

COMFORT INN OF UTICA [MOT] *Mount Clemens, MI*

COMFORT INN O'HARE [MOT] *Chicago O'Hare Airport Area, IL*

COMFORT INN SOUTH [MOT] *Joliet, IL*

COMFORT INN WEST [MOT] *Akron, OH*

COMFORT INN WEST [MOT] *Indianapolis, IN*

COMFORT SUITES [MOT] *Aurora, IL*

COMFORT SUITES [MOT] *Cincinnati, OH*

COMFORT SUITES [MOT] *Effingham, IL*

COMFORT SUITES [MOT] *Marion, IN*

COMFORT SUITES [MOT] *Mason, OH*

COMFORT SUITES [MOT] *Oak Brook, IL*

COMFORT SUITES [MOT] *Peoria, IL*

COMFORT SUITES [MOT] *Stevens Point, WI*

COMFORT SUITES-AIRPORT [MOT] *Columbus, OH*

CONCOURSE HOTEL [HOT] *Columbus, OH*

CONGRESS PLAZA [HOT] *Chicago, IL*

CORNERSTONE INN [BB] *Nashville, IN*

COUNTRY HEARTH INN [MOT] *Auburn, IN*

COUNTRY HEARTH INN [MOT] *Chillicothe, OH*

COUNTRY HEARTH INN [MOT] *Findlay, OH*

COUNTRY HEARTH INN [MOT] *Indianapolis, IN*

COUNTRY HEARTH INN [MOT] *Jackson, MI*

COUNTRY HOUSE [BB] *New Glarus, WI*

COUNTRY HOUSE [MOT] *Spooner, WI*

COUNTRY HOUSE RESORT [MOT] *Sister Bay (Door County), WI*

COUNTRY INN [MOT] *Chippewa Falls, WI*

COUNTRY INN AND SUITES [MOT] *Hayward, WI*

COUNTRY INN BY CARLSON [MOT] *Holland, MI*

COUNTRY INN BY CARLSON [MOT] *Sparta, WI*

COUNTRY PRIDE INN [MOT] *Oconomowoc, WI*

COUNTRYSIDE INN [MOT] *La Grange, IL*

COURTYARD BY MARRIOTT [MOT] *Ann Arbor, MI*

COURTYARD BY MARRIOTT [MOT] *Arlington Heights, IL*

COURTYARD BY MARRIOTT [MOT] *Beachwood, OH*

COURTYARD BY MARRIOTT [MOT] *Bloomington, IN*

COURTYARD BY MARRIOTT [MOT] *Chicago, IL*

COURTYARD BY MARRIOTT [MOT] *Chicago, IL*

COURTYARD BY MARRIOTT [MOT] *Cincinnati, OH*

COURTYARD BY MARRIOTT [MOT] *Columbus, OH*

COURTYARD BY MARRIOTT [MOT] *Columbus, OH*

COURTYARD BY MARRIOTT [MOT] *Dearborn, MI*

COURTYARD BY MARRIOTT [MOT] *Detroit Wayne County Airport Area, MI*

COURTYARD BY MARRIOTT [MOT] *Elmhurst, IL*

COURTYARD BY MARRIOTT [MOT] *Fort Wayne, IN*

COURTYARD BY MARRIOTT [MOT] *Glenview, IL*

COURTYARD BY MARRIOTT [MOT] *Goshen, IN*

COURTYARD BY MARRIOTT [MOT] *Highland Park, IL*

COURTYARD BY MARRIOTT [MOT] *Indianapolis, IN*

COURTYARD BY MARRIOTT [MOT] *Indianapolis, IN*

COURTYARD BY MARRIOTT [MOT] *Lansing, MI*

COURTYARD BY MARRIOTT [MOT] *Miamisburg, OH*

COURTYARD BY MARRIOTT [MOT] *Northbrook, IL*

COURTYARD BY MARRIOTT [MOT] *Oak Brook, IL*

COURTYARD BY MARRIOTT [MOT] *Pontiac, MI*

COURTYARD BY MARRIOTT [MOT] *Rockford, IL*

COURTYARD BY MARRIOTT [MOT] *Southfield, MI*

COURTYARD BY MARRIOTT [MOT] *Springfield, IL*

COURTYARD BY MARRIOTT [MOT] *St. Joseph, MI*

COURTYARD BY MARRIOTT [MOT] *Toledo, OH*

COURTYARD BY MARRIOTT [MOT] *Troy, MI*

COURTYARD BY MARRIOTT [MOT] *Valparaiso, IN*

COURTYARD BY MARRIOTT [MOT] *Warren, MI*

COURTYARD BY MARRIOTT [MOT] *Wheeling, IL*

COURTYARD BY MARRIOTT DETROIT DOWNTOWN [MOT] *Detroit, MI*

COURTYARD BY MARRIOTT DETROIT LIVONIA [MOT] *Detroit, MI*

COURTYARD BY MARRIOTT NAPERVILLE [MOT] *Naperville, IL*

COURTYARD BY MARRIOTT O'HARE [MOT] *Chicago O'Hare Airport Area, IL*

COURTYARD BY MARRIOTT WAUKEGAN [MOT] *Waukegan, IL*

CREEKWOOD INN [BB] *Michigan City, IN*

CROSS COUNTRY INN [MOT] *Cincinnati, OH*

CROSS COUNTRY INN [MOT] *Columbus, OH*

CROSS COUNTRY INN [MOT] *Dayton, OH*

CROSS COUNTRY INN- CINCINNATI [MOT] *Cincinnati, OH*

CROSS COUNTRY INN- CLEVELAND SOUTH [MOT] *Cleveland, OH*

CROSS COUNTRY INN- DAYTON [MOT] *Vandalia, OH*

CROSS COUNTRY INN- FINDLAY [MOT] *Findlay, OH*

CROWNE PLAZA [HOT] *Ann Arbor, MI*

CROWNE PLAZA [HOT] *Cincinnati, OH*

CROWNE PLAZA [HOT] *Columbus, OH*

CROWNE PLAZA [HOT] *Dayton, OH*

CROWNE PLAZA [HOT] *Grand Rapids, MI*

CROWNE PLAZA CHICAGO - THE SILVERSMITH [HOT] *Chicago, IL*

CROWNE PLAZA DETROIT METRO [HOT] *Detroit Wayne County Airport Area, MI*

CROWNE PLAZA HOTEL UNION STATION [HOT] *Indianapolis, IN*

CROWN INN [MOT] *Toledo, OH*

CRYSTAL MOUNTAIN RESORT [RST] *Traverse City, MI*

CULVER COVE RESORT & CONFERENCE CENTER [MOT] *Plymouth, IN*

CURRIER'S LAKEVIEW MOTEL [MOT] *Rice Lake, WI*

DAHLMANN CAMPUS INN, THE [HOT] *Ann Arbor, MI*

DALE MOTEL [MOT] *Tawas City, MI*

DALLES HOUSE MOTEL [MOT] *St. Croix Falls, WI*

DAYS INN [MOT] *Athens, OH*

DAYS INN [MOT] *Battle Creek, MI*

DAYS INN [MOT] *Benton, IL*

DAYS INN [MOT] *Bowling Green, OH*

DAYS INN [MOT] *Cadillac, MI*

DAYS INN [MOT] *Cambridge, OH*

DAYS INN [MOT] *Charleston, IL*

DAYS INN [MOT] *Cheboygan, MI*

DAYS INN [MOT] *Chillicothe, OH*

DAYS INN [MOT] *Danville, IL*

DAYS INN [MOT] *Dayton, OH*

DAYS INN [MOT] *Defiance, OH*

DAYS INN [MOT] *Delaware, OH*

DAYS INN [MOT] *Eagle River, WI*

DAYS INN [MOT] *Effingham, IL*

DAYS INN [MOT] *Elgin, IL*

DAYS INN [MOT] *Elyria, OH*

DAYS INN [MOT] *Escanaba, MI*

DAYS INN [MOT] *Evansville, IN*

DAYS INN [MOT] *Fond du Lac, WI*

DAYS INN [MOT] *Fremont, OH*

DAYS INN [MOT] *Gaylord, MI*

DAYS INN [MOT] *Grand Haven, MI*

DAYS INN [MOT] *Grand Rapids, MI*

DAYS INN [MOT] *Green Bay, WI*

DAYS INN [MOT] *Jasper, IN*

DAYS INN [MOT] *Kalamazoo, MI*

DAYS INN [MOT] *Kent, OH*

DAYS INN [MOT] *Libertyville, IL*

DAYS INN [MOT] *Mackinaw City, MI*

DAYS INN [MOT] *Macomb, IL*

DAYS INN [MOT] *Marquette, MI*

DAYS INN [MOT] *Mason, OH*

DAYS INN [MOT] *McHenry, IL*

DAYS INN [MOT] *Monroe, MI*

DAYS INN [MOT] *Muncie, IN*

DAYS INN [MOT] *Munising, MI*

DAYS INN [MOT] *Muskegon, MI*

DAYS INN [MOT] *Newberry, MI*

DAYS INN [MOT] *Port Clinton, OH*

DAYS INN [MOT] *Sault Ste. Marie, MI*

DAYS INN [MOT] *South Bend, IN*

DAYS INN [MOT] *Springfield, IL*

DAYS INN [MOT] *St. Charles, IL*

DAYS INN [MOT] *St. Clairsville, OH*

DAYS INN [MOT] *St. Ignace, MI*

DAYS INN [MOT] *St. Joseph, MI*

DAYS INN [MOT] *Terre Haute, IN*

DAYS INN [MOT] *Toledo, OH*

DAYS INN [MOT] *Traverse City, MI*

DAYS INN [MOT] *Vandalia, IL*

DAYS INN [MOT] *Wisconsin Dells, WI*

DAYS INN [MOT] *Woodstock, IL*

DAYS INN [MOT] *Zanesville, OH*

DAYS INN-BLACK RIVER FALLS [MOT] *Black River Falls, WI*

DAYS INN HOTEL AND CONFERENCE CENTER [MOT] *La Crosse, WI*

DAYS INN-MANISTEE [MOT] *Manistee, MI*

DEER PATH INN [BB] *Highwood, IL*

DESOTO HOUSE HOTEL [HOT] *Galena, IL*
DILLMAN'S BAY PROPERTIES [RST] *Lac du Flambeau, WI*
DOHERTY HOTEL [MOT] *Clare, MI*
DON HALL'S GUESTHOUSE [MOT] *Fort Wayne, IN*
DON Q INN [MOT] *Dodgeville, WI*
DORAL ENGLEWOOD CONFERENCE RESORT AND SPA [RST] *Itasca, IL*
DORAL MOTEL [MOT] *Sault Ste. Marie, MI*
DOUBLETREE [HOT] *Farmington, MI*
DOUBLETREE [HOT] *Skokie, IL*
DOUBLETREE GUEST SUITES [AS] *Chicago, IL*
DOUBLETREE GUEST SUITES [AS] *Columbus, OH*
DOUBLETREE GUEST SUITES [AS] *Dayton, OH*
DOUBLETREE GUEST SUITES [AS] *Downers Grove, IL*
DOUBLETREE GUEST SUITES [AS] *Glenview, IL*
DOUBLETREE GUEST SUITES HOTEL [HOT] *Indianapolis, IN*
DOWNTOWN MOTEL [MOT] *Sparta, WI*
DRAKE, THE [HOT] *Chicago, IL*
DRURY INN [MOT] *Collinsville, IL*
DRURY INN [MOT] *Evansville, IN*
DRURY INN [MOT] *Indianapolis, IN*
DRURY INN [MOT] *Mount Vernon, IL*
DRURY INN [MOT] *Terre Haute, IN*
DRURY INN [MOT] *Troy, MI*
DUNE LAND BEACH INN [BB] *Michigan City, IN*
DUTCH COLONIAL INN [BB] *Holland, MI*
DU WAYNE [MOT] *St. Charles, IL*
EAGLE HARBOR INN [BB] *Ephraim (Door County), WI*
EAGLE RIDGE INN & RESORT [RST] *Galena, IL*
EAGLE RIVER INN AND RESORT [MOT] *Eagle River, WI*
EASTLAND SUITES [MOT] *Bloomington, IL*
EAST LAND SUITES [MOT] *Champaign/Urbana, IL*
ECONO LODGE [MOT] *Collinsville, IL*
ECONO LODGE [MOT] *Elkhart, IN*
ECONO LODGE [MOT] *Fond du Lac, WI*
ECONO LODGE [MOT] *Homewood, IL*
ECONO LODGE [MOT] *Madison, WI*
ECONO LODGE [MOT] *Manistique, MI*
ECONO LODGE [MOT] *Marietta, OH*
ECONO LODGE [MOT] *Peru, IL*

ECONO LODGE [MOT] *Petoskey, MI*
ECONO LODGE [MOT] *St. Ignace, MI*
ECONO LODGE [MOT] *Wisconsin Rapids, WI*
ECONO LODGE [MOT] *Wooster, OH*
ECONO LODGE AND SUITES [MOT] *South Haven, MI*
EDGE OF TOWN MOTEL [MOT] *Sister Bay (Door County), WI*
EDGEWATER, THE [MOT] *Madison, WI*
EDGEWATER INN [AS] *Charlevoix, MI*
EDGEWATER RESORT MOTEL [MOT] *Ephraim (Door County), WI*
EGG HARBOR LODGE [MOT] *Egg Harbor (Door County), WI*
ELK RAPIDS BEACH RESORT [MOT] *Traverse City, MI*
EL RANCHO STEVENS [RST] *Gaylord, MI*
EMBASSY SUITES [AS] *Beachwood, OH*
EMBASSY SUITES [AS] *Downers Grove, IL*
EMBASSY SUITES [AS] *Indianapolis, IN*
EMBASSY SUITES [AS] *Indianapolis, IN*
EMBASSY SUITES [AS] *Northbrook, IL*
EMBASSY SUITES [AS] *Troy, MI*
EMBASSY SUITES CHICAGO - DOWNTOWN [AS] *Chicago, IL*
EMBASSY SUITES CINCINNATI NORTHEAST [AS] *Cincinnati, OH*
EMBASSY SUITES-DOWNTOWN [AS] *Cleveland, OH*
EMBASSY SUITES HOTEL [AS] *Columbus, OH*
EMBASSY SUITES HOTEL [AS] *Detroit, MI*
EMBASSY SUITES HOTEL O'HARE-ROSEMONT [AS] *Chicago O'Hare Airport Area, IL*
EMBASSY SUITES-MILWAUKEE WEST [AS] *Milwaukee, WI*
EMBASSY SUITES SCHAUMBURG [HOT] *Schaumburg, IL*
ENGLISH INN, THE [BB] *Lansing, MI*
EPHRAIM GUEST HOUSE [MOT] *Ephraim (Door County), WI*
EPHRAIM INN [BB] *Ephraim (Door County), WI*
EPHRAIM MOTEL [MOT] *Ephraim (Door County), WI*
EPHRAIM SHORES MOTEL [MOT] *Ephraim (Door County), WI*
ESCH'S SERENITY BAY [CC] *St. Germain, WI*
ESSENHAUS COUNTRY INN [BB] *Goshen, IN*
EUCLID [MOT] *Bay City, MI*
EVERGREEN BEACH [MOT] *Ephraim (Door County), WI*

EVERGREEN MOTEL [MOT]
 Ladysmith, WI
EXECUTIVE HOTEL & SUITES [MOT]
 Farmington, MI
EXEL INN [MOT] *Appleton, WI*
EXEL INN [MOT] *Chicago O'Hare
 Airport Area, IL*
EXEL INN [MOT] *Eau Claire, WI*
EXEL INN [MOT] *Grand Rapids, MI*
EXEL INN [MOT] *Green Bay, WI*
EXEL INN [MOT] *La Crosse, WI*
EXEL INN [MOT] *Madison, WI*
EXEL INN [MOT] *Milwaukee, WI*
EXEL INN [MOT] *Milwaukee, WI*
EXEL INN [MOT] *Naperville, IL*
EXEL INN [MOT] *Oak Lawn, IL*
EXEL INN [MOT] *Rockford, IL*
EXEL INN [MOT] *Wausau, WI*
EXEL INN [MOT] *Wauwatosa, WI*
EXEL INN [MOT] *Wheeling, IL*
FAIRFIELD INN [MOT] *Ann Arbor, MI*
FAIRFIELD INN [MOT] *Bloomington,
 IL*
FAIRFIELD INN [MOT] *Chicago, IL*
FAIRFIELD INN [MOT] *Cincinnati, OH*
FAIRFIELD INN [MOT] *Columbus, OH*
FAIRFIELD INN [MOT] *Danville, IL*
FAIRFIELD INN [MOT] *Dayton, OH*
FAIRFIELD INN [MOT] *Decatur, IL*
FAIRFIELD INN [MOT] *Evansville, IN*
FAIRFIELD INN [MOT] *Findlay, OH*
FAIRFIELD INN [MOT] *Glenview, IL*
FAIRFIELD INN [MOT] *Green Bay, WI*
FAIRFIELD INN [MOT] *Gurnee, IL*
FAIRFIELD INN [MOT] *Hinsdale, IL*
FAIRFIELD INN [MOT] *Indianapolis,
 IN*
FAIRFIELD INN [MOT] *Kalamazoo, MI*
FAIRFIELD INN [MOT] *Kokomo, IN*
FAIRFIELD INN [MOT] *Lafayette, IN*
FAIRFIELD INN [MOT] *Lansing, MI*
FAIRFIELD INN [MOT] *Madison, WI*
FAIRFIELD INN [MOT] *Merrillville, IN*
FAIRFIELD INN [MOT] *Middletown
 (Butler County), OH*
FAIRFIELD INN [MOT] *Oshkosh, WI*
FAIRFIELD INN [MOT] *Peoria, IL*
FAIRFIELD INN [MOT] *Pontiac, MI*
FAIRFIELD INN [MOT] *Port Clinton,
 OH*
FAIRFIELD INN [MOT] *Rockford, IL*
FAIRFIELD INN [MOT] *Sandusky, OH*
FAIRFIELD INN [MOT] *Springfield, OH*
FAIRFIELD INN [MOT] *Terre Haute, IN*
FAIRFIELD INN [MOT] *Troy, MI*
FAIRFIELD INN [MOT] *Warren, MI*
FAIRFIELD INN [MOT] *Waukesha, WI*
FAIRFIELD INN [MOT] *Zanesville, OH*
FAIRFIELD INN - CLEVELAND
 AIRPORT [MOT] *Cleveland, OH*
FAIRFIELD INN DETROIT WEST
 CANTON [MOT] *Plymouth, MI*

FAIRFIELD INN EAST [MOT]
 Evansville, IN
FAIRMONT CHICAGO, THE [HOT]
 Chicago, IL
FANNY HILL VICTORIAN INN [BB]
 Eau Claire, WI
52 STAFFORD [BB] *Elkhart Lake, WI*
FINDLAY INN & CONFERENCE
 CENTER [MOT] *Findlay, OH*
FINDLAY'S HOLIDAY INN AND
 VIKING VILLAGE [MOT]
 *Washington Island (Door
 County), WI*
FITZPATRICK CHICAGO HOTEL [AS]
 Chicago, IL
FLETCHER [MOT] *Alpena, MI*
FORTY WINKS INN [MOT]
 Wauwatosa, WI
FOUNTAIN INN [MOT] *Grand Haven,
 MI*
FOUR POINTS BY SHERATON [MOT]
 Brecksville, OH
FOUR POINTS BY SHERATON [MOT]
 Canton, OH
FOUR POINTS BY SHERATON
 AIRPORT [MOT] *Milwaukee, WI*
FOUR POINTS BY SHERATON
 BARCELO HOTEL [MOT] *Oak
 Brook, IL*
FOUR POINTS BY SHERATON [MOT]
 Saginaw, MI
FOUR SEASONS HOTEL CHICAGO
 [HOT] *Chicago, IL*
FOUR SEASONS MOTEL [MOT]
 Crandon, WI
FOUR SEASONS MOTEL [MOT]
 Ludington, MI
FRANKENMUTH BAVARIAN INN
 LODGE [MOT] *Frankenmuth,
 MI*
FRENCH COUNTRY INN [BB] *Lake
 Geneva, WI*
FRENCH COUNTRY INN BED AND
 BREAKFAST [BB] *Ephraim (Door
 County), WI*
FRENCH LICK SPRINGS RESORT
 [RST] *French Lick, IN*
FROELICH'S SAYNER LODGE [RST]
 Sayner, WI
GARFIELD SUITES HOTEL [AS]
 Cincinnati, OH
GARLAND RESORT & GOLF COURSE
 [RST] *Gaylord, MI*
GATEWAY MOTEL [MOT] *Newberry,
 MI*
GEORGIAN INN [MOT] *Warren, MI*
GIANT CITY STATE PARK LODGE
 [CC] *Carbondale, IL*
GLENLAUREL [BB] *Lancaster, OH*
GLEN LOCH MOTEL [MOT]
 Chippewa Falls, WI

GOLD COAST GUEST HOUSE [BB] *Chicago, IL*
GOLDEN LAMB [BB] *Lebanon, OH*
GORDON LODGE [RST] *Baileys Harbor (Door County), WI*
GOSHEN INN & CONFERENCE CENTER [MOT] *Goshen, IN*
GRAND BEACH RESORT HOTEL [MOT] *Traverse City, MI*
GRAND GENEVA RESORT AND SPA [RST] *Lake Geneva, WI*
GRAND HOTEL [RST] *Mackinac Island, MI*
GRAND MACKINAW INN AND SUITES [MOT] *Mackinaw City, MI*
GRAND TRAVERSE RESORT [RST] *Traverse City, MI*
GRAND VICTORIA CASINO & RESORT BY HYATT [RST] *Aurora, IN*
GRAND VIEW [MOT] *Beaver Dam, WI*
GRAND VIEW MOTEL [MOT] *Ellison Bay (Door County), WI*
GRAY GOOSE BED AND BREAKFAST [BB] *Sturgeon Bay (Door County), WI*
GREAT NORTHERN [MOT] *Manitowish Waters, WI*
GREEN ACRES MOTEL [MOT] *Spooner, WI*
GREENCREST MANOR [BB] *Battle Creek, MI*
GUESTHOUSE HOTEL [MOT] *Freeport, IL*
GYPSY VILLA RESORT [RST] *Eagle River, WI*
HALL HOUSE BED & BREAKFAST [BB] *Kalamazoo, MI*
HAMILTONIAN [HOT] *Hamilton, OH*
HAMPTON INN [MOT] *Ann Arbor, MI*
HAMPTON INN [MOT] *Belleville, IL*
HAMPTON INN [MOT] *Bloomington, IL*
HAMPTON INN [MOT] *Bloomington, IN*
HAMPTON INN [MOT] *Cadillac, MI*
HAMPTON INN [MOT] *Canton, OH*
HAMPTON INN [MOT] *Chicago O'Hare Airport Area, IL*
HAMPTON INN [MOT] *Cincinnati, OH*
HAMPTON INN [MOT] *Columbus, OH*
HAMPTON INN [MOT] *Dayton, OH*
HAMPTON INN [MOT] *Dearborn, MI*
HAMPTON INN [MOT] *Detroit Wayne County Airport Area, MI*
HAMPTON INN [MOT] *Eau Claire, WI*
HAMPTON INN [MOT] *Effingham, IL*
HAMPTON INN [MOT] *Evansville, IN*

HAMPTON INN [MOT] *Farmington, MI*
HAMPTON INN [MOT] *Grand Rapids, MI*
HAMPTON INN [MOT] *Gurnee, IL*
HAMPTON INN [MOT] *Indianapolis, IN*
HAMPTON INN [MOT] *La Crosse, WI*
HAMPTON INN [MOT] *Lansing, MI*
HAMPTON INN [MOT] *Madison, WI*
HAMPTON INN [MOT] *Milwaukee, WI*
HAMPTON INN [MOT] *Moline, IL*
HAMPTON INN [MOT] *Naperville, IL*
HAMPTON INN [MOT] *Oak Brook, IL*
HAMPTON INN [MOT] *Oak Brook, IL*
HAMPTON INN [MOT] *Oak Lawn, IL*
HAMPTON INN [MOT] *Oxford, OH*
HAMPTON INN [MOT] *Peoria, IL*
HAMPTON INN [MOT] *Pontiac, MI*
HAMPTON INN [MOT] *Rockford, IL*
HAMPTON INN [MOT] *Saginaw, MI*
HAMPTON INN [MOT] *Schaumburg, IL*
HAMPTON INN [MOT] *Southfield, MI*
HAMPTON INN [MOT] *Springfield, IL*
HAMPTON INN [MOT] *Traverse City, MI*
HAMPTON INN [MOT] *Troy, MI*
HAMPTON INN [MOT] *Warren, MI*
HAMPTON INN [MOT] *Waukesha, WI*
HAMPTON INN & SUITES [MOT] *Chillicothe, OH*
HAMPTON INN AND SUITES [MOT] *Kokomo, IN*
HAMPTON INN AT MIDWAY AIRPORT [MOT] *Chicago, IL*
HAMPTON INN COUNTRYSIDE [MOT] *La Grange, IL*
HAMPTON INN DAYTON SOUTH [MOT] *Dayton, OH*
HAMPTON INN EAST [MOT] *Indianapolis, IN*
HAMPTON INN NORTH [MOT] *Ann Arbor, MI*
HAMPTON INN NW [MOT] *Indianapolis, IN*
HAMPTON INN TOLEDO SOUTH/MAUMEE [MOT] *Toledo, OH*
HANNAFORD INN & SUITES [MOT] *Mason, OH*
HARBOR GUEST HOUSE [BB] *Fish Creek (Door County), WI*
HARBOR HOUSE INN [BB] *Ellison Bay (Door County), WI*
HARBOR HOUSE INN [BB] *Grand Haven, MI*
HARBOR LIGHTS MOTEL & CONDOS [MOT] *Frankfort, MI*

HARBOR SPRINGS COTTAGE INN
[MOT] *Harbor Springs, MI*
HARBOUR POINTE MOTOR INN
[MOT] *St. Ignace, MI*
HARELEY HOTEL [MOT] *Lansing, MI*
HAWTHORN SUITE HOTEL &
CONFERENCE CENTER [MOT]
Champaign/Urbana, IL
HAWTHORN SUITES [MOT] *Grand
Rapids, MI*
HAWTHORN SUITES [MOT]
Wheeling, IL
HEARTLAND INN [MOT] *Eau Claire,
WI*
HEIDEL HOUSE [RST] *Green Lake, WI*
HELLMAN GUEST HOUSE [BB]
Galena, IL
HELMS FOUR SEASONS RESORT
[MOT] *Sister Bay (Door County),
WI*
HERITAGE INN [MOT] *Traverse City,
MI*
HERRINGTON INN, THE [BB] *Geneva,
IL*
HILLENDALE BED & BREAKFAST [BB]
Dixon, IL
HILTON [HOT] *Brecksville, OH*
HILTON [HOT] *Canton, OH*
HILTON [HOT] *Fort Wayne, IN*
HILTON [HOT] *Milwaukee, WI*
HILTON [HOT] *Naperville, IL*
HILTON [HOT] *Springfield, IL*
HILTON [HOT] *Toledo, OH*
HILTON CHICAGO [HOT] *Chicago, IL*
HILTON GRAND RAPIDS AIRPORT
[HOT] *Grand Rapids, MI*
HILTON INN [HOT] *Akron, OH*
HILTON INN [HOT] *Milwaukee, WI*
HILTON INN SOUTHFIELD [HOT]
Southfield, MI
HILTON NORTHBROOK [HOT]
Northbrook, IL
HILTON NORTHFIELD [HOT] *Troy,
MI*
HILTON NOVI [HOT] *Farmington, MI*
HILTON OAK LAWN [HOT] *Oak
Lawn, IL*
HILTON QUAKER SQUARE [HOT]
Akron, OH
HILTON SUITES [AS] *Oak Brook, IL*
HILTON SUITES [AS] *Pontiac, MI*
HILTON SUITES DETROIT METRO
AIRPORT [AS] *Detroit Wayne
County Airport Area, MI*
HISTORIC CURTIS INN THE SQUARE
[MOT] *Mount Vernon, OH*
HOLIDAY ACRES RESORT [RST]
Rhinelander, WI
HOLIDAY INN [MOT] *Akron, OH*
HOLIDAY INN [MOT] *Akron, OH*
HOLIDAY INN [MOT] *Alpena, MI*
HOLIDAY INN [MOT] *Anderson, IN*

HOLIDAY INN [MOT] *Ann Arbor, MI*
HOLIDAY INN [MOT] *Appleton, WI*
HOLIDAY INN [MOT] *Bay City, MI*
HOLIDAY INN [MOT] *Beachwood, OH*
HOLIDAY INN [MOT] *Beloit, WI*
HOLIDAY INN [MOT] *Big Rapids, MI*
HOLIDAY INN [MOT] *Bloomington, IN*
HOLIDAY INN [MOT] *Brecksville, OH*
HOLIDAY INN [MOT] *Cambridge, OH*
HOLIDAY INN [HOT] *Chicago, IL*
HOLIDAY INN [HOT] *Chicago, IL*
HOLIDAY INN [HOT] *Chicago O'Hare
Airport Area, IL*
HOLIDAY INN [MOT] *Cincinnati, OH*
HOLIDAY INN [MOT] *Columbus, IN*
HOLIDAY INN [MOT] *Columbus, OH*
HOLIDAY INN [MOT] *Crawfordsville,
IN*
HOLIDAY INN [MOT] *Dayton, OH*
HOLIDAY INN [MOT] *Detroit, MI*
HOLIDAY INN [MOT] *Elmhurst, IL*
HOLIDAY INN [MOT] *Evanston, IL*
HOLIDAY INN [MOT] *Evansville, IN*
HOLIDAY INN [MOT] *Flint, MI*
HOLIDAY INN [MOT] *Fond du Lac,
WI*
HOLIDAY INN [MOT] *Fort Wayne, IN*
HOLIDAY INN [MOT] *Gallipolis, OH*
HOLIDAY INN [MOT] *Gaylord, MI*
HOLIDAY INN [MOT] *Glen Ellyn, IL*
HOLIDAY INN [MOT] *Grand Rapids,
MI*
HOLIDAY INN [MOT] *Grand Rapids,
MI*
HOLIDAY INN [MOT] *Grayling, MI*
HOLIDAY INN [MOT] *Green Bay, WI*
HOLIDAY INN [MOT] *Gurnee, IL*
HOLIDAY INN [MOT] *Hammond, IN*
HOLIDAY INN [MOT] *Hillside, IL*
HOLIDAY INN [MOT] *Hinsdale, IL*
HOLIDAY INN [MOT] *Holland, MI*
HOLIDAY INN [MOT] *Jackson, MI*
HOLIDAY INN [MOT] *Jasper, IN*
HOLIDAY INN [MOT] *Kalamazoo, MI*
HOLIDAY INN [MOT] *Kent, OH*
HOLIDAY INN [MOT] *Lafayette, IN*
HOLIDAY INN [MOT] *Lansing, MI*
HOLIDAY INN [MOT] *Lima, OH*
HOLIDAY INN [MOT] *Logansport, IN*
HOLIDAY INN [MOT] *Mansfield, OH*
HOLIDAY INN [MOT] *Marietta, OH*
HOLIDAY INN [MOT] *Marquette, MI*
HOLIDAY INN [MOT] *McHenry, IL*
HOLIDAY INN [MOT] *Midland, MI*
HOLIDAY INN [MOT] *Milwaukee, WI*
HOLIDAY INN [MOT] *Morris, IL*
HOLIDAY INN [MOT] *Mount Pleasant,
MI*
HOLIDAY INN [MOT] *Mount Vernon,
IL*
HOLIDAY INN [MOT] *Muskegon, MI*

HOLIDAY INN [MOT] *New Philadelphia, OH*
HOLIDAY INN [MOT] *Oak Lawn, IL*
HOLIDAY INN [MOT] *Petoskey, MI*
HOLIDAY INN [MOT] *Rhinelander, WI*
HOLIDAY INN [MOT] *Rockford, IL*
HOLIDAY INN [MOT] *Sandusky, OH*
HOLIDAY INN [MOT] *Schaumburg, IL*
HOLIDAY INN [MOT] *Sidney, OH*
HOLIDAY INN [MOT] *Skokie, IL*
HOLIDAY INN [MOT] *South Bend, IN*
HOLIDAY INN [MOT] *Southfield, MI*
HOLIDAY INN [MOT] *Steubenville, OH*
HOLIDAY INN [MOT] *Stevens Point, WI*
HOLIDAY INN [MOT] *Terre Haute, IN*
HOLIDAY INN [MOT] *Toledo, OH*
HOLIDAY INN [MOT] *Tomah, WI*
HOLIDAY INN [MOT] *Traverse City, MI*
HOLIDAY INN [MOT] *Troy, MI*
HOLIDAY INN [MOT] *Zanesville, OH*
HOLIDAY INN AIRPORT [MOT] *Green Bay, WI*
HOLIDAY INN - ALTON [MOT] *Alton, IL*
HOLIDAY INN AQUA DOME [MOT] *Wisconsin Dells, WI*
HOLIDAY INN CANTON [MOT] *Canton, OH*
HOLIDAY INN CITY CENTER [MOT] *Columbus, OH*
HOLIDAY INN CITY CENTER [MOT] *South Bend, IN*
HOLIDAY INN CITY CENTRE [HOT] *Peoria, IL*
HOLIDAY INN COLLINSVILLE/ ST. LOUIS [MOT] *Collinsville, IL*
HOLIDAY INN COLUMBUS EAST I-70 [HOT] *Columbus, OH*
HOLIDAY INN COUNTRYSIDE - LAGRANGE [MOT] *La Grange, IL*
HOLIDAY INN DAYTON MALL [MOT] *Miamisburg, OH*
HOLIDAY INN EAST [MOT] *Indianapolis, IN*
HOLIDAY INN EASTGATE [HOT] *Cincinnati, OH*
HOLIDAY INN ELYRIA [MOT] *Elyria, OH*
HOLIDAY INN EXECUTIVE CONFERENCE CENTER [MOT] *Michigan City, IN*
HOLIDAY INN EXPRESS [MOT] *Arlington Heights, IL*
HOLIDAY INN EXPRESS [MOT] *Auburn, IN*
HOLIDAY INN EXPRESS [MOT] *Beloit, WI*

HOLIDAY INN EXPRESS [MOT] *Birmingham, MI*
HOLIDAY INN EXPRESS [MOT] *Chillicothe, OH*
HOLIDAY INN EXPRESS [MOT] *Downers Grove, IL*
HOLIDAY INN EXPRESS [MOT] *Effingham, IL*
HOLIDAY INN EXPRESS [MOT] *Evansville, IN*
HOLIDAY INN EXPRESS [MOT] *Flint, MI*
HOLIDAY INN EXPRESS [MOT] *Kokomo, IN*
HOLIDAY INN EXPRESS [MOT] *Mackinaw City, MI*
HOLIDAY INN EXPRESS [MOT] *Middletown (Butler County), OH*
HOLIDAY INN EXPRESS [MOT] *Valparaiso, IN*
HOLIDAY INN EXPRESS [MOT] *Warren, MI*
HOLIDAY INN EXPRESS [MOT] *Waukegan, IL*
HOLIDAY INN EXPRESS [MOT] *Wauwatosa, WI*
HOLIDAY INN EXPRESS [MOT] *Wilmington, OH*
HOLIDAY INN EXPRESS HARBORSIDE [MOT] *Kenosha, WI*
HOLIDAY INN EXPRESS HOTEL [MOT] *Monroe, MI*
HOLIDAY INN EXPRESS HOTEL AND SUITES [MOT] *Oshkosh, WI*
HOLIDAY INN LAKEVIEW [MOT] *Jeffersonville, IN*
HOLIDAY INN MARION [MOT] *Marion, IN*
HOLIDAY INN-NORMAL [MOT] *Bloomington, IL*
HOLIDAY INN NORTH [HOT] *Grand Rapids, MI*
HOLIDAY INN SELECT [HOT] *Chicago O'Hare Airport Area, IL*
HOLIDAY INN SELECT [MOT] *Decatur, IL*
HOLIDAY INN SELECT [MOT] *Indianapolis, IN*
HOLIDAY INN SELECT [HOT] *Naperville, IL*
HOLIDAY INN WORTHINGTON [MOT] *Columbus, OH*
HOLIDAY MOTEL [MOT] *Manistique, MI*
HOLIDAY MOTEL [MOT] *Prairie du Chien, WI*
HOLIDAY MOTEL [MOT] *Sturgeon Bay (Door County), WI*
HOMERIDGE BED AND BREAKFAST, THE [BB] *Alton, IL*

HOMESTEAD [MOT] *Fish Creek (Door County), WI*

HOMESTEAD, THE [RST] *Glen Arbor, MI*

HOMEWOOD SUITES [MOT] *Columbus, OH*

HOMEWOOD SUITES [MOT] *Dayton, OH*

HOMEWOOD SUITES [MOT] *Indianapolis, IN*

HOMEWOOD SUITES [MOT] *Warren, MI*

HOMEWOOD SUITES BY HILTON [MOT] *Lafayette, IN*

HOMEWOOD SUITES BY HILTON [HOT] *Schaumburg, IL*

HONEYMOON MANSION BED & BREAKFAST [BB] *New Albany, IN*

HOSPITALITY HOUSE [MOT] *Grayling, MI*

HOSPITALITY INN [MOT] *Milwaukee, WI*

HOTEL ALLEGRO [HOT] *Chicago, IL*

HOTEL BARONETTE, THE [MOT] *Farmington, MI*

HOTEL BURNHAM [HOT] *Chicago, IL*

HOTEL DU NORD [MOT] *Sister Bay (Door County), WI*

HOTEL INTER-CONTINENTAL [HOT] *Chicago, IL*

HOTEL MEAD [MOT] *Wisconsin Rapids, WI*

HOTEL MONACO CHICAGO [HOT] *Chicago, IL*

HOTEL NAUVOO [BB] *Nauvoo, IL*

HOTEL PERE MARQUETTE [HOT] *Peoria, IL*

HOTEL WISCONSIN [HOT] *Milwaukee, WI*

HOUSE OF BLUES [HOT] *Chicago, IL*

HOUSTON MOTEL [MOT] *Lebanon, OH*

HOWARD JOHNSON [MOT] *Dayton, OH*

HOWARD JOHNSON [MOT] *Mackinaw City, MI*

HOWARD JOHNSON [MOT] *Rockford, IL*

HOWARD JOHNSON EXPRESS INN [MOT] *Collinsville, IL*

HOWARD JOHNSON EXPRESS INN [MOT] *De Kalb, IL*

HOWARD JOHNSON EXPRESS INN [MOT] *St. Ignace, MI*

HOWARD JOHNSON HOTEL [MOT] *Skokie, IL*

HOWARD JOHNSON INN [MOT] *Oshkosh, WI*

HOWARD JOHNSON PLAZA HOTEL [MOT] *Madison, WI*

HUESTON WOODS RESORT [MOT] *Oxford, OH*

HYATT [HOT] *Naperville, IL*

HYATT AT UNIVERSITY VILLAGE [HOT] *Chicago, IL*

HYATT DEERFIELD [HOT] *Northbrook, IL*

HYATT ON CAPITOL SQUARE [HOT] *Columbus, OH*

HYATT ON PRINTER'S ROW [HOT] *Chicago, IL*

HYATT REGENCY [HOT] *Chicago, IL*

HYATT REGENCY [HOT] *Columbus, OH*

HYATT REGENCY [HOT] *Indianapolis, IN*

HYATT REGENCY [HOT] *Milwaukee, WI*

HYATT REGENCY CINCINNATI [HOT] *Cincinnati, OH*

HYATT REGENCY CLEVELAND [HOT] *Cleveland, OH*

HYATT REGENCY DEARBORN [HOT] *Dearborn, MI*

HYATT REGENCY MCCORMICK PLACE [HOT] *Chicago, IL*

HYATT REGENCY OAK BROOK [HOT] *Oak Brook, IL*

HYATT REGENCY O'HARE [HOT] *Chicago O'Hare Airport Area, IL*

HYATT REGENCY WOODFIELD [HOT] *Schaumburg, IL*

HYATT ROSEMONT [HOT] *Chicago O'Hare Airport Area, IL*

ILLINOIS BEACH RESORT AND CONFRENCE CENTER [MOT] *Illinois Beach State Park, IL*

IMA INDIANHEAD [MOT] *Chippewa Falls, WI*

IMPERIAL HOUSE HOTEL [MOT] *Cincinnati, OH*

IMPERIAL MOTEL [MOT] *Marquette, MI*

INDIANAPOLIS MARRIOTT NORTH [HOT] *Indianapolis, IN*

INDIAN CREEK BED & BREAKFAST [BB] *Goshen, IN*

INDIANHEAD MOUNTAIN RESORT [RST] *Wakefield, MI*

INDIAN LAKES RESORT [RST] *Itasca, IL*

INDIAN OAK RESORT & SPA [RST] *Valparaiso, IN*

INDIAN TRAIL MOTEL [MOT] *Wisconsin Dells, WI*

INN AT AMISH ACRES, THE [MOT] *Nappanee, IN*

INN AT BAY HARBOR, THE [RST] *Petoskey, MI*

INN AT CEDAR CROSSING [BB] *Sturgeon Bay (Door County), WI*

INN AT HONEY RUN [BB] *Wooster, OH*

INN AT LITTLE SISTER HILL, THE [MOT] *Sister Bay (Door County), WI*

INN AT PINE TERRACE [BB] *Oconomowoc, WI*

INN AT ROSCOE VILLAGE, THE [MOT] *Coshocton, OH*

INN AT SIX FLAGS, THE [MOT] *Aurora, OH*

INN AT ST. MARYS [MOT] *South Bend, IN*

INN OF BURR RIDGE, THE [MOT] *Hinsdale, IL*

INN OF KENT [MOT] *Kent, OH*

INN ON WOODLAKE [HOT] *Kohler, WI*

INN TOWN [MOT] *Waupun, WI*

INTER-CONTINENTAL SUITE HOTEL [HOT] *Cleveland, OH*

INTERLAKEN RESORT AND COUNTRY SPA [MOT] *Lake Geneva, WI*

INTERNATIONAL MOTEL [MOT] *Wisconsin Dells, WI*

IROQUOIS MOTEL [HOT] *Mackinac Island, MI*

ISLAND HOUSE [HOT] *Mackinac Island, MI*

IVY INN HOTEL [MOT] *Madison, WI*

JAMES STREET INN [BB] *Green Bay, WI*

JAY'S INN [MOT] *Vandalia, IL*

JULIE'S PARK CAFE AND MOTEL [MOT] *Fish Creek (Door County), WI*

JUMER CHATEAU [HOT] *Bloomington, IL*

JUMERS CASTLE LODGE [HOT] *Champaign/Urbana, IL*

JUMER'S CASTLE LODGE [HOT] *Peoria, IL*

JUMERS CONTINENTAL INN [MOT] *Galesburg, IL*

JUSTIN TRAILS COUNTRY INN [BB] *Sparta, WI*

KAFKA'S RESORT [RST] *Rhinelander, WI*

KALAHARI RESORT [RST] *Wisconsin Dells, WI*

K AND K MOTEL [MOT] *Mauston, WI*

KARAKAHL COUNTRY INN [MOT] *Mount Horeb, WI*

KEWADIN [MOT] *Mackinaw City, MI*

KEWADIN INN [MOT] *St. Ignace, MI*

KEWANEE MOTOR LODGE [MOT] *Kewanee, IL*

KIMBERLY COUNTRY ESTATE [BB] *Harbor Springs, MI*

KINGS ISLAND RESORT & CONFERENCE CENTER [MOT] *Mason, OH*

KINGSLEY [MOT] *Bloomfield Hills, MI*

KINGSLEY HOUSE BED & BREAKFAST [BB] *Saugatuck, MI*

KINTNER HOUSE INN [BB] *Corydon, IN*

KNIGHTS INN [MOT] *Elkhart, IN*

KNIGHTS INN [MOT] *Kenosha, WI*

KNIGHTS INN [MOT] *Lancaster, OH*

KNIGHTS INN [MOT] *Lebanon, OH*

KNIGHTS INN [MOT] *Mansfield, OH*

KNIGHTS INN [MOT] *Marietta, OH*

KNIGHTS INN [MOT] *Michigan City, IN*

KNIGHTS INN [MOT] *Monroe, WI*

KNIGHTS INN [MOT] *Port Huron, MI*

KNIGHTS INN [MOT] *Racine, WI*

KNIGHTS INN [MOT] *Richmond, IN*

KNIGHTS INN [MOT] *South Bend, IN*

KNIGHTS INN [MOT] *St. Clairsville, OH*

K ROYALE MOTOR INN [MOT] *St. Ignace, MI*

LAFAYETTE [HOT] *Marietta, OH*

LAKE BLUFF [MOT] *South Haven, MI*

LAKE SHORE RESORT [MOT] *Saugatuck, MI*

LAKE TRAIL [MOT] *Oscoda, MI*

LAKE VIEW [HOT] *Mackinac Island, MI*

LAMP POST INN [MOT] *Ann Arbor, MI*

LANDING RESORT [MOT] *Egg Harbor (Door County), WI*

LANDS INN [MOT] *Ludington, MI*

LANE MOTEL [MOT] *French Lick, IN*

L'ANSE MOTEL AND SUITES [MOT] *Houghton, MI*

LA QUINTA INN [MOT] *Arlington Heights, IL*

LA QUINTA INN [MOT] *Champaign/Urbana, IL*

LA QUINTA INN [MOT] *Chicago O'Hare Airport Area, IL*

LA QUINTA INN [MOT] *Indianapolis, IN*

LA QUINTA INN [MOT] *Kalamazoo, MI*

LA QUINTA INN [MOT] *Moline, IL*

LA QUINTA INN [MOT] *Oak Brook, IL*

LA QUINTA INN [MOT] *Schaumburg, IL*

LARK INN [MOT] *Tomah, WI*

LAUERMAN GUEST HOUSE INN [BB] *Marinette, WI*

LAWSON MOTEL [MOT] *Sault Ste. Marie, MI*

LEATHEM SMITH LODGE AND MARINA [MOT] *Sturgeon Bay (Door County), WI*

LEES INN [MOT] *Anderson, IN*

LEES INN [MOT] *Greenfield, IN*

LEES INN [MOT] *Lafayette, IN*

LEES INN [MOT] *Muncie, IN*

LEES INN [MOT] *Richmond, IN*

LELAND LODGE [MOT] *Leland, MI*
LE MERIDIEN CHICAGO [HOT]
Chicago, IL
LENOX INN [MOT] *Columbus, OH*
LENOX SUITES HOTEL [AS] *Chicago, IL*
LEXINGTON HOTEL SUITES [MOT]
Grand Rapids, MI
LIGHTHOUSE VIEW [MOT]
Mackinaw City, MI
LILAC TREE HOTEL [HOT] *Mackinac Island, MI*
LINCOLN LODGE [MOT]
Champaign/Urbana, IL
LITTLE SISTER RESORT AT PEBBLE
[RST] *Sister Bay (Door County), WI*
LODGE [MOT] *Charlevoix, MI*
LOEB HOUSE B & B [BB] *Lafayette, IN*
LOFTS HOTEL & SUITES [HOT]
Columbus, OH
LOGAN HOUSE [BB] *Galena, IL*
LONGHOLLOW POINT RESORT
[MOT] *Galena, IL*
LULL-ABI MOTEL [MOT] *Egg Harbor (Door County), WI*
LUNA INN AND SUITES [MOT]
Wisconsin Dells, WI
MADISON CONCOURSE HOTEL
AND GOVERNOR'S CLUB
[HOT] *Madison, WI*
MAGGIE'S BED & BREAKFAST [BB]
Collinsville, IL
MAIN STREET INN [MOT] *Traverse City, MI*
MAJESTIC HOTEL [HOT] *Chicago, IL*
MANCHESTER INN AND
CONFERENCE CENTER, THE
[MOT] *Middletown (Butler County), OH*
MANCHESTER SUITES-AIRPORT
[MOT] *Milwaukee, WI*
MANCHESTER SUITES NORTHWEST
[MOT] *Milwaukee, WI*
MANISTEE INN & MARINA [MOT]
Manistee, MI
MANITOU MANOR BED &
BREAKFAST [BB] *Leland, MI*
MANOR MOTEL [MOT] *Joliet, IL*
MANOR MOTEL [MOT] *Newberry, MI*
MAPLE MANOR MOTEL [MOT] *Eau Claire, WI*
MAPLES MOTELS [MOT] *Wisconsin Rapids, WI*
MAPLEWOOD HOTEL [BB]
Saugatuck, MI
MARGARITA EUROPEAN, THE [BB]
Evanston, IL
MARINA BAY MOTOR LODGE [MOT]
Ludington, MI
MARINER MOTEL [MOT] *Green Bay, WI*
MARK III [MOT] *Bedford, IN*

MARK TWAIN HOTEL [MOT] *Peoria, IL*
MARRIOTT [HOT] *Schaumburg, IL*
MARRIOTT [HOT] *South Bend, IN*
MARRIOTT AT EAGLE CREST
YPSILANTI [HOT] *Ypsilanti, MI*
MARRIOTT AT UNIVERSITY PLACE
EAST LANSING [HOT] *Lansing, MI*
MARRIOTT CHICAGO O'HARE
[HOT] *Chicago O'Hare Airport Area, IL*
MARRIOTT CINCINNATI AIRPORT
[HOT] *Cincinnati, OH*
MARRIOTT CLEVELAND AIRPORT
[HOT] *Cleveland, OH*
MARRIOTT DAYTON [HOT] *Dayton, OH*
MARRIOTT DETROIT METRO
AIRPORT [HOT] *Detroit, MI*
MARRIOTT DOWNTOWN AT KEY
CENTER [HOT] *Cleveland, OH*
MARRIOTT DOWNTOWN CHICAGO
[HOT] *Chicago, IL*
MARRIOTT DOWNTOWN
INDIANAPOLIS [HOT]
Indianapolis, IN
MARRIOTT EAST [HOT] *Beachwood, OH*
MARRIOTT EVANSVILLE AIRPORT
[HOT] *Evansville, IN*
MARRIOTT FORT WAYNE [HOT] *Fort Wayne, IN*
MARRIOTT HOTEL, THE DEARBORN
INN [HOT] *Dearborn, MI*
MARRIOTT INDIANAPOLIS [HOT]
Indianapolis, IN
MARRIOTT LIVONIA DETROIT
[HOT] *Detroit, MI*
MARRIOTT MADISON WEST [HOT]
Madison, WI
MARRIOTT NORTH [HOT] *Columbus, OH*
MARRIOTT NORTH CINCINNATI
[HOT] *Cincinnati, OH*
MARRIOTT NORTHEAST
CINCINNATI [HOT] *Mason, OH*
MARRIOTT NORTHWEST
COLUMBUS [HOT] *Columbus, OH*
MARRIOTT OAK BROOK CHICAGO
[HOT] *Oak Brook, IL*
MARRIOTT PONTIAC AT
CENTERPOINT DETROIT
[HOT] *Pontiac, MI*
MARRIOTT RACINE [HOT] *Racine, WI*
MARRIOTT RENAISSANCE CENTER
[HOT] *Detroit, MI*
MARRIOTT ROMULUS DETROIT
[HOT] *Detroit Wayne County Airport Area, MI*

MARRIOTT'S LINCOLNSHIRE
    RESORT [RST] *Wheeling, IL*
MARRIOTT SOUTHFIELD DETROIT
    [HOT] *Southfield, MI*
MARRIOTT SUITES [AS] *Downers
    Grove, IL*
MARRIOTT SUITES [AS] *Northbrook,
    IL*
MARRIOTT SUITES CHICAGO
    O'HARE [AS] *Chicago O'Hare
    Airport Area, IL*
MARRIOTT TROY [HOT] *Troy, MI*
MARRIOTT WAUKESHA [HOT]
    Waukesha, WI
MARSH RIDGE RESORT [RST]
    Gaylord, MI
MARTEN HOUSE HOTEL AND LILLY
    CONFERENCE CENTER [MOT]
    Indianapolis, IN
MARVIN'S GARDEN INN [MOT]
    Southfield, MI
MAYFLOWER [MOT] *Wisconsin Dells,
    WI*
MAYVILLE INN [MOT] *Beaver Dam,
    WI*
MCCAMLY PLAZA [HOT] *Battle Creek,
    MI*
MCCARTHY'S BEAR CREEK INN [BB]
    Marshall, MI
MCGUIRE'S RESORT &
    CONFERENCE CENTER [MOT]
    Cadillac, MI
MEADOW BROOKE RESORT [CC]
    Wisconsin Dells, WI
MELINGS [MOT] *Monmouth, IL*
MENDON COUNTRY INN [BB] *Three
    Rivers, MI*
MILLENIUM HOTEL [HOT]
    Cincinnati, OH
MILLENNIUM KNICKERBOCKER
    [HOT] *Chicago, IL*
MILLERS LAKESIDE MOTEL [MOT]
    Ludington, MI
MISSION POINT RESORT [RST]
    Mackinac Island, MI
MISSISSIPPI MEMORIES BED &
    BREAKFAST [BB] *Nauvoo, IL*
MONTAGUE INN [BB] *Saginaw, MI*
MORRIS INN, THE [MOT] *South Bend,
    IN*
MORRIS' NORTHERNAIRE RESORT
    [CC] *Houghton Lake, MI*
MOTEL 6 [MOT] *Columbus, OH*
MOTEL 6 [MOT] *Kokomo, IN*
MOTEL 6 [MOT] *Mackinaw City, MI*
MOTEL 6 [MOT] *Youngstown, OH*
MOTEL 6 SOUTH [MOT] *Joliet, IL*
MOTEL CENTRALIA [MOT] *Centralia,
    IL*
MOTEL NAUVOO [MOT] *Nauvoo, IL*

MOUNTAIN VIEW LODGES [MOT]
    Ontonagon, MI
MROCZER INN [MOT] *Paw Paw, MI*
NAPPANEE INN, THE [MOT]
    Nappanee, IN
NATIONAL HOUSE INN [BB]
    Marshall, MI
NAUVOO FAMILY MOTEL [MOT]
    Nauvoo, IL
NEW CONCORD INN [MOT]
    Dodgeville, WI
NEW CONCORD INN [MOT]
    Minocqua, WI
NEW HARMONY INN [MOT] *New
    Harmony, IN*
NICKERSON INN [BB] *Ludington, MI*
NIGHT SAVER INN [MOT] *La Crosse,
    WI*
NORDIC LODGE [MOT] *Sister Bay
    (Door County), WI*
NOR-GATE [MOT] *Indian River, MI*
NORTH COUNTRY LODGE [MOT]
    Grayling, MI
NORTH SHORE INN [MOT] *Traverse
    City, MI*
NORTHSHORE MOTOR INN [MOT]
    Manistique, MI
NORTHWAY MOTEL [MOT] *Fond du
    Lac, WI*
NORTHWOODS MOTEL [MOT]
    Hayward, WI
OAK BROOK HILLS HOTEL &
    RESORT [RST] *Oak Brook, IL*
OAKS, THE [BB] *Petersburg, IL*
OAKWOOD INN & CONFERENCE
    CENTER [MOT] *Nappanee, IN*
OAKWOOD LODGE [BB] *Green Lake,
    WI*
OBERLIN INN [MOT] *Oberlin, OH*
OHIO UNIVERSITY INN AND
    CONFERENCE CENTER, THE
    [MOT] *Athens, OH*
OLD RITTENHOUSE INN [BB]
    Bayfield, WI
OLD TOWN BED & BREAKFAST [BB]
    Chicago, IL
OLIVER INN BED & BREAKFAST [BB]
    South Bend, IN
OLYMPIA RESORT AND SPA [RST]
    Oconomowoc, WI
OMNI AMBASSADOR EAST [HOT]
    Chicago, IL
OMNI CHICAGO HOTEL [HOT]
    Chicago, IL
OMNI DETROIT HOTEL AT RIVER
    PLACE [HOT] *Detroit, MI*
OMNI INDIANAPOLIS NORTH
    HOTEL [HOT] *Indianapolis, IN*
OMNI NETHERLAND PLAZA [HOT]
    Cincinnati, OH

OMNI ORRINGTON HOTEL [HOT]
Evanston, IL
OMNI SEVERIN HOTEL [HOT]
Indianapolis, IN
OPEN HEARTH LODGE [MOT] *Sister Bay (Door County), WI*
OSTHOFF RESORT [RST] *Elkhart Lake, WI*
OTTAWA INN SUITES [MOT] *Ottawa, IL*
OXBOW BED & BREAKFAST [BB] *Du Quoin, IL*
PALMER HOUSE HILTON [HOT]
Chicago, IL
PAPER VALLEY HOTEL AND CONFERENCE CENTER [HOT]
Appleton, WI
PARADISE MOTEL [MOT] *Wisconsin Dells, WI*
PARK AVENUE GUEST HOUSE [BB]
Galena, IL
PARKCREST INN [MOT] *Detroit, MI*
PARK EAST [HOT] *Milwaukee, WI*
PARK HOTEL [HOT] *Warren, OH*
PARK HOUSE BED & BREAKFAST [BB]
Saugatuck, MI
PARK HYATT CHICAGO [HOT]
Chicago, IL
PARK INN [MOT] *Chippewa Falls, WI*
PARK PLACE [HOT] *Traverse City, MI*
PARK PLAZA INTERNATIONAL [HOT]
Oshkosh, WI
PARKSIDE [MOT] *Mackinaw City, MI*
PEAR TREE INN [MOT] *Terre Haute, IN*
PENINSULA CHICAGO, THE [HOT]
Chicago, IL
PENRODS AUSABLE RIVER RESORT [CC] *Grayling, MI*
PERE MARQUETTE LODGE [MOT]
Alton, IL
PETERSON'S CHALET COTTAGES [MOT] *Ontonagon, MI*
PETTICOAT INN [MOT] *Alma, MI*
PFISTER, THE [HOT] *Milwaukee, WI*
PHIPPS INN [BB] *Hudson, WI*
PINEAIRE RESORT MOTEL [MOT]
Land O' Lakes, WI
PINECREST [MOT] *Traverse City, MI*
PINE GROVE MOTEL [MOT] *Ephraim (Door County), WI*
PINE HOLLOW INN BED & BREAKFAST [BB] *Galena, IL*
PINES AT PATOKA LAKE VILLAGE [CC] *French Lick, IN*
PIONEER RESORT AND MARINA [RST] *Oshkosh, WI*
POINTE NORTH OF GRAYLING MOTEL [MOT] *Grayling, MI*
POINTES NORTH INN [MOT] *Traverse City, MI*

POINT MOTEL [MOT] *Stevens Point, WI*
POTAWATOMI INN [RST] *Angola, IN*
PRAIRIE HOUSE MOTEL [MOT]
Spring Green, WI
PRAIRIE MOTEL [MOT] *Prairie du Chien, WI*
PRIMERATE INN [MOT] *Superior, WI*
QUALITY INN [MOT] *Baraboo, WI*
QUALITY INN [MOT] *Cincinnati, OH*
QUALITY INN [MOT] *Dayton, OH*
QUALITY INN [MOT] *Dearborn, MI*
QUALITY INN [MOT] *Defiance, OH*
QUALITY INN [MOT] *Detroit Wayne County Airport Area, MI*
QUALITY INN [MOT] *Eau Claire, WI*
QUALITY INN [MOT] *Effingham, IL*
QUALITY INN [MOT] *Gaylord, MI*
QUALITY INN [MOT] *Plymouth, MI*
QUALITY INN [MOT] *Sault Ste. Marie, MI*
QUALITY INN [MOT] *Wisconsin Rapids, WI*
QUALITY INN & CONFERENCE CENTER [MOT] *Toledo, OH*
QUALITY INN AND CONVENTION CENTER [MOT] *Coldwater, MI*
QUALITY INN AND SUITES [MOT]
Elkhart, IN
QUALITY INN & SUITES BEACHFRONT [MOT]
Mackinaw City, MI
QUALITY INN TERRACE CLUB [MOT] *Grand Rapids, MI*
QUALITY SUITES [MOT] *Lansing, MI*
QUEEN ANNE INN [BB] *South Bend, IN*
RADISSON [HOT] *Lansing, MI*
RADISSON AIRPORT [HOT]
Cleveland, OH
RADISSON AIRPORT HOTEL [HOT]
Columbus, OH
RADISSON AKRON FAIRLAWN [HOT]
Akron, OH
RADISSON HARBOUR INN [HOT]
Sandusky, OH
RADISSON HOTEL [HOT] *Arlington Heights, IL*
RADISSON HOTEL [HOT] *Farmington, MI*
RADISSON HOTEL [HOT] *Oak Lawn, IL*
RADISSON HOTEL & CONFERENCE CENTER CLEVELAND-EASTLAKE [HOT] *Mentor, OH*
RADISSON HOTEL & SUITES [AS]
Chicago, IL
RADISSON HOTEL AT STAR PLAZA [HOT] *Merrillville, IN*
RADISSON HOTEL - BEACHWOOD [HOT] *Beachwood, OH*

RADISSON HOTEL CITY CENTRE [HOT] *Indianapolis, IN*
RADISSON HOTEL LA CROSSE [HOT] *La Crosse, WI*
RADISSON HOTEL MILWAUKEE AIRPORT [HOT] *Milwaukee, WI*
RADISSON HOTEL MILWAUKEE WEST [HOT] *Milwaukee, WI*
RADISSON HOTEL ROBERTS [HOT] *Muncie, IN*
RADISSON INN [HOT] *Green Bay, WI*
RADISSON INN [HOT] *Lafayette, IN*
RADISSON PLAZA [HOT] *Kalamazoo, MI*
RAMADA [MOT] *Indianapolis, IN*
RAMADA INN [MOT] *Appleton, WI*
RAMADA INN [MOT] *Danville, IL*
RAMADA INN [MOT] *Elkhart, IN*
RAMADA INN [MOT] *Elyria, OH*
RAMADA INN [MOT] *Galesburg, IL*
RAMADA INN [MOT] *Hurley, WI*
RAMADA INN [MOT] *Janesville, WI*
RAMADA INN [MOT] *Jeffersonville, IN*
RAMADA INN [MOT] *Kokomo, IN*
RAMADA INN [MOT] *La Porte, IN*
RAMADA INN [MOT] *Lafayette, IN*
RAMADA INN [MOT] *Mackinaw City, MI*
RAMADA INN [MOT] *Marquette, MI*
RAMADA INN [MOT] *McHenry, IL*
RAMADA INN [MOT] *Milan, OH*
RAMADA INN [MOT] *Milwaukee, WI*
RAMADA INN [MOT] *Muncie, IN*
RAMADA INN [MOT] *Oshkosh, WI*
RAMADA INN [MOT] *Plymouth, IN*
RAMADA INN [MOT] *Portsmouth, OH*
RAMADA INN [MOT] *Richmond, IN*
RAMADA INN [MOT] *Springfield, IL*
RAMADA INN [MOT] *Waukegan, IL*
RAMADA INN [MOT] *Wausau, WI*
RAMADA INN & CONFERENCE CENTER [MOT] *Hammond, IN*
RAMADA INN AND CONFERENCE CENTER [MOT] *Mentor, OH*
RAMADA INN AND CONVENTION CENTER [MOT] *Effingham, IL*
RAMADA INN & PLAZA HOTEL [MOT] *Columbus, IN*
RAMADA INN CONFERENCE CENTER [MOT] *Eau Claire, WI*
RAMADA INN - FAIRVIEW HEIGHTS [MOT] *Belleville, IL*
RAMADA INN HOTEL & CONFERENCE CENTER [MOT] *Mattoon, IL*
RAMADA INN INDIANAPOLIS AIRPORT [MOT] *Indianapolis, IN*
RAMADA INN LAKESHORE [MOT] *Chicago, IL*

RAMADA LIMITED [MOT] *Belleville, IL*
RAMADA LIMITED [MOT] *Port Clinton, OH*
RAMADA LIMITED [MOT] *Springfield, IL*
RAMADA LIMITED OF NOVI [MOT] *Farmington, MI*
RAMADA LIMITED VANDALIA [MOT] *Vandalia, IL*
RAMADA LIMITED WATERFRONT [MOT] *Mackinaw City, MI*
RAMADA LIMITED WAUKESHA-MILWAUKEE WEST [MOT] *Waukesha, WI*
RAMADA PLAZA [MOT] *Fond du Lac, WI*
RAMADA PLAZA [MOT] *Warsaw, IN*
RAMADA PLAZA HOTEL & CONFERENCE CENTER [MOT] *Columbus, OH*
RAMADA PLAZA HOTEL O'HARE [MOT] *Chicago O'Hare Airport Area, IL*
RAMADA PLAZA HOTEL OJIBWAY [MOT] *Sault Ste. Marie, MI*
RAPHAEL [HOT] *Chicago, IL*
RED ROOF INN [MOT] *Akron, OH*
RED ROOF INN [MOT] *Canton, OH*
RED ROOF INN [MOT] *Champaign/Urbana, IL*
RED ROOF INN [HOT] *Chicago, IL*
RED ROOF INN [MOT] *Cincinnati, OH*
RED ROOF INN [MOT] *Dayton, OH*
RED ROOF INN [MOT] *Dearborn, MI*
RED ROOF INN [MOT] *Downers Grove, IL*
RED ROOF INN [MOT] *Elkhart, IN*
RED ROOF INN [MOT] *Farmington, MI*
RED ROOF INN [MOT] *Flint, MI*
RED ROOF INN [MOT] *Grand Rapids, MI*
RED ROOF INN [MOT] *Hinsdale, IL*
RED ROOF INN [MOT] *Kalamazoo, MI*
RED ROOF INN [MOT] *Miamisburg, OH*
RED ROOF INN [MOT] *Michigan City, IN*
RED ROOF INN [MOT] *Milwaukee, WI*
RED ROOF INN [MOT] *Naperville, IL*
RED ROOF INN [MOT] *Peoria, IL*
RED ROOF INN [MOT] *Plymouth, MI*
RED ROOF INN [MOT] *Rockford, IL*
RED ROOF INN [MOT] *Schaumburg, IL*
RED ROOF INN [MOT] *Springfield, IL*
RED ROOF INN [MOT] *Warren, MI*
RED ROOF INN COLUMBUS NORTH [MOT] *Columbus, OH*

RED ROOF INN LANSING EAST [MOT] *Lansing, MI*
RED ROOF INN MERRILLVILLE [MOT] *Merrillville, IN*
RED ROOF INN - NORTH [MOT] *Ann Arbor, MI*
RED ROOF INN TROY [MOT] *Troy, MI*
RED ROOF-KINGS ISLAND [MOT] *Mason, OH*
REDWOOD MOTEL [MOT] *Mineral Point, WI*
REDWOOD MOTOR LODGE [MOT] *Oscoda, MI*
REGAL COUNTRY INN [MOT] *Wakefield, MI*
RENAISSANCE CHICAGO HOTEL [HOT] *Chicago, IL*
RENAISSANCE CHICAGO NORTH SHORE HOTEL [HOT] *Northbrook, IL*
RENAISSANCE CLEVELAND [HOT] *Cleveland, OH*
RENAISSANCE OAK BROOK HOTEL [HOT] *Oak Brook, IL*
RENAISSANCE QUAIL HOLLOW [RST] *Painesville, OH*
RENAISSANCE SPRINGFIELD [HOT] *Springfield, IL*
RENAISSANCE TOWER [HOT] *Indianapolis, IN*
REND LAKE RESORT [RST] *Benton, IL*
RESIDENCE INN BY MARRIOTT [EX] *Ann Arbor, MI*
RESIDENCE INN BY MARRIOTT [EX] *Chicago, IL*
RESIDENCE INN BY MARRIOTT [EX] *Chicago O'Hare Airport Area, IL*
RESIDENCE INN BY MARRIOTT [EX] *Cincinnati, OH*
RESIDENCE INN BY MARRIOTT [EX] *Cleveland, OH*
RESIDENCE INN BY MARRIOTT [EX] *Fort Wayne, IN*
RESIDENCE INN BY MARRIOTT [EX] *Grand Rapids, MI*
RESIDENCE INN BY MARRIOTT [EX] *Kalamazoo, MI*
RESIDENCE INN BY MARRIOTT EAST LANSING [EX] *Lansing, MI*
RESIDENCE INN BY MARRIOTT [EX] *Madison, WI*
RESIDENCE INN BY MARRIOTT [EX] *Miamisburg, OH*
RESIDENCE INN BY MARRIOTT [EX] *Northbrook, IL*
RESIDENCE INN BY MARRIOTT [EX] *Rockford, IL*
RESIDENCE INN BY MARRIOTT [EX] *South Bend, IN*
RESIDENCE INN BY MARRIOTT [EX] *Troy, MI*
RESIDENCE INN BY MARRIOTT [EX] *Warren, MI*
REST WELL MOTEL [MOT] *Tomah, WI*
RIB MOUNTAIN INN [MOT] *Wausau, WI*
RIDERS 1812 [BB] *Painesville, OH*
RIDGE MOTOR INN [MOT] *Portage, WI*
RITZ-CARLTON, CHICAGO, THE [HOT] *Chicago, IL*
RITZ-CARLTON, CLEVELAND, THE [HOT] *Cleveland, OH*
RITZ-CARLTON, DEARBORN, THE [HOT] *Dearborn, MI*
RIVER HILLS MOTEL [MOT] *Algoma, WI*
RIVER INN [MOT] *Wisconsin Dells, WI*
RIVERSIDE DAYS INN [MOT] *Racine, WI*
RIVIERA MOTEL AND SUITES [MOT] *Wisconsin Dells, WI*
ROADSTAR INN [MOT] *Appleton, WI*
ROADSTAR INN [MOT] *Eau Claire, WI*
ROAD STAR INN [MOT] *Green Bay, WI*
ROADSTAR INN [MOT] *La Crosse, WI*
ROSEMONT INN RESORT [BB] *Saugatuck, MI*
ROSENBERRY INN [BB] *Wausau, WI*
ROUND BARN LODGE [MOT] *Spring Green, WI*
ROYAL PONTALUNA BED & BREAKFAST, THE [BB] *Grand Haven, MI*
ST. CLAIR INN [MOT] *St. Clair, MI*
SALT CREEK INN [MOT] *Nashville, IN*
SALT FORK RESORT & CONFERENCE CENTER [RST] *Cambridge, OH*
SANCTUARY AT WILDWOOD [BB] *Three Rivers, MI*
SANTA'S LODGE [MOT] *Santa Claus, IN*
SAWMILL CREEK RESORT [RST] *Sandusky, OH*
SCANDIA COTTAGES [MOT] *Sister Bay (Door County), WI*
SCOFIELD HOUSE BED AND BREAKFAST [BB] *Sturgeon Bay (Door County), WI*
SEASONS LODGE, THE [MOT] *Nashville, IN*
SEAWAY MOTEL [MOT] *Sault Ste. Marie, MI*
SELECT INN [MOT] *Madison, WI*
SELECT INN [MOT] *Waukesha, WI*
SENECA [HOT] *Chicago, IL*
SETTLEMENT COURTYARD INN [BB] *Fish Creek (Door County), WI*
SHAKER INN [MOT] *Lebanon, OH*

SHANGRA-LA MOTEL [MOT] *Saugatuck, MI*

SHANTY CREEK RESORT [RST] *Bellaire, MI*

SHERATON [HOT] *Madison, WI*

SHERATON AIRPORT [HOT] *Cleveland, OH*

SHERATON ARLINGTON PARK [HOT] *Arlington Heights, IL*

SHERATON BROOKFIELD [HOT] *Milwaukee, WI*

SHERATON CHICAGO HOTEL & TOWERS [HOT] *Chicago, IL*

SHERATON CLEVELAND CITY CENTRE HOTEL [HOT] *Cleveland, OH*

SHERATON FOUR POINTS [MOT] *Chicago, IL*

SHERATON GATEWAY SUITES [AS] *Chicago O'Hare Airport Area, IL*

SHERATON HOTEL [HOT] *Lansing, MI*

SHERATON INDIANAPOLIS HOTEL & SUITES [HOT] *Indianapolis, IN*

SHERATON INN [HOT] *Milwaukee, WI*

SHERATON INN ANN HARBOR [HOT] *Ann Arbor, MI*

SHERATON SUITES [AS] *Chicago O'Hare Airport Area, IL*

SHERATON SUITES [HOT] *Columbus, OH*

SHERMAN HOUSE [BB] *Batesville, IN*

SHERWOOD FOREST BED & BREAKFAST [BB] *Saugatuck, MI*

SHORECREST MOTOR INN, THE [MOT] *Detroit, MI*

SHORELINE RESORT [MOT] *Ellison Bay (Door County), WI*

SIGNATURE INN [MOT] *Cincinnati, OH*

SIGNATURE INN [MOT] *Columbus, OH*

SIGNATURE INN [MOT] *Elkhart, IN*

SIGNATURE INN [MOT] *Evansville, IN*

SIGNATURE INN [MOT] *Fort Wayne, IN*

SIGNATURE INN [MOT] *Kokomo, IN*

SIGNATURE INN [MOT] *Lafayette, IN*

SIGNATURE INN [MOT] *Muncie, IN*

SIGNATURE INN [MOT] *Peoria, IL*

SIGNATURE INN [MOT] *South Bend, IN*

SIGNATURE INN [MOT] *Terre Haute, IN*

SIGNATURE INN SOUTH [MOT] *Indianapolis, IN*

SKY LITE [MOT] *Green Bay, WI*

SLEEP INN CHICAGO/MIDWAY [MOT] *Chicago, IL*

SNYDER'S SHORELINE INN [MOT] *Ludington, MI*

SOARING EAGLE CASINO & RESORT [RST] *Mount Pleasant, MI*

SOFITEL CHICAGO O'HARE [HOT] *Chicago O'Hare Airport Area, IL*

SOMERSET INN [MOT] *Troy, MI*

SOMERSET INN AND SUITES [MOT] *Ephraim (Door County), WI*

SONIC MOTEL [MOT] *Galesville, WI*

SPINNING WHEEL MOTEL [MOT] *Baraboo, WI*

SPRINGFIELD INN [HOT] *Springfield, OH*

STAFFORD'S BAY VIEW INN [BB] *Petoskey, MI*

STAFFORD'S PERRY HOTEL [HOT] *Petoskey, MI*

STAGECOACH INN BED AND BREAKFAST [BB] *Cedarburg, WI*

STARLITE BUDGET INN [MOT] *Mackinaw City, MI*

STARVED ROCK LODGE AND CONFERENCE CENTER [RST] *Starved Rock State Park, IL*

STONE HARBOR RESORT [RST] *Sturgeon Bay (Door County), WI*

STONEHENGE LODGE [MOT] *Bedford, IN*

STUART AVENUE INN BED & BREAKFAST [BB] *Kalamazoo, MI*

STUDIO PLUS [MOT] *Evansville, IN*

SUGAR BEACH RESORT HOTEL [MOT] *Traverse City, MI*

SUGAR LOAF RESORT [RST] *Traverse City, MI*

SUN-N-SNOW MOTEL [MOT] *Cadillac, MI*

SUNRISE LODGE [RST] *Land O' Lakes, WI*

SUNSET RESORT MOTEL [MOT] *Munising, MI*

SUPER 8 [MOT] *Alton, IL*

SUPER 8 [MOT] *Ashland, WI*

SUPER 8 [MOT] *Bayfield, WI*

SUPER 8 [MOT] *Cadillac, MI*

SUPER 8 [MOT] *Carbondale, IL*

SUPER 8 [MOT] *Effingham, IL*

SUPER 8 [MOT] *Grayling, MI*

SUPER 8 [MOT] *Green Bay, WI*

SUPER 8 [MOT] *Hayward, WI*

SUPER 8 [MOT] *Houghton, MI*

SUPER 8 [MOT] *Iron Mountain, MI*

SUPER 8 [MOT] *La Crosse, WI*

SUPER 8 [MOT] *Midland, MI*

SUPER 8 [MOT] *Mount Pleasant, MI*

SUPER 8 [MOT] *Munising, MI*

SUPER 8 [MOT] *Muskegon, MI*

SUPER 8 [MOT] *Rice Lake, WI*

SUPER 8 [MOT] *Sault Ste. Marie, MI*

SUPER 8 [MOT] *South Bend, IN*
SUPER 8 [MOT] *Superior, WI*
SUPER 8 [MOT] *Tomah, WI*
SUPER 8 [MOT] *Wausau, WI*
SUPER 8 FORT ATKINSON [MOT] *Fort Atkinson, WI*
SUPER 8 MOTEL [MOT] *Altamont, IL*
SUPER 8 MOTEL [MOT] *Battle Creek, MI*
SUPER 8 MOTEL [MOT] *Champaign/Urbana, IL*
SUPER 8 MOTEL [MOT] *Cincinnati, OH*
SUPER 8 MOTEL [MOT] *De Kalb, IL*
SUPER 8 MOTEL [MOT] *Flint, MI*
SUPER 8 MOTEL [MOT] *Holland, MI*
SUPER 8 MOTEL [MOT] *Houghton, MI*
SUPER 8 MOTEL [MOT] *Joliet, IL*
SUPER 8 MOTEL [MOT] *Kalamazoo, MI*
SUPER 8 MOTEL [MOT] *Mackinaw City, MI*
SUPER 8 MOTEL [MOT] *Marinette, WI*
SUPER 8 MOTEL [MOT] *Menomonee Falls, WI*
SUPER 8 MOTEL [MOT] *Peru, IL*
SUPER 8 MOTEL [MOT] *Saginaw, MI*
SUPER 8 MOTEL [MOT] *Sandusky, OH*
SUPER 8 MOTEL [MOT] *Springfield, IL*
SUPER 8 MOTEL [MOT] *St. Joseph, MI*
SUPER 8 MOTEL [MOT] *Waukegan, IL*
SUPER 8 MOTEL [MOT] *Wisconsin Dells, WI*
SUPER 8 - PLATTEVILLE [MOT] *Platteville, WI*
SUTTON PLACE [HOT] *Chicago, IL*
SWAN INN [MOT] *Grand Rapids, MI*
SWAN'S COURT BED & BREAKFAST [BB] *Belleville, IL*
SWEDEN HOUSE LODGE [MOT] *Rockford, IL*
SWEET BASIL HILL BED & BREAKFAST [BB] *Gurnee, IL*
SWISS-AIRE MOTEL [MOT] *New Glarus, WI*
SWISSOTEL CHICAGO [HOT] *Chicago, IL*
TALBOTT HOTEL, THE [HOT] *Chicago, IL*
TAWAS BAY HOLIDAY INN RESORT [MOT] *Tawas City, MI*
TAWAS MOTEL - RESORT [MOT] *Tawas City, MI*
TERRACE BLUFF BAY INN [MOT] *Escanaba, MI*
THOMAS EDISON INN [MOT] *Port Huron, MI*
THUNDERBIRD MOTOR INN [MOT] *St. Ignace, MI*
TIMBERLINE [MOT] *Saugatuck, MI*
TIMBERS MOTOR LODGE [MOT] *Iron Mountain, MI*

TIROLER HOF INN [MOT] *Marquette, MI*
TOWN HOUSE MOTEL [MOT] *Belleville, IL*
TOWNSEND HOTEL, THE [HOT] *Birmingham, MI*
TRADEWINDS [MOT] *St. Ignace, MI*
TRAVELODGE [MOT] *Cambridge, OH*
TRAVELODGE [MOT] *Delaware, OH*
TRAVELODGE [MOT] *Mansfield, OH*
TRAVELODGE [MOT] *Marion, OH*
TRAVELODGE [MOT] *New Philadelphia, OH*
TRAVELODGE [MOT] *Quincy, IL*
TRAVELODGE [MOT] *Vandalia, IL*
TRAVELODGE OF NEW LISBON [MOT] *Mauston, WI*
TRAVERSE BAY INN [MOT] *Traverse City, MI*
TREETOPS RESORT [RST] *Gaylord, MI*
TREMONT [HOT] *Chicago, IL*
TROLLHAUGEN LODGE [MOT] *Ephraim (Door County), WI*
TRUEMAN CLUB [MOT] *Columbus, OH*
TURKEY RUN INN [MOT] *Turkey Run State Park, IN*
TWIN GABLES INN [BB] *Saugatuck, MI*
UNIVERSITY INN [MOT] *Kent, OH*
UNIVERSITY INN & CONFERENCE CENTER [MOT] *Lafayette, IN*
UNIVERSITY PLACE [HOT] *Indianapolis, IN*
UNIVERSITY PLAZA HOTEL [MOT] *Columbus, OH*
VACATIONLAND MOTEL [MOT] *Houghton, MI*
VAL HALLA MOTEL [MOT] *Houghton Lake, MI*
VALUE HOST MOTOR INN [MOT] *Escanaba, MI*
VALUE HOST MOTOR INN [MOT] *Marquette, MI*
VARNS GUEST HOUSE [BB] *Goshen, IN*
VENTURE INN MOTEL [MOT] *Houghton Lake, MI*
VERNON MANOR HOTEL, THE [HOT] *Cincinnati, OH*
VICTORIAN ROSE GARDEN BED & BREAKFAST [BB] *Dundee, IL*
VICTORIAN VILLAGE ON ELKHART LAKE [RST] *Elkhart Lake, WI*
VIKING ARMS INN [MOT] *Ludington, MI*
VIKING VILLAGE MOTEL [MOT] *Washington Island (Door County), WI*
VILLAGE PRMIER [MOT] *Mount Vernon, IL*

VOYAGER INN AT DOOR COUNTY [MOT] *Sister Bay (Door County), WI*

WAGON TRAIL [RST] *Ellison Bay (Door County), WI*

WALDEN INN [BB] *Greencastle, IN*

WASHINGTON HOUSE INN [BB] *Cedarburg, WI*

WATERFRONT INN [MOT] *Mackinaw City, MI*

WATER STREET INN [MOT] *Boyne City, MI*

W CHICAGO - CITY CENTER [HOT] *Chicago, IL*

W CHICAGO - LAKESHORE [HOT] *Chicago, IL*

WEATHERVANE TERRACE HOTEL [MOT] *Charlevoix, MI*

WEBER'S INN [MOT] *Ann Arbor, MI*

WELKER'S LODGE [MOT] *Grand Marais, MI*

WEST BEND FANTASUITES [MOT] *Port Washington, WI*

WESTIN [HOT] *Chicago O'Hare Airport Area, IL*

WESTIN [HOT] *Cincinnati, OH*

WESTIN GREAT SOUTHERN, THE [HOT] *Columbus, OH*

WESTIN INDIANAPOLIS [HOT] *Indianapolis, IN*

WESTIN MICHIGAN AVENUE [HOT] *Chicago, IL*

WESTIN RIVER NORTH CHICAGO [HOT] *Chicago, IL*

WESTIN SOUTHFIELD-DETROIT, THE [HOT] *Southfield, MI*

WESTON PLAZA HOTEL [MOT] *Elkhart, IN*

WESTWOOD INN HOTEL & SUITES [MOT] *Milwaukee, WI*

WHISTLING SWAN INN, THE [BB] *Fish Creek (Door County), WI*

WHITE BIRCH INN [MOT] *Sturgeon Bay (Door County), WI*

WHITE BIRCH VILLAGE [CC] *Boulder Junction, WI*

WHITE EAGLE [MOT] *Eagle River, WI*

WHITE GULL INN [BB] *Fish Creek (Door County), WI*

WHITEHALL HOTEL, THE [HOT] *Chicago, IL*

WHITE LACE INN [BB] *Sturgeon Bay (Door County), WI*

WHITE OAK INN [BB] *Mount Vernon, OH*

WICKWOOD INN [BB] *Saugatuck, MI*

WILLOWS, THE [HOT] *Chicago, IL*

WILMINGTON INN [MOT] *Wilmington, OH*

WINDFIELD INN [MOT] *Bayfield, WI*

WINTERGREEN RESORT AND CONFERENCE CENTER [MOT] *Wisconsin Dells, WI*

WISCONSIN HOUSE [BB] *Platteville, WI*

WOODBINE VILLA [CC] *Houghton Lake, MI*

WOODFIELD SUITES [MOT] *Appleton, WI*

WOODFIELD SUITES [MOT] *Cincinnati, OH*

WOODFIN SUITE HOTEL [AS] *Columbus, OH*

WOODSIDE RANCH TRADING POST [RAN] *Mauston, WI*

WOOSTER INN [BB] *Wooster, OH*

WORTHINGTON INN [BB] *Columbus, OH*

WYNDHAM [HOT] *Naperville, IL*

WYNDHAM CHICAGO [HOT] *Chicago, IL*

WYNDHAM CLEVELAND HOTEL [HOT] *Cleveland, OH*

WYNDHAM DRAKE HOTEL [HOT] *Oak Brook, IL*

WYNDHAM DUBLIN HOTEL [HOT] *Columbus, OH*

WYNDHAM GARDEN [MOT] *Indianapolis, IN*

WYNDHAM GARDEN [MOT] *Schaumburg, IL*

WYNDHAM GARDEN HOTEL [MOT] *Arlington Heights, IL*

WYNDHAM GARDEN HOTEL [MOT] *Farmington, MI*

WYNDHAM GARDEN HOTEL [MOT] *Naperville, IL*

WYNDHAM GARDEN HOTEL [MOT] *Waukesha, WI*

WYNDHAM HOTEL [HOT] *Milwaukee, WI*

WYNDHAM NORTHWEST CHICAGO [HOT] *Itasca, IL*

WYNDHAM TOLEDO HOTEL [HOT] *Toledo, OH*

YANKEE HILL INN BED AND BREAK-FAST [BB] *Elkhart Lake, WI*

YELTON MANOR BED & BREAKFAST [BB] *South Haven, MI*

YESTERDAY'S MEMORIES BED AND BREAKFAST [BB] *Peru, IL*

ZASTROWS LYNX LAKE LODGE [CC] *Boulder Junction, WI*

ZELLAR'S VILLAGE INN [MOT] *Newberry, MI*

ZENDER'S BAVARIAN HAUS [MOT] *Frankenmuth, MI*

RESTAURANT LIST

Establishment names are listed in alphabetical order followed by a symbol identifying their classification and then city and state. The symbols for classification are: [RES] for Restaurants and [URD] for Unrated Dining Spots.

ABRUZZI'S CAFE 422 [RES] *Warren, OH*
ADMIRALTY [RES] *Madison, WI*
ADOBO GRILL [RES] *Chicago, IL*
AGLAMESIS BROS [URD] *Cincinnati, OH*
AH-WOK [RES] *Farmington, MI*
ALBERINI'S [RES] *Youngstown, OH*
ALBERT'S CAFE & PATISSERIE [RES] *Chicago, IL*
ALEX'S [RES] *Miamisburg, OH*
ALEX'S BISTRO [RES] *Columbus, OH*
ALFRED'S SUPPER CLUB [RES] *Green Lake, WI*
AL JOHNSON'S SWEDISH RESTAURANT [RES] *Sister Bay (Door County), WI*
ALPENROSE [RES] *Holland, MI*
ALVIE'S GATEWAY GRILLE [URD] *Cleveland, OH*
AMAR INDIA [RES] *Dayton, OH*
AMBER ROSE [RES] *Dayton, OH*
AMBRIA [RES] *Chicago, IL*
AMERICAN GIRL PLACE CAFE [URD] *Chicago, IL*
AMISH ACRES [RES] *Nappanee, IN*
ANDANTE [RES] *Petoskey, MI*
ANDIAMO ITALIA [RES] *Warren, MI*
ANDRIS WAUNEE FARM [RES] *Kewanee, IL*
ANELLO'S TORCHLIGHT [RES] *Shawano, IL*
ANN SATHER [URD] *Chicago, IL*
ANTLER'S [RES] *Sault Ste. Marie, MI*
ARBOREAL INN [RES] *Grand Haven, MI*
ARCO DE CUCHILLEROS [URD] *Chicago, IL*
ARISTOCRAT PUB [RES] *Indianapolis, IN*
ARNIE'S [RES] *Grand Rapids, MI*
ART'S PLACE [RES] *Akron, OH*
ARUN'S [RES] *Chicago, IL*
ATHENIAN ROOM [RES] *Chicago, IL*
ATLANTIQUE [RES] *Chicago, IL*
ATWATER'S [RES] *Geneva, IL*
ATWOOD CAFE [RES] *Chicago, IL*
AU BON APPETIT [RES] *Milwaukee, WI*
AUBRIOT [RES] *Chicago, IL*

AUNTIE PASTA'S [RES] *Traverse City, MI*
AURELIO'S PIZZA [RES] *Homewood, IL*
BAERTSCHY'S PINE GABLES SUPPER CLUB [RES] *Eagle River, WI*
BALISTRERI'S BLUE MOUND INN [RES] *Milwaukee, WI*
BANDERA [RES] *Chicago, IL*
BARICELLI INN [RES] *Cleveland, OH*
BAR LOUIE [RES] *Chicago, IL*
BARNSIDER [RES] *Dayton, OH*
BARON'S STEAKHOUSE [RES] *Detroit, MI*
BARRINGTON COUNTRY BISTRO [RES] *Schaumburg, IL*
BARTOLOTTA'S [RES] *Wauwatosa, WI*
BARTOLOTTA'S LAKE PARK BISTRO [RES] *Milwaukee, WI*
BASIL'S LE FRANKLIN RESTAURANT [RES] *Michigan City, IN*
BASS LAKE TAVERN [RES] *Chardon, OH*
BASTA PASTA [RES] *Chicago, IL*
BAVARIAN INN [RES] *Milwaukee, WI*
BAY HARBOR INN [RES] *Sandusky, OH*
BELLA CIAO [RES] *Ann Arbor, MI*
BELLA NOTTE [RES] *Chicago, IL*
BELTLINE CAFE [RES] *Freeport, IL*
BEN PAO [RES] *Chicago, IL*
BERGHOFF [RES] *Chicago, IL*
BETISE [RES] *Wilmette, IL*
BEXLEY'S MONK [RES] *Columbus, OH*
BICE [RES] *Chicago, IL*
BIG BOWL CAFE [RES] *Chicago, IL*
BIG DOWNTOWN [RES] *Chicago, IL*
BIGGS [RES] *Chicago, IL*
BIN 36 [RES] *Chicago, IL*
BISTRO 110 [RES] *Chicago, IL*
BISTRO BANLIEUE [RES] *Downers Grove, IL*
BISTROT ZINC [RES] *Chicago, IL*
BLACKBIRD [RES] *Chicago, IL*
BLACK CAT [RES] *Tiffin, OH*
BLACK FOREST [RES] *Cincinnati, OH*
BLACKHAWK LOUNGE [RES] *Chicago, IL*
BLACKJACK STEAK HOUSE [RES] *Antigo, WI*
BLACK RAM [RES] *Chicago O'Hare Airport Area, IL*

BLACK SWAN [RES] *Kalamazoo, MI*
BLUE BIRD [RES] *Leland, MI*
BLUE MESA [RES] *Chicago, IL*
BLUE POINT OYSTER BAR [RES]
  Chicago, IL
BOB CHINN'S CRAB HOUSE [RES]
  Wheeling, IL
BODER'S ON THE RIVER [RES]
  Cedarburg, WI
BOOBY'S [URD] *Carbondale, IL*
BOULEVARD INN [RES] *Milwaukee,
  WI*
BOWERS HARBOR INN [RES] *Traverse
  City, MI*
BRANDING IRON [RES] *Delaware, OH*
BRASSERIE JO [RES] *Chicago, IL*
BRAVO [RES] *Kalamazoo, MI*
BRAVO! ITALIAN KITCHEN [RES]
  Columbus, OH
BRAVO! ITALIAN KITCHEN [RES]
  Dayton, OH
BRAXTON SEAFOOD GRILL [RES]
  Oak Brook, IL
BRETT'S [RES] *Chicago, IL*
BRICKS [RES] *Chicago, IL*
BROOKSIDE INN [RES] *Beulah, MI*
B R SCOTESE'S [RES] *Dayton, OH*
BUBBA GUMP'S [RES] *Galena, IL*
BUCA DI BEPPO [RES] *Chicago, IL*
BUCA DI BEPPO [RES] *Milwaukee, WI*
BUCA DI BEPPO [RES] *Wheeling, IL*
BUCHEL'S COLONIAL HOUSE [RES]
  Port Washington, WI
BUCKINGHAM'S [RES] *Chicago, IL*
BUGGY WHEEL BUFFET [RES]
  Goshen, IN
BULLWINKLE'S TOP HAT BISTRO
  [RES] *Miamisburg, OH*
BUNGALOW [RES] *Crawfordsville, IN*
BUN'S OF DELAWARE [RES] *Delaware,
  OH*
BURNSTAD'S [RES] *Tomah, WI*
BUTTERFLY CLUB [RES] *Beloit, WI*
BUXTON INN DINING ROOM [RES]
  Newark, OH
CABIN CLUB [RES] *Cleveland, OH*
CAFE ABSINTHE [RES] *Chicago, IL*
CAFE BA-BA-REEBA! [RES] *Chicago, IL*
CAFE BERNARD [RES] *Chicago, IL*
CAFE BON HOMME [RES] *Plymouth,
  MI*
CAFE CENTRAL [RES] *Highland Park,
  IL*
CAFE ITALIA/TWISTED TACO CAFE
  [RES] *Galena, IL*
CAFE JOHNELL [RES] *Fort Wayne, IN*
CAFE LA CAVE [RES] *Chicago O'Hare
  Airport Area, IL*
CAFE PATOU [RES] *Rockford, IL*
CAFE SAUSALITO [RES] *Cleveland, OH*
CAFI IBERICO [RES] *Chicago, IL*

CALITERRA [RES] *Chicago, IL*
CAMPAGNOLA [RES] *Evanston, IL*
C AND C SUPPER CLUB [RES] *Fish
  Creek (Door County), WI*
CAP CITY DINER-GRANDVIEW [RES]
  Columbus, OH
CAPE COD ROOM [RES] *Chicago, IL*
CAPITAL GRILLE, THE [RES] *Chicago,
  IL*
CAPTAIN'S COVE BAR AND GRILL
  [RES] *Ottawa, IL*
CAPTAIN'S TABLE [RES] *Algoma, WI*
CARLOS' [RES] *Highland Park, IL*
CARLUCCI [RES] *Chicago O'Hare
  Airport Area, IL*
CARMELO'S [RES] *Wausau, WI*
CARMEN'S [URD] *Evanston, IL*
CARMINE'S [RES] *Chicago, IL*
CARRIAGE HOUSE [RES] *Mackinac
  Island, MI*
CARRIAGE HOUSE DINING ROOM,
  THE [RES] *South Bend, IN*
CARVER'S ON THE LAKE [RES] *Green
  Lake, WI*
CASEY'S [RES] *Springfield, OH*
CAUCUS CLUB [RES] *Detroit, MI*
CEILING ZERO [RES] *Northbrook, IL*
CELEBRITY CAFE [RES] *Chicago, IL*
CELESTIAL, THE [RES] *Cincinnati, OH*
CELLAR [RES] *Kewanee, IL*
CENTRALIA HOUSE [RES] *Centralia,
  IL*
CENTRAL STATION CAFE [RES]
  Bloomington, IL
CENTRO [RES] *Chicago, IL*
C'EST MICHELE [RES] *Moline, IL*
CHA CHA CHA [RES] *Dundee, IL*
CHARLEY'S CRAB [RES] *Beachwood,
  OH*
CHARLIE TROTTER'S [RES] *Chicago,
  IL*
CHATEAU POMIJE [RES] *Cincinnati,
  OH*
CHECKERBERRY [RES] *Goshen, IN*
CHENG-1 CUISINE [RES] *Cincinnati,
  OH*
CHEQUERS [RES] *Saugatuck, MI*
CHERRINGTON'S [RES] *Cincinnati,
  OH*
CHERRY HUT [RES] *Beulah, MI*
CHERRY VALLEY LODGE DINING
  ROOM [RES] *Newark, OH*
CHESANING HERITAGE HOUSE
  [RES] *Flint, MI*
CHESAPEAKE SEAFOOD HOUSE
  [RES] *Springfield, IL*
CHESTER'S ROAD HOUSE [RES]
  Cincinnati, OH
CHEZ FRANCOIS [RES] *Vermilion, OH*
CHEZ JOEL [RES] *Chicago, IL*

CHICAGO CHOP HOUSE [RES] *Chicago, IL*

CHINA BUFFET [RES] *Effingham, IL*

CHINA COTTAGE [RES] *Dayton, OH*

CHINA GOURMET [RES] *Cincinnati, OH*

CHINA HOUSE [RES] *Madison, WI*

CHOCOLATE SWAN, THE [URD] *Milwaukee, WI*

CIELO [RES] *Chicago, IL*

CITY STREETS RIVERSIDE [RES] *Sheboygan, WI*

CLARMONT [RES] *Columbus, OH*

CLEMENTINE'S [RES] *South Haven, MI*

CLUB GENE & GEORGETTI [RES] *Chicago, IL*

CLUB ISABELLA [RES] *Cleveland, OH*

CLUB LUCKY [RES] *Chicago, IL*

COACHMAN'S GOLF RESORT [RES] *Madison, WI*

COCO PAZZO [RES] *Chicago, IL*

COLORADO STEAKHOUSE [RES] *Bloomington, IN*

COMMON HOUSE [RES] *Baileys Harbor (Door County), WI*

CONVITO ITALIANO [URD] *Wilmette, IL*

COOKER [RES] *Columbus, OH*

COOKERY [RES] *Fish Creek (Door County), WI*

CORNWELL'S TURKEYVILLE [URD] *Marshall, MI*

COUNTRY SQUIRE [RES] *Grayslake, IL*

COUNTY CLARE [RES] *Milwaukee, WI*

COVE [RES] *Leland, MI*

COYLES [RES] *Houghton Lake, MI*

CRAWDADDY BAYOU [RES] *Wheeling, IL*

CROFTON ON WELLS [RES] *Chicago, IL*

CUISINES [RES] *Chicago, IL*

CYRANO'S BISTRO AND WINE BAR [RES] *Chicago, IL*

DADDY JACK'S [RES] *Indianapolis, IN*

DAMON'S [RES] *Chillicothe, OH*

DAMON'S [RES] *Middletown (Butler County), OH*

DAMON'S [RES] *Newark, OH*

DAMON'S [RES] *Wilmington, OH*

DAMON'S THE PLACE FOR RIBS [RES] *South Bend, IN*

DAM SITE INN [RES] *Mackinaw City, MI*

DANIELS ON LIBERTY AND THE MOVEABLE FEAST [RES] *Ann Arbor, MI*

DAPPER'S [RES] *Glenview, IL*

DEL-BAR [RES] *Wisconsin Dells, WI*

DEL RIO [RES] *Highwood, IL*

DESHA'S [RES] *Cincinnati, OH*

DIFFERENT DRUMMER [RES] *Greencastle, IN*

DINER ON SYCAMORE, THE [RES] *Cincinnati, OH*

DINING ROOM AT KENDALL COLLEGE, THE [RES] *Evanston, IL*

DINNER BELL DINER [RES] *Painesville, OH*

DOC PIERCE'S [RES] *Mishawaka, IN*

DOHERTY [RES] *Clare, MI*

DON HALL'S-THE FACTORY [RES] *Fort Wayne, IN*

DON JUAN [RES] *Chicago, IL*

DON ROTH'S [RES] *Wheeling, IL*

DON'S FISHMARKET [RES] *Skokie, IL*

DON'S LIGHTHOUSE GRILLE [RES] *Cleveland, OH*

DOS BANDIDOS [RES] *Milwaukee, WI*

DRAGON INN [RES] *Homewood, IL*

DRAGON INN NORTH [RES] *Glenview, IL*

DUBA'S [RES] *Grand Rapids, MI*

DURAN'S OF DUNDEE [RES] *Dundee, IL*

DUTCH KITCHEN [RES] *Arcola, IL*

EAGAN'S [RES] *Milwaukee, WI*

EARLE [RES] *Ann Arbor, MI*

ED DEBEVIC'S [URD] *Chicago, IL*

EDELWEISS STEAK HOUSE AND MOTEL [RES] *Chippewa Falls, WI*

EGG HARBOR CAFE [RES] *Highwood, IL*

EGG HARBOR CAFE [RES] *Hinsdale, IL*

84 EAST PASTA ETC [RES] *Holland, MI*

EL GRANDE [RES] *Ashtabula, OH*

ELIASON'S SOME PLACE ELSE [RES] *St. Germain, WI*

ELI'S THE PLACE FOR STEAK [RES] *Chicago, IL*

ELLA'S DELI [URD] *Madison, WI*

EL MESON [RES] *Dayton, OH*

ELM GROVE INN [RES] *Milwaukee, WI*

EL RANCHERITO [RES] *Effingham, IL*

EL RANCHERITO [RES] *Mount Vernon, IL*

ELSA'S ON THE PARK [RES] *Milwaukee, WI*

EL ZOCALO [RES] *Detroit, MI*

EMBERS [RES] *Mackinaw City, MI*

EMBERS [RES] *Mount Pleasant, MI*

EMILIO'S TAPAS [RES] *Chicago, IL*

EMPEROR'S CHOICE [RES] *Chicago, IL*

ENGINE HOUSE NO. 5 [RES] *Columbus, OH*

ENGLISH ROOM [RES] *Highwood, IL*

ENGLISH ROOM [RES] *Milwaukee, WI*

ENTRE NOUS [RES] *Chicago, IL*
ERNESTO'S [RES] *Plymouth, MI*
ERWIN'S [RES] *Chicago, IL*
ESCOFFIER [RES] *Ann Arbor, MI*
ESSEN HAUS [RES] *Madison, WI*
EVEREST [RES] *Chicago, IL*
EVE'S SUPPER CLUB [RES] *Green Bay, WI*
FAHRENHEIT [RES] *Chicago, IL*
FAIRINGTON [RES] *Sidney, OH*
FANNY HILL INN AND DINNER THEATRE [RES] *Eau Claire, WI*
FERRARI'S LITTLE ITALY [RES] *Cincinnati, OH*
FIFI'S [RES] *Toledo, OH*
FILLING STATION ANTIQUE EATERY [RES] *St. Charles, IL*
FINDLAY'S HOLIDAY INN [RES] *Washington Island (Door County), WI*
FIN 'N FEATHER SHOWBOATS [RES] *Oshkosh, WI*
FISCHER'S [RES] *Belleville, IL*
FISCHER'S [RES] *Wisconsin Dells, WI*
FISHBONE'S RHYTHM KITCHEN CAFE [RES] *Detroit, MI*
FIVE LAKES GRILL [RES] *Farmington, MI*
FLANAGAN'S [RES] *Fort Wayne, IN*
FLORIAN II [RES] *Baileys Harbor (Door County), WI*
FOGCUTTER [RES] *Port Huron, MI*
FOND DE LA TOUR [RES] *Oak Brook, IL*
FORE & AFT [RES] *Cincinnati, OH*
FOREST VIEW GARDENS [RES] *Cincinnati, OH*
FORTE' [RES] *Birmingham, MI*
FORUM, THE [RES] *Cambridge, OH*
FOX AND HOUNDS [RES] *Menomonee Falls, WI*
FRANCESCA'S NORTH [RES] *Northbrook, IL*
FRANCESCO'S HOLE IN THE WALL [RES] *Northbrook, IL*
FRANKENMUTH BAVARIAN INN [RES] *Frankenmuth, MI*
FREIGHTERS [RES] *Sault Ste. Marie, MI*
FREIGHTHOUSE [RES] *La Crosse, WI*
FRIED GREEN TOMATOES [RES] *Galena, IL*
FROGGY'S [RES] *Highwood, IL*
FRONTERA GRILL [RES] *Chicago, IL*
GABRIEL'S [RES] *Highwood, IL*
GALE STREET INN [RES] *Libertyville, IL*
GANDY DANCER [RES] *Ann Arbor, MI*
GARDEN AT THE LIGHTHOUSE [RES] *Port Clinton, OH*
GEJA'S CAFE [RES] *Chicago, IL*

GENII'S FINE FOODS [RES] *Tawas City, MI*
GEORGE'S STEAK HOUSE [RES] *Appleton, WI*
GERMANO'S [RES] *Cincinnati, OH*
GIBBS COUNTRY HOUSE [RES] *Ludington, MI*
GIBSON'S [RES] *Grand Rapids, MI*
GIBSON'S STEAKHOUSE [RES] *Chicago, IL*
GILARDI'S [RES] *Wheeling, IL*
GILBERT'S STEAK HOUSE [RES] *Jackson, MI*
GIOCO [RES] *Chicago, IL*
GIOVANNI'S [RES] *Rockford, IL*
GLASS CHIMNEY [RES] *Indianapolis, IN*
GOLDEN LAMB INN [RES] *Lebanon, OH*
GOLDEN MAST INN [RES] *Oconomowoc, WI*
GOLDEN MUSHROOM [RES] *Southfield, MI*
GOVNOR'S LOUNGE [RES] *Mackinac Island, MI*
GRACE [RES] *Chicago, IL*
GRAND FINALE [RES] *Cincinnati, OH*
GRANDPA JOHN'S [URD] *Nauvoo, IL*
GRAND RIVER SALOON [RES] *Grand Rapids, MI*
GRANT'S OLDE STAGE STATION TAVERN [RES] *Egg Harbor (Door County), WI*
GREAT LAKES BREWING CO [RES] *Cleveland, OH*
GREAT WALL [RES] *Racine, WI*
GREAT WALL [RES] *Rockford, IL*
GREEK ISLANDS [RES] *Chicago, IL*
GREEK ISLANDS WEST [RES] *Glen Ellyn, IL*
GRENADIER'S [RES] *Milwaukee, WI*
GRILLE ROOM, THE [RES] *Dearborn, MI*
GRISANTI'S [RES] *Bloomington, IN*
GUARINO'S [RES] *Cleveland, OH*
GUIDE'S INN [RES] *Boulder Junction, WI*
GULLIVER'S LANDING [RES] *Wausau, WI*
GUN ROOM, THE [RES] *Marietta, OH*
HAAB'S [RES] *Ypsilanti, MI*
HACK-MA-TACK INN [RES] *Cheboygan, MI*
HANDKE'S CUISINE [RES] *Columbus, OH*
HARD ROCK CAFE [URD] *Chicago, IL*
HARRY CARAY'S [RES] *Chicago, IL*
HARVEST DINING ROOM [RES] *Nashville, IN*
HARVEST ON HURON [RES] *Chicago, IL*

HATCHERY [RES] *Angola, IN*
HATSUHANA [RES] *Chicago, IL*
HERITAGE [RES] *Cincinnati, OH*
HERITAGE HOUSE [URD] *Springfield, IL*
HERMANN'S EUROPEAN CAFE [RES] *Cadillac, MI*
HISTORIC HOLLY HOTEL [RES] *Holly, MI*
HISTORIC NICKERSON INN [RES] *Ludington, MI*
HOB NOB [RES] *Racine, WI*
HOLIDAY ON THE LAKE [RES] *Houghton Lake, MI*
HOLLYHOCK HILL [RES] *Indianapolis, IN*
HOMESTEAD INN [RES] *Milan, OH*
HOTEL DU NORD [RES] *Sister Bay (Door County), WI*
HOTEL FRANKFORT [RES] *Frankfort, MI*
HOTEL NAUVOO [RES] *Nauvoo, IL*
HOUSE OF CHAN [RES] *Muskegon, MI*
HOUSE OF GERHARD [RES] *Kenosha, WI*
HOUSE OF HUNAN [RES] *Akron, OH*
HOUSE OF TAM [RES] *Cincinnati, OH*
HOUSTON INN [RES] *Mason, OH*
HUNAN HOUSE [RES] *Columbus, OH*
HUNAN LION [RES] *Columbus, OH*
IMMIGRANT, THE [RES] *Kohler, WI*
INDIAN GARDEN [RES] *Chicago, IL*
INN AT CEDAR CROSSING [RES] *Sturgeon Bay (Door County), WI*
INN AT FOWLER'S MILL, THE [RES] *Chardon, OH*
INTERMEZZO [RES] *Detroit, MI*
IRON HORSE INN [RES] *Cincinnati, OH*
IXCAPUZALCO [RES] *Chicago, IL*
IZUMI'S [RES] *Milwaukee, WI*
JACK PANDL'S WHITEFISH BAY INN [RES] *Milwaukee, WI*
JAKE'S [RES] *Wauwatosa, WI*
J ALEXANDER'S [RES] *Dayton, OH*
JANE'S [RES] *Chicago, IL*
JAY'S [RES] *Dayton, OH*
JENNY'S [RES] *McHenry, IL*
JERY'S OLD TOWN INN [RES] *Menomonee Falls, WI*
JILLY'S CAFE [RES] *Evanston, IL*
JIMBO'S CLUB 70 [RES] *Spooner, WI*
JIM'S STEAK HOUSE [RES] *Bloomington, IL*
JOE'S BE-BOP CAFE [RES] *Chicago, IL*
JOHN BRANN'S STEAKHOUSE [RES] *Grand Rapids, MI*
JOHNNY'S BAR [RES] *Cleveland, OH*
JOHN Q'S STEAKHOUSE [RES] *Cleveland, OH*
JOHN'S [RES] *Canton, OH*

JOHN'S PLACE [RES] *Chicago, IL*
JUMER'S CASTLE [RES] *Peoria, IL*
JUNCTION [RES] *Bowling Green, OH*
K2U [RES] *Columbus, OH*
KARIBALIS [RES] *Hayward, WI*
KARL RATZSCH'S [RES] *Milwaukee, WI*
KATZINGER'S [URD] *Columbus, OH*
KAUFMAN'S [RES] *Bowling Green, OH*
KERRYTOWN BISTRO [RES] *Ann Arbor, MI*
KEY WEST SHRIMP HOUSE [RES] *Madison, IN*
KIERNAN'S STEAK HOUSE [RES] *Dearborn, MI*
KIKI'S BISTRO [RES] *Chicago, IL*
KING AND I [RES] *Milwaukee, WI*
KLAY OVEN [RES] *Chicago, IL*
KLOSTERMAN'S DERR ROAD INN [RES] *Springfield, OH*
KNICK, THE [RES] *Milwaukee, WI*
KNIGHT'S STEAKHOUSE & GRILL [RES] *Jackson, MI*
KORTES' ENGLISH INN [RES] *Fish Creek (Door County), WI*
KOWLOON [RES] *Cedarburg, WI*
KUNI'S JAPANESE RESTAURANT [RES] *Evanston, IL*
LA BECASSE [RES] *Glen Arbor, MI*
LA BOCCA DELLA VERITA [RES] *Chicago, IL*
LAKESIDE CHARLIE'S [RES] *Cadillac, MI*
LAMBS FARM COUNTRY INN, THE [RES] *Libertyville, IL*
LANDMARK CAFE & CREPERIE [RES] *Galesburg, IL*
LANNING'S [RES] *Akron, OH*
LA NORMANDIE TAVERN & CHOPHOUSE [RES] *Cincinnati, OH*
L'ANTIBES [RES] *Columbus, OH*
LA PAILLOTTE [RES] *Chicago, IL*
LARK, THE [RES] *Bloomfield Hills, MI*
LA SALLE GRILL [RES] *South Bend, IN*
LA SARDINE [RES] *Chicago, IL*
LAS BELLAS ARTES [RES] *Elmhurst, IL*
LA SENORITA [RES] *Traverse City, MI*
LAS PALMAS [RES] *Evanston, IL*
LA STRADA [RES] *Chicago, IL*
L'AUBERGE [RES] *Dayton, OH*
LAWRY'S PRIME RIB [RES] *Chicago, IL*
LE BOUCHON [RES] *Chicago, IL*
LE BOX CAFE [RES] *Cincinnati, OH*
LEELANAU COUNTRY INN [RES] *Leland, MI*
LE FRANCAIS [RES] *Wheeling, IL*
LEGGS INN [RES] *Harbor Springs, MI*
LEMON GRASS [RES] *Cleveland, OH*
LENHARDT'S [RES] *Cincinnati, OH*
LE PETIT CAFE [RES] *Bloomington, IN*

LES NOMADES [RES] *Chicago, IL*
LE TITI DE PARIS [RES] *Arlington Heights, IL*
L'ETOILE [RES] *Madison, WI*
LE VICHYSSOIS [RES] *McHenry, IL*
LINCOLN PARK GRILLE [RES] *Dayton, OH*
LINDEN HOF [RES] *Bay City, MI*
LINDEY'S [RES] *Columbus, OH*
LINDSAY'S ON GRAND [RES] *Chippewa Falls, WI*
LION & LAMB [RES] *Beachwood, OH*
LITTLE BOHEMIA [RES] *Manitowish Waters, WI*
LITTLE ITALY [RES] *Farmington, MI*
LITTLE SZECHWAN [RES] *Highland Park, IL*
LITTLE TRAVELER ATRIUM CAFE [URD] *Geneva, IL*
LOG CABIN [RES] *Galena, IL*
LOG CABIN SUPPER CLUB [RES] *Escanaba, MI*
LOHMANN'S STEAK HOUSE [RES] *Menomonee Falls, WI*
LOLLI'S [RES] *Canton, OH*
LONZEROTTI'S [RES] *Jacksonville, IL*
LOTAWATA CREEK [RES] *Belleville, IL*
LOUIS' BON APPETIT [RES] *Merrillville, IN*
LOUISIANA KITCHEN [RES] *Chicago, IL*
LUCKY PLATTER [RES] *Evanston, IL*
LUTZ'S CONTINENTAL CAFE & PASTRY SHOP [URD] *Chicago, IL*
L. WOODS TAP & PINE LODGE [RES] *Skokie, IL*
MACKINNON'S [RES] *Farmington, MI*
MADER'S [RES] *Milwaukee, WI*
MAGDALENA'S [RES] *Corydon, IN*
MAGGIANO'S [RES] *Chicago, IL*
MAGNOLIA GRILLE/IDLER RIVERBOAT [RES] *South Haven, MI*
MAHOGANY'S [RES] *Charlevoix, MI*
MAISONETTE [RES] *Cincinnati, OH*
MAJESTIC OYSTER [RES] *Indianapolis, IN*
MAKUCH'S RED ROOSTER [RES] *Flint, MI*
MALDANER'S [RES] *Springfield, IL*
MANCY'S [RES] *Toledo, OH*
MANGIA TRATTORIA [RES] *Kenosha, WI*
MANIACI'S CAFE SICILIANO [RES] *Milwaukee, WI*
MANITOU [RES] *Frankfort, MI*
MAPLES, THE [RES] *Peru, IL*
MARCHE [RES] *Chicago, IL*
MARCO POLO'S [RES] *Brecksville, OH*

MARIA ADORNETTO [RES] *Zanesville, OH*
MARINER'S INN [RES] *Madison, WI*
MARK'S [RES] *Rice Lake, WI*
MARY LOU'S GRILL [RES] *Carbondale, IL*
MATHON'S [RES] *Waukegan, IL*
MATTERHORN [RES] *Elkhart, IN*
MAZA [RES] *Chicago, IL*
MCCLAIN'S [RES] *Bellevue, OH*
MECKLENBURG GARDENS [RES] *Cincinnati, OH*
MELTING POT [RES] *Oak Brook, IL*
MERITAGE [RES] *Chicago, IL*
MERLE'S #1 BARBECUE [URD] *Evanston, IL*
MESON SABIKA [RES] *Naperville, IL*
MIA FRANCESCA [RES] *Chicago, IL*
MICHAEL'S [RES] *Wausau, WI*
MIKE DITKA'S [RES] *Chicago, IL*
MILK PAIL [RES] *Dundee, IL*
MILLIE'S [RES] *Delavan, WI*
MILL RACE INN [RES] *Geneva, IL*
MILLROSE [RES] *Schaumburg, IL*
MILL SUPPER CLUB [RES] *Sturgeon Bay (Door County), WI*
MIMMA'S CAFE [RES] *Milwaukee, WI*
MIRAI SUSHI [RES] *Chicago, IL*
MK [RES] *Chicago, IL*
MOD [RES] *Chicago, IL*
MOLINARI'S [RES] *Mentor, OH*
MON AMI GABI [RES] *Chicago, IL*
MON JIN LAU [RES] *Troy, MI*
MONTE'S RIVERSIDE INN [RES] *Ottawa, IL*
MONTGOMERY INN [RES] *Cincinnati, OH*
MONTGOMERY INN BOATHOUSE [RES] *Cincinnati, OH*
MONTPARNASSE [RES] *Naperville, IL*
MORO'S [RES] *Dearborn, MI*
MORRIS INN [RES] *South Bend, IN*
MORTON'S OF CHICAGO [RES] *Chicago, IL*
MORTON'S OF CHICAGO [RES] *Cleveland, OH*
MORTON'S OF CHICAGO [RES] *Columbus, OH*
MORTON'S OF CHICAGO [RES] *Oak Brook, IL*
MORTON'S OF CHICAGO [RES] *Rosemont, IL*
MORTON'S OF CHICAGO [RES] *Southfield, MI*
MOSSANT BISTRO [RES] *Chicago, IL*
MYKONOS [RES] *Glenview, IL*
MYRON & PHIL'S [RES] *Skokie, IL*
NASHVILLE HOUSE [RES] *Nashville, IN*
NATIONAL EXEMPLAR [RES] *Cincinnati, OH*

NATOMA [RES] *Newark, OH*
NAU-TI-GAL [RES] *Madison, WI*
'NEATH THE BIRCHES [RES]
　　Mackinaw City, MI
NED KELLY'S [RES]
　　Champaign/Urbana, IL
NEW GLARUS HOTEL [RES] *New
　　Glarus, WI*
NEW JAPAN [RES] *Evanston, IL*
NEW YORK, THE [RES] *Harbor
　　Springs, MI*
NEW YORK SPAGHETTI HOUSE [RES]
　　Cleveland, OH
NICK'S FISHMARKET [RES] *Chicago,
　　IL*
NICK'S FISHMARKET [RES] *Chicago
　　O'Hare Airport Area, IL*
NICOLA'S [RES] *Cincinnati, OH*
NIEMERG'S STEAK HOUSE [RES]
　　Effingham, IL
NINE [RES] *Chicago, IL*
94TH AERO SQUADRON [RES]
　　Wheeling, IL
NIX [RES] *Chicago, IL*
N.N. SMOKEHOUSE [RES] *Chicago, IL*
NOMI [RES] *Chicago, IL*
NORSKE NOOK [RES] *Rice Lake, WI*
NORTHERN GRILL AND PIZZA [RES]
　　Sister Bay (Door County), WI
NORTH POND CAFE [RES] *Chicago,
　　IL*
NORTH SHORE BISTRO [RES]
　　Milwaukee, WI
NORTHSIDE CAFE [RES] *Chicago, IL*
NORTHWOODS SUPPER CLUB [RES]
　　Marquette, MI
NORTON'S MARINE DINING ROOM
　　[RES] *Green Lake, WI*
NORWOOD PINES [RES] *Minocqua,
　　WI*
OAK TREE [RES] *Chicago, IL*
OAKWOOD CLUB [RES] *Dayton, OH*
OCEANIQUE [RES] *Evanston, IL*
OLD BARN [RES] *Oak Lawn, IL*
OLDE RICHMOND INN [RES]
　　Richmond, IN
OLD MARKET HOUSE INN [RES]
　　Zanesville, OH
OLD MOHAWK [RES] *Columbus, OH*
OLD POST OFFICE RESTAURANT
　　[RES] *Ephraim (Door County),
　　WI*
OLD RITTENHOUSE [RES] *Bayfield,
　　WI*
OLD TOWN SERBIAN GOURMET
　　HOUSE [RES] *Milwaukee, WI*
OLD WAREHOUSE [RES] *Coshocton,
　　OH*
ONE SIXTYBLUE [RES] *Chicago, IL*
OOGIE'S [RES] *Galesburg, IL*
OPUS ONE [RES] *Detroit, MI*

ORDINARY, THE [RES] *Nashville, IN*
O SOLE MIO [RES] *Bay City, MI*
OSTERIA DEL MONDO [RES]
　　Milwaukee, WI
PACIFIC MOON [RES] *Cincinnati, OH*
PACKINGHOUSE [RES] *Galesburg, IL*
PAESANO'S [RES] *Ann Arbor, MI*
PALACE, THE [RES] *Cincinnati, OH*
PALM [RES] *Chicago, IL*
PALM COURT [RES] *Arlington Heights,
　　IL*
PANCAKE CHEF [RES] *Mackinaw City,
　　MI*
PANDA PANDA SZECHWAN [RES]
　　Highland Park, IL
PANDL'S BAYSIDE [RES] *Milwaukee,
　　WI*
PAPAGUS GREEK TAVERNA [RES]
　　Chicago, IL
PAPARAZZI [RES] *Peoria, IL*
PARK AVENUE CAFE [RES] *Chicago, IL*
PARKER'S [RES] *Cleveland, OH*
PARTHENON [RES] *Chicago, IL*
PASTEUR [RES] *Chicago, IL*
PAT'S COLONIAL PUB [RES]
　　Mishawaka, IN
PAUL BUNYAN'S [RES] *Minocqua, WI*
PAULSON'S OLD ORCHARD INN
　　[RES] *Ephraim (Door County),
　　WI*
PEERLESS MILL INN [RES]
　　Miamisburg, OH
PEGASUS TAVERNA [RES] *Detroit, MI*
PELLETIER'S [RES] *Fish Creek (Door
　　County), WI*
PENNY'S NOODLE SHOP [RES]
　　Chicago, IL
PEPPER MILL [RES] *Oak Brook, IL*
PEREDDIE'S [RES] *Holland, MI*
PERIYALI GREEK TAVERN [RES]
　　Glenview, IL
PETE MILLER'S STEAKHOUSE [RES]
　　Evanston, IL
PETER'S [RES] *Indianapolis, IN*
PETERSEN'S [RES] *Cincinnati, OH*
PHIL SMIDT'S [RES] *Hammond, IN*
PHOENIX, THE [RES] *Cincinnati, OH*
PICANO'S [RES] *Troy, MI*
PICCOLO MONDO [RES] *Cleveland,
　　OH*
PIETRO'S BACK DOOR PIZZERIA
　　[RES] *Grand Rapids, MI*
PIGGY'S [RES] *La Crosse, WI*
PINE CLUB [RES] *Dayton, OH*
PIPER [RES] *Holland, MI*
PIPPINS [RES] *Boyne City, MI*
PIZZA D.O.C [RES] *Chicago, IL*
PIZZERIA UNO [URD] *Chicago, IL*
PLAYERS ON MADISON [RES]
　　Cleveland, OH

PLEASANT VALLEY INN [RES] *Milwaukee, WI*
POCKETS [URD] *Chicago, IL*
POLARIS [RES] *Milwaukee, WI*
POPEYE'S GALLEY AND GROG [RES] *Lake Geneva, WI*
PORT EDWARD [RES] *Dundee, IL*
PORTERHOUSE [RES] *Milwaukee, WI*
POST HOUSE [RES] *Spring Green, WI*
PRAIRIE [RES] *Chicago, IL*
PRECINCT [RES] *Cincinnati, OH*
PRIMAVISTA [RES] *Cincinnati, OH*
PRINTER'S ROW [RES] *Chicago, IL*
PUBLIC LANDING [RES] *Lockport, IL*
PUFFERBELLY LTD [RES] *Kent, OH*
PUMP ROOM [RES] *Chicago, IL*
QUINCY GRILLE ON THE RIVER [RES] *Chicago, IL*
QUIVEY'S GROVE [RES] *Madison, WI*
RAFFERTY'S DOCKSIDE [RES] *Muskegon, MI*
RATTLESNAKE CLUB [RES] *Detroit, MI*
RAY RADIGAN'S [RES] *Kenosha, WI*
RED CIRCLE INN [RES] *Oconomowoc, WI*
RED DOOR INN [RES] *Peru, IL*
REDFISH [RES] *Chicago, IL*
RED GERANIUM [RES] *New Harmony, IN*
REDLIGHT [RES] *Chicago, IL*
RED ROCK CAFE [RES] *Milwaukee, WI*
RED STEER [RES] *Minocqua, WI*
REED'S STATE STREET PUB [RES] *La Porte, IN*
REFECTORY [RES] *Columbus, OH*
REFLECTIONS [RES] *Traverse City, MI*
RESTAURANT AND PAGLIACCI'S, THE [RES] *Stevens Point, WI*
RESTAURANT AT THE CANTERBURY [RES] *Indianapolis, IN*
RESTAURANT AT THE PALM COURT, THE [RES] *Cincinnati, OH*
RETRO BISTRO [RES] *Arlington Heights, IL*
RHINELANDER CAFE AND PUB [RES] *Rhinelander, WI*
RHONDA'S WHARFSIDE [RES] *Frankfort, MI*
RICHARD'S [RES] *Sheboygan, WI*
RIDER'S INN [RES] *Painesville, OH*
RIGSBY'S CUISINE VOLATILE [RES] *Columbus, OH*
RISTORANTE BRISSAGO [RES] *Lake Geneva, WI*
RISTORANTE GIOVANNI [RES] *Beachwood, OH*
RITZ-CARLTON DINING ROOM, THE [RES] *Chicago, IL*
RIVA [RES] *Chicago, IL*
RIVER CRAB [RES] *St. Clair, MI*

RIVER LANE INN [RES] *Milwaukee, WI*
RIVER'S BEND [RES] *Green Bay, WI*
RIVERSITE [RES] *Cedarburg, WI*
RIVERVIEW ROOM [RES] *Cleveland, OH*
RJ SNAPPERS [RES] *Columbus, OH*
ROBBINS [RES] *Oshkosh, WI*
ROCKOME FAMILY STYLE [RES] *Arcola, IL*
ROCKWELL INN [RES] *Morris, IL*
ROCKY'S OF NORTHVILLE [RES] *Farmington, MI*
RON SANTO'S AMERICAN ROTISSERIE [RES] *Schaumburg, IL*
ROOKWOOD POTTERY [RES] *Cincinnati, OH*
ROSEBUD [RES] *Chicago, IL*
ROWE INN [RES] *Charlevoix, MI*
ROYAL INDIA [RES] *Milwaukee, WI*
R-PLACE FAMILY EATERY [RES] *Morris, IL*
RUGBY GRILLE [RES] *Birmingham, MI*
RUSSIAN TEA CAFE [RES] *Chicago, IL*
RUSTY'S [RES] *Edwardsville, IL*
SA-BAI THONG [RES] *Madison, WI*
SAFE HOUSE [URD] *Milwaukee, WI*
SAIL INN [RES] *Beulah, MI*
ST. CLAIR INN [RES] *St. Clair, MI*
ST. ELMO STEAK HOUSE [RES] *Indianapolis, IN*
ST. MORITZ [RES] *Lake Geneva, WI*
SALOON [RES] *Chicago, IL*
SALPICON [RES] *Chicago, IL*
SALTY'S SEAFOOD AND SPIRITS [RES] *Fond du Lac, WI*
SAMBA [RES] *Naperville, IL*
SANDPIPER [RES] *Baileys Harbor (Door County), WI*
SANFORD [RES] *Milwaukee, WI*
SANS SOUCI [RES] *Cleveland, OH*
SANTORINI [RES] *Chicago, IL*
SAYAT NOVA [RES] *Chicago, IL*
SAYFEE'S [RES] *Grand Rapids, MI*
SAZ'S STATE HOUSE [RES] *Milwaukee, WI*
SCHELDE'S [RES] *Traverse City, MI*
SCHLANG'S BAVARIAN INN [RES] *Gaylord, MI*
SCHMIDT'S SAUSAGE HAUS [RES] *Columbus, OH*
SCHNITZELBANK [RES] *Grand Rapids, MI*
SCHNITZELBANK [RES] *Jasper, IN*
SCHREINER'S [RES] *Fond du Lac, WI*
SCHULER'S OF MARSHALL [RES] *Marshall, MI*
SCHULER'S OF STEVENSVILLE [RES] *St. Joseph, MI*
SCOOZI [RES] *Chicago, IL*

SCOTTY'S [RES] *Ludington, MI*
SEAFOOD 32 [RES] *Cincinnati, OH*
SEASONS [RES] *Chicago, IL*
SECRETS RIBS & MORE [RES] *Joliet, IL*
SELENSKY'S GRAND CHAMPION GRILL [RES] *Milwaukee, WI*
SEVEN SAUCES [RES] *Athens, OH*
SEVEN SEAS [RES] *Waukesha, WI*
SEVEN STARS DINING ROOM [RES] *Columbus, OH*
SHACK SMOKEHOUSE AND GRILLE [RES] *Superior, WI*
SHALLOTS [RES] *Chicago, IL*
SHANGHAI GARDEN [RES] *Grand Rapids, MI*
SHAW'S [RES] *Lancaster, OH*
SHAW'S CRAB HOUSE [RES] *Chicago, IL*
SHERMAN HOUSE [RES] *Batesville, IN*
SHORELINE [RES] *Ellison Bay (Door County), WI*
SHUHEI [RES] *Beachwood, OH*
SIAM SQUARE [RES] *Evanston, IL*
SIGNATURE ROOM AT THE 95TH [RES] *Chicago, IL*
SINGHA THAI [RES] *Milwaukee, WI*
SMITH BROTHERS' FISH SHANTY [RES] *Port Washington, WI*
SOUK [RES] *Chicago, IL*
SOUL KITCHEN [RES] *Chicago, IL*
SOUTH GATE CAFE [RES] *Highwood, IL*
SPAGO [RES] *Chicago, IL*
SPANG'S [RES] *Minocqua, WI*
SPANG'S [RES] *St. Germain, WI*
SPIAGGIA [RES] *Chicago, IL*
STAFFORD'S BAY VIEW INN [RES] *Petoskey, MI*
STAFFORD'S ONE WATER STREET [RES] *Boyne City, MI*
STAFFORD'S PIER [RES] *Harbor Springs, MI*
STAFFORD'S WEATHERVANE [RES] *Charlevoix, MI*
STEAK HOUSE, THE [RES] *Galesburg, IL*
STETSON'S CHOPHOUSE [RES] *Chicago, IL*
STEVE KAO'S [RES] *Dayton, OH*
STEVEN WADE'S CAFE [RES] *Milwaukee, WI*
STONEHOUSE [RES] *Escanaba, MI*
STREETERVILLE GRILLE [RES] *Chicago, IL*
SU CASA [RES] *Chicago, IL*
SUGAR BOWL [RES] *Gaylord, MI*
SUMMER KITCHEN [RES] *Ephraim (Door County), WI*
SUMMERTIME [RES] *Fish Creek (Door County), WI*
SUSHI WABI [RES] *Chicago, IL*

SWANBERG'S BAVARIAN INN [RES] *Manitowish Waters, WI*
SWEET LORRAINE'S CAFE [RES] *Southfield, MI*
SYCAMORE GRILLE [RES] *Kokomo, IN*
SYDNEY'S [RES] *Munising, MI*
SZECHWAN EAST [RES] *Chicago, IL*
TALLGRASS [RES] *Lockport, IL*
TAMARACK INN [RES] *Copper Harbor, MI*
TANDOOR'S [RES] *Cincinnati, OH*
TANGIER [RES] *Akron, OH*
TANGLEWOOD [RES] *Wilmette, IL*
TAPATIO [RES] *Columbus, OH*
TAPAWINGO [RES] *Charlevoix, MI*
TASTE OF THE TOWN [RES] *Richmond, IN*
TAVERN IN THE TOWN [RES] *Libertyville, IL*
TAZA [URD] *Chicago, IL*
TEAK [RES] *Cincinnati, OH*
THAT PLACE ON BELLFLOWER [RES] *Cleveland, OH*
THEO'S [RES] *Cambridge, OH*
THOMATO'S [RES] *Dayton, OH*
THREE BROTHERS [RES] *Milwaukee, WI*
302 WEST [RES] *Geneva, IL*
312 CHICAGO [RES] *Chicago, IL*
TILL MIDNIGHT [RES] *Holland, MI*
TIMBERS [RES] *Platteville, WI*
TIMBERS CHARHOUSE [RES] *Highland Park, IL*
TIMPONE'S [RES] *Champaign/Urbana, IL*
TIPPECANOE PLACE [RES] *South Bend, IN*
TIZI MELLOUL [RES] *Chicago, IL*
TJ'S [RES] *Wooster, OH*
TOM'S OYSTER BAR [RES] *Southfield, MI*
TONELLI'S [RES] *Northbrook, IL*
TONY PACKO'S CAFE [RES] *Toledo, OH*
TONY'S [RES] *Alton, IL*
TONY'S [RES] *Columbus, OH*
TONY'S [RES] *Muskegon, MI*
TONY'S STEAK HOUSE [RES] *Marion, IL*
TOO CHEZ [RES] *Farmington, MI*
TO PERFECTION [RES] *Du Quoin, IL*
TOPOLOBAMPO [RES] *Chicago, IL*
TOULOUSE [RES] *Saugatuck, MI*
TRAFFIC JAM & SNUG [URD] *Detroit, MI*
TRATTORIA NO. 10 [RES] *Chicago, IL*
TRATTORIA PARMA [RES] *Chicago, IL*
TRES HERMANOS [RES] *Milwaukee, WI*
TRES HOMBRES [RES] *Carbondale, IL*
TRIBUTE [RES] *Farmington, MI*

TRIO [RES] *Evanston, IL*
TRIPLE CROWN [RES] *Akron, OH*
TRU [RES] *Chicago, IL*
TUCCI BENUCCH [RES] *Chicago, IL*
TUDOR'S [RES] *Lima, OH*
TULA'S [RES] *Rhinelander, WI*
TUSCANY [RES] *Chicago, IL*
UPTOWN GRILL [RES] *Peru, IL*
VA PENSIERO [RES] *Evanston, IL*
VIKING [RES] *Ellison Bay (Door County), WI*
VILLAGE CAFE [RES] *Egg Harbor (Door County), WI*
VINCI [RES] *Chicago, IL*
VIVERE [RES] *Chicago, IL*
VIVO [RES] *Chicago, IL*
WAGON WHEEL SUPPER CLUB [RES] *Wausau, WI*
WALKER BROTHERS ORIGINAL PANCAKE HOUSE [URD] *Wilmette, IL*
WALLY'S HOUSE OF EMBERS [RES] *Wisconsin Dells, WI*
WALTER'S [RES] *Chicago O'Hare Airport Area, IL*
WATER LILY [RES] *Mount Pleasant, MI*
WATERMARK [RES] *Cleveland, OH*
WATUSI [RES] *Chicago, IL*
WAUSAU MINE CO. [RES] *Wausau, WI*
WEBER GRILL [RES] *Wheeling, IL*
WEBSTER'S [RES] *Kalamazoo, MI*
WEISSGERBER'S 3RD STREET PIER [RES] *Milwaukee, WI*
WEISSGERBER'S GASTHAUS INN [RES] *Waukesha, WI*
WELLINGTON [RES] *Green Bay, WI*
WELSHFIELD INN [RES] *Aurora, OH*
WELTON'S [RES] *Dayton, OH*
WEST BANK CAFE [RES] *Milwaukee, WI*
WESTERN AVENUE GRILL [RES] *Glen Arbor, MI*
WHISKY'S [RES] *Aurora, IN*
WHITE FENCE FARM [RES] *Joliet, IL*
WHITE GULL INN [RES] *Fish Creek (Door County), WI*
WHITNEY, THE [RES] *Detroit, MI*
WHITNEY'S BAR AND GRILL [RES] *Oak Lawn, IL*
WILLOW ON WAGNER [RES] *Glenview, IL*
WINDOWS [RES] *Traverse City, MI*
WINTERGREEN GRILLE [RES] *Wisconsin Dells, WI*
WISCONSIN FARMS [RES] *Oshkosh, WI*
WISHBONE [RES] *Chicago, IL*
WOOSTER INN [RES] *Wooster, OH*
WYOMING CATTLE CO [RES] *Grand Rapids, MI*

YEN CHING [RES] *Milwaukee, WI*
ZEALOUS [RES] *Chicago, IL*
ZEHNDER'S [RES] *Frankenmuth, MI*
ZINFANDEL [RES] *Chicago, IL*
ZINGERMAN'S DELICATESSEN [URD] *Ann Arbor, MI*

CITY INDEX

Akron, OH, 391
Algoma, WI, 512
Alliance, OH, 395
Alma, MI, 250
Alpena, MI, 250
Altamont, IL, 7
Alton, IL, 7
Anderson, IN, 168
Angola, IN, 169
Ann Arbor, MI, 251
Antigo, WI, 512
Antioch, IL, 8
Appleton, WI, 512
Arcola, IL, 9
Arlington Heights, IL, 10
Ashland, WI, 514
Ashtabula, OH, 395
Athens, OH, 396
Auburn, IN, 170
Aurora, IL, 12
Aurora, IN, 171
Aurora, OH, 397
Baileys Harbor (Door County), WI, 515
Baraboo, WI, 516
Batesville, IN, 171
Battle Creek, MI, 255
Bay City, MI, 257
Bayfield, WI, 517
Beachwood, OH, 398
Beaver Dam, WI, 519
Bedford, IN, 172
Bellaire, MI, 258
Bellefontaine, OH, 399
Belleville, IL, 13
Bellevue, OH, 400
Beloit, WI, 519
Benton, IL, 14
Benton Harbor, MI, 259
Beulah, MI, 259
Big Rapids, MI, 260
Birmingham, MI, 260
Bishop Hill, IL, 15
Black River Falls, WI, 520
Bloomfield Hills, MI, 261
Bloomington, IL, 16
Bloomington, IN, 173
Boulder Junction, WI, 521
Bowling Green, OH, 401
Boyne City, MI, 262
Brazil, IN, 175
Brecksville, OH, 402
Brookfield, IL, 18
Brown County State Park, IN, 175
Burlington, WI, 522

Cable, WI, 523
Cadillac, MI, 263
Cahokia, IL, 18
Cairo, IL, 19
Calumet, MI, 265
Cambridge, OH, 402
Canton, OH, 404
Carbondale, IL, 20
Cedarburg, WI, 523
Celina, OH, 406
Centralia, IL, 21
Champaign/Urbana, IL, 21
Chardon, OH, 407
Charleston, IL, 24
Charlevoix, MI, 265
Cheboygan, MI, 267
Chicago, IL, 25
Chicago O'Hare Airport Area, IL, 67
Chillicothe, OH, 408
Chippewa Falls, WI, 524
Cicero, IL, 71
Cincinnati, OH, 410
Clare, MI, 268
Cleveland, OH, 423
Coldwater, MI, 268
Collinsville, IL, 71
Columbus, IN, 176
Columbus, OH, 435
Conneaut, OH, 443
Connersville, IN, 176
Copper Harbor, MI, 270
Corydon, IN, 177
Coshocton, OH, 443
Crandon, WI, 526
Crawfordsville, IN, 178
Danville, IL, 72
Dayton, OH, 444
Dearborn, MI, 271
Decatur, IL, 73
Defiance, OH, 449
De Kalb, IL, 75
Delavan, WI, 526
Delaware, OH, 450
Des Plaines, IL, 76
Detroit, MI, 274
Detroit Wayne County Airport Area, MI, 284
Devil's Lake State Park, WI, 526
Dixon, IL, 76
Dodgeville, WI, 527
Door County, WI, 528
Downers Grove, IL, 77
Dundee, IL, 78
Du Quoin, IL, 79
Eagle River, WI, 528

East Lansing, MI, 285
East Liverpool, OH, 451
Eau Claire, WI, 530
Edwardsville, IL, 79
Effingham, IL, 80
Egg Harbor (Door County), WI, 532
Elgin, IL, 81
Elk Grove Village, IL, 82
Elkhart, IN, 180
Elkhart Lake, WI, 533
Elkhorn, WI, 535
Ellison Bay (Door County), WI, 535
Elmhurst, IL, 82
Elyria, OH, 452
Ephraim (Door County), WI, 537
Escanaba, MI, 285
Evanston, IL, 83
Evansville, IN, 181
Farmington, MI, 287
Findlay, OH, 453
Fish Creek (Door County), WI, 539
Flint, MI, 289
Fond du Lac, WI, 541
Fontana, WI, 543
Fort Ancient State Memorial, OH, 454
Fort Atkinson, WI, 544
Fort Hill State Memorial, OH, 454
Fort Kaskaskia State Historic Site, IL, 87
Fort Wayne, IN, 184
Frankenmuth, MI, 291
Frankfort, MI, 292
Freeport, IL, 87
Fremont, OH, 454
French Lick, IN, 187
Galena, IL, 88
Galesburg, IL, 92
Galesville, WI, 544
Gallipolis, OH, 455
Gaylord, MI, 293
Geneva, IL, 93
Geneva (Adams County), IN, 188
Geneva-on-the-Lake, OH, 455
George Rogers Clark National Historical Park, IN, 188
Glen Arbor, MI, 295
Glen Ellyn, IL, 94
Glenview, IL, 95
Gnadenhutten, OH, 456
Goshen, IN, 188
Grand Haven, MI, 296
Grand Marais, MI, 298
Grand Rapids, MI, 298
Grayling, MI, 303
Grayslake, IL, 97
Green Bay, WI, 545
Greencastle, IN, 190
Greenfield, IN, 190
Green Lake, WI, 548
Greenville, IL, 97

Gurnee, IL, 98
Hamilton, OH, 456
Hammond, IN, 191
Hancock, MI, 304
Harbor Springs, MI, 305
Harrison, MI, 307
Havana, IL, 99
Hayward, WI, 549
Highland Park, IL, 99
Highwood, IL, 100
Hillside, IL, 101
Hinsdale, IL, 102
Hocking Hills State Park, OH, 457
Holland, MI, 307
Holly, MI, 309
Homewood, IL, 103
Houghton, MI, 310
Houghton Lake, MI, 311
Hudson, WI, 551
Hulbert, MI, 312
Huntington, IN, 192
Hurley, WI, 551
Illinois Beach State Park, IL, 103
Indiana Dunes National Lakeshore, IN, 192
Indiana Dunes State Park, IN, 193
Indianapolis, IN, 193
Indian River, MI, 312
Iron Mountain, MI, 313
Iron River, MI, 314
Ironton, OH, 457
Ironwood, MI, 315
Ishpeming, MI, 316
Isle Royale National Park, MI, 316
Itasca, IL, 104
Jackson, MI, 317
Jacksonville, IL, 104
Janesville, WI, 552
Jasper, IN, 205
Jeffersonville, IN, 206
Joliet, IL, 105
Kalamazoo, MI, 319
Kankakee, IL, 106
Kelleys Island, OH, 458
Kenosha, WI, 553
Kent, OH, 459
Kewanee, IL, 107
Kohler, WI, 555
Kokomo, IN, 207
Lac du Flambeau, WI, 556
La Crosse, WI, 556
Ladysmith, WI, 558
Lafayette, IN, 208
La Grange, IL, 108
Lake Geneva, WI, 559
Lancaster, OH, 460
Land O' Lakes, WI, 561
Lansing, MI, 322
La Porte, IN, 211
Lebanon, OH, 462
Leland, MI, 325

Libertyville, IL, 109
Lima, OH, 463
Lincoln, IL, 110
Lincoln Boyhood National Memorial
    & Lincoln State Park, IN, 212
Lincoln's New Salem State Historic
    Site, IL, 111
Lockport, IL, 111
Logansport, IN, 212
Lorain, OH, 463
Ludington, MI, 326
Mackinac Island, MI, 328
Mackinaw City, MI, 331
Macomb, IL, 112
Madison, IN, 213
Madison, WI, 561
Manistee, MI, 335
Manistique, MI, 336
Manitowish Waters, WI, 566
Manitowoc, WI, 567
Mansfield, OH, 464
Marietta, OH, 466
Marinette, WI, 567
Marion, IL, 113
Marion, IN, 214
Marion, OH, 468
Marquette, MI, 337
Marshall, IL, 114
Marshall, MI, 339
Marshfield, WI, 568
Mason, OH, 469
Massillon, OH, 470
Mattoon, IL, 114
Mauston, WI, 569
McHenry, IL, 115
Menasha, WI, 569
Menominee, MI, 340
Menomonee Falls, WI, 569
Menomonie, WI, 570
Mentor, OH, 471
Merrillville, IN, 215
Miamisburg, OH, 471
Michigan City, IN, 216
Middletown (Butler County), OH,
    473
Midland, MI, 341
Milan, OH, 473
Milwaukee, WI, 571
Mineral Point, WI, 583
Minocqua, WI, 584
Mishawaka, IN, 217
Moline, IL, 116
Monmouth, IL, 117
Monroe, MI, 342
Monroe, WI, 585
Morris, IL, 117
Mount Clemens, MI, 343
Mount Gilead, OH, 475
Mount Horeb, WI, 587
Mount Pleasant, MI, 343
Mount Vernon, IL, 118
Mount Vernon, OH, 475

Muncie, IN, 218
Munising, MI, 345
Muskegon, MI, 346
Naperville, IL, 119
Nappanee, IN, 220
Nashville, IN, 221
Nauvoo, IL, 121
Neenah-Menasha, WI, 587
New Albany, IN, 222
Newark, OH, 475
Newberry, MI, 349
New Buffalo, MI, 350
New Castle, IN, 223
New Glarus, WI, 588
New Harmony, IN, 224
New Philadelphia, OH, 477
Niles, MI, 350
Normal, IL, 123
Northbrook, IL, 123
Oak Brook, IL, 125
Oak Lawn, IL, 128
Oak Park, IL, 130
Oberlin, OH, 479
Oconomowoc, WI, 589
Oconto, WI, 590
Olney, IL, 131
Ontonagon, MI, 350
Oregon, IL, 131
Oscoda, MI, 351
Oshkosh, WI, 590
Ottawa, IL, 132
Owosso, MI, 352
Oxford, OH, 480
Painesville, OH, 481
Park Falls, WI, 593
Paw Paw, MI, 352
Peoria, IL, 133
PÈre Marquette State Park, IL, 136
Peru, IL, 137
Peru, IN, 225
Peshtigo, WI, 594
Petersburg, IL, 139
Petoskey, MI, 353
Piqua, OH, 482
Platteville, WI, 594
Plymouth, IN, 226
Plymouth, MI, 355
Pontiac, MI, 355
Portage, WI, 595
Port Austin, MI, 357
Port Clinton, OH, 482
Port Huron, MI, 357
Portsmouth, OH, 483
Port Washington, WI, 596
Prairie du Chien, WI, 596
Prairie du Sac, WI, 598
Put-in-Bay, OH, 484
Quincy, IL, 139
Racine, WI, 598
Reedsburg, WI, 599
Rhinelander, WI, 600
Rice Lake, WI, 602

Richland Center, WI, 603
Richmond, IN, 227
Rockford, IL, 140
Rock Island, IL, 143
Rockville, IN, 228
Romulus, MI, 358
Rosemont, IL, 144
Saginaw, MI, 359
St. Charles, IL, 144
St. Clair, MI, 360
St. Clairsville, OH, 485
St. Croix Falls, WI, 603
St. Germain, WI, 604
St. Ignace, MI, 361
St. Joseph, MI, 363
Salem, IL, 145
Sandusky, OH, 485
Santa Claus, IN, 229
Saugatuck, MI, 365
Sault Ste. Marie, MI, 367
Sayner, WI, 605
Schaumburg, IL, 146
Schiller Park, IL, 148
Serpent Mound State Memorial, OH, 488
Shakamak State Park, IN, 230
Shawano, WI, 605
Sheboygan, WI, 606
Sidney, OH, 488
Sister Bay (Door County), WI, 607
Skokie, IL, 148
Sleeping Bear Dunes National Lakeshore, MI, 369
Soo Junction, MI, 370
South Bend, IN, 230
Southfield, MI, 370
South Haven, MI, 372
Sparta, WI, 609
Spooner, WI, 610
Springfield, IL, 149
Springfield, OH, 488
Spring Green, WI, 611
Spring Mill State Park, IN, 235
Starved Rock State Park, IL, 154
Steubenville, OH, 490
Stevens Point, WI, 612
Strongsville, OH, 490
Sturgeon Bay (Door County), WI, 613
Superior, WI, 616
Tawas City, MI, 373

Terre Haute, IN, 235
Three Lakes, WI, 618
Three Rivers, MI, 374
Tiffin, OH, 491
Tippecanoe River State Park, IN, 237
Toledo, OH, 491
Tomah, WI, 619
Traverse City, MI, 374
Troy, MI, 379
Turkey Run State Park, IN, 237
Two Rivers, WI, 620
Union, IL, 154
Urbana, IL, 155
Valparaiso, IN, 238
Vandalia, IL, 155
Vandalia, OH, 495
Van Wert, OH, 495
Vermilion, OH, 496
Vincennes, IN, 239
Wabash, IN, 240
Wakefield, MI, 381
Wapakoneta, OH, 496
Warren, MI, 382
Warren, OH, 496
Warsaw, IN, 241
Washington Island (Door County), WI, 620
Watertown, WI, 621
Waukegan, IL, 156
Waukesha, WI, 622
Waupaca, WI, 623
Waupun, WI, 624
Wausau, WI, 625
Wauseon, OH, 497
Wautoma, WI, 627
Wauwatosa, WI, 627
Wheaton, IL, 157
Wheeling, IL, 158
Whitehall, MI, 383
Wilmette, IL, 160
Wilmington, OH, 498
Wisconsin Dells, WI, 628
Wisconsin Rapids, WI, 632
Woodruff, WI, 633
Woodstock, IL, 161
Wooster, OH, 499
Wyandotte, IN, 242
Youngstown, OH, 500
Ypsilanti, MI, 384
Zanesville, OH, 502

Notes

Notes

Notes

Notes

Notes

Notes

Notes

Notes

Notes

Notes

Mobil
Travel Guide®

New England
Eastern Canada
Connecticut
Maine
Massachusetts
New Hampshire
Rhode Island
Vermont
New Brunswick
Nova Scotia
Ontario
Prince Edward
Island
Quebec

Northwest
Idaho
Montana
Oregon
Washington
Wyoming
Alberta
British Columbia
Manitoba

Great Plains
Iowa
Kansas
Minnesota
Missouri
Nebraska
North Dakota
Oklahoma
South Dakota

Great Lakes
Illinois
Indiana
Michigan
Ohio
Wisconsin

California

New York
New Jersey

Southwest
Arizona
Colorado
Nevada
New Mexico
Texas
Utah

Southeast
Alabama
Arkansas
Georgia
Kentucky
Louisiana
Mississippi
North Carolina
South Carolina
Tennessee

Florida

Mid-Atlantic
Delaware
Maryland
Pennsylvania
Virginia
Washington, D.C.
West Virginia

Notes

Add your opinion!

Help make the Guides even more useful. Tell us about your experiences with the hotels and restaurants listed in the Guides (or ones that should be added).

Find us on the Internet at **www.mobiltravelguide.com/feedback**

Or copy the form below and mail to Mobil Travel Guides, 1460 Renaissance Drive, Suite 401, Park Ridge, IL 60068. All information will be kept confidential.

Your name _____   Were children with you on trip? ▨ Yes ▨ No

Street _____   Number of people in your party _____

City/State/Zip _____   Your occupation _____

▨ Hotel ▨ Resort ▨ Restaurant
▨ Motel ▨ Inn ▨ Other

Establishment name _____

Street_____ City_____ State _____

Do you agree with our description? ▨ Yes ▨ No If not, give reason_____

Please give us your opinion of the following:

Decor	Cleanliness	Service	Food
▨ Excellent	▨ Spotless	▨ Excellent	▨ Excellent
▨ Good	▨ Clean	▨ Good	▨ Good
▨ Fair	▨ Unclean	▨ Fair	▨ Fair
▨ Poor	▨ Dirty	▨ Poor	▨ Poor

2003 Guide rating _____ ★
Check your suggested rating
▨ ★
▨ ★★
▨ ★★★
▨ ★★★★
▨ ★★★★★
✓ unusually good value

Date of visit _____   First visit? ▨ Yes ▨ No

Comments _____

▨ Hotel ▨ Resort ▨ Restaurant
▨ Motel ▨ Inn ▨ Other

Establishment name_____

Street_____ City_____ State _____

Do you agree with our description? ▨ Yes ▨ No If not, give reason_____

Please give us your opinion of the following:

Decor	Cleanliness	Service	Food
▨ Excellent	▨ Spotless	▨ Excellent	▨ Excellent
▨ Good	▨ Clean	▨ Good	▨ Good
▨ Fair	▨ Unclean	▨ Fair	▨ Fair
▨ Poor	▨ Dirty	▨ Poor	▨ Poor

2003 Guide rating _____ ★
Check your suggested rating
▨ ★
▨ ★★
▨ ★★★
▨ ★★★★
▨ ★★★★★
✓ unusually good value

Date of visit _____   First visit? ▨ Yes ▨ No

Comments _____